BUSINESS LAW TODAY

Standard Volume I

Hudson Valley Community College

Roger LeRoy Miller I Gaylord A. Jentz

CENGAGE
Learning™

Australia • Brazil • Japan • Korea • Mexico • Singapore • Spain • United Kingdom • United States

CENGAGE
Learning™

BUSINESS LAW TODAY
Standard Volume I
Hudson Valley Community College

Roger LeRoy Miller I Gaylord A. Jentz

Executive Editors:
 Michele Baird

 Maureen Staudt

 Michael Stranz

Project Development Manager:
 Linda deStefano

Senior Marketing Coordinators:
 Sara Mercurio

 Lindsay Shapiro

Senior Production / Manufacturing Manager:
 Donna M. Brown

PreMedia Services Supervisor:
 Rebecca A. Walker

Rights & Permissions Specialist:
 Kalina Hintz

Cover Image:
 Getty Images*

* Unless otherwise noted, all cover images used
by Custom Solutions, a part of Cengage
Learning, have been supplied courtesy of Getty
Images with the exception of the Earthview
cover image, which has been supplied by the
National Aeronautics and Space Administration
(NASA).

For product information and technology assistance, contact us at
Cengage Learning Customer & Sales Support, 1-800-354-9706

For permission to use material from this text or product,
submit all requests online at **cengage.com/permissions**
Further permissions questions can be emailed to
permissionrequest@cengage.com

ISBN-13: 978-0-324-83025-5

ISBN-10: 0-324-83025-4

Cengage Learning
5191 Natorp Boulevard
Mason, Ohio 45040
USA

Cengage Learning is a leading provider of customized learning solutions with
office locations around the globe, including Singapore, the United Kingdom,
Australia, Mexico, Brazil, and Japan. Locate your local office at:
international.cengage.com/region

Cengage Learning products are represented in Canada by Nelson Education, Ltd.

For your lifelong learning solutions, visit **custom.cengage.com**

Visit our corporate website at **cengage.com**

Printed in the United States of America

Contents in Brief

Contents*

UNIT THREE
Sales and
Lease
Contracts   399

UNIT FOUR
Negotiable
Instruments 505

UNIT NINE

**The International
Legal
Environment 1097**

APPENDICES

UNIT ONE The Legal Environment of Business

UNIT CONTENTS

CHAPTER 1
The Legal Environment

LEARNING OBJECTIVES

AFTER READING THIS CHAPTER, YOU SHOULD BE ABLE TO ANSWER THE FOLLOWING QUESTIONS:

1 What is the Uniform Commercial Code?

2 What is the common law tradition?

3 What is a precedent? When might a court depart from precedent?

4 What is the difference between remedies at law and remedies in equity?

5 What are some important differences between civil law and criminal law?

> **❝**The law is of as much interest to the layman as it is to the lawyer.**❞**
>
> Lord Balfour, 1848–1930
> (British prime minister,
> 1902–1905)

L ord Balfour's assertion in the chapter-opening quotation emphasizes the underlying theme of every page in this book—that law is of interest to all persons, not just to lawyers. Those entering the world of business will find themselves subject to numerous laws and government regulations. A basic knowledge of these laws and regulations is beneficial— if not essential—to anyone contemplating a successful career in today's business world.

In this introductory chapter, we first look at the nature of law and at some concepts that have significantly influenced how jurists (those skilled in the law, including judges, lawyers, and legal scholars) view the nature and function of law. We then look at an important question for any student reading this text: How does the legal environment affect business decision making? We next describe the basic sources of American law, the common law tradition, and the importance of the common law today. We conclude the chapter with a discussion of some general classifications of law.

THE NATURE OF LAW

LAW
A body of enforceable rules governing relationships among individuals and between individuals and their society.

Law has had and will continue to have different definitions. Although the definitions vary in their particulars, they all are based on the general observation that, at a minimum, **law** consists of *enforceable rules governing relationships among individuals and between individuals and their society.* These "enforceable rules" may consist of unwritten principles of behavior established by a nomadic tribe. They may be set forth in an ancient or a contemporary law code. They may consist of written laws and court decisions created by modern legislative and judicial bodies, as in the United States. Regardless of how such rules are created, they all have one thing in common: they establish rights, duties, and privileges that are consistent with the values and beliefs of their society or its ruling group.

Those who embark on a study of law will find that these broad statements leave unanswered some important questions concerning the nature of law. Part of the study of law, often referred to as **jurisprudence,** involves learning about different schools of legal thought and discovering how each school's approach to law can affect judicial decision making.

You may think that legal philosophy is far removed from the practical study of business law and the legal environment. In fact, it is not. As you will learn in the chapters of this text, how judges apply the law to specific disputes, including disputes relating to the business world, depends in part on their philosophical approaches to law. We look now at some of the significant schools of legal, or jurisprudential, thought that have evolved over time.

The Natural Law Tradition

An age-old question about the nature of law has to do with the finality of a nation's laws, such as the laws of the United States at the present time. For example, what if a substantial number of that nation's citizens consider a particular law to be a "bad" law? Must a citizen obey the law if doing so goes against his or her conscience? Is there a higher or universal law to which individuals can appeal? One who adheres to the natural law tradition would answer this question in the affirmative. **Natural law** denotes a system of moral and ethical principles that are inherent in human nature and thus can be discovered through the use of people's own native intelligence.

The natural law tradition is one of the oldest and most significant schools of jurisprudence. It dates back to the days of the Greek philosopher Aristotle (384–322 B.C.E.), who distinguished between natural law and the laws governing a particular nation. According to Aristotle, natural law applies universally to all humankind.

The notion that people have "natural rights" stems from the natural law tradition. Those who claim that a specific foreign government is depriving certain citizens of their human rights are implicitly appealing to a higher law that has universal applicability. The question of the universality of basic human rights also comes into play in the context of international business operations. For example, U.S. companies that have operations abroad often hire foreign workers as employees. Should the same laws that protect U.S. employees apply to these foreign employees? This question is rooted implicitly in a concept of universal rights that has its origins in the natural law tradition.

Legal Positivism

In contrast, **positive law,** or national law (the written law of a given society at a particular point in time), applies only to the citizens of that nation or society. Those who adhere to **legal positivism** believe that there can be no higher law than a nation's positive law. According to the positivist school, there is no such thing as "natural rights." Rather, human rights exist solely because of laws. If the laws are not enforced, anarchy will result. Thus, whether a law is "bad" or "good" is irrelevant. The law is the law and must be obeyed until it is changed—in an orderly manner through a legitimate lawmaking process. A judge with positivist leanings probably would be more inclined to defer to an existing law than would a judge who adheres to the natural law tradition.

The Historical School

The **historical school** of legal thought emphasizes the evolutionary process of law by concentrating on the origin and history of the legal system. Thus, this school looks to the past

Was Aristotle a proponent of the natural or positive law tradition?
(Collection of The Louvre/Photo by Eric Gaba/Wikimedia Commons)

JURISPRUDENCE
The science or philosophy of law.

NATURAL LAW
The belief that government and the legal system should reflect universal moral and ethical principles that are inherent in human nature. The natural law school is the oldest and one of the most significant schools of legal thought.

POSITIVE LAW
The body of conventional, or written, law of a particular society at a particular point in time.

LEGAL POSITIVISM
A school of legal thought centered on the assumption that there is no law higher than the laws created by a national government. Laws must be obeyed, even if they are unjust, to prevent anarchy.

HISTORICAL SCHOOL
A school of legal thought that emphasizes the evolutionary process of law and looks to the past to discover what the principles of contemporary law should be.

to discover what the principles of contemporary law should be. The legal doctrines that have withstood the passage of time—those that have worked in the past—are deemed best suited for shaping present laws. Hence, law derives its legitimacy and authority from adhering to the standards that historical development has shown to be workable. Followers of the historical school are more likely than those of other schools to adhere strictly to decisions made in past cases.

Legal Realism

LEGAL REALISM
A school of legal thought of the 1920s and 1930s that generally advocated a less abstract and more realistic approach to the law, an approach that takes into account customary practices and the circumstances in which transactions take place. This school left a lasting imprint on American jurisprudence.

SOCIOLOGICAL SCHOOL
A school of legal thought that views the law as a tool for promoting justice in society.

In the 1920s and 1930s, a number of jurists and scholars, known as *legal realists*, rebelled against the historical approach to law. **Legal realism** is based on the idea that law is just one of many institutions in society and that it is shaped by social forces and needs. The law is a human enterprise, and judges should take social and economic realities into account when deciding cases. Legal realists also believe that the law can never be applied with total uniformity. Given that judges are human beings with unique personalities, value systems, and intellects, obviously different judges will bring different reasoning processes to the same case.

Legal realism strongly influenced the growth of what is sometimes called the **sociological school** of jurisprudence. This school views law as a tool for promoting justice in society. In the 1960s, for example, the justices of the United States Supreme Court played a leading role in the civil rights movement by upholding long-neglected laws calling for equal treatment for all Americans, including African Americans and other minorities. Generally, jurists who adhere to the sociological school are more likely to depart from past decisions than are those jurists who adhere to the other schools of legal thought.

BUSINESS ACTIVITIES AND THE LEGAL ENVIRONMENT

As those entering the world of business will learn, laws and government regulations affect virtually all business activities—hiring and firing decisions, workplace safety, the manufacturing and marketing of products, and business financing, to name just a few. To make good business decisions, a basic knowledge of the laws and regulations governing these activities is beneficial, if not essential. In today's world, though, a knowledge of "black-letter" law is not enough. Businesspersons are also pressured to make ethical decisions. Thus, the study of business law necessarily involves an ethical dimension.

Many Different Laws May Affect a Single Business Transaction

BREACH
The failure to perform a legal obligation.

As you will note, each chapter in this text covers a specific area of the law and shows how the legal rules in that area affect business activities. Although compartmentalizing the law in this fashion facilitates learning, it does not indicate the extent to which many different laws may apply to just one transaction. **■EXAMPLE 1.1** Suppose that you are the president of NetSys, Inc., a company that creates and maintains computer network systems for its clients, including business firms. NetSys also markets software for customers who require an internal computer network. One day, Janet Hernandez, an operations officer for Southwest Distribution Corporation (SDC), contacts you by e-mail about a possible contract involving SDC's computer network. In deciding whether to enter into a contract with SDC, you need to consider, among other things, the legal requirements for an enforceable contract. Are the requirements different for a contract for services and a contract for products? What are your options if SDC **breaches** (breaks, or fails to perform) the contract? The answers to these questions are part of contract law and sales law.

Other questions might concern payment under the contract. How can you guarantee that NetSys will be paid? For example, if SDC pays with a check that is returned for insufficient funds, what are your options? Answers to these questions can be found in the laws that relate to negotiable instruments (such as checks) and creditors' rights. Also, a dispute may arise over the rights to NetSys's software, or there may be a question of liability if the software is defective. There may be an issue as to whether you and Hernandez had the authority to make the deal in the first place, or an accountant's evaluation of the contract may lead to a dispute. Resolutions of these questions may be found in the laws that relate to intellectual property, e-commerce, torts, product liability, agency, business organizations, or professional liability. ▣

Finally, if any dispute cannot be resolved amicably, then the laws and the rules concerning courts and court procedures spell out the steps of a lawsuit. Exhibit 1–1 illustrates the various areas of the law that may influence business decision making.

To prevent potential legal disputes, businesspersons need to be aware of the many different laws that may apply to a single business transaction. It is equally important for businesspersons to understand enough about the law to know when to turn to an expert for advice. For information on how to choose an attorney, see the *Application* feature at the end of this chapter.

PREVENTING LEGAL DISPUTES

▣

Ethics and Business Decision Making

Merely knowing the areas of law that may affect a business decision is not sufficient in today's business world. Businesspersons must also take ethics into account. As you will learn in Chapter 7, *ethics* is generally defined as the study of what constitutes right or wrong behavior. Today, business decision makers need to consider not just whether a decision is legal, but also whether it is ethical.

EXHIBIT 1–1 Areas of the Law That May Affect Business Decision Making

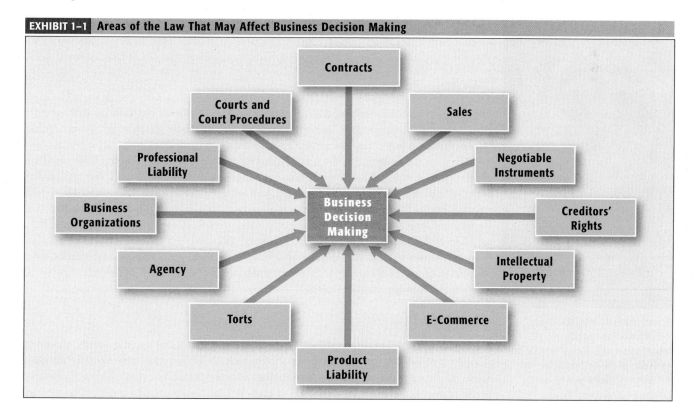

PRIMARY SOURCE OF LAW
A document that establishes the law on a particular issue, such as a constitution, a statute, an administrative rule, or a court decision.

SECONDARY SOURCE OF LAW
A publication that summarizes or interprets the law, such as a legal encyclopedia, a legal treatise, or an article in a law review.

CONSTITUTIONAL LAW
The body of law derived from the U.S. Constitution and the constitutions of the various states.

STATUTORY LAW
The body of law enacted by legislative bodies (as opposed to constitutional law, administrative law, or case law).

Young students view the U.S. Constitution on display in Washington, D.C. Can a law be in violation of the Constitution and still be enforced? Why or why not?
(Michael Evans/Zuma Press)

Throughout this text, you will learn about the relationship between the law and ethics, as well as about some of the types of ethical questions that often arise in the business context. Not only is Chapter 7 devoted solely to an examination of the importance of ethical considerations in business decision making, but various other elements in every chapter of this text are designed to help you become aware of the ethical aspects of questions that businesspersons may face. For example, the *Ethical Issue* features in each chapter of the text explore the ethical dimensions of topics treated within that chapter. In addition, the case problems at the end of each chapter include *A Question of Ethics* designed to introduce you to the ethical aspects of a specific case involving a real-life situation.

SOURCES OF AMERICAN LAW

There are numerous sources of American law. **Primary sources of law,** or sources that establish the law, include the following:

- The U.S. Constitution and the constitutions of the various states.
- Statutes, or laws, passed by Congress and by state legislatures.
- Regulations created by administrative agencies, such as the federal Food and Drug Administration.
- Case law (court decisions).

We describe each of these important primary sources of law in the following pages. (See the appendix at the end of this chapter for a discussion of how to find statutes, regulations, and case law.)

Secondary sources of law are books and articles that summarize and clarify the primary sources of law. Legal encyclopedias, compilations (such as *Restatements of the Law,* which summarize court decisions on a particular topic), official comments to statutes, treatises, articles in law reviews published by law schools, and articles in other legal journals are examples of secondary sources of law. Courts often refer to secondary sources of law for guidance in interpreting and applying the primary sources of law discussed here.

Constitutional Law

The federal government and the states have separate written constitutions that set forth the general organization, powers, and limits of their respective governments. **Constitutional law** is the law as expressed in these constitutions.

The U.S. Constitution is the supreme law of the land. As such, it is the basis of all law in the United States. A law in violation of the Constitution, if challenged, will be declared unconstitutional and will not be enforced no matter what its source. Because of its paramount importance in the American legal system, we discuss the U.S. Constitution at length in Chapter 2 and present the complete text of the Constitution in Appendix B.

The Tenth Amendment to the U.S. Constitution reserves to the states all powers not granted to the federal government. Each state in the union has its own constitution. Unless it conflicts with the U.S. Constitution or a federal law, a state constitution is supreme within the state's borders.

Statutory Law

Laws enacted by legislative bodies at any level of government, such as the statutes passed by Congress or by state legislatures, make up the body of law generally referred to as **statutory law.** When a legislature passes a statute, that statute ultimately is included in the federal code of laws or the relevant state code of laws. Whenever a particular statute is mentioned in this text, we usually provide a footnote showing its **citation** (a reference to a publication in which a legal authority—such as a statute or a court decision—or other source can be found). In the appendix following this chapter, we explain how you can use these citations to find statutory law.

Statutory law also includes local **ordinances**—statutes (laws, rules, or orders) passed by municipal or county governing units to govern matters not covered by federal or state law. Ordinances commonly have to do with city or county land use (zoning ordinances), building and safety codes, and other matters affecting the local governing unit.

A federal statute, of course, applies to all states. A state statute, in contrast, applies only within the state's borders. State laws thus may vary from state to state. No federal statute may violate the U.S. Constitution, and no state statute or local ordinance may violate the U.S. Constitution or the relevant state constitution.

Uniform Laws   During the 1800s, the differences among state laws frequently created difficulties for businesspersons conducting trade and commerce among the states. To counter these problems, a group of legal scholars and lawyers formed the National Conference of Commissioners on Uniform State Laws (NCCUSL) in 1892 to draft **uniform laws** ("model statutes") for the states to consider adopting. The NCCUSL still exists today and continues to issue uniform laws.

Each state has the option of adopting or rejecting a uniform law. *Only if a state legislature adopts a uniform law does that law become part of the statutory law of that state.* Note that a state legislature may adopt all or part of a uniform law as it is written, or the legislature may rewrite the law however the legislature wishes. Hence, even though many states may have adopted a uniform law, those states' laws may not be entirely "uniform."

The earliest uniform law, the Uniform Negotiable Instruments Law, was completed by 1896 and was adopted in every state by the early 1920s (although not all states used exactly the same wording). Over the following decades, other acts were drawn up in a similar manner. In all, the NCCUSL has issued more than two hundred uniform acts since its inception. The most ambitious uniform act of all, however, was the Uniform Commercial Code.

The Uniform Commercial Code (UCC)   The Uniform Commercial Code (UCC), which was created through the joint efforts of the NCCUSL and the American Law Institute,[1] was first issued in 1952. The UCC has been adopted in all fifty states,[2] the District of Columbia, and the Virgin Islands. The UCC facilitates commerce among the states by providing a uniform, yet flexible, set of rules governing commercial transactions. The UCC assures businesspersons that their contracts, if validly entered into, normally will be enforced.

As you will read in later chapters, from time to time the NCCUSL revises the articles contained in the UCC and submits the revised versions to the states for adoption. During the 1990s, for example, four articles (Articles 3, 4, 5, and 9) were revised, and two new articles (Articles 2A and 4A) were added. Because of its importance in the area of commercial law, we cite the UCC frequently in this text. We also present excerpts of the UCC in Appendix C. (For a discussion of the creation of the UCC, see the *Landmark in the Law* feature in Chapter 15.)

Administrative Law

Another important source of American law is **administrative law,** which consists of the rules, orders, and decisions of administrative agencies. An **administrative agency** is a federal, state,

---

1. This institute was formed in the 1920s and consists of practicing attorneys, legal scholars, and judges.
2. Louisiana has adopted only Articles 1, 3, 4, 5, 7, 8, and 9.

CITATION
A reference to a publication in which a legal authority—such as a statute or a court decision—or other source can be found.

ORDINANCE
A regulation enacted by a city or county legislative body that becomes part of that state's statutory law.

ON THE WEB

To find state compilations (codes) of statutory laws, go to

findlaw.com/casecode/state.html.

UNIFORM LAW
A model law created by the National Conference of Commissioners on Uniform State Laws and/or the American Law Institute for the states to consider adopting. If the state adopts the law, it becomes statutory law in that state. Each state has the option of adopting or rejecting all or part of a uniform law.

ADMINISTRATIVE LAW
The body of law created by administrative agencies (in the form of rules, regulations, orders, and decisions) in order to carry out their duties and responsibilities.

ADMINISTRATIVE AGENCY
A federal or state government agency established to perform a specific function. Administrative agencies are authorized by legislative acts to make and enforce rules in order to administer and enforce the acts.

or local government agency established to perform a specific function. Rules issued by various administrative agencies now affect virtually every aspect of a business's operations, including the firm's capital structure and financing, its hiring and firing procedures, its relations with employees and unions, and the way it manufactures and markets its products.

Federal Agencies   At the national level, numerous **executive agencies** exist within the cabinet departments of the executive branch. For example, the Food and Drug Administration is within the U.S. Department of Health and Human Services. Executive agencies are subject to the authority of the president, who has the power to appoint and remove officers of federal agencies. There are also major **independent regulatory agencies** at the federal level, including the Federal Trade Commission, the Securities and Exchange Commission, and the Federal Communications Commission. The president's power is less pronounced in regard to independent agencies, whose officers serve for fixed terms and cannot be removed without just cause.

State and Local Agencies   There are administrative agencies at the state and local levels as well. Commonly, a state agency (such as a state pollution-control agency) is created as a parallel to a federal agency (such as the Environmental Protection Agency). Just as federal statutes take precedence over conflicting state statutes, so do federal agency regulations take precedence over conflicting state regulations. Because the rules of state and local agencies vary widely, we focus here exclusively on federal administrative law.

Agency Creation   Because Congress cannot possibly oversee the actual implementation of all the laws it enacts, it must delegate such tasks to others, especially when the legislation involves highly technical matters, such as air and water pollution. Congress creates an administrative agency by enacting **enabling legislation,** which specifies the name, composition, purpose, and powers of the agency being created.

   ■EXAMPLE 1.2   The Federal Trade Commission (FTC) was created in 1914 by the Federal Trade Commission Act.[3] This act prohibits unfair and deceptive trade practices. It also describes the procedures the agency must follow to charge persons or organizations with violations of the act, and it provides for judicial review (review by the courts) of agency orders. Other portions of the act grant the agency powers to "make rules and regulations for the purpose of carrying out the Act," to conduct investigations of business practices, to obtain reports from interstate corporations concerning their business practices, to investigate possible violations of the act, to publish findings of its investigations, and to recommend new legislation. The act also empowers the FTC to hold trial-like hearings and to **adjudicate** (resolve judicially) certain kinds of disputes that involve FTC regulations. **■**

   Note that the powers granted to the FTC incorporate functions associated with the legislative branch of government (rulemaking), the executive branch (investigation and enforcement), and the judicial branch (adjudication). Taken together, these functions constitute **administrative process,** which is the administration of law by administrative agencies.

Rulemaking   One of the major functions of an administrative agency is **rulemaking**—creating or modifying rules, or regulations, pursuant to its enabling legislation. The Administrative Procedure Act of 1946[4] imposes strict procedural requirements that agencies must follow in their rulemaking and other functions.

EXECUTIVE AGENCY
An administrative agency within the executive branch of government. At the federal level, executive agencies are those within the cabinet departments.

INDEPENDENT REGULATORY AGENCY
An administrative agency that is not considered part of the government's executive branch and is not subject to the authority of the president. Independent agency officials cannot be removed without cause.

ENABLING LEGISLATION
A statute enacted by Congress that authorizes the creation of an administrative agency and specifies the name, composition, purpose, and powers of the agency being created.

ADJUDICATE
To render a judicial decision. In the administrative process, adjudication is the trial-like proceeding in which an administrative law judge hears and decides issues that arise when an administrative agency charges a person or a firm with violating a law or regulation enforced by the agency.

ADMINISTRATIVE PROCESS
The procedure used by administrative agencies in the administration of law.

RULEMAKING
The process undertaken by an administrative agency when formally adopting a new regulation or amending an old one. Rulemaking involves notifying the public of a proposed rule or change and receiving and considering the public's comments.

---

3. 15 U.S.C. Sections 45–58.
4. 5 U.S.C. Sections 551–706.

The most common rulemaking procedure involves three steps. First, the agency must give public notice of the proposed rulemaking proceedings, where and when the proceedings will be held, the agency's legal authority for the proceedings, and the terms or subject matter of the proposed rule. The notice must be published in the *Federal Register*, a daily publication of the U.S. government. Second, following this notice, the agency must allow ample time for interested parties to comment in writing on the proposed rule. After the comments have been received and reviewed, the agency takes them into consideration when drafting the final version of the regulation. The third and last step is the drafting of the final rule and its publication in the *Federal Register*. (See the appendix at the end of this chapter for an explanation of how to find agency regulations.)

ON THE WEB

You can find proposed and final rules issued by administrative agencies by accessing the *Federal Register* online at www.gpoaccess.gov/fr/index.html.

Investigation and Enforcement   Agencies have both investigatory and prosecutorial powers. An agency can request that individuals or organizations hand over specified books, papers, electronic records, or other documents. In addition, agencies may conduct on-site inspections, although a search warrant is normally required for such inspections. Sometimes, a search of a home, an office, or a factory is the only means of obtaining evidence needed to prove a regulatory violation. Agencies investigate a wide range of activities, including coal mining, automobile manufacturing, and the industrial discharge of pollutants into the environment.

After conducting its own investigation of a suspected rule violation, an agency may decide to take action against an individual or a business. Most administrative actions are resolved through negotiated settlement at their initial stages without the need for formal adjudication. If a settlement cannot be reached, though, the agency may issue a formal complaint and proceed to adjudication.

Adjudication   Agency adjudication involves a trial-like hearing before an **administrative law judge (ALJ).** Hearing procedures vary widely from agency to agency. After the hearing, the ALJ renders a decision in the case. The ALJ can compel the charged party to pay a fine or can prohibit the party from carrying on some specified activity. Either side may appeal the ALJ's decision to the commission or board that governs the agency. If the party fails to get relief there, appeal can be made to a federal court. If no party appeals the case, the ALJ's decision becomes final.

ADMINISTRATIVE LAW JUDGE (ALJ)
One who presides over an administrative agency hearing and has the power to administer oaths, take testimony, rule on questions of evidence, and make determinations of fact.

Do administrative agencies exercise too much authority? Administrative agencies, such as the FTC, combine functions normally divided among the three branches of government in a single governmental entity. The broad range of authority that agencies exercise sometimes poses questions of fairness. After all, agencies create rules that are as legally binding as the laws passed by Congress—the only federal government institution authorized by the Constitution to make laws. To be sure, arbitrary rulemaking by agencies is checked by the procedural requirements set forth in the Administrative Procedure Act (APA), as well as by the courts, to which agency decisions may be appealed. Yet some people claim that these checks are not enough.

ETHICAL ISSUE 1.1

Consider that in addition to *legislative rules,* which are subject to the procedural requirements of the APA, agencies also create *interpretive rules*—rules that specify how the agency will interpret and apply its regulations. The APA does not apply to interpretive rulemaking. Moreover, although a firm that challenges an agency's rule may appeal the agency's decision in the matter to a court, the courts generally defer to agency rules, including interpretive rules, and to agency decisions.

Case Law and Common Law Doctrines

The rules of law announced in court decisions constitute another basic source of American law. These rules of law include interpretations of constitutional provisions, of statutes enacted by legislatures, and of regulations created by administrative agencies. Today, this body of judge-made law is referred to as **case law.** Case law—the doctrines and principles announced in cases—governs all areas not covered by statutory law or administrative law and is part of our common law tradition. We look at the origins and characteristics of the common law tradition in some detail in the pages that follow.

THE COMMON LAW TRADITION

Because of our colonial heritage, much of American law is based on the English legal system. A knowledge of this tradition is crucial to understanding our legal system today because judges in the United States still apply common law principles when deciding cases.

Early English Courts

After the Normans conquered England in 1066, William the Conqueror and his successors began the process of unifying the country under their rule. One of the means they used to do this was the establishment of the king's courts, or *curiae regis.* Before the Norman Conquest, disputes had been settled according to the local legal customs and traditions in various regions of the country. The king's courts sought to establish a uniform set of rules for the country as a whole. What evolved in these courts was the beginning of the **common law**—a body of general rules that applied throughout the entire English realm. Eventually, the common law tradition became part of the heritage of all nations that were once British colonies, including the United States.

Courts developed the common law rules from the principles underlying judges' decisions in actual legal controversies. Judges attempted to be consistent, and whenever possible, they based their decisions on the principles suggested by earlier cases. They sought to decide similar cases in a similar way and considered new cases with care, because they knew that their decisions would make new law. Each interpretation became part of the law on the subject and served as a legal **precedent**—that is, a decision that furnished an example or authority for deciding subsequent cases involving similar legal principles or facts.

In the early years of the common law, there was no single place or publication where court opinions, or written decisions, could be found. Beginning in the late thirteenth and early fourteenth centuries, however, each year portions of significant decisions of that year were gathered together and recorded in *Year Books.* The *Year Books* were useful references for lawyers and judges. In the sixteenth century, the *Year Books* were discontinued, and other reports of cases became available. (See the appendix to this chapter for a discussion of how cases are reported, or published, in the United States today.)

Stare Decisis

The practice of deciding new cases with reference to former decisions, or precedents, eventually became a cornerstone of the English and U.S. judicial systems. The practice forms a doctrine called ***stare decisis***[5] ("to stand on decided cases").

The court of chancery in the reign of King George I. Early English court decisions formed the basis of what type of law? (From a painting by Benjamin Ferrers in the National Portrait Gallery/Photo by Corbis Bettmann)

CASE LAW
  The rules of law announced in court decisions. Case law includes the aggregate of reported cases that interpret judicial precedents, statutes, regulations, and constitutional provisions.

COMMON LAW
  The body of law developed from custom or judicial decisions in English and U.S. courts, not attributable to a legislature.

PRECEDENT
  A court decision that furnishes an example or authority for deciding subsequent cases involving identical or similar facts.

STARE DECISIS
  A common law doctrine under which judges are obligated to follow the precedents established in prior decisions.

---

5. Pronounced *stahr*-ee dih-*si*-sis.

The Importance of Precedents in Judicial Decision Making Under the doctrine of *stare decisis*, once a court has set forth a principle of law as being applicable to a certain set of facts, that court and courts of lower rank must adhere to that principle and apply it in future cases involving similar fact patterns. *Stare decisis* has two aspects: first, that decisions made by a higher court are binding on lower courts; and second, that a court should not overturn its own precedents unless there is a strong reason to do so.

Controlling precedents in a *jurisdiction* (an area in which a court or courts have the power to apply the law—see Chapter 3) are referred to as binding authorities. A **binding authority** is any source of law that a court must follow when deciding a case. Binding authorities include constitutions, statutes, and regulations that govern the issue being decided, as well as court decisions that are controlling precedents within the jurisdiction. United States Supreme Court case decisions, no matter how old, remain controlling until they are overruled by a subsequent decision of the Supreme Court, by a constitutional amendment, or by congressional legislation.

Stare Decisis **and Legal Stability** The doctrine of *stare decisis* helps the courts to be more efficient because if other courts have carefully reasoned through a similar case, their legal reasoning and opinions can serve as guides. *Stare decisis* also makes the law more stable and predictable. If the law on a given subject is well settled, someone bringing a case to court can usually rely on the court to make a decision based on what the law has been.

Departures from Precedent Although courts are obligated to follow precedents, sometimes a court will depart from the rule of precedent if it decides that a given precedent should no longer be followed. If a court decides that a precedent is simply incorrect or that technological or social changes have rendered the precedent inapplicable, the court might rule contrary to the precedent. Cases that overturn precedent often receive a great deal of publicity.

■EXAMPLE 1.3 In *Brown v. Board of Education of Topeka*,[6] the United States Supreme Court expressly overturned precedent when it concluded that separate educational facilities for whites and blacks, which had been upheld as constitutional in numerous previous cases,[7] were inherently unequal. The Supreme Court's departure from precedent in *Brown* received a tremendous amount of publicity as people began to realize the ramifications of this change in the law. ■

When There Is No Precedent At times, a court hears a case for which there are no precedents within its jurisdiction on which to base its decision. When hearing such cases, called "cases of first impression," courts often look at precedents established in other jurisdictions for guidance. Precedents from other jurisdictions, because they are not binding on the court, are referred to as **persuasive authorities.** A court may also consider various other factors, including legal principles and policies underlying previous court decisions or existing statutes, fairness, social values and customs, public policy, and data and concepts drawn from the social sciences.

Can a court consider unpublished decisions as persuasive precedent? See this chapter's *Adapting the Law to the Online Environment* feature on the following pages for a discussion of this issue.

In a 1954 photo, Nettie Hunt sits on the steps of the United States Supreme Court building with her daughter after the Court's landmark ruling in Brown v. Board of Education of Topeka. (Library of Congress, Prints & Photographs Division/*U.S. News & World Report* Magazine Collection)

BINDING AUTHORITY
Any source of law that a court must follow when deciding a case. Binding authorities include constitutions, statutes, and regulations that govern the issue being decided, as well as court decisions that are controlling precedents within the jurisdiction.

ON THE WEB

To learn how the Supreme Court justified its departure from precedent in the 1954 *Brown* decision, you can access the Court's opinion online by going to **findlaw.com/casecode/supreme.html**, entering "347" and "483" in the boxes below the "Citation Search" heading, and clicking on "get it."

PERSUASIVE AUTHORITY
Any legal authority or source of law that a court may look to for guidance but on which it need not rely in making its decision. Persuasive authorities include cases from other jurisdictions and secondary sources of law.

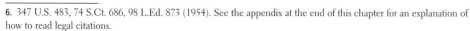

6. 347 U.S. 483, 74 S.Ct. 686, 98 L.Ed. 873 (1954). See the appendix at the end of this chapter for an explanation of how to read legal citations.
7. See *Plessy v. Ferguson*, 163 U.S. 537, 16 S.Ct. 1138, 41 L.Ed. 256 (1896).

ADAPTING THE LAW TO THE ONLINE ENVIRONMENT

How the Internet Is Expanding Precedent

The notion that courts should rely on precedents to decide the outcome of similar cases has long been a cornerstone of U.S. law. But what precisely is *precedent?* Today, the availability of "unpublished opinions" over the Internet is changing what the law considers to be precedent. An *unpublished opinion* is a decision issued by an appellate court that is not intended for publication in a reporter (the bound books that contain court opinions).[a] Courts traditionally have not considered unpublished opinions to be "precedents," binding or persuasive, and often have not allowed attorneys to refer to these decisions in their arguments.

Even though certain decisions are not intended for publication, they are posted ("published") almost immediately on online legal databases, such as Westlaw and Lexis. Moreover, with the proliferation of free legal databases and court Web sites, the general public also has almost instant access to the unpublished decisions of most courts. This has caused considerable debate during the last few years over whether unpublished opinions should be given the same precedential effect as published opinions. Some have even argued that

categorizing some decisions as not establishing precedent is unconstitutional.[b]

What Is the Difference between Published and Unpublished Opinions?

In recent years, the number of court decisions not published in printed books has risen dramatically, causing many to wonder why some opinions are published and therefore precedential, whereas others are not. Commentators have suggested a number of reasons why so many decisions are not designated for publication. Some say it is because the courts are overloaded and judges do not have time to write detailed opinions in every case. Others say that because the cost of publishing is so high, judges must determine which decisions are significant enough to appear in official books. The unpublished cases are the ones that courts deem to be less important. Others say judges refrain from publishing the decisions in difficult cases and deem them nonprecedential because they do not wish to set a bad precedent.

Whatever the reason, most decisions made by today's courts are not printed in the case reporters. By some estimates, nearly 80 percent of the decisions issued by federal

a. Recently decided cases that are not yet published are also sometimes called *unpublished opinions,* but because these decisions will eventually be printed in reporters, we do not include them here.

b. See, for example, *Anastasoff v. United States,* 235 F.3d 1054 (2001), in which the U.S. Court of Appeals for the Eighth Circuit vacated its prior ruling that denying precedential effect to unpublished opinions was unconstitutional.

Equitable Remedies and Courts of Equity

REMEDY
The relief given to an innocent party to enforce a right or compensate for the violation of a right.

A **remedy** is the means given to a party to enforce a right or to compensate for the violation of a right. **■EXAMPLE 1.4** Suppose that Shem is injured because of Rowan's wrongdoing. A court may order Rowan to compensate Shem for the harm by paying Shem a certain amount. ■

In the early king's courts of England, the kinds of remedies that could be granted were severely restricted. If one person wronged another, the king's courts could award as compensation either money or property, including land. These courts became known as *courts of law,* and the remedies were called *remedies at law.* Even though this system introduced uniformity in the settling of disputes, when plaintiffs wanted a remedy other than economic compensation, the courts of law could do nothing, so "no remedy, no right."

Remedies in Equity   *Equity* refers to a branch of the law, founded in justice and fair dealing, that seeks to supply a fair and adequate remedy when no remedy is available at law. In medieval England, when individuals could not obtain an adequate remedy in a court of law, they petitioned the king for relief. Most of these petitions were decided by an adviser to the king called the *chancellor.* The chancellor was said to be the "keeper of the king's conscience." When the chancellor thought that the claim was a fair one, new

appellate courts are unpublished. The number is equally high in some state court systems. California's intermediate appellate courts, for example, publish only about 7 percent of their decisions. Given the situation, why should the courts not be able to consider prior rulings in unpublished decisions?

Should Unpublished Decisions Establish Precedent?

Prior to the Internet, one might have been able to justify not considering unpublished decisions as precedent on the grounds of fairness. How could lawyers know about unpublished decisions if they were not printed in the case reporters? Because only the wealthiest clients could afford to pay their attorneys to research unpublished decisions, treating them as precedent would have led to inequality in justice. Now that opinions are available with the click of a mouse, however, this justification is no longer valid.

A more significant argument against allowing unpublished decisions to be precedent has to do with who authors these opinions. Staff attorneys and law clerks frequently write unpublished opinions so that judges can spend more time shaping and editing the opinions intended for publication. Consequently, allowing unpublished decisions to establish precedent could result in bad precedents because the reasoning in these unpublished decisions may not be up to par. Others counter that if the decision is considered merely as persuasive precedent, judges who disagree with the reasoning are free to reject the conclusion.

The United States Supreme Court Changes Federal Rules on Unpublished Opinions after 2007

In spite of objections from several hundred judges and lawyers, the United States Supreme Court made history in 2006 when it announced that it would allow lawyers to refer to (cite) unpublished decisions in all federal courts. The new rule, Rule 32.1 of the Federal Rules of Appellate Procedure, states that federal courts may not prohibit or restrict the citation of federal judicial opinions that have been designated as "not for publication," "nonprecedential," or "not precedent." The rule applies only to federal courts and only to unpublished opinions issued after January 1, 2007. It does not specify what weight a court must give to its own unpublished opinions or to those from another court. Basically, Rule 32.1 simply establishes a uniform rule for all of the federal courts that allows attorneys to cite—and judges to consider as persuasive precedent—unpublished decisions as of 2007.

The impact of this new rule remains to be seen. At present, the majority of the states do not allow their state courts to consider unpublished cases as persuasive precedent, and this rule does not affect the states. The Supreme Court's decision, however, provides an example of how technology—the availability of unpublished opinions over the Internet—has affected the law.

 FOR CRITICAL ANALYSIS *Now that the Supreme Court is allowing unpublished decisions to be used as persuasive precedent in federal courts, should state courts follow? Why or why not?*

and unique remedies were granted. In this way, a new body of rules and remedies came into being, and eventually formal *chancery courts*, or *courts of equity*, were established. The remedies granted by these courts were called *remedies in equity*. Thus, two distinct court systems were created, each having its own set of judges and its own set of remedies.

Plaintiffs (those bringing lawsuits) had to specify whether they were bringing an "action at law" or an "action in equity," and they chose their courts accordingly. **EXAMPLE 1.5** A plaintiff might ask a court of equity to order a **defendant** (a person against whom a lawsuit is brought) to perform within the terms of a contract. A court of law could not issue such an order because its remedies were limited to payment of money or property as compensation for damages. A court of equity, however, could issue a decree for *specific performance*—an order to perform what was promised. A court of equity could also issue an *injunction*, directing a party to do or refrain from doing a particular act. In certain cases, a court of equity could allow for the *rescission* (cancellation) of the contract, thereby returning the parties to the positions that they held prior to the contract's formation. ■ Equitable remedies will be discussed in greater detail in Chapter 13.

PLAINTIFF
One who initiates a lawsuit.

DEFENDANT
One against whom a lawsuit is brought; the accused person in a criminal proceeding.

The Merging of Law and Equity Today, in most states, the courts of law and equity have merged, and thus the distinction between the two courts has largely disappeared. A plaintiff may now request both legal and equitable remedies in the same action, and the

REMEMBER Even though, in most states, courts of law and equity have merged, the principles of equity still apply.

EXHIBIT 1–2 Procedural Differences between an Action at Law and an Action in Equity		
PROCEDURE	ACTION AT LAW	ACTION IN EQUITY
Initiation of lawsuit	By filing a complaint	By filing a petition
Decision	By jury or judge	By judge (no jury)
Result	Judgment	Decree
Remedy	Monetary damages	Injunction, specific performance, or rescission

trial court judge may grant either form—or both forms—of relief. The merging of law and equity, however, does not diminish the importance of distinguishing legal remedies from equitable remedies. To request the proper remedy, a businessperson (or her or his attorney) must know what remedies are available for the specific kinds of harms suffered. Today, as a rule, courts will grant an equitable remedy only when the remedy at law (money damages) is inadequate. Exhibit 1–2 summarizes the procedural differences (applicable in most states) between an action at law and an action in equity.

Equitable Principles and Maxims   Over time, the courts have developed a number of **equitable principles and maxims** that provide guidance in deciding whether plaintiffs should be granted equitable relief. Because of their importance, both historically and in our judicial system today, these principles and maxims are set forth in this chapter's *Landmark in the Law* feature.

EQUITABLE PRINCIPLES AND MAXIMS
General propositions or principles of law that have to do with fairness (equity).

CLASSIFICATIONS OF LAW

The huge body of the law may be broken down according to several classification systems. For example, one classification system divides law into **substantive law** (all laws that define, describe, regulate, and create legal rights and obligations) and **procedural law** (all laws that establish the methods of enforcing the rights established by substantive law). Other classification systems divide law into federal law and state law or private law (dealing with relationships between persons) and public law (addressing the relationship between persons and their governments).

SUBSTANTIVE LAW
Law that defines, describes, regulates, and creates legal rights and obligations.

PROCEDURAL LAW
Law that establishes the methods of enforcing the rights established by substantive law.

CYBERLAW
An informal term used to refer to all laws governing electronic communications and transactions, particularly those conducted via the Internet.

Frequently, people use the term **cyberlaw** to refer to the emerging body of law that governs transactions conducted via the Internet. Cyberlaw is not really a classification of law, nor is it a new *type* of law. Rather, it is an informal term used to describe traditional legal principles that have been modified and adapted to fit situations that are unique to the online world. Of course, in some areas new statutes have been enacted, at both the federal and state levels, to cover specific types of problems stemming from online communications. Throughout this book, you will read how the law in a given area is evolving to govern specific legal issues that arise in the online context.

Civil Law and Criminal Law

CIVIL LAW
The branch of law dealing with the definition and enforcement of all private or public rights, as opposed to criminal matters.

Civil law spells out the rights and duties that exist between persons and between persons and their governments, and the relief available when a person's rights are violated. Typically, in a civil case, a private party sues another private party (although the government can also sue a party for a civil law violation) to make that other party comply with a duty or pay for the damage caused by the failure to comply with a duty. **EXAMPLE 1.6** If a seller fails to perform a contract with a buyer, the buyer may bring a lawsuit against the seller. The purpose of the lawsuit will be either to compel the seller to perform as

LANDMARK IN THE LAW — Equitable Principles and Maxims

In medieval England, courts of equity had the responsibility of using discretion in supplementing the common law. Even today, when the same court can award both legal and equitable remedies, it must exercise discretion. Courts often invoke equitable principles and maxims when making their decisions. Here are some of the most significant equitable principles and maxims:

1 *Whoever seeks equity must do equity.* (Anyone who wishes to be treated fairly must treat others fairly.)
2 *Where there is equal equity, the law must prevail.* (The law will determine the outcome of a controversy in which the merits of both sides are equal.)
3 *One seeking the aid of an equity court must come to the court with clean hands.* (Plaintiffs must have acted fairly and honestly.)
4 *Equity will not suffer a wrong to be without a remedy.* (Equitable relief will be awarded when there is a right to relief and there is no adequate remedy at law.)
5 *Equity regards substance rather than form.* (Equity is more concerned with fairness and justice than with legal technicalities.)
6 *Equity aids the vigilant, not those who rest on their rights.* (Equity will not help those who neglect their rights for an unreasonable period of time.)

The last maxim has become known as the *equitable doctrine of laches.* The doctrine arose to encourage people to bring lawsuits while the evidence was fresh; if they failed to do so, they would not be allowed to bring a lawsuit. What constitutes a reasonable time, of course, varies according to the circumstances of the case. Time periods for different types of cases are now usually fixed by **statutes of limitations.** After the time allowed under a statute of limitations has expired, no action can be brought, no matter how strong the case was originally.

STATUTE OF LIMITATIONS
A federal or state statute setting the maximum time period during which a certain action can be brought or certain rights enforced.

APPLICATION TO TODAY'S WORLD *The equitable maxims listed above underlie many of the legal rules and principles that are commonly applied by the courts today— and that you will read about in this book. For example, in Chapter 9 you will read about the* doctrine of promissory estoppel. *Under this doctrine, a person who has reasonably and substantially relied on the promise of another may be able to obtain some measure of recovery, even though no enforceable contract, or agreement, exists. The court will* estop *(bar, or impede) the one making the promise from asserting the lack of a valid contract as a defense. The rationale underlying the doctrine of promissory estoppel is similar to that expressed in the fourth and fifth maxims above.*

RELEVANT WEB SITES *To locate information on the Web concerning* equitable principles and maxims, *go to this text's Web site at* **www.thomsonedu.com/westbuslaw/blt**, *select "Chapter 1," and click on "URLs for Landmarks."*

BEYOND OUR BORDERS   National Law Systems

Despite their varying cultures and customs, virtually all countries have laws governing torts, contracts, employment, and other areas, just as the United States does. In part, this is because two types of legal systems predominate around the globe today. One is the common law system of England and the United States, which we have discussed elsewhere. The other system is based on Roman civil law, or "code law." The term *civil law*, as used here, refers not to civil as opposed to criminal law but to codified law—an ordered grouping of legal principles enacted into law by a legislature or governing body. In a *civil law system*, the primary source of law is a statutory code, and case precedents are not judicially binding, as they normally are in a common law system. Although judges in a civil law system commonly refer to previous decisions as sources of legal guidance, they are not bound by precedent; in other words, the doctrine of *stare decisis* does not apply.

A third, less prevalent, legal system is common in Islamic countries, where the law is often influenced by *sharia*, the religious law of Islam. *Sharia* is a comprehensive code of principles that governs both the public and private lives of Islamic persons, directing many aspects of day-to-day life, including politics, economics, banking, business law, contract law, and social issues. Although *sharia* affects the legal codes of many Muslim countries, the extent of its impact and its interpretation vary widely. In some Middle Eastern nations, aspects of *sharia* have been codified in modern legal codes and are enforced by national judicial systems.

The accompanying exhibit lists some countries that today follow either the common law system or the civil law system. Generally, those countries that were once colonies of Great Britain retained their English common law heritage after they achieved independence. Similarly, the civil law system, which is followed in most continental European nations, was retained in the Latin American, African, and Asian countries that were once colonies of those nations. Japan and South Africa also have civil law systems.

CIVIL LAW SYSTEM
A system of law derived from that of the Roman Empire and based on a code rather than case law; the predominant system of law in the nations of continental Europe and the nations that were once their colonies. In the United States, Louisiana, because of its historical ties to France, has in part a civil law system.

CRIMINAL LAW
Law that defines and governs actions that constitute crimes. Generally, criminal law has to do with wrongful actions committed against society for which society demands redress.

promised or, more commonly, to obtain money damages for the seller's failure to perform. ■

Much of the law that we discuss in this text is civil law. Contract law, for example, which we discuss in Chapters 8 through 14, is civil law. The whole body of tort law (see Chapter 4) is civil law. Note that *civil law* is not the same as a *civil law system*. As you will read shortly, a **civil law system** is a legal system based on a written code of laws.

Criminal law has to do with wrongs committed against society for which society demands redress. Criminal acts are proscribed by local, state, or federal government statutes. Thus, criminal defendants are prosecuted by public officials, such as a district attorney (D.A.), on behalf of the state, not by their victims or other private parties. Whereas in a civil case the object is to obtain remedies (such as money damages) to compensate the injured party, in a criminal case the object is to punish the wrongdoer in an attempt to deter others from similar actions. Penalties for violations of criminal statutes consist of fines and/or imprisonment—and, in some cases, death. We will discuss the differences between civil and criminal law in greater detail in Chapter 6.

National and International Law

Although the focus of this book is U.S. business law, increasingly businesspersons in this country engage in transactions that extend beyond our national borders. In these situa-

In the United States, the state of Louisiana, because of its historical ties to France, has in part a civil law system. The legal systems of Puerto Rico, Québec, and Scotland are similarly characterized as having elements of the civil law system.

Realize that although national law systems share many commonalities, they also have distinct differences. Even when the basic principles are fundamentally similar (as they are in contract law, for example), significant variations exist in the practical application and effect of these laws across countries. Therefore, those persons who plan to do business in another nation would be wise to become familiar with the laws of that nation.

 FOR CRITICAL ANALYSIS *Does the civil law system offer any advantages over the common law system, or vice versa? Explain.*

THE LEGAL SYSTEMS OF SELECTED NATIONS			
CIVIL LAW		**COMMON LAW**	
Argentina	Indonesia	Australia	Nigeria
Austria	Iran	Bangladesh	Singapore
Brazil	Italy	Canada	United Kingdom
Chile	Japan	Ghana	United States
China	Mexico	India	Zambia
Egypt	Poland	Israel	
Finland	South Korea	Jamaica	
France	Sweden	Kenya	
Germany	Tunisia	Malaysia	
Greece	Venezuela	New Zealand	

ON THE WEB
The Library of Congress offers extensive information on national and international law at www.loc.gov.

tions, the laws of other nations or the laws governing relationships among nations may come into play. For this reason, those who pursue a career in business today should have an understanding of the global legal environment.

National Law   The law of a particular nation, such as the United States or Sweden, is **national law**. National law, of course, varies from country to country because each country's law reflects the interests, customs, activities, and values that are unique to that nation's culture. Even though the laws and legal systems of various countries differ substantially, broad similarities do exist, as discussed in this chapter's *Beyond Our Borders* feature.

International Law   In contrast to national law, international law applies to more than one nation. **International law** can be defined as a body of written and unwritten laws observed by independent nations and governing the acts of individuals as well as governments. International law is an intermingling of rules and constraints derived from a variety of sources, including the laws of individual nations, the customs that have evolved among nations in their relations with one another, and treaties and international organizations. In essence, international law is the result of centuries-old attempts to reconcile the traditional need of each nation to be the final authority over its own affairs with the desire of nations to benefit economically from trade and harmonious relations with one another.

NATIONAL LAW
Law that pertains to a particular nation (as opposed to international law).

INTERNATIONAL LAW
The law that governs relations among nations. National laws, customs, treaties, and international conferences and organizations are generally considered to be the most important sources of international law.

The key difference between national law and international law is that government authorities can enforce national law. If a nation violates an international law, however, the most that other countries or international organizations can do (if persuasive tactics fail) is to resort to coercive actions against the violating nation. Coercive actions range from the severance of diplomatic relations and boycotts to, as a last resort, war. We examine the laws governing international business transactions in later chapters (including parts of Chapters 15 through 18, which cover contracts for the sale of goods, and all of Chapter 39).

REVIEWING The Legal Environment

Suppose the California legislature passes a law that severely restricts carbon dioxide emissions from automobiles in that state. A group of automobile manufacturers file suit against the state of California to prevent the enforcement of the law. The automakers claim that a federal law already sets fuel economy standards nationwide and that these standards are essentially the same as carbon dioxide emission standards. According to the automobile manufacturers, it is unfair to allow California to impose more stringent regulations than those set by the federal law. Using the information presented in the chapter, answer the following questions.

1 Who are the parties (the plaintiffs and the defendant) in this lawsuit?

2 Are the plaintiffs seeking a legal remedy or an equitable remedy? Why?

3 What is the primary source of the law that is at issue here?

4 Read through the appendix that follows this chapter, and then answer the following question: Where would you look to find the relevant California and federal laws?

APPLICATION How Can You Choose and Use a Lawyer?

If you are contemplating a career in the business world, sooner or later you will probably face the question, "Do I need a lawyer?" The answer will likely be "Yes," at least at some time during your career. Today, it is virtually impossible for nonexperts to keep up with the myriad rules and regulations that govern the conduct of business in the United States. It is also increasingly possible for businesspersons to incur penalties for violating laws or regulations of which they are totally unaware.

Although lawyers may seem expensive—anywhere from $100 to $500 or more per hour—cautious businesspersons will make sure that they are not "penny wise and pound foolish." The consultation fee paid to an attorney can be insignificant compared with the potential liability facing a businessperson. Obtaining competent legal advice *before* a dispute arises may enable a busi-

nessperson to avoid potentially costly mistakes. Also, keep in mind that sometimes higher-priced attorneys from larger firms may be worth the extra expense because they may have more clout in the local legal community to wield on your behalf.

Selecting an Attorney

In selecting an attorney, you can ask friends, relatives, or business associates to recommend someone. Alternatively, you can call the local or state bar association to obtain the names of several lawyers or check the Yellow Pages in your local telephone directory for listings. West Group has an online database containing biographies of attorneys throughout the country, listed by area of specialty and by state. You can find attorneys in your area by accessing West's Legal Directory online at **directory.findlaw.com**. You might also investigate legal clinics and prepaid legal service plans.

For your initial meeting with an attorney you are considering hiring, prepare a written list of your questions and a brief summary of the problem for which you need legal advice. Also, bring copies of any relevant documents that the lawyer might need to see. While at the meeting, ask about legal fees, discuss the legal problem you are facing (or anticipate facing), and clarify the scope of what you want the lawyer to do for you. Remember that virtually everything you say at this meeting is protected by the attorney-client privilege of confidentiality.

Evaluating Your Attorney

Before hiring the attorney, ask yourself the following questions after your first meeting: Did the attorney seem knowledgeable about what is needed to address your concerns? Did he or she seem willing to investigate the law and the facts further to ensure an accurate understanding of your legal situation? Did you communicate well with each other? Did the attorney perceive what issues were of foremost concern to you and address those issues to your satisfaction? Did the attorney "speak your language" when explaining the legal implications of those issues?

Even after you hire the attorney, continue to evaluate the relationship over time. For many businesspersons, relationships with attorneys last for decades. Make sure that your relationship with your attorney will be a fruitful one.

CHECKLIST FOR CHOOSING AND USING A LAWYER

1 If you ever think that you need legal advice, you probably do.
2 When choosing an attorney, try to get recommendations from friends, relatives, or business associates who have had long-standing relationships with their attorneys. If that fails, check with your local or state bar association, West Group's online directory, or the Yellow Pages.
3 When you initially consult with an attorney, bring a written list of questions to which you want answers, perhaps a summary of your problem, and copies of relevant documents.
4 Do not hesitate to ask about the legal fees that your attorney will charge, and be sure to clarify the scope of the work to be undertaken by the attorney. Ask any and all questions that you feel are necessary to ensure that you understand your legal options.

KEY TERMS

adjudicate 8
administrative agency 7
administrative law 7
administrative law judge (ALJ) 9
administrative process 8
binding authority 11
breach 4
case law 10
citation 7
civil law 14
civil law system 16
common law 10
constitutional law 6
criminal law 16
cyberlaw 14

defendant 13
enabling legislation 8
equitable principles and maxims 14
executive agency 8
historical school 3
independent regulatory agency 8
international law 17
jurisprudence 3
law 2
legal positivism 3
legal realism 4
national law 17
natural law 3
ordinance 7

persuasive authority 11
plaintiff 13
positive law 3
precedent 10
primary source of law 6
procedural law 14
remedy 12
rulemaking 8
secondary source of law 6
sociological school 4
stare decisis 10
statute of limitations 15
statutory law 6
substantive law 14
uniform law 7

CHAPTER SUMMARY — The Legal Environment

The Nature of Law (See pages 2–4.)	Law can be defined as a body of enforceable rules governing relationships among individuals and between individuals and their society. Four important schools of legal thought, or legal philosophies, are the following: 1. *Natural law tradition*—One of the oldest and most significant schools of legal thought. Those who believe in natural law hold that there is a universal law applicable to all human beings and that this law is of a higher order than positive, or conventional, law.

(Continued)

CHAPTER SUMMARY   The Legal Environment—Continued

The Nature of Law—Continued	2. *Legal positivism*—A school of legal thought centered on the assumption that there is no law higher than the laws created by the government. Laws must be obeyed, even if they are unjust, to prevent anarchy.
	3. *Historical school*—A school of legal thought that stresses the evolutionary nature of law and looks to doctrines that have withstood the passage of time for guidance in shaping present laws.
	4. *Legal realism*—A school of legal thought, popular during the 1920s and 1930s, that left a lasting imprint on American jurisprudence. Legal realists generally advocated a less abstract and more realistic approach to the law, an approach that would take into account customary practices and the circumstances in which transactions take place.
Sources of American Law (See pages 6–10.)	1. *Constitutional law*—The law as expressed in the U.S. Constitution and the various state constitutions. The U.S. Constitution is the supreme law of the land. State constitutions are supreme within state borders to the extent that they do not violate the U.S. Constitution or a federal law.
	2. *Statutory law*—Laws or ordinances created by federal, state, and local legislatures and governing bodies. None of these laws can violate the U.S. Constitution or the relevant state constitutions. Uniform laws, when adopted by a state legislature, become statutory law in that state.
	3. *Administrative law*—The rules, orders, and decisions of federal or state government administrative agencies. Federal administrative agencies are created by enabling legislation enacted by the U.S. Congress. Agency functions include rulemaking, investigation and enforcement, and adjudication.
	4. *Case law and common law doctrines*—Judge-made law, including interpretations of constitutional provisions, of statutes enacted by legislatures, and of regulations created by administrative agencies. The common law—the doctrines and principles embodied in case law—governs all areas not covered by statutory law (or agency regulations issued to implement various statutes).
The Common Law Tradition (See pages 10–14.)	1. *Common law*—Law that originated in medieval England with the creation of the king's courts, or *curiae regis,* and the development of a body of rules that were common to (or applied throughout) the land.
	2. *Stare decisis*—A doctrine under which judges "stand on decided cases"—or follow the rule of precedent—in deciding cases. *Stare decisis* is the cornerstone of the common law tradition.
	3. *Remedies—*
	a. Remedies at law—Money or something else of value.
	b. Remedies in equity—Remedies that are granted when the remedies at law are unavailable or inadequate. Equitable remedies include specific performance, an injunction, and contract rescission (cancellation).
Classifications of Law (See pages 14–18.)	The law may be broken down according to several classification systems, such as substantive or procedural law, federal or state law, and private or public law. Two broad classifications are civil and criminal law, and national and international law. Cyberlaw is not really a classification of law but a term that is used for the growing body of case law and statutory law that applies to Internet transactions.

FOR REVIEW

Answers for the even-numbered questions in this **For Review** *section can be found in Appendix E at the end of this text.*

1 What is the Uniform Commercial Code?

2 What is the common law tradition?

3 What is a precedent? When might a court depart from precedent?

4 What is the difference between remedies at law and remedies in equity?

5 What are some important differences between civil law and criminal law?

 The following multiple-choice question is representative of the types of questions available in one of the four sections of ThomsonNOW for *Business Law Today*. ThomsonNOW also provides feedback for each response option, whether correct or incorrect, and refers to the location within the chapter where the correct answer can be found.

Civil law can best be described as

a the law that governs relations between persons and between persons and the government.

b the common law of taxes.

c federal, not state, law.

d the law governing the relations among nations.

QUESTIONS AND CASE PROBLEMS

HYPOTHETICAL SCENARIOS

1.1 Binding versus Persuasive Authority. A county court in Illinois is deciding a case involving an issue that has never been addressed before in that state's courts. The Iowa Supreme Court, however, recently decided a case involving a very similar fact pattern. Is the Illinois court obligated to follow the Iowa Supreme Court's decision on the issue? If the United States Supreme Court had decided a similar case, would that decision be binding on the Illinois court? Explain.

1.2 Remedies. Arthur Rabe is suing Xavier Sanchez for breaching a contract in which Sanchez promised to sell Rabe a Van Gogh painting for $150,000.

1 In this lawsuit, who is the plaintiff, and who is the defendant?

2 If Rabe wants Sanchez to perform the contract as promised, what remedy should Rabe seek?

3 Suppose that Rabe wants to cancel the contract because Sanchez fraudulently misrepresented the painting as an original Van Gogh when in fact it is a copy. In this situation, what remedy should Rabe seek?

4 Will the remedy Rabe seeks in either situation be a remedy at law or a remedy in equity?

5 Suppose that the court finds in Rabe's favor and grants one of these remedies. Sanchez then appeals the decision to a higher court. Read through the subsection entitled "Appellants and Appellees" in the appendix following this chapter. On appeal, which party in the Rabe-Sanchez case will be the appellant (or petitioner), and which party will be the appellee (or respondent)?

1.3 Legal Systems. What are the key differences between a common law system and a civil law system? Why do some countries have common law systems and others have civil law systems?

1.4 Hypothetical Question with Sample Answer. This chapter discussed a number of sources of American law. Which source of law takes priority in each of the following situations, and why?

1 A federal statute conflicts with the U.S. Constitution.

2 A federal statute conflicts with a state constitution.

3 A state statute conflicts with the common law of that state.

4 A state constitutional amendment conflicts with the U.S. Constitution.

5 A federal administrative regulation conflicts with a state constitution.

For a sample answer to Question 1.4, go to Appendix F at the end of this text.

1.5 Philosophy of Law. After World War II ended in 1945, an international tribunal of judges convened at Nuremberg, Germany. The judges convicted several Nazi war criminals of "crimes against humanity." Assuming that the Nazis who were convicted had not disobeyed any law of their country and had merely been following their government's (Hitler's) orders, what law had they violated? Explain.

1.6 Reading Citations. Assume that you want to read the court's entire opinion in the case of *Menashe v. V Secret Catalogue, Inc.*, 409 F.Supp.2d 412 (S.D.N.Y. 2006). The case focuses on whether "SEXY LITTLE THINGS" is a suggestive or descriptive trademark and which of the parties to the suit used the mark first in commerce. (Note that this case is presented in Chapter 5 of this text as Case 5.2.) Read the section entitled "Finding Case Law" in the appendix that follows this chapter, and then explain specifically where you would find the court's opinion.

1.7 *Stare Decisis.* In the text of this chapter, we stated that the doctrine of *stare decisis* "became a cornerstone of the English and U.S. judicial systems." What does *stare decisis* mean, and why has this doctrine been so fundamental to the development of our legal tradition?

1.8 **Court Opinions.** Read through the subsection entitled "Case Titles and Terminology" in the appendix following this chapter. What is the difference between a concurring opinion and a majority opinion? Between a concurring opinion and a dissenting opinion? Why do judges and justices write concurring and dissenting opinions, given that these opinions will not affect the outcome of the case at hand, which has already been decided by majority vote?

1.9 **A Question of Ethics.** On July 5, 1884, Dudley, Stephens, and Brooks—"all able-bodied English seamen"—and a teenage English boy were cast adrift in a lifeboat following a storm at sea. They had no water with them in the boat, and all they had for sustenance were two one-pound tins of turnips. On

July 24, Dudley proposed that one of the four in the lifeboat be sacrificed to save the others. Stephens agreed with Dudley, but Brooks refused to consent—and the boy was never asked for his opinion. On July 25, Dudley killed the boy, and the three men then fed on the boy's body and blood. Four days later, the men were rescued by a passing vessel. They were taken to England and tried for the murder of the boy. If the men had not fed on the boy's body, they would probably have died of starvation within the four-day period. The boy, who was in a much weaker condition, would likely have died before the rest. [Regina v. Dudley and Stephens, 14 Q.B.D. (Queen's Bench Division, England) 273 (1884)]

1 The basic question in this case is whether the survivors should be subject to penalties under English criminal law, given the men's unusual circumstances. You be the judge, and decide the issue. Give the reasons for your decision.

2 Should judges ever have the power to look beyond the written "letter of the law" in making their decisions? Why or why not?

CRITICAL THINKING
AND WRITING ASSIGNMENTS

1.10 **Critical Legal Thinking.** Courts of equity tend to follow general rules or maxims rather than following common law precedents, as courts of law do. Some of these maxims were listed in this chapter's *Landmark in the Law* feature on page 15. Why do equity courts give credence to such general maxims rather than to a hard-and-fast body of law?

1.11 **Critical Thinking and Writing Assignment for Business.** John's company is involved in a lawsuit with a customer, Beth. John

argues that for fifty years, in cases involving circumstances similar to this case, judges have ruled in a way that indicates that the judge in this case should rule in favor of John's company. Is this a valid argument? If so, must the judge in this case rule as those other judges have? What argument could Beth use to counter John's reasoning?

ONLINE ACTIVITIES

PRACTICAL
INTERNET EXERCISES

Go to this text's Web site at **www.thomsonedu.com/westbuslaw/blt**, select "Chapter 1," and click on "Practical Internet Exercises." There you will find the following Internet research exercises that you can perform to learn more about the topics covered in this chapter.

PRACTICAL INTERNET EXERCISE 1-1 LEGAL PERSPECTIVE—Internet Sources of Law

PRACTICAL INTERNET EXERCISE 1-2 MANAGEMENT PERSPECTIVE—Online Assistance from Government Agencies

BEFORE THE TEST

Go to this text's Web site at **www.thomsonedu.com/westbuslaw/blt**, select "Chapter 1," and click on "Interactive Quizzes." You will find a number of interactive questions relating to this chapter.

APPENDIX TO CHAPTER 1

The statutes, agency regulations, and case law referred to in this text establish the rights and duties of businesspersons engaged in various types of activities. The cases presented in the following chapters provide you with concise, real-life illustrations of how the courts interpret and apply these laws. Because of the importance of knowing how to find statutory, administrative, and case law, this appendix offers a brief introduction to how these laws are published and to the legal "shorthand" employed in referencing these legal sources.

FINDING STATUTORY AND ADMINISTRATIVE LAW

When Congress passes laws, they are collected in a publication titled *United States Statutes at Large*. When state legislatures pass laws, they are collected in similar state publications. Most frequently, however, laws are referred to in their codified form—that is, the form in which they appear in the federal and state codes. In these codes, laws are compiled by subject.

United States Code

The *United States Code* (U.S.C.) arranges all existing federal laws of a public and permanent nature by subject. Each of the fifty subjects into which the U.S.C. arranges the laws is given a title and a title number. For example, laws relating to commerce and trade are collected in "Title 15, Commerce and Trade." Titles are subdivided by sections. A citation to the U.S.C. includes title and section numbers. Thus, a reference to "15 U.S.C. Section 1" means that the statute can be found in Section 1 of Title 15. ("Section" may also be designated by the symbol §, and "Sections" by §§.)

Sometimes a citation includes the abbreviation *et seq.*—as in "15 U.S.C. Sections 1 *et seq.*" The term is an abbreviated form of *et sequitur*, which is Latin for "and the following"; when used in a citation, it refers to sections that concern the same subject as the numbered section and follow it in sequence.

Commercial publications of these laws and regulations are available and are widely used. For example, West Group publishes the *United States Code Annotated* (U.S.C.A.). The U.S.C.A. contains the complete text of laws included in the U.S.C., notes of court decisions that interpret and apply specific sections of the statutes, and the text of presidential proclamations and executive orders. The U.S.C.A. also includes research aids, such as cross-references to related statutes, historical notes, and library references. A citation to the U.S.C.A. is similar to a citation to the U.S.C.: "15 U.S.C.A. Section 1."

State Codes

State codes follow the U.S.C. pattern of arranging law by subject. The state codes may be called codes, revisions, compilations, consolidations, general statutes, or statutes, depending on the preferences of the states. In some codes, subjects are designated by number. In others, they are designated by name. For example, "13 Pennsylvania Consolidated Statutes Section 1101" means that the statute can be found in Title 13, Section 1101, of the Pennsylvania code. "California Commercial Code Section 1101" means the statute

ON THE WEB

You can search the *United States Code* online at **www.law.cornell.edu/uscode**.

can be found in Section 1101 under the subject heading "Commercial Code" of the California code. Abbreviations may be used. For example, "13 Pennsylvania Consolidated Statutes Section 1101" may be abbreviated "13 Pa. C.S. § 1101," and "California Commercial Code Section 1101" may be abbreviated "Cal. Com. Code § 1101."

Administrative Rules

Rules and regulations adopted by federal administrative agencies are compiled in the *Code of Federal Regulations* (C.F.R.). Like the U.S.C., the C.F.R. is divided into fifty titles. Rules within each title are assigned section numbers. A full citation to the C.F.R. includes title and section numbers. For example, a reference to "17 C.F.R. Section 230.504" means that the rule can be found in Section 230.504 of Title 17.

FINDING CASE LAW

Before discussing the case reporting system, we need to look briefly at the court system (which will be discussed in detail in Chapter 3). There are two types of courts in the United States, federal courts and state courts. Both the federal and state court systems consist of several levels, or tiers, of courts. *Trial courts*, in which evidence is presented and testimony given, are on the bottom tier (which also includes lower courts handling specialized issues). Decisions from a trial court can be appealed to a higher court, which commonly would be an intermediate *court of appeals*, or an *appellate court*. Decisions from these intermediate courts of appeals may be appealed to an even higher court, such as a state supreme court or the United States Supreme Court.

State Court Decisions

Most state trial court decisions are not published. Except in New York and a few other states that publish selected opinions of their trial courts, decisions from state trial courts are merely filed in the office of the clerk of the court, where the decisions are available for public inspection. (Sometimes, they can be found online as well.) Written decisions of the appellate, or reviewing, courts, however, are published and distributed. As you will note, most of the state court cases presented in this book are from state appellate courts. The reported appellate decisions are published in volumes called *reports* or *reporters*, which are numbered consecutively. State appellate court decisions are found in the state reporters of that particular state.

Additionally, state court opinions appear in regional units of the *National Reporter System*, published by West Group. Most lawyers and libraries have the West reporters because they report cases more quickly and are distributed more widely than the state-published reports. In fact, many states have eliminated their own reporters in favor of West's National Reporter System. The National Reporter System divides the states into the following geographic areas: *Atlantic* (A. or A.2d), *North Eastern* (N.E. or N.E.2d), *North Western* (N.W. or N.W.2d), *Pacific* (P., P.2d, or P.3d), *South Eastern* (S.E. or S.E.2d), *South Western* (S.W., S.W.2d, or S.W.3d), and *Southern* (So. or So.2d). (The *2d* and *3d* in the abbreviations refer to *Second Series* and *Third Series*, respectively.) The states included in each of these regional divisions are indicated in Exhibit 1A–1, which illustrates West's National Reporter System.

After appellate decisions have been published, they are normally referred to (cited) by the name of the case; the volume, name, and page number of the state's official reporter (if different from West's National Reporter System); the volume, name, and page number of the *National Reporter*; and the volume, name, and page number of any other selected reporter. This information is included in the *citation*. (Citing a reporter by volume number,

EXHIBIT 1A–1 **West's National Reporter System—Regional/Federal**

Regional Reporters	Coverage Beginning	Coverage
Atlantic Reporter (A. or A.2d)	1885	Connecticut, Delaware, District of Columbia, Maine, Maryland, New Hampshire, New Jersey, Pennsylvania, Rhode Island, and Vermont.
North Eastern Reporter (N.E. or N.E.2d)	1885	Illinois, Indiana, Massachusetts, New York, and Ohio.
North Western Reporter (N.W. or N.W.2d)	1879	Iowa, Michigan, Minnesota, Nebraska, North Dakota, South Dakota, and Wisconsin.
Pacific Reporter (P., P.2d, or P.3d)	1883	Alaska, Arizona, California, Colorado, Hawaii, Idaho, Kansas, Montana, Nevada, New Mexico, Oklahoma, Oregon, Utah, Washington, and Wyoming.
South Eastern Reporter (S.E. or S.E.2d)	1887	Georgia, North Carolina, South Carolina, Virginia, and West Virginia.
South Western Reporter (S.W., S.W.2d, or S.W.3d)	1886	Arkansas, Kentucky, Missouri, Tennessee, and Texas.
Southern Reporter (So. or So.2d)	1887	Alabama, Florida, Louisiana, and Mississippi.

Federal Reporters

	Coverage Beginning	Coverage
Federal Reporter (F., F.2d, or F.3d)	1880	U.S. Circuit Courts from 1880 to 1912; U.S. Commerce Court from 1911 to 1913; U.S. District Courts from 1880 to 1932; U.S. Court of Claims (now called U.S. Court of Federal Claims) from 1929 to 1932 and since 1960; U.S. Courts of Appeals since 1891; U.S. Court of Customs and Patent Appeals since 1929; U.S. Emergency Court of Appeals since 1943.
Federal Supplement (F.Supp. or F.Supp.2d)	1932	U.S. Court of Claims from 1932 to 1960; U.S. District Courts since 1932; U.S. Customs Court since 1956.
Federal Rules Decisions (F.R.D.)	1939	U.S. District Courts involving the Federal Rules of Civil Procedure since 1939 and Federal Rules of Criminal Procedure since 1946.
Supreme Court Reporter (S.Ct.)	1882	United States Supreme Court since the October term of 1882.
Bankruptcy Reporter (Bankr.)	1980	Bankruptcy decisions of U.S. Bankruptcy Courts, U.S. District Courts, U.S. Courts of Appeals, and the United States Supreme Court.
Military Justice Reporter (M.J.)	1978	U.S. Court of Military Appeals and Courts of Military Review for the Army, Navy, Air Force, and Coast Guard.

NATIONAL REPORTER SYSTEM MAP

name, and page number, in that order, is common to all citations.) When more than one reporter is cited for the same case, each reference is called a *parallel citation*. For example, consider the following case: *Buell-Wilson v. Ford Motor Co.*, 141 Cal.App.4th 525, 46 Cal.Rptr.3d 147 (2006). We see that the opinion in this case may be found in Volume 141 of the official *California Appellate Reports, Fourth Series*, on page 525. The parallel citation is to Volume 46 of the *California Reporter, Third Series*, page 147. In presenting appellate opinions in this text, in addition to the reporter, we give the name of the court hearing the case and the year of the court's decision.

A few states—including those with intermediate appellate courts, such as California, Illinois, and New York—have more than one reporter for opinions issued by their courts. Sample citations from these courts, as well as others, are listed and explained in Exhibit 1A–2.

Federal Court Decisions

ON THE WEB

To find links to Supreme Court opinions and opinions issued by the federal appellate courts, a good starting point is FindLaw's guide at

findlaw.com/10fedgov/judicial.

Federal district court decisions are published unofficially in West's *Federal Supplement* (F. Supp. or F.Supp.2d), and opinions from the circuit courts of appeals (federal reviewing courts) are reported unofficially in West's *Federal Reporter* (F., F.2d, or F.3d). Cases concerning federal bankruptcy law are published unofficially in West's *Bankruptcy Reporter* (Bankr.). The official edition of United States Supreme Court decisions is the *United States Reports* (U.S.), which is published by the federal government. Unofficial editions of Supreme Court cases include West's *Supreme Court Reporter* (S.Ct.) and the *Lawyers' Edition of the Supreme Court Reports* (L.Ed. or L.Ed.2d). Sample citations for federal court decisions are also listed and explained in Exhibit 1A–2.

Unpublished Opinions and Old Cases

Many court opinions that are not yet published or that are not intended for publication can be accessed through Westlaw® (abbreviated in citations as "WL"), an online legal database maintained by West Group. When no citation to a published reporter is available for cases cited in this text, we give the WL citation (see Exhibit 1A–2 for an example).

On a few occasions, this text cites opinions from old, classic cases dating to the nineteenth century or earlier; some of these are from the English courts. The citations to these cases may not conform to the descriptions given above because the reporters in which they were published have since been replaced.

READING AND UNDERSTANDING CASE LAW

The cases in this text have been condensed from the full text of the courts' opinions and paraphrased by the authors. For those wishing to review court cases for future research projects or to gain additional legal information, the following sections will provide useful insights into how to read and understand case law.

Case Titles and Terminology

The title of a case, such as *Adams v. Jones*, indicates the names of the parties to the lawsuit. The *v.* in the case title stands for *versus*, which means "against." In the trial court, Adams was the plaintiff—the person who filed the suit. Jones was the defendant. If the case is appealed, however, the appellate court will sometimes place the name of the party appealing the decision first, so the case may be called *Jones v. Adams*. Because some reviewing courts retain the trial court order of names, it is often impossible to distinguish the plaintiff from the defendant in the title of a reported appellate court decision. You must carefully read the facts of each case to identify the parties.

EXHIBIT 1A–2 How to Read Citations

STATE COURTS

271 Neb. 454, 712 N.W.2d 280 (2006)[a]

N.W. is the abbreviation for West's publication of state court decisions rendered in the *North Western Reporter* of the National Reporter System. *2d* indicates that this case was included in the *Second Series* of that reporter. The number 712 refers to the volume number of the reporter; the number 280 refers to the page in that volume on which this case begins.

Neb. is an abbreviation for *Nebraska Reports*, Nebraska's official reports of the decisions of its highest court, the Nebraska Supreme Court.

125 Cal.App.4th 949, 23 Cal.Rptr.3d 233 (2005)

Cal.Rptr. is the abbreviation for West's unofficial reports—titled *California Reporter*—of the decisions of California courts.

1 N.Y.3d 280, 803 N.E.2d 757, 771 N.Y.S.2d 484 (2003)

N.Y.S. is the abbreviation for West's unofficial reports—titled *New York Supplement*—of the decisions of New York courts.

N.Y. is the abbreviation for *New York Reports*, New York's official reports of the decisions of its court of appeals. The New York Court of Appeals is the state's highest court, analogous to other states' supreme courts. In New York, a supreme court is a trial court.

267 Ga.App. 832, 600 S.E.2d 800 (2004)

Ga.App. is the abbreviation for *Georgia Appeals Reports*, Georgia's official reports of the decisions of its court of appeals.

FEDERAL COURTS

547 U.S. 71, 126 S.Ct. 1503, 164 L.Ed.2d 179 (2006)

L.Ed. is an abbreviation for *Lawyers' Edition of the Supreme Court Reports*, an unofficial edition of decisions of the United States Supreme Court.

S.Ct. is the abbreviation for West's unofficial reports—titled *Supreme Court Reporter*—of decisions of the United States Supreme Court.

U.S. is the abbreviation for *United States Reports*, the official edition of the decisions of the United States Supreme Court.

a. The case names have been deleted from these citations to emphasize the publications. It should be kept in mind, however, that the name of a case is as important as the specific page numbers in the volumes in which it is found. If a citation is incorrect, the correct citation may be found in a publication's index of case names. In addition to providing a check on errors in citations, the date of a case is important because the value of a recent case as an authority is likely to be greater than that of older cases.

(Continued)

EXHIBIT 1A–2 **How to Read Citations—Continued**

FEDERAL COURTS (Continued)

439 F.3d 884 (8th Cir. 2006)

8th Cir. is an abbreviation denoting that this case was decided in the United States Court of Appeals for the Eighth Circuit.

340 F.Supp.2d 1051 (D. S.D. 2004)

D. S.D. is an abbreviation indicating that the United States District Court for the District of South Dakota decided this case.

ENGLISH COURTS

9 Exch. 341, 156 Eng.Rep. 145 (1854)

Eng.Rep. is an abbreviation for *English Reports, Full Reprint,* a series of reports containing selected decisions made in English courts between 1378 and 1865.

Exch. is an abbreviation for *English Exchequer Reports*, which includes the original reports of cases decided in England's Court of Exchequer.

STATUTORY AND OTHER CITATIONS

18 U.S.C. Section 1961(1)(A)

U.S.C. denotes *United States Code*, the codification of *United States Statutes at Large*. The number 18 refers to the statute's U.S.C. title number and 1961 to its section number within that title. The number 1 in parentheses refers to a subsection within the section, and the letter A in parentheses to a subdivision within the subsection.

UCC 2–206(1)(b)

UCC is an abbreviation for *Uniform Commercial Code*. The first number 2 is a reference to an article of the UCC, and 206 to a section within that article. The number 1 in parentheses refers to a subsection within the section, and the letter b in parentheses to a subdivision within the subsection.

Restatement (Second) of Torts, Section 568

Restatement (Second) of Torts refers to the second edition of the American Law Institute's *Restatement of the Law of Torts*. The number 568 refers to a specific section.

17 C.F.R. Section 230.505

C.F.R. is an abbreviation for *Code of Federal Regulations*, a compilation of federal administrative regulations. The number 17 designates the regulation's title number, and 230.505 designates a specific section within that title.

EXHIBIT 1A–2 | **How to Read Citations—Continued**

Westlaw® Citations[b]

2006 WL 1193212

WL is an abbreviation for Westlaw. The number 2006 is the year of the document that can be found with this citation in the Westlaw database. The number 1193212 is a number assigned to a specific document. A higher number indicates that a document was added to the Westlaw database later in the year.

Uniform Resource Locators (URLs)

http://www.westlaw.com[c]

The suffix *com* is the top level domain (TLD) for this Web site. The TLD *com* is an abbreviation for "commercial," which usually means that a for-profit entity hosts (maintains or supports) this Web site.

westlaw is the host name—the part of the domain name selected by the organization that registered the name. In this case, West Group registered the name. This Internet site is the Westlaw database on the Web.

www is an abbreviation for "World Wide Web." The Web is a system of Internet servers that support documents formatted in *HTML* (hypertext markup language). HTML supports links to text, graphics, and audio and video files.

http://www.uscourts.gov

This is "The Federal Judiciary Home Page." The host is the Administrative Office of the U.S. Courts. The TLD *gov* is an abbreviation for "government." This Web site includes information and links from, and about, the federal courts.

http://www.law.cornell.edu/index.html

This part of a URL points to a Web page or file at a specific location within the host's domain. This page is a menu with links to documents within the domain and to other Internet resources.

This is the host name for a Web site that contains the Internet publications of the Legal Information Institute (LII), which is a part of Cornell Law School. The LII site includes a variety of legal materials and links to other legal resources on the Internet. The TLD *edu* is an abbreviation for "educational institution" (a school or a university).

http://www.ipl.org/div/news

This part of the Web site points to a static *news* page at this Web site, which provides links to online newspapers from around the world.

div is an abbreviation for "division," which is the way that the Internet Public Library tags the content on its Web site as relating to a specific topic.

ipl is an abbreviation for "Internet Public Library," which is an online service that provides reference resources and links to other information services on the Web. The IPL is supported chiefly by the School of Information at the University of Michigan. The TLD *org* is an abbreviation for "organization" (normally nonprofit).

b. Many court decisions that are not yet published or that are not intended for publication can be accessed through Westlaw®, an online legal database.
c. The basic form for a URL is "service://hostname/path." The Internet service for all of the URLs in this text is *http* (hypertext transfer protocol). Because most Web browsers add this prefix automatically when a user enters a host name or a hostname/path, we have omitted the http:// from the URLs listed in this text.

The following terms and phrases are frequently encountered in court opinions and legal publications. Because it is important to understand what these terms and phrases mean, we define and discuss them here.

Plaintiffs and Defendants   As mentioned in Chapter 1, the plaintiff in a lawsuit is the party that initiates the action. The defendant is the party against which a lawsuit is brought. Lawsuits frequently involve more than one plaintiff and/or defendant.

Appellants and Appellees   The *appellant* is the party that appeals a case to another court or jurisdiction from the court or jurisdiction in which the case was originally brought. Sometimes, an appellant is referred to as the *petitioner*. The *appellee* is the party against which the appeal is taken. Sometimes, the appellee is referred to as the *respondent*.

Judges and Justices   The terms *judge* and *justice* are usually synonymous and represent two designations given to judges in various courts. All members of the United States Supreme Court, for example, are referred to as justices. And justice is the formal title usually given to judges of appellate courts, although this is not always the case. In New York, a justice is a judge of the trial court (which is called the Supreme Court), and a member of the Court of Appeals (the state's highest court) is called a judge. The term *justice* is commonly abbreviated to J., and *justices* to JJ. A Supreme Court case might refer to Justice Ginsburg as Ginsburg, J., or to Chief Justice Roberts as Roberts, C.J.

Decisions and Opinions   Most decisions reached by reviewing, or appellate, courts are explained in written *opinions*. The opinion contains the court's reasons for its decision, the rules of law that apply, and the judgment. When all judges or justices unanimously agree on an opinion, the opinion is written for the entire court and can be deemed a *unanimous opinion*. When there is not unanimous agreement, a *majority opinion* is written, outlining the views of the majority of the judges or justices deciding the case.

Often, a judge or justice who feels strongly about making or emphasizing a point that was not made or emphasized in the unanimous or majority opinion will write a *concurring opinion*. That means the judge or justice agrees (concurs) with the judgment given in the unanimous or majority opinion but for different reasons. When there is not a unanimous opinion, a *dissenting opinion* is usually written by a judge or justice who does not agree with the majority. (See the *Extended Case Study* following Chapter 7 for an example of a dissenting opinion.) The dissenting opinion is important because it may form the basis of the arguments used years later in overruling the precedential majority opinion. Occasionally, a court issues a *per curiam* (Latin for "of the court") opinion, which does not indicate which judge or justice authored the opinion.

A Sample Court Case

Knowing how to read and analyze a court opinion is an essential step in undertaking accurate legal research. A further step involves "briefing" the case. Legal researchers routinely brief cases by summarizing and reducing the texts of the opinions to their essential elements. (For instructions on how to brief a case, go to Appendix A at the end of this text.) The cases contained within the chapters of this text have already been analyzed and briefed by the authors, and the essential aspects of each case are presented in a convenient format consisting of four basic sections: *Facts*, *Issue*, *Decision*, and *Reason*, as shown in Exhibit 1A–3 on pages 32 and 33, which has also been annotated to illustrate the kind of information that is contained in each section.

The United States Supreme Court building in Washington, D.C. In what reporters are Supreme Court opinions published? (PhotoDisc)

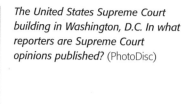

Throughout this text, in addition to this basic format, we sometimes include a special introductory section entitled *Historical and Social* [*Economic, Technological, Political*, or other] *Setting*. In some instances, a *Company Profile* is included in place of the introductory setting. These profiles provide background on one of the parties to the lawsuit. Each case is followed by either a brief *For Critical Analysis* section, which, as in Exhibit 1A–3, presents a question regarding some issue raised by the case; a *Why Is This Case Important?* section, which explains the significance of the case; or a *What If the Facts Were Different?* question, which alters the facts slightly and asks you to consider how this would change the outcome. A section entitled *Impact of This Case on Today's Law* concludes the *Landmark and Classic Cases* that appear throughout the text to indicate the significance of the case for today's legal landscape.

EXHIBIT 1A–3 A Sample Court Case

1

SAMPLE CASE Nunez v. Carrabba's Italian Grill, Inc.

Supreme Judicial Court of Massachusetts, 448 Mass. 170, 859 N.E.2d 801 (2007).

2

FACTS At about 7 P.M. on May 10, 2002, Robert Nunez, who was then eighteen years old, went to Carrabba's Italian Grill, Inc., a restaurant in Peabody, where he had worked as a waiter. He ate dinner and drank six alcoholic beverages served to him by a bartender whom he knew. About 9:30 P.M., he drove home. Two hours later, he went to the Palace, a nightclub in Saugus. He had done promotional work for the club and had otherwise visited at least thirty times, gaining entry with false identification. At the Palace, he was served one or two alcoholic beverages by a bartender whom he knew.

4 After midnight, as he drove home, his vehicle approached an intersection with a green traffic light, and he accelerated to get through the light before it turned red. In the intersection, his car was struck by another car that failed to stop at the red light for the opposite direction. Nunez was thrown from his car and seriously injured. To recover for his injuries, he filed a suit in a Massachusetts state court against Carrabba's and the Palace, claiming in part that they were negligent in serving alcoholic beverages to him, an "intoxicated underage adult," contributing to his injuries. The court issued a summary judgment partly in the defendants' favor. All of the parties appealed to the Supreme Judicial Court, Massachusetts' highest court.

ISSUE Does a commercial establishment licensed to sell alcohol to the public owe the same duty of care **5** to a person who is between eighteen and twenty-one years old as it does to a person who is less than eighteen years old?

DECISION Yes. The Supreme Judicial Court affirmed the lower court's judgment and remanded the case to **6** that court for further proceedings. The duty of care that a licensed commercial establishment selling alcoholic beverages owes to an underage adult is the same as its duty to a minor.

3

REASON To persons under eighteen years of age (minors), a licensed establishment owes a duty to refrain from serving them any alcohol. In this case, the court pointed out that the Massachusetts State legislature has identified in many statutes the dangers of furnishing alcohol to underage adults (persons between eighteen and twenty-one years of age). "In light of these clear legislative concerns," the court concluded that the duty of care owed to minors applies "with equal force when the person to whom the alcohol is served is between the ages of eighteen and twenty-one years." In either circumstance, the person is under the legal drinking age. A certain statute forbids the serving of alcoholic beverages to **7** anyone under the age of twenty-one years because "they are thought to be peculiarly susceptible to the effects of alcohol and less able to make decisions about what amount of alcohol they may safely consume in various situations." The court reasoned, "If the Legislature had deemed these concerns less significant for individuals between the ages of eighteen and twenty-one years, then it could have lowered the legal drinking age." Since 1984, however, the legal drinking age in Massachusetts has been twenty-one. To hold the defendants liable, the plaintiff need only show that they served him alcoholic beverages aware that he was under twenty-one and that, as a consequence, he was injured.

FOR CRITICAL ANALYSIS–Social Consideration *Should the duty applied in this* **8** *case to certain commercial establishments apply with "equal force" to a social host serving alcohol to guests when one of those being served is an adult, but underage, individual? Why or why not?*

Review of Sample Court Case

1 The name of the case is *Nunez v. Carrabba's Italian Grill, Inc.* The injured underage adult at the center of this case is the plaintiff; one of the commercial establishments at which the plaintiff was served alcohol is the named defendant.

2 The court deciding this case is the Supreme Judicial Court of Massachusetts.

3 The case citation includes citations to the official *Massachusetts Reports* and to the unofficial *North Eastern Reporter, Second Series.* The case can be found in volume 448 of the *Massachusetts Reports* at page 170, and in volume 859 of the *North Eastern Reporter, Second Series,* at page 801.

4 The **FACTS** section identifies the plaintiff and the defendants, describes the events leading up to the lawsuit, and indicates what the plaintiff sought to obtain by bringing the action. Because this is a case before an appellate court, the ruling of the lower court is also included here.

5 The **ISSUE** section presents the central issue (or issues) to be decided by the court. In this case, the court is faced with an issue that has not yet been decided by any Massachusetts state court. Most cases concern more than one issue, but the authors of this textbook have edited each case to focus on just one issue.

6 The **DECISION** section, as the term indicates, contains the court's decision on the issue or issues before the court. The decision reflects the opinion of the judge, or the majority of the judges or justices, hearing the case. In this particular case, the court affirmed the lower court's judgment. Decisions by appellate courts are frequently phrased in reference to the lower court's decision—that is, the appellate court may "affirm" the lower court's ruling or "reverse" it. In either situation, the appellate court may "remand," or send back, the case for further proceedings.

7 The **REASON** section indicates what relevant laws and judicial principles were applied in forming the particular conclusion arrived at in the case at bar ("before the court"). In this case, the principle that was applied concerned the duty that a commercial establishment licensed to serve alcohol to the public owes to underage patrons. The court determined that such an establishment owes the same duty to all underage patrons, whether they are minors or adults.

8 The **FOR CRITICAL ANALYSIS—Social Consideration** section raises a question to be considered in relation to the case just presented. Here the question involves a "social" consideration. In other cases presented in this text, the "consideration" may involve a cultural, economic, environmental, ethical, international, political, or technological consideration.

CHAPTER 3
Courts and Alternative Dispute Resolution

"The Judicial Department comes home in its effects to every man's fireside: it passes on his property, his reputation, his life, his all.**"**

John Marshall, 1755–1835
(Chief justice of the United States Supreme Court, 1801–1835)

LEARNING OBJECTIVES

AFTER READING THIS CHAPTER, YOU SHOULD BE ABLE TO ANSWER THE FOLLOWING QUESTIONS:

1 What is judicial review? How and when was the power of judicial review established?

2 Before a court can hear a case, it must have jurisdiction. Over what must it have jurisdiction? How are the courts applying traditional jurisdictional concepts to cases involving Internet transactions?

3 What is the difference between a trial court and an appellate court?

4 In a lawsuit, what are the pleadings? What is discovery, and how does electronic discovery differ from traditional discovery? What is electronic filing?

5 How are online forums being used to resolve disputes?

As Chief Justice John Marshall remarked in the chapter-opening quotation, ultimately, we are all affected by what the courts say and do. This is particularly true in the business world—nearly every businessperson will face either a potential or an actual lawsuit at some time or another. For this reason, anyone contemplating a career in business will benefit from an understanding of court systems in the United States, including the mechanics of lawsuits.

In this chapter, after examining the judiciary's overall role in the American governmental scheme, we discuss some basic requirements that must be met before a party may bring a lawsuit before a particular court. We then look at the court systems of the United States in some detail and, to clarify judicial procedures, follow a hypothetical case through a state court system. Even though there are fifty-two court systems in the United States—one for each of the fifty states, one for the District of Columbia, plus a federal system—similarities abound. Keep in mind that the federal courts are not superior to the state courts; they are simply an independent system of courts, which derives its authority from Article III, Sections 1 and 2, of the U.S. Constitution. The chapter concludes with an overview of some alternative methods of settling disputes, including methods for settling disputes in online forums.

Note that technological developments are affecting court procedures just as they are affecting all other areas of the law. In this chapter, we will also indicate how court doctrines and procedures, as well as alternative methods of dispute settlement, are being adapted to the needs of a cyber age.

In New York City, the federal courthouse (left), and the New York State Court of Appeals (right). Are the federal courts superior to the state courts? (Left: Wally Gobetz/ Flickr/Creative Commons; right: Courtesy of New York State Court of Appeals)

THE JUDICIARY'S ROLE IN AMERICAN GOVERNMENT

As you learned in Chapter 1, the body of American law includes the federal and state constitutions, statutes passed by legislative bodies, administrative law, and the case decisions and legal principles that form the common law. These laws would be meaningless, however, without the courts to interpret and apply them. This is the essential role of the judiciary—the courts—in the American governmental system: to interpret and apply the law.

Judicial Review

As the branch of government entrusted with interpreting the laws, the judiciary can decide, among other things, whether the laws or actions of the other two branches are constitutional. The process for making such a determination is known as **judicial review.** The power of judicial review enables the judicial branch to act as a check on the other two branches of government, in line with the checks-and-balances system established by the U.S. Constitution. (Judicial review can also be found in other countries—see this chapter's *Beyond Our Borders* feature on the following page.)

JUDICIAL REVIEW
The process by which a court decides on the constitutionality of legislative enactments and actions of the executive branch.

The Origins of Judicial Review in the United States

The power of judicial review was not mentioned in the Constitution, but the concept was not new at the time the nation was founded. Indeed, before 1789 state courts had already overturned state legislative acts that conflicted with state constitutions. Additionally, many of the founders expected the United States Supreme Court to assume a similar role with respect to the federal Constitution. Alexander Hamilton and James Madison both emphasized the importance of judicial review in their essays urging the adoption of the new Constitution. When was the doctrine of judicial review established? See this chapter's *Landmark in the Law* feature on page 65 for the answer.

BASIC JUDICIAL REQUIREMENTS

Before a court can hear a lawsuit, certain requirements must first be met. These requirements relate to jurisdiction, venue, and standing to sue. We examine each of these important concepts here.

BEYOND OUR BORDERS | Judicial Review in Other Nations

The concept of judicial review was pioneered by the United States. Some maintain that one of the reasons the doctrine was readily accepted in this country was that it fit well with the checks and balances designed by the founders. Today, all established constitutional democracies have some form of judicial review—the power to rule on the constitutionality of laws—but its form varies from country to country.

For example, Canada's Supreme Court can exercise judicial review but is barred from doing so if a law includes a provision explicitly prohibiting such review. In France, the Constitutional Council rules on the constitutionality of laws *before* the laws take effect. Laws can be referred to the council for prior review by the president, the prime minister, and the heads of the two chambers of parliament. Prior review is also an option in Germany and Italy, if requested by the national or a regional government. In contrast, the United States Supreme Court does not give advisory opinions; the Supreme Court will render a decision only when there is an actual dispute concerning an issue.

Members of the Constitutional Council of France. The Council rules on the constitutionality of laws before the laws take effect. Does the United States have a similar system? (Photo Courtesy of the Conseil Constitutionnel)

FOR CRITICAL ANALYSIS *In any country in which a constitution sets forth the basic powers and structure of government, some governmental body has to decide whether laws enacted by the government are consistent with that constitution. Why might the courts be best suited to handle this task? What might be a better alternative?*

■

Jurisdiction

JURISDICTION
The authority of a court to hear and decide a specific case.

In Latin, *juris* means "law," and *diction* means "to speak." Thus, "the power to speak the law" is the literal meaning of the term **jurisdiction.** Before any court can hear a case, it must have jurisdiction over the person (or company) against whom the suit is brought (the defendant) or over the property involved in the suit. The court must also have jurisdiction over the subject matter.

Jurisdiction over Persons   Generally, a court can exercise personal jurisdiction (*in personam* jurisdiction) over any person or business that resides in a certain geographic area. A state trial court, for example, normally has jurisdictional authority over residents (including businesses) in a particular area of the state, such as a county or district. A state's highest court (often called the state supreme court)[1] has jurisdiction over all residents of that state.

LONG ARM STATUTE
A state statute that permits a state to obtain personal jurisdiction over nonresident defendants. A defendant must have certain "minimum contacts" with that state for the statute to apply.

Jurisdiction over Nonresident Defendants.   In addition, under the authority of a state **long arm statute,** a court can exercise personal jurisdiction over certain out-of-state defendants based on activities that took place within the state. Before exercising long arm jurisdiction over a nonresident, however, the court must be convinced that the defendant had sufficient contacts, or *minimum contacts*, with the state to justify the jurisdiction.[2]

---

1. As will be discussed shortly, a state's highest court is frequently referred to as the state supreme court, but there are exceptions. For example, in New York, the supreme court is a trial court.
2. The minimum-contacts standard was established in *International Shoe Co. v. State of Washington,* 326 U.S. 310, 66 S.Ct. 154, 90 L.Ed. 95 (1945).

The *Marbury v. Madison*[a] decision is widely viewed as a cornerstone of constitutional law. When Thomas Jefferson defeated John Adams in the presidential election of 1800, Adams feared the Jeffersonians' antipathy toward business and also toward a strong national government. Adams thus rushed to "pack" the judiciary with loyal Federalists (those who believed in a strong national government) by appointing what came to be called "midnight judges" just before Jefferson took office. All of the fifty-nine judicial appointment letters had to be certified and delivered, but Adams's secretary of state (John Marshall) was only able to deliver forty-two of them by the time Jefferson took over as president. Jefferson refused to order his secretary of state, James Madison, to deliver the remaining commissions.

Marshall's Dilemma   William Marbury and three others to whom the commissions had not been delivered sought a writ of *mandamus* (an order directing a government official to fulfill a duty) from the United States Supreme Court, as authorized by the Judiciary Act of 1789. As fate would have it, John Marshall (Adams's secretary of state) had just been appointed as chief justice of the Supreme Court. Marshall faced a dilemma: If he ordered the commissions delivered, the new secretary of state (Madison) could simply refuse to deliver them—and the Court had no way to compel action. At the same time, if Marshall simply allowed the new administration to do as it wished, the Court's power would be severely eroded.

Marshall's Decision   Marshall masterfully fashioned his decision to enlarge the power of the Supreme Court by affirming the Court's power of judicial review. He stated, "It is emphatically the province and duty of the Judicial Department to say what the law is. . . . If two laws conflict with each other, the courts must decide on the operation of each. . . . So if the law be in opposition to the Constitution . . . [t]he Court must determine which of these conflicting rules governs the case."

Marshall's decision did not require anyone to do anything. He concluded that the highest court did not have the power to issue a writ of *mandamus* in this particular case. Although the Judiciary Act of 1789 specified that the Supreme Court could issue writs of *mandamus* as part of its original jurisdiction, Article III of the U.S. Constitution, which spelled out the Court's original jurisdiction, did not mention writs of *mandamus*. Because Congress did not have the right to expand the Supreme Court's jurisdiction, this section of the Judiciary Act was unconstitutional—and thus void. The decision still stands today as a judicial and political masterpiece.

APPLICATION TO TODAY'S WORLD   *Since the* Marbury v. Madison *decision, the power of judicial review has remained unchallenged and today is exercised by both federal and state courts. If the courts did not have the power of judicial review, the constitutionality of Congress's acts could not be challenged in court—a congressional statute would remain law until changed by Congress. The courts of other countries that have adopted a constitutional democracy often cite this decision as a justification for judicial review.*

RELEVANT WEB SITES   *To locate information on the Web concerning the* Marbury v. Madison *decision, go to this text's Web site at* **www.thomsonedu.com/westbuslaw/blt**, *select "Chapter 3," and click on "URLs for Landmarks."*

a. 5 U.S. (1 Cranch) 137, 2 L.Ed. 60 (1803).

Generally, this means that the defendant must have enough of a connection to the state for the judge to conclude that it is fair for the state to exercise power over the defendant. If an out-of-state defendant caused an automobile accident or sold defective goods within the state, for instance, a court will usually find that minimum contacts exist to exercise jurisdiction over that defendant.

Similarly, a state may exercise personal jurisdiction over a nonresident defendant who is sued for breaching a contract that was formed within the state, even when that contract was negotiated over the phone or through correspondence. **■EXAMPLE 3.1** Nick Mileti, a resident of California, co-produced a movie called *Streamers* and organized a corporation, Streamers International Distributors, Inc., to distribute the film. Joseph Cole, a resident of Ohio, bought two hundred shares of Streamers stock and loaned the firm $475,000, which he borrowed from an Ohio bank. The film was unsuccessful. Mileti agreed to repay Cole's loan in a contract arranged through phone calls and correspondence between California and Ohio. When Mileti did not repay the loan, the bank sued Cole, who in turn filed a suit against Mileti in a federal district court in Ohio. The court held that Mileti—through phone calls and letters—had sufficient contacts with the state of Ohio for the court to exercise jurisdiction over him.[3] ■

Personal Jurisdiction over Corporations. Because corporations are considered legal persons,[4] courts use the same principles to determine whether it is fair to exercise jurisdiction over a corporation. Usually, a corporation has met the minimum-contacts requirement if it does business within the state or has an office or branch within the state. **■EXAMPLE 3.2** Suppose that a Maine corporation has a branch office or a manufacturing plant in Georgia. Does this Maine corporation have sufficient minimum contacts with the state of Georgia to allow a Georgia court to exercise jurisdiction over it? Yes, it does. If the Maine corporation advertises and sells its products in Georgia, those activities will also likely suffice to meet the minimum-contacts requirement, even if the corporate headquarters are located in a different state. ■

The following case involved a lawsuit filed by a California resident against a Nevada hotel and others for failing to provide notice of an energy surcharge imposed on the guests. Although the hotel had no bank accounts or employees in California, it advertised heavily in that state and obtained a significant percentage of its business from California residents. Based on these activities, could a California state court exercise personal jurisdiction over the hotel?

---

3. *Cole v. Mileti*, 133 F.3d 433 (6th Cir. 1998).
4. In the eyes of the law, corporations are "legal persons"—entities that can sue and be sued. See Chapter 28.

CASE 3.1 **Snowney v. Harrah's Entertainment, Inc.**

California Supreme Court, 35 Cal.4th 1054, 112 P.3d 28, 29 Cal.Rptr.3d 33 (2005).

FACTS Harrah's Entertainment, Inc., owns and operates hotels in Nevada. In 2001, Frank Snowney, a California resident, reserved a room in one of Harrah's hotels by phone from his home. The reservations clerk told him that the cost was $50 per night plus the room tax. When Snowney checked out, however, the bill included a $3 energy surcharge. Snowney filed a suit in a California state court against Harrah's and other hotel owners, alleging in part fraud for levying the surcharge without notice. The defendants filed a motion to dismiss for lack of personal jurisdiction, claiming that they did not do business in California. Snowney argued in part that the hotels advertised extensively to California residents through billboards, newspapers, and radio and television stations in the state and through an interactive Web site that accepted reservations from state residents. The court granted the

CASE 3.1–Continued

defendants' motion, but on Snowney's appeal, a state intermediate appellate court reversed this ruling. The hotels appealed to the California Supreme Court.

ISSUE Could a California state court exercise personal jurisdiction over out-of-state hotels, based on the hotels' in-state advertising and significant business with California residents?

DECISION Yes. The California Supreme Court affirmed the judgment of the state intermediate appellate court, holding that the Nevada defendants were subject to personal jurisdiction in California state courts.

REASON The state supreme court identified three requirements for a court's exercise of jurisdiction over a nonresident defendant: the defendant must avail itself of "forum benefits," the case must relate to the defendant's contacts with the state, and the assertion of jurisdiction must be fair. The court reasoned that through a Web site, the hotels

had "availed" themselves "of forum benefits. * * * By touting the proximity of their hotels to California and providing driving directions from California to their hotels, defendants' site specifically targeted residents of California. Defendants also concede that many of their patrons come from California and that some of these patrons undoubtedly made reservations using their Web site." The hotels advertised extensively in the state through direct mail, billboards, newspapers, and radio and television stations located in the state. "Given the intensity of defendants' activities in California, we * * * have little difficulty in finding a substantial connection between the two." Finally, "defendants do not contend the exercise of jurisdiction would be unfair or unreasonable, and we see no reason to conclude otherwise."

WHAT IF THE FACTS WERE DIFFERENT?
If the Nevada hotels had not extensively advertised for California residents' business, would the outcome in this case have been the same? Why or why not?

Jurisdiction over Property A court can also exercise jurisdiction over property that is located within its boundaries. This kind of jurisdiction is known as *in rem* jurisdiction, or "jurisdiction over the thing." ▪**EXAMPLE 3.3** Suppose that a dispute arises over the ownership of a boat in dry dock in Fort Lauderdale, Florida. The boat is owned by an Ohio resident, over whom a Florida court normally cannot exercise personal jurisdiction. The other party to the dispute is a resident of Nebraska. In this situation, a lawsuit concerning the boat could be brought in a Florida state court on the basis of the court's *in rem* jurisdiction. ▪

Jurisdiction over Subject Matter Jurisdiction over subject matter is a limitation on the types of cases a court can hear. In both the federal and state court systems, there are courts of *general* (unlimited) *jurisdiction* and courts of *limited jurisdiction*. An example of a court of general jurisdiction is a state trial court or a federal district court. An example of a state court of limited jurisdiction is a probate court. **Probate courts** are state courts that handle only matters relating to the transfer of a person's assets and obligations after that person's death, including matters relating to the custody and guardianship of children. An example of a federal court of limited subject-matter jurisdiction is a bankruptcy court. **Bankruptcy courts** handle only bankruptcy proceedings, which are governed by federal bankruptcy law (discussed in Chapter 23). In contrast, a court of general jurisdiction can decide a broad array of cases.

A court's jurisdiction over subject matter is usually defined in the statute or constitution creating the court. In both the federal and state court systems, a court's subject-matter jurisdiction can be limited not only by the subject of the lawsuit but also by the amount in controversy, by whether a case is a felony (a more serious type of crime) or a misdemeanor (a less serious type of crime), or by whether the proceeding is a trial or an appeal.

PROBATE COURT
A state court of limited jurisdiction that conducts proceedings relating to the settlement of a deceased person's estate.

BANKRUPTCY COURT
A federal court of limited jurisdiction that handles only bankruptcy proceedings, which are governed by federal bankruptcy law.

Original and Appellate Jurisdiction   The distinction between courts of original jurisdiction and courts of appellate jurisdiction normally lies in whether the case is being heard for the first time. Courts having original jurisdiction are courts of the first instance, or trial courts—that is, courts in which lawsuits begin, trials take place, and evidence is presented. In the federal court system, the *district courts* are trial courts. In the various state court systems, the trial courts are known by various names, as will be discussed shortly.

The key point here is that any court having original jurisdiction is normally known as a trial court. Courts having appellate jurisdiction act as reviewing courts, or appellate courts. In general, cases can be brought before appellate courts only on appeal from an order or a judgment of a trial court or other lower court.

Jurisdiction of the Federal Courts   Because the federal government is a government of limited powers, the jurisdiction of the federal courts is limited. Article III of the U.S. Constitution establishes the boundaries of federal judicial power. Section 2 of Article III states that "[t]he judicial Power shall extend to all Cases, in Law and Equity, arising under this Constitution, the Laws of the United States, and Treaties made, or which shall be made, under their Authority."

Federal Questions.   Whenever a plaintiff's cause of action is based, at least in part, on the U.S. Constitution, a treaty, or a federal law, then a **federal question** arises, and the case comes under the judicial power of the federal courts. Any lawsuit involving a federal question can originate in a federal court. People who claim that their rights under the U.S. Constitution have been violated can begin their suits in a federal court. Note that most cases involving a federal question do not have to be tried in a federal court. The plaintiff can file the action in either a federal court or a state trial court (because the federal and state courts have *concurrent jurisdiction* over many matters, as will be discussed shortly).

Diversity of Citizenship.   Federal district courts can also exercise original jurisdiction over cases involving **diversity of citizenship.** Such cases may arise between (1) citizens of different states, (2) a foreign country and citizens of a state or of different states, or (3) citizens of a state and citizens or subjects of a foreign country. The amount in controversy must be more than $75,000 before a federal court can take jurisdiction in such cases. For purposes of diversity jurisdiction, a corporation is a citizen of both the state in which it is incorporated and the state in which its principal place of business is located. A case involving diversity of citizenship can be filed in the appropriate federal district court, or, if the case starts in a state court, it can sometimes be transferred to a federal court. A large percentage of the cases filed in federal courts each year are based on diversity of citizenship.

Note that in a case based on a federal question, a federal court will apply federal law. In a case based on diversity of citizenship, however, a federal court will apply the relevant state law (which is often the law of the state in which the court sits).

Exclusive versus Concurrent Jurisdiction   When both federal and state courts have the power to hear a case, as is true in suits involving diversity of citizenship, **concurrent jurisdiction** exists. When cases can be tried only in federal courts or only in state courts, exclusive jurisdiction exists. Federal courts have **exclusive jurisdiction** in cases involving federal crimes, bankruptcy, patents, and copyrights; in suits against the United States; and in some areas of admiralty law (law governing transportation on the seas and ocean waters). States also have exclusive jurisdiction over certain subject matter—for example,

FEDERAL QUESTION
A question that pertains to the U.S. Constitution, acts of Congress, or treaties. A federal question provides a basis for federal jurisdiction.

DIVERSITY OF CITIZENSHIP
Under Article III, Section 2, of the U.S. Constitution, a basis for federal district court jurisdiction over a lawsuit between (1) citizens of different states, (2) a foreign country and citizens of a state or of different states, or (3) citizens of a state and citizens or subjects of a foreign country. The amount in controversy must be more than $75,000 before a federal district court can take jurisdiction in such cases.

CONCURRENT JURISDICTION
Jurisdiction that exists when two different courts have the power to hear a case. For example, some cases can be heard in a federal or a state court.

EXCLUSIVE JURISDICTION
Jurisdiction that exists when a case can be heard only in a particular court or type of court.

EXHIBIT 3–1 Exclusive and Concurrent Jurisdiction

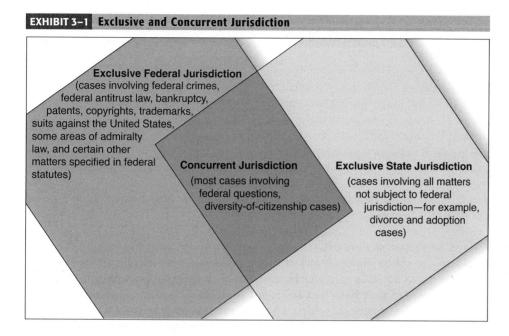

Exclusive Federal Jurisdiction
(cases involving federal crimes,
federal antitrust law, bankruptcy,
patents, copyrights, trademarks,
suits against the United States,
some areas of admiralty
law, and certain other
matters specified in federal
statutes)

Concurrent Jurisdiction
(most cases involving
federal questions,
diversity-of-citizenship cases)

Exclusive State Jurisdiction
(cases involving all matters
not subject to federal
jurisdiction—for example,
divorce and adoption
cases)

divorce and adoption. The concepts of exclusive and concurrent jurisdiction are illustrated in Exhibit 3–1.

When concurrent jurisdiction exists, a party has a choice of whether to bring a suit in, for example, a federal or a state court. The party's lawyer will consider several factors in counseling the party as to which choice is preferable. The lawyer may prefer to litigate the case in a state court because he or she is more familiar with the state court's procedures, or perhaps the attorney believes that the state's judge or jury would be more sympathetic to the client and the case. Alternatively, the lawyer may advise the client to sue in federal court. Perhaps the state court's **docket** (the court's schedule listing the cases to be heard) is crowded, and the case could come to trial sooner in a federal court. Perhaps some feature of federal practice or procedure could offer an advantage in the client's case. Other important considerations include the law in the particular jurisdiction, how that law has been applied in the jurisdiction's courts, and what the results in similar cases have been in that jurisdiction.

DOCKET
The list of cases entered on a court's calendar and thus scheduled to be heard by the court.

Jurisdiction in Cyberspace

The Internet's capacity to bypass political and geographic boundaries undercuts the traditional basic limitations on a court's authority to exercise jurisdiction. These limits include a party's contacts with a court's geographic jurisdiction. As already discussed, for a court to compel a defendant to come before it, there must be at least minimum contacts—the presence of a salesperson within the state, for example. Are there sufficient minimum contacts if the defendant's only connection to a jurisdiction is an ad on the Web originating from a remote location?

The "Sliding-Scale" Standard   Gradually, the courts are developing a standard—called a "sliding-scale" standard—for determining when the exercise of jurisdiction over an out-of-state defendant is proper. In developing this standard, the courts have identified three types of Internet business contacts: (1) substantial business conducted over the Internet (with contracts and sales, for example), (2) some interactivity through a Web site, and (3) passive advertising. Jurisdiction is proper for the first category, improper for the third, and may or may not be appropriate for the second.[5] An Internet communication is typically considered passive if people have to voluntarily access it to read the message, and active if it is sent to specific individuals.

In certain situations, even a single contact can satisfy the minimum-contacts requirement. **■EXAMPLE 3.4** A Texas resident, Davis, sent an unsolicited e-mail message to numerous Mississippi residents advertising a pornographic Web site. Davis falsified the "from" header in the e-mail so that it appeared that Internet Doorway had sent the mail. Internet Doorway filed a lawsuit against Davis in Mississippi claiming that its reputation and goodwill in the community had been harmed. The U.S. district court in Mississippi held that Davis's single e-mail to Mississippi residents satisfied the minimum-contacts requirement for jurisdiction. The court concluded that Davis, by sending the e-mail solicitation, should reasonably have expected that she could be "haled into court in a distant jurisdiction to answer for the ramifications."[6] ■

PREVENTING LEGAL DISPUTES

Today's entrepreneurs are often eager to establish Web sites to promote their products and solicit orders. Many of these individuals may not be aware that defendants can be sued in states in which they have never been physically present, provided they have had sufficient contacts with that state's residents over the Internet. Businesspersons who contemplate making their Web sites the least bit interactive should consult an attorney to find out whether by doing so they will be subjecting themselves to jurisdiction in every state. Becoming informed about the extent of potential exposure to lawsuits in various locations is an important part of preventing litigation.

■

International Jurisdictional Issues   Because the Internet is international in scope, international jurisdictional issues understandably have come to the fore. What seems to be emerging in the world's courts is a standard that echoes the "minimum-contacts" requirement applied by the U.S. courts. Most courts are indicating that minimum contacts—doing business within the jurisdiction, for example—are enough to compel a defendant to appear and that a physical presence is not necessary. The effect of this standard is that a business firm has to comply with the laws in any jurisdiction in which it targets customers for its products. This situation is complicated by the fact that many countries' laws on particular issues—free speech, for example—are very different from U.S. laws.

■EXAMPLE 3.5 To understand some of the problems created by Internet commerce, consider a French court's judgment against the U.S.-based Internet company Yahoo!, Inc. Yahoo operates an online auction site on which Nazi memorabilia have been offered for sale. In France, the display of any objects representing symbols of Nazi ideology subjects the person or entity displaying such objects to both criminal and civil liability. The International League against Racism and Anti-Semitism filed a lawsuit in Paris against Yahoo for displaying Nazi memorabilia and offering them for sale via its Web site.

The French court asserted jurisdiction over Yahoo on the ground that the materials on the company's U.S.-based servers could be viewed on a Web site accessible in France. The French court ordered Yahoo to eliminate all Internet access in France to the Nazi memorabilia offered for sale through its online auctions. Yahoo then took the case to a federal district court in the United States, claiming that the French court's order violated the First Amendment. Although the federal district court ruled in favor of Yahoo, the U.S. Court of

---

5. For a leading case on this issue, see *Zippo Manufacturing Co. v. Zippo Dot Com, Inc.*, 952 F.Supp. 1119 (W.D.Pa. 1997).

6. *Internet Doorway, Inc. v. Parks*, 138 F.Supp.2d 773 (S.D.Miss. 2001).

Appeals for the Ninth Circuit reversed. According to the appellate court, U.S. courts lacked personal jurisdiction over the French groups involved. The ruling leaves open the possibility that Yahoo, and anyone else who posts anything on the Internet, could be held answerable to the laws of any country in which the message might be received.[7] ▣

Venue

Jurisdiction has to do with whether a court has authority to hear a case involving specific persons, property, or subject matter. **Venue**[8] is concerned with the most appropriate physical location for a trial. Two state courts (or two federal courts) may have the authority to exercise jurisdiction over a case, but it may be more appropriate or convenient to hear the case in one court than in the other.

Basically, the concept of venue reflects the policy that a court trying a suit should be in the geographic neighborhood (usually the county) where the incident leading to the lawsuit occurred or where the parties involved in the lawsuit reside. Venue in a civil case typically is where the defendant resides, whereas venue in a criminal case normally is where the crime occurred. Pretrial publicity or other factors, though, may require a change of venue to another community, especially in criminal cases when the defendant's right to a fair and impartial jury has been impaired. **■EXAMPLE 3.6** A change of venue from Oklahoma City to Denver, Colorado, was ordered for the trials of Timothy McVeigh and Terry Nichols, who had been indicted in connection with the 1995 bombing of the Alfred P. Murrah Federal Building in Oklahoma City. (At trial, both McVeigh and Nichols were convicted. McVeigh received the death penalty and was put to death by lethal injection in early 2001. Nichols was sentenced to life imprisonment.) ▣

VENUE
The geographic district in which a legal action is tried and from which the jury is selected.

STANDING TO SUE
The requirement that an individual must have a sufficient stake in a controversy before he or she can bring a lawsuit. The plaintiff must demonstrate that he or she has been either injured or threatened with injury.

JUSTICIABLE CONTROVERSY
A controversy that is not hypothetical or academic but real and substantial; a requirement that must be satisfied before a court will hear a case.

Standing to Sue

Before a person can bring a lawsuit before a court, the party must have **standing to sue,** or a sufficient "stake" in the matter to justify seeking relief through the court system. In other words, to have standing, a party must have a legally protected and tangible interest at stake in the litigation. The party bringing the lawsuit must have suffered a harm, or have been threatened by a harm, as a result of the action about which she or he has complained. Standing to sue also requires that the controversy at issue be a **justiciable**[9] **controversy**—a controversy that is real and substantial, as opposed to hypothetical or academic.

■EXAMPLE 3.7 To persuade DaimlerChrysler Corporation to build a $1.2 billion Jeep assembly plant in the area, the city of Toledo, Ohio, gave the company an exemption from local property tax for ten years, as well as a state franchise tax credit. Toledo taxpayers filed a lawsuit in state court claiming that the tax breaks violated the commerce clause in the U.S. Constitution. The taxpayers alleged that the tax exemption and credit injured them because they would have to pay higher taxes to cover the shortfall in tax revenues. In 2006, the United States Supreme Court ruled that the taxpayers lacked standing to sue over the incentive program because their alleged injury was "conjectural or hypothetical" and, therefore, there was no justiciable controversy.[10] ▣

The Jeep assembly plant in Toledo, Ohio, which was built after the makers of Jeep, the DaimlerChrysler Corporation, received substantial tax breaks and tax credits from state and city governments. Ohio residents complained that the tax breaks given to DaimlerChrysler would result in a higher tax burden for individuals. What did the United States Supreme Court conclude about whether taxpayers in this situation have standing to sue?
(AP Photo/J.D. Pooley)

---

7. *Yahoo!, Inc. v. La Ligue Contre le Racisme et l'Antisemitisme,* 379 F.3d 1120 (9th Cir. 2004); on rehearing, *Yahoo!, Inc. v. La Ligue Contre le Racisme et l'Antisemitisme,* 433 F.3d 1199 (9th Cir. 2006); *cert.* denied, ___ U.S. ___, 126 S.Ct. 2332, 164 L.Ed.2d 848 (2006).

8. Pronounced *ven*-yoo.

9. Pronounced jus-*tish*-uh-bul.

10. *DaimlerChrysler v. Cuno,* ___ U.S. ___, 126 S.Ct.1854, 164 L.Ed.2d 589 (2006).

EXHIBIT 3–2 Federal Courts and State Court Systems

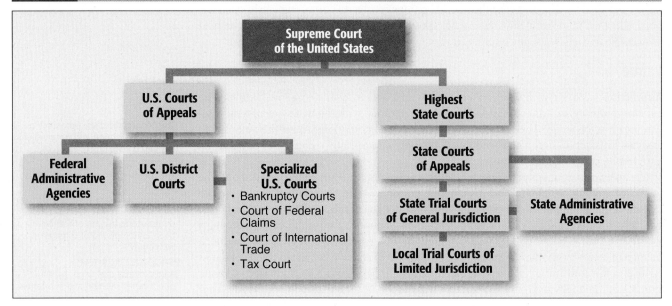

Note that in some situations a person may have standing to sue on behalf of another person, such as a minor or a mentally incompetent person. **EXAMPLE 3.8** Suppose that three-year-old Emma suffers serious injuries as a result of a defectively manufactured toy. Because Emma is a minor, her parent or legal guardian can bring a lawsuit on her behalf. ▣

THE STATE AND FEDERAL COURT SYSTEMS

As mentioned earlier in this chapter, each state has its own court system. Additionally, there is a system of federal courts. Although state court systems differ, Exhibit 3–2 illustrates the basic organizational structure characteristic of the court systems in many states. The exhibit also shows how the federal court system is structured. We turn now to an examination of these court systems, beginning with the state courts.

State Court Systems

Typically, a state court system will include several levels, or tiers, of courts. As indicated in Exhibit 3–2, state courts may include (1) trial courts of limited jurisdiction, (2) trial courts of general jurisdiction, (3) appellate courts, and (4) the state's highest court (often called the state supreme court). Generally, any person who is a party to a lawsuit has the opportunity to plead the case before a trial court and then, if he or she loses, before at least one level of appellate court. Finally, if the case involves a federal statute or federal constitutional issue, the decision of the state supreme court on that issue may be further appealed to the United States Supreme Court.

The states use various methods to select judges for their courts. Usually, voters elect judges, but sometimes judges are appointed. In Iowa, for example, the governor appoints judges, and then the general population decides whether to confirm their appointment in the next general election. The states usually specify the number of years that the judge will serve. In contrast, as you will read shortly, judges in the federal court system are appointed by the president of the United States and, if they are confirmed by the Senate, hold office for life—unless they engage in blatantly illegal conduct.

Does the use of private judges threaten our system of justice? The use of private judges has gained popularity in some states. In California, for example, a number of celebrity divorces—such as that of Brad Pitt and Jennifer Aniston—have taken place in private forums out of the public eye. Unlike a divorce mediator, a private judge (usually a retired judge who charges the parties a hefty fee) has the power to conduct trials and grant legal resolutions, such as divorce decrees.

ETHICAL ISSUE 3.1

    In 2006, private judging came under fire in Ohio because private judges were conducting jury trials and using county courtrooms at the expense of taxpayers. Under an Ohio statute, parties to any civil action can have their dispute tried by a retired judge of their choosing who will make a decision in the matter.[11] Although the parties in one case had opted for a jury trial before a private judge, a public judge, Nancy Margaret Russo, refused to give up jurisdiction over the case on the ground that private judges are not authorized to conduct jury trials. Ultimately, the Ohio Supreme Court agreed with Judge Russo, holding that while the legislature had authorized private judges, they were not allowed to conduct jury trials and must reimburse the county for the use of courtrooms. As the court noted, private judging raises significant public-policy issues that the legislature needs to consider.[12] Some litigants may be willing and able to pay the extra cost to have their dispute heard by a private judge long before they would be able to set a trial date in a regular court. But is such a system fair for those who cannot afford private judges? What are the ethical implications of allowing parties to avoid the public scrutiny of a normal trial by opting to pay extra for a private judge and secret proceedings? Could allowing private judges to hear the cases of wealthier litigants lead to two different systems of justice?

Trial Courts   Trial courts are exactly what their name implies—courts in which trials are held and testimony taken. State trial courts have either general or limited jurisdiction. Trial courts that have general jurisdiction as to subject matter may be called county, district, superior, or circuit courts.[13] The jurisdiction of these courts is often determined by the size of the county in which the court sits. State trial courts of general jurisdiction have jurisdiction over a wide variety of subjects, including both civil disputes and criminal prosecutions. (In some states, trial courts of general jurisdiction may hear appeals from courts of limited jurisdiction.)

    Some courts of limited jurisdiction are called special inferior trial courts or minor judiciary courts. **Small claims courts** are inferior trial courts that hear only civil cases involving claims of less than a certain amount, such as $5,000 (the amount varies from state to state). Suits brought in small claims courts are generally conducted informally, and lawyers are not required (in a few states, lawyers are not even allowed). Another example of an inferior trial court is a local municipal court that hears mainly traffic cases. Decisions of small claims courts and municipal courts may sometimes be appealed to a

SMALL CLAIMS COURT
A special court in which parties may litigate small claims (such as $5,000 or less). Attorneys are not required in small claims courts and, in some states, are not allowed to represent the parties.

---

11. See Ohio Revised Code Section 2701.10.
12. *State ex rel. Russo v. McDonnell*, 110 Ohio St.3d 144, 852 N.E.2d 145 (2006). (*Ex rel.* is Latin for *ex relatione*. The phrase refers to an action brought on behalf of the state, by the attorney general, at the instigation of an individual who has a private interest in the matter.)
13. The name in Ohio is court of common pleas; the name in New York is supreme court.

Child custody cases sometimes make national news, as this one did in 2007. After the death of Anna Nicole Smith—a former Playboy Playmate and actress—a number of disputes erupted over who would take custody of Smith's infant daughter. In this photo, attorneys ask the court for a DNA sample to be taken from Smith's body to assist the court in determining the identify of the child's father. Are child custody disputes normally heard by courts of general jurisdiction or courts of limited jurisdiction?
(AP Photo/Lou Toman/Pool)

state trial court of general jurisdiction. Other courts of limited jurisdiction as to subject matter include domestic relations courts, which handle primarily divorce actions and child-custody disputes, and probate courts, as mentioned earlier.

Appellate, or Reviewing, Courts   Every state has at least one court of appeals (appellate court, or reviewing court), which may be an intermediate appellate court or the state's highest court. About three-fourths of the states have intermediate appellate courts. Generally, courts of appeals do not conduct new trials, in which evidence is submitted to the court and witnesses are examined. Rather, an appellate court panel of three or more judges reviews the record of the case on appeal, which includes a transcript of the trial proceedings, and determines whether the trial court committed an error.

QUESTION OF FACT
In a lawsuit, an issue that involves only disputed facts, and not what the law is on a given point. Questions of fact are decided by the jury in a jury trial (by the judge if there is no jury).

QUESTION OF LAW
In a lawsuit, an issue involving the application or interpretation of a law. Only a judge, not a jury, can rule on questions of law.

Usually, appellate courts focus on questions of law, not questions of fact. A **question of fact** deals with what really happened in regard to the dispute being tried—such as whether a party actually burned a flag. A **question of law** concerns the application or interpretation of the law—such as whether flag-burning is a form of speech protected by the First Amendment to the Constitution. Only a judge, not a jury, can rule on questions of law. Appellate courts normally defer to a trial court's findings on questions of fact because the trial court judge and jury were in a better position to evaluate testimony by directly observing witnesses' gestures, demeanor, and nonverbal behavior during the trial. At the appellate level, the judges review the written transcript of the trial, which does not include these nonverbal elements.

An appellate court will challenge a trial court's finding of fact only when the finding is clearly erroneous (that is, when it is contrary to the evidence presented at trial) or when there is no evidence to support the finding. **■EXAMPLE 3.9** Suppose that a jury concluded that a manufacturer's product harmed the plaintiff but no evidence was submitted to the court to support that conclusion. In that situation, the appellate court would hold that the trial court's decision was erroneous. The options exercised by appellate courts will be discussed further later in this chapter. ■

BE CAREFUL   The decisions of a state's highest court are final on questions of state law.

Highest State Courts   The highest appellate court in a state is usually called the supreme court but may be called by some other name. For example, in both New York and Maryland, the highest state court is called the court of appeals. The decisions of each state's highest court are final on all questions of state law. Only when issues of federal law are involved can a decision made by a state's highest court be overruled by the United States Supreme Court.

The Federal Court System

The federal court system is basically a three-tiered model consisting of (1) U.S. district courts (trial courts of general jurisdiction) and various courts of limited jurisdiction, (2) U.S. courts of appeals (intermediate courts of appeals), and (3) the United States Supreme Court. Unlike state court judges, who are usually elected, federal court judges—including the justices of the Supreme Court—are appointed by the president of the United States and confirmed by the U.S. Senate. All federal judges receive lifetime appointments (because under Article III they "hold their offices during Good Behavior").

U.S. District Courts   At the federal level, the equivalent of a state trial court of general jurisdiction is the district court. There is at least one federal district court in every state. The number of judicial districts can vary over time, primarily owing to population changes and corresponding caseloads. Currently, there are ninety-four federal judicial districts.

U.S. district courts have original jurisdiction in federal matters. Federal cases typically originate in district courts. There are other courts with original, but special (or limited), jurisdiction, such as the federal bankruptcy courts and others shown in Exhibit 3–2.

U.S. Courts of Appeals   In the federal court system, there are thirteen U.S. courts of appeals—also referred to as U.S. circuit courts of appeals. The federal courts of appeals for twelve of the circuits, including the U.S. Court of Appeals for the District of Columbia Circuit, hear appeals from the federal district courts located within their respective judicial circuits. The Court of Appeals for the Thirteenth Circuit, called the Federal Circuit, has national appellate jurisdiction over certain types of cases, such as cases involving patent law and cases in which the U.S. government is a defendant.

The decisions of the circuit courts of appeals are final in most cases, but appeal to the United States Supreme Court is possible. Exhibit 3–3 on the following page shows the geographic boundaries of the U.S. circuit courts of appeals and the boundaries of the U.S. district courts within each circuit.

The United States Supreme Court   The highest level of the three-tiered model of the federal court system is the United States Supreme Court. According to the language of Article III of the U.S. Constitution, there is only one national Supreme Court. All other courts in the federal system are considered "inferior." Congress is empowered to create other inferior courts as it deems necessary. The inferior courts that Congress has created include the second tier in our model—the U.S. courts of appeals—as well as the district courts and any other courts of limited, or specialized, jurisdiction.

The United States Supreme Court consists of nine justices. Although the Supreme Court has original, or trial, jurisdiction in rare instances (set forth in Article III, Section 2), most of its work is as an appeals court. The Supreme Court can review any case decided by any of the federal courts of appeals, and it also has appellate authority over some cases decided in the state courts.

Appeals to the Supreme Court.   To bring a case before the Supreme Court, a party requests that the Court issue a writ of *certiorari*. A **writ of *certiorari***[14] is an order issued by the Supreme Court to a lower court requiring the latter to send it the record of the case for review. The Court will not issue a writ unless at least four of the nine justices approve of it. This is called the **rule of four.** Whether the Court will issue a writ of *certiorari* is entirely within its discretion. The Court is not required to issue one, and most petitions

---

14. Pronounced sur-shee-uh-*rah*-ree.

ON THE WEB

To find information about the federal court system and links to all federal courts, go to the home page of the federal judiciary at

www.uscourts.gov.

ON THE WEB

To access Supreme Court opinions, as well as information about the history and function of the Court, go to the Court's official Web site at

www.supremecourtus.gov.

WRIT OF *CERTIORARI*
A writ from a higher court asking the lower court for the record of a case.

RULE OF FOUR
A rule of the United States Supreme Court under which the Court will not issue a writ of *certiorari* unless at least four justices approve of the decision to issue the writ.

EXHIBIT 3–3 Boundaries of the U.S. Courts of Appeals and U.S. District Courts

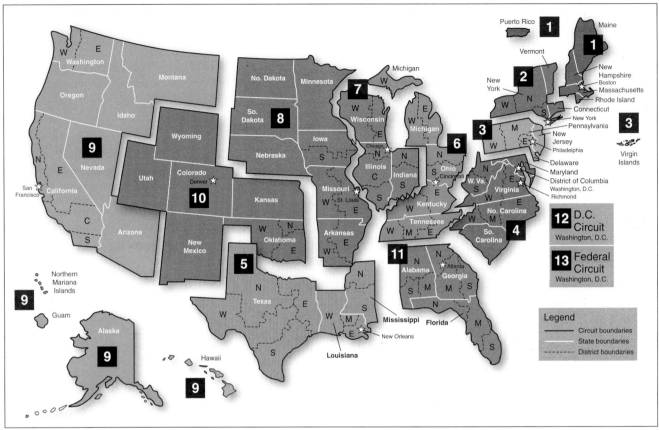

Source: Administrative Office of the United States Courts.

for writs are denied. (Thousands of cases are filed with the Supreme Court each year; yet it hears, on average, fewer than one hundred of these cases.)[15] A denial is not a decision on the merits of a case, nor does it indicate agreement with the lower court's opinion. Furthermore, a denial of the writ has no value as a precedent.

Petitions Granted by the Court. Typically, the Court grants petitions when cases raise important constitutional questions or when the lower courts are issuing conflicting decisions on a significant issue. The justices, however, never explain their reasons for hearing certain cases and not others, so it is difficult to predict which type of case the Court might select.

FOLLOWING A STATE COURT CASE

To illustrate the procedures that would be followed in a civil lawsuit brought in a state court, we present a hypothetical case and follow it through the state court system. The case involves an automobile accident in which Kevin Anderson, driving a Mercedes, struck Lisa Marconi, driving a Ford Taurus. The accident occurred at the intersection of Wilshire Boulevard and Rodeo Drive in Beverly Hills, California. Marconi suffered personal injuries, incurring medical and hospital expenses as well as lost wages for four months.

---

15. From the mid-1950s through the early 1990s, the United States Supreme Court reviewed more cases per year than it has in the last few years. In the Court's 1982–1983 term, for example, the Court issued opinions in 151 cases. In contrast, in its 2005–2006 term, the Court issued opinions in only 87 cases.

The justices of the United States Supreme Court (as of 2007). Does the fact that these justices are appointed for life have any effect on the decisions they reach in the cases they hear? Why or why not? (Photos from collection of the Supreme Court of the United States)

Anderson and Marconi are unable to agree on a settlement, and Marconi sues Anderson. Marconi is the plaintiff, and Anderson is the defendant. Both are represented by lawyers.

During each phase of the **litigation** (the process of working a lawsuit through the court system), Marconi and Anderson will have to observe strict procedural requirements. A large body of law—procedural law—establishes the rules and standards for determining disputes in courts. Procedural rules are very complex, and they vary from court to court and from state to state. There is a set of federal rules of procedure as well as various sets of rules for state courts. Additionally, the applicable procedures will depend on whether the case is a civil or criminal proceeding. Generally, the Marconi-Anderson civil lawsuit will involve the procedures discussed in the following subsections. Keep in mind that attempts to settle the case may be ongoing throughout the trial.

LITIGATION
The process of resolving a dispute through the court system.

The Pleadings

The complaint and answer (and the counterclaim and reply)—all of which are discussed below—taken together are called the **pleadings.** The pleadings inform each party of the other's claims and specify the issues (disputed questions) involved in the case. Because the rules of procedure vary depending on the jurisdiction of the court, the style and form of the pleadings may be quite different in different states.

The Plaintiff's Complaint Marconi's suit against Anderson commences when her lawyer files a **complaint** with the appropriate court. The complaint contains a statement

PLEADINGS
Statements made by the plaintiff and the defendant in a lawsuit that detail the facts, charges, and defenses involved in the litigation. The complaint and answer are part of the pleadings.

COMPLAINT
The pleading made by a plaintiff alleging wrongdoing on the part of the defendant; the document that, when filed with a court, initiates a lawsuit.

alleging (asserting to the court, in a pleading) the facts necessary for the court to take jurisdiction, a brief summary of the facts necessary to show that the plaintiff is entitled to a remedy, and a statement of the remedy the plaintiff is seeking. Complaints may be lengthy or brief, depending on the complexity of the case and the rules of the jurisdiction.

After the complaint has been filed, the sheriff, a deputy of the county, or another *process server* (one who delivers a complaint and summons) serves a **summons** and a copy of the complaint on defendant Anderson. The summons notifies Anderson that he must file an answer to the complaint with both the court and the plaintiff's attorney within a specified time period (usually twenty to thirty days). The summons also informs Anderson that failure to answer may result in a **default judgment** for the plaintiff, meaning the plaintiff could be awarded the damages alleged in her complaint.

Service of process is essential in our legal system. No case can proceed to a trial unless the plaintiff can prove that he or she has properly served the defendant. Did the plaintiff in the following case effect proper service of the summons and the complaint on an out-of-state corporation?

SUMMONS
A document informing a defendant that a legal action has been commenced against him or her and that the defendant must appear in court on a certain date to answer the plaintiff's complaint.

DEFAULT JUDGMENT
A judgment entered by a court against a defendant who has failed to appear in court to answer or defend against the plaintiff's claim.

CASE 3.2   **Cruz v. Fagor America, Inc.**

California Court of Appeal, Fourth District, Division 1, 146 Cal.App.4th 488, 52 Cal.Rptr.3d 862 (2007).

FACTS At the San Diego County Fair in California in the summer of 2001, Alan Cruz's parents bought a pressure cooker distributed by Fagor America, Inc. On September 10, sixteen-year-old Cruz tried to take the lid off of the pressure cooker and was burned on the left side of his torso and thigh. Cruz's parents e-mailed Fagor to alert the company to what had happened. Fagor denied liability. Cruz filed a suit in a California state court against Fagor, alleging negligence and product liability (see Chapters 4 and 18). Cruz mailed a summons and a copy of the complaint to Fagor by certified mail, return receipt requested. The envelope was addressed to "Patricio Barriga, Chairman of the Board, FAGOR AMERICA, INC., A Delaware Corporation, 1099 Wall Street, Lyndhurst, NJ 07071-3678." The receipt was returned with the signature of "Tina Hayes." When Fagor did not file an answer to Cruz's complaint, Cruz obtained a default judgment and was awarded damages of $259,114.50. More than nine months later, Barriga claimed that he had not been notified of the suit, and Fagor filed a motion to set aside the judgment. The court granted the motion, in part, on the ground that Cruz's service of process had not been effective. Cruz appealed to a state intermediate appellate court.

ISSUE Was Cruz's service of process effective?

DECISION Yes. The state intermediate appellate court reversed the decision of the lower court, ruling that it erred in concluding that the judgment against Fagor was void for the lack of a valid service of process.

REASON The appellate court concluded that Cruz met all of the requirements for serving an out-of-state corporation. In compliance with a California state statute, Cruz sent the summons and a copy of the complaint via first-class mail, return receipt requested. Significantly, Cruz addressed the service to Barriga, Fagor's president, not to the corporation itself. Barriga did not sign the receipt, but Hayes did. Under a state statute, service is proper when the summons and a copy of the complaint are delivered to "a person authorized by the corporation to receive service." According to a representative of the U.S. Postal Service, Hayes was a Fagor employee who regularly received mail on her employer's behalf. "The only reasonable inference from the evidence in the record is that Hayes was authorized to accept mail on behalf of Fagor's president at the time she signed the return receipt for the summons and complaint." Furthermore, reasoned the court, "By virtue of her authority to accept mail on Fagor's behalf, Hayes's notice of the action is imputed to Fagor and its officers. * * * To hold otherwise would be to ignore the realities of corporate life, in which the duty to sign for mail received often resides with a designated mailroom employee, a receptionist, a secretary, or an assistant."

 FOR CRITICAL ANALYSIS–Social Consideration
Should a plaintiff be required to serve a defendant with a summons and a copy of a complaint more than once? Why or why not?

The Defendant's Answer   The defendant's **answer** either admits the statements or allegations set forth in the complaint or denies them and outlines any defenses that the defendant may have. If Anderson admits to all of Marconi's allegations in his answer, the court will enter a judgment for Marconi. If Anderson denies any of Marconi's allegations, the litigation will go forward.

Anderson can deny Marconi's allegations and set forth his own claim that Marconi was in fact negligent and therefore owes him compensation for the damage to his Mercedes. This is appropriately called a **counterclaim.** If Anderson files a counterclaim, Marconi will have to answer it with a pleading, normally called a **reply,** which has the same characteristics as an answer.

Anderson can also admit the truth of Marconi's complaint but raise new facts that may result in dismissal of the action. This is called raising an *affirmative defense.* For example, Anderson could assert the expiration of the time period under the relevant *statute of limitations* (a state or federal statute that sets the maximum time period during which a certain action can be brought or rights enforced) as an affirmative defense.

Motion to Dismiss   A **motion to dismiss** requests the court to dismiss the case for stated reasons. Grounds for dismissal of a case include improper delivery of the complaint and summons, improper venue, and the plaintiff's failure to state a claim for which a court could grant relief (a remedy). For example, if Marconi had suffered no injuries or losses as a result of Anderson's negligence, Anderson could move to have the case dismissed because Marconi had not stated a claim for which relief could be granted.

If the judge grants the motion to dismiss, the plaintiff generally is given time to file an amended complaint. If the judge denies the motion, the suit will go forward, and the defendant must then file an answer. Note that if Marconi wishes to discontinue the suit because, for example, an out-of-court settlement has been reached, she can likewise move for dismissal. The court can also dismiss the case on its own motion.

Pretrial Motions

Either party may attempt to get the case dismissed before trial through the use of various pretrial motions. We have already mentioned the motion to dismiss. Two other important pretrial motions are the motion for judgment on the pleadings and the motion for summary judgment.

At the close of the pleadings, either party may make a **motion for judgment on the pleadings,** or on the merits of the case. The judge will grant the motion only when there is no dispute over the facts of the case and the sole issue to be resolved is a question of law. In deciding on the motion, the judge may consider only the evidence contained in the pleadings.

In contrast, in a **motion for summary judgment,** the court may consider evidence outside the pleadings, such as sworn statements (affidavits) by parties or witnesses, or other documents relating to the case. A motion for summary judgment can be made by either party. As with the motion for judgment on the pleadings, a motion for summary judgment will be granted only if there are no genuine questions of fact and the sole question is a question of law. Pretrial motions, including summary judgment motions and motions for judgment on the pleadings, are listed and described in Exhibit 3–4 on the next page.

Discovery

Before a trial begins, each party can use a number of procedural devices to obtain information and gather evidence about the case from the other party or from third parties. The process of obtaining such information is known as **discovery.** Discovery includes gaining access to witnesses, documents, records, and other types of evidence.

ANSWER
Procedurally, a defendant's response to the plaintiff's complaint.

COUNTERCLAIM
A claim made by a defendant in a civil lawsuit against the plaintiff. In effect, the defendant is suing the plaintiff.

REPLY
Procedurally, a plaintiff's response to a defendant's answer.

MOTION TO DISMISS
A pleading in which a defendant asserts that the plaintiff's claim fails to state a cause of action (that is, has no basis in law) or that there are other grounds on which a suit should be dismissed. Although the defendant normally is the party requesting a dismissal, either the plaintiff or the court can also make a motion to dismiss the case.

MOTION FOR JUDGMENT ON THE PLEADINGS
A motion by either party to a lawsuit at the close of the pleadings requesting the court to decide the issue solely on the pleadings without proceeding to trial. The motion will be granted only if no facts are in dispute.

MOTION FOR SUMMARY JUDGMENT
A motion requesting the court to enter a judgment without proceeding to trial. The motion can be based on evidence outside the pleadings and will be granted only if no facts are in dispute.

DISCOVERY
A phase in the litigation process during which the opposing parties may obtain information from each other and from third parties prior to trial.

EXHIBIT 3–4 Pretrial Motions

MOTION TO DISMISS

A motion normally filed by the defendant in which the defendant asks the court to dismiss the case for a specified reason, such as improper service, lack of personal jurisdiction, or the plaintiff's failure to state a claim for which relief can be granted.

MOTION TO STRIKE

A motion filed by the defendant in which the defendant asks the court to strike (delete) from the complaint certain paragraphs contained in the complaint. Motions to strike help to clarify the underlying issues that form the basis for the complaint by removing paragraphs that are redundant or irrelevant to the action.

MOTION TO MAKE MORE DEFINITE AND CERTAIN

A motion filed by the defendant to compel the plaintiff to clarify the basis of the plaintiff's cause of action. The motion is filed when the defendant believes that the complaint is too vague or ambiguous for the defendant to respond to it in a meaningful way.

MOTION FOR JUDGMENT ON THE PLEADINGS

A motion that may be filed by either party in which the party asks the court to enter a judgment in his or her favor based on information contained in the pleadings. A judgment on the pleadings will be made only if there are no facts in dispute and the only question is how the law applies to a set of undisputed facts.

MOTION TO COMPEL DISCOVERY

A motion that may be filed by either party in which the party asks the court to compel the other party to comply with a discovery request. If a party refuses to allow the opponent to inspect and copy certain documents, for example, the party requesting the documents may make a motion to compel production of those documents.

MOTION FOR SUMMARY JUDGMENT

A motion that may be filed by either party in which the party asks the court to enter judgment in her or his favor without a trial. Unlike a motion for judgment on the pleadings, a motion for summary judgment can be supported by evidence outside the pleadings, such as witnesses' affidavits, answers to interrogatories, and other evidence obtained prior to or during discovery.

The Federal Rules of Civil Procedure and similar rules in the states set forth the guidelines for discovery activity. The rules governing discovery are designed to make sure that a witness or a party is not unduly harassed, that privileged material (communications that need not be presented in court) is safeguarded, and that only matters relevant to the case at hand are discoverable.

Discovery prevents surprises at trial by giving parties access to evidence that might otherwise be hidden. This allows both parties to learn as much as they can about what to expect at a trial before they reach the courtroom. It also serves to narrow the issues so that trial time is spent on the main questions in the case.

DEPOSITION
The testimony of a party to a lawsuit or a witness taken under oath before a trial.

Depositions and Interrogatories Discovery can involve the use of depositions or interrogatories, or both. **Depositions** are sworn testimony by a party to the lawsuit or any witness.

The person being deposed (the deponent) answers questions asked by the attorneys, and the questions and answers are recorded by an authorized court official and sworn to and signed by the deponent. (Occasionally, written depositions are taken when witnesses are unable to appear in person.) The answers given to depositions will, of course, help the attorneys prepare their cases. They can also be used in court to impeach (challenge the credibility of) a party or a witness who changes his or her testimony at the trial. In addition, the answers given in a deposition can be used as testimony if the witness is not available at trial.

Interrogatories are written questions for which written answers are prepared and then signed under oath. The main difference between interrogatories and written depositions is that interrogatories are directed to a party to the lawsuit (the plaintiff or the defendant), not to a witness, and the party can prepare answers with the aid of an attorney. The scope of interrogatories is broader because parties are obligated to answer the questions, even if that means disclosing information from their records and files.

INTERROGATORIES
A series of written questions for which written answers are prepared by a party to a lawsuit, usually with the assistance of the party's attorney, and then signed under oath.

Requests for Other Information   A party can serve a written request on the other party for an admission of the truth of matters relating to the trial. Any matter admitted under such a request is conclusively established for the trial. For example, Marconi can ask Anderson to admit that he was driving at a speed of forty-five miles an hour. A request for admission saves time at trial because the parties will not have to spend time proving facts on which they already agree.

A party can also gain access to documents and other items not in her or his possession in order to inspect and examine them. Likewise, a party can gain "entry upon land" to inspect the premises. Anderson's attorney, for example, normally can gain permission to inspect and photocopy Marconi's car repair bills.

When the physical or mental condition of one party is in question, the opposing party can ask the court to order a physical or mental examination. If the court is willing to make the order, which it will do only if the need for the information outweighs the right to privacy of the person to be examined, the opposing party can obtain the results of the examination.

Electronic Discovery   Any relevant material, including information stored electronically, can be the object of a discovery request. Electronic evidence, or **e-evidence,** includes all types of computer-generated or electronically recorded information, such as e-mail, voice mail, spreadsheets, word-processing documents, and other data. E-evidence is important because it can reveal significant facts that are not discoverable by other means. For example, whenever a person is working on a computer, information is being recorded on the hard drive disk without ever being saved by the user. This information includes the file's location, path, creator, date created, date last accessed, concealed notes, earlier versions, passwords, and formatting. It reveals information about how, when, and by whom a document was created, accessed, modified, and transmitted. This information can be obtained only from the file in its electronic format—not from printed-out versions.

E-EVIDENCE
Evidence that consists of computer-generated or electronically recorded information, including e-mail, voice mail, spreadsheets, word-processing documents, and other data.

The federal rules and most state rules (as well as court decisions) allow parties to obtain discovery of electronic data (or e-evidence). In fact, amendments to the Federal Rules of Civil Procedure that took effect in December 2006 specifically deal with the preservation, retrieval, and production of electronic data. Traditional means, such as interrogatories and depositions, are still used to find out about the e-evidence, but the parties must usually hire an expert to retrieve evidence in its electronic format. Using special software, the expert can reconstruct e-mail exchanges to establish who knew what and when they knew it. The expert can even recover files from a computer that the user thought had been deleted. Reviewing back-up copies of documents and e-mail can provide useful—and often quite damaging—information about how a particular matter progressed over several weeks or months. Data stored on back-up tapes, however, become usable only when fragmented data contained on the tapes are joined together and erased data are reconstructed.

Electronic Discovery and Document Retention

Under the Federal Rules of Civil Procedure (FRCP), the party responding to a discovery request has traditionally been required to pay the expenses involved in obtaining the requested materials. Only if compliance was too burdensome or costly could a judge limit the scope of the request or shift some or all of the costs to the requesting party. Today, however, electronic discovery has dramatically increased the costs associated with complying with discovery requests. Electronic discovery typically involves hiring computer forensics experts to make "image" copies of desktop, laptop, and server hard drives. Experts are also needed to retrieve and reconstruct data from removable storage media (such as DVDs, CD-ROMs, and pen drives), back-up tapes, voice mail, cell phones, and any other devices that digitally store data. Consequently, both providing electronic data discovery and failing to preserve electronic data for discovery can prove costly for today's businesspersons.

Courts May Shift the Costs of Electronic Data Discovery

As mentioned in the text, the process of electronic data discovery is expensive and can easily run into thousands—if not millions—of dollars. In one case, for example, a court found that restoring the back-up tapes of just one of the many defendants in the case would cost $9.75 million. Acquiring 200,000 e-mail messages from another defendant could cost as much as $84,000, with an additional $247,000 to have an attorney review the retrieved documents.[a]

Increasingly, the courts are shifting part of the costs of obtaining e-evidence to the party requesting it (usually the plaintiff), particularly if the electronic data are in a relatively inaccessible form, such as in back-up tapes or deleted files. If the data are in an accessible format, the usual rules of discovery apply: the responding party pays the costs of producing responsive data. Cost-shifting is appropriate only when the electronic discovery imposes an undue burden or expense on the responding party. In deciding whether to shift the costs, the courts also consider other factors, such as the availability of the information from other sources, the total cost of production compared with the amount in controversy, and each party's ability to pay the costs. Sometimes, a court may require the responding party to restore and produce representative documents from a small sample of the requested medium to verify the relevance of the data before the party incurs significant expenses.[b]

a. *Rowe Entertainment, Inc. v. William Morris Agency,* 2002 WL 975713 (S.D.N.Y. 2002).
b. See, for example, *Zubulake v. UBS Warburg, LLC,* 2003 WL 21087884 (S.D.N.Y. 2003); and *Quinby v. WestLB AG,* 2006 WL 2597900 (S.D.N.Y. 2006).

Although electronic discovery has significant advantages over paper discovery, it is also time consuming and expensive. These costs are amplified when the parties involved in the lawsuit are large corporations with many offices and employees. Moreover, as some businesses are finding out, failure to retain electronic data or to comply with electronic discovery requests can also be costly. This chapter's *Adapting the Law to the Online Environment* feature discusses how the law pertaining to electronic discovery is evolving.

Pretrial Conference

Either party or the court can request a pretrial conference, or hearing. Usually, the hearing consists of an informal discussion between the judge and the opposing attorneys after discovery has taken place. The purpose of the hearing is to explore the possibility of a settlement without trial and, if this is not possible, to identify the matters that are in dispute and to plan the course of the trial.

Jury Selection

A trial can be held with or without a jury. The Seventh Amendment to the U.S. Constitution guarantees the right to a jury trial for cases in *federal* courts when the amount in controversy exceeds $20, but this guarantee does not apply to state courts. Most states have similar guarantees in their own constitutions (although the threshold dollar

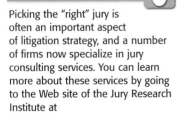

The Need to Preserve Electronic Data

Many companies have no written document-preservation policies and routinely delete data from servers and overwrite e-mails. Whenever there is a "reasonable anticipation of litigation," however, the law requires that all relevant documents must be preserved. In addition, newly amended Rule 26(b)(2) of the FRCP states that even though a party is not required to produce "inaccessible" data (unless the court has granted a motion to compel), the data must still be preserved. Preserving data can be a challenge, particularly for large companies that have electronic data scattered across multiple networks, servers, desktops, laptops, handheld devices, and even home computers or other off-site locations. Nevertheless, it is a necessity. Given that most documents today are in electronic form and are never printed out to hard copy, litigation success can hinge on electronic discovery.

The Consequences of Failing to Preserve or Provide E-Evidence Discovery

As an example of the serious consequences of failing to preserve electronic data, consider what happened to Morgan Stanley & Company, Inc.[c] Coleman Holdings sued Morgan Stanley (MS) for fraud in connection with a stock sale transaction that took place in 1998 and 1999. After receiving notice of the suit in 2003, MS directed its investment bankers to preserve paper documents but continued its practice of overwriting e-mails, even though Coleman had requested e-mail discovery. In April 2004, the court ordered MS to search the

c. *Coleman (Parent) Holdings, Inc. v. Morgan Stanley & Co., Inc.,* 2005 WL 679071 (Fla.Cir.Ct. 2005).

back-up tapes relating to the thirty-six employees involved in the transaction. One month later, MS produced 1,300 pages of e-mails, but it did not search or disclose the existence of more than 1,700 back-up tapes at its various offices.

Six months after the discovery deadline set by the court, MS notified Coleman that it had discovered additional e-mail back-up tapes and provided an additional 8,000 pages of e-mails and attachments. The court concluded that MS had willfully ignored its discovery obligations and imposed sanctions on the firm. The court also authorized the jury to be instructed that a reasonable person could conclude that evidence of MS's discovery misconduct demonstrated its consciousness of guilt. The court reasoned that MS had a duty to preserve and maintain e-mails in readily accessible form.

In other cases, failure to preserve e-evidence or provide electronic discovery has led a firm to settle the case. For instance, Gateway's failure to preserve and produce a single damaging e-mail caused that firm to settle a dispute on the evening before trial.[d]

 FOR CRITICAL ANALYSIS *Given the significant and often burdensome costs associated with electronic discovery, should courts consider cost-shifting in every case involving electronic discovery? Why or why not? How might a large corporation protect itself from allegations that it intentionally failed to preserve electronic data? What should companies do to be proactive in preserving electronic data for discovery?*

d. *Adams v. Gateway, Inc.,* 2006 WL 2563418 (D. Utah 2006).

---

amount is higher than $20). The right to a trial by jury does not have to be exercised, and many cases are tried without a jury. In most states and in federal courts, one of the parties must request a jury in a civil case, or the right is presumed to be waived.

Before a jury trial commences, a jury must be selected. The jury selection process is known as ***voir dire***.[16] During *voir dire* in most jurisdictions, attorneys for the plaintiff and the defendant ask prospective jurors oral questions to determine whether a potential jury member is biased or has any connection with a party to the action or with a prospective witness. In some jurisdictions, the judge may do all or part of the questioning based on written questions submitted by counsel for the parties.

During *voir dire*, a party may challenge a certain number of prospective jurors *peremptorily*—that is, ask that an individual not be sworn in as a juror without providing any reason. Alternatively, a party may challenge a prospective juror *for cause*—that is, provide a reason why an individual should not be sworn in as a juror. If the judge grants the challenge, the individual is asked to step down. A prospective juror may not be excluded from the jury by the use of discriminatory challenges, however, such as those based on racial criteria[17] or gender.[18]

VOIR DIRE
Old French phrase meaning "to speak the truth." In legal language, the phrase refers to the process in which the attorneys question prospective jurors to learn about their backgrounds, attitudes, biases, and other characteristics that may affect their ability to serve as impartial jurors.

TAKE NOTE A prospective juror cannot be excluded solely on the basis of his or her race or gender.

---

16. Pronounced vwahr *deehr.*
17. *Batson v. Kentucky,* 476 U.S. 79, 106 S.Ct. 1712, 90 L.Ed.2d 69 (1986).
18. *J.E.B. v. Alabama ex rel. T.B.,* 511 U.S. 127, 114 S.Ct. 1419, 128 L.Ed.2d 89 (1994).

At the Trial

At the beginning of the trial, the attorneys present their opening arguments, setting forth the facts that they expect to provide during the trial. Then the plaintiff's case is presented. In our hypothetical case, Marconi's lawyer would introduce evidence (relevant documents, exhibits, and the testimony of witnesses) to support Marconi's position. The defendant has the opportunity to challenge any evidence introduced and to cross-examine any of the plaintiff's witnesses.

At the end of the plaintiff's case, the defendant's attorney has the opportunity to ask the judge to direct a verdict for the defendant on the ground that the plaintiff has presented no evidence that would justify the granting of the plaintiff's remedy. This is called a **motion for a directed verdict** (known in federal courts as a *motion for judgment as a matter of law*). If the motion is not granted (it seldom is granted), the defendant's attorney then presents the evidence and witnesses for the defendant's case. At the conclusion of the defendant's case, the defendant's attorney has another opportunity to make a motion for a directed verdict. The plaintiff's attorney can challenge any evidence introduced and cross-examine the defendant's witnesses.

After the defense concludes its presentation, the attorneys present their closing arguments, each urging a verdict in favor of her or his client. The judge instructs the jury in the law that applies to the case (these instructions are often called *charges*), and the jury retires to the jury room to deliberate a verdict. In the Marconi-Anderson case, the jury will not only decide for the plaintiff or for the defendant but, if it finds for the plaintiff, will also decide on the amount of the **award** (the compensation to be paid to her).

MOTION FOR A DIRECTED VERDICT
In a jury trial, a motion for the judge to take the decision out of the hands of the jury and to direct a verdict for the party who filed the motion on the ground that the other party has not produced sufficient evidence to support her or his claim.

AWARD
In litigation, the amount of monetary compensation awarded to a plaintiff in a civil lawsuit as damages. In the context of alternative dispute resolution, the decision rendered by an arbitrator.

MOTION FOR JUDGMENT *N.O.V.*
A motion requesting the court to grant judgment in favor of the party making the motion on the ground that the jury's verdict against him or her was unreasonable and erroneous.

MOTION FOR A NEW TRIAL
A motion asserting that the trial was so fundamentally flawed (because of error, newly discovered evidence, prejudice, or another reason) that a new trial is necessary to prevent a miscarriage of justice.

Posttrial Motions

After the jury has rendered its verdict, either party may make a posttrial motion. If Marconi wins and Anderson's attorney has previously moved for a directed verdict, Anderson's attorney may make a **motion for judgment *n.o.v.*** (from the Latin *non obstante veredicto*, which means "notwithstanding the verdict"—called a *motion for judgment as a matter of law* in the federal courts). Such a motion will be granted only if the jury's verdict was unreasonable and erroneous. If the judge grants the motion, the jury's verdict will be set aside, and a judgment will be entered in favor of the opposite party (Anderson).

Alternatively, Anderson could make a **motion for a new trial,** asking the judge to set aside the adverse verdict and to hold a new trial. The motion will be granted if, after looking at all the evidence, the judge is convinced that the jury was in error but does not feel it is appropriate to grant judgment for the other side. A judge can also grant a new trial on the basis of newly discovered evidence, misconduct by the participants or the jury during the trial, or error by the judge.

The Appeal

Assume here that any posttrial motion is denied and that Anderson appeals the case. (If Marconi wins but receives a smaller monetary award than she sought, she can appeal also.) Keep in mind, though, that a party cannot appeal a trial court's decision simply because he or she is dissatisfied with the outcome of the trial. A party must have legitimate grounds to file an appeal; that is, he or she must be able to claim that the lower court committed an error. If Anderson has grounds to appeal the case, a notice of appeal must be filed with the clerk of the trial court within a prescribed time. Anderson now becomes the appellant, or petitioner, and Marconi becomes the appellee, or respondent.

Filing the Appeal Anderson's attorney files with the appellate court the record on appeal, which includes the pleadings, the trial transcript, the judge's rulings on motions made by the parties, and other trial-related documents. Anderson's attorney will also provide a condensation of the record, known as an *abstract*, which is filed with the reviewing court along with the brief. The **brief** is a formal legal document outlining the facts and issues of the case, the judge's rulings or jury's findings that should be reversed or modified, the applicable law, and arguments on Anderson's behalf (citing applicable statutes and relevant cases as precedents).

Marconi's attorney will file an answering brief. Anderson's attorney can file a reply to Marconi's brief, although it is not required. The reviewing court then considers the case.

Appellate Review As mentioned earlier, a court of appeals does not hear evidence. Rather, it reviews the record for errors of law. Its decision concerning a case is based on the record on appeal, the abstracts, and the attorneys' briefs. The attorneys can present oral arguments, after which the case is taken under advisement. In general, appellate courts do not reverse findings of fact unless the findings are unsupported or contradicted by the evidence.

If the reviewing court believes that an error was committed during the trial or that the jury was improperly instructed, the judgment will be *reversed*. Sometimes, the case will be *remanded* (sent back to the court that originally heard the case) for a new trial. Even when a case is remanded to a trial court for further proceedings, however, the appellate court normally spells out how the relevant law should be interpreted and applied to the case.

A case may be remanded for several reasons. For instance, if the appellate court decides that a judge improperly granted summary judgment, the case will be remanded for a trial. If the appellate court decides that the trial judge erroneously applied the law, the case will be remanded for a new trial, with instructions to the trial court to apply the law as clarified by the appellate court. If the appellate court decides that the trial jury's award of damages was too high, the case will be remanded with instructions to reduce the damages award. In most cases, the judgment of the lower court is *affirmed*, resulting in the enforcement of the court's judgment or decree.

Appeal to a Higher Appellate Court If the reviewing court is an intermediate appellate court, the losing party may decide to appeal to the state supreme court (the highest state court). Such a petition corresponds to a petition for a writ of *certiorari* from the United States Supreme Court. Although the losing party has a right to ask (petition) a higher court to review the case, the party does not have a right to have the case heard by the higher appellate court. Appellate courts normally have discretionary power and can accept or reject an appeal. Like the United States Supreme Court, in general state supreme courts deny most appeals. If the appeal is granted, new briefs must be filed before the state supreme court, and the attorneys may be allowed or requested to present oral arguments. Like the intermediate appellate court, the supreme court may reverse or affirm the appellate court's decision or remand the case. At this point, the case typically has reached its end (unless a federal question is at issue and one of the parties has legitimate grounds to seek review by a federal appellate court).

Enforcing the Judgment

The uncertainties of the litigation process are compounded by the lack of guarantees that any judgment will be enforceable. Even if a plaintiff wins an award of damages in court, the defendant may not have sufficient assets or insurance to cover that amount. Usually, one of the factors considered before a lawsuit is initiated is whether the defendant has sufficient assets to cover the amount of damages sought, should the plaintiff win the case. What other factors should be considered when deciding whether to initiate a lawsuit? See the *Application* feature at the end of this chapter for answers to this question.

BRIEF
A formal legal document prepared by a party's attorney (in answer to the appellant's brief) and submitted to an appellate court when a case is appealed. The appellant's brief outlines the facts and issues of the case, the judge's rulings or jury's findings that should be reversed or modified, the applicable law, and the arguments on the client's behalf.

THE COURTS ADAPT TO THE ONLINE WORLD

We have already mentioned that the courts have attempted to adapt traditional jurisdictional concepts to the online world. Not surprisingly, the Internet has also brought about changes in court procedures and practices, including new methods for filing pleadings and other documents and issuing decisions and opinions. Some jurisdictions are exploring the possibility of cyber courts, in which legal proceedings could be conducted totally online.

Electronic Filing

The federal court system first experimented with an electronic filing system in January 1996, and its Case Management/Electronic Case Files (CM/ECF) system has now been implemented in nearly all of the federal appellate courts and bankruptcy courts, as well as a majority of the district courts. The CM/ECF system allows federal courts to accept documents filed electronically in PDF format via the Internet. A few federal bankruptcy courts now even *require* some documents to be filed electronically.

Nearly half of the states have some form of electronic filing. These states include Arizona, California, Colorado, Connecticut, Delaware, Georgia, Kansas, Maryland, Michigan, New Hampshire, New Jersey, New Mexico, New York, North Carolina, North Dakota, Ohio, Pennsylvania, Utah, Texas, Virginia, Washington, and Wisconsin, as well as the District of Columbia. Some of these states, including Arizona, California, Colorado, Delaware, and New York, offer statewide e-filing systems. Generally, when electronic filing is made available, it is optional. Nonetheless, some state courts have now made e-filing mandatory in certain types of disputes, such as complex civil litigation.

The expenses associated with an appeal can be considerable, and e-filing can add substantially to the cost. In some cases, appellants who successfully appeal a judgment are entitled to be awarded their costs, including an amount for printing the copies of the record on appeal and the briefs. In other cases, the courts have refused to award e-filing costs to the successful party even though the court encouraged the parties to submit briefs and other documents in an electronic format.[19]

Courts Online

Most courts today have sites on the Web. Of course, each court decides what to make available at its site. Some courts display only the names of court personnel and office phone numbers. Others add court rules and forms. Many appellate court sites include judicial decisions, although the decisions may remain online for only a limited time period. In addition, in some states, such as California and Florida, court clerks offer docket information and other searchable databases online.

Appellate court decisions are often posted online immediately after they are rendered. Recent decisions of the U.S. courts of appeals, for example, are available online at their Web sites. The United States Supreme Court also has an official Web site and publishes its opinions there immediately after they are announced to the public. (These Web sites are listed elsewhere in this chapter in the *On the Web* features.) In fact, even decisions that are designated as unpublished opinions by the appellate courts are often published online (as discussed in the *Adapting the Law to the Online Environment* feature in Chapter 1 on pages 12 and 13).

ON THE WEB

For a list of the federal courts that accept electronic filing, go to the following page at a Web site maintained by the Administrative Office of the U.S. Courts:

www.uscourts.gov/cmecf/cmecf_court.html.

ON THE WEB

For links to state court rules addressing e-filing issues, go to the following site, which is provided by the American Bar Association:

www.abanet.org/tech/ltrc/research/ efiling/rules.html.

---

19. See, for example, *Phansalkar v. Andersen Weinroth & Co.*, 356 F.3d 188 (2d Cir. 2004).

Cyber Courts and Proceedings

Someday, litigants may be able to use cyber courts, in which judicial proceedings take place only on the Internet. The parties to a case could meet online to make their arguments and present their evidence. This might be done with e-mail submissions, through video cameras, in designated "chat" rooms, at closed sites, or through the use of other Internet facilities. These courtrooms could be efficient and economical. We might also see the use of virtual lawyers, judges, and juries—and possibly the replacement of court personnel with computer software. Already the state of Michigan has passed legislation creating cyber courts that will hear cases involving technology issues and high-tech businesses. Many lawyers predict that other states will follow suit.

The courts may also use the Internet in other ways. In a groundbreaking decision in early 2001, for example, a Florida county court granted "virtual" visitation rights in a couple's divorce proceeding. Although the court granted custody of the couple's ten-year-old daughter to the father, the court also ordered each parent to buy a computer and a video-conferencing system so that the mother could "visit" with her child via the Internet at any time.[20]

ON THE WEB

To read about Michigan's cyber court legislation, go to the following Web page sponsored by Matthew R. Halpin & Associates, P.C.:

www.michigancyberlaw.com.

How will online access to courts affect privacy? In the past, trial court records, although normally available to the public, remained obscure because they were difficult to access: a person had to travel to the courthouse in person and ask to see the documents. As online access to court records increases and electronic filing becomes the norm, this "practical obscurity," as lawyers call it, may soon disappear. Electronic filing on a nationwide basis would open up all court documents to anyone with an Internet connection and a Web browser. Utilizing special "data-mining" software, anyone could go online and within just a few minutes access information—ranging from personal health records to financial reports to criminal violations—from dozens of courts. This means that serious privacy issues are at stake. Many courts are struggling with the issue of whether to restrict public access to certain types of documents and have taken a myriad of different approaches. Some courts make civil case information available but restrict Internet access to criminal case information. Other courts, such as those in Florida, have deemed certain types of documents and court proceedings confidential and no longer post this information online.[21] Still other courts, such as those in South Dakota, Vermont, and Washington, have developed policies to prevent the parties' confidential data and Social Security numbers from being released on public documents.

ETHICAL ISSUE 3.2

ALTERNATIVE DISPUTE RESOLUTION

Litigation is expensive. It is also time consuming. Because of the backlog of cases pending in many courts, several years may pass before a case is actually tried. For these and other reasons, more and more businesspersons are turning to **alternative dispute resolution (ADR)** as a means of settling their disputes.

The great advantage of ADR is its flexibility. Methods of ADR range from the parties sitting down together and attempting to work out their differences to multinational corporations agreeing to resolve a dispute through a formal hearing before a panel of experts. Normally, the parties themselves can control how the dispute will be settled, what procedures will be

ALTERNATIVE DISPUTE RESOLUTION (ADR)
The resolution of disputes in ways other than those involved in the traditional judicial process. Negotiation, mediation, and arbitration are forms of ADR.

---

20. For a discussion of this case, see Shelley Emling, "After the Divorce, Internet Visits?" *Austin American-Statesman,* January 30, 2001, pp. A1 and A10.
21. *In re Report of Supreme Court Workgroup on Public Records,* 825 So.2d 889 (Fla. 2002). See also *Brennan v. Giles County Board of Education,* ___ S.W.3d ___ (Tenn.Ct.App. 2005).

used, whether a neutral third party will be present or make a decision, and whether that decision will be legally binding or nonbinding.

Today, more than 90 percent of cases are settled before trial through some form of ADR. Indeed, most states either require or encourage parties to undertake ADR prior to trial. Many federal courts have instituted ADR programs as well. In the following pages, we examine the basic forms of ADR. Keep in mind, though, that new methods of ADR—and new combinations of existing methods—are constantly being devised and employed.

Negotiation

NEGOTIATION
A process in which parties attempt to settle their dispute informally, with or without attorneys to represent them.

The simplest form of ADR is **negotiation,** a process in which the parties attempt to settle their dispute informally, with or without attorneys to represent them. Attorneys frequently advise their clients to negotiate a settlement voluntarily before they proceed to trial. Parties may even try to negotiate a settlement during a trial, or after the trial but before an appeal. Negotiation traditionally involves just the parties themselves and (typically) their attorneys. The attorneys, though, are advocates—they are obligated to put their clients' interests first.

Mediation

MEDIATION
A method of settling disputes outside of court by using the services of a neutral third party, who acts as a communicating agent between the parties and assists them in negotiating a settlement.

In **mediation,** a neutral third party acts as a mediator and works with both sides in the dispute to facilitate a resolution. The mediator talks with the parties separately as well as jointly and emphasizes their points of agreement in an attempt to help the parties evaluate their options. Although the mediator may propose a solution (called a mediator's proposal), he or she does not make a decision resolving the matter. States that require parties to undergo ADR before trial often offer mediation as one of the ADR options or (as in Florida) the only option.

One of the biggest advantages of mediation is that it is not as adversarial as litigation. In trials, the parties "do battle" with each other in the courtroom, trying to prove one another wrong, while the judge is usually a passive observer. In mediation, the mediator takes an active role and attempts to bring the parties together so that they can come to a mutually satisfactory resolution. The mediation process tends to reduce the hostility between the disputants, allowing them to resume their former relationship without bad feelings. For this reason, mediation is often the preferred form of ADR for disputes involving business partners, employers and employees, or other parties involved in long-term relationships.

■**EXAMPLE 3.10** Suppose that two business partners have a dispute over how the profits of their firm should be distributed. If the dispute is litigated, the parties will be adversaries, and their respective attorneys will emphasize how the parties' positions differ, not what they have in common. In contrast, when a dispute is mediated, the mediator emphasizes the common ground shared by the parties and helps them work toward agreement. The business partners can work out the distribution of profits without damaging their continuing relationship as partners. ■

ON THE WEB

For a collection of information and links related to alternative dispute resolution, mediation, and arbitration, go to the Web site of Hieros Gamos at

www.hg.org/adr.html.

Arbitration

ARBITRATION
The settling of a dispute by submitting it to a disinterested third party (other than a court), who renders a decision that is (most often) legally binding.

A more formal method of ADR is **arbitration,** in which an arbitrator (a neutral third party or a panel of experts) hears a dispute and imposes a resolution on the parties. Arbitration is unlike other forms of ADR because the third party hearing the dispute makes a decision for the parties. Exhibit 3–5 outlines the basic differences among the three traditional forms of ADR. Usually, the parties in arbitration agree that the third party's decision will be *legally binding,* although the parties can also agree to *nonbinding* arbitration. (Additionally, arbitration that is mandated by the courts often is not binding on the parties.) In nonbinding arbitration, the parties can go forward with a lawsuit if they do not agree with the arbitrator's decision.

In some respects, formal arbitration resembles a trial, although usually the procedural rules are much less restrictive than those governing litigation. In the typical arbitration, the parties present opening arguments and ask for specific remedies. Evidence is then presented, and witnesses may be called and examined by both sides. The arbitrator then renders a decision, which is called an *award*.

An arbitrator's award is usually the final word on the matter. Although the parties may appeal an arbitrator's decision, a court's review of the decision will be much more restricted in scope than an appellate court's review of a trial court's decision. The general view is that because the parties were free to frame the issues and set the powers of the arbitrator at the outset, they cannot complain about the results. The award will be set aside only if the arbitrator's conduct or "bad faith" substantially prejudiced the rights of one of the parties, if the award violates an established public policy, or if the arbitrator exceeded her or his powers (arbitrated issues that the parties did not agree to submit to arbitration).

Arbitration Clauses and Statutes Virtually any commercial matter can be submitted to arbitration. Frequently, parties include an **arbitration clause** in a contract (a written agreement—see Chapter 8); the clause provides that any dispute that arises under the contract will be resolved through arbitration rather than through the court system. Parties can also agree to arbitrate a dispute after a dispute arises.

Most states have statutes (often based in part on the Uniform Arbitration Act of 1955) under which arbitration clauses will be enforced, and some state statutes compel arbitration of certain types of disputes, such as those involving public employees. At the federal level, the Federal Arbitration Act (FAA), enacted in 1925, enforces arbitration clauses in contracts involving maritime activity and interstate commerce (though its applicability to employment contracts has been controversial, as discussed in a later subsection). Because of the breadth of the commerce clause (see Chapter 2), arbitration agreements involving transactions only slightly connected to the flow of interstate commerce may fall under the FAA.

The question in the following case was whether a court or an arbitrator should consider a claim that an entire contract, including its arbitration clause, is rendered void by the alleged illegality of a separate provision in the contract.

Supporters of a union that represents firefighters and paramedics stage a protest during a contract dispute with the city of Philadelphia. An arbitration panel ruled in favor of the union and ordered a wage increase, and the city appealed. On what grounds can a court, on appeal, set aside the decision of an arbitration panel?
(Photo Courtesy of the Philadelphia Fire Fighters' Union–IAFF Local 22. All rights reserved.)

ARBITRATION CLAUSE
A clause in a contract that provides that, in the event of a dispute, the parties will submit the dispute to arbitration rather than litigate the dispute in court.

EXHIBIT 3–5	Basic Differences in the Traditional Forms of ADR		
TYPE OF ADR	**DESCRIPTION**	**NEUTRAL THIRD PARTY PRESENT**	**WHO DECIDES THE RESOLUTION**
Negotiation	The parties meet informally with or without their attorneys and attempt to agree on a resolution.	No	The parties themselves reach a resolution.
Mediation	A neutral third party meets with the parties and emphasizes points of agreement to help them resolve their dispute.	Yes	The parties, but the mediator may suggest or propose a resolution.
Arbitration	The parties present their arguments and evidence before an arbitrator at a hearing, and the arbitrator renders a decision resolving the parties' dispute.	Yes	The arbitrator imposes a resolution on the parties that may be either binding or nonbinding.

CASE 3.3 **Buckeye Check Cashing, Inc. v. Cardegna**

Supreme Court of the United States, 546 U.S. 440, 126 S.Ct. 1204, 163 L.Ed.2d 1038 (2006).
www.law.cornell.edu/supct/index.html[a]

FACTS Buckeye Check Cashing, Inc., cashes personal checks for consumers in Florida. Buckeye agrees to delay submitting a check for payment in exchange for a consumer's payment of a "finance charge." For each transaction, the consumer signs a "Deferred Deposit and Disclosure Agreement," which states, "By signing this Agreement, you agree that i[f] a dispute of any kind arises out of this Agreement * * * th[e]n either you or we or third parties involved can choose to have that dispute resolved by binding arbitration." John Cardegna and others filed a suit in a Florida state court against Buckeye, alleging that the "finance charge" represented an illegally high interest rate in violation of Florida state laws, thereby rendering the agreement "criminal on its face." Buckeye filed a motion to compel arbitration. The court denied the motion. On Buckeye's appeal, a state intermediate appellate court reversed this denial, but on the plaintiffs' appeal, the Florida Supreme Court reversed the lower appellate court's decision. Buckeye appealed to the United States Supreme Court.

ISSUE Can a court consider a claim that an entire contract, including its arbitration clause, is rendered void by the alleged illegality of a separate provision in the contract?

DECISION No. The United States Supreme Court reversed the judgment of the Florida Supreme Court and remanded the case for further proceedings. The Court ruled that a challenge to the validity of a contract as a whole, and not specifically to an arbitration clause contained in the contract, must be resolved by an arbitrator.

a. In the "Supreme Court Collection" menu at the top of the page, click on "Search." When that page opens, in the "Search for:" box, type "Buckeye," choose "All decisions" in the accompanying list, and click on "Search." In the result, scroll to the name of the case and click on the appropriate link to access the opinion.

REASON The Court set out three propositions. "First, as a matter of substantive federal arbitration law, an arbitration provision is severable [capable of being legally separated] from the remainder of the contract. Second, unless the challenge is to the arbitration clause itself, the issue of the contract's validity is considered by the arbitrator in the first instance. Third, this arbitration law applies in state as well as federal courts." The Court concluded that here, because the plaintiffs challenged the contract's "finance charge," but not its arbitration provisions, those provisions were enforceable apart from the remainder of the contract. "The challenge should therefore be considered by an arbitrator, not a court." The plaintiffs also argued that the only arbitration agreements to which the Federal Arbitration Act (FAA) applies are those involving contracts and that the Buckeye agreement was not a contract because it was "void *ab initio*" (from the beginning). The FAA allows a challenge to an arbitration provision "upon such grounds as exist at law or in equity for the revocation [cancellation] of any contract." The Court reasoned that this includes contracts that later prove to be void. "Otherwise, the grounds for revocation would be limited to those that rendered a contract voidable—which would mean (implausibly) that an arbitration agreement could be challenged as voidable but not as void."

  WHY IS THIS CASE IMPORTANT TO BUSINESSPERSONS? *The result illustrates the rule that the Federal Arbitration Act can be the basis for severing an arbitration clause from a contract and separately enforcing the clause. The holding in the* Buckeye *case makes this possible even if the remainder of the contract is later held to be invalid and even if a state law otherwise prohibits the enforcement of an arbitration clause in a contract that is unenforceable under state law.*

▣

KEEP IN MIND Litigation—even of a dispute over whether a particular matter should be submitted to arbitration—can be time consuming and expensive.

The Issue of Arbitrability When a dispute arises as to whether the parties have agreed in an arbitration clause to submit a particular matter to arbitration, one party may file suit to compel arbitration. The court before which the suit is brought will decide *not* the basic controversy but rather the issue of arbitrability—that is, whether the matter is one that must be resolved through arbitration. If the court finds that the subject matter in controversy is covered by the agreement to arbitrate, then a party may be compelled to arbitrate the dispute. Even when a claim involves a violation of a statute passed to protect a certain class of people, such as employees, a court may determine that the parties must nonetheless abide by their agreement to arbitrate the dispute. Usually, a court will allow the claim to be arbitrated if the court, in interpreting the statute, can find no legislative intent to the contrary.

No party, however, will be ordered to submit a particular dispute to arbitration unless the court is convinced that the party consented to do so.[22] Additionally, the courts will not compel arbitration if it is clear that the prescribed arbitration rules and procedures are inherently unfair to one of the parties. **■EXAMPLE 3.11** In one case, an employer asked a court to issue an order compelling a former employee to submit to arbitration in accordance with an arbitration agreement that the parties had signed. Under that agreement, the employer was to establish the procedure and the rules for the arbitration. The court held that the employee did not have to submit her claim to arbitration because "the rules were so one sided that their only possible purpose is to undermine the neutrality of the proceeding." According to the court, the biased rules created "a sham system unworthy even of the name of arbitration" in violation of the parties' agreement to arbitrate.[23] ■

Mandatory Arbitration in the Employment Context   A significant question in the last several years has concerned mandatory arbitration clauses in employment contracts. Many claim that employees' rights are not sufficiently protected when the workers are forced, as a condition of being hired, to agree to arbitrate all disputes and thus waive their rights under statutes specifically designed to protect employees. The United States Supreme Court, however, has generally held that mandatory arbitration clauses in employment contracts are enforceable.

■EXAMPLE 3.12 In a landmark 1991 decision, *Gilmer v. Interstate/Johnson Lane Corp.*,[24] the Supreme Court held that a claim brought under a federal statute prohibiting age discrimination (see Chapter 34) could be subject to arbitration. The Court concluded that the employee had waived his right to sue when he agreed, as part of a required registration application to be a securities representative with the New York Stock Exchange, to arbitrate "any dispute, claim, or controversy" relating to his employment. ■

The *Gilmer* decision was controversial and generated much discussion during the 1990s. By the early 2000s, some lower courts began to question whether Congress intended the FAA—which expressly excludes the employment contracts of seamen, railroad employees, or any other class of workers engaged in foreign or interstate commerce—to apply to any employment contracts. In 2001, however, the United States Supreme Court clarified that the act applies to most employment contracts, except those that involve interstate transportation workers.[25]

The United States Supreme Court has made it clear that arbitration clauses in employment contracts are enforceable under the FAA. Nevertheless, to prevent future disputes, business owners and managers would be wise to exercise caution when drafting such clauses and requiring employees to sign them. It is especially important to make certain that the terms of the agreement (including how the parties will split the costs of the arbitration procedure, for example) are not so one sided and unfair that a court could declare the entire agreement unenforceable.

PREVENTING
LEGAL DISPUTES

---

22. See, for example, *Wright v. Universal Maritime Service Corp.*, 525 U.S. 70, 119 S.Ct. 391, 142 L.Ed.2d 361 (1998).

23. *Hooters of America, Inc. v. Phillips*, 173 F.3d 933 (4th Cir. 1999).

24. 500 U.S. 20, 111 S.Ct. 1647, 114 L.Ed.2d 26 (1991).

25. *Circuit City Stores, Inc. v. Adams*, 532 U.S. 105, 121 S.Ct. 1302, 149 L.Ed.2d 234 (2001). See also *Circuit City Stores, Inc. v. Adams*, 279 F.3d 889 (9th Cir. 2002). The Supreme Court's *Circuit City* decision is the basis for the *Case Analysis Question* at the end of this chapter.

Other Types of ADR

The three forms of ADR just discussed are the oldest and traditionally the most commonly used. In recent years, a variety of new types of ADR have emerged. Some parties today are using *assisted negotiation*, in which a third party participates in the negotiation process. The third party may be an expert in the subject matter of the dispute. In *early neutral case evaluation*, the parties explain the situation to the expert, and the expert assesses the strengths and weaknesses of each party's claims. Another form of assisted negotiation is the *mini-trial*, in which the parties present arguments before the third party (usually an expert), who renders an advisory opinion on how a court would likely decide the issue. This proceeding is designed to assist the parties in determining whether they should settle or take the dispute to court.

Other types of ADR combine characteristics of mediation with those of arbitration. In *binding mediation*, for example, the parties agree that if they cannot resolve the dispute, the mediator can make a legally binding decision on the issue. In *mediation-arbitration*, or "med-arb," the parties agree to first attempt to settle their dispute through mediation. If no settlement is reached, the dispute will be arbitrated.

Today's courts are also experimenting with a variety of ADR alternatives to speed up (and reduce the cost of) justice. Numerous federal courts now hold **summary jury trials (SJTs)**, in which the parties present their arguments and evidence and the jury renders a verdict. The jury's verdict is not binding, but it does act as a guide to both sides in reaching an agreement during the mandatory negotiations that immediately follow the trial. Other alternatives being employed by the courts include summary procedures for commercial litigation and the appointment of special masters to assist judges in deciding complex issues.

Providers of ADR Services

ADR services are provided by both government agencies and private organizations. A major provider of ADR services is the American Arbitration Association (AAA), which was founded in 1926 and now handles more than 200,000 claims a year in its numerous offices worldwide. Most of the largest U.S. law firms are members of this nonprofit association.

Cases brought before the AAA are heard by an expert or a panel of experts in the area relating to the dispute and are usually settled quickly. Generally, about half of the panel members are lawyers. To cover its costs, the AAA charges a fee, paid by the party filing the claim. In addition, each party to the dispute pays a specified amount for each hearing day, as well as a special additional fee for cases involving personal injuries or property loss. The AAA has a special team devoted to resolving large complex disputes across a wide range of industries.

Hundreds of for-profit firms around the country also provide various forms of dispute-resolution services. Typically, these firms hire retired judges to conduct arbitration hearings or otherwise assist parties in settling their disputes. The judges follow procedures similar to those of the federal courts and use similar rules. Usually, each party to the dispute pays a filing fee and a designated fee for a hearing session or conference.

ONLINE DISPUTE RESOLUTION

An increasing number of companies and organizations offer dispute-resolution services using the Internet. The settlement of disputes in these online forums is known as **online dispute resolution (ODR)**. The disputes resolved in these forums have most commonly involved disagreements over the rights to domain names (Web site addresses—see Chapter 5) or over the quality of goods sold via the Internet, including goods sold through Internet auction sites.

SUMMARY JURY TRIAL (SJT)
A method of settling disputes, used in many federal courts, in which a trial is held, but the jury's verdict is not binding. The verdict acts only as a guide to both sides in reaching an agreement during the mandatory negotiations that immediately follow the summary jury trial.

ON THE WEB

To obtain information on the services offered by the American Arbitration Association (AAA), as well as forms that are used to submit a case for arbitration, go to the AAA's Web site at

www.adr.org.

ONLINE DISPUTE RESOLUTION (ODR)
The resolution of disputes with the assistance of organizations that offer dispute-resolution services via the Internet.

ODR may be best for resolving small- to medium-sized business liability claims, which may not be worth the expense of litigation or traditional ADR. Rules being developed in online forums, however, may ultimately become a code of conduct for everyone who does business in cyberspace. Most online forums do not automatically apply the law of any specific jurisdiction. Instead, results are often based on general, universal legal principles. As with most offline methods of dispute resolution, any party may appeal to a court at any time.

Negotiation and Mediation Services

The online negotiation of a dispute is generally simpler and more practical than litigation. Typically, one party files a complaint, and the other party is notified by e-mail. Password-protected access is possible twenty-four hours a day, seven days a week. Fees are generally low (often 2 to 4 percent, or less, of the disputed amount).

CyberSettle.com, National Arbitration and Mediation (NAM), and other Web-based firms offer online forums for negotiating monetary settlements. Even the Better Business Bureau now provides online dispute settlement (**www.bbbonline.org**). The parties to a dispute may agree to submit offers; if the offers fall within a previously agreed-on range, they will end the dispute. Special software keeps secret any offers that are not within the range. If there is no agreed-on range, typically an offer includes a deadline when the offer will expire, and the other party must respond before then. The parties can drop the negotiations at any time.

Mediation providers have also tried resolving disputes online. SquareTrade, for example, provides mediation services for the online auction site eBay as well as other parties. It has resolved more than 2 million disputes between merchants and consumers in 120 countries. SquareTrade uses Web-based software that walks participants through a five-step e-resolution process. Disputing parties first attempt to negotiate directly on a secure page within SquareTrade's Web site. There is no fee for negotiation. If the parties cannot reach an agreement, they can consult with a mediator. The entire process takes as little as ten to fourteen days.

Arbitration Programs

A number of organizations, including the American Arbitration Association, offer online arbitration programs. The Internet Corporation for Assigned Names and Numbers (ICANN), a nonprofit corporation that the federal government set up to oversee the distribution of domain names, has issued special rules for the resolution of domain name disputes.[26] ICANN has also authorized several organizations to arbitrate domain name disputes in accordance with ICANN's rules.

Resolution Forum, Inc. (RFI), a nonprofit organization associated with the Center for Legal Responsibility at South Texas College of Law, offers arbitration services through its CAN-WIN conferencing system. Using standard browser software and an RFI password, the parties to a dispute access an online conference room.

The Virtual Magistrate (VMAG) is a program provided through Chicago-Kent College of Law. VMAG offers arbitration for disputes involving online activities, including torts such as spamming and defamation (discussed in Chapter 4), wrongful messages and postings, and online contract or property disputes. VMAG attempts to resolve a dispute quickly (within seventy-two hours) and inexpensively. A VMAG arbitrator's decision is issued in a written opinion and may be appealed to a court.

ON THE WEB

To read about the policies and goals of the Virtual Magistrate program, go to

www.vmag.org.

---

26. ICANN's Rules for Uniform Domain Name Dispute Resolution Policy are online at **www.icann.org/dndr/udrp/ uniform-rules.htm**. Domain names will be discussed in more detail in Chapter 5, in the context of trademark law.

REVIEWING Courts and Alternative Dispute Resolution

Stan Garner resides in Illinois and promotes boxing matches for SuperSports, Inc., an Illinois corporation. Garner created the promotional concept of the "Ages" fights—a series of three boxing matches pitting an older fighter (George Foreman) against a younger fighter, such as John Ruiz or Riddick Bowe. The concept included titles for each of the three fights ("Challenge of the Ages," "Battle of the Ages," and "Fight of the Ages"), as well as promotional epithets to characterize the two fighters ("the Foreman Factor"). Garner contacted George Foreman and his manager, who both reside in Texas, to sell the idea, and they arranged a meeting at Caesar's Palace in Las Vegas, Nevada. At some point in the negotiations, Foreman's manager signed a nondisclosure agreement prohibiting him from disclosing Garner's promotional concepts unless they signed a contract. Nevertheless, after negotiations between Garner and Foreman fell through, Foreman used Garner's "Battle of the Ages" concept to promote a subsequent fight. Garner filed a lawsuit against Foreman and his manager in a federal district court located in Illinois, alleging breach of contract. Using the information presented in the chapter, answer the following questions.

1 On what basis might the federal district court in Illinois exercise jurisdiction in this case?

2 Does the federal district court have original or appellate jurisdiction?

3 Suppose that Garner had filed his action in an Illinois state court. Could an Illinois state court exercise personal jurisdiction over Foreman or his manager? Why or why not?

4 Assume that Garner had filed his action in a Nevada state court. Would that court have personal jurisdiction over Foreman or his manager? Explain.

APPLICATION To Sue or Not to Sue?[*]

W rongs are committed every minute of every day in the United States. These wrongs may be committed inadvertently or intentionally. Sometimes, businesspersons believe that wrongs have been committed against them by other businesspersons; by consumers; or by the local, state, or federal government. If you are deciding whether or not to sue for a wrong that has been committed against you or your business, you must consider many issues.

The Question of Cost

Competent legal advice is not inexpensive. Good commercial business law attorneys charge $100 to $600 an hour, plus expenses. It is almost always worthwhile to make an initial visit to an attorney who has skills in the area in which you are going to sue to get an estimate of the expected costs of pursuing redress for your grievance. You may be charged for the initial visit as well.

Note that less than 10 percent of all corporate lawsuits go to trial—the rest are settled beforehand. You may end up settling for far less than you think you are "owed" simply because of the length of time it will take for your case to come to trial and the cost of going to court. And then you might not win, anyway!

Basically, then, you must do a cost-benefit analysis to determine whether you should sue. Your attorney can give you an estimate of the dollar costs involved in litigating the dispute. Realize, though, that litigation also involves nondollar costs. These costs include time away from your business, stress, inconvenience, and publicity—to name but a few. You need to weigh all of these costs against the benefits. You can "guesstimate" the benefits by multiplying the probable size of the award by the probability of obtaining that award.

The Alternatives before You

Another method of settling your grievance is by alternative dispute resolution (ADR). Negotiation, mediation, arbitration, and other ADR forms are becoming increasingly attractive alternatives to court litigation (and private judges) because

[*] This *Application* is not meant to substitute for the services of an attorney who is licensed to practice law in your state.

they usually yield quick results at a comparatively low cost. Most disputes relating to business can be mediated or arbitrated through the American Arbitration Association (AAA), which can be accessed online at **www.adr.org**.

There are numerous other ADR providers as well. You can obtain information on ADR from the AAA, courthouses, chambers of commerce, law firms, state bar associations, or the American Bar Association. The Yellow Pages in large metropolitan areas usually list agencies and firms that can help you settle your dispute out of court (look under "Mediation"). You can also locate providers on the Web by using a general search engine, such as Google, and searching for arbitration providers in a specific city, such as "arbitration providers in Portland, Oregon."

Depending on the nature of the dispute and the amount of damages you seek, you might wish to contact one of the organizations that offer online dispute-resolution services, such as those discussed in this chapter.

CHECKLIST FOR DECIDING WHETHER TO SUE

1. Are you prepared to pay for going to court? Make this decision only after you have consulted an attorney to get an estimate of the costs of litigating the dispute.
2. Do you have the patience to follow a court case through the judicial system, even if it takes several years?
3. Is there a way for you to settle your grievance without going to court? Even if the settlement is less than you think you are owed—in net terms corrected for future expenses, lost time, and frustration—you may be better off settling now for the smaller figure.
4. Can you use some form of alternative dispute resolution? Before you say no, investigate these alternatives—they are usually cheaper and quicker to use than the standard judicial process.

KEY TERMS

alternative dispute
   resolution (ADR) 87
answer 79
arbitration 88
arbitration clause 89
award 84
bankruptcy court 67
brief 85
complaint 77
concurrent jurisdiction 68
counterclaim 79
default judgment 78
deposition 80
discovery 79
diversity of citizenship 68
docket 69
e-evidence 81

exclusive jurisdiction 68
federal question 68
interrogatories 81
judicial review 63
jurisdiction 64
justiciable controversy 71
litigation 77
long arm statute 64
mediation 88
motion for a directed verdict 84
motion for a new trial 84
motion for judgment *n.o.v.* 84
motion for judgment on the
   pleadings 79
motion for summary judgment 79
motion to dismiss 79
negotiation 88

online dispute
   resolution (ODR) 92
pleadings 77
probate court 67
question of fact 74
question of law 74
reply 79
rule of four 75
small claims court 73
standing to sue 71
summary jury trial (SJT) 92
summons 78
venue 71
voir dire 83
writ of *certiorari* 75

CHAPTER SUMMARY Courts and Alternative Dispute Resolution

The Judiciary's Role in American Government (See page 63.)	The role of the judiciary—the courts—in the American governmental system is to interpret and apply the law. Through the process of judicial review—determining the constitutionality of laws—the judicial branch acts as a check on the executive and legislative branches of government.
Basic Judicial Requirements (See pages 63–72.)	1. *Jurisdiction*—Before a court can hear a case, it must have jurisdiction over the person against whom the suit is brought or the property involved in the suit, as well as jurisdiction over the subject matter.

(Continued)

CHAPTER SUMMARY Courts and Alternative Dispute Resolution–Continued

Basic Judicial Requirements– Continued	a. Limited versus general jurisdiction—Limited jurisdiction exists when a court is limited to a specific subject matter, such as probate or divorce. General jurisdiction exists when a court can hear any kind of case.
	b. Original versus appellate jurisdiction—Original jurisdiction exists when courts have authority to hear a case for the first time (trial courts). Appellate jurisdiction exists with courts of appeals, or reviewing courts; generally, appellate courts do not have original jurisdiction.
	c. Federal jurisdiction—Arises (1) when a federal question is involved (when the plaintiff's cause of action is based, at least in part, on the U.S. Constitution, a treaty, or a federal law) or (2) when a case involves diversity of citizenship (citizens of different states, for example) and the amount in controversy exceeds $75,000.
	d. Concurrent versus exclusive jurisdiction—Concurrent jurisdiction exists when two different courts have authority to hear the same case. Exclusive jurisdiction exists when only state courts or only federal courts have authority to hear a case.
	2. *Jurisdiction in cyberspace*—Because the Internet does not have physical boundaries, traditional jurisdictional concepts have been difficult to apply in cases involving activities conducted via the Web. Gradually, the courts are developing standards to use in determining when jurisdiction over a Web site owner or operator located in another state is proper.
	3. *Venue*—Venue has to do with the most appropriate location for a trial, which is usually the geographic area where the event leading to the dispute took place or where the parties reside.
	4. *Standing to sue*—A requirement that a party must have a legally protected and tangible interest at stake sufficient to justify seeking relief through the court system. The controversy at issue must also be a justiciable controversy—one that is real and substantial, as opposed to hypothetical or academic.
The State and Federal Court Systems (See pages 72–76.)	1. *Trial courts*—Courts of original jurisdiction, in which legal actions are initiated.
	a. State—Courts of general jurisdiction can hear any case; courts of limited jurisdiction include domestic relations courts, probate courts, traffic courts, and small claims courts.
	b. Federal—The federal district court is the equivalent of the state trial court. Federal courts of limited jurisdiction include the U.S. Tax Court, the U.S. Bankruptcy Court, and the U.S. Court of Federal Claims.
	2. *Intermediate appellate courts*—Courts of appeals, or reviewing courts; generally without original jurisdiction. Many states have an intermediate appellate court; in the federal court system, the U.S. circuit courts of appeals are the intermediate appellate courts.
	3. *Supreme (highest) courts*—Each state has a supreme court, although it may be called by some other name; appeal from the state supreme court to the United States Supreme Court is possible only if the case involves a federal question. The United States Supreme Court is the highest court in the federal court system and the final arbiter of the U.S. Constitution and federal law.
Following a State Court Case (See pages 76–85.)	Rules of procedure prescribe the way in which disputes are handled in the courts. Rules differ from court to court, and separate sets of rules exist for federal and state courts, as well as for criminal and civil cases. A sample civil court case in a state court would involve the following procedures:
	1. *The pleadings*—
	a. Complaint—Filed by the plaintiff with the court to initiate the lawsuit; served with a summons on the defendant.
	b. Answer—A response to the complaint in which the defendant admits or denies the allegations made by the plaintiff; may assert a counterclaim or an affirmative defense.

CHAPTER SUMMARY Courts and Alternative Dispute Resolution—Continued

Following a State Court Case—Continued	c. Motion to dismiss—A request to the court to dismiss the case for stated reasons, such as the plaintiff's failure to state a claim for which relief can be granted.
	
	2. *Pretrial motions (in addition to the motion to dismiss)*—
	
	    a. Motion for judgment on the pleadings—May be made by either party; will be granted if the parties agree on the facts and the only question is how the law applies to the facts. The judge bases the decision solely on the pleadings.
	
	    b. Motion for summary judgment—May be made by either party; will be granted if the parties agree on the facts. The judge applies the law in rendering a judgment. The judge can consider evidence outside the pleadings when evaluating the motion.
	
	3. *Discovery*—The process of gathering evidence concerning the case. Discovery involves depositions (sworn testimony by a party to the lawsuit or any witness), interrogatories (written questions and answers to these questions made by parties to the action with the aid of their attorneys), and various requests (for admissions, documents, and medical examinations, for example). Discovery may also involve electronically recorded information, such as e-mail, voice mail, word-processing documents, and other data compilations. Although electronic discovery has significant advantages over paper discovery, it is also more time consuming and expensive and often requires the parties to hire experts.
	
	4. *Pretrial conference*—Either party or the court can request a pretrial conference to identify the matters in dispute after discovery has taken place and to plan the course of the trial.
	
	5. *Trial*—Following jury selection (*voir dire*), the trial begins with opening statements from both parties' attorneys. The following events then occur:
	
	    a. The plaintiff's introduction of evidence (including the testimony of witnesses) supporting the plaintiff's position. The defendant's attorney can challenge evidence and cross-examine witnesses.
	
	    b. The defendant's introduction of evidence (including the testimony of witnesses) supporting the defendant's position. The plaintiff's attorney can challenge evidence and cross-examine witnesses.
	
	    c. Closing arguments by the attorneys in favor of their respective clients, the judge's instructions to the jury, and the jury's verdict.
	
	6. *Posttrial motions*—
	
	    a. Motion for judgment *n.o.v.* ("notwithstanding the verdict")—Will be granted if the judge is convinced that the jury was in error.
	
	    b. Motion for a new trial—Will be granted if the judge is convinced that the jury was in error; can also be granted on the grounds of newly discovered evidence, misconduct by the participants during the trial, or error by the judge.
	
	7. *Appeal*—Either party can appeal the trial court's judgment to an appropriate court of appeals. After reviewing the record on appeal, the abstracts, and the attorneys' briefs, the appellate court holds a hearing and renders its opinion.

The Courts Adapt to the Online World (See pages 86–87.)	A number of state and federal courts now allow parties to file litigation-related documents with the courts via the Internet or other electronic means. Nearly all of the federal appellate courts and bankruptcy courts and a majority of the federal district courts have implemented electronic filing systems. Almost every court now has a Web page offering information about the court and its procedures, and increasingly courts are publishing their opinions online. In the future, we may see "cyber courts," in which all trial proceedings are conducted online.
Alternative Dispute Resolution (See pages 87–92.)	1. *Negotiation*—The parties come together, with or without attorneys to represent them, and try to reach a settlement without the involvement of a third party.

(Continued)

CHAPTER SUMMARY Courts and Alternative Dispute Resolution—Continued

Alternative Dispute Resolution—Continued	2. *Mediation*—The parties themselves reach an agreement with the help of a neutral third party, called a mediator, who proposes solutions. At the parties' request, a mediator may make a legally binding decision.
	3. *Arbitration*—A more formal method of ADR in which the parties submit their dispute to a neutral third party, the arbitrator, who renders a decision. The decision may or may not be legally binding, depending on the circumstances.
	4. *Other types of ADR*—These include early neutral case evaluation, mini-trials, and summary jury trials (SJTs); generally, these are forms of "assisted negotiation."
	5. *Providers of ADR services*—The leading nonprofit provider of ADR services is the American Arbitration Association. Hundreds of for-profit firms also provide ADR services.
Online Dispute Resolution (See pages 92–93.)	A number of organizations and firms are now offering negotiation, mediation, and arbitration services through online forums. To date, these forums have been a practical alternative for the resolution of domain name disputes and e-commerce disputes in which the amount in controversy is relatively small.

FOR REVIEW

Answers for the even-numbered questions in this **For Review** *section can be found in Appendix E at the end of this text.*

1 What is judicial review? How and when was the power of judicial review established?

2 Before a court can hear a case, it must have jurisdiction. Over what must it have jurisdiction? How are the courts applying traditional jurisdictional concepts to cases involving Internet transactions?

3 What is the difference between a trial court and an appellate court?

4 In a lawsuit, what are the pleadings? What is discovery, and how does electronic discovery differ from traditional discovery? What is electronic filing?

5 How are online forums being used to resolve disputes?

 The following multiple-choice question is representative of the types of questions available in one of the four sections of ThomsonNOW for *Business Law Today.* **ThomsonNOW also provides feedback for each response option, whether correct or incorrect, and refers to the location within the chapter where the correct answer can be found.**

A long arm statute allows a court to exercise jurisdiction over

a an in-state resident.

b any nonresident defendant.

c a nonresident defendant who has minimum contacts with the state in which the court is located.

d the citizens of any neighboring state.

◼

QUESTIONS AND CASE PROBLEMS

 **HYPOTHETICAL SCENARIOS**

3.1 Arbitration. In an arbitration proceeding, the arbitrator need not be a judge or even a lawyer. How, then, can the arbitrator's decision have the force of law and be binding on the parties involved?

3.2 Hypothetical Question with Sample Answer. Marya Callais, a citizen of Florida, was walking along a busy street in Tallahassee when a large crate flew off a passing truck and hit her, causing numerous injuries to Callais. She incurred a great deal of pain and suffering plus significant medical expenses, and she could not work for six months. She wishes to sue the trucking firm for $300,000 in damages. The firm's headquarters are in Georgia, although the company does business in Florida. In what court may Callais bring suit—a Florida state court, a Georgia state court, or a federal court? What factors might influence her decision?

 For a sample answer to Question 3.2, go to Appendix F at the end of this text.

CASE PROBLEMS

3.3 Standing. Blue Cross and Blue Shield insurance companies (the Blues) provide 68 million Americans with health-care financing. The Blues have paid billions of dollars for care attributable to illnesses related to tobacco use. In an attempt to recover some of this amount, the Blues filed a suit in a federal district court against tobacco companies and others, alleging fraud, among other things. The Blues claimed that beginning in 1953, the defendants conspired to addict millions of Americans, including members of Blue Cross plans, to cigarettes and other tobacco products. The conspiracy involved misrepresentation about the safety of nicotine and its addictive properties, marketing efforts targeting children, and agreements not to produce or market safer cigarettes. As a result of the defendants' efforts, many tobacco users developed lung, throat, and other cancers, as well as heart disease, stroke, emphysema, and other illnesses. The defendants asked the court to dismiss the case on the ground that the plaintiffs did not have standing to sue. Do the Blues have standing in this case? Why or why not? [*Blue Cross and Blue Shield of New Jersey, Inc. v. Philip Morris, Inc.*, 36 F.Supp.2d 560 (E.D.N.Y. 1999)]

3.4 Case Problem with Sample Answer. Ms. Thompson filed a suit in a federal district court against her employer, Altheimer & Gray, seeking damages for alleged racial discrimination in violation of federal law. During *voir dire*, the judge asked the prospective jurors whether "there is something about this kind of lawsuit for monetary damages that would start any of you leaning for or against a particular party?" Ms. Leiter, one of the prospective jurors, raised her hand and explained that she had "been an owner of a couple of businesses and am currently an owner of a business, and I feel that as an employer and owner of a business that will definitely sway my judgment in this case." She explained, "I am constantly faced with people that want various benefits or different positions in the company or better contacts or, you know, a myriad of issues that employers face on a regular basis, and I have to decide whether or not that person should get them." Asked by Thompson's lawyer whether "you believe that people file lawsuits just because they don't get something they want," Leiter answered, "I believe there are some people that do." In answer to another question, she said, "I think I bring a lot of background to this case, and I can't say that it's not going to cloud my judgment. I can try to be as fair as I can, as I do every day." Thompson filed a motion to strike Leiter for cause. Should the judge grant the motion? Explain. [*Thompson v. Altheimer & Gray*, 248 F.3d 621 (7th Cir. 2001)]

After you have answered Problem 3.4, compare your answer with the sample answer given on the Web site that accompanies this text. Go to www.thomsonedu.com/westbuslaw/blt, select "Chapter 3," and click on "Case Problem with Sample Answer."

3.5 Arbitration. Alexander Little worked for Auto Stiegler, Inc., an automobile dealership in Los Angeles County, California, eventually becoming the service manager. While employed, Little signed an arbitration agreement that required all employment-related disputes to be submitted to arbitration. The agreement also provided that any award over $50,000 could be appealed to a second arbitrator. Little was later demoted and terminated. Alleging that these actions were in retaliation for investigating and reporting warranty fraud and thus were in violation of public policy, Little filed a suit in a California state court against Auto Stiegler. The defendant filed a motion with the court to compel arbitration. Little responded that the arbitration agreement should not be enforced because, among other things, the appeal provision was unfairly one sided. Is this provision enforceable? Should the court grant Auto Stiegler's motion? Why or why not? [*Little v. Auto Stiegler, Inc.*, 29 Cal.4th 1064, 63 P.3d 979, 130 Cal.Rptr.2d 892 (2003)]

3.6 Standing to Sue. Lamar Advertising of Penn, LLC, an outdoor advertising business, wanted to erect billboards of varying sizes in a multiphase operation throughout the town of Orchard Park, New York. An Orchard Park ordinance restricted the signs to certain sizes in certain areas, to advertising products and services available for sale only on the premises, and to other limits. Lamar asked Orchard Park for permission to build signs in some areas larger than the ordinance allowed in those locations (but not as large as allowed in other areas). When the town refused, Lamar filed a suit in a federal district court, claiming that the ordinance violated the First Amendment. Did Lamar have standing to challenge the ordinance? If the court could sever the provisions of the ordinance restricting a sign's content from the provisions limiting a sign's size, would your answer be the same? Explain. [*Lamar Advertising of Penn, LLC v. Town of Orchard Park, New York*, 356 F.3d 365 (2d Cir. 2004)]

3.7 Jurisdiction. Xcentric Ventures, LLC, is an Arizona firm that operates the Web sites RipOffReport.com and BadBusinessBureau.com. Visitors to the sites can buy a copy of a book titled *Do-It-Yourself Guide: How to Get Rip-Off Revenge.* The price ($21.95) includes shipping to anywhere in the United States, including Illinois, to which thirteen copies have been shipped. The sites accept donations and feature postings by individuals who claim to have been "ripped off." Some visitors posted comments about George S. May International Co., a management-consulting firm. The postings alleged fraud, larceny, possession of child pornography, and possession of controlled substances (illegal drugs). May filed a suit against Xcentric and others in a federal district court in Illinois, alleging in part "false descriptions and representations." The defendants filed a motion to dismiss for lack of jurisdiction. What is the standard for exercising jurisdiction over a party whose only connection to a jurisdiction is over the Web? How would that standard apply in this case? Explain. [*George S. May International Co. v. Xcentric Ventures, LLC,* 409 F.Supp.2d 1052 (N.D.Ill. 2006)]

3.8 Appellate Review. BSH Home Appliances Corp. makes appliances under the Bosch, Siemens, Thermador, and Gaggenau brands. To make and market the "Pro 27 Stainless Steel Range," a restaurant-quality range for home use, BSH gave specifications for its burner to Detroit Radiant Products Co. and requested a price for 30,000 units. Detroit quoted $28.25 per unit, offering to absorb all tooling and research and development costs. In 2001 and 2003, BSH sent Detroit two purchase orders, for 15,000 and 16,000 units, respectively. In 2004, after Detroit had shipped 12,886 units, BSH stopped scheduling deliveries. Detroit filed a suit against BSH, alleging breach of contract. BSH argued, in part, that the second purchase order had not added to the first but had replaced it. After a trial, a federal district court issued its "Findings of Fact and Conclusions of Law." The court found that the two purchase orders "required BSH to purchase 31,000 units of the burner at $28.25 per unit." The court ruled that Detroit was entitled to $418,261 for 18,114 unsold burners. BSH

appealed to the U.S. Court of Appeals for the Sixth Circuit. Can an appellate court set aside a trial court's findings of fact? Can an appellate court come to its own conclusions of law? What should the court rule in this case? Explain. [*Detroit Radiant Products Co. v. BSH Home Appliances Corp.,* 473 F.3d 623 (6th Cir. 2007)]

3.9 **A Question of Ethics.** *Narnia Investments, Ltd., filed a suit in a Texas state court against several defendants, including Harvestons Securities, Inc., a securities dealer. (Securities are documents evidencing the ownership of a corporation, in the form of stock, or debts owed by it, in the form of bonds.) Harvestons is registered with the state of Texas and thus may be served with a summons and a copy of a complaint delivered to the Texas Securities Commissioner. In this case, the return of service indicated that process was served on the commissioner "by delivering to JoAnn Kocerek, defendant, in person, a true copy of this [summons] together with the accompanying copy(ies) of the [complaint]." Harvestons did not file an answer, and Narnia obtained a default judgment against the defendant for $365,000, plus attorneys' fees and interest. Five months after this judgment, Harvestons filed a motion for a new trial, which the court denied. Harvestons appealed to a state intermediate appellate court, claiming that it had not been served in strict compliance with the rules governing service of process.* [Harvestons Securities, Inc. v. Narnia Investments, Ltd., 218 S.W.3d 126 (Tex.App.—Houston [14 Dist.] 2007)]

1 Harvestons asserted that Narnia's service was invalid in part because "the return of service states that process was delivered to 'JoAnn Kocerek'" and did not show that she "had the authority to accept process on behalf of Harvestons or the Texas Securities Commissioner." Should such a detail, if it is required, be strictly construed and applied? Should it apply in this case? Explain.

2 Whose responsibility is it to see that service of process is accomplished properly? Was it accomplished properly in this case? Why or why not?

CRITICAL THINKING AND WRITING ASSIGNMENTS

3.10 Critical Legal Thinking. Suppose that a state statute requires that all civil lawsuits involving damages of less than $50,000 be arbitrated and allows such a case to be tried in court only if a party is dissatisfied with the arbitrator's decision. Suppose further that the statute also provides that if a trial does not result in an improvement of more than 10 percent in the position of the party who demanded the trial, that party must pay the entire costs of the arbitration proceeding. Would such a statute violate litigants' rights of access to the courts and to

trial by jury? Would it matter if the statute was part of a pilot program and affected only a few judicial districts in the state?

3.11 Case Analysis Question. Go to Appendix G at the end of this text and examine Case No. 1 [*Circuit City Stores, Inc. v. Adams,* 532 U.S. 105, 121 S.Ct. 1302, 149 L.Ed.2d 234 (2001)]. This case has been excerpted there in great detail. Review and then brief the case, making sure that your brief answers the following questions.

1 What was Adams's primary complaint against Circuit City in the state court, and how did the case end up in the federal court system?

2 Did the U.S. Court of Appeals for the Ninth Circuit decide that Adams's employment contract was subject to the mandatory arbitration provisions of the Federal Arbitration Act?

3 What reasons did the United States Supreme Court cite for reversing the decision of the U.S. Court of Appeals for the Ninth Circuit?

4 How did the dissent evaluate the Court's use of the rules of statutory construction?

5 Did Adams end up having to arbitrate the case against Circuit City after all? Why or why not?

3.12 **Video Question.** Go to this text's Web site at **www. thomsonedu.com/westbuslaw/blt** and select "Chapter 3." Click on "Video Questions" and view the video titled *Jurisdiction in Cyberspace.* Then answer the following questions.

1 What standard would a court apply to determine whether it has jurisdiction over the out-of-state computer firm in the video?

2 What factors is a court likely to consider in assessing whether sufficient contacts exist when the only connection to the jurisdiction is through a Web site?

3 How do you think a court would resolve the issue in this case?

ONLINE ACTIVITIES

PRACTICAL INTERNET EXERCISES

Go to this text's Web site at **www.thomsonedu.com/westbuslaw/blt**, select "Chapter 3," and click on "Practical Internet Exercises." There you will find the following Internet research exercises that you can perform to learn more about the topics covered in this chapter.

PRACTICAL INTERNET EXERCISE 3–1   LEGAL PERSPECTIVE—The Judiciary's Role in American Government

PRACTICAL INTERNET EXERCISE 3–2   MANAGEMENT PERSPECTIVE—Alternative Dispute Resolution

PRACTICAL INTERNET EXERCISE 3–3   SOCIAL PERSPECTIVE—Resolve a Dispute Online

BEFORE THE TEST

Go to this text's Web site at **www.thomsonedu.com/westbuslaw/blt**, select "Chapter 3," and click on "Interactive Quizzes." You will find a number of interactive questions relating to this chapter.

CHAPTER 4
Torts and Cyber Torts

LEARNING OBJECTIVES

AFTER READING THIS CHAPTER, YOU SHOULD BE ABLE TO ANSWER THE FOLLOWING QUESTIONS:

1 What is a tort?

2 What is the purpose of tort law? What are two basic categories of torts?

3 What are the four elements of negligence?

4 What is meant by strict liability? In what circumstances is strict liability applied?

5 What is a cyber tort, and how are tort theories being applied in cyberspace?

> **❝** 'Tort' more or less means 'wrong' . . . . One of my friends [in law school] said that Torts is the course which proves that your mother was right.**❞**
>
> Scott Turow, 1949–present
> (American lawyer and author)

TORT
A civil wrong not arising from a breach of contract; a breach of a legal duty that proximately causes harm or injury to another.

BUSINESS TORT
Wrongful interference with another's business rights.

DAMAGES
Money sought as a remedy for a breach of contract or a tortious action.

As Scott Turow's statement in the chapter-opening quotation indicates, **torts** are wrongful actions.[1] Through tort law, society compensates those who have suffered injuries as a result of the wrongful conduct of others. Although some torts, such as assault and trespass, originated in the English common law, the field of tort law continues to expand. As new ways to commit wrongs are discovered, such as the use of the Internet to commit wrongful acts, the courts are extending tort law to cover these wrongs.

As you will see in later chapters of this book, many of the lawsuits brought by or against business firms are based on the tort theories discussed in this chapter. Some of the torts examined here can occur in any context, including the business environment. Others, traditionally referred to as **business torts,** involve wrongful interference with the business rights of others. Business torts include such vague concepts as *unfair competition* and *wrongfully interfering with the business relations of another.*

THE BASIS OF TORT LAW

Two notions serve as the basis of all torts: wrongs and compensation. Tort law is designed to compensate those who have suffered a loss or injury due to another person's wrongful act. In a tort action, one person or group brings a personal suit against another person or group to obtain compensation (money **damages**) or other relief for the harm suffered.

---

1. The word *tort* is French for "wrong."

The Purpose of Tort Law

Generally, the purpose of tort law is to provide remedies for the invasion of various *protected interests*. Society recognizes an interest in personal physical safety, and tort law provides remedies for acts that cause physical injury or interfere with physical security and freedom of movement. Society recognizes an interest in protecting real and personal property, and tort law provides remedies for acts that cause destruction or damage to property. Society also recognizes an interest in protecting certain intangible interests, such as personal privacy, family relations, reputation, and dignity, and tort law provides remedies for invasion of these protected interests.

Damages Available in Tort Actions

Because the purpose of tort law is to compensate the injured party for the damage suffered, it is important to have a basic understanding of the types of damages that plaintiffs seek in tort actions.

Compensatory Damages **Compensatory damages** are intended to compensate or reimburse a plaintiff for actual losses—to make the plaintiff whole and put her or him in the same position that she or he would have been in had the tort not occurred. Compensatory damages awards are often broken down into special damages and general damages. *Special damages* compensate the plaintiff for quantifiable monetary losses, such as medical expenses, lost wages and benefits (now and in the future), extra costs, the loss of irreplaceable items, and the costs of repairing or replacing damaged property. *General damages* compensate individuals (not companies) for the nonmonetary aspects of the harm suffered, such as pain and suffering. A court might award general damages for physical or emotional pain and suffering, loss of companionship, loss of consortium (losing the emotional and physical benefits of a spousal relationship), disfigurement, loss of reputation, or loss or impairment of mental or physical capacity.

> **COMPENSATORY DAMAGES**
> A monetary award equivalent to the actual value of injuries or damage sustained by the aggrieved party.

Punitive Damages Occasionally, **punitive damages** may also be awarded in tort cases to punish the wrongdoer and deter others from similar wrongdoing. Punitive damages are appropriate only when the defendant's conduct was particularly egregious [bad] or reprehensible [unacceptable]. Usually, this means that punitive damages are available mainly in intentional tort actions and only rarely in negligence lawsuits (*intentional torts* and *negligence* are explained later in the chapter). They may be awarded, however, in suits involving *gross negligence,* which can be defined as an intentional failure to perform a manifest duty in reckless disregard of the consequences of such a failure for the life or property of another.

> **PUNITIVE DAMAGES**
> Monetary damages that may be awarded to a plaintiff to punish the defendant and deter future similar conduct.

Great judicial restraint is exercised in granting punitive damages to plaintiffs in tort actions, because punitive damages are subject to the limitations imposed by the due process clause of the U.S. Constitution (discussed in Chapter 2). In *State Farm Mutual Automobile Insurance Co. v. Campbell,*[2] the United States Supreme Court held that to the extent an award of punitive damages is grossly excessive, it furthers no legitimate purpose and violates due process requirements. Although this case dealt with intentional torts (fraud and intentional infliction of emotional distress), the Court's holding applies equally to punitive damages awards in gross negligence cases (as well as to product liability cases, which will be discussed in Chapter 18). (What types of damages do other nations award in tort cases? See this chapter's *Beyond Our Borders* feature on the following page for a discussion of tort liability in other countries.)

---

2. 538 U.S. 408, 123 S.Ct. 1513, 155 L.Ed.2d 585 (2003).

BEYOND OUR BORDERS Tort Liability and Damages in Other Nations

In contrast to U.S. courts, courts in Europe generally limit damages to compensatory damages; punitive damages are virtually unheard of in European countries. Even when plaintiffs do win compensatory damages, they generally receive much less than would be awarded in a similar case brought in the United States. In part, this is because citizens of European countries usually receive government-provided health care and relatively generous social security benefits. Another reason, though, is that European courts tend to view the duty of care and the concept of risk differently than U.S. courts do. In the United States, if a swimmer falls off a high diving board and is injured, a court may decide that the pool owner should be held liable, given that such a fall is a foreseeable risk. If punitive damages are awarded, they could total millions of dollars. In a similar situation in Europe, a court might hold that the plaintiff, not the pool owner, was responsible for the injury.

Tort laws in other nations also differ in the way damages are calculated. For example, under Swiss law and Turkish law, a court is permitted to reduce the amount of damages if an award of full damages would cause undue hardship for the party who was found negligent. In the United States, in contrast, the courts normally do not take a party's economic circumstances into consideration.

 FOR CRITICAL ANALYSIS *What impact might the typically greater damages awards in the United States have on a businessperson's decision about whether to keep the firm's operations in the United States or move them to another country? Does the potential cost of paying damages encourage large corporations to outsource jobs to other nations? Why or why not?*

Classifications of Torts

ON THE WEB

You can find cases and articles on torts in the tort law library at the Internet Law Library's Web site. Go to

www.lawguru.com/ilawlib.

CYBER TORT
A tort committed in cyberspace.

INTENTIONAL TORT
A wrongful act knowingly committed.

TORTFEASOR
One who commits a tort.

There are two broad classifications of torts: *intentional torts* and *unintentional torts* (torts involving negligence). The classification of a particular tort depends largely on how the tort occurs (intentionally or negligently) and the surrounding circumstances. In the following pages, you will read about these two classifications of torts.

Torts committed via the Internet are sometimes referred to as **cyber torts.** We look at how the courts have applied traditional tort law to wrongful actions in the online environment in the concluding pages of this chapter.

INTENTIONAL TORTS AGAINST PERSONS

An **intentional tort,** as the term implies, requires *intent*. The **tortfeasor** (the one committing the tort) must intend to commit an act, the consequences of which interfere with the personal or business interests of another in a way not permitted by law. An evil or harmful motive is not required—in fact, the actor may even have a beneficial motive for committing what turns out to be a tortious act. In tort law, intent means only that the actor intended the consequences of his or her act or knew with substantial certainty that certain consequences would result from the act. The law generally assumes that individuals intend the *normal* consequences of their actions. Thus, forcefully pushing another—even if done in jest and without any evil motive—is an intentional tort (if injury results), because the object of a strong push can ordinarily be expected to fall down.

This section discusses intentional torts against persons, which include assault and battery, false imprisonment, infliction of emotional distress, defamation, invasion of the right to privacy, appropriation, misrepresentation, and wrongful interference.

Assault and Battery

Any intentional, unexcused act that creates in another person a reasonable apprehension of immediate harmful or offensive contact is an **assault.** Apprehension is not the same as fear. If a contact is such that a reasonable person would want to avoid it, and if there is a reasonable basis for believing that the contact will occur, then the plaintiff suffers apprehension whether or not he or she is afraid. The interest protected by tort law concerning assault is the freedom from having to expect harmful or offensive contact. The arousal of apprehension is enough to justify compensation.

The *completion* of the act that caused the apprehension, if it results in harm to the plaintiff, is a **battery,** which is defined as an unexcused and harmful or offensive physical contact *intentionally* performed. Suppose that Ivan threatens Jean with a gun, then shoots her. The pointing of the gun at Jean is an assault; the firing of the gun (if the bullet hits Jean) is a battery. The interest protected by tort law concerning battery is the right to personal security and safety. The contact can be harmful, or it can be merely offensive (such as an unwelcome kiss). Physical injury need not occur. The contact can involve any part of the body or anything attached to it—for example, a hat or other item of clothing, a purse, or a chair or an automobile in which one is sitting. Whether the contact is offensive or not is determined by the *reasonable person standard.*[3] The contact can be made by the defendant or by some force the defendant sets in motion—for example, a rock thrown, food poisoned, or a stick swung.

Compensation   If the plaintiff shows that there was contact, and the jury (or judge, if there is no jury) agrees that the contact was offensive, the plaintiff has a right to compensation. There is no need to show that the defendant acted out of malice; the person could have just been joking or playing around. The underlying motive does not matter, only the intent to bring about the harmful or offensive contact to the plaintiff. In fact, proving a motive is never necessary (but is sometimes relevant). A plaintiff may be compensated for the emotional harm or loss of reputation resulting from a battery, as well as for physical harm.

Defenses to Assault and Battery   A defendant who is sued for assault, battery, or both can raise any of the following legally recognized **defenses** (reasons why plaintiffs should not obtain what they are seeking) :

1 *Consent.* When a person consents to the act that is allegedly tortious, this may be a complete or partial defense to liability (legal responsibility).

2 *Self-defense.* An individual who is defending her or his life or physical well-being can claim self-defense. In situations of both *real* and *apparent* danger, a person may use whatever force is *reasonably* necessary to prevent harmful contact.

3 *Defense of others.* An individual can act in a reasonable manner to protect others who are in real or apparent danger.

4 *Defense of property.* Reasonable force may be used in attempting to remove intruders from one's home, although force that is likely to cause death or great bodily injury can never be used just to protect property.

ASSAULT
Any word or action intended to make another person fearful of immediate physical harm; a reasonably believable threat.

BATTERY
The unprivileged, intentional touching of another.

DEFENSE
A reason offered and alleged by a defendant in an action or suit as to why the plaintiff should not recover or establish what she or he seeks.

BE AWARE   Some of these same four defenses can be raised by a defendant who is sued for other torts.

---

3. The reasonable person standard is an "objective" test of how a reasonable person would have acted under the same circumstances. See "The Duty of Care and Its Breach" later in this chapter.

False Imprisonment

False imprisonment is the intentional confinement or restraint of another person's activities without justification. False imprisonment interferes with the freedom to move without restraint. The confinement can be accomplished through the use of physical barriers, physical restraint, or threats of physical force. Moral pressure or threats of future harm do not constitute false imprisonment. It is essential that the person being restrained would not willingly wish to be restrained.

Businesspersons are often confronted with suits for false imprisonment after they have attempted to confine a suspected shoplifter for questioning. Under the "privilege to detain" granted to merchants in some states, a merchant can use the defense of *probable cause* to justify delaying a suspected shoplifter. In this context, probable cause exists when there is sufficient evidence to support the belief that a person is guilty (as you will read in Chapter 6, *probable cause* is defined differently in the context of criminal law). Although laws pertaining to the privilege to detain vary from state to state, generally they require that any detention be conducted in a *reasonable* manner and for only a *reasonable* length of time.

PREVENTING LEGAL DISPUTES

Businesspersons who operate retail establishments need to make sure that their employees are aware of the limitations on the privilege to detain. Even if someone is suspected of shoplifting, businesspersons (and employees) must have probable cause to stop and question the person and must behave reasonably and detain the person for only a sensible amount of time. Undue force or unreasonable detention can lead to liability for the business.

Intentional Infliction of Emotional Distress

The tort of *intentional infliction of emotional distress* can be defined as an intentional act that amounts to extreme and outrageous conduct resulting in severe emotional distress to another. **EXAMPLE 4.1** A prankster telephones Jesse and says that Jesse's spouse has just been in a horrible accident. As a result, Jesse suffers intense mental pain or anxiety. The caller's behavior is deemed to be extreme and outrageous conduct that exceeds the bounds of decency accepted by society and is therefore **actionable** (capable of serving as the ground for a lawsuit). ■

ACTIONABLE
Capable of serving as the basis of a lawsuit. An actionable claim can be pursued in a lawsuit or other court action.

Emotional distress claims pose several problems. One major problem is that such claims must be subject to some limitation, or the courts could be flooded with lawsuits alleging emotional distress. A society in which individuals are rewarded if they are unable to endure the normal emotional stresses of day-to-day living is obviously undesirable. Therefore, the law usually focuses on the nature of the acts that fall under this tort. Indignity or annoyance alone is usually not sufficient to support a lawsuit based on intentional infliction of emotional distress.

Many times, however, repeated annoyances (such as those experienced by a person who is being stalked), coupled with threats, are enough. In a business context, for example, the repeated use of extreme methods to collect an overdue debt may be actionable. Because it is difficult to prove the existence of emotional suffering, a court may require that the emotional distress be evidenced by some physical symptom or illness. Alternatively, a court might require evidence of a specific emotional disturbance that can be documented by a psychiatric consultant or other medical professional.

Defamation

As discussed in Chapter 2, the freedom of speech guaranteed by the First Amendment to the U.S. Constitution is not absolute. In interpreting the First Amendment, the courts must balance free speech rights against other strong social interests, including society's interest in preventing and redressing attacks on reputation.

Defamation of character involves wrongfully hurting a person's good reputation. The law has imposed a general duty on all persons to refrain from making *false*, defamatory *statements of fact* about others. Breaching this duty in writing or other permanent form (such as a digital recording) involves the tort of **libel.** Breaching this duty orally involves the tort of **slander.** As you will read later in this chapter, the tort of defamation can also arise when a false statement of fact is made about a person's product, business, or legal ownership rights to property.

Often at issue in defamation lawsuits (including online defamation, discussed later in this chapter) is whether the defendant made a statement of fact or a *statement of opinion.* Statements of opinion are normally not actionable because they are protected under the First Amendment. In other words, making a negative statement about another person is not defamation unless the statement is false and represents something as a fact (for example, "Vladik cheats on his taxes") rather than a personal opinion (for example, "Vladik is a jerk").

The Publication Requirement   The basis of the tort of defamation is the publication of a statement or statements that hold an individual up to contempt, ridicule, or hatred. *Publication* here means that the defamatory statements are communicated to persons other than the defamed party. ■**EXAMPLE 4.2** If Thompson writes Andrews a private letter accusing him of embezzling funds, the action does not constitute libel. If Peters calls Gordon dishonest and incompetent when no one else is around, the action does not constitute slander. In neither instance was the message communicated to a third party. ■

The courts have generally held that even dictating a letter to a secretary constitutes publication, although the publication may be privileged (privileged communications will be discussed shortly). Moreover, if a third party overhears defamatory statements by chance, the courts usually hold that this also constitutes publication. Defamatory statements made via the Internet are also actionable, as you will read later in this chapter. Note further that any individual who republishes or repeats defamatory statements is liable even if that person reveals the source of such statements.

Damages for Libel   Once a defendant's liability for libel is established, *general damages* are presumed as a matter of law. As mentioned earlier, general damages are designed to compensate the plaintiff for nonspecific harms such as disgrace or dishonor in the eyes of the community, humiliation, injured reputation, and emotional distress—harms that are difficult to measure. In other words, to recover damages in a libel case, the plaintiff need not prove that she or he was actually injured in any way as a result of the libelous statement.

Damages for Slander   In contrast to cases alleging libel, in a case alleging slander, the plaintiff must prove *special damages* to establish the defendant's liability. In other words, the plaintiff must show that the slanderous statement caused the plaintiff to suffer actual economic or monetary losses. Unless this initial hurdle of proving special damages is overcome, a plaintiff alleging slander normally cannot go forward with the suit and recover any damages. This requirement is imposed in cases involving slander because slanderous statements have a temporary quality. In contrast, a libelous (written) statement has the quality of permanence, can be circulated widely, and usually results from some degree of deliberation on the part of the author.

Exceptions to the burden of proving special damages in cases alleging slander are made for certain types of slanderous statements. If a false statement constitutes "slander *per se*," no proof of special damages is required for it to be actionable. The following four types of utterances are considered to be slander *per se*:

DEFAMATION
Anything published or publicly spoken that causes injury to another's good name, reputation, or character.

LIBEL
Defamation in writing or other form having the quality of permanence (such as a digital recording).

SLANDER
Defamation in oral form.

1 A statement that another has a loathsome disease (historically, leprosy and sexually transmitted diseases, but now also including allegations of mental illness).

2 A statement that another has committed improprieties while engaging in a business, profession, or trade.

3 A statement that another has committed or has been imprisoned for a serious crime.

4 A statement that a person (usually only unmarried persons and sometimes only women) is unchaste or has engaged in serious sexual misconduct.

PRIVILEGE
A legal right, exemption, or immunity granted to a person or a class of persons. In the context of defamation, an absolute privilege immunizes the person making the statements from a lawsuit, regardless of whether the statements were malicious.

Defenses against Defamation Truth is normally an absolute defense against a defamation charge. In other words, if the defendant in a defamation suit can prove that his or her allegedly defamatory statements were true, normally no tort has been committed. Other defenses to defamation may exist if the statement is privileged or concerns a public figure. Note that the majority of defamation actions in the United States are filed in state courts, and the states may differ in how they define both defamation and the particular defenses they allow, such as privilege (discussed next).

Privileged Communications. In some circumstances, a person will not be liable for defamatory statements because she or he enjoys a **privilege,** or immunity. Privileged communications are of two types: absolute and qualified.[4] Only in judicial proceedings and certain government proceedings is an *absolute* privilege granted. For example, statements made in the courtroom by attorneys and judges during a trial are absolutely privileged. So are statements made by government officials during legislative debate, even if the officials make such statements maliciously—that is, knowing them to be untrue. An absolute privilege is granted in these situations because government personnel deal with matters that are so much in the public interest that the parties involved should be able to speak out fully and freely without restriction.

In other situations, a person will not be liable for defamatory statements because he or she has a *qualified*, or conditional, privilege. An employer's statements in written evaluations of employees are an example of a qualified privilege. Generally, if the statements are made in good faith and the publication is limited to those who have a legitimate interest in the communication, the statements fall within the area of qualified privilege. **EXAMPLE 4.3** Jorge applies for membership at the local country club. After the country club's board rejects his application, Jorge sues the club's office manager for making allegedly defamatory statements to the board concerning a conversation she had with Jorge. Assuming that the office manager had simply relayed what she thought was her duty to convey to the club's board, her statements would likely be protected by qualified privilege.[5] ■

The concept of conditional privilege rests on the assumption that in some situations, the right to know or speak is paramount to the right not to be defamed. Only if the privilege is abused or the statement is knowingly false or malicious will the person be liable for damages.

Public Figures. Public officials who exercise substantial governmental power and any persons in the public limelight are consid-

The British edition of the National Enquirer *agreed to pay actress Kate Hudson an undisclosed amount in damages and to print an apology to settle a libel lawsuit she had filed in England. The tabloid had published an article stating that Hudson was "way too thin" and "looked like skin and bones." Would these statements be considered libel under U.S. defamation laws?* (Katie Kiehn/Creative Commons)

---

4. Note that the term *privileged communication* in this context is not the same as privileged communication between a professional, such as an attorney, and his or her client. The latter type of privilege will be discussed in Chapter 35, in the context of the liability of professionals.
5. For a case involving a qualified privilege, see *Hickson Corp. v. Northern Crossarm Co.*, 357 F.3d 1256 (11th Cir. 2004).

ered *public figures.* In general, public figures are considered fair game, and false and defamatory statements about them that are published in the press will not constitute defamation unless the statements are made with **actual malice.**[6] To be made with actual malice, a statement must be made *with either knowledge of falsity or a reckless disregard of the truth.* Statements made about public figures, especially when the statements are made via a public medium, are usually related to matters of general interest; they are made about people who substantially affect all of us. Furthermore, public figures generally have some access to a public medium for answering disparaging (belittling, discrediting) false-hoods about themselves; private individuals do not. For these reasons, public figures have a greater burden of proof in defamation cases (they must prove actual malice) than do private individuals.

Invasion of the Right to Privacy

A person has a right to solitude and freedom from prying public eyes—in other words, to privacy. As discussed in Chapter 2, the Supreme Court has held that a fundamental right to privacy is also implied by various amendments to the U.S. Constitution. Some state constitutions explicitly provide for privacy rights. In addition, a number of federal and state statutes have been enacted to protect individual rights in specific areas. Tort law also safeguards these rights through the tort *invasion of privacy.* Four acts qualify as an invasion of privacy:

1 *Appropriation of identity.* Under the common law, using a person's name, picture, or other likeness for commercial purposes without permission is a tortious invasion of privacy. Most states today have also enacted statutes prohibiting appropriation (discussed further in the next subsection).

2 *Intrusion into an individual's affairs or seclusion.* For example, invading someone's home or illegally searching someone's briefcase is an invasion of privacy. The tort has been held to extend to eavesdropping by wiretap, the unauthorized scanning of a bank account, compulsory blood testing, and window peeping.

3 *False light.* Publication of information that places a person in a false light is another category of invasion of privacy. This could be a story attributing to the person ideas not held or actions not taken by the person. (Publishing such a story could involve the tort of defamation as well.)

4 *Public disclosure of private facts.* This type of invasion of privacy occurs when a person publicly discloses private facts about an individual that an ordinary person would find objectionable or embarrassing. A newspaper account of a private citizen's sex life or financial affairs could be an actionable invasion of privacy, even if the information revealed is true, because it is not of public concern.

Appropriation

The use by one person of another person's name, likeness, or other identifying characteristic, without permission and for the benefit of the user, constitutes the tort of **appropriation.** Under the law, an individual's right to privacy normally includes the right to the exclusive use of her or his identity.

■EXAMPLE 4.4 Vanna White, the hostess of the popular television game show *Wheel of Fortune,* brought a case against Samsung Electronics America, Inc. Without White's permission, Samsung included in an advertisement for its videocassette recorders (VCRs)

ACTUAL MALICE
The deliberate intent to cause harm, which exists when a person makes a statement either knowing that it is false or showing a reckless disregard for whether it is true. In a defamation suit, a statement made about a public figure normally must be made with actual malice for the plaintiff to recover damages.

ON THE WEB

You can find information and cases relating to employee privacy rights with respect to electronic monitoring at the Web site of the American Civil Liberties Union (ACLU). Go to

www.aclu.org/privacy/workplace/ index.html.

APPROPRIATION
In tort law, the use by one person of another person's name, likeness, or other identifying characteristic without permission and for the benefit of the user.

---

6. *New York Times Co. v. Sullivan,* 376 U.S. 254, 84 S.Ct. 710, 11 L.Ed.2d 686 (1964).

a depiction of a robot dressed in a wig, gown, and jewelry, posed in a scene that resembled the *Wheel of Fortune* set, in a stance for which White is famous. The court held in White's favor, holding that the tort of appropriation does not require the use of a celebrity's name or likeness. The court stated that Samsung's robot ad left "little doubt" as to the identity of the celebrity whom the ad was meant to depict.[7] ■

Cases of wrongful appropriation, or misappropriation, may also involve the rights of those who invest time and funds in the creation of a special system, such as a method of broadcasting sports events. Commercial misappropriation may also occur when a person takes and uses the property of another for the sole purpose of capitalizing unfairly on the goodwill or reputation of the property owner.

Fraudulent Misrepresentation

A misrepresentation leads another to believe in a condition that is different from the condition that actually exists. This is often accomplished through a false or incorrect statement. Although persons sometimes make misrepresentations accidentally because they are unaware of the existing facts, the tort of **fraudulent misrepresentation,** or fraud, involves *intentional* deceit for personal gain. The tort includes several elements:

1 The misrepresentation of facts or conditions with knowledge that they are false or with reckless disregard for the truth.

2 An intent to induce another to rely on the misrepresentation.

3 Justifiable reliance by the deceived party.

4 Damages suffered as a result of the reliance.

5 A causal connection between the misrepresentation and the injury suffered.

For fraud to occur, more than mere **puffery,** or *seller's talk,* must be involved. Fraud exists only when a person represents as a fact something she or he knows is untrue. For example, it is fraud to claim that a roof does not leak when one knows it does. Facts are objectively ascertainable, whereas seller's talk is not. "I am the best accountant in town" is seller's talk. The speaker is not trying to represent something as fact because *best* is a subjective, not an objective, term.[8]

Normally, the tort of misrepresentation or fraud occurs only when there is reliance on a *statement of fact.* Sometimes, however, reliance on a *statement of opinion* may involve the tort of misrepresentation if the individual making the statement of opinion has a superior knowledge of the subject matter. For example, when a lawyer makes a statement of opinion about the law in a state in which the lawyer is licensed to practice, a court would construe reliance on such a statement to be equivalent to reliance on a statement of fact. We examine fraudulent misrepresentation in further detail in Chapter 11, in the context of contract law.

Wrongful Interference

Business torts involving wrongful interference are generally divided into two categories: wrongful interference with a contractual relationship and wrongful interference with a business relationship.

Wrongful Interference with a Contractual Relationship   The body of tort law relating to *intentional interference with a contractual relationship* has expanded greatly in recent years.

FRAUDULENT MISREPRESENTATION
Any misrepresentation, either by misstatement or by omission of a material fact, knowingly made with the intention of deceiving another and on which a reasonable person would and does rely to his or her detriment.

PUFFERY
A salesperson's often exaggerated claims concerning the quality of property offered for sale. Such claims involve opinions rather than facts and are not considered to be legally binding promises or warranties.

ON THE WEB

The 'Lectric Law Library's Legal Lexicon includes a useful discussion of the elements of fraud, as well as different types of fraud. To access this page, go to

www.lectlaw.com/def/1079.htm.

---

7. *White v. Samsung Electronics America, Inc.,* 971 F.2d 1395 (9th Cir. 1992).

8. In contracts for the sale of goods, Article 2 of the Uniform Commercial Code distinguishes, for warranty purposes, between statements of opinion (puffery) and statements of fact. See Chapter 18 for a further discussion of this issue.

A landmark case involved an opera singer, Joanna Wagner, who was under contract to sing for a man named Lumley for a specified period of years. A man named Gye, who knew of this contract, nonetheless "enticed" Wagner to refuse to carry out the agreement, and Wagner began to sing for Gye. Gye's action constituted a tort because it wrongfully interfered with the contractual relationship between Wagner and Lumley.[9] (Of course, Wagner's refusal to carry out the agreement also entitled Lumley to sue Wagner for breach of contract.)

Three elements are necessary for wrongful interference with a contractual relationship to occur:

1 A valid, enforceable contract must exist between two parties.

2 A third party must know that this contract exists.

3 The third party must *intentionally* induce a party to breach the contract.

In principle, any lawful contract can be the basis for an action of this type. The contract could be between a firm and its employees or a firm and its customers. Sometimes, a competitor of a firm draws away one of the firm's key employees. Only if the original employer can show that the competitor knew of the contract's existence and intentionally induced the breach can damages be recovered from the competitor.

■EXAMPLE 4.5 Carlin has a contract with Sutter that calls for Sutter to do gardening work on Carlin's large estate every week for fifty-two weeks at a specified price per week. Mellon, who needs gardening services and knows nothing about the Sutter-Carlin contract, contacts Sutter and offers to pay Sutter a wage that is substantially higher than that offered by Carlin. Sutter breaches his contract with Carlin so that he can work for Mellon. Carlin cannot sue Mellon because Mellon knew nothing of the Sutter-Carlin contract and was totally unaware that the higher wage he offered induced Sutter to breach that contract. ■

> **REMEMBER** It is the intent to do an act that is important in tort law, not the motive behind the intent.

ETHICAL ISSUE 4.1

Can a person whose marriage breaks up file a tort action against the person who "stole" his or her spouse? The answer is "yes"—at least in some states, such as North Carolina. These states recognize a tort that is somewhat analogous (similar) to a wrongful interference claim except that it arises in a personal rather than a business context. "Alienation of affection" claims allow a plaintiff whose marriage has broken up due to adultery to file a lawsuit against the "other woman" or "other man." This tort has existed since the early days of the common law, but at that time only a husband could file an alienation suit against a man who stole his wife. As times changed, a wife was also given the right to sue the woman who caused her husband to be unfaithful. Today, most states have abolished the tort of alienation of affection because it treats a person's spouse as a piece of property.

Nevertheless, the tort still exists in a handful of states and is being used by former spouses to get sizable damage awards. In one case, for example, Cindy Harrell discovered that her husband was having an affair with Beth Anne Carroccio. Harrell sent several letters telling Carroccio to leave her husband alone, but the extramarital relations continued, so Harrell filed a lawsuit. In 2006, a court ordered Carroccio to pay $500,000 to Harrell for the loss of future financial support, humiliation, and emotional distress. Such cases are not rare in North Carolina, where more than two hundred alienation of affection cases are filed each year.[10] Alienation suits are often brought to gain leverage in divorce or custody proceedings and can even be filed years later after the ex-spouse has married the person who alienated him or her from the previous marriage.[11]

■

---

9. *Lumley v. Gye*, 118 Eng.Rep. 749 (1853).

10. *Harrell v. Carroccio*, decided June 8, 2006, by the Superior Court in Greensboro, North Carolina; facts as reported by Natalie White, "N.C. Woman Ordered to Pay $500,000 for Stealing Another Woman's Husband," *Lawyers USA*, July 17, 2006, p. 8.

11. See, for example, *McCutchen v. McCutchen*, 360 N.C. 280, 624 S.E.2d 620 (2006).

PREDATORY BEHAVIOR
Business behavior that is undertaken with the intention of unlawfully driving competitors out of the market.

Wrongful Interference with a Business Relationship   Businesspersons devise countless schemes to attract customers, but they are prohibited from unreasonably interfering with another's business in their attempts to gain a share of the market. There is a difference between competitive methods and **predatory behavior**—actions undertaken with the intention of unlawfully driving competitors completely out of the market. The distinction usually depends on whether a business is attempting to attract customers in general or to solicit only those customers who have shown an interest in a similar product or service of a specific competitor.

■**EXAMPLE 4.6**   A shopping mall contains two athletic shoe stores: Joe's and SneakerSprint. Joe's cannot station an employee at the entrance of SneakerSprint to divert customers to Joe's and tell them that Joe's will beat SneakerSprint's prices. This type of activity constitutes the tort of wrongful interference with a business relationship, which is commonly considered to be an unfair trade practice. If this type of activity were permitted, Joe's would reap the benefits of SneakerSprint's advertising. ■

Defenses to Wrongful Interference   A person will not be liable for the tort of wrongful interference with a contractual or business relationship if it can be shown that the interference was justified, or permissible. Bona fide competitive behavior is a permissible interference even if it results in the breaking of a contract. ■**EXAMPLE 4.7**   If Antonio's Meats advertises so effectively that it induces Sam's Restaurant to break its contract with Burke's Meat Company, Burke's Meat Company will be unable to recover against Antonio's Meats on a wrongful interference theory. After all, the public policy that favors free competition in advertising outweighs any possible instability that such competitive activity might cause in contractual relations. ■ Although luring customers away from a competitor through aggressive marketing and advertising strategies obviously interferes with the competitor's relationship with its customers, courts typically allow such activities in the spirit of competition.

REMEMBER   What society and the law consider permissible often depends on the circumstances.

INTENTIONAL TORTS AGAINST PROPERTY

Intentional torts against property include trespass to land, trespass to personal property, conversion, and disparagement of property. These torts are wrongful actions that interfere with individuals' legally recognized rights with regard to their land or personal property. The law distinguishes real property from personal property (see Chapters 36 and 37). *Real property* is land and things "permanently" attached to the land. *Personal property* consists of all other items, which are basically movable. Thus, a house and lot are real property, whereas the furniture inside a house is personal property. Cash and stocks and bonds are also personal property.

Trespass to Land

TRESPASS TO LAND
The entry onto, above, or below the surface of land owned by another without the owner's permission or legal authorization.

A **trespass to land** occurs whenever a person, without permission, enters onto, above, or below the surface of land that is owned by another; causes anything to enter onto the land; remains on the land; or permits anything to remain on it. Actual harm to the land is not an essential element of this tort because the tort is designed to protect the right of an owner to exclusive possession of her or his property. Common types of trespass to land include walking or driving on someone else's land, shooting a gun over the land, throwing rocks at a building that belongs to someone else, building a dam across a river and thereby causing water to back up on someone else's land, and constructing a building so that part of it is on an adjoining landowner's property.

Trespass Criteria, Rights, and Duties   Before a person can be a trespasser, the owner of the real property (or other person in actual and exclusive possession of the property) must establish that person as a trespasser. For example, "posted" trespass signs expressly establish

as a trespasser a person who ignores these signs and enters onto the property. A guest in your home is not a trespasser—unless she or he has been asked to leave but refuses. Any person who enters onto your property to commit an illegal act (such as a thief entering a lumberyard at night to steal lumber) is established impliedly as a trespasser, without posted signs.

At common law, a trespasser is liable for damages caused to the property and generally cannot hold the owner liable for injuries sustained on the premises. This common law rule is being abandoned in many jurisdictions in favor of a *reasonable duty of care* rule that varies depending on the status of the parties; for example, a landowner may have a duty to post a notice that the property is patrolled by guard dogs. Also, under the *attractive nuisance* doctrine, children do not assume the risks of the premises if they are attracted to the property by some object, such as a swimming pool, an abandoned building, or a sand pile. Trespassers normally can be removed from the premises through the use of reasonable force without the owner's being liable for assault, battery, or false imprisonment.

Defenses against Trespass to Land   Trespass to land involves wrongful interference with another person's real property rights. One defense to this claim is to show that the trespass was warranted—for example, that the trespasser entered the property to assist someone in danger. Another defense exists when the trespasser can show that he or she had a license to come onto the land. A *licensee* is one who is invited (or allowed to enter) onto the property of another for the licensee's benefit. A person who enters another's property to read an electric meter, for example, is a licensee. When you purchase a ticket to attend a movie or sporting event, you are licensed to go onto the property of another to view that movie or event. Note that licenses to enter onto another's property are *revocable* by the property owner. If a property owner asks a meter reader to leave and the meter reader refuses to do so, the meter reader at that point becomes a trespasser.

Trespass to Personal Property

Whenever an individual wrongfully takes or harms the personal property of another or otherwise interferes with the lawful owner's possession of personal property, **trespass to personal property** occurs (also called *trespass to chattels* or *trespass to personalty*[12]). In

TRESPASS TO PERSONAL PROPERTY
The unlawful taking or harming of another's personal property; interference with another's right to the exclusive possession of his or her personal property.

---

12. Pronounced *per-sun-ul-tee*.

this context, harm means not only destruction of the property, but also anything that diminishes its value, condition, or quality. Trespass to personal property involves intentional meddling with a possessory interest, including barring an owner's access to personal property. **■EXAMPLE 4.8** If Kelly takes Ryan's business law book as a practical joke and hides it so that Ryan is unable to find it for several days prior to the final examination, Kelly has engaged in a trespass to personal property. (Kelly has also committed the tort of *conversion*—to be discussed shortly.) ■

If it can be shown that the trespass to personal property was warranted, then a complete defense exists. Most states, for example, allow automobile repair shops to hold a customer's car (under what is called an *artisan's lien*, discussed in Chapter 23) when the customer refuses to pay for repairs already completed.

Conversion

CONVERSION
Wrongfully taking or retaining possession of an individual's personal property and placing it in the service of another.

Whenever a person wrongfully possesses or uses the personal property of another without permission, the tort of **conversion** occurs. Any act that deprives an owner of personal property or the use of that property without that owner's permission and without just cause can be conversion. Often, when conversion occurs, a trespass to personal property also occurs because the original taking of the personal property from the owner was a trespass, and wrongfully retaining it is conversion. Conversion is the civil side of crimes related to theft, but it is not limited to theft. Even if the rightful owner consented to the initial taking of the property, so there was no theft or trespass, a failure to return the personal property may still be conversion. **■EXAMPLE 4.9** Chen borrows Marik's iPod to use while traveling home from school for the holidays. When Chen returns to school, Marik asks for his iPod back. Chen tells Marik that she gave it to her little brother for Christmas. In this situation, Marik can sue Chen for conversion, and Chen will have to either return the iPod or pay damages equal to its value. ■

KEEP IN MIND In tort law, the underlying motive for an act does not matter. What matters is the intent to do the act that results in the tort.

Even if a person mistakenly believed that she or he was entitled to the goods, the tort of conversion may occur. In other words, good intentions are not a defense against conversion; in fact, conversion can be an entirely innocent act. Someone who buys stolen goods, for example, can be liable for conversion even if he or she did not know that the goods were stolen. If the true owner brings a tort action against the buyer, the buyer must either return the property to the owner or pay the owner the full value of the property, despite having already paid the purchase price to the thief.

A successful defense against the charge of conversion is that the purported owner does not, in fact, own the property or does not have a right to possess it that is superior to the right of the holder.

Disparagement of Property

DISPARAGEMENT OF PROPERTY
An economically injurious falsehood made about another's product or property; a general term for torts that are more specifically referred to as *slander of quality* or *slander of title*.

Disparagement of property occurs when economically injurious falsehoods are made about another's product or property, not about another's reputation. Disparagement of property is a general term for torts that can be more specifically referred to as *slander of quality* or *slander of title*.

SLANDER OF QUALITY (TRADE LIBEL)
The publication of false information about another's product, alleging that it is not what its seller claims.

Slander of Quality Publication of false information about another's product, alleging that it is not what its seller claims, constitutes the tort of **slander of quality**, or **trade libel**. The plaintiff must prove that actual damages proximately resulted from the slander of quality. In other words, the plaintiff must show not only that a third person refrained from dealing with the plaintiff because of the improper publication but also that there were associated damages. The economic calculation of such damages—they are, after all, conjectural—is often extremely difficult.

An improper publication may be both a slander of quality and defamation of character. For example, a statement that disparages the quality of a product may also, by implication, disparage the character of the person who would sell such a product.

Slander of Title   When a publication denies or casts doubt on another's legal ownership of any property, and this results in financial loss to that property's owner, the tort of **slander of title** may exist. Usually, this is an intentional tort in which someone knowingly publishes an untrue statement about property with the intent of discouraging a third person from dealing with the person slandered. For example, it would be difficult for a car dealer to attract customers after competitors published a notice that the dealer's stock consisted of stolen autos.

SLANDER OF TITLE
The publication of a statement that denies or casts doubt on another's legal ownership of any property, causing financial loss to that property's owner.

UNINTENTIONAL TORTS (NEGLIGENCE)

The tort of **negligence** occurs when someone suffers injury because of another's failure to live up to a required *duty of care*. In contrast to intentional torts, in torts involving negligence, the tortfeasor neither wishes to bring about the consequences of the act nor believes that they will occur. The actor's conduct merely creates a *risk* of such consequences. If no risk is created, there is no negligence. Moreover, the risk must be foreseeable—that is, it must be such that a reasonable person engaging in the same activity

NEGLIGENCE
The failure to exercise the standard of care that a reasonable person would exercise in similar circumstances.

Drawing by Maslin; © 1990 The New Yorker Magazine, Inc.

"To answer your question. Yes, if you shoot an arrow into the air and it falls to earth you should know not where, you could be liable for any damage it may cause."

would anticipate the risk and guard against it. In determining what is reasonable conduct, courts consider the nature of the possible harm.

Many of the actions discussed earlier in the chapter in the section on intentional torts constitute negligence if the element of intent is missing. **■EXAMPLE 4.10** Suppose that Juarez walks up to Natsuyo and intentionally shoves her. Natsuyo falls and breaks an arm as a result. In this situation, Juarez has committed an intentional tort (assault and battery). If Juarez carelessly bumps into Natsuyo, however, and she falls and breaks an arm as a result, Juarez's action will constitute negligence. In either situation, Juarez has committed a tort. ■

To succeed in a negligence action, the plaintiff must prove each of the following:

1 That the defendant owed a duty of care to the plaintiff.

2 That the defendant breached that duty.

3 That the plaintiff suffered a legally recognizable injury.

4 That the defendant's breach caused the plaintiff's injury.

We discuss here each of these four elements of negligence.

The Duty of Care and Its Breach

DUTY OF CARE
The duty of all persons, as established by tort law, to exercise a reasonable amount of care in their dealings with others. Failure to exercise due care, which is normally determined by the reasonable person standard, constitutes the tort of negligence.

Central to the tort of negligence is the concept of a **duty of care.** The idea is that if we are to live in society with other people, some actions can be tolerated and some cannot; some actions are right and some are wrong; and some actions are reasonable and some are not. The basic principle underlying the duty of care is that people are free to act as they please so long as their actions do not infringe on the interests of others.

When someone fails to comply with the duty to exercise reasonable care, a potentially tortious act may have been committed. Failure to live up to a standard of care may be an act (setting fire to a building) or an omission (neglecting to put out a campfire). It may be a careless act or a carefully performed but nevertheless dangerous act that results in injury. Courts consider the nature of the act (whether it is outrageous or commonplace), the manner in which the act is performed (cautiously versus heedlessly), and the nature of the injury (whether it is serious or slight) in determining whether the duty of care has been breached.

REASONABLE PERSON STANDARD
The standard of behavior expected of a hypothetical "reasonable person"; the standard against which negligence is measured and that must be observed to avoid liability for negligence.

The Reasonable Person Standard   Tort law measures duty by the **reasonable person standard.** In determining whether a duty of care has been breached, the courts ask how a reasonable person would have acted in the same circumstances. The reasonable person standard is said to be (though in an absolute sense it cannot be) objective. It is not necessarily how a particular person would act. It is society's judgment on how people *should* act. If the so-called reasonable person existed, he or she would be careful, conscientious, even tempered, and honest. The courts frequently use this hypothetical reasonable person in decisions relating to other areas of law as well. That individuals are required to exercise a reasonable standard of care in their activities is a pervasive concept in business law, and many of the issues discussed in subsequent chapters of this text have to do with this duty.

In negligence cases, the degree of care to be exercised varies, depending on the defendant's occupation or profession, her or his relationship with the plaintiff, and other factors. Generally, whether an action constitutes a breach of the duty of care is determined on a case-by-case basis. The outcome depends on how the judge (or jury, if it is a jury trial) decides a reasonable person in the position of the defendant would act in the particular circumstances of the case.

Does a person's duty of care include a duty to come to the aid of a stranger in peril?
Suppose that you are walking down a city street and notice that a pedestrian is about to step directly in front of an oncoming bus. Do you have a legal duty to warn that individual? No. Although most people would probably concede that the observer has an *ethical* or moral duty to warn the other in this situation, tort law does not impose a general duty to rescue others in peril. People involved in special relationships, however, have been held to have a duty to rescue other parties within the relationship. A person has a duty to rescue his or her child or spouse if either is in danger, for example. Other special relationships, such as those between teachers and students or hiking and hunting partners, may also give rise to a duty to rescue. In addition, if a person who has no duty to rescue undertakes to rescue another, then the rescuer is charged with a duty to follow through with due care in the rescue attempt.

ETHICAL ISSUE 4.2

■

The Duty of Landowners   Landowners are expected to exercise reasonable care to protect persons coming onto their property from harm. As mentioned earlier, in some jurisdictions, landowners are held to owe a duty to protect even trespassers against certain risks. Landowners who rent or lease premises to tenants (see Chapter 37) are expected to exercise reasonable care to ensure that the tenants and their guests are not harmed in common areas, such as stairways, entryways, and laundry rooms.

Duty to Warn Business Invitees of Risks.   Retailers and other firms that explicitly or implicitly invite persons to come onto their premises are usually charged with a duty to exercise reasonable care to protect those persons, who are considered **business invitees.** For example, if you entered a supermarket, slipped on a wet floor, and sustained injuries as a result, the owner of the supermarket would be liable for damages if, when you slipped, there was no sign warning that the floor was wet. A court would hold that the business owner was negligent because the owner failed to exercise a reasonable degree of care in protecting the store's customers against foreseeable risks about which the owner knew or *should have known.* That a patron might slip on the wet floor and be injured as a result was a foreseeable risk, and the owner should have taken care to avoid this risk or to warn the customer of it.

The landowner also has a duty to discover and remove any hidden dangers that might injure a customer or other invitee. Store owners have a duty to protect customers from potentially slipping and injuring themselves on merchandise that has fallen off the shelves. In one case, for example, Wal-Mart was held liable because a customer was injured when he slipped on shotgun shell pellets that had fallen off a display and were on the floor.[13]

BUSINESS INVITEE
A person, such as a customer or a client, who is invited onto business premises by the owner of those premises for business purposes.

Obvious Risks Provide an Exception.   Some risks, of course, are so obvious that the owner need not warn of them. For instance, a business owner does not need to warn customers to open a door before attempting to walk through it. Other risks, however, may seem obvious to a business owner but may not be so in the eyes of another, such as a child. For example, a hardware store owner may think it is unnecessary to warn customers not to climb a stepladder leaning against the back wall of the store. It is possible, though, that a child could climb up and tip the ladder over and be hurt as a result and that the store could be held liable.

The issue in the following case was whether the obviousness of the existence of wet napkins on the floor of a nightclub obviated the owner's duty to its customers to maintain the premises in a safe condition.

A sign in a merchant's window warns business invitees about slippery floors. If a customer subsequently slips on a wet floor and is injured, can the merchant be held liable? (Debaird/Creative Commons)

---

13. *Martin v. Wal-Mart Stores, Inc.*, 183 F.3d 770 (1999).

CASE 4.1   Izquierdo v. Gyroscope, Inc.

District Court of Appeal of Florida, Fourth District, 946 So.2d 115 (2007).

FACTS Giorgio's Grill in Hollywood, Florida, is a restaurant that becomes a nightclub after hours. At those times, traditionally, as the manager of Giorgio's knew, the staff and customers threw paper napkins into the air as the music played. The napkins landed on the floor, but no one picked them up. If they became too deep, customers pushed them to the side. Because drinks were occasionally spilled, sometimes the napkins were wet. One night, Jane Izquierdo went to Giorgio's to meet a friend. She had been to the club five or six times and knew of the napkin-throwing tradition. She had one drink and went to the restroom. On her return, she slipped and fell, breaking her leg. After surgery, she relied on a wheelchair for three months and continued to suffer pain. She filed a suit in a Florida state court against Gyroscope, Inc., the owner of Giorgio's, alleging negligence. A jury returned a verdict in favor of the defendant, and Izquierdo filed a motion for a new trial, which the court denied. She appealed to a state intermediate appellate court.

ISSUE Does the obviousness of a risk discharge a business owner's duty to its invitees to maintain the premises in a safe condition?

DECISION No. The state intermediate appellate court reversed the lower court's decision, concluding that "the trial court abused its discretion" in denying Izquierdo's motion. The appellate court remanded the case for a new trial.

REASON The court reasoned that "the uncontroverted evidence shows at least some negligence on the part of the restaurant." The court emphasized, "[I]mportantly, the manager of the restaurant admitted that permitting the wet napkins to remain on the floor was a hazardous condition." Izquierdo testified that she slipped, fell down on a wet floor, and found napkins on her shoes. "The inference that the wet napkins on the floor caused her fall clearly was the only reasonable inference which could be drawn from the facts." Izquierdo knew of the napkin-throwing tradition, and the existence of napkins on the floor was obvious, but these circumstances "merely discharge[d] the landowner's duty to warn. It does not discharge the landowner's duty to maintain the premises in a reasonably safe condition."

FOR CRITICAL ANALYSIS–Social Consideration
Should the result in this case have been different if, in all the years that the napkin-throwing tradition existed, no one had ever fallen on them before Izquierdo did?

PREVENTING LEGAL DISPUTES

It can sometimes be difficult for business owners to determine whether risks are obvious. Because the law imposes liability on business owners who fail to discover hidden dangers on the premises and protect patrons from being injured, it is advisable to post warnings of any potential risks on the property. Businesspersons should train their employees to be on the lookout for possibly dangerous conditions on the premises at all times and to notify a superior immediately if they notice something. Making the business premises as safe as possible for all persons who might be there, including children, the elderly, and individuals with disabilities, is one of the best ways to prevent potential legal disputes.

ON THE WEB

You can locate the professional standards for various organizations at
www.lib.uwaterloo.ca/society/standards.html.

The Duty of Professionals If an individual has knowledge, skill, or intelligence superior to that of an ordinary person, the individual's conduct must be consistent with that status. Professionals—including physicians, dentists, architects, engineers, accountants, lawyers, and others—are required to have a standard minimum level of special knowledge and ability. Therefore, in determining whether professionals have exercised reasonable care, their training and expertise are taken into account. In other words, an accountant cannot defend against a lawsuit for negligence by stating, "But I was not familiar with that principle of accounting."

If a professional violates her or his duty of care toward a client, the professional may be sued for **malpractice,** which is essentially professional negligence. For example, a patient might sue a physician for *medical malpractice*. A client might sue an attorney for *legal malpractice*.

The Injury Requirement and Damages

For a tort to have been committed, the plaintiff must have suffered a *legally recognizable* injury. To recover damages (receive compensation), the plaintiff must have suffered some loss, harm, wrong, or invasion of a protected interest. Essentially, the purpose of tort law is to compensate for legally recognized injuries resulting from wrongful acts. If no harm or injury results from a given negligent action, there is nothing to compensate—and no tort exists. **■EXAMPLE 4.11** If you carelessly bump into a passerby, who stumbles and falls as a result, you may be liable in tort if the passerby is injured in the fall. If the person is unharmed, however, there normally could be no suit for damages because no injury was suffered. Although the passerby might be angry and suffer emotional distress, few courts recognize negligently inflicted emotional distress as a tort unless it results in some physical disturbance or dysfunction. **■**

Compensatory damages are the norm in negligence cases. As noted earlier, a court will award punitive damages only if the defendant's conduct was grossly negligent, reflecting an intentional failure to perform a duty with reckless disregard of the consequences to others.

Causation

Another element necessary to a tort is *causation*. If a person fails in a duty of care and someone suffers an injury, the wrongful activity must have caused the harm for the activity to be considered a tort. In deciding whether there is causation, the court must address two questions:

1 *Is there causation in fact?* Did the injury occur because of the defendant's act, or would it have occurred anyway? If an injury would not have occurred without the defendant's act, then there is causation in fact. **Causation in fact** can usually be determined by the use of the *but for* test: "but for" the wrongful act, the injury would not have occurred. Theoretically, causation in fact is limitless. One could claim, for example, that "but for" the creation of the world, a particular injury would not have occurred. Thus, as a practical matter, the law has to establish limits, and it does so through the concept of proximate cause.

2 *Was the act the proximate cause of the injury?* **Proximate cause,** or legal cause, exists when the connection between an act and an injury is strong enough to justify imposing liability. **■EXAMPLE 4.12** Ackerman carelessly leaves a campfire burning. The fire not only burns down the forest but also sets off an explosion in a nearby chemical plant that spills chemicals into a river, killing all the fish for a hundred miles downstream and ruining the economy of a tourist resort. Should Ackerman be liable to the resort owners? To the tourists whose vacations were ruined? These are questions of proximate cause that a court must decide. **■**

Both questions must be answered in the affirmative for liability in tort to arise. If a defendant's action constitutes causation in fact but a court decides that the action is not the proximate cause of the plaintiff's injury, the causation requirement has not been met—and the defendant normally will not be liable to the plaintiff.

Questions of proximate cause are linked to the concept of foreseeability because it would be unfair to impose liability on a defendant unless the defendant's actions created a foreseeable risk of injury. Probably the most cited case on proximate cause is the *Palsgraf* case, discussed in this chapter's *Landmark in the Law* feature on page 120. In determining

MALPRACTICE
Professional misconduct or the lack of the requisite degree of skill as a professional. Negligence—the failure to exercise due care—on the part of a professional, such as a physician, is commonly referred to as malpractice.

CAUSATION IN FACT
An act or omission without which an event would not have occurred.

PROXIMATE CAUSE
Legal cause; exists when the connection between an act and an injury is strong enough to justify imposing liability.

NOTE Proximate cause can be thought of as a question of social policy. Should the defendant be made to bear the loss instead of the plaintiff?

LANDMARK IN THE LAW — *Palsgraf v. Long Island Railroad Co.* (1928)

In 1928, the New York Court of Appeals (that state's highest court) issued its decision in *Palsgraf v. Long Island Railroad Co.*,[a] a case that has become a landmark in negligence law and proximate cause.

The Facts of the Case   The plaintiff, Helen Palsgraf, was waiting for a train on a station platform. A man carrying a small package wrapped in newspaper was rushing to catch a train that had begun to move away from the platform. As the man attempted to jump aboard the moving train, he seemed unsteady and about to fall. A railroad guard on the train car reached forward to grab him, and another guard on the platform pushed him from behind to help him board the train. In the process, the man's package fell on the railroad tracks and exploded, because it contained fireworks. The repercussions of the explosion caused scales at the other end of the train platform to fall on Palsgraf, who was injured as a result. She sued the railroad company for damages in a New York state court.

The Question of Proximate Cause   At the trial, the jury found that the railroad guards were negligent in their conduct. On appeal, the question before the New York Court of Appeals was whether the conduct of the railroad guards was the proximate cause of Palsgraf's injuries. In other words, did the guards' duty of care extend to Palsgraf, who was outside the zone of danger and whose injury could not reasonably have been foreseen?

The court stated that the question of whether the guards were negligent *with respect to Palsgraf* depended on whether her injury was *reasonably foreseeable* to the railroad guards. Although the guards may have acted negligently with respect to the man boarding the train, this had no bearing on the question of their negligence with respect to Palsgraf. This was not a situation in which a person commited an act so potentially harmful (for example, firing a gun at a building) that he or she would be held responsible for any harm that resulted. The court stated that here "there was nothing in the situation to suggest to the most cautious mind that the parcel wrapped in newspaper would spread wreckage through the station." The court thus concluded that the railroad guards were not negligent with respect to Palsgraf because her injury was not reasonably foreseeable.

APPLICATION TO TODAY'S WORLD   *The Palsgraf case established foreseeability as the test for proximate cause. Today, the courts continue to apply this test in determining proximate cause—and thus tort liability for injuries. Generally, if the victim of a harm or the consequences of a harm done are unforeseeable, there is no proximate cause. Note, though, that in the online environment, distinctions based on physical proximity, such as the "zone of danger" cited by the court in this case, are largely inapplicable.*

RELEVANT WEB SITES   *To locate information on the Web concerning the* Palsgraf *decision, go to this text's Web site at* **www.thomsonedu.com/westbuslaw/blt**, *select "Chapter 4," and click on "URLs for Landmarks."*

a. 248 N.Y. 339, 162 N.E. 99 (1928).

ASSUMPTION OF RISK
A doctrine under which a plaintiff may not recover for injuries or damage suffered from risks he or she knows of and has voluntarily assumed.

the issue of proximate cause, the court addressed the following question: Does a defendant's duty of care extend only to those who may be injured as a result of a foreseeable risk, or does it extend also to a person whose injury could not reasonably be foreseen?

Defenses to Negligence

Defendants often defend against negligence claims by asserting that the plaintiffs failed to prove the existence of one or more of the required elements for negligence. Additionally, there are three basic *affirmative* defenses in negligence cases (defenses that a defendant can use to avoid liability even if the facts are as the plaintiff state): (1) assumption of risk, (2) superseding cause, and (3) contributory and comparative negligence.

Assumption of Risk   A plaintiff who voluntarily enters into a risky situation, knowing the risk involved, will not be allowed to recover. This is the defense of **assumption of risk**. The requirements of this defense are (1) knowledge of the risk and (2) voluntary assumption of the risk. This defense is frequently asserted when the plaintiff is injured during recreational activities that involve known risk, such as skiing and parachuting.

The risk can be assumed by express agreement, or the assumption of risk can be implied by the plaintiff's knowledge of the risk and subsequent conduct. For example, a driver entering a race knows that there is a risk of being killed or injured in a crash. Of course, the plaintiff does not assume a risk different from or greater than the risk normally carried by the activity. In our example, the race driver would not assume the risk that the banking in the curves of the racetrack will give way during the race because of a construction defect.

Risks are not deemed to be assumed in situations involving emergencies. Neither are they assumed when a statute protects a class of people from harm and a member of the class is injured by the harm. For example, employees are protected by statute from harmful working conditions and therefore do not assume the risks associated with the workplace. An employee who is injured will generally be compensated regardless of fault under state workers' compensation statutes (discussed in Chapter 33).

In the following case, a ball kicked by a player practicing on a nearby field injured a man who was attending his son's soccer tournament. The question before the court was whether a bystander who was not watching a soccer match at the time of the injury had nevertheless assumed the risk of being struck by a wayward ball.

Two bungee jumpers leap from a platform. If they are injured and sue the operator of the jump for negligence, what defenses might the operator use to avoid liability?
(Mark Setchell/Creative Commons)

CASE 4.2   **Sutton v. Eastern New York Youth Soccer Association, Inc.**

New York Supreme Court, Appellate Division, Third Department, 8 A.D.3d 855, 779 N.Y.S.2d 149 (2004).

FACTS   On May 30, 1999, James Sutton's son, a member of the Latham Circle Soccer Club, was participating in the Highland Soccer Club Tournament at Maalyck Park in Glenville, New York. Sutton attended as a spectator. After watching his son's second game from the sidelines, Sutton walked to the end of the field to a tent that his son's team had put up thirty to forty yards behind the goal line to provide shade for the players when they were not engaged on the field. Half a dozen players from the Guilderland Soccer Club were on the field warming up for the next game. In the tent, while taking a sandwich from a cooler, Sutton was struck in the chest and knocked off his feet by a ball kicked from the field by a Guilderland player, Ian Goss. Sutton filed a suit in a New York state court against the Eastern New York Youth Soccer Association and others sponsoring or participating in the tournament, as well as Goss, seeking to recover damages for injuries he sustained to his knee as a result of the accident. The court found that Sutton had assumed the risk of being struck by a soccer ball, issued a summary judgment in favor of

CASE 4.2—Continues next page

CASE 4.2–Continued

all of the defendants, and dismissed the complaint. Sutton appealed this order to a state intermediate appellate court.

ISSUE Does a bystander or a spectator who is not watching a soccer match assume the risk of being struck by an errant ball?

DECISION Yes. The state intermediate appellate court affirmed the order of the lower court. "The doctrine of assumption of risk can apply not only to participants of sporting events, but to spectators and bystanders who are not actively engaged in watching the event at the time of their injury."

REASON The state intermediate appellate court emphasized that "the spectator at a sporting event, no less than the participant, accepts the dangers that inhere in it so far as they are obvious and necessary." This "tournament involved hundreds of players with teams playing at various times on at least five fields and plaintiff had been at the

tournament all morning, surrounded by this activity." Sutton argued that the "defendants unreasonably enhanced the risk of injury * * * by essentially inviting him to stand at the end of the field through their placement of the team tent." The court reasoned, however, that "just as the owner of a baseball park is not responsible for the spectator who leaves his or her seat and walks through a potentially more hazardous zone to reach a bathroom or concession stand, thereby assuming the open and obvious risk of being hit by a ball, defendants here cannot be held responsible for the risk assumed by plaintiff when he, aware that players were active on the field, left the sidelines and stood in the tent positioned in the arguably more dangerous zone behind the goal line." Also, Sutton "was familiar with the game of soccer having admittedly been a frequent spectator of the game for over 14 years."

 FOR CRITICAL ANALYSIS–Cultural Consideration
What is the basis underlying the defense of assumption of risk, and how does that basis support the court's decision in the Sutton *case?*

Superseding Cause An unforeseeable intervening event may break the connection between a wrongful act and an injury to another. If so, the event acts as a *superseding cause*—that is, it relieves a defendant of liability for injuries caused by the intervening event. **■EXAMPLE 4.13** Derrick, while riding his bicycle, negligently hits Julie, who is walking on the sidewalk. As a result of the impact, Julie falls and fractures her hip. While she is waiting for help to arrive, a small aircraft crashes nearby and explodes, and some of the fiery debris hits her, causing her to sustain severe burns. Derrick will be liable for the damages caused by Julie's fractured hip because the risk was foreseeable. Normally, Derrick will not be liable for the burns caused by the plane crash—because the risk of a plane's crashing nearby and injuring Julie was not foreseeable. ■

CONTRIBUTORY NEGLIGENCE
A rule in tort law that completely bars the plaintiff from recovering any damages if the damage suffered is partly the plaintiff's own fault; used in a minority of states.

COMPARATIVE NEGLIGENCE
A rule in tort law that reduces the plaintiff's recovery in proportion to the plaintiff's degree of fault, rather than barring recovery completely; used in the majority of states.

Contributory and Comparative Negligence All individuals are expected to exercise a reasonable degree of care in looking out for themselves. In the past, under the common law doctrine of **contributory negligence,** a plaintiff who was also negligent (failed to exercise a reasonable degree of care) could not recover anything from the defendant. Under this rule, no matter how insignificant the plaintiff's negligence was relative to the defendant's negligence, the plaintiff would be precluded from recovering any damages. Today, only a few jurisdictions still hold to this doctrine.

In the majority of states, the doctrine of contributory negligence has been replaced by a **comparative negligence** standard. Under the comparative negligence standard, both the plaintiff's and the defendant's negligence are computed, and the liability for damages is distributed accordingly. Some jurisdictions have adopted a "pure" form of comparative negligence that allows the plaintiff to recover, even if the extent of his or her fault is greater than that of the defendant. For example, if the plaintiff was 80 percent at fault and the defendant 20 percent at fault, the plaintiff may recover 20 percent of his or her damages. Many states' comparative negligence statutes, however, contain a "50 percent" rule under which the plaintiff recovers nothing if she or he was more than 50 percent at fault. Following this rule, a plaintiff who is 35 percent at fault could recover 65 percent of his or her damages, but a plaintiff who is 65 percent (more than 50 percent) at fault could recover nothing.

Special Negligence Doctrines and Statutes

There are a number of special doctrines and statutes relating to negligence. We examine a few of them here.

Res Ipsa Loquitur   Generally, in lawsuits involving negligence, the plaintiff has the burden of proving that the defendant was negligent. In certain situations, however, under the doctrine of **res ipsa loquitur**[14] (meaning "the facts speak for themselves"), the courts may infer that negligence has occurred. Then the burden of proof rests on the defendant to prove she or he was *not* negligent. This doctrine is applied only when the event creating the damage or injury is one that ordinarily would occur only as a result of negligence. **■EXAMPLE 4.14** A person undergoes abdominal surgery and following the surgery has nerve damage in her spine near the area of the operation. In this situation, the person can sue the surgeon under a theory of *res ipsa loquitur,* because the injury would never have occurred in the absence of the surgeon's negligence.[15] ▣

RES IPSA LOQUITUR
A doctrine under which negligence may be inferred simply because an event occurred, if it is the type of event that would not occur in the absence of negligence. Literally, the term means "the facts speak for themselves."

Negligence *Per Se*   Certain conduct, whether it consists of an action or a failure to act, may be treated as **negligence *per se*** (*per se* means "in or of itself"). Negligence *per se* may occur if an individual violates a statute or ordinance and thereby causes the kind of harm that the statute was intended to prevent. The injured person must prove (1) that the statute clearly sets out what standard of conduct is expected, when and where it is expected, and of whom it is expected; (2) that he or she is in the class intended to be protected by the statute; and (3) that the statute was designed to prevent the type of injury that he or she suffered. The standard of conduct required by the statute is the duty that the defendant owes to the plaintiff, and a violation of the statute is the breach of that duty. **■EXAMPLE 4.15** A statute requires a landowner to maintain a building in safe condition and to keep all electrical, plumbing, and heating installations in good working order. The statute is meant to protect tenants and those who are rightfully in the building. Irving, a landlord, violates the statute by failing to keep the lighting in his building's stairwell in working order. A tenant, Swan, falls down the stairs and is injured due to the lack of lighting. In this situation, a majority of courts will hold that the violation of the statute conclusively establishes Irving's breach of a duty of care—that is, that Irving is negligent *per se*. ▣

NEGLIGENCE *PER SE*
An action or failure to act in violation of a statutory requirement.

"Danger Invites Rescue" Doctrine   Sometimes, a person who is trying to avoid harm—such as an individual who swerves to avoid colliding with an oncoming car—ends up causing harm to another as a result (the driver of the other car). In those situations, the original wrongdoer is liable to anyone who is injured, even if the injury actually resulted from another person's attempt to escape harm. The "danger invites rescue" doctrine extends the same protection to a person who is trying to rescue another from harm—the original wrongdoer is liable for injuries to an individual attempting a rescue. The idea is that the rescuer should not be held liable for any damages because he or she did not cause the danger and because danger invites rescue. **■EXAMPLE 4.16** Ludlam, while driving down a street, fails to see a stop sign because he is trying to stop a squabble between his two young children in the car's back seat. Salter, on the curb near the stop sign, realizes that Ludlam is about to hit a pedestrian and runs into the street to push the pedestrian out of the way. If Ludlam's vehicle hits Salter instead, Ludlam will be liable for Salter's injury, as well as for any injuries the other pedestrian sustained. ▣ Rescuers may injure themselves, or the person rescued, or even a stranger, but the original wrongdoer will still be liable.

---

14. Pronounced *rehz ihp*-suh *low*-kwuh-tuhr.
15. See, for example, *Gubbins v. Hurson*, 885 A.2d 269 (D.C. 2005).

An automobile struck a man who was crossing the street near a shopping mall in Columbus, Ohio. The woman in the photo was a passerby who rushed to his assistance. Suppose that the woman drags the man out of the street so that he will not be hit by another car, and in doing so, she makes his injuries worse. Can she be held liable for damages? (AP Photo/Jack Kustron)

GOOD SAMARITAN STATUTE
A state statute stipulating that persons who provide emergency services to, or rescue, someone in peril cannot be sued for negligence, unless they act recklessly, thereby causing further harm.

DRAM SHOP ACT
A state statute that imposes liability on the owners of bars and taverns, as well as those who serve alcoholic drinks to the public, for injuries resulting from accidents caused by intoxicated persons when the sellers or servers of alcoholic drinks contributed to the intoxication.

STRICT LIABILITY
Liability regardless of fault. In tort law, strict liability is imposed on a manufacturer or seller that introduces into commerce a good that is unreasonably dangerous when in a defective condition.

Special Negligence Statutes A number of states have enacted statutes prescribing duties and responsibilities in certain circumstances. For example, most states now have what are called **Good Samaritan statutes.**[16] Under these statutes, someone who is aided voluntarily by another cannot turn around and sue the "Good Samaritan" for negligence. These laws were passed largely to protect physicians and medical personnel who voluntarily render services in emergency situations to those in need, such as individuals hurt in car accidents.

Many states have also passed **dram shop acts,**[17] under which a tavern owner or bartender may be held liable for injuries caused by a person who became intoxicated while drinking at the bar or who was already intoxicated when served by the bartender. Some states' statutes also impose liability on *social hosts* (persons hosting parties) for injuries caused by guests who became intoxicated at the hosts' homes. Under these statutes, it is unnecessary to prove that the tavern owner, bartender, or social host was negligent.

STRICT LIABILITY

Another category of torts is called **strict liability,** or *liability without fault.* Intentional torts and torts of negligence involve acts that depart from a reasonable standard of care and cause injuries. Under the doctrine of strict liability, liability for injury is imposed for reasons other than fault. Strict liability for damages proximately caused by an abnormally dangerous or exceptional activity is one application of this doctrine. Courts apply the doctrine of strict liability in such cases because of the extreme risk of the activity. Even if blasting with dynamite is performed with all reasonable care, there is still a risk of injury. Balancing that risk against the potential for harm, it seems reasonable to ask the person engaged in the activity to pay for injuries caused by that activity. Although there is no fault, there is still responsibility because of the dangerous nature of the undertaking.

There are other applications of the strict liability principle. Persons who keep dangerous animals, for example, are strictly liable for any harm inflicted by the animals. A significant application of strict liability is in the area of *product liability*—liability of manufacturers and sellers for harmful or defective products. Liability here is a matter of social policy and is based on two factors: (1) the manufacturer or seller can better bear the cost of injury because it can spread the cost throughout society by increasing prices of goods and services, and (2) the manufacturer or seller is making a profit from its activities and therefore should bear the cost of injury as an operating expense. We will discuss product liability in greater detail in Chapter 18.

CYBER TORTS

Torts can also be committed in the online environment. Torts committed via the Internet are often called *cyber torts.* Over the last ten years, the courts have had to decide how to apply traditional tort law to torts committed in cyberspace. Consider, for example, issues of proof. How can it be proved that an online defamatory remark was "published" (which requires that a third party see or hear it)? How can the identity of the person who made the remark be discovered? Can an Internet service provider (ISP), such as America Online, Inc. (AOL), be forced to reveal the source of an anonymous comment made by one of its subscribers? We explore some of these questions in this section, as well as some of the legal questions that have arisen with respect to bulk e-mail advertising.

---

16. These laws derive their name from the Good Samaritan story in the Bible. In the story, a traveler who had been robbed and beaten lay along the roadside, ignored by those passing by. Eventually, a man from the country of Samaria (the "Good Samaritan") stopped to render assistance to the injured person.

17. Historically, a *dram* was a small unit of liquid, and spirits were sold in drams. Thus, a dram shop was a place where liquor was sold in drams.

Defamation Online

Recall from the discussion of defamation earlier in this chapter that one who repeats or otherwise republishes a defamatory statement can be subject to liability as if she or he had originally published it. Thus, publishers generally can be held liable for defamatory contents in the books and periodicals that they publish. Now consider online forums. These forums allow anyone—customers, employees, or crackpots—to complain about a firm's personnel, policies, practices, or products. Whatever the truth of the complaint is, it might have an impact on the business of the firm. One of the early questions in the online legal arena was whether the providers of such forums could be held liable, as publishers, for defamatory statements made in those forums.

Liability of Internet Service Providers   Newspapers, magazines, and television and radio stations may be held liable for defamatory remarks that they disseminate, even if those remarks are prepared or created by others. Prior to the passage of the Communications Decency Act (CDA) of 1996, the courts grappled with the question of whether ISPs should be held liable for defamatory messages made by users of their services. The CDA resolved the issue by stating that "[n]o provider or user of an interactive computer service shall be treated as the publisher or speaker of any information provided by another information content provider."[18] The CDA has been invoked to shield ISPs from liability for defamatory postings on their bulletin boards.

■EXAMPLE 4.17   In a leading case on this issue, America Online, Inc. (AOL, now part of Time Warner, Inc.), was not held liable even though it did not promptly remove defamatory messages of which it had been made aware. A federal appellate court stated that the CDA "plainly immunizes computer service providers like AOL from liability for information that originates with third parties." The court explained that the purpose of the statute is "to maintain the robust nature of Internet communication and, accordingly, to keep government interference in the medium to a minimum."[19] ■ Courts have reached similar conclusions in subsequent cases[20] and have also extended the immunity to liability to online auction providers, such as eBay.[21]

Is an Internet dating service liable for a false profile of an actual person—in this case, an actress who has appeared in *Star Trek: Deep Space Nine* and other television shows and movies—posted by an identity thief who provided the content? That was the question in the following case.

---

18. 47 U.S.C. Section 230.
19. *Zeran v. America Online, Inc.*, 129 F.3d 327 (4th Cir. 1997); *cert.* denied, 524 U.S. 937, 118 S.Ct. 2341, 141 L.Ed.2d 712 (1998).
20. See, for example, *Noah v. AOL Time Warner, Inc.*, 261 F.Supp.2d 532 (E.D.Va. 2003).
21. *Stoner v. eBay, Inc.*, 2000 WL 1705637 (Cal.Super.Ct. 2000).

CASE 4.3   **Carafano v. Metrosplash.com, Inc.**

United States Court of Appeals, Ninth Circuit, 339 F.3d 1119 (2003).

FACTS   Matchmaker.com is a commercial Internet dating service. For a fee, members post anonymous profiles and view profiles of other members, contacting them via e-mail sent through Matchmaker. In October 1999, someone posted a profile of Christianne Carafano without her knowledge or consent. Under the stage name Chase Masterson, Carafano has appeared in films and television shows, including *Star Trek: Deep Space Nine* and *General Hospital.* Contacting the profile's e-mail address produced an automatic reply that

CASE 4.3–Continues next page

CASE 4.3–Continued

included Carafano's home address and phone number. She began to receive messages responding to the profile, some of which were threatening. Alarmed, she contacted the police. She felt unsafe in her home and stayed away for several months. Meanwhile, Siouxzan Perry, who handled Carafano's e-mail, learned of the false profile and demanded that Matchmaker remove it immediately. Carafano filed a suit in a California state court against Matchmaker and its owner, Metrosplash.com, Inc., alleging invasion of privacy, appropriation, defamation, and other torts. The case was moved to a federal district court, which issued a summary judgment in the defendants' favor. Carafano appealed to the U.S. Court of Appeals for the Ninth Circuit.

ISSUE Does an online dating service qualify for the same immunity as an Internet service provider (ISP) for the defamatory posting of a false profile using a celebrity's personal information?

DECISION Yes. The U.S. Court of Appeals for the Ninth Circuit affirmed the lower court's decision. The appellate court held that under the Communications Decency Act (CDA), Matchmaker was not responsible for the "underlying

misinformation" that characterized the false profile of Carafano.

REASON The court reasoned that in the CDA, "Congress granted most Internet services immunity from liability for publishing false or defamatory material so long as the information was provided by another party * * * for two basic policy reasons: to promote the free exchange of information and ideas over the Internet and to encourage voluntary monitoring for offensive or obscene material." In light of these concerns, the courts have adopted "a relatively expansive definition of 'interactive computer service' and a relatively restrictive definition of 'information content provider.'" An "interactive computer service" qualifies for immunity "so long as it does not also function as an 'information content provider' for the portion of the statement or publication at issue. * * * Thus, despite the serious and utterly deplorable consequences that occurred in this case, we conclude that Congress intended that service providers such as Matchmaker be afforded immunity from suit."

WHY IS THIS CASE IMPORTANT? *The holding in this case shows that courts will go out of their way to grant immunity from liability for online defamation under the CDA—even when the consequences in a given case are "utterly deplorable."*

Piercing the Veil of Anonymity A threshold barrier to anyone who seeks to bring an action for online defamation is discovering the identity of the person who posted the defamatory message online. ISPs can disclose personal information about their customers only when ordered to do so by a court. Consequently, businesses and individuals are increasingly resorting to lawsuits against "John Does." Then, using the authority of the courts, they can obtain from the ISPs the identities of the persons responsible for the messages.

EXAMPLE 4.18 Eric Hvide, a former chief executive of a company called Hvide Marine, sued a number of "John Does" who had posted allegedly defamatory statements about his company on various online message boards. Hvide sued the John Does for libel in a Florida court. The court ruled that Yahoo and AOL had to reveal the identities of the defendant Does.[22] ■

In some other cases, however, the rights of plaintiffs in such situations have been balanced against the defendants' rights to free speech. For example, a New Jersey court refused to compel Yahoo to disclose the identity of a person who had posted an allegedly defamatory message on Yahoo's message board. The court reasoned that more than a bare allegation of defamation is required to outweigh an individual's "competing right of anonymity in the exercise of [the] right of free speech."[23]

---

22. *Does v. Hvide*, 770 So.2d 1237 (Fla.App.3d 2000).
23. *Dendrite International, Inc. v. Doe No. 3*, 342 N.J.Super. 134, 775 A.2d 756 (2001).

Spam

Bulk, unsolicited e-mail ("junk" e-mail) sent to all of the users on a particular e-mailing list is often called **spam**.[24] Typically, spam consists of a product ad sent to all of the users on an e-mailing list or all of the members of a newsgroup. Spam can waste user time and network bandwidth (the amount of data that can be transmitted within a certain time). It also imposes a burden on an ISP's equipment as well as on an e-mail recipient's computer system. Because of the problems associated with spam, a majority of the states now have laws regulating its transmission. In 2003, the U.S. Congress also enacted a law to regulate spam, but the volume of spam has actually increased since the law was enacted. (See this chapter's *Beyond Our Borders* feature on page 128 for a discussion of another law passed by Congress in 2006 attempting to address spam originating outside the United States.)

State Regulation of Spam   In an attempt to combat spam, thirty-six states have enacted laws that prohibit or regulate its use. Many state laws regulating spam require the senders of e-mail ads to instruct the recipients on how they can "opt out" of further e-mail ads from the same sources. For instance, in some states an unsolicited e-mail ad must include a toll-free phone number or return e-mail address through which the recipient can contact the sender to request that no more ads be e-mailed. The most stringent state law is California's antispam law, which went into effect on January 1, 2004. That law follows the "opt-in" model favored by consumer groups and antispam advocates. In other words, the law prohibits any person or business from sending e-mail ads to or from any e-mail address in California unless the recipient has expressly agreed to receive e-mails from the sender. An exemption is made for e-mail sent to consumers with whom the advertiser has a "preexisting or current business relationship."

The Federal CAN-SPAM Act   In 2003, Congress enacted the Controlling the Assault of Non-Solicited Pornography and Marketing (CAN-SPAM) Act, which took effect on January 1, 2004. The legislation applies to any "commercial electronic mail messages" that are sent to promote a commercial product or service. Significantly, the statute preempts state antispam laws except for those provisions in state laws that prohibit false and deceptive e-mailing practices.

Generally, the act permits the use of unsolicited commercial e-mail but prohibits certain types of spamming activities, including the use of a false return address and the use of false, misleading, or deceptive information when sending e-mail. The statute also prohibits the use of "dictionary attacks"—sending messages to randomly generated e-mail addresses—and the "harvesting" of e-mail addresses from Web sites through the use of specialized software. Additionally, the law requires senders of commercial e-mail to do the following:

1 Include a return address on the e-mail.

2 Include a clear notification that the message is an ad and provide a valid physical postal address.

3 Provide a mechanism that allows recipients to "opt out" of further e-mail ads from the same source.

4 Take action on a recipient's "opt-out" request within ten days.

5 Label any sexually oriented materials as such.

ON THE WEB

The Center for Democracy and Technology conducted a study on spam. The report and the center's recommendations on how to avoid receiving spam are available online at

www.cdt.org/speech/spam/
030319spamreport.shtml.

---

24. The term *spam* is said to come from a skit by Monty Python, a popular group of British comedians in the 1970s and 1980s, in which they sang a song with the lyrics, "Spam spam spam spam, spam spam spam spam, lovely spam, wonderful spam." Like these lyrics, spam online is often considered to be a repetition of worthless text.

BEYOND OUR BORDERS Cross-Border Spam

Spam is a serious problem in the United States, but enforcing antispam laws has been complicated by the fact that many spammers are located outside U.S. borders. After the CAN-SPAM Act of 2003 prohibited false and deceptive e-mails originating in the United States, spamming from other nations increased, and the wrongdoers generally were able to escape detection and legal sanctions.

Prior to 2006, the Federal Trade Commission (FTC) lacked the authority to investigate cross-border spamming activities and to communicate with foreign nations concerning spam and other deceptive practices conducted via the Internet. In 2006, however, Congress passed the U.S. Safe Web Act (also known as the Undertaking Spam, Spyware, and Fraud Enforcement with Enforcers Beyond Borders Act),[a] which increased the FTC's ability to combat spam on a global level.

The act allows the FTC to cooperate and share information with foreign agencies in investigating and prosecuting those involved in Internet fraud and deception, including spamming, spyware, and various Internet scams. Although the FTC and foreign agencies can provide investigative assistance to one another, the act exempts foreign agencies from U.S. public disclosure laws. In other words, the activities undertaken by the foreign agency (even if requested by the FTC) will be kept secret.

FOR CRITICAL ANALYSIS *A provision in the U.S. Safe Web Act provides Internet service providers (ISPs) with a "safe harbor" (immunity from liability) for supplying information to the FTC concerning possible unfair or deceptive conduct in foreign jurisdictions. Is this provision fair? Why or why not?*

a. Pub. L. No. 109-455, 120 Stat. 3372 (December 22, 2006), which enacted 15 U.S.C.A. Sections 57b-2a, 57b-2b, 57c-1, and 57c-2, and amended various other sections of the *United States Code*.

REVIEWING Torts and Cyber Torts

Two sisters, Darla and Irene, are partners in an import business located in a small town in Rhode Island. Irene is also campaigning to be the mayor of their town. Both sisters travel to other countries to purchase the goods they sell at their retail store. Irene buys Indonesian goods, and Darla buys goods from Africa. After a tsunami (tidal wave) destroys many of the cities in Indonesia to which Irene usually travels, she phones one of her contacts there and asks him to procure some items and ship them to her. He informs her that it will be impossible to buy these items now because the townspeople are being evacuated due to a water shortage. Irene is angry and tells the man that if he cannot purchase the goods, he should just take them without paying for them after the town has been evacuated. Darla overhears her sister's instructions and is outraged. They have a falling-out, and Darla decides that she no longer wishes to be in business with her sister. Using the information presented in the chapter, answer the following questions.

1 Suppose that Darla tells several of her friends about Irene's instructing the man to take goods without paying for them from the people of Indonesia after the tsunami disaster. If Irene files a tort action against Darla alleging slander, will her suit be successful? Why or why not?

2 Now suppose that Irene wins the election and becomes the city's mayor. Darla then writes a letter to the editor of the local newspaper disclosing Irene's misconduct. If Irene accuses Darla of committing libel, what defenses could Darla assert?

3 If Irene accepts goods shipped from Indonesia that were wrongfully obtained, has she committed an intentional tort against property? Explain.

4 Suppose now that Darla was in the store one day with an elderly customer, Betty Green, who was looking for a unique gift for her granddaughter's graduation present. When the phone rang, Darla left the customer and walked to the counter to answer the phone. Green wandered around the store and eventually went through an open door into the stockroom area, where she fell over some boxes on the floor and fractured her hip. Green files a negligence action against the store. Did Darla breach her duty of care? Why or why not?

APPLICATION

How Important Is Tort Liability to Business?*

A lthough there are more claims for breach of contract than any other category of lawsuits, the dollar amount of damages awarded in tort actions is typically much higher than the awards in contract claims. Furthermore, tort claims are commonplace for businesses. Large companies (those grossing more than $1 billion per year) face an average of 556 pending tort claims and spend an average of $19.8 million on litigation each year.

Because of the potential for large damages awards for intentional and unintentional acts, businesspersons should take preventive measures to avoid tort liability as much as possible. Remember that injured persons can bring most tort actions against a business as well as against another person. In fact, if given a choice, plaintiffs often sue a business rather than an individual because the business is more likely to have "deep pockets" (the ability to pay large damages awards). Moreover, sometimes tort liability exists for businesses when it would not exist for individuals—for example, in situations involving business invitees, negligent hiring or supervision, trade libel, and often strict liability and cyber tort claims.

The Extent of Business Negligence Liability

A business can be exposed to negligence liability in a wide variety of instances. Consider just a few examples. Is a business that fails to warn invitees that its floor is slippery after a rainstorm liable to an injured customer? Is a grocery store liable when a customer slips and falls on a piece of fruit dropped by a previous customer? What about liability for injuries that occur in the parking lot in front of a business when conditions are icy due to the weather or there is a hole in the pavement? What if a patron falls and is injured due to a defect in the carpeting inside a store? The possibilities are almost endless, but nevertheless a business should try to anticipate circumstances that could lead to negligence actions and take preventive measures.

Even the hiring of employees can lead to negligence liability. For example, a business can be liable if it fails to do a criminal background check before hiring a person to supervise a child-care center when an investigation would have revealed that the person had previously been convicted of sexual assault. Failing to properly supervise or instruct employees can also lead to liability for a business.

Professionals such as doctors, lawyers, engineers, and accountants have a duty to their clients to exercise the skills, knowledge, and intelligence they profess to have or the standards expected of their profession. Providing anything less to the client or patient is a special type of negligence called malpractice.

Liability for Torts of Employees and Agents

A business can also be held liable for the negligence or intentional torts of its employees and agents. You will learn more about the law of agency and employment in later chapters of this text (especially in Chapters 24, 33, and 34). For now, it is sufficient to realize that a business is liable for the torts committed by an employee who is acting within the scope of his or her employment or an agent who is acting with the authority of the business. Therefore, if a sales agent commits fraud while acting within the scope of her or his employment, the business will be held liable. Similarly, if a corporate executive posts defamatory messages about a competing firm on the company Web site, the corporation can be held liable.

* This *Application* is not meant to substitute for the services of an attorney who is licensed to practice law in your state.

(Continued)

CHECKLIST FOR MINIMIZING BUSINESS TORT LIABILITY

1 Constantly inspect the premises and look for areas where customers or employees might trip, slide, or fall. Take corrective action whenever you find a problem.
2 Make sure that employee training includes a segment on the importance of periodic safety inspections and procedures for reporting unsafe conditions.
3 Routinely maintain all business equipment (including vehicles) and make sure that the business has complied with any applicable administrative regulations.
4 Check with your liability insurance company for suggestions on improving the safety of your premises and operations. By following its advice, you may be able to lower your insurance premium and ensure that the company will continue to provide coverage.
5 Make sure that your general liability policy will adequately cover the potential exposure of the business. Reassess the amount of coverage annually, particularly if the business has expanded.
6 Carefully review the background and qualifications of individuals you are considering hiring as employees or agents, and eliminate candidates who may increase the business's exposure to tort liability.
7 Investigate and review all negligence claims promptly. Most claims can be settled at low cost without a filed lawsuit, and frequently it is good public relations to do so.

KEY TERMS

actionable 106
actual malice 109
appropriation 109
assault 105
assumption of risk 120
battery 105
business invitee 117
business tort 102
causation in fact 119
comparative negligence 122
compensatory damages 103
contributory negligence 122
conversion 114
cyber tort 104
damages 102

defamation 107
defense 105
disparagement of property 114
dram shop act 124
duty of care 116
fraudulent misrepresentation 110
Good Samaritan statute 124
intentional tort 104
libel 107
malpractice 119
negligence 115
negligence *per se* 123
predatory behavior 112
privilege 108
proximate cause 119

puffery 110
punitive damages 103
reasonable person standard 116
res ipsa loquitur 123
slander 107
slander of quality (trade libel) 114
slander of title 115
spam 127
strict liability 124
tort 102
tortfeasor 104
trade libel 114
trespass to land 112
trespass to personal property 113

CHAPTER SUMMARY Torts and Cyber Torts

Intentional Torts against Persons
(See pages 104–112.)

1. *Assault and battery*—An assault is an unexcused and intentional act that causes another person to be apprehensive of immediate harm. A battery is an assault that results in physical contact.

2. *False imprisonment*—The intentional confinement or restraint of another person's movement without justification.

3. *Intentional infliction of emotional distress*—An intentional act that amounts to extreme and outrageous conduct resulting in severe emotional distress to another.

4. *Defamation (libel or slander)*—A false statement of fact, not made under privilege, that is communicated to a third person and that causes damage to a person's reputation. For public figures, the plaintiff must also prove actual malice.

5. *Invasion of the right to privacy*—The use of a person's name or likeness for commercial purposes without permission, wrongful intrusion into a person's private activities, publication

CHAPTER SUMMARY Torts and Cyber Torts–Continued

Intentional Torts against Persons—Continued	of information that places a person in a false light, or disclosure of private facts that an ordinary person would find objectionable. 6. *Appropriation*—The use of another person's name, likeness, or other identifying characteristic, without permission and for the benefit of the user. 7. *Misrepresentation (fraud)*—A false representation made by one party, through misstatement of facts or through conduct, with the intention of deceiving another and on which the other reasonably relies to his or her detriment. 8. *Wrongful interference*—The knowing, intentional interference by a third party with an enforceable contractual relationship or an established business relationship between other parties for the purpose of advancing the economic interests of the third party.
Intentional Torts against Property (See pages 112–115.)	1. *Trespass to land*—The invasion of another's real property without consent or privilege. Specific rights and duties apply once a person is expressly or impliedly established as a trespasser. 2. *Trespass to personal property*—Unlawfully damaging or interfering with the owner's right to use, possess, or enjoy her or his personal property. 3. *Conversion*—Wrongfully taking personal property from its rightful owner or possessor and placing it in the service of another. 4. *Disparagement of property*—Any economically injurious falsehood that is made about another's product or property; an inclusive term for the torts of *slander of quality* and *slander of title.*

Unintentional Torts (Negligence)
(See pages 115–124.)
	1. *Negligence*—The careless performance of a legally required duty or the failure to perform a legally required act. Elements that must be proved are that a legal duty of care exists, that the defendant breached that duty, and that the breach caused damage or injury to another.
	
	2. *Defenses to negligence*—The basic affirmative defenses in negligence cases are (a) assumption of risk, (b) superseding cause, and (c) contributory or comparative negligence.
	
	3. *Special negligence doctrines and statutes*—
	
	  a. *Res ipsa loquitur*—A doctrine under which a plaintiff need not prove negligence on the part of the defendant because "the facts speak for themselves."
	
	  b. Negligence *per se*—A type of negligence that may occur if a person violates a statute or an ordinance and the violation causes another to suffer the kind of injury that the statute or ordinance was intended to prevent.
	
	  c. Special negligence statutes—State statutes that prescribe duties and responsibilities in certain circumstances. Dram shop acts and Good Samaritan statutes are examples of special negligence statutes.

Strict Liability (See page 124.)	Under the doctrine of strict liability, a person may be held liable, regardless of the degree of care exercised, for damages or injuries caused by her or his product or activity. Strict liability includes liability for harms caused by abnormally dangerous activities, by dangerous animals, and by defective products (product liability).
Cyber Torts (See pages 124–128.)	General tort principles are being extended to cover cyber torts, or torts that occur in cyberspace, such as online defamation and spamming (which may constitute trespass to personal property). Federal and state statutes may also apply to certain forms of cyber torts. For example, under the federal Communications Decency Act of 1996, Internet service providers (ISPs) are not liable for defamatory messages posted by their subscribers. A majority of the states and the federal government now regulate unwanted e-mail ads (spam).

FOR REVIEW

Answers for the even-numbered questions in this For Review *section can be found in Appendix E at the end of this text.*

1 What is a tort?

2 What is the purpose of tort law? What are two basic categories of torts?

3 What are the four elements of negligence?

4 What is meant by strict liability? In what circumstances is strict liability applied?

5 What is a cyber tort, and how are tort theories being applied in cyberspace?

 The following multiple-choice question is representative of the types of questions available in one of the four sections of ThomsonNOW for *Business Law Today.* **ThomsonNOW also provides feedback for each response option, whether correct or incorrect, and refers to the location within the chapter where the correct answer can be found.**

If your actions harm someone else but you never intended to cause that harm, you may nevertheless be liable for the tort of

a conversion.

b nuisance.

c negligence.

d trespass.

QUESTIONS AND CASE PROBLEMS

 **HYPOTHETICAL SCENARIOS**

4.1 Defenses to Negligence. Corinna was riding her bike on a city street. While she was riding, she frequently looked back to verify that the books that she had fastened to the rear part of her bike were still attached. On one occasion while she was looking behind her, she failed to notice a car that was entering an intersection just as she was crossing it. The car hit her, causing her to sustain numerous injuries. Three eye-witnesses stated that the driver of the car had failed to stop at the stop sign before entering the intersection. Corinna sued the driver of the car for negligence. What defenses might the defendant driver raise in this lawsuit? Discuss fully.

4.2 Hypothetical Question with Sample Answer. In which of the following situations will the acting party be liable for the tort of negligence? Explain fully.

1 Mary goes to the golf course on Sunday morning, eager to try out a new set of golf clubs she has just purchased. As she tees off on the first hole, the head of her club flies off and injures a nearby golfer.

2 Mary's doctor gives her some pain medication and tells her not to drive after she takes it, as the medication induces

drowsiness. In spite of the doctor's warning, Mary decides to drive to the store while on the medication. Owing to her lack of alertness, she fails to stop at a traffic light and crashes into another vehicle, injuring a passenger.

 **For a sample answer to Question 4.2, go to Appendix F at the end of this text.**

4.3 Liability to Business Invitees. Kim went to Ling's Market to pick up a few items for dinner. It was a rainy, windy day, and the wind had blown water through the door of Ling's Market each time the door opened. As Kim entered through the door, she slipped and fell in the approximately one-half inch of rainwater that had accumulated on the floor. The manager knew of the weather conditions but had not posted any sign to warn customers of the water hazard. Kim injured her back as a result of the fall and sued Ling's for damages. Can Ling's be held liable for negligence in this situation? Discuss.

 CASE
PROBLEMS

4.4 Duty of Care. As pedestrians exited at the close of an arts and crafts show, Jason Davis, an employee of the show's producer, stood near the exit. Suddenly and without warning, Davis turned around and collided with Yvonne Esposito, an eighty-year-old woman. Esposito was knocked to the ground, fracturing her hip. After hip-replacement surgery, she was left with a permanent physical impairment. Esposito filed a suit in a federal district court against Davis and others, alleging negligence. What are the factors that indicate whether Davis owed Esposito a duty of care? What do those factors indicate in these circumstances? [*Esposito v. Davis*, 47 F.3d 164 (5th Cir. 1995)]

4.5 Invasion of Privacy. During the spring and summer of 1999, Edward and Geneva Irvine received numerous "hang up" phone calls, including three calls in the middle of the night. With the help of their local phone company, the Irvines learned that many of the calls were from the telemarketing department of the *Akron Beacon Journal* in Akron, Ohio. The *Beacon's* sales force was equipped with an automatic dialing machine. During business hours, the dialer was used to maximize productivity by calling multiple phone numbers at once and connecting a call to a sales representative only after it was answered. After business hours, the dialer was used to dial a list of disconnected numbers to determine whether they had been reconnected. If the dialer detected a ring, it recorded the information and dropped the call. If the automated dialing system crashed, which it did frequently, it redialed the entire list. The Irvines filed a suit in an Ohio state court against the *Beacon* and others, alleging in part invasion of privacy. In whose favor should the court rule, and why? [*Irvine v. Akron Beacon Journal*, 147 Ohio App.3d 428, 770 N.E.2d 1105 (9 Dist. 2002)]

4.6 Case Problem with Sample Answer. New Hampshire International Speedway, Inc., owned the New Hampshire International Speedway, a racetrack next to Route 106 in Loudon, New Hampshire. In August 1998, on the weekend before the Winston Cup race, Speedway opened its parking facility to recreational vehicles (RVs). Speedway stationed its employee Frederick Neergaard at the entrance to the parking area at a "stop-bar" gate as a security guard. Leslie Wheeler, who was planning to attend the race, drove south in an RV on Route 106 toward Speedway. Meanwhile, Dennis Carignan was also driving south on Route 106 on a motorcycle, on which Mary Carignan was a passenger. As Wheeler approached the parking area, he saw Neergaard signaling him to turn left, which he began to do. At the same time, Carignan attempted to pass the RV on its left side, and the two vehicles collided. Mary sustained an injury to her right knee, lacerations on her ankle, and a broken hip. She filed a negligence action in a New Hampshire state court against Speedway and others. Which element of negligence is at the center of this dispute? How is a court likely to rule in this case, and why? [*Carignan v. New Hampshire International Speedway, Inc.*, 151 N.H. 409, 858 A.2d 536 (N.H. 2004)]

After you have answered Problem 4.6, compare your answer with the sample answer given on the Web site that accompanies this text. Go to www.thomsonedu.com/westbuslaw/blt, select "Chapter 4," and click on "Case Problem with Sample Answer."

4.7 Defamation. Lydia Hagberg went to her bank, California Federal Bank, FSB, to cash a check made out to her by Smith Barney (SB), an investment-services firm. Nolene Showalter, a bank employee, suspected that the check was counterfeit. Showalter phoned SB and was told that the check was not valid. As she phoned the police, Gary Wood, a bank security officer, contacted SB again and was told that its earlier statement was "erroneous" and that the check was valid. Meanwhile, a police officer arrived, drew Hagberg away from the teller's window, spread her legs, patted her down, and handcuffed her. The officer searched her purse, asked her whether she had any weapons or stolen property and whether she was driving a stolen vehicle, and arrested her. Hagberg filed a suit in a California state court against the bank and others, alleging, among other things, slander. Should the absolute privilege for communications made in judicial or other official proceedings apply to statements made when a citizen contacts the police to report suspected criminal activity? Why or why not? [*Hagberg v. California Federal Bank, FSB*, 32 Cal.4th 350, 81 P.3d 244, 7 Cal.Rptr.3d 803 (2004)]

4.8 Emotional Distress. Between 1996 and 1998, Donna Swanson received several anonymous, handwritten letters that, among other things, accused her husband, Alan, of infidelity. In 1998, John Grisham, Jr., the author of *The Firm* and many other best-selling novels, received an anonymous letter that appeared to have been written by the same person. Grisham and the Swansons suspected Katherine Almy, who soon filed a suit in a Virginia state court against them, alleging in part intentional infliction of emotional distress. According to Almy, Grisham intended to have her "really, really, suffer" for writing the letters, and the three devised a scheme to falsely accuse her. They gave David Liebman, a handwriting analyst, samples of Almy's handwriting. These included copies of confidential documents from her children's files at St. Anne's-Belfield School in Charlottesville, Virginia, where Alan taught and Grisham served on the board of directors. In Almy's view, Grisham influenced Liebman to report that Almy might have written the letters and misrepresented this report as conclusive, which led the police to confront Almy. She claimed that she then suffered severe emotional distress and depression, causing "a complete disintegration of virtually every aspect of her life" and requiring her "to undergo extensive therapy." In response, the defendants asked the court to dismiss the complaint for failure to state a claim. Should the court grant this request? Explain. [*Almy v. Grisham*, 639 S.E.2d 182 (Va. 2007)]

4.9 **A Question of Ethics.** *Intel Corp. has an e-mail system for its employees. Ken Hamidi, a former Intel employee, sent a series of six e-mail messages to 35,000 Intel employees over a twenty-one-month period. In the messages, Hamidi criticized the company's labor practices and urged employees to leave the company. Intel sought a court order to stop the e-mail campaign, arguing that Hamidi's actions constituted a trespass to chattels (personal property) because the e-mail significantly interfered with productivity, thereby causing economic damage. The state trial court granted Intel's motion for summary judgment and ordered Hamidi to stop sending messages. When the case reached the California Supreme Court, however, the court held that under California law, the tort of trespass to chattels required some evidence of injury to the plaintiff's personal property. Because Hamidi's e-mail had neither damaged Intel's computer system nor impaired its functioning, the court ruled that Hamidi's actions*

did not amount to a trespass to chattels. The court did not reject the idea that trespass theory could apply to cyberspace. Rather, the court simply held that to succeed in a lawsuit for trespass to chattels, a plaintiff must demonstrate that some concrete harm resulted from the unwanted e-mail. [Intel Corp. v. Hamidi, 30 Cal.4th 1342, 71 P.3d 296, 1 Cal.Rptr.3d 32 (2003)]

1 Should a court require that spam cause actual physical damage or impairment of the computer system (by over-burdening it, for example) to establish that a spammer has committed trespass? Why or why not?

2 The content of Hamidi's messages caused much discussion among employees and managers, diverting workers' time and attention and thus interfering with productivity. Why did the court not consider this disruption to be sufficient evidence of harm? Do you agree with the court?

 CRITICAL THINKING AND WRITING ASSIGNMENTS

4.10 Critical Legal Thinking. What general principle underlies the common law doctrine that business owners have a duty of care toward their customers? Does the duty of care unfairly burden business owners? Why or why not?

4.11 **Video Question.** Go to this text's Web site at **www.thomsonedu.com/westbuslaw/blt** and select "Chapter 4." Click on "Video Questions" and view the video titled *Jaws.* Then answer the following questions.

1 In the video, the mayor (Murray Hamilton) and a few other men try to persuade Chief Brody (Roy Scheider) not to close the town's beaches. If Chief Brody keeps the beaches open and a swimmer is injured or killed because

he failed to warn swimmers about the potential shark danger, has he committed a tort? If so, what kind of tort (intentional tort against persons, intentional tort against property, or negligence)? Explain your answer.

2 Can Chief Brody be held liable for any injuries or deaths to swimmers under the doctrine of strict liability? Why or why not?

3 Suppose that Chief Brody goes against the mayor's instructions and warns people to stay out of the water. Nevertheless, several swimmers do not heed his warning and are injured as a result. What defense or defenses could Chief Brody raise under these circumstances if he is sued for negligence?

ONLINE ACTIVITIES

PRACTICAL INTERNET EXERCISES

Go to this text's Web site at **www.thomsonedu.com/westbuslaw/blt**, select "Chapter 4," and click on "Practical Internet Exercises." There you will find the following Internet research exercises that you can perform to learn more about the topics covered in this chapter.

PRACTICAL INTERNET EXERCISE 4–1 LEGAL PERSPECTIVE—Online Defamation

PRACTICAL INTERNET EXERCISE 4–2 SOCIAL PERSPECTIVE—Legal and Illegal Uses of Spam

PRACTICAL INTERNET EXERCISE 4–3 MANAGEMENT PERSPECTIVE—The Duty to Warn

BEFORE THE TEST

Go to this text's Web site at **www.thomsonedu.com/westbuslaw/blt**, select "Chapter 4," and click on "Interactive Quizzes." You will find a number of interactive questions relating to this chapter.

CHAPTER 5
Intellectual Property and Internet Law

LEARNING OBJECTIVES

AFTER READING THIS CHAPTER, YOU SHOULD BE ABLE TO ANSWER THE FOLLOWING QUESTIONS:

1 What is intellectual property?

2 Why are trademarks and patents protected by the law?

3 What laws protect authors' rights in the works they generate?

4 What are trade secrets, and what laws offer protection for this form of intellectual property?

5 What steps have been taken to protect intellectual property rights in today's digital age?

> **"** The Internet, by virtue of its ability to mesh what will be hundreds of millions of people together, . . . is . . . a profoundly different capability that by and large human beings have not had before. **"**
>
> Tony Rutkowski, 1943–present
> (Executive director of the
> Internet Society, 1994–1996)

INTELLECTUAL PROPERTY
Property resulting from intellectual, creative processes.

Of significant concern to businesspersons today is the need to protect their rights in intellectual property. **Intellectual property** is any property resulting from intellectual, creative processes—the products of an individual's mind. Although it is an abstract term for an abstract concept, intellectual property is nonetheless familiar to almost everyone. The information contained in books and computer files is intellectual property. The software you use, the movies you see, and the music you listen to are all forms of intellectual property. In fact, in today's information age, it should come as no surprise that the value of the world's intellectual property probably now exceeds the value of physical property, such as machines and houses.

The need to protect creative works was recognized by the framers of the U.S. Constitution more than two hundred years ago: Article I, Section 8, of the Constitution authorized Congress "[t]o promote the Progress of Science and useful Arts, by securing for limited Times to Authors and Inventors the exclusive Right to their respective Writings and Discoveries." Laws protecting patents, trademarks, and copyrights are explicitly designed to protect and reward inventive and artistic creativity. Exhibit 5–1 on the following page offers a comprehensive summary of these forms of intellectual property, as well as intellectual property that consists of *trade secrets*.

An understanding of intellectual property law is important because intellectual property has taken on increasing significance, not only in the United States but globally as well. Today, the prosperity of many U.S. companies depends more on their ownership rights in intangible intellectual property than on their tangible assets. As you will read in

EXHIBIT 5–1 Forms of Intellectual Property

	DEFINITION	HOW ACQUIRED	DURATION	REMEDY FOR INFRINGEMENT
Patent	A grant from the government that gives an inventor exclusive rights to an invention.	By filing a patent application with the U.S. Patent and Trademark Office and receiving its approval.	Twenty years from the date of the application; for design patents, fourteen years.	Monetary damages, including royalties and lost profits, *plus* attorneys' fees. Damages may be tripled for intentional infringements.
Copyright	The right of an author or originator of a literary or artistic work, or other production that falls within a specified category, to have the exclusive use of that work for a given period of time.	Automatic (once the work or creation is put in tangible form). Only the *expression* of an idea (and not the idea itself) can be protected by copyright.	For authors: the life of the author plus 70 years. For publishers: 95 years after the date of publication or 120 years after creation.	Actual damages plus profits received by the party who infringed *or* statutory damages under the Copyright Act, *plus* costs and attorneys' fees in either situation.
Trademark (service mark and trade dress)	Any distinctive word, name, symbol, or device (image or appearance), or combination thereof, that an entity uses to distinguish its goods or services from those of others. The owner has the exclusive right to use that mark or trade dress.	1. At common law, ownership created by use of the mark. 2. Registration with the appropriate federal or state office gives notice and is permitted if the mark is currently in use or will be within the next six months.	Unlimited, as long as it is in use. To continue notice by registration, the owner must renew by filing between the fifth and sixth years, and thereafter, every ten years.	1. Injunction prohibiting the future use of the mark. 2. Actual damages plus profits received by the party who infringed (can be increased under the Lanham Act). 3. Destruction of articles that infringed. 4. *Plus* costs and attorneys' fees.
Trade secret	Any information that a business possesses and that gives the business an advantage over competitors (including formulas, lists, patterns, plans, processes, and programs).	Through the originality and development of the information and processes that constitute the business secret and are unknown to others.	Unlimited, so long as not revealed to others. Once revealed to others, it is no longer a trade secret.	Monetary damages for misappropriation (the Uniform Trade Secrets Act also permits punitive damages if willful), *plus* costs and attorneys' fees.

TRADEMARK
A distinctive mark, motto, device, or emblem that a manufacturer stamps, prints, or otherwise affixes to the goods it produces so that they may be identified on the market and their origins made known. Once a trademark is established (under the common law or through registration), the owner is entitled to its exclusive use.

this chapter, protecting these assets in today's online world has proved particularly challenging. This is because, as indicated in the chapter-opening quotation, the Internet's capability is "profoundly different" from anything we have had in the past.

TRADEMARKS AND RELATED PROPERTY

A **trademark** is a distinctive mark, motto, device, or emblem that a manufacturer stamps, prints, or otherwise affixes to the goods it produces so that they may be identified on the market and their origins made known. At common law, the person who used a symbol or mark to identify a business or product was protected in the use of that trademark. Clearly, by using another's trademark, a business could lead consumers to believe that its goods were made by the other business. The law seeks to avoid this kind of confusion. In the following classic case concerning Coca-Cola, the defendants argued that the Coca-Cola trademark was entitled to no protection under the law because the term did not accurately represent the product.

CASE 5.1 **The Coca-Cola Co. v. Koke Co. of America**

LANDMARK AND CLASSIC CASES

Supreme Court of the United States, 254 U.S. 143, 41 S.Ct. 113, 65 L.Ed. 189 (1920).
www.findlaw.com/casecode/supreme.html[a]

COMPANY PROFILE *John Pemberton, an Atlanta pharmacist, invented a caramel-colored, carbonated soft drink in 1886. His bookkeeper, Frank Robinson, named the beverage Coca-Cola after two of the ingredients, coca leaves and kola nuts. Asa Candler bought the Coca-Cola Company in 1891 and, within seven years, had made the soft drink available in all of the United States, as well as in parts of Canada and Mexico. Candler continued to sell Coke aggressively and to open up new markets, reaching Europe before 1910. In doing so, however, he attracted numerous competitors, some of whom tried to capitalize directly on the Coke name.*

FACTS The Coca-Cola Company brought an action in a federal district court to enjoin other beverage companies from using the words *Koke* and *Dope* for the defendants' products. The defendants contended that the Coca-Cola trademark was a fraudulent representation and that Coca-Cola was therefore not entitled to any help from the courts. By use of the Coca-Cola name, the defendants alleged, the Coca-Cola Company represented that the beverage contained cocaine (from coca leaves). The district court granted the injunction, but the federal appellate court reversed. The Coca-Cola Company appealed to the United States Supreme Court.

ISSUE Did the marketing of products called Koke and Dope by the Koke Company of America and other firms constitute an infringement on Coca-Cola's trademark?

DECISION Yes for Koke, but no for Dope. The United States Supreme Court enjoined the competing beverage companies from calling their products Koke but did not prevent them from calling their products Dope.

a. This is the "U.S. Supreme Court Opinions" page within the Web site of the "FindLaw Internet Legal Resources" database. This page provides several options for accessing an opinion. Because you know the citation for this case, you can go to the "Citation Search" box, type in the appropriate volume and page numbers for the *United States Reports* ("254" and "143," respectively, for the *Coca-Cola* case), and click on "Get It."

REASON The Court noted that, to be sure, prior to 1900 the Coca-Cola beverage had contained a small amount of cocaine. This ingredient had been deleted from the formula by 1906 at the latest, however, and the Coca-Cola Company had advertised to the public that no cocaine was present in its drink. Coca-Cola was a widely popular drink "to be had at almost any soda fountain." Because of the public's widespread familiarity with Coca-Cola, the retention of the name of the beverage (referring to coca leaves and kola nuts) was not misleading: "Coca-Cola probably means to most persons the plaintiff's familiar product to be had everywhere rather than a compound of particular substances." The name *Coke* was found to be so common a term for the trademarked product Coca-Cola that the defendants' use of the similar-sounding *Koke* as a name for their beverages was disallowed. The Court could find no reason to restrain the defendants from using the name *Dope*, however.

 WHAT IF THE FACTS WERE DIFFERENT? *Suppose that Coca-Cola had been trying to make the public believe that its product contained cocaine. Would the result in the case likely have been different?*

IMPACT OF THIS CASE ON TODAY'S LAW *In this early case, the United States Supreme Court made it clear that trademarks and trade names (and nicknames for those marks and names, such as "Coke" for "Coca-Cola") that are in common use receive protection under the common law. This holding is significant historically because it is the predecessor to the federal statute later passed to protect trademark rights (the Lanham Act of 1946, to be discussed shortly). In many ways, that statute represented a codification of common law principles governing trademarks.*

RELEVANT WEB SITES *To locate information on the Web concerning the Coca-Cola decision, go to this text's Web site at* **www.thomsonedu.com/westbuslaw/blt**, *select "Chapter 5," and click on "URLs for Landmarks."*

Statutory Protection of Trademarks

Statutory protection of trademarks and related property is provided at the federal level by the Lanham Act of 1946.[1] The Lanham Act was enacted in part to protect manufacturers from losing business to rival companies that used confusingly similar trademarks. The Lanham Act incorporates the common law of trademarks and provides remedies for owners of trademarks who wish to enforce their claims in federal court. Many states also have trademark statutes.

Trademark Dilution In 1995, Congress amended the Lanham Act by passing the Federal Trademark Dilution Act,[2] which extended the protection available to trademark owners by allowing them to bring a suit in federal court for trademark *dilution*. Until the passage of this amendment, federal trademark law prohibited only the unauthorized use of the same mark on competing—or on noncompeting but "related"—goods or services when such use would likely confuse consumers as to the origin of those goods and services. Trademark dilution laws protect "distinctive" or "famous" trademarks (such as Jergens, McDonald's, Dell, and Apple) from certain unauthorized uses even when the use is on noncompeting goods or is unlikely to confuse. More than half of the states have also enacted trademark dilution laws.

Use of a Similar Mark May Constitute Trademark Dilution A famous mark may be diluted not only by the use of an *identical* mark but also by the use of a *similar* mark provided that it reduces the value of the famous mark. ▪**EXAMPLE 5.1** Well-known lingerie maker Victoria's Secret brought a trademark dilution action against "Victor's Little Secret," a small retail store that sold adult videos, lingerie, and other items. Although the lower courts granted Victoria's Secret an injunction prohibiting the adult store from using a similar mark, the United States Supreme Court reversed the decision. According to the Court, the likelihood of dilution is not enough to establish dilution. The plaintiff must present some evidence that the allegedly infringing user's mark actually reduces the value of the famous mark or lessens its capacity to identify goods and services.[3] ▪

Trademark Registration

Trademarks may be registered with the state or with the federal government. To register for protection under federal trademark law, a person must file an application with the U.S. Patent and Trademark Office in Washington, D.C. Under present law, a mark can be registered (1) if it is currently in commerce or (2) if the applicant intends to put the mark into commerce within six months.

In special circumstances, the six-month period can be extended by thirty months, giving the applicant a total of three years from the date of notice of trademark approval to make use of the mark and file the required use statement. Registration is postponed until the mark is actually used. Nonetheless, during this waiting period, any applicant can legally protect his or her

Various billboards and neon signs in New York City's Times Square. Why are trademarks protected by the law?
(Rusty Haskell/Creative Commons)

1. 15 U.S.C. Sections 1051–1128.
2. 15 U.S.C. Section 1125.
3. *Moseley v. V Secret Catalogue, Inc.*, 537 U.S. 418, 123 S.Ct. 1115, 155 L.Ed.2d 1 (2003).

trademark against a third party who previously has neither used the mark nor filed an application for it. Registration is renewable between the fifth and sixth years after the initial registration and every ten years thereafter (every twenty years for trademarks registered before 1990).

Trademark Infringement

Registration of a trademark with the U.S. Patent and Trademark Office gives notice on a nationwide basis that the trademark belongs exclusively to the registrant. The registrant is also allowed to use the symbol ® to indicate that the mark has been registered. Whenever that trademark is copied to a substantial degree or used in its entirety by another, intentionally or unintentionally, the trademark has been *infringed* (used without authorization). When a trademark has been infringed, the owner of the mark has a cause of action against the infringer. To sue for trademark infringement, a person need not have registered the trademark, but registration does furnish proof of the date of inception of the trademark's use.

The purple and orange colors displayed on FedEx envelopes, packets, and delivery vehicles, including this airplane, are a distinctive feature of that company. If a start-up company specializing in courier delivery services used those same colors, would the new company be infringing on FedEx's trademark? (Adrian Pingstone/ Wikipedia Commons)

Only those trademarks that are deemed sufficiently distinctive from all competing trademarks will be protected, however. The trademarks must be sufficiently distinct to enable consumers to identify the manufacturer of the goods easily and to differentiate among competing products.

Strong Marks   Fanciful, arbitrary, or suggestive trademarks are generally considered to be the most distinctive (strongest) trademarks because they are normally taken from outside the context of the particular product and thus provide the best means of distinguishing one product from another.

■EXAMPLE 5.2   Fanciful trademarks include invented words, such as "Xerox" for one manufacturer's copiers and "Kodak" for another company's photographic products. Arbitrary trademarks use common words in a fictitious or arbitrary manner to create a distinctive mark that identifies the source of the product, such as "Dutch Boy" as a name on a can of paint. Suggestive trademarks suggest something about a product without describing the product directly. For instance, "Dairy Queen" suggests an association between its products and milk, but it does not directly describe ice cream. ▣

Secondary Meaning   Descriptive terms, geographic terms, and personal names are not inherently distinctive and do not receive protection under the law *until* they acquire a secondary meaning. A secondary meaning may arise when customers begin to associate a specific term or phrase, such as "London Fog," with specific trademarked items (coats with "London Fog" labels). Whether a secondary meaning becomes attached to a term or name usually depends on how extensively the product is advertised, the market for the product, the number of sales, and other factors. The United States Supreme Court has held that even a color can qualify for trademark protection.[4] Once a secondary meaning is attached to a term or name, a trademark is considered distinctive and is protected. In one recent case, a federal court ruled that trademark law protects the particular color schemes used by four state university sports teams, including Ohio State University and Louisiana State University.[5]

At issue in the following case was whether a certain mark was suggestive or descriptive.

4. *Qualitex Co. v. Jacobson Products Co.*, 514 U.S. 159, 115 S.Ct. 1300, 131 L.Ed.2d 248 (1995).
5. *Board of Supervisors of LA State University v. Smack Apparel Co.*, 438 F.Supp.2d 653 (2006).

CASE 5.2   Menashe v. V Secret Catalogue, Inc.

United States District Court, Southern District of New York, 409 F.Supp.2d 412 (2006).

FACTS In autumn 2002, Victoria's Secret Stores, Inc., and its affiliated companies, including V Secret Catalogue, Inc., began to develop a panty collection to be named "SEXY LITTLE THINGS." In spring 2004, Ronit Menashe, a publicist, and Audrey Quock, a fashion model and actress, began to plan a line of women's underwear also called "SEXY LITTLE THINGS." Menashe and Quock designed their line, negotiated for its manufacture, registered the domain name **www.sexylittlethings.com**, and filed an intent-to-use (ITU) application with the U.S. Patent and Trademark Office (USPTO). In July 2004, Victoria's Secret's collection appeared in its stores in Ohio, Michigan, and California and, in less than three months, was prominently displayed in all its stores, in its catalogues, and on its Web site. By mid-November, more than 13 million units of the line had been sold, accounting for 4 percent of the company's sales for the year. When the firm applied to register "SEXY LITTLE THINGS" with the USPTO, it learned of Menashe and Quock's ITU application. The firm warned the pair that their use of the phrase constituted trademark infringement. Menashe and Quock filed a suit in a federal district court against V Secret Catalogue and others, asking the court to, among other things, declare "noninfringement of the trademark."

ISSUE Is "SEXY LITTLE THINGS" a descriptive term for lingerie that had not attained secondary meaning by the time the plaintiffs filed their ITU application, or is it a suggestive mark that qualifies for trademark protection without proof of secondary meaning?

DECISION The court concluded that "SEXY LITTLE THINGS" was a suggestive mark that Victoria's Secret used in commerce prior to the time the plaintiffs filed their ITU application. For this reason, Victoria's Secret had "priority in the Mark," and Menashe and Quock were not entitled to a judgment of "noninfringement."

REASON The court explained that "to merit trademark protection, a mark must be capable of distinguishing the products it marks from those of others." A descriptive term conveys an immediate idea of the ingredients, qualities, or characteristics of the goods. In contrast, a suggestive term requires imagination, thought, and perception to reach a conclusion as to the nature of the goods. Suggestive marks are automatically protected because they are inherently distinctive; that is, their intrinsic nature serves to identify a particular source of a product. Descriptive marks are not inherently distinctive and may only be protected on a showing of secondary meaning—that is, that the purchasing public associates the mark with a particular source. In this case, the court held that the mark "SEXY LITTLE THINGS" was suggestive because it calls to mind the phrase "sexy little things" popularly used to refer to attractive young women. The court observed that because of this suggestive nature, the mark prompts the purchaser to mentally associate the lingerie with its targeted twenty- to thirty-year-old consumers. Courts have classified marks that both describe the product and evoke other associations as inherently distinctive. In addition, the court reasoned that Victoria's Secret's use of the mark does not deprive competitors of ways to describe their lingerie products. "Indeed, Victoria's Secret's own descriptions of its lingerie in its catalogues and Web site illustrate that there are numerous ways to describe provocative underwear."

WHY IS THIS CASE IMPORTANT? *This case is notable for the court's characterization of the plaintiffs' suit as "defensive." ITU applicants may defend against other parties' claims of infringement, but they do not have the right to charge others with infringement. In this case, however, the court allowed the plaintiffs to preemptively defend themselves against Victoria's Secret's efforts to stop the use of the "SEXY LITTLE THINGS" mark.*

Generic Terms Generic terms are terms that refer to an entire class of products, such as *bicycle* and *computer*. Generic terms receive no protection, even if they acquire secondary meanings. A particularly thorny problem arises when a trademark acquires generic use. For instance, *aspirin* and *thermos* were originally trademarked products, but today the words are used generically. Other examples are *escalator, trampoline, raisin bran, dry ice, lanolin, linoleum, nylon,* and *corn flakes.*

Note that a generic term will not be protected under trademark law even if the term has acquired a secondary meaning. **▪EXAMPLE 5.3** In one case, America Online, Inc. (AOL), sued AT&T Corporation, claiming that AT&T's use of "You Have Mail" on its WorldNet Service infringed AOL's trademark rights in the same phrase. The court ruled, however, that because each of the three words in the phrase was a generic term, the phrase as a whole was generic. Although the phrase had become widely associated with AOL's e-mail notification service, and thus may have acquired a secondary meaning, this issue was of no significance in this case. The court stated that it would not consider whether the mark had acquired any secondary meaning because "generic marks with secondary meaning are still not entitled to protection."[6] ▪

Service, Certification, and Collective Marks

A **service mark** is essentially a trademark that is used to distinguish the *services* (rather than the products) of one person or company from those of another. For instance, each airline has a particular mark or symbol associated with its name. Titles and character names used in radio and television are frequently registered as service marks.

Other marks protected by law include certification marks and collective marks. A **certification mark** is used by one or more persons, other than the owner, to certify the region, materials, mode of manufacture, quality, or other characteristic of specific goods or services. **▪EXAMPLE 5.4** Certification marks include such marks as "Good Housekeeping Seal of Approval" and "UL Tested." ▪ When used by members of a cooperative, association, union, or other organization, a certification mark is referred to as a **collective mark.** **▪EXAMPLE 5.5** Collective marks appear at the ends of the credits of movies to indicate the various associations and organizations that participated in making the movie. The union marks found on the tags of certain products are also collective marks. ▪

Trade Names

Trademarks apply to *products*. The term **trade name** is used to indicate part or all of a business's name, whether the business is a sole proprietorship, a partnership, or a corporation. Generally, a trade name is directly related to a business and its goodwill. Trade names may be protected as trademarks if the trade name is the same as the company's trademarked product—for example, Coca-Cola. Unless also used as a trademark or service mark, a trade name cannot be registered with the federal government. Trade names are protected under the common law, however. As with trademarks, words must be unusual or fancifully used if they are to be protected as trade names. The word *Safeway*, for instance, was held by the courts to be sufficiently fanciful to obtain protection as a trade name for a grocery chain.[7]

Trade Dress

The term **trade dress** refers to the image and overall appearance of a product. Trade dress is a broad concept and can include either all or part of the total image or overall impression created by a product or its packaging. **▪EXAMPLE 5.6** The distinctive decor, menu, layout, and style of service of a particular restaurant may be regarded as the restaurant's trade dress. Similarly, trade dress can include the layout and appearance of a mail-order catalog, the use of a lighthouse as part of the design of a golf hole, the fish shape of a cracker, or the G-shaped design of a Gucci watch. ▪

---

6. *America Online, Inc. v. AT&T Corp.,* 243 F.3d 812 (4th Cir. 2001).
7. *Safeway Stores v. Suburban Foods,* 130 F.Supp. 249 (E.D.Va. 1955).

SERVICE MARK
A mark used in the sale or the advertising of services to distinguish the services of one person from those of others. Titles, character names, and other distinctive features of radio and television programs may be registered as service marks.

CERTIFICATION MARK
A mark used by one or more persons, other than the owner, to certify the region, materials, mode of manufacture, quality, or other characteristic of specific goods or services.

COLLECTIVE MARK
A mark used by members of a cooperative, association, union, or other organization to certify the region, materials, mode of manufacture, quality, or other characteristic of specific goods or services.

TRADE NAME
A term that is used to indicate part or all of a business's name and that is directly related to the business's reputation and goodwill. Trade names are protected under the common law (and under trademark law, if the name is the same as the firm's trademarked product).

TRADE DRESS
The image and overall appearance of a product—for example, the distinctive decor, menu, layout, and style of service of a particular restaurant. Basically, trade dress is subject to the same protection as trademarks.

A "UL" certification mark. How does a certification mark differ from a trademark?

Basically, trade dress is subject to the same protection as trademarks. In cases involving trade dress infringement, as in trademark infringement cases, a major consideration is whether consumers are likely to be confused by the allegedly infringing use.

CYBER MARKS

CYBER MARK
A trademark in cyberspace.

In cyberspace, trademarks are sometimes referred to as **cyber marks.** We turn now to a discussion of trademark-related issues in cyberspace and how new laws and the courts are addressing these issues. One concern relates to the rights of a trademark's owner to use the mark as part of a domain name (Internet address). Other issues have to do with cybersquatting, meta tags, and trademark dilution on the Web. In some instances, licensing can be a way to avoid liability for infringing on another's intellectual property rights in cyberspace.

Domain Names

DOMAIN NAME
The last part of an Internet address, such as "westlaw.edu." The top level (the part of the name to the right of the period) indicates the type of entity that operates the site ("edu" is an abbreviation for "educational"). The second level (the part of the name to the left of the period) is chosen by the entity.

Conflicts over rights to domain names emerged as e-commerce expanded on a worldwide scale. By using the same, or a similar, domain name, parties have attempted to profit from the goodwill of a competitor, to sell pornography, to offer for sale another party's domain name, and to otherwise infringe on others' trademarks. A **domain name** is part of an Internet address, such as "westlaw.edu." Every domain name ends with a top level domain (TLD), which is the part to the right of the period that indicates the type of entity that operates the site (for example, "edu" is an abbreviation for "educational"). The second level domain (SLD) is the part of the name to the left of the period, which is chosen by the business entity or individual registering the domain name. Competition among firms with similar names and products preceding the *.com* TLD caused numerous disputes over domain name rights. As noted in Chapter 3, the Internet Corporation for Assigned Names and Numbers (ICANN), a nonprofit corporation, oversees the distribution of domain names. ICANN also facilitates the settlement of domain name disputes and operates an online arbitration system.

Anticybersquatting Legislation

CYBERSQUATTING
The act of registering a domain name that is the same as, or confusingly similar to, the trademark of another and then offering to sell that domain name back to the trademark owner.

Cybersquatting occurs when a person registers a domain name that is the same as, or confusingly similar to, the trademark of another and then offers to sell the domain name back to the trademark owner. During the 1990s, cybersquatting led to so much litigation that Congress passed the Anticybersquatting Consumer Protection Act of 1999 (ACPA), which amended the Lanham Act—the federal law protecting trademarks discussed earlier.

The ACPA makes it illegal for a person to "register, traffic in, or use" a domain name (1) if the name is identical or confusingly similar to the trademark of another and (2) if the one registering, trafficking in, or using the domain name has a "bad faith intent" to profit from that trademark. The act does not define what constitutes bad faith. Instead, it lists several factors that courts can consider in deciding whether bad faith exists. Some of these factors are whether there is an intent to divert consumers in a way that could harm the goodwill represented by the trademark, whether there is an offer to transfer or sell the domain name to the trademark owner, and whether there is an intent to use the domain name to offer goods and services.

The ACPA applies to all domain name registrations of trademarks, even domain names registered before the passage of the act. Successful plaintiffs in suits brought under the act can collect actual damages and profits or elect to receive statutory damages of $1,000 to $100,000.

Meta Tags

Search engines compile their results by looking through a Web site's key-word field. *Meta tags,* or key words (see Chapter 2), may be inserted into this field to increase the likelihood that a site will be included in search engine results, even though the site may have nothing to do with the inserted words. Using this same technique, one site may appropriate the key words of other sites with more frequent hits so that the appropriating site appears in the same search engine results as the more popular sites. Using another's trademark in a meta tag without the owner's permission, however, normally constitutes trademark infringement.

Some uses of another's trademark as a meta tag may be permissible if the use is reasonably necessary and does not suggest that the owner authorized or sponsored the use. **EXAMPLE 5.7** Terri Welles, a former model who had been "Playmate of the Year" in *Playboy* magazine, established a Web site that used the terms *Playboy* and *Playmate* as meta tags. Playboy Enterprises, Inc., which publishes *Playboy*, filed suit seeking to prevent Welles from using these meta tags. The court determined that Welles's use of Playboy's meta tags to direct users to her Web site was permissible because it did not suggest sponsorship and there were no descriptive substitutes for the terms *Playboy* and *Playmate*.[8] ▣

Dilution in the Online World

As discussed earlier, trademark *dilution* occurs when a trademark is used, without authorization, in a way that diminishes the distinctive quality of the mark. Unlike trademark infringement, a claim of dilution does not require proof that consumers are likely to be confused by a connection between the unauthorized use and the mark. For this reason, the products involved do not have to be similar. In the first case alleging dilution on the Web, a court precluded the use of "candyland.com" as the URL for an adult site. The suit was brought by the maker of the Candyland children's game and owner of the Candyland mark. Although consumers were not likely to connect candyland.com with the children's game, the court reasoned that the sexually explicit adult site would dilute the value of the Candyland mark.[9]

Licensing

One of the ways to make use of another's trademark or other form of intellectual property, while avoiding litigation, is to obtain a license to do so. A **license** in this context is essentially an agreement permitting the use of a trademark, copyright, patent, or trade secret for certain limited purposes. The party that owns the intellectual property rights and issues the license is the *licensor*, and the party obtaining the license is the *licensee*. A license grants only the rights expressly described in the license agreement. A licensor might, for example, allow the licensee to use the trademark as part of its company name, or as part of its domain name, but not otherwise use the mark on any products or services. Typically, license agreements are very detailed and should be carefully drafted. Disputes frequently arise over licensing agreements, particularly when the license involves Internet uses, such as a license allowing a trademark to be used in domain names.

EXAMPLE 5.8 Morton and Tigrett founded the Hard Rock Café, which became a popular chain of restaurants internationally. Years later they had a falling out and split their Hard Rock Café properties throughout the world into two territories. Eventually, Tigrett sold his interests to another company, and Morton opened the Hard Rock Hotel and Casino in Las Vegas. The hotel was licensed to use some of the same trademark logos as the Hard Rock Café. When Morton later used the logos on the Web site for the hotel and on merchandise advertised on the Web site, he was sued for breaching the licensing agreement.

LICENSE
In the context of intellectual property law, an agreement permitting the use of a trademark, copyright, patent, or trade secret for certain limited purposes.

---

8. *Playboy Enterprises, Inc. v. Welles*, 279 F.3d 796 (9th Cir. 2002).
9. *Hasbro, Inc. v. Internet Entertainment Group, Ltd.*, 1996 WL 84858 (W.D.Wash. 1996).

The licensor claimed that Morton had exceeded the rights granted under the license because the Internet site reached beyond the territory specified in the agreement.

After several years of costly litigation, the court concluded that the licensing agreement was broad enough to allow Morton to use the logos as the Hard Rock Hotel's trademark. The court held, however, that advertising merchandise with the Hard Rock Café's logos on the hotel's Web site constituted infringement and ordered Morton to cease the advertisements. Despite the infringement, the plaintiffs were not entitled to monetary damages because they had not proved that the Web site had caused consumer confusion or that Morton had acted in bad faith or willfully deceived consumers.[10] ▣

PREVENTING LEGAL DISPUTES

To avoid litigation, anyone signing a licensing contract should consult with an attorney to make sure that the specific wording in the contract is very clear as to what rights are or are not being conveyed. Moreover, to prevent misunderstandings over the scope of the rights being acquired, the licensee should determine whether any other parties hold licenses to use that particular intellectual property and the extent of those rights.

▣

PATENTS

PATENT
A government grant that gives an inventor the exclusive right or privilege to make, use, or sell his or her invention for a limited time period.

A **patent** is a grant from the government that gives an inventor the exclusive right to make, use, and sell an invention for a period of twenty years from the date of filing the application for a patent. Patents for designs, as opposed to inventions, are given for a fourteen-year period. For either a regular patent or a design patent, the applicant must demonstrate to the satisfaction of the U.S. Patent and Trademark Office that the invention, discovery, process, or design is *novel, useful,* and *not obvious* in light of current technology.

In contrast to patent law in many other countries, in the United States the first person to invent a product or process gets the patent rights rather than the first person to file for a patent on that product or process. Because it is difficult to prove who invented an item first, however, the first person to file an application is often deemed the first to invent (unless the inventor has detailed research notes or other evidence). An inventor can publish the invention or offer it for sale prior to filing a patent application but must apply for a patent within one year of doing so or forfeit the patent rights. The period of patent protection begins on the date the patent application was filed, rather than when it was issued, which can sometimes be years later. After the patent period ends (either fourteen or twenty years later), the product or process enters the public domain, and anyone can make, sell, or use the invention without paying the patent holder.

Searchable Patent Databases

A significant development relating to patents is the availability online of the world's patent databases. The Web site of the U.S. Patent and Trademark Office provides searchable databases covering U.S. patents granted since 1976. The Web site of the European Patent Office provides online access to fifty million patent documents in more than seventy nations through a searchable network of databases. Businesses use these searchable databases in many ways. Because patents are valuable assets, businesses may need to perform patent searches to list or inventory their assets. Patent searches may also be conducted to study trends and patterns in a specific technology or to gather information about competi-

---

10. *Hard Rock Café International (USA), Inc. v. Morton,* 1999 WL 717995 (S.D.N.Y. 1999).

tors in the industry. In addition, a business might search patent databases to develop a business strategy in a particular market or to evaluate a job applicant's contributions to a technology. Although online databases are accessible to anyone, businesspersons might consider hiring a specialist to perform advanced patent searches.

What Is Patentable?

Under federal law, "[w]hoever invents or discovers any new and useful process, machine, manufacture, or composition of matter, or any new and useful improvement thereof, may obtain a patent therefor, subject to the conditions and requirements of this title."[11] At one time, it was difficult for developers and manufacturers of software to obtain patent protection because many software products simply automate procedures that can be performed manually. In other words, it was thought that computer programs did not meet the "novel" and "not obvious" requirements previously mentioned. Also, the basis for software is often a mathematical equation or formula, which is not patentable. In 1981, however, the United States Supreme Court held that it is possible to obtain a patent for a *process* that incorporates a computer program—providing, of course, that the process itself is patentable.[12] Subsequently, many patents have been issued for software-related inventions.

In 1998, in a landmark case, *State Street Bank & Trust Co. v. Signature Financial Group, Inc.,*[13] the U.S. Court of Appeals for the Federal Circuit ruled that business processes were patentable. After this decision, numerous technology firms applied for business process patents. Walker Digital applied for a business process patent for its "Dutch auction" system, which allowed consumers to make offers for airline tickets on the Internet and led to the creation of Priceline.com. Amazon.com obtained a business process patent for its "one-click" ordering system, a method of processing credit-card orders securely. Indeed, since the *State Street* decision, the number of Internet-related patents issued by the U.S. Patent and Trademark Office has increased dramatically.

In sum, almost anything is patentable, except (1) the laws of nature, (2) natural phenomena, and (3) abstract ideas (including algorithms). Even artistic methods, certain works of art, and the structure of storylines are patentable, provided that they are novel and not obvious. Plants that are reproduced asexually (by means other than from seed), such as hybrid or genetically engineered plants, are patentable in the United States, as are genetically engineered (or cloned) microorganisms and animals.

Should a software program that allows consumers to make offers for vacation packages via the Internet be considered a "new and useful" process that can be the subject of a business process patent? Why or why not?

ON THE WEB

You can access the European Patent Office's Web site at

www.european-patent-office.org.

Is it an abuse of patent law for a company to sue farmers whose crops were accidentally contaminated by genetically modified seed? Monsanto, Inc., has been selling genetically modified (GM) seeds to farmers in the United States and throughout the world as a way to achieve higher yields using fewer pesticides. Monsanto requires farmers who buy GM seeds to sign licensing agreements promising to plant the seeds for only one crop and to pay a technology fee for each acre planted. To ensure that the farmers comply with the restrictions, Monsanto has set aside $10 million a year and a staff of seventy-five individuals to investigate and prosecute farmers who use the GM seeds illegally. If the company receives an anonymous tip about a farmer, it sends its "seed police" to investigate, take samples from the farmer's field for testing, interview neighbors, and even conduct surveillance of the farmer's family and operation.

ETHICAL ISSUE 5.1

11. 35 U.S.C. 101.
12. *Diamond v. Diehr*, 450 U.S. 175, 101 S.Ct. 1048, 67 L.Ed.2d 155 (1981).
13. 149 F.3d 1368 (Fed. Cir. 1998).

How might a farmer—like Percy Schmeiser, shown in the photo—unknowingly commit patent infringement? (Photo Courtesy of Percy Schmeiser)

The problem is that the patented GM seeds, like ordinary seeds, reproduce if they are scattered by the wind or transferred on farm equipment. Thus, they can contaminate neighboring fields. Consider, for example, the situation faced by a Canadian canola farmer, Percy Schmeiser. Schmeiser had not purchased any GM seeds or signed any licensing agreement, but on investigation Monsanto found that some of his crop contained evidence of a Monsanto genetic trait. Schmeiser refused to pay royalties to Monsanto because he had not planted any GM seeds. It turned out that Schmeiser's crop had been contaminated with the GM seed, likely by seed escaping from passing trucks. Nevertheless, the Canadian Supreme Court ruled that Schmeiser had committed patent infringement and ordered him to destroy the crops containing evidence of the patented seed.[14] Schmeiser's plight is not unusual. Monsanto has filed more than ninety lawsuits against nearly 150 farmers in the United States and has been awarded more than $15 million in damages (not including out-of-court settlement amounts).[15] Farmers claim that Monsanto has acted unethically by intimidating them and threatening to pursue them in court for years if they refuse to settle out of court by paying royalties.

Patent Infringement

If a firm makes, uses, or sells another's patented design, product, or process without the patent owner's permission, it commits the tort of patent infringement. Patent infringement may occur even though the patent owner has not put the patented product in commerce. Patent infringement may also occur even though not all features or parts of an invention are copied. (With respect to a patented process, however, all steps or their equivalent must be copied for infringement to exist.)

Remedies for Patent Infringement

If a patent is infringed, the patent holder may sue for relief in federal court. The patent holder can seek an injunction against the infringer and can also request damages for royalties and lost profits. In some cases, the court may grant the winning party reimbursement for attorneys' fees and costs. If the court determines that the infringement was willful, the court can triple the amount of damages awarded (treble damages).

In the past, permanent injunctions were routinely granted to prevent future infringement. In 2006, however, the United States Supreme Court ruled that patent holders are not automatically entitled to a permanent injunction against future infringing activities—the federal courts have discretion to decide whether equity requires it. According to the Supreme Court, a patent holder must prove that it has suffered irreparable injury and that the public interest would not be disserved by a permanent injunction.[16]

This decision gives courts discretion to decide what is equitable in the circumstances and allows them to consider what is in the public interest rather than just the interests of the parties. For example, in the first case applying this rule, a court found that although Microsoft had infringed on the patent of a small software company, the latter was not entitled to an injunction. According to the court, the small company was not irreparably harmed and could be adequately compensated by damages. Also, the public might suffer negative effects from an injunction because the infringement involved part of Microsoft's widely used Office suite software.[17]

---

14. *Monsanto Canada, Inc. v. Schmeiser,* 1 S.C.R. 902, 2004 SCC 34 (CanLII). Note that in contrast to most cases in the United States, the Canadian court did not award damages for the infringement and only ordered Schmeiser to stop the infringing activity.

15. See, for example, *Monsanto Co. v. Scruggs,* 459 F.3d 1328 (2006); *Monsanto Co. v. McFarling,* ___ F.Supp.2d ___ (E.D.Mo. 2005) and *Sample v. Monsanto Co.,* 283 F.Supp.2d 1088 (2003).

16. *eBay, Inc. v. MercExchange, LLC,* 126 U.S. 1837, 126 S.Ct. 1837, 164 L.Ed.2d 641 (2006).

17. *Z4 Technologies, Inc. v. Microsoft Corp.,* 434 F.Supp.2d 437 (2006).

Litigation over whether a patent has been infringed is typically expensive and often requires a team of experts to investigate and analyze the commercial, technical, and legal aspects of the case. Because of these costs, a businessperson facing patent infringement litigation—either as the patent holder or as the alleged infringer—should carefully evaluate the evidence as well as the various settlement options. If both sides appear to have good arguments as to whether the patent was infringed or whether it was valid, it may be in a firm's best interest to settle the case. This is particularly true if the firm is not certain that the court would grant an injunction. Similarly, if the patented technology is not commercially significant to one's business, it might be best to consider a nonexclusive license as a means of resolving the dispute. This option is more important for patent holders now that injunctions may be harder to obtain. Settlement may be as simple as an agreement that one party will stop making, using, or selling the patented product or process, or it may involve monetary compensation for past activities and/or licensing for future activities.

PREVENTING LEGAL DISPUTES

COPYRIGHTS

A **copyright** is an intangible property right granted by federal statute to the author or originator of certain literary or artistic productions. Currently, copyrights are governed by the Copyright Act of 1976,[18] as amended. Works created after January 1, 1978, are automatically given statutory copyright protection for the life of the author plus 70 years. For copyrights owned by publishing houses, the copyright expires 95 years from the date of publication or 120 years from the date of creation, whichever is first. For works by more than one author, the copyright expires 70 years after the death of the last surviving author.

These time periods reflect the extensions of the length of copyright protection enacted by Congress in the Copyright Term Extension Act of 1998.[19] Critics challenged this act as overstepping the bounds of Congress's power and violating the constitutional requirement that copyrights endure for only a limited time. In 2003, however, the United States Supreme Court upheld the act in *Eldred v. Ashcroft*.[20] This ruling obviously favored copyright holders by preventing copyrighted works from the 1920s and 1930s from losing protection and falling into the public domain for an additional two decades.

Copyrights can be registered with the U.S. Copyright Office in Washington, D.C. A copyright owner no longer needs to place a © or *Copr.* or *Copyright* on the work, however, to have the work protected against infringement. Chances are that if somebody created it, somebody owns it.

COPYRIGHT
The exclusive right of an author or originator of a literary or artistic production to publish, print, or sell that production for a statutory period of time. A copyright has the same monopolistic nature as a patent or trademark, but it differs in that it applies exclusively to works of art, literature, and other works of authorship (including computer programs).

ON THE WEB

For information on copyrights, go to the U.S. Copyright Office at

www.copyright/gov.

What Is Protected Expression?

Works that are copyrightable include books, records, films, artworks, architectural plans, menus, music videos, product packaging, and computer software. To be protected, a work must be "fixed in a durable medium" from which it can be perceived, reproduced, or communicated. Protection is automatic. Registration is not required.

To obtain protection under the Copyright Act, a work must be original and fall into one of the following categories:

1 Literary works (including newspaper and magazine articles, computer and training manuals, catalogues, brochures, and print advertisements).

BE CAREFUL If a creative work does not fall into a certain category, it might not be copyrighted, but it may be protected by other intellectual property law.

---

18. 17 U.S.C. Sections 101 *et seq.*
19. 17 U.S.C.A. Section 302.
20. 537 U.S. 186, 123 S.Ct. 769, 154 L.Ed.2d 683 (2003).

A sign in New York City warns audience members about to attend an improv theatrical performance. Can a live performance, especially one that is improvisational in nature, be copyrighted? (Photo by W. Seltzer, Creative Commons)

2 Musical works and accompanying words (including advertising jingles).

3 Dramatic works and accompanying music.

4 Pantomimes and choreographic works (including ballets and other forms of dance).

5 Pictorial, graphic, and sculptural works (including cartoons, maps, posters, statues, and even stuffed animals).

6 Motion pictures and other audiovisual works (including multimedia works).

7 Sound recordings.

8 Architectural works.

Section 102 Exclusions Section 102 of the Copyright Act specifically excludes copyright protection for any "idea, procedure, process, system, method of operation, concept, principle, or discovery, regardless of the form in which it is described, explained, illustrated, or embodied." Note that it is not possible to copyright an *idea*. The underlying ideas embodied in a work may be freely used by others. What is copyrightable is the particular way in which an idea is *expressed*. Whenever an idea and an expression are inseparable, the expression cannot be copyrighted. Generally, anything that is not an original expression will not qualify for copyright protection. Facts widely known to the public are not copyrightable. Page numbers are not copyrightable because they follow a sequence known to everyone. Mathematical calculations are not copyrightable.

ETHICAL ISSUE 5.2

Should the federal Copyright Act preempt plaintiffs from bringing "idea-submission" claims under state law? Prior to 2004, federal courts generally held that the Copyright Act preempted (or superseded—see Chapter 2) claims in state courts alleging the theft of ideas. The decision in the case *Grosso v. Miramax Film Corp.,*[21] however, opened the door to such claims. In that case, Jeff Grosso, who wrote a screenplay called *The Shell Game,* claimed that Miramax stole the ideas and themes of his work when it made the movie *Rounders.* Both the screenplay and the movie have poker settings, and the characters in both use similar poker jargon.

Grosso filed a copyright claim in a federal court and also asserted a claim under state law alleging the existence of an implied contract (a contract that may be implied even in the absence of an express promise—see Chapter 9). Ultimately, the U.S. Court of Appeals for the Ninth Circuit ruled that, although Grosso had failed to prove his claim under copyright law, the Copyright Act did not preempt the state contract law claim. Since the *Grosso* decision, numerous cases have been filed in state courts alleging that an idea that was pitched to a television network or movie producer was "stolen" and that the person whose idea it was should be compensated. In California, idea-submission lawsuits have been filed over television series, such as *Project Runway* and *The 4400,* as well as motion pictures, including *The Last Samurai, Broken Flowers,* and *The Wedding Crashers.* The question is, given that these plaintiffs were unable to maintain a copyright action because the law does not protect ideas (only expressions of ideas), should they be allowed to sue over the same ideas in state courts?

Compilations of Facts Unlike ideas, *compilations* of facts are copyrightable. Under Section 103 of the Copyright Act, a compilation is work formed by the collection and assembling of preexisting materials or of data that are selected, coordinated, or arranged in such a way that the resulting work as a whole constitutes an original work of authorship." The key requirement for the copyrightability of a compilation is originality. **EXAMPLE 5.9** The white

---

21. 383 F.3d 965 (9th Cir. 2004); *cert.* denied, 126 S.Ct. 361, 163 L.Ed.2d 68 (2005).

pages of a telephone directory do not qualify for copyright protection when the information that makes up the directory (names, addresses, and telephone numbers) is not selected, coordinated, or arranged in an original way.[22] In one case, even the Yellow Pages of a telephone directory did not qualify for copyright protection.[23] ▣

Copyright Infringement

Whenever the form or expression of an idea is copied, an infringement of copyright occurs. The reproduction does not have to be exactly the same as the original, nor does it have to reproduce the original in its entirety. If a substantial part of the original is reproduced, there is copyright infringement.

Damages for Copyright Infringement   Those who infringe copyrights may be liable for damages or criminal penalties. These range from actual damages or statutory damages, imposed at the court's discretion, to criminal proceedings for willful violations. Actual damages are based on the harm caused to the copyright holder by the infringement, while statutory damages, not to exceed $150,000, are provided for under the Copyright Act. In addition, criminal proceedings may result in fines and/or imprisonment.

The "Fair Use" Exception   An exception to liability for copyright infringement is made under the "fair use" doctrine. In certain circumstances, a person or organization can reproduce copyrighted material without paying royalties (fees paid to the copyright holder for the privilege of reproducing the copyrighted material). Section 107 of the Copyright Act provides as follows:

> [T]he fair use of a copyrighted work, including such use by reproduction in copies or phonorecords or by any other means specified by [Section 106 of the Copyright Act,] for purposes such as criticism, comment, news reporting, teaching (including multiple copies for classroom use), scholarship, or research, is not an infringement of copyright. In determining whether the use made of a work in any particular case is a fair use the factors to be considered shall include—
>
> (1) the purpose and character of the use, including whether such use is of a commercial nature or is for nonprofit educational purposes;
> (2) the nature of the copyrighted work;
> (3) the amount and substantiality of the portion used in relation to the copyrighted work as a whole; and
> (4) the effect of the use upon the potential market for or value of the copyrighted work.

Because these guidelines are very broad, the courts determine whether a particular use is fair on a case-by-case basis. Thus, anyone reproducing copyrighted material may be committing a violation. In determining whether a use is fair, courts have often considered the fourth factor to be the most important.

Copyright Protection for Software

In 1980, Congress passed the Computer Software Copyright Act, which amended the Copyright Act of 1976 to include computer programs in the list of creative works protected by federal copyright law. The 1980 statute, which classifies computer programs as "literary works," defines a computer program as a "set of statements or instructions to be used directly or indirectly in a computer in order to bring about a certain result."

ON THE WEB

You can find a host of information on copyright law, including the Copyright Act and significant United States Supreme Court cases in the area of copyright law, at

www.law.cornell.edu/supct/cases/ copyrt.htm.

---

22. *Feist Publications, Inc. v. Rural Telephone Service Co.*, 499 U.S. 340, 111 S.Ct. 1282, 113 L.Ed.2d 358 (1991).
23. *Bellsouth Advertising & Publishing Corp. v. Donnelley Information Publishing, Inc.*, 999 F.2d 1436 (11th Cir. 1993).

Legal Issues Facing Bloggers and Podcasters

C ompanies increasingly are using blogs (Web logs) and podcasts (essentially audio blogs, sometimes with video clips) internally to encourage communication among employees and externally to communicate with customers. Blogs offer many advantages, not the least of which is that setting up a blog and keeping it current (making "posts") costs next to nothing because so much easy-to-use free software is available. Podcasts, even those including video, require only a little more sophistication. Nonetheless, both blogs and podcasts also carry some legal risks for the companies that sponsor them.

Benefits of Blogs and Podcasts

Internal blogs used by a company's employees can offer a number of benefits. Blogs provide an open communications platform, potentially allowing new ways of coordinating activities among employees. For example, a team of production workers might use a blog to move a new product idea forward: the team starts a blog, one worker posts a proposal, and other team members quickly post comments in response. The blog can be an excellent way to generate new ideas. Internal blogs also allow for team learning and encourage dialogue. When workers are spread out across the country or around the world, blogging provides a cheap means of communication that does not require sophisticated project management software.

Many companies are also creating external blogs, which are available to clients and customers. External blogs can be used to push products, obtain feedback from customers, and shape the image that the company presents to outsiders. Even some company chief executive officers (CEOs), including the CEOs of McDonald's, Boeing, and Hewlett-Packard, have started blogs.

Potential Legal Risks

Despite their many advantages, blogs and podcasts can also expose a company to a number of legal risks, including the following.

- **Tort Liability** Internal blogs and podcasts can lead to claims of defamation or sexual harassment if an employee posts racist or sexually explicit comments. At the same time, if a company monitors its employees' blogs and podcasts, it may find itself facing claims of invasion of privacy (see Chapter 33 for a discussion of similar issues involving employees' e-mail).

Because of the unique nature of computer programs, the courts have had many problems applying and interpreting the 1980 act. Generally, though, the courts have held that copyright protection extends not only to those parts of a computer program that can be read by humans, such as the high-level language of a source code, but also to the binary-language object code of a computer program, which is readable only by the computer.[24] Additionally, such elements as the overall structure, sequence, and organization of a program have been deemed copyrightable.[25] The courts have disagreed as to whether the "look and feel"—the general appearance, command structure, video images, menus, windows, and other screen displays—of computer programs should also be protected by copyright. The courts have tended, however, not to extend copyright protection to look-and-feel aspects of computer programs.

Copyrights in Digital Information

Copyright law is probably the most important form of intellectual property protection on the Internet. This is because much of the material on the Internet consists of works of authorship (including multimedia presentations, software, and database information), which are the traditional focus of copyright law. Copyright law is also important because the nature of the Internet requires that data be "copied" to be transferred online. Copies

---

24. See *Stern Electronics, Inc. v. Kaufman*, 669 F.2d 852 (2d Cir. 1982); and *Apple Computer, Inc. v. Franklin Computer Corp.*, 714 F.2d 1240 (3d Cir. 1983).
25. *Whelan Associates, Inc. v. Jaslow Dental Laboratory, Inc.*, 797 F.2d 1222 (3d Cir. 1986).

- **Security of Information** Blogs may also be susceptible to security breaches. If an outsider obtains access to an internal blog, a company's trade secrets could be lost. Outsiders could also potentially gain access to blogs containing financial information.

- **Discovery Issues** As explained in Chapter 3, litigation today frequently involves electronic discovery. This can extend to blog posts and comments as well as to e-mail. Thus, a company should be aware that anything posted on its blogs can be used as evidence during litigation. A company will therefore need to preserve and retain blog postings related to any dispute likely to go to trial.

- **Compliance Issues** Many corporations are regulated by one or more agencies and required to comply with various statutes. Laws that require compliance may also apply to blog postings. For example, the Securities and Exchange Commission (SEC) has regulations establishing the information a company must disclose to potential investors and the public in connection with its stock. A company regulated by the SEC will find that these rules apply to blogs. The same is true for companies regulated under the Sarbanes-Oxley Act, which will be discussed in Chapters 7, 30, and 35.

- **Copyright Infringement** Blogs can also expose a company to charges of copyright infringement. Suppose, for example, that an employee posts a long passage from a

magazine article on the company's blog, either internal or external, without the author's permission. Similarly, photos taken from other blogs or Web sites cannot be posted without prior permission. Note, also, that copyright infringement can occur even if the blog was created without any pecuniary (monetary) motivation. Typically, though, a blogger can claim "fair use" if she or he posts a passage from someone else's work along with an electronic link to the complete version.

External blogs carry most of the same risks as internal blogs and others as well. Not only can external blogs lead to charges of invasion of privacy, defamation, or copyright infringement related to what the company and its employees post, but they can also expose the company to liability for what visitors post. If a company's blog allows visitors to post comments and a visitor makes a defamatory statement, the company that created the blog could be held liable for publishing it. Thus, any company considering establishing blogs and podcasts, whether internal or external, should be aware of the risks and take steps to guard against them.

 FOR CRITICAL ANALYSIS *Do individuals who create blogs face the same risks as companies that use blogs? Explain.*

have traditionally been a significant part of the controversies arising in this area of the law. (See this chapter's *Adapting the Law to the Online Environment* feature for a discussion of how blogs and podcasts can expose a company to legal risks including lawsuits for copyright infringement.)

The Copyright Act of 1976 When Congress drafted the principal U.S. law governing copyrights, the Copyright Act of 1976, cyberspace did not exist for most of us, and the primary threat to copyright owners was from persons making unauthorized *tangible* copies of works. Because of the nature of cyberspace, however, one of the early controversies was determining at what point an intangible, electronic "copy" of a work has been made. The courts held that loading a file or program into a computer's random access memory, or RAM, constitutes the making of a "copy" for purposes of copyright law.[26] RAM is a portion of a computer's memory into which a file, for instance, is loaded so that it can be accessed (read or written over). Thus, a copyright is infringed when a party downloads software into RAM without owning the software or otherwise having a right to download it.[27]

Today, technology has vastly increased the potential for copyright infringement. The question in the following case was whether a musician commits copyright infringement when he or she copies any part—even as little as two seconds—of a copyrighted sound recording without the permission of the copyright's owner.

 ON THE WEB

The University of Michigan provides information on copyrights generally and copyrights in digital information at

www.copyright.umich.edu/law.html.

---

26. *MAI Systems Corp. v. Peak Computer, Inc.*, 991 F.2d 511 (9th Cir. 1993).
27. *DSC Communications Corp. v. Pulse Communications, Inc.*, 170 F.3d 1354 (Fed. Cir. 1999).

CASE 5.3   Bridgeport Music, Inc. v. Dimension Films

United States Court of Appeals, Sixth Circuit, 410 F.3d 792 (2005).
www.findlaw.com/casecode/courts/6th.html[a]

FACTS Bridgeport Music, Inc., is in the business of publishing music and exploiting copyrights of musical compositions. Westbound Records, Inc., is in the business of recording and distributing sound recordings. Bridgeport and Westbound own the composition and recording copyrights to "Get Off Your Ass and Jam" by George Clinton, Jr., and the Funkadelics. The recording "Get Off" opens with a three-note solo guitar riff that lasts four seconds. The rap song "100 Miles and Runnin" contains a two-second sample from the guitar solo, at a lower pitch, looped and extended to sixteen beats, in five places in the song, with each looped segment lasting about seven seconds. "100 Miles" was included in the sound track of the movie *I Got the Hook Up*, which was distributed by No Limit Films. Bridgeport, Westbound, and others filed a suit in a federal district court against No Limit and others, alleging copyright infringement. No Limit did not dispute that it digitally sampled a copyrighted sound recording. The court found, however, that no reasonable juror, even one familiar with the works of George Clinton, would recognize the source of the sample. Accordingly, the court issued a summary judgment in the defendants' favor. Westbound appealed the judgment to the U.S. Court of Appeals for the Sixth Circuit.

ISSUE Can a person use a few seconds of another's copyrighted sound recording in his or her own music recording without infringing on the copyright?

a. In the "Docket Number Search" box, type "02-6521pv," and click on "get it." In the result, click on the case name to access the opinion.

DECISION No. The U.S. Court of Appeals for the Sixth Circuit reversed the lower court's summary judgment on Westbound's claims against No Limit and remanded the case.

REASON The appellate court held that digitally sampling a copyrighted sound recording of any length constitutes copyright infringement. The court noted that under the Copyright Act, the owner of the copyright in a sound recording has the exclusive rights to sample his or her own recording. In this instance, the court said that it was possible to articulate a bright line rule—"[g]et a license or do not sample." The court felt that this rule would not stifle creativity in any significant way. "[I]f an artist wants to incorporate a 'riff' from another work in his or her recording, he is free to duplicate the sound of that 'riff' in the studio." Or the artist can get a license to use the original recording. The court also emphasized that "sampling is never accidental. * * * When you sample a sound recording you know you are taking another's work product."

WHAT IF THE FACTS WERE DIFFERENT? *Suppose that rather than taking a few notes from another's musical composition, No Limit had played the exact same notes in the studio when recording. In other words, the band would not have "sampled" the copyrighted work of another. How would this change the outcome of the case? Could Bridgeport and Westbound still prove copyright infringement? Why or why not?*

Further Developments in Copyright Law   Prior to 1997, criminal penalties under copyright law could be imposed only if unauthorized copies were exchanged for financial gain. Yet much piracy of copyrighted materials was "altruistic" in nature; unauthorized copies were made and distributed not for financial gain but simply for reasons of generosity—to share the copies with others.

To combat altruistic piracy and for other reasons, Congress passed the No Electronic Theft (NET) Act of 1997. This act extends criminal liability for the piracy of copyrighted materials to persons who exchange unauthorized copies of copyrighted works, such as software, even though they realize no profit from the exchange. The act also imposes penalties on those who make unauthorized electronic copies of books, magazines, movies, or music for *personal* use, thus altering the traditional "fair use" doctrine. The criminal penalties for violating the act are steep; they include fines as high as $250,000 and incarceration for up to five years.

153 **CHAPTER 5**
INTELLECTUAL PROPERTY
AND INTERNET LAW

In 1998, Congress passed further legislation to protect copyright holders—the Digital Millennium Copyright Act. Because of its significance in protecting against the piracy of copyrighted materials in the online environment, this act is presented as this chapter's *Landmark in the Law* feature on pages 154 and 155.

MP3 and File-Sharing Technology

Soon after the Internet became popular, a few enterprising programmers created software to compress large data files, particularly those associated with music. The reduced file sizes make transmitting music over the Internet feasible. The most widely known compression and decompression system is MP3, which enables music fans to download songs or entire CDs onto their computers or onto a portable listening device, such as an iPod. The MP3 system also made it possible for music fans to access other music fans' files by engaging in file-sharing via the Internet.

File-sharing via the Internet is accomplished through what is called **peer-to-peer (P2P) networking.** The concept is simple. Rather than going through a central Web server, P2P involves numerous personal computers (PCs) that are connected to the Internet. Files stored on one PC can be accessed by other individuals who are members of the same network. Sometimes this is called a **distributed network.** In other words, parts of the network are distributed all over the country or the world. File-sharing offers an unlimited number of uses for distributed networks. For instance, thousands of researchers allow their home computers' computing power to be simultaneously accessed through file-sharing software so that very large mathematical problems can be solved quickly. Additionally, persons scattered throughout the country or the world can work together on the same project by using file-sharing programs.

Sharing Stored Music Files   When file-sharing is used to download others' stored music files, copyright issues arise. Recording artists and their labels stand to lose large amounts of royalties and revenues if relatively few CDs are purchased and then made available on distributed networks, from which everyone can get them for free. The issue of file-sharing infringement has been the subject of an ongoing debate for some time.

EXAMPLE 5.10 In the highly publicized case of *A&M Records, Inc. v. Napster, Inc.,*[28] several firms in the recording industry sued Napster, Inc., the owner of the then-popular Napster Web site. The Napster site provided registered users with free software that enabled them to transfer exact copies of the contents of MP3 files from one computer to another via the Internet. Napster also maintained centralized search indices so that users could locate specific titles or artists' recordings on the computers of other members. The firms argued that Napster should be liable for contributory and vicarious[29] (indirect) copyright infringement because it assisted others in obtaining copies of copyrighted music without the copyright owners' permission. Both the federal district court and the U.S. Court of Appeals for the Ninth Circuit agreed and held Napster liable for violating copyright laws. The court reasoned that Napster was liable for its users' infringement because the technology that Napster had used was centralized and gave it "the ability to locate infringing material listed on its search indices and the right to terminate users' access to the system." ▣

DON'T GET SUED OR IMPRISONED:
You can't afford the long arm of the RIAA

Forewarned is Forearmed

Recently, the RIAA (Recording Industry Association of America) has been conducting comprehensive audits on university networks. The Information Technology Division warns students that those illegally downloading and/or distributing copyrighted music, videos, or other works are at a high risk of prosecution. You will be held personally liable for such illegal activities.

You will be held personally liable for such illegal activities.

AS A REMINDER:

- *It is illegal to make, use, or pass along unauthorized copies of software, graphics, music or any other creative art or intellectual property for multimedia projects or any other use. This includes the copying of software programs, etc., required in a class.*

- *Illegal file sharing of copyrighted materials over Texas Tech Networks is strictly prohibited.*

- *It is illegal for anyone to upload or download full-length sound recordings or DVDs without permission of the copyright owners.*

For more detailed information concerning copyright and related laws, please visit http://www.ttu.edu/safecomputing/ttu/riaa/ (eRaider username and password required).

Know the law, protect yourself.

TEXAS TECH UNIVERSITY
Information Technology Division

Texas Tech University sent a notice to its students warning them of the legal risks involved in sharing stored music files. What other types of electronic files do college students share that might be a violation of copyright laws? (Wesley Fryer/ Creative Commons)

PEER-TO-PEER (P2P) NETWORKING
The sharing of resources (such as files, hard drives, and processing styles) among multiple computers without necessarily requiring a central network server.

DISTRIBUTED NETWORK
A network that can be used by persons located (distributed) around the country or the globe to share computer files.

---

28. 239 F.3d 1004 (9th Cir. 2001).

29. *Vicarious (indirect) liability* exists when one person is subject to liability for another's actions. A common example occurs in the employment context, when an employer is held vicariously liable by third parties for torts committed by employees in the course of their employment.

LANDMARK IN THE LAW **The Digital Millennium Copyright Act of 1998**

The United States leads the world in the production of creative products, including books, films, videos, recordings, and software. In fact, as indicated earlier in this chapter, the creative industries are more important to the U.S. economy than the traditional product industries are. Exports of U.S. creative products, for example, surpass those of every other U.S. industry in value. Creative industries are growing at nearly three times the rate of the economy as a whole.

Steps have been taken, both nationally and internationally, to protect ownership rights in intellectual property, including copyrights. In 1996, to curb unauthorized copying of copyrighted materials, the World Intellectual Property Organization (WIPO) enacted a treaty to upgrade global standards of copyright protection, particularly for the Internet.

Implementing the WIPO Treaty   In 1998, Congress implemented the provisions of the WIPO treaty by updating U.S. copyright law. The law—the Digital Millennium Copyright Act of 1998—is a landmark step in the protection of copyright owners and, because of the leading position of the United States in the creative industries, serves as a model for other nations. Among other things, the act established civil and criminal penalties for anyone who circumvents (bypasses, or gets around—through clever maneuvering, for example) encryption software or other technological antipiracy protection. Also prohibited are the manufacture, import, sale, and distribution of devices or services for circumvention.

The act provides for exceptions to fit the needs of libraries, scientists, universities, and others. In general, the law does not restrict the "fair use" of circumvention methods for educational and other noncommercial purposes. For example, circumvention is allowed to test computer security, conduct encryption research, protect personal privacy, and enable parents to monitor their children's use of the Internet. The exceptions are to be reconsidered every three years.

Limiting the Liability of Internet Service Providers   The 1998 act also limited the liability of Internet service providers (ISPs). Under the act, an ISP is not liable for

After the *Napster* decision, the recording industry filed and won numerous lawsuits against companies that distribute online file-sharing software. The courts held these companies liable based on two theories: contributory infringement, which applies if the company had reason to know about a user's infringement and failed to stop it; and vicarious liability, which exists if the company was able to control the users' activities and stood to benefit financially from their infringement.

The Evolution of File-Sharing Technologies   In the wake of the *Napster* decision, other companies developed technologies that allow P2P network users to share stored music files, without paying a fee, more quickly and efficiently than ever. Software such as Morpheus, KaZaA, and LimeWire, for example, provides users with an interface that is similar to a Web browser.[30] Instead of the company's locating songs for users on other members' computers, the software automatically annotates files with descriptive informa-

---

30. Note that in 2005, KaZaA entered a settlement agreement with four major music companies that had alleged copyright infringement. KaZaA agreed to offer only legitimate, fee-based music downloads in the future.

any copyright infringement by its customer *unless* the ISP is aware of the subscriber's violation. An ISP may be held liable only if it fails to take action to shut the subscriber down after learning of the violation. A copyright holder has to act promptly, however, by pursuing a claim in court, or the subscriber has the right to be restored to online access.

APPLICATION TO TODAY'S WORLD *The application of the Digital Millennium Copyright Act of 1998 to today's world is fairly self-evident. If Congress had not enacted this legislation, copyright owners would have a far more difficult time obtaining legal redress against those who, without authorization, decrypt and/or copy copyrighted materials. Of course, problems remain, particularly because of the global nature of the Internet. From a practical standpoint, the degree of protection afforded to copyright holders depends on the extent to which other nations that have signed the WIPO treaty actually implement its provisions and agree on the interpretation of terms, such as what constitutes an electronic copy.*

FOR CRITICAL ANALYSIS *Critics of the 1998 act claim that it has not been used as Congress originally envisioned and that it has had the unintended consequences of chilling free speech and scientific research. In one case, for example, a Russian scientist was arrested after speaking at a conference in the United States because he had worked on a software program that enabled owners of Adobe e-books to convert the files to PDF format. The scientist, who was not charged with copyright infringement, was ultimately cleared of any wrongdoing, but the incident has prompted a number of foreign scientists to refuse to attend conferences in the United States. In what other ways might the act chill free speech? Is there any way to amend the act to avoid this potential problem? Explain.*

RELEVANT WEB SITES *To locate information on the Web concerning the Digital Millennium Copyright Act of 1998, go to this text's Web site at* **www.thomsonedu.com/ westbuslaw/blt**, *select "Chapter 5," and click on "URLs for Landmarks."*

---

tion so that the music can easily be categorized and cross-referenced (by artist and title, for instance). When a user performs a search, the software is able to locate a list of peers that have the file available for downloading. Also, to expedite the P2P transfer, the software distributes the download task over the entire list of peers simultaneously. By downloading even one file, the user becomes a point of distribution for that file, which is then automatically shared with others on the network.

Because the file-sharing software was decentralized and did not use search indices, the companies had no ability to supervise or control which music (or other media files) their users exchanged. In addition, it was difficult for courts to apply the traditional doctrines of contributory and vicarious liability to these new technologies.

The Supreme Court's *Grokster* Decision In 2005, the United States Supreme Court expanded the liability of file-sharing companies in its decision in *Metro-Goldwyn-Mayer Studios, Inc. v. Grokster, Ltd.*[31] In that case, organizations in the music and film industry

---

31. 545 U.S. 913, 125 S.Ct. 2764, 162 L.Ed.2d 781 (2005).

Will holding the companies that make file-sharing software legally responsible for the copyright infringement of their end-users stifle innovation and technology, as these demonstrators suggest?
(Beatrice Murch/Creative Commons)

(the plaintiffs) sued several companies that distribute file-sharing software used in P2P networks, including Grokster, Ltd., and StreamCast Networks, Inc. (the defendants). The plaintiffs claimed that the companies were contributorily and vicariously liable for the infringement of their end users. The Supreme Court held that "one who distributes a device [software] with the object of promoting its use to infringe the copyright, as shown by clear expression or other affirmative steps taken to foster infringement, is liable for the resulting acts of infringement by third parties."

Although the Supreme Court did not specify what kind of affirmative steps are necessary to establish liability, it did note that there was ample evidence that the defendants had acted with the intent to cause copyright violations. (Grokster later settled this dispute out of court and stopped distributing its software.) Essentially, this means that file-sharing companies that have taken affirmative steps to promote copyright infringement can be held secondarily liable for millions of infringing acts that their users commit daily. Because the Court did not define exactly what is necessary to impose liability, however, a substantial amount of legal uncertainty remains concerning this issue. Although some file-sharing companies have been shut down, illegal file-sharing—and lawsuits against file-sharing companies and the individuals who use them—has continued in the years since this decision.

In the following case, six recording companies filed a suit against an individual user, charging her with copyright infringement for downloading eight songs without the owners' consent.

CASE 5.4   Sony BMG Music Entertainment v. Villarreal

United States District Court, Middle District of Georgia, Macon Division, ___ F.Supp.2d ___ (2007).

FACTS Sony BMG Music Entertainment, UMG Recordings, Inc., Warner Bros. Records Inc., Virgin Records America, Inc., Capitol Records, Inc., and BMG Music are the copyright owners or licensees of rights to certain sound recordings. In September 2006, these companies filed a suit in a federal district court against Sharon Villarreal, alleging copyright infringement. The plaintiffs complained that Villarreal "has, without the permission or consent of Plaintiffs, used (and continues to use) an online media distribution system to download Plaintiffs' copyrighted recordings, to distribute the copyrighted recordings to the public, and/or to make the copyrighted recordings available for distribution to others." The plaintiffs claimed that Villarreal had downloaded and distributed, or made available for distribution, eight of their recordings, including "Goodbye Earl" by the Dixie Chicks, "I Got a Girl" by Lou Bega, "A Long December" by the Counting Crows, "Black Balloon" by the Goo Goo Dolls, "Like a Virgin" by Madonna, "Steal My Kisses" by Ben Harper, "Another Brick in the Wall, Pt. 2" by Pink Floyd, and "I Might Get Over You" by Kenny Chesney. Villarreal was notified of the complaint but did not respond. The plaintiffs asked the court to enter a default judgment in their favor, to award damages and costs, and to issue an injunction against Villarreal.

ISSUE Were the copyright owners and licensees entitled to a judgment in their favor and the relief that they sought?

DECISION Yes. "Having considered Plaintiffs' well-pleaded allegations in this case, the Court does find a sufficient basis in the Complaint for a judgment to be entered in Plaintiffs' favor for violations of the Copyright Act."

REASON The court recognized that a defendant's failure to respond to a complaint or appear before a court should not be "treated as an absolute confession of the defendant of [her] liability and of the plaintiff's right to recover." In this case, the plaintiffs' complaint was clear, their allegations stated a claim for copyright infringement, "[a]nd, of course, by her default in this case, Defendant has admitted these allegations as true." The court determined that the plaintiffs were entitled to $6,000 in damages under the Copyright Act—the minimum

CASE 5.4—Continued

statutory provision of $750 for each of the eight songs infringed—plus $490 for the costs of bringing the suit. Villarreal was also enjoined from "directly or indirectly" infringing on the plaintiffs' rights in their recordings through the use of "the Internet or any online media distribution system" and ordered to destroy all of her copies of the downloaded songs. "Defendant's past and current conduct has and will, unless enjoined, cause Plaintiffs irreparable injury that cannot be fully compensated or

measured in money." Thus "an injunction barring Defendant from infringing upon all of Plaintiffs' copyrighted recordings, and not just those eight recordings listed herein, is appropriate. For the same reasons, * * * the injunction entered in this case should likewise cover works created in the future."

 FOR CRITICAL ANALYSIS—Social Consideration *What interest does the public have in upholding copyright law and granting the sort of relief that was awarded in this case? Explain.*

TRADE SECRETS

The law of trade secrets protects some business processes and information that are not or cannot be patented, copyrighted, or trademarked against appropriation by a competitor. **Trade secrets** include customer lists, plans, research and development, pricing information, marketing techniques, production methods, and generally anything that makes an individual company unique and that would have value to a competitor.

Unlike copyright and trademark protection, protection of trade secrets extends both to ideas and to their expression. (For this reason, and because a trade secret involves no registration or filing requirements, trade secret protection may be well suited for software.) Of course, the secret formula, method, or other information must be disclosed to some persons, particularly to key employees. Businesses generally attempt to protect their trade secrets by having all employees who use the process or information agree in their contracts, or in confidentiality agreements, never to divulge it. See the *Application* feature at the end of this chapter for more advice on how a business can protect its trade secrets.

> **TRADE SECRETS**
> Information or processes that give a business an advantage over competitors that do not know the information or processes.

State and Federal Law on Trade Secrets

Under Section 757 of the *Restatement of Torts*, those who disclose or use another's trade secret, without authorization, are liable to that other party if (1) they discovered the secret by improper means or (2) their disclosure or use constitutes a breach of a duty owed to the other party. The theft of confidential business data by industrial espionage, as when a business taps into a competitor's computer, is a theft of trade secrets without any contractual violation and is actionable in itself.

Until nearly thirty years ago, virtually all law with respect to trade secrets was common law. In an effort to reduce the unpredictability of the common law in this area, a model act, the Uniform Trade Secrets Act, was presented to the states for adoption in 1979. Parts of this act have been adopted in more than thirty states. Typically, a state that has adopted parts of the act has adopted only those parts that encompass its own existing common law. Additionally, in 1996 Congress passed the Economic Espionage Act, which made the theft of trade secrets a federal crime. We will examine the provisions and significance of this act in Chapter 6, in the context of crimes related to business.

Trade Secrets in Cyberspace

The nature of new computer technology undercuts a business firm's ability to protect its confidential information, including trade secrets.[32] For instance, a dishonest employee could

> **ON THE WEB**
>
> The Cyberspace Law Institute offers articles and information on such topics as trade secrets at
>
> **www.cli.org**.

---

32. Note that the courts have even found that customers' e-mail addresses may constitute trade secrets. See *T-N-T Motorsports, Inc. v. Hennessey Motorsports, Inc.*, 965 S.W.2d 18 (Tex.App.—Houston [1 Dist.] 1998); rehearing overruled (1998); petition dismissed (1998).

e-mail trade secrets in a company's computer to a competitor or a future employer. If e-mail is not an option, the employee might walk out with the information on a flash pen drive.

INTERNATIONAL PROTECTION FOR INTELLECTUAL PROPERTY

For many years, the United States has been a party to various international agreements relating to intellectual property rights. For example, the Paris Convention of 1883, to which about 169 countries are signatory, allows parties in one country to file for patent and trademark protection in any of the other member countries. Other international agreements include the Berne Convention and the Trade-Related Aspects of Intellectual Property Rights, or, more simply, TRIPS agreement. For a discussion of a treaty that allows a company to register its trademark in foreign nations with a single application, see this chapter's *Beyond Our Borders* feature.

The Berne Convention

Under the Berne Convention of 1886, an international copyright agreement, if a U.S. citizen writes a book, every country that has signed the convention must recognize the U.S. author's copyright in the book. Also, if a citizen of a country that has not signed the convention first publishes a book in one of the 162 countries that have signed, all other countries that have signed the convention must recognize that author's copyright. Copyright notice is not needed to gain protection under the Berne Convention for works published after March 1, 1989.

This convention and other international agreements have given some protection to intellectual property on a worldwide level. None of them, however, has been as significant and far reaching in scope as the agreement discussed next.

The TRIPS Agreement

Representatives from more than one hundred nations signed the TRIPS agreement in 1994. The agreement established, for the first time, standards for the international protection of intellectual property rights, including patents, trademarks, and copyrights for movies, computer programs, books, and music. The TRIPS agreement provides that each member country must include in its domestic laws broad intellectual property rights and effective remedies (including civil and criminal penalties) for violations of those rights.

Members Cannot Discriminate against Foreign Intellectual Property Owners
Generally, the TRIPS agreement forbids member nations from discriminating against foreign owners of intellectual property rights (in the administration, regulation, or adjudication of such rights). In other words, a member nation cannot give its own nationals (citizens) favorable treatment without offering the same treatment to nationals of all member countries. For instance, if a U.S. software manufacturer brings a suit for the infringement of intellectual property rights under a member nation's national laws, the U.S. manufacturer is entitled to receive the same treatment as a domestic manufacturer. Each member nation must also ensure that legal procedures are available for parties who wish to bring actions for infringement of intellectual property rights. Additionally, a related document established a mechanism for settling disputes among member nations.

Despite the Chinese government's periodic crackdowns, imitation designer goods are openly sold at the Xiangyang Fashion Market in Shanghai. What agreement has been the most significant in the effort to protect intellectual property rights internationally? (Emily Walker/ Creative Commons)

 **BEYOND OUR BORDERS** The Madrid Protocol

In the past, one of the difficulties in protecting U.S. trademarks internationally was that it was time consuming and expensive to apply for trademark registration in foreign countries. The filing fees and procedures for trademark registration vary significantly among individual countries. The Madrid Protocol, however, which President George W. Bush signed into law in the fall of 2003, may help to resolve these problems. The Madrid Protocol is an international treaty that has been signed by sixty-eight countries. Under its provisions, a U.S. company wishing to register its trademark abroad can submit a single application and designate other member countries in which it would like to register the mark. The treaty is designed to reduce the costs of obtaining international trademark protection by more than 60 percent, according to proponents.

Although the Madrid Protocol may simplify and reduce the cost of trademark registration in foreign nations, it remains to be seen whether it will provide significant benefits to trademark owners. Even with an easier registration process, the issue of whether member countries will enforce the law and protect the mark still remains.

 FOR CRITICAL ANALYSIS *What are some of the pros and cons of having an international standard for trademark protection?*

Covers All Types of Intellectual Property Particular provisions of the TRIPS agreement relate to patent, trademark, and copyright protection for intellectual property. The agreement specifically provides copyright protection for computer programs by stating that compilations of data, databases, or other materials are "intellectual creations" and that they are to be protected as copyrightable works. Other provisions relate to trade secrets and the rental of computer programs and cinematographic works.

REVIEWING **Intellectual Property and Internet Law**

 Two computer science majors, Trent and Xavier, have an idea for a new video game, which they propose to call "Hallowed." They form a business and begin developing their idea. Several months later, Trent and Xavier run into a problem with their design and consult with a friend, Brad, who is an expert in creating computer source codes. After the software is completed but before Hallowed is marketed, a video game called Halo 2 is released for both the Xbox and Game Cube systems. Halo 2 uses source codes similar to those of Hallowed and imitates Hallowed's overall look and feel, although not all the features are alike. Using the information presented in the chapter, answer the following questions.

1 Would the name "Hallowed" receive protection as a trademark or as trade dress?

2 If Trent and Xavier had obtained a business process patent on Hallowed, would the release of Halo 2 infringe on their patent? Why or why not?

3 Based only on the facts described above, could Trent and Xavier sue the makers of Halo 2 for copyright infringement? Why or why not?

4 Suppose that Trent and Xavier discover that Brad took the idea of Hallowed and sold it to the company that produced Halo 2. Which type of intellectual property issue does this raise?

Most successful businesses have trade secrets. The law protects trade secrets indefinitely, provided that the information is not generally known, is kept secret, and has commercial value. Sometimes, of course, a business needs to disclose secret information to a party in the course of conducting business. For example, a company may need to hire a consultant to revamp a computer system, an engineer to design a manufacturing system, or a marketing firm to implement a sales program. In addition, the company may also wish to expand its operations and will need a foreign agent or distributor. All of these individuals or firms may need access to some of the company's trade secrets. One way to protect against the unauthorized disclosure of such information is through confidentiality agreements.

Confidentiality Agreements

In a confidentiality agreement, one party promises not to divulge information about the other party to anyone else or to use the other party's confidential information for his or her own benefit. Confidentiality agreements are often included in licensing and employment contracts, but they can also be separate contracts. The key is to make sure that the agreement adequately protects the trade secrets and applies to any related transactions between the parties. For instance, if you execute a separate confidentiality agreement with a marketing firm, you need to make sure that it refers to any other contracts you have made with that firm prior to the confidentiality agreement. Also, subsequent contracts with the firm should either refer back to the confidentiality agreement or include a new confidentiality provision.

Defining the Scope of the Agreement

Confidentiality agreements must be reasonable. Business-persons should consider what information needs to be

protected and for how long. Make certain to define what you mean by *confidential information* in the agreement. Do you want to protect just your customer list or all financial, technical, and other business information? Think ahead, cover the bases, and be specific.

The duration of the agreement usually depends on the nature of the information. Very important secret information should remain confidential for a longer time than less important secrets. Sometimes, as with an advertising campaign, the time period for confidentiality may be self-evident (if the campaign ends in six months, for example). Tailor the agreement to your needs as much as possible. If the party to whom you are disclosing information will no longer need the information after a certain date—such as when the project is completed—include a provision requiring the return of confidential information after that date. This will alleviate concerns that your confidential trade secrets might later fall into the hands of a stranger.

CHECKLIST FOR THE
OWNER OF TRADE SECRETS

1. Determine what your trade secrets are and who may need access to them.
2. Make sure that confidentiality agreements define, in an all-inclusive manner, what information should be considered confidential.
3. Specify a time period that is reasonable under the circumstances.
4. Identify the agreements to which the confidentiality provisions apply.
5. Require that the confidential materials be returned to you after the project ends.

* This *Application* is not meant to substitute for the services of an attorney who is licensed to practice law in your state.

CHAPTER SUMMARY	Intellectual Property and Internet Law
Trademarks and Related Property (See pages 136–142.)	1. A *trademark* is a distinctive mark, motto, device, or emblem that a manufacturer stamps, prints, or otherwise affixes to the goods it produces so that they may be identified on the market and their origin vouched for. 2. The major federal statutes protecting trademarks and related property are the Lanham Act of 1946 and the Federal Trademark Dilution Act of 1995. Generally, to be protected, a trademark must be sufficiently distinctive from all competing trademarks. 3. *Trademark infringement* occurs when one uses a mark that is the same as, or confusingly similar to, the protected trademark, service mark, trade name, or trade dress of another without permission when marketing goods or services.
Cyber Marks (See pages 142–144.)	A *cyber mark* is a trademark in cyberspace. Trademark infringement in cyberspace occurs when one person uses, in a domain name or in meta tags, a name that is the same as, or confusingly similar to, the protected mark of another.
Patents (See pages 144–147.)	1. A *patent* is a grant from the government that gives an inventor the exclusive right to make, use, and sell an invention for a period of twenty years (fourteen years for a design patent) from the date of filing the application for a patent. To be patentable, an invention (or a discovery, process, or design) must be genuine, novel, useful, and not obvious in light of current technology. Computer software may be patented. 2. Almost anything is patentable, except (1) the laws of nature, (2) natural phenomena, and (3) abstract ideas (including algorithms). 3. *Patent infringement* occurs when one uses or sells another's patented design, product, or process without the patent owner's permission. The patent holder can sue the infringer in federal court and request an injunction, but must prove irreparable injury to obtain a permanent injunction against the infringer. The patent holder can also request damages and attorneys' fees; if the infringement was willful, the court can grant treble damages.
Copyrights (See pages 147–157.)	1. A *copyright* is an intangible property right granted by federal statute to the author or originator of certain literary or artistic productions. Computer software may be copyrighted. 2. *Copyright infringement* occurs whenever the form or expression of an idea is copied without the permission of the copyright holder. An exception applies if the copying is deemed a "fair use." 3. Copyrights are governed by the Copyright Act of 1976, as amended. To protect copyrights in digital information, Congress passed the No Electronic Theft Act of 1997 and the Digital Millennium Copyright Act of 1998. 4. Technology that allows users to share files via the Internet on distributed networks often raises copyright infringement issues. 5. The United States Supreme Court has ruled that companies that provide file-sharing software to users can be held liable for contributory and vicarious copyright liability if they take affirmative steps to promote copyright infringement.
Trade Secrets (See pages 157–158.)	*Trade secrets* include customer lists, plans, research and development, and pricing information, for example. Trade secrets are protected under the common law and, in some states, under statutory law against misappropriation by competitors. The Economic Espionage Act of 1996 made the theft of trade secrets a federal crime (see Chapter 6).

(Continued)

CHAPTER SUMMARY Intellectual Property and Internet Law–Continued

International Protection for Intellectual Property (See pages 158–159.)	Various international agreements provide international protection for intellectual property. A landmark agreement is the 1994 agreement on Trade-Related Aspects of Intellectual Property Rights (TRIPS), which provides for enforcement procedures in all countries signatory to the agreement.

FOR REVIEW

Answers for the even-numbered questions in this **For Review** *section can be found in Appendix E at the end of this text.*

1 What is intellectual property?

2 Why are trademarks and patents protected by the law?

3 What laws protect authors' rights in the works they generate?

4 What are trade secrets, and what laws offer protection for this form of intellectual property?

5 What steps have been taken to protect intellectual property rights in today's digital age?

 The following multiple-choice question is representative of the types of questions available in one of the four sections of ThomsonNOW for *Business Law Today.* **ThomsonNOW also provides feedback for each response option, whether correct or incorrect, and refers to the location within the chapter where the correct answer can be found.**

Trademark dilution laws protect against the

   a unauthorized use of a mark by a competitor only.

   b unauthorized use of a mark regardless of whether the user is a competitor.

   c unauthorized use of a patent.

   d authorized use of trade dress, in some cases.

QUESTIONS AND CASE PROBLEMS

 **HYPOTHETICAL SCENARIOS**

5.1 Patent Infringement. John and Andrew Doney invented a hard-bearing device for balancing rotors. Although they registered their invention with the U.S. Patent and Trademark Office, it was never used as an automobile wheel balancer. Some time later, Exetron Corp. produced an automobile wheel balancer that used a hard-bearing device with a support plate similar to that of the Doneys. Given that the Doneys had not used their device for automobile wheel balancing, does Exetron's use of a similar hard-bearing device infringe on the Doneys' patent?

5.2 Hypothetical Question with Sample Answer. In which of the following situations would a court likely hold Maruta liable for copyright infringement?

   1 At the library, Maruta photocopies ten pages from a scholarly journal relating to a topic on which she is writing a term paper.

   2 Maruta makes leather handbags and sells them in her small leather shop. She advertises her handbags as "Vutton handbags," hoping that customers might mistakenly assume that they were made by Vuitton, the well-known maker of high-quality luggage and handbags.

   3 Maruta owns a video store. She purchases one copy of several popular movie DVDs from various distributors. Then, using blank DVDs, she burns copies of the movies to rent or sell to her customers.

   4 Maruta teaches Latin American history at a small university. She has a videocassette recorder and frequently tapes television programs relating to Latin America. She then takes the videos to her classroom so that her students can watch them.

 **For a sample answer to Question 5.2, go to Appendix F at the end of this text.**

CASE PROBLEMS

5.3 Trademark Infringement. Elvis Presley Enterprises, Inc. (EPE), owns all of the trademarks of the Elvis Presley estate. None of these marks is registered for use in the restaurant business. Barry Capece registered "The Velvet Elvis" as a service mark for a restaurant and tavern with the U.S. Patent and Trademark Office. Capece opened a nightclub called "The Velvet Elvis" with a menu, decor, advertising, and promotional events that evoked Elvis Presley and his music. EPE filed a suit in a federal district court against Capece and others, claiming, among other things, that "The Velvet Elvis" service mark infringed on EPE's trademarks. During the trial, witnesses testified that they thought the bar was associated with Elvis Presley. Should Capece be ordered to stop using "The Velvet Elvis" mark? Why or why not? [*Elvis Presley Enterprises, Inc. v. Capece*, 141 F.3d 188 (5th Cir. 1998)]

5.4 Trademark Infringement. A&H Sportswear, Inc., a swimsuit maker, obtained a trademark for its MIRACLESUIT in 1992. The MIRACLESUIT design makes the wearer appear slimmer. The MIRACLESUIT was widely advertised and discussed in the media. The MIRACLESUIT was also sold for a brief time in the Victoria's Secret (VS) catalogue, which is published by Victoria's Secret Catalogue, Inc. In 1993, Victoria's Secret Stores, Inc., began selling a cleavage-enhancing bra, which was named THE MIRACLE BRA and for which a trademark was obtained. The next year, THE MIRACLE BRA swimwear debuted in the VS catalogue and stores. A&H filed a suit in a federal district court against VS Stores and VS Catalogue, alleging in part that the miracle bra mark, when applied to swimwear, infringed on the miraclesuit mark. A&H argued that there was a "possibility of confusion" between the marks. The VS entities contended that the appropriate standard was "likelihood of confusion" and that, in this case, there was no likelihood of confusion. In whose favor will the court rule, and why? [*A&H Sportswear, Inc. v. Victoria's Secret Stores, Inc.*, 166 F.3d 197 (3d Cir. 1999)]

5.5 Patent Infringement. As a cattle rancher in Nebraska, Gerald Gohl used handheld searchlights to find and help calving animals (animals giving birth) in harsh blizzard conditions. Gohl thought that it would be more helpful to have a portable searchlight mounted on the outside of a vehicle and remotely controlled. He and Al Gebhardt developed and patented practical applications of this idea—the Golight and the wireless, remote-controlled Radio Ray, which could rotate 360 degrees—and formed Golight, Inc., to make and market these products. In 1997, Wal-Mart Stores, Inc., began selling a portable, wireless, remote-controlled searchlight that was identical to the Radio Ray except for a stop piece that prevented the light from rotating more than 351 degrees. Golight sent Wal-Mart a letter, claiming that its device infringed Golight's patent. Wal-Mart sold its remaining inventory of the devices and stopped carrying the product. Golight filed a suit in a federal district court against Wal-Mart, alleging patent infringement. How should the court rule? Explain. [*Golight, Inc. v. Wal-Mart Stores, Inc.*, 355 F.3d 1327 (Fed. Cir. 2004)]

5.6 Case Problem with Sample Answer. Gateway, Inc., sells computers, computer products, computer peripherals, and computer accessories throughout the world. By 1988, Gateway had begun its first national advertising campaign using black-and-white cows and black-and-white cow spots. By 1991, black-and-white cows and spots had become Gateway's symbol. The next year, Gateway registered a black-and-white cow-spots design in association with computers and computer peripherals as its trademark. Companion Products, Inc. (CPI), sells stuffed animals trademarked as "Stretch Pets." Stretch Pets have an animal's head and an elastic body that can wrap around the edges of computer monitors, computer cases, or televisions. CPI produces sixteen Stretch Pets, including a polar bear, a moose, several dogs, and a penguin. One of CPI's top-selling products is a black-and-white cow that CPI identifies as "Cody Cow," which was first sold in 1999. Gateway filed a suit in a federal district court against CPI, alleging trade dress infringement and related claims. What is "trade dress"? What is the major factor in cases involving trade dress infringement? Does that factor exist in this case? Explain. [*Gateway, Inc. v. Companion Products, Inc.*, 384 F.3d 503 (8th Cir. 2004)]

After you have answered Problem 5.6, compare your answer with the sample answer given on the Web site that accompanies this text. Go to www.thomsonedu.com/westbuslaw/blt, select "Chapter 5," and click on "Case Problem with Sample Answer."

5.7 Trade Secrets. Briefing.com offers Internet-based analyses of investment opportunities to investors. Richard Green is the company's president. One of Briefing.com's competitors is StreetAccount, LLC (limited liability company), whose owners include Gregory Jones and Cynthia Dietzmann. Jones worked for Briefing.com for six years until he quit in March 2003, and he was a member of its board of directors until April 2003. Dietzmann worked for Briefing.com for seven years until she quit in March 2003. As Briefing.com employees, Jones and Dietzmann had access to confidential business data. For instance, Dietzmann developed a list of contacts through which Briefing.com obtained market information to display online. When Dietzmann quit, however, she did not return all of the contact information to the company. Briefing.com and Green filed a suit in a federal district court against Jones, Dietzmann, and StreetAccount, alleging that they appropriated these data and other "trade secrets" to form a competing business. What are trade secrets? Why are they protected? Under what circumstances is a party liable at common law for their appropriation? How should these principles apply in this case? [*Briefing.com v. Jones*, 2006 WY 16, 126 P.3d 928 (2006)]

5.8 Trademarks. In 1969, Jack Masquelier, a professor of pharmacology, discovered a chemical antioxidant made from the bark of a French pine tree. The substance supposedly assists in nutritional distribution and blood circulation. Horphag Research, Ltd., began to sell the product under the name Pycnogenol, which Horphag registered as a trademark in 1993. Pycnogenol became one of the fifteen best-selling herbal supplements in the United States. In 1999, through the Web site **healthierlife.com**, Larry Garcia began to sell Masquelier's Original OPCs, a supplement derived from grape pits. Claiming that this product was the "true Pycnogenol," Garcia used the mark as a meta tag and a generic term, attributing the results of research on Horphag's product to Masquelier's and altering quotes in scientific literature to substitute the name of Masquelier's product for Horphag's. Customers contacted Horphag, after buying Garcia's product, to learn that it was not Horphag's product. Others called Horphag to ask whether Garcia "was selling . . . real Pycnogenol." Horphag filed a suit in a federal district court against Garcia, alleging in part that he was diluting Horphag's mark. What is trademark dilution? Did it occur here? Explain. [*Horphag Research, Ltd. v. Garcia,* 475 F.3d 1029 (9th Cir. 2007)]

5.9 **A Question of Ethics.** *Custom Copies, Inc., in Gainesville, Florida, is a copy shop, reproducing and distributing, for profit, on request, material published and owned by others. One of the copy shop's primary activities is the preparation and sale of coursepacks, which contain compi-*lations of readings for college courses. For a particular coursepack, a teacher selects the readings and delivers a syllabus to the copy shop, which obtains the materials from a library and copies them, and then binds and sells the copies. Blackwell Publishing, Inc., in Malden, Massachusetts, publishes books and journals in medicine and other fields and owns the copyrights to these publications. Blackwell and others filed a suit in a federal district court against Custom Copies, alleging copyright infringement for its "routine and systematic reproduction of materials from plaintiffs' publications, without seeking permission," to compile coursepacks for classes at the University of Florida. The plaintiffs asked the court to issue an injunction and award them damages, as well as the profit from the infringement. The defendant filed a motion to dismiss the complaint. [Blackwell Publishing, Inc. v. Custom Copies, Inc., __ F.Supp.2d __ (N.D. Fla. 2007)]*

1 Custom Copies argued in part that it did not "distribute" the coursepacks. Does a copy shop violate copyright law if it only copies materials for coursepacks? Does the copying fall under the "fair use" exception? Should the court grant the defendants' motion? Why or why not?

2 What is the potential impact if copies of a book or journal are created and sold without the permission of, and the payment of royalties or a fee to, the copyright owner? Explain.

 CRITICAL THINKING AND WRITING ASSIGNMENTS

5.10 Critical Legal Thinking. In the United States, patent protection is granted to the first person to invent a given product or process, even though another person may be the first to file for a patent on the same product or process. What are the advantages of this patenting procedure? Can you think of any disadvantages? Explain.

5.11 Critical Thinking and Writing Assignment for Business. Delta Computers, Inc., makes computer-related products under the brand name "Delta," which the company registers as a trademark. Without Delta's permission, E-Product Corp. embeds the Delta mark in E-Product's Web site, in black type on a blue background. This tag causes the E-Product site to be returned at the top of the list of results on a search engine query for "Delta." Does E-Product's use of the Delta mark as a meta tag without Delta's permission constitute trademark infringement? Explain.

5.12 Case Analysis Question. Go to Appendix G at the end of this text and examine Case No. 2 [*New York Times v. Tasini,* 533 U.S. 483, 121 S.Ct. 2381, 150 L.Ed.2d 500 (2001)]. This case has been excerpted there in great detail. Review and then brief the case, making sure that your brief answers the following questions.

1 What was at the center of the dispute between the parties in the case?

2 Which side do you think has the better argument in this case? Why?

3 According to the United States Supreme Court, do publishers that want to put the contents of periodicals into e-databases and onto CD-ROMs or DVDs need to obtain the permission of the writers whose contributions are included?

4 The Copyright Act of 1976 was enacted before the Internet and online databases became widely used. Should the act apply to the uses of copyrighted materials at issue in this case? Explain.

5 When rights such as those in this case become more valuable as a result of new technology, should the law be changed to redistribute the economic benefit of those rights? Why or why not?

5.13 **Video Question.** Go to this text's Web site at <u>www.thomsonedu.com/westbuslaw/blt</u> and select "Chapter 5." Click on "Video Questions" and view the video titled *The Jerk.* Then answer the following questions.

1 In the video, Navin (Steve Martin) creates a special handle for Fox's (Bill Macy's) glasses. Can Navin obtain a patent or a copyright protecting his invention? Explain your answer.

2 Suppose that after Navin legally protects his idea, Fox steals it and decides to develop it for himself, without Navin's permission. Has Fox committed infringement? If so, what kind: trademark, patent, or copyright?

3 Suppose that after Navin legally protects his idea, he realizes he doesn't have the funds to mass-produce the special handle. Navin therefore agrees to allow Fox to manufacture the product. Has Navin granted Fox a license? Explain.

4 Assume that Navin is able to manufacture his invention. What might Navin do to ensure that his product is identifiable and can be distinguished from other products on the market?

ONLINE ACTIVITIES

PRACTICAL INTERNET EXERCISES

Go to this text's Web site at **www.thomsonedu.com/westbuslaw/blt**, select "Chapter 5," and click on "Practical Internet Exercises." There you will find the following Internet research exercises that you can perform to learn more about the topics covered in this chapter.

PRACTICAL INTERNET EXERCISE 5-1 LEGAL PERSPECTIVE—Unwarranted Legal Threats

PRACTICAL INTERNET EXERCISE 5-2 TECHNOLOGICAL PERSPECTIVE—File-Sharing

PRACTICAL INTERNET EXERCISE 5-3 MANAGEMENT PERSPECTIVE—Protecting Intellectual Property across Borders

BEFORE THE TEST

Go to this text's Web site at **www.thomsonedu.com/westbuslaw/blt**, select "Chapter 5," and click on "Interactive Quizzes." You will find a number of interactive questions relating to this chapter.

CHAPTER 6
Criminal Law and Cyber Crimes

66 No state shall
. . . deprive any
person of life,
liberty, or
property without
due process of
law, nor deny to
any person
within its
jurisdiction the
equal protection
of the laws. **99**

Fourteenth Amendment to the
U.S. Constitution, July 28, 1868

LEARNING OBJECTIVES

AFTER READING THIS CHAPTER, YOU SHOULD BE ABLE TO
ANSWER THE FOLLOWING QUESTIONS:

1 What two elements must exist before a person can
be held liable for a crime? Can a corporation
commit crimes?

2 What are five broad categories of crimes? What is
white-collar crime?

3 What defenses might be raised by criminal
defendants to avoid liability for criminal acts?

4 What constitutional safeguards exist to protect
persons accused of crimes? What are the basic
steps in the criminal process?

5 What is cyber crime? What laws apply to crimes
committed in cyberspace?

V arious sanctions are used to bring about a society in which individuals engaging in
business can compete and flourish. These sanctions include damages for various
types of tortious conduct (as discussed in Chapter 4), damages for breach of contract (to
be discussed in Chapter 13), and the equitable remedies discussed in Chapter 1.
Additional sanctions are imposed under criminal law. Many statutes regulating business
provide for criminal as well as civil sanctions. Therefore, criminal law joins civil law as an
important element in the legal environment of business.

In this chapter, following a brief summary of the major differences between criminal
and civil law, we look at how crimes are classified and what elements must be present for
criminal liability to exist. We then examine various categories of crimes, the defenses that
can be raised to avoid liability for criminal actions, and criminal procedural law. Criminal
procedural law attempts to ensure that a criminal defendant's right to "due process of law"
is enforced. This right is guaranteed by the Fourteenth Amendment to the U.S.
Constitution, as stated in the chapter-opening quotation.

Since the advent of computer networks and, more recently, the Internet, new types of
crimes or new variations of traditional crimes have been committed in cyberspace. For
that reason, they are often referred to as **cyber crimes.** Generally, cyber crime refers more
to the way particular crimes are committed than to a new category of crimes. We devote
the concluding pages of this chapter to a discussion of this increasingly significant area of
criminal activity.

CYBER CRIME
A crime that occurs online, in the
virtual community of the Internet,
as opposed to the physical world.

CIVIL LAW AND CRIMINAL LAW

Remember from Chapter 1 that *civil law* spells out the duties that exist between persons or between persons and their governments, excluding the duty not to commit crimes. Contract law, for example, is part of civil law. The whole body of tort law, which deals with the infringement by one person on the legally recognized rights of another, is also an area of civil law.

Criminal law, in contrast, has to do with crime. A **crime** can be defined as a wrong against society proclaimed in a statute and, if committed, punishable by society through fines and/or imprisonment—and, in some cases, death. As mentioned in Chapter 1, because crimes are *offenses against society as a whole*, they are prosecuted by a public official, such as a district attorney (D.A.), not by victims. Victims often report the crime to the police, but it is ultimately the D.A.'s office that decides whether to file criminal charges and to what extent to pursue the prosecution or carry out additional investigation.

CRIME
A wrong against society proclaimed in a statute and, if committed, punishable by society through fines and/or imprisonment—and, in some cases, death.

Key Differences between Civil Law and Criminal Law

Because the state has extensive resources at its disposal when prosecuting criminal cases, there are numerous procedural safeguards to protect the rights of defendants. We look here at one of these safeguards—the higher burden of proof that applies in a criminal case—as well as the harsher sanctions for criminal acts as compared to civil wrongs. Exhibit 6–1 summarizes these and other key differences between civil law and criminal law.

Burden of Proof   In a civil case, the plaintiff usually must prove his or her case by a *preponderance of the evidence*. Under this standard, the plaintiff must convince the court that, based on the evidence presented by both parties, it is more likely than not that the plaintiff's allegation is true.

In a criminal case, in contrast, the state must prove its case **beyond a reasonable doubt.** If the jury views the evidence in the case as reasonably permitting either a guilty or a not guilty verdict, then the jury's verdict must be *not* guilty. In other words, the government (prosecutor) must prove beyond a reasonable doubt that the defendant has committed every essential element of the offense with which she or he is charged. If the jurors are not convinced of the defendant's guilt beyond a reasonable doubt, they must find the defendant not guilty. Note also that in a criminal case, the jury's verdict normally must be unanimous—agreed to by all members of the jury—to convict the defendant. (In a civil trial by jury, in contrast, typically only three-fourths of the jurors need to agree.)

The higher burden of proof in criminal cases reflects a fundamental social value—the belief that it is worse to convict an innocent individual than to let a guilty person go free. We will look at other safeguards later in the chapter, in the context of criminal procedure.

BEYOND A REASONABLE DOUBT
The standard of proof used in criminal cases. If there is any reasonable doubt that a criminal defendant committed the crime with which she or he has been charged, then the verdict must be "not guilty."

EXHIBIT 6–1	Key Differences between Civil Law and Criminal Law	
ISSUE	**CIVIL LAW**	**CRIMINAL LAW**
Party who brings suit	Person who suffered harm	The state
Wrongful act	Causing harm to a person or to a person's property	Violating a statute that prohibits some type of activity
Burden of proof	Preponderance of the evidence	Beyond a reasonable doubt
Verdict	Three-fourths majority (typically)	Unanimous
Remedy	Damages to compensate for the harm or a decree to achieve an equitable result	Punishment (fine, imprisonment, or death)

Criminal Sanctions The sanctions imposed on criminal wrongdoers are also harsher than those that are applied in civil cases. Remember from Chapter 4 that the purpose of tort law is to allow persons harmed by the wrongful acts of others to obtain compensation from the wrongdoer rather than to punish the wrongdoer. In contrast, criminal sanctions are designed to punish those who commit crimes and to deter others from committing similar acts in the future. Criminal sanctions include fines as well as the much harsher penalty of the loss of one's liberty by incarceration in a jail or prison. The harshest criminal sanction is, of course, the death penalty.

Civil Liability for Criminal Acts

Some torts, such as assault and battery, provide a basis for a criminal prosecution as well as a tort action. **EXAMPLE 6.1** Joe is walking down the street, minding his own business, when suddenly a person attacks him. In the ensuing struggle, the attacker stabs Joe several times, seriously injuring him. A police officer restrains and arrests the wrongdoer. In this situation, the attacker may be subject both to criminal prosecution by the state and to a tort lawsuit brought by Joe. ■ Exhibit 6–2 illustrates how the same act can result in both a tort action and a criminal action against the wrongdoer.

CRIMINAL LIABILITY

Two elements must exist simultaneously for a person to be convicted of a crime: (1) the performance of a prohibited act and (2) a specified state of mind or intent on the part of the actor. Additionally, to establish criminal liability, there must be a *concurrence* between the act and the intent. In other words, these two elements must occur together.

EXHIBIT 6–2 Tort Lawsuit and Criminal Prosecution for the Same Act

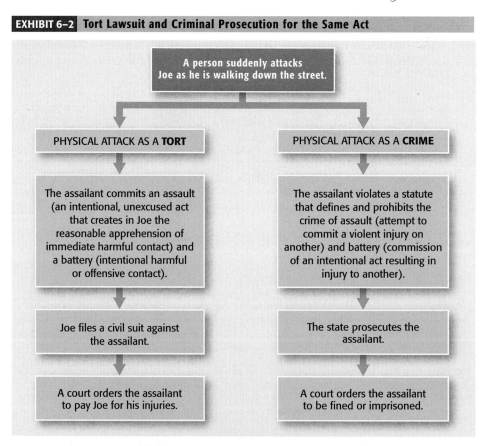

The Criminal Act

Every criminal statute prohibits certain behavior. Most crimes require an act of *commission*; that is, a person must *do* something in order to be accused of a crime. In criminal law, a prohibited act is referred to as the ***actus reus***,[1] or guilty act. In some situations, an act of *omission* can be a crime, but only when a person has a legal duty to perform the omitted act, such as failing to file a tax return. For instance, in 2005 the federal government filed a criminal action against the former winner of the reality TV show *Survivor* for failing to report to the Internal Revenue Service more than $1 million in winnings.

The *guilty act* requirement is based on one of the premises of criminal law—that a person is punished for harm done to society. For a crime to exist, the guilty act must cause some harm to a person or to property. Thinking about killing someone or about stealing a car may be wrong, but the thoughts do no harm until they are translated into action. Of course, a person can be punished for attempting murder or robbery, but normally only if he or she took substantial steps toward the criminal objective.

State of Mind

A wrongful mental state (***mens rea***)[2] is generally required to establish criminal liability. What constitutes such a mental state varies according to the wrongful action. For murder, the act is the taking of a life, and the mental state is the intent to take life. For theft, the guilty act is the taking of another person's property, and the mental state involves both the knowledge that the property belongs to another and the intent to deprive the owner of it.

A guilty mental state can be attributed to acts of negligence or recklessness as well. *Criminal negligence* involves the mental state in which the defendant takes an unjustified, substantial, and foreseeable risk that results in harm. Under the Model Penal Code, a defendant is negligent even if she or he was not actually aware of the risk but *should have been aware* of it.[3] A defendant is criminally reckless if he or she consciously disregards a substantial and unjustifiable risk.

CORPORATE CRIMINAL LIABILITY

As will be discussed in Chapter 28, a *corporation* is a legal entity created under the laws of a state. Both the corporation as an entity and the individual directors and officers of the corporation are potentially subject to liability for criminal acts.

Liability of the Corporate Entity

At one time, it was thought that a corporation could not incur criminal liability because, although a corporation is a legal person, it can act only through its agents (corporate directors, officers, and employees). Therefore, the corporate entity itself could not "intend" to commit a crime. Under modern criminal law, however, a corporation may be held liable for crimes. Obviously, corporations cannot be imprisoned, but they can be fined or denied certain legal privileges (such as a license).

Today, corporations are normally liable for the crimes committed by their agents and employees within the course and scope of their employment.[4] For such criminal liability to be imposed, the prosecutor normally must show that the corporation could have prevented the act or that there was authorized consent to, or knowledge of, the act by persons

ACTUS REUS
A guilty (prohibited) act. The commission of a prohibited act is one of the two essential elements required for criminal liability, the other element being the intent to commit a crime.

MENS REA
Mental state, or intent. A wrongful mental state is as necessary as a wrongful act to establish criminal liability. What constitutes a mental state varies according to the wrongful action. Thus, for murder, the *mens rea* is the intent to take a life.

ON THE WEB

Many state criminal codes are now online. To find your state's code, go to **www.findlaw.com** and select "State" under the link to "US Laws: Cases and Codes."

---

1. Pronounced *ak*-tuhs *ray*-uhs.
2. Pronounced *mehns ray*-uh.
3. Model Penal Code Section 2.02(2)(d).
4. See Model Penal Code Section 2.07.

in supervisory positions within the corporation. In addition, corporations can be criminally liable for failing to perform specific duties imposed by law (such as duties under environmental laws or securities laws).

Liability of Corporate Officers and Directors

Corporate directors and officers are personally liable for the crimes they commit, regardless of whether the crimes were committed for their personal benefit or on the corporation's behalf. Additionally, corporate directors and officers may be held liable for the actions of employees under their supervision. Under what has become known as the *responsible corporate officer doctrine*, a court may impose criminal liability on a corporate officer regardless of whether she or he participated in, directed, or even knew about a given criminal violation.

■**EXAMPLE 6.2** In *United States v. Park*,[5] the chief executive officer of a national supermarket chain was held personally liable for sanitation violations in corporate warehouses, in which the food was exposed to contamination by rodents. The United States Supreme Court upheld the imposition of personal liability on the corporate officer not because he intended the crime or even knew about it but because he was in a "responsible relationship" to the corporation and had the power to prevent the violation. ■ Since the *Park* decision, courts have applied the responsible corporate officer doctrine on a number of occasions to hold corporate officers liable for their employees' statutory violations.

PREVENTING LEGAL DISPUTES

Because corporate officers and directors can be held liable for the crimes of their subordinates, the former should always be aware of any criminal statutes relevant to their particular industry or trade. In addition, firms would be wise to train their employees in how to comply with the multitude of applicable laws, particularly environmental laws and health and safety regulations, which frequently involve criminal sanctions.

■

TYPES OF CRIMES

The number of acts that are defined as criminal is nearly endless. Federal, state, and local laws provide for the classification and punishment of hundreds of thousands of different criminal acts. Traditionally, though, crimes have been grouped into five broad categories, or types: violent crime (crimes against persons), property crime, public order crime, white-collar crime, and organized crime. Within each of these categories, crimes may also be separated into more than one classification. Cyber crime—which consists of crimes committed in cyberspace with the use of computers—is, as mentioned earlier in this chapter, less a category of crime than a new way to commit crime. We will examine cyber crime later in this chapter.

Violent Crime

Crimes against persons, because they cause others to suffer harm or death, are referred to as *violent crimes*. Murder is a violent crime. So is sexual assault, or rape. Assault and battery, which were discussed in Chapter 4 in the context of tort law, are also classified as violent crimes. **Robbery**—defined as the taking of cash, personal property, or any other article of value from a person by means of force or fear—is another violent crime. Typically, states have more severe penalties for *aggravated robbery*—robbery with the use of a deadly weapon.

ROBBERY
The act of forcefully and unlawfully taking personal property of any value from another. Force or intimidation is usually necessary for an act of theft to be considered robbery.

—————————————

5. 421 U.S. 658, 95 S.Ct. 1903, 44 L.Ed.2d 489 (1975).

Each of these violent crimes is further classified by degree, depending on the circumstances surrounding the criminal act. These circumstances include the intent of the person committing the crime, whether a weapon was used, and (in cases other than murder) the level of pain and suffering experienced by the victim.

Property Crime

The most common type of criminal activity is property crime—crimes in which the goal of the offender is some form of economic gain or the damaging of property. Robbery is a form of property crime, as well as a violent crime, because the offender seeks to gain the property of another. We look here at a number of other crimes that fall within the general category of property crime.

This is a crime scene in Brockton, Massachusetts, a few years ago. The victim, a fifteen-year-old high school student, was shot and killed on a city street. Violent crime is the type of crime about which the public is most concerned, but is it the most common kind of crime committed? (AP Photo/Craig Murray/*The Enterprise*)

Burglary Traditionally, **burglary** was defined under the common law as breaking and entering the dwelling of another at night with the intent to commit a felony. Originally, the definition was aimed at protecting an individual's home and its occupants. Most state statutes have eliminated some of the requirements found in the common law definition. The time of day at which the breaking and entering occurs, for example, is usually immaterial. State statutes frequently omit the element of breaking, and some states do not require that the building be a dwelling. When a deadly weapon is used in a burglary, the person can be charged with *aggravated burglary* and punished more severely.

BURGLARY
The unlawful entry or breaking into a building with the intent to commit a felony. (Some state statutes expand this to include the intent to commit any crime.)

Larceny Under the common law, the crime of **larceny** involved the unlawful taking and carrying away of someone else's personal property with the intent to permanently deprive the owner of possession. Put simply, larceny is stealing or theft. Whereas robbery involves force or fear, larceny does not. Therefore, picking pockets is larceny. Similarly, taking company products and supplies home for personal use, if one is not authorized to do so, is larceny. (Note that a person who commits larceny generally can also be sued under tort law because the act of taking possession of another's property involves a trespass to personal property.)

LARCENY
The wrongful taking and carrying away of another person's personal property with the intent to permanently deprive the owner of the property. Some states classify larceny as either grand or petit, depending on the property's value.

Most states have expanded the definition of property that is subject to larceny statutes. Stealing computer programs may constitute larceny even though the "property" consists of magnetic impulses. Stealing computer time can also constitute larceny. So, too, can the theft of natural gas or Internet and television cable service. Trade secrets can be subject to larceny statutes.

A home damaged by Hurricane Katrina and subsequently looted. The sign facetiously thanks the perpetrator for "robbing" the property. Given the circumstances, is the crime committed here robbery, burglary, or some lesser property crime? (Goatling/Trista B/ Creative Commons)

This home in Florida was damaged by arson. If the owner of the home hired someone else to burn it down, what crimes has the owner committed? (Justin Griffith/Creative Commons)

ARSON
The intentional burning of another's dwelling. Some statutes have expanded this to include any real property regardless of ownership and the destruction of property by other means—for example, by explosion.

FORGERY
The fraudulent making or altering of any writing in a way that changes the legal rights and liabilities of another.

The common law distinguished between grand and petit larceny depending on the value of the property taken. Many states have abolished this distinction, but in those that have not, grand larceny (or theft) is a felony and petit larceny (or theft), is a misdemeanor.

Obtaining Goods by False Pretenses   It is a criminal act to obtain goods by means of false pretenses, such as buying groceries with a check knowing that one has insufficient funds to cover it or offering to sell someone a digital camera knowing that one does not actually own the camera. Statutes dealing with such illegal activities vary widely from state to state.

Receiving Stolen Goods   It is a crime to receive stolen goods. The recipient of such goods need not know the true identity of the owner or the thief. All that is necessary is that the recipient knows or should have known that the goods are stolen, which implies an intent to deprive the owner of those goods.

Arson   The willful and malicious burning of a building (and, in some states, personal property) owned by another is the crime of **arson.** At common law, arson traditionally applied only to burning down another person's house. The law was designed to protect human life. Today, arson statutes have been extended to cover the destruction of any building, regardless of ownership, by fire or explosion.

Every state has a special statute that covers the act of burning a building for the purpose of collecting insurance. **■EXAMPLE 6.3** If Smith owns an insured apartment building that is falling apart and sets fire to it himself or pays someone else to do so, he is guilty not only of arson but also of defrauding the insurer, which is attempted larceny. ■ Of course, the insurer need not pay the claim when insurance fraud is proved.

Forgery   The fraudulent making or altering of any writing in a way that changes the legal rights and liabilities of another is **forgery.** **■EXAMPLE 6.4** Without authorization, Severson signs Bennett's name to the back of a check made out to Bennett and attempts to cash it. Severson has committed the crime of forgery. ■ Forgery also includes changing trademarks, falsifying public records, counterfeiting, and altering a legal document.

Public Order Crime

Historically, societies have always outlawed activities that are considered to be contrary to public values and morals. Today, the most common public order crimes include public drunkenness, prostitution, gambling, and illegal drug use. These crimes are sometimes referred to as victimless crimes because they normally harm only the offender. From a broader perspective, however, they are deemed detrimental to society as a whole because they may create an environment that gives rise to property and violent crimes.

White-Collar Crime

WHITE-COLLAR CRIME
Nonviolent crime committed by individuals or corporations to obtain a personal or business advantage.

Crimes that typically occur only in the business context are popularly referred to as **white-collar crimes.** Although there is no official definition of white-collar crime, the term is commonly used to mean an illegal act or series of acts committed by an individual or business entity using some nonviolent means. Usually, this kind of crime is committed in the course of a legitimate occupation. Corporate crimes fall into this category. In addition,

When Dennis Kozlowski was running Tyco International, he often threw lavish parties. On the left, he is shown at one such party for his wife's birthday on the island of Sardinia. Of the $2 million spent on the party, Tyco International—that is, the shareholders—paid for half of it. Eventually, Kozlowski was convicted of twenty-two counts of grand larceny, totaling more than $150 million in unauthorized bonuses. In addition, he was convicted of fraud involving more than $400 million. In 2005, he was sentenced to eight and one-third years in prison, and he could serve up to twenty-five years. What general type of crime did he commit?
(Left photo, AP Photo; Right photo, The Smoking Gun)

certain property crimes, such as larceny and forgery, may also be white-collar crimes if they occur within the business context.

Embezzlement When a person who is entrusted with another person's property or money fraudulently appropriates it, **embezzlement** occurs. Typically, embezzlement is carried out by an employee who steals funds. Banks are particularly prone to this problem, but embezzlement can occur in any firm. In a number of businesses, corporate officers or accountants have fraudulently converted funds for their own benefit and then "jimmied" the books to cover up their crime. Embezzlement is not larceny, because the wrongdoer does not physically take the property from the possession of another, and it is not robbery, because force or fear is not used.

It does not matter whether the accused takes the funds from the victim or from a third person. If the financial officer of a large corporation pockets checks from third parties that were given to her to deposit into the corporate account, she is embezzling. Frequently, an embezzler takes a relatively small amount at one time but does so repeatedly over a long period. This might be done by underreporting income or deposits and embezzling the remaining amount, for example, or by creating fictitious persons or accounts and writing checks to them from the corporate account.

Practically speaking, an embezzler who returns what has been taken might not be prosecuted because the owner is unwilling to take the time to make a complaint, cooperate with the state's investigative efforts, and appear in court. Also, the owner may not want the crime to become public knowledge. Nevertheless, the intent to return the embezzled property is not a defense to the crime of embezzlement.

EMBEZZLEMENT
The fraudulent appropriation of funds or other property by a person to whom the funds or property has been entrusted.

To avoid potential embezzlement by corporate officers and employees, businesspersons should limit access to the firm's financial information and accounts. In addition, because embezzlement often takes place over a prolonged period of time, businesses should regularly conduct audits to discover and account for any discrepancies in the company's financial records.

PREVENTING LEGAL DISPUTES

Mail and Wire Fraud One of the most potent weapons against white-collar criminals is the Mail Fraud Act of 1990.[6] Under this act, it is a federal crime (mail fraud) to use the mails to defraud the public. Illegal use of the mails must involve (1) mailing or causing someone else to mail a writing—something written, printed, or photocopied—for the purpose of executing a scheme to defraud and (2) a contemplated or an organized scheme to defraud by false pretenses. If, for example, Johnson advertises by mail the sale of a cure for cancer that he knows to be fraudulent because it has no medical validity, he can be prosecuted for fraudulent use of the mails.

Federal law also makes it a crime to use wire (for example, the telephone), radio, or television transmissions to defraud.[7] Violators may be fined up to $1,000, imprisoned for up to five years, or both. If the violation affects a financial institution, the violator may be fined up to $1 million, imprisoned for up to thirty years, or both.

The following case involved charges of mail fraud in which funds misrepresented to support charities were acquired through telemarketing. The question was whether the prosecution could offer proof of the telemarketers' commission rate when no one had lied about it.

---

6. 18 U.S.C. Sections 1341–1342.
7. 18 U.S.C. Section 1343.

CASE 6.1 **United States v. Lyons**

United States Court of Appeals, Ninth Circuit, 472 F.3d 1055 (2007).

FACTS In 1994, in California, Gabriel Sanchez formed the First Church of Life (FCL), which had no congregation, services, or place of worship. Sanchez's friend Timothy Lyons formed a fundraising company called North American Acquisitions (NAA). Through FCL, Sanchez and Lyons set up six charities—AIDS Research Association, Children's Assistance Foundation, Cops and Sheriffs of America, Handicapped Youth Services, U.S. Firefighters, and U.S. Veterans League. NAA hired telemarketers to solicit donations on the charities' behalf. Over time, more than $6 million was raised, of which less than $5,000 was actually spent on charitable causes. The telemarketers kept 80 percent of the donated funds as commissions, and NAA took 10 percent. Most of the rest of the funds went to Sanchez, who spent it on himself. In 2002, Lyons and Sanchez were charged in a federal district court with mail fraud and other crimes. Throughout the trial, the prosecution referred to the high commissions paid to the telemarketers. The defendants were convicted, and each was sentenced to fifteen years' imprisonment. They asked the U.S. Court of Appeals for the Ninth Circuit to overturn their convictions, asserting that the prosecution had used the high cost of fundraising as evidence of fraud even though the defendants had not lied about the cost.

ISSUE Could evidence of the commissions paid to the telemarketers be introduced when those from whom the funds were solicited were not lied to about the commissions?

DECISION Yes. The U.S. Court of Appeals for the Ninth Circuit upheld the convictions. The defendants' "undoing was not that the commissions were large but that their charitable web was a scam. Donors were told their contributions went to specific charitable activities when, in reality, almost no money did."

REASON The court acknowledged that a failure to reveal the high cost of fundraising to potential donors does not establish fraud. "[T]he mere fact that a telemarketer keeps [80 percent] of contributions it solicits cannot be the basis of a fraud conviction, and neither can the fact that a telemarketer fails to volunteer this information to would-be donors." But when "nondisclosure is accompanied by intentionally misleading statements designed to deceive the listener," the high cost of fundraising may be introduced as evidence of fraud. "[T]he State may vigorously enforce its antifraud laws to prohibit professional fundraisers from obtaining money on false pretenses or by making false statements." Here, in addition to the proof of the telemarketers' commissions, the prosecution offered evidence of Lyons and Sanchez's specific

CASE 6.1–Continued

misrepresentations and omissions regarding the defendants' use of the donated funds. All of this "evidence underscored the fact that virtually none of the money that ended up in the bank accounts of the six FCL charities went to any charitable activities at all, let alone the specific charitable activities mentioned in the telemarketers' calls. * * * [A]dmission of evidence regarding the fundraising costs was essential to understanding the overall scheme and the shell game of the multiple charities."

 FOR CRITICAL ANALYSIS–Ethical Consideration *It may have been legal in this case, but was it ethical for the prosecution to repeatedly emphasize the size of the telemarketers' commissions? Why or why not?*

Bribery   Basically, three types of bribery are considered crimes: bribery of public officials, commercial bribery, and bribery of foreign officials. The attempt to influence a public official to act in a way that serves a private interest is a crime. As an element of this crime, intent must be present and proved. The bribe can be anything the recipient considers to be valuable. Realize that *the crime of bribery occurs when the bribe is offered.* It does not matter whether the person to whom the bribe is offered accepts the bribe or agrees to perform whatever action is desired by the person offering the bribe. *Accepting a bribe* is a separate crime.

Bribing foreign officials to obtain favorable business contracts is a crime. The Foreign Corrupt Practices Act of 1977, which will be discussed in Chapter 7, was passed to curb the use of bribery by U.S. businesspersons in securing foreign contracts.

Bankruptcy Fraud   Federal bankruptcy law (see Chapter 23) allows individuals and businesses to be relieved of oppressive debt through bankruptcy proceedings. Numerous white-collar crimes may be committed during the many phases of a bankruptcy proceeding. A creditor, for example, may file a false claim against the debtor, which is a crime. Also, a debtor may fraudulently transfer assets to favored parties before or after the petition for bankruptcy is filed. For example, a company-owned automobile may be "sold" at a bargain price to a trusted friend or relative. Closely related to the crime of fraudulent transfer of property is the crime of fraudulent concealment of property, such as hiding gold coins.

The Theft of Trade Secrets   As discussed in Chapter 5, trade secrets constitute a form of intellectual property that for many businesses can be extremely valuable. The Economic Espionage Act of 1996[8] made the theft of trade secrets a federal crime. The act also made it a federal crime to buy or possess trade secrets of another person, knowing that the trade secrets were stolen or otherwise acquired without the owner's authorization.

Violations of the act can result in steep penalties. An individual who violates the act can be imprisoned for up to ten years and fined up to $500,000. If a corporation or other organization violates the act, it can be fined up to $5 million. Additionally, the law provides that any property acquired as a result of the violation, such as airplanes and automobiles, and any property used in the commission of the violation, such as computers and other electronic devices, are subject to criminal *forfeiture*—meaning that the government can take the property. A theft of trade secrets conducted via the Internet, for example, could result in the forfeiture of every computer or other device used in the commission of the crime, as well as any assets gained from the stolen trade secrets.

---

8. 18 U.S.C. Sections 1831–1839.

Mister M, an American magician, was featured on a television show during which he revealed how magic tricks are performed. As a result, some magicians in Brazil sued the Brazilian television network that aired the show. The magicians claimed that the network aided Mister M in exposing their trade secrets. They won their case. Would such a lawsuit have been successful in a U.S. court? Why or why not?
(AP Photo/Katia Tamahara)

INSIDER TRADING
The purchase or sale of securities on the basis of *inside information* (information that has not been made available to the public).

Insider Trading An individual who obtains "inside information" about the plans of a publicly listed corporation can often make stock-trading profits by purchasing or selling corporate securities based on the information. **Insider trading** is a violation of securities law and will be considered more fully in Chapter 30. Generally, the rule is that a person who possesses inside information and has a duty not to disclose it to outsiders may not profit from the purchase or sale of securities based on that information until the information is made available to the public.

Organized Crime

ON THE WEB

You can find a wealth of information on famous criminal trials at a Web site maintained by the University of Missouri–Kansas City law school. Go to

www.law.umkc.edu/faculty/projects/ftrials/ftrials.html.

As mentioned, white-collar crime takes place within the confines of the legitimate business world. *Organized crime,* in contrast, operates *illegitimately* by, among other things, providing illegal goods and services. For organized crime, the traditional preferred markets are gambling, prostitution, illegal narcotics, and loan sharking (lending at higher than legal interest rates), along with more recent ventures into counterfeiting and credit-card scams.

Money Laundering The profits from organized crime and illegal activities amount to billions of dollars a year, particularly the profits from illegal drug transactions and, to a lesser extent, from racketeering, prostitution, and gambling. Under federal law, banks, savings and loan associations, and other financial institutions are required to report currency transactions involving more than $10,000. Consequently, those who engage in illegal activities face difficulties in depositing their cash profits from illegal transactions.

As an alternative to simply storing cash from illegal transactions in a safe-deposit box, wrongdoers and racketeers have invented ways to launder "dirty" money to make it "clean." This **money laundering** is done through legitimate businesses.

MONEY LAUNDERING
Falsely reporting income that has been obtained through criminal activity as income obtained through a legitimate business enterprise—in effect, "laundering" the "dirty money."

■**EXAMPLE 6.5** Matt, a successful drug dealer, becomes a partner with a restaurateur. Little by little, the restaurant shows increasing profits. As a partner in the restaurant, Matt is able to report the "profits" of the restaurant as legitimate income on which he pays federal and state taxes. He can then spend those funds without worrying that his lifestyle may exceed the level possible with his reported income. ■

The Racketeer Influenced and Corrupt Organizations Act In 1970, in an effort to curb the apparently increasing entry of organized crime into the legitimate business world, Congress passed the Racketeer Influenced and Corrupt Organizations Act (RICO).[9] The statute, which was enacted as part of the Organized Crime Control Act, makes it a federal crime to (1) use income obtained from racketeering activity to purchase any interest in an enterprise, (2) acquire or maintain an interest in an enterprise through racketeering activity, (3) conduct or participate in the affairs of an enterprise through racketeering activity, or (4) conspire to do any of the preceding activities.

RICO incorporates by reference twenty-six separate types of federal crimes and nine types of state felonies[10] and declares that if a person commits two of these offenses, he or she is guilty of "racketeering activity." Under the criminal provisions of RICO, any individual found guilty is subject to a fine of up to $25,000 per violation, imprisonment for up to twenty years, or both. Additionally, the statute provides that those who violate RICO may be required to forfeit (give up) any assets, in the form of property or cash, that were acquired as a result of the illegal activity or that were "involved in" or an "instrumentality of" the activity.

The broad language of RICO has allowed it to be applied in cases that have little or nothing to do with organized crime. In fact, today the statute is more often used to attack white-collar crimes than organized crime. In addition, RICO creates civil as well as criminal liability. The government can seek civil penalties, including the divestiture of a defendant's interest in a business (called forfeiture) or the dissolution of the business. Moreover, in some cases, the statute allows private individuals to sue violators and potentially recover three times their actual losses (treble damages), plus attorneys' fees, for business injuries caused by a violation of the statute. This is perhaps the most controversial aspect of RICO and one that continues to cause debate in the nation's federal courts.

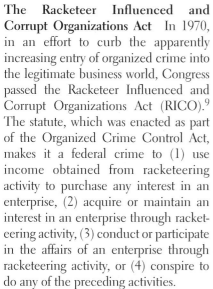

The Godfather *series of classic movies depicted the actions of the U.S. mafia (a secret criminal organization) as well as its Sicilian origins. The Federal Bureau of Investigation (FBI) is responsible for pursuing mafia members. Since the terrorist attacks of September 11, 2001, however, much of the FBI's resources have shifted to tracking terrorist activity. What do you think has happened to the size of the U.S. mafia as a result of this switch? Why?* (Bradley Newman/Creative Commons)

Should courts allow private parties to file RICO actions against their employers based on a pattern of hiring illegal immigrants? The civil sanctions authorized by RICO have given plaintiffs a tremendous financial incentive to pursue businesses and employers for RICO violations. In one recent case, for example, a group of employees sued their employer, Mohawk Industries, Inc. The employees claimed that Mohawk had engaged in a pattern of hiring illegal immigrants willing to work for lower wages in an effort to drive down the wages of legal employees. Mohawk, the second-largest carpet manufacturer in the United States with over 30,000 employees, allegedly conspired with recruiting agencies to hire undocumented workers and even provided illegal aliens with transportation from the border. The plaintiffs claimed

ETHICAL ISSUE 6.1

---

9. 18 U.S.C. Sections 1961–1968.
10. See 18 U.S.C. Section 1961(1)(A).

that this pattern of illegal hiring expanded Mohawk's hourly workforce and resulted in lower wages for the plaintiffs (and other legal employees). Mohawk filed a motion to dismiss for lack of evidence of racketeering activity, which the federal court denied, and the case was appealed.

The United States Supreme Court initially granted a *writ of certiorari* in this case but later dismissed the writ as "improvidently granted" and remanded the case to the U.S. Court of Appeals for the Eleventh Circuit. In September 2006, the federal appellate court ruled that the plaintiffs had presented sufficient evidence of racketeering activity to go forward with the RICO suit.[11] Although the merits of the case have not yet been resolved, the potential treble (triple) damages award against Mohawk could be substantial. In addition, the case is likely to open the door to other actions against employers that have a history of employing illegal immigrants and thereby causing injury to the economic interests of other employees.

Classification of Crimes

Depending on their degree of seriousness, crimes typically are classified as felonies or misdemeanors. **Felonies** are serious crimes punishable by death or by imprisonment for more than a year. **Misdemeanors** are less serious crimes, punishable by a fine or by confinement for up to a year. In most jurisdictions, **petty offenses** are considered to be a subset of misdemeanors. Petty offenses are minor violations, such as jaywalking or violations of building codes. Even for petty offenses, however, a guilty party can be put in jail for a few days, fined, or both, depending on state or local law.

Whether a crime is a felony or a misdemeanor can determine in which court the case is tried and, in some states, whether the defendant has a right to a jury trial. Many states also define different degrees of felony offenses (first, second, and third degree murder, for example) and vary the punishment according to the degree. Some states also have different classes (degrees) of misdemeanors.

DEFENSES TO CRIMINAL LIABILITY

In certain circumstances, the law may allow a person to be excused from criminal liability because she or he lacks the required mental state. Criminal defendants may also be relieved of criminal liability if they can show that their criminal actions were justified, given the circumstances. Among the most important defenses to criminal liability are infancy, intoxication, insanity, mistake, consent, duress, justifiable use of force, entrapment, and the statute of limitations. Also, in some cases, defendants are given immunity and thus relieved, at least in part, of criminal liability for crimes they committed. We look at each of these defenses here.

Note that procedural violations, such as obtaining evidence without a valid search warrant, may operate as defenses also. As you will read later in this chapter, evidence obtained in violation of a defendant's constitutional rights normally may not be admitted in court. If the evidence is suppressed, then there may be no basis for prosecuting the defendant.

---

11. *Williams v. Mohawk Industries, Inc.*, 465 F.3d 1277 (11th Cir. 2006); *cert.* granted ___ U.S. ___, 126 S.Ct. 830, 163 L.Ed.2d 705 (2005); and *cert.* dismissed at ___ U.S. ___, 126 S.Ct. 2016, 164 L.Ed.2d 776 (2006). The holding in this case conflicts with a decision in another federal circuit; see *Baker v. IBP, Inc.*, 357 F.3d 685 (7th Cir. 2004).

CONCEPT SUMMARY	Types of Crimes
CRIME CATEGORY	**DEFINITION AND EXAMPLES**
Violent Crime	1. *Definition*—Crimes that cause others to suffer harm or death. 2. *Examples*—Murder, assault and battery, sexual assault (rape), and robbery.
Property Crime	1. *Definition*—Crimes in which the goal of the offender is some form of economic gain or the damaging of property; the most common form of crime. 2. *Examples*—Burglary, larceny, obtaining goods by false pretenses, receiving stolen goods, arson, and forgery.
Public Order Crime	1. *Definition*—Crimes contrary to public values and morals. 2. *Examples*—Public drunkenness, prostitution, gambling, and illegal drug use.
White-Collar Crime	1. *Definition*—An illegal act or series of acts committed by an individual or business entity using some nonviolent means to obtain a personal or business advantage; usually committed in the course of a legitimate occupation. 2. *Examples*—Embezzlement, mail and wire fraud, bribery, bankruptcy fraud, the theft of trade secrets, and insider trading.
Organized Crime	1. *Definition*—A form of crime conducted by groups operating illegitimately to satisfy the public's demand for illegal goods and services (such as gambling or illegal narcotics). 2. *Money laundering*—The establishment of legitimate enterprises through which "dirty" money (obtained through criminal activities, such as organized crime) can be "laundered" (made to appear to be legitimate income). 3. *RICO*—The Racketeer Influenced and Corrupt Organizations Act (RICO) of 1970 makes it a federal crime to (a) use income obtained from racketeering activity to purchase any interest in an enterprise, (b) acquire or maintain an interest in an enterprise through racketeering activity, (c) conduct or participate in the affairs of an enterprise through racketeering activity, or (d) conspire to do any of the preceding activities. RICO provides for both civil and criminal liability.

Infancy

The term *infant*, as used in the law, refers to any person who has not yet reached the age of majority (see Chapter 10). In all states, certain courts handle cases involving children who are alleged to have violated the law. In some states, juvenile courts handle children's cases exclusively. In other states, however, courts that handle children's cases may also have jurisdiction over additional matters. In most states, a child may be treated as an adult and tried in a regular court if she or he is above a certain age (usually fourteen) and is charged with a felony, such as rape or murder.

Intoxication

The law recognizes two types of intoxication, whether from drugs or from alcohol: *involuntary* and *voluntary*. Involuntary intoxication occurs when a person either is physically forced to ingest or inject an intoxicating substance or is unaware that a substance contains drugs or alcohol. Involuntary intoxication is a defense to a crime if its effect was to make a person incapable of obeying the law or of understanding that the act committed was wrong. Voluntary intoxication is rarely a defense, but it may be effective in cases in which the defendant was so *extremely* intoxicated as to negate the state of mind that a crime requires.

These two brothers were only thirteen and fourteen years old when they killed their father with a baseball bat and then set their Florida house on fire. In court, they did not deny their wrongdoing. They were sentenced to terms of seven to eight years for third-degree murder and arson. Under what circumstances should they not be held responsible for their reprehensible actions? (The Smoking Gun)

COMPARE   "Ignorance" is a lack of information. "Mistake" is a confusion of information.

CONSENT
Voluntary agreement to a proposition or an act of another; a concurrence of wills.

Insanity

Just as a child is often judged to be incapable of the state of mind required to commit a crime, so also may someone suffering from a mental illness. Thus, insanity may be a defense to a criminal charge. The courts have had difficulty deciding what the test for legal insanity should be, however, and psychiatrists as well as lawyers are critical of the tests used. Almost all federal courts and some states use the relatively liberal standard set forth in the Model Penal Code:

> A person is not responsible for criminal conduct if at the time of such conduct as a result of mental disease or defect he [or she] lacks substantial capacity either to appreciate the wrongfulness of his [or her] conduct or to conform his [or her] conduct to the requirements of the law.

Some states use the *M'Naghten* test,[12] under which a criminal defendant is not responsible if, at the time of the offense, he or she did not know the nature and quality of the act or did not know that the act was wrong. Other states use the irresistible-impulse test. A person operating under an irresistible impulse may know an act is wrong but cannot refrain from doing it. Under any of these tests, proving insanity is extremely difficult. For this reason, the insanity defense is rarely used and usually is not successful.

Mistake

Everyone has heard the saying "Ignorance of the law is no excuse." Ordinarily, ignorance of the law or a mistaken idea about what the law requires is not a valid defense. In some states, however, that rule has been modified. Criminal defendants who claim that they honestly did not know that they were breaking a law may have a valid defense if (1) the law was not published or reasonably made known to the public or (2) the defendant relied on an official statement of the law that was erroneous.

A *mistake of fact,* as opposed to a *mistake of law,* operates as a defense if it negates the mental state necessary to commit a crime. **EXAMPLE 6.6** If Oliver Wheaton mistakenly walks off with Julie Tyson's briefcase because he thinks it is his, there is no theft. Theft requires knowledge that the property belongs to another. (If Wheaton's act causes Tyson to incur damages, however, Wheaton may be subject to liability for trespass to personal property or conversion, torts that were discussed in Chapter 4.) ■

Consent

What if a victim consents to a crime or even encourages the person intending a criminal act to commit it? Ordinarily, **consent** does not operate as a bar to criminal liability. In some rare circumstances, however, the law may allow consent to be used as a defense. In each case, the question is whether the law forbids an act that was committed against the victim's will or forbids the act without regard to the victim's wish. The law forbids murder, prostitution, and drug use regardless of whether the victim consents to it. Also, if the act causes harm to a third person who has not consented, there is no escape from criminal liability. Consent or forgiveness given after a crime has been committed is not really a defense, though it can affect the likelihood of prosecution or the severity of the sentence. Consent operates most successfully as a defense in crimes against property.

EXAMPLE 6.7 Barry gives Phong permission to stay in Barry's lakeside cabin and hunt for deer on the adjoining land. After observing Phong carrying a gun into the cabin at

---

12. A rule derived from *M'Naghten's Case,* 8 Eng.Rep. 718 (1843).

night, a neighbor calls the police, and an officer subsequently arrests Phong. If charged with burglary (or aggravated burglary, because he had a weapon), Phong can assert the defense of consent. He had obtained Barry's consent to enter the premises. ▪

Duress

Duress exists when the *wrongful threat* of one person induces another person to perform an act that she or he would not otherwise perform. In such a situation, duress is said to negate the mental state necessary to commit a crime. For duress to qualify as a defense, the following requirements must be met:

1 The threat must be of serious bodily harm or death.

2 The harm threatened must be greater than the harm caused by the crime.

3 The threat must be immediate and inescapable.

4 The defendant must have been involved in the situation through no fault of his or her own.

DURESS
Unlawful pressure brought to bear on a person, causing the person to perform an act that she or he would not otherwise perform.

Justifiable Use of Force

Probably the best-known defense to criminal liability is **self-defense.** Other situations, however, also justify the use of force: the defense of one's dwelling, the defense of other property, and the prevention of a crime. In all of these situations, it is important to distinguish between deadly and nondeadly force. *Deadly force* is likely to result in death or serious bodily harm. *Nondeadly force* is force that reasonably appears necessary to prevent the imminent use of criminal force.

Generally speaking, people can use the amount of nondeadly force that seems necessary to protect themselves, their dwellings, or other property or to prevent the commission of a crime. Deadly force can be used in self-defense if the defender *reasonably believes* that imminent death or grievous bodily harm will otherwise result, if the attacker is using unlawful force (an example of lawful force is that exerted by a police officer), and if the defender has not initiated or provoked the attack. Deadly force normally can be used to defend a dwelling only if the unlawful entry is violent and the person believes deadly force is necessary to prevent imminent death or great bodily harm or—in some jurisdictions—if the person believes deadly force is necessary to prevent the commission of a felony (such as arson) in the dwelling.

SELF-DEFENSE
The legally recognized privilege to protect oneself or one's property against injury by another. The privilege of self-defense usually applies only to acts that are reasonably necessary to protect oneself, one's property, or another person.

Entrapment

Entrapment is a defense designed to prevent police officers or other government agents from enticing persons to commit crimes in order to later prosecute them for criminal acts. In the typical entrapment case, an undercover agent *suggests* that a crime be committed and somehow pressures or induces an individual to commit it. The agent then arrests the individual for the crime.

For entrapment to be considered a defense, both the suggestion and the inducement must take place. The defense is intended not to prevent law enforcement agents from setting a trap for an unwary criminal but rather to prevent them from pushing the individual into it. The crucial issue is whether the person who committed a crime was predisposed to commit the illegal act or did so because the agent induced it.

ENTRAPMENT
In criminal law, a defense in which the defendant claims that he or she was induced by a public official—usually an undercover agent or police officer—to commit a crime that he or she would otherwise not have committed.

Statute of Limitations

With some exceptions, such as for the crime of murder, statutes of limitations apply to crimes just as they do to civil wrongs. In other words, the state must initiate criminal prosecution within a certain number of years. If a criminal action is brought after the statutory time period has expired, the accused person can raise the statute of limitations as a defense.

Immunity

At times, the state may wish to obtain information from a person accused of a crime. Accused persons are understandably reluctant to give information if it will be used to prosecute them, and they cannot be forced to do so. The privilege against **self-incrimination** is granted by the Fifth Amendment to the U.S. Constitution, which reads, in part, "nor shall [any person] be compelled in any criminal case to be a witness against himself." In cases in which the state wishes to obtain information from a person accused of a crime, the state can grant *immunity* from prosecution or agree to prosecute for a less serious offense in exchange for the information. Once immunity is given, the person can no longer refuse to testify on Fifth Amendment grounds because he or she now has an absolute privilege against self-incrimination.

Often, a grant of immunity from prosecution for a serious crime is part of the **plea bargaining** between the defendant and the prosecuting attorney. The defendant may be convicted of a lesser offense, while the state uses the defendant's testimony to prosecute accomplices for serious crimes carrying heavy penalties.

CONSTITUTIONAL SAFEGUARDS AND CRIMINAL PROCEDURES

Criminal law brings the power of the state, with all its resources, to bear against the individual. Criminal procedures are designed to protect the constitutional rights of individuals and to prevent the arbitrary use of power on the part of the government.

The U.S. Constitution provides specific safeguards for those accused of crimes. Most of these safeguards protect individuals against state government actions, as well as federal government actions, by virtue of the due process clause of the Fourteenth Amendment. These protections are set forth in the Fourth, Fifth, Sixth, and Eighth Amendments.

Fourth Amendment Protections

The Fourth Amendment protects the "right of the people to be secure in their persons, houses, papers, and effects." Before searching or seizing private property, law enforcement officers must obtain a **search warrant**—an order from a judge or other public official authorizing the search or seizure.

Search Warrants and Probable Cause   To obtain a search warrant, law enforcement officers must convince a judge that they have reasonable grounds, or **probable cause**, to believe a search will reveal a specific illegality. Probable cause requires the officers to have trustworthy evidence that would convince a reasonable person that the proposed search or seizure is more likely justified than not. Furthermore, the Fourth Amendment prohibits general warrants. It requires a particular description of what is to be searched or seized. General searches through a person's belongings are impermissible. The search cannot extend beyond what is described in the warrant. Although search warrants require specificity, if a search warrant is issued for a person's residence, items that are in that residence may be searched even if they do not belong to that individual.

■EXAMPLE 6.8   Paycom Billing Services, Inc., facilitates payments from Internet users to its client Web sites and stores vast amounts of credit-card information in the process. Three partners at Paycom received a letter from an employee, Christopher Adjani, threatening to sell Paycom's confidential client information if the company did not pay him $3 million. Pursuant to an investigation, the Federal Bureau of Investigation (FBI) obtained

---

SELF-INCRIMINATION
The giving of testimony that may subject the testifier to criminal prosecution. The Fifth Amendment to the Constitution protects against self-incrimination by providing that no person "shall be compelled in any criminal case to be a witness against himself."

PLEA BARGAINING
The process by which a criminal defendant and the prosecutor in a criminal case work out a mutually satisfactory disposition of the case, subject to court approval; usually involves the defendant's pleading guilty to a lesser offense in return for a lighter sentence.

SEARCH WARRANT
An order granted by a public authority, such as a judge, that authorizes law enforcement personnel to search a particular premise or property.

PROBABLE CAUSE
Reasonable grounds for believing that a person should be arrested or searched.

a search warrant to search Adjani's person, automobile, and residence, including computer equipment. When the FBI agents served the warrant, they discovered evidence of the criminal scheme in the e-mail communications on a computer in the residence. The computer belonged to Adjani's live-in girlfriend. Adjani filed a motion to suppress this evidence, claiming that because he did not own the computer, it was beyond the scope of the warrant. Although the federal trial court granted the defendant's motion and suppressed the incriminating e-mails, in 2006 the U.S. Court of Appeals for the Ninth Circuit reversed. According to the appellate court, despite the novel Fourth Amendment issues raised in the case, the search of the computer was proper given the alleged involvement of computers in the crime.[13] ▣

Searches and Seizures in the Business Context   The constitutional protection against unreasonable searches and seizures also extends to businesses and professionals. At the same time, though, the federal and state governments have an interest in regulating commercial activities to protect the public. As government regulation of business increased, government inspectors conducted frequent and unannounced inspections to ensure compliance with the regulations. Such inspections could be extremely disruptive. In 1978, the United States Supreme Court held that government inspectors do not have the right to enter business premises without a warrant, although the standard of probable cause is not the same as that required in nonbusiness contexts.[14] The existence of a general and neutral plan of enforcement will justify the issuance of a warrant.

Lawyers and accountants frequently possess the business records of their clients, and inspecting these documents while they are out of the hands of their true owners also requires a warrant. No warrant is required, however, for seizures of spoiled or contaminated food. Nor are warrants required for searches of businesses in such highly regulated industries as liquor, guns, and strip mining. General manufacturing is not considered to be one of these highly regulated industries, however.

The standard used for highly regulated industries is sometimes applied in other contexts as well. In the following case, the court considered whether the standard applies to airports and thus permits a suspicionless checkpoint search to be conducted in an airport to screen airline passengers.

ON THE WEB

You can learn about some of the constitutional questions raised by various criminal laws and procedures by going to the Web site of the American Civil Liberties Union at

www.aclu.org.

---

13. *United States v. Adjani*, 452 F.3d 1140 (9th Cir. 2006). The parties have filed a petition to have the United States Supreme Court review the case.
14. *Marshall v. Barlow's, Inc.*, 436 U.S. 307, 98 S.Ct. 1816, 56 L.Ed.2d 305 (1978).

Passengers and their carry-on items are searched at an airport security checkpoint. Do such searches violate passengers' Fourth Amendment rights. (Ralf Roletschek/Wikimedia Commons)

CASE 6.2 United States v. Hartwell

United States Court of Appeals, Third Circuit, 436 F.3d 174 (2006).

FACTS Christian Hartwell arrived at the Philadelphia International Airport on May 17, 2003, to catch a flight to Phoenix, Arizona. He reached the security checkpoint, placed his hand luggage on a conveyor belt to be X-rayed, and approached the metal detector. Hartwell's luggage was scanned without incident, but when he walked through the checkpoint, he set off the magnetometer. He was told to remove all items from his pockets and try again. Hartwell removed several items from his pocket but still set off the alarm. Carlos Padua, a federal Transportation Security Administration (TSA) agent, took Hartwell aside and scanned him with a handheld magnetometer. The wand revealed a solid object in Hartwell's pants pocket. Padua asked what it was, but Hartwell did not respond. Escorted to a private screening room, Hartwell refused several requests to empty his pocket. By Hartwell's account, Padua then reached into the pocket and removed two packages of crack cocaine. Hartwell was arrested and convicted on charges related to the possession of the drugs. He appealed to the U.S. Court of Appeals for the Third Circuit, arguing that the search violated the Fourth Amendment.

ISSUE Does a checkpoint search conducted in an airport to screen airline passengers violate the Fourth Amendment?

DECISION No. The U.S. Court of Appeals for the Third Circuit held that Hartwell's search was permissible under the Fourth Amendment, "even though it was initiated without individualized suspicion and was conducted without a warrant. It is permissible * * * because the State has an overwhelming interest in preserving air travel safety, and the procedure is tailored to advance that interest while proving to be only minimally invasive."

REASON The court balanced "the gravity of the public concerns" that have given rise to airport searches, the extent to which the searches advance the public interest, and the impact of the searches on "individual liberty." The court identified the public concern as "preventing terrorist attacks on airplanes," which "is of paramount importance." With respect to advancing the public interest, "absent a search, there is no effective means of detecting which airline passengers are reasonably likely to hijack an airplane." The court added that airport checkpoints and searches have been effective. As for any interference with liberty, the procedures in this case were "minimally intrusive. They were well tailored to protect personal privacy, escalating in invasiveness only after a lower level of screening disclosed a reason to conduct a more probing search." Besides, every airline passenger is subject to a supervised search "not far from the scrutiny" of the other passengers, who—particularly since "[t]he events of September 11, 2001"—are all on notice that they will be searched, too.

 WHY IS THIS CASE IMPORTANT? *In this case, the U.S. Court of Appeals for the Third Circuit applied the administrative search doctrine that applies to highly regulated industries. The United States Supreme Court developed this standard for analyzing suspicionless vehicle checkpoints, such as those used to determine the sobriety of randomly selected drivers. The Supreme Court has not ruled on the legality of airport screenings, however.*

Fifth Amendment Protections

The Fifth Amendment offers significant protections for accused persons. One is the guarantee that no one can be deprived of "life, liberty, or property without due process of law." Two other important Fifth Amendment provisions protect persons against double jeopardy and self-incrimination.

Due Process of Law   Remember from Chapter 2 that *due process of law* has both procedural and substantive aspects. Procedural due process requirements underlie criminal procedures. Basically, the law must be carried out in a fair and orderly way. In criminal cases, due process means that defendants should have an opportunity to object to the charges against them before a fair, neutral decision maker, such as a judge. Defendants must also be given the opportunity to confront and cross-examine witnesses and accusers and to present their own witnesses.

DOUBLE JEOPARDY
A situation occurring when a person is tried twice for the same criminal offense; prohibited by the Fifth Amendment to the Constitution.

Double Jeopardy   The Fifth Amendment also protects persons from **double jeopardy** (being tried twice for the same criminal offense). The prohibition against double jeopardy means that once a criminal defendant is acquitted (found "not guilty") of a particular crime, the government may not retry him or her for the same crime.

The prohibition against double jeopardy does not preclude the crime victim from bringing a civil suit against that same person to recover damages, however. Additionally, a state's prosecution of a crime will not prevent a separate federal prosecution relating to the same activity, and vice versa. **■EXAMPLE 6.9** A person found "not guilty" of assault and battery in a criminal case may be sued by the victim in a civil tort case for damages. A person who is prosecuted for assault and battery in a state court may be prosecuted in a federal court for civil rights violations resulting from the same action. ▣

Self-Incrimination As explained earlier, the Fifth Amendment grants a privilege against self-incrimination. Thus, in any criminal proceeding, an accused person cannot be compelled to give testimony that might subject her or him to any criminal prosecution.

The Fifth Amendment's guarantee against self-incrimination extends only to natural persons. Because a corporation is a legal entity and not a natural person, the privilege against self-incrimination does not apply to it. Similarly, the business records of a partnership do not receive Fifth Amendment protection.[15] When a partnership is required to produce these records, it must do so even if the information incriminates the persons who constitute the business entity. Sole proprietors and sole practitioners (those who fully own their businesses) who have not incorporated normally cannot be compelled to produce their business records. These individuals have full protection against self-incrimination because they function in only one capacity; there is no separate business entity (see Chapter 25).

BE AWARE The Fifth Amendment protection against self-incrimination does not cover partnerships or corporations.

Protections under the Sixth and Eighth Amendments

The Sixth Amendment guarantees several important rights for criminal defendants: the right to a speedy trial, the right to a jury trial, the right to a public trial, the right to confront witnesses, and the right to counsel. The Eighth Amendment prohibits excessive bail and fines, as well as cruel and unusual punishment.

The Sixth Amendment right to counsel is one of the rights of which a suspect must be advised when he or she is arrested under the *Miranda* rule (discussed later in this chapter). In many cases, a statement that a criminal suspect makes in the absence of counsel is not admissible at trial unless the suspect has knowingly and voluntarily waived this right. Is this right to counsel triggered when judicial proceedings are initiated through any preliminary step? Or is this right triggered only when a suspect is "interrogated" by the police? In the following case, the court considered these questions.

---

15. The privilege has been applied to some small family partnerships. See *United States v. Slutsky*, 352 F.Supp. 1105 (S.D.N.Y. 1972).

CASE 6.3   **Fellers v. United States**

Supreme Court of the United States, 540 U.S. 519, 124 S.Ct. 1019, 157 L.Ed.2d 1016 (2004).
www.law.cornell.edu/supct/index.html[a]

FACTS In February 2000, an indictment was issued charging John Fellers, a resident of Lincoln, Nebraska, with conspiracy to distribute methamphetamine. Police officers Michael Garnett

a. Click on "Search" in the top menu bar, and type "Fellers" in the "Search" box that appears. In the result, click on the name of the case under Supreme Court case names to access the opinion. The Legal Information Institute of Cornell Law School in Ithaca, New York, maintains this Web site.

and Jeff Bliemeister went to Fellers's home to arrest him. They told Fellers that the purpose of their visit was to discuss his use and distribution of methamphetamine. They said that they had a warrant for his arrest and that the charges referred to his involvement with four individuals. Fellers responded that he knew the persons and had used methamphetamine with them. The officers took Fellers to jail and advised him for the first time of his right to counsel. He waived this right and repeated

CASE 6.3–Continues next page

CASE 6.3–Continued

his earlier statements. Before Fellers's trial, the court ruled that his "jailhouse statements" could be admitted at his trial because he had waived his right to counsel before making them. After Fellers's conviction, he appealed to the U.S. Court of Appeals for the Eighth Circuit, arguing that the officers had elicited his incriminating "home statements" without advising him of his right to counsel and that his "jailhouse statements" should thus have been excluded from his trial as "fruits" of his earlier statements. The appellate court affirmed the lower court's judgment, holding that Fellers had not had a right to counsel at his home because he had not been subject to police "interrogation." Fellers appealed to the United States Supreme Court.

ISSUE Did Garnett and Bliemeister violate Fellers's right to counsel by deliberately eliciting information from him during their visit to his home without advising him of his right to counsel?

DECISION Yes. The United States Supreme Court reversed the lower court's decision and remanded the case for the determination of a different issue. The Supreme Court held that the Sixth Amendment bars the use at trial of a suspect's incriminating words, deliberately elicited by police after an indictment, in the absence of either counsel or a waiver of the right to counsel, regardless of whether police conduct constitutes an "interrogation."

REASON The Court explained, "The Sixth Amendment right to counsel is triggered at or after the time that judicial proceedings have been initiated * * * . [A]n accused is denied the basic protections of the Sixth Amendment when there is used against him at his trial evidence of his own incriminating words, which federal agents * * * deliberately elicited from him after he had been indicted and in the absence of his counsel." In this case, "there is no question that the officers * * * deliberately elicited information from petitioner [Fellers]. Indeed, the officers, upon arriving at petitioner's house, informed him that their purpose in coming was to discuss his involvement in the distribution of methamphetamine and his association with certain charged co-conspirators. * * * [T]he ensuing discussion took place after petitioner had been indicted [formally charged], outside the presence of counsel, and in the absence of any waiver of petitioner's Sixth Amendment rights."

 FOR CRITICAL ANALYSIS–Social Consideration
Should Fellers's "jailhouse statements" also have been excluded from his trial? Why or why not?

The Exclusionary Rule and the *Miranda* Rule

Two other procedural protections for criminal defendants are the exclusionary rule and the *Miranda* rule.

EXCLUSIONARY RULE
In criminal procedure, a rule under which any evidence that is obtained in violation of the accused's constitutional rights guaranteed by the Fourth, Fifth, and Sixth Amendments, as well as any evidence derived from illegally obtained evidence, will not be admissible in court.

The Exclusionary Rule Under what is known as the **exclusionary rule,** all evidence obtained in violation of the constitutional rights spelled out in the Fourth, Fifth, and Sixth Amendments, as well as all evidence derived from illegally obtained evidence, normally must be excluded from the trial. Evidence derived from illegally obtained evidence is known as the "fruit of the poisonous tree." For example, if a confession is obtained after an illegal arrest, the arrest is "the poisonous tree," and the confession, if "tainted" by the arrest, is the "fruit."

The purpose of the exclusionary rule is to deter police from conducting warrantless searches and engaging in other misconduct. The rule is sometimes criticized because it can lead to injustice. Many a defendant has "gotten off on a technicality" because law enforcement personnel failed to observe procedural requirements. Even though a defendant may be obviously guilty, if the evidence of that guilt was obtained improperly (without a valid search warrant, for example), it normally cannot be used against the defendant in court.

REMEMBER Once a suspect has been informed of his or her rights, anything that person says can be used as evidence in a trial.

The *Miranda* Rule In *Miranda v. Arizona*, a case decided in 1966, the United States Supreme Court established the rule that individuals who are arrested must be informed of certain constitutional rights, including their Fifth Amendment right to remain silent and their Sixth Amendment right to counsel. If the arresting officers fail to inform a criminal suspect of these constitutional rights, any statements the suspect makes normally will not be admissible in court. Although the Supreme Court's *Miranda* decision was controversial, it has survived attempts by Congress to overrule the decision.[16] Because of its importance in criminal procedure, the *Miranda* case is presented as this chapter's *Landmark in the Law* feature on the following page.

Exceptions to the *Miranda* Rule Over time, as part of a continuing attempt to balance the rights of accused persons against the rights of society, the United States Supreme Court has carved out numerous exceptions to the *Miranda* rule. For example, the Court has recognized a "public safety" exception, holding that certain statements—such as statements concerning the location of a weapon—are admissible even if the defendant was not given *Miranda* warnings.[17] The Court has also clarified that in certain circumstances, a defendant's confession need not be excluded as evidence even if the police failed to inform the defendant of his or her *Miranda* rights.[18] If other, legally obtained evidence admitted at trial is strong enough to justify the conviction without the confession, then the fact that the confession was obtained illegally can be, in effect, ignored.[19]

The Supreme Court has also ruled that a suspect must unequivocally and assertively request to exercise his or her right to counsel in order to stop police questioning. Saying "Maybe I should talk to a lawyer" during an interrogation after being taken into custody is not enough. The Court held that police officers are not required to decipher the suspect's intentions in such situations.[20]

> **MIRANDA WARNING**
> 1. YOU HAVE THE RIGHT TO REMAIN SILENT.
> 2. ANYTHING YOU SAY CAN AND WILL BE USED AGAINST YOU IN A COURT OF LAW.
> 3. YOU HAVE THE RIGHT TO TALK TO A LAWYER AND HAVE HIM PRESENT WITH YOU WHILE YOU ARE BEING QUESTIONED.
> 4. IF YOU CANNOT AFFORD TO HIRE A LAWYER, ONE WILL BE APPOINTED TO REPRESENT YOU BEFORE ANY QUESTIONING IF YOU WISH.
> 5. YOU CAN DECIDE AT ANY TIME TO EXERCISE THESE RIGHTS AND NOT ANSWER ANY QUESTIONS OR MAKE ANY STATEMENTS.
> **WAIVER**
> DO YOU UNDERSTAND EACH OF THESE RIGHTS I HAVE EXPLAINED TO YOU? HAVING THESE RIGHTS IN MIND, DO YOU WISH TO TALK TO US NOW?

The Miranda warning that law enforcement must explain to suspects to inform them of their rights under the Fifth and Sixth Amendments.

ON THE WEB

If you are interested in reading the Supreme Court's opinion in *Miranda v. Arizona,* go to **www.supct.law.cornell.edu/supct/cases/name.htm**. Select "M" from the menu at the top of the page, and scroll down the page that opens to the *Miranda v. Arizona* case.

CRIMINAL PROCESS

As mentioned, a criminal prosecution differs significantly from a civil case in several respects. These differences reflect the desire to safeguard the rights of the individual against the state. Exhibit 6–3 on page 189 summarizes the major procedural steps in processing a criminal case. Here we discuss three phases of the criminal process—arrest, indictment or information, and trial—in more detail.

Arrest

Before a warrant for arrest can be issued, there must be probable cause for believing that the individual in question has committed a crime. As discussed earlier, *probable cause* can be defined as a substantial likelihood that the person has committed or is about to commit a crime. Note that probable cause involves a likelihood, not just a possibility. An arrest may sometimes be made without a warrant if there is no time to get one, as when a police officer observes a crime taking place, but the action of the arresting officer is still judged by the standard of probable cause.

Indictment or Information

Individuals must be formally charged with having committed specific crimes before they can be brought to trial. If issued by a grand jury, this charge is called an **indictment**.[21]

INDICTMENT
A charge by a grand jury that a named person has committed a crime.

---

16. *Dickerson v. United States,* 530 U.S. 428, 120 S.Ct. 2326, 147 L.Ed.2d 405 (2000).
17. *New York v. Quarles,* 467 U.S. 649, 104 S.Ct. 2626, 81 L.Ed.2d 550 (1984).
18. *Moran v. Burbine,* 475 U.S. 412, 106 S.Ct. 1135, 89 L.Ed.2d 410 (1986).
19. *Arizona v. Fulminante,* 499 U.S. 279, 111 S.Ct. 1246, 113 L.Ed.2d 302 (1991).
20. *Davis v. United States,* 512 U.S. 452, 114 S.Ct. 2350, 129 L.Ed.2d 362 (1994).
21. Pronounced in-*dyte*-ment.

LANDMARK IN THE LAW *Miranda v. Arizona* (1966)

The United States Supreme Court's decision in *Miranda v. Arizona*[a] has been cited in more court decisions than any other case in the history of American law. Through television shows and other media, the case has also become familiar to most of the adult population in the United States.

The case arose after Ernesto Miranda was arrested in his home, on March 13, 1963, for the kidnapping and rape of an eighteen-year-old woman. Miranda was taken to a police station in Phoenix, Arizona, and questioned by two police officers. Two hours later, the officers emerged from the interrogation room with a written confession signed by Miranda.

Rulings by the Lower Courts   The confession was admitted into evidence at the trial, and Miranda was convicted and sentenced to prison for twenty to thirty years. Miranda appealed the decision, claiming that he had not been informed of his constitutional rights. He did not claim that he was innocent of the crime or that his confession was false or made under duress. He claimed only that he would not have confessed to the crime if he had been advised of his right to remain silent and to have an attorney. The Supreme Court of Arizona held that Miranda's constitutional rights had not been violated and affirmed his conviction. In forming its decision, the court emphasized that Miranda had not specifically requested an attorney.

The Supreme Court's Decision   The *Miranda* case was subsequently consolidated with three other cases involving similar issues and reviewed by the United States Supreme Court. In its decision, the Supreme Court stated that whenever an individual is taken into custody, "the following measures are required: He must be warned prior to any questioning that he has the right to remain silent, that anything he says can be used against him in a court of law, that he has the right to the presence of an attorney, and that if he cannot afford an attorney one will be appointed for him prior to any questioning if he so desires." If the accused waives his or her rights to remain silent and to have counsel present, the government must be able to demonstrate that the waiver was made knowingly, intelligently, and voluntarily.

APPLICATION TO TODAY'S WORLD   *Today, both on television and in the real world, police officers routinely advise suspects of their "Miranda rights" on arrest. When Ernesto Miranda himself was later murdered, the suspected murderer was "read his Miranda rights." Despite Congress's attempt to overrule the Miranda requirements the Supreme Court has affirmed the decision as constitutional. Interestingly, this decision has also had ramifications for criminal procedure in Great Britain. British police officers are required, when making arrests, to inform suspects, "You do not have to say anything. But if you do not mention now something which you later use in your defense, the court may decide that your failure to mention it now strengthens the case against you. A record will be made of everything you say, and it may be given in evidence if you are brought to trial."*

RELEVANT WEB SITES   *To locate information on the Web concerning the Miranda decision, go to this text's Web site at* **www.thomsonedu.com/westbuslaw/blt**, *select "Chapter 6," and click on "URLs for Landmarks."*

a. 384 U.S. 436, 86 S.Ct. 1602, 16 L.Ed.2d 694 (1966).

EXHIBIT 6–3 **Major Procedural Steps in a Criminal Case**

ARREST

Police officer takes suspect into custody. Most arrests are made without a warrant. After the arrest, the officer searches the suspect, who is then taken to the police station.

BOOKING

At the police station, the suspect is searched again, photographed, fingerprinted, and allowed at least one telephone call. After the booking, charges are reviewed, and if they are not dropped, a complaint is filed and a magistrate (judge) reviews the case for probable cause.

INITIAL APPEARANCE

The defendant appears before the judge, who informs the defendant of the charges and of his or her rights. If the defendant requests a lawyer and cannot afford one, a lawyer is appointed. The judge sets bail (conditions under which a suspect can obtain release pending disposition of the case).

GRAND JURY

A grand jury determines if there is probable cause to believe that the defendant committed the crime. The federal government and about half of the states require grand jury indictments for at least some felonies.

PRELIMINARY HEARING

In a court proceeding, a prosecutor presents evidence, and the judge determines if there is probable cause to hold the defendant over for trial.

INDICTMENT

An *indictment* is a written document issued by the grand jury to formally charge the defendant with a crime.

INFORMATION

An *information* is a formal criminal charge made by the prosecutor.

ARRAIGNMENT

The defendant is brought before the court, informed of the charges, and asked to enter a plea.

PLEA BARGAIN

A plea bargain is a prosecutors promise to make concessions (or promise to seek concessions) in return for a defendant's guilty plea. Concessions may include a reduced charge or a lesser sentence.

GUILTY PLEA

In many jurisdictions, most cases that reach the arraignment stage do not go to trial but are resolved by a guilty plea, often as a result of a plea bargain. The judge sets the case for sentencing.

TRIAL

Trials can be either jury trials or bench trials. (In a bench trial, there is no jury, and the judge decides questions of fact as well as questions of law.) If the verdict is "guilty," the judge sets a date for the sentencing. Everyone convicted of a crime has the right to an appeal.

GRAND JURY
A group of citizens called to decide, after hearing the state's evidence, whether a reasonable basis (probable cause) exists for believing that a crime has been committed and that a trial ought to be held.

INFORMATION
A formal accusation or complaint (without an indictment) issued in certain types of actions (usually criminal actions involving lesser crimes) by a government prosecutor.

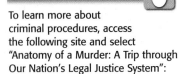

ON THE WEB

To learn more about criminal procedures, access the following site and select "Anatomy of a Murder: A Trip through Our Nation's Legal Justice System":

library.thinkquest.org/2760/home.htm.

A **grand jury** usually consists of more jurors than the ordinary trial jury. A grand jury does not determine the guilt or innocence of an accused party; rather, its function is to hear the state's evidence and determine whether a reasonable basis (probable cause) exists for believing that a crime has been committed and that a trial ought to be held.

Usually, grand juries are used in cases involving serious crimes, such as murder. For lesser crimes, an individual may be formally charged with a crime by what is called an **information,** or criminal complaint. An information will be issued by a government prosecutor if the prosecutor determines that there is sufficient evidence to justify bringing the individual to trial.

Trial

At a criminal trial, the accused person does not have to prove anything; the entire burden of proof is on the prosecutor (the state). As mentioned earlier, the prosecution must show that, based on all the evidence presented, the defendant's guilt is established *beyond a reasonable doubt.* If there is a reasonable doubt as to whether a criminal defendant did, in fact, commit the crime with which she or he has been charged, then the verdict must be "not guilty." Note that giving a verdict of "not guilty" is not the same as stating that the defendant is innocent; it merely means that not enough evidence was properly presented to the court to prove guilt beyond a reasonable doubt.

Courts have complex rules about what types of evidence may be presented and how the evidence may be brought out in criminal cases. These rules are designed to ensure that evidence in trials is relevant, reliable, and not prejudicial toward the defendant. For example, under the Sixth Amendment, persons accused of a crime have the right to confront the witnesses against them in open court. If the prosecutor wishes to present a witness's testimony by means of a document obtained in an *ex parte* examination, the prosecutor must show that the witness is unavailable to testify in court and that the defendant had a prior opportunity to cross-examine her or him. (In this context, an *ex parte* examination is a proceeding for the benefit of the prosecution without notice to the defendant.)

Sentencing Guidelines

In 1984, Congress passed the Sentencing Reform Act. This act created the U.S. Sentencing Commission, which was charged with the task of standardizing sentences for federal crimes. The commission's guidelines, which became effective in 1987, established a range of possible penalties for each federal crime and required the judge to select a sentence from within that range. In other words, the guidelines originally established a mandatory system because judges were not allowed to deviate from the specified sentencing range. Some federal judges felt uneasy about imposing long prison sentences on certain criminal defendants, particularly first-time offenders, and in illegal substances cases involving small quantities of drugs.[22]

In 2005, the Supreme Court held that certain provisions of the federal sentencing guidelines were unconstitutional.[23] The case involved Freddie Booker, who was arrested with 92.5 grams of crack cocaine in his possession. During questioning by police, he signed a written statement in which he admitted to selling an additional quantity—566 grams of crack cocaine—elsewhere. The additional 566 grams of crack were not brought up at trial. Nevertheless, under the federal sentencing guidelines the judge was required to sentence Booker to twenty-two years in prison. Ultimately, the Supreme Court ruled that this sentence was unconstitutional because a jury did not find beyond a reasonable doubt that Booker had possessed the additional 566 grams of crack.

---

22. See, for example, *United States v. Angelos,* 345 F.Supp.2d 1227 (D. Utah 2004).
23. *United States v. Booker,* 543 U.S. 220, 125 S.Ct. 738, 160 L.Ed.2d 621 (2005).

The Supreme Court's ruling in 2005 essentially changed the federal sentencing guidelines from mandatory to advisory. Depending on the circumstances of the case, a federal trial judge may now depart from the guidelines if he or she believes that it is reasonable to do so. Note, however, that the sentencing guidelines still exist and provide for enhanced punishment for certain types of crimes, including white-collar crimes, violations of the Sarbanes-Oxley Act (to be discussed in Chapter 7), and violations of securities laws.[24]

CYBER CRIME

Some years ago, the American Bar Association defined **computer crime** as any act that is directed against computers and computer parts, that uses computers as instruments of crime, or that involves computers and constitutes abuse. Today, because much of the crime committed with the use of computers occurs in cyberspace, many computer crimes fall under the broad label of cyber crime. Here we look at several types of activity that constitute cyber crimes against persons or property. Other cyber crimes will be discussed in later chapters of this text as they relate to particular topics, such as banking or consumer law. For a discussion of how some states are passing laws making spamming a crime, see this chapter's *Adapting the Law to the Online Environment* feature on pages 192 and 193.

Cyber Theft

In cyberspace, thieves are not subject to the physical limitations of the "real" world. A thief can steal data stored in a networked computer with Internet access from anywhere on the globe. Only the speed of the connection and the thief's computer equipment limit the quantity of data that can be stolen.

Financial Crimes   Computer networks also provide opportunities for employees to commit crimes that can involve serious economic losses. For example, employees of a company's accounting department can transfer funds among accounts with little effort and often with less risk than would be involved in transactions evidenced by paperwork.

Generally, the dependence of businesses on computer operations has left firms vulnerable to sabotage, fraud, embezzlement, and the theft of proprietary data, such as trade secrets or other intellectual property. As noted in Chapter 5, the piracy of intellectual property via the Internet is one of the most serious legal challenges facing lawmakers and the courts today.

Identity Theft   A form of cyber theft that has become particularly troublesome in recent years is **identity theft.** Identity theft occurs when the wrongdoer steals a form of identification—such as a name, date of birth, or Social Security number—and uses the information to access the victim's financial resources. This crime existed to a certain extent before the widespread use of the Internet. Thieves would "steal" calling-card numbers by watching people using public telephones, or they would rifle through garbage to find bank account or credit-card numbers. The identity thieves would then use the calling-card or credit-card numbers or would withdraw funds from the victims' accounts. The Internet, however, has turned identity theft into perhaps the fastest-growing financial crime in the United States. See the *Application* feature at the end of this chapter for information on how businesspersons can prevent identity theft.

Three federal statutes deal specifically with identity theft. The Identity Theft and Assumption Deterrence Act of 1998[25] made identity theft a federal crime and directed the U.S. Sentencing Commission to incorporate the crime into its sentencing guidelines. The Fair

COMPUTER CRIME
Any act that is directed against computers and computer parts, that uses computers as instruments of crime, or that involves computers and constitutes abuse.

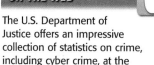 **BE AWARE**   Technological change is one of the primary factors that lead to new types of crime.

IDENTITY THEFT
The act of stealing another's identifying information—such as a name, date of birth, or Social Security number—and using that information to access the victim's financial resources.

---

24. The sentencing guidelines were amended in 2003, as required under the Sarbanes-Oxley Act of 2002, to impose stiffer penalties for corporate securities fraud—see Chapter 30.
25. 18 U.S.C. Section 1028.

ADAPTING THE LAW TO THE ONLINE ENVIRONMENT — When Spamming Is a Crime

A significant issue today is whether persons who send spam (bulk unsolicited e-mail) over the Internet can be charged with a crime. As discussed in Chapter 4, spamming has become a major problem for businesses. At the time the federal CAN-SPAM Act was passed in 2003, the U.S. Senate found that spam constituted more than half of all e-mail traffic and projected that it would cost corporations more than $113 billion by 2007. By all accounts, though, the amount of spam has actually increased since the federal CAN-SPAM Act was enacted. Given that the CAN-SPAM Act has failed to reduce the amount of spam, some states have taken matters into their own hands and have now passed laws making spamming a crime.

A Few States Have Enacted Criminal Spamming Statutes

A few states, such as Maryland and Virginia, have passed groundbreaking laws that make spamming a crime.[a] Under

a. See, for example, Maryland Code, Criminal Law, Section 3-805.1; and Virginia Criminal Code Sections 18.2–152.3:1.

the Virginia Computer Crimes Act (VCCA), it is a crime against property to use a computer or computer network "with the intent to falsify or forge electronic mail transmission information or other routing information in any manner." The law further provides that attempting to send spam to more than ten thousand recipients in any twenty-four-hour period is a felony. The VCCA also includes provisions allowing authorities to seize the assets or proceeds obtained through an illegal spamming operation.

Maryland's antispamming law similarly prohibits sending commercial e-mail to recipients using false information about the identity of the sender, the origin, transmission path, or subject of the message. Under the Maryland law, however, the number of spam messages required to convict a person of the offense is much lower. Sending ten illegal messages in twenty-four hours violates the statute, and the more spam sent, the more severe the punishment will be, up to a maximum of ten years in prison and a $25,000 fine.

America's First Conviction for Felony Spamming

In the biggest case on criminal spamming to date, a Virginia appellate court in 2006 upheld the conviction of Jeremy Jaynes, a spammer who had sent more than ten thousand junk messages a day using sixteen Internet connections and a

---

HACKER
A person who uses one computer to break into another. Professional computer programmers refer to such persons as "crackers."

CYBERTERRORIST
A hacker whose purpose is to exploit a target computer for a serious impact, such as corrupting a program to sabotage a business.

and Accurate Credit Transactions Act of 2003[26] gives victims of identity theft certain rights in working with creditors and credit bureaus to remove negative information from their credit reports. This act will be discussed in detail in Chapter 32 in the context of consumer law. The Identity Theft Penalty Enhancement Act of 2004[27] authorized more severe penalties in aggravated cases in which the identity theft was committed in connection with the thief's employment or with other serious crimes (such as terrorism or firearms or immigration offenses).

Hacking and Cyberterrorism

Persons who use one computer to break into another are sometimes referred to as **hackers.** Hackers who break into computers without authorization often commit cyber theft. Sometimes, however, their principal aim is to prove how smart they are by gaining access to others' password-protected computers and causing random data errors or making unpaid-for telephone calls.[28] **Cyberterrorists** are hackers who, rather than trying to gain attention, strive to remain undetected so that they can exploit computers for a serious impact. Just as "real" terrorists destroyed the World Trade Center towers and a portion of the Pentagon in September 2001, cyberterrorists might explode "logic bombs" to shut down central computers. Such activities can pose a danger to national security.

Businesses may be targeted by cyberterrorists as well as hackers. The goals of a hacking operation might include a wholesale theft of data, such as a merchant's customer files,

---

26. 15 U.S.C. Sections 1681 *et seq.*
27. 18 U.S.C. Section 1028A.
28. The total cost of crime on the Internet is estimated to be many billions of dollars annually, but two-thirds of that total is said to consist of unpaid-for toll calls.

number of aliases (such as Gaven Stubberfield). Jaynes, a resident of North Carolina, had used a variety of business names as fronts for his spam and had sent some of the messages through servers in Virginia.

Prior to his 2004 arrest, Jaynes was widely recognized as the eighth most prolific spammer in the world. He had accumulated a personal fortune of $24 million and was earning $750,000 a month spamming get-rich-quick schemes, pornography, and sham products and services. Jaynes's sister, Jessica DeGroot, was also involved in the criminal scheme, and her name was on the credit card used to purchase domain names for Jaynes's spamming operation. During the search of Jaynes's residence, police found a compact disc containing at least 176 million full e-mail addresses and more than 1.3 billion user names, as well as Zip disks containing 107 million e-mail addresses. Jaynes also had a DVD containing not only e-mail addresses, but also other personal account information for millions of individuals. All of this information had been stolen from America Online.

Jaynes was convicted of three counts of felony spamming based on the fact that he had sent more than ten thousand pieces of spam per day on three separate days, using false Internet addresses and aliases. The jury sentenced him to nine years in prison (although prosecutors had asked for a fifteen-year sentence). The trial court postponed his prison sentence, however, until after the appeal. On appeal, Jaynes argued that Virginia did not have jurisdiction over him and that the state's criminal spamming statute violated his First Amendment rights to free speech. The state appellate court concluded that jurisdiction was proper because Jaynes had utilized servers within the state. On the First Amendment issue, the court held that the VCCA did not proscribe speech at all, because it only prohibited "intentional falsity as a machination [plot] to make massive, uncompensated use of the private property of an ISP [Internet service provider]."[b] This was the first felony conviction for spamming in the United States.

FOR CRITICAL ANALYSIS *How might criminal spamming statutes, which are likely to vary among the states, affect legitimate businesspersons who advertise on the Internet? If a business discovers that a spammer is using the business's name in connection with spam, what recourse does that business have?*

b. *Jaynes v. Commonwealth of Virginia,* 48 Va.App. 673, 634 S.E.2d 357 (2006).

---

or the monitoring of a computer to discover a business firm's plans and transactions. A cyberterrorist might also want to insert false codes or data. For example, the processing control system of a food manufacturer could be changed to alter the levels of ingredients so that consumers of the food would become ill.

A cyberterrorist attack on a major financial institution such as the New York Stock Exchange or a large bank could leave securities or money markets in flux and seriously affect the daily lives of millions of citizens. Similarly, any prolonged disruption of computer, cable, satellite, or telecommunications systems due to the actions of expert hackers would have serious repercussions on business operations—and national security—on a global level. Computer viruses are another tool that can be used by cyberterrorists to cripple communications networks.

Prosecuting Cyber Crimes

The "location" of cyber crime (cyberspace) has raised new issues in the investigation of crimes and the prosecution of offenders. A threshold issue is, of course, jurisdiction. A person who commits an act against a business in California, where the act is a cyber crime, might never have set foot in California but might instead reside in New York, or even in Canada, where the act may not be a crime. If the crime was committed via e-mail, the question arises as to whether the e-mail would constitute sufficient "minimum contacts" (see Chapter 3) for the victim's state to exercise jurisdiction over the perpetrator.

The brand name SPAM® comes from canned meat that contains pork. In this scene from a Monty Python comedy series, a small restaurant has a menu with only SPAM written on it. Various states have criminalized some online spamming. What arguments are used to justify passing criminal statutes relating to spam on the Internet? (Wikipedia Commons)

Identifying the wrongdoer can also be difficult. Cyber criminals do not leave physical traces, such as fingerprints or DNA samples, as evidence of their crimes. Even electronic "footprints" can be hard to find and follow. For example, e-mail may be sent through a remailer, an online service that guarantees that a message cannot be traced to its source.

For these reasons, laws written to protect physical property are difficult to apply in cyberspace. Nonetheless, governments at both the state and federal levels have taken significant steps toward controlling cyber crime, both by applying existing criminal statutes and by enacting new laws that specifically address wrongs committed in cyberspace.

The Computer Fraud and Abuse Act

Perhaps the most significant federal statute specifically addressing cyber crime is the Counterfeit Access Device and Computer Fraud and Abuse Act of 1984 (commonly known as the Computer Fraud and Abuse Act, or CFAA). This act, as amended by the National Information Infrastructure Protection Act of 1996,[29] provides, among other things, that a person who accesses a computer online, without authority, to obtain classified, restricted, or protected data, or attempts to do so, is subject to criminal prosecution. Such data could include financial and credit records, medical records, legal files, military and national security files, and other confidential information in government or private computers. The crime has two elements: accessing a computer without authority and taking the data.

This theft is a felony if it is committed for a commercial purpose or for private financial gain, or if the value of the stolen data (or computer time) exceeds $5,000. Penalties include fines and imprisonment for up to twenty years. A victim of computer theft can also bring a civil suit against the violator to obtain damages, an injunction, and other relief.

PREVENTING LEGAL DISPUTES

Although outside hackers are a threat to businesses, employees, former employees, and other "insiders" are responsible for most computer abuse, including breaches of information security. Therefore, businesspersons need to be cautious about which employees have access to computer data and to give employees access only to information that they need to know. Another important preventive measure is to have employees agree, in a written contract, not to disclose confidential information during or after employment without the employer's consent. Business owners should also make sure that they use the latest methods available to secure their computer systems, including firewalls and encryption techniques, for example.

---

29. 18 U.S.C. Section 1030.

REVIEWING Criminal Law and Cyber Crimes

Edward Hanousek worked for Pacific & Arctic Railway and Navigation Company (P&A) as a roadmaster of the White Pass & Yukon Railroad in Alaska. As an officer of the corporation, Hanousek was responsible "for every detail of the safe and efficient maintenance and construction of track, structures, and marine facilities of the entire railroad," including special projects. One project was a rock quarry, known as "6-mile," above the Skagway River. Next to the quarry, and just beneath the surface, ran a high-pressure oil pipeline owned by Pacific & Arctic Pipeline, Inc., P&A's sister company. When the quarry's backhoe operator punctured the pipeline, an estimated 1,000 to 5,000 gallons of oil were discharged into the river. Hanousek was charged with negligently discharging a harmful quantity of oil into a navigable water of the United States in violation of the criminal provisions of the Clean Water Act (CWA). Using the information presented in the chapter, answer the following questions.

1 Did Hanousek have the required mental state (*mens rea*) to be convicted of a crime? Why or why not?

2 Which theory discussed in the chapter would enable a court to hold Hanousek criminally liable for violating the statute regardless of whether he participated in, directed, or even knew about the specific violation?

3 Could the quarry's backhoe operator who punctured the pipeline also be charged with a crime in this situation? Explain.

4 Suppose that at trial, Hanousek argued that he could not be convicted because he was not aware of the requirements of the CWA. Would this defense be successful? Why or why not?

APPLICATION How Can You Protect against Identity Theft?*

Identity theft is probably the fastest-growing crime in the United States. The Federal Trade Commission received 686,683 complaints of consumer fraud in 2005. Of these, 255,000 (about 37 percent) were for identity fraud. It is estimated that identity theft occurs every seventy-nine seconds and that annual losses due to this crime will have exceeded $70 billion by 2008.

Dollar loss is not the only cost. Victims of identity theft spend, on average, about six hundred hours resolving the situation after someone has fraudulently used their names to purchase goods or services, open accounts, or make unauthorized charges to their accounts. Moreover, businesses typically are unable to recoup the costs of these unauthorized purchases because they usually can hold only the thief responsible.

Sources of Information That Might Be Used

The rise in identity theft has been fueled by the vast amount of personal information stored in databases. Educational institutions, governments, and businesses all store vast quantities of information about their students, clients, and customers. As a number of recent incidents demonstrate, unless measures are taken to secure these databases, they are vulnerable to thieves.

For example, personal information was stolen from numerous universities (including Georgetown University, Ohio University, the University of Texas, and Vermont State College). Even more disturbing is the number of U.S. government databases that have been breached. For example, a laptop computer containing confidential information for about 26.5 million veterans was stolen from an employee at the Department of Veteran Affairs. The U.S. Navy reported that the records of seventy-five thousand student loan recipients, employees, and military personnel and their families were breached.

Cities, counties, Internet sources (such as Hotels.com and Neinet), insurance companies (such as Aetna), manufacturing

firms (such as Honeywell), nonprofit organizations, and even newspapers (such as the *Boston Globe*) have lost copious amounts of personal information in the last few years. In 2005, Bank of America reportedly lost tapes containing records of 1.2 million federal employees. Businesses sometimes do not publicly report incidents of theft, so the list is probably even longer. Although not all of the lost data will ultimately be used for identity theft, the potential is huge.

CHECKLIST FOR THE BUSINESS OWNER

1 Review what personal information is kept in your computer databases. Wherever possible, eliminate Social Security numbers and other personal information and code all account numbers to limit access to the account holder.

2 Review employee access to databases containing personal account information. Some employees should have no access, some limited access, some full access. Instruct your employees in how computers and personal information are to be used and not used.

3 Establish policies on what types of information may be stored on portable sources, such as laptop computers. Monitoring is important. Also maintain accurate records of where confidential data are kept and who has access to the data.

4 Consider using passwords and digital signatures to protect your computer system and data against unauthorized use.

5 Shred paper documents as much as possible—remember that theft can come from rummaging through your trash.

6 Be prepared for possible identity theft when your wallet, purse, credit card, checks, or mail is stolen—report the loss immediately to credit-card companies, banks, and credit bureaus. Do not keep passwords or personal identification numbers in your wallet.

7 Avoid giving any personal information over the telephone and always verify the identity of the caller.

---

* This *Application* is not meant to substitute for the services of an attorney who is licensed to practice law in your state.

KEY TERMS

actus reus 169
arson 172
beyond a reasonable doubt 167
burglary 171
computer crime 191
consent 180
crime 167
cyber crime 166
cyberterrorist 192
double jeopardy 184
duress 181
embezzlement 173

entrapment 181
exclusionary rule 186
felony 178
forgery 172
grand jury 190
hacker 192
identity theft 191
indictment 187
information 190
insider trading 176
larceny 171
mens rea 169

misdemeanor 178
money laundering 176
petty offense 178
plea bargaining 182
probable cause 182
robbery 170
search warrant 182
self-defense 181
self-incrimination 182
white-collar crime 172

CHAPTER SUMMARY　Criminal Law and Cyber Crimes

**Civil Law
and Criminal Law**
(See pages 167–168.)

1. *Civil law*—Spells out the duties that exist between persons or between citizens and their governments, excluding the duty not to commit crimes.

2. *Criminal law*—Has to do with crimes, which are defined as wrongs against society proclaimed in statutes and, if committed, punishable by society through fines and/or imprisonment—and, in some cases, death. Because crimes are *offenses against society as a whole*, they are prosecuted by a public official, not by victims.

3. *Key differences*—An important difference between civil and criminal law is that the standard of proof is higher in criminal cases (see Exhibit 6–1 on page 167 for other differences between civil and criminal law).

4. *Civil liability for criminal acts*—A criminal act may give rise to both criminal liability and tort liability (see Exhibit 6–2 on page 168 for an example of criminal and tort liability for the same act).

Criminal Liability
(See pages 168–169.)

1. *Guilty act*—In general, some form of harmful act must be committed for a crime to exist.

2. *Intent*—An intent to commit a crime, or a wrongful mental state, is generally required for a crime to exist.

**Corporate
Criminal Liability**
(See pages 169–170.)

1. *Liability of corporations*—Corporations normally are liable for the crimes committed by their agents and employees within the course and scope of their employment. Corporations cannot be imprisoned, but they can be fined or denied certain legal privileges.

2. *Liability of corporate officers and directors*—Corporate directors and officers are personally liable for the crimes they commit and may be held liable for the actions of employees under their supervision.

Types of Crimes
(See pages 170–178.)

1. Crimes fall into five general categories: violent crime, property crime, public order crime, white-collar crime, and organized crime.

   a. Violent crimes are those that cause others to suffer harm or death, including murder, assault and battery, sexual assault (rape), and robbery.

   b. Property crimes are the most common form of crime. The offender's goal is to obtain some economic gain or to damage property. This category includes burglary, larceny, obtaining goods by false pretenses, receiving stolen property, arson, and forgery.

   c. Public order crimes are acts, such as public drunkenness, prostitution, gambling, and illegal drug use, that a statute has established are contrary to public values and morals.

   d. White-collar crimes are illegal acts committed by a person or business using nonviolent means to obtain a personal or business advantage. Usually, such crimes are committed in the

CHAPTER SUMMARY Criminal Law and Cyber Crimes—Continued

Types of Crimes— Continued	course of a legitimate occupation. Embezzlement, mail and wire fraud, bribery, bankruptcy fraud, the theft of trade secrets, and insider trading are examples of this category of crime.
	e. Organized crime is a form of crime conducted by groups operating illegitimately to satisfy the public's demand for illegal goods and services (such as gambling or illegal narcotics). This category of crime also includes money laundering and racketeering (RICO) violations.
	2. Each type of crime may also be classified according to its degree of seriousness. Felonies are serious crimes punishable by death or by imprisonment for more than one year. Misdemeanors are less serious crimes punishable by fines or by confinement for up to one year.
Defenses to Criminal Liability (See pages 178–182.)	Defenses to criminal liability include infancy, intoxication, insanity, mistake, consent, duress, justifiable use of force, entrapment, and the statute of limitations. Also, in some cases defendants may be relieved of criminal liability, at least in part, if they are given immunity.
Constitutional Safeguards and Criminal Procedures (See pages 182–187.)	1. *Fourth Amendment*—Provides protection against unreasonable searches and seizures and requires that probable cause exist before a warrant for a search or an arrest can be issued.
	2. *Fifth Amendment*—Requires due process of law, prohibits double jeopardy, and protects against self-incrimination.
	3. *Sixth Amendment*—Provides guarantees of a speedy trial, a trial by jury, a public trial, the right to confront witnesses, and the right to counsel.
	4. *Eighth Amendment*—Prohibits excessive bail and fines, and cruel and unusual punishment.
	5. *Exclusionary rule*—A criminal procedural rule that prohibits the introduction at trial of all evidence obtained in violation of constitutional rights, as well as any evidence derived from the illegally obtained evidence.
	6. *Miranda rule*—A rule set forth by the Supreme Court in *Miranda v. Arizona* holding that individuals who are arrested must be informed of certain constitutional rights, including their right to counsel.
Criminal Process (See pages 187–191.)	1. *Arrest, indictment, and trial*—Procedures governing arrest, indictment, and trial for a crime are designed to safeguard the rights of the individual against the state. See Exhibit 6–3 on page 189 for a summary of the procedural steps involved in prosecuting a criminal case.
	2. *Sentencing guidelines*—The federal government has established sentencing laws or guidelines. The federal sentencing guidelines indicate a range of penalties for each federal crime; federal judges consider these guidelines when imposing sentences on those convicted of federal crimes.
Cyber Crime (See pages 191–194.)	Cyber crimes occur in cyberspace. Examples include cyber theft (financial crimes committed with the aid of computers, as well as identity theft), hacking, and cyberterrorism. The Computer Fraud and Abuse Act of 1984, as amended by the National Information Infrastructure Protection Act of 1996, is a significant federal statute that addresses cyber crime.

FOR REVIEW

Answers for the even-numbered questions in this **For Review** *section can be found in Appendix E at the end of this text.*

1 What two elements must exist before a person can be held liable for a crime? Can a corporation commit crimes?

2 What are five broad categories of crimes? What is white-collar crime?

3 What defenses might be raised by criminal defendants to avoid liability for criminal acts?

4 What constitutional safeguards exist to protect persons accused of crimes? What are the basic steps in the criminal process?

5 What is cyber crime? What laws apply to crimes committed in cyberspace?

Thomson **The following multiple-choice question is representative of the types of questions available in one of the four sections of
NOW!** **ThomsonNOW for *Business Law Today*. ThomsonNOW also provides feedback for each response option, whether correct or
incorrect, and refers to the location within the chapter where the correct answer can be found.**

Under the "responsible corporate officer" doctrine, corporate officers

a are responsible for their own actions but are not responsible for the actions of employees under their supervision.

b are responsible only for crimes from which they personally benefit.

c are not personally responsible for any crimes committed by the corporation.

d are responsible for their own actions and also for the actions of employees under their supervision.

QUESTIONS AND CASE PROBLEMS

 ## HYPOTHETICAL SCENARIOS

6.1 Criminal versus Civil Trials. In criminal trials, the defendant must be proved guilty beyond a reasonable doubt, whereas in civil trials, the defendant need only be proved guilty by a preponderance of the evidence. Discuss why a higher standard of proof is required in criminal trials.

6.2 Hypothetical Question with Sample Answer. The following situations are similar (all involve the theft of Makoto's laptop computer), yet they represent three different crimes. Identify the three crimes, noting the differences among them.

1 While passing Makoto's house one night, Sarah sees a laptop computer left unattended on Makoto's porch. Sarah takes the computer, carries it home, and tells everyone she owns it.

2 While passing Makoto's house one night, Sarah sees Makoto outside with a laptop computer. Holding Makoto at gunpoint, Sarah forces him to give up the computer. Then Sarah runs away with it.

3 While passing Makoto's house one night, Sarah sees a laptop computer on a desk near a window. Sarah breaks the lock on the front door, enters, and leaves with the computer.

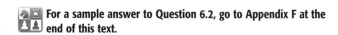 **For a sample answer to Question 6.2, go to Appendix F at the end of this text.**

6.3 Types of Crimes. Which, if any, of the following crimes necessarily involve illegal activity on the part of more than one person?

1 Bribery.

2 Forgery.

3 Embezzlement.

4 Larceny.

5 Receiving stolen property.

6.4 Double Jeopardy. Armington, while robbing a drugstore, shot and seriously injured Jennings, a drugstore clerk. Armington was subsequently convicted of armed robbery and assault and battery in a criminal trial. Jennings later brought a civil tort suit against Armington for damages. Armington contended that he could not be tried again for the same crime, as that would constitute double jeopardy, which is prohibited by the Fifth Amendment to the U.S. Constitution. Is Armington correct? Explain.

 ## CASE PROBLEMS

6.5 Fifth Amendment. The federal government was investigating a corporation and its employees. The alleged criminal wrongdoing, which included the falsification of corporate books and records, occurred between 1993 and 1996 in one division of the corporation. In 1999, the corporation pleaded guilty and agreed to cooperate in an investigation of the individuals who might have been involved in the improper corporate activities. "Doe I," "Doe II," and "Doe III" were officers of the corporation during the period when the illegal activities occurred and worked in the division where the wrongdoing took place. They were no longer working for the corporation, however, when, as part of the subsequent investigation, the government asked them to provide specific corporate documents in their possession. All three asserted the Fifth Amendment privilege against self-incrimination. The government asked a federal district court to order the three to produce the records. Corporate employees can be compelled to produce corporate records in a criminal proceeding because they hold the records as representatives of the corporation, to which the Fifth Amendment privilege against self-incrimination does not apply. Should *former* employees also be compelled to produce corporate records in their possession? Why or why not? [*In re Three Grand Jury Subpoenas Duces Tecum Dated January 29, 1999,* 191 F.3d 173 (2d Cir. 1999)]

6.6 Larceny. In February 2001, a homeowner hired Jimmy Smith, a contractor claiming to employ a crew of thirty workers, to build a garage. The homeowner paid Smith $7,950 and agreed to make additional payments as needed to complete the project, up to $15,900. Smith promised to start the next day and finish within eight weeks. Nearly a month passed with no work, while Smith lied to the homeowner that materials were on "back order." During a second month, footings were created for the foundation, and a subcontractor poured the concrete slab, but Smith did not return the homeowner's phone calls. After eight weeks, the homeowner confronted Smith, who promised to complete the job, worked on the site that day until lunch, and never returned. Three months later, the homeowner again confronted Smith, who promised to "pay [him] off" later that day but did not do so. In March 2002, the state of Georgia filed criminal charges against Smith. While his trial was pending, he promised to pay the homeowner "next week," but again failed to refund any money. The value of the labor performed before Smith abandoned the project was between $800 and $1,000, the value of the materials was $367, and the subcontractor was paid $2,270. Did Smith commit larceny? Explain. [*Smith v. State of Georgia,* 265 Ga.App.57, 592 S.E.2d 871 (2004)]

6.7 Case Problem with Sample Answer. The Sixth Amendment guarantees to a defendant who faces possible imprisonment the right to counsel at all critical stages of the criminal process, including the arraignment and the trial. In 1996, Felipe Tovar, a twenty-one-year-old college student, was arrested in Ames, Iowa, for operating a motor vehicle while under the influence of alcohol (OWI). Tovar was informed of his right to apply for court-appointed counsel and waived it. At his arraignment, he pleaded guilty. Six weeks later, he appeared for sentencing, again waived his right to counsel, and was sentenced to two days' imprisonment. In 1998, Tovar was convicted of OWI again, and in 2000, he was charged with OWI for a third time. In Iowa, a third OWI offense is a felony. Tovar asked the court not to use his first OWI conviction to enhance the third OWI charge. He argued that his 1996 waiver of counsel was not "intelligent" because the court did not make him aware of "the dangers and disadvantages of self-representation." What determines whether a person's choice in any situation is "intelligent"? What should determine whether a defendant's waiver of counsel is "intelligent" at critical stages of a criminal proceeding? [*Iowa v. Tovar,* 541 U.S. 77, 124 S.Ct. 1379, 158 L.Ed.2d 209 (2004)]

After you have answered Problem 6.7, compare your answer with the sample answer given on the Web site that accompanies this text. Go to **www.thomsonedu.com/westbuslaw/blt**, select "Chapter 6," and click on "Case Problem with Sample Answer."

6.8 Trial. Robert Michels met Allison Formal through an online dating Web site in 2002. Michels represented himself as the retired chief executive officer of a large company that he had sold for millions of dollars. In January 2003, Michels proposed that he and Formal create a limited liability company (a special form of business organization discussed in Chapter 27)— Formal Properties Trust, LLC—to "channel their investments in real estate." Formal agreed to contribute $100,000 to the company and wrote two $50,000 checks to "Michels and Associates, LLC." Six months later, Michels told Formal that their LLC had been formed in Delaware. Later, Formal asked Michels about her investments. He responded evasively, and she demanded that an independent accountant review the firm's records. Michels refused. Formal contacted the police. Michels was charged in a Virginia state court with obtaining money by false pretenses. The Delaware secretary of state verified, in two certified documents, that "Formal Properties Trust, L.L.C." and "Michels and Associates, L.L.C." did not exist in Delaware. Did the admission of the Delaware secretary of state's certified documents at Michels's trial violate his rights under the Sixth Amendment? Why or why not? [*Michels v. Commonwealth of Virginia,* 47 Va.App. 461, 624 S.E.2d 675 (2006)]

6.9 White-Collar Crime. Helm Instruction Co. in Maumee, Ohio, makes custom electrical control systems. Helm hired Patrick Walsh in September 1998 to work as comptroller. Walsh soon developed a close relationship with Richard Wilhelm, Helm's president, who granted Walsh's request to hire Shari Price as Walsh's assistant. Wilhelm was not aware that Walsh and Price were engaged in an extramarital affair. Over the next five years, Walsh and Price spent more than $200,000 of Helm's funds on themselves. Among other things, Walsh drew unauthorized checks on Helm's accounts to pay his personal credit cards, and issued to Price and himself unauthorized salary increases, overtime payments, and tuition reimbursement payments, altering Helm's records to hide the payments. After an investigation, Helm officials confronted Walsh. He denied the affair with Price, claimed that his unauthorized use of Helm's funds was an "interest-free loan" and argued that it was less of a burden on the company to pay his credit cards than to give him the salary increases to which he felt he was entitled. Did Walsh commit a crime? If so, what crime did he commit? Discuss. [*State v. Walsh,* __ Ohio App.3d __, __ N.E.2d __ (6 Dist. 2007)]

6.10 A Question of Ethics. *A troublesome issue concerning the constitutional privilege against self-incrimination has to do with the extent to which trickery by law enforcement officers during an interrogation may overwhelm a suspect's will to avoid self-incrimination. For example, in one case two officers questioned Charles McFarland, who was incarcerated in a state prison, about his connection to a handgun that had been used to shoot two other officers. McFarland was advised of his rights but was not asked whether he was willing to waive those rights. Instead, to induce McFarland to speak, the officers deceived him into believing that "[n]obody is going to give you* *charges," and he made incriminating admissions. He was indicted for possessing a handgun as a convicted felon.* [United States v. McFarland, 424 F.Supp.2d 427 (N.D.N.Y. 2006)]

1 Review the discussion of *Miranda v. Arizona* in this chapter's *Landmark in the Law* feature on page 188. Should McFarland's statements be suppressed—that is, not be admissible at trial—because he was not asked whether he

was willing to waive his rights before he made his self-incriminating statements? Does *Miranda* apply to McFarland's situation?

2 Do you think that it is fair for the police to resort to trickery and deception to bring those who may have committed crimes to justice? Why or why not? What rights or public policies must be balanced in deciding this issue?

CRITICAL THINKING AND WRITING ASSIGNMENTS

6.11 For Critical Analysis. Do you think that criminal procedure in this country is weighted too heavily in favor of accused persons? Can you think of a fairer way to balance the constitutional rights of accused persons against the right of society to be protected against criminal behavior? Should different criminal procedures be used when terrorism is involved? Explain.

6.12 Critical Legal Thinking. Ray steals a purse from an unattended car at a gas station. Because the purse contains money and a handgun, Ray is convicted of grand theft of property (cash) and grand theft of a firearm. On appeal, Ray claims that he is not guilty of grand theft of a firearm because he did not know that the purse contained a gun. Can Ray be convicted of the crime of grand theft of a firearm even though he did not know that the gun was in the purse?

6.13 **Video Question.** Go to this text's Web site at **www. thomsonedu.com/westbuslaw/blt** and select "Chapter 6." Click on "Video Questions" and view the video titled *Casino.* Then answer the following questions.

1 In the video, a casino manager, Ace (Robert De Niro), discusses how politicians "won their 'comp life' when they got elected." "Comps" are the free gifts that casinos give to high-stakes gamblers to keep their business. If an elected official accepts comps, is he or she committing a crime? If so, what type of crime? Explain your answers.

2 Assume that Ace committed a crime by giving politicians comps. Can the casino, Tangiers Corporation, be held liable for that crime? Why or why not? How could a court punish the corporation?

3 Suppose that the Federal Bureau of Investigation (FBI) wants to search the premises of Tangiers for evidence of criminal activity. If casino management refuses to consent to the search, what constitutional safeguards and criminal procedures, if any, protect Tangiers?

ONLINE ACTIVITIES

PRACTICAL INTERNET EXERCISES

Go to this text's Web site at **www.thomsonedu.com/westbuslaw/blt**, select "Chapter 6," and click on "Practical Internet Exercises." There you will find the following Internet research exercises that you can perform to learn more about the topics covered in this chapter.

PRACTICAL INTERNET EXERCISE 6-1 LEGAL PERSPECTIVE—Revisiting *Miranda*

PRACTICAL INTERNET EXERCISE 6-2 MANAGEMENT PERSPECTIVE—Hackers

PRACTICAL INTERNET EXERCISE 6-3 INTERNATIONAL PERSPECTIVE—Fighting Cyber Crime Worldwide

BEFORE THE TEST

Go to this text's Web site at **www.thomsonedu.com/westbuslaw/blt**, select "Chapter 6," and click on "Interactive Quizzes." You will find a number of interactive questions relating to this chapter.

CHAPTER 8
Nature and Classification

" The social order rests upon the stability and predictability of conduct, of which keeping promises is a large item.**"**

Roscoe Pound, 1870–1964
(American jurist)

LEARNING OBJECTIVES

AFTER READING THIS CHAPTER, YOU SHOULD BE ABLE TO ANSWER THE FOLLOWING QUESTIONS:

1 What is a contract? What is the objective theory of contracts?

2 What are the four basic elements necessary to the formation of a valid contract?

3 What is the difference between an implied-in-fact contract and an implied-in-law contract (quasi contract)?

4 How does a void contract differ from a voidable contract? What is an unenforceable contract?

5 Why have plain language laws been enacted? What rules guide the courts in interpreting contracts?

A s the eminent jurist Roscoe Pound observed in the chapter-opening quotation, "keeping promises" is important to a stable social order. Contract law deals with, among other things, the formation and keeping of promises. A **promise** is an assertion that something either will or will not happen in the future.

Like other types of law, contract law reflects our social values, interests, and expectations at a given point in time. It shows, for example, what kinds of promises our society thinks should be legally binding. It distinguishes between promises that create only *moral* obligations (such as a promise to take a friend to lunch) and promises that are legally binding (such as a promise to pay for merchandise purchased). Contract law also demonstrates what excuses our society accepts for breaking certain types of promises. In addition, it shows what promises are considered to be contrary to public policy—against the interests of society as a whole—and therefore legally invalid. When the person making a promise is a child or is mentally incompetent, for example, a question will arise as to whether the promise should be enforced. Resolving such questions is the essence of contract law.

PROMISE
An assertion that something either will or will not happen in the future.

AN OVERVIEW OF CONTRACT LAW

Before we look at the numerous rules that courts use to determine whether a particular promise will be enforced, it is necessary to understand some fundamental concepts of contract law. In this section, we describe the sources and general function of contract law. We also provide the definition of a contract and introduce the objective theory of contracts.

Sources of Contract Law

The common law governs all contracts except when it has been modified or replaced by statutory law, such as the Uniform Commercial Code (UCC),[1] or by administrative agency regulations. Contracts relating to services, real estate, employment, and insurance, for example, generally are governed by the common law of contracts.

Contracts for the sale and lease of goods, however, are governed by the UCC—to the extent that the UCC has modified general contract law. The relationship between general contract law and the law governing sales and leases of goods will be explored in detail in Chapter 15. In this unit covering the common law of contracts (Chapters 8 through 14), we indicate briefly in footnotes the areas in which the UCC has significantly altered common law contract principles.

The Function of Contracts

No aspect of modern life is entirely free of contractual relationships. You acquire rights and obligations, for example, when you borrow funds, when you buy or lease a house, when you obtain insurance, when you form a business, and when you purchase goods or services. Contract law is designed to provide stability and predictability for both buyers and sellers in the marketplace.

Contract law assures the parties to private agreements that the promises they make will be enforceable. Clearly, many promises are kept because the parties involved feel a moral obligation to do so or because keeping a promise is in their mutual self-interest. The **promisor** (the person making the promise) and the **promisee** (the person to whom the promise is made) may decide to honor their agreement for other reasons. Nevertheless, the rules of contract law are often followed in business agreements to avoid potential problems.

By supplying procedures for enforcing private agreements, contract law provides an essential condition for the existence of a market economy. Without a legal framework of reasonably assured expectations within which to plan and venture, businesspersons would be able to rely only on the good faith of others. Duty and good faith are usually sufficient, but when dramatic price changes or adverse economic conditions make it costly to comply with a promise, these elements may not be enough. Contract law is necessary to ensure compliance with a promise or to entitle the innocent party to some form of relief.

Definition of a Contract

A **contract** is an agreement that can be enforced in court. It is formed by two or more parties who agree to perform or to refrain from performing some act now or in the future. Generally, contract disputes arise when there is a promise of future performance. If the contractual promise is not fulfilled, the party who made it is subject to the sanctions of a court (see Chapter 13). That party may be required to pay monetary damages for failing to perform the contractual promise; in limited instances, the party may be required to perform the promised act.

The Objective Theory of Contracts

In determining whether a contract has been formed, the element of intent is of prime importance. In contract law, intent is determined by what is referred to as the **objective theory of contracts,** not by the personal or subjective intent, or belief, of a party. The theory is that a party's intention to enter into a contract is judged by outward, objective facts as interpreted

PROMISOR
A person who makes a promise.
PROMISEE
A person to whom a promise is made.

CONTRACT
An agreement that can be enforced in court; formed by two or more competent parties who agree, for consideration, to perform or to refrain from performing some legal act now or in the future.
OBJECTIVE THEORY OF CONTRACTS
A theory under which the intent to form a contract will be judged by outward, objective facts (what the party said when entering into the contract, how the party acted or appeared, and the circumstances surrounding the transaction) as interpreted by a reasonable person, rather than by the party's own secret, subjective intentions.

ON THE WEB

An extensive definition of the term *contract* is offered by the 'Lectric Law Library at www.lectlaw.com/def/c123.htm.

---

1. See Chapter 1 and Chapter 20 for further discussions of the significance and coverage of the Uniform Commercial Code (UCC). Excerpts from the UCC are presented in Appendix C at the end of this book.

The manager of a Toyota dealership in Glendora, California, displays the same contract written in four different Asian languages (Chinese, Korean, Vietnamese, and Tagalog). A consumer protection law in California requires certain businesses, such as car dealers and apartment owners, that have employees who orally negotiate contracts in these languages to provide written contracts in that same language. Why might it be important to the enforceability of a written contract that the consumer actually be able to read its provisions?
(AP Photo/Damian Dovarganes)

by a *reasonable person*, rather than by the party's own secret, subjective intentions. Objective facts include (1) what the party said when entering into the contract, (2) how the party acted or appeared, and (3) the circumstances surrounding the transaction. As will be discussed later in this chapter, in the section on express versus implied contracts, intent to form a contract may be manifested by conduct, as well as by words, oral or written.

Freedom of Contract and Freedom from Contract

As a general rule, the law recognizes everyone's ability to enter freely into contractual arrangements. This recognition is called *freedom of contract*, a freedom protected by the U.S. Constitution in Article I, Section 10. Because freedom of contract is a fundamental public policy of the United States, courts rarely interfere with contracts that have been voluntarily made.

Of course, as in other areas of the law, there are many exceptions to the general rule that contracts voluntarily negotiated will be enforced. For example, illegal bargains, agreements that unreasonably restrain trade, and certain unfair contracts made between one party with a great amount of bargaining power and another with little power are generally not enforced. In addition, as you will read in Chapter 10, certain contracts and clauses may not be enforceable if they are contrary to public policy, fairness, and justice. These exceptions provide *freedom from contract* for persons who may have been forced into making contracts unfavorable to themselves.

ELEMENTS OF A CONTRACT

The many topics that will be discussed in the following chapters on contract law require an understanding of the basic elements of a valid contract and the way in which the contract was created. The topics to be covered in this unit on contracts also require an understanding of the types of circumstances in which even legally valid contracts will not be enforced.

Requirements of a Valid Contract

The following list briefly describes the four requirements that must be met for a valid contract to exist. If any of these elements is lacking, no contract will have been formed. (Each item will be explained more fully in subsequent chapters.)

1 *Agreement.* An agreement to form a contract includes an *offer* and an *acceptance*. One party must offer to enter into a legal agreement, and another party must accept the terms of the offer (see Chapter 9).

2 *Consideration.* Any promises made by parties must be supported by legally sufficient and bargained-for consideration (something of value received or promised to convince a person to make a deal) (see Chapter 9).

3 *Contractual capacity.* Both parties entering into the contract must have the contractual capacity to do so; the law must recognize them as possessing characteristics that qualify them as competent parties (see Chapter 10).

4 *Legality.* The contract's purpose must be to accomplish some goal that is legal and not against public policy (see Chapter 10).

Defenses to the Enforceability of a Contract

Even if all of the elements of a valid contract are present, a contract may be unenforceable if the following requirements are not met.

1 *Genuineness of assent.* The consent of both parties must be genuine. For example, if a contract was formed as a result of fraud, mistake, or duress, the contract may not be enforceable.

2 *Form.* The contract must be in whatever form the law requires; for example, some contracts must be in writing to be enforceable.

The failure to fulfill either requirement may be raised as a *defense* to the enforceability of an otherwise valid contract. Both requirements will be explained in more detail in Chapter 11.

TYPES OF CONTRACTS

There are numerous types of contracts. They are categorized based on legal distinctions as to their formation, performance, and enforceability. Exhibit 8–1 illustrates three classifications, or categories, of contracts based on their mode of formation.

Contract Formation

As you can see in Exhibit 8–1, three classifications, or categories, of contracts are based on how and when a contract is formed. The best way to explain each type of contract is to compare one type with another, as we do in the following pages.

Bilateral versus Unilateral Contracts   Every contract involves at least two parties. The **offeror** is the party making the offer. The **offeree** is the party to whom the offer is made. The offeror always promises to do or not to do something and thus is also a promisor. Whether the contract is classified as *bilateral* or *unilateral* depends on what the offeree must do to accept the offer and bind the offeror to a contract.

Bilateral Contracts. If the offeree can accept the offer simply by promising to perform, the contract is a **bilateral contract.** Hence, a bilateral contract is a "promise for a promise." An example of a bilateral contract is a contract in which one person agrees to buy another person's automobile for a specified price. No performance, such as the payment

OFFEROR
A person who makes an offer.

OFFEREE
A person to whom an offer is made.

BILATERAL CONTRACT
A type of contract that arises when a promise is given in exchange for a return promise.

EXHIBIT 8–1	Classifications Based on Contract Formation

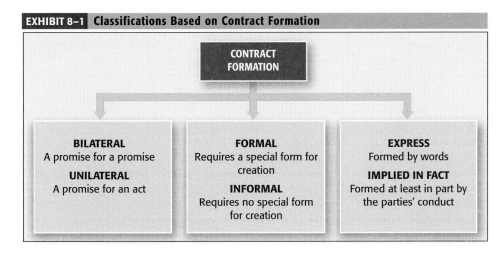

CONTRACT FORMATION

BILATERAL	**FORMAL**	**EXPRESS**
A promise for a promise	Requires a special form for creation	Formed by words
UNILATERAL	**INFORMAL**	**IMPLIED IN FACT**
A promise for an act	Requires no special form for creation	Formed at least in part by the parties' conduct

of funds or delivery of goods, need take place for a bilateral contract to be formed. The contract comes into existence at the moment the promises are exchanged.

■EXAMPLE 8.1 Jeff offers to buy Ann's digital camera for $200. Jeff tells Ann that he will give her the cash for the camera on the following Friday, when he gets paid. Ann accepts Jeff's offer and promises to give him the camera when he pays her on Friday. Jeff and Ann have formed a bilateral contract. ■

Unilateral Contracts. If the offer is phrased so that the offeree can accept only by completing the contract performance, the contract is a **unilateral contract.** Hence, a unilateral contract is a "promise for an act." In other words, the contract is formed not at the moment when promises are exchanged but rather when the contract is *performed.*

■EXAMPLE 8.2 Reese says to Celia, "If you drive my car from New York to Los Angeles, I'll give you $1,000." Only on Celia's completion of the act—bringing the car to Los Angeles—does she fully accept Reese's offer to pay $1,000. If she chooses not to accept the offer to drive the car to Los Angeles, there are no legal consequences. ■

Contests, lotteries, and other competitions offering prizes are also examples of offers for unilateral contracts. If a person complies with the rules of the contest—such as by submitting the right lottery number at the right place and time—a unilateral contract is formed, binding the organization offering the prize to a contract to perform as promised in the offer.

Can a school's, or an employer's, letter of tentative acceptance to a prospective student, or a possible employee, qualify as a unilateral contract? That was the issue in the following case.

UNILATERAL CONTRACT
A contract that results when an offer can be accepted only by the offeree's performance.

CASE 8.1 Ardito v. City of Providence

United States District Court, District of Rhode Island, 263 F.Supp.2d 358 (2003).

FACTS In 2001, the city of Providence, Rhode Island, decided to begin hiring police officers to fill vacancies in its police department. Because only individuals who had graduated from the Providence Police Academy were eligible, the city also decided to conduct two training sessions, the "60th and 61st Police Academies." To be admitted, an applicant had to pass a series of tests and be deemed qualified by members of the department after an interview. The applicants judged most qualified were sent a letter informing them that they had been selected to attend the academy if they successfully completed a medical checkup and a psychological examination. The letter for the applicants to the 61st Academy, dated October 15, stated that it was "a conditional offer of employment." Meanwhile, a new chief of police, Dean Esserman, decided to revise the selection process, which caused some of those who had received the letter to be rejected. Derek Ardito and thirteen other newly rejected applicants filed a suit in a federal district court against the city, seeking a halt to the 61st Academy unless they were allowed to attend. They alleged in part that the city was in breach of contract.

ISSUE Was the October 15 letter a unilateral offer that the plaintiffs had accepted by passing the required medical and psychological examinations?

DECISION Yes. The court issued an injunction to prohibit the city from conducting the 61st Police Academy unless the plaintiffs were included.

REASON The court found the October 15 letter to be "a classic example of an offer to enter into a unilateral contract. The October 15 letter expressly stated that it was a 'conditional offer of employment' and the message that it conveyed was that the recipient would be admitted into the 61st Academy if he or she successfully completed the medical and psychological examinations." The court contrasted the letter with "notices sent to applicants by the City at earlier stages of the selection process. Those notices merely informed applicants that they had completed a step in the process and remained eligible to be considered for admission into the Academy. Unlike the October 15 letter, the prior notices did not purport to extend a 'conditional offer' of admission." The court concluded that "[t]he plaintiffs accepted the City's offer

CASE 8.1–Continued

of admission into the Academy by satisfying the specified conditions. Each of the plaintiffs submitted to and passed lengthy and intrusive medical and psychological examinations."

 WHAT IF THE FACTS WERE DIFFERENT?
Suppose that the October 15 letter had used the phrase potential offer of employment *rather than the word* conditional. *Would the court in this case still have considered the letter to be a unilateral contract?*

Revocation of Offers for Unilateral Contracts. A problem arises in unilateral contracts when the promisor attempts to *revoke* (cancel) the offer after the promisee has begun performance but before the act has been completed. **■EXAMPLE 8.3** Suppose that Roberta offers to buy Ed's sailboat, moored in San Francisco, on delivery of the boat to Roberta's dock in Newport Beach, three hundred miles south of San Francisco. Ed rigs the boat and sets sail. Shortly before his arrival at Newport Beach, Ed receives a radio message from Roberta withdrawing her offer. Roberta's offer is to form a unilateral contract, and only Ed's delivery of the sailboat at her dock is an acceptance. ■

In contract law, offers are normally *revocable* (capable of being taken back, or canceled) until accepted. Under the traditional view of unilateral contracts, Roberta's revocation would terminate the offer. Because of the harsh effect on the offeree of the revocation of an offer to form a unilateral contract, the modern-day view is that once performance has been *substantially* undertaken, the offeror cannot revoke the offer. Thus, in our example, even though Ed has not yet accepted the offer by complete performance, Roberta is prohibited from revoking it. Ed can deliver the boat and bind Roberta to the contract.

Formal versus Informal Contracts   Another classification system divides contracts into formal contracts and informal contracts. **Formal contracts** are contracts that require a special form or method of creation (formation) to be enforceable.[2] *Contracts under seal* are a type of formal contract that involves a formalized writing with a special seal attached.[3] In the past, the seals were often made of wax and impressed on the paper document. Today, the significance of the seal in contract law has lessened, though standard-form contracts still sometimes include a place for a seal next to the signature lines. Letters of credit, which are frequently used in international sales contracts, are another type of formal contract. As will be discussed in Chapter 39, letters of credit are agreements to pay contingent on the purchaser's receipt of invoices and bills of lading (documents evidencing receipt of, and title to, goods shipped).

Informal contracts (also called *simple contracts*) include all other contracts. No special form is required (except for certain types of contracts that must be in writing), as the contracts are usually based on their substance rather than their form. Typically, businesspersons put their contracts in writing to ensure that there is some proof of a contract's existence should problems arise.

Express versus Implied Contracts   Contracts may also be formed and categorized as express or implied by the conduct of the parties. We look here at the differences between these two types of contracts.

ON THE WEB

For easy-to-understand definitions of legal terms and concepts, including terms and concepts relating to contract law, go to **dictionary.law.com** and key in a term, such as *contract* or *consideration.*

FORMAL CONTRACT
A contract that by law requires a specific form, such as being executed under seal, for its validity.

INFORMAL CONTRACT
A contract that does not require a specified form or formality to be valid.

KEEP IN MIND Not every contract is a document with "Contract" printed in block letters at the top. A contract can be expressed in a letter, a memo, or another document.

---

2. See *Restatement (Second) of Contracts*, Section 6, which explains that formal contracts include (1) contracts under seal, (2) recognizances, (3) negotiable instruments, and (4) letters of credit. As mentioned in Chapter 1, *Restatements of the Law* are books that summarize court decisions on a particular topic and that courts often refer to for guidance.
3. A seal may be actual (made of wax or some other durable substance), impressed on the paper, or indicated simply by the word *seal* or the letters *L.S.* at the end of the document. *L.S.* stands for *locus sigilli*, which means "the place for the seal."

What determines whether a contract for accounting, tax preparation, or any other service is an express contract or an implied-in-fact contract? (Getty Images)

EXPRESS CONTRACT
A contract in which the terms of the agreement are stated in words, oral or written.

Express Contracts. In an **express contract,** the terms of the agreement are fully and explicitly stated in words, oral or written. A signed lease for an apartment or a house is an express written contract. If a classmate accepts your offer to sell your textbooks from last semester for $75, an express oral contract has been made.

IMPLIED-IN-FACT CONTRACT
A contract formed in whole or in part from the conduct of the parties (as opposed to an express contract).

Implied Contracts. A contract that is implied from the conduct of the parties is called an **implied-in-fact contract,** or an implied contract. This type of contract differs from an express contract in that the *conduct* of the parties, rather than their words, creates and defines at least some of the terms of the contract. (Note that a contract can be a mixture of an express contract and an implied-in-fact contract. In other words, a contract may contain some express terms, while others are implied.)

Requirements for an Implied-in-Fact Contract. For an implied-in-fact contract to arise, certain requirements must be met. Normally, if the following conditions exist, a court will hold that an implied contract was formed:

1 The plaintiff furnished some service or property.
2 The plaintiff expected to be paid for that service or property, and the defendant knew or should have known that payment was expected (by using the objective-theory-of-contracts test discussed on pages 231 and 232).
3 The defendant had a chance to reject the services or property and did not.

■**EXAMPLE 8.4** Suppose that you need an accountant to fill out your tax return this year. You look through the Yellow Pages and find an accounting firm located in your neighborhood. You drop by the firm's office, explain your problem to an accountant, and learn what fees will be charged. The next day you return and give the receptionist all of the necessary information and documents, such as canceled checks and W-2 forms. Then you walk out the door without saying anything expressly to the accountant.

In this situation, you have entered into an implied-in-fact contract to pay the accountant the usual and reasonable fees for her accounting services. The contract is implied by your conduct and by hers. She expects to be paid for completing your tax return. By bringing in the records she will need to do the work, you have implied an intent to pay for her services. ■ (For another example of how an implied-in-fact contract can arise, see the *Application* feature at the end of this chapter.)

Contract Performance

Contracts are also classified according to their state of performance. A contract that has been fully performed on both sides is called an **executed contract.** A contract that has not been fully performed on either side is called an **executory contract.** If one party has fully performed but the other has not, the contract is said to be executed on the one side and executory on the other, but the contract is still classified as executory.

■**EXAMPLE 8.5** Assume that you agree to buy ten tons of coal from Western Coal Company. Further assume that Western has delivered the coal to your steel mill, where it is now being burned. At this point, the contract is an executory contract—it is executed on the part of Western and executory on your part. After you pay Western for the coal, the contract will be executed on both sides. ■

Contract Enforceability

A **valid contract** has the four elements necessary for contract formation: (1) an agreement (offer and acceptance) (2) supported by legally sufficient consideration (3) for a legal purpose and (4) made by parties who have the legal capacity to enter into the contract. As mentioned, we will discuss each of these elements in the following chapters. As you can see in Exhibit 8–2, valid contracts may be enforceable, voidable, or unenforceable. Additionally, a contract may be referred to as a *void contract.* We look next at the meaning of the terms *voidable, unenforceable,* and *void* in relation to contract enforceability.

Voidable Contracts   A **voidable contract** is a *valid* contract but one that can be avoided at the option of one or both of the parties. The party having the option can elect either to

EXECUTED CONTRACT
A contract that has been completely performed by both parties.

EXECUTORY CONTRACT
A contract that has not as yet been fully performed.

VALID CONTRACT
A contract that results when the elements necessary for contract formation (agreement, consideration, legal purpose, and contractual capacity) are present.

VOIDABLE CONTRACT
A contract that may be legally avoided (canceled, or annulled) at the option of one or both of the parties.

EXHIBIT 8–2 Enforceable, Voidable, Unenforceable, and Void Contracts

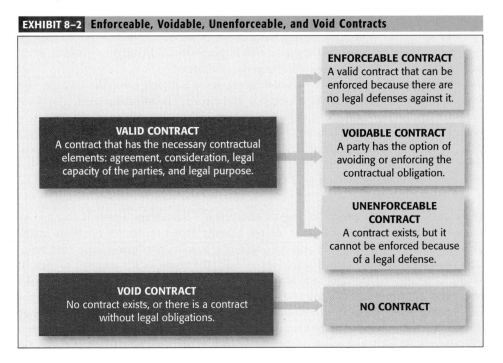

ENFORCEABLE CONTRACT
A valid contract that can be enforced because there are no legal defenses against it.

VALID CONTRACT
A contract that has the necessary contractual elements: agreement, consideration, legal capacity of the parties, and legal purpose.

VOIDABLE CONTRACT
A party has the option of avoiding or enforcing the contractual obligation.

UNENFORCEABLE CONTRACT
A contract exists, but it cannot be enforced because of a legal defense.

VOID CONTRACT
No contract exists, or there is a contract without legal obligations.

NO CONTRACT

avoid any duty to perform or to *ratify* (make valid) the contract. If the contract is avoided, both parties are released from it. If it is ratified, both parties must fully perform their respective legal obligations.

As you will read in Chapter 10, contracts made by minors, insane persons, and intoxicated persons may be voidable. As a general rule, for example, contracts made by minors are voidable at the option of the minor. Additionally, contracts entered into under fraudulent conditions are voidable at the option of the defrauded party. Contracts entered into under legally defined duress or undue influence are voidable (see Chapter 11).

UNENFORCEABLE CONTRACT
A valid contract rendered unenforceable by some statute or law.

Unenforceable Contracts   An **unenforceable contract** is one that cannot be enforced because of certain legal defenses against it. It is not unenforceable because a party failed to satisfy a legal requirement of the contract; rather, it is a valid contract rendered unenforceable by some statute or law. For example, some contracts must be in writing (see Chapter 11), and if they are not, they will not be enforceable except in certain exceptional circumstances.

VOID CONTRACT
A contract having no legal force or binding effect.

Void Contracts   A **void contract** is no contract at all. The terms *void* and *contract* are contradictory. None of the parties has any legal obligations if a contract is void. A contract can be void because, for example, one of the parties was previously determined by a court to be legally insane (and thus lacked the legal capacity to enter into a contract) or because the purpose of the contract was illegal.

QUASI CONTRACTS

QUASI CONTRACT
A fictional contract imposed on the parties by a court in the interests of fairness and justice; usually imposed to avoid the unjust enrichment of one party at the expense of another.

Quasi contracts, or contracts *implied in law*, are wholly different from actual contracts. Express contracts and implied-in-fact contracts are actual or true contracts formed by the words or actions of the parties. The word *quasi* is Latin for "as if" or "analogous to." Quasi contracts are not true contracts because they do not arise from any agreement, express or implied, between the parties themselves. Rather, quasi contracts are fictional contracts that courts can impose on the parties "as if" the parties had entered into an actual contract. They are equitable rather than legal contracts. Usually, quasi contracts are imposed to avoid the *unjust enrichment* of one party at the expense of another. The doctrine of unjust enrichment is based on the theory that individuals should not be allowed to profit or enrich themselves inequitably at the expense of others.

■EXAMPLE 8.6 Suppose that a vacationing physician is driving down the highway and finds Emerson lying unconscious on the side of the road. The physician renders medical aid that saves Emerson's life. Although the injured, unconscious Emerson did not solicit the medical aid and was not aware that the aid had been rendered, Emerson received a valuable benefit, and the requirements for a quasi contract were fulfilled. In such a situation, the law normally will impose a quasi contract, and Emerson will have to pay the physician for the reasonable value of the medical services provided. ■

ETHICAL ISSUE 8.1

When does enrichment qualify as "unjust enrichment"? Sometimes a party is enriched by (benefits from) the actions of another, yet the benefits do not necessarily constitute unjust enrichment. For example, in one case the owner of a building (the lessor) leased the building to a commercial tenant (the lessee) for five years. The lessee, which assumed all responsibility for repairs, maintenance, and alterations, hired DCB Construction Company to make alterations to the premises at a cost of about $300,000. The lessor told DCB that it would not be responsible for any of the costs. Nonetheless, when the lessee quit paying rent, was evicted, and failed to pay DCB for the completed work, DCB sued the lessor for the amount still owing ($280,000). In this case, clearly the lessor had benefited from DCB's work. Yet did this benefit amount to unjust enrichment under the law? No, stated the court. The court pointed out that DCB did the work for the lessee and was notified by the lessor that it would not be liable for the costs of the work. Further, no fraud or mistake was involved. The court noted that the courts almost always reject unjust enrichment claims such as this one.[4]

◼

Limitations on Quasi-Contractual Recovery

Although quasi contracts exist to prevent unjust enrichment, the party who obtains a benefit is not liable for the fair value in some situations. Basically, a party who has conferred a benefit on someone else unnecessarily or as a result of misconduct or negligence cannot invoke the doctrine of quasi contract. The enrichment in those situations will not be considered "unjust."

◼ **EXAMPLE 8.7** You take your car to the local car wash and ask to have it run through the washer and to have the gas tank filled. While your car is being washed, you go to a nearby shopping center for two hours. In the meantime, one of the workers at the car wash mistakenly assumes that your car is the one that he is supposed to hand wax. When you come back, you are presented with a bill for a full tank of gas, a wash job, and a hand wax. Clearly, a benefit has been conferred on you. But this benefit occurred because of a mistake by the car wash employee. You have not been *unjustly* enriched under these circumstances. People normally cannot be forced to pay for benefits "thrust" on them. ◼

When an Actual Contract Exists

The doctrine of quasi contract generally cannot be used when an actual contract covers the area in controversy. This is because a remedy already exists if a party is unjustly enriched as a result of a breach of contract: the nonbreaching party can sue the breaching party for breach of contract. In this instance, a court does not need to impose a quasi contract to achieve justice. ◼ **EXAMPLE 8.8** Fung contracts with Cameron to deliver a furnace to a building owned by Bateman. Fung delivers the furnace, but Cameron never pays Fung. Bateman has been unjustly enriched in this situation, to be sure. Nevertheless, Fung cannot recover from Bateman in quasi contract because Fung had an actual contract with Cameron. Fung already has a remedy—he can sue for breach of contract to recover the price of the furnace from Cameron. No quasi contract need be imposed by the court in this situation to achieve justice. ◼

INTERPRETATION OF CONTRACTS

Sometimes parties agree that a contract has been formed but disagree on its meaning or legal effect. One reason that this may happen is that one of the parties is not familiar with the legal terminology used in the contract. To an extent, *plain language laws* have helped to avoid this difficulty. Sometimes, though, a dispute may still arise over the meaning of a contract simply because the rights or obligations under the contract are not expressed clearly—no matter how "plain" the language used.

In this section, we look at some common law rules of contract interpretation. These rules, including the *plain meaning rule* and various other rules that have evolved over time, provide the courts with guidelines for deciding disputes over how contract terms or provisions should be interpreted. Exhibit 8–3 on the following page provides a brief graphic summary of how these rules are applied.

---
4. *DCB Construction Co. v. Central City Development Co.*, 940 P.2d 958 (Colo.App. 1997).

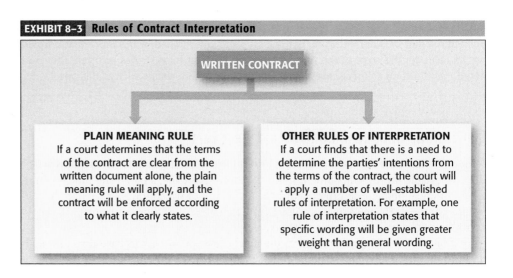

EXHIBIT 8-3 Rules of Contract Interpretation

WRITTEN CONTRACT

PLAIN MEANING RULE
If a court determines that the terms of the contract are clear from the written document alone, the plain meaning rule will apply, and the contract will be enforced according to what it clearly states.

OTHER RULES OF INTERPRETATION
If a court finds that there is a need to determine the parties' intentions from the terms of the contract, the court will apply a number of well-established rules of interpretation. For example, one rule of interpretation states that specific wording will be given greater weight than general wording.

PREVENTING LEGAL DISPUTES

To avoid disputes over contract interpretation, business managers should make sure that their intentions are clearly expressed in their contracts. Careful drafting of contracts not only helps prevent potential disputes over the meaning of certain terms but may also be crucial if the firm brings or needs to defend against a lawsuit for breach of contract. By using simple, clear language and avoiding legalese, managers take a major step toward avoiding contract disputes.

Plain Language Laws

DON'T FORGET Most laws, like most contracts, can be expressed in plain English.

Today, the federal government and a majority of the states have enacted plain language laws to regulate legal writing. All federal agencies are required to use plain language in most of their forms and written communications. Plain language requirements have been extended to agency rulemaking as well.

At the state level, plain language laws frequently apply to consumer contracts that are primarily for personal, family, or household purposes. For example, a New York law requires residential leases and other consumer contracts to be (1) "written in a clear and coherent manner using words with common and everyday meanings" and (2) "appropriately divided and captioned by [the] various sections."[5] If a party to a contract, such as an insurance company, violates a plain language statute, a consumer can sue that party for damages if she or he suffers harm (unless the party can show that it made a good faith effort to comply with the statute). Some state statutes even allow parties to submit proposed contracts to the state attorney general, whose approval then eliminates any liability for damages because of a supposed violation of the plain language statute.

The legal profession is also moving toward plain English, and court rules in many jurisdictions require attorneys to use plain language in court documents. At times, judges have refused to accept motions that are incoherent due to their highly technical legal language. A number of states have also rewritten their jury instructions. Generally, the revised instructions are phrased in simpler language, use the active voice more often, and avoid "legalese" to the extent that it is possible to do so.

---

5. New York General Obligations Law Section 5-702.

This spacecraft at Astrotech Corporation in Florida is designed to collect information on conditions in space that can cause damage to communication systems, power grids, and satellites. Suppose that a visiting engineer suggests a design modification that the company incorporates into later models of the spacecraft. Should that engineer receive compensation for the modification even though she or he had no written contract with the company? Why or why not? Under what doctrine could a court impose a fictional contract to compensate the visiting engineer? (AP Photo/ John Raoux)

The Plain Meaning Rule

When a contract's writing is clear and unequivocal, a court will enforce it according to its obvious terms. The meaning of the terms must be determined from the *face of the instrument*—from the written document alone. This is sometimes referred to as the *plain meaning rule.*

Under this rule, if a contract's words appear to be clear and unambiguous, a court cannot consider *extrinsic evidence*, which is any evidence not contained in the document itself. Admissibility of extrinsic evidence can significantly affect how a court interprets ambiguous contractual provisions and thus can affect the outcome of litigation. The following case illustrates these points.

NOTE No one can avoid contractual obligations by claiming that she or he did not read the contract. A contract normally is interpreted as if each party read every word carefully.

CASE 8.2 | **Wagner v. Columbia Pictures Industries, Inc.**

California Court of Appeal, Second District, Division 7, 146 Cal.App.4th 586, 52 Cal.Rptr.3d 898 (2007).

FACTS Actor Robert Wagner entered into an agreement with Spelling-Goldberg Productions (SGP) "relating to Charlie's Angels (herein called the 'series')." The contract entitled Wagner to 50 percent of the net profits that SGP received "for the right to exhibit photoplays of the series and from the exploitation of all ancillary, music and subsidiary rights in connection therewith." SGP hired Ivan Goff and Ben Roberts to write the series, under a contract subject to the Writers Guild

of America Minimum Basic Agreement (MBA).[a] The MBA stipulates that the writer of a television show retains the right to make and market films based on the material, subject to the producer's right to buy this right if the writer decides to sell it within five years. The first "Charlie's Angels" episode aired in 1976. In 1982, SGP sold its rights to the series to

a. The Writers Guild of America is an association of screen and television writers that negotiates industry-wide agreements with motion picture and television producers to cover the rights of its members.

CASE 8.2–Continues next page

CASE 8.2–Continued

Columbia Pictures Industries, Inc. Thirteen years later, Columbia bought the movie rights to the material from Goff's and Roberts's heirs. In 2000 and 2003, Columbia produced and distributed two "Charlie's Angels" films. Wagner filed a suit in a California state court against Columbia, claiming a share of the profits from the films. The court granted Columbia's motion for summary judgment. Wagner appealed to a state intermediate appellate court.

ISSUE Does the language of the Wagner contract with SGP entitle Columbia to all of the profits from the two "Charlie's Angels" films?

DECISION Yes. The state intermediate appellate court affirmed the lower court's judgment. The contract "unambiguously" stated the conditions under which the parties were to share the films' profits, and those conditions had not occurred.

REASON Wagner offered evidence to show that a previous contract with SGP had been intended to give him half of the net profits from a property titled "Love Song" received from all sources without limitation as to source or time. Wagner argued that the "Charlie's Angels" agreement used identical language in its profits provision, which thus should be interpreted to give him the same share. The court stated that an "agreement is the writing itself." Extrinsic evidence is not admissible "to show intention independent of an unambiguous written instrument." In this case, even if the parties intended Wagner to share in the profits from all sources, "they did not say so in their contract." Under the language of the contract, Wagner was entitled to share in the profits from the exercise of the movie rights to "Charlie's Angels" if those rights were exploited as "ancillary" or "subsidiary" to the primary "right to exhibit photoplays of the series" but not if those rights were acquired separately. SGP's contract with Goff and Roberts was subject to the MBA, under which the writers kept the movie rights, which the producer could buy if the writers opted to sell them within five years. SGP did not acquire the movie rights to "Charlie's Angels" by exercising this right within the five-year period. Columbia obtained those rights independently more than five years later.

 FOR CRITICAL ANALYSIS–Legal Question *How might the result in this case have been different if the court had allowed Wagner's extrinsic evidence of a prior contract regarding "Love Song" to be used as evidence in this dispute?*

Other Rules of Interpretation

Generally, a court will interpret the language to give effect to the parties' intent *as expressed in their contract.* This is the primary purpose of the rules of interpretation—to determine the parties' intent from the language used in their agreement and to give effect to that intent. A court normally will not make or remake a contract, nor will it normally interpret the language according to what the parties *claim* their intent was when they made the contract.[6] The courts use the following rules in interpreting contractual terms:

1 Insofar as possible, a reasonable, lawful, and effective meaning will be given to all of a contract's terms.

2 A contract will be interpreted as a whole; individual, specific clauses will be considered subordinate to the contract's general intent. All writings that are a part of the same transaction will be interpreted together.

3 Terms that were the subject of separate negotiation will be given greater consideration than standardized terms and terms that were not negotiated separately.

4 A word will be given its ordinary, commonly accepted meaning, and a technical word or term will be given its technical meaning, unless the parties clearly intended something else.

5 Specific and exact wording will be given greater consideration than general language.

---

6. Nevertheless, if a court finds that, even after applying the rules of interpretation, the terms are susceptible to more than one meaning, the court may permit extrinsic evidence to prove what the parties intended. See, for example, *Langdon v. United Restaurants, Inc.,* 105 S.W.3d 882 (Mo.Ct.App. 2003).

6 Written or typewritten terms prevail over preprinted terms.

7 Because a contract should be drafted in clear and unambiguous language, a party that uses ambiguous expressions is held to be responsible for the ambiguities. Thus, when the language has more than one meaning, it will be interpreted *against* the party that drafted the contract.

8 Evidence of trade usage, prior dealing, and course of performance may be admitted to clarify the meaning of an ambiguously worded contract. (We define and discuss these terms in Chapter 15.) What each of the parties does pursuant to the contract will be interpreted as consistent with what the other does and with any relevant usage of trade and course of dealing or performance. Express terms (terms expressly stated in the contract) are given the greatest weight, followed by course of performance, course of dealing, and custom and usage of trade—in that order. When considering custom and usage, a court will look at the trade customs and usage common to the particular business or industry and to the locale in which the contract was made or is to be performed.

In the following case, the ordinary meaning of a word was at the heart of a significant dispute.

> "How many a dispute could have been deflated into a single paragraph if the disputants had dared define their terms."
>
> ARISTOTLE,
> 384–322 B.C.E.
> (Greek philosopher)

CASE 8.3 **Citizens Communications Co. v. Trustmark Insurance**

United States District Court, District of Connecticut, 303 F.Supp.2d 197 (2004).

FACTS Citizens Communications Company is one of the largest telecommunications companies in the United States and is the parent company to Frontier Telephone, which offers services in thirty states. Citizens provides health insurance to its nearly five thousand employees under a self-funded health plan. Under such a plan, a company normally buys an insurance policy to cover claims that exceed a certain amount. Citizens bought a policy from Trustmark Insurance to cover claims that exceeded $100,000, subject to a $1 million maximum benefit per employee. In November 1999, Garry Lonquist, a Citizens employee, experienced complications from heart surgery that required intensive care. By January, Lonquist's medical bills exceeded $1 million. Trustmark refused to renew Citizens' policy unless, among other things, it included an amendment providing a separate $1 million deductible for Lonquist, effectively removing him from coverage. This amendment was referred to as the "Lonquist Laser." Citizens accepted this offer in a letter dated March 6, 2000. Later, Citizens filed a suit in a federal district court against Trustmark and others, seeking damages and other relief for an alleged breach of contract. Citizens claimed in part that the "Lonquist Laser" was not valid. Both parties filed motions for summary judgment.

ISSUE Was the Lonquist Laser an effective amendment of the parties' insurance contract?

DECISION Yes. The court granted Trustmark's motion for summary judgment on this issue.

REASON The court recognized that "[a]lthough the policy defines many of its terms, it does not define the term 'amendment'; nor does anything in the policy specify precisely what an amendment must look like, other than that it must be approved by Trustmark and signed by Citizens, both of which occurred here." The court further explained that "courts have consistently referred to dictionary definitions to interpret words used in insurance contracts." The court noted that according to *Webster's Unabridged Dictionary* (Random House, 2001), the ordinary meaning of the term *amendment* is " 'a change made by correction, addition, or deletion.' That is precisely what occurred here, when the parties knowingly agreed * * * to alter or change the terms" of the policy "by deleting or removing the Lonquist claim * * * . Accordingly, under the plain language of the contract, the Court concludes that any agreement that meets the requirements necessary to form a contract under state law and that is signed and approved by both parties satisfies the requirements of the policy and is a valid and enforceable amendment. Because the Lonquist Laser set forth in the March 6 Agreement unquestionably meets that standard, it is a valid amendment of the parties' insurance contract."

FOR CRITICAL ANALYSIS–Social Consideration *What might the parties have done to avoid this litigation?*

REVIEWING Nature and Classification

Grant Borman, who was engaged in a construction project, leased a crane from Allied Equipment and hired Crosstown Trucking Co. to deliver the crane to the construction site. Crosstown, while the crane was in its possession and without permission from either Borman or Allied Equipment, used the crane to install a transformer for a utility company, which paid Crosstown for the job. Crosstown then delivered the crane to Borman's construction site at the appointed time of delivery. When Allied Equipment learned of the unauthorized use of the crane by Crosstown, it sued Crosstown for damages, seeking to recover the rental value of Crosstown's use of the crane. Using the information presented in the chapter, answer the following questions.

1 What are the four requirements of a valid contract?

2 Did Crosstown have a valid contract with Borman concerning the use of the crane? If so, was it a bilateral or unilateral contract? Explain.

3 Can Allied Equipment obtain damages from Crosstown based on an implied-in-fact contract? Why or why not?

4 Should a court impose a quasi contract on the parties in this situation to allow Allied to recover damages from Crosstown? Why or why not?

APPLICATION How Can You Avoid Unintended Employment Contracts?*

Employers have learned many lessons from court decisions. In recent years, for example, the message has been clear that employers should be cautious about what they say in their employment manuals.

Employment Manuals and Implied-in-Fact Contracts

Promises made in an employment manual may create an implied-in-fact employment contract. If an employment handbook states that employees will be fired only for specific causes, the employer may be held to that "promise." This is true even if, by state law, employment is "at will"—that is, the employer is allowed to hire and fire employees at will, with or without cause. The at-will doctrine will not apply if the terms of employment are subject to an implied contract between the employer and the employee. If a court holds that an implied employment contract exists—on the basis of promises made in an employment manual—the employment is no longer at will. The employer will be bound by the contract and liable for damages for breaching the contract.

Taking Precautions

Employers who wish to avoid potential liability for breaching unintended employment contracts should therefore make it clear to employees that the policies expressed in an employment manual are not to be interpreted as contractual promises. An effective way to do this is to inform employees, when initially giving them the handbook or discussing its contents with them, that the handbook is not intended as a contract and to include a disclaimer to that effect in the employment manual. The disclaimer might read as follows: "This policy manual describes the basic personnel policies and practices of our Company. You should understand that the manual does not modify our Company's 'at-will' employment doctrine or provide employees with any kind of contractual rights."

The employer should make the disclaimer clear and prominent so that the applicant cannot later claim that it was the employer's fault that the employee did not see the disclaimer. A disclaimer will be clear and prominent if it is set off from the surrounding text by the use of larger type, a different color, all capital letters, or some other device that calls the reader's attention to it.

The employer should also avoid including in the handbook any definite promises such as that employees will be fired only

* This *Application* is not meant to substitute for the services of an attorney who is licensed to practice law in your state.

for cause or that after they have worked for a specific length of time, they will not be fired except for certain reasons. The handbook itself should contain a clear and prominent disclaimer of contractual liability for its contents.

CHECKLIST FOR THE EMPLOYER

1 Inform new employees that statements in an employment handbook are not intended as contractual terms.
2 Include clear and prominent disclaimers to this effect in employment applications and in the employment handbook.

3 Ask employees to sign a statement that they have read the disclaimer and understand that the employment handbook is not a contract and does not create any legally binding obligations.
4 Avoid including in the handbook any definite promises relating to job security, and include a clear and prominent disclaimer of contractual liability for any statements made within the handbook.

KEY TERMS

bilateral contract 233
contract 231
executed contract 237
executory contract 237
express contract 236
formal contract 235
implied-in-fact contract 236

informal contract 235
objective theory of contracts 231
offeree 233
offeror 233
promise 230
promisee 231
promisor 231

quasi contract 238
unenforceable contract 238
unilateral contract 234
valid contract 237
void contract 238
voidable contract 237

CHAPTER SUMMARY Nature and Classification

An Overview of Contract Law
(See pages 230–232.)

1. *Sources of contract law*—The common law governs all contracts except when it has been modified or replaced by statutory law, such as the Uniform Commercial Code (UCC), or by administrative agency regulations. The UCC governs contracts for the sale or lease of goods (see Chapter 15).

2. *The function of contracts*—Contract law establishes what kinds of promises will be legally binding and supplies procedures for enforcing legally binding promises, or agreements.

3. *The definition of a contract*—A contract is an agreement that can be enforced in court. It is formed by two or more competent parties who agree to perform or to refrain from performing some act now or in the future.

4. *Objective theory of contracts*—In contract law, intent is determined by objective facts, not by the personal or subjective intent, or belief, of a party.

Elements of a Contract
(See pages 232–233.)

1. *Requirements of a valid contract*—The four requirements of a valid contract are agreement, consideration, contractual capacity, and legality.

2. *Defenses to the enforceability of a contract*—Even if the four requirements of a valid contract are met, a contract may be unenforceable if it lacks genuineness of assent or is not in the required form.

(Continued)

CHAPTER SUMMARY Nature and Classification–Continued

Types of Contracts (See pages 233–238.)	1. *Bilateral*—A promise for a promise.
	2. *Unilateral*—A promise for an act (acceptance is the completed—or substantial—performance of the contract by the offeree).
	3. *Formal*—Requires a special form for contract formation.
	4. *Informal*—Requires no special form for contract formation.
	5. *Express*—Formed by words (oral, written, or a combination).
	6. *Implied in fact*—Formed at least in part by the conduct of the parties.
	7. *Executed*—A fully performed contract.
	8. *Executory*—A contract not yet fully performed.
	9. *Valid*—A contract that has the necessary contractual elements of offer and acceptance, consideration, parties with legal capacity, and a legal purpose.
	10. *Voidable*—A contract that a party has the option of avoiding or enforcing.
	11. *Unenforceable*—A valid contract that cannot be enforced because of a legal defense.
	12. *Void*—No contract exists, or there is a contract without legal obligations.
Quasi Contracts (See pages 238–239.)	A quasi contract, or a contract implied in law, is a contract that is imposed by law to prevent unjust enrichment.
Interpretation of Contracts (See pages 239–243.)	Increasingly, plain language laws are requiring private contracts to be written in plain language so that the terms are clear and understandable to the parties. Under the plain meaning rule, a court will enforce the contract according to its plain terms, the meaning of which must be determined from the written document alone. Other rules applied by the courts when interpreting contracts include the following:
	1. A reasonable, lawful, and effective meaning will be given to all contract terms.
	2. A contract will be interpreted as a whole, specific clauses will be considered subordinate to the contract's general intent, and all writings that are a part of the same transaction will be interpreted together.
	3. Terms that were negotiated separately will be given greater consideration than standardized terms and terms not negotiated separately.
	4. Words will be given their commonly accepted meanings and technical words their technical meanings, unless the parties clearly intended otherwise.
	5. Specific wording will be given greater consideration than general language.
	6. Written or typewritten terms prevail over preprinted terms.
	7. A party that uses ambiguous expressions is held to be responsible for the ambiguities.
	8. Evidence of prior dealing, course of performance, or usage of trade is admissible to clarify an ambiguously worded contract.

FOR REVIEW

Answers for the even-numbered questions in this **For Review** *section can be found in Appendix E at the end of this text.*

1 What is a contract? What is the objective theory of contracts?

2 What are the four basic elements necessary to the formation of a valid contract?

3 What is the difference between an implied-in-fact contract and an implied-in-law contract (quasi contract)?

4 How does a void contract differ from a voidable contract? What is an unenforceable contract?

5 Why have plain language laws been enacted? What rules guide the courts in interpreting contracts?

 The following multiple-choice question is representative of the types of questions available in one of the four sections of ThomsonNOW for *Business Law Today*. ThomsonNOW also provides feedback for each response option, whether correct or incorrect, and refers to the location within the chapter where the correct answer can be found.

Ambiguous terms in a contract are generally

a interpreted against the party with greater bargaining power.

b not enforced.

c interpreted according to what the parties claim their intent was when they drafted the contract.

d interpreted against the party who drafted the contract containing ambiguous language.

■

QUESTIONS AND CASE PROBLEMS

 HYPOTHETICAL SCENARIOS

8.1 Express versus Implied Contracts. Suppose that a local businessperson, McDougal, is a good friend of Krunch, the owner of a local candy store. Every day on his lunch hour McDougal goes into Krunch's candy store and spends about five minutes looking at the candy. After examining Krunch's candy and talking with Krunch, McDougal usually buys one or two candy bars. One afternoon, McDougal goes into Krunch's candy shop, looks at the candy, and picks up a $1 candy bar. Seeing that Krunch is very busy, he catches Krunch's eye, waves the candy bar at Krunch without saying a word, and walks out. Is there a contract? If so, classify it within the categories presented in this chapter.

8.2 Hypothetical Question with Sample Answer. Janine was hospitalized with severe abdominal pain and placed in an intensive care unit. Her doctor told the hospital personnel to order around-the-clock nursing care for Janine. At the hospital's request, a nursing services firm, Nursing Services Unlimited, provided two weeks of in-hospital care and, after Janine was sent home, an additional two weeks of at-home care. During the at-home period of care, Janine was fully aware that she was receiving the benefit of the nursing services. Nursing Services later billed Janine $4,000 for the nursing care, but Janine refused to pay on the ground that she had never contracted for the services, either orally or in writing. In view of the fact that no express contract was ever formed, can Nursing Services recover the $4,000 from Janine? If so, under what legal theory? Discuss.

 For a sample answer to Question 8.2, go to Appendix F at the end of this text.

8.3 Contract Classification. High-Flying Advertising, Inc., contracted with Big Burger Restaurants to fly an advertisement above the Connecticut beaches. The advertisement offered $5,000 to any person who could swim from the Connecticut beaches to Long Island across the Long Island Sound in less than a day. McElfresh saw the streamer and accepted the challenge. He started his marathon swim that same day at 10 A.M. After he had been swimming for four hours and was about halfway across the sound, McElfresh saw another plane pulling a streamer that read, "Big Burger revokes." Is there a contract between McElfresh and Big Burger? If there is a contract, what type(s) of contract is (are) formed?

■

 **CASE PROBLEMS**

8.4 Implied Contract. Thomas Rinks and Joseph Shields developed Psycho Chihuahua, a caricature of a Chihuahua dog with a "do-not-back-down" attitude. They promoted and marketed the character through their company, Wrench, L.L.C. Ed Alfaro and Rudy Pollak, representatives of Taco Bell Corp., learned of Psycho Chihuahua and met with Rinks and Shields to talk about using the character as a Taco Bell "icon." Wrench sent artwork, merchandise, and marketing ideas to Alfaro, who promoted the character within Taco Bell. Alfaro asked Wrench to propose terms for Taco Bell's use of Psycho Chihuahua. Taco Bell did not accept Wrench's terms, but Alfaro continued to promote the character within the company. Meanwhile, Taco Bell hired a new advertising agency, which proposed an advertising campaign involving a Chihuahua. When Alfaro learned of this proposal, he sent the Psycho Chihuahua materials to the agency. Taco Bell made a Chihuahua the focus of its marketing but paid nothing to Wrench. Wrench filed a suit against Taco Bell in a federal district court, claiming in part that it had an implied contract with Taco Bell, which the latter breached. Do these facts satisfy the requirements for an implied contract? Why or why not? [*Wrench, L.L.C. v. Taco Bell Corp.*, 256 F.3d 446 (6th Cir.2001), *cert. denied*, 534 U.S. 1114, 122 S.Ct. 921, 151 L.Ed.2d 885 (2002)]

8.5 Interpretation of Contracts. East Mill Associates (EMA) was developing residential "units" in East Brunswick, New Jersey, within the service area of the East Brunswick Sewerage Authority (EBSA). The sewer system required an upgrade to the Ryder's Lane Pumping Station to accommodate the new units. EMA agreed to pay "fifty-five percent (55%) of the total cost" of the upgrade. At the time, the estimated cost to EMA was $150,000 to $200,000. Impediments to the project arose, however, substantially increasing the cost. Among other things, the pumping station had to be moved to accommodate a widened road nearby. The upgrade was delayed for almost three years. When it was completed, EBSA asked EMA for $340,022.12, which represented 55 percent of the total cost. EMA did not pay. EBSA filed a suit in a New Jersey state court against EMA for breach of contract. What rule should the court apply to interpret the parties' contract? How should that rule be applied? Why? [*East Brunswick Sewerage Authority v. East Mill Associates, Inc.*, 365 N.J.Super. 120, 838 A.2d 494 (A.D. 2004)]

8.6 Case Problem with Sample Answer. In December 2000, Nextel South Corp., a communications firm, contacted R. A. Clark Consulting, Ltd., an executive search firm, about finding an employment manager for Nextel's call center in Atlanta, Georgia. Over the next six months, Clark screened, evaluated, and interviewed more than three hundred candidates. Clark provided Nextel with more than fifteen candidate summaries, including one for Dan Sax. Nextel hired Sax for the position at an annual salary of $75,000. Sax started work on June 25, 2001, took two weeks' vacation, and quit on July 31 in the middle of a project. Clark spent the next six weeks looking for a replacement, until Nextel asked Clark to stop. Clark billed Nextel for its service, but Nextel refused to pay, asserting in part that the parties had not signed an agreement. Nextel's typical agreement specified payment to an employment agency of 20 percent of an employee's salary. Clark filed a suit in a Georgia state court against Nextel to recover the reasonable value of its services. What is a quasi contract? What would Clark have to show to recover on this basis? Should the court rule in Clark's favor? Explain. [*Nextel*

South Corp. v. R. A. Clark Consulting, Ltd., 266 Ga.App. 85, 596 S.E.2d 416 (2004)]

After you have answered Problem 8.6, compare your answer with the sample answer given on the Web site that accompanies this text. Go to www.thomsonedu.com/westbuslaw/blt, select "Chapter 8," and click on "Case Problem with Sample Answer."

8.7 Contract Enforceability. California's Subdivision Map Act (SMA) prohibits the sale of real property until a map of its subdivision is filed with, and approved by, the appropriate state agency. In November 2004, Black Hills Investments, Inc., entered into two contracts with Albertson's, Inc., to buy two parcels of property in a shopping center development. Each contract required that "all governmental approvals relating to any lot split [or] subdivision" be obtained before the sale but permitted Albertson's to waive this condition. Black Hills made a $133,000 deposit on the purchase. A few weeks later, before the sales were complete, Albertson's filed with a local state agency a map that subdivided the shopping center into four parcels, including the two that Black Hills had agreed to buy. In January 2005, Black Hills objected to concessions that Albertson's had made to a buyer of one of the other parcels, told Albertson's that it was terminating its deal, and asked for a return of its deposit. Albertson's refused. Black Hills filed a suit in a California state court against Albertson's, arguing that the contracts were void. Are these contracts valid, voidable, unenforceable, or void? Explain. [*Black Hills Investments, Inc. v. Albertson's, Inc.*, 146 Cal.App.4th 883, 53 Cal.Rptr.3d 263 (4 Dist. 2007)]

8.8 A Question of Ethics. *International Business Machines Corp. (IBM) hired Niels Jensen in 2000 as a software sales representative. In 2001, IBM presented a new "Software Sales Incentive Plan" (SIP) at a conference for its sales employees. A brochure given to the attendees stated, "[T]here are no caps to your earnings; the more you sell, * * * the more earnings for you." The brochure outlined how the plan worked and referred the employees to the "Sales Incentives" section of IBM's corporate intranet for more details. Jensen was given a "quota letter" that said he would be paid $75,000 as a base salary and, if he attained his quota, an additional $75,000 as incentive pay. In September, Jensen closed a deal with the U.S. Department of the Treasury's Internal Revenue Service worth more than $24 million to IBM. Relying on the SIP brochure, Jensen estimated his commission to be $2.6 million. IBM paid him less than $500,000, however. Jensen filed a suit in a federal district court against IBM, contending the SIP brochure and quota letter constituted a unilateral offer that became a binding contract when Jensen closed the sale. In view of these facts, consider the following questions.* [*Jensen v. International Business Machines Corp.*, 454 F.3d 382 (4th Cir. 2006)]

1 Would it be fair to the employer in this case to hold that the SIP brochure and the quota letter created a unilateral contract if IBM did not *intend* to create such a contract? Would it be fair to the employee to hold that *no* contract was created? Explain.

2 The "Sales Incentives" section of IBM's intranet included a clause providing that "[m]anagement will decide if an adjustment to the payment is appropriate" when an employee closes a large transaction. Jensen's quota letter stated, "[The SIP] program does not constitute a promise by IBM to make any distributions under it. IBM reserves the right to adjust the program terms or to cancel or otherwise modify the program at any time." How do these statements affect your answers to the above questions? From an ethical perspective, would it be fair to hold that a contract exists despite these statements?

CRITICAL THINKING
AND WRITING ASSIGNMENTS

8.9 Critical Legal Thinking. Review the list of basic requirements for contract formation given at the beginning of this chapter. In view of those requirements, analyze the relationship entered into when a student enrolls in a college or university. Has a contract been formed? If so, is it a bilateral contract or a unilateral contract? Discuss.

8.10 Case Analysis Question. Go to Appendix G at the end of this text and examine Case No. 3 [*AmeriPro Search, Inc. v. Fleming Steel Co.*, 2001 Pa.Super. 325, 787 A.2d 988 (2001)]. This case has been excerpted there in great detail. Review and then brief the case, making sure that your brief answers the following questions.

1 Did Brauninger (the employment agent) and Kohn (the president of Fleming) agree on how much money AmeriPro would be paid if Fleming hired an engineer recommended by the agency?

2 How did Barracchini (the employee) originally find out about the job opportunity with Fleming Steel in 1993?

3 Who arranged the interview in April 1994, and why did Fleming fail to hire Barracchini at that time? What about the interview in 1995?

4 What was the trial court's ruling on the question of whether a quasi contract existed?

5 Did the appellate court uphold the lower court's ruling? Why or why not?

8.11 **Video Question.** Go to this text's Web site at **www. thomsonedu.com/westbuslaw/blt** and select "Chapter 8." Click on "Video Questions" and view the video titled *Bowfinger*. Then answer the following questions.

1 In the video, Renfro (Robert Downey, Jr.) says to Bowfinger (Steve Martin), "You bring me this script and Kit Ramsey and you've got yourself a 'go' picture." Assume for the purposes of this question that their agreement is a contract. Is the contract bilateral or unilateral? Is it express or implied? Is it formal or informal? Is it executed or executory? Explain your answers.

2 What criteria would a court rely on to interpret the terms of the contract?

3 Recall from the video that the contract between Bowfinger and the producer was oral. Suppose that a statute requires contracts of this type to be in writing. In that situation would the contract be void, voidable, or unenforceable? Explain.

PRACTICAL
INTERNET EXERCISES

Go to this text's Web site at **www.thomsonedu.com/westbuslaw/blt**, select "Chapter 8," and click on "Practical Internet Exercises." There you will find the following Internet research exercises that you can perform to learn more about the topics covered in this chapter.

PRACTICAL INTERNET EXERCISE 8-1 LEGAL PERSPECTIVE—Contracts and Contract Provisions

PRACTICAL INTERNET EXERCISE 8-2 MANAGEMENT PERSPECTIVE—Implied Employment Contracts

PRACTICAL INTERNET EXERCISE 8-3 HISTORICAL PERSPECTIVE—Contracts in Ancient Mesopotamia

BEFORE THE TEST

Go to this text's Web site at **www.thomsonedu.com/westbuslaw/blt**, select "Chapter 8," and click on "Interactive Quizzes." You will find a number of interactive questions relating to this chapter.

CHAPTER 9
Agreement and Consideration

CHAPTER OUTLINE

—AGREEMENT

—CONSIDERATION AND
ITS REQUIREMENTS

—CONTRACTS THAT
LACK CONSIDERATION

—SETTLEMENT OF CLAIMS

—PROMISSORY ESTOPPEL

LEARNING OBJECTIVES

AFTER READING THIS CHAPTER, YOU SHOULD BE ABLE TO
ANSWER THE FOLLOWING QUESTIONS:

1 What elements are necessary for an effective offer?
What are some examples of nonoffers?

2 In what circumstances will an offer be irrevocable?

3 What are the elements that are necessary for an
effective acceptance?

4 What is consideration? What is required for
consideration to be legally sufficient?

5 In what circumstances might a promise be enforced
despite a lack of consideration?

Voltaire's statement that it is "necessity that makes laws" is certainly true in regard to contracts. In Chapter 8, we pointed out that promises and agreements, and the knowledge that some of those promises and agreements will be legally enforced, are essential to civilized society. The homes we live in, the food we eat, the clothes we wear, the cars we drive, the books we read, the videos and recordings we watch and listen to—all of these have been purchased through contractual agreements. Contract law developed over time, through the common law tradition, to meet society's need to know with certainty what kinds of promises, or contracts, will be enforced and the point at which a valid and binding contract is formed.

For a contract to be considered valid and enforceable, the requirements listed in Chapter 8 must be met. In this chapter, we look closely at two of these requirements, *agreement* and *consideration*. As you read through this chapter, keep in mind that the requirements of agreement and consideration apply to all contracts, regardless of how they are formed. Many contracts continue to be formed in the traditional way—through the exchange of paper documents. Increasingly, though, contracts are also being formed online—through the exchange of electronic messages or documents. We discuss online contracts to a limited extent in this chapter and will look at them more closely in Chapter 14.

AGREEMENT

An essential element for contract formation is **agreement**—the parties must agree on the terms of the contract. Ordinarily, agreement is evidenced by two events: an *offer* and an

AGREEMENT
A meeting of two or more minds in regard to the terms of a contract; usually broken down into two events—an offer by one party to form a contract and an acceptance of the offer by the person to whom the offer is made.

acceptance. One party offers a certain bargain to another party, who then accepts that bargain.

Because words often fail to convey the precise meaning intended, the law of contracts generally adheres to the *objective theory of contracts,* as discussed in Chapter 8. Under this theory, a party's words and conduct are held to mean whatever a reasonable person in the offeree's position would think they meant. The court will give words their usual meanings even if "it were proved by twenty bishops that [the] party . . . intended something else."[1]

Requirements of the Offer

An **offer** is a promise or commitment to perform or refrain from performing some specified act in the future. As discussed in Chapter 8, the party making an offer is called the *offeror,* and the party to whom the offer is made is called the *offeree.*

Three elements are necessary for an offer to be effective:

1 There must be a serious, objective intention by the offeror.

2 The terms of the offer must be reasonably certain, or definite, so that the parties and the court can ascertain the terms of the contract.

3 The offer must be communicated to the offeree.

Once an effective offer has been made, the offeree's acceptance of that offer creates a legally binding contract (providing the other essential elements for a valid and enforceable contract are present).

In today's e-commerce world, offers are frequently made online. Essentially, the requirements for traditional offers apply to online offers as well, as you will read in Chapter 14.

Intention   The first requirement for an effective offer to exist is a serious, objective intention on the part of the offeror. Intent is not determined by the *subjective* intentions, beliefs, or assumptions of the offeror. Rather, it is determined by what a reasonable person in the offeree's position would conclude the offeror's words and actions meant. Offers made in obvious anger, jest, or undue excitement do not meet the serious-and-objective-intent test. Because these offers are not effective, an offeree's acceptance does not create an agreement.

■EXAMPLE 9.1 You and three classmates ride to school each day in Julio's new automobile, which has a market value of $18,000. One cold morning, the four of you get into the car, but Julio cannot get it started. He yells in anger, "I'll sell this car to anyone for $500!" You drop $500 in his lap. A reasonable person, taking into consideration Julio's frustration and the obvious difference in value between the car's market price and the purchase price, would declare that Julio's offer was not made with serious and objective intent and that you do not have an agreement. ■

In the subsections that follow, we examine the concept of intention further as we look at the distinctions between offers and nonoffers. In the following classic case in the area of contractual agreement, the court had to decide whether an offer was intended when boasts, brags, and dares "after a few drinks" resulted in a contract to sell certain property.

OFFER
A promise or commitment to perform or refrain from performing some specified act in the future.

---

1. Judge Learned Hand in *Hotchkiss v. National City Bank of New York,* 200 F. 287 (2d Cir. 1911); aff'd 231 U.S. 50, 34 S.Ct. 20, 58 L.Ed. 115 (1913). (The term *aff'd* is an abbreviation for *affirmed;* an appellate court can affirm a lower court's judgment, decree, or order, thereby declaring that it is valid and must stand as rendered.)

CASE 9.1 Lucy v. Zehmer

LANDMARK AND CLASSIC CASES

Supreme Court of Appeals of Virginia, 196 Va. 493, 84 S.E.2d 516 (1954).

FACTS Lucy and Zehmer had known each other for fifteen to twenty years. For some time, Lucy had been wanting to buy Zehmer's farm. Zehmer had always told Lucy that he was not interested in selling. One night, Lucy stopped in to visit with the Zehmers at a restaurant they operated. Lucy said to Zehmer, "I bet you wouldn't take $50,000 for that place." Zehmer replied, "Yes, I would, too; you wouldn't give fifty." Throughout the evening, the conversation returned to the sale of the farm. At the same time, the parties were drinking whiskey. Eventually, Zehmer wrote up an agreement, on the back of a restaurant check, for the sale of the farm, and he asked his wife to sign it—which she did. When Lucy brought an action in a Virginia state court to enforce the agreement, Zehmer argued that he had been "high as a Georgia pine" at the time and that the offer had been made in jest: "two doggoned drunks bluffing to see who could talk the biggest and say the most." Lucy claimed that he had not been intoxicated and did not think Zehmer had been, either, given the way Zehmer handled the transaction. The trial court ruled in favor of the Zehmers, and Lucy appealed.

ISSUE Can the agreement be avoided on the basis of intoxication?

DECISION No. The agreement to sell the farm was binding.

REASON The court held that the evidence given about the nature of the conversation, the appearance and completeness of the agreement, and the signing all tended to show that a serious business transaction, not a casual jest, was intended. The court had to look into the objective meaning of the words and acts of the Zehmers: "An agreement or mutual assent is of course essential to a valid contract, but the law imputes to a person an intention corresponding to the reasonable meaning of his words and acts. If his words and acts, judged by a reasonable standard, manifest an intention to agree, it is immaterial what may be the real but unexpressed state of mind."

WHAT IF THE FACTS WERE DIFFERENT? *Suppose that the day after Lucy signed the real estate sales agreement, he decided that he did not want the farm after all, and Zehmer sued Lucy to perform the contract. Would this change in the facts alter the court's decision that Lucy and Zehmer had created an enforceable contract? Why or why not?*

IMPACT OF THIS CASE ON TODAY'S LAW *This is a classic case in contract law because it so clearly illustrates the objective theory of contracts with respect to determining whether an offer was intended. Today, the objective theory of contracts continues to be applied by the courts, and* Lucy v. Zehmer *is routinely cited as a significant precedent in this area.*

RELEVANT WEB SITES *To locate information on the Web concerning the* Lucy v. Zehmer *decision, go to this text's Web site at* **www.thomsonedu.com/westbuslaw/blt**, *select "Chapter 9," and click on "URLs for Landmarks."*

Expressions of Opinion. An expression of opinion is not an offer. It does not demonstrate an intention to enter into a binding agreement. **EXAMPLE 9.2** In *Hawkins v. McGee*,[2] Hawkins took his son to McGee, a physician, and asked McGee to operate on the son's hand. McGee said that the boy would be in the hospital three or four days and that the hand would *probably* heal a few days later. The son's hand did not heal for a month, but nonetheless the father did not win a suit for breach of contract. The court held that McGee did not make an offer to heal the son's hand in three or four days. He merely expressed an opinion as to when the hand would heal. ■

BE CAREFUL An opinion is not an offer and not a contract term. Goods or services can be "perfect" in one party's opinion and "poor" in another's.

Statements of Future Intent. A statement of an *intention* to do something in the future is not an offer. **EXAMPLE 9.3** If Ari says, "I *plan* to sell my stock in Novation, Inc., for $150 per share," a contract is not created if John "accepts" and tenders $150 per share for the stock. Ari has merely expressed his intention to enter into a future contract for the sale of the stock. If John accepts and tenders the $150 per share, no contract is formed, because

---

2. 84 N.H. 114, 146 A. 641 (1929).

a reasonable person would conclude that Ari was only *thinking about* selling his stock, not promising to sell it. ■

Preliminary Negotiations.   A request or invitation to negotiate is not an offer; it only expresses a willingness to discuss the possibility of entering into a contract. Examples are statements such as "Will you sell Forest Acres?" and "I wouldn't sell my car for less than $8,000." A reasonable person in the offeree's position would not conclude that such a statement indicated an intention to enter into a binding obligation. Likewise, when the government and private firms need to have construction work done, they invite contractors to submit bids. The *invitation* to submit bids is not an offer, and a contractor does not bind the government or private firm by submitting a bid. (The bids that the contractors submit are offers, however, and the government or private firm can bind the contractor by accepting the bid.)

Advertisements, Catalogues, and Circulars.   In general, advertisements, mail-order catalogues, price lists, and circular letters (meant for the general public) are treated as invitations to negotiate, not as offers to form a contract.[3] **■EXAMPLE 9.4** Suppose that you put an ad in the classified section of your local newspaper offering to sell your guitar for $275. Seven people call and "accept" your "offer" before you can remove the ad from the newspaper. If the ad were truly an offer, you would be bound by seven contracts to sell your guitar. Because *initial* advertisements are treated as *invitations* to make offers rather than offers, however, you will have seven offers to choose from, and you can accept the best one without incurring any liability for the six you reject. ■ On some occasions, though, courts have construed advertisements to be offers because the ads contained definite terms that invited acceptance (such as an ad offering a reward for the return of a lost dog).[4]

Price lists are another form of invitation to negotiate or trade. A seller's price list is not an offer to sell at that price; it merely invites the buyer to offer to buy at that price. In fact, the seller usually puts "prices subject to change" on the price list. Only in rare circumstances will a price quotation be construed as an offer.[5]

KEEP IN MIND Advertisements are not binding, but they cannot be deceptive.

Should promises of prizes made in ads and circulars always be enforced? Businesses and other organizations commonly promote their products or services by offering prizes, rewards, and the like for the performance of specific actions. Ordinarily, these ads for prizes present few problems. At times, though, people perform whatever is necessary to win an advertised prize only to learn that the offer was made in jest—that is, the ad's sponsor had no real intention of giving anyone the prize. Consider an example. PepsiCo launched an ad campaign that said consumers could use "Pepsi Points"—which could be found on specially marked packages of Pepsi or purchased for ten cents each—to obtain T-shirts and other merchandise with the Pepsi logo. One of the ads featured a Harrier fighter jet, which was listed at 7 million Pepsi Points. When a consumer, John Leonard, raised $700,000, purchased 7 million Pepsi Points, and laid claim to the prize, however, PepsiCo contended that the Harrier jet in the commercial was "fanciful" and that the offer was made in jest.

In the lawsuit that followed, the court agreed, stating that "no objective person could reasonably have concluded that the commercial actually offered consumers a Harrier jet."[6] Yet Leonard obviously did draw that conclusion, and in a number of other cases, individuals have undertaken serious efforts to win nonexistent prizes. Some claim that not enforcing such promises is unfair to individuals who rely on the promises, as John Leonard did in this case.

ETHICAL ISSUE 9.1

■

---

3. *Restatement (Second) of Contracts*, Section 26, Comment b.

4. The classic example is *Lefkowitz v. Great Minneapolis Surplus Store, Inc.*, 251 Minn. 188, 86 N.W.2d 689 (1957).

5. See, for example, *Fairmount Glass Works v. Grunden-Martin Woodenware Co.*, 106 Ky. 659, 51 S.W. 196 (1899).

6. *Leonard v. PepsiCo*, 88 F.Supp.2d 116 (S.D.N.Y. 1999); aff'd 210 F.3d 88 (2d Cir. 2000).

A $27 million Harrier fighter jet that was offered as a prize in PepsiCo's "Drink Pepsi—Get Stuff" ad campaign. Although the jet was a fanciful jest to PepsiCo, one consumer took the offer seriously and attempted to fulfill the terms of the prize. Is PepsiCo's "offer" of the jet enforceable? (Paul Friel/Creative Commons)

Auctions. In an auction, a seller "offers" goods for sale through an auctioneer, but this is not an offer to form a contract. Rather, it is an invitation asking bidders to submit offers. In the context of an auction, a bidder is the offeror, and the auctioneer is the offeree. The offer is accepted when the auctioneer strikes the hammer. Before the fall of the hammer, a bidder may revoke (take back) her or his bid, or the auctioneer may reject that bid or all bids. Typically, an auctioneer will reject a bid that is below the price the seller is willing to accept.

When the auctioneer accepts a higher bid, he or she rejects all previous bids. Because rejection terminates an offer (as will be discussed later), those bids represent offers that have been terminated. Thus, if the highest bidder withdraws his or her bid before the hammer falls, none of the previous bids is reinstated. If the bid is not withdrawn or rejected, the contract is formed when the auctioneer announces, "Going once, going twice, sold!" (or something similar) and lets the hammer fall.

Traditionally, auctions have been either "with reserve" or "without reserve." In an auction with reserve, the seller (through the auctioneer) may withdraw the goods at any time before the auctioneer closes the sale by announcement or by the fall of the hammer. All auctions are assumed to be auctions with reserve unless the terms of the auction are explicitly stated to be *without reserve*. In an auction without reserve, the goods cannot be withdrawn by the seller and must be sold to the highest bidder. In auctions with reserve, the seller may reserve the right to confirm or reject the sale even after "the hammer has fallen." In this situation, the seller is obligated to notify those attending the auction that sales of goods made during the auction are not final until confirmed by the seller.[7]

How do these rules apply to an online auction of rights to a domain name? For a discussion of a case involving this issue, see this chapter's *Adapting the Law to the Online Environment* feature on pages 256 and 257.

Agreements to Agree. Traditionally, agreements to agree—that is, agreements to agree to the material terms of a contract at some future date—were not considered to be binding contracts. The modern view, however, is that agreements to agree may be enforceable agreements (contracts) if it is clear that the parties intend to be bound by the agreements. In other words, under the modern view the emphasis is on the parties' intent rather than on form.

■**EXAMPLE 9.5** When the Pennzoil Company discussed with the Getty Oil Company the possible purchase of Getty's stock, a memorandum of agreement was drafted to reflect the terms of the conversations. After more negotiations over the price, both companies issued press releases announcing an agreement in principle on the terms of the memorandum. The next day, Texaco, Inc., offered to buy all of Getty's stock at a higher price. The day after that, Getty's board of directors voted to accept Texaco's offer, and Texaco and Getty signed a merger agreement. When Pennzoil sued Texaco for tortious interference with its "contractual" relationship with Getty, a jury concluded that Getty and Pennzoil had intended to form a binding contract, with only the details left to be worked out, before Texaco made its offer. Texaco was held liable for wrongfully interfering with this contract.[8] ■

---

7. These rules apply under both the common law of contracts and the Uniform Commercial Code, or UCC. See UCC 2–328.

8. *Texaco, Inc. v. Pennzoil Co.*, 729 S.W.2d 768 (Tex.App.—Houston [1st Dist.] 1987, writ ref'd n.r.e.). (Generally, a complete Texas Court of Appeals citation includes the writ-of-error history showing the Texas Supreme Court's disposition of the case. In this case, *writ ref'd n.r.e.* is an abbreviation for "writ refused, no reversible error," which means that Texas's highest court refused to grant the appellant's request to review the case, because the court did not think there was any reversible error.)

In an auction, such as this one in Boonville, Missouri, is the party selling the goods the "offeror" for purposes of contract law? Why or why not? (AP Photo/L. G. Patterson)

Suppose that two parties draw up a brief, handwritten memorandum of agreement, intending to set forth their decisions in a more formal document later. If the arrangements are never formalized, can the memorandum constitute a binding contract? Increasingly, the courts are holding that a preliminary agreement constitutes a binding contract if the parties have agreed on all essential terms and no disputed issues remain to be resolved.[9] In contrast, if the parties agree on certain major terms but leave other terms open for further negotiation, a preliminary agreement is binding only in the sense that the parties have committed themselves to negotiate the undecided terms in good faith in an effort to reach a final agreement.

PREVENTING LEGAL DISPUTES

To avoid potential legal disputes, businesspersons should be cautious when drafting a memorandum outlining a preliminary agreement or understanding with another party. If all the major terms are included, a court might hold that the agreement is binding even though it was intended to be only a tentative agreement. One approach to avoid being bound to the terms of a preliminary agreement is to include in the writing not only the points on which the parties agree, but also the points of disagreement. Alternatively, a person might add a note or disclaimer to the memorandum stating that, although the parties anticipate entering a contract in the future, neither party intends to be legally bound to the terms that were discussed. That way, the other party cannot claim that you have already reached an agreement on all essential terms.

Definiteness The second requirement for an effective offer involves the definiteness of its terms. An offer must have reasonably definite terms so that a court can determine if a breach has occurred and give an appropriate remedy.[10]

---

9. See, for example, *Fluorine On Call, Ltd. v. Fluorogas Limited,* No. 01-CV-186 (W.D.Tex. 2002), contract issue affirmed on appeal at 380 F.3d 849 (5th Cir. 2004).

10. *Restatement (Second) of Contracts,* Section 33. The UCC has relaxed the requirements regarding the definiteness of terms in contracts for the sale of goods. See UCC 2–204(3).

ADAPTING THE LAW TO THE ONLINE ENVIRONMENT — Can an Online Bid Constitute an Acceptance?

Under the Uniform Commercial Code, or UCC (see Chapter 15), a bid at an auction constitutes an offer. The offer (the highest bid) is accepted when the auctioneer's hammer falls. The UCC also states that auctions are "with reserve" unless the seller specifies otherwise. As noted in the text, in an auction with reserve, the seller reserves the right *not* to sell the goods to the highest bidder. Hence, even after the hammer falls, the contract for sale remains conditioned on the seller's approval. The question of how these rules should be applied to an online auction of a domain name, in which no hammer falls, came before a California court.

The Bid (or Offer?)

The case involved an online auction conducted by The.TV Corporation International (DotTV) on its Web site. DotTV posted an announcement on its Web site asking for bids for rights to the "Golf.tv" domain name and stating that the name would go to the highest bidder. Je Ho Lim submitted a bid for $1,010 and authorized DotTV to charge that amount to his credit card if his bid was the highest. Later, DotTV sent Lim an e-mail message stating that he had "won the auction" and charged the bid price of $1,010 to Lim's credit card. When DotTV subsequently refused to transfer the name, Lim sued DotTV for, among other things, breach of contract. Lim argued that his bid constituted an acceptance of DotTV's offer to sell the name. DotTV contended that Lim's bid was an offer, which it had not accepted. Furthermore, even if it had accepted Lim's offer, because the auction was "with reserve,"

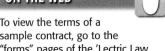
An offer may invite an acceptance to be worded in such specific terms that the contract is made definite. **EXAMPLE 9.6** Suppose that Marcus Business Machines contacts your corporation and offers to sell "from one to ten MacCool copying machines for $1,600 each; state number desired in acceptance." Your corporation agrees to buy two copiers. Because the quantity is specified in the acceptance, the terms are definite, and the contract is enforceable. ■

Communication A third requirement for an effective offer is communication—the offer must be communicated to the offeree. **EXAMPLE 9.7** Suppose that Tolson advertises a reward for the return of her lost cat. Dirlik, not knowing of the reward, finds the cat and returns it to Tolson. Ordinarily, Dirlik cannot recover the reward because an essential element of a reward contract is that the one who claims the reward must have known it was offered. A few states would allow recovery of the reward, but not on contract principles—Dirlik would be allowed to recover on the basis that it would be unfair to deny him the reward just because he did not know about it. ■

Termination of the Offer

The communication of an effective offer to an offeree gives the offeree the power to transform the offer into a binding, legal obligation (a contract) by an acceptance. This power of acceptance does not continue forever, though. It can be terminated by action of the parties or by operation of law.

Termination by Action of the Parties An offer can be terminated by the action of the parties in any of three ways: by revocation, by rejection, or by counteroffer.

Revocation of the Offer. The offeror's act of withdrawing an offer is referred to as **revocation.** Unless an offer is irrevocable, the offeror usually can revoke the offer (even if he or she has promised to keep the offer open), as long as the revocation is communicated to the offeree before the offeree accepts. Revocation may be accomplished by an express repudiation of the offer (for example, with a statement such as "I withdraw my previous

DotTV could withdraw the domain name from the auction even after acceptance. The trial court held for DotTV, and Lim appealed.

The Court's Analysis

The appellate court first explained that the UCC's provisions concerning auctions did not apply in this case because the UCC applies only to "goods" and domain names are not goods. The court then looked at common law principles as codified in the *Restatement (Second) of Contracts*. The rules under the *Restatement* are similar to those of the UCC: a bid in an auction is an offer that is accepted when the "hammer falls," and an auction is with reserve unless otherwise specified by the seller.

The court also pointed out, however, that DotTV's charging of the bid price to Lim's credit card was inconsistent with DotTV's claim that it could withdraw the domain name from the bidding because the auction was with reserve.

Furthermore, stated the court, even if it concluded that Lim's bid was an offer and not an acceptance, DotTV had accepted the offer by its e-mail to Lim stating that he had won the auction. In all, held the court, there was no evidence that a contract between DotTV and Lim had *not* been formed, and Lim had stated a valid claim against DotTV for breach of contract. The court thus reversed the lower court's decision and remanded the case for further deliberation consistent with the appellate court's opinion.[a]

FOR CRITICAL ANALYSIS *Should the UCC rules governing auctions apply to items sold on online auction sites, such as eBay? Why or why not? How can you know whether eBay's auctions are "with reserve" or "without reserve"?*

a. *Lim v. The.TV Corp. International,* 99 Cal.App.4th 684, 121 Cal.Rptr.2d 333 (2d Dist. 2002).

offer of October 17") or by the performance of acts that are inconsistent with the existence of the offer and that are made known to the offeree.

■EXAMPLE 9.8 Geraldine offers to sell some land to Gary. A week passes, and Gary, who has not yet accepted the offer, learns from his friend Konstantine that Geraldine has in the meantime sold the property to Nunan. Gary's knowledge of Geraldine's sale of the land to Nunan, even though he learned of it through a third party, effectively revokes Geraldine's offer to sell the land to Gary. Geraldine's sale of the land to Nunan is inconsistent with the continued existence of the offer to Gary, and thus the offer to Gary is revoked. ■

The general rule followed by most states is that a revocation becomes effective when the offeree or the offeree's agent (a person who acts on behalf of another) actually receives it. Therefore, a letter of revocation mailed on April 1 and delivered at the offeree's residence or place of business on April 3 becomes effective on April 3.

An offer made to the general public can be revoked in the same manner in which the offer was originally communicated. **■EXAMPLE 9.9** Suppose that a department store offers a $10,000 reward to anyone providing information leading to the apprehension of the persons who burglarized its downtown store. The offer is published in three local papers and in four papers in neighboring communities. To revoke the offer, the store must publish the revocation in all seven papers for the same number of days it published the offer. The revocation is then accessible to the general public, and the offer is revoked even if some particular offeree does not know about the revocation. ■

Irrevocable Offers. Although most offers are revocable, some can be made irrevocable. Increasingly, courts refuse to allow an offeror to revoke an offer when the offeree has changed position because of justifiable reliance on the offer (under the doctrine of *detrimental reliance,* or *promissory estoppel,* discussed later in this chapter). In some circumstances, "firm offers" made by merchants may also be considered irrevocable. We discuss these offers in Chapter 15.

Another form of irrevocable offer is an option contract. An **option contract** is created when an offeror promises to hold an offer open for a specified period of time in return for

OPTION CONTRACT
A contract under which the offeror cannot revoke the offer for a stipulated time period. During this period, the offeree can accept or reject the offer without fear that the offer will be made to another person. The offeree must give consideration for the option (the irrevocable offer) to be enforceable.

A billboard offers a reward for the capture of the killer of this woman's husband. How can this offer be revoked? (AP Photo/Denis Poroy)

a payment (consideration) given by the offeree. An option contract takes away the offeror's power to revoke an offer for the period of time specified in the option. If no time is specified, then a reasonable period of time is implied. **■EXAMPLE 9.10** Suppose that you are in the business of writing movie scripts. Your agent contacts the head of development at New Line Cinema and offers to sell New Line your new movie script. New Line likes your script and agrees to pay you $25,000 for a six-month option. In this situation, you (through your agent) are the offeror, and New Line is the offeree. You cannot revoke your offer to sell New Line your script for the next six months. After six months, if no contract has been formed, New Line loses the $25,000, and you are free to sell your script to another movie studio. ■

Option contracts are also frequently used in conjunction with the sale of real estate. **■EXAMPLE 9.11** You might agree with a landowner to lease a house and include in the lease contract a clause stating that you will pay $15,000 for an option to purchase the property within a specified period of time. If you decide not to purchase the home after the specified period has lapsed, you lose the $15,000, and the landlord is free to sell the property to another buyer. ■

Rejection of the Offer by the Offeree. If the offeree rejects the offer, the offer is terminated. Any subsequent attempt by the offeree to accept will be construed as a new offer, giving the original offeror (now the offeree) the power of acceptance. A rejection is ordinarily accomplished by words or by conduct indicating an intent not to accept the offer.

As with a revocation, a rejection of an offer is effective only when it is actually received by the offeror or the offeror's agent. **■EXAMPLE 9.12** Suppose that Growgood Farms mails a letter to Campbell Soup Company offering to sell carrots at ten cents a pound. (Of course, today, such offers tend to be sent electronically rather than by mail, as will be discussed in Chapter 14.) Campbell Soup Company could reject the offer either by sending or faxing a letter to Growgood Farms expressly rejecting the offer or by mailing the offer back to Growgood, indicating an intent to reject it. Alternatively, Campbell could offer to buy the carrots at eight cents per pound (a counteroffer), necessarily rejecting the original offer. ■

BE CAREFUL The way in which a response to an offer is phrased can determine whether the offer is accepted or rejected.

Merely inquiring about an offer does not constitute rejection. **■EXAMPLE 9.13** A friend offers to buy your DVD movie collection for $300. You respond, "Is this your best offer?" or "Will you pay me $375 for it?" A reasonable person would conclude that you did not reject the offer but merely made an inquiry for further consideration of the offer. You can still accept and bind your friend to the $300 purchase price. When the offeree merely inquires as to the firmness of the offer, there is no reason to presume that she or he intends to reject it. ■

Counteroffer by the Offeree. A **counteroffer** is a rejection of the original offer and the simultaneous making of a new offer. **■EXAMPLE 9.14** Suppose that Burke offers to sell his home to Lang for $270,000. Lang responds, "Your price is too high. I'll offer to purchase your house for $250,000." Lang's response is called a counteroffer because it rejects Burke's offer to sell at $270,000 and creates a new offer by Lang to purchase the home at a price of $250,000. ■

At common law, the **mirror image rule** requires that the offeree's acceptance match the offeror's offer exactly. In other words, the terms of the acceptance must "mirror" those of the offer. If the acceptance materially changes or adds to the terms of the original offer, it will be considered not an acceptance but a counteroffer—which, of course, need not be accepted. The original offeror can, however, accept the terms of the counteroffer and create a valid contract.[11]

Termination by Operation of Law The offeree's power to transform an offer into a binding, legal obligation can be terminated by operation of law if any of four conditions occur: lapse of time, destruction of the specific subject matter, death or incompetence of the offeror or offeree, or supervening illegality of the proposed contract.

Lapse of Time. An offer terminates automatically by law when the period of time *specified in the offer* has passed. If the offer states that it will be left open until a particular date, then the offer will terminate at midnight on that day. If the offer states that it will be left open for a number of days, such as ten days, this time period normally begins to run when the offer is actually received by the offeree, not when it is formed or sent. When the offer is delayed (through the misdelivery of mail, for example), the period begins to run from the date the offeree would have received the offer, but only if the offeree knows or should know that the offer is delayed.[12]

■EXAMPLE 9.15 Suppose that Beth offers to sell her boat to Jonah, stating that the offer will remain open until May 20. Unless Jonah accepts the offer by midnight on May 20, the offer will lapse (terminate). Now suppose that Beth writes a letter to Jonah, offering to sell him her boat if Jonah accepts the offer within twenty days of the letter's date, which is May 1. Jonah must accept within twenty days after May 1, or the offer will terminate. Suppose that instead of including the date May 1 in her letter, Beth had simply written to Jonah offering to sell him her boat if Jonah accepted within twenty days. In this instance, Jonah must accept within twenty days of receiving the letter. The same rule would apply if Beth used insufficient postage and Jonah received the letter ten days late without knowing that it had been delayed. If, however, Jonah knew that the letter was delayed, the offer would lapse twenty days after the day he ordinarily would have received the offer had Beth used sufficient postage. ■

COUNTEROFFER
An offeree's response to an offer in which the offeree rejects the original offer and at the same time makes a new offer.

MIRROR IMAGE RULE
A common law rule that requires that the terms of the offeree's acceptance adhere exactly to the terms of the offeror's offer for a valid contract to be formed.

ON THE WEB

For answers to some common questions about contract law, go to the Web site of the Legal Information Network, Inc., at **www.contract-law.com/TheLaw.htm**.

---

11. The mirror image rule has been greatly modified in regard to sales contracts. Section 2–207 of the UCC provides that a contract is formed if the offeree makes a definite expression of acceptance (such as signing the form in the appropriate location), even though the terms of the acceptance modify or add to the terms of the original offer (see Chapter 15).

12. *Restatement (Second) of Contracts*, Section 49.

If the offer does not specify a time for acceptance, the offer terminates at the end of a *reasonable* period of time. A reasonable period of time is determined by the subject matter of the contract, business and market conditions, and other relevant circumstances. An offer to sell farm produce, for example, will terminate sooner than an offer to sell farm equipment because farm produce is perishable and subject to greater fluctuations in market value.

Destruction of the Subject Matter. An offer is automatically terminated if the specific subject matter of the offer is destroyed before the offer is accepted. For example, if Bekins offers to sell his prize cow to Yatsen, but the cow is struck by lightning and dies before Yatsen can accept, the offer is automatically terminated. (Note that if Yatsen accepted the offer just before lightning struck the cow, a contract would have been formed, but, because of the cow's death, a court would likely excuse Bekins's obligation to perform the contract on the basis of impossibility of performance—see Chapter 12.)

Death or Incompetence of the Offeror or Offeree. An offeree's power of acceptance is terminated when the offeror or offeree dies or is deprived of legal capacity to enter into the proposed contract, *unless the offer is irrevocable.*[13] A revocable offer is personal to both parties and normally cannot pass to a decedent's heirs or estate or to the guardian of a mentally incompetent person. This rule applies whether or not one party had notice of the death or incompetence of the other party. **■EXAMPLE 9.16** Kapola, who is quite ill, writes to her friend Amanda, offering to sell Amanda her grand piano for only $400. That night, Kapola dies. The next day, Amanda, not knowing of Kapola's death, writes a letter to Kapola, accepting the offer and enclosing a check for $400. Is there a contract? No. There is no contract because the offer automatically terminated on Kapola's death. ■

Supervening Illegality of the Proposed Contract. A statute or court decision that makes an offer illegal automatically terminates the offer. **■EXAMPLE 9.17** Suppose that Acme Finance Corporation offers to lend Jack $20,000 at 15 percent interest annually, but before Jack can accept, the state legislature enacts a statute prohibiting loans at interest rates greater than 12 percent. In this situation, the offer is automatically terminated. (If the statute is enacted after Jack accepts the offer, a valid contract is formed, but the contract may still be unenforceable—see Chapter 10.) ■

Acceptance

ACCEPTANCE
A voluntary act by the offeree that shows assent, or agreement, to the terms of an offer; may consist of words or conduct.

An **acceptance** is a voluntary act by the offeree that shows assent, or agreement, to the terms of an offer. The offeree's act may consist of words or conduct. The acceptance must be unequivocal and must be communicated to the offeror.

Who Can Accept? Generally, a third person cannot substitute for the offeree and effectively accept the offer. After all, the identity of the offeree is as much a condition of a bargaining offer as any other term contained therein. Thus, except in special circumstances, only the person to whom the offer is made or that person's agent can accept the offer and create a binding contract. For example, Lottie makes an offer to Paul. Paul is not interested, but his friend José accepts the offer. No contract is formed.

Unequivocal Acceptance To exercise the power of acceptance effectively, the offeree must accept unequivocally. This is the *mirror image rule* previously discussed. If the

---

13. *Restatement (Second) of Contracts*, Section 48. If the offer is irrevocable, it is not terminated when the offeror dies.

acceptance is subject to new conditions or if the terms of the acceptance materially change the original offer, the acceptance may be deemed a counteroffer that implicitly rejects the original offer.

Certain terms, when added to an acceptance, will not qualify the acceptance sufficiently to constitute rejection of the offer. **EXAMPLE 9.18** Suppose that in response to a person offering to sell a painting by a well-known artist, the offeree replies, "I accept; please send a written contract." The offeree is requesting a written contract but is not making it a condition for acceptance. Therefore, the acceptance is effective without the written contract. In contrast, if the offeree replies, "I accept *if* you send a written contract," the acceptance is expressly conditioned on the request for a writing, and the statement is not an acceptance but a counteroffer. (Notice how important each word is!)[14] ▣

Silence as Acceptance Ordinarily, silence cannot constitute acceptance, even if the offeror states, "By your silence and inaction, you will be deemed to have accepted this offer." This general rule applies because an offeree should not be put under a burden of liability to act affirmatively in order to reject an offer. No consideration—that is, nothing of value—has passed to the offeree to impose such a liability.

In some instances, however, the offeree does have a duty to speak; if so, his or her silence or inaction will operate as an acceptance. Silence may be an acceptance when an offeree takes the benefit of offered services even though he or she had an opportunity to reject them and knew that they were offered with the expectation of compensation. **EXAMPLE 9.19** Suppose that John, a college student who earns extra income by washing store windows, taps on the window of a store and catches the attention of the store's manager. John points to the window and raises his cleaner, signaling that he will be washing the window. The manager does nothing to stop him. Here, the store manager's silence constitutes an acceptance, and an implied-in-fact contract is created. The store is bound to pay a reasonable value for John's work. ▣

Silence can also operate as an acceptance when the offeree has had prior dealings with the offeror. If a merchant, for example, routinely receives shipments from a supplier and in the past has always notified the supplier when defective goods are rejected, then silence

---

14. As noted in footnote 11, in regard to sales contracts, the UCC provides that an acceptance may still be effective even if some terms are added. The new terms are simply treated as proposals for additions to the contract, unless both parties are merchants. If the parties are merchants, the additional terms (with some exceptions) become part of the contract [UCC 2–207(2)].

CALL
1-800-262-2001
OR ORDER
ONLINE AT
www.columbiahouse.com

THE **LORD** OF THE **RINGS**
THE RETURN OF THE KING

will be sent to you and charged to your Discover Card account unless we receive other instructions by 05/21/07.

Check the box that applies
Mark "X"

Order Regular Priced Selections below and Earn 2 FunCash Dollars on each
Selections at Regular Price & Discount Sets   W=DVD

YES, send my Director's Selection immediately

NO, do not send my Director's Selection

This photo shows a letter from a DVD club that was sent to a club member. If the recipient (offeree) does nothing, has he or she accepted the offer? Why or why not?

constitutes acceptance. Also, if a buyer solicits an offer specifying that certain terms and conditions are acceptable, and the seller makes the offer in response to the solicitation, the buyer has a duty to reject—that is, a duty to tell the seller that the offer is not acceptable. Failure to reject (silence) will operate as an acceptance.

REMEMBER A bilateral contract is a promise for a promise, and a unilateral contract is performance for a promise.

Communication of Acceptance   Whether the offeror must be notified of the acceptance depends on the nature of the contract. In a bilateral contract, communication of acceptance is necessary because acceptance is in the form of a promise (not performance), and the contract is formed when the promise is made (rather than when the act is performed). Communication of acceptance is not necessary, however, if the offer dispenses with the requirement. Also, if the offer can be accepted by silence, no communication is necessary.[15]

Because a unilateral contract calls for the full performance of some act, acceptance is usually evident, and notification is unnecessary. Nevertheless, exceptions do exist, such as when the offeror requests notice of acceptance or has no way of determining whether the requested act has been performed. In addition, sometimes the law (such as Article 2 of the UCC) requires notice of acceptance, and thus notice is necessary.[16]

Mode and Timeliness of Acceptance   Acceptance in bilateral contracts must be timely. The general rule is that acceptance in a bilateral contract is timely if it is made before the offer is terminated. Problems may arise, though, when the parties involved are not dealing face to face. In such situations, the offeree should use an authorized mode of communication.

The Mailbox Rule.   Acceptance takes effect, thus completing formation of the contract, at the time the offeree sends or delivers the communication via the mode expressly or impliedly authorized by the offeror. This is the so-called **mailbox rule,** also called the *deposited acceptance rule,* which the majority of courts uphold. Under this rule, if the authorized mode of communication is the mail, then an acceptance becomes valid when it is dispatched (placed in the control of the U.S. Postal Service)—*not* when it is received by the offeror.

MAILBOX RULE
A rule providing that an acceptance of an offer becomes effective on dispatch (on being placed in an official mailbox), if mail is, expressly or impliedly, an authorized means of communication of acceptance to the offeror.

The mailbox rule was formed to prevent the confusion that arises when an offeror sends a letter of revocation but, before it arrives, the offeree sends a letter of acceptance. Thus, whereas a revocation becomes effective only when it is *received* by the offeree, an acceptance becomes effective on *dispatch* (when sent, even if it is never received), provided that an *authorized* means of communication is used.

Authorized Means of Communication.   A means of communicating acceptance can be either expressly authorized—that is, expressly stipulated in the offer—or impliedly authorized by the facts and circumstances surrounding the situation or by law.[17] An acceptance sent by means not expressly or impliedly authorized normally is not effective until it is received by the offeror.

---

15. Under UCC 2–206(1)(b), an order or other offer to buy goods that are to be promptly shipped may be treated as either a bilateral or a unilateral offer and can be accepted by a promise to ship or by actual shipment.

16. UCC 2–206(2).

17. *Restatement (Second) of Contracts,* Section 30, provides that an offer invites acceptance "by any medium reasonable in the circumstances," unless the offer is specific about the means of acceptance. Under Section 65, a medium is reasonable if it is one used by the offeror or one customary in similar transactions, unless the offeree knows of circumstances that would argue against the reasonableness of a particular medium (the need for speed because of rapid price changes, for example).

When an offeror specifies how acceptance should be made (for example, by overnight delivery), *express authorization* is said to exist. Moreover, both the offeror and the offeree are bound in contract the moment that such a mode of acceptance is employed. **■EXAMPLE 9.20** Shaylee & Perkins, a Massachusetts firm, offers to sell a container of antique furniture to Leaham's Antiques in Colorado. The offer states that Leaham's must accept the offer via FedEx overnight delivery. The acceptance is effective (and a binding contract is formed) the moment that Leaham's gives the overnight envelope containing the acceptance to the FedEx driver. ■

Most offerors do not expressly specify the means of communication by which the offeree is to accept. Thus, the common law recognizes the following implied authorized means of acceptance[18]:

1 The offeror's choice of a particular mode of communication in making the offer implies that the offeree is authorized to use the same mode *or a faster* one for acceptance.

2 When two parties are at a distance, mailing is impliedly authorized.

Exceptions. There are three basic exceptions to the rule that a contract is formed when acceptance is sent by authorized means:

1 If the acceptance is not properly dispatched (if a letter is incorrectly addressed, for example, or lacks sufficient postage), in most states it will not be effective until it is received by the offeror.

2 The offeror can stipulate in the offer that an acceptance will not be effective until it is received (usually by a specified time) by the offeror.

3 Sometimes an offeree sends a rejection first, then later changes his or her mind and sends an acceptance. Obviously, this chain of events could cause confusion and even detriment to the offeror, depending on whether the rejection or the acceptance arrives first. In such situations, the law cancels the rule of acceptance on dispatch, and the first communication received by the offeror determines whether a contract is formed. If the rejection arrives first, there is no contract.[19]

PREVENTING LEGAL DISPUTES

An effective way to avoid legal disputes over contracts is to communicate your intentions clearly to the other party and express every detail in writing, even when a written contract is not legally required. If you are the offeror, be explicit in your offer about how long the offer will remain open and stipulate the authorized means of communicating the acceptance. Include a provision requiring the offeree to notify you of acceptance regardless of whether a bilateral or unilateral contract will be formed. (See the *Application* feature at the end of this chapter for additional suggestions on controlling the terms of an offer.) If you are the offeree, make sure that the language you use for any counteroffer, negotiation, or acceptance is absolutely clear and unambiguous. A simple "I accept" is best in most situations. Providing notice of the acceptance can lessen the potential for problems arising due to revocation or lost communications.

---

18. Note that UCC 2–206(1)(a) states specifically that an acceptance of an offer for the sale of goods can be made by any medium that is *reasonable* under the circumstances.
19. *Restatement (Second) of Contracts*, Section 40.

If an offer expressly authorizes acceptance of the offer by first-class mail or express delivery, can the offeree accept by a faster means, such as by fax or e-mail? Why or why not? (Chiaki Hayashi/Creative Commons)

CONSIDERATION
  Generally, the value given in return for a promise; involves two elements—the giving of something of legally sufficient value and a bargained-for exchange. The consideration must result in a detriment to the promisee or a benefit to the promisor.

FORBEARANCE
  The act of refraining from an action that one has a legal right to undertake.

Technology and Acceptances   Technology, and particularly the Internet, has all but eliminated the need for the mailbox rule because online acceptances typically are communicated instantaneously to the offeror. As you will learn in Chapter 14, although online offers are not significantly different from traditional offers contained in paper documents, online acceptances have posed some unusual problems.

CONSIDERATION AND ITS REQUIREMENTS

In every legal system, some promises will be enforced, and other promises will not be enforced. The simple fact that a party has made a promise, then, does not mean the promise is enforceable. Under the common law, a primary basis for the enforcement of promises is consideration. **Consideration** is usually defined as the value given in return for a promise. We look here at the basic elements of consideration and then at some other contract doctrines relating to consideration.

Elements of Consideration

Often, consideration is broken down into two parts: (1) something of *legally sufficient value* must be given in exchange for the promise, and (2) there must be a *bargained-for exchange.*

Legal Value   The "something of legally sufficient value" may consist of (1) a promise to do something that one has no prior legal duty to do (to pay on receipt of certain goods, for example), (2) the performance of an action that one is otherwise not obligated to undertake (such as providing accounting services), or (3) the refraining from an action that one has a legal right to undertake (called a **forbearance**).

Consideration in bilateral contracts normally consists of a promise in return for a promise, as explained in Chapter 8. ■**EXAMPLE 9.21** Suppose that in a contract for the sale of goods, the seller promises to ship specific goods to the buyer, and the buyer promises to pay for those goods when they are received. Each of these promises constitutes consideration for the contract. ■ In contrast, unilateral contracts involve a promise in return for a performance. ■**EXAMPLE 9.22** Suppose that Anita says to her neighbor, "If you paint my garage, I will pay you $800." Anita's neighbor paints the garage. The act of painting the garage is the consideration that creates Anita's contractual obligation to pay her neighbor $800. ■

What if, in return for a promise to pay, a person refrains from pursuing harmful habits, such as the use of tobacco and alcohol? Does such forbearance create consideration for the contract? This was the issue in *Hamer v. Sidway,* a classic case concerning consideration that we present as this chapter's *Landmark in the Law* feature on pages 266 and 267.

Bargained-for Exchange   The second element of consideration is that it must provide the basis for the bargain struck between the contracting parties. The promise given by the promisor must induce the promisee to incur a legal detriment either now or in the future, and the detriment incurred must induce the promisor to make the promise. This element of bargained-for exchange distinguishes contracts from gifts.

■**EXAMPLE 9.23** Suppose that Roberto says to his son, "In consideration of the fact that you are not as wealthy as your brothers, I will pay you $5,000." This promise is not enforceable because Roberto's son has not given any return consideration for the $5,000 promised.[20] The son (the promisee) incurs no legal detriment; he does not have to promise anything or undertake (or refrain from undertaking) any action to receive the $5,000.

---

20. See *Fink v. Cox,* 18 Johns. 145, 9 Am.Dec. 191 (N.Y. 1820).

Here, Roberto has simply stated his motive for giving his son a gift. The fact that the word *consideration* is used does not, by itself, mean that consideration has been given.

Legal Sufficiency and Adequacy of Consideration

Legal sufficiency of consideration involves the requirement that consideration be something of value in the eyes of the law. Adequacy of consideration involves "how much" consideration is given. Essentially, adequacy of consideration concerns the fairness of the bargain. On the surface, fairness would appear to be an issue when the items exchanged are of unequal value. In general, however, courts do not question the adequacy of consideration if the consideration is legally sufficient. Under the doctrine of freedom of contract, parties are usually free to bargain as they wish. If people could sue merely because they had entered into an unwise contract, the courts would be overloaded with frivolous suits.

Nevertheless, in rare situations a court will consider whether the amount or value of the consideration is adequate. This is because apparently inadequate consideration can indicate that fraud, duress, or undue influence was involved. It might also indicate that a gift was made (if a father "sells" a $100,000 house to his daughter for only $1,000, for example). When the consideration is grossly inadequate, a court may declare the contract unenforceable on the ground that it is unconscionable,[21] meaning that, generally speaking, it is so one sided under the circumstances as to be clearly unfair. (*Unconscionability* will be discussed further in Chapter 10.)

The determination of whether consideration exists does not depend on the comparative value of the things exchanged. Something need not be of direct economic or financial value to be considered legally sufficient consideration. In many situations, the exchange of promises and potential benefits is deemed sufficient as consideration.

CONTRACTS THAT LACK CONSIDERATION

Sometimes, one or both of the parties to a contract may think that they have exchanged consideration when in fact they have not. Here we look at some situations in which the parties' promises or actions do not qualify as contractual consideration.

Preexisting Duty

Under most circumstances, a promise to do what one already has a legal duty to do does not constitute legally sufficient consideration because no legal detriment is incurred.[22] The preexisting legal duty may be imposed by law or may arise out of a previous contract. A sheriff, for example, cannot collect a reward for information leading to the capture of a criminal if the sheriff already has a legal duty to capture the criminal. Likewise, if a party is already bound by contract to perform a certain duty, that duty cannot serve as consideration for a second contract.

EXAMPLE 9.24 Suppose that Bauman-Bache, Inc., begins construction on a seven-story office building and after three months demands an extra $75,000 on its contract. If the extra $75,000 is not paid, the firm will stop working. The owner of the land, having no one else to complete construction, agrees to pay the extra $75,000. The agreement is not enforceable because it is not supported by legally sufficient consideration; Bauman-Bache had a preexisting contractual duty to complete the building. ■

ON THE WEB

The New Hampshire Attorney General's Consumer's Sourcebook provides information on contract law from a consumer's perspective. You can access this book online at **www.doj.nh.gov/consumer/sourcebook**.

BE AWARE A consumer's signature on a contract does not always guarantee that the contract will be enforced. Ultimately, the terms must be fair.

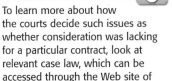

ON THE WEB

To learn more about how the courts decide such issues as whether consideration was lacking for a particular contract, look at relevant case law, which can be accessed through the Web site of Cornell University's School of Law at **www.law.cornell.edu/wex/index.php/Contracts**.

---

21. Pronounced un-*kon*-shun-uh-bul.
22. See *Foakes v. Beer*, 9 App.Cas. 605 (1884).

LANDMARK IN THE LAW — *Hamer v. Sidway* (1891)

In *Hamer v. Sidway,*[a] the issue before the court arose from a contract created in 1869 between William Story, Sr., and his nephew, William Story II. The uncle promised his nephew that if the nephew refrained from drinking alcohol, using tobacco, and playing billiards and cards for money until he reached the age of twenty-one, the uncle would pay him $5,000 (about $75,000 in today's dollars). The nephew, who indulged occasionally in all of these "vices," agreed to refrain from them and did so for the next six years. Following his twenty-first birthday in 1875, the nephew wrote to his uncle that he had performed his part of the bargain and was thus entitled to the promised $5,000. A few days later, the uncle wrote the nephew a letter stating, "[Y]ou shall have the five thousand dollars, as I promised you." The uncle said that the money was in the bank and that the nephew could "consider this money on interest."

The Issue of Consideration   The nephew left the money in the care of his uncle, who held it for the next twelve years. When the uncle died in 1887, however, the executor of the uncle's estate refused to pay the $5,000 claim brought by Hamer, a third party to whom the promise had been *assigned.* (The law allows parties to assign, or transfer, rights in contracts to third parties; see Chapter 12.) The executor, Sidway, contended that the contract was invalid because there was insufficient consideration to support it. The

a. 124 N.Y. 538, 27 N.E. 256 (1891).

Unforeseen Difficulties   The rule regarding preexisting duty is meant to prevent extortion and the so-called holdup game. What happens, though, when an honest contractor, who has contracted with a landowner to build a house, runs into extraordinary difficulties that were totally unforeseen at the time the contract was formed? In the interests of fairness and equity, the courts sometimes allow exceptions to the preexisting duty rule. In the example just mentioned, if the landowner agrees to pay extra compensation to the contractor for overcoming the unforeseen difficulties (such as having to use dynamite and special equipment to remove an unexpected rock formation to excavate for a basement), the court may refrain from applying the preexisting duty rule and enforce the agreement. When the "unforeseen difficulties" that give rise to a contract modification are the types of risks ordinarily assumed in business, however, the courts will usually assert the preexisting duty rule.[23]

RESCISSION
A remedy whereby a contract is canceled and the parties are returned to the positions they occupied before the contract was made; may be effected through the mutual consent of the parties, by the parties' conduct, or by court decree.

Rescission and New Contract   The law recognizes that two parties can mutually agree to rescind their contract, at least to the extent that it is executory (still to be carried out). Rescission[24] is the unmaking of a contract so as to return the parties to the positions they

---

23. Note that under the UCC, any agreement modifying a contract within Article 2 on sales needs no consideration to be binding. See UCC 2–209(1).
24. Pronounced reh-*sih*-zhen.

uncle had received nothing, and the nephew had actually benefited by fulfilling the uncle's wishes. Therefore, no contract existed.

The Court's Conclusion   Although a lower court upheld Sidway's position, the New York Court of Appeals reversed and ruled in favor of the plaintiff, Hamer. "The promisee used tobacco, occasionally drank liquor, and he had a legal right to do so," the court stated. "That right he abandoned for a period of years upon the strength of the promise of the testator [one who makes a will] that for such forbearance he would give him $5,000. We need not speculate on the effort which may have been required to give up the use of those stimulants. It is sufficient that he restricted his lawful freedom of action within certain prescribed limits upon the faith of his uncle's agreement."

APPLICATION TO TODAY'S WORLD   *Although this case was decided more than a century ago, the principles enunciated by the court remain applicable to contracts formed today, including online contracts. For a contract to be valid and binding, consideration must be given, and that consideration must be something of legally sufficient value.*

RELEVANT WEB SITES   *To locate information on the Web concerning the* Hamer v. Sidway *decision, go to this text's Web site at* **www.thomsonedu.com/westbuslaw/blt**, *select "Chapter 9," and click on "URLs for Landmarks."*

occupied before the contract was made. Sometimes, parties rescind a contract and make a new contract at the same time. When this occurs, it is often difficult to determine whether there was consideration for the new contract or whether the parties had a pre-existing duty under the previous contract. If a court finds there was a preexisting duty, then the new contract will be invalid because there was no consideration.

Past Consideration

Promises made in return for actions or events that have already taken place are unenforceable. These promises lack consideration in that the element of bargained-for exchange is missing. In short, you can bargain for something to take place now or in the future but not for something that has already taken place. Therefore, **past consideration** is no consideration.

EXAMPLE 9.25   Suppose that Elsie, a real estate agent, does her friend Judy a favor by selling Judy's house and not charging any commission. Later, Judy says to Elsie, "In return for your generous act, I will pay you $6,000." This promise is made in return for past consideration and is thus unenforceable; in effect, Judy is stating her intention to give Elsie a gift.

Is a party's suggestion that a professional athlete use a certain nickname for marketing products sufficient consideration for the athlete's later promise to pay the party a portion of the profits? That was the question in the following case.

PAST CONSIDERATION
An act that takes place before the contract is made and that ordinarily, by itself, cannot be consideration for a later promise to pay for the act.

CASE 9.2 Blackmon v. Iverson

United States District Court, Eastern District of Pennsylvania, 324 F.Supp.2d 602 (2003).

FACTS Jamil Blackmon became friends with Allen Iverson in 1987 when Iverson was a high school student who showed tremendous promise as an athlete. Blackmon began to provide financial and other support to Iverson and his family. One evening in 1994, Blackmon suggested that Iverson use "The Answer" as a nickname in the summer league basketball tournaments. Blackmon said that Iverson would be "The Answer" to all of the National Basketball Association's woes. Later that night, Iverson said that he would give Blackmon 25 percent of any proceeds from the merchandising of products that used "The Answer" as a logo or slogan. Blackmon invested time, funds, and effort in refining the concept of "The Answer." In 1996, just before being drafted by the Philadelphia 76ers, Iverson told Blackmon that Iverson intended to use "The Answer" under a contract with Reebok. In 1997, Reebok began to sell, and continues to sell, products bearing "The Answer" slogan. None of the products uses any of Blackmon's designs, however, and Iverson does not share any of his profits with Blackmon. In 1998, Iverson persuaded Blackmon to move to Philadelphia. Blackmon subsequently filed a suit in a federal district court against Iverson, alleging breach of contract, among other things. Iverson filed a motion for summary judgment.

ISSUE Was Blackmon's suggestion that Iverson use "The Answer" as a nickname valid consideration for Iverson's subsequent promise to pay Blackmon 25 percent of the profits from sales of products that used "The Answer" as a slogan?

DECISION No. The court held that Blackmon's suggestion of a nickname for Iverson was gratuitous and took place before Iverson's promise to pay Blackmon for the idea.

Therefore, the court held that it was not sufficient consideration.

REASON The court granted Iverson's motion to dismiss Blackmon's complaint. The alleged contract between the parties was not supported by sufficient consideration. "Consideration confers a benefit upon the promisor or causes a detriment to the promisee and must be an act, forbearance, or return promise bargained for and given in exchange for the original promise. Under [the] law, past consideration is insufficient to support a subsequent promise." The disclosure of the idea for the use of "The Answer" as a marketing tool occurred before the formation of a promise to pay for the use of the idea. Blackmon expressed the idea one evening in 1994. The same night, Iverson made a promise to pay, but he did not tell Blackmon that he would use "The Answer" in connection with the Reebok contract until two years later, and no sales of goods occurred until the following year. Under these circumstances, the disclosure of the idea was past consideration and insufficient to create a binding contract. Likewise, Blackmon's support of Iverson, which began in 1987 and continued in 1994, 1996, and 1997, preceded any promise to pay. With respect to Blackmon's move to Philadelphia, "there is no allegation that the move was required in exchange for any promise by the defendant to pay."

WHAT IF THE FACTS WERE DIFFERENT? *Suppose that only five minutes had elapsed between Blackmon's suggestion that Iverson use "The Answer" as a marketing slogan and Iverson's promise to give Blackmon a percentage of the proceeds. Would the court's ruling in this case have been any different? Why or why not?*

Illusory Promises

If the terms of the contract express such uncertainty of performance that the promisor has not definitely promised to do anything, the promise is said to be *illusory*—without consideration and unenforceable. **EXAMPLE 9.26** The president of Tuscan Corporation says to his employees, "All of you have worked hard, and if profits remain high, a 10 percent bonus at the end of the year will be given—if management thinks it is warranted." This is an *illusory promise*, or no promise at all, because performance depends solely on the discretion of the president (the management). There is no bargained-for consideration. The statement declares merely that management may or may not do something in the future. ■

Option-to-cancel clauses in contracts for specified time periods sometimes present problems in regard to consideration. **EXAMPLE 9.27** Abe contracts to hire Chris for one year at $5,000 per month, reserving the right to cancel the contract at any time. On close examination of these words, you can see that Abe has not actually agreed to hire Chris, as Abe could cancel without liability before Chris started performance. Abe has not given up the opportunity of hiring someone else. This contract is therefore illusory. Now suppose that Abe contracts to hire Chris for a one-year period at $5,000 per month, reserving the right to cancel the contract at any time after Chris has begun performance by giving Chris thirty days' notice. Abe, by saying that he will give Chris thirty days' notice, is relinquishing the opportunity (legal right) to hire someone else instead of Chris for a thirty-day period. If Chris works for one month, at the end of which Abe gives him thirty days' notice, Chris has a valid and enforceable contractual claim for $10,000 in salary. ◼

SETTLEMENT OF CLAIMS

Businesspersons or others can settle legal claims in several ways. It is important to understand the nature of the consideration given in these settlement agreements, or contracts. Claims are commonly settled through an *accord and satisfaction*, in which a debtor offers to pay a lesser amount than the creditor purports is owed. Two other methods that are also often used to settle claims are the *release* and the *covenant not to sue*.

REMEMBER Businesspersons should consider settling potential legal disputes to save both their own time and resources and those of the courts.

Accord and Satisfaction

In an **accord and satisfaction,** a debtor offers to pay, and a creditor accepts, a lesser amount than the creditor originally claimed was owed. Thus, in an accord and satisfaction, the debtor attempts to terminate an existing obligation. The *accord* is the settlement agreement. In an accord, the debtor offers to give or perform something less than the parties originally agreed on, and the creditor accepts that offer in satisfaction of the claim. *Satisfaction* is the performance (usually payment), which takes place after the accord is executed. A basic rule is that there can be no satisfaction unless there is first an accord.

For accord and satisfaction to occur, the amount of the debt *must be in dispute*. If it is a **liquidated debt,** then accord and satisfaction cannot take place. A debt is liquidated if its amount has been ascertained, fixed, agreed on, settled, or exactly determined. An example of a liquidated debt is a loan contract in which the borrower agrees to pay a stipulated amount every month until the amount of the loan is paid. In the majority of states, acceptance of (an accord for) a lesser sum than the entire amount of a liquidated debt is not satisfaction, and the balance of the debt is still legally owed. The rationale for this rule is that the debtor has given no consideration to satisfy the obligation of paying the balance to the creditor—because the debtor has a preexisting legal obligation to pay the entire debt.

An *unliquidated debt* is the opposite of a liquidated debt. Here, reasonable persons may differ over the amount owed. It is *not* settled, fixed, agreed on, ascertained, or determined. In these circumstances, acceptance of payment of the lesser sum operates as a satisfaction, or discharge, of the debt. One argument to support this rule is that the parties give up a legal right to contest the amount in dispute, and thus consideration is given.

ACCORD AND SATISFACTION
A common means of settling a disputed claim, whereby a debtor offers to pay a lesser amount than the creditor purports is owed. The creditor's acceptance of the offer creates an accord (agreement), and when the accord is executed, satisfaction occurs.

LIQUIDATED DEBT
A debt for which the amount has been ascertained, fixed, agreed on, settled, or exactly determined. If the amount of the debt is in dispute, the debt is considered unliquidated.

Release

A **release** is a contract in which one party forfeits the right to pursue a legal claim against the other party. Releases will generally be binding if they are (1) given in good faith, (2) stated in a signed writing (required by many states), and (3) accompanied by consideration.[25] Clearly, parties are better off if they know the extent of their injuries or damages before signing releases.

RELEASE
A contract in which one party forfeits the right to pursue a legal claim against the other party.

---

25. Under the UCC, a written, signed waiver or renunciation by an aggrieved party discharges any further liability for a breach, even without consideration [UCC 1–107].

■EXAMPLE 9.28 Suppose that you are involved in an automobile accident caused by Raoul's negligence. Raoul offers to give you $2,000 if you will release him from further liability resulting from the accident. You believe that this amount will cover your damages, so you agree to and sign the release. Later you discover that the repairs to your car will cost $4,200. Can you collect the balance from Raoul? The answer is normally no; you are limited to the $2,000 in the release. Why? The reason is that a valid contract existed. You and Raoul both assented to the bargain (hence, agreement existed), and sufficient consideration was present. Your consideration for the contract was the legal detriment you suffered (by releasing Raoul from liability, you forfeited your right to sue to recover damages, should they be more than $2,000). This legal detriment was induced by Raoul's promise to give you the $2,000. Raoul's promise was, in turn, induced by your promise not to pursue your legal right to sue him for damages. ■

Before agreeing to a release, a party should be certain of its terms. The following case emphasizes this point.

CASE 9.3   BP Products North America, Inc. v. Oakridge at Winegard, Inc.

United States District Court, Middle District of Florida, 469 F.Supp.2d 1128 (2007).

FACTS Oakridge at Winegard, Inc., and Mahammad Qureshi operated a gas station and convenience store in Orlando, Florida, subject to an exclusive fuel supply agreement with BP Products North America, Inc. Under the agreement, BP had a "right to first refusal" with respect to the sale of the premises if Oakridge received an offer. In November 2005, without notifying BP, Oakridge contracted to sell the premises to Pacific Energy, Inc., and Arooj Ahmed. Pacific wanted to sell Citgo, not BP, fuel. Qureshi told Ahmed that terminating the agreement with BP would cost $100,000—the amount that BP had provided to build the station—and agreed to reduce its price by that amount. Several months later, when BP learned of the sale and switch to Citgo fuel, it filed a suit in a federal district court against Oakridge and the others to void the deal. The parties filed claims, counterclaims, and cross-claims, and attempted unsuccessfully to mediate a resolution. Later, during a phone conference, Oakridge offered BP $263,616.95 to cover its advance of funds under the fuel supply agreement, with ownership of the premises to be retained by Pacific and all of the other claims among the parties to be released. Everyone agreed. Two weeks later, however, Oakridge refused to sign the release. BP and Pacific asked the court to order its enforcement.

ISSUE Was the settlement and release negotiated in the phone conference among the parties enforceable?

DECISION Yes. The court concluded that "there was a meeting of the minds and the parties entered into an enforceable settlement agreement" during the conference call. The court entered a judgment in favor of BP and against Oakridge and Qureshi for $263,616.95, plus interest. The court also allowed Pacific to remain in possession of the premises and dismissed the other claims.

REASON The court found that "while the exact language of the releases was not crafted during the * * * conference call, the evidence clearly establishes that the parties all agreed to release all of their claims against one another." Oakridge argued in part that the negotiations had been informal. Oakridge asserted that the agreement should not release Pacific from its alleged obligation to indemnify the seller for $100,000 of the amount to be paid to BP. Oakridge contended that "BP and Pacific knew or had reason to know that Oakridge inadvertently omitted discussion of the $100,000 reimbursement amount allegedly owed by Pacific to Oakridge for early termination of the fuel supply agreement." The court found no evidence, however, that "BP and Pacific knew or should have known that the $100,000 reimbursement amount had been inadvertently omitted." Furthermore, the court emphasized, "the evidence clearly demonstrates that the parties all agreed to release all claims against each other arising out of the instant [present] litigation during the * * * conference call."

FOR CRITICAL ANALYSIS–Social Consideration *Why are settlement and release agreements encouraged and readily enforced?*

Covenant Not to Sue

Unlike a release, a **covenant not to sue** does not always bar further recovery. The parties simply substitute a contractual obligation for some other type of legal action based on a valid claim. Suppose (following the earlier example) that you agree with Raoul not to sue for damages in a tort action if he will pay for the damage to your car. If Raoul fails to pay, you can bring an action for breach of contract.

COVENANT NOT TO SUE
An agreement to substitute a contractual obligation for some other type of legal action based on a valid claim.

PROMISSORY ESTOPPEL

Sometimes, individuals rely on promises, and such reliance may form a basis for contract rights and duties. Under the doctrine of **promissory estoppel** (also called *detrimental reliance*), a person who has reasonably relied on the promise of another can often obtain some measure of recovery. When the doctrine of promissory estoppel is applied, the promisor (the offeror) is **estopped** (barred or impeded) from revoking the promise. For the doctrine of promissory estoppel to be applied, the following elements are required:

PROMISSORY ESTOPPEL
A doctrine that applies when a promisor makes a clear and definite promise on which the promisee justifiably relies. Such a promise is binding if justice will be better served by the enforcement of the promise.

ESTOPPED
Barred, impeded, or precluded.

1 There must be a clear and definite promise.

2 The promisee must justifiably rely on the promise.

3 The reliance normally must be of a substantial and definite character.

4 Justice will be better served by the enforcement of the promise.

■EXAMPLE 9.29 Your uncle tells you, "I'll pay you $1,500 a week so that you won't have to work anymore." In reliance on your uncle's promise, you quit your job, but your uncle refuses to pay you. Under the doctrine of promissory estoppel, you may be able to enforce his promise.[26] Now your uncle makes a promise to give you $20,000 to buy a car. If you buy the car with your own funds and he does not pay you, you may once again be able to enforce the promise under this doctrine. ■

---

26. A classic example is *Ricketts v. Scothorn*, 57 Neb. 51, 77 N.W. 365 (1898).

REVIEWING Agreement and Consideration

Shane Durbin wanted to have a recording studio custom built in his home. He sent invitations to a number of local contractors to submit bids on the project. Rory Amstel submitted the lowest bid, which was $20,000 less than any of the other bids Durbin received. Durbin then called Amstel to ascertain the type and quality of the materials that were included in the bid and to find out if he could substitute a superior brand of acoustic tiles for the same bid price. Amstel said he would have to check into the price difference. The parties also discussed a possible start date for construction. Two weeks later, Durbin changed his mind and decided not to go forward with his plan to build a recording studio. Amstel filed a suit against Durbin for breach of contract. Using the information presented in the chapter, answer the following questions.

1 Did Amstel's bid meet the requirements of an offer? Explain.

2 Was there an acceptance of the offer? Why or why not?

3 Suppose that the court determines that the parties did not reach an agreement. Further suppose that Amstel, in anticipation of building Durbin's studio, had purchased materials and refused other jobs so that he would have time in his schedule for Durbin's project. Under what theory discussed in the chapter might Amstel attempt to recover these costs?

4 Now suppose that Durbin had gone forward with his plan to build the studio and immediately accepted Amstel's bid

(Continued)

without discussing the type or quality of materials. After Amstel began construction, Durbin asked Amstel to substitute a superior brand of acoustic tiles for the tiles that Amstel had intended to use at the time that he bid on the project. Amstel installed the tiles, then asked Durbin to pay the difference in price, but Durbin refused. Can Amstel sue to obtain the price differential from Durbin in this situation? Why or why not?

APPLICATION   Controlling the Terms of the Offer*

T he courts normally attempt to "save" contracts whenever feasible, but sometimes it is impossible to do so. Two common reasons that contracts fail are that (1) the terms of the offer were too unclear or indefinite to constitute a binding contract on the offer's acceptance, and (2) the acceptance was not timely. If you are an offeror, you can control both of these factors: you can determine what the terms of the future contract will be, as well as the time and mode of acceptance.

Include Clear and Definite Terms

If a contract's terms are too unclear or indefinite, the contract will fail. Unless a court can ascertain exactly what the rights and duties of the parties are under a particular contract, the court cannot enforce those rights and duties. Therefore, as an offeror, make sure that the terms of your offer are sufficiently definite to constitute a binding contract if the offer is accepted. A statement such as "Quantity to be determined later" may allow the offeree, after acceptance, to claim that a contract was never formed because the quantity term was not specified or is ambiguous. (Note, however, that sales and lease contracts governed by the Uniform Commercial Code may be formed even though terms are missing or ambiguous.)

Another reason an offeror should make sure that the offer's terms are clear and definite is that if a contract results, any ambiguous provision may be interpreted against the party that drafted the contract (see Chapter 8).

Specify the Time and Mode of Acceptance

Problems concerning contract formation also arise when it is unclear whether an acceptance is effective or at what time it became effective. To avoid such problems, you should take some precautions when phrasing the offer. Whether your offer is made via the Internet, fax, express delivery, or mail, you can specify that the offer must be accepted (or even that you must receive the acceptance) by a certain time, and if it is not, the offer will terminate. Similarly, you can specify the mode of acceptance. In online offers, you can indicate that to accept the offer, the user must click on a certain box on the screen. If you make an offer and want the acceptance to be faxed to you, make sure that you clearly indicate that the acceptance must be faxed to you at a given fax number by a specific time, or it will not be effective.

CHECKLIST FOR THE OFFEROR

1 Make sure that the terms of the offer are sufficiently clear and definite to allow both the parties and a court to determine the specific rights and obligations of the parties. Otherwise, the contract may fail for indefiniteness.
2 Specify in the offer the date on which the offer will terminate and the authorized mode of acceptance. For example, you can indicate that an acceptance, to be effective, must be faxed to you at a specific fax number by a specific time or date. You can even specify that the acceptance will not be effective until you receive it.

* This *Application* is not meant to substitute for the services of an attorney who is licensed to practice law in your state.

KEY TERMS

mailbox rule 262
mirror image rule 259
offer 251

option contract 257
past consideration 267
promissory estoppel 271

release 269
rescission 266
revocation 256

CHAPTER SUMMARY	Agreement and Consideration
Requirements of the Offer (See pages 251–256.)	1. *Intent*—There must be a serious, objective intention by the offeror to become bound by the offer. Nonoffer situations include (a) expressions of opinion; (b) statements of intention; (c) preliminary negotiations; (d) generally, advertisements, catalogues, price lists, and circulars; (e) solicitations for bids made by an auctioneer; and (f) traditionally, agreements to agree in the future. 2. *Definiteness*—The terms of the offer must be sufficiently definite to be ascertainable by the parties or by a court. 3. *Communication*—The offer must be communicated to the offeree.
Termination of the Offer (See pages 256–260.)	1. *By action of the parties*— a. Revocation—Unless the offer is irrevocable, it can be revoked at any time before acceptance without liability. Revocation is not effective until received by the offeree or the offeree's agent. Some offers, such as a merchant's firm offer and option contracts, are irrevocable. b. Rejection—Accomplished by words or actions that demonstrate a clear intent not to accept the offer; not effective until received by the offeror or the offeror's agent. c. Counteroffer—A rejection of the original offer and the making of a new offer. 2. *By operation of law*— a. Lapse of time—The offer terminates (1) at the end of the time period specified in the offer or (2) if no time period is stated in the offer, at the end of a reasonable time period. b. Destruction of the specific subject matter of the offer—Automatically terminates the offer. c. Death or incompetence of the offeror or offeree—Terminates the offer unless the offer is irrevocable. d. Illegality—Supervening illegality terminates the offer.
Acceptance (See pages 260–264.)	1. Can be made only by the offeree or the offeree's agent. 2. Must be unequivocal. Under the common law (mirror image rule), if new terms or conditions are added to the acceptance, it will be considered a counteroffer. 3. Acceptance of a unilateral offer is effective on full performance of the requested act. Generally, no communication is necessary. 4. Acceptance of a bilateral offer can be communicated by the offeree by any authorized mode of communication and is effective on dispatch. Unless the offeror expressly specifies the mode of communication, the following methods are impliedly authorized: a. The same mode used by the offeror or a faster mode. b. Mail, when the two parties are at a distance. c. In sales contracts, by any reasonable medium.
Elements of Consideration (See pages 264–265.)	Consideration is broken down into two parts: (1) something of *legally sufficient value* must be given in exchange for the promise, and (2) there must be a *bargained-for exchange*.

(Continued)

CHAPTER SUMMARY Agreement and Consideration—Continued

Legal Sufficiency and Adequacy of Consideration (See page 265.)	Legal sufficiency of consideration relates to the first element of consideration—something of legal value must be given in exchange for a promise. Adequacy of consideration relates to "how much" consideration is given and whether a fair bargain was reached. Courts will inquire into the adequacy of consideration (whether the consideration is legally sufficient) only when fraud, undue influence, duress, or unconscionability may be involved.
Contracts That Lack Consideration (See pages 265–269.)	Consideration is lacking in the following situations: 1. *Preexisting duty*—Consideration is not legally sufficient if one is either by law or by contract under a *preexisting duty* to perform the action being offered as consideration for a new contract. 2. *Past consideration*—Actions or events that have already taken place do not constitute legally sufficient consideration. 3. *Illusory promises*—When the nature or extent of performance is too uncertain, the promise is rendered illusory (without consideration and unenforceable).
Settlement of Claims (See pages 269–271.)	1. *Accord and satisfaction*—An *accord* is an agreement in which a debtor offers to pay a lesser amount than the creditor claims is owed. *Satisfaction* may take place when the accord is executed. 2. *Release*—An agreement in which, for consideration, a party forfeits the right to seek further recovery beyond the terms specified in the release. 3. *Covenant not to sue*—An agreement not to sue on a present, valid claim.
Promissory Estoppel (See page 271.)	The equitable doctrine of promissory estoppel applies when a promisor reasonably expects a promise to induce definite and substantial action or forbearance by the promisee, and the promisee does act in reliance on the promise. Such a promise is binding if injustice can be avoided only by enforcement of the promise. Also known as the doctrine of *detrimental reliance*.

FOR REVIEW

Answers for the even-numbered questions in this **For Review** *section can be found in Appendix E at the end of this text.*

1 What elements are necessary for an effective offer? What are some examples of nonoffers?

2 In what circumstances will an offer be irrevocable?

3 What are the elements that are necessary for an effective acceptance?

4 What is consideration? What is required for consideration to be legally sufficient?

5 In what circumstances might a promise be enforced despite a lack of consideration?

 The following multiple-choice question is representative of the types of questions available in one of the four sections of ThomsonNOW for *Business Law Today*. ThomsonNOW also provides feedback for each response option, whether correct or incorrect, and refers to the location within the chapter where the correct answer can be found.

In the interests of fairness and equity, the courts may allow an exception to the preexisting duty rule when

a the consideration given for a contract is past consideration.

b the promise is illusory.

c the consideration is inadequate.

d contract performance involves unforeseen difficulties.

QUESTIONS AND CASE PROBLEMS

HYPOTHETICAL SCENARIOS

9.1 Agreement. Ball writes to Sullivan and inquires how much Sullivan is asking for a specific forty-acre tract of land Sullivan owns. In a letter received by Ball, Sullivan states, "I will not take less than $60,000 for the forty-acre tract as specified." Ball immediately sends Sullivan a telegram stating, "I accept your offer for $60,000 for the forty-acre tract as specified." Discuss whether Ball can hold Sullivan to a contract for sale of the land.

9.2 Hypothetical Question with Sample Answer. Chernek, the sole owner of a small business, has a large piece of used farm equipment for sale. He offers to sell the equipment to Bollow for $10,000. Discuss the legal effects of the following events on the offer:

1 Chernek dies prior to Bollow's acceptance, and at the time she accepts, Bollow is unaware of Chernek's death.

2 The night before Bollow accepts, a fire destroys the equipment.

3 Bollow pays $100 for a thirty-day option to purchase the equipment. During this period, Chernek dies, and Bollow accepts the offer, knowing of Chernek's death.

4 Bollow pays $100 for a thirty-day option to purchase the equipment. During this period, Bollow dies, and Bollow's estate accepts Chernek's offer within the stipulated time period.

 For a sample answer to Question 9.2, go to Appendix F at the end of this text.

9.3 Offer and Acceptance. Carrie offered to sell a set of legal encyclopedias to Antonio for $300. Antonio said that he would think about her offer and let her know his decision the next day. Norvel, who had overheard the conversation between Carrie and Antonio, said to Carrie, "I accept your offer" and gave her $300. Carrie gave Norvel the books. The next day, Antonio, who had no idea that Carrie had already sold the books to Norvel, told Carrie that he accepted her offer. Has Carrie breached a valid contract with Antonio? Explain.

9.4 Consideration. Daniel, a recent college graduate, is on his way home for the Christmas holidays from his new job. He gets caught in a snowstorm and is taken in by an elderly couple, who provide him with food and shelter. After the snowplows have cleared the road, Daniel proceeds home. Daniel's father, Fred, is most appreciative of the elderly couple's action and in a letter promises to pay them $500. The elderly couple, in need of funds, accept Fred's offer. Then, because of a dispute with Daniel, Fred refuses to pay the elderly couple the $500. Discuss whether the couple can hold Fred liable in contract for the services rendered to Daniel.

CASE PROBLEMS

9.5 Intention. Music that is distributed on compact discs and similar media generates income in the form of "mechanical" royalties. Music that is publicly performed, such as when a song is played on the radio, included in a movie or commercial, or sampled in another song, produces "performance" royalties. Both types of royalties are divided between the songwriter and the song's publisher. Vincent Cusano is a musician and songwriter who performed under the name "Vinnie Vincent" as a guitarist with the group KISS in the early 1980s. Cusano co-wrote three songs entitled "Killer," "I Love It Loud," and "I Still Love You," which KISS recorded and released in 1982 on an album titled *Creatures of the Night.* Cusano left KISS in 1984. Eight years later, Cusano sold to Horipro Entertainment Group "one hundred (100%) percent undivided interest" of his rights in the songs "other than Songwriter's share of performance income." Later, Cusano filed a suit in a federal district court against Horipro, claiming in part that he never intended to sell the writer's share of

the mechanical royalties. Horipro filed a motion for summary judgment. Should the court grant the motion? Explain. [*Cusano v. Horipro Entertainment Group*, 301 F.Supp.2d 272 (S.D.N.Y. 2004)]

9.6 Case Problem with Sample Answer. As a child, Martha Carr once visited her mother's 108-acre tract of unimproved land in Richland County, South Carolina. In 1968, Betty and Raymond Campbell leased the land. Carr, a resident of New York, was diagnosed as having schizophrenia and depression in 1986, was hospitalized five or six times, and takes prescription drugs for the illnesses. In 1996, Carr inherited the Richland property and, two years later, contacted the Campbells about selling the land. Carr asked Betty about the value of the land, and Betty said that the county tax assessor had determined that the land's *agricultural value* was $54,000. The Campbells knew at the time that the county had assessed the total property value at $103,700 for tax purposes. On

August 6, Carr signed a contract to sell the land to the Campbells for $54,000. Believing the price to be unfair, however, Carr did not deliver the deed. The Campbells filed a suit in a South Carolina state court against Carr, seeking specific performance of the contract. At trial, an expert real estate appraiser testified that the *real market value* of the property was $162,000 at the time of the contract. Under what circumstances will a court examine the adequacy of consideration? Are those circumstances present in this case? Should the court enforce the contract between Carr and the Campbells? Explain. [*Campbell v. Carr*, 361 S.C. 258, 603 S.E.2d 625 (2004)]

After you have answered Problem 9.6, compare your answer with the sample answer given on the Web site that accompanies this text. Go to www.thomsonedu.com/westbuslaw/blt, select "Chapter 9," and click on "Case Problem with Sample Answer."

9.7 Agreement. In 2000, David and Sandra Harless leased 2.3 acres of real property at 2801 River Road S.E. in Winnabow, North Carolina, to their son-in-law and daughter, Tony and Jeanie Connor. The Connors planned to operate a "general store/variety store" on the premises. They agreed to lease the property for sixty months with an option to renew for an additional sixty months. The lease included an option to buy the property for "fair market value at the time of such purchase (based on at least two appraisals)." In March 2003, Tony told David that the Connors wanted to buy the property. In May, Tony gave David an appraisal that estimated the property's value at $140,000. In July, the Connors presented a second appraisal that put the value at $160,000. The Connors offered $150,000. The Harlesses replied that "under no circumstances would they ever agree to sell their old store building and approximately 2.5 acres to their daughter . . . and their son-in-law." The Connors filed a suit in a North Carolina state court against the Harlesses, alleging breach of contract. Did these parties have a contract to sell the property? If so, what were its terms? If not, why not? [*Connor v. Harless*, 176 N.C.App. 402, 626 S.E.2d 755 (2006)]

9.8 Offer. In August 2000, in California, Terry Reigelsperger sought treatment for pain in his lower back from chiropractor James Siller. Reigelsperger felt better after the treatment and did not intend to return for more, although he did not mention this to Siller. Before leaving the office, Reigelsperger signed an "informed consent" form that read, in part, "I intend this consent form to cover the entire course of treatment for my present condition and for any future condition(s) for which I seek treatment." He also signed an agreement that required the parties to submit to arbitration "any

dispute as to medical malpractice. . . .This agreement is intended to bind the patient and the health care provider . . . who now or in the future treat[s] the patient." Two years later, Reigelsperger sought treatment from Siller for a different condition relating to his cervical spine and shoulder. Claiming malpractice with respect to the second treatment, Reigelsperger filed a suit in a California state court against Siller. Siller asked the court to order the submission of the dispute to arbitration. Does Reigelsperger's lack of intent to return to Siller after his first treatment affect the enforceability of the arbitration agreement and consent form? Why or why not? [*Reigelsperger v. Siller*, 40 Cal.4th 574, 53 Cal.Rptr.3d 887, 150 P.3d 764 (2007)]

9.9 A Question of Ethics. *John Sasson and Emily Springer met in January 2002. John worked for the U.S. Army as an engineer. Emily was an attorney with a law firm. When, six months later, John bought a townhouse in Randolph, New Jersey, he asked Emily to live with him. She agreed, but retained the ownership of her home in Monmouth Beach. John paid the mortgage and the other expenses on the townhouse. He urged Emily to quit her job and work from "our house." In May 2003, Emily took John's advice and started her own law practice. In December, John made her the beneficiary of his $150,000 individual retirement account (IRA) and said that he would give her his 2002 BMW M3 car before the end of the next year. He proposed to her in September 2004, giving her a diamond engagement ring and promising to "take care of her" for the rest of her life. Less than a month later, John was critically injured by an accidental blow to his head during a basketball game and died. On behalf of John's estate, which was valued at $1.1 million, his brother Steven filed a complaint in a New Jersey state court to have Emily evicted from the townhouse. Given these facts, consider the following questions.* [*In re Estate of Sasson*, 387 N.J.Super. 459, 904 A.2d 769 (App.Div. 2006)]

1 Based on John's promise to "take care of her" for the rest of her life, Emily claimed that she was entitled to the townhouse, the BMW, and an additional portion of John's estate. Under what circumstances would such a promise constitute a valid, enforceable contract? Does John's promise meet these requirements? Why or why not?

2 Whether or not John's promise is legally binding, is there an ethical basis on which it should be enforced? Is there an ethical basis for *not* enforcing it? Are there any circumstances under which a promise of support should be—or should *not* be—enforced? Discuss.

CRITICAL THINKING
AND WRITING ASSIGNMENTS

9.10 Critical Legal Thinking. Under what circumstances should courts examine the adequacy of consideration?

9.11 **Video Question.** Go to this text's Web site at **www. thomsonedu.com/westbuslaw/blt** and select "Chapter 9." Click on "Video Questions" and view the video titled *Offer and Acceptance.* Then answer the following questions.

1 On the video, Vinny indicates that he can't sell his car to Oscar for four thousand dollars; then he says, "maybe five . . . ." Discuss whether Vinny has made an offer or a counteroffer.

2 Oscar then says to Vinny, "Okay, I'll take it. But you gotta let me pay you four thousand now and the other thousand in two weeks." According to the chapter, do Oscar and Vinny have an agreement? Why or why not?

3 When Maria later says to Vinny, "I'll take it," has she accepted an offer? Why or why not?

ONLINE ACTIVITIES

PRACTICAL
INTERNET EXERCISES

Go to this text's Web site at **www.thomsonedu.com/westbuslaw/blt**, select "Chapter 9," and click on "Practical Internet Exercises." There you will find the following Internet research exercises that you can perform to learn more about the topics covered in this chapter.

PRACTICAL INTERNET EXERCISE 9–1   LEGAL PERSPECTIVE—Contract Terms

PRACTICAL INTERNET EXERCISE 9–2   ETHICAL PERSPECTIVE—Offers and Advertisements

PRACTICAL INTERNET EXERCISE 9–3   MANAGEMENT PERSPECTIVE—Promissory Estoppel

BEFORE THE TEST

Go to this text's Web site at **www.thomsonedu.com/westbuslaw/blt**, select "Chapter 9," and click on "Interactive Quizzes." You will find a number of interactive questions relating to this chapter.

CHAPTER 10
Capacity and Legality

CHAPTER OUTLINE

—CONTRACTUAL CAPACITY

—LEGALITY

—THE EFFECT OF ILLEGALITY

LEARNING OBJECTIVES

AFTER READING THIS CHAPTER, YOU SHOULD BE ABLE TO ANSWER THE FOLLOWING QUESTIONS:

1 What are some exceptions to the rule that a minor can disaffirm (avoid) any contract?

2 Does an intoxicated person have the capacity to enter into an enforceable contract?

3 Does the mental incompetence of one party necessarily make a contract void?

4 Under what circumstances will a covenant not to compete be enforceable? When will such covenants not be enforced?

5 What is an exculpatory clause? In what circumstances might exculpatory clauses be enforced? When will they not be enforced?

C ourts generally want contracts to be enforceable, and much of the law is devoted to aiding the enforceability of contracts. Nonetheless, as indicated in the chapter-opening quotation, "liberty of contract" is not absolute. In other words, not all people can make legally binding contracts at all times. Contracts entered into by persons lacking the capacity to do so may be voidable. Similarly, contracts calling for the performance of an illegal act are illegal and thus void—they are not contracts at all. In this chapter, we examine contractual capacity and some aspects of illegal bargains.

CONTRACTUAL CAPACITY

CONTRACTUAL CAPACITY
The threshold mental capacity required by law for a party who enters into a contract to be bound by that contract.

Contractual capacity is the legal ability to enter into a contractual relationship. Courts generally presume the existence of contractual capacity, but in some situations, capacity is lacking or may be questionable. A person who has been determined by a court to be mentally incompetent, for example, cannot form a legally binding contract with another party. In other situations, a party may have the capacity to enter into a valid contract but may also have the right to avoid liability under it. For example, minors—or *infants*, as they are commonly referred to in the law—usually are not legally bound by contracts. In this section, we look at the effect of youth, intoxication, and mental incompetence on contractual capacity.

Minors

Today, in virtually all states, the *age of majority* (when a person is no longer a minor) for contractual purposes is eighteen years—the so-called coming of age. (The age of majority may still be twenty-one for other purposes, however, such as the purchase and consumption of alcohol.) In addition, some states provide for the termination of minority on marriage. Minority status may also be terminated by a minor's **emancipation,** which occurs when a child's parent or legal guardian relinquishes the legal right to exercise control over the child. Normally, minors who leave home to support themselves are considered emancipated. Several jurisdictions permit minors to petition a court for emancipation themselves. For business purposes, a minor may petition a court to be treated as an adult.

The general rule is that a minor can enter into any contract an adult can, provided that the contract is not one prohibited by law for minors (for example, the sale of alcoholic beverages or tobacco). A contract entered into by a minor, however, is voidable at the option of that minor, subject to certain exceptions (to be discussed shortly). To exercise the option to avoid a contract, a minor need only manifest an intention not to be bound by it. The minor "avoids" the contract by disaffirming it.

Disaffirmance   The legal avoidance, or setting aside, of a contractual obligation is referred to as **disaffirmance.** To disaffirm, a minor must express, through words or conduct, his or her intent not to be bound to the contract. The minor must disaffirm the entire contract, not merely a portion of it. For instance, a minor cannot decide to keep part of the goods purchased under a contract and return the remaining goods. When a minor disaffirms a contract, the minor can recover any property that she or he transferred to the adult as consideration for the contract, even if it is then in the possession of a third party.[1]

A contract can ordinarily be disaffirmed at any time during minority[2] or for a reasonable time after the minor comes of age. What constitutes a "reasonable" time may vary. Two months would probably be considered reasonable, but except in unusual circumstances, a court may not find it reasonable to wait a year or more after coming of age to disaffirm. If an individual fails to disaffirm an executed contract within a reasonable time after reaching the age of majority, a court will likely hold that the contract has been ratified (*ratification* will be discussed shortly).

Note that an adult who enters into a contract with a minor cannot avoid his or her contractual duties on the ground that the minor can do so. Unless the minor exercises the option to disaffirm the contract, the adult party normally is bound by it.

A Minor's Obligations on Disaffirmance   Although all states' laws permit minors to disaffirm contracts (with certain exceptions), including executed contracts, state laws differ on the extent of a minor's obligations on disaffirmance.

Majority Rule.   Courts in a majority of states hold that the minor need only return the goods (or other consideration) subject to the contract, provided the goods are in the minor's possession or control.
EXAMPLE 10.1 Jim Garrison, a seventeen-year-old, purchases a computer from Radio Shack. While transporting the computer to his home, Garrison, through no fault of his own, is involved in a car accident. As a result of the accident, the plastic casing of the computer is broken. The next day, he returns the computer to Radio Shack and disaffirms the contract. Under the majority view, this return fulfills Garrison's duty

EMANCIPATION
In regard to minors, the act of being freed from parental control; occurs when a child's parent or legal guardian relinquishes the legal right to exercise control over the child. Normally, a minor who leaves home to support himself or herself is considered emancipated.

DISAFFIRMANCE
The legal avoidance, or setting aside, of a contractual obligation.

This minor is discussing the purchase of a used car with a salesperson. When a minor disaffirms a contract, such as a contract to buy a car, most states require the minor to return whatever he or she purchased, if it is within his or her control. Why do some states require more?
(Michael Newman/PhotoEdit)

---

1. The Uniform Commercial Code, in Section 2–403(1), allows an exception if the third party is a "good faith purchaser for value." See Chapter 16.

2. In some states, however, a minor who enters into a contract for the sale of land cannot disaffirm the contract until she or he reaches the age of majority.

even though the computer is now damaged. Garrison is entitled to receive a refund of the purchase price (if paid in cash) or to be relieved of any further obligations under an agreement to purchase the computer on credit. ▣

Minority Rule. A growing number of states, either by statute or by court decision, place an additional duty on the minor—the duty to restore the adult party to the position she or he held before the contract was made. **EXAMPLE 10.2** Sixteen-year-old Joseph Dodson bought a pickup truck for $4,900 from a used-car dealer. Although the truck developed mechanical problems nine months later, Dodson continued to drive it until the engine blew up and it stopped running. Then Dodson disaffirmed the contract and attempted to return the truck to the dealer for a refund of the full purchase price. The dealer refused to accept the pickup or refund the money. Dodson filed suit. Ultimately, the Tennessee Supreme Court allowed Dodson to disaffirm the contract but required him to compensate the seller for the depreciated value—not the purchase price—of the pickup.[3] ▣ This example illustrates the trend among today's courts to hold a minor responsible for damage, ordinary wear and tear, and depreciation of goods that the minor used prior to disaffirmance.

Exceptions to the Minor's Right to Disaffirm State courts and legislatures have carved out several exceptions to the minor's right to disaffirm. Some contracts cannot be avoided simply as a matter of law, on the ground of public policy. For example, marriage contracts and contracts to enlist in the armed services fall into this category. Other contracts may not be disaffirmed for different reasons, including those discussed here.

Misrepresentation of Age. Suppose that a minor tells a seller she is twenty-one years old when she is really seventeen. Ordinarily, the minor can disaffirm the contract even though she has misrepresented her age. Moreover, in some jurisdictions the minor is not liable for the tort of fraudulent misrepresentation, the rationale being that such a tort judgment might indirectly force the minor to perform the contract.

In many jurisdictions, however, a minor who has misrepresented his or her age can be bound by a contract under certain circumstances. First, several states have enacted statutes for precisely this purpose. In these states, misrepresentation of age is enough to prohibit disaffirmance. Other statutes prohibit disaffirmance by a minor who has engaged in business as an adult. Second, some courts refuse to allow minors to disaffirm executed (fully performed) contracts unless they can return the consideration received. The combination of the minors' misrepresentations and their unjust enrichment has persuaded these courts to *estop* (prevent) the minors from asserting contractual incapacity.

Contracts for Necessaries. A minor who enters into a contract for necessaries may disaffirm the contract but remains liable for the reasonable value of the goods used. **Necessaries** are basic needs, such as food, clothing, shelter, and medical services, at a level of value required to maintain the minor's standard of living or financial and social status. Thus, what will be considered a necessary for one person may be a luxury for another. Additionally, what is considered a necessary depends on whether the minor is under the care or control of his or her parents, who are required by law to provide necessaries for the minor. If a minor's parents provide the minor with shelter, for example, then a contract to lease shelter (such as an apartment) normally will not be regarded as a contract for necessaries.

Generally, then, to qualify as a contract for necessaries, (1) the item contracted for must be necessary to the minor's existence, (2) the value of the necessary item may be up to a level required to maintain the minor's standard of living or financial and social sta-

NECESSARIES
Necessities required for life, such as food, shelter, clothing, and medical attention; may include whatever is believed to be necessary to maintain a person's standard of living or financial and social status.

BE AWARE A minor's station in life (including financial and social status and lifestyle) is important in determining whether an item is a necessary or a luxury. For example, clothing is a necessary, but if a minor from a low-income family contracts for the purchase of a $2,000 leather coat, a court may deem the coat a luxury. In this situation, the contract would not be for "necessaries."

---

3. *Dodson v. Shrader,* 824 S.W.2d 545 (Tenn. 1992).

tus, and (3) the minor must not be under the care of a parent or guardian who is required to supply this item. Unless these three criteria are met, the minor can normally disaffirm the contract *without* being liable for the reasonable value of the goods used.

The issue in the following case was whether a medical services provider could collect from a minor, as a contract for necessaries, the cost of emergency services rendered to the minor when his mother did not pay.

CASE 10.1   **Yale Diagnostic Radiology v. Estate of Harun Fountain**

Supreme Court of Connecticut, 267 Conn. 351, 838 A.2d 179 (2004).

FACTS In March 1996, Harun Fountain was shot in the back of the head at point-blank range by a playmate. Fountain required extensive life-saving medical services from a variety of providers, including Yale Diagnostic Radiology. Yale billed Fountain's mother, Vernetta Turner-Tucker, for the cost of its services, $17,694, but she did not pay. Instead, in January 2001, Turner-Tucker filed for bankruptcy (see Chapter 23), and all of her debts, including the amount owed to Yale, were discharged. Meanwhile, she filed a suit in a Connecticut state court against the boy who shot Fountain and obtained payment for Fountain's medical care. These funds were deposited in an account—sometimes referred to as an "estate"—established on Fountain's behalf. Yale filed a suit against Fountain's estate, asking the court to order the estate to pay Yale's bill, but the court refused to grant the order. Yale appealed to a state intermediate appellate court, which reversed this ruling and ordered the payment. The estate appealed to the state supreme court.

ISSUE Can a party that provides emergency medical services to a minor collect for those services from the minor if his or her parents do not pay?

DECISION Yes. The Connecticut Supreme Court affirmed the judgment of the appellate court. Yale could collect from

Fountain's estate for the cost of its services under the doctrine of necessaries.

REASON The state supreme court explained that while Connecticut has long recognized the rule that a minor's contracts are voidable, a minor cannot avoid a contract for goods or services necessary for the minor's health. The court reasoned that this principle is based on the theory of quasi contract (also known as *implied-in-law contracts*—see Chapter 8). According to the court, two contracts arise when a necessary medical service is provided to a minor. The primary contract is between the provider and the minor's parents and is based on the parents' duty to pay for the child's necessary health expenses. A secondary contract is implied in law between the provider and the minor to prevent unjust enrichment. "Therefore," stated the court, "where necessary medical services are rendered to a minor whose parents do not pay for them, equity and justice demand that a secondary implied-in-law contract arise between the medical services provider and the minor who has received the benefits of those services."

 FOR CRITICAL ANALYSIS–Social Consideration *What might have happened in future cases if the court had held that there was no implied-in-law contract between Fountain and Yale?*

Insurance and Loans. Traditionally, insurance has not been viewed as a necessary, so minors can ordinarily disaffirm their insurance contracts and recover all premiums paid. Nevertheless, some jurisdictions prohibit disaffirming insurance contracts—for example, when minors contract for life insurance on their own lives. Financial loans are seldom considered to be necessaries, even if the minor spends the borrowed funds on necessaries. If, however, a lender makes a loan to a minor for the express purpose of enabling the minor to purchase necessaries, and the lender personally makes sure the funds are so spent, the minor normally is obligated to repay the loan.

Ratification In contract law, **ratification** is the act of accepting and giving legal force to an obligation that previously was not enforceable. A minor who has reached the age of

RATIFICATION
The act of accepting and giving legal force to an obligation that previously was not enforceable.

majority can ratify a contract expressly or impliedly. *Express* ratification occurs when the individual, on reaching the age of majority, states orally or in writing that she or he intends to be bound by the contract. *Implied* ratification takes place when the minor, on reaching the age of majority, indicates an intent to abide by the contract.

■EXAMPLE 10.3 Lin enters a contract to sell her laptop to Arturo, a minor. If Arturo does not disaffirm the contract and, on reaching the age of majority, writes a letter to Lin stating that he still agrees to buy the laptop, he has expressly ratified the contract. If, instead, Arturo takes possession of the laptop as a minor and continues to use it well after reaching the age of majority, he has impliedly ratified the contract. ■

If a minor fails to disaffirm a contract within a reasonable time after reaching the age of majority, then a court must determine whether the conduct constitutes implied ratification or disaffirmance. Generally, courts presume that a contract that is *executed* (fully performed by both sides) was ratified. A contract that is still *executory* (not yet performed by both parties) is normally considered to be disaffirmed.

Parents' Liability   As a general rule, parents are not liable for the contracts made by minor children acting on their own, except contracts for necessaries, which the parents are legally required to provide. This is why businesses ordinarily require parents to cosign any contract made with a minor. The parents then become personally obligated to perform the conditions of the contract, even if their child avoids liability.

Normally, minors are personally liable for their own torts. The parents of the minor can *also* be held liable in certain situations. In some states, parents may be liable if they failed to exercise proper parental control when they knew or should have known that this lack of control posed an unreasonable risk of harm to others. **■EXAMPLE 10.4** Suppose that parents allow their eleven-year-old child to drive a car on public roads. If the child drives negligently and causes someone else to be injured, the parents may be held liable for the minor's tort (negligence). ■ Other states have enacted statutes that impose liability on parents for certain kinds of tortious acts committed by their children, such as those that are willful and malicious.

The *Concept Summary* on this page summarizes the rules relating to contracts by minors. See the *Application* feature at the end of this chapter for factors that businesspersons should consider before forming contracts with minors.

CONCEPT SUMMARY	**Contracts by Minors**
General Rule	Contracts entered into by minors are voidable at the option of the minor.
Rules of Disaffirmance	A minor may disaffirm a contract at any time while still a minor and within a reasonable time after reaching the age of majority. Most states only require that the minor return the goods that were subject to the contract, regardless of any damage, wear and tear, or depreciation of those goods. Some states require that the minor pay for any damage to, or depreciation of, the goods being returned.
Exceptions to Basic Rules of Disaffirmance	1. *Necessaries*—Minors may disaffirm contracts for necessaries but remain liable for the reasonable value of the goods or services. 2. *Ratification*—After reaching the age of majority, a person can ratify a contract that he or she formed as a minor, thereby becoming fully liable on the contract. 3. *Fraud or misrepresentation*—In many jurisdictions, a minor who misrepresents her or his age is denied the right of disaffirmance.

Intoxicated Persons

Contractual capacity also becomes an issue when a party to a contract was intoxicated at the time the contract was made. Intoxication is a condition in which a person's normal capacity to act or think is inhibited by alcohol or some other drug. If the person was sufficiently intoxicated to lack mental capacity, the contract may be voidable even if the intoxication was purely voluntary. For the contract to be voidable, however, the person must prove that the intoxication impaired her or his reason and judgment so severely that she or he did not comprehend the legal consequences of entering into the contract. In addition, to avoid the contract in the majority of states, the person claiming intoxication must be able to return all consideration received.

If, despite intoxication, the person understood the legal consequences of the agreement, the contract is enforceable. The fact that the terms of the contract are foolish or obviously favor the other party does not make the contract voidable (unless the other party fraudulently induced the person to become intoxicated). As a practical matter, courts rarely permit contracts to be avoided on the ground of intoxication, because it is difficult to determine whether a party was sufficiently intoxicated to avoid legal duties. Rather than inquire into the intoxicated person's mental state, many courts instead focus on objective indications of capacity to determine whether the contract is voidable owing to intoxication.[4]

Mentally Incompetent Persons

Contracts made by mentally incompetent persons can be void, voidable, or valid. We look here at the circumstances that determine when these classifications apply.

When the Contract Will Be Void   If a court has previously determined that a person is mentally incompetent and has appointed a guardian to represent the person, any contract made by that mentally incompetent person is *void*—no contract exists. Only the guardian can enter into a binding contract on behalf of the mentally incompetent person.

When the Contract Will Be Voidable   If a court has not previously judged a person to be mentally incompetent but in fact the person was incompetent at the time, the contract may be *voidable*. A contract is voidable if the person did not know he or she was entering into the contract or lacked the mental capacity to comprehend its nature, purpose, and consequences. In such situations, the contract is voidable at the option of the mentally incompetent person but not the other party. The contract may then be disaffirmed or ratified (if the person regains mental competence). Like intoxicated persons, mentally incompetent persons must return any consideration and pay for the reasonable value of any necessaries they receive.

■EXAMPLE 10.5 Milo, a mentally incompetent man who had not been previously declared incompetent by a judge, agrees to sell twenty lots in a prime residential neighborhood to Anastof. At the time of entering the contract, Milo is confused over which lots he is selling and how much they are worth. As a result, he contracts to sell the properties for substantially less than their market value. If the court finds that Milo was unable to understand the nature and consequences of the contract, the contract is voidable. Milo can avoid the sale, provided that he returns any consideration he received. ■

---

4. See, for example, the court's decision in *Lucy v. Zehmer*, presented as Case 9.1 in Chapter 9.

Payday loans are popular with individuals who do not have regular banking relationships. A client writes a check for some relatively small amount to be cashed at "pay day," usually in two weeks. About 10 million U.S. residents apply for these loans in any given year. The implicit interest rates are extremely high, sometimes more than 100 percent on an annualized basis. Why would anyone agree to pay so much for such a short-term loan? (Seth Anderson/Creative Commons)

USURY
Charging an illegal rate of interest.

When the Contract Will Be Valid   A contract entered into by a mentally incompetent person (whom a court has not previously declared incompetent) may also be *valid* if the person had capacity *at the time the contract was formed*. For instance, a person may be able to understand the nature and effect of entering into a certain contract yet simultaneously lack capacity to engage in other activities. In such cases, the contract ordinarily will be valid because the person is not legally mentally incompetent for contractual purposes.[5] Similarly, an otherwise mentally incompetent person may have a *lucid interval*—a temporary restoration of sufficient intelligence, judgment, and will to enter into contracts—during which she or he will be considered to have full legal capacity.

LEGALITY

To this point, we have discussed three of the requirements for a valid contract to exist—agreement, consideration, and contractual capacity. Now we examine the fourth—legality. For a contract to be valid and enforceable, it must be formed for a legal purpose. A contract to do something that is prohibited by federal or state statutory law is illegal and, as such, void from the outset and thus unenforceable. Additionally, a contract to commit a tortious act or to commit an action that is contrary to public policy is illegal and unenforceable.

Contracts Contrary to Statute

Statutes often set forth rules specifying which terms and clauses may be included in contracts and which are prohibited. We examine here several ways in which contracts may be contrary to a statute and thus illegal.

Contracts to Commit a Crime   Any contract to commit a crime is a contract in violation of a statute. Thus, a contract to sell an illegal drug (the sale of which is prohibited by statute) is not enforceable. If the object or performance of the contract is rendered illegal by statute *after* the contract has been entered into, the contract is considered to be discharged by law. (See the discussion of *impossibility of performance* in Chapter 12.)

Usury   Virtually every state has a statute that sets the maximum rate of interest that can be charged for different types of transactions, including ordinary loans. A lender who makes a loan at an interest rate above the lawful maximum commits **usury.** The maximum rate of interest varies from state to state, as do the consequences for lenders who make usurious loans. Some states allow the lender to recover only the principal of a loan along with interest up to the legal maximum. In effect, the lender is denied recovery of the excess interest. In other states, the lender can recover the principal amount of the loan but no interest.

Although usury statutes place a ceiling on allowable rates of interest, exceptions are made to facilitate business transactions. For example, many states exempt corporate loans from the usury laws. In addition, almost all states have special statutes allowing much higher interest rates on small loans to help those borrowers who need funds and could not otherwise obtain loans.

Gambling   All states have statutes that regulate gambling—defined as any scheme that involves the distribution of property by chance among persons who have paid valuable

---

5. Modern courts no longer require a person to be completely irrational to disaffirm contracts on the basis of mental incompetence. A contract may be voidable if, by reason of a mental illness or defect, an individual was unable to act reasonably with respect to the transaction and the other party had reason to know of the condition.

Adults gamble at a casino. Would this same activity be illegal if it were conducted online? If so, could it be prevented? How? (Marc Levin/Creative Commons)

consideration for the opportunity (chance) to receive the property.[6] Gambling is the creation of risk for the purpose of assuming it. Traditionally, the states have deemed gambling contracts illegal and thus void.

In several states, however, including Louisiana, Michigan, Nevada, and New Jersey, casino gambling is legal. In other states, certain forms of gambling are legal. California, for example, has not defined draw poker as a crime, although criminal statutes prohibit numerous other types of gambling games. A number of states allow gambling on horse races, and the majority of states have legalized state-operated lotteries, as well as lotteries (such as bingo) conducted for charitable purposes. Many states also allow gambling on Indian reservations.

Sometimes, it is difficult to distinguish a gambling contract from the risk sharing inherent in almost all contracts. ■EXAMPLE 10.6 In one case, five co-workers each received a free lottery ticket from a customer and agreed to split the winnings if one of the tickets turned out to be the winning one. At first glance, this may seem entirely legal. The court, however, noted that the oral contract in this case "was an exchange of promises to share winnings from the parties' individually owned lottery tickets upon the happening of the uncertain event" that one of the tickets would win. Consequently, concluded the court, the agreement at issue was "founded on a gambling consideration" and therefore was void.[7] ■

Online Gambling   A significant issue today is how gambling laws can be applied in the Internet context. Because state laws pertaining to gambling differ, online gambling raises a number of unique issues. For example, in those states that do not allow casino gambling or offtrack betting, what can a state government do if residents of the state place bets online? Also, where does the actual act of gambling occur? For example, suppose that a

---

6. See *Wishing Well Club v. Akron,* 112 N.E.2d 41 (Ohio Com.Pl. 1951).
7. *Dickerson v. Deno,* 770 So.2d 63 (Ala. 2000).

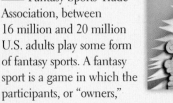

ADAPTING THE LAW TO THE ONLINE ENVIRONMENT — Are Online Fantasy Sports Just Another Form of Real-Life Gambling?

According to the Fantasy Sports Trade Association, between 16 million and 20 million U.S. adults play some form of fantasy sports. A fantasy sport is a game in which the participants, or "owners," build a team composed of real-life players from different real-life teams. For example, an owner might include a quarterback from the New England Patriots and a running back from the San Diego Chargers. The fantasy team then competes against other fantasy sports teams with different owners. Each week during the season for the particular sport, the statistical performances of the real-life players are translated into points, and the points of all the players on an owner's fantasy team are totaled. Although fantasy baseball, basketball, golf, hockey, and other sports—even professional wrestling—are available, most participants play fantasy football.

Enter the Internet

Although the origin of fantasy sports supposedly can be traced back to 1962, when an owner of the Oakland Raiders football team and four other football fans created the Greater Oakland Professional Pigskin Prognosticators League, or GOPPPL, fantasy sports did not become big business until access to the Internet became widespread in the 1990s. Today, the number of players is increasing at a rate of 7 to 10 percent per year, and the game contributes as much as $4 billion annually to the U.S. economy. Fantasy sports sites have proliferated on the Internet, as have fantasy sports news sites, such as RotoWire.com and Fantasyfootballnews.com.

One of the appeals of online fantasy sports is that the participants can gamble on the outcome. In a fantasy football league, for example, each participant-owner adds a given amount to the pot and then "drafts" his or her fantasy team from the actual National Football League (NFL) players. Each week, as described earlier, the owner receives points based on his or her players' statistical performances. At the end of the season, the weekly points are totaled, and the owner with the most points wins the pot.

Exemption from Online Gambling Prohibitions

As online gambling has expanded, Congress has stepped in to attempt to regulate it. In October 2006, Congress passed and President George W. Bush signed into law a bill that, in essence, outlaws Internet gambling by making it illegal for

resident of New York places bets via the Internet at a gambling site located in Antigua. Is the actual act of "gambling" taking place in New York or in Antigua? According to a New York court in one case, "if the person engaged in gambling is located in New York, then New York is the location where the gambling occurred."[8] Courts of other states may take a different view, however.

Another issue that is being debated is whether entering contracts that involve gambling on sports teams that do not really exist—fantasy sports—is a form of gambling. For a discussion of this issue, see this chapter's *Adapting the Law to the Online Environment* feature.

Sabbath (Sunday) Laws Statutes referred to as Sabbath (Sunday) laws prohibit the formation or performance of certain contracts on a Sunday. These laws, which date back to colonial times, are often called **blue laws**, as mentioned in Chapter 2. Blue laws get their name from the blue paper on which New Haven, Connecticut, printed its town ordinance in 1781 that prohibited work and required businesses to close on Sunday. According to a few state and local laws, all contracts entered into on a Sunday are illegal. Laws in other states or municipalities prohibit only the sale of certain types of merchandise, such as alcoholic beverages, on a Sunday.

In most states with such statutes, contracts that were entered into on a Sunday can be ratified during a weekday. Also, if a contract that was entered into on a Sunday has been

BLUE LAWS
State or local laws that prohibit the performance of certain types of commercial activities on Sunday.

---

8. *United States v. Cohen*, 260 F.3d. 68 (2d Cir. 2001).

credit-card companies and banking institutions to engage in transactions with Internet gambling companies.[a] Note that the act does not prohibit individuals from placing bets online, but rather focuses on restricting their ability to obtain financing for online gambling. Although the legislation seems comprehensive, it specifically exempts Internet wagers on horse racing, state lotteries, and fantasy sports. In other words, Congress explicitly determined that fantasy sports do *not* constitute a prohibited Internet gambling activity.

But Aren't Participants in Fantasy Sports Leagues Really Gambling?

In a lawsuit filed in the U.S. District Court for the District of New Jersey, Charles E. Humphrey, Jr., alleges that many media companies, including CBS, ESPN, and *The Sporting News*, are engaging in illegal gambling by hosting pay-to-play fantasy leagues.[b] The lawsuit centers on Web-based fantasy games that require payment and are offered by CBS, Sportsline.com, ESPN.com, and SportingNews.com.

a. Security and Accountability for Every Port Act, Public Law No. 109-347, Sections 5361–5367, ___ Stat. ___ (2006). (A version of the Unlawful Internet Gambling Enforcement Act of 2006 was incorporated into this statute as Title VIII.)

b. *Humphrey v. Viacom, Inc.,* No. 2:33-av-0001 (D.N.J. filed June 20, 2006).

In the offline world, federal law prohibits any games of chance—sweepstakes or drawings—that require entrants to submit consideration in order to play. *Consideration* has been defined as the purchase of a product or the payment of money. Thus, Humphrey must establish that fantasy sports leagues are games of chance and not games of skill. If he prevails, it would then be illegal under existing federal law for fantasy sports leagues to collect entrance fees.

 FOR CRITICAL ANALYSIS *What arguments can be used to support the idea that playing fantasy sports requires skill?*

---

fully performed (executed), normally it cannot be rescinded (canceled). Exceptions to Sunday laws permit contracts for necessities (such as food) and works of charity. Many states do not enforce Sunday laws, and some state courts have held these laws to be unconstitutional because they interfere with the freedom of religion.

Licensing Statutes All states require that members of certain professions obtain licenses allowing them to practice. Physicians, lawyers, real estate brokers, architects, electricians, and stockbrokers are but a few of the people who must be licensed. Some licenses are obtained only after extensive schooling and examinations, which indicate to the public that a special skill has been acquired. Others require only that the particular person be of good moral character and pay a fee.

The Purpose of Licensing Statutes. Generally, business licenses provide a means of regulating and taxing certain businesses and protecting the public against actions that could threaten the general welfare. For example, in nearly all states, a stockbroker must be licensed and must file a bond with the state to protect the public from fraudulent transactions in stocks. Similarly, a plumber must be licensed and bonded to protect the public against incompetent plumbers and to protect the public health. Only persons or businesses possessing the qualifications and complying with the conditions required by statute are entitled to licenses. For instance, the owner of a bar can be required to sell food as a condition of obtaining a license to serve liquor.

ON THE WEB

If you are interested in reading the earliest legislation regulating activities on the Sabbath in colonial America (and about some of the punishments meted out for failing to obey these regulations), go to

www.natreformassn.org/statesman/99/colfound.html.

Contracts with Unlicensed Practitioners. A contract with an unlicensed practitioner may still be enforceable, depending on the nature of the licensing statute. Some states expressly provide that the lack of a license in certain occupations bars the enforcement of work-related contracts. If the statute does not expressly state this, one must look to the underlying purpose of the licensing requirements for a particular occupation. If the purpose is to protect the public from unauthorized practitioners, a contract involving an unlicensed individual is illegal and unenforceable. If, however, the underlying purpose of the statute is to raise government revenues, a contract with an unlicensed practitioner is enforceable—although the unlicensed person is usually fined.

Contracts Contrary to Public Policy

Although contracts involve private parties, some are not enforceable because of the negative impact they would have on society. These contracts are said to be *contrary to public policy*. Examples include a contract to commit an immoral act, such as selling a child, and a contract that prohibits marriage. **■EXAMPLE 10.7** Everett offers a young man $10,000 if he refrains from marrying Everett's daughter. If the young man accepts, no contract is formed (the contract is void) because it is contrary to public policy. Thus, if the man marries Everett's daughter, Everett cannot sue him for breach of contract. ■ Business contracts that may be contrary to public policy include contracts in restraint of trade and unconscionable contracts or clauses.

Contracts in Restraint of Trade Contracts in restraint of trade (anticompetitive agreements) usually adversely affect the public policy that favors competition in the economy. Typically, such contracts also violate one or more federal or state statutes.[9] An exception is recognized when the restraint is reasonable and is part of, or supplemental to, a contract for the sale of a business or an **employment contract** (a contract stating the terms and conditions of employment). Many such exceptions involve a type of restraint called a **covenant not to compete,** or a restrictive covenant.

EMPLOYMENT CONTRACT
A contract between an employer and an employee in which the terms and conditions of employment are stated.

COVENANT NOT TO COMPETE
A contractual promise of one party to refrain from conducting business similar to that of another party for a certain period of time and within a specified geographic area. Courts commonly enforce such covenants if they are reasonable in terms of time and geographic area and are part of, or supplemental to, a contract for the sale of a business or an employment contract.

Covenants Not to Compete and the Sale of an Ongoing Business. Covenants (promises) not to compete are often contained as ancillary (secondary, or subordinate) clauses in contracts concerning the sale of an ongoing business. A covenant not to compete is created when a seller agrees not to open a new store in a certain geographic area surrounding the old store. Such agreements enable the seller to sell, and the purchaser to buy, the goodwill and reputation of an ongoing business. If, for example, a well-known merchant sells his or her store and opens a competing business a block away, many of the merchant's customers will likely do business at the new store. This renders less valuable the good name and reputation sold to the other merchant for a price. If a covenant not to compete is not ancillary to a sales agreement, however, it will be void because it unreasonably restrains trade and is contrary to public policy.

Covenants Not to Compete in Employment Contracts. Agreements not to compete can also be included in employment contracts. People in middle-level and upper-level management positions commonly agree not to work for competitors or not to start a competing business for a specified period of time after terminating employment. Such agreements are generally legal so long as the specified period of time is not excessive in duration and the geographic restriction is reasonable. Basically, the restriction on compe-

---

9. Federal statutes prohibiting anticompetitive agreements include the Sherman Antitrust Act, the Clayton Act, and the Federal Trade Commission Act. See Chapter 31.

tition must be reasonable—that is, not any greater than necessary to protect a legitimate business interest. Although a court might find that a time restriction of one year is reasonable, a time restriction of two, three, or five years may not be considered reasonable.

Determining what constitutes "reasonable" time and geographic restrictions in the online environment is a more difficult issue that is being addressed by the courts. The Internet environment has no physical borders, so geographic restrictions are no longer relevant. Also, a reasonable time period may be shorter in the online environment than in conventional employment contracts because the restrictions would apply worldwide.

■EXAMPLE 10.8 Mark Schlack was a Web site manager and vice president for EarthWeb, Inc., an information technology firm. Schlack had signed a covenant not to compete promising not to work for any competing company for one year after his employment was terminated. When Schlack later accepted an offer from another company to design a Web site, EarthWeb sued to enforce the covenant not to compete. The federal district court hearing the case decided that the covenant was unreasonable because it prohibited Schlack from working for a competitor anywhere in the world for one year.[10] ■

Enforcement Problems. The laws governing the enforceability of covenants not to compete vary significantly from state to state. In some states, such as Texas, such a covenant will not be enforced unless the employee has received some benefit in return for signing the noncompete agreement. This is true even if the covenant is reasonable as to time and area. If the employee receives no benefit, the covenant will be deemed void. California prohibits the enforcement of covenants not to compete altogether.

Occasionally, depending on the jurisdiction, courts will *reform* covenants not to compete. If a covenant is found to be unreasonable in time or geographic area, the court may convert the terms into reasonable ones and then enforce the reformed covenant. This presents a problem, however, in that the judge has implicitly become a party to the contract. Consequently, courts usually resort to contract **reformation** only when necessary to prevent undue burdens or hardships.

A business clearly has a legitimate interest in having employees sign covenants not to compete and in preventing them from using the valuable skills and training provided by the business for the benefit of a competitor. The problem is that these covenants frequently lead to litigation. Moreover, it is difficult to predict what a court will consider reasonable in a given situation. Therefore, businesspersons need to be aware of the difficulties in enforcing noncompete agreements. When drafting covenants not to compete, seek the advice of counsel in the relevant jurisdiction, and avoid overreaching in terms of time and geographic restrictions. Consider using noncompete clauses only for key employees and, if necessary, offer some compensation (consideration) for signing the agreement. In addition, for high-tech companies and Web-based businesses, the time restriction should be narrowed considerably to compensate for the extensive geographic restriction (worldwide). If an employee signed a noncompete clause when he or she was hired, it is wise to revisit the meaning of that clause with the employee at the time of termination. Sometimes, simply discussing one another's expectations and understanding of a contract provision can help to stave off legal disputes in the future.

■

ON THE WEB

For more information on restrictive covenants in employment contracts, you can access an article written by attorneys at Loose Brown & Associates, P.C., at **www.loosebrown.com/Articles/bl2.htm**.

REFORMATION
A court-ordered correction of a written contract so that it reflects the true intentions of the parties.

PREVENTING
LEGAL DISPUTES

10. *EarthWeb, Inc. v. Schlack,* 71 F.Supp.2d 299 (S.D.N.Y. 1999).

Unconscionable Contracts or Clauses Ordinarily, a court does not look at the fairness or equity of a contract; for example, a court normally will not inquire into the adequacy of consideration. Persons are assumed to be reasonably intelligent, and the court does not come to their aid just because they have made unwise or foolish bargains. In certain circumstances, however, bargains are so oppressive that the courts relieve innocent parties of part or all of their duties. Such a bargain is called an **unconscionable contract** (or **unconscionable clause**). Both the Uniform Commercial Code (UCC) and the Uniform Consumer Credit Code (UCCC) embody the unconscionability concept—the former with regard to the sale of goods and the latter with regard to consumer loans and the waiver of rights.[11] A contract can be unconscionable on either procedural or substantive grounds, as discussed in the following subsections and illustrated graphically in Exhibit 10–1.

Procedural Unconscionability. Procedural unconscionability has to do with how a term becomes part of a contract and relates to factors bearing on a party's lack of knowledge or understanding of the contract terms because of inconspicuous print, unintelligible language ("legalese"), lack of opportunity to read the contract, lack of opportunity to ask questions about the contract's meaning, and other factors. Procedural unconscionability sometimes relates to purported lack of voluntariness because of a disparity in bargaining power between the two parties. Contracts entered into because of one party's vastly superior bargaining power may be deemed unconscionable. Such contracts are often referred to as **adhesion contracts.** An adhesion contract is written exclusively by one party (the dominant party, usually the seller or creditor) and presented to the other (the adhering party, usually the buyer or borrower) on a take-it-or-leave-it basis.[12] In other words, the adhering party has no opportunity to negotiate the terms of the contract.

---

11. See, for example, UCC 2–302 and 2–719, and UCCC 5–108 and 1–107.
12. See, for example, *Henningsen v. Bloomfield Motors, Inc.*, 32 N.J. 358, 161 A.2d 69 (1960).

> **UNCONSCIONABLE CONTRACT (OR UNCONSCIONABLE CLAUSE)**
> A contract or clause that is void on the basis of public policy because one party, as a result of disproportionate bargaining power, is forced to accept terms that are unfairly burdensome and that unfairly benefit the dominating party.

> **ADHESION CONTRACT**
> A "standard-form" contract, such as that between a large retailer and a consumer, in which the stronger party dictates the terms.

EXHIBIT 10–1 | **Unconscionability**

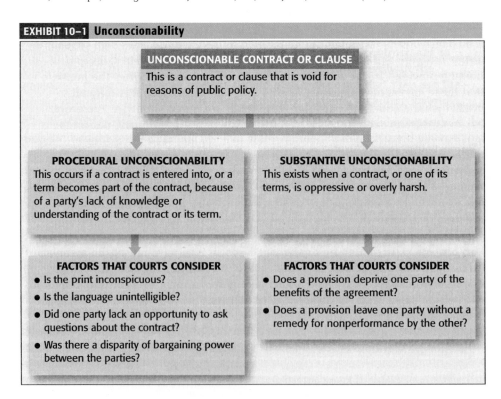

UNCONSCIONABLE CONTRACT OR CLAUSE
This is a contract or clause that is void for reasons of public policy.

PROCEDURAL UNCONSCIONABILITY
This occurs if a contract is entered into, or a term becomes part of the contract, because of a party's lack of knowledge or understanding of the contract or its term.

SUBSTANTIVE UNCONSCIONABILITY
This exists when a contract, or one of its terms, is oppressive or overly harsh.

FACTORS THAT COURTS CONSIDER
- Is the print inconspicuous?
- Is the language unintelligible?
- Did one party lack an opportunity to ask questions about the contract?
- Was there a disparity of bargaining power between the parties?

FACTORS THAT COURTS CONSIDER
- Does a provision deprive one party of the benefits of the agreement?
- Does a provision leave one party without a remedy for nonperformance by the other?

Standard-form contracts often contain fine-print provisions that shift a risk naturally borne by one party to the other. A variety of businesses use such contracts. Life insurance policies, residential leases, loan agreements, and employment agency contracts are often standard-form contracts. To avoid enforcement of the contract or of a particular clause, the aggrieved party must show that the parties had substantially unequal bargaining positions and that enforcement would be manifestly unfair or oppressive. If the required showing is made, the contract or particular term is deemed unconscionable and is not enforced.

In the following case, the question was whether a standard-form contract clause that mandated individual arbitration of any dispute and precluded class action[13] was unconscionable.

---

13. A *class action* is a means by which one or more individuals of a large group of persons interested in a dispute can sue as a class without every member of the group needing to appear in court.

CASE 10.2   Thibodeau v. Comcast Corp.

Superior Court of Pennsylvania, Philadelphia County, 2006 PA Super. 346, 912 A.2d 874 (2006).

FACTS Philip Thibodeau was a subscriber to Comcast Corporation's cable-television service in Pennsylvania. As part of his subscription, Thibodeau rented two converter boxes and two remote controls, which he thought were needed to receive the broadcasts. At the time, Comcast did not tell its customers that nonpremium programming could be viewed without the boxes and that the remotes were wholly unnecessary. In 2002, Comcast mailed Thibodeau and others a "customer agreement" that mandated the individual arbitration of all disputes and precluded class action. Meanwhile, also in Pennsylvania, Lorena Afroilan bought a Panasonic Corporation cell phone and contracted with the AT&T Wireless network for service. With the purchase, Afroilan was given a "Welcome Guide," which required the individual arbitration of all disputes and precluded class action. When Afroilan tried to switch providers, she discovered that her phone had a lock preventing its use on any network other than AT&T's. Thibodeau, Afroilan, and others filed class-action suits in a Pennsylvania state court against Comcast, AT&T, and Panasonic, alleging violations of state law. The trial court combined the suits and denied the defendants' requests to dismiss the complaints and compel individual arbitration. The defendants appealed.

ISSUE Should the court enforce the arbitration clauses that were part of the adhesion contracts and compel the plaintiffs to arbitrate their disputes?

DECISION No. The state appellate court affirmed the lower court's decision not to compel individual arbitration of these disputes. The court held that the preclusion of all class action in the defendants' "customer agreement" and "Welcome Guide" was "unconscionable and unenforceable."

REASON The court noted that "[n]ot every contract of adhesion contains unconscionable provisions. A contract of adhesion is only unconscionable if it unreasonably favors the drafter." In this case, the customer contracts of both Comcast and AT&T attempted to require all customers to arbitrate all claims as individuals and to prevent them from filing class actions. According to the court, class-action suits are particularly important for consumers because they provide a means for those with limited financial resources and time to join together and assert their lawful rights. The individual members of a class often suffer only minimal damages, and no consumer would expend the time, fees, and costs of litigation for this small potential recovery. For example, defendant Thibodeau alleged that he was overcharged $9.60 per month. The court reasoned that to enforce the provisions requiring arbitration and prohibiting class actions would effectively immunize Comcast and AT&T from liability for any minor consumer claims. Because it is clearly contrary to public policy to immunize large corporations from liability, the court held that the provisions of the adhesion contracts were unconscionable and unenforceable.

WHAT IF THE FACTS WERE DIFFERENT?
If the "customer agreement" and "Welcome Guide" had precluded only class litigation and mandated class arbitration, would the court have considered the provisions unconscionable? Why or why not?

■

Substantive Unconscionability. Substantive unconscionability characterizes those contracts, or portions of contracts, that are oppressive or overly harsh. Courts generally focus on provisions that deprive one party of the benefits of the agreement or leave that party without remedy for nonperformance by the other. For example, suppose that a person with little income and only a fourth-grade education agrees to purchase a refrigerator for $3,000 and signs a two-year installment contract. The same type of refrigerator usually sells for $900 on the market. Despite the general rule that the courts will not inquire into the adequacy of the consideration, some courts have held that this type of contract is unconscionable because the contract terms are so oppressive as to "shock the conscience" of the court.[14]

Exculpatory Clauses Often closely related to the concept of unconscionability are **exculpatory clauses,** which release a party from liability in the event of monetary or physical injury, *no matter who is at fault.* Indeed, courts frequently refuse to enforce such clauses because they deem them to be unconscionable. Exculpatory clauses found in rental agreements for commercial property are normally held to be contrary to public policy. Such clauses are almost universally held to be illegal and unenforceable when they are included in residential property leases. Depending on the situation, exculpatory clauses in the employment context may be deemed unconscionable.

EXAMPLE 10.9 Suppose, for example, that Madison Manufacturing Company requires all of its employees to sign an employment contract with a clause stating that employees bear the risks incident to the position. Specifically, the contract states that the employer (Madison) is not responsible for any injury or damage that an employee may suffer as a result of accidents, carelessness, or misconduct of that employee or any other Madison worker. In this situation, because the exculpatory clause attempts to remove the employer's potential liability for any injuries to its employees, a court would usually find that the clause is contrary to public policy and unenforceable.[15] ■

Exculpatory clauses may be enforced, however, when the parties seeking their enforcement are not involved in businesses considered important to the public interest. Businesses such as health clubs, amusement parks, horse-rental concessions, golf-cart concessions, and skydiving organizations frequently use exculpatory clauses to limit their liability for patrons' injuries. Because these services are not essential, the firms offering them are sometimes considered to have no relative advantage in bargaining strength, and anyone contracting for their services is considered to do so voluntarily.

EXCULPATORY CLAUSE
A clause that releases a contractual party from liability in the event of monetary or physical injury, no matter who is at fault.

REMEMBER Nearly everyone is liable for her or his own torts, and this responsibility cannot be contracted away.

ETHICAL ISSUE 10.1

Should exculpatory clauses allow the signer an opportunity to bargain? Before you may engage in a variety of activities, such as joining a gym or taking a lap around a miniature car racecourse, you may be asked to sign an agreement containing a clause releasing the owner of the operation from liability for any injury that you may suffer. Such exculpatory clauses are common. Nevertheless, courts frequently refuse to enforce them.

The Wisconsin Supreme Court, for example, has invalidated every exculpatory clause brought before it in the last twenty-five years. A recent case involved the death of a woman who drowned in a private swimming and fitness facility after signing a general waiver release statement.[16] The Wisconsin Supreme Court ruled that the exculpatory agreement was invalid because, among other things, the signer did not have "any opportunity to bargain." Indeed,

---

14. See, for example, *Jones v. Star Credit Corp.*, 59 Misc.2d 189, 298 N.Y.S.2d 264 (1969). This case will be presented in Chapter 15 as Case 15.3.
15. For a case with similar facts, see *Little Rock & Fort Smith Railway Co. v. Eubanks*, 48 Ark. 460, 3 S.W. 808 (1887). In such a case, the exculpatory clause may also be illegal because it violates a state workers' compensation law.
16. *Atkins v. Swimwest Family Fitness Center*, 2005 WI 4, 277 Wis.2d 303, 691 N.W.2d 334 (2005).

waiver-of-liability agreements are almost always presented on a take-it-or-leave-it basis. Thus, if all courts were to make "an opportunity to bargain" a requirement for a valid agreement, virtually all exculpatory clauses would be deemed invalid. That would mean that under no circumstances could the creator of the waiver-of-liability agreement avoid liability—even if the signer of the agreement was 100 percent at fault and negligent. The result would be higher liability insurance rates for all businesses dealing with the public. Such higher insurance rates would be ultimately passed on to consumers in the form of higher prices for those who engage in downhill skiing, go to gyms, and do bungee jumping. Is this a fair outcome?

THE EFFECT OF ILLEGALITY

In general, an illegal contract is void: the contract is deemed never to have existed, and the courts will not aid either party. In most illegal contracts, both parties are considered to be equally at fault—*in pari delicto*. If the contract is executory (not yet fulfilled), neither party can enforce it. If it has been executed, there can be neither contractual nor quasi-contractual recovery.

That one wrongdoer in an illegal contract is unjustly enriched at the expense of the other is of no concern to the law—except under certain circumstances (to be discussed shortly). The major justification for this hands-off attitude is that it is improper to place the machinery of justice at the disposal of a plaintiff who has broken the law by entering into an illegal bargain. Another justification is the hoped-for deterrent effect of this general rule. A plaintiff who suffers a loss because of an illegal bargain will presumably be deterred from entering into similar illegal bargains in the future.

There are exceptions to the general rule that neither party to an illegal bargain can sue for breach and neither party can recover for performance rendered. We look at these exceptions here.

Justifiable Ignorance of the Facts

When one of the parties to a contract is relatively innocent (has no reason to know that the contract is illegal), that party can often recover any benefits conferred in a partially executed contract. In this situation, the courts will not enforce the contract but will allow the parties to return to their original positions.

A court may sometimes permit an innocent party who has fully performed under a contract to enforce the contract against the guilty party. **EXAMPLE 10.10** A trucking company contracts with Gillespie to carry crated goods to a specific destination for a normal fee of $5,000. The trucker delivers the crates and later finds out that they contained illegal goods. Although the shipment, use, and sale of the goods are illegal under the law, the trucker, being an innocent party, can normally still legally collect the $5,000 from Gillespie.

Members of Protected Classes

When a statute protects a certain class of people, a member of that class can enforce an illegal contract even though the other party cannot. **EXAMPLE 10.11** Statutes prohibit certain employees (such as flight attendants) from working more than a specified number of hours per month. These employees thus constitute a class protected by statute. An employee who is required to work more than the maximum can recover for those extra hours of service.

Other examples of statutes designed to protect a particular class of people are **blue sky laws**—state laws that regulate the offering and sale of securities for the protection of the

BLUE SKY LAWS
State laws that regulate the offering and sale of securities for the protection of the public.

public (see Chapter 30)—and state statutes regulating the sale of insurance. If an insurance company violates a statute when selling insurance, the purchaser can nevertheless enforce the policy and recover from the insurer.

Withdrawal from an Illegal Agreement

If the illegal part of a bargain has not yet been performed, the party rendering performance can withdraw from the contract and recover the performance or its value. ■EXAMPLE 10.12 Suppose that Marta and Amil decide to wager (illegally) on the outcome of a boxing match. Each deposits money with a stakeholder, who agrees to pay the winner of the bet. At this point, each party has performed part of the agreement, but the illegal part of the agreement will not occur until the money is paid to the winner. Before such payment occurs, either party is entitled to withdraw from the agreement by giving notice to the stakeholder of his or her withdrawal. ■

Severable, or Divisible, Contracts

A contract that is *severable*, or divisible, consists of distinct parts that can be performed separately, with separate consideration provided for each part. With an *indivisible* contract, in contrast, the parties intended that complete performance by each party would be essential, even if the contract contains a number of seemingly separate provisions.

   If a contract is divisible into legal and illegal portions, a court may enforce the legal portion but not the illegal one, so long as the illegal portion does not affect the essence of the bargain. This approach is consistent with the basic policy of enforcing the legal intentions of the contracting parties whenever possible. ■EXAMPLE 10.13 Suppose that Cole signs an employment contract that includes an overly broad and thus illegal covenant not to compete. In that situation, the court might allow the employment contract to be enforceable but reform the unreasonably broad covenant by converting its terms into reasonable ones. Alternatively, the court could declare the covenant illegal (and thus void) and enforce the remaining employment terms. ■

ETHICAL ISSUE 10.2

How do courts decide when a contract is severable? Severability frequently arises in cases involving arbitration clauses. Should a court strike out illegal portions of an arbitration clause and enforce the remaining provisions? That is the fairest solution, according to the U.S. Court of Appeals for the Third Circuit in *Spinetti v. Service Corp. International.*[17] In that case, a woman sued her former employer for age and gender discrimination (see Chapter 34). The woman had signed a contract in which she agreed to arbitrate any disputes with the employer. Part of the arbitration clause required the employee to pay a substantial amount in fees for the arbitration ($500 plus $3,750 in filing fees, $150 per day, and half of the arbitrator's hourly fee of $250). Because these provisions would make arbitration prohibitively expensive for employees, the court held that they were unenforceable and illegal. The court noted that two competing public policies were involved here: first, the policy of protecting employees' ability to enforce their statutory rights against workplace discrimination; and second, the strong policy favoring arbitration agreements. By striking out the illegal portions of the arbitration clause but still requiring the dispute to be arbitrated, the court reasoned that it could further both goals.

■

---

17. 324 F.3d 212 (3d Cir. 2003).

Contracts Illegal through Fraud, Duress, or Undue Influence

Often, one party to an illegal contract is more at fault than the other. When a party has been induced to enter into an illegal bargain through fraud, duress, or undue influence on the part of the other party to the agreement, the first party will be allowed to recover for the performance or its value.

REVIEWING **Capacity and Legality**

Renee Beaver started racing go-karts competitively in 2005, when she was fourteen. Many of the races required her to sign an exculpatory clause to participate, which she or her parents regularly signed. In 2008, right before her birthday, she participated in the annual Elkhart Grand Prix, a series of races in Elkhart, Indiana. During the event in which she drove, a piece of foam padding used as a course barrier was torn from its base and ended up on the track. A portion of the padding struck Beaver in the head, and another portion was thrown into oncoming traffic, causing a multikart collision during which she sustained severe injuries. Beaver filed an action against the race organizers for negligence. The organizers could not locate the exculpatory clause that Beaver was supposed to have signed. Race organizers argued that she must have signed one to enter the race, but even if she had not signed one, her actions showed her intent to be bound by its terms. Using the information presented in the chapter, answer the following questions.

1 Did Beaver have the contractual capacity to enter a contract with an exculpatory clause? Why or why not?

2 Assuming that Beaver did, in fact, sign the exculpatory clause, did she later disaffirm or ratify the contract? Explain.

3 Now assume that Beaver had stated that she was eighteen years old at the time that she signed the exculpatory clause. How might this affect Beaver's ability to disaffirm or ratify the contract?

4 If Beaver did not actually sign the exculpatory clause, could a court conclude that she impliedly accepted its terms by participating in the race? Why or why not?

APPLICATION **Should Retailers Enter into Contracts with Minors and Intoxicated Persons?***

Sales personnel, particularly those who are paid on a commission basis, are often eager to make contracts. Sometimes, however, these salespersons must deal with minors and intoxicated persons, both of whom have limited contractual capacity. Therefore, if you are a retailer, you should make sure that your employees are acquainted with the law governing contracts with minors and intoxicated persons.

Contracts with Minors

If your business involves selling consumer durables, such as large-screen televisions, entertainment centers, appliances, furniture, or automobiles, your sales personnel must be careful in forming contracts with minors and should heed the adage, "When in doubt, check." Remember that a contract signed by a minor (unless it is for necessaries) normally is voidable, and the minor may exercise the option to disaffirm the contract. Employees should demand proof of legal age when they have any doubt about whether a customer is a minor. If the customer is a minor, the employees should insist that an adult (such as a parent) be the purchaser or at least cosign any sales contract.

In addition, because the law governing minors' rights varies substantially from state to state, you should check with your attorney concerning the laws governing disaffirmance in your state. You and those you hire to sell your products should know, for example, what the consequences will be if a minor

---

* This *Application* is not meant to substitute for the services of an attorney who is licensed to practice law in your state.

(Continued)

disaffirms the sale or has misrepresented his or her age when forming a sales contract. Similarly, you need to find out whether and in what circumstances a minor, on disaffirming a contract, can be required to pay for damage to goods sold under the contract.

Dealing with Intoxicated Persons

Little need be said about a salesperson's dealings with obviously intoxicated persons. If the customer, despite intoxication, understands the legal consequences of the contract being signed, the contract is enforceable. Nonetheless, it may be extremely difficult to establish that the intoxicated customer understood the consequences of entering into the contract if the customer claims that she or he did not understand. Therefore, the best advice is, "When in doubt, don't." In other words, if you suspect a customer may be intoxicated, do not sign a contract with that customer.

CHECKLIST FOR THE RETAILER

1 When in doubt about the age of a customer to whom you are about to sell major consumer durable goods or anything other than necessaries, require proof of legal age.
2 If such proof is not forthcoming, require that a parent or guardian sign the contract.
3 Check with an attorney about the laws governing minors' contracts in your state.
4 Do not sign contracts with intoxicated customers.

KEY TERMS

adhesion contract 290
blue laws 286
blue sky laws 293
contractual capacity 278
covenant not to compete 288

disaffirmance 279
emancipation 279
employment contract 288
exculpatory clause 292
necessaries 280

ratification 281
reformation 289
unconscionable contract
   or clause 290
usury 284

CHAPTER SUMMARY   Capacity and Legality

CONTRACTUAL CAPACITY

Minors
(See pages 278–282.)

A minor is a person who has not yet reached the age of majority. In most states, the age of majority is eighteen for contract purposes. Contracts with minors are voidable at the option of the minor.

1. *Disaffirmance*—The legal avoidance of a contractual obligation.

   a. Disaffirmance can take place (in most states) at any time during minority and within a reasonable time after the minor has reached the age of majority.

   b. If a minor disaffirms part of a contract, the entire contract must be disaffirmed.

   c. When disaffirming executed contracts, the minor has a duty to return received goods if they are still in the minor's control or (in some states) to pay their reasonable value.

   d. A minor who has committed an act of fraud (such as misrepresentation of age) will be denied the right to disaffirm by some courts.

   e. A minor may disaffirm a contract for necessaries but remains liable for the reasonable value of the goods.

2. *Ratification*—The acceptance, or affirmation, of a legal obligation; may be express or implied.

   a. Express ratification—Exists when the minor, through a writing or an oral agreement, explicitly assumes the obligations imposed by the contract.

CHAPTER SUMMARY **Capacity and Legality–Continued**

Minors–Continued	b. *Implied ratification*—Exists when the conduct of the minor is inconsistent with disaffirmance or when the minor fails to disaffirm an executed contract within a reasonable time after reaching the age of majority.
	3. *Parents' liability*—Generally, except for contracts for necessaries, parents are not liable for the contracts made by minor children acting on their own, nor are parents liable for minors' torts except in certain circumstances.
	4. *Emancipation*—Occurs when a child's parent or legal guardian relinquishes the legal right to exercise control over the child. Normally, a minor who leaves home to support himself or herself is considered emancipated. In some jurisdictions, minors themselves are permitted to petition for emancipation for limited purposes.
Intoxicated Persons (See page 283.)	1. A contract entered into by an intoxicated person is voidable at the option of the intoxicated person if the person was sufficiently intoxicated to lack mental capacity, even if the intoxication was voluntary.
	2. A contract with an intoxicated person is enforceable if, despite being intoxicated, the person understood the legal consequences of entering into the contract.
Mentally Incompetent Persons (See pages 283–284.)	1. A contract made by a person previously judged by a court to be mentally incompetent is void.
	2. A contract made by a mentally incompetent person whom a court has not previously declared to be mentally incompetent is voidable at the option of the mentally incompetent person.

LEGALITY

Contracts Contrary to Statute (See pages 284–288.)	1. *Usury*—Usury occurs when a lender makes a loan at an interest rate above the lawful maximum. The maximum rate of interest varies from state to state.
	2. *Gambling*—Gambling contracts that contravene (go against) state statutes are deemed illegal and thus void.
	3. *Sabbath (Sunday) laws*—These laws prohibit the formation or performance of certain contracts on Sunday. Such laws vary widely from state to state, and many states do not enforce them.
	4. *Licensing statutes*—Contracts entered into by persons who do not have a license, when one is required by statute, will not be enforceable *unless* the underlying purpose of the statute is to raise government revenues (and not to protect the public from unauthorized practitioners).
Contracts Contrary to Public Policy (See pages 288–293.)	1. *Contracts in restraint of trade*—Contracts to reduce or restrain free competition are illegal and prohibited by statutes. An exception is a *covenant not to compete*. It is usually enforced by the courts if the terms are secondary to a contract (such as a contract for the sale of a business or an employment contract) and are reasonable as to time and area of restraint. Courts tend to scrutinize covenants not to compete closely and, at times, may reform them if they are overbroad rather than declaring the entire covenant unenforceable.
	2. *Unconscionable contracts and clauses*—When a contract or contract clause is so unfair that it is oppressive to one party, it may be deemed unconscionable; as such, it is illegal and cannot be enforced.
	3. *Exculpatory clauses*—An exculpatory clause is a clause that releases a party from liability in the event of monetary or physical injury, no matter who is at fault. In certain situations, exculpatory clauses may be contrary to public policy and thus unenforceable.

EFFECT OF ILLEGALITY

General Rule (See page 293.)	In general, an illegal contract is void, and the courts will not aid either party when both parties are considered to be equally at fault (*in pari delicto*). If the contract is executory, neither party can

(Continued)

CHAPTER SUMMARY Capacity and Legality–Continued

General Rule—Continued	enforce it. If the contract is executed, there can be neither contractual nor quasi-contractual recovery.
Exceptions (See pages 293–295.)	Several exceptions exist to the general rule that neither party to an illegal bargain will be able to recover. In the following situations, the court may grant recovery:

1. *Justifiable ignorance of the facts*—When one party to the contract is relatively innocent.

2. *Members of protected classes*—When one party to the contract is a member of a group of persons protected by statute, such as employees.

3. *Withdrawal from an illegal agreement*—When either party seeks to recover consideration given for an illegal contract before the illegal act is performed.

4. *Severable, or divisible, contracts*—When the court can divide the contract into illegal and legal portions and the illegal portion is not essential to the bargain.

5. *Fraud, duress, or undue influence*—When one party was induced to enter into an illegal bargain through fraud, duress, or undue influence.

FOR REVIEW

Answers for the even-numbered questions in this **For Review** *section can be found in Appendix E at the end of this text.*

1 What are some exceptions to the rule that a minor can disaffirm (avoid) any contract?

2 Does an intoxicated person have the capacity to enter into an enforceable contract?

3 Does the mental incompetence of one party necessarily make a contract void?

4 Under what circumstances will a covenant not to compete be enforceable? When will such covenants not be enforced?

5 What is an exculpatory clause? In what circumstances might exculpatory clauses be enforced? When will they not be enforced?

 The following multiple-choice question is representative of the types of questions available in one of the four sections of ThomsonNOW for *Business Law Today*. **ThomsonNOW also provides feedback for each response option, whether correct or incorrect, and refers to the location within the chapter where the correct answer can be found.**

The general rule with regard to minors who enter into contracts is that

a all such contracts are void.

b all such contracts are enforceable.

c some contracts can be avoided by the minor.

d such contracts can be avoided by the adult party to the contract.

■

QUESTIONS AND CASE PROBLEMS

 **HYPOTHETICAL SCENARIOS**

10.1 Contracts by Minors. Kalen is a seventeen-year-old minor who has just graduated from high school. He is attending a university two hundred miles from home and has contracted to rent an apartment near the university for one year at $500 per month. He is working at a convenience store to earn enough income to be self-supporting. After living in the apartment and paying monthly rent for four months, he becomes involved in a dispute with his landlord. Kalen, still a minor, moves out and returns the key to the landlord. The landlord wants to hold Kalen liable for the balance of the payments due under the lease. Discuss fully Kalen's liability in this situation.

10.2 Hypothetical Question with Sample Answer. A famous New York City hotel, Hotel Lux, is noted for its food as well as its luxury accommodations. Hotel Lux contracts with a famous chef, Chef Perlee, to become its head chef at $6,000 per month. The contract states that should Perlee leave the employment of Hotel Lux for any reason, he will not work as a chef for any hotel or restaurant in New York, New Jersey, or Pennsylvania for a period of one year. During the first six months of the contract, Hotel Lux extensively advertises Perlee as its head chef, and business at the hotel is excellent. Then a dispute arises between the hotel management and Perlee, and Perlee terminates his employment. One month later, he is hired by a famous New Jersey restaurant just across the New York state line. Hotel Lux learns of Perlee's employment through a large advertisement in a New York City newspaper. It seeks to enjoin (prevent) Perlee from

working in that restaurant as a chef for one year. Discuss how successful Hotel Lux will be in its action.

 For a sample answer to Question 10.2, go to Appendix F at the end of this text.

10.3 Mental Incompetence. Joanne is a seventy-five-year-old widow who survives on her husband's small pension. Joanne has become increasingly forgetful, and her family worries that she may have Alzheimer's disease (a brain disorder that seriously affects a person's ability to carry out daily activities). No physician has diagnosed her, however, and no court has ruled on Joanne's legal competence. One day while out shopping, Joanne stops by a store that is having a sale on pianos and enters into a fifteen-year installment contract to buy a grand piano. When the piano arrives the next day, Joanne seems confused and repeatedly asks the deliveryperson why a piano is being delivered. Joanne claims that she does not recall buying a piano. Explain whether this contract is void, voidable, or valid. Can Joanne avoid her contractual obligation to buy the piano? If so, how?

CASE PROBLEMS

10.4 Exculpatory Clause. Norbert Eelbode applied for a job with Travelers Inn in the state of Washington. As part of the application process, Eelbode was sent to Laura Grothe, a physical therapist at Chec Medical Centers, Inc., for a preemployment physical exam. Before the exam, Eelbode signed a document that stated in part, "I hereby release Chec and the Washington Readicare Medical Group and its physicians from all liability arising from any injury to me resulting from my participation in the exam." During the exam, Grothe asked Eelbode to lift an item while bending from the waist using only his back with his knees locked. Eelbode experienced immediate sharp and burning pain in his lower back and down the back of his right leg. Eelbode filed a suit in a Washington state court against Grothe and Chec, claiming that he was injured because of an improperly administered back torso strength test. Citing the document that Eelbode signed, Grothe and Chec filed a motion for summary judgment. Should the court grant the motion? Why or why not? [*Eelbode v. Chec Medical Centers, Inc.*, 97 Wash.App. 462, 984 P.2d 436 (1999)]

10.5 Case Problem with Sample Answer. In 1993, Mutual Service Casualty Insurance Co. and its affiliates (collectively, MSI) hired Thomas Brass as an insurance agent. Three years later, Brass entered into a career agent's contract with MSI. This contract contained provisions regarding Brass's activities after termination. These provisions stated that, for a period of not less than one year, Brass could not solicit any MSI customers to "lapse, cancel, or replace" any insurance contract in force

with MSI in an effort to take that business to a competitor. If he did, MSI could at any time refuse to pay the commissions that it otherwise owed him. The contract also restricted Brass from working for American National Insurance Co. for three years after termination. In 1998, Brass quit MSI and immediately went to work for American National, soliciting MSI customers. MSI filed a suit in a Wisconsin state court against Brass, claiming that he had violated the noncompete terms of his MSI contract. Should the court enforce the covenant not to compete? Why or why not? [*Mutual Service Casualty Insurance Co. v. Brass*, 242 Wis.2d 733, 625 N.W.2d 648 (App. 2001)]

After you have answered Problem 10.5, compare your answer with the sample answer given on the Web site that accompanies this text. Go to www.thomsonedu.com/westbuslaw/blt, select "Chapter 10," and click on "Case Problem with Sample Answer."

10.6 Misrepresentation of Age. Millennium Club, Inc., operates a tavern in South Bend, Indiana. In January 2003, Pamela Avila and other minors gained admission by misrepresenting that they were at least twenty-one years old. According to Millennium's representatives, the minors used false driver's licenses, "fraudulent transfer of a stamp used to gain admission by another patron or other means of false identification." To gain access, the minors also signed affidavits falsely attesting to the fact that they were twenty-one or older. When the state filed criminal charges against the Millennium Club,

Millennium filed a suit in an Indiana state court against Avila and more than two hundred others, seeking damages of $3,000 each for misrepresenting their ages. The minors filed a motion to dismiss the complaint. Should the court grant the motion? What are the competing policy interests in this case? If the Millennium Club was not careful in checking the minors' identification, should it be allowed to recover? If Millennium Club reasonably relied on the minors' representations, should the minors be allowed to avoid liability? Discuss. [*Millennium Club, Inc. v. Avila*, 809 N.E.2d 906 (Ind.App. 2004)]

10.7 Covenant Not to Compete. Gary Forsee was an executive officer with responsibility for the U.S. operations of BellSouth Corp., a company providing global telecommunications services. Under a covenant not to compete, Forsee agreed that for a period of eighteen months after termination from employment, he would not provide services in competition with BellSouth "to any person or entity which provides products or services identical or similar to products and services provided by [BellSouth]" within the territory. *Territory* was defined to include the geographic area in which Forsee provided services to BellSouth. The *services* included "management, strategic planning, business planning, administration, or other participation in or providing advice with respect to the communications services business." Forsee announced his intent to resign and accept a position as chief executive officer of Sprint Corp., a competitor of BellSouth. BellSouth filed a suit in a Georgia state court against Forsee, claiming in part that his acceptance of employment with Sprint would violate the covenant not to compete. Is the covenant legal? Should it be enforced? Why or why not? [*BellSouth Corp. v. Forsee*, 265 Ga.App. 589, 595 S.E.2d 99 (2004)]

10.8 Licensing Statutes. Under California law, a contract to manage a professional boxer must be in writing and the manager must be licensed by the state athletic commission. Marco Antonio Barrera is a professional boxer and two-time world champion. In May 2003, Jose Castillo, who was not licensed by the state, orally agreed to assume Barrera's management. He "understood" that he would be paid in accord with the "practice in the professional boxing industry, but in no case less than ten percent (10%) of the gross revenue" that Barrera generated as a boxer and through endorsements. Among

other accomplishments, Castillo negotiated an exclusive promotion contract for Barrera with Golden Boy Promotions, Inc., which is owned and operated by Oscar De La Hoya. Castillo also helped Barrera settle three lawsuits and resolve unrelated tax problems so that Barrera could continue boxing. Castillo did not train Barrera, pick his opponents, or arrange his fights, however. When Barrera abruptly stopped communicating with Castillo, the latter filed a suit in a California state court against Barrera and others, alleging breach of contract. Under what circumstances is a contract with an unlicensed practitioner enforceable? Is the alleged contract in this case enforceable? Why or why not? [*Castillo v. Barrera*, 146 Cal.App.4th 1317, 53 Cal.Rptr.3d 494 (2 Dist. 2007)]

10.9 **A Question of Ethics.** *Dow AgroSciences, LLC (DAS), makes and sells agricultural seed products. In 2000, Timothy Glenn, a DAS sales manager, signed a covenant not to compete. He agreed that for two years from the date of his termination, he would not "engage in or contribute my knowledge to any work or activity involving an area of technology or business that is then competitive with a technology or business with respect to which I had access to Confidential Information during the five years immediately prior to such termination." Working with DAS business, operations, and research and development personnel, and being a member of high-level teams, Glenn had access to confidential DAS information, including agreements with DAS's business partners, marketing plans, litigation details, product secrets, new product development, future plans, and pricing strategies. In 2006, Glenn resigned to work for Pioneer Hi-Bred International, Inc., a DAS competitor. DAS filed a suit in an Indiana state court against Glenn, asking that he be enjoined from accepting any "position that would call on him to use confidential DAS information."* [Glenn v. Dow AgroSciences, LLC, 861 N.E.2d 1 (Ind.App. 2007)]

1 Generally, what interests are served by enforcing covenants not to compete? What interests are served by refusing to enforce them?

2 What argument could be made in support of reforming (and then enforcing) illegal covenants not to compete? What argument could be made against this practice?

3 How should the court rule in this case? Why?

CRITICAL THINKING AND WRITING ASSIGNMENTS

10.10 Critical Legal Thinking. Are legalized forms of gambling, such as state-operated lotteries, consistent with a continuing public policy against the enforcement of gambling contracts? Why or why not?

10.11 **Video Question.** Go to this text's Web site at **www.thomsonedu.com/westbuslaw/blt** and select

"Chapter 10." Click on "Video Questions" and view the video titled *The Money Pit*. Then answer the following questions.

1 Assume that a valid contract exists between Walter (Tom Hanks) and the plumber. Recall from the video that the plumber had at least two drinks before agreeing to take on

the plumbing job. If the plumber was intoxicated, is the contract voidable? Why or why not?

2 Suppose that state law requires plumbers in Walter's state to have a plumber's license and that this plumber does not have a license. Would the contract be enforceable? Why or why not?

3 In the video, the plumber suggests that Walter has been "turned down by every other plumber in the valley."

Although the plumber does not even look at the house's plumbing, he agrees to do the repairs if Walter gives him a check for $5,000 right then "before he changes his mind." If Walter later seeks to void the contract because it is contrary to public policy, what should he argue?

ONLINE ACTIVITIES

 **PRACTICAL INTERNET EXERCISES**

Go to this text's Web site at **www.thomsonedu.com/westbuslaw/blt**, select "Chapter 10," and click on "Practical Internet Exercises." There you will find the following Internet research exercises that you can perform to learn more about the topics covered in this chapter.

PRACTICAL INTERNET EXERCISE 10-1 MANAGEMENT PERSPECTIVE—Minors and the Law

PRACTICAL INTERNET EXERCISE 10-2 SOCIAL PERSPECTIVE—Online Gambling

PRACTICAL INTERNET EXERCISE 10-3 LEGAL PERSPECTIVE—Covenants Not to Compete

BEFORE THE TEST

Go to this text's Web site at **www.thomsonedu.com/westbuslaw/blt**, select "Chapter 10," and click on "Interactive Quizzes." You will find a number of interactive questions relating to this chapter.

CHAPTER 11
Defenses to Contract Enforceability

CHAPTER OUTLINE

- GENUINENESS OF ASSENT
- THE STATUTE OF FRAUDS— REQUIREMENT OF A WRITING
- THE STATUTE OF FRAUDS— SUFFICIENCY OF THE WRITING
- THE PAROL EVIDENCE RULE

LEARNING OBJECTIVES

AFTER READING THIS CHAPTER, YOU SHOULD BE ABLE TO ANSWER THE FOLLOWING QUESTIONS:

1 In what types of situations might genuineness of assent to a contract's terms be lacking?

2 What is the difference between a mistake of value or quality and a mistake of fact?

3 What elements must exist for fraudulent misrepresentation to occur?

4 What contracts must be in writing to be enforceable?

5 What is parol evidence? When is it admissible to clarify the terms of a written contract?

A n otherwise valid contract may still be unenforceable if the parties have not genuinely assented to its terms. As mentioned in Chapter 8, lack of genuine assent is a *defense* to the enforcement of a contract. As Aristotle stated in the chapter-opening quotation, the law seeks to ensure that "the citizens of a state will do justice to one another." If the law were to enforce contracts not genuinely assented to by the contracting parties, injustice would result. The first part of this chapter focuses on the kinds of factors that indicate that genuineness of assent to a contract may be lacking.

A contract that is otherwise valid may also be unenforceable if it is not in the proper form. For example, if a contract is required by law to be in writing and there is no written evidence of the contract, it may not be enforceable. In the second part of this chapter, we examine the kinds of contracts that require a writing under what is called the *Statute of Frauds*. The chapter concludes with a discussion of the parol evidence rule, under which courts determine the admissibility at trial of evidence extraneous (external) to written contracts.

GENUINENESS OF ASSENT

Genuineness of assent may be lacking because of mistake, fraudulent misrepresentation, undue influence, or duress. Generally, a party who demonstrates that he or she did not genuinely assent (agree) to the terms of a contract can choose either to carry out the contract or to rescind (cancel) it and thus avoid the entire transaction.

Mistakes

We all make mistakes, so it is not surprising that mistakes are made when contracts are created. In certain circumstances, contract law allows a contract to be avoided on the basis of mistake. It is important to distinguish between *mistakes of fact* and *mistakes of value or quality*. Only a mistake of fact may allow a contract to be avoided.

EXAMPLE 11.1 Suppose that Paco buys a violin from Beverly for $250. Although the violin is very old, neither party believes that it is extremely valuable. Later, however, an antiques dealer informs the parties that the violin is rare and worth thousands of dollars. Here, both parties were mistaken, but the mistake is a mistake of *value* rather than a mistake of *fact* that warrants contract rescission. Therefore, Paco cannot rescind the contract. ▣

Mistakes of fact occur in two forms—*unilateral* and *bilateral (mutual)*. A unilateral mistake is made by only one of the contracting parties; a mutual mistake is made by both. We look next at these two types of mistakes and illustrate them graphically in Exhibit 11–1.

Unilateral Mistakes A unilateral mistake occurs when only one party is mistaken as to a *material fact*—that is, a fact important to the subject matter of the contract. Generally, a unilateral mistake does not give the mistaken party any right to relief from the contract. In other words, the contract normally is enforceable against the mistaken party. **EXAMPLE 11.2** Elena intends to sell her motor home for $17,500. When she learns that Chin is interested in buying a used motor home, she faxes a letter offering to sell the vehicle to him. When typing the fax, however, she mistakenly keys in the price of $15,700. Chin immediately sends Elena a fax accepting her offer. Even though Elena intended to sell her motor home for $17,500, she has made a unilateral mistake and is bound by contract to sell the vehicle to Chin for $15,700. ▣

There are at least two exceptions to this rule.[1] First, if the *other* party to the contract knows or should have known that a mistake of fact was made, the contract may not be enforceable. **EXAMPLE 11.3** In the above example, if Chin knew that Elena intended to sell her motor home for $17,500, then Elena's unilateral mistake (stating $15,700 in her offer) may render the resulting contract unenforceable. ▣ The second exception arises when a unilateral mistake of fact was due to a mathematical mistake in addition, subtraction, division, or multiplication and was made inadvertently and without gross (extreme)

> "Mistakes are the inevitable lot of mankind."
>
> SIR GEORGE JESSEL,
> 1824–1883
> (English jurist)

BE CAREFUL What a party to a contract knows or should know can determine whether the contract is enforceable.

---

1. The *Restatement (Second) of Contracts*, Section 153, liberalizes the general rule to take into account the modern trend of allowing avoidance in some circumstances even though only one party has been mistaken.

EXHIBIT 11–1 Mistakes of Fact

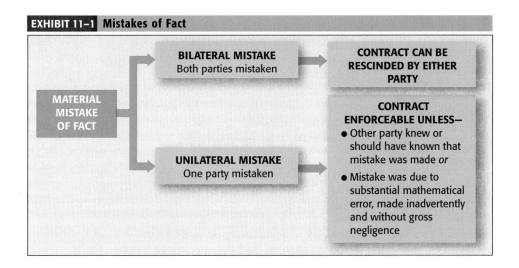

negligence. If a contractor's bid was significantly low because he or she made a mistake in addition when totaling the estimated costs, any contract resulting from the bid normally may be rescinded. Of course, in both situations, the mistake must still involve some *material fact.*

Bilateral (Mutual) Mistakes   When both parties are mistaken about the same material fact, the contract can be rescinded by either party.[2] Note that, as with unilateral mistakes, the mistake must be about a *material fact* (one that is important and central to the contract). **■EXAMPLE 11.4** Keeley buys a landscape painting from Umberto's art gallery. Both Umberto and Keeley believe that the painting is by the artist Vincent van Gogh. Later, Keeley discovers that the painting is a very clever fake. Because neither Umberto nor Keeley was aware of this fact when they made their deal, Keeley can rescind the contract and recover the purchase price of the painting. ■

A word or term in a contract may be subject to more than one reasonable interpretation. In that situation, if the parties to the contract attach materially different meanings to the term, their mutual misunderstanding may allow the contract to be rescinded. **■EXAMPLE 11.5** In a classic case, *Raffles v. Wichelhaus,*[3] Wichelhaus purchased a shipment of cotton from Raffles to arrive on a ship called the *Peerless* from Bombay, India. Wichelhaus meant a ship called *Peerless* sailing from Bombay in October; Raffles meant a different ship called *Peerless* sailing from Bombay in December. When the goods arrived on the December *Peerless* and Raffles tried to deliver them, Wichelhaus refused to accept them. The British court held for Wichelhaus, concluding that no mutual assent existed because the parties had attached materially different meanings to an essential term of the contract (which ship *Peerless* was to transport the goods). ■

In the following case, an injured worker sought to set aside a settlement agreement entered into with his employer, arguing that the agreement was based on a mutual mistake of fact—a physician's mistaken diagnosis of the worker's injury.

---

2. *Restatement (Second) of Contracts,* Section 152.
3. 159 Eng.Rep. 375 (1864).

CASE 11.1   **Roberts v. Century Contractors, Inc.**

Court of Appeals of North Carolina, 162 N.C.App. 688, 592 S.E.2d 215 (2004).
www.aoc.state.nc.us/www/public/html/opinions.htm[a]

FACTS   Bobby Roberts was an employee of Century Contractors, Inc., in July 1993, when a pipe struck him in a work-related accident, causing trauma to his neck and back. Dr. James Markworth of Southeastern Orthopaedic Clinic diagnosed Roberts's injuries. After surgery and treatment, Markworth concluded that Roberts was at maximum medical improvement (MMI) and stopped treating him. Roberts agreed with Century to accept $125,000 and payment of related

medical expenses, and to waive any right to make further claims in regard to his injury. In June 1998, still experiencing pain, Roberts saw Dr. Allen Friedman, who determined that Roberts was not at MMI. Markworth then admitted that his diagnosis was a mistake. Roberts filed a claim for workers' compensation (see Chapter 33), seeking compensation and medical benefits for his injury. He alleged that his agreement with Century should be set aside due to a mutual mistake of fact. The North Carolina state administrative agency authorized to rule on workers' compensation claims awarded Roberts what he sought. Century appealed to a state intermediate appellate court.

ISSUE   Should the agreement between Roberts and Century be set aside on the basis of a mutual mistake of fact?

---

a. In the "Keywords" box, type "Roberts." In the "What" pull-down menu, select "Title." In the "Additional Search Options" section, choose "Court of Appeals Opinions Only." Click on "Search." In the result, scroll to the name of the case and click on it to access the opinion. The North Carolina Administrative Office of the Courts maintains this Web site.

CASE 11.1–Continued

DECISION Yes. The state intermediate appellate court affirmed the award of compensation and medical benefits to Roberts.

REASON The court explained that compromise settlement agreements, including settlement agreements in workers' compensation cases, are governed by general principles of contract law. The court stated that it is a well-settled principle of contract law that a valid contract exists only where there has been a meeting of the minds as to all essential terms of the agreement. "Therefore," said the court, "where a mistake is common to both parties and concerns a material past or presently existing fact, such that there is no meeting of the minds, a contract may be avoided." The mistake "must be as to a fact which enters into and forms the basis of the contract * * * and must be such that it animates and controls the conduct of the parties." Also, "relief from a contract due to mistake of fact will be had only where *both* parties to an agreement are mistaken." The court pointed out that Markworth's MMI diagnosis was "material to the settlement of this claim" and that both parties relied on this information in entering into settlement negotiations. Later, however, "Dr. Friedman testified, and the [state agency found] as fact, that plaintiff was not at maximum medical improvement." Thus, the court concluded that there was a mutual mistake with regard to the plaintiff's medical condition at the time of the signing of the settlement agreement.

 FOR CRITICAL ANALYSIS–Social Consideration *Why did the court consider Markworth's misdiagnosis a bilateral mistake rather than a unilateral mistake?*

Fraudulent Misrepresentation

Although fraud is a tort, the presence of fraud also affects the genuineness of the innocent party's consent to a contract. When an innocent party consents to a contract with fraudulent terms, the contract usually can be avoided because she or he has not *voluntarily* consented to the terms.[4] Normally, the innocent party can either rescind (cancel) the contract and be restored to her or his original position or enforce the contract and seek damages for injuries resulting from the fraud.

Typically, fraud involves three elements:

1 A misrepresentation of a material fact must occur.

2 There must be an intent to deceive.

3 The innocent party must justifiably rely on the misrepresentation.

Additionally, to collect damages, a party must have been injured as a result of the misrepresentation.

Fraudulent misrepresentation can also occur in the online environment. For a case involving allegations that Yahoo fraudulently posted online personal ads, see this chapter's *Adapting the Law to the Online Environment* feature on pages 306 and 307. Because curbing Internet fraud is a major challenge in today's world, we also explore the topic further in Chapter 32, in the context of consumer law.

Misrepresentation Must Occur The first element of proving fraud is to show that misrepresentation of a material fact has occurred. This misrepresentation can take the form of words or actions. For example, an art gallery owner's statement, "This painting is a Picasso" is a misrepresentation of fact if the painting was done by another artist.

A statement of opinion is generally not subject to a claim of fraud. For example, claims such as "This computer will never break down" and "This car will last for years and years"

A woman browses through some online personal ads. Individuals who post their profiles on an Internet dating site may tend to exaggerate their attractive traits and may even make statements about themselves that they know to be false. But what happens when an Internet service provider makes fraudulent misrepresentations about its users? (Photo by Bill Stryker)

REMEMBER To collect damages in almost any lawsuit, there must be some sort of injury.

---

4. *Restatement (Second) of Contracts*, Sections 163 and 164.

Online Personals—Fraud and Misrepresentation Issues

Keying the words *online personals* into the Google search engine will return more than 35 million hits, including Match.com, Chanceforlove.com, Widowsorwidowers.com, Makefriendsonline.com, and Yahoo! Personals. Yahoo! Personals, which calls itself the "top online dating site," offers two options. One is for people looking for casual dates. It allows users to create their own profiles, browse member profiles, and exchange e-mail or instant messages. The second option, called Yahoo! Personals Primer, is for people who want serious relationships. Users must take a relationship test. Then they can use Yahoo's computerized matching system to "zero in on marriage material." With this service, users can chat on the phone, as well as exchange e-mail.

The Thorny Problem of Misrepresentation

When singles (and others) create their profiles for online dating services, they tend to exaggerate their more appealing features and downplay or omit their less attractive attributes. All users of such services are aware that the profiles may not correspond exactly with reality, but they do assume that the profiles are not complete misrepresentations. In 2006, however, Robert Anthony, individually and on behalf of others, brought a suit against Yahoo in federal district court, alleging fraud and negligent misrepresentation, among other things.

In his complaint, Anthony claimed that Yahoo was not just posting fictitious or exaggerated profiles submitted by users but was deliberately and intentionally originating, creating, and perpetuating false and/or nonexistent profiles. According to Anthony, many profiles used the exact same phrases "with such unique dictation and vernacular [language] that such a random occurrence would not be possible." Anthony also argued that some photo images had multiple identities—that is, the same photo appeared in several different profiles. He

---

are statements of opinion, not fact, and contracting parties should recognize them as such and not rely on them. A fact is objective and verifiable; an opinion is usually subject to debate. Therefore, a seller is allowed to "huff and puff his [or her] wares" without being liable for fraud. In certain cases, however, particularly when a naïve purchaser relies on an expert's opinion, the innocent party may be entitled to *rescission* (cancellation) or *reformation* (an equitable remedy granted by a court in which the terms of a contract are altered to reflect the true intentions of the parties).

Misrepresentation by Conduct. Misrepresentation can occur by conduct, as well as through express oral or written statements. For example, if a seller, by her or his actions, prevents a buyer from learning of some fact that is material to the contract, such behavior constitutes misrepresentation by conduct.[5] **EXAMPLE 11.6** Cummings contracts to purchase a racehorse from Garner. The horse is blind in one eye, but when Garner shows the horse, he skillfully conceals this fact by keeping the horse's head turned so that Cummings does not see the defect. The concealment constitutes fraud. ■ Another example of misrepresentation by conduct is the untruthful denial of knowledge or information concerning facts that are material to the contract when such knowledge or information is requested.

Misrepresentation of Law. Misrepresentation of law *ordinarily* does not entitle a party to be relieved of a contract. **EXAMPLE 11.7** Debbie has a parcel of property that she is trying to sell to Barry. Debbie knows that a local ordinance prohibits building anything higher than three stories on the property. Nonetheless, she tells Barry, "You can build a condominium fifty stories high if you want to." Barry buys the land and later discovers that Debbie's statement is false. Normally, Barry cannot avoid the contract because under the common law, people are assumed to know state and local laws. ■ Exceptions to this rule

---

5. *Restatement (Second) of Contracts,* Section 160.

also alleged that Yahoo continued to circulate profiles of "actual, legitimate former subscribers whose subscriptions had expired." Finally, Anthony claimed that when a subscription neared its end date, Yahoo would send the subscriber a fake profile, heralding it a "potential 'new match.'"

Did Yahoo Have Immunity?

Yahoo asked the court to dismiss the complaint on the grounds that the lawsuit was barred by the Communications Decency Act (CDA) of 1996.[a] As discussed in Chapter 4, the CDA shields Internet service providers (ISPs) from liability for any information submitted by another information content provider. In other words, an interactive computer service cannot be held liable under state law as a publisher of information that originates from a third party information content provider. The CDA defines an information content provider as "any person or entity that is responsible, in whole or in part, for the creation or development of information provided through the Internet or any other interactive computer service."[b]

a. 47 U.S.C. Section 230.
b. 47 U.S.C. Section 230(f)(3).

The court rejected Yahoo's claim that it had immunity under the CDA and held that Yahoo had become an information content provider itself when it created bogus user profiles. The court observed that "no case of which this court is aware has immunized a defendant from allegations that *it* created tortious content."[c] Thus, the court denied Yahoo's motion to dismiss and allowed Anthony's claims of fraud and negligent misrepresentation to proceed to trial.[d]

 FOR CRITICAL ANALYSIS *Assume that Anthony had contacted various users of Yahoo's online dating service only to discover that each user's profile exaggerated the user's physical appearance, intelligence, and occupation. Would Anthony prevail if he brought a lawsuit for fraudulent misrepresentation against Yahoo in that situation? Why or why not?*

c. For an example of the type of cases that have been brought against Internet dating services, see *Carafano v. Metrosplash.com, Inc.,* 339 F.3d 1119 (9th Cir. 2003), presented as Case 4.3 in Chapter 4.
d. *Anthony v. Yahoo!, Inc.,* 421 F.Supp.2d 1257 (N.D.Cal. 2006).

occur, however, when the misrepresenting party is in a profession known to require greater knowledge of the law than the average citizen possesses.

Misrepresentation by Silence. Ordinarily, neither party to a contract has a duty to come forward and disclose facts, and a contract normally will not be set aside because certain pertinent information has not been volunteered. **■EXAMPLE 11.8** Suppose that you are selling a car that has been in an accident and has been repaired. You do not need to volunteer this information to a potential buyer. If, however, the purchaser asks you if the car has had extensive bodywork and you lie, you have committed a fraudulent misrepresentation. ■

Generally, if the seller knows of a serious defect or a serious potential problem about which the buyer cannot reasonably be expected to know, the seller may have a duty to speak. Normally, the seller must disclose only "latent" defects—that is, defects that could not readily be discovered. Thus, termites in a house may not be a latent defect because a buyer could normally discover their presence through a termite inspection. Also, when the parties are in a *fiduciary relationship* (one of trust, such as partners, physician and patient, or attorney and client), there is a duty to disclose material facts; failure to do so may constitute fraud.

Intent to Deceive The second element of fraud is knowledge on the part of the misrepresenting party that facts have been misrepresented. This element, usually called *scienter,*[6] or "guilty knowledge," generally signifies that there was an intent to deceive. *Scienter* clearly exists if a party knows that a fact is not as stated. *Scienter* also exists if a party makes a statement that he or she believes not to be true or makes a statement recklessly, without regard to whether it is true or false. Finally, this element is met if a party says or implies that a statement is made on some basis, such as personal knowledge or personal investigation, when it is not.

SCIENTER
Knowledge by the misrepresenting party that material facts have been falsely represented or omitted with an intent to deceive.

6. Pronounced *sy-en-*ter.

Suppose that a city solicited bids from contractors to expand its public transportation system on this strip of land without disclosing the existence of a subsoil condition that would greatly increase the project's cost. Assuming that the city was aware of the situation, would it have had a duty to disclose the condition to bidders? What effect would the city's silence have on the resulting contract?
(Michael McCauslin/Creative Commons)

REMEMBER An opinion is neither a contract offer, nor a contract term, nor fraud.

ETHICAL ISSUE 11.1

■EXAMPLE 11.9 A convicted felon, Robert Sarvis, applied for a position as an adjunct professor two weeks after his release from prison. On his résumé, he lied about his past work history by representing that he had been the president of a corporation for fourteen years and had taught business law at another college. At his interview, Sarvis stated that he was "well equipped to teach" business law and ethics and that he had "a great interest and knowledge of business law." After he was hired and began working, Sarvis's probation officer alerted the school to his criminal history. The school immediately fired Sarvis, and he brought a lawsuit against the school for breaching his employment contract. The school claimed that it was not liable for the breach because of Sarvis's fraudulent misrepresentations during the hiring process. The court agreed. Sarvis had not fully disclosed his personal history, he clearly had an intent to deceive, and the school had justifiably relied on his misrepresentations. Therefore, the school could rescind Sarvis's employment contract.[7] ■

Reliance on the Misrepresentation The third element of fraud is *justifiable reliance* on the misrepresentation of fact. The deceived party must have a justifiable reason for relying on the misrepresentation, and the misrepresentation must be an important factor (but not necessarily the sole factor) in inducing the party to enter into the contract.

Reliance is not justified if the innocent party knows the true facts or relies on obviously extravagant statements. **■EXAMPLE 11.10** If a used-car dealer tells you, "This old Cadillac will get over sixty miles to the gallon," you normally would not be justified in relying on this statement. Suppose, however, that Merkel, a bank director, induces O'Connell, a co-director, to sign a statement that the bank has sufficient assets to meet its liabilities by telling O'Connell, "We have plenty of assets to satisfy our creditors." This statement is false. If O'Connell knows the true facts or, as a bank director, should know the true facts, he is not justified in relying on Merkel's statement. If O'Connell does not know the true facts, however, *and has no way of finding them out,* he may be justified in relying on the statement. ■

How much information must employers disclose to prospective employees? One of the problems employers face is that it is not always clear what information they should disclose to prospective employees. To lure qualified workers, employers are often tempted to "promise the moon" and paint their companies' prospects as bright. Employers must be careful, though, to avoid any conduct that could be interpreted by a court as intentionally deceptive. In particular, they must avoid making any statements about their companies' future prospects or financial health that they know to be false. If they do make a false statement on which a prospective employee relies to her or his detriment, they may be sued for fraudulent misrepresentation.

In one case, for example, an employee accepted a job with a brokerage firm, relying on assurances that the firm was not about to be sold. In fact, as the employee was later able to prove in his lawsuit against the firm for fraud, negotiations to sell the firm were underway at the time he was hired. The trial court awarded the employee more than $6 million in damages, a decision that was affirmed on appeal.[8] Generally, employers must be truthful in their hiring to avoid possible lawsuits for fraudulent misrepresentation.

---

7. *Sarvis v. Vermont State Colleges,* 172 Vt. 76, 772 A.2d 494 (2001).
8. *McConkey v. AON Corp.,* 354 N.J.Super. 25, 804 A.2d 572 (A.D. 2002).

Injury to the Innocent Party   Most courts do not require a showing of injury when the action is to rescind (cancel) the contract—these courts hold that because rescission returns the parties to the positions they held before the contract was made, a showing of injury to the innocent party is unnecessary.[9]

To recover damages caused by fraud, however, proof of an injury is universally required. The measure of damages is ordinarily equal to the property's value had it been delivered as represented, less the actual price paid for the property. In actions based on fraud, courts often award *punitive,* or *exemplary, damages,* which are granted to a plaintiff over and above the compensation for the actual loss. As pointed out in Chapter 4, punitive damages are based on the public-policy consideration of punishing the defendant or setting an example to deter similar wrongdoing by others.

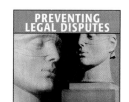

PREVENTING
LEGAL DISPUTES

To avoid making comments that might later be construed as a misrepresentation of material fact, business owners and managers should be careful what they say to clients and customers. Those in the business of selling products or services should assume that all customers are naïve and are relying on the seller's representations. Instruct employees to phrase their comments so that customers understand that any statements that are not factual are the employee's opinion. If someone asks a question that is beyond the employee's knowledge, it is better to say that he or she does not know than to guess and have the customer rely on a representation that turns out to be false. This can be particularly important when the questions concern topics such as compatibility or speed of electronic and digital goods, software, or related services.

Businesspersons should also be prudent about what they say when interviewing potential employees. Do not speculate on the financial health of the firm or exaggerate the company's future prospects. Exercising caution in one's statements to others in a business context is the best way to avoid potential legal actions for fraudulent misrepresentation.

◼

Undue Influence

Undue influence arises from relationships in which one party can greatly influence another party, thus overcoming that party's free will. Minors and elderly people, for example, are often under the influence of guardians. If a guardian induces a young or elderly ward (a person placed by a court under the care of a guardian) to enter into a contract that benefits the guardian, the guardian may have exerted undue influence.

Undue influence can arise from a number of confidential or fiduciary relationships, including attorney-client, physician-patient, guardian-ward, parent-child, husband-wife, and trustee-beneficiary relationships. The essential feature of undue influence is that the party being taken advantage of does not, in reality, exercise free will in entering into a contract. A contract entered into under excessive or undue influence lacks genuine assent and is therefore voidable.[10]

Duress

Assent to the terms of a contract is not genuine if one of the parties is forced into the agreement. Forcing a party to enter into a contract because of the fear created by threats is referred to as *duress.*[11] Inducing consent to a contract through blackmail or extortion also

ON THE WEB

To read more about contesting contracts on the grounds of fraud and duress, go to

**www.lawyers.com/lawyers/A~1001073~
LDC/CONTESTING+CONTRACT.html.**

---

9. For a leading case on this issue, see *Kaufman v. Jaffe,* 244 App.Div. 344, 279 N.Y.S. 392 (1935).
10. *Restatement (Second) of Contracts,* Section 177.
11. *Restatement (Second) of Contracts,* Sections 174 and 175.

constitutes duress. Duress is both a defense to the enforcement of a contract and a ground for rescission of a contract. Therefore, a party who signs a contract under duress can choose to carry out the contract or to avoid the entire transaction. (The wronged party usually has this choice in cases in which assent is not real or genuine.)

Economic need is generally not sufficient to constitute duress, even when one party exacts a very high price for an item the other party needs. If the party exacting the price also creates the need, however, economic duress may be found. **■EXAMPLE 11.11** The Internal Revenue Service (IRS) assessed a large tax and penalty against Weller. Weller retained Eyman to contest the assessment. Two days before the deadline for filing a reply with the IRS, Eyman declined to represent Weller unless he agreed to pay a very high fee for Eyman's services. The agreement was held to be unenforceable.[12] Although Eyman had threatened only to withdraw his services, something that he was legally entitled to do, he was responsible for delaying his withdrawal until just before the deadline. Because Weller was forced into either signing the contract or losing his right to challenge the IRS assessment, the agreement was secured under duress. ■

THE STATUTE OF FRAUDS–REQUIREMENT OF A WRITING

STATUTE OF FRAUDS
A state statute under which certain types of contracts must be in writing to be enforceable.

Today, every state has a statute that stipulates what types of contracts must be in writing or be evidenced by a record. In this text, we refer to such a statute as the **Statute of Frauds.** The primary purpose of the statute is to ensure that, for certain types of contracts, there is reliable evidence of the contracts and their terms. These types of contracts are those historically deemed to be important or complex. Although the statutes vary slightly from state to state, the following types of contracts are normally required to be in writing or evidenced by a written memorandum:

KEEP IN MIND Although only certain types of contracts must be in writing to be enforceable, it is good practice to put other contracts in writing as well to prevent disputes over contract terms.

1 Contracts involving interests in land.

2 Contracts that cannot by their terms be performed within one year from the date of formation.

3 Collateral contracts, such as promises to answer for the debt or duty of another.

4 Promises made in consideration of marriage.

5 Contracts for the sale of goods priced at $500 or more (under the Uniform Commercial Code, or UCC—see Chapter 15).

Agreements or promises that fit into one or more of these categories are said to "fall under" or "fall within" the Statute of Frauds. (Certain exceptions are made to the Statute of Frauds, however, as you will read later in this section.)

The actual name of the Statute of Frauds is misleading because it does not apply to fraud. Rather, the statute denies enforceability to certain contracts that do not comply with its requirements. The name derives from an English act passed in 1677, which is presented as this chapter's *Landmark in the Law* feature.

Contracts Involving Interests in Land

Land is a form of *real property*, or real estate, which includes not only land but all physical objects that are permanently attached to the soil, such as buildings, plants, trees, and the soil itself. Under the Statute of Frauds, a contract involving an interest in land must be evidenced by a writing to be enforceable.[13] If Carol, for example, contracts orally to sell Seaside Shelter

---

12. *Thompson Crane & Trucking Co. v. Eyman*, 123 Cal.App.2d 904, 267 P.2d 1043 (1954).

13. In some states, the contract will be enforced if each party admits to the existence of the oral contract in court or admits to its existence during discovery before trial (see Chapter 3).

LANDMARK IN THE LAW · The Statute of Frauds

On April 12, 1677, the English Parliament passed "An Act for the Prevention of Frauds and Perjuries." Four days later, the act was signed by King Charles II and became the law of the land. The act contained twenty-five sections and stipulated that certain types of contracts would henceforth have to be in writing or evidenced by a written memorandum if they were to be enforceable by the courts.[a]

Enforcement of Oral Promises The English act was enacted specifically to prevent the many frauds that were being perpetrated through the perjured testimony of witnesses in cases involving breached oral agreements, for which no written evidence existed. During the early history of the common law in England, the courts generally did not enforce oral contracts, but in the fourteenth century, they began to be enforced in certain *assumpsit* actions.[b] These actions, to which the origins of modern contract law are traced, allowed a party to sue and obtain relief when a promise or contract had been breached. During the next two centuries, the king's courts commonly enforced oral promises in actions in *assumpsit.*

Problems with Oral Contracts Because the courts enforced oral contracts on the strength of oral testimony by witnesses, it was not too difficult to evade justice by alleging that a contract had been breached and then procuring "convincing" witnesses to support the claim. The possibility of fraud in such actions was enhanced by the fact that seventeenth-century English courts did not allow oral testimony to be given by the parties to a lawsuit—or by any parties with an interest in the litigation, such as husbands or wives. Defenses against actions for breach of contract were thus limited to written evidence and the testimony given by third parties. The Statute of Frauds was enacted to minimize the possibility of fraud in oral contracts relating to certain types of transactions.

APPLICATION TO TODAY'S WORLD *Essentially, the Statute of Frauds offers a defense against contracts that fall under the statute. Indeed, some have criticized the statute because, although it was created to protect the innocent, it can also be used as a technical defense by a party who has breached a genuine, mutually agreed-on oral contract—if the contract falls within the Statute of Frauds. For this reason, some legal scholars believe the act has caused more fraud than it has prevented. Nonetheless, U.S. courts continue to apply the Statute of Frauds to disputes involving oral contracts. The definitions of such terms as* writing *and* signature, *however, have changed to accommodate electronic documents—as you will read in Chapter 14, which covers e-contracts.*

RELEVANT WEB SITES *To locate information on the Web concerning the Statute of Frauds, go to this text's Web site at* **www.thomsonedu.com/westbuslaw/blt**, *select "Chapter 11," and click on "URLs for Landmarks."*

a. These contracts are discussed in the text of this chapter.
b. *Assumpsit* is Latin for "he or she undertook" or "he or she promised." The emergence of remedies for breached promises and duties dates to these actions. One of the earliest cases occurred in 1370, when the court allowed an individual to sue a person who, in trying to cure the plaintiff's horse, had acted so negligently that the horse died. Another such action was permitted in 1375, when a plaintiff obtained relief for having been maimed by a surgeon hired to cure him.

to Axel but later decides not to sell, Axel cannot enforce the contract. Similarly, if Axel refuses to close the deal, Carol cannot force Axel to pay for the land by bringing a lawsuit. The Statute of Frauds is a *defense* to the enforcement of this type of oral contract.

A contract for the sale of land ordinarily involves the entire interest in the real property, including buildings, growing crops, vegetation, minerals, timber, and anything else affixed to the land. Therefore, a *fixture* (personal property so affixed or so used as to become a part of the realty—see Chapter 37) is treated as real property.

The Statute of Frauds requires written contracts not just for the sale of land but also for the transfer of other interests in land, such as mortgages and leases. We describe these other interests in Chapter 37.

The One-Year Rule

Contracts that cannot, *by their own terms,* be performed within one year *from the day after* the contract is formed must be in writing to be enforceable. Because disputes over such contracts are unlikely to occur until some time after the contracts are made, resolution of these disputes is difficult unless the contract terms have been put in writing. The one-year period begins to run *the day after the contract is made.*

■EXAMPLE 11.12 Suppose that Superior University forms a contract with Kimi San stating that San will teach three courses in history during the coming academic year (September 15 through June 15). If the contract is formed in March, it must be in writing to be enforceable—because it cannot be performed within one year. If the contract is not formed until July, however, it will not have to be in writing to be enforceable—because it can be performed within one year. ■ Exhibit 11–2 graphically illustrates the one-year rule.

Normally, the test for determining whether an oral contract is enforceable under the one-year rule of the Statute of Frauds is whether performance is *possible* within one year from the day after the date of contract formation—not whether the agreement is *likely* to be performed within one year. When performance of a contract is objectively impossible during the one-year period, the oral contract will be unenforceable.

EXHIBIT 11–2 **The One-Year Rule**

Under the Statute of Frauds, contracts that by their terms are impossible to perform within one year from the day after the date of contract formation must be in writing to be enforceable. Put another way, if it is at all possible to perform an oral contract within one year from the day after the contract is made, the contract will fall outside the Statute of Frauds and be enforceable.

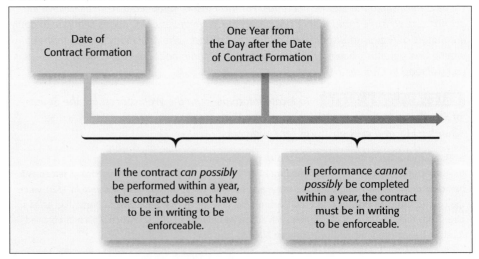

Collateral Promises

A **collateral promise,** or secondary promise, is one that is ancillary (subsidiary) to a principal transaction or primary contractual relationship. In other words, a collateral promise is one made by a third party to assume the debts or obligations of a primary party to a contract if that party does not perform. Any collateral promise of this nature falls under the Statute of Frauds and therefore must be in writing to be enforceable. To understand this concept, it is important to distinguish between primary and secondary promises and obligations.

Primary versus Secondary Obligations   A contract in which a party assumes a primary obligation normally does not need to be in writing to be enforceable. ▮**EXAMPLE 11.13** Suppose that Kenneth orally contracts with Joanne's Floral Boutique to send his mother a dozen roses for Mother's Day. Kenneth promises to pay the boutique when he receives the bill for the flowers. Kenneth is a direct party to this contract and has incurred a *primary* obligation under the contract. Because he is a party to the contract and has a primary obligation to Joanne's Floral Boutique, this contract does not fall under the Statute of Frauds and does not have to be in writing to be enforceable. If Kenneth fails to pay the florist and the florist sues him for payment, Kenneth cannot raise the Statute of Frauds as a defense. He cannot claim that the contract is unenforceable because it was not in writing. ▮

In contrast, a contract in which a party assumes a secondary obligation does have to be in writing to be enforceable. ▮**EXAMPLE 11.14** Suppose that Kenneth's mother borrows $10,000 from the Medford Trust Company on a promissory note payable six months later. Kenneth promises the bank officer handling the loan that he will pay the $10,000 *if his mother does not pay the loan on time.* Kenneth, in this situation, becomes what is known as a *guarantor* on the loan. He is guaranteeing to the bank (the creditor) that he will pay the loan if his mother fails to do so. This kind of collateral promise, in which the guarantor states that he or she will become responsible only if the primary party does not perform, must be in writing to be enforceable. ▮ We return to the concept of guaranty and the distinction between primary and secondary obligations in Chapter 23, in the context of creditors' rights.

An Exception—The "Main Purpose" Rule   An oral promise to answer for the debt of another is covered by the Statute of Frauds *unless* the guarantor's purpose in accepting secondary liability is to secure a personal benefit. Under the "main purpose" rule, this type of contract need not be in writing.[14] The assumption is that a court can infer from the circumstances of a case whether a "leading objective" of the promisor was to secure a personal benefit.

▮**EXAMPLE 11.15** Carrie Oswald contracts with Machine Manufacturing Company to have some machines custom made for her factory. To ensure that Machine Manufacturing will have the supplies it needs to make the machines, Oswald promises Allrite Materials Supply Company, Machine Manufacturing's supplier, that if Allrite continues to deliver materials to Machine Manufacturing, she will guarantee payment. This promise need not be in writing, even though the effect may be to pay the debt of another, because Oswald's main purpose is to secure a benefit for herself. ▮

Another typical application of the so-called main purpose doctrine occurs when one creditor guarantees the debtor's debt to another creditor to forestall litigation. This allows the debtor to remain in business long enough to generate profits sufficient to pay *both* creditors. In this situation, the guaranty does not need to be in writing to be enforceable.

COLLATERAL PROMISE
A secondary promise that is ancillary (subsidiary) to a principal transaction or primary contractual relationship, such as a promise made by one person to pay the debts of another if the latter fails to perform. A collateral promise normally must be in writing to be enforceable.

---

14. *Restatement (Second) of Contracts,* Section 116.

*"Now, according to this agreement, his problems will be your
problems, and your problems will be your problems."*

Promises Made in Consideration of Marriage

A unilateral promise to make a monetary payment or to give property
in consideration of marriage must be in writing. If Mr. Baumann promises to pay Joe Villard $10,000 if Villard marries Baumann's daughter,
the promise must be in writing to be enforceable. The same rule
applies to **prenuptial agreements**—agreements made before marriage
(also called *antenuptial agreements*) that define each partner's ownership rights in the other partner's property. A prospective wife or husband may wish to limit the amount the prospective spouse can obtain
if the marriage ends in divorce. Prenuptial agreements made in consideration of marriage must be in writing to be enforceable.

PRENUPTIAL AGREEMENT
An agreement made before
marriage that defines each
partner's ownership rights in
the other partner's property.
Prenuptial agreements must be
in writing to be enforceable.

Generally, courts tend to give more credence to prenuptial agreements that are accompanied by consideration. ▣**EXAMPLE 11.16**
Maureen, who is not wealthy, marries Kaiser, who has a net worth of $300 million. Kaiser
has several children, and he wants them to receive most of his wealth on his death. Prior
to their marriage, Maureen and Kaiser draft and sign a prenuptial agreement in which
Kaiser promises to give Maureen $100,000 per year for the rest of her life if they divorce.
As consideration for consenting to this amount, Kaiser offers Maureen $1 million. If
Maureen consents to the agreement and accepts the $1 million, very likely a court would
hold that this prenuptial agreement is valid, should it ever be contested. ▣

ETHICAL ISSUE 11.2

What happens to the prenuptial agreement when an engagement is broken? Sometimes,
parties include in their prenuptial agreements terms that have to do with premarital activities.
For example, in one case a couple agreed that the bride-to-be (Virginia DeFina) would pay for
all expenses relating to the wedding. In return, the groom-to-be (Stephen Scott) promised to
transfer a one-half interest in the real property that was to be the marital abode. Then the
couple broke their engagement, and the wedding was canceled. By this time, DeFina had
already incurred $16,000 in wedding expenses. Given that the wedding was canceled, did
DeFina have any claim on Scott's property? Scott claimed that she did not because their
agreement assumed that they would marry. Furthermore, Scott maintained that traditionally
the bride and/or her family pay the wedding expenses anyway.

When this question came before a New York court, the court first noted that women are
usually the economic losers in broken engagements. Not only have they traditionally had to
bear the wedding expenses, but under the laws of some states, they are also required to
return the engagement ring. The court, referring to this "regime" as "both unequal and unjustified," decided that contract principles should apply. The court pointed out that Scott and
DeFina were "well-established professional adults" who formed clear plans regarding their
engagement and their eventual marriage. Indeed, Scott was an attorney who had been married twice before. Thus, the court concluded that DeFina had a lien (a claim—see Chapter 23)
on Scott's property in the amount of $16,000.[15]

▣

Contracts for the Sale of Goods

The Uniform Commercial Code (UCC) includes Statute of Frauds provisions that require
written evidence of a contract. Section 2–201 contains the major provision, which generally requires a writing or memorandum for the sale of goods priced at $500 or more under
the UCC (see Chapter 15). A writing that will satisfy the UCC requirement need only state

---

15. *DeFina v. Scott*, 195 Misc.2d 75, 755 N.Y.S.2d 587 (N.Y.Sup. 2003).

the quantity term; other terms agreed on need not be stated "accurately" in the writing, as long as they adequately reflect both parties' intentions. The contract will not be enforceable, however, for any quantity greater than that set forth in the writing. In addition, the writing must be signed by the person against whom enforcement is sought. Beyond these two requirements, the writing need not designate the buyer or the seller, the terms of payment, or the price. (See this chapter's *Beyond Our Borders* feature to learn whether other countries have requirements similar to those in the Statute of Frauds.)

Exceptions to the Statute of Frauds

Exceptions to the applicability of the Statute of Frauds are made in certain situations. We describe those situations here.

Partial Performance   In cases involving oral contracts for the transfer of interests in land, if the purchaser has paid part of the price, taken possession, and made valuable improvements to the property, and if the parties cannot be returned to their positions prior to the contract, a court may grant *specific performance* (performance of the contract according to its precise terms). Whether a court will enforce an oral contract for an interest in land when partial performance has taken place is usually determined by the degree of injury that would be suffered if the court chose *not* to enforce the oral contract. In some states, mere reliance on certain types of oral contracts is enough to remove them from the Statute of Frauds.

Under the UCC, an oral contract for goods priced at $500 or more is enforceable to the extent that a seller accepts payment or a buyer accepts delivery of the goods.[16]

ON THE WEB

The online version of UCC Section 2–201 on the Statute of Frauds includes links to definitions of certain terms used in the section. To access this text, go to

www.law.cornell.edu/ucc/2/2-201.html.

---

16. UCC 2–201(3)(c). See Chapter 15.

■EXAMPLE 11.17 If the president of Ajax Corporation orders by telephone thirty crates of bleach from Cloney, Inc., and repudiates the contract after ten crates have been delivered and accepted, Cloney can enforce the contract to the extent of the ten crates accepted by Ajax. ■

The existence and extent of a contract to supply computer kiosks for use in school cafeterias was in dispute in the following case.

CASE 11.2   **School-Link Technologies, Inc. v. Applied Resources, Inc.**

United States District Court, District of Kansas, 471 F.Supp.2d 1101 (2007).

FACTS Applied Resources, Inc. (ARI), makes computer hardware for point-of-sale systems: kiosks that consist of computers encased in chassis on which card readers or other payment devices are mounted. School-Link Technologies, Inc. (SLT), sells food-service technology to schools. In August 2003, the New York City Department of Education (NYCDOE) asked SLT to propose a cafeteria payment system that included kiosks. SLT asked ARI to participate in a pilot project, orally promising ARI that it would be the exclusive supplier of as many as 1,500 kiosks if NYCDOE awarded the contract to SLT. ARI agreed. SLT intended to cut ARI out of the deal, however, and told NYCDOE that SLT would be making its own kiosks. Meanwhile, SLT paid ARI in advance for a certain number of goods, but insisted on onerous terms for a written contract to which ARI would not agree. ARI suspended production of the prepaid items and refused to refund over $55,000 of SLT's funds. SLT filed a suit in a federal district court against ARI. ARI responded in part with a counterclaim for breach of contract, asserting that SLT failed to use ARI as an exclusive supplier as promised. ARI sought the expenses it incurred for the pilot project and the amount of profit that it would have realized on the entire deal. SLT filed a motion for summary judgment on this claim.

ISSUE Was the oral agreement for the kiosks enforceable to the extent to which it had been performed?

DECISION Yes. The court denied SLT's motion for summary judgment on ARI's counterclaim for breach of contract "with respect to goods which SLT already received and accepted, i.e., the goods for the pilot program with the NYCDOE."

REASON The court acknowledged that, according to the Uniform Commercial Code, a contract for a sale of goods for a price of $500 or more generally must be in writing and must be signed by the party against whom enforcement is sought. The court reasoned that "[b]ecause the NYCDOE contract undisputedly involved the sale of goods in excess of $500, the parties' oral contract that ARI would be the exclusive supplier of kiosks for the project is not enforceable in the absence of an applicable exception to this general rule." Under the partial performance exception to the rule, an oral contract for a sale of goods over $500 that would otherwise be unenforceable for the lack of a writing is enforceable to the extent that the seller delivers the goods and the buyer accepts them. In that situation, the performance serves as a substitute for the required writing. Thus, in this case, the court concluded that the alleged oral contract between SLT and ARI, to the effect that ARI would be the exclusive supplier of kiosks for SLT's contract with NYCDOE, was enforceable to the extent that ARI had delivered the kiosks for the pilot project and SLT had accepted them. The court added, however, that "the remaining aspect of that claim is barred by the [S]tatute of [F]rauds."

 FOR CRITICAL ANALYSIS–Social Consideration *Could ARI successfully assert a claim against SLT based on fraudulent misrepresentation? Explain.*

■

Admissions   In some states, if a party against whom enforcement of an oral contract is sought admits in pleadings, testimony, or otherwise in court proceedings that a contract for sale was made, the contract will be enforceable.[17] A contract subject to the UCC will be enforceable, but only to the extent of the quantity admitted.[18] **■EXAMPLE 11.18** Suppose

---

17. *Restatement (Second) of Contracts*, Section 133.
18. UCC 2–201(3)(b). See Chapter 15.

that the president of Ajax Corporation in the previous example admits under oath that an oral agreement was made with Cloney, Inc., for twenty crates of bleach. In this situation, even if Cloney, Inc., claims that Ajax had contracted for thirty crates, the agreement will be enforceable only to the extent admitted (for twenty rather than thirty crates of bleach). ▣

Promissory Estoppel   In some states, an oral contract that would otherwise be unenforceable under the Statute of Frauds may be enforced under the doctrine of promissory estoppel, or detrimental reliance. Recall from Chapter 9 that if a promisor makes a promise on which the promisee justifiably relies to her or his detriment, a court may *estop* (prevent) the promisor from denying that a contract exists. Section 139 of the *Restatement (Second) of Contracts* provides that in these circumstances, an oral promise can be enforceable, notwithstanding the Statute of Frauds, if the reliance was foreseeable to the person making the promise and if injustice can be avoided only by enforcing the promise.

Special Exceptions under the UCC   Special exceptions to the applicability of the Statute of Frauds exist for sales contracts. Oral contracts for customized goods may be enforced in certain circumstances. Another exception has to do with oral contracts between merchants that have been confirmed in writing. We will examine these exceptions in Chapter 15. Exhibit 11–3 graphically summarizes the types of contracts that fall under the Statute of Frauds and the various exceptions that apply.

ON THE WEB

For information on the *Restatements of the Law,* including the *Restatement (Second) of Contracts,* go to the American Law Institute's Web site at

www.ali.org.

THE STATUTE OF FRAUDS—SUFFICIENCY OF THE WRITING

A written contract will satisfy the writing requirement of the Statute of Frauds. A *written memorandum* (written evidence of the oral contract) signed by the party against whom enforcement is sought will also satisfy the writing requirement.[19] The signature need not

---

19. As mentioned earlier, under the UCC's Statute of Frauds, a writing is required only for contracts for the sale of goods priced at $500 or more (see Chapter 15).

EXHIBIT 11–3 **Contracts Subject to the Statute of Frauds**

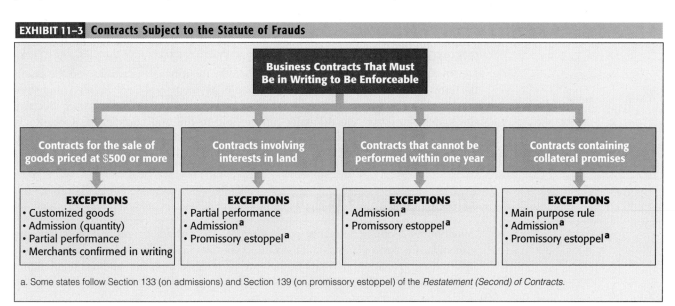

Business Contracts That Must Be in Writing to Be Enforceable			
Contracts for the sale of goods priced at $500 or more	**Contracts involving interests in land**	**Contracts that cannot be performed within one year**	**Contracts containing collateral promises**
EXCEPTIONS	**EXCEPTIONS**	**EXCEPTIONS**	**EXCEPTIONS**
• Customized goods • Admission (quantity) • Partial performance • Merchants confirmed in writing	• Partial performance • Admission[a] • Promissory estoppel[a]	• Admission[a] • Promissory estoppel[a]	• Main purpose rule • Admission[a] • Promissory estoppel[a]

a. Some states follow Section 133 (on admissions) and Section 139 (on promissory estoppel) of the *Restatement (Second) of Contracts.*

be placed at the end of the document but can be anywhere in the writing; it can even be initials rather than the full name. (See the *Application* feature at the end of this chapter for suggestions on how to prevent problems with oral contracts.)

A significant issue in today's business world has to do with how "signatures" can be created and verified on electronic contracts and other documents. We will examine electronic signatures in Chapter 14.

What Constitutes a Writing?

A writing can consist of any confirmation, invoice, sales slip, check, fax, or e-mail—or such items in combination. The written contract need not consist of a single document to constitute an enforceable contract. One document may incorporate another document by expressly referring to it. Several documents may form a single contract if they are physically attached, such as by staple, paper clip, or glue. Several documents may form a single contract even if they are only placed in the same envelope.

EXAMPLE 11.19 Sam orally agrees to sell some land next to a shopping mall to Terry. Sam gives Terry an unsigned memo that contains a legal description of the property, and Terry gives Sam an unsigned first draft of their contract. Sam sends Terry a signed letter that refers to the memo and to the first and final drafts of the contract. Terry sends Sam an unsigned copy of the final draft of the contract with a signed check stapled to it. Together, the documents can constitute a writing sufficient to satisfy the Statute of Frauds and bind both parties to the terms of the contract as evidenced by the writings. ■

What Must Be Contained in the Writing?

A memorandum evidencing the oral contract need only contain the essential terms of the contract. Under most provisions of the Statute of Frauds, the writing must name the parties and identify the subject matter, consideration, and quantity. With respect to contracts for the sale of land, some states require that the memorandum also set forth the essential terms of the contract, such as location and price, with sufficient clarity to allow the terms to be determined from the memo itself, without reference to any outside sources.[20] Under the UCC, in regard to the sale of goods, the writing need only state the quantity and be signed by the party against whom enforcement is sought.

Because only the party against whom enforcement is sought must have signed the writing, a contract may be enforceable by one of its parties but not by the other. **EXAMPLE 11.20** Rock orally agrees to buy Betty Devlin's lake house and lot for $350,000. Devlin writes Rock a letter confirming the sale by identifying the parties and the essential terms of the sales contract—price, method of payment, and legal address—and signs the letter. Devlin has made a written memorandum of the oral land contract. Because she signed the letter, she normally can be held to the oral contract by Rock. Rock, however, because he has not signed or entered into a written contract or memorandum, can plead the Statute of Frauds as a defense, and Devlin cannot enforce the contract against him. ■

THE PAROL EVIDENCE RULE

Sometimes, a written contract does not include—or contradicts—an oral understanding reached by the parties before or at the time of contracting. For example, suppose a person signs a lease agreement that says no pets are allowed because the landlord orally represented at the time of the lease contract that tenants were allowed to have cats. Can the

---

20. *Rhodes v. Wilkins*, 83 N.M. 782, 498 P.2d 311 (1972).

tenant have a cat despite what the lease agreement says? In determining the outcome of such disputes, the courts look to a common law rule governing the admissibility in court of oral evidence, or *parol evidence.*

Under the **parol evidence rule,** if a court finds that a written contract represents the complete and final statement of the parties' agreement, then it will not allow either party to present parol evidence (testimony or other evidence of communications between the parties that are not contained in the contract itself). In other words, a party cannot introduce in court evidence of the parties' prior negotiations, prior agreements, or contemporaneous oral agreements if that evidence contradicts or varies the terms of the parties' written contract.[21]

Does a football team's agreement with its fans to sell "stadium builder licenses" (SBLs) for seats represent the parties' entire contract, or can an SBL brochure explain or vary the agreement? That was the question in the following case.

PAROL EVIDENCE RULE
A substantive rule of contracts, as well as a procedural rule of evidence, under which a court will not receive into evidence the parties' prior negotiations, prior agreements, or contemporaneous oral agreements if that evidence contradicts or varies the terms of the parties' written contract.

---

21. *Restatement (Second) of Contracts,* Section 213.

CASE 11.3 **Yocca v. Pittsburgh Steelers Sports, Inc.**

Supreme Court of Pennsylvania, 578 Pa. 479, 854 A.2d 425 (2004).

FACTS In October 1998, Pittsburgh Steelers Sports, Inc., and others (collectively, the Steelers) sent Ronald Yocca a brochure that advertised a new stadium to be built for the Pittsburgh Steelers football team. The brochure publicized the opportunity to buy stadium builder licenses (SBLs), which grant the right to buy annual season tickets to the games. Prices varied, depending on the seats' locations, which were indicated by small diagrams. Yocca applied for an SBL, listing his seating preferences. The Steelers sent him a letter notifying him of the section in which his seat was located. A diagram that was included with the letter showed different parameters of the seating section than shown in the brochure's diagrams. The Steelers also sent Yocca documents setting out the terms of the SBL and requiring his signature. These documents included a clause that read, "This Agreement contains the entire agreement of the parties." Yocca signed the documents, and the Steelers told him the specific location of his seat. When he arrived at the stadium, however, the seat was not where he expected it to be. Yocca and other SBL buyers filed a suit in a Pennsylvania state court against the Steelers, alleging, among other things, breach of contract. The court ordered the dismissal of the complaint. The plaintiffs appealed to a state intermediate appellate court, which reversed this order. The defendants appealed to the state supreme court.

ISSUE Did the documents that the Steelers sent to Yocca setting forth the terms of the SBL constitute the parties' entire agreement and preclude the introduction of parol evidence?

DECISION Yes. The Pennsylvania Supreme Court reversed the lower court's judgment and ruled in favor of the Steelers.

REASON The state supreme court held that the SBL documents constituted the parties' entire contract and under the parol evidence rule could not be supplemented by previous negotiations or agreements. Because the plaintiffs' complaint was based on the claim that the defendants violated the terms of the brochure, and the brochure was not part of the contract, the complaint was properly dismissed. The court explained that "the SBL Brochure did not represent a promise by the Steelers to sell SBLs to Appellees. Rather, the Brochure was merely an offer by the Steelers to sell Appellees the right to be assigned an unspecified seat in an unspecified section of the new stadium and the right to receive a contract to buy an SBL for that later-assigned seat. * * * [T]he SBL Agreement clearly represented the parties' contract concerning the sale of SBLs. Unlike the SBL Brochure, the SBL Agreement reflected a promise by the Steelers to actually sell Appellees a specific number of SBL seats in a specified section. Furthermore, the SBL Agreement * * * explicitly stated that it represented the parties' entire contract regarding the sale of SBLs."

WHAT IF THE FACTS WERE DIFFERENT?
Suppose that the Steelers had not sent Yocca a diagram with the letter notifying him of his seat's section and that the SBL documents had not included a clause stating that the documents contained the entire agreement of the parties. Would the result have been different? Why or why not?

Exceptions to the Parol Evidence Rule

Because of the rigidity of the parol evidence rule, courts make several exceptions. These exceptions include the following:

1 Evidence of a *subsequent modification* of a written contract can be introduced in court. Keep in mind that the oral modifications may not be enforceable if they come under the Statute of Frauds—for example, if they increase the price of the goods for sale to $500 or more or increase the term for performance to more than one year. Also, oral modifications will not be enforceable if the original contract provides that any modification must be in writing.[22]

2 Oral evidence can be introduced in all cases to show that the contract was voidable or void (for example, induced by mistake, fraud, or misrepresentation). In this situation, if deception led one of the parties to agree to the terms of a written contract, oral evidence indicating fraud should not be excluded. Courts frown on bad faith and are quick to allow the introduction at trial of parol evidence when it establishes fraud.

3 When the terms of a written contract are ambiguous, evidence is admissible to show the meaning of the terms.

4 Evidence is admissible when the written contract is incomplete in that it lacks one or more of the essential terms. The courts allow evidence to "fill in the gaps" in the contract.

5 Under the UCC, evidence can be introduced to explain or supplement a written contract by showing a prior dealing, course of performance, or usage of trade.[23] We discuss these terms in further detail in Chapter 15, in the context of sales contracts. Here, it is sufficient to say that when buyers and sellers deal with each other over extended periods of time, certain customary practices develop. These practices are often overlooked in the writing of the contract, so courts allow the introduction of evidence to show how the parties have acted in the past. Usage of trade—practices and customs generally followed in a particular industry—can also shed light on the meaning of certain contract provisions, and thus evidence of trade usage may be admissible.

6 The parol evidence rule does not apply if the existence of the entire written contract is subject to an orally agreed-on condition. Proof of the condition does not alter or modify the written terms but affects the *enforceability* of the written contract. **■EXAMPLE 11.21** Jelek orally agrees to purchase Armand's car for $8,000, but only if Jelek's mechanic, Frank, inspects the car and approves of the purchase. Frank cannot do an inspection for another week, and Armand is leaving town for the weekend. Jelek wants to use the car right away, so he drafts a contract of sale that does not include the agreed-on condition of a mechanical inspection. Both parties sign the contract. The following week Frank, the mechanic, inspects the car but does not recommend its purchase. When Jelek does not buy the car, Armand sues him for breach of contract. In this case, Jelek's oral agreement did not alter or modify the terms of the written agreement but concerned whether the contract existed at all. Therefore, the parol evidence rule does not apply. ■

7 When an *obvious* or *gross* clerical (or typographic) error exists that clearly would not represent the agreement of the parties, parol evidence is admissible to correct the error. **■EXAMPLE 11.22** Sempter agrees to lease 1,000 square feet of office space from Stone Enterprises at the current monthly rate of $3 per square foot. The signed written lease provides for a monthly lease payment of $300 rather than the $3,000 agreed to by the parties. Because the error is obvious, Stone Enterprises would be allowed to admit parol evidence to correct the mistake. ■

NOTE The parol evidence rule and its exceptions relate to the rules concerning the *interpretation* of contracts.

---

22. UCC 2–209(2), (3). See Chapter 15.
23. UCC 1–205, 2–202. See Chapter 15.

Integrated Contracts

The determination of whether evidence will be allowed basically depends on whether the written contract is intended to be a complete and final statement of the terms of the agreement. If it is so intended, it is referred to as an **integrated contract,** and extraneous evidence (evidence from outside the contract) is excluded.

An integrated contract can be either completely or partially integrated. If it contains all of the terms of the parties' agreement, then it is completely integrated. If it contains only some of the terms that the parties agreed on and not others, it is partially integrated. If the contract is only partially integrated, evidence of consistent additional terms is admissible to supplement the written agreement.[24] Note that for both completely and partially integrated contracts, courts exclude any evidence that *contradicts* the writing and allow parol evidence only to add to the terms of a partially integrated contract. Exhibit 11–4 illustrates the relationship between integrated contracts and the parol evidence rule.

INTEGRATED CONTRACT
A written contract that constitutes the final expression of the parties' agreement. If a contract is integrated, evidence extraneous to the contract that contradicts or alters the meaning of the contract in any way is inadmissible.

---

24. *Restatement (Second) of Contracts,* Section 216.

EXHIBIT 11-4 **Parol Evidence Rule**

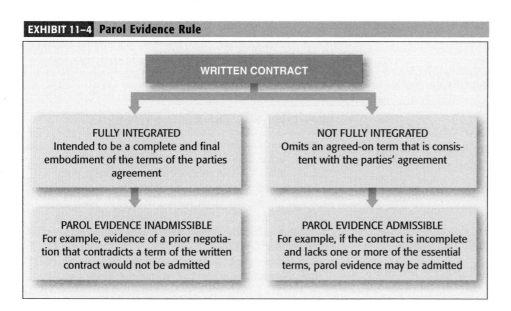

REVIEWING **Defenses to Contract Enforceability**

Charter Golf, Inc., manufactures and sells golf apparel and supplies. Ken Odin had worked as a Charter sales representative for six months when he was offered a position with a competing firm. Charter's president, Jerry Montieth, offered Odin a 10 percent commission "for the rest of his life" if Ken would turn down the offer and stay on with Charter. He also promised that Odin would not be fired unless he was dishonest. Odin turned down the competitor's offer and stayed with Charter. Three years later, Charter fired Odin for no reason. Odin sued, alleging breach of contract. Using the information presented in the chapter, answer the following questions.

1 Would a court likely decide that Montieth's employment contract falls within the Statute of Frauds? Why or why not?

2 Assume that the court does find that the contract falls within the Statute of Frauds and that the state in which the court sits recognizes every exception to the Statute of Frauds discussed in the chapter. What exception provides Odin with the best chance of enforcing the oral contract in this situation?

(Continued)

3 Now suppose that Montieth had taken out a pencil, written "10 percent for life" on the back of a register receipt, and handed it to Odin. Would this satisfy the Statute of Frauds? Why or why not?

4 Assume that Odin had signed a written employment contract at the time he was hired to work for Charter, but it was not completely integrated. Would a court allow Odin to present parol evidence of Montieth's subsequent promises?

As a general rule, most business contracts should be in writing even when they fall outside the Statute of Frauds. Businesspersons frequently make oral contracts over the telephone, however, particularly when the parties have done business with each other in the past.

chant receiving the confirmation objects in writing within ten days of its receipt. This law (discussed in Chapter 15) clearly points out the need for the merchant receiving the confirmation to review it carefully to ascertain that the confirmation conforms to the oral contract. If the writing does not so conform, the merchant can object in writing (the Statute of Frauds still applies), and the parties can resolve misunderstandings without legal liability. If the merchant fails to object, the written confirmation can be used as evidence to prove the terms of the oral contract. Note, however, that this ten-day rule does not apply to contracts for interests in realty or for services, to which the UCC does not apply.

Confirm the Agreement in Writing

Any time an oral contract is made, it is advisable for one of the parties to send either a written memorandum or a confirmation of the oral agreement by fax or e-mail to the other party. This accomplishes two purposes: (1) it demonstrates the party's clear intention to form a contract, and (2) it provides the terms of the contract as that party understood them. If the party receiving the memorandum or confirmation then disagrees with the terms as described, the issue can be addressed before performance begins.

Special Rules for Contracts between Merchants

What about the sale of goods between merchants? Under the UCC, written confirmation received by one merchant removes the Statute of Frauds requirement of a writing unless the mer-

CHECKLIST FOR THE BUSINESSPERSON

1 When feasible, use written contracts.
2 If you enter into an oral contract over the telephone, fax or e-mail a written confirmation outlining your understanding of the oral contract.
3 If you receive the other party's written or faxed confirmation, read it carefully to make sure that it states the terms already agreed to in the oral contract, as you understand them.
4 If you have any objections, notify the other party of these objections, in writing, within ten days.

* This Application is not meant to substitute for the services of an attorney who is licensed to practice law in your state.

CHAPTER SUMMARY Defenses to Contract Enforceability

GENUINENESS OF ASSENT

Mistakes (See pages 302–305.)	1. *Unilateral*—Generally, the mistaken party is bound by the contract *unless* (a) the other party knows or should have known of the mistake or (b) the mistake is an inadvertent mathematical error—such as an error in addition or subtraction—committed without gross negligence.

CHAPTER SUMMARY Defenses to Contract Enforceability–Continued

Mistakes—Continued	2. *Bilateral (mutual)*—When both parties are mistaken about the same material fact, such as identity, either party can avoid the contract.
Fraudulent Misrepresentation (See pages 305–309.)	When fraud occurs, usually the innocent party can enforce or avoid the contract. The elements necessary to establish fraud are as follows: 1. A misrepresentation of a material fact must occur. 2. There must be an intent to deceive. 3. The innocent party must justifiably rely on the misrepresentation.
Undue Influence (See page 309.)	Undue influence arises from special relationships, such as fiduciary or confidential relationships, in which one party's free will has been overcome by the undue influence exerted by the other party. Usually, the contract is voidable.
Duress (See pages 309–310.)	Duress is the tactic of forcing a party to enter a contract under the fear of a threat—for example, the threat of violence or serious economic loss. The party forced to enter the contract can rescind the contract.

FORM

The Statute of Frauds—Requirement of a Writing (See pages 310–317.)	1. *Applicability*—The following types of contracts fall under the Statute of Frauds and must be in writing to be enforceable:
	   a. Contracts involving interests in land—The statute applies to any contract for an interest in realty, such as a sale, a lease, or a mortgage.
	   b. Contracts that cannot by their terms be performed within one year—The statute applies only to contracts that are objectively impossible to perform fully within one year from (the day after) the contract's formation.
	   c. Collateral promises—The statute applies only to express contracts made between the guarantor and the creditor that make the guarantor secondarily liable. Exception: the main purpose rule.
	   d. Promises made in consideration of marriage—The statute applies to promises to make a monetary payment or give property in consideration of a promise to marry and to prenuptial agreements made in consideration of marriage.
	   e. Contracts for the sale of goods priced at $500 or more—See the Statute of Frauds provision in Section 2–201 of the Uniform Commercial Code (UCC).
	 2. *Exceptions*—Partial performance, admissions, and promissory estoppel.

The Statute of Frauds—Sufficiency of the Writing (See pages 317–318.)	To constitute an enforceable contract under the Statute of Frauds, a writing must be signed by the party against whom enforcement is sought, name the parties, identify the subject matter, and state with reasonable certainty the essential terms of the contract. In a sale of land, the price and a description of the property may need to be stated with sufficient clarity to allow them to be determined without reference to outside sources. Under the UCC, a contract for a sale of goods is not enforceable beyond the quantity of goods shown in the contract.
The Parol Evidence Rule (See pages 318–321.)	The parol evidence rule prohibits the introduction at trial of evidence of the parties' prior negotiations, prior agreements, or contemporaneous oral agreements that contradicts or varies the terms of the parties' written contract. The written contract is assumed to be the complete embodiment of the parties' agreement. Exceptions are made in the following circumstances: 1. To show that the contract was subsequently modified. 2. To show that the contract was voidable or void. 3. To clarify the meaning of ambiguous terms.

(Continued)

CHAPTER SUMMARY Defenses to Contract Enforceability—Continued

The Parol Evidence Rule—Continued

4. To clarify the terms of the contract when the written contract lacks one or more of its essential terms.

5. Under the UCC, to explain the meaning of contract terms in light of a prior dealing, course of performance, or usage of trade.

6. To show that the entire contract is subject to an orally agreed-on condition.

7. When an obvious clerical or typographic error was made.

FOR REVIEW

Answers for the even-numbered questions in this For Review *section can be found in Appendix E at the end of this text.*

1 In what types of situations might genuineness of assent to a contract's terms be lacking?

2 What is the difference between a mistake of value or quality and a mistake of fact?

3 What elements must exist for fraudulent misrepresentation to occur?

4 What contracts must be in writing to be enforceable?

5 What is parol evidence? When is it admissible to clarify the terms of a written contract?

 Thomson NOW! **The following multiple-choice question is representative of the types of questions available in one of the four sections of ThomsonNOW for** *Business Law Today.* **ThomsonNOW also provides feedback for each response option, whether correct or incorrect, and refers to the location within the chapter where the correct answer can be found.**

Misrepresentations of material facts can be made by

a actions alone.

b words alone.

c words or actions.

d writings alone.

■

QUESTIONS AND CASE PROBLEMS

 **HYPOTHETICAL SCENARIOS**

11.1 Genuineness of Assent. Jerome is an elderly man who lives with his nephew, Philip. Jerome is totally dependent on Philip's support. Philip tells Jerome that unless Jerome transfers a tract of land he owns to Philip for a price 30 percent below market value, Philip will no longer support and take care of him. Jerome enters into the contract. Discuss fully whether Jerome can set aside this contract.

11.2 Hypothetical Question with Sample Answer. Gemma promises a local hardware store that she will pay for a lawn mower that her brother is purchasing on credit if the brother fails to pay the debt. Must this promise be in writing to be enforceable? Why or why not?

 **For a sample answer to Question 11.2, go to Appendix F at the end of this text.**

11.3 Fraudulent Misrepresentation. Larry offered to sell Stanley his car and told Stanley that the car had been driven only 25,000 miles and had never been in an accident. Stanley hired Cohen, a mechanic, to appraise the condition of the car, and Cohen said that the car probably had at least 50,000 miles on it and probably had been in an accident. In spite of this information, Stanley still thought the car would be a good buy for the price, so he purchased it. Later, when the car developed numerous mechanical problems, Stanley sought to rescind the contract on the basis of Larry's fraudulent misrepresentation of the auto's condition. Will Stanley be able to rescind his contract? Discuss.

■

CASE PROBLEMS

11.4 Fraudulent Misrepresentation. William Meade, Leland Stewart, Doug Vierkant, and David Girard applied for, and were offered, jobs at the El-Jay Division of Cedarapids, Inc., in Eugene, Oregon. During the interviews, each applicant asked about El-Jay's future. They were told, among other things, that El-Jay was a stable company with few downsizings and layoffs, sales were up and were expected to increase, and production was expanding. Cedarapids management had already planned to close El-Jay, however. Each applicant signed an at-will employment agreement. To take the job at El-Jay, each new employee either quit the job he was doing or passed up other employment opportunities. Each employee and his family then moved to Eugene. When El-Jay closed soon after they started their new jobs, Meade and the others filed a suit in a federal district court against Cedarapids, alleging, in part, fraudulent misrepresentation. Were the plaintiffs justified in relying on the statements made to them during their job interviews? Explain. [*Meade v. Cedarapids, Inc.*, 164 F.3d 1218 (9th Cir. 1999)]

11.5 Oral Contracts. Robert Pinto, doing business as Pinto Associates, hired Richard MacDonald as an independent contractor in March 1992. The parties orally agreed on the terms of employment, including payment to MacDonald of a share of the company's income, but they did not put anything in writing. In March 1995, MacDonald quit. Pinto then told MacDonald that he was entitled to $9,602.17—25 percent of the difference between the accounts receivable and the accounts payable as of MacDonald's last day. MacDonald disagreed and demanded more than $83,500—25 percent of the revenue from all invoices, less the cost of materials and outside processing, for each of the years that he worked for Pinto. Pinto refused. MacDonald filed a suit in a Connecticut state court against Pinto, alleging breach of contract. In Pinto's response and at the trial, he testified that the parties had an oral contract under which MacDonald was entitled to 25 percent of the difference between accounts receivable and payable as of the date of MacDonald's termination. Did the parties have an enforceable contract? How should the court rule, and why? [*MacDonald v. Pinto*, 62 Conn.App. 317, 771 A.2d 156 (2001)]

11.6 Case Problem with Sample Answer. Novell, Inc., owned the source code for DR DOS, a computer operating system that Microsoft Corp. targeted with anticompetitive practices in the early 1990s. Novell worried that if it filed a suit, Microsoft would retaliate with further unfair practices. Consequently, Novell sold DR DOS to Caldera, Inc., the predecessor in interest to Canopy Group. The purposes of the sale were to obligate Canopy to bring an action against Microsoft and to allow Novell to share in the recovery without revealing its role. Novell and Canopy signed two documents: a contract of sale, obligating Canopy to pay $400,000 for rights to the source code, and a temporary license, obligating Canopy to pay at least $600,000 in royalties, which

included a percentage of any recovery from the suit. Canopy settled the dispute with Microsoft, deducted its expenses, and paid Novell its percentage. Novell filed a suit in a Utah state court against Canopy, alleging breach of contract for Canopy's deduction of expenses. Canopy responded that it could show that the parties had an oral agreement on this point. On what basis might the court refuse to consider this evidence? Is that the appropriate course in this case? Explain. [*Novell, Inc. v. Canopy Group, Inc.*, 2004 UT App. 162, 92 P.3d 768 (2004)]

 **After you have answered Problem 11.6, compare your answer with the sample answer given on the Web site that** accompanies this text. Go to www.thomsonedu.com/westbuslaw/blt, select "Chapter 11," and click on "Case Problem with Sample Answer."

11.7 The Parol Evidence Rule. Carlin Krieg owned a dairy farm in St. Joe, Indiana, that was appraised at $154,000 in December 1997. In August 1999, Krieg told Donald Hieber that he intended to sell the farm for $106,000. Hieber offered to buy it. Krieg also told Hieber that he wanted to retain a "right of residency" for life in the farm. In October, Krieg and Hieber executed a "Purchase Agreement" that provided that Krieg "shall transfer full and complete possession" of the farm "subject to [his] right of residency." The agreement also contained an integration clause that stated "there are no conditions, representations, warranties, or agreements not stated in this instrument." In November 2000, the house was burned in a fire, rendering it unlivable. Hieber filed an insurance claim for the damage and received the proceeds, but he did not fix the house. Krieg filed a suit in an Indiana state court against Hieber, alleging breach of contract. Is there any basis on which the court can consider evidence regarding the parties' negotiations prior to their agreement for the sale of the farm? Explain. [*Krieg v. Hieber*, 802 N.E.2d 938 (Ind.App. 2004)]

11.8 Fraudulent Misrepresentation. According to the student handbook at Cleveland Chiropractic College (CCC) in Missouri, *academic misconduct* includes "selling . . . any copy of any material intended to be used as an instrument of academic evaluation in advance of its initial administration." Leonard Verni was enrolled at CCC in Dr. Aleksandr Makarov's dermatology class. Before the first examination, Verni was reported to be selling copies of the test. CCC investigated and concluded that Verni had committed academic misconduct. Verni was dismissed from CCC, which informed him of his right to an appeal. According to the handbook, at the hearing on appeal a student could have an attorney or other advisor, present witnesses' testimony and other evidence, and "question any testimony . . . against him/her." At his hearing, however, Verni did not bring his attorney, present evidence on his behalf, nor question any adverse witnesses. When the dismissal was upheld, Verni filed a suit in a Missouri state court against CCC and others, claiming, in part, fraudulent misrepresentation. Verni argued that because he "relied" on the handbook's "representation" that CCC would follow its appeal procedure, he was unable to properly refute the charges against him. Can Verni succeed with this argument? Explain. [*Verni v. Cleveland Chiropractic College,* 212 S.W.3d 150 (Mo. 2007)]

11.9 **A Question of Ethics.** *The law firm of Traystman, Coric and Keramidas represented Andrew Daigle in a divorce in Norwich, Connecticut. Scott McGowan, an attorney with the firm, handled the proceedings' two-day trial. After the first day of the trial, McGowan told Daigle to sign a promissory note in the amount of $26,973 (the amount that Daigle then owed to the firm). If Daigle did not sign the note, McGowan said that he would withdraw from the case, forcing Daigle to*

get another attorney or continue to trial by himself. Daigle said that he wanted another attorney, Martin Rutchik, to see the note. McGowan urged Daigle to sign it and assured him that a copy would be sent to Rutchik. Feeling that he had no other choice, Daigle signed the note. When he did not pay, the law firm filed a suit in a Connecticut state court against him. Daigle asserted that the note was unenforceable because he had signed it under duress. [*Traystman, Coric and Keramidas v. Daigle, 84 Conn.App. 843, 855 A.2d 996 (2004)*]

1 What are the requirements for the use of duress as a defense to a contract? Are the requirements met here?

2 What might the law firm argue in response to Daigle's assertion? Did the law firm act unethically? Explain.

 # CRITICAL THINKING AND WRITING ASSIGNMENTS

11.10 Critical Legal Thinking. Describe the types of individuals who might be capable of exerting undue influence on others.

11.11 **Video Question.** Go to this text's Web site at **www.thomsonedu.com/westbuslaw/blt** and select "Chapter 11." Click on "Video Questions" and view the video titled *Mistake.* Then answer the following questions.

1 What kind of mistake is involved in the dispute shown in the video (bilateral or unilateral, mistake of fact or mistake of value)?

2 According to the chapter, in what two situations would the supermarket be able to rescind a contract to sell peppers to Melnick at the incorrectly advertised price?

3 Does it matter if the price that was advertised was a reasonable price for the peppers? Why or why not?

ONLINE ACTIVITIES

PRACTICAL INTERNET EXERCISES

Go to this text's Web site at **www.thomsonedu.com/westbuslaw/blt**, select "Chapter 11," and click on "Practical Internet Exercises." There you will find the following Internet research exercises that you can perform to learn more about the topics covered in this chapter.

PRACTICAL INTERNET EXERCISE 11–1 LEGAL PERSPECTIVE—Promissory Estoppel and the Statute of Frauds

PRACTICAL INTERNET EXERCISE 11–2 MANAGEMENT PERSPECTIVE—Fraudulent Misrepresentation

PRACTICAL INTERNET EXERCISE 11–3 HISTORICAL PERSPECTIVE—The English Act for the Prevention of Frauds and Perjuries

BEFORE THE TEST

Go to this text's Web site at **www.thomsonedu.com/westbuslaw/blt**, select "Chapter 11," and click on "Interactive Quizzes." You will find a number of interactive questions relating to this chapter.

CHAPTER 12
Third Party Rights and Discharge

LEARNING OBJECTIVES

AFTER READING THIS CHAPTER, YOU SHOULD BE ABLE TO ANSWER THE FOLLOWING QUESTIONS:

1 What is the difference between an assignment and a delegation?

2 What rights can be assigned despite a contract clause expressly prohibiting assignment?

3 What factors indicate that a third party beneficiary is an intended beneficiary?

4 How are most contracts discharged?

5 What is a contractual condition, and how might a condition affect contractual obligations?

> **❝**The laws of a state change with the changing times.**❞**
>
> Aeschylus, 525–456 B.C.E.
> (Greek dramatist)

Because a contract is a private agreement between the parties who have entered into it, it is fitting that these parties alone should have rights and liabilities under the contract. This concept is referred to as **privity of contract,** and it establishes the basic principle that third parties have no rights in contracts to which they are not parties.

You may be convinced by now that for every rule of contract law, there is an exception. As times change, so must the laws, as indicated in the chapter-opening quotation. When justice cannot be served by adherence to a rule of law, exceptions to the rule must be made. In this chapter, we look at some exceptions to the rule of privity of contract. These exceptions include *assignments* and *delegations*, as well as *third party beneficiary contracts*. We also examine how contractual obligations can be *discharged*. Normally, contract discharge is accomplished by both parties performing the acts promised in the contract. In the latter part of this chapter, we look at the degree of performance required to discharge a contractual obligation, as well as at some other ways in which contract discharge can occur.

PRIVITY OF CONTRACT
The relationship that exists between the promisor and the promisee of a contract.

ASSIGNMENTS

In a bilateral contract, the two parties have corresponding rights and duties. One party has a *right* to require the other to perform some task, and the other has a *duty* to perform it. Sometimes, though, a party will transfer her or his rights under the contract to someone else. The transfer of contract *rights* to a third person is known as an **assignment.** (The transfer of contract duties is a *delegation*, as discussed later in this chapter.)

ASSIGNMENT
The act of transferring to another all or part of one's rights arising under a contract.

Assignments are important because they are utilized in much business financing. Lending institutions, such as banks, frequently assign the rights to receive payments under their loan contracts to other firms, which pay for those rights. If you obtain a loan from your local bank to purchase a car, you may later receive in the mail a notice stating that your bank has transferred (assigned) its rights to receive payments on the loan to another firm and that, when the time comes to repay your loan, you must make the payments to that other firm.

Lenders that make *mortgage loans* (loans to allow prospective home buyers to purchase land or a home) often assign their rights to collect the mortgage payments to a third party, such as GMAC Mortgage Corporation. Following an assignment, the home buyer is notified that future payments must be made to the third party, rather than to the original lender. Billions of dollars change hands daily in the business world in the form of assignments of rights in contracts.

Effect of an Assignment

ASSIGNOR
A party who transfers (assigns) his or her rights under a contract to another party (called the *assignee*).

ASSIGNEE
A party to whom the rights under a contract are transferred, or assigned.

OBLIGEE
One to whom an obligation is owed.

OBLIGOR
One who owes an obligation to another.

In an assignment, the party assigning the rights to a third party is known as the **assignor,** and the party receiving the rights is the **assignee.** Other traditional terminology used to describe the parties in assignment relationships are the **obligee** (the person to whom a duty, or obligation, is owed) and the **obligor** (the person who is obligated to perform the duty).

When rights under a contract are assigned unconditionally, the rights of the *assignor* (the party making the assignment) are extinguished.[1] The third party (the *assignee,* or the party receiving the assignment) has a right to demand performance from the other original party to the contract (the *obligor,* the person who is obligated to perform). ■**EXAMPLE 12.1** Brent (the obligor) owes Alex $1,000, and Alex, the obligee, assigns to Carmen the right to receive the $1,000 (thus, Alex is now the assignor). Here, a valid assignment of a debt exists. Carmen, the assignee, can enforce the contract against Brent, the obligor, if Brent fails to perform (pay the $1,000). ■ Exhibit 12–1 illustrates assignment relationships.

The assignee obtains only those rights that the assignor originally had. Also, the assignee's rights are subject to the defenses that the obligor has against the assignor.

---

1. *Restatement (Second) of Contracts,* Section 317.

EXHIBIT 12–1 **Assignment Relationships**

In the assignment relationship illustrated here, Alex assigns his *rights* under a contract that he made with Brent to a third party, Carmen. Alex thus becomes the *assignor* and Carmen the *assignee* of the contractual rights. Brent, the *obligor* (the party owing performance under the contract), now owes performance to Carmen instead of Alex. Alex's original contract rights are extinguished after assignment.

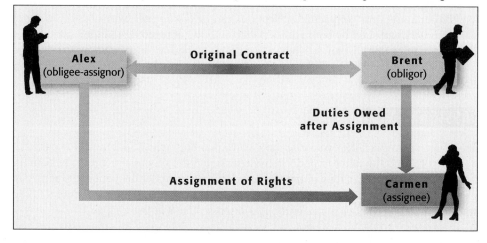

EXAMPLE 12.2 Brent owes Alex $1,000 under a contract in which Brent agreed to buy Alex's MacBook Pro laptop. Alex assigns his right to receive the $1,000 to Carmen. Brent, in deciding to purchase the laptop, relied on Alex's fraudulent misrepresentation that the computer had 2 gigabytes of memory. When Brent discovers that the computer has only 1 gigabyte of memory, he tells Alex that he is going to return the laptop and cancel the contract. Even though Alex has assigned his "right" to receive the $1,000 to Carmen, Brent need not pay Carmen the $1,000—Brent can raise the defense of Alex's fraudulent misrepresentation to avoid payment. ■

Rights That Cannot Be Assigned

As a general rule, all rights can be assigned. Exceptions are made, however, in the following special circumstances.

When a Statute Expressly Prohibits Assignment If a statute expressly prohibits assignment, the particular right in question cannot be assigned. **EXAMPLE 12.3** Marn is a new employee of CompuFuture, Inc. CompuFuture is an employer under workers' compensation statutes (see Chapter 33) in this state, so Marn is a covered employee. Marn has a relatively high-risk job. In need of a loan, she borrows from Stark, assigning to Stark all workers' compensation benefits due her should she be injured on the job. A state statute prohibits the assignment of *future* workers' compensation benefits, and thus such rights cannot be assigned. ■

When a Contract Is Personal in Nature When a contract is for personal services, the rights under the contract normally cannot be assigned unless all that remains is a monetary payment.[2] **EXAMPLE 12.4** Brent signs a contract to be a tutor for Alex's children. Alex then attempts to assign to Carmen his right to Brent's services. Carmen cannot enforce the contract against Brent. Brent may not like Carmen's children or for some other reason may not want to tutor them. Because personal services are unique to the person rendering them, rights to receive personal services cannot be assigned. ■

When an Assignment Will Significantly Change the Risk or Duties of the Obligor A right cannot be assigned if assignment will significantly increase or alter the risks or the duties of the obligor (the party owing performance under the contract).[3] **EXAMPLE 12.5** Alex has a hotel, and to insure it, he takes out a policy with Northwest Insurance Company. The policy insures against fire, theft, floods, and vandalism. Alex attempts to assign the insurance policy to Carmen, who also owns a hotel. The assignment is ineffective because it may substantially alter the insurance company's duty of performance and the risk that the company undertakes. An insurance company evaluates the particular risk of a certain party and tailors its policy to fit that risk. If the policy is assigned to a third party, the insurance risk is materially altered. ■

When the Contract Prohibits Assignment If a contract stipulates that the right cannot be assigned, then *ordinarily*

ON THE WEB

You can find a number of forms that can be used in the assignment of different types of contracts, at www.ilrg.com/forms/#transfers.

This site is maintained by the Internet Legal Research Group.

A music teacher instructs his pupil. Assuming that the boy's mother, Katherine, contracted with the teacher for his services, can Katherine assign the right to receive music lessons to another party? Why or why not? (Buccina Studios/PhotoDisc Green)

---

2. *Restatement (Second) of Contracts*, Sections 317 and 318.
3. See Section 2–210(2) of the Uniform Commercial Code (UCC).

it cannot be assigned. ▣EXAMPLE 12.6 Brent agrees to build a house for Alex. The contract between Brent and Alex states, "This contract cannot be assigned by Alex without Brent's consent. Any assignment without such consent renders this contract void, and all rights hereunder will thereupon terminate." Alex then assigns his rights to Carmen, without first obtaining Brent's consent. Carmen cannot enforce the contract against Brent. ▣ This rule has several exceptions:

1 A contract cannot prevent an assignment of the right to receive funds. This exception exists to encourage the free flow of funds and credit in modern business settings.

2 The assignment of ownership rights in real estate often cannot be prohibited because such a prohibition is contrary to public policy in most states. Prohibitions of this kind are called restraints against **alienation** (the voluntary transfer of land ownership).

3 The assignment of negotiable instruments (see Chapter 19) cannot be prohibited.

4 In a contract for the sale of goods, the right to receive damages for breach of contract or for payment of an account owed may be assigned even though the sales contract prohibits such an assignment.[4]

ALIENATION
The process of transferring land out of one's possession (thus "alienating" the land from oneself).

Notice of Assignment

Once a valid assignment of rights has been made to a third party, the third party should notify the obligor of the assignment (for example, in Exhibit 12–1 on page 328, Carmen should notify Brent). Giving notice is not legally necessary to establish the validity of the assignment because an assignment is effective immediately, whether or not notice is given. Two major problems arise, however, when notice of the assignment is *not* given to the obligor:

1 If the assignor assigns the same right to two different persons, the question arises as to which one has priority—that is, which one has the right to the performance by the obligor. Although the rule most often observed in the United States is that the first assignment in time is the first in right, some states follow the English rule, which basically gives priority to the first assignee who gives notice. ▣EXAMPLE 12.7 Brent owes Alex $5,000 on a contractual obligation. On May 1, Alex assigns this monetary claim to Carmen, but she does not give notice of the assignment to Brent. On June 1, for services Dorman has rendered to Alex, Alex assigns the same monetary claim (to collect $5,000 from Brent) to Dorman. Dorman immediately notifies Brent of the assignment. In the majority of states, Carmen would have priority because the assignment to her was first in time. In some states, however, Dorman would have priority because he gave first notice. ▣

2 Until the obligor has notice of an assignment, the obligor can discharge his or her obligation by performance to the assignor, and this performance constitutes a discharge to the assignee. Once the obligor receives proper notice, only performance to the assignee can discharge the obligor's obligations. ▣EXAMPLE 12.8 Suppose that Alex, in the above example, assigns to Carmen his right to collect $5,000 from Brent, and Carmen does not give notice to Brent. Brent subsequently pays Alex the $5,000. Although the assignment was valid, Brent's payment to Alex is a discharge of the debt, and Carmen's failure to notify Brent of the assignment causes her to lose the right to collect the $5,000 from Brent. (Note that Carmen still has a claim against Alex for the $5,000.) If Carmen had given Brent notice of the assignment, however, Brent's payment to Alex would not have discharged the debt. ▣

---

4. UCC 2–210(2).

In a business context, the importance of notifying the obligor (the party that is obligated to perform the duty) of an assignment cannot be overemphasized. Providing notice of assignment, though not legally required, is one of the best ways to avoid potential legal disputes over assignments. Whether the businessperson is the assignee or the assignor, she or he should inform the obligor of the assignment. As already described, an assignee who does not give notice may lose the right to performance, but failure to notify the obligor may have repercussions for the assignor as well. Consider what would happen if no notice is given by either the assignor or the assignee, and the obligor performs the duty for the assignor. In this situation, the assignee, to whom the right to receive performance was assigned, can sue the assignor for breach of contract. The assignor will also likely be involved in litigation if he or she has assigned a right to two different parties, which can happen when assigning rights that overlap somewhat (such as rights to receive profits from a given enterprise). Assignments of rights are extremely useful in business, but to prevent legal problems, businesspersons should be careful to assign the same rights only once and should always give the obligor notice of the assignment.

PREVENTING
LEGAL DISPUTES

DELEGATIONS

Just as a party can transfer rights to a third party through an assignment, a party can also transfer duties. Duties are not assigned, however; they are *delegated*. Normally, a **delegation of duties** does not relieve the party making the delegation (the **delegator**) of the obligation to perform in the event that the party to whom the duty has been delegated (the **delegatee**) fails to perform. No special form is required to create a valid delegation of duties. As long as the delegator expresses an intention to make the delegation, it is effective; the delegator need not even use the word *delegate*. Exhibit 12–2 graphically illustrates delegation relationships.

DELEGATION OF DUTIES
The act of transferring to another all or part of one's duties arising under a contract.

DELEGATOR
A party who transfers (delegates) her or his obligations under a contract to another party (called the *delegatee*).

DELEGATEE
A party to whom contractual obligations are transferred, or delegated.

EXHIBIT 12–2 Delegation Relationships

In the delegation relationship illustrated here, Brent delegates his *duties* under a contract that he made with Alex to a third party, Carmen. Brent thus becomes the *delegator* and Carmen the *delegatee* of the contractual duties. Carmen now owes performance of the contractual duties to Alex. Note that a delegation of duties normally does not relieve the delegator (Brent) of liability if the delegatee (Carmen) fails to perform the contractual duties.

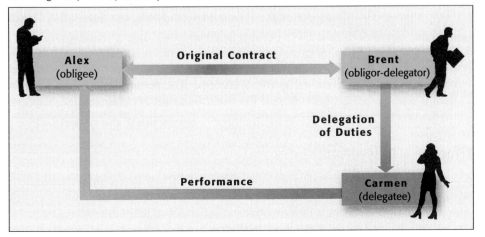

Duties That Cannot Be Delegated

As a general rule, any duty can be delegated. This rule has some exceptions, however. Delegation is prohibited in the following circumstances:

1 When performance depends on the personal skill or talents of the obligor.

2 When special trust has been placed in the obligor.

3 When performance by a third party will vary materially from that expected by the obligee (the one to whom performance is owed) under the contract.

4 When the contract expressly prohibits delegation.

The following examples will help to clarify the kinds of duties that can and cannot be delegated:

1 Brent contracts with Alex to tutor Alex in various aspects of financial underwriting and investment banking. Brent, an experienced businessperson known for his expertise in finance, delegates his duties to a third party, Carmen. This delegation is ineffective because Brent contracted to render a service that is founded on Brent's *expertise* and Alex placed *special trust* in Brent's teaching ability. The delegation changes Alex's expectancy under the contract.

2 Brent, a famous musician, contracts with Alex to *personally* perform at a concert. Then Brent receives a better offer elsewhere and delegates his duty to perform to another musician, Miles. Regardless of Miles's exceptional musical talents, the delegation is not effective without Alex's consent because the contract was for *personal* performance.

3 Brent, an accountant, contracts to perform annual audits of Alex's business records for the next five years. The contract states that Brent must provide the services himself and cannot delegate these duties to another. Two years later, Brent is busy on other projects and delegates his obligations to perform Alex's audit to Arianna, who is a certified public accountant at the same firm. This delegation is not effective because the contract *expressly prohibited* delegation.

4 Alex is a wealthy philanthropist who just created a charitable foundation. Alex has known Brent for twenty years and knows that Brent shares his beliefs on many humanitarian issues. He contracts with Brent to be in charge of allocating funds among various charitable causes. Six months later, Brent is experiencing health problems and delegates his duties to Drew. Alex does not approve of Drew as a replacement. In this situation, Alex can claim the delegation was not effective because it *materially altered his expectations* under the contract. Alex had reasonable expectations about the types of charities to which Brent would give the foundation's funds, and substituting Drew's performance materially changes those expectations.

5 Brent contracts with Alex to pick up and deliver heavy construction machinery to Alex's property. Brent delegates this duty to Carmen, who is in the business of delivering heavy machinery. This delegation is effective. The performance required is of a routine and nonpersonal nature, and the delegation does not change Alex's expectations under the contract.

Effect of a Delegation

If a delegation of duties is enforceable, the *obligee* (the one to whom performance is owed) must accept performance from the delegatee (the one to whom the duties are delegated). **■EXAMPLE 12.9** In the fifth example in the above list, Brent delegates his duty (to pick up and deliver heavy construction machinery to Alex's property) to Carmen. In that situation, Alex (the obligee) must accept performance from Carmen (the delegatee) because the delegation was effective. The obligee can legally refuse performance from the delegatee only if the duty is one that cannot be delegated. ▣

A valid delegation of duties does not relieve the delegator of obligations under the contract.[5] In the above example, if Carmen (the delegatee) fails to perform, Brent (the delegator) is still liable to Alex (the obligee). The obligee can also hold the delegatee liable if the delegatee made a promise of performance that will directly benefit the obligee. In this situation, there is an "assumption of duty" on the part of the delegatee, and breach of this duty makes the delegatee liable to the obligee. For example, if Carmen (the delegatee) promises Brent (the delegator), in a contract, to pick up and deliver the construction equipment to Alex's property but fails to do so, Alex (the obligee) can sue Brent, Carmen, or both. Although there are many exceptions, the general rule today is that the obligee can sue both the delegatee and the delegator.

The *Concept Summary* below summarizes the basic principles of the laws governing assignments and delegations.

"Assignment of All Rights"

Sometimes, a contract provides for an "assignment of all rights." The traditional view was that under this type of assignment, the assignee did not assume any duties. This view was based

COMPARE In an assignment, the assignor's original contract rights are extinguished after the assignment. In a delegation, the delegator remains liable for performance under the contract if the delegatee fails to perform.

---

5. For a classic case on this issue, see *Crane Ice Cream Co. v. Terminal Freezing & Heating Co.*, 147 Md. 588, 128 A. 280 (1925).

CONCEPT SUMMARY Assignments and Delegations

Which rights can be assigned, and which duties can be delegated?	All rights can be assigned *unless:* 1. A statute expressly prohibits assignment. 2. The assignment will materially alter the obligor's risk or duties. 3. The contract is for personal services. 4. The contract prohibits assignment.	All duties can be delegated *unless:* 1. Performance depends on the obligor's personal skills or talents. 2. Special trust has been placed in the obligor. 3. Performance by a third party will materially vary from that expected by the obligee. 4. The contract prohibits delegation.
What if the contract prohibits assignment or delegation?	No rights can be assigned *except:* 1. Rights to receive money. 2. Ownership rights in real estate. 3. Rights to negotiable instruments. 4. Rights to payments under a sales contract or damages for breach of a sales contract.	No duties can be delegated.
What is the effect on the original party's rights?	On a valid assignment, effective immediately, the original party (assignor) no longer has any rights under the contract.	On a valid delegation, if the delegatee fails to perform, the original party (delegator) is liable to the obligee (who may also hold the delegatee liable).

on the theory that the assignee's agreement to accept the benefits of the contract was not sufficient to imply a promise to assume the duties of the contract.

Modern authorities, however, take the view that the probable intent in using such general words is to create both an assignment of rights and an assumption of duties.[6] Therefore, when general words are used (for example, "I assign the contract" or "all my rights under the contract"), the contract is construed as implying both an assignment of rights and an assumption of duties. (See the *Application* feature at the end of this chapter for factors that businesspersons should consider when dealing with assignments and delegations.)

THIRD PARTY BENEFICIARIES

THIRD PARTY BENEFICIARY
One for whose benefit a promise is made in a contract but who is not a party to the contract.

INTENDED BENEFICIARY
A third party for whose benefit a contract is formed. An intended beneficiary can sue the promisor if such a contract is breached.

As mentioned earlier in this chapter, to have contractual rights, a person normally must be a party to the contract. In other words, privity of contract must exist. An exception to the doctrine of privity exists when the original parties to the contract intend, at the time of contracting, that the contract performance directly benefit a third person. In this situation, the third person becomes a **third party beneficiary** of the contract. As an **intended beneficiary** of the contract, the third party has legal rights and can sue the promisor directly for breach of the contract.

Who, though, is the promisor? In bilateral contracts, both parties to the contract are promisors because they both make promises that can be enforced. In third party beneficiary contracts, courts determine the identity of the promisor by asking which party made the promise that benefits the third party—that person is the promisor. Allowing the third party to sue the promisor directly in effect circumvents the "middle person" (the promisee) and thus reduces the burden on the courts. Otherwise, the third party would sue the promisee, who would then sue the promisor.

A classic case in the area of third party beneficiary contracts is *Lawrence v. Fox*—a case decided in 1859. In *Lawrence*, which is presented as this chapter's *Landmark in the Law* feature, the court set aside the traditional requirement of privity and allowed a third party to bring a suit directly against the promisor.

Types of Intended Beneficiaries

ON THE WEB

A *New York Law Journal* article discussing leading decisions from the New York Court of Appeals is online at

www.courts.state.ny.us/history/elecbook/thereshallbe/pg51.htm.

The law distinguishes between *intended* beneficiaries and *incidental* beneficiaries. Only intended beneficiaries acquire legal rights in a contract. One type of intended beneficiary is a *creditor beneficiary*. Like the plaintiff in *Lawerence v. Fox*, a creditor beneficiary benefits from a contract in which one party (the promisor) promises another party (the promisee) to pay a debt that the promisee owes to a third party (the creditor beneficiary). As an intended beneficiary, the creditor beneficiary can sue the promisor directly to enforce the contract.

Another type of intended beneficiary is a *donee* beneficiary. When a contract is made for the express purpose of giving a *gift* to a third party, the third party (the donee beneficiary) can sue the promisor directly to enforce the promise.[7] The most common donee beneficiary contract is a life insurance contract. **■EXAMPLE 12.10** Akins (the promisee) pays premiums to Standard Life, a life insurance company, and Standard Life (the promisor) promises to pay a certain amount on Akins's death to anyone Akins designates as a beneficiary. The designated beneficiary is a donee beneficiary under the life insurance policy and can enforce the promise made by the insurance company to pay her or him on Akins's death. **■**

---

6. See UCC 2–210(1), (4); and *Restatement (Second) of Contracts*, Section 328.
7. This principle was first enunciated in *Seaver v. Ransom*, 224 N.Y. 233, 120 N.E. 639 (1918).

LANDMARK IN THE LAW — *Lawrence v. Fox* (1859)

In 1859, the New York Court of Appeals (that state's highest court) decided a case, *Lawrence v. Fox*,[a] in which the court departed from the doctrine of privity of contract and allowed a third party to sue the promisor directly. Prior to that time, contractual liability had always been limited to the parties to the contract.

Case Background   The case involved three parties—Holly, Lawrence, and Fox. Holly had borrowed $300 from Lawrence. Shortly thereafter, Holly loaned $300 to Fox, who in return promised Holly that he would pay Holly's debt to Lawrence on the following day. When Lawrence failed in his attempts to obtain the $300 from Fox, he sued Fox to recover the funds.

Why didn't Lawrence sue Holly directly, rather than pursue the unusual route of suing Fox, which meant that his chances at recovery were much slimmer? According to one scholar, the answer to this question is that the "Holly" in this case was probably Merwin Spencer Hawley. Both Hawley and the defendant, Arthur Wellesley Fox, were prominent members of the business community in Buffalo, New York. Evidence at trial suggested that the debt Hawley owed Lawrence was a gambling debt. Because gambling was illegal under New York law, Lawrence could not recover directly from Hawley in court, as the contract would have been deemed illegal.[b]

The Issue before the Court and the Court's Ruling   In any event, the issue before the court was whether Lawrence, who was not a party to the Holly-Fox contract, could sue Fox directly to recover the $300. The court held that Lawrence could do so. It was manifestly "just," declared the court, to allow Lawrence to recover the funds from Fox. The court enunciated the principle of law that "[in the case of] a promise made for the benefit of another, he for whose benefit it is made may bring an action for its breach."

APPLICATION TO TODAY'S WORLD   *At the time this decision was rendered, allowing a third party to sue a promisor directly was a novel idea and represented a radical departure from contract law. Although privity of contract remained the guiding principle until after the turn of the century, in two leading cases decided in 1916[c] and 1918,[d] the New York Court of Appeals cited* Lawrence v. Fox *in justifying its departure from the principle of privity of contract. Since then, the third party beneficiary rule has been continuously expanded in scope.*

RELEVANT WEB SITES   *To locate information on the Web concerning the* Lawrence v. Fox *decision, go to this text's Web site at* **www.thomsonedu.com/westbuslaw/blt**, *select "Chapter 12," and click on "URLs for Landmarks."*

a. 20 N.Y. 268 (1859).
b. See Antony Jon Waters, "The Property in the Promise: A Study of the Third Party Beneficiary Rule," 98 *Harvard Law Review* 1109, 1168 (1985).
c. *MacPherson v. Buick Motor Co.,* 217 N.Y. 382, 111 N.E. 1050 (1916). This case will be discussed in Chapter 18 in the *Landmark in the Law* feature.
d. *Seaver v. Ransom,* 224 N.Y. 233, 120 N.E. 639 (1918).

As the law concerning third party beneficiaries evolved, numerous cases arose in which the third party beneficiary did not fit readily into either the creditor beneficiary or the donee beneficiary category. Thus, the modern view, and the one adopted by the *Restatement (Second) of Contracts*, does not draw such clear lines and distinguishes only between intended beneficiaries (who can sue to enforce contracts made for their benefit) and incidental beneficiaries (who cannot sue, as will be discussed shortly).

When the Rights of an Intended Beneficiary Vest

An intended third party beneficiary cannot enforce a contract against the original parties until the rights of the third party have *vested*, meaning that the rights have taken effect and cannot be taken away. Until these rights have vested, the original parties to the contract—the promisor and the promisee—can modify or rescind the contract without the consent of the third party. When do the rights of third parties vest? Generally, the rights vest when one of the following occurs:

1 When the third party demonstrates manifest assent to the contract, such as sending a letter or note acknowledging awareness of and consent to a contract formed for her or his benefit.

2 When the third party materially alters his or her position in detrimental reliance on the contract, such as when a donee beneficiary contracts to have a home built in reliance on the receipt of funds promised to him or her in a donee beneficiary contract.

3 When the conditions for vesting are satisfied. For example, the rights of a beneficiary under a life insurance policy vest when the insured person dies.

If the contract expressly reserves to the contracting parties the right to cancel, rescind, or modify the contract, the rights of the third party beneficiary are subject to any changes that result. In such a situation, the vesting of the third party's rights does not terminate the power of the original contracting parties to alter their legal relationships.[8]

Incidental Beneficiaries

INCIDENTAL BENEFICIARY
A third party who incidentally benefits from a contract but whose benefit was not the reason the contract was formed. An incidental beneficiary has no rights in a contract and cannot sue to have the contract enforced.

The benefit that an **incidental beneficiary** receives from a contract between two parties is unintentional. Therefore, an incidental beneficiary cannot enforce a contract to which he or she is not a party.

■**EXAMPLE 12.11** In one case, spectators at a Mike Tyson boxing match in which Tyson was disqualified for biting his opponent's ear sued Tyson and the fight's promoters for a refund of their money on the basis of breach of contract. The spectators claimed that they had standing to sue the defendants as third party beneficiaries of the contract between Tyson and the fight's promoters. The court, however, held that the spectators did not have standing to sue because they were not in contractual privity with any of the defendants. Furthermore, any benefits they received from the contract were incidental to the contract. The court noted that the spectators got what they paid for: "the right to view whatever event transpired."[9] ■

Is a person who benefits from a contract between another party and a government entity an incidental beneficiary or an intended beneficiary? For a discussion of a case raising this question, see this chapter's *Adapting the Law to the Online Environment* feature.

---

8. Defenses raised against third party beneficiaries are given in the *Restatement (Second) of Contracts*, Section 309.
9. *Castillo v. Tyson*, 268 A.D.2d 336, 701 N.Y.S.2d 423 (Sup.Ct.App.Div. 2000).

ADAPTING THE LAW TO THE ONLINE ENVIRONMENT **Government Contracts and Third Party Beneficiaries**

Government entities often contract with private organizations to provide certain services to the public. Are those who benefit under such contracts intended beneficiaries? This question came before the court in a case involving a person who had registered a domain name with an organization that had contracted with the federal government to provide domain name registration services.

The Domain Name Conflict

In 1994, in the early days of the Internet (as a public surfing/shopping vehicle), domain names were free for the asking. At that time, Network Solutions, Inc. (NSI), was the sole registrar of domain names. NSI had a contract with a federal government agency stating that NSI had the primary responsibility for "ensuring the quality, timeliness, and effective management" of domain name registration services.

Gary Kremen, seeing what he felt was a great opportunity, registered the name "sex.com" with NSI. Unfortunately for Kremen, Stephen Cohen also saw the potential of that domain name. Cohen, who had just gotten out of prison for impersonating a bankruptcy lawyer, knew that Kremen had already registered the name. That fact, however, in the words of the court, "was only a minor impediment for a man of Cohen's boundless resource and bounded integrity." Through forgery and deceit, Cohen succeeded in having NSI transfer the domain name to his company. When Kremen later contacted NSI, he was told that it was too late to undo the transfer. Kremen then turned to the courts for assistance.

The Legal Issues

Kremen sued Cohen, seeking as damages the substantial profits that Cohen had made by using the name. The court held in Kremen's favor and awarded him millions of dollars in damages. Kremen could not collect the judgment, however, because Cohen had disappeared—after first transferring large sums to offshore accounts. Kremen then tried to hold NSI responsible for his losses by alleging, among other things, that he was an intended third party beneficiary of NSI's contract with the government. He claimed that because NSI had not "effectively managed" its duties, as it was obligated to do under the contract, his domain name had been wrongfully transferred.

Was Kremen an intended third party beneficiary of the contract? When the case ultimately reached the U.S. Court of Appeals for the Ninth Circuit, the court held that Kremen was not an intended third party beneficiary of the contract. The court noted that a third party can enforce a contract if the contract reflects an "express or implied intention of the parties to the contract to benefit the third party." The court emphasized, however, that when a contract is with a government entity, a more stringent test applies: for a third party to be an intended beneficiary, *the contract must express a clear intent to benefit the third party*. If it does not express this clear intent, then anyone who benefits under the contract is regarded as an incidental beneficiary and, as such, cannot sue to enforce the contract.[a]

 FOR CRITICAL ANALYSIS *Kremen also alleged that NSI had breached an implied-in-fact contract with him, but the court dismissed this claim. Why would the court hold that no contract existed between Kremen and NSI? Was a required element for a valid contract lacking?*

a. *Kremen v. Cohen*, 337 F.3d 1024 (9th Cir. 2003).

Intended versus Incidental Beneficiaries

In determining whether a third party beneficiary is an intended or an incidental beneficiary, the courts generally use the *reasonable person* test. Under this test, a beneficiary will be considered an intended beneficiary if a reasonable person in the position of the beneficiary would believe that the promisor *intended* to confer on the beneficiary the right to bring suit to enforce the contract.

In determining whether a party is an intended or an incidental beneficiary, the courts also look at a number of other factors. As you can see in Exhibit 12–3 on the next page, which graphically illustrates the distinction between intended and incidental beneficiaries, the presence of one or more of the following factors strongly indicates that the third party is an intended (rather than an incidental) beneficiary to the contract:

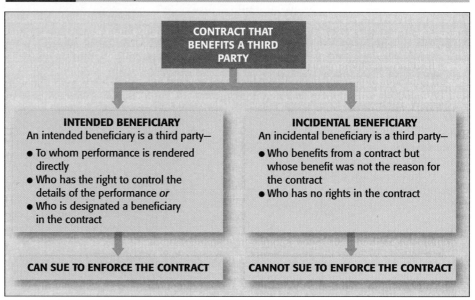

EXHIBIT 12–3 **Third Party Beneficiaries**

CONTRACT THAT BENEFITS A THIRD PARTY

INTENDED BENEFICIARY
An intended beneficiary is a third party—
● To whom performance is rendered directly
● Who has the right to control the details of the performance *or*
● Who is designated a beneficiary in the contract

CAN SUE TO ENFORCE THE CONTRACT

INCIDENTAL BENEFICIARY
An incidental beneficiary is a third party—
● Who benefits from a contract but whose benefit was not the reason for the contract
● Who has no rights in the contract

CANNOT SUE TO ENFORCE THE CONTRACT

1 Performance is rendered directly to the third party.

2 The third party has the right to control the details of performance.

3 The third party is expressly designated as a beneficiary in the contract.

In the following case, a subcontractor claimed to be an intended beneficiary of the general contractor's contractual promise to obtain property insurance after the construction of an addition to a building was completed.

CASE 12.1 **Midwestern Indemnity Co. v. Systems Builders, Inc.**

Court of Appeals of Indiana, 801 N.E.2d 661 (2004).

FACTS Action Steel, Inc., entered into a contract with Systems Builders, Inc., a general contractor, to construct an addition to a commercial building in Indianapolis, Indiana. The contract provided that Action Steel would obtain, after the addition's completion, insurance, which "shall include the interest of * * * subcontractors." The parties would then "waive all rights against * * * any of their subcontractors." Varco-Pruden Building, a subcontractor, designed the addition and supplied the premade building system for it. The addition was completed in the summer of 1995. Action Steel obtained an insurance policy from Midwestern Indemnity Company. In January 1996, a snowstorm hit the Indianapolis area and the new addition collapsed. Midwestern paid more than $1.3 million to Action Steel for the loss. Because Midwestern paid for the loss, it stood in Action Steel's place in a suit filed in an

Indiana state court against Varco-Pruden and others to recover this amount. Varco-Pruden filed a motion for summary judgment, arguing, in part, that it was a third party beneficiary of the waiver clause in the contract between Action Steel and Systems Builders. The court issued a summary judgment in favor of Varco-Pruden on this point. Midwestern appealed to a state intermediate appellate court, arguing that Varco-Pruden was not a third party beneficiary of the contract.

ISSUE Was the subcontractor, Varco-Pruden, a third party beneficiary of the contract clause between Action Steel and Systems Builders?

DECISION Yes. The state intermediate appellate court affirmed the lower court's judgment.

CASE 12.1—Continued

REASON The appellate court first explained that one who is not a party to a contract can enforce the contract as a third party beneficiary if (1) the contracting parties intended to benefit the third party, (2) the contract imposed a duty on one of the parties in favor of the third party, and (3) the performance of the terms of the contract rendered a direct benefit to the third party. According to the court, a "plain reading" of the construction contract indicated that Action Steel intended to benefit Varco-Pruden. Under the contract's terms, when Action Steel bought property insurance after the project was completed, Action Steel intended that subcontractors, such as Varco-Pruden, would benefit from the waiver clause. The contract provided that the insurance "shall include the interest of * * * subcontractors." Furthermore, the contract imposed a duty on Action Steel, providing that if it

acquired insurance after the completion of the project, it "shall * * * waive all rights against * * * any of [the parties'] subcontractors." Finally, the court concluded that the performance of these clauses in the contract rendered a direct benefit—Action Steel's waiver—to Varco-Pruden.

 WHY IS THIS CASE IMPORTANT TO BUSINESSPERSONS? *This case illustrates how resolving the issue of whether a beneficiary is intended or incidental can have serious consequences for the beneficiary's liability. In this situation, Varco-Pruden designed and supplied the building system for the addition, which collapsed during a major snowstorm resulting in millions of dollars in damages. Nevertheless, because Varco-Pruden was the intended beneficiary of a contract clause waiving liability, Varco-Pruden could not be held liable for even one cent of the damages.*

CONTRACT DISCHARGE

The most common way to **discharge**, or terminate, one's contractual duties is by the **performance** of those duties. The duty to perform under a contract may be *conditioned* on the occurrence or nonoccurrence of a certain event, or the duty may be *absolute*. As shown in Exhibit 12–4 on page 340, in addition to performance, a contract can be discharged in numerous other ways, including discharge by agreement of the parties and discharge by operation of law.

Conditions of Performance

In most contracts, promises of performance are not expressly conditioned or qualified. Instead, they are *absolute promises*. They must be performed, or the party promising the act will be in breach of contract. **■EXAMPLE 12.12** JoAnne contracts to sell Alfonso a painting for $10,000. The parties' promises are unconditional: JoAnne's transfer of the painting to Alfonso and Alfonso's payment of $10,000 to JoAnne. The payment does not have to be made if the painting is not transferred. ■

In some situations, however, contractual promises are conditioned. A **condition** is a possible future event, the occurrence or nonoccurrence of which will trigger the performance of a legal obligation or terminate an existing obligation under a contract. If the condition is not satisfied, the obligations of the parties are discharged. **■EXAMPLE 12.13** Suppose that Alfonso, in the above example, offers to purchase JoAnne's painting only if an independent appraisal indicates that it is worth at least $10,000. JoAnne accepts Alfonso's offer. Their obligations (promises) are conditioned on the outcome of the appraisal. Should this condition not be satisfied (for example, if the appraiser deems the value of the painting to be only $5,000), their obligations to each other are discharged and cannot be enforced. ■

We look here at three types of conditions that can be present in any given contract: *conditions precedent, conditions subsequent,* and *concurrent conditions.*

Conditions Precedent A condition that must be fulfilled before a party's promise becomes absolute is called a **condition precedent.** The condition precedes the absolute duty to perform, as in the JoAnne-Alfonso example just given. Real estate contracts

DISCHARGE
The termination of an obligation. In contract law, discharge occurs when the parties have fully performed their contractual obligations or when events, conduct of the parties, or operation of law releases the parties from performance.

PERFORMANCE
In contract law, the fulfillment of one's duties arising under a contract with another; the normal way of discharging one's contractual obligations.

CONDITION
A qualification, provision, or clause in a contractual agreement, the occurrence or nonoccurrence of which creates, suspends, or terminates the obligations of the contracting parties.

CONDITION PRECEDENT
In a contractual agreement, a condition that must be met before a party's promise becomes absolute.

EXHIBIT 12–4 Contract Discharge

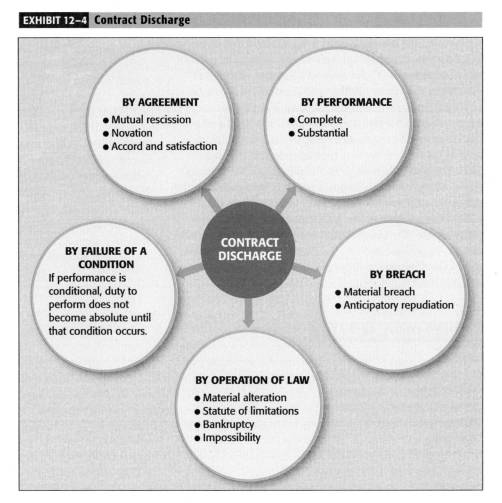

frequently are conditioned on the buyer's ability to obtain financing. **EXAMPLE 12.14** Fisher promises to buy Calvin's house if Salvation Bank approves Fisher's mortgage application. The Fisher-Calvin contract is therefore subject to a condition precedent—the bank's approval of Fisher's mortgage application. If the bank does not approve the application, the contract will fail because the condition precedent was not met. ▪ Insurance contracts frequently specify that certain conditions, such as passing a physical examination, must be met before the insurance company will be obligated to perform under the contract.

Conditions Subsequent When a condition operates to terminate a party's absolute promise to perform, it is called a **condition subsequent.** The condition follows, or is subsequent to, the absolute duty to perform. If the condition occurs, the party need not perform any further. **EXAMPLE 12.15** A law firm hires Julia Darby, a recent law school graduate and a newly licensed attorney. Their contract provides that the firm's obligation to continue employing Darby is discharged if she fails to maintain her license to practice law. This is a condition subsequent because a failure to maintain the license will discharge a duty that has already arisen.[10] ▪

CONDITION SUBSEQUENT
A condition in a contract that, if not fulfilled, operates to terminate a party's absolute promise to perform.

10. The difference between conditions precedent and conditions subsequent is relatively unimportant from a substantive point of view but very important procedurally. Usually, the plaintiff must prove conditions precedent, because typically it is the plaintiff who claims that there is a duty to be performed. Similarly, the defendant must normally prove conditions subsequent, because typically it is the defendant who claims that a duty no longer exists.

Generally, conditions precedent are common, and conditions subsequent are rare. The *Restatement (Second) of Contracts* deletes the terms *condition subsequent* and *condition precedent* and refers to both simply as "conditions."[11]

Concurrent Conditions   When each party's absolute duty to perform is conditioned on the other party's absolute duty to perform, **concurrent conditions** are present. These conditions exist only when the parties expressly or impliedly are to perform their respective duties *simultaneously*. ■**EXAMPLE 12.16** if a buyer promises to pay for goods when they are delivered by the seller, each party's absolute duty to perform is conditioned on the other party's absolute duty to perform. The buyer's duty to pay for the goods does not become absolute until the seller either delivers or attempts to deliver the goods. Likewise, the seller's duty to deliver the goods does not become absolute until the buyer pays or attempts to pay for the goods. Therefore, neither can recover from the other for breach without first tendering performance. ■

CONCURRENT CONDITIONS
Conditions that must occur or be performed at the same time; they are mutually dependent. No obligations arise until these conditions are simultaneously performed.

Discharge by Performance

The contract comes to an end when both parties fulfill their respective duties by performing the acts they have promised. Performance can also be accomplished by tender. **Tender** is an unconditional offer to perform by a person who is ready, willing, and able to do so. Therefore, a seller who places goods at the disposal of a buyer has tendered delivery and can demand payment according to the terms of the agreement. A buyer who offers to pay for goods has tendered payment and can demand delivery of the goods.

Once performance has been tendered, the party making the tender has done everything possible to carry out the terms of the contract. If the other party then refuses to perform, the party making the tender can consider the duty discharged and sue for breach of contract.

TENDER
An unconditional offer to perform an obligation by a person who is ready, willing, and able to do so.

Complete Performance   When a party performs exactly as agreed, there is no question as to whether the contract has been performed. When a party's performance is perfect, it is said to be complete.

Normally, conditions expressly stated in the contract must fully occur in all aspects for complete performance (strict performance) of the contract to take place. Any deviation breaches the contract and discharges the other party's obligations to perform. For example, most construction contracts require the builder to meet certain specifications. If the specifications are conditions, complete performance is required to avoid material breach. (*Material breach* will be discussed shortly.) If the conditions are met, the other party to the contract must then fulfill her or his obligation to pay the builder. If the specifications are not conditions and if the builder, without the other party's permission, fails to meet the specifications, performance is not complete. What effect does such a failure have on the other party's obligation to pay? The answer is part of the doctrine of *substantial performance*.

A woman shakes hands with a salesperson after agreeing to purchase a car. Suppose that the agreement is conditioned on the dealer's installing certain optional equipment. When the woman returns to the dealership the following day, she discovers that the optional features that were agreed on have not been added to the car. Is she still obligated to buy the car? Why or why not? What type of condition is this? (Brian Teutsch/ Creative Commons)

Substantial Performance   A party who in good faith performs substantially all of the terms of a contract can enforce the contract against the other party under the doctrine of substantial performance. Note that good faith is required. Intentionally failing to comply with the terms is a breach of the contract.

To qualify as *substantial performance*, the performance must not vary greatly from the performance promised in the contract, and it must create substantially the same benefits as those promised in the contract. If the omission, variance, or defect in performance is unimportant and can easily be compensated for by awarding damages, a court is likely to

---

11. *Restatement (Second) of Contracts*, Section 224.

hold that the contract has been substantially performed. Courts decide whether the performance was substantial on a case-by-case basis, examining all of the facts of the particular situation. If performance is substantial, the other party's duty to perform remains absolute (except that the party can sue for damages due to the minor deviations).

■EXAMPLE 12.17 A couple contracts with a construction company to build a house. The contract specifies that Brand X plasterboard be used for the walls. The builder cannot obtain Brand X plasterboard, and the buyers are on holiday in the mountains of Peru and virtually unreachable. The builder decides to install Brand Y instead, which he knows is identical in quality and durability to Brand X plasterboard. All other aspects of construction conform to the contract. In this situation, a court will likely hold that the builder had substantially performed his end of the bargain, and therefore the couple will be obligated to pay the builder. The court might, however, award the couple damages for the use of a different brand of plasterboard, but the couple would still have to pay the contractor the contract price, less the amount of damages. ■

ON THE WEB

For a summary of how contracts may be discharged and other principles of contract law, go to **contracts.lawyers.com**, and click on the "Terminating a Contract" link.

Performance to the Satisfaction of Another Contracts often state that completed work must personally satisfy one of the parties or a third person. The question is whether this satisfaction becomes a condition precedent, requiring actual personal satisfaction or approval for discharge, or whether the test of satisfaction is performance that would satisfy a *reasonable person* (substantial performance).

When the subject matter of the contract is *personal*, a contract to be performed to the satisfaction of one of the parties is conditioned, and performance must actually satisfy that party. For example, contracts for portraits, works of art, and tailoring are considered personal. Therefore, only the personal satisfaction of the party fulfills the condition—unless a court finds the party is expressing dissatisfaction only to avoid payment or otherwise is not acting in good faith.

Most other contracts need to be performed only to the satisfaction of a reasonable person unless they *expressly state otherwise*. When such contracts require performance to the satisfaction of a third party (for example, "to the satisfaction of Robert Ames, the supervising engineer"), the courts are divided. A majority of courts require the work to be satisfactory to a reasonable person, but some courts hold that the personal satisfaction of the third party designated in the contract (Robert Ames, in this example) must be met. Again, the personal judgment must be made honestly, or the condition will be excused.

BREACH OF CONTRACT
The failure, without legal excuse, of a promisor to perform the obligations of a contract.

Material Breach of Contract A **breach of contract** is the nonperformance of a contractual duty. A breach is *material* when performance is not at least substantial.[12] If there is a material breach, the nonbreaching party is excused from the performance of contractual duties and can sue for damages caused by the breach. If the breach is *minor* (not material), the nonbreaching party's duty to perform may sometimes be suspended until the breach is remedied, but the duty is not entirely excused. Once the minor breach is cured, the nonbreaching party must resume performance of the contractual obligations that had been undertaken.

Any breach entitles the nonbreaching party to sue for damages, but only a material breach discharges the nonbreaching party from the contract. The policy underlying these rules is that contracts should go forward when only minor problems occur, but contracts should be terminated if major problems arise.[13]

Did a seller's failure to repair the plumbing in an apartment building within the eight-month period specified in a contract with the buyers constitute a material breach of the parties' contract? That was the issue in the following case.

---

12. *Restatement (Second) of Contracts*, Section 241.
13. See UCC 2–612, which deals with installment contracts for the sale of goods.

CASE 12.2 Kim v. Park

Court of Appeals of Oregon, 192 Or.App. 365, 86 P.3d 63 (2004).
www.publications.ojd.state.or.us/appeals.htm[a]

FACTS Su Yong Kim sold an apartment building in Portland, Oregon, to Chon Sik Park, Bok Soon Park, Johan Cen, William Itzineag, Johnny Perea, and Patricia Maldonado. At the time, the building's plumbing violated the Portland Housing Code. The contract provided the following: "Seller shall correct the plumbing code violation * * * within eight months * * * . Buyer shall cooperate with seller in * * * providing access to the premises to complete repairs." Kim did not make the repairs within eight months, but twelve months after the date of the contract, Kim cut holes in the walls of the apartments to expose the plumbing. Seven weeks later, early one morning, Kim sent plumbers to the building without notice to the owners, apparently in an attempt to make repairs. The owners ordered the plumbers to leave, refused to allow Kim to send others, and stopped making payments under the contract. Kim filed a suit in an Oregon state court against the buyers, seeking the amount due. The buyers asserted that Kim's failure to repair the plumbing was a material breach that excused the performance of their obligations and counterclaimed for damages for the breach. The court concluded that Kim's breach was not material and ordered relief in his favor. The buyers appealed to a state intermediate appellate court.

ISSUE Was the seller's failure to repair the plumbing according to the parties' contract a material breach excusing the buyers' performance?

DECISION Yes. The state intermediate appellate court reversed the decision of the lower court on this issue and

a. Click on "Cases decided in 2004," and scroll to the name of the case under the date 3/3/04. Then click on the case name to access the opinion. The state of Oregon's judicial branch maintains this Web site.

remanded the case for a determination of the amount of damages.

REASON The appellate court reasoned that a breach is material if it "goes to the very substance of the contract and defeats the object of the parties entering into the contract." In this case, as a result of the code violations, "the City of Portland continued to assess fines against defendants and defendants lost some tenants." The court pointed out that the requirement that the seller repair the plumbing within eight months was intended to ensure that the building's plumbing would satisfy the city code within a reasonable time after the sale. Also, the buyers had purchased the building from the seller so that they could rent out the apartments in it. According to the court, "[a]lthough the repairs to the plumbing in the building would have caused some temporary inconvenience to the tenants, the failure of plaintiff to make the repairs in accordance with the contract ultimately prevented defendants from using the building as intended by the parties' agreement. In light of that evidence, we hold that as a matter of law the plaintiff's [seller's] failure to perform as promised was a material breach of the contract." The court added that because the seller's breach was material, the buyers were not obligated to continue to perform their obligation to make the payments under the contract.

 WHY IS THIS CASE IMPORTANT? *This case emphasizes that when one party's failure to perform a contractual obligation causes another to suffer significant harm, the other party normally is entitled to a remedy. Recall from Chapters 8 and 9 that even when no contract exists, someone who justifiably relies to her or his detriment on the promise of another may be able to obtain relief under the doctrine of quasi contract or promissory estoppel.*

Anticipatory Repudiation of a Contract Before either party to a contract has a duty to perform, one of the parties may refuse to perform her or his contractual obligations. This is called **anticipatory repudiation**.[14] When anticipatory repudiation occurs, it is treated as a material breach of contract, and the nonbreaching party is permitted to bring an action for damages immediately, even though the scheduled time for performance under the contract may still be in the future.[15] Until the nonbreaching party treats this early

ANTICIPATORY REPUDIATION
An assertion or action by a party indicating that he or she will not perform an obligation that the party is contractually obligated to perform at a future time.

---

14. *Restatement (Second) of Contracts*, Section 253; and UCC 2–610.
15. The doctrine of anticipatory repudiation first arose in the landmark case of *Hochster v. De La Tour*, 2 Ellis and Blackburn Reports 678 (1853), when an English court recognized the delay and expense inherent in a rule requiring a nonbreaching party to wait until the time of performance before suing on an anticipatory repudiation.

repudiation as a breach, however, the breaching party can retract the anticipatory repudiation by proper notice and restore the parties to their original obligations.[16]

An anticipatory repudiation is treated as a present, material breach for two reasons. First, the nonbreaching party should not be required to remain ready and willing to perform when the other party has already repudiated the contract. Second, the nonbreaching party should have the opportunity to seek a similar contract elsewhere and may have the duty to do so to minimize his or her loss.

Quite often, an anticipatory repudiation occurs when a sharp fluctuation in market prices creates a situation in which performance of the contract would be extremely unfavorable to one of the parties. **■EXAMPLE 12.18** Martin Corporation contracts to manufacture and sell ten thousand personal computers to ComAge, a retailer of computer equipment that has five hundred outlet stores. Delivery is to be made six months from the date of the contract. The contract price is based on Martin's present costs of purchasing inventory parts from others. One month later, three suppliers of computer parts raise their prices to Martin. Because of these higher prices, Martin stands to lose $500,000 if it sells the computers to ComAge at the contract price. Martin writes to ComAge, stating that it cannot deliver the ten thousand computers at the contract price. Martin's letter is an anticipatory repudiation of the contract. ComAge has the option of treating the repudiation as a material breach and proceeding immediately to pursue remedies, even though the contract delivery date is still five months away. ■

Discharge by Agreement

Any contract can be discharged by agreement of the parties. The agreement can be contained in the original contract, or the parties can form a new contract for the express purpose of discharging the original contract.

Discharge by Rescission   As mentioned in previous chapters, rescission is the process in which the parties cancel the contract and are returned to the positions they occupied prior to the contract's formation. For *mutual rescission* to take place, the parties must make another agreement that also satisfies the legal requirements for a contract—there must be an *offer*, an *acceptance*, and *consideration*. Ordinarily, if the parties agree to rescind the original contract, their promises not to perform those acts promised in the original contract will be legal consideration for the second contract.

Mutual rescission can occur in this manner when the original contract is executory on both sides (that is, neither party has completed performance). Agreements to rescind most executory contracts (with the exception of real estate contracts) are enforceable even if they are made orally and even if the original agreement was in writing.[17] When one party has fully performed, however, an agreement to rescind the original contract usually is not enforceable unless additional consideration or restitution is made.[18]

Discharge by Novation   The process of **novation** substitutes a third party for one of the original parties. Essentially, the parties to the original contract and one or more new parties all get together and agree to the substitution. The requirements of a novation are as follows:

---

16. See UCC 2–611.
17. Agreements to rescind contracts involving transfers of realty, however, must be evidenced by a writing. Another exception has to do with the sale of goods under the UCC, when the sales contract requires written rescission.
18. Under UCC 2–209(1), however, no consideration is needed to modify a contract for a sale of goods; see also UCC 1–107. See Chapter 15 for an extended discussion of the UCC.

1 The existence of a previous, valid obligation.

2 Agreement by all of the parties to a new contract.

3 The extinguishing of the old obligation (discharge of the prior party).

4 A new, valid contract.

A novation may appear to be similar to an assignment or delegation. Nevertheless, there is an important distinction: a novation involves a new contract, and an assignment or delegation involves the old contract.

■EXAMPLE 12.19 Suppose that you contract with Logan Enterprises to sell it your office equipment business. Logan later decides that it should not expand at this time but learns of another party, MBI Corporation, that is interested in purchasing your business. All three of you get together and agree to a novation. As long as the new contract is supported by consideration, the novation discharges the original contract between you and Logan and replaces it with the new contract between you and MBI Corporation. Logan prefers the novation because it discharges Logan's liabilities under the contract with you. If the original contract had been an installment sales contract requiring twelve monthly payments, and Logan had merely assigned the contract (assigned its rights and delegated its duties under the contract) to MBI Corporation, Logan would have remained liable to you for the payments if MBI Corporation defaulted. ■

Discharge by Accord and Satisfaction   As Chapter 9 explained, in an *accord and satisfaction,* the parties agree to accept performance different from the performance originally promised. An *accord* is an executory contract (one that has not yet been performed) to perform some act to satisfy an existing contractual duty that is not yet discharged.[19] A *satisfaction* is the performance of the accord agreement. An *accord* and its *satisfaction* discharge the original contractual obligation.

Once the accord has been made, the original obligation is merely suspended until the accord agreement is fully performed. If it is not performed, the party to whom performance is owed can bring an action on the original obligation or for breach of the accord. **■EXAMPLE 12.20** Shea obtains a judgment against Marla for $8,000. Later, both parties agree that the judgment can be satisfied by Marla's transfer of her automobile to Shea. This agreement to accept the auto in lieu of $8,000 in cash is the accord. If Marla transfers her automobile to Shea, the accord agreement is fully performed, and the $8,000 debt is discharged. If Marla refuses to transfer her car, the accord is breached. Because the original obligation is merely suspended, Shea can sue to enforce the judgment for $8,000 in cash or bring an action for breach of the accord. ■

Discharge by Operation of Law

Under some circumstances, contractual duties may be discharged by operation of law. These circumstances include material alteration of the contract, the running of the relevant statute of limitations, bankruptcy, and impossibility of performance.

Contract Alteration   To discourage parties from altering written contracts, the law allows an innocent party to be discharged when one party has materially altered a written contract without the knowledge or consent of the other party. For example, if a party alters a material term of the contract—such as the quantity term or the price term—without the knowledge or consent of the other party, the party who was unaware of the alteration can treat the contract as discharged or terminated.

"Law is a practical matter."

ROSCOE POUND,
1870–1964
(American jurist)

---

19. *Restatement (Second) of Contracts,* Section 281.

Statutes of Limitations As mentioned earlier in this text, statutes of limitations limit the period during which a party can sue on a particular cause of action. After the applicable limitations period has passed, a suit can no longer be brought. For example, the limitations period for bringing lawsuits for breach of oral contracts is usually two to three years; for written contracts, four to five years; and for recovery of amounts awarded in judgment, ten to twenty years, depending on state law. Lawsuits for breach of a contract for the sale of goods must be brought within four years after the cause of action has accrued. By original agreement, the parties can agree to reduce this four-year period to not less than a one-year period. They cannot, however, agree to extend it beyond the four-year limitations period.

Bankruptcy A proceeding in bankruptcy attempts to allocate the debtor's assets to the creditors in a fair and equitable fashion. Once the assets have been allocated, the debtor receives a *discharge in bankruptcy* (see Chapter 23). A discharge in bankruptcy ordinarily bars the creditors from enforcing most of the debtor's contracts.

When Performance Is Impossible After a contract has been made, performance may become impossible in an objective sense. This is known as **impossibility of performance** and may discharge the contract.[20] Performance may also become so difficult or costly due to some unforeseen event that a court will consider it commercially unfeasible, or impracticable, as discussed later in the chapter.

Objective Impossibility. Objective impossibility ("It can't be done") must be distinguished from subjective impossibility ("I'm sorry, I simply can't do it"). An example of subjective impossibility is the inability to pay funds on time because the bank is closed.[21] In effect, the nonperforming party is saying, "It is impossible for *me* to perform," rather than "It is impossible for *anyone* to perform." Accordingly, such excuses do not discharge a contract, and the nonperforming party is normally held in breach of contract. Three basic types of situations will generally qualify as grounds for the discharge of contractual obligations based on impossibility of performance[22]:

1 *When a party whose personal performance is essential to the completion of the contract dies or becomes incapacitated prior to performance.* **■EXAMPLE 12.21** Fred, a famous dancer, contracts with Ethereal Dancing Guild to play a leading role in its new ballet. Before the ballet can be performed, Fred becomes ill and dies. His personal performance was essential to the completion of the contract. Thus, his death discharges the contract and his estate's liability for his nonperformance. **■**

2 *When the specific subject matter of the contract is destroyed.* **■EXAMPLE 12.22** A-1 Farm Equipment agrees to sell Gudgel the green tractor on its lot and promises to have the tractor ready for Gudgel to pick up on Saturday. On Friday night, however, a truck veers off the nearby highway and smashes into the tractor, destroying it beyond repair. Because the contract was for this specific tractor, A-1's performance is rendered impossible owing to the accident. **■**

3 *When a change in the law renders performance illegal.* An example is a contract to build an apartment building, when the zoning laws are changed to prohibit the construction of residential rental property at this location. This change renders the contract impossible to perform.

IMPOSSIBILITY OF PERFORMANCE
A doctrine under which a party to a contract is relieved of her or his duty to perform when performance becomes objectively impossible or totally impracticable (through no fault of either party).

If a fire incapacitated a commercial bakery's oven, would the bakery be excused from performing its contracts until the oven was fixed? If the bakery had a contract for a special holiday order and the oven could not be fixed until after the holiday, would that contract be discharged? Why or why not?
(Matt Biddulph/Creative Commons)

---

20. *Restatement (Second) of Contracts*, Section 261.
21. *Ingham Lumber Co. v. Ingersoll & Co.*, 93 Ark. 447, 125 S.W. 139 (1910).
22. *Restatement (Second) of Contracts*, Sections 262–266; and UCC 2–615.

Temporary Impossibility.   An occurrence or event that makes performance temporarily impossible operates to suspend performance until the impossibility ceases. Then, ordinarily, the parties must perform the contract as originally planned. If, however, the lapse of time and the change in circumstances surrounding the contract make it substantially more burdensome for the parties to perform the promised acts, the contract is discharged.

■EXAMPLE 12.23 The leading case on the subject, *Autry v. Republic Productions,*[23] involved an actor who was drafted into the army in 1942. Being drafted rendered the actor's contract temporarily impossible to perform, and it was suspended until the end of the war. When the actor got out of the army, the purchasing power of the dollar had so diminished that performance of the contract would have been substantially burdensome to him. Therefore, the contract was discharged. ■

Should the courts allow the defense of impossibility of performance to be used more often? The doctrine of impossibility of performance is applied only when the parties could not have reasonably foreseen, at the time the contract was formed, the event or events that rendered performance impossible. In some cases, the courts may seem to go too far in holding that the parties should have foreseen certain events or conditions, thus precluding the parties from avoiding contractual obligations under the doctrine of impossibility of performance. Even though the courts rarely excuse parties from performance under the doctrine of impossibility, they allow parties to raise this defense more often than they once did. Indeed, until the latter part of the nineteenth century, courts were reluctant to discharge a contract even when performance appeared to be literally impossible. Generally, the courts must balance the freedom of parties to contract (and assume the risks involved) against the injustice that may result when certain contractual obligations are enforced. If the courts allowed parties to raise impossibility of performance as a defense to contractual obligations more often, freedom of contract would suffer.

■

Commercial Impracticability   Courts may excuse parties from their performance obligations when the performance becomes much more difficult or expensive than originally contemplated at the time the contract was formed. For someone to invoke the doctrine of **commercial impracticability** successfully, however, the anticipated performance must become *extremely* difficult or costly.[24]

The added burden of performing not only must be extreme but also *must not have been known by the parties when the contract was made.* For example, in one case, a court held that a contract could be discharged because a party would have to pay ten times more than the original estimate to excavate a certain amount of gravel.[25] In another case, the court allowed a party to rescind a contract for the sale of land because of a potential problem with contaminated groundwater under the land. The court found that "the potential for substantial and unbargained-for" liability made contract performance economically impracticable. Interestingly, the court in that case also noted that the possibility of "environmental degradation with consequences extending well beyond the parties' land sale" was just as important to its decision as the economic considerations.[26] (See this chapter's *Beyond Our Borders* feature on page 349 for a discussion of Germany's approach to impracticability and impossibility of performance.)

COMMERCIAL IMPRACTICABILITY
A doctrine under which a seller may be excused from performing a contract when (1) a contingency occurs, (2) the contingency's occurrence makes performance impracticable, and (3) the nonoccurrence of the contingency was a basic assumption on which the contract was made. Despite the fact that UCC Section 2–615 expressly frees only sellers under this doctrine, courts have not distinguished between buyers and sellers in applying it.

NOTE   The doctrine of commercial impracticability does not provide relief from such events as ordinary price increases or easily predictable changes in the weather.

23. 30 Cal.2d 144, 180 P.2d 888 (1947).
24. *Restatement (Second) of Contracts,* Section 264.
25. *Mineral Park Land Co. v. Howard,* 172 Cal. 289, 156 P. 458 (1916).
26. *Cape-France Enterprises v. Estate of Peed,* 305 Mont. 513, 29 P.3d 1011 (2001).

The contract dispute in the following case arose out of the cancellation of a wedding reception due to a power failure. Is a power failure sufficient to invoke the doctrine of commercial impracticability?

CASE 12.3   Facto v. Pantagis

Superior Court of New Jersey, Appellate Division, 390 N.J.Super. 227, 915 A.2d 59 (2007).
lawlibrary.rutgers.edu/search.shtml[a]

FACTS Leo and Elizabeth Facto contracted with Snuffy Pantagis Enterprise, Inc., for the use of Pantagis Renaissance, a banquet hall in Scotch Plains, New Jersey, for a wedding reception in August 2002. The Factos paid the $10,578 price in advance. The contract excused Pantagis from performance "if it is prevented from doing so by an act of God (e.g., flood, power failure, etc.), or other unforeseen events or circumstances." Soon after the reception began, there was a power failure. The lights and the air conditioning shut off. The band hired for the reception refused to play without electricity to power their instruments, and the lack of lighting prevented the photographer and videographer from taking pictures. The temperature was in the 90s, the humidity was high, and the guests quickly became uncomfortable. Three hours later, after a fight between a guest and a Pantagis employee, the emergency lights began to fade, and the police evacuated the hall. The Factos filed a suit in a New Jersey state court against Pantagis, alleging breach of contract, among other things. The Factos sought to recover their prepayment, plus amounts paid to the band, the photographer, and the videographer. The court concluded that Pantagis did not breach the contract and dismissed the complaint. The Factos appealed to a state intermediate appellate court.

ISSUE Can a power failure constitute the kind of unexpected occurrence that relieves a party of the duty to perform a contract?

DECISION Yes. The state intermediate appellate court agreed that the power failure relieved Pantagis of its

contractual obligation, but held that Pantagis's inability to perform also relieved the Factos of their obligation. The court reversed the dismissal and remanded the case for an award to the Factos of the amount of their prepayment less the value of the services they received.

REASON The appellate court did not attribute any significance to the contract's reference to a power failure as "an act of God." The court reasoned that "even if a power failure caused by circumstances other than a natural event [was] not considered to be 'an act of God,' it still would constitute an unforeseen event or circumstance that would excuse performance." Of course, a power failure is not absolutely unforeseeable during hot summer months. But "absolute unforeseeability of a condition is not a prerequisite to the defense of impracticability." It is "the destruction or * * * deterioration of a specific thing necessary for the performance of the contract [that] makes performance impracticable." In this case, the power failure was area-wide and beyond the control of Pantagis, which was prevented from performing its contract. Because Pantagis was not in breach, however, did not mean that the Factos could not recover the amount they prepaid for the reception. When "one party to a contract is excused from performance as a result of an unforeseen event that makes performance impracticable, the other party is also generally excused from performance." Therefore, the power failure that relieved Pantagis of its obligation to the Factos also relieved the Factos of their obligation to Pantagis.

FOR CRITICAL ANALYSIS–Social Consideration *If Pantagis offered to reschedule the reception, should it be absolved of the obligation to refund the Factos' prepayment? Explain.*

---

a. In the "Search for Cases by Party Name" section, select the "Appellate Division," type "Pantagis" in the "First Name:" box, and click on "Submit Form." In the result, click on the "click here to get this case" link to access the opinion. The Rutgers University School of Law in Camden, New Jersey, maintains this Web site.

FRUSTRATION OF PURPOSE
A court-created doctrine under which a party to a contract will be relieved of her or his duty to perform when the objective purpose for performance no longer exists (due to reasons beyond that party's control).

Frustration of Purpose   Closely allied with the doctrine of commercial impracticability is the doctrine of **frustration of purpose**. In principle, a contract will be discharged if supervening circumstances make it impossible to attain the purpose both parties had in mind when making the contract. As with commercial impracticability, the supervening event must not have been foreseeable at the time of the contracting.

BEYOND OUR BORDERS Impossibility or Impracticability of Performance in Germany

In the United States, when a party alleges that contract performance is impossible or impracticable because of circumstances unforeseen at the time the contract was formed, a court will either discharge the party's contractual obligations or hold the party to the contract. In other words, if a court agrees that the contract is impossible or impracticable to perform, the remedy is to rescind (cancel) the contract. Under German law, however, a court may adjust the terms of (reform) a contract in light of economic developments. If an unforeseen event affects the foundation of the agreement, the court can alter the contract's terms in view of the disruption in expectations, thus making the contract fair to the parties.

 FOR CRITICAL ANALYSIS *When a contract becomes impossible or impracticable to perform, which remedy would a businessperson prefer—rescission or reformation? Why?*

REVIEWING Third Party Rights and Discharge

Val's Foods signs a contract to buy 1,500 pounds of basil from Sun Farms, a small organic herb grower, as long as an independent organization inspects and certifies that the crop contains no pesticide or herbicide residue. Val's has a contract with several restaurant chains to supply pesto and intends to use Sun Farms' basil in the pesto to fulfill these contracts. When Sun Farms is preparing to harvest the basil, an unexpected hailstorm destroys half the crop. Sun Farms attempts to purchase additional basil from other farms, but it is late in the season and the price is twice the normal market price. Sun Farms is too small to absorb this cost and immediately notifies Val's that it will not fulfill the contract. Using the information presented in the chapter, answer the following questions.

1 Suppose that the basil does not pass the chemical-residue inspection. Which concept discussed in the chapter might allow Val's to refuse to perform the contract in this situation?

2 Under which legal theory or theories might Sun Farms claim that its obligation under the contract has been discharged by operation of law? Discuss fully.

3 Suppose that Sun Farms contacts every basil grower in the country and buys the last remaining chemical-free basil anywhere. Nevertheless, Sun Farms is able to ship only 1,475 pounds to Val's. Would this fulfill Sun Farms' obligations to Val's? Why or why not?

4 Now suppose that Sun Farms sells its operations to Happy Valley Farms. As a part of the sale, all three parties agree that Happy Valley will provide the basil as stated under the original contract. What is this type of agreement called?

APPLICATION Dealing with Third Party Rights*

Assignments of contractual rights and delegations of duties are common in the business world. As you discovered in this chapter, third party rights and duties stem from the law on assignments, delegations, and third party beneficiaries. A third party may even be unaware that he or she has rights in a contract, as can happen when a person is the beneficiary of a life insurance policy. In certain situations, businesses may wish to attempt to prohibit a third party from acquiring such rights.

The general rule, though, is that any contractual right or duty can be assigned or delegated unless the assignment or

* This *Application* is not meant to substitute for the services of an attorney who is licensed to practice law in your state.

delegation is prohibited by (1) the contract, (2) a statute, or (3) other limitations.

For example, a tenant under a long-term lease contract may assign the lease to another party. To avoid such assignments, property owners often prohibit the assignment of the balance of a lease term unless the property owner's consent is obtained.

In the manufacture and sale of goods, manufacturers can assign or delegate the production of such goods to a third party unless prohibited by contract. Consequently, most purchase orders (contracts) have a clause that prohibits such assignments or delegations without the buyer's consent.

CHECKLIST FOR THE BUSINESSPERSON

1 Determine whether you can assign or delegate your rights or duties under a contract to a third party.

2 If you can assign or delegate your contract rights or performance, attempt to determine your benefits and obligations, such as notice to customers, if you do make the assignment or delegation.

3 If you do not want your contract rights or duties to be assigned or delegated, insert a contract clause that prohibits assignment or delegation without your consent.

4 Whenever you might be a third party beneficiary to a contract, such as a creditor beneficiary, take steps to determine your rights.

KEY TERMS

alienation 330
anticipatory repudiation 343
assignee 328
assignment 327
assignor 328
breach of contract 342
commercial impracticability 347
concurrent conditions 341
condition 339

condition precedent 339
condition subsequent 340
delegatee 331
delegation of duties 331
delegator 331
discharge 339
frustration of purpose 348
impossibility of performance 346
incidental beneficiary 336

intended beneficiary 334
novation 344
obligee 328
obligor 328
performance 339
privity of contract 327
tender 341
third party beneficiary 334

CHAPTER SUMMARY   Third Party Rights and Discharge

THIRD PARTY RIGHTS

Assignments
(See pages 327–331.)

1. An assignment is the transfer of rights under a contract to a third party. The person assigning the rights is the *assignor,* and the party to whom the rights are assigned is the *assignee.* The assignee has a right to demand performance from the other original party to the contract.

2. Generally, all rights can be assigned, except in the following circumstances:

   a. When assignment is expressly prohibited by statute (for example, workers' compensation benefits).

   b. When a contract calls for the performance of personal services.

   c. When the assignment will materially increase or alter the risks or duties of the *obligor* (the party that is obligated to perform).

   d. When the contract itself stipulates that the rights cannot be assigned (with some exceptions).

CHAPTER SUMMARY   *Third Party Rights and Discharge—Continued*

Assignments— Continued	3. The assignee should notify the obligor of the assignment. Although not legally required, notification avoids two potential problems:
	a. If the assignor assigns the same right to two different persons, generally the first assignment in time is the first in right, but in some states the first assignee to give notice takes priority.
	b. Until the obligor is notified of the assignment, the obligor can tender performance to the assignor. If the assignor accepts the performance, the obligor's duties under the contract are discharged without benefit to the assignee.
Delegations (See pages 331–334.)	1. A delegation is the transfer of duties under a contract to a third party (the *delegatee*), who then assumes the obligation of performing the contractual duties previously held by the one making the delegation (the *delegator*).
	2. As a general rule, any duty can be delegated, except in the following circumstances:
	a. When performance depends on the personal skill or talents of the obligor.
	b. When special trust has been placed in the obligor.
	c. When performance by a third party will vary materially from that expected by the obligee (the one to whom the duty is owed) under the contract.
	d. When the contract expressly prohibits delegation.
	3. A valid delegation of duties does not relieve the delegator of obligations under the contract. If the delegatee fails to perform, the delegator is still liable to the obligee.
	4. An "assignment of all rights" or an "assignment of the contract" is often construed to mean that both the rights and the duties arising under the contract are transferred to a third party.
Third Party Beneficiaries (See pages 334–339.)	A third party beneficiary contract is one made for the purpose of benefiting a third party.
	1. *Intended beneficiary*—One for whose benefit a contract is created. When the promisor (the one making the contractual promise that benefits a third party) fails to perform as promised, the third party can sue the promisor directly. Examples of third party beneficiaries are creditor and donee beneficiaries.
	2. *Incidental beneficiary*—A third party who indirectly (incidentally) benefits from a contract but for whose benefit the contract was not specifically intended. Incidental beneficiaries have no rights to the benefits received and cannot sue to have the contract enforced.
	<div align="center">**CONTRACT DISCHARGE**</div>
Conditions of Performance (See pages 339–341.)	Contract obligations may be subject to the following types of conditions:
	1. *Condition precedent*—A condition that must be fulfilled before a party's promise becomes absolute.
	2. *Condition subsequent*—A condition that operates to terminate a party's absolute promise to perform.
	3. *Concurrent conditions*—Conditions that must be performed simultaneously. Each party's absolute duty to perform is conditioned on the other party's absolute duty to perform.
Discharge by Performance (See pages 341–344.)	A contract may be discharged by complete (strict) performance or by substantial performance. In some instances, performance must be to the satisfaction of another. Totally inadequate performance constitutes a material breach of the contract. An anticipatory repudiation of a contract allows the other party to sue immediately for breach of contract.
Discharge by Agreement (See pages 344–345.)	Parties may agree to discharge their contractual obligations in several ways:
	1. *By rescission*—The parties mutually agree to rescind (cancel) the contract.

(Continued)

CHAPTER SUMMARY   Third Party Rights and Discharge–Continued

Discharge by Agreement–Continued	2. *By novation*–A new party is substituted for one of the primary parties to a contract.
	3. *By accord and satisfaction*–The parties agree to render and accept performance different from that on which they originally agreed.
Discharge by Operation of Law (See pages 345–349.)	Parties' obligations under contracts may be discharged by operation of law owing to one of the following:
	1. Contract alteration.
	2. Statutes of limitations.
	3. Bankruptcy.
	4. Impossibility of performance.
	5. Impracticability of performance.
	6. Frustration of purpose.

FOR REVIEW

Answers for the even-numbered questions in this **For Review** *section can be found in Appendix E at the end of this text.*

1 What is the difference between an assignment and a delegation?

2 What rights can be assigned despite a contract clause expressly prohibiting assignment?

3 What factors indicate that a third party beneficiary is an intended beneficiary?

4 How are most contracts discharged?

5 What is a contractual condition, and how might a condition affect contractual obligations?

 The following multiple-choice question is representative of the types of questions available in one of the four sections of ThomsonNOW for *Business Law Today.* **ThomsonNOW also provides feedback for each response option, whether correct or incorrect, and refers to the location within the chapter where the correct answer can be found.**

Anticipatory repudiation often occurs when

a one party to the contract dies.

b one party to the contract experiences a sudden increase in investment income.

c market price fluctuations make it extremely difficult to perform the contract as promised.

d a discharge by agreement is fully accepted.

■

QUESTIONS AND CASE PROBLEMS

 **HYPOTHETICAL SCENARIOS**

12.1 Third Party Beneficiaries. Wilken owes Rivera $2,000. Howie promises Wilken that he will pay Rivera the $2,000 in return for Wilken's promise to give Howie's children guitar lessons. Is Rivera an intended beneficiary of the Howie-Wilken contract? Explain.

12.2 Anticipatory Repudiation. ABC Clothiers, Inc., has a contract with Taylor & Sons, a retailer, to deliver one thousand summer suits to Taylor's place of business on or before May 1. On April 1, Taylor senior receives a letter from ABC informing him that ABC will not be able to make the delivery as scheduled. Taylor is very upset, as he had planned a big ad campaign. He wants to file a suit against ABC immediately (April 2). Taylor's son, Tom, tells his father that filing a lawsuit is not proper until ABC actually fails to deliver the suits on May 1. Discuss fully who is correct, Taylor senior or Tom.

12.3 Hypothetical Question with Sample Answer. Aron, a college student, signs a one-year lease agreement that runs from September 1 to August 31. The lease agreement specifies that the lease cannot be assigned without the landlord's consent. In late May, Aron decides not to go to summer school and assigns the balance of the lease (three months) to a close friend, Erica. The landlord objects to the assignment and denies Erica access to the apartment. Aron claims that Erica

is financially sound and should be allowed the full rights and privileges of an assignee. Discuss fully whether the landlord or Aron is correct.

 **For a sample answer to Question 12.3, go to Appendix F at the end of this text.**

12.4 Impossibility of Performance. Millie contracted to sell Frank 1,000 bushels of corn to be grown on Millie's farm. Owing to a drought during the growing season, Millie's yield was much less than anticipated, and she could deliver only 250 bushels to Frank. Frank accepted the lesser amount but sued Millie for breach of contract. Can Millie defend successfully on the basis of objective impossibility of performance? Explain.

■

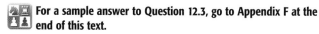

CASE PROBLEMS

12.5 Performance. In May 1996, O'Brien-Sheipe Funeral Home, Inc., in Hempstead, New York, hired Teramo & Co. to build an addition to O'Brien's funeral home. The parties' contract did not specify a date for the completion of the work. The city of Hempstead issued a building permit for the project on June 14, and Teramo began work about two weeks later. There was some delay in construction because O'Brien asked that no work be done during funeral services, but by the end of March 1997, the work was substantially complete. The city of Hempstead issued a "Certificate of Completion" on April 15. During the construction, O'Brien made periodic payments to Teramo, but there was a balance due of $17,950, which O'Brien did not pay. To recover this amount, Teramo filed a suit in a New York state court against O'Brien. O'Brien filed a counterclaim to recover lost profits for business allegedly lost due to the time Teramo took to build the addition, and for $6,180 spent to correct problems caused by poor work. Which, if any, party is entitled to an award in this case? Explain. [*Teramo & Co. v. O'Brien-Sheipe Funeral Home, Inc.*, 283 A.D.2d 635, 725 N.Y.S.2d 87 (2001)]

12.6 Substantial Performance. Adolf and Ida Krueger contracted with Pisani Construction, Inc., to erect a metal building as an addition to an existing structure. The two structures were to share a common wall, and the frames and panel heights of the new building were to match those of the existing structure. Shortly before completion of the project, however, it was apparent that the roofline of the new building was approximately three inches higher than that of the existing structure. Pisani modified the ridge caps of the buildings to blend the rooflines. The discrepancy had other consequences, however, including misalignment of the gutters and windows of the two buildings, which resulted in an icing problem in the winter. The Kruegers occupied the new structure but refused to make the last payment under the contract.

Pisani filed a suit in a Connecticut state court to collect. Did Pisani substantially perform its obligations? Should the Kruegers be ordered to pay? Why or why not? [*Pisani Construction, Inc. v. Krueger*, 68 Conn.App. 361, 791 A.2d 634 (2002)]

12.7 Case Problem with Sample Answer. The National Collegiate Athletic Association (NCAA) regulates intercollegiate amateur athletics among more than 1,200 colleges and universities with which it contracts. Among other things, the NCAA maintains rules of eligibility for student participation in intercollegiate athletic events. Jeremy Bloom, a high school football and track star, was recruited to play football at the University of Colorado (CU). Before enrolling, he competed in Olympic and professional World Cup skiing events, becoming the World Cup champion in freestyle moguls. During the Olympics, Bloom appeared on MTV and was offered other paid entertainment opportunities, including a chance to host a show on Nickelodeon. Bloom was also paid to endorse certain ski equipment and contracted to model clothing for Tommy Hilfiger. On Bloom's behalf, CU asked the NCAA to waive its rules restricting student-athlete endorsement and media activities. The NCAA refused, and Bloom quit the activities to play football for CU. He filed a suit in a Colorado state court against the NCAA, however, asserting breach of contract on the ground that its rules permitted these activities if they were needed to support a professional athletic career. The NCAA responded that Bloom did not have standing to pursue this claim. What contract has allegedly been breached in this case? Is Bloom a party to this contract? If not, is he a third party beneficiary of it, and if so, is his status intended or incidental? Explain. [*Bloom v. National Collegiate Athletic Association*, 93 P.3d 621 (Colo.App. 2004)]

After you have answered Problem 12.7, compare your answer with the sample answer given on the Web site that accompanies this text. Go to www.thomsonedu.com/westbuslaw/blt, select "Chapter 12," and click on "Case Problem with Sample Answer."

12.8 Discharge by Operation of Law. Train operators and other railroad personnel use signaling systems to ensure safe train travel. Reading Blue Mountain & Northern Railroad Co. (RBMN) and Norfolk Southern Railway Co. entered into a contract for the maintenance of a signaling system that serviced a stretch of track near Jim Thorpe, Pennsylvania. The system included a series of poles, similar to telephone poles, suspending wires above the tracks. The contract provided that "the intent of the parties is to maintain the existing . . . facilities" and split the cost equally. In December 2002, a severe storm severed the wires and destroyed most of the poles. RBMN and Norfolk discussed replacing the old system, which they agreed was antiquated, inefficient, dangerous to rebuild, and expensive, but they could not agree on an alternative. Norfolk installed an entirely new system and filed a suit in a federal district court against RBMN to recover half of the cost. RBMN filed a motion for summary judgment, asserting, in part, the doctrine of frustration of purpose. What is this doctrine? Does it apply in this case? How should the court rule on RBMN's motion? Explain. [*Norfolk Southern Railway Co. v. Reading Blue Mountain & Northern Railroad Co.*, 346 F.Supp.2d 720 (M.D.Pa. 2004)]

12.9 Material Breach. Kermit Johnson formed FB & I Building Products, Inc., in Watertown, South Dakota, to sell building materials. In December 1998, FB & I contracted with Superior Truss & Components in Minneota, Minnesota, "to exclusively sell Superior's open-faced wall panels, floor panels, roof trusses and other miscellaneous products." In March 2000, FB & I agreed to exclusively sell Component Manufacturing Co.'s building products in Colorado. Two months later, Superior learned of FB & I's deal with Component and terminated its contract with FB & I. That contract provided that on cancellation, "FB & I will be entitled to retain the customers that they continue to sell and service with Superior products." Superior refused to honor this provision. Between the cancellation of FB & I's contract and 2004, Superior made $2,327,528 in sales to FB & I customers without paying a commission. FB & I filed a suit in a South Dakota state court against Superior, alleging in part, breach of contract and seeking the unpaid commissions. Superior insisted that FB & I had materially breached their

contract, excusing Superior from performing. In whose favor should the court rule and why? [*FB & I Building Products, Inc. v. Superior Truss & Components, a Division of Banks Lumber, Inc.*, 727 N.W.2d 474 (S.D. 2007)]

12.10 A Question of Ethics. *King County, Washington, hired Frank Coluccio Construction Co. (FCCC) to act as general contractor for a public works project involving the construction of a small utility tunnel under the Duwamish Waterway. FCCC hired Donald B. Murphy Contractors, Inc. (DBM), as a subcontractor. DBM was responsible for constructing an access shaft at the eastern end of the tunnel. Problems arose during construction, including a "blow in" of the access shaft when it filled with water, soil, and debris. FCCC and DBM incurred substantial expenses from the repairs and delays. Under the project contract, King County was supposed to buy an insurance policy to "insure against physical loss or damage by perils included under an 'All Risk' Builder's Risk policy." Any claim under this policy was to be filed through the insured. King County, which had general property damage insurance, did not obtain an all-risk builder's risk policy. For the losses attributable to the blow-in, FCCC and DBM submitted builder's risk claims, which the county denied. FCCC filed a suit in a Washington state court against King County, alleging, among other claims, breach of contract. [Frank Coluccio Construction Co. v. King County, 136 Wash.App. 751, 150 P.3d 1147 (Div. 1 2007)]*

1 King County's property damage policy specifically excluded, at the county's request, coverage of tunnels. The county drafted its contract with FCCC to require the all-risk builder's risk policy and authorize itself to "sponsor" claims. When FCCC and DBM filed their claims, the county secretly colluded with its property damage insurer to deny payment. What do these facts indicate about the county's ethics and legal liability in this situation?

2 Could DBM, as a third party to the contract between King County and FCCC, maintain an action on the contract against King County? Discuss.

3 All-risk insurance is a promise to pay on the "fortuitous" happening of a loss or damage from any cause except those that are specifically excluded. Payment is not usually made on a loss that, at the time the insurance was obtained, the claimant subjectively knew would occur. If a loss results from faulty workmanship on the part of a contractor, should the obligation to pay under an all-risk policy be discharged? Explain.

CRITICAL THINKING AND WRITING ASSIGNMENTS

12.11 Critical Legal Thinking. The concept of substantial performance permits a party to be discharged from a contract even though the party has not fully performed her or his obliga-

tions according to the contract's terms. Is this fair? What policy interests are at issue here?

12.12 **Video Question.** Go to this text's Web site at www. thomsonedu.com/westbuslaw/blt and select

"Chapter 12." Click on "Video Questions" and view the video titled *Third Party Beneficiaries*. Then answer the following questions.

1 Discuss whether a valid contract was formed when Oscar and Vinny bet on the outcome of a football game. Would Vinny be able to enforce the contract in court?

2 Is the Fresh Air Fund an incidental or an intended beneficiary? Why?

3 Can Maria sue to enforce Vinny's promise to donate Oscar's winnings to the Fresh Air Fund?

ONLINE ACTIVITIES

PRACTICAL INTERNET EXERCISES

Go to this text's Web site at **www.thomsonedu.com/westbuslaw/blt**, select "Chapter 12," and click on "Practical Internet Exercises." There you will find the following Internet research exercises that you can perform to learn more about the topics covered in this chapter.

PRACTICAL INTERNET EXERCISE 12–1 LEGAL PERSPECTIVE—Anticipatory Repudiation

PRACTICAL INTERNET EXERCISE 12–2 MANAGEMENT PERSPECTIVE—Commercial Impracticability

BEFORE THE TEST

Go to this text's Web site at **www.thomsonedu.com/westbuslaw/blt**, select "Chapter 12," and click on "Interactive Quizzes." You will find a number of interactive questions relating to this chapter.

CHAPTER 13
Breach and Remedies

CHAPTER OUTLINE

- DAMAGES
- EQUITABLE REMEDIES
- RECOVERY BASED ON QUASI CONTRACT
- CONTRACT PROVISIONS LIMITING REMEDIES
- ELECTION OF REMEDIES

LEARNING OBJECTIVES

AFTER READING THIS CHAPTER, YOU SHOULD BE ABLE TO ANSWER THE FOLLOWING QUESTIONS:

1 What is the difference between compensatory damages and consequential damages? What are nominal damages, and when do courts award nominal damages?

2 What is the standard measure of compensatory damages when a contract is breached? How are damages computed differently in construction contracts?

3 Under what circumstances is the remedy of rescission and restitution available?

4 When do courts grant specific performance as a remedy?

5 What is the rationale underlying the doctrine of election of remedies?

As the Athenian political leader Solon instructed centuries ago in the chapter-opening quotation, a contract will not be broken so long as "it is to the advantage of both" parties to fulfill their contractual obligations. Normally, a person enters into a contract with another to secure an advantage. When it is no longer advantageous for a party to fulfill her or his contractual obligations, that party may breach the contract. As discussed in Chapter 12, a *breach of contract* occurs when a party fails to perform part or all of the required duties under a contract.[1] Once a party fails to perform or performs inadequately, the other party—the nonbreaching party—can choose one or more of several remedies.

The most common remedies available to a nonbreaching party under contract law include damages, rescission and restitution, specific performance, and reformation. As discussed in Chapter 1, courts distinguish between *remedies at law* and *remedies in equity*. Today, the remedy at law is normally monetary damages. We discuss this remedy in the first part of this chapter. Equitable remedies include rescission and restitution, specific performance, and reformation, all of which we examine later in the chapter. Usually, a court will not award an equitable remedy unless the remedy at law is inadequate. In the final pages of this chapter, we look at some special legal doctrines and concepts relating to remedies.

1. *Restatement (Second) of Contracts*, Section 235(2).

DAMAGES

A breach of contract entitles the nonbreaching party to sue for monetary damages. As you read in Chapter 4, damages are designed to compensate a party for harm suffered as a result of another's wrongful act. In the context of contract law, damages are designed to compensate the nonbreaching party for the loss of the bargain. Often, courts say that innocent parties are to be placed in the position they would have occupied had the contract been fully performed.[2]

Types of Damages

There are basically four broad categories of damages:

1 Compensatory (to cover direct losses and costs).

2 Consequential (to cover indirect and foreseeable losses).

3 Punitive (to punish and deter wrongdoing).

4 Nominal (to recognize wrongdoing when no monetary loss is shown).

Compensatory and punitive damages were discussed in Chapter 4 in the context of tort law. Here, we look at these types of damages, as well as consequential and nominal damages, in the context of contract law.

Compensatory Damages   Damages compensating the nonbreaching party for the *loss of the bargain* are known as *compensatory damages*. These damages compensate the injured party only for damages actually sustained and proved to have arisen directly from the loss of the bargain caused by the breach of contract. They simply replace what was lost because of the wrong or damage.

The standard measure of compensatory damages is the difference between the value of the breaching party's promised performance under the contract and the value of her or his actual performance. This amount is reduced by any loss that the injured party has avoided.
EXAMPLE 13.1 You contract with Marinot Industries to perform certain personal services exclusively for Marinot during August for a payment of $4,000. Marinot cancels the contract and is in breach. You are able to find another job during August but can earn only $3,000. You normally can sue Marinot for breach and recover $1,000 as compensatory damages. You may also recover from Marinot the amount that you spent to find the other job. ▪ Expenses that are directly incurred because of a breach of contract—such as those incurred to obtain performance from another source—are called **incidental damages.**

The measurement of compensatory damages varies by type of contract. Certain types of contracts deserve special mention—contracts for the sale of goods, contracts for the sale of land, and construction contracts.

Sale of Goods.   In a contract for the sale of goods, the usual measure of compensatory damages is the difference between the contract price and the market price.[3]
EXAMPLE 13.2 MediQuick Laboratories contracts with Cal Computer Industries to purchase ten model UTS 400 network servers for $8,000 each. If Cal Computer fails to deliver the ten servers, and the current market price of the servers is $8,950, MediQuick's measure of damages is $9,500 (10 × $950), plus any incidental damages (expenses) caused by the breach. ▪ If the buyer breaches and the seller has not yet produced the goods,

REMEMBER The terms of a contract must be sufficiently definite for a court to determine the amount of damages to award.

INCIDENTAL DAMAGES
Damages awarded to compensate for expenses that are directly incurred because of a breach of contract—such as those incurred to obtain performance from another source.

---

2. *Restatement (Second) of Contracts,* Section 347; and Section 1–106(1) of the Uniform Commercial Code (UCC).
3. This is the difference between the contract price and the market price at the time and place at which the goods were to be delivered or tendered. [See UCC 2–708, 2–713, and 2–715(1), discussed in Chapter 16.]

ON THE WEB

For a summary of how contracts may be breached and other information on contract law, go to

consumer-law.lawyers.com/
Contract-Termination.html.

compensatory damages normally equal the seller's lost profits on the sale, rather than the difference between the contract price and the market price.

Sale of Land.   Ordinarily, because each parcel of land is unique, the remedy for a seller's breach of a contract for a sale of real estate is specific performance—that is, the buyer is awarded the parcel of property for which he or she bargained (*specific performance* is discussed more fully later in this chapter). When this remedy is unavailable (because the property has been sold, for example) or when the buyer is the party in breach, the measure of damages is typically the difference between the contract price and the market price of the land. The majority of states follow this rule.

Construction Contracts.   The measure of damages in a building or construction contract varies depending on which party breaches and when the breach occurs. The owner can breach at three different stages of the construction:

1 Before performance has begun.

2 During performance.

3 After performance has been completed.

If the owner breaches *before performance has begun,* the contractor can recover only the profits that would have been made on the contract (that is, the total contract price less the cost of materials and labor). If the owner breaches *during performance,* the contractor can recover the profits plus the costs incurred in partially constructing the building. If the owner breaches *after the construction has been completed,* the contractor can recover the entire contract price plus interest.

When the contractor breaches the construction contract—either by failing to begin construction or by stopping work partway through the project—the measure of damages is the cost of completion, which includes reasonable compensation for any delay in performance. If the contractor finishes late, the measure of damages is the loss of use. The *Concept Summary* below summarizes the rules concerning the measurement of damages in breached construction contracts. (The *Application* feature at the end of this chapter offers some suggestions for a contractor who cannot perform.)

CONSEQUENTIAL DAMAGES
Special damages that compensate for a loss that does not directly or immediately result from the breach (for example, lost profits). For the plaintiff to collect consequential damages, they must have been reasonably foreseeable at the time the breach or injury occurred.

Consequential Damages   Foreseeable damages that result from a party's breach of contract are referred to as **consequential damages,** or *special damages.* Consequential damages differ from compensatory damages in that they are caused by special circumstances beyond the contract itself. They flow from the consequences, or results, of a breach. When a seller fails to deliver goods, knowing that the buyer is planning to use or resell

CONCEPT SUMMARY **Measurement of Damages—Breach of Construction Contracts**

PARTY IN BREACH	TIME OF BREACH	MEASUREMENT OF DAMAGES
Owner	Before construction has begun	Profits (contract price less cost of materials and labor)
Owner	During construction	Profits plus costs incurred up to time of breach
Owner	After construction is completed	Contract price plus interest
Contractor	Before construction has begun	Cost above contract price to complete work
Contractor	Before construction is completed	Generally, all costs incurred by owner to complete

those goods immediately, consequential damages are awarded for the loss of profits from the planned resale.

■EXAMPLE 13.3 Gilmore contracts to have a specific item shipped to her—one that she desperately needs to repair her printing press. In her contract with the shipper, Gilmore states that she must receive the item by Monday, or she will not be able to print her paper and will lose $3,000. If the shipper is late, Gilmore normally can recover the consequential damages caused by the delay (that is, the $3,000 in losses). ■

To recover consequential damages, the breaching party must know (or have reason to know) that special circumstances will cause the nonbreaching party to suffer an additional loss.[4] See this chapter's *Landmark in the Law* feature on pages 360 and 361 for a discussion of *Hadley v. Baxendale*, a case decided in England in 1854.

> **NOTE** A seller who does not wish to take on the risk of consequential damages can limit the buyer's remedies via contract.

Business owners and managers should realize that it is sometimes impossible to prevent contract disputes. They should also understand that collecting damages through a court judgment requires litigation, which can be expensive and time consuming. Furthermore, court judgments are often difficult to enforce, particularly if the breaching party does not have sufficient assets to pay the damages awarded.[5] For these reasons, parties generally choose to settle their contract disputes before trial rather than litigate in hopes of being awarded—and being able to collect—damages (or other remedies). In sum, there is wisdom in the old saying, "a bird in the hand is worth two in the bush."

PREVENTING
LEGAL DISPUTES

Punitive Damages Recall from Chapter 4 that punitive damages are designed to punish a wrongdoer and to set an example to deter similar conduct in the future. Punitive damages, or *exemplary damages*, generally are not awarded in an action for breach of contract. Such damages have no legitimate place in contract law because they are, in essence, penalties, and a breach of contract is not unlawful in a criminal sense. A contract is simply a civil relationship between the parties. The law may compensate one party for the loss of the bargain—no more and no less.

In a few situations, a person's actions can cause both a breach of contract and a tort. **■EXAMPLE 13.4** Two parties establish by contract a certain reasonable standard or duty of care. Failure to live up to that standard is a breach of the contract. The same act that breached the contract may also constitute negligence, or it may be an intentional tort if, for example, the breaching party committed fraud. In such a situation, it is possible for the nonbreaching party to recover punitive damages for the tort in addition to compensatory and consequential damages for the breach of contract. ■

Nominal Damages When no actual damage or financial loss results from a breach of contract and only a technical injury is involved, the court may award **nominal damages** to the innocent party. Nominal damages awards are often small, such as one dollar, but they do establish that the defendant acted wrongfully. Most lawsuits for nominal damages are brought as a matter of principle under the theory that a breach has occurred and some damages must be imposed regardless of actual loss.

NOMINAL DAMAGES
A small monetary award (often one dollar) granted to a plaintiff when no actual damage was suffered.

---

4. UCC 2–715(2). See Chapter 17.

5. Courts dispose of cases, after trials, by entering judgments. A judgment may order the losing party to pay monetary damages to the winning party. Collecting a judgment, however, can pose problems. For example, the judgment debtor may be insolvent (unable to pay his or her bills when they come due) or have only a small net worth, or exemption laws may prevent a creditor from seizing the debtor's assets to satisfy a debt (see Chapter 23).

LANDMARK IN THE LAW — *Hadley v. Baxendale* (1854)

The rule that notice of special ("consequential") circumstances must be given if consequential damages are to be recovered was first enunciated in *Hadley v. Baxendale,*[a] a landmark case decided in 1854.

Case Background   This case involved a broken crankshaft used in a flour mill run by the Hadley family in Gloucester, England. The crankshaft attached to the steam engine in the mill broke, and the shaft had to be sent to a foundry located in Greenwich so that a new shaft could be made to fit the other parts of the engine.

The Hadleys hired Baxendale, a common carrier, to transport the shaft from Gloucester to Greenwich. Baxendale received payment in advance and promised to deliver the shaft the following day. It was not delivered for several days, however. As a consequence, the mill was closed during those days because the Hadleys had no extra crankshaft on hand to use. The Hadleys sued Baxendale to recover the profits they lost during that time. Baxendale contended that the loss of profits was "too remote."

In the mid-1800s, it was common knowledge that large mills, such as that run by the Hadleys, normally had more than one crankshaft in case the main one broke and had to be repaired, as happened in this case. It is against this background that the parties argued their respective positions on whether the damages resulting from loss of profits while the crankshaft was out for repair were "too remote" to be recoverable.

The Issue before the Court and the Court's Ruling   The crucial issue before the court was whether the Hadleys had informed the carrier, Baxendale, of the special

a. 9 Exch. 341, 156 Eng.Rep. 145 (1854).

■EXAMPLE 13.5 Hernandez contracts to buy potatoes at fifty cents a pound from Lentz. Lentz breaches the contract and does not deliver the potatoes. Meanwhile, the price of potatoes falls. Hernandez is able to buy them in the open market at half the price he agreed to pay Lentz. Hernandez is clearly better off because of Lentz's breach. Thus, in a suit for breach of contract, Hernandez may be awarded only nominal damages for the technical injury he sustained, as no monetary loss was involved. ■

Mitigation of Damages

MITIGATION OF DAMAGES
A rule requiring a plaintiff to do whatever is reasonable to minimize the damages caused by the defendant.

In most situations, when a breach of contract occurs, the injured party is held to a duty to mitigate, or reduce, the damages that he or she suffers. Under this doctrine of **mitigation of damages,** the required action depends on the nature of the situation.

■EXAMPLE 13.6 Some states require a landlord to use reasonable means to find a new tenant if a tenant abandons the premises and fails to pay rent. If an acceptable tenant becomes available, the landlord is required to lease the premises to this tenant to mitigate the damages recoverable from the former tenant. The former tenant is still liable for the difference between the amount of the rent under the original lease and the rent received from the new tenant. If the landlord has not taken the reasonable steps necessary to find a new tenant, a court will likely reduce any award by the amount of rent the landlord could have received had such reasonable means been used. ■

In the majority of states, a person whose employment has been wrongfully terminated has a duty to mitigate damages incurred because of the employer's breach of the employ-

circumstances surrounding the crankshaft's repair, in particular that the mill would have to shut down while the crankshaft was being repaired. If Baxendale had been notified of this circumstance at the time the contract was formed, then the remedy for breaching the contract would have been the amount of damages that would reasonably follow from the breach—including the Hadleys' lost profits.

In the court's opinion, however, the only circumstances communicated by the Hadleys to Baxendale at the time the contract was made were that the item to be transported was a broken crankshaft of a mill and that the Hadleys were the owners and operators of that mill. The court concluded that these circumstances did not reasonably indicate that the mill would have to stop operations if the delivery of the crankshaft was delayed.

APPLICATION TO TODAY'S WORLD *Today, the rule enunciated by the court in this case still applies. When damages are awarded, compensation is given only for those injuries that the defendant could reasonably have foreseen as a probable result of the usual course of events following a breach. If the injury complained of is outside the usual and foreseeable course of events, the plaintiff must show specifically that the defendant had reason to know the facts and foresee the injury. This rule applies to contracts in the online environment as well. For example, suppose that a Web merchant loses business (and profits) due to a computer system's failure. If the failure was caused by malfunctioning software, the merchant normally may recover the lost profits from the software maker if these consequential damages were foreseeable.*

RELEVANT WEB SITES *To locate information on the Web concerning the* Hadley v. Baxendale *decision, go to this text's Web site at* **www.thomsonedu.com/westbuslaw/blt***, select "Chapter 13," and click on "URLs for Landmarks."*

---

ment contract. In other words, wrongfully terminated employees have a duty to take similar jobs if they are available. If the employees fail to do this, the damages they receive will be equivalent to their salaries less the incomes they would have received in similar jobs obtained by reasonable means. The employer has the burden of proving that such jobs existed and that the employee could have been hired. Normally, the employee is under no duty to take a job that is not of the same type and rank.

Whether a tenant farmer acceptably attempted to mitigate his damages on his landlord's breach of their lease was at issue in the following case.

CASE 13.1   **Hanson v. Boeder**

Supreme Court of North Dakota, 2007 ND 20, 727 N.W.2d 280 (2007).
www.ndcourts.com/court/opinions.htm[a]

FACTS In 1998, Paul Hanson signed a five-year lease to farm 1,350 acres of Donald Boeder's land in Steele County, North Dakota, for $50 per acre beginning with the 1999 crop year. Under the lease, Hanson could use grain bins with a capacity of 93,000 bushels and two machine sheds on the property. The rent was $67,515 per year, with half due on April 1 and the balance due on November 1. In 2003, Boeder and Hanson renewed the lease for a second five-year period. During both

a. Click on the "By ND citation" link. In the result, click on "2007" and then the name of the case to access the opinion. The North Dakota Supreme Court maintains this Web site.

CASE 13.1–Continues next page

CASE 13.1–Continued

terms, Boeder and Hanson disagreed about Hanson's farming practices, but during the second term, their disagreement escalated. In August 2005, Boeder told Hanson that their lease was over. Boeder also told Hanson not to till the land in the fall because it had been leased to a new tenant who wanted to do it himself. Hanson continued to work Boeder's land, however, while running ads in the local newspapers for other farmland to rent. Unable to find other land, Hanson filed a suit in a North Dakota state court against Boeder for breach of contract, asking the court to assess damages. The court awarded Hanson $315,194.26 to cover his lost profits, the lost use of the bins and sheds, and the value of the fall tillage. Boeder appealed to the North Dakota Supreme Court, arguing in part that Hanson failed to mitigate his damages.

ISSUE Did Hanson take appropriate steps to mitigate his damages?

DECISION Yes. The Supreme Court of North Dakota affirmed the lower court's award of damages to Hanson.

REASON The state supreme court explained that normally, "[f]or the breach of an obligation arising from contract, the

measure of damages * * * is the amount which will compensate the party aggrieved for all the detriment proximately caused thereby or which in the ordinary course of things would be likely to result therefrom." The court recognized that "[a] person injured by the wrongful acts of another has a duty to mitigate or minimize the damages and must protect himself if he can do so with reasonable exertion or at trifling expense, and can recover from the delinquent party only such damages as he could not, with reasonable effort, have avoided." In this case, Hanson had not been aware of any farmland available for lease, and he had run ads in the local newspapers seeking other farmland to rent. That Hanson was unsuccessful affected the amount of his recovery, but it did not point to a failure to mitigate his damages.

FOR CRITICAL ANALYSIS–Social Consideration
During the trial, Boeder tried to retract his repudiation of the lease to allow Hanson to continue farming for the rest of the lease term. Should the court have considered this an acceptable substitute to mitigate Hanson's damages?

Liquidated Damages versus Penalties

LIQUIDATED DAMAGES
An amount, stipulated in a contract, that the parties to the contract believe to be a reasonable estimation of the damages that will occur in the event of a breach.

PENALTY
A contractual clause that states that a certain amount of monetary damages will be paid in the event of a future default or breach of contract. The damages are a punishment for a default and not a measure of compensation for the contract's breach. The agreement as to the penalty amount will not be enforced, and recovery will be limited to actual damages.

A **liquidated damages** provision in a contract specifies that a certain dollar amount is to be paid in the event of a future default or breach of contract. (*Liquidated* means determined, settled, or fixed.) For example, a provision requiring a construction contractor to pay $300 for every day he or she is late in completing the project is a liquidated damages provision. Liquidated damages differ from penalties. A **penalty** specifies a certain amount to be paid in the event of a default or breach of contract and is designed to penalize the breaching party. Liquidated damages provisions normally are enforceable. In contrast, if a court finds that a provision calls for a penalty, the agreement as to the amount will not be enforced, and recovery will be limited to actual damages.[6]

To determine whether a particular provision is for liquidated damages or for a penalty, the court must answer two questions:

1 At the time the contract was formed, was it apparent that damages would be difficult to estimate in the event of a breach?

2 Was the amount set as damages a reasonable estimate of those potential damages and not excessive?[7]

If the answers to both questions are yes, the provision normally will be enforced. If either answer is no, the provision normally will not be enforced. Liquidated damages provisions are frequently used in construction contracts because it is difficult to estimate the amount of damages that would be caused by a delay in completing the work.

---

6. This is also the rule under the UCC. See UCC 2–718(1).
7. *Restatement (Second) of Contracts*, Section 356(1).

ETHICAL ISSUE 13.1

Should a court enforce a liquidated damages clause when the amount due under that clause exceeds the actual value of the contracted goods so significantly that it seems unfair? A court had to answer this question in a case involving leased equipment. Eaton Hydraulics, Inc., entered a contract to lease nearly $9 million of computer equipment from Winthrop Resources Corporation, a computer leasing company. Four years later, Winthrop sued Eaton for breach of contract, alleging that Eaton had failed to meet numerous payment obligations (often because the payments were late), failed to properly maintain the equipment, and failed to properly pack and ship the equipment back to Winthrop. The parties' contract included a liquidated damages clause that provided a formula for calculating the "Casualty Loss Value (CLV)," which would be the damages in the event of a breach.

Based on this clause, Winthrop claimed that Eaton was liable for more than $4 million in damages. Eaton argued that the CLV was an unreasonable and unenforceable penalty. Eaton presented evidence showing that when the lease ended and the computers were returned to Winthrop, each had a fair market value of about $75. The value calculated under the CLV, however, was between $500 and $700—considerably more than four times their market value. The court rejected Eaton's argument, noting that the provision was "clearly not a fair market value calculation." The court held that the liquidated damages provision was proper because of "the speculative nature of the value of the computers at termination of the lease schedules." The court reasoned that Winthrop and Eaton were both sophisticated international companies that had negotiated this contract knowing that the damages for breaching it could be several times the fair market value of the equipment. In essence, the court would not consider whether the amount due under the liquidated damages clause was fair because the parties were sophisticated businesses that had agreed on the method of calculation.[8]

The *Concept Summary* below summarizes the rules on the availability of the different types of damages.

---

8. *Winthrop Resources Corp. v. Eaton Hydraulics, Inc.*, 361 F.3d 465 (8th Cir. 2004).

CONCEPT SUMMARY Damages

REMEDY	AVAILABILITY	RESULT
Compensatory Damages	A party sustains and proves an injury arising directly from the loss of the bargain.	The injured party is compensated for the loss of the bargain.
Consequential Damages	Special circumstances, of which the breaching party is aware or should be aware, cause the injured party additional loss.	The injured party is given the entire *benefit* of the bargain, such as forgone profits.
Punitive Damages	Damages are normally available only when a tort is also involved.	The wrongdoer is punished, and others are deterred from committing similar acts.
Nominal Damages	There is no financial loss.	Wrongdoing is established without actual damages being suffered. The plaintiff is awarded a nominal amount (such as $1) in damages.
Liquidated Damages	A contract provides a specific amount to be paid as damages in the event that the contract is later breached.	The nonbreaching party is paid the amount stipulated in the contract for the breach, unless the amount is construed as a penalty.

American cyclist Tyler Hamilton, leading a race, was suspended from competitive cycling for two years for transfusing himself with another person's blood. Hamilton had a contract to compete on the Phonak team, but the team terminated its contract with Hamilton after his suspension. (Jarrett Campbell/ Creative Commons)

RESTITUTION
An equitable remedy under which a person is restored to his or her original position prior to loss or injury, or placed in the position he or she would have been in had the breach not occurred.

SPECIFIC PERFORMANCE
An equitable remedy requiring exactly the performance that was specified; usually granted only when monetary damages would be an inadequate remedy and the subject matter of the contract is unique.

CONTRAST Restitution offers several advantages over traditional damages. Restitution may be available in situations when damages cannot be proved or are difficult to prove. Restitution can be used to recover specific property. Restitution sometimes results in a greater overall award.

EQUITABLE REMEDIES

In some situations, damages are an inadequate remedy for a breach of contract. In these cases, the nonbreaching party may ask the court for an equitable remedy. Equitable remedies include rescission and restitution, specific performance, and reformation.

Rescission and Restitution

As discussed in Chapter 12, *rescission* is essentially an action to undo, or cancel, a contract—to return nonbreaching parties to the positions that they occupied prior to the transaction. When fraud, mistake, duress, or failure of consideration is present, rescission is available. The failure of one party to perform under a contract entitles the other party to rescind the contract.[9] The rescinding party must give prompt notice to the breaching party.

Restitution To rescind a contract, both parties generally must make **restitution** to each other by returning goods, property, or funds previously conveyed.[10] If the physical property or goods can be returned, they must be. If the property or goods have been consumed, restitution must be made in an equivalent dollar amount.

Essentially, restitution involves the recapture of a benefit conferred on the defendant that has unjustly enriched her or him. **EXAMPLE 13.7** Andrea pays $32,000 to Myles in return for his promise to design a house for her. The next day, Myles calls Andrea and tells her that he has taken a position with a large architectural firm in another state and cannot design the house. Andrea decides to hire another architect that afternoon. Andrea can require restitution of $32,000 because Myles has received an unjust benefit of $32,000. ■

Restitution Is Not Limited to Rescission Cases Restitution may be required when a contract is rescinded, but the right to restitution is not limited to rescission cases. Restitution may be sought in actions for breach of contract, tort actions, and other actions at law or in equity. Usually, restitution can be obtained when funds or property has been transferred by mistake or because of fraud. An award in a case may include restitution of funds or property obtained through embezzlement, conversion, theft, copyright infringement, or misconduct by a party in a confidential or other special relationship.

Specific Performance

The equitable remedy of **specific performance** calls for the performance of the act promised in the contract. This remedy is often attractive to a nonbreaching party because it provides the exact bargain promised in the contract. It also avoids some of the problems inherent in a suit for monetary damages. First, the nonbreaching party need not worry about collecting the judgment. Second, the nonbreaching party need not look around for another contract. Third, the actual performance may be more valuable than the monetary damages.

Normally, however, specific performance will not be granted unless the party's legal remedy (monetary damages) is inadequate.[11] For this reason, contracts for the sale of goods rarely qualify for specific performance. Monetary damages ordinarily are adequate

---

9. The rescission discussed here refers to *unilateral* rescission, in which only one party wants to undo the contract. In *mutual* rescission, both parties agree to undo the contract. Mutual rescission discharges the contract; unilateral rescission is generally available as a remedy for breach of contract.
10. *Restatement (Second) of Contracts*, Section 370.
11. *Restatement (Second) of Contracts*, Section 359.

in such situations because substantially identical goods can be bought or sold in the market. Only if the goods are unique will a court grant specific performance. For instance, paintings, sculptures, and rare books and coins are often unique, and monetary damages will not enable a buyer to obtain substantially identical substitutes in the market.

Sale of Land A court will grant specific performance to a buyer in an action for a breach of contract involving the sale of land. In this situation, the legal remedy of monetary damages will not compensate the buyer adequately because every parcel of land is unique; obviously, the buyer cannot obtain the same land in the same location elsewhere. Only when specific performance is unavailable (for example, when the seller has sold the property to someone else) will damages be awarded instead.

Is specific performance warranted when one of the parties has substantially—but not *fully*—performed under the contract? That was the question in the following case.

Suppose that a seller contracts to sell some valuable coins to a buyer. If the seller breaches the contract, would specific performance be an appropriate remedy for the buyer to seek? Why or why not? (PhotoDisc/ Getty Images)

CASE 13.2   Stainbrook v. Low

Court of Appeals of Indiana, 842 N.E.2d 386 (2006).

FACTS In April 2004, Howard Stainbrook agreed to sell to Trent Low forty acres of land in Jennings County, Indiana, for $45,000. Thirty-two of the acres were wooded and eight were tillable. Under the agreement, Low was to pay for a survey of the property and other costs, including a tax payment due in November. Low gave Stainbrook a check for $1,000 to show his intent to fulfill the contract. They agreed to close the deal on May 11, and Low made financial arrangements to meet his obligations. On May 8, a tractor rolled over on Stainbrook, and he died. Stainbrook's son David became the executor of his father's estate. David asked Low to withdraw his offer to buy the forty acres. Low refused and filed a suit in an Indiana state court against David, seeking to enforce the contract. The court ordered specific performance. David appealed to a state intermediate appellate court, arguing, in part, that his father's contract with Low was "ambiguous and inequitable."

ISSUE Is complete performance of a contract required for the party to be entitled to the remedy of specific performance?

DECISION No. A party who has substantially performed or offered to perform his or her obligations under a contract is entitled to pursue specific performance as a remedy. The state intermediate appellate court held that specific performance was an appropriate remedy in this case and affirmed the lower court's order.

REASON The appellate court explained that a contracting party's substantial performance is sufficient to support a court's order for specific performance. Here, "Low both offered to perform and substantially performed his contractual obligations." The appellate court found that Low had offered to make the tax payment that was due, but Stainbrook's estate refused the offer. Also, Low had obtained financing before the closing date, and there was nothing to indicate that he was not prepared to meet his financial obligations and go forward with the sale. Moreover, although the survey had not yet been arranged, there was no evidence that Low would not have paid for the survey of the land as required by the contract. Because Low had substantially performed under the terms of the contract, the court held that Low was entitled to the remedy of specific performance.

WHY IS THIS CASE IMPORTANT? The court reaffirmed the principle that "[s]pecific performance is a matter of course when it involves contracts to purchase real estate." The court also emphasized that "[a] party seeking specific performance of a real estate contract must prove that he has substantially performed his contract obligations or offered to do so." The court's reasoning underscores the importance of focusing on the elements of a principle to resolve a case fairly.

Contracts for Personal Services Personal-service contracts require one party to work personally for another party. Courts normally refuse to grant specific performance of contracts for personal services. This is because to order a party to perform personal services against his or her will amounts to a type of involuntary servitude, which is contrary to the public policy expressed in the Thirteenth Amendment to the U.S. Constitution. Moreover, the courts do not want to monitor contracts for personal services.

■**EXAMPLE 13.8** If you contract with a brain surgeon to perform brain surgery on you and the surgeon refuses to perform, the court will not compel (and you certainly would not want) the surgeon to perform under these circumstances. There is no way the court can assure meaningful performance in such a situation.[12] ■

Reformation

Reformation is an equitable remedy used when the parties have *imperfectly* expressed their agreement in writing. Reformation allows a court to rewrite the contract to reflect the parties' true intentions. Courts order reformation most often when fraud or mutual mistake is present. ■**EXAMPLE 13.9** If Keshan contracts to buy a forklift from Shelley but the written contract refers to a crane, a mutual mistake has occurred. Accordingly, a court could reform the contract so that the writing conforms to the parties' original intention as to which piece of equipment is being sold. ■

Courts frequently reform contracts in two other situations. The first occurs when two parties who have made a binding oral contract agree to put the oral contract in writing but, in doing so, make an error in stating the terms. Universally, the courts allow into evidence the correct terms of the oral contract, thereby reforming the written contract. The second situation occurs when the parties have executed a written covenant not to compete (see Chapter 10). If the covenant not to compete is for a valid and legitimate purpose (such as the sale of a business) but the area or time restraints are unreasonable, some courts will reform the restraints by making them reasonable and will enforce the entire contract as reformed. Other courts, however, will throw the entire restrictive covenant out as illegal. Exhibit 13–1 graphically presents the remedies, including reformation, that are available to the nonbreaching party.

---

12. Similarly, courts often refuse to order specific performance of construction contracts because courts are not set up to operate as construction supervisors or engineers.

EXHIBIT 13–1 **Remedies for Breach of Contract**

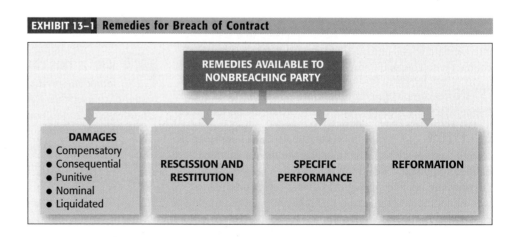

RECOVERY BASED ON QUASI CONTRACT

Recall from Chapter 8 that a quasi contract is not a true contract but rather a fictional contract that is imposed on the parties to prevent unjust enrichment. Hence, a quasi contract provides a basis for relief when no enforceable contract exists. The legal obligation arises because the law considers that the party accepting the benefits has made an implied promise to pay for them. Generally, when one party confers a benefit on another party, justice requires that the party receiving the benefit pay a reasonable value for it.

When Quasi Contracts Are Used

Quasi contract is a legal theory under which an obligation is imposed in the absence of an agreement. It allows the courts to act as if a contract exists when there is no actual contract or agreement between the parties. The courts can also use this theory when the parties have a contract, but it is unenforceable for some reason.

Quasi-contractual recovery is often granted when one party has partially performed under a contract that is unenforceable. It provides an alternative to suing for damages and allows the party to recover the reasonable value of the partial performance. **EXAMPLE 13.10** Ericson contracts to build two oil derricks for Petro Industries. The derricks are to be built over a period of three years, but the parties do not create a written contract. Therefore, the Statute of Frauds will bar the enforcement of the contract.[13] After Ericson completes one derrick, Petro Industries informs him that it will not pay for the derrick. Ericson can sue Petro Industries under the theory of quasi contract. ■

DON'T FORGET The function of a quasi contract is to impose a legal obligation on a party who made no actual promise.

The Requirements of Quasi Contract

To recover on a quasi contract theory, the party seeking recovery must show the following:

1 The party conferred a benefit on the other party.
2 The party conferred the benefit with the reasonable expectation of being paid.
3 The party did not act as a volunteer in conferring the benefit.
4 The party receiving the benefit would be unjustly enriched by retaining the benefit without paying for it.

EXAMPLE 13.11 In Example 13.10, Ericson can sue in quasi contract because all of the conditions for quasi-contractual recovery have been fulfilled. Ericson built the oil derrick with the expectation of being paid. The derrick conferred an obvious benefit on Petro Industries, and Petro Industries would be unjustly enriched if it was allowed to keep the derrick without paying Ericson for the work. Therefore, Ericson should be able to recover the reasonable value of the oil derrick that was built (under the theory of *quantum meruit*[14]—"as much as he or she deserves"). The reasonable value is ordinarily equal to the fair market value. ■

CONTRACT PROVISIONS LIMITING REMEDIES

A contract may include provisions stating that no damages can be recovered for certain types of breaches or that damages will be limited to a maximum amount. The contract may also provide that the only remedy for breach is replacement, repair, or refund of the

---

13. Contracts that by their terms cannot be performed within one year from the day after the date of contract formation must be in writing to be enforceable (see Chapter 11).
14. Pronounced *kwahn*-tuhm *mehr*-oo-wuht.

RECALL Exculpatory clauses may be held unconscionable, depending on the relative bargaining positions of the parties and the importance to the public interest of the business seeking to enforce the clause.

purchase price. Provisions stating that no damages can be recovered are called *exculpatory clauses* (see Chapter 10). Provisions that affect the availability of certain remedies are called *limitation-of-liability clauses.*

Whether these contract provisions and clauses will be enforced depends on the type of breach that is excused by the provision. For example, a clause excluding liability for negligence may be enforced in some cases. When an exculpatory clause for negligence is contained in a contract made between parties who have roughly equal bargaining power, the clause usually will be enforced. The Uniform Commercial Code (UCC) specifically allows limitation-of-liability clauses to be included in contracts for the sale of goods, as will be discussed in detail in Chapter 17.[15] A provision excluding liability for fraudulent or intentional injury, however, will not be enforced. Likewise, a clause excluding liability for illegal acts or violations of the law will not be enforced.

At issue in the following case was the enforceability of a limitation-of-liability clause in a home-inspection contract.

---

15. UCC 2–719.

CASE 13.3 **Lucier v. Williams**

Superior Court of New Jersey, Appellate Division, 366 N.J.Super. 485, 841 A.2d 907 (2004).
lawlibrary.rutgers.edu/search.shtml[a]

FACTS Eric Lucier and Karen Haley, first-time home buyers, contracted to buy a single-family home for $128,500 from James and Angela Williams in Berlin Township, New Jersey. The buyers asked Cambridge Associates, Limited (CAL), to perform a home inspection. CAL presented the buyers with a contract that limited CAL's liability to "$500, or 50% of fees actually paid to CAL by Client, whichever sum is smaller. Such causes include, but are not limited to, CAL's negligence, errors, omissions, * * * [or] breach of contract." Lucier reluctantly signed the contract. On CAL's behalf, Al Vasys performed the inspection and issued a report. The buyers paid CAL $385. Shortly after Lucier and Haley moved into the house, they noticed leaks, which required roof repairs estimated to cost $8,000 to $10,000. They filed a suit in a New Jersey state court against CAL and others, seeking damages for the loss. CAL filed a motion for summary judgment, claiming that under the limitation-of-liability clause, its liability, if any, was limited to one-half of the contract price, or $192.50. The court granted the motion. The plaintiffs appealed to a state intermediate appellate court.

a. Click on the link to "Search by party name." Select "Appellate Division," and type "Lucier" in the first box and "Williams" in the second box. Click on "Submit Form" to access the opinion. Rutgers University School of Law in Camden, New Jersey, maintains this Web site.

ISSUE Did the limitation-of-liability clause in the CAL contract limit the plaintiffs' recovery?

DECISION No. The state intermediate appellate court held that the provision was unenforceable. The court reversed the ruling of the lower court and remanded the case for further proceedings.

REASON The appellate court held that the limitation-of-liability clause was unenforceable for three reasons: (1) the contract was an adhesion contract prepared by the home inspector (an *adhesion contract* is a standard-form contract presented on a take-it-or-leave-it basis—see Chapter 10); (2) the parties had grossly unequal bargaining power; and (3) the provision undermined the fundamental purpose of the contract, having "the practical effect of avoiding almost all responsibility for the professional's negligence." Additionally, the court explained that limiting liability in home-inspection contracts is contrary to the state's public policy of requiring "reliable evaluation of a home's fitness for purchase and holding professionals to certain industry standards." The court added that "[t]he foisting [forcing] of a contract of this type in this setting on an inexperienced consumer clearly demonstrates a lack of fair dealing by the professional. * * * If, upon the occasional dereliction, the home inspector's only

CASE 13.3–Continued

consequence is the obligation to refund a few hundred dollars (the smaller of 50 percent of the inspection contract price or $500), there is no meaningful incentive to act diligently in the performance of home inspection contracts."

 FOR CRITICAL ANALYSIS–Social Consideration *What is the difference between the limitation-of-liability clause in this case and an exculpatory clause (discussed in Chapter 10 on page 292)?*

ELECTION OF REMEDIES

In many cases, a nonbreaching party has several remedies available. Because the remedies may be inconsistent with one another, the common law of contracts requires the party to choose which remedy to pursue. This is called *election of remedies.* The purpose of the doctrine of election of remedies is to prevent double recovery. **■EXAMPLE 13.12** Jefferson agrees to sell his land to Adams. Then Jefferson changes his mind and repudiates the contract. Adams can sue for compensatory damages or for specific performance. If Adams receives damages as a result of the breach, she should not also be granted specific performance of the sales contract because that would mean she would unfairly end up with both the land and the damages. The doctrine of election of remedies requires Adams to choose the remedy she wants, and it eliminates any possibility of double recovery. ■

In contrast, remedies under the UCC are cumulative. They include all of the remedies available under the UCC for breach of a sales or lease contract.[16] We will examine the UCC provisions on limited remedies in Chapter 17, in the context of the remedies available on the breach of a contract for the sale or lease of goods.

BE AWARE Which remedy a plaintiff elects depends on the subject of the contract, the defenses of the breaching party, any tactical advantages of choosing a particular remedy, and what the plaintiff can prove with respect to the remedy sought.

---

16. See UCC 2–703 and 2–711.

REVIEWING **Breach and Remedies**

 Suppose that Kyle Bruno enters a contract with X Entertainment to be a stuntman in a movie being produced. Bruno is widely known as the best motorcycle stuntman in the business, and the movie to be produced, *Xtreme Riders,* has numerous scenes involving high-speed freestyle street-bike stunts. Filming is set to begin August 1 and end by December 1 so that the film can be released the following summer. Both parties to the contract have stipulated that the filming must end on time in order to capture the profits from the summer movie market. The contract states that Bruno will be paid 10 percent of the net proceeds from the movie for his stunts. The contract also includes a liquidated damages provision, which specifies that if Bruno breaches the contract, he will owe X Entertainment $1 million. In addition, the contract includes a limitation-of-liability clause stating that if Bruno is injured during filming, X Entertainment's liability is limited to nominal damages.

Using the information presented in the chapter, answer the following questions.

1 One day, while Bruno is preparing for a difficult stunt, he gets into an argument with the director and refuses to perform any stunts. Can X Entertainment seek specific performance of the contract? Why or why not?

2 Suppose that while performing a high-speed wheelie on a motorcycle, Bruno is injured by an intentionally reckless act of an X Entertainment employee. Will a court be likely to enforce the limitation-of-liability clause? Why or why not?

3 What factors would a court consider to determine if the $1 million liquidated damages clause is valid or is a penalty?

4 Suppose that there was no liquidated damages clause (or the court refused to enforce it) and X Entertainment breached the contract. The breach caused the release of the film to be delayed until after summer. Could Bruno seek consequential (special) damages for lost profits from the summer movie market in that situation? Explain.

Not every contract can be performed. If you are a contractor, you may take on a job that, for one reason or another, you cannot or do not wish to perform. Simply walking away from the job and hoping for the best normally is not the most effective way to avoid litigation—which can be costly, time consuming, and emotionally draining. Instead, you should consider various options that may reduce the likelihood of litigation.

For example, suppose that you are a building contractor and you sign a contract to build a home for the Andersons according to a set of plans that they provided. Performance is to begin on June 15. On June 1, Central Enterprises offers you a position that will yield you two and a half times the amount of net income you could earn as an independent builder. To take the job, you have to start on June 15. You cannot be in two places at the same time, so to accept the new position, you must breach the contract with the Andersons.

Consider Your Options

What can you do in this situation? One option is to subcontract the work to another builder and oversee the work yourself to make sure it conforms to the contract. Another option is to negotiate with the Andersons for a release. You can offer to find another qualified builder who will build a house of the same quality at the same price. Alternatively, you can offer to pay any additional costs if another builder takes the job and is

more expensive. In any event, this additional cost would be one measure of damages that a court would impose on you if the Andersons prevailed in a suit for breach of contract (in addition to any costs the Andersons suffer as a result of the breach, such as costs due to the delay in construction). Thus, by making the offer, you might be able to avoid the expense of litigation—if the Andersons accept your offer.

Settlement Offers

Often, parties are reluctant to propose compromise settlements because they fear that what they say will be used against them in court if litigation ensues. Generally, however, offers for settlement will not be admitted in court to prove that you are liable for a breach of contract (though they are at times admissible to prove a party breached the duty of good faith).

CHECKLIST FOR THE CONTRACTOR WHO CANNOT PERFORM

1 Consider a compromise.
2 Subcontract out the work and oversee it.
3 Offer to find an alternative contractor to fulfill your obligation.
4 Make a cash offer to "buy" a release from your contract. Work with an attorney in making the offer, unless only an insignificant amount is involved.

* This *Application* is not meant to substitute for the services of an attorney who is licensed to practice law in your state.

KEY TERMS

consequential damages 358
incidental damages 357
liquidated damages 362

mitigation of damages 360
nominal damages 359
penalty 362

restitution 364
specific performance 364

CHAPTER SUMMARY   Breach and Remedies

COMMON REMEDIES AVAILABLE TO NONBREACHING PARTY

Damages
(See pages 357–363.)

The legal remedy designed to compensate the nonbreaching party for the loss of the bargain. By awarding monetary damages, the court tries to place the parties in the positions that they would have occupied had the contract been fully performed. The nonbreaching party frequently has a duty to *mitigate* (lessen or reduce) the damages incurred as a result of the contract's breach. There are five broad categories of damages:

CHAPTER SUMMARY Breach and Remedies–Continued

Damages–Continued	1. *Compensatory damages*—Damages that compensate the nonbreaching party for injuries actually sustained and proved to have arisen directly from the loss of the bargain resulting from the breach of contract.
	a. In breached contracts for the sale of goods, the usual measure of compensatory damages is the difference between the contract price and the market price.
	b. In breached contracts for the sale of land, the measure of damages is ordinarily the same as in contracts for the sale of goods.
	c. In breached construction contracts, the measure of damages depends on which party breaches and at what stage of construction the breach occurs.
	2. *Consequential damages*—Damages resulting from special circumstances beyond the contract itself; the damages flow only from the consequences of a breach. For a party to recover consequential damages, the damages must be the foreseeable result of a breach of contract, and the breaching party must have known at the time the contract was formed that special circumstances existed that would cause the nonbreaching party to incur additional loss on breach of the contract. Also called *special damages*.
	3. *Punitive damages*—Damages awarded to punish the breaching party. Usually not awarded in an action for breach of contract unless a tort is involved.
	4. *Nominal damages*—Damages small in amount (such as one dollar) that are awarded when a breach has occurred but no actual injury has been suffered. Awarded only to establish that the defendant acted wrongfully.
	5. *Liquidated damages*—Damages that may be specified in a contract as the amount to be paid to the nonbreaching party in the event the contract is breached in the future. Clauses providing for liquidated damages are enforced if the damages were difficult to estimate at the time the contract was formed and if the amount stipulated is reasonable. If the amount is construed to be a penalty, the clause will not be enforced.
Rescission and Restitution (See page 364.)	1. *Rescission*—A remedy whereby a contract is canceled and the parties are restored to the original positions that they occupied prior to the transaction. Available when fraud, a mistake, duress, or failure of consideration is present. The rescinding party must give prompt notice of the rescission to the breaching party.
	2. *Restitution*—When a contract is rescinded, both parties must make restitution to each other by returning the goods, property, or funds previously conveyed. Restitution prevents the unjust enrichment of the parties.
Specific Performance (See pages 364–366.)	An equitable remedy calling for the performance of the act promised in the contract. This remedy is available only in special situations—such as those involving contracts for the sale of unique goods or land—and when monetary damages would be an inadequate remedy. Specific performance is not available as a remedy for breached contracts for personal services.
Reformation (See page 366.)	An equitable remedy allowing a contract to be "reformed," or rewritten, to reflect the parties' true intentions. Available when an agreement is imperfectly expressed in writing.
Recovery Based on Quasi Contract (See page 367.)	An equitable theory imposed by the courts to obtain justice and prevent unjust enrichment in a situation in which no enforceable contract exists. The party seeking recovery must show the following:
	1. A benefit was conferred on the other party.
	2. The party conferring the benefit did so with the expectation of being paid.
	3. The benefit was not volunteered.

(Continued)

CHAPTER SUMMARY Breach and Remedies–Continued

Recovery Based on Quasi Contract–Continued	4. Retaining the benefit without paying for it would result in the unjust enrichment of the party receiving the benefit.
	CONTRACT DOCTRINES RELATING TO REMEDIES
Contract Provisions Limiting Remedies (See pages 367–369.)	A contract may provide that no damages (or only a limited amount of damages) can be recovered in the event the contract is breached. Clauses excluding liability for fraudulent or intentional injury or for illegal acts cannot be enforced. Clauses excluding liability for negligence may be enforced if both parties hold roughly equal bargaining power. Under the Uniform Commercial Code (UCC), remedies may be limited in contracts for the sale of goods.
Election of Remedies (See page 369.)	A common law doctrine under which a nonbreaching party must choose one remedy from those available. This doctrine prevents double recovery. Under the UCC, remedies are cumulative for the breach of a contract for the sale of goods.

FOR REVIEW

Answers for the even-numbered questions in this For Review *section can be found in Appendix E at the end of this text.*

1 What is the difference between compensatory damages and consequential damages? What are nominal damages, and when do courts award nominal damages?

2 What is the standard measure of compensatory damages when a contract is breached? How are damages computed differently in construction contracts?

3 Under what circumstances is the remedy of rescission and restitution available?

4 When do courts grant specific performance as a remedy?

5 What is the rationale underlying the doctrine of election of remedies?

 The following multiple-choice question is representative of the types of questions available in one of the four sections of ThomsonNOW for *Business Law Today.* ThomsonNOW also provides feedback for each response option, whether correct or incorrect, and refers to the location within the chapter where the correct answer can be found.

Consequential damages are

a very small (usually one dollar) and meant simply to show that the defendant acted wrongfully.

b foreseeable damages that are caused by circumstances beyond the contract itself but that arise as a consequence of the contract's breach.

c damages that compensate a party for actual losses directly resulting from the breach of contract.

d damages that punish a breaching party.

QUESTIONS AND CASE PROBLEMS

 **HYPOTHETICAL SCENARIOS**

13.1 Liquidated Damages. Carnack contracts to sell his house and lot to Willard for $100,000. The terms of the contract call for Willard to pay 10 percent of the purchase price as a deposit toward the purchase price, or as a down payment. The terms further stipulate that should the buyer breach the contract, Carnack will retain the deposit as liquidated damages. Willard pays the deposit, but because her expected financing of the $90,000 balance falls through, she breaches the contract. Two weeks later, Carnack sells the house and lot to Balkova for $105,000. Willard demands her $10,000 back, but Carnack refuses, claiming that Willard's breach and the contract terms entitle him to keep the deposit. Discuss who is correct.

13.2 Hypothetical Question with Sample Answer. In which of the following situations might a court grant specific performance as a remedy for the breach of the contract?

1 Tarrington contracts to sell her house and lot to Rainier. Then, on finding another buyer willing to pay a higher purchase price, she refuses to deed the property to Rainier.

2 Marita contracts to sing and dance in Horace's nightclub for one month, beginning June 1. She then refuses to perform.

3 Juan contracts to purchase a rare coin from Edmund, who is breaking up his coin collection. At the last minute, Edmund decides to keep his coin collection intact and refuses to deliver the coin to Juan.

4 Astro Computer Corp. has three shareholders: Coase, who owns 48 percent of the stock; De Valle, who owns 48 percent; and Cary, who owns 4 percent. Cary contracts to sell his 4 percent to De Valle but later refuses to transfer the shares to him.

 For a sample answer to Question 13.2, go to Appendix F at the end of this text.

13.3 Measure of Damages. Johnson contracted to lease a house to Fox for $700 a month, beginning October 1. Fox stipulated in the contract that before he moved in, the interior of the house had to be completely repainted. On September 9, Johnson hired Keever to do the required painting for $1,000. He told Keever that the painting had to be finished by October 1 but did not explain why. On September 28, Keever quit for no reason, having completed approximately 80 percent of the work. Johnson then paid Sam $300 to finish the painting, but Sam did not finish until October 4. When Fox found that the painting had not been completed as stipulated in his contract with Johnson, he leased another home. Johnson found another tenant who would lease the property at $700 a month, beginning October 15. Johnson then sued Keever for breach of contract, claiming damages of $650. This amount included the $300 Johnson paid Sam to finish the painting and $350 for rent for the first half of October, which Johnson had lost as a result of Keever's breach. Johnson had not yet paid Keever anything for Keever's work. Can Johnson collect the $650 from Keever? Explain.

CASE PROBLEMS

13.4 Mitigation of Damages. Lauren Vuylsteke, a single mother with three children, lived in Portland, Oregon. Cynthia Broan also lived in Oregon until she moved to New York City to open and operate an art gallery. Broan asked Vuylsteke to manage the gallery under a one-year contract for an annual salary of $72,000. To begin work, Vuylsteke relocated to New York. As part of the move, Vuylsteke transferred custody of her children to her husband, who lived in London, England. In accepting the job, Vuylsteke also forfeited her husband's alimony and child-support payments, including unpaid amounts of nearly $30,000. Before Vuylsteke started work, Broan repudiated the contract. Unable to find employment for more than an annual salary of $25,000, Vuylsteke moved to London to be near her children. Vuylsteke filed a suit in an Oregon state court against Broan, seeking damages for breach of contract. Should the court hold, as Broan argued, that Vuylsteke did not take reasonable steps to mitigate her damages? Why or why not? [*Vuylsteke v. Broan*, 172 Or.App. 74, 17 P.3d 1072 (2001)]

13.5 Liquidated Damages versus Penalties. Every homeowner in the Putnam County, Indiana, subdivision of Stardust Hills must be a member of the Stardust Hills Owners Association, Inc., and must pay annual dues of $200 for the maintenance of common areas and other community services. Under the association's rules, dues paid more than ten days late "shall bear a delinquent fee at a rate of $2.00 per day." Phyllis Gaddis failed to pay the dues on a Stardust Hills lot that she owned. Late fees began to accrue. Nearly two months later, the association filed a suit in an Indiana state court to collect the unpaid dues and the late fees. Gaddis argued in response that the delinquent fee was an unenforceable penalty. What questions should be considered in determining the status of this fee? Should the association's rule regarding assessment of the fee be enforced? Explain. [*Gaddis v. Stardust Hills Owners Association, Inc.*, 804 N.E.2d 231 (Ind.App. 2004)]

13.6 Case Problem with Sample Answer. Tyna Ek met Russell Peterson in Seattle, Washington. Peterson persuaded Ek to buy a boat that he had once owned, the *O'Hana Kai*, which was in Juneau, Alaska. Ek paid the boat's current owner $43,000 for the boat, and in January 2000, she and Peterson entered into a contract, under which Peterson agreed to make the vessel seaworthy so that within one month it could be transported to Seattle, where he would pay its moorage costs. He would renovate the boat at his own expense in return for a portion of the profit on its resale in 2001. On the sale, Ek would recover her costs, and then Peterson would be reimbursed for his. Ek loaned Peterson her cell phone so that they could communicate while he prepared the vessel for the trip to Seattle. In March, Peterson, who was still in Alaska, borrowed $4,000 from Ek. Two months later, Ek began to receive unanticipated, unauthorized bills for vessel parts and moorage, the use of her phone, and charges on her credit card. She went to Juneau to take possession of the boat. Peterson moved it to Petersburg, Alaska, where he registered it under a false name, and then to Taku Harbor, where the police seized it. Ek filed a suit in an Alaska state court against Peterson, alleging breach of contract and seeking damages. If the court finds in Ek's favor, what should her damages include? Discuss. [*Peterson v. Ek*, 93 P.3d 458 (Alaska 2004)]

After you have answered Problem 13.6, compare your answer with the sample answer given on the Web site that accompanies this text. Go to www.thomsonedu.com/westbuslaw/blt, select "Chapter 13," and click on "Case Problem with Sample Answer."

13.7 Remedies. On July 7, 2000, Frances Morelli agreed to sell to Judith Bucklin a house at 126 Lakedell Drive in Warwick, Rhode Island, for $77,000. Bucklin made a deposit on the house. The closing at which the parties would exchange the deed for the price was scheduled for September 1. The agreement did not state that "time is of the essence," but it did provide, in "Paragraph 10" that "[i]f Seller is unable to [convey good, clear, insurable, and marketable title], Buyer shall have the option to: (a) accept such title as Seller is able to convey without abatement or reduction of the Purchase Price, or (b) cancel this Agreement and receive a return of all Deposits." An examination of the public records revealed that the house did not have marketable title. Wishing to be flexible, Bucklin offered Morelli time to resolve the problem, and the closing did not occur as scheduled. Morelli decided "the deal is over" and offered to return the deposit. Bucklin refused and, in mid-October, decided to exercise her option under Paragraph 10(a). She notified Morelli, who did not respond. Bucklin filed a suit in a Rhode Island state court against Morelli. In whose favor should the court rule? Should damages be awarded? If not, what is the appropriate remedy? Why? [*Bucklin v. Morelli*, 912 A.2d 931 (R.I. 2007)]

13.8 A Question of Ethics. *Julio Garza was employed by the Texas Animal Health Commission (TAHC) as a health inspector in 1981. His responsibilities included bleeding and tagging cattle, vaccinating and tattooing calves, and working livestock markets. Garza was injured on the job in 1988 and underwent surgery in January 1989. When his paid leave was exhausted, he asked TAHC for light-duty work, specifically the job of tick inspector, but his supervisor refused the request. In September, TAHC notified Garza that he was fired. Garza sued TAHC and others, alleging, in part, wrongful termination, and an important issue before the court was whether Garza had mitigated his damages. The court found that in the seven years between his termination and his trial date, Garza had held only one job—an unpaid job on his parents' ranch. When asked how often he looked for work during that time, Garza responded that he did not know, but he had looked in "several" places. The last time he looked for work was three or four months before the trial. That effort was merely an informal inquiry to his neighbors about working on their ranch. In view of these facts, consider the following questions. [Texas Animal Health Commission v. Garza, 27 S.W.3d 54 (Tex.App.—San Antonio 2000)]*

1 The court in this case stated that the "general rule as to mitigation of damages in breach of employment suits is that the discharged employee must use reasonable diligence to mitigate damages by seeking other employment." In your opinion, did Garza fulfill this requirement? If you were the judge, how would you rule in this case?

2 Assume for the moment that Garza had indeed been wrongfully terminated. In this situation, would it be fair to Garza to require him to mitigate his damages? Why or why not?

3 Generally, what are the ethical underpinnings of the rule that employees seeking damages for breach of employment contracts must mitigate their damages?

CRITICAL THINKING
AND WRITING ASSIGNMENTS

13.9 Critical Legal Thinking. Review the discussion of the doctrine of election of remedies in this chapter. What are some of the advantages and disadvantages of this doctrine?

13.10 Video Question. Go to this text's Web site at www.thomsonedu.com/westbuslaw/blt and select "Chapter 13." Click on "Video Questions" and view the video titled *Midnight Run*. Then answer the following questions.

1 In the video, Eddie (Joe Pantoliano) and Jack (Robert De Niro) negotiate a contract for Jack to find "the Duke," a mob accountant who embezzled funds, and bring him back

for trial. Assume that the contract is valid. If Jack breaches the contract by failing to bring in the Duke, what kinds of remedies, if any, can Eddie seek? Explain your answer.

2 Would the equitable remedy of specific performance be available to either Jack or Eddie in the event of a breach? Why or why not?

3 Now assume that the contract between Eddie and Jack is unenforceable. Nevertheless, Jack performs his side of the bargain by bringing in the Duke. Does Jack have any legal recourse in this situation? Explain.

ONLINE ACTIVITIES

PRACTICAL INTERNET EXERCISES

Go to this text's Web site at **www.thomsonedu.com/westbuslaw/blt**, select "Chapter 13," and click "Practical Internet Exercises." There you will find the following Internet research exercises that can perform to learn more about the topics covered in this chapter.

PRACTICAL INTERNET EXERCISE 13-1 LEGAL PERSPECTIVE—Contract Damages and Contract Theo

PRACTICAL INTERNET EXERCISE 13-2 MANAGEMENT PERSPECTIVE—The Duty to Mitigate

BEFORE THE TEST

Go to this text's Web site at **www.thomsonedu.com/westbuslaw/blt**, select "Chapter 13," and click "Interactive Quizzes." You will find a number of interactive questions relating to this chapter.

CHAPTER 24
Agency Relationships in Business

AGENCY
A relationship between two parties in which one party (the agent) agrees to represent or act for the other (the principal).

CHAPTER OUTLINE

– AGENCY RELATIONSHIPS

– HOW AGENCY RELATIONSHIPS ARE FORMED

– DUTIES OF AGENTS AND PRINCIPALS

– AGENT'S AUTHORITY

– LIABILITY IN AGENCY RELATIONSHIPS

– HOW AGENCY RELATIONSHIPS ARE TERMINATED

LEARNING OBJECTIVES

AFTER READING THIS CHAPTER, YOU SHOULD BE ABLE TO ANSWER THE FOLLOWING QUESTIONS:

1 What is the difference between an employee and an independent contractor?

2 How do agency relationships arise?

3 What duties do agents and principals owe to each other?

4 When is a principal liable for the agent's actions with respect to third parties? When is the agent liable?

5 What are some of the ways in which an agency relationship can be terminated?

O ne of the most common, important, and pervasive legal relationships is that of **agency.** As discussed in Chapter 20, in an agency relationship between two parties, one of the parties, called the *agent*, agrees to represent or act for the other, called the *principal*. The principal has the right to control the agent's conduct in matters entrusted to the agent, and the agent must exercise his or her powers "for the benefit of the principal only," as Justice Joseph Story indicated in the chapter-opening quotation. By using agents, a principal can conduct multiple business operations simultaneously in various locations. Thus, for example, contracts that bind the principal can be made at different places with different persons at the same time.

Agency relationships permeate the business world. Indeed, agency law is essential to the existence and operation of a corporate entity, because only through its agents can a corporation function and enter into contracts. A familiar example of an agent is a corporate officer who serves in a representative capacity for the owners of the corporation. In this capacity, the officer has the authority to bind the principal (the corporation) to a contract.

AGENCY RELATIONSHIPS

Section 1(1) of the *Restatement (Second) of Agency*[1] defines agency as "the fiduciary relation which results from the manifestation of consent by one person to another that the other shall act in his [or her] behalf and subject to his [or her] control, and consent by the other so to act." In other words, in a principal-agent relationship, the parties have

---

1. The *Restatement (Second) of Agency* is an authoritative summary of the law of agency and is often referred to by judges and other legal professionals.

agreed that the agent will act *on behalf and instead of* the principal in negotiating and transacting business with third parties.

The term **fiduciary** is at the heart of agency law. The term can be used both as a noun and as an adjective. When used as a noun, it refers to a person having a duty created by her or his undertaking to act primarily for another's benefit in matters connected with the undertaking. When used as an adjective, as in "fiduciary relationship," it means that the relationship involves trust and confidence.

Agency relationships commonly exist between employers and employees. Agency relationships may sometimes also exist between employers and independent contractors who are hired to perform special tasks or services.

FIDUCIARY
As a noun, a person having a duty created by his or her undertaking to act primarily for another's benefit in matters connected with the undertaking. As an adjective, a relationship founded on trust and confidence.

Employer-Employee Relationships

Normally, all employees who deal with third parties are deemed to be agents. A salesperson in a department store, for instance, is an agent of the store's owner (the principal) and acts on the owner's behalf. Any sale of goods made by the salesperson to a customer is binding on the principal. Similarly, most representations of fact made by the salesperson with respect to the goods sold are binding on the principal.

Because employees who deal with third parties are normally deemed to be agents of their employers, agency law and employment law overlap considerably. Agency relationships, though, as will become apparent, can exist outside an employer-employee relationship and thus have a broader reach than employment laws do. Additionally, bear in mind that agency law is based on the common law. In the employment realm, many common law doctrines have been displaced by statutory law and government regulations relating to employment relationships.

Employment laws (state and federal) apply only to the employer-employee relationship. Statutes governing Social Security, withholding taxes, workers' compensation, unemployment compensation, workplace safety, employment discrimination, and the like (see Chapters 33 and 34) are applicable only if employer-employee status exists. *These laws do not apply to an independent contractor.*

ON THE WEB

For information on the *Restatements of the Law,* including planned revisions, go to the American Law Institute's Web site at

www.ali.org.

Employer–Independent Contractor Relationships

Independent contractors are not employees because, by definition, those who hire them have no control over the details of their physical performance. Section 2 of the *Restatement (Second) of Agency* defines an **independent contractor** as follows:

> [An independent contractor is] a person who contracts with another to do something for him [or her] but who is not controlled by the other nor subject to the other's right to control with respect to his [or her] physical conduct in the performance of the undertaking. *He [or she] may or may not be an agent.* [Emphasis added.]

Building contractors and subcontractors are independent contractors; a property owner does not control the acts of either of these professionals. Truck drivers who own their equipment and hire themselves out on a per-job basis are independent contractors, but truck drivers who drive company trucks on a regular basis are usually employees.

The relationship between a person or firm and an independent contractor may or may not involve an agency relationship. To illustrate: An owner of real estate who hires a real estate broker to negotiate a sale of his or her property not only has contracted with an independent contractor (the real estate broker) but also has established an agency relationship for the specific purpose of assisting in the sale of the property. Another example is an insurance agent, who is both

INDEPENDENT CONTRACTOR
One who works for, and receives payment from, an employer but whose working conditions and methods are not controlled by the employer. An independent contractor is not an employee but may be an agent.

An independent contractor communicates from a building site. What are some significant differences between employees and independent contractors? (Greg Younger/ Creative Commons)

an independent contractor and an agent of the insurance company for which she or he sells policies. (Note that an insurance *broker*, in contrast, normally is an agent of the person obtaining insurance and not of the insurance company.)

Determining Employee Status

The courts are frequently asked to determine whether a particular worker is an employee or an independent contractor. How a court decides this issue can have a significant effect on the rights and liabilities of the parties. For example, employers are required to pay certain taxes, such as Social Security and unemployment taxes, for employees but not for independent contractors.

Criteria Used by the Courts In determining whether a worker has the status of an employee or an independent contractor, the courts often consider the following questions:

1 How much control can the employer exercise over the details of the work? (If an employer can exercise considerable control over the details of the work, this would indicate employee status. This is perhaps the most important factor weighed by the courts in determining employee status.)

2 Is the worker engaged in an occupation or business distinct from that of the employer? (If so, this points to independent-contractor status, not employee status.)

3 Is the work usually done under the employer's direction or by a specialist without supervision? (If the work is usually done under the employer's direction, this would indicate employee status.)

4 Does the employer supply the tools at the place of work? (If so, this would indicate employee status.)

5 For how long is the person employed? (If the person is employed for a long period of time, this would indicate employee status.)

6 What is the method of payment—by time period or at the completion of the job? (Payment by time period, such as once every two weeks or once a month, would indicate employee status.)

7 What degree of skill is required of the worker? (If little skill is required, this may indicate employee status.)

Sometimes, workers may benefit from having employee status—for tax purposes and to be protected under certain employment laws, for example. As mentioned earlier, federal statutes governing employment discrimination apply only when an employer-employee relationship exists. The question in the following case was whether, for the purpose of applying one of these statutes, a television show's co-host was an employee or an independent contractor.

CASE 24.1 **Alberty-Vélez v. Corporación de Puerto Rico**

United States Court of Appeals, First Circuit, 361 F.3d 1 (2004).
www.ca1.uscourts.gov[a]

FACTS In July 1993, Victoria Lis Alberty-Vélez (Alberty) began to co-host a new television show, *Desde Mi Pueblo,* on WIPR,

a. In the right-hand column, click on "Opinions." When that page opens, under "General Search," in the "Opinion Number begins with" box, type "02-2187" and click on "Submit Search." In the result, click on the appropriate link to access the opinion. The U.S. Court of Appeals for the First Circuit maintains this Web site.

a television station in Puerto Rico. The show profiled Puerto Rican cities and towns. Instead of signing a single contract, Alberty signed a new contract for each episode. Each contract obligated her to work a certain number of days. She was not obliged to do other work for WIPR, and WIPR was not obliged to contract with her for other work. During the filming, Alberty was responsible for providing her clothing, shoes, accessories,

CASE 24.1–Continued

hairstylist, and other services and materials. She was paid a lump sum, ranging from $400 to $550, for each episode. WIPR did not withhold income or Social Security taxes and did not provide health insurance, life insurance, a retirement plan, paid sick leave, maternity leave, or vacation time. Alberty became pregnant, and after November 1994, WIPR stopped contracting with her. She filed a suit in a federal district court against WIPR's owner, Corporación de Puerto Rico para la Difusión Pública, alleging, among other things, discrimination on the basis of her pregnancy in violation of a federal statute. The court issued a judgment in the defendant's favor. Alberty appealed to the U.S. Court of Appeals for the First Circuit.

ISSUE Was Alberty an independent contractor and therefore outside the application of the federal statute restricting employment discrimination on the basis of pregnancy?

DECISION Yes. The U.S. Court of Appeals for the First Circuit affirmed the lower court's judgment in WIPR's favor.

REASON The appellate court explained that in determining whether a party is an independent contractor, a court considers the employer's right to control the manner and means by which the party does the job for which he or she is

hired. Important factors include the required skills, the source of the tools for the job, the location of the work, the duration of the relationship between the parties, whether the employer has the right to assign other projects to the hired party, the parties' discretion over when and how long the work is done, the method of payment, whether the work is part of the employer's regular business, whether the employer is in business, the provision of employee benefits, and the tax treatment of the hired party. In this case, the court found that "[t]he parties structured their relationship through the use of set length contracts that permitted Alberty the freedom to pursue other opportunities and assured WIPR that it would not have to pay Alberty for the weeks that it was not filming. Further, the lack of benefits, the method of payment, and the parties' own description of their relationship in tax documents all indicate independent-contractor status."

 WHAT IF THE FACTS WERE DIFFERENT?
Suppose that Alberty had been a full-time, hourly worker and that such status was common among television hosts, but WIPR had manipulated the benefits and tax withholdings to favor independent-contractor status. Would the result have been different? Why or why not?

Criteria Used by the IRS Businesspersons should be aware that the Internal Revenue Service (IRS) has established its own criteria for determining whether a worker is an independent contractor or an employee. Although the IRS once considered twenty factors in determining a worker's status, guidelines that took effect in 1997 encourage IRS examiners to focus on just one of those factors—the degree of control the business exercises over the worker.

The IRS tends to closely scrutinize a firm's classification of its workers because, as mentioned, employers can avoid certain tax liabilities by hiring independent contractors instead of employees. Even when a firm classifies a worker as an independent contractor, if the IRS decides that the worker is actually an employee, the employer will be responsible for paying any applicable Social Security, withholding, and unemployment taxes.

■EXAMPLE 24.1 Microsoft Corporation had required a number of workers to become associated with employment agencies so that they could work for Microsoft as temporary workers. The workers sued, alleging that they were actually employees of Microsoft (rather than independent contractors) and thus entitled to participate in the company's stock option plan. The IRS determined that the workers were employees because Microsoft had exercised significant control over their work performance. A court affirmed this decision on appeal. Ultimately, Microsoft was required to pay back payroll taxes for hundreds of workers who had contractually agreed to work for Microsoft as independent contractors.[2] ■

---

2. *Vizcaino v. U.S. District Court for the Western District of Washington*, 173 F.3d 713 (9th Cir. 1999).

PREVENTING LEGAL DISPUTES

Businesspersons should be aware that the mere designation of a person as an independent contractor does not mean the employer can necessarily avoid tax liability. The courts and the IRS look behind the label to ascertain the true relationship between the worker and the business entity. Control is the most significant factor. Because of the potentially significant tax liability if the IRS determines that independent contractors are actually employees, businesspersons should seek the advice of an attorney when classifying workers as independent contractors. The *Application* feature at the end of the chapter offers more suggestions for using independent contractors.

Employee Status and "Works for Hire"   Under the Copyright Act of 1976, any copyrighted work created by an employee within the scope of her or his employment at the request of the employer is a "work for hire," and the employer owns the copyright to the work. When an employer hires an independent contractor—a freelance artist, writer, or computer programmer, for example—the independent contractor owns the copyright *unless* the parties agree in writing that the work is a "work for hire" and the work falls into one of nine specific categories, including audiovisual and other works.

EXAMPLE 24.2 Graham marketed CD-ROM discs containing compilations of software programs that are available free to the public. Graham hired James to create a file-retrieval program that allowed users to access the software on the CDs. James built into the final version of the program a notice stating that he was the author of the program and owned the copyright. Graham removed the notice. When James sold the program to another CD-ROM publisher, Graham filed a suit claiming that James's file-retrieval program was a "work for hire" and that Graham owned the copyright to the program. The court, however, decided that James—a skilled computer programmer who controlled the manner and method of his work—was an independent contractor and not an employee for hire. Thus, James owned the copyright to the file-retrieval program.[3]

HOW AGENCY RELATIONSHIPS ARE FORMED

Agency relationships normally are consensual; that is, they come about by voluntary consent and agreement between the parties. Generally, the agreement need not be in writing,[4] and consideration is not required.

A person must have contractual capacity to be a principal.[5] Those who cannot legally enter into contracts directly should not be allowed to do so indirectly through an agent. Any person can be an agent, though, regardless of whether he or she has the capacity to enter a contract. Because an agent derives the authority to enter into contracts from the principal and because a contract made by an agent is legally viewed as a contract of the principal, it is immaterial whether the agent personally has the legal capacity to make that contract. Thus, even a minor or a person who is legally incompetent can be appointed as an agent (but generally cannot be a principal).

---

3. *Graham v. James,* 144 F.3d 229 (2d Cir. 1998).
4. There are two main exceptions to the statement that agency agreements need not be in writing: (1) Whenever agency authority empowers the agent to enter into a contract that the Statute of Frauds requires to be in writing, the agent's authority from the principal must likewise be in writing (this is called the *equal dignity rule,* to be discussed later in this chapter). (2) A power of attorney, which confers authority to an agent, must be in writing.
5. Note that some states allow a minor to be a principal. When a minor is permitted to be a principal, however, any resulting contracts will be voidable by the minor principal but not by the adult third party.

An agency relationship can be created for any legal purpose. An agency relationship that is created for an illegal purpose or that is contrary to public policy is unenforceable. **EXAMPLE 24.3** Sharp (as principal) contracts with Blesh (as agent) to sell illegal narcotics. This agency relationship is unenforceable because selling illegal narcotics is a felony and is contrary to public policy. ■ It is also illegal for physicians and other licensed professionals to employ unlicensed agents to perform professional actions.

Generally, an agency relationship can arise in four ways: by agreement of the parties, by ratification, by estoppel, and by operation of law. Here we look at each of these possibilities, and they are summarized in the *Concept Summary* on page 681.

Agency by Agreement

Most agency relationships are based on an express or implied agreement that the agent will act for the principal and that the principal agrees to have the agent so act. An agency agreement can take the form of an express written contract. **EXAMPLE 24.4** Renato enters into a written agreement with Troy, a real estate agent, to sell Renato's house. An agency relationship exists between Renato and Troy for the sale of the house and is detailed in a document that both parties sign. ■

Many express agency relationships are created by oral agreements rather than written contracts. **EXAMPLE 24.5** Reese asks Cary, a gardener, to contract with others for the care of his lawn on a regular basis. Cary agrees. In this situation, an agency relationship exists between Reese and Cary for the lawn care. ■

An agency agreement can also be implied by conduct. **EXAMPLE 24.6** A hotel expressly allows only Boris Koontz to park cars, but Boris has no employment contract there. The hotel's manager tells Boris when to work, as well as where and how to park the cars. The hotel's conduct amounts to a manifestation of its willingness to have Boris park its customers' cars, and Boris can infer from the hotel's conduct that he has authority to act as a parking valet. It can be inferred that Boris is an agent-employee for the hotel, his purpose being to provide valet parking services for hotel guests. ■

Agency by Ratification

On occasion, a person who is in fact not an agent (or who is an agent acting outside the scope of her or his authority) may make a contract on behalf of another (a principal). If the principal approves or affirms that contract by word or by action, an agency relationship is created by **ratification.** Ratification involves a question of intent, and intent can be expressed by either words or conduct. The basic requirements for ratification are discussed later in this chapter.

Agency by Estoppel

When a principal causes a third person to believe that another person is his or her agent, and the third person deals with the supposed agent, the principal is "estopped to deny" the agency relationship. In such a situation, the principal's actions create the *appearance* of an agency that does not in fact exist. The third person must prove that she or he *reasonably* believed that an agency relationship existed, though.[6] Facts and circumstances must show that an ordinary, prudent person familiar with business practice and custom would have been justified in concluding that the agent had authority.

EXAMPLE 24.7 Andrew accompanies Grant, a seed sales representative, to call on a customer, Steve, the proprietor of the General Seed Store. Andrew has done independent

---

6. These concepts also apply when a person who is in fact an agent undertakes an action that is beyond the scope of her or his authority, as will be discussed later in this chapter.

ON THE WEB

An excellent source for information on agency, including court cases involving agency concepts, is the Legal Information Institute (LII) at Cornell University. You can access the LII's Web page on this topic at

www.law.cornell.edu/wex/index.php/ Agency.

RATIFICATION
The act of accepting and giving legal force to an obligation that previously was not enforceable.

A restaurant offers valet parking services. Can it be inferred that the parking attendant shown here is an agent of the restaurant? Why or why not? (Valerie Everett/Creative Commons)

sales work but has never signed an employment agreement with Grant. Grant boasts to Steve that he wishes he had three more assistants "just like Andrew." By making this representation, Grant creates the impression that Andrew is his agent and has authority to solicit orders. Steve has reason to believe from Grant's statements that Andrew is an agent for Grant. Steve then places seed orders with Andrew. If Grant does not correct the impression that Andrew is an agent, Grant will be bound to fill the orders just as if Andrew were really his agent. Grant's representation to Steve created the impression that Andrew was Grant's agent and had authority to solicit orders. ▣

Note that the acts or declarations of a purported *agent* in and of themselves do not create an agency by estoppel. Rather, it is the deeds or statements *of the principal* that create an agency by estoppel. **■EXAMPLE 24.8** If Andrew walks into Steve's store and claims to be Grant's agent, when in fact he is not, and Grant has no knowledge of Andrew's representations, Grant will not be bound to any deal struck by Andrew and Steve. Andrew's acts and declarations alone do not create an agency by estoppel. ▣

Under what other circumstances might a third party reasonably believe that an agent has the authority to act for a principal when the agent actually does not have this authority? The following case provides an illustration.

CASE 24.2   **Motorsport Marketing, Inc. v. Wiedmaier, Inc.**

Missouri Court of Appeals, Western District, 195 S.W.3d 492 (2006).
www.courts.mo.gov[a]

FACTS Wiedmaier, Inc., owns and operates Wiedmaier Truck Stop in St. Joseph, Missouri. The owners are Marsha Wiedmaier and her husband, Jerry. Their son Michael does not own an interest in the firm, but in 2002 and 2003, he worked for it as a fuel truck operator. Motorsport Marketing, Inc., sells racing collectibles and memorabilia to retail outlets. In April 2003, Michael faxed a credit application to Motorsport's sales manager, Lesa James. Michael's mother, Marsha, signed the form as "Secretary-Owner" of Wiedmaier; after she signed, Michael added himself to the list of owners. Motorsport approved a credit line. Michael formed Extreme Diecast, LLC, which he told Motorsport was part of Wiedmaier, and began ordering Motorsport merchandise. By early 2004, however, Michael had stopped making payments on the account, quit his job, and moved to Columbus, Ohio. Patrick Rainey, the president of Motorsport, contacted Marsha. She refused to pay. Motorsport filed a suit in a Missouri state court against Wiedmaier and others to collect the unpaid amount. The court entered a judgment in favor of Motorsport, assessing liability against the defendants for the outstanding balance of

a. In the "Quick Links" box, click on "Opinion & Minutes." When that page opens, click on the "Missouri Court of Appeals, Western District opinions" link. At the bottom of the next page, click on the "Search Opinions" link. In that page's "Search for" box, type "Wiedmaier" and click on "Search." In the result, click on the name of the case to access the opinion. The Missouri state courts maintain this Web site.

$93,388.58, plus $13,406.38 in interest and $25,165.93 in attorneys' fees. The defendants appealed to a state intermediate appellate court.

ISSUE Did Motorsport reasonably believe that Michael acted as Wiedmaier's agent in ordering merchandise?

DECISION Yes. The state intermediate appellate court affirmed the judgment of the lower court, echoing the conclusion that "Michael acted as an apparent agent of Wiedmaier, Inc., in its dealings with Motorsport."

REASON The appellate court emphasized that "[t]he credit application constituted a direct communication from Wiedmaier, Inc. (through Marsha) to Motorsport causing Motorsport to reasonably believe that Michael had authority to act for Wiedmaier, Inc." Marsha signed the application, on which Michael was listed as an owner. The defendants argued that Michael paid Motorsport with checks drawn on Extreme Diecast's account, which should have led Motorsport to investigate further. In response, the court pointed out that, as Motorsport was aware, "it is a common practice for a truck stop to have a separate division with a separate name to handle its diecast and other related merchandise, and that Michael represented that this is exactly what Extreme Diecast was." In good faith reliance on the credit application and Michael's representations, Motorsport extended credit to Wiedmaier and filled Michael's orders. "If the transaction[s]

CASE 24.2–Continued

executed by Michael [do] not bind Wiedmaier, Inc., Motorsport will suffer the loss of the balance due on the account."

 WHAT IF THE FACTS WERE DIFFERENT?
Suppose that Motorsport's sales manager had telephoned Marsha Wiedmaier rather than just faxing the credit

application. Further suppose that Marsha had vouched for Michael's creditworthiness but informed Motorsport that she and her husband owned Wiedmaier and that Michael worked for them. How might the outcome of this case have been different in that situation?

Agency by Operation of Law

The courts may find an agency relationship in the absence of a formal agreement in other situations as well. This can occur in family relationships. For instance, suppose that one spouse purchases certain basic necessaries and charges them to the other spouse's charge account. The courts will often rule that the latter is liable to pay for the necessaries, either because of a social policy of promoting the general welfare of the spouse or because of a legal duty to supply necessaries to family members.

Agency by operation of law may also occur in emergency situations, when the agent's failure to act outside the scope of his or her authority would cause the principal substantial loss. If the agent is unable to contact the principal, the courts will often grant this emergency power. For instance, a railroad engineer may contract on behalf of her or his employer for medical care for an injured motorist hit by the train. The *Concept Summary* reviews the various ways that agencies are formed.

DUTIES OF AGENTS AND PRINCIPALS

Once the principal-agent relationship has been created, both parties have duties that govern their conduct. As discussed previously, an agency relationship is *fiduciary*—one of trust. In a fiduciary relationship, each party owes the other the duty to act with the utmost good faith. We now examine the various duties of agents and principals.

CONCEPT SUMMARY **How Agency Relationships Are Formed**

METHOD OF FORMATION	DESCRIPTION
By Agreement	The agency relationship is formed through express consent (oral or written) or implied by conduct.
By Ratification	The principal either by act or by agreement ratifies the conduct of a person who is not in fact an agent.
By Estoppel	The principal causes a third person to believe that another person is the principal's agent, and the third person acts to his or her detriment in reasonable reliance on that belief.
By Operation of Law	The agency relationship is based on a social duty (such as the need to support family members) or formed in emergency situations when the agent is unable to contact the principal and failure to act outside the scope of the agent's authority would cause the principal substantial loss.

BE AWARE An agent's disclosure of confidential information could constitute the business tort of misappropriation of trade secrets.

In general, for every duty of the principal, the agent has a corresponding right, and vice versa. When one party to the agency relationship violates his or her duty to the other party, the remedies available to the nonbreaching party arise out of contract and tort law. These remedies include monetary damages, termination of the agency relationship, an injunction, and required accountings.

Agent's Duties to the Principal

Generally, the agent owes the principal five duties—performance, notification, loyalty, obedience, and accounting.

Performance An implied condition in every agency contract is the agent's agreement to use reasonable diligence and skill in performing the work. When an agent fails entirely to perform her or his duties, liability for breach of contract normally will result. The degree of skill or care required of an agent is usually that expected of a reasonable person under similar circumstances. Generally, this is interpreted to mean ordinary care. If an agent has represented himself or herself as possessing special skills, however, the agent is expected to exercise the degree of skill or skills claimed. Failure to do so constitutes a breach of the agent's duty.

Not all agency relationships are based on contract. In some situations, an agent acts gratuitously—that is, not for monetary compensation. A gratuitous agent cannot be liable for breach of contract, as there is no contract; he or she is subject only to tort liability. Once a gratuitous agent has begun to act in an agency capacity, he or she has the duty to continue to perform in that capacity in an acceptable manner and is subject to the same standards of care and duty to perform as other agents.

Notification An agent is required to notify the principal of all matters that come to her or his attention concerning the subject matter of the agency. This is the *duty of notification*, or the duty to inform. **■EXAMPLE 24.9** Lang, an artist, is about to negotiate a contract to sell a series of paintings to Barber's Art Gallery for $25,000. Lang's agent learns that Barber is insolvent and will be unable to pay for the paintings. Lang's agent has a duty to inform Lang of this fact because it is relevant to the subject matter of the agency—the sale of Lang's paintings. ■ Generally, the law assumes that the principal knows of any information acquired by the agent that is relevant to the agency—regardless of whether the agent actually passes on this information to the principal. It is a basic tenet of agency law that notice to the agent is notice to the principal.

Loyalty Loyalty is one of the most fundamental duties in a fiduciary relationship. Basically, the agent has the duty to act *solely for the benefit of his or her principal* and not in the interest of the agent or a third party. For example, an agent cannot represent two principals in the same transaction unless both know of the dual capacity and consent to it. The duty of loyalty also means that any information or knowledge acquired through the agency relationship is considered confidential. It would be a breach of loyalty to disclose such information either during the agency relationship or after its termination. Typical examples of confidential information are trade secrets and customer lists compiled by the principal.

In short, the agent's loyalty must be undivided. The agent's actions must be strictly for the benefit of the principal and must not result in any secret profit for the agent. The following case involved a real estate agent who discovered, while working for a principal, that a property owner would

A real estate agent meets with clients in her office. Suppose that the agent knows a buyer who is willing to pay more than the asking price for a property. What duty would the agent breach if she bought the property from the seller and sold it at a profit to that buyer? (Yoon Hernandez/Creative Commons)

only sell the desired property as a package deal with another parcel. One of the questions the court had to decide was whether the agent breached the duty of loyalty by buying the property to resell it to the principal.

CASE 24.3   **Cousins v. Realty Ventures, Inc.**

Court of Appeal of Louisiana, Fifth Circuit, 844 So.2d 860 (2003).

FACTS   Don Cousins, an insurance agent, sought commercial real estate in Metairie, Louisiana, for Eagle Ventures, Inc., to buy as an investment. Cousins engaged the services of Leo Hodgins, a real estate agent and the owner of Realty Ventures, Inc. (RVI). In June 1991, on Eagle's behalf, Hodgins submitted an offer of $90,000 to Westinghouse Credit Corporation to buy an 8,000-square-foot office building at 3330 Lake Villa Drive. Westinghouse responded that it could not sell the property immediately due to an agreement with its property management company. Through Hodgins, Eagle resubmitted the offer in October. Hodgins learned that Westinghouse would sell the building only with its neighboring property, a 33,000-square-foot office building at 4141 Veterans Boulevard, for $425,000. Hodgins estimated the two properties' worth to be about $1 million. Without telling Eagle about the package, Hodgins, his brother Paul, and RVI formed 4141 Vets Limited Partnership to buy the two buildings on May 7, 1992, for $420,000. Hodgins then offered to sell 3330 Lake Villa to Eagle for $175,000. Cousins and others filed a suit in a Louisiana state court against RVI and others, alleging breach of fiduciary duties. A jury returned a verdict in favor of the plaintiffs and awarded damages in the amount of $1.75 million. The defendants appealed to a state intermediate appellate court.

ISSUE   Did Hodgins breach the agent's duty of loyalty?

DECISION   Yes. The state intermediate appellate court affirmed the judgment of the lower court. "Leo Hodgins'

failure to communicate the package sale to plaintiffs the moment he learned of it constituted a breach of his fiduciary duties to them."

REASON   The appellate court specified that "Hodgins' duty was to give plaintiffs the information that Westinghouse rejected their offer for a single property sale and allow them to decide whether they wished to purchase both properties." The court explained that an agent's "precise duties" are defined by "the nature of the task the * * * agent undertakes to perform and the agreements he makes with the involved parties." Here, Cousins engaged Hodgins to find commercial investment property for Eagle to buy, and Hodgins called the principal's attention to Westinghouse's office building at 3330 Lake Villa Drive. Despite Eagle's offer to buy the property, submitted through Hodgins, and Westinghouse's response, Hodgins arranged a sale of the property to his firm, 4141 Vets Limited Partnership. The court pointed out that a real estate agent has "a duty to communicate to his principal all offers received and may be liable in damages for failure to do so. Moreover, a realtor has a duty to relay accurate information about property, a duty which extends to both vendor and purchaser, and may be held liable if such duty is breached."

 FOR CRITICAL ANALYSIS–Social Consideration *What steps do the facts in the* Cousins *case indicate that an investor might want to consider when dealing through an agent?*

Obedience   When acting on behalf of a principal, an agent has a duty to follow all lawful and clearly stated instructions of the principal. Any deviation from such instructions is a violation of this duty. During emergency situations, however, when the principal cannot be consulted, the agent may deviate from the instructions without violating this duty. Whenever instructions are not clearly stated, the agent can fulfill the duty of obedience by acting in good faith and in a manner reasonable under the circumstances.

Accounting   Unless an agent and a principal agree otherwise, the agent has the duty to keep and make available to the principal an account of all property and funds received and paid out on behalf of the principal. This includes gifts from third parties in connection with the agency. For example, a gift from a customer to a salesperson for prompt deliveries made by the salesperson's firm, in the absence of a company policy to the contrary, belongs to the firm. The agent has a duty to maintain separate accounts for the principal's funds and for the agent's personal funds, and the agent must not intermingle these accounts.

Principal's Duties to the Agent

The principal also owes certain duties to the agent. These duties relate to compensation, reimbursement and indemnification, cooperation, and safe working conditions.

Compensation   In general, when a principal requests certain services from an agent, the agent reasonably expects payment. The principal therefore has a duty to pay the agent for services rendered. For example, when an accountant or an attorney is asked to act as an agent, an agreement to compensate the agent for such service is implied. The principal also has a duty to pay that compensation in a timely manner. Except in a gratuitous agency relationship, in which an agent does not act for payment in return, the principal must pay the agreed-on value for an agent's services. If no amount has been expressly agreed on, the principal owes the agent the customary compensation for such services.

PREVENTING LEGAL DISPUTES

Many disputes arise because the principal and agent did not specify how much the agent would be paid. To avoid such disputes, businesspersons should always state in advance, and in writing, the amount or rate of compensation that they will pay their agents. Even when dealing with salespersons, such as real estate agents, who customarily are paid a percentage of the value of the sale, it is best to explicitly state the rate of compensation. When the parties are clear up front about the terms of their agency relationship, a dispute is less likely to surface.

◼

REMEMBER   An agent who signs a negotiable instrument on behalf of a principal may be personally liable on the instrument. Liability depends in part on whether the identity of the principal is disclosed and whether the parties intend the agent to be bound by her or his signature.

Reimbursement and Indemnification   Whenever an agent disburses funds to fulfill the request of the principal or to pay for necessary expenses in the course of a reasonable performance of his or her agency duties, the principal has the duty to reimburse the agent for these payments. Agents cannot recover for expenses incurred through their own misconduct or negligence, though.

Subject to the terms of the agency agreement, the principal has the duty to compensate, or *indemnify*, an agent for liabilities incurred because of authorized and lawful acts and transactions. For instance, if the principal fails to perform a contract formed by the agent with a third party and the third party then sues the agent, the principal is obligated to compensate the agent for any costs incurred in defending against the lawsuit.

Additionally, the principal must indemnify (pay) the agent for the value of benefits that the agent confers on the principal. The amount of indemnification is usually specified in the agency contract. If it is not, the courts will look to the nature of the business and the type of loss to determine the amount. Note that this rule applies to acts by gratuitous agents as well. If the finder of a dog that becomes sick takes the dog to a veterinarian and pays the required fees for the veterinarian's services, the agent is entitled to be reimbursed by the owner of the dog for those fees.

Cooperation   A principal has a duty to cooperate with the agent and to assist the agent in performing her or his duties. The principal must do nothing to prevent such performance. When a principal grants an agent an exclusive territory, for example, the principal creates an *exclusive agency* and cannot compete with the agent or appoint or allow another agent to so compete. If the principal does so, she or he will be exposed to liability for the agent's lost sales or profits. **EXAMPLE 24.10** Akers (the principal) creates an exclusive agency by granting Johnson (the agent) an exclusive territory within which Johnson may sell Akers's products. In this situation, Akers cannot compete with Johnson within that territory—or appoint or allow another agent to so compete—because this would violate the exclusive agency. If Akers does so, he can be held liable for Johnson's lost sales or profits. ■

Safe Working Conditions   Under the common law, a principal is required to provide safe working premises, equipment, and conditions for all agents and employees. The principal has a duty to inspect the working conditions and to warn agents and employees about any unsafe areas. When the agent is an employee, the employer's liability is frequently covered by state workers' compensation insurance, and federal and state statutes often require the employer to meet certain safety standards (to be discussed in Chapter 33).

AGENT'S AUTHORITY

An agent's authority to act can be either *actual* (express or implied) or *apparent*. If an agent contracts outside the scope of his or her authority, the principal may still become liable by ratifying the contract.

Actual Authority

As indicated, an agent's actual authority can be express or implied. We look here at both of these forms of actual authority.

Express Authority   *Express authority* is authority declared in clear, direct, and definite terms. Express authority can be given orally or in writing. In most states, the **equal dignity rule** requires that if the contract being executed is or must be in writing, then the agent's authority must also be in writing. Failure to comply with the equal dignity rule can make a contract voidable *at the option of the principal*. The law regards the contract at that point as a mere offer. If the principal decides to accept the offer, acceptance must be ratified, or affirmed, in writing.

EXAMPLE 24.11 Klee (the principal) orally asks Parkinson (the agent) to sell a ranch that Klee owns. Parkinson finds a buyer and signs a sales contract (a contract for an interest in realty must be in writing) on behalf of Klee to sell the ranch. The buyer cannot enforce the contract unless Klee subsequently ratifies Parkinson's agency status *in writing*. Once Parkinson's agency status is ratified, either party can enforce rights under the contract. ■

Modern business practice allows an exception to the equal dignity rule. An executive officer of a corporation normally is not required to obtain written authority from the corporation to conduct *ordinary* business transactions. The equal dignity rule does not apply when an agent acts in the presence of a principal or when the agent's act of signing is merely perfunctory. Thus, if Dickens (the principal) negotiates a contract but is called out of town the day it is to be signed and orally authorizes Santini to sign the contract, the oral authorization is sufficient.

Power of Attorney   Giving an agent a **power of attorney** confers express authority.[7] The power of attorney normally is a written document and is usually notarized. (A document is notarized when a **notary public**—a public official authorized to attest to the authenticity of signatures—signs and dates the document and imprints it with his or her seal of authority.) Most states have statutory provisions for creating a power of attorney. A power

EQUAL DIGNITY RULE
In most states, a rule stating that express authority given to an agent must be in writing if the contract to be made on behalf of the principal is required to be in writing.

POWER OF ATTORNEY
A written document, which is usually notarized, authorizing another to act as one's agent; can be special (permitting the agent to do specified acts only) or general (permitting the agent to transact all business for the principal).

NOTARY PUBLIC
A public official authorized to attest to the authenticity of signatures.

---

7. An agent who holds the power of attorney is called an *attorney-in-fact* for the principal. The holder does not have to be an attorney-at-law (and often is not).

EXHIBIT 24–1 **A Sample General Power of Attorney**

GENERAL POWER OF ATTORNEY

Know All Men by These Present:

That I, _____ , hereinafter referred to as PRINCIPAL, in the County of _____
State of _____ , do(es) appoint _____ as my true and lawful attorney.

In principal's name, and for principal's use and benefit, said attorney is authorized hereby;

(1) To demand, sue for, collect, and receive all money, debts, accounts, legacies, bequests, interest, dividends, annuities, and demands as are now or shall hereafter become due, payable, or belonging to principal, and take all lawful means, for the recovery thereof and to compromise the same and give discharges for the same;
(2) To buy and sell land, make contracts of every kind relative to land, any interest therein or the possession thereof, and to take possession and exercise control over the use thereof;
(3) To buy, sell, mortgage, hypothecate, assign, transfer, and in any manner deal with goods, wares and merchandise, choses in action, certificates or shares of capital stock, and other property in possession or in action, and to make, do, and transact all and every kind of business of whatever nature;
(4) To execute, acknowledge, and deliver contracts of sale, escrow instructions, deeds, leases including leases for minerals and hydrocarbon substances and assignments of leases, covenants, agreements and assignments of agreements, mortgages and assignments of mortgages, conveyances in trust, to secure indebtedness or other obligations, and assign the beneficial interest thereunder, subordinations of liens or encumbrances, bills of lading, receipts, evidences of debt, releases, bonds, notes, bills, requests to reconvey deeds of trust, partial or full judgments, satisfactions of mortgages, and other debts, and other written instruments of whatever kind and nature, all upon such terms and conditions as said attorney shall approve.

GIVING AND GRANTING to said attorney full power and authority to do all and every act and thing whatsoever requisite and necessary to be done relative to any of the foregoing as fully to all intents and purposes as principal might or could do if personally present.

All that said attorney shall lawfully do or cause to be done under the authority of this power of attorney is expressly approved.

Dated: _____   /s/_____

State of _____ } SS.
County of _____

On _____ , before me, the undersigned, a Notary Public in and for said State, personally appeared _____

known to me to be the person _____ whose name _____ subscribed
to the within instrument and acknowledged that _____ executed the same.
Witness my hand and official seal.   (Seal) _____
                                                                      Notary Public in and for said State.

of attorney can be special (permitting the agent to do specified acts only), or it can be general (permitting the agent to transact all business for the principal). Because a general power of attorney grants extensive authority to an agent to act on behalf of the principal in many ways (see Exhibit 24–1), it should be used with great caution. Ordinarily, a power of attorney terminates on the incapacity or death of the person giving the power.[8]

Implied Authority   An agent has the *implied authority* to do what is reasonably necessary to carry out express authority and accomplish the objectives of the agency. Authority

---

8. A *durable* power of attorney, however, continues to be effective despite the principal's incapacity. An elderly person, for example, might grant a durable power of attorney to provide for the handling of property and investments or specific health-care needs should she or he become incompetent.

can also be implied by custom or inferred from the position the agent occupies.
■EXAMPLE 24.12 Mueller is employed by Al's Supermarket to manage one of its stores. Al's has not expressly stated that Mueller has authority to contract with third persons. In this situation, though, authority to manage a business implies authority to do what is reasonably required (as is customary or can be inferred from a manager's position) to operate the business. This includes forming contracts to hire employees, to buy merchandise and equipment, and to advertise the products sold in the store. ■

ETHICAL ISSUE 24.1

Does an agent's breach of loyalty terminate the agent's authority? Suppose that an employee-agent who is authorized to access company trade secrets contained in computer files takes those secrets to a competitor for whom the employee is about to begin working. Clearly, in this situation the agent has violated the ethical—and legal—duty of loyalty to the principal. Does this breach of loyalty mean that the employee's act of accessing the trade secrets was unauthorized? The question has significant implications because if the act was unauthorized, the employee will be subject to state and federal laws prohibiting unauthorized access to computer information and data. If the act was authorized, the employee will not be subject to such laws. Although one court has held that the moment the employee accessed trade secrets for the purpose of divulging them to a competitor, the employee's authority as an agent terminated,[9] most courts have held that an agent's authority continues.

In one case, for example, three employees of Lockheed Martin Corporation copied confidential information and trade secrets from Lockheed's computer network onto compact discs and BlackBerries (personal digital assistants). Lockheed had authorized the employee-agents to access these files but was understandably upset when the three resigned and went to work for a competitor, taking the trade secrets with them. Lockheed sued the former agents under the Computer Fraud and Abuse Act (discussed in Chapter 6), arguing that they accessed the data without authorization. The federal district court, however, held that the individuals did have authorization to access the computer network and did not lose this authorization when they breached the duty of loyalty. Therefore, the court dismissed the case.[10] This ruling is important for businesspersons because it means that an employee-agent who steals confidential data or trade secrets may not be liable for unauthorized access.

> "The law is not a series of calculating machines where definitions and answers come tumbling out when the right levers are pushed."
> WILLIAM O. DOUGLAS,
> 1898–1980
> (Associate justice of the United States
> Supreme Court, 1939–1975)

Apparent Authority

Actual authority (express or implied) arises from what the principal manifests *to the agent*. An agent has **apparent authority** when the principal, by either words or actions, causes a *third party* reasonably to believe that an agent has authority to act, even though the agent has no express or implied authority. If the third party changes her or his position in reliance on the principal's representations, the principal may be *estopped* (prevented) from denying that the agent had authority.

■EXAMPLE 24.13 A traveling salesperson, Ling (the agent), is authorized to take customers' orders. Ling does not deliver the ordered goods and is not authorized to collect payments for the goods. A customer, Byron, pays Ling for a solicited order. Ling then takes the payment to the principal's accounting department, and an accountant accepts the payment and sends Byron a receipt. This procedure is thereafter followed for other orders solicited from and paid for by Byron. Later, Ling solicits an order, and Byron pays her as before. This time, however, Ling absconds with the payment. Can Byron claim that the payment to the agent was authorized and was thus, in effect, a payment to the principal?

APPARENT AUTHORITY
Authority that is only apparent, not real. In agency law, a person may be deemed to have had the power to act as an agent for another party if the other party's manifestations to a third party led the third party to believe that an agency existed when, in fact, it did not.

---

9. *Shurgard Storage Centers, Inc. v. Safeguard Self Storage, Inc.,* 119 F.Supp.2d 1121 (W.D.Wash. 2000).
10. *Lockheed Martin Corp. v. Speed,* ___ F.Supp.2d ___ (M.D.Fla. 2006).

The answer is normally yes, because the principal's *repeated* acts of accepting Byron's payment led him reasonably to expect that Ling had authority to receive payments for goods solicited. Although Ling did not have express or implied authority, the principal's conduct gave Ling *apparent* authority to collect. In this situation, the principal would be estopped from denying that Ling had authority to collect payments. ▣

Ratification

As already mentioned, ratification occurs when the principal affirms an agent's *unauthorized* act. When ratification occurs, the principal is bound to the agent's act, and the act is treated as if it had been authorized by the principal *from the outset*. Ratification can be either express or implied.

If the principal does not ratify the contract, the principal is not bound, and the third party's agreement with the agent is viewed as merely an unaccepted offer. Because the third party's agreement is an unaccepted offer, the third party can revoke the offer at any time, without liability, before the principal ratifies the contract.

The requirements for ratification can be summarized as follows:

1 The agent must have acted on behalf of an identified principal who subsequently ratifies the action.

2 The principal must know of all material facts involved in the transaction. If a principal ratifies a contract without knowing all of the facts, the principal can rescind (cancel) the contract.

3 The principal must affirm the agent's act in its entirety.

4 The principal must have the legal capacity to authorize the transaction at the time the agent engages in the act and at the time the principal ratifies. The third party must also have the legal capacity to engage in the transaction.

5 The principal's affirmation must occur before the third party withdraws from the transaction.

6 The principal must observe the same formalities when approving the act done by the agent as would have been required to authorize it initially.

The *Concept Summary* outlines the rules concerning an agent's authority to bind the principal and a third party.

LIABILITY IN AGENCY RELATIONSHIPS

Frequently, a question arises as to which party, the principal or the agent, should be held liable for contracts formed by the agent or for torts or crimes committed by the agent. We look here at these aspects of agency law.

Liability for Contracts

Liability for contracts formed by an agent depends on how the principal is classified and on whether the actions of the agent were authorized or unauthorized. Principals are classified as disclosed, partially disclosed, or undisclosed.[11]

A **disclosed principal** is a principal whose identity is known by the third party at the time the contract is made by the agent. A **partially disclosed principal** is a principal

BE AWARE An agent who exceeds his or her authority and enters into a contract that the principal does not ratify may be liable to the third party on the ground of misrepresentation.

DISCLOSED PRINCIPAL
A principal whose identity is known to a third party at the time the agent makes a contract with the third party.

PARTIALLY DISCLOSED PRINCIPAL
A principal whose identity is unknown by a third party, but the third party knows that the agent is or may be acting for a principal at the time the agent and the third party form a contract.

11. *Restatement (Second) of Agency*, Section 4.

CONCEPT SUMMARY — Authority of Agent to Bind Principal and Third Party

AUTHORITY OF AGENT	DEFINITION	EFFECT ON PRINCIPAL AND THIRD PARTY
Express Authority	Authority expressly given by the principal to the agent.	Principal and third party are bound in contract.
Implied Authority	Authority implied (1) because such authority is necessary if the agent is to carry out expressly authorized duties and responsibilities, (2) by custom, or (3) from the position in which the principal has placed the agent.	Principal and third party are bound in contract.
Apparent Authority	Authority created when the conduct of the principal leads a third party to believe that the principal's agent has authority.	Principal and third party are bound in contract.
Unauthorized Acts	Acts committed by an agent that are outside the scope of his or her express, implied, or apparent authority.	Principal and third party are not bound in contract—*unless* the principal ratifies prior to the third party's withdrawal.

whose identity is not known by the third party, but the third party knows that the agent is or may be acting for a principal at the time the contract is made. **EXAMPLE 24.14** Sarah has contracted with a real estate agent to sell certain property. She wishes to keep her identity a secret, but the agent makes it perfectly clear to potential buyers of the property that the agent is acting in an agency capacity. In this situation, Sarah is a partially disclosed principal. ■ An **undisclosed principal** is a principal whose identity is totally unknown by the third party, and the third party has no knowledge that the agent is acting in an agency capacity at the time the contract is made.

Authorized Acts   If an agent acts within the scope of her or his authority, normally the principal is obligated to perform the contract regardless of whether the principal was disclosed, partially disclosed, or undisclosed. Whether the agent may also be held liable under the contract, however, depends on the disclosed, partially disclosed, or undisclosed status of the principal.

Disclosed or Partially Disclosed Principal.   A disclosed or partially disclosed principal is liable to a third party for a contract made by an agent who is acting within the scope of her or his authority. If the principal is disclosed, an agent has no contractual liability for the nonperformance of the principal or the third party. If the principal is partially disclosed, in most states the agent is also treated as a party to the contract, and the third party can hold the agent liable for contractual nonperformance.[12]

EXAMPLE 24.15 Walgreens leased commercial property to operate a drugstore at a mall owned by Kedzie Plaza Associates. A property management company, Taxman Corporation, signed the lease on behalf of the principal, Kedzie. The lease required the landlord to keep the sidewalks free of snow and ice, so Taxman, on behalf of Kedzie, contracted with another

UNDISCLOSED PRINCIPAL
A principal whose identity is unknown by a third person, and the third person has no knowledge that the agent is acting for a principal at the time the agent and the third person form a contract.

---

12. *Restatement (Second) of Agency*, Section 321.

company to remove ice and snow from the sidewalks surrounding the Walgreens store. When a Walgreens employee slipped on ice outside the store and was injured, she sued Taxman for negligence. Because the principal's identity (Kedzie) was fully disclosed in the snow-removal contract, however, the Illinois court ruled that the agent, Taxman, could not be held liable. Taxman did not assume a contractual obligation to remove the snow but merely retained a contractor to do so on behalf of the owner.[13] ▣

Undisclosed Principal.   When neither the fact of agency nor the identity of the principal is disclosed, the undisclosed principal is bound to perform just as if the principal had been fully disclosed at the time the contract was made. The agent is also liable as a party to the contract.

When a principal's identity is undisclosed and the agent is forced to pay the third party, the agent is entitled to be indemnified (compensated) by the principal. The principal had a duty to perform, even though his or her identity was undisclosed, and failure to do so will make the principal ultimately liable. Once the undisclosed principal's identity is revealed, the third party generally can elect to hold either the principal or the agent liable on the contract. Conversely, the undisclosed principal can require the third party to fulfill the contract, *unless* (1) the undisclosed principal was expressly excluded as a party in the contract; (2) the contract is a negotiable instrument signed by the agent with no indication of signing in a representative capacity; or (3) the performance of the agent is personal to the contract, allowing the third party to refuse the principal's performance.

Unauthorized Acts   If an agent has no authority but nevertheless contracts with a third party, the principal cannot be held liable on the contract. It does not matter whether the principal was disclosed, partially disclosed, or undisclosed. The *agent* is liable, however.
EXAMPLE 24.16 Scranton signs a contract for the purchase of a truck, purportedly acting as an agent under authority granted by Johnson. In fact, Johnson has not given Scranton any such authority. Johnson refuses to pay for the truck, claiming that Scranton had no authority to purchase it. The seller of the truck is entitled to hold Scranton liable for payment. ▣

If the principal is disclosed or partially disclosed, the agent is liable to the third party as long as the third party relied on the agency status. The agent's liability here is based on the breach of an *implied warranty of authority* (an agent impliedly warrants that he or she has the authority to enter a contract on behalf of the principal), not on breach of the contract itself.[14] If the third party knows at the time the contract is made that the agent does not have authority—or if the agent expresses to the third party *uncertainty* as to the extent of her or his authority—then the agent is not personally liable.

Liability for E-Agents   Although in the past standard agency principles applied only to *human* agents, today these same principles are being applied to electronic agents. An electronic agent, or **e-agent,** is a semiautonomous computer program that is capable of executing specific tasks. E-agents used in e-commerce include software that can search through many databases and retrieve only information that is relevant for the user.

The Uniform Electronic Transactions Act (UETA), which was discussed in detail in Chapter 14 and has been adopted by the majority of the states, contains several provisions relating to the principal's liability for the actions of

E-AGENT
A computer program that by electronic or other automated means can independently initiate an action or respond to electronic messages or data without review by an individual.

Today, one can buy an array of products, including groceries, online. What act has taken steps to apply traditional agency principles to online transactions? (Photo by Bill Stryker)

---

13. *McBride v. Taxman Corp.,* 327 Ill.App.3d 992, 765 N.E.2d 51 (2002).
14. The agent is not liable on the contract because the agent was never intended personally to be a party to the contract.

e-agents. Section 15 of the UETA states that e-agents may enter into binding agreements on behalf of their principals. Presumably, then—at least in those states that have adopted the act—the principal will be bound by the terms in a contract entered into by an e-agent. Thus, if you place an order over the Internet, the company (principal) whose system took the order via an e-agent cannot claim that it did not receive your order.

The UETA also stipulates that if an e-agent does not provide an opportunity to prevent errors at the time of the transaction, the other party to the transaction can avoid the transaction. For instance, if an e-agent fails to provide an on-screen confirmation of a purchase or sale, the other party can avoid the effect of any errors.

Liability for Torts and Crimes

Obviously, any person, including an agent, is liable for her or his own torts and crimes. Whether a principal can also be held liable for an agent's torts and crimes depends on several factors, which we examine here. In some situations, a principal may be held liable not only for the torts of an agent but also for the torts committed by an independent contractor.

Principal's Tortious Conduct A principal conducting an activity through an agent may be liable for harm resulting from the principal's own negligence or recklessness. Thus, a principal may be liable for giving improper instructions, authorizing the use of improper materials or tools, or establishing improper rules that resulted in the agent's committing a tort. **■EXAMPLE 24.17** Jack knows that Suki cannot drive but nevertheless tells her to use the company truck to deliver some equipment to a customer. In this situation, Jack (the principal) will be liable for his own negligence to anyone injured by Suki's negligent driving. ■

Principal's Authorization of Agent's Tortious Conduct A principal who authorizes an agent to commit a tort may be liable to persons or property injured thereby, because the act is considered to be the principal's. **■EXAMPLE 24.18** Selkow directs his agent, Warren, to cut the corn on specific acreage, which neither of them has the right to do. The harvest is therefore a trespass (a tort), and Selkow is liable to the owner of the corn. ■

Note also that an agent acting at the principal's direction can be liable as a *tortfeasor* (one who commits a wrong, or tort), along with the principal, for committing the tortious act even if the agent was unaware of the wrongfulness of the act. Assume in the above example that Warren, the agent, did not know that Selkow had no right to harvest the corn. Warren can be held liable to the owner of the field for damages, along with Selkow, the principal.

Liability for Agent's Misrepresentation A principal is exposed to tort liability whenever a third person sustains a loss due to the agent's misrepresentation. The principal's liability depends on whether the agent was actually or apparently authorized to make representations and whether such representations were made within the scope of the agency. The principal is always directly responsible for an agent's misrepresentation made within the scope of the agent's authority. **■EXAMPLE 24.19** Bassett is a demonstrator for Moore's products. Moore sends Bassett to a home show to demonstrate the products and to answer questions from consumers. Moore has given Bassett authority to make statements about the products. If Bassett makes only true representations, all is fine; but if he makes false claims, Moore will be liable for any injuries or damages sustained by third parties in reliance on Bassett's false representations. ■

A serious ski accident occurs under the supervised instruction of a ski resort employee. Are there any circumstances under which the principal (the resort) will not be liable? (Rob Lee/Creative Commons)

Liability for Agent's Negligence   As mentioned, an agent is liable for his or her own torts. A principal may also be liable for harm an agent caused to a third party under the doctrine of *respondeat superior,*[15] a Latin term meaning "let the master respond." This doctrine, which is discussed in this chapter's *Landmark in the Law* feature, is similar to the theory of strict liability discussed in Chapter 4. The doctrine imposes **vicarious liability,** or indirect liability, on the employer—that is, liability without regard to the personal fault of the employer for torts committed by an employee in the course or scope of employment.

Determining the Scope of Employment.   The key to determining whether a principal may be liable for the torts of an agent under the doctrine of *respondeat superior* is whether the torts are committed within the scope of the agency or employment. The *Restatement (Second) of Agency,* Section 229, indicates the factors that today's courts will consider in determining whether a particular act occurred within the course and scope of employment. These factors are as follows:

1 Whether the employee's act was authorized by the employer.

2 The time, place, and purpose of the act.

3 Whether the act was one commonly performed by employees on behalf of their employers.

4 The extent to which the employer's interest was advanced by the act.

5 The extent to which the private interests of the employee were involved.

6 Whether the employer furnished the means or instrumentality (for example, a truck or a machine) by which the injury was inflicted.

7 Whether the employer had reason to know that the employee would do the act in question and whether the employee had ever done it before.

8 Whether the act involved the commission of a serious crime.

Suppose that the driver of the overturned truck in this photo caused a traffic accident that resulted in property damages and personal injuries. If the driver's employer (the principal) learns that the driver had been drinking alcohol during a break right before the incident, can the principal avoid liability? Why or why not? (Sister72/Creative Commons)

The Distinction between a "Detour" and a "Frolic."   A useful insight into the "scope of employment" concept may be gained from the judge's classic distinction between a "detour" and a "frolic" in the case of *Joel v. Morison* (1834).[16] In this case, the English court held that if a servant merely took a detour from his master's business, the master will be responsible. If, however, the servant was on a "frolic of his own" and not in any way "on his master's business," the master will not be liable.

EXAMPLE 24.20 Mandel, a traveling salesperson, while driving his employer's vehicle to call on a customer, decides to stop at the post office—which is one block off his route—to mail a personal letter. As Mandel approaches the post office, he negligently runs into a parked vehicle owned by Chan. In this situation, because Mandel's detour from the employer's business is not substantial, he is still acting within the scope of employment, and the employer is liable. The result would be different, though, if Mandel had decided to pick up a few friends for cocktails in another city and in the process had negligently run into Chan's vehicle. In that circumstance, the departure from the employer's business would be substantial, and the employer normally would not be liable to Chan for damages. Mandel would be considered to have been on a "frolic" of his own. ■

---

15. Pronounced ree-*spahn*-dee-uht soo-*peer*-ee-your.
16. 6 Car. & P. 501, 172 Eng. Reprint 1338 (1834).

LANDMARK IN THE LAW The Doctrine of *Respondeat Superior*

The idea that a master (employer) must respond to third persons for losses negligently caused by the master's servant (employee) first appeared in Lord Holt's opinion in *Jones v. Hart* (1698).[a] By the early nineteenth century, this maxim had been adopted by most courts and was referred to as the doctrine of *respondeat superior.*

Theories of Liability   The vicarious (indirect) liability of the master for the acts of the servant has been supported primarily by two theories. The first theory rests on the issue of *control,* or *fault:* the master has control over the acts of the servant and is thus responsible for injuries arising out of such service. The second theory is economic in nature: because the master takes the benefits or profits of the servant's service, he or she should also suffer the losses; moreover, the master is better able than the servant to absorb such losses.

The *control* theory is clearly recognized in the *Restatement (Second) of Agency,* which defines a master as "a principal who employs an agent to perform service in his [or her] affairs and who controls, or has the right to control, the physical conduct of the other in the performance of the service." Accordingly, a servant is defined as "an agent employed by a master to perform service in his [or her] affairs whose physical conduct in his [or her] performance of the service is controlled, or is subject to control, by the master."

Limitations on the Employer's Liability   There are limitations on the master's liability for the acts of the servant, however. An employer (master) is responsible only for the wrongful conduct of an employee (servant) that occurs in "the scope of employment." The criteria used by the courts in determining whether an employee is acting within the scope of employment are set forth in the *Restatement (Second) of Agency* and discussed in the text. Generally, the act must be of a kind the servant was employed to do; must have occurred within "authorized time and space limits"; and must have been "activated, at least in part, by a purpose to serve the master."

APPLICATION TO TODAY'S WORLD   *The courts have accepted the doctrine of* respondeat superior *for nearly two centuries. This theory of vicarious liability is laden with practical implications in all situations in which a principal-agent (master-servant, employer-employee) relationship exists. Today, the small-town grocer with one clerk and the multinational corporation with thousands of employees are equally subject to the doctrinal demand of "let the master respond." (For a further discussion of employers' liability for wrongs committed by their employees, including wrongs committed in the online employment environment, see Chapter 33.)*

RELEVANT WEB SITES   *To locate information on the Web concerning the doctrine of* respondeat superior, *go to this text's Web site at* **www.thomsonedu.com/westbuslaw/blt**, *select "Chapter 24," and click on "URLs for Landmarks."*

a. K.B. 642, 90 Eng. Reprint 1255 (1698).

NOTE An agent-employee going to or from work or meals usually is not considered to be within the scope of employment. An agent-employee whose job requires travel, however, is considered to be within the scope of employment for the entire trip, including the return.

Employee Travel Time. An employee going to and from work or to and from meals is usually considered outside the scope of employment. If travel is part of a person's position, however, such as a traveling salesperson or a regional representative of a company, then travel time is normally considered within the scope of employment. Thus, the duration of the business trip, including the return trip home, is within the scope of employment unless there is a significant departure from the employer's business.

Notice of Dangerous Conditions. The employer is charged with knowledge of any dangerous conditions discovered by an employee and pertinent to the employment situation. **■EXAMPLE 24.21** Chad, a maintenance employee in Martin's apartment building, notices a lead pipe protruding from the ground in the building's courtyard. The employee neglects either to fix the pipe or to inform the employer of the danger. John falls on the pipe and is injured. The employer is charged with knowledge of the dangerous condition regardless of whether or not Chad actually informed the employer. That knowledge is imputed to the employer by virtue of the employment relationship. ■

Liability for Agent's Intentional Torts Most intentional torts that employees commit have no relation to their employment; thus, their employers will not be held liable. Nevertheless, under the doctrine of *respondeat superior*, the employer can be liable for intentional torts of the employee that are committed within the course and scope of employment, just as the employer is liable for negligence. For instance, an employer is liable when an employee (such as a "bouncer" at a nightclub or a security guard at a department store) commits the tort of assault and battery or false imprisonment while acting within the scope of employment.

In addition, an employer who knows or should know that an employee has a propensity for committing tortious acts is liable for the employee's acts even if they would not ordinarily be considered within the scope of employment. For example, if the employer hires a bouncer knowing that he has a history of arrests for assault and battery, the employer may be liable if the employee viciously attacks a patron in the parking lot after hours.

An employer may also be liable for permitting an employee to engage in reckless actions that can injure others. **■EXAMPLE 24.22** An employer observes an employee smoking while filling containerized trucks with highly flammable liquids. Failure to stop the employee will cause the employer to be liable for any injuries that result if a truck explodes. ■ (See this chapter's *Beyond Our Borders* feature for a discussion of another approach to an employer's liability for an employee's acts.)

Liability for Independent Contractor's Torts Generally, an employer is not liable for physical harm caused to a third person by the negligent act of an independent contractor in the performance of the contract. This is because the employer does not have *the right to control* the details of an independent contractor's performance. Exceptions to this rule are made in certain situations, though, such as when unusually hazardous activities are involved. Typical examples of such activities include blasting operations, the transportation of highly volatile chemicals, or the use of poisonous gases. In these situations, an employer cannot be shielded from liability merely by using an independent contractor. Strict liability is imposed on the employer-principal as a matter of law. Also, in some states, strict liability may be imposed by statute.

Liability for Agent's Crimes An agent is liable for his or her own crimes. A principal or employer is not liable for an agent's crime even if the crime was committed within the scope of authority or employment—unless the principal participated by conspiracy or

BEYOND OUR BORDERS Islamic Law and *Respondeat Superior*

The doctrine of *respondeat superior* is well established in the legal systems of the United States and most Western countries. As you have already read, under this doctrine employers can be held liable for the acts of their agents, including employees. The doctrine of *respondeat superior* is not universal, however. Middle Eastern countries, for example, do not follow this doctrine. Islamic law, as codified in the *sharia,* holds to a strict belief that responsibility for human actions lies with the individual and cannot be vicariously extended to others. This belief and other concepts of Islamic law are based on the writings of Muhammad, a seventh-century prophet whose revelations formed the basis of the Islamic religion and, by extension, the *sharia.* Muhammad's prophecies are documented in the Qur'an (Koran), which is the principal source of the *sharia.*

FOR CRITICAL ANALYSIS *How would U.S. society be affected if employers could not be held vicariously liable for their employees' torts?*

■

other action. In some jurisdictions, under specific statutes, a principal may be liable for an agent's violation, in the course and scope of employment, of regulations, such as those governing sanitation, prices, weights, and the sale of liquor.

HOW AGENCY RELATIONSHIPS ARE TERMINATED

Agency law is similar to contract law in that both an agency and a contract can be terminated by an act of the parties or by operation of law. Once the relationship between the principal and the agent has ended, the agent no longer has the right (*actual* authority) to bind the principal. For an agent's *apparent* authority to be terminated, though, third persons may also need to be notified that the agency has been terminated.

Termination by Act of the Parties

An agency may be terminated by act of the parties in several ways, including those discussed here.

Lapse of Time An agency agreement may specify the time period during which the agency relationship will exist. If so, the agency ends when that time period expires. For instance, if the parties agree that the agency will begin on January 1, 2008, and end on December 31, 2009, the agency is automatically terminated on December 31, 2009. If no definite time is stated, then the agency continues for a reasonable time and can be terminated at will by either party. What constitutes a "reasonable time" depends, of course, on the circumstances and the nature of the agency relationship.

Purpose Achieved An agent can be employed to accomplish a particular objective, such as the purchase of stock for a cattle rancher. In that situation, the agency automatically ends after the cattle have been purchased. If more than one agent is employed to accomplish the same purpose, such as the sale of real estate, the first agent to complete the sale automatically terminates the agency relationship for all the others.

Occurrence of a Specific Event   An agency can be created to terminate on the happening of a certain event. If Posner appoints Rubik to handle her business affairs while she is away, the agency automatically terminates when Posner returns.

Mutual Agreement   Recall from the chapters on contract law that parties can cancel (rescind) a contract by mutually agreeing to terminate the contractual relationship. The same holds true in agency law regardless of whether the agency contract is in writing or whether it is for a specific duration.

Termination by One Party   As a general rule, either party can terminate the agency relationship (the act of termination is called *revocation* if done by the principal and *renunciation* if done by the agent). Although both parties have the *power* to terminate the agency, they may not possess the *right*. Wrongful termination can subject the canceling party to a suit for breach of contract. ■**EXAMPLE 24.23** Rawlins has a one-year employment contract with Munro to act as an agent in return for $65,000. Munro has the *power* to discharge Rawlins before the contract period expires. If Munro discharges Rawlins, however, Munro can be sued for breaching the contract and will be liable to Rawlins for damages because he had no *right* to terminate the agency. ■

A special rule applies in an *agency coupled with an interest*. This type of agency is not an agency in the usual sense because it is created for the agent's benefit instead of the principal's benefit. ■**EXAMPLE 24.24** Julie borrows $5,000 from Rob, giving Rob some of her jewelry and signing a letter giving Rob the power to sell the jewelry as her agent if she fails to repay the loan. After receiving the $5,000 from Rob, Julie attempts to revoke Rob's authority to sell the jewelry as her agent. Julie would not succeed in this attempt because a principal cannot revoke an agency created for the agent's benefit. ■

Notice of Termination   When an agency has been terminated by act of the parties, it is the principal's duty to inform any third parties who know of the existence of the agency that it has been terminated (although notice of the termination may be given by others). Although an agent's actual authority ends when the agency is terminated, an agent's *apparent authority* continues until the third party receives notice (from any source) that such authority has been terminated. If the principal knows that a third party has dealt with the agent, the principal is expected to notify that person *directly*. For third parties who have heard about the agency but have not yet dealt with the agent, *constructive notice* is sufficient.[17]

No particular form is required for notice of agency termination to be effective. The principal can personally notify the agent, or the agent can learn of the termination through some other means. ■**EXAMPLE 24.25** Manning bids on a shipment of steel, and Stone is hired as an agent to arrange transportation of the shipment. When Stone learns that Manning has lost the bid, Stone's authority to make the transportation arrangement terminates. ■ If the agent's authority is written, however, it normally must be revoked in writing.

Termination by Operation of Law

Termination of an agency by operation of law occurs in the circumstances discussed here. Note that when an agency terminates by operation of law, there is no duty to notify third persons.

---

17. *Constructive notice* is information or knowledge of a fact imputed by law to a person if he or she could have discovered the fact by proper diligence. Constructive notice is often accomplished by newspaper publication.

Death or Insanity   The general rule is that the death or mental incompetence of either the principal or the agent automatically and immediately terminates the ordinary agency relationship. Knowledge of the death is not required. **■EXAMPLE 24.26** Geer sends Pyron to China to purchase a rare painting. Before Pyron makes the purchase, Geer dies. Pyron's agent status is terminated at the moment of Geer's death, even though Pyron does not know that Geer has died. ■ Some states, however, have enacted statutes changing this common law rule to make knowledge of the principal's death a requirement for agency termination.

An agent's transactions that occur after the death of the principal are not binding on the principal's estate.[18] **■EXAMPLE 24.27** Carson is hired by Perry to collect a debt from Thomas (a third party). Perry dies, but Carson, not knowing of Perry's death, still collects the funds from Thomas. Thomas's payment to Carson is no longer legally sufficient to discharge the debt to Perry because Carson's authority to collect ended on Perry's death. If Carson absconds with the funds, Thomas is still liable for the debt to Perry's estate. ■

Impossibility   When the specific subject matter of an agency is destroyed or lost, the agency terminates. **■EXAMPLE 24.28** Bullard employs Gonzalez to sell Bullard's house. Prior to any sale, the house is destroyed by fire. In this situation, Gonzalez's agency and authority to sell Bullard's house terminate. ■ Similarly, when it is impossible for the agent to perform the agency lawfully because of a change in the law, the agency terminates.

Changed Circumstances   When an event occurs that has such an unusual effect on the subject matter of the agency that the agent can reasonably infer that the principal will not want the agency to continue, the agency terminates. **■EXAMPLE 24.29** Roberts hires Mullen to sell a tract of land for $20,000. Subsequently, Mullen learns that there is oil under the land and that the land is worth $1 million. The agency and Mullen's authority to sell the land for $20,000 are terminated. ■

Bankruptcy   If either the principal or the agent petitions for bankruptcy, the agency is *usually* terminated. In certain circumstances, as when the agent's financial status is irrelevant to the purpose of the agency, the agency relationship may continue. Insolvency (defined as the inability to pay debts when they become due or when liabilities exceed assets), as distinguished from bankruptcy, does not necessarily terminate the relationship.

War   When the principal's country and the agent's country are at war with each other, the agency is terminated. In this situation, the agency is automatically suspended or terminated because there is no way to enforce the legal rights and obligations of the parties.

---

18. Recall from Chapter 21 that special rules apply when the agent is a bank. Banks can continue to exercise specific types of authority even after a customer has died or become mentally incompetent unless they have knowledge of the death or incompetence [Section 4–405 of the Uniform Commercial Code]. Even with knowledge of the customer's death, the bank has authority to honor checks for ten days following the customer's death in the absence of a stop-payment order.

REVIEWING **Agency Relationships in Business**

Lynne Meyer, on her way to a business meeting and in a hurry, stopped by a Buy-Mart store for a new pair of nylons to wear to the meeting. There was a long line at one of the checkout counters, but a cashier, Valerie Watts, opened another counter and began loading the cash drawer. Meyer told Watts that she was in a hurry and asked Watts to work faster. Watts, however, only slowed her pace.

At this point, Meyer hit Watts. It is not clear from the record whether Meyer hit Watts intentionally or, in an attempt to retrieve the nylons, hit her inadvertently. In response, Watts grabbed Meyer by the hair and hit her repeatedly in the back of the head, while Meyer screamed for help. Management personnel separated the two women and questioned them about the incident. Watts was immediately fired for violating the store's no-fighting policy. Meyer subsequently sued Buy-Mart, alleging that the store was liable for the tort (assault and battery) committed by its employee. Using the information presented in the chapter, answer the following questions.

1 Under what doctrine discussed in this chapter might Buy-Mart be held liable for the tort committed by Watts?

2 What is the key factor in determining whether Buy-Mart is liable under this doctrine?

3 How is Buy-Mart's potential liability affected depending on whether Watts's behavior constituted an intentional tort or a tort of negligence?

4 Suppose that when Watts applied for the job at Buy-Mart, she disclosed in her application that she had previously been convicted of felony assault and battery. Nevertheless, Buy-Mart hired Watts as a cashier. How might this fact affect Buy-Mart's liability for Watts's actions?

APPLICATION | How Can an Employer Use Independent Contractors?*

As an employer, you may at some time consider hiring an independent contractor. Hiring workers as independent contractors instead of as employees may help you reduce both your potential tort liability and your tax liability.

Minimizing Potential Tort Liability

One reason for using an independent contractor is that employers are usually not liable for torts that an independent contractor commits against third parties. Nevertheless, there are exceptions. If an employer exercises significant control over the activities of the independent contractor, for example, the contractor may be considered an employee, and the employer can then be liable for the contractor's torts.

To minimize even the possibility of being liable for the negligence of an independent contractor, you should check the contractor's qualifications before hiring him or her. The degree to which you should investigate depends, of course, on the nature of the work. For example, hiring an independent contractor to maintain the landscaping around your building should require less investigation than employing an independent contractor to install the electrical systems that you sell. Also, a more thorough investigation is necessary when the contractor's activities present a potential danger to the public (as in delivering explosives).

Generally, it is a good idea to have the independent contractor assume, in a written contract, liability for harms caused to third parties by the contractor's negligence. You should also require the independent contractor to purchase liability insurance to cover the costs of potential lawsuits for harms caused to third persons by the independent contractor's hazardous activities or negligence.

Reducing Tax Liability and Other Costs

Another reason for hiring independent contractors is that you do not need to pay or withhold Social Security, income, or unemployment taxes on their behalf. The independent contractor is responsible for paying these taxes. Additionally, the independent contractor is not eligible for any retirement or medical plans or other fringe benefits that you provide for yourself and your employees, and this is a cost saving to you.

A word of caution, though: simply designating a person as an independent contractor does not make her or him one. The Internal Revenue Service (IRS) will reclassify individuals as employees if it determines that they are "in fact" employees, regardless of how you have designated them. Thus, the IRS will not treat an office assistant as an independent contractor simply because you designate him or her as such. If the IRS determines that you exercise significant control over the assistant, the IRS may decide that the assistant is, in fact, an employee.

If you improperly designate an employee as an independent contractor, the penalty may be high. Usually, you will be liable for back Social Security and unemployment taxes, plus interest and penalties. When in doubt, seek professional assistance in such matters.

---

* This Application is not meant to substitute for the services of an attorney who is licensed to practice law in your state.

CHECKLIST FOR THE EMPLOYER

1 Check the qualifications of any independent contractor you plan to use to reduce the possibility that you might be legally liable for the contractor's negligence.

2 It is best to require in any contract with an independent contractor that the contractor assume liability for harm to a third person caused by the contractor's negligence.

3 In your contracts with independent contractors, require that they carry liability insurance. Examine the policy to make sure that it is current, particularly

when the contractor will be undertaking actions that are more than normally hazardous to the public.

4 Do not do anything that would lead a third person to believe that an independent contractor is your employee, and do not allow independent contractors to represent themselves as your employees.

5 Regularly inspect the work of the independent contractor to make sure that it is being performed in accordance with contract specifications. Such supervision on your part will not change the worker's status as an independent contractor.

KEY TERMS

agency 674
apparent authority 687
disclosed principal 689
e-agent 690
equal dignity rule 685

fiduciary 675
independent contractor 675
notary public 685
partially disclosed principal 689
power of attorney 685

ratification 679
respondeat superior 692
undisclosed principal 689
vicarious liability 692

CHAPTER SUMMARY Agency Relationships in Business

Agency Relationships (See pages 674–678.)	In a *principal-agent* relationship, an agent acts on behalf of and instead of the principal in dealing with third parties. An employee who deals with third parties is normally an agent. An independent contractor is not an employee, and the employer has no control over the details of physical performance. An independent contractor may or may not be an agent.
How Agency Relationships Are Formed (See pages 678–681.)	Agency relationships may be formed by agreement, by ratification, by estoppel, and by operation of law—see the *Concept Summary* on page 681.
Duties of Agents and Principals (See pages 681–685.)	1. *Duties of the agent—* a. Performance—The agent must use reasonable diligence and skill in performing her or his duties or use the special skills that the agent has represented to the principal that the agent possesses. b. Notification—The agent is required to notify the principal of all matters that come to his or her attention concerning the subject matter of the agency. c. Loyalty—The agent has a duty to act solely for the benefit of the principal and not in the interest of the agent or a third party. d. Obedience—The agent must follow all lawful and clearly stated instructions of the principal. e. Accounting—The agent has a duty to make available to the principal records of all property and funds received and paid out on behalf of the principal. 2. *Duties of the principal—* a. Compensation—Except in a gratuitous agency relationship, the principal must pay the agreed-on value (or reasonable value) for an agent's services.

(Continued)

CHAPTER SUMMARY Agency Relationships in Business–Continued

Duties of Agents and Principals–Continued	b. Reimbursement and indemnification–The principal must reimburse the agent for all funds disbursed at the request of the principal and for all funds the agent disburses for necessary expenses in the course of reasonable performance of his or her agency duties.
	c. Cooperation–A principal must cooperate with and assist an agent in performing her or his duties.
	d. Safe working conditions–A principal must provide safe working conditions for the agent-employee.
Agent's Authority (See pages 685–688.)	1. *Express authority*–Can be oral or in writing. Authorization must be in writing if the agent is to execute a contract that must be in writing.
	2. *Implied authority*–Authority customarily associated with the position of the agent or authority that is deemed necessary for the agent to carry out expressly authorized tasks.
	3. *Apparent authority*–Exists when the principal, by word or action, causes a third party reasonably to believe that an agent has authority to act, even though the agent has no express or implied authority.
	4. *Ratification*–The affirmation by the principal of an agent's unauthorized action or promise. For the ratification to be effective, the principal must be aware of all material facts.
Liability in Agency Relationships (See pages 688–695.)	1. *Liability for contracts*–If the principal's identity is disclosed or partially disclosed at the time the agent forms a contract with a third party, the principal is liable to the third party under the contract if the agent acted within the scope of his or her authority. If the principal's identity is undisclosed at the time of contract formation, the agent is personally liable to the third party, but if the agent acted within the scope of his or her authority, the principal is also bound by the contract.
	2. *Liability for agent's negligence*–Under the doctrine of *respondeat superior,* the principal is liable for any harm caused to another through the agent's torts if the agent was acting within the scope of her or his employment at the time the harmful act occurred.
	3. *Liability for agent's intentional torts*–Usually, employers are not liable for the intentional torts that their agents commit, *unless:*
	a. The acts are committed within the scope of employment, and thus the doctrine of *respondeat superior* applies.
	b. The employer allowed an employee to engage in reckless acts that caused injury to another.
	c. The agent's misrepresentation causes a third party to sustain damage, and the agent had either actual or apparent authority to act.
	4. *Liability for independent contractor's torts*–A principal is not liable for harm caused by an independent contractor's negligence, unless hazardous activities are involved (in this situation, the principal is strictly liable for any resulting harm) or other exceptions apply.
	5. *Liability for agent's crimes*–An agent is responsible for his or her own crimes, even if the crimes were committed while the agent was acting within the scope of authority or employment. A principal will be liable for an agent's crime only if the principal participated by conspiracy or other action or (in some jurisdictions) if the agent violated certain government regulations in the course of employment.
How Agency Relationships Are Terminated (See pages 695–697.)	1. *By act of the parties*–
	a. Lapse of time (if the parties specified a definite time for the duration of the agency when the agency was established).
	b. Purpose achieved.
	c. Occurrence of a specific event.
	d. Mutual rescission (requires mutual consent of principal and agent).

CHAPTER SUMMARY Agency Relationships in Business—Continued

How Agency Relationships Are Terminated— Continued	e. Termination by act of either the principal (revocation) or the agent (renunciation). (A principal cannot revoke an agency coupled with an interest.)
	
	f. Notice to third parties is required when an agency is terminated by act of the parties. Direct notice is required for those who have previously dealt with the agency; constructive notice will suffice for all other third parties.
	
	2. *By operation of law*—
	
	  a. Death or mental incompetence of either the principal or the agent.
	
	  b. Impossibility (when the purpose of the agency cannot be achieved because of an event beyond the parties' control).
	
	  c. Changed circumstances (in which it would be inequitable to require that the agency be continued).
	
	  d. Bankruptcy of the principal or the agent, or war between the principal's and agent's countries.
	
	  e. Notice to third parties is not required when an agency is terminated by operation of law.

FOR REVIEW

Answers for the even-numbered questions in this **For Review** *section can be found in Appendix E at the end of this text.*

1 What is the difference between an employee and an independent contractor?

2 How do agency relationships arise?

3 What duties do agents and principals owe to each other?

4 When is a principal liable for the agent's actions with respect to third parties? When is the agent liable?

5 What are some of the ways in which an agency relationship can be terminated?

 The following multiple-choice question is representative of the types of questions available in one of the four sections of ThomsonNOW for *Business Law Today*. ThomsonNOW also provides feedback for each response option, whether correct or incorrect, and refers to the location within the chapter where the correct answer can be found.

When determining whether a worker is an employee or an independent contractor, a key factor to consider is the

  a length of time necessary to finish a job.

  b number of hours worked by the worker.

  c degree to which the worker is computer literate.

  d extent to which the employer controls the actions of the worker.

◾

QUESTIONS AND CASE PROBLEMS

HYPOTHETICAL SCENARIOS

24.1 Ratification by Principal. Springer was a political candidate running for Congress. He was operating on a tight budget and instructed his campaign staff not to purchase any campaign materials without his explicit authorization. In spite of these instructions, one of his campaign workers ordered Dubychek Printing Co. to print some promotional materials for Springer's campaign. When the printed materials arrived, Springer did not return them but instead used them during his campaign. When Springer failed to pay for the materials, Dubychek sued for recovery of the price. Springer contended that he was not liable on the sales contract because he had not authorized his agent to purchase the printing services. Dubychek argued that the campaign worker was Springer's agent and that the worker had authority to make the printing contract. Additionally, Dubychek claimed that even if the purchase was unauthorized, Springer's use of the materials constituted ratification of his agent's unauthorized purchase. Is Dubychek correct? Explain.

24.2 Hypothetical Question with Sample Answer. Paul Gett is a well-known, wealthy financial expert living in the city of Torris. Adam Wade, Gett's friend, tells Timothy Brown that he is Gett's agent for the purchase of rare coins. Wade even shows Brown a local newspaper clipping mentioning Gett's interest in coin collecting. Brown, knowing of Wade's friendship with Gett, contracts with Wade to sell a rare coin valued at $25,000 to Gett. Wade takes the coin and disappears with it. On the payment due date, Brown seeks to collect from Gett, claiming that Wade's agency made Gett

liable. Gett does not deny that Wade was a friend, but he claims that Wade was never his agent. Discuss fully whether an agency was in existence at the time the contract for the rare coin was made.

For a sample answer to Question 24.2, go to Appendix F at the end of this text.

24.3 Employee versus Independent Contractor. Stephen Hemmerling was a driver for the Happy Cab Co. Hemmerling paid certain fixed expenses and abided by a variety of rules relating to the use of the cab, the hours that could be worked, and the solicitation of fares, among other things. Rates were set by the state. Happy Cab did not withhold taxes from Hemmerling's pay. While driving the cab, Hemmerling was injured in an accident and filed a claim against Happy Cab in a Nebraska state court for workers' compensation benefits. Such benefits are not available to independent contractors. On what basis might the court hold that Hemmerling is an employee? Explain.

CASE PROBLEMS

24.4 Agency Formation. Ford Motor Credit Co. is a subsidiary of Ford Motor Co. with its own offices, officers, and directors. Ford Credit buys contracts and leases of automobiles entered into by dealers and consumers. Ford Credit also provides inventory financing for dealers' purchases of Ford and non-Ford vehicles and makes loans to Ford and non-Ford dealers. Dealers and consumers are not required to finance their purchases or leases of Ford vehicles through Ford Credit. Ford Motor is not a party to the agreements between Ford Credit and its customers and does not directly receive any payments under those agreements. Also, Ford Credit is not subject to any agreement with Ford Motor "restricting or conditioning" its ability to finance the dealers' inventories or the consumers' purchases or leases of vehicles. A number of plaintiffs filed a product liability suit in a Missouri state court against Ford Motor. Ford Motor claimed that the court did not have venue. The plaintiffs asserted that Ford Credit, which had an office in the jurisdiction, acted as Ford's "agent for the transaction of its usual and customary business" there. Is Ford Credit an agent of Ford Motor? Discuss. [*State ex rel. Ford Motor Co. v. Bacon*, 63 S.W.3d 641 (Mo. 2002)]

24.5 Liability for Independent Contractor's Torts. Greif Brothers Corp., a steel drum manufacturer, owned and operated a manufacturing plant in Youngstown, Ohio. In 1987, Lowell Wilson, the plant superintendent, hired Youngstown Security Patrol, Inc. (YSP), a security company, to guard Greif property and "deter thieves and vandals." Some YSP security guards, as Wilson knew, carried firearms. Eric Bator, a YSP security guard, was not certified as an armed guard but nevertheless took his gun, in a briefcase, to work.

While working at the Greif plant on August 12, 1991, Bator fired his gun at Derrell Pusey, in the belief that Pusey was an intruder. The bullet struck and killed Pusey. Pusey's mother filed a suit in an Ohio state court against Greif and others, alleging, in part, that her son's death was the result of YSP's negligence, for which Greif was responsible. Greif filed a motion for a directed verdict. What is the plaintiff's best argument that Greif is responsible for YSP's actions? What is Greif's best defense? Explain. [*Pusey v. Bator*, 94 Ohio St.3d 275, 762 N.E.2d 968 (2002)]

24.6 Case Problem with Sample Answer. Sam and Theresa Daigle decided to build a home in Cameron Parish, Louisiana. To obtain financing, they contacted Trinity United Mortgage Co. In a meeting with Joe Diez on Trinity's behalf, on July 18, 2001, the Daigles signed a temporary loan agreement with Union Planters Bank. Diez assured them that they did not need to make payments on this loan until their house was built and that permanent financing had been secured. Because the Daigles did not make payments on the Union loan, Trinity declined to make the permanent loan. Meanwhile, Diez left Trinity's employ. On November 1, the Daigles moved into their new house. They tried to contact Diez at Trinity but were told that he was unavailable and would get back to them. Three weeks later, Diez came to the Daigles' home and had them sign documents that they believed were to secure a permanent loan but that were actually an application with Diez's new employer. Union filed a suit in a Louisiana state court against the Daigles for failing to pay on its loan. The Daigles paid Union, obtained permanent financing through another source, and filed a suit against Trinity to recover the cost. Who should have told the Daigles that Diez was no longer Trinity's agent? Could Trinity be liable to the Daigles on this basis? Explain. [*Daigle v. Trinity United Mortgage, L.L.C.*, 890 So.2d 583 (La.App. 3 Cir. 2004)]

 After you have answered Problem 24.6, compare your answer with the sample answer given on the Web site that accompanies this text. Go to www.thomsonedu.com/westbuslaw/blt, select "Chapter 24," and click on "Case Problem with Sample Answer."

24.7 Principal's Duties to Agent. Josef Boehm was an officer and the majority shareholder of Alaska Industrial Hardware, Inc. (AIH), in Anchorage, Alaska. In August 2001, Lincolnshire Management, Inc., in New York, created AIH Acquisition Corp. to buy AIH. The three firms signed a "commitment letter" to negotiate "a definitive stock purchase agreement" (SPA). In September, Harold Snow and Ronald Braley began to work, on Boehm's behalf, with Vincent Coyle, an agent for AIH Acquisition, to produce an SPA. They exchanged many drafts and dozens of e-mails. Finally, in February 2002, Braley told Coyle that Boehm would sign the SPA "early next week." That did not occur, however, and at the end of March, after more negotiations and drafts, Boehm demanded a higher price. AIH Acquisition agreed, and following more work by the agents, another SPA was drafted. In April, the parties met in Anchorage. Boehm still refused to sign. AIH Acquisition and others filed a suit in a federal district court against AIH. Did Boehm violate any of the duties that principals owe to their agents? If so, which duty, and how was it violated? Explain. [*AIH Acquisition Corp. v. Alaska Industrial Hardware, Inc.*, __ F.Supp.2d __ (S.D.N.Y. 2004)]

24.8 Agent's Duties to Principal. In July 2001, John Warren viewed a condominium in Woodland Hills, California, as a potential buyer. Hildegard Merrill was the agent for the seller. Because Warren's credit rating was poor, Merrill told him he needed a co-borrower to obtain a mortgage at a reasonable rate. Merrill said that her daughter Charmaine would "go on title" until the loan and sale were complete if Warren would pay her $10,000. Merrill also offered to defer her commission on the sale as a loan to Warren so that he could make a 20 percent down payment on the property. He agreed to both plans. Merrill applied for and secured the mortgage in Charmaine's name alone by misrepresenting her daughter's address, business, and income. To close the

sale, Merrill had Warren remove his name from the title to the property. In October, Warren moved into the condominium, repaid Merrill the amount of her deferred commission, and began paying the mortgage. Within a few months, Merrill had Warren evicted. Warren filed a suit in a California state court against Merrill and Charmaine. Who among these parties was in an agency relationship? What is the basic duty that an agent owes a principal? Was the duty breached here? Explain. [*Warren v. Merrill*, 143 Cal.App.4th 96, 49 Cal.Rptr.3d 122 (2 Dist. 2006)]

24.9 **A Question of Ethics.** *Emergency One, Inc. (EO), makes fire and rescue vehicles. Western Fire Truck, Inc., contracted with EO to be its exclusive dealer in Colorado and Wyoming through December 2003. James Costello, a Western salesperson, was authorized to order EO vehicles for his customers. Without informing Western, Costello e-mailed EO about Western's difficulties in obtaining cash to fund its operations. He asked about the viability of Western's contract and his possible employment with EO. On EO's request, and in disregard of Western's instructions, Costello sent some payments for EO vehicles directly to EO. In addition, Costello, with EO's help, sent a competing bid to a potential Western customer. EO's representative e-mailed Costello, "You have my permission to kick [Western's] ass." In April 2002, EO terminated its contract with Western, which, after reviewing Costello's e-mail, fired Costello. Western filed a suit in a Colorado state court against Costello and EO, alleging, among other things, that Costello breached his duty as an agent and that EO aided and abetted the breach. [*Western Fire Truck, Inc. v. Emergency One, Inc.*, 134 P.3d 570 (Colo.App. 2006)]*

1 Was there an agency relationship between Western and Costello? Western required monthly reports from its sales staff, but Costello did not report regularly. Does this indicate that Costello was *not* Western's agent? In determining whether an agency relationship exists, is the *right* to control or the *fact* of control more important? Explain.

2 Did Costello owe Western a duty? If so, what was the duty? Did Costello breach it? How?

3 A Colorado state statute allows a court to award punitive damages in "circumstances of fraud, malice, or willful and wanton conduct." Did any of these circumstances exist in this case? Should punitive damages be assessed against either defendant? Why or why not?

CRITICAL THINKING AND WRITING ASSIGNMENTS

24.10 Critical Legal Thinking. What policy is served by the law that employers do not have copyright ownership in works created by independent contractors (unless there is a written "work for hire" agreement)?

24.11 **Video Question.** Go to this text's Web site at www.thomsonedu.com/westbuslaw/blt and select

"Chapter 24." Click on "Video Questions" and view the video titled *Fast Times at Ridgemont High*. Then answer the following questions.

1 Recall from the video that Brad (Judge Reinhold) is told to deliver an order of Captain Hook Fish and Chips to IBM. Is Brad an employee or an independent contractor? Why?

2 Assume that Brad is an employee and agent of Captain Hook Fish and Chips. What duties does he owe Captain Hook Fish and Chips? What duties does Captain Hook Fish and Chips, as principal, owe to Brad?

3 In the video, Brad throws part of his uniform and several bags of the food that he is supposed to deliver out of his car window while driving. If Brad is an agent-employee and his actions cause injury to a person or property, can Captain Hook Fish and Chips be held liable? Why or why not? What should Captain Hook argue to avoid liability for Brad's actions?

ONLINE ACTIVITIES

PRACTICAL INTERNET EXERCISES

Go to this text's Web site at **www.thomsonedu.com/westbuslaw/blt**, select "Chapter 24," and click on "Practical Internet Exercises." There you will find the following Internet research exercises that you can perform to learn more about the topics covered in this chapter.

PRACTICAL INTERNET EXERCISE 24–1   LEGAL PERSPECTIVE—Employees or Independent Contractors?

PRACTICAL INTERNET EXERCISE 24–2   MANAGEMENT PERSPECTIVE—Liability in Agency Relationships

BEFORE THE TEST

Go to this text's Web site at **www.thomsonedu.com/westbuslaw/blt**, select "Chapter 24," and click on "Interactive Quizzes." You will find a number of interactive questions relating to this chapter.

CHAPTER 25
Sole Proprietorships and Private Franchises

LEARNING OBJECTIVES

AFTER READING THIS CHAPTER, YOU SHOULD BE ABLE TO ANSWER THE FOLLOWING QUESTIONS:

1 What advantages and disadvantages are associated with the sole proprietorship?

2 What is a franchise? What are the most common types of franchises?

3 What laws govern a franchising relationship?

4 What terms and conditions are typically included in a franchise contract?

5 What is wrongful termination? In what types of situations do courts typically find that a franchisor has wrongfully terminated a franchise?

> **"[E]veryone thirsteth after gaine."**
>
> Sir Edward Coke, 1552–1634
> (English jurist and politician)

Many Americans would agree with Sir Edward Coke's comment in the chapter-opening quotation that most people, at least, "thirsteth after gaine." Certainly, an entrepreneur's primary motive for undertaking a business enterprise is to make profits. An **entrepreneur** is by definition one who initiates and assumes the financial risks of a new enterprise and undertakes to provide or control its management.

One of the questions faced by anyone who wishes to start up a business is what form of business organization should be chosen for the business endeavor. In making this determination, the entrepreneur needs to consider a number of factors. Four important factors are (1) ease of creation, (2) the liability of the owners, (3) tax considerations, and (4) the need for capital. In studying this unit on business organizations, keep these factors in mind as you read about the various business organizational forms available to entrepreneurs.

Traditionally, entrepreneurs have used three major forms to structure their business enterprises—the sole proprietorship, the partnership, and the corporation. In this chapter, we examine the sole proprietorship as well as franchises. Although the franchise is not really a business organizational form, it is widely used today by entrepreneurs seeking to make profits. In Chapter 26, we will examine the second major traditional business form, the partnership, as well as some newer variations on partnerships. The third major traditional form—the corporation—is discussed in detail in Chapters 28 through 30. We will also look at the limited liability company—a relatively new and increasingly popular form of business enterprise—in Chapter 27. In Chapter 30, the concluding chapter in this unit on business organizations, we discuss investor protection, insider trading, and corporate governance.

ENTREPRENEUR
One who initiates and assumes the financial risk of a new business enterprise and undertakes to provide or control its management.

Sometimes, individuals want to run their own businesses. They can do this as a sole proprietor or as a partnership. They can get a head start on a business by buying a franchise of a well-known product, such as Domino's Pizza.
("The Consumerist"/Creative Commons)

SOLE PROPRIETORSHIPS

SOLE PROPRIETORSHIP
The simplest form of business organization, in which the owner is the business. The owner reports business income on his or her personal income tax return and is legally responsible for all debts and obligations incurred by the business.

The simplest form of business organization is a **sole proprietorship.** In this form, the owner is the business; thus, anyone who does business without creating a separate business organization has a sole proprietorship. More than two-thirds of all U.S. businesses are sole proprietorships. They are usually small enterprises—about 99 percent of the sole proprietorships in the United States have revenues of less than $1 million per year. Sole proprietors can own and manage any type of business, ranging from an informal, home-office undertaking to a large restaurant or construction firm. Today, a number of online businesses that sell goods and services on a nationwide basis are organized as sole proprietorships.

Advantages of the Sole Proprietorship

A major advantage of the sole proprietorship is that the proprietor owns the entire business and has a right to receive all of the profits (because he or she assumes all of the risk). In addition, it is often easier and less costly to start a sole proprietorship than to start any other kind of business, as few legal formalities are involved.[1] One does not need to file any documents with the government to start a sole proprietorship (though a state business license may be required to operate certain businesses).

This type of business organization also entails more flexibility than does a partnership or a corporation. The sole proprietor is free to make any decision she or he wishes concerning the business—including whom to hire, when to take a vacation, and what kind of business to pursue, for example. In addition, the proprietor can sell or transfer all or part of the business to another party at any time and does not need approval from anyone else (as would be required from partners in a partnership or normally from shareholders in a corporation).

A sole proprietor pays only personal income taxes (including Social Security, or self-employment, tax) on the business's profits, which are reported as personal income on the

---

1. Although starting up a sole proprietorship involves relatively few legal formalities compared to other business organizational forms, even small sole proprietorships may need to comply with certain zoning requirements, obtain appropriate licenses, and the like.

proprietor's personal income tax return. Sole proprietors are also allowed to establish certain tax-exempt retirement accounts.

Disadvantages of the Sole Proprietorship

The major disadvantage of the sole proprietorship is that the proprietor alone bears the burden of any losses or liabilities incurred by the business enterprise. In other words, the sole proprietor has unlimited liability, or legal responsibility, for all obligations incurred in doing business. Any lawsuit against the business or its employees can lead to unlimited personal liability for the owner of a sole proprietorship. Creditors can go after the owner's personal assets to satisfy any business debts. This unlimited liability is a major factor to be considered in choosing a business form.

■**EXAMPLE 25.1** Sheila Fowler operates a golf shop business as a sole proprietorship. The shop is located near one of the best golf courses in the country. A professional golfer, Dean Maheesh, is seriously injured when a display of golf clubs, which one of Fowler's employees had failed to secure, falls on him. If Maheesh sues Fowler's shop (a sole proprietorship) and wins, Fowler's personal liability could easily exceed the limits of her insurance policy. In this situation, not only might Fowler lose her business, but she could also lose her house, car, and any other personal assets that can be attached to pay the judgment. ■

This woman creates floral arrangements. She owns the business by herself. What are the advantages of doing business as a sole proprietorship? (Salim Fadhley/ Creative Commons)

The sole proprietorship also has the disadvantage of lacking continuity on the death of the proprietor. When the owner dies, so does the business—it is automatically dissolved. Another disadvantage is that the proprietor's opportunity to raise capital is limited to personal funds and the funds of those who are willing to make loans.

The personal liability of the owner of a sole proprietorship was at issue in the following case. The case involved the federal Cable Communications Act, which prohibits a commercial establishment from broadcasting television programs to its patrons without authorization. The court had to decide whether the owner of a sole proprietorship that installed a satellite television system was personally liable for violating this act by identifying a restaurant as a "residence" for billing purposes.

CASE 25.1 **Garden City Boxing Club, Inc. v. Dominguez**

United States District Court, Northern District of Illinois, Eastern Division, __ F.Supp.2d __ (2006).

FACTS Garden City Boxing Club, Inc. (GCB), which is based in San Jose, California, owned the exclusive right to broadcast via closed-circuit television several prizefights, including the match between Oscar De La Hoya and Fernando Vargas on September 14, 2002. GCB sold the right to receive the broadcasts to bars and other commercial venues. The fee was $20 multiplied by an establishment's maximum fire code occupancy. Antenas Enterprises in Chicago, Illinois, sells and installs satellite television systems under a contract with DISH Network. After installing a system, Antenas sends the buyer's address and other identifying information to DISH. In January 2002, Luis Garcia, an Antenas employee, identified a new customer as José Melendez at 220 Hawthorn Commons in Vernon Hills. The address was a

restaurant—Mundelein Burrito—but Garcia designated the account as residential. Mundelein's patrons watched the De La Hoya–Vargas match on September 14, as well as three other fights on other dates, for which the restaurant paid only the residential rate to DISH and nothing to GCB. GCB filed a suit in a federal district court against Luis Dominguez, the sole proprietor of Antenas, to collect the fee.

ISSUE Is Dominguez personally liable for the amount of Mundelein's fee?

DECISION Yes. The court issued a summary judgment in GCB's favor, holding that the plaintiff was entitled to the amount of the fee, plus damages and attorneys' fees.

CASE 25.1—Continues next page

CASE 25.1–Continued

REASON The court found that Mundelein was clearly a commercial establishment. "The structure of the building, an exterior identification sign, and its location in a strip mall made this obvious." Under the Cable Communications Act, "[a]n authorized intermediary of a communication violates the Act when it divulges communication through an electronic channel to one other than the addressee." Antenas's improper designation of Mundelein as residential allowed the unauthorized broadcast of four prizefights to the restaurant. Antenas is a sole proprietorship. A sole proprietorship has no legal identity apart from that of the individual who owns it.

Furthermore, a sole proprietor is personally responsible for the acts that his or her employees commit within the scope of their employment. Dominguez owns Antenas, and Garcia is Dominguez's employee. "Accordingly, Dominguez is personally liable for the damages caused by the violation of * * * the [Cable Communications] Act."

 WHAT IF THE FACTS WERE DIFFERENT? *If Mundelein had identified itself as a residence when ordering the satellite system, how might the result in this case have been different?*

ETHICAL ISSUE 25.1

Should online sole proprietors be treated the same as corporations for the purpose of determining venue? The Internet has expanded the ability of sole proprietorships to market their products nationwide without greatly increasing their costs. As a result, many small sole proprietorships market their goods online on a national basis. Does this mean that sole proprietorships should now be considered the equivalent of corporations for certain purposes, such as venue? As explained in Chapter 3, venue is the most appropriate location for trial. Unlike jurisdiction, which involves the court's power to hear a particular case, questions of venue often require a court to determine whether a particular forum is fair for the parties and witnesses in a case.

Consider, for example, a suit for alleged trademark infringement brought by a New York corporation (the plaintiff) against a sole proprietorship (the defendant) based in Kansas. The federal district court, which was located in New York, had to decide whether that venue was proper. Under the relevant statute, if the defendant had been a corporation, venue would have been proper in any district where the court had personal jurisdiction, and thus, the court could have heard the dispute. The plaintiff asserted that the defendant did business in forty-seven states and resembled a corporation in all respects except for its legal structure. Thus, argued the plaintiff, the defendant should be treated as the functional equivalent of a corporation for venue purposes. To hold otherwise would be unfair. The court, though, was not convinced. In the court's view, the fact that an online business has a broad geographic distribution does not convert a sole proprietorship into the functional equivalent of a corporation.[2]

FRANCHISE
Any arrangement in which the owner of a trademark, trade name, or copyright licenses another to use that trademark, trade name, or copyright in the selling of goods or services.

FRANCHISEE
One receiving a license to use another's (the franchisor's) trademark, trade name, or copyright in the sale of goods and services.

FRANCHISOR
One licensing another (the franchisee) to use the owner's trademark, trade name, or copyright in the selling of goods or services.

FRANCHISES

Instead of setting up a business form through which to market their own products or services, many entrepreneurs opt to purchase a franchise. A **franchise** is defined as any arrangement in which the owner of a trademark, a trade name, or a copyright licenses others to use the trademark, trade name, or copyright in the selling of goods or services. A **franchisee** (a purchaser of a franchise) is generally legally independent of the **franchisor** (the seller of the franchise). At the same time, the franchisee is economically dependent on the franchisor's integrated business system. In other words, a franchisee can operate as an independent businessperson but still obtain the advantages of a regional or national organization.

---

2. *Hsin Ten Enterprise USA, Inc. v. Clark Enterprises*, 138 F.Supp.2d 449 (S.D.N.Y. 2000).

Today, it is estimated that franchising companies and their franchisees account for a significant portion of all retail sales in this country. Well-known franchises include McDonald's, 7-Eleven, and Burger King. Franchising has also become a popular way for businesses to expand their operations internationally, as will be discussed in this chapter's *Beyond Our Borders* feature on page 713.

Types of Franchises

Because the franchising industry is so extensive and so many different types of businesses sell franchises, it is difficult to summarize the many types of franchises that now exist. Generally, though, the majority of franchises fall into one of three classifications: distributorships, chain-style business operations, or manufacturing or processing-plant arrangements. We briefly describe these types of franchises here.

Distributorship   A *distributorship* arises when a manufacturing concern (franchisor) licenses a dealer (franchisee) to sell its product. Often, a distributorship covers an exclusive territory. An example of this type of franchise is an automobile dealership or beer distributorship.

■EXAMPLE 25.2 Anheuser-Busch distributes its brands of beer through a network of authorized wholesale distributors, each with an assigned territory. Marik signs a distributorship contract for the area from Gainesville to Ocala, Florida. If the contract states that Marik is the exclusive distributor in that area, then no other franchisee may distribute Anheuser-Busch beer in that region. ■

Chain-Style Business Operation   In a *chain-style business operation*, a franchise operates under a franchisor's trade name and is identified as a member of a select group of dealers that engage in the franchisor's business. The franchisee is generally required to follow standardized or prescribed methods of operation. Often, the franchisor requires that the franchisee maintain certain standards of operation. In addition, sometimes the franchisee is obligated to obtain materials and supplies exclusively from the franchisor. Examples of this type of franchise are McDonald's and most other fast-food chains. Chain-style franchises are also common in service-related businesses, including real estate brokerage firms, such as Century 21, and tax-preparing services, such as H & R Block, Inc.

Manufacturing or Processing-Plant Arrangement   In a *manufacturing or processing-plant arrangement*, the franchisor transmits to the franchisee the essential ingredients or formula to make a particular product. The franchisee then markets the product either at wholesale or at retail in accordance with the franchisor's standards. Examples of this type of franchise are Coca-Cola and other soft-drink bottling companies.

Laws Governing Franchising

Because a franchise relationship is primarily a contractual relationship, it is governed by contract law. If the franchise exists primarily for the sale of products manufactured by the franchisor, the law governing sales contracts as expressed in Article 2 of the Uniform Commercial Code applies (see Chapters 15 through 18). Additionally, the federal government and most states have enacted laws governing certain aspects of franchising. Generally, these laws are designed to protect prospective franchisees from dishonest franchisors and to prohibit franchisors from terminating franchises without good cause.

Because of the protections given to franchisees, sometimes a person who is not in fact a franchisee tries to claim franchisee status. **■EXAMPLE 25.3** Janet Isbell was a sales representative for Mary Kay cosmetics. When she lost her job, Isbell sued Mary Kay, Inc., claiming that she was a franchisee and, as such, was entitled to the protections of the state

KEEP IN MIND Because a franchise involves the licensing of a trademark, a trade name, or a copyright, the law governing intellectual property may apply in some cases.

franchising law. Mary Kay responded that Isbell was an independent contractor and not a franchisee. The case eventually reached the Arkansas Supreme Court, which held that to be entitled to protection under Arkansas law, a franchisee had "to establish or maintain a place of business in the state." Although Isbell had rented storefront space in a Little Rock mall to use as a training center, Isbell's contract with Mary Kay did not require her to do so. Therefore, Isbell was an independent contractor, not a franchisee.[3] ■

PREVENTING LEGAL DISPUTES

Businesspersons should realize that federal and state laws control the franchising relationship. Ultimately, it falls to the courts to interpret the laws and determine whether a franchise relationship exists. In some cases, courts have held that even though the parties signed a franchising agreement, the franchisees are in fact employees because of the degree of control exercised over them by the franchisors. In other cases, courts have held that a franchising relationship exists even in the absence of a franchising contract. Because of the myriad of federal laws that apply, and because state laws on franchising vary dramatically, businesspersons should seek the advice of counsel within the state prior to entering a franchising relationship.

■

Federal Regulation of Franchising The federal government has enacted laws that protect franchisees in certain industries, such as automobile dealerships and service stations. These laws protect the franchisee from unreasonable demands and bad faith terminations of the franchise by the franchisor. If an automobile manufacturer-franchisor terminates a franchise because of a dealer-franchisee's failure to comply with unreasonable demands (for example, failure to attain an unrealistically high sales quota), the manufacturer may be liable for damages.[4] Similarly, federal law prescribes the conditions under which a franchisor of service stations can terminate the franchise.[5] Federal antitrust laws (to be discussed in Chapter 31) also apply in certain circumstances to prohibit certain types of anticompetitive agreements.

Additionally, the Franchise Rule of the Federal Trade Commission (FTC) requires franchisors to disclose material facts that a prospective franchisee needs to make an informed decision concerning the purchase of a franchise.[6] The rule was designed to enable potential franchisees to weigh the risks and benefits of an investment. The rule requires the franchisor to make numerous written disclosures to prospective franchisees. For example, a franchisor is required to disclose whether the projected earnings figures are based on actual data or hypothetical examples. If a franchisor makes sales or earnings projections based on actual data for a specific franchise location, the franchisor must disclose the number and percentage of its actual franchises that have achieved this result. All representations made to a prospective franchisee must have a reasonable basis. Franchisors are also required to explain termination, cancellation, and renewal provisions of the franchise contract to potential franchisees before the agreement is signed. Those who violate the Franchise Rule are subject to substantial civil penalties, and the FTC can sue on behalf of injured parties to recover damages.

Can a franchisor satisfy the Franchise Rule by providing disclosures via the Internet? See this chapter's *Adapting the Law to the Online Environment* feature for a discussion of this topic.

---

3. *Mary Kay, Inc. v. Isbell*, 338 Ark. 556, 999 S.W.2d 669 (1999).
4. Automobile Dealers' Franchise Act of 1965, also known as the Automobile Dealers' Day in Court Act, 15 U.S.C. Sections 1221 *et seq.*
5. Petroleum Marketing Practices Act (PMPA) of 1979,15 U.S.C. Sections 2801 *et seq.*
6. 16 C.F.R. Part 436.

ADAPTING THE LAW TO THE ONLINE ENVIRONMENT **Satisfying the FTC's Franchise Rule in the Internet Age**

The Federal Trade Commission (FTC) issued its Franchise Rule in 1978, when the normal medium for transmission of information in a permanent form was on paper. When the Internet became a reality for a large number of people in the 1990s, the FTC was faced with the possibility that franchisors might use Web sites to provide downloadable information to prospective franchisees. Is such online information the equivalent of an offer that requires compliance with the FTC's Franchise Rule? The FTC said yes.

Prior to the Internet age, the FTC had already issued advisory opinions allowing electronic disclosures by CD-ROM. Basically, the FTC permits a franchisor to provide the required disclosures via a CD-ROM or DVD only if the prospective franchisee is given the option of receiving the disclosure in electronic or paper format and chooses electronic. The CD-ROM or DVD itself must have a label indicating that it contains the disclosures required by the FTC and the date when it was issued.

Disclosures Exclusively on a Web Site?

In October 1999, the FTC published for comment a proposed rule that would allow franchisors to provide disclosure documents through the Internet as long as they followed certain instructions. (In doing this, the FTC was following its standard procedure for changing its regulations—see Chapter 1 for a discussion of agency rulemaking procedures.)[a] Among other things, the proposed instructions require that prospective franchisees be able to download or otherwise preserve all electronic disclosure documents.

The comment period closed at the end of January 2000. Since 2000, the FTC has solicited demonstration projects for electronic dissemination of disclosure documents.[b] In the years since the FTC solicitation, only a few franchisors have applied for demonstration status by offering to use their Web sites for franchise disclosure purposes.

Franchise.com Gets the Green Light

In 2001, Franchise.com, a marketer of existing franchises, became the first Web-based franchise operation to win the FTC's approval of its plan to provide electronic disclosure services for all of its franchisor advertisers. Franchise.com requires any franchisor that wishes to advertise on its Web site to provide a disclosure document containing the FTC's proposed cover-page statement regarding electronic disclosures. When a prospective franchisee comes to the Franchise.com Web site, he or she must agree to receive disclosures electronically by clicking on the appropriate button. The prospect can then obtain information on a particular franchise through the Web site. Whenever prospective franchisees access their accounts at the Web site, there are hyperlinks to written summary documents. Each time a prospective franchisee clicks on the hyperlinks, she or he is advised to download or print the disclosure document for future reference.

The FTC determined that Franchise.com's system was consistent with the Franchise Rule and issued an informal staff advisory to that effect in 2001. In 2003, McGarry Internet, Ltd., of Dublin, Ireland, received similar approval. This company sends each prospective franchisee a Uniform Franchise Offering Circular via e-mail. In 2005, the FTC approved the request of VaultraNet, which had developed an Internet-based file delivery and signature system that it uses to provide disclosure documents to prospective franchisees. After the FTC evaluates the experiences of these and other Internet-based companies, it will issue final rules governing the use of the Internet to offer franchises.

FOR CRITICAL ANALYSIS *Why do you think it has taken so long for the FTC to issue final rules about franchisors using the Internet?*

a. 16 C.F.R. Part 436, 64 Fed.Reg. 57,294 (October 22, 1999).
b. 65 Fed.Reg. 44,484 (July 18, 2000).

State Regulation of Franchising State legislation varies but often is aimed at protecting franchisees from unfair practices and bad faith terminations by franchisors. Approximately fifteen states have laws similar to the federal rules requiring franchisors to provide presale disclosures to prospective franchisees.[7] Some states also require a disclosure document (known as an *offering circular*) to be filed with a state official. To protect franchisees, a state law might require the disclosure of information such as the actual costs

ON THE WEB

For information about the FTC's regulations on franchising, as well as state laws regulating franchising, go to

www.ftc.gov/bcp/franchise/netfran.htm.

---

7. These states include California, Hawaii, Illinois, Indiana, Maryland, Michigan, Minnesota, New York, North Dakota, Oregon, Rhode Island, South Dakota, Virginia, Washington, and Wisconsin.

of operation, recurring expenses, and profits earned, along with data substantiating these figures. To protect franchisees against arbitrary or bad faith terminations, the law might also require that certain procedures be followed in terminating a franchising relationship. State deceptive trade practices acts (see Chapter 32) may also apply and prohibit certain types of actions on the part of franchisors.

■EXAMPLE 25.4 The Illinois Franchise Disclosure Act prohibits any untrue statement of a material fact in connection with the offer or sale of any franchise. Miyamoto, a franchisor of bagel restaurants, understates the start-up costs and exaggerates the anticipated yearly profits from operating a bagel shop when meeting with prospective buyers. After the sale, the buyers discover that Miyamoto's statements were not true. Because these statements were false and materially influenced the franchisee's decision to buy, Miyamoto has violated state law.[8] ■

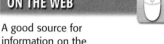

ON THE WEB

A good source for information on the purchase and sale of franchises is Franchising.org, which is online at

www.franchising.org.

THE FRANCHISE CONTRACT

The franchise relationship is defined by a contract between the franchisor and the franchisee. The franchise contract specifies the terms and conditions of the franchise and spells out the rights and duties of the franchisor and the franchisee. If either party fails to perform the contractual duties, that party may be subject to a lawsuit for breach of contract. Generally, statutes and case law governing franchising tend to emphasize the importance of good faith and fair dealing in franchise relationships.

Because each type of franchise relationship has its own characteristics, it is difficult to describe the broad range of details a franchising contract may include. In the remaining pages of this chapter, we look at some of the major issues that typically are addressed in a franchise contract. The *Application* feature at the end of this chapter further describes some steps a franchisee can take to avoid problems common in franchise agreements.

Payment for the Franchise

The franchisee ordinarily pays an initial fee or lump-sum price for the franchise license (the privilege of being granted a franchise). This fee is separate from the various products that the franchisee purchases from or through the franchisor. In some industries, the franchisor relies heavily on the initial sale of the franchise for realizing a profit. In other industries, the continued dealing between the parties brings profit to both. In most situations, the franchisor will receive a stated percentage of the annual sales or annual volume of business done by the franchisee. The franchise agreement may also require the franchisee to pay a percentage of advertising costs and certain administrative expenses.

Franchises can extend to foreign countries, even for very American brands such as Disney. In 2006, the RJ Corporation of India signed a franchise agreement with Disney Consumer Products. What do you think some of the elements of that agreement were? (AP Photo/ Saurabh Das)

Business Premises

The franchise agreement may specify whether the premises for the business must be leased or purchased outright. In some cases, a building must be constructed or remodeled to meet the terms of the agreement. The agreement usually will specify whether the franchisor supplies equipment and furnishings for the premises or whether this is the responsibility of the franchisee.

Location of the Franchise

Typically, the franchisor will determine the territory to be served. Some franchise contracts give the franchisee exclusive rights, or "territorial rights," to a certain geographic area. Other franchise contracts, though they define the

---

8. *Bixby's Food Systems, Inc. v. McKay,* 193 F.Supp.2d 1053 (N.D.Ill. 2002).

BEYOND OUR BORDERS Franchising in Foreign Nations

In the last twenty years, many U.S. companies (particularly fast-food chains and coffeehouses) have successfully expanded through franchising in nations around the globe. Franchises offer businesses a way to expand internationally without violating the legal restrictions that many nations impose on foreign ownership of businesses. Although Canada has been the most popular location for franchises in the past, during the last few years, franchisors have expanded their target locations to Asia, South America, Central America, and Mexico.

Businesspersons must exercise caution when entering international franchise relationships—perhaps even more so than when entering other types of international contracts. Differences in language, culture, laws, and business practices can seriously complicate the franchising relationship. If a U.S. franchisor has quality control standards that do not mesh with local business practices, for example, how can the franchisor maintain the quality of its product and protect its good reputation? If the law in China, for example, does not provide for the same level of intellectual property protection, how can a U.S. franchisor protect its trademark rights or prevent its "secret recipe or formula" from being copied?

Because of the complexities of international franchising, successful franchisors recommend that a company seeking to franchise overseas conduct thorough research to determine whether its particular type of business will be well received in that location. It is important to know the political and cultural climate of the target country, as well as the economic trends. Marketing surveys to assess the potential success of the franchise location are crucial in international markets. Also, because complying with U.S. disclosure laws may not satisfy the legal requirements of other nations, most successful franchisors retain counsel knowledgeable in the laws of the target location. Competent counsel can draft dispute-settlement provisions (such as an arbitration clause) for international franchising contracts and advise the parties about the tax implications of operating a foreign franchise (such as import taxes and customs duties).

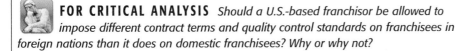

FOR CRITICAL ANALYSIS *Should a U.S.-based franchisor be allowed to impose different contract terms and quality control standards on franchisees in foreign nations than it does on domestic franchisees? Why or why not?*

---

territory allotted to a particular franchise, either specifically state that the franchise is nonexclusive or are silent on the issue of territorial rights.

Many franchise cases involve disputes over territorial rights, and the implied covenant of good faith and fair dealing often comes into play in this area of franchising. For example, suppose that the franchise contract either does not give a franchisee exclusive territorial rights or is silent on the issue. If the franchisor allows a competing franchise to be established nearby, the franchisee may suffer a significant loss in profits. In this situation, a court may hold that the franchisor's actions breached an implied covenant of good faith and fair dealing.

Business Organization of the Franchisee

The business organization of the franchisee is of great concern to the franchisor. Depending on the terms of the franchise agreement, the franchisor may specify particular requirements for the form and capital structure of the business. The franchise agreement may also require that the franchisee adhere to certain standards of operation in such aspects of the business as sales quotas, quality, and record keeping. Furthermore, a franchisor may wish to retain stringent control over the training of personnel involved in the operation and over administrative aspects of the business.

Quality Control by the Franchisor

Although the day-to-day operation of the franchise business is normally left to the franchisee, the franchise agreement may provide for the amount of supervision and control agreed on by the parties. When the franchisee prepares a product, such as food, or provides a service, such as a motel, the contract often provides that the franchisor will establish certain standards for the facility. Typically, the contract will state that the franchisor is permitted to make periodic inspections to ensure that the standards are being maintained so as to protect the franchise's name and reputation.

As a general rule, the validity of a provision permitting the franchisor to establish and enforce certain quality standards is unquestioned. Because the franchisor has a legitimate interest in maintaining the quality of the product or service to protect its name and reputation, it can exercise greater control in this area than would otherwise be tolerated. Increasingly, however, franchisors are finding that if they exercise too much control over the operations of their franchisees, they may incur vicarious (indirect) liability under agency theory for the acts of their franchisees' employees. The actual exercise of control, or at least the right to control, is the key consideration. If the franchisee controls the day-to-day operations of the business to a significant degree, the franchisor may be able to avoid liability, as the following case illustrates.

RECALL Under the doctrine of *respondeat superior,* an employer may be liable for the torts of employees if they occur within the scope of employment, without regard to the personal fault of the employer.

CASE 25.2 **Kerl v. Dennis Rasmussen, Inc.**

Wisconsin Supreme Court, 273 Wis.2d 106, 682 N.W.2d 328 (2004).

FACTS Arby's, Inc., is a national franchisor of fast-food restaurants. Dennis Rasmussen, Inc. (DRI), is an Arby's franchisee. Under the terms of their franchise contract, DRI agreed to follow Arby's specifications for several aspects of operating the business. DRI hired Cathy Propp as manager for its Arby's restaurant in 1994. In early 1999, Propp hired Harvey Pierce, a local county jail inmate with work-release privileges after a conviction for sexual assault. On June 11, Pierce left his shift at the restaurant without permission, walked half a mile to a discount store parking lot, and shot his former girlfriend Robin Kerl, her fiancé David Jones, and himself. Pierce and Jones died. Kerl survived but is permanently disabled. Kerl and others filed a suit in a Wisconsin state court against DRI and Arby's, claiming, among other things, that Arby's was vicariously liable for DRI's allegedly negligent hiring and supervision of Pierce. Arby's filed a motion for summary judgment, which the court granted. A state intermediate appellate court affirmed this judgment. The plaintiffs appealed to the Wisconsin Supreme Court.

ISSUE Was Arby's vicariously liable for DRI's actions?

DECISION No. The Wisconsin Supreme Court affirmed the lower court's decision, holding that Arby's was not vicariously liable for DRI's actions. Arby's had neither a right of control nor actual control over DRI's allegedly negligent actions.

REASON The state supreme court pointed out that "[v]icarious liability under the doctrine of *respondeat superior* depends upon the existence of a master/servant agency relationship," but "the license agreement between Arby's and DRI contains a provision that disclaims any agency relationship." Further, the "plethora of general controls on the operation of DRI's restaurant" in the parties' franchise contract "are consistent with the quality and operational standards commonly contained in franchise agreements to achieve product and marketing uniformity and to protect the franchisor's trademark. They are insufficient to establish a master/servant relationship. More particularly, they do not establish that Arby's controlled or had the right to control

CASE 25.2–Continued

DRI's hiring and supervision of employees." And "a franchisor may be subject to vicarious liability for the tortious conduct of its franchisee only if the franchisor had control or a right of control over the daily operation of the specific aspect of the franchisee's business that is alleged to have caused the harm."

 WHY IS THIS CASE IMPORTANT TO BUSINESSPERSONS? *This case addresses an important issue for franchisors—vicarious (indirect) liability for*

franchisees' actions. Many franchisors understandably want to exercise enough control over the franchisee to protect the identity and reputation of the franchise. Yet the more control a franchisor exercises, the more likely it is that a court will hold the franchisor liable for any injuries sustained at the franchise or as a result of the franchisee's conduct.

Pricing Arrangements

Franchises provide the franchisor with an outlet for the firm's goods and services. Depending on the nature of the business, the franchisor may require the franchisee to purchase certain supplies from the franchisor at an established price.[9] A franchisor cannot, however, set the prices at which the franchisee will resell the goods because such price setting may be a violation of state or federal antitrust laws, or both. A franchisor can suggest retail prices but cannot mandate them.

TERMINATION OF THE FRANCHISE

The duration of the franchise is a matter to be determined between the parties. Sometimes, a franchise will start out for a short period, such as a year, so that the franchisor can determine whether it wants to stay in business with the franchisee. Other times, the duration of the franchise contract correlates with the term of the lease for the business premises and both are renewable at the end of that period. Usually, the franchise agreement will specify that termination must be "for cause," such as death or disability of the franchisee, insolvency of the franchisee, breach of the franchise agreement, or failure to meet specified sales quotas. Most franchise contracts provide that notice of termination must be given. If no set time for termination is specified, then a reasonable time, with notice, will be implied. A franchisee must be given reasonable time to wind up the business—that is, to do the accounting and return the copyright or trademark or any other property of the franchisor.

Wrongful Termination

Because a franchisor's termination of a franchise often has adverse consequences for the franchisee, much franchise litigation involves claims of wrongful termination. Generally, the termination provisions of contracts are more favorable to the franchisor. This means that the franchisee, who normally invests a substantial amount of time and funds to make the franchise operation successful, may receive little or nothing for the business on termination. The franchisor owns the trademark and hence the business.

It is in this area that statutory and case law become important. The federal and state laws discussed earlier attempt, among other things, to protect franchisees from the arbitrary or unfair termination of their franchises by the franchisors. Generally, both statutory

9. Although a franchisor can require franchisees to purchase supplies from it, requiring a franchisee to purchase exclusively from the franchisor may violate federal antitrust laws (see Chapter 31). For two landmark cases in this area, see *United States v. Arnold, Schwinn & Co.*, 388 U.S. 365, 87 S.Ct. 1856, 18 L.Ed.2d 1249 (1967); and *Fortner Enterprises, Inc. v. U.S. Steel Corp.*, 394 U.S. 495, 89 S.Ct. 1252, 22 L.Ed.2d 495 (1969).

and case law emphasize the importance of good faith and fair dealing in terminating a franchise relationship.

PREVENTING LEGAL DISPUTES

To avoid potential disputes regarding franchise termination, a prospective franchisee should always do preliminary research on a franchisor before agreeing to enter into a franchise contract. Find out whether the franchisor has terminated franchises in the past, how many times, and for what reasons. Contact five to ten franchisees of the same franchisor and ask questions about their relationships and any problems. Learning whether the franchisor has been honest, reliable, and reasonable with its franchisees in the past can be invaluable in preventing disputes over termination and bad faith actions of a franchisor.

The Importance of Good Faith and Fair Dealing

In determining whether a franchisor has acted in good faith when terminating a franchise agreement, the courts generally try to balance the rights of both parties. If a court perceives that a franchisor has arbitrarily or unfairly terminated a franchise, the franchisee will be provided with a remedy for wrongful termination. If a franchisor's decision to terminate a franchise was made in the normal course of the franchisor's business operations, however, and reasonable notice of termination was given to the franchisee, generally a court will not consider the termination wrongful.

At issue in the following case was whether General Motors Corporation acted wrongfully in terminating its franchise with a motor vehicle dealer in Connecticut.

CASE 25.3 **Chic Miller's Chevrolet, Inc. v. General Motors Corp.**

United States District Court, District of Connecticut, 352 F.Supp.2d 251 (2005).

FACTS Chapin Miller began work as a mail clerk with General Motors Acceptance Corporation (GMAC). By 1967, Miller had succeeded sufficiently within the organization to acquire Chic Miller's Chevrolet, a General Motors Corporation (GM) dealership, in Bristol, Connecticut. As part of its operations, Chic Miller's entered into lending agreements, commonly known as floor plan financing, to enable it to buy new vehicles from GM. At first, the dealership had floor plan financing through GMAC. In 2001, however, Miller believed that GMAC was charging interest "at an inappropriately high rate" and negotiated a lower rate from Chase Manhattan Bank. In November 2002, Chase declined to provide further financing. Unable to obtain a loan from any other lender, Chic Miller's contacted GMAC, which also refused to make a deal. Under the parties' "Dealer Sales and Service Agreement," GM could terminate a dealership for "Failure of Dealer to maintain the line of credit." GM sent several notices of termination, but Chic Miller's remained open until March 2003, when it closed for seven days. GM sent a final termination notice. Chic Miller's

filed a suit in a federal district court against GM, alleging, among other things, a failure to act in good faith in terminating the franchise. GM filed a motion for summary judgment.

ISSUE Did GM act wrongfully in terminating its franchise with Chic Miller's?

DECISION No. The court granted GM's motion for summary judgment. GM acted in good faith, with good cause under the applicable state statute, in terminating Chic Miller's franchise.

REASON The court stated that to terminate a franchise under the Connecticut Franchise Act, "a franchisor must: provide notice that complies with statutory requirements; have 'good cause' for the termination; and act 'in good faith.'" The court explained that there is "good cause" under the statute "if there is a failure by the dealer to comply with a provision of the franchise which is both reasonable and of material significance to the franchise relationship." In this case, the

CASE 25.3—Continued

dealer failed to maintain floor plan financing, a material requirement under the franchise agreement. "[W]ithout floor plan financing, a dealership is unable to purchase motor vehicle inventory, which, in turn, severely limits a dealership's ability to earn income from vehicle sales." The dealership "will eventually lose its ability to generate revenues and become financially insolvent, and will not be able to conduct customary sales and service operations." Here, the dealer also failed to conduct sales and service operations for seven consecutive business days, another material requirement under the parties' contract.

 WHAT IF THE FACTS WERE DIFFERENT? *Suppose that in March 2003, Chic Miller's had placed one newspaper ad promoting its services and had sold one car. Would the result have been different? Why or why not?*

REVIEWING **Sole Proprietorships and Private Franchises**

Carlos Del Rey decided to open a fast-food Mexican restaurant and signed a franchise contract with a national chain called La Grande Enchilada. Under the franchise agreement, Del Rey purchased the building and La Grande Enchilada supplied the equipment. The contract required the franchisee to strictly follow the franchisor's operating manual and stated that failure to do so would be grounds for terminating the franchise contract. The manual set forth detailed operating procedures and safety standards, and provided that a La Grande Enchilada representative would inspect the restaurant monthly to ensure compliance. Nine months after Del Rey began operating his La Grande Enchilada, a spark from the grill ignited an oily towel in the kitchen. No one was injured, but by the time firefighters were able to put out the fire, the kitchen had sustained extensive damage. The cook told the fire department that the towel was "about two feet from the grill" when it caught fire, which was in compliance with the franchisor's manual that required towels to be at least one foot from the grills. Nevertheless, the next day La Grande Enchilada notified Del Rey that his franchise would terminate in thirty days for failure to follow the prescribed safety procedures. Using the information presented in the chapter, answer the following questions.

1 What type of franchise was Del Rey's La Grande Enchilada restaurant?

2 If Del Rey operates the restaurant as a sole proprietorship, who bears the loss for the damaged kitchen? Explain.

3 Assume that Del Rey files a lawsuit against La Grande Enchilada, claiming that his franchise was wrongfully terminated. What is the main factor a court would consider in determining whether the franchise was wrongfully terminated?

4 Would a court be likely to rule that La Grande Enchilada had good cause to terminate Del Rey's franchise in this situation? Why or why not?

APPLICATION **What Problems Can a Franchisee Anticipate?***

A franchise arrangement appeals to many prospective businesspersons for several reasons. Entrepreneurs who purchase franchises can operate independently and without the risks associated with products that have never before been marketed. Additionally, the franchisee can usually rely on the assistance and guidance of a management network that is regional or national in scope and has been in place for some time. Franchisees do face potential problems, however. Generally, to avoid possibly significant economic and legal difficulties, it is imperative that you obtain all relevant details about the business and that you have an attorney evaluate the franchise contract for possible pitfalls.

* This *Application* is not meant to substitute for the services of an attorney who is licensed to practice law in your state.

(Continued)

The Franchise Fee

Virtually all franchise contracts require a franchise fee payable up front or in installments. This fee often ranges between $10,000 and $50,000. For nationally known franchises, such as McDonald's, the fee may be $500,000 or more. To calculate the true cost of the franchise, however, you must also include the fees that are paid once the franchise opens for business. For example, as a franchisee, you would probably pay 2 to 8 percent of your gross sales as royalties to the franchisor (for the use of the franchisor's trademark, for example). Another 1 to 2 percent of gross sales might go to the franchisor to cover advertising costs. Although your business would benefit from the advertising, the cost of that advertising might exceed the benefits you would realize.

Electronic Encroachment and Termination Provisions

Even when the franchise contract gives the franchisee exclusive territorial rights, a problem that many franchisees do not anticipate is the adverse effects on their businesses of so-called electronic encroachment. For example, suppose that a franchise contract gives the franchisee exclusive rights to operate a franchise in a certain territory. Nothing in the contract, though, indicates what will happen if the franchisor sells its products to customers located within the franchisee's territory via telemarketing, mail-order catalogues, or online services over the Internet. As a prospective franchisee, you should make sure that your franchise contract covers such contingencies and protects you against any losses you might incur if you face these types of competition in your area.

A major economic consequence, usually of a negative nature, will occur if the franchisor can or does terminate your franchise agreement. Before you sign a franchise contract, make sure that the contract provisions regarding termination are reasonable, clearly specified, and provide you with adequate notice and sufficient time to wind up business.

CHECKLIST FOR THE FRANCHISEE

1. Find out all you can about the franchisor: How long has the franchisor been in business? How profitable is the business? Is there a healthy market for the product?
2. Obtain the most recent financial statement from the franchisor and a complete description of the business.
3. Obtain a clear and complete statement of all fees that you will be required to pay.
4. Determine whether the franchisor will help you find a suitable location, train management and employees, assist with promotion and advertising, and supply capital or credit.
5. Visit other franchisees in the same business. Ask them about their profitability and their experiences with the product, the market, and the franchisor.
6. Evaluate your training and experience in the business on which you are about to embark. Are they sufficient to ensure success as a franchisee?
7. Carefully examine the franchise contract provisions relating to termination of the franchise agreement. Are they specific enough to allow you to sue for breach of contract in the event the franchisor wrongfully terminates the contract? Find out how many franchises have been terminated in the past several years.
8. Will you have an exclusive geographic territory and, if so, for how many years? Does the franchisor have a right to engage in telemarketing, electronic marketing, and Internet or mail-order sales to customers within this territory?
9. Finally, the most important way to protect yourself is to have an attorney familiar with franchise law examine the contract before you sign it.

KEY TERMS

entrepreneur 705
franchise 708

franchisee 708
franchisor 708

sole proprietorship 706

CHAPTER SUMMARY Sole Proprietorships and Private Franchises

Sole Proprietorships (See pages 706–708.)	The simplest form of business organization; used by anyone who does business without creating a separate organization. The owner is the business. The owner pays personal income taxes on all profits and is personally liable for all business debts.
Franchises (See pages 708–712.)	1. *Types of franchises*— a. Distributorship (for example, automobile dealerships). b. Chain-style operation (for example, fast-food chains).

CHAPTER SUMMARY Sole Proprietorships and Private Franchises—Continued

Franchises—Continued	c. Manufacturing/processing-plant arrangement (for example, soft-drink bottling companies, such as Coca-Cola).
	2. *Laws governing franchising—*
	a. Franchises are governed by contract law.
	b. Franchises are also governed by federal and state statutory and regulatory laws, as well as agency law.
The Franchise Contract (See pages 712–715.)	The franchise relationship is defined by a contract between the franchisor and the franchisee. The contract normally spells out the following terms:
	1. *Payment for the franchise*—Ordinarily, the contract requires the franchisee (purchaser) to pay an initial fee or lump-sum price for the franchise license.
	2. *Business premises*—Specifies whether the business premises will be leased or purchased by the franchisee.
	3. *Location of the franchise*—Specifies the territory to be served by the franchisee.
	4. *Business organization*—The franchisor may specify particular requirements for the form and capital structure of the business.
	5. *Quality control*—The franchisor may require the franchisee to abide by certain standards of quality relating to the product or service offered.
	6. *Pricing arrangements*—The franchisor may require the franchisee to purchase certain supplies from the franchisor at an established price but cannot set retail resale prices.
Termination of the Franchise (See pages 715–717.)	Usually, the contract provides for the date and/or conditions of termination of the franchise arrangement. Both federal and state statutes attempt to protect franchisees from franchisors who unfairly or arbitrarily terminate franchises.

FOR REVIEW

Answers for the even-numbered questions in this For Review *section can be found in Appendix E at the end of this text.*

1 What advantages and disadvantages are associated with the sole proprietorship?

2 What is a franchise? What are the most common types of franchises?

3 What laws govern a franchising relationship?

4 What terms and conditions are typically included in a franchise contract?

5 What is wrongful termination? In what types of situations do courts typically find that a franchisor has wrongfully terminated a franchise?

 The following multiple-choice question is representative of the types of questions available in one of the four sections of ThomsonNOW for *Business Law Today*. **ThomsonNOW also provides feedback for each response option, whether correct or incorrect, and refers to the location within the chapter where the correct answer can be found.**

When a franchise agreement contains no set time for winding up a franchisee's business, a franchisee

a must wind up the business within seven working days.

b must wind up the business by whatever date the franchisor decides—whether that be one day, ten days, or three months later.

c must be given a reasonable time to wind up the business.

d normally must comply with state franchise winding-up statutes.

QUESTIONS AND CASE PROBLEMS

HYPOTHETICAL SCENARIOS

25.1 Control of a Franchise. National Foods, Inc., sells franchises to its fast-food restaurants, known as Chicky-D's. Under the franchise agreement, franchisees agree to hire and train employees strictly according to Chicky-D's standards. The regional supervisors at Chicky-D's are required to approve all job candidates before they are hired and all general policies affecting those employees. Chicky-D's reserves the right to terminate a franchise for violating the franchisor's rules. In practice, however, Chicky-D's regional supervisors routinely approve new employees and individual franchisees' policies. After several incidents of racist comments and conduct by Tim, a recently hired assistant manager at a Chicky-D's, Sharon, a counterperson at the restaurant, resigns. Sharon files a suit in a federal district court against National. National files a motion for summary judgment, arguing that it is not liable for harassment by franchise employees. Will the court grant National's motion? Why or why not?

25.2 Hypothetical Question with Sample Answer. Omega Computers, Inc., is a franchisor that grants exclusive physical territories to its franchisees with retail locations, including Pete's Digital Products. Omega sells more than two hundred of the franchises before establishing an interactive Web site. On the site, a customer can order Omega's products directly from the franchisor. When Pete's sets up a Web site through which a customer can also order Omega's products, Omega and Pete's file suits against each other, alleging that each is in violation of the franchise relationship. To decide this issue, what factors should the court consider? How might these parties have avoided this conflict? Discuss.

 **For a sample answer to Question 25.2, go to Appendix F at the end of this text.**

■

CASE PROBLEMS

25.3 Franchise Termination. C.B. Management Co. operated McDonald's restaurants in Cleveland, Ohio, under a franchise agreement with McDonald's Corp. The agreement required C.B. to make monthly payments of, among other things, certain percentages of the gross sales to McDonald's. If any payment was more than thirty days late, McDonald's had the right to terminate the franchise. The agreement stated, "No waiver by [McDonald's] of any breach . . . shall constitute a waiver of any subsequent breach." McDonald's sometimes accepted C.B.'s late payments, but when C.B. defaulted on the payments in July 1997, McDonald's gave notice of thirty days to comply or surrender possession of the restaurants. C.B. missed the deadline. McDonald's demanded that C.B. vacate the restaurants. C.B. refused. McDonald's filed a suit in a federal district court against C.B., alleging violations of the franchise agreement. C.B. counterclaimed, alleging, among other things, that McDonald's had breached the implied covenant of good faith and fair dealing. McDonald's filed a motion to dismiss C.B.'s counterclaim. On what did C.B. base its claim? Will the court agree? Why or why not? [*McDonald's Corp. v. C.B. Management Co.*, 13 F.Supp.2d 705 (N.D.Ill. 1998)]

25.4 Franchise Termination. Heating & Air Specialists, Inc., doing business as A/C Service Co., marketed heating and air-conditioning products. A/C contracted with Lennox Industries, Inc., to be a franchised dealer of Lennox products. The parties signed a standard franchise contract drafted by Lennox. The contract provided that either party could terminate the agreement with or without cause on thirty days' notice and that the agreement would terminate immediately if A/C opened another facility at a different location. At the time, A/C operated only one location in Arkansas. A few months later, A/C opened a second location in Tulsa, Oklahoma. Lennox's district sales manager gave A/C oral authorization to sell Lennox products in Tulsa, at least on a temporary basis, but nothing was put in writing. Several of Lennox's other dealers in Tulsa complained to Lennox about A/C's presence. Lennox gave A/C notice that it was terminating A/C's Tulsa franchise. Meanwhile, A/C had failed to keep its Lennox account current and owed the franchisor more than $200,000. Citing this delinquency, Lennox notified A/C that unless it paid its account within ten days, Lennox would terminate both franchises. A/C did not pay. Lennox terminated the franchises. A/C filed a suit in a federal district court against Lennox, alleging, in part, breach of the franchise agreement for terminating the Tulsa franchise. Is A/C correct? Explain. [*Heating & Air Specialists, Inc. v. Jones*, 180 F.3d 923 (8th Cir. 1999)]

25.5 Franchise Termination. In 1985, Bruce Byrne, with his sons Scott and Gordon, opened Lone Star R.V. Sales, Inc., a motor home dealership in Houston, Texas. In 1994, Lone Star became a franchised dealer for Winnebago Industries, Inc., a manufacturer of recreational vehicles. The parties renewed the franchise in 1995, but during the next year, their relationship began to deteriorate. Lone Star did not maintain a current inventory, its sales did not meet goals agreed to between the parties, and Lone Star disparaged Winnebago products to consumers and otherwise failed to actively promote them. Several times, the Byrnes subjected Winnebago employees to verbal abuse. During one phone conversation, Bruce threatened to throw a certain Winnebago sales manager off Lone Star's lot if he appeared at the dealership. Bruce was physically incapable of carrying out the threat, however. In 1998, Winnebago terminated the franchise, claiming, among many other things, that it was concerned for the safety of its employees. Lone Star filed a protest with the Texas Motor Vehicle Board. Did Winnebago have good cause to terminate Lone Star's franchise? Discuss. [*Lone Star R.V. Sales, Inc. v. Motor Vehicle Board of the Texas Department of Transportation*, 49 S.W.3d 492 (Tex.App.—Austin, 2001)]

25.6 Franchise Termination. In the automobile industry, luxury-car customers are considered the most demanding segment of the market with respect to customer service. Jaguar Cars, a division of Ford Motor Co., is the exclusive U.S. distributor of Jaguar luxury cars. Jaguar Cars distributes its products through franchised dealers. In April 1999, Dave Ostrem Imports, Inc., an authorized Jaguar dealer in Des Moines, Iowa, contracted to sell its dealership to Midwest Automotive III, LLC. A Jaguar franchise generally cannot be sold without Jaguar Cars' permission. Jaguar Cars asked Midwest Auto to submit three years of customer satisfaction index (CSI) data for all franchises with which its owners had been associated. CSI data are intended to measure how well dealers treat their customers and satisfy their customers' needs. Jaguar Cars requires above-average CSI ratings for its dealers. Most of Midwest Auto's scores fell below the national average. Jaguar Cars rejected Midwest Auto's application and sought to terminate the franchise, claiming that a transfer of the dealership would be "substantially detrimental" to the distribution of Jaguar vehicles in the community. Is Jaguar Cars' attempt to terminate this franchise reasonable? Why or why not? [*Midwest Automotive III, LLC v. Iowa Department of Transportation*, 646 N.W.2d 417 (Iowa 2002)]

25.7 The Franchise Contract. On August 23, 1995, Climaco Guzman entered into a commercial janitorial services franchise agreement with Jan-Pro Cleaning Systems, Inc., in Rhode Island for a franchise fee of $3,285. In the agreement, Jan-Pro promised to furnish Guzman with "one (1) or more customer account(s) . . . amounting to $8,000.00 gross volume per year. . . . No portion of the franchise fee is refundable except and to the extent that the Franchisor, within 120 business days following the date of execution of the Franchise Agreement, fails to provide accounts." By February 19, Guzman had not received any accounts and demanded a full refund. Jan-Pro then promised "two accounts grossing $12,000 per year in income." Despite the promises, Jan-Pro did not have the ability to furnish accounts that met the requirements. In September, Guzman filed a suit in a Rhode Island state court against

Jan-Pro, alleging, in part, fraudulent misrepresentation. Should the court rule in Guzman's favor? Why or why not? [*Guzman v. Jan-Pro Cleaning Systems, Inc.*, 839 A.2d 504 (R.I. 2003)]

25.8 Case Problem with Sample Answer. Walik Elkhatib, a Palestinian Arab, emigrated to the United States in 1971 and became a U.S. citizen. Eight years later, Elkhatib bought a Dunkin' Donuts, Inc., franchise in Bellwood, Illinois. Dunkin' Donuts began offering breakfast sandwiches with bacon, ham, or sausage through its franchises in 1984, but Elkhatib refused to sell these items at his store on the ground that his religion forbade the handling of pork. In 1995, Elkhatib opened a second franchise in Berkeley, Illinois, at which he also refused to sell pork products. The next year, at both locations, Elkhatib began selling meatless sandwiches. In 1998, Elkhatib opened a third franchise in Westchester, Illinois. When he proposed to relocate this franchise, Dunkin' Donuts refused to approve the new location and added that it would not renew any of his franchise agreements because he did not carry the full sandwich line. Elkhatib filed a suit in a federal district court against Dunkin' Donuts and others. The defendants filed a motion for summary judgment. Did Dunkin' Donuts act in good faith in its relationship with Elkhatib? Explain. [*Elkhatib v. Dunkin' Donuts, Inc.*, __ F.Supp.2d __ (N.D.Ill. 2004)]

After you have answered Problem 25.8, compare your answer with the sample answer given on the Web site that accompanies this text. Go to www.thomsonedu.com/westbuslaw/blt, select "Chapter 25," and click on "Case Problem with Sample Answer."

25.9 Sole Proprietorship. James Ferguson operates "Jim's 11-E Auto Sales" in Jonesborough, Tennessee, as a sole proprietorship. In 1999, Consumers Insurance Co. issued a policy to "Jim Ferguson, Jim's 11E Auto Sales" covering "Owned 'Autos' Only." *Auto* was defined to include "a land motor vehicle," which was not further explained in the policy. Coverage extended to damages caused by the owner or driver of an underinsured motor vehicle. In 2000, Ferguson bought and titled in his own name a 1976 Harley-Davidson motorcycle, intending to repair and sell the cycle through his dealership. In October 2001, while driving the motorcycle, Ferguson was struck by an auto driven by John Jenkins. Ferguson filed a suit in a Tennessee state court against Jenkins—who was underinsured with respect to Ferguson's medical bills—and Consumers. The insurer argued, among other things, that because the motorcycle was bought and titled in Ferguson's own name, and he was driving it at the time of the accident, it was his personal vehicle and thus was not covered under the dealership's policy. What is the relationship between a sole proprietor and a sole proprietorship? How might this status affect the court's decision in this case? [*Ferguson v. Jenkins*, 204 S.W.3d 779 (Tenn.App. 2006)]

25.10 A Question of Ethics. *In August 2004, Ralph Vilardo contacted Travel Center, Inc., in Cincinnati, Ohio, to buy a trip to Florida in December for his family to celebrate his fiftieth wedding anniversary. Vilardo paid $6,900 to*

David Sheets, the sole proprietor of Travel Center. Vilardo also paid $195 to Sheets for a separate trip to Florida in February 2005. Sheets assured Vilardo that everything was set, but in fact no arrangements were made. Later, two unauthorized charges for travel services totaling $1,182.35 appeared on Vilardo's credit-card statement. Vilardo filed a suit in an Ohio state court against Sheets and his business, alleging, among other things, fraud and violations of the state consumer protection law. Vilardo served Sheets and Travel Center with copies of the complaint, the summons, a request for admissions, and other documents filed with the court, including a motion for summary judgment. Responses to each of these filings were subject to certain time limits. Sheets responded once on his own behalf with a denial of all of Vilardo's claims. Travel Center did not respond. [Vilardo v. Sheets, __ Ohio App.3d __, __ N.E.2d __ (12 Dist. 2006)]

1 Almost four months after Vilardo filed his complaint, Sheets decided that he was unable to adequately represent himself and retained an attorney who asked the court for more time. Should the court grant this request? Why or why not? Ultimately, what should the court rule in this case?

2 Sheets admitted that "Travel Center, Inc." was a sole proprietorship, He also argued that liability might be imposed on his business but not on himself. How would you rule with respect to this argument? Why? Would there be anything unethical about allowing Sheets to avoid liability on this basis? Explain.

CRITICAL THINKING
AND WRITING ASSIGNMENTS

25.11 Critical Legal Thinking. Suppose that a franchisor requires the franchisee to purchase a particular type of van that will be used to deliver the franchised carpet-cleaning services to the public. If the van is involved in an accident that causes injury to a person, should the franchisor be held liable for the injuries? What are the arguments for and against holding the franchisor liable under the circumstances? Would it be better if the law established a clear rule regarding the degree of control a franchisor must exert before being subjected to liability for the franchisee's actions? Why or why not?

25.12 Critical Thinking and Writing Assignment for Business. Jordan Mendelson is interested in starting a kitchen franchise business. Customers will come to the business to assemble gourmet dinners and then take the prepared meals to their homes for cooking. The franchisor requires each store to use a specific layout and provides the recipes for various dinners, but the franchisee is not required to purchase the food products from the franchisor. What general factors should Mendelson consider before entering a contract to start such a franchise? Is location important? Are there any laws that Mendelson should consider due to the fact that this franchise involves food preparation and sales? If the franchisor does not insist on a specific type of business entity, should Mendelson operate this business as a sole proprietorship? Why or why not?

ONLINE ACTIVITIES

PRACTICAL
INTERNET EXERCISES

Go to this text's Web site at **www.thomsonedu.com/westbuslaw/blt**, select "Chapter 25," and click on "Practical Internet Exercises." There you will find the following Internet research exercises that you can perform to learn more about the topics covered in this chapter.

PRACTICAL INTERNET EXERCISE 25–1 LEGAL PERSPECTIVE—Starting a Business

PRACTICAL INTERNET EXERCISE 25–2 MANAGEMENT PERSPECTIVE—Franchises

BEFORE THE TEST

Go to this text's Web site at **www.thomsonedu.com/westbuslaw/blt**, select "Chapter 25," and click on "Interactive Quizzes." You will find a number of interactive questions relating to this chapter.

CHAPTER 26
Partnerships

LEARNING OBJECTIVES

AFTER READING THIS CHAPTER, YOU SHOULD BE ABLE TO ANSWER THE FOLLOWING QUESTIONS:

1 What are the three essential elements of a partnership?

2 What are the rights and duties of partners in an ordinary partnership?

3 What is meant by joint and several liability? Why is this often considered to be a disadvantage of the partnership form of business?

4 What advantages do limited liability partnerships offer to businesspersons that are not offered by general partnerships?

5 What are the key differences between the rights and liabilities of general partners and those of limited partners?

> " All gains . . .
> are the fruit of
> venturing. "
>
> Herodotus, fifth century B.C.E.
> (Greek historian)

T raditionally, the two most common forms of business organization selected by two or more persons entering into business together are the partnership and the corporation. A *partnership* arises from an agreement, express or implied, between two or more persons to carry on a business for profit. Partners are co-owners of a business and have joint control over its operation and the right to share in its profits. In this chapter, we focus on partnerships (corporations will be discussed in Chapters 28 through 30).

We open the chapter with an examination of ordinary partnerships, or *general partnerships*, and the rights and duties of partners in this traditional business entity. We then examine some special forms of partnerships known as *limited liability partnerships* and *limited partnerships*, which receive different treatment under the law. As the chapter-opening quotation indicates, all gains are the "fruit of venturing," and partnerships—to the extent that they encourage business ventures—contribute to those gains.

BASIC PARTNERSHIP CONCEPTS

Partnerships are governed both by common law concepts—in particular, those relating to agency—and by statutory law. As in so many other areas of business law, the National Conference of Commissioners on Uniform State Laws has drafted uniform laws for partnerships, and these uniform laws have been widely adopted by the states.

Agency Concepts and Partnership Law

When two or more persons agree to do business as partners, they enter into a special relationship with one another. To an extent, their relationship is similar to an agency relationship because each partner is deemed to be the agent of the other partners and of the partnership. The common law agency concepts outlined in Chapter 24 thus apply—specifically, the imputation of knowledge of, and responsibility for, acts done within the scope of the partnership relationship. In their relations with one another, partners, like agents, are bound by fiduciary ties.

In one important way, however, partnership law is distinct from agency law. A partnership is based on a voluntary contract between two or more competent persons who agree to place financial capital, labor, and skill in a business with the understanding that profits and losses will be shared. In a nonpartnership agency relationship, the agent usually does not have an ownership interest in the business, nor is he or she obliged to bear a portion of the ordinary business losses.

The Uniform Partnership Act

The Uniform Partnership Act (UPA) governs the operation of partnerships *in the absence of express agreement* and has done much to reduce controversies in the law relating to partnerships. In other words, the partners are free to establish rules for their partnership that differ from those stated in the UPA. The UPA was originally set forth by the National Conference of Commissioners on Uniform State Laws in 1914 and has undergone several major revisions. Except for Louisiana, every state has adopted the UPA. The majority of states have adopted the most recent version of the UPA, which was issued in 1994 and amended in 1997 to provide limited liability for partners in a limited liability partnership.[1] We therefore base our discussion of the UPA in this chapter on the 1997 version of the act and refer to older versions of the UPA in footnotes when appropriate. Whenever relevant, we include bracketed references to specific UPA provisions.

Definition of Partnership

Conflicts commonly arise over whether a business enterprise is legally a partnership, especially in the absence of a formal, written partnership agreement. The UPA defines a **partnership** as "an association of two or more persons to carry on as co-owners a business for profit" [UPA 101(6)]. The *intent* to associate is a key element of a partnership, and a person cannot join a partnership unless all of the other partners consent [UPA 401(i)].

Do partners have to be human beings, or could an entity such as a corporation become a partner? At one time, many states had restrictions on corporations becoming partners, but such restrictions have become less common over the years. The Revised Model Business Corporation Act (to be discussed in Chapter 28) allows corporations generally to make contracts and incur liabilities, and the UPA specifically permits a corporation to be a partner. By definition, "a partnership is an association of two or more persons," and the UPA defines *person* as including corporations [UPA 101(10)].

Partnership Status

In resolving disputes over whether partnership status exists, courts will usually look for the following three essential elements, which are implicit in the UPA's definition of a partnership:

PARTNERSHIP
An agreement by two or more persons to carry on, as co-owners, a business for profit.

KEEP IN MIND Two or more persons are required to form a partnership. Other forms of business can be organized by a single individual.

---

1. At the time this book went to press, more than half of the states, as well as the District of Columbia, Puerto Rico, and the U.S. Virgin Islands, had adopted the UPA with the 1997 amendments. Excerpts from the latest version of the UPA are presented on the Web site that accompanies this text.

Partnerships create benefits, but they have costs—the main one being the unlimited personal liability of all partners. Some large accounting firms have therefore gone to great lengths to reduce potential partner liability problems. Shown here is an annual meeting of Ernst & Young, a firm with more than 140,000 employees in 140 countries. This accounting services business has created separate legal entities to provide services to clients, thereby reducing liability exposure to those working in other countries for other clients. (Rob Lee/Creative Commons)

1 A sharing of profits and losses.

2 A joint ownership of the business.

3 An equal right to be involved in the management of the business.

If the evidence in a particular case is insufficient to establish all three factors, the UPA provides a set of guidelines to be used. For example, the sharing of profits and losses from a business is considered *prima facie* ("on the face of it") evidence that a partnership has been created. No such presumption is made, however, if the profits were received as payment of any of the following [UPA 202(c)(3)]:

1 A debt by installments or interest on a loan.

2 Wages of an employee or for the services of an independent contractor.

3 Rent to a landlord.

4 An annuity to a surviving spouse or representative of a deceased partner.

5 A sale of goodwill of a business or property.

■EXAMPLE 26.1 A debtor owes a creditor $5,000 on an unsecured debt. To repay the debt, the debtor agrees to pay (and the creditor, to accept) 10 percent of the debtor's monthly business profits until the loan with interest has been paid. Although the creditor is sharing profits from the business, the debtor and creditor are not presumed to be partners. ■

Joint Property Ownership and Partnership Status

Joint ownership of property, obviously, does not in and of itself create a partnership. Therefore, if persons own real property as joint tenants or as tenants in common (forms of joint ownership, to be discussed in Chapter 36), this does not mean that they are partners in a partnership. In fact, the sharing of gross revenues and even profits from such ownership is usually not enough to create a partnership [UPA 202(c)(1), (2)].

■EXAMPLE 26.2 Chiang and Burke jointly own a piece of rural property. They lease the land to a farmer, with the understanding that—in lieu of set rental payments—they will receive a share of the profits from the farming operation conducted by the farmer. This arrangement normally would not make Chiang, Burke, and the farmer partners. ■

Note, though, that although the sharing of profits from ownership of property does not prove the existence of a partnership, sharing *both profits and losses* usually does. **■EXAMPLE 26.3** Two sisters, Zoe and Cienna, buy a restaurant together, open a joint bank account from which they pay for expenses and supplies, and share the net profits that the restaurant generates. Zoe manages the restaurant and Cienna handles the bookkeeping. After eight years, Cienna stops doing the bookkeeping and does no other work for the restaurant. Zoe, who is now operating the restaurant by herself, no longer wants to share the profits with Cienna. She offers to buy her sister out, but the two cannot agree on a fair price. When Cienna files a lawsuit, a question arises as to whether the two sisters were partners in the restaurant. In this situation, a court would find that a partnership existed because the sisters shared management responsibilities, had joint accounts, and shared the profits and the losses of the restaurant equally. ■

Entity versus Aggregate Theory of Partnerships

At common law, a partnership was treated only as an aggregate of individuals and never as a separate legal entity. Thus, at common law a suit could never be brought by or against the firm in its own name; each individual partner had to sue or be sued.

Today, in contrast, a majority of the states follow the UPA and treat a partnership as an entity for most purposes. For example, a partnership usually can sue or be sued, collect judgments, and have all accounting procedures in the name of the partnership entity [UPA 201, 307(a)]. As an entity, a partnership may hold the title to real or personal property in its name rather than in the names of the individual partners. Additionally, federal procedural laws permit the partnership to be treated as an entity in suits in federal courts and bankruptcy proceedings.

For federal income tax purposes, however, the partnership is treated as an aggregate of the individual partners rather than a separate legal entity. The partnership is a pass-through entity and not a taxpaying entity. A **pass-through entity** is a business entity that has no tax liability; the entity's income is passed through to the owners of the entity, who pay taxes on it. Thus, the income or losses the partnership incurs are "passed through" the entity framework and attributed to the partners on their individual tax returns. The partnership itself has no tax liability and is responsible only for filing an **information return** with the Internal Revenue Service. In other words, the firm itself pays no taxes. A partner's profit from the partnership (whether distributed or not) is taxed as individual income to the individual partner.

PASS-THROUGH ENTITY
A business entity that has no tax liability. The entity's income is passed through to the owners, and the owners pay taxes on the income.

INFORMATION RETURN
A tax return submitted by a partnership that only reports the income and losses earned by the business. The partnership as an entity does not pay taxes on the income received by the partnership. A partner's profit from the partnership (whether distributed or not) is taxed as individual income to the individual partner.

PARTNERSHIP FORMATION

As a general rule, agreements to form a partnership can be *oral, written,* or *implied by conduct*. Some partnership agreements, however, must be in writing to be legally enforceable under the Statute of Frauds (see Chapter 11 for details). For example, when a partnership agreement authorizes the partners to deal in transfers of real property, it must be evidenced by a sufficient writing.

The Partnership Agreement

ARTICLES OF PARTNERSHIP
A written agreement that sets forth each partner's rights and obligations with respect to the partnership.

A partnership agreement, called **articles of partnership,** can include virtually any terms that the parties wish, unless they are illegal or contrary to public policy or statute [UPA 103]. The agreement usually specifies the name and location of the business, the duration of the partnership, the purpose of the business, each partner's share of the profits, how the partnership will be managed, how assets will be distributed on dissolution, and other provisions. The

BEYOND OUR BORDERS   Doing Business with Foreign Partners

Businesspersons from the United States who wish to operate a partnership in another country often discover that the country requires local participation. Such a requirement means that nationals of the host country must own a specific share of the business. In other words, the U.S. businesspersons would need to admit to the partnership a partner or partners who live in the host country.

Sometimes, U.S. businesspersons are reluctant to establish partnerships in a country that requires local participation. They fear that if the partnership breaks up, the technology and expertise developed by the partnership business may end up in the hands of a future competitor. In that event, the U.S. parties may have little recourse under the host country's law against their former partners' use of the intellectual property.

 FOR CRITICAL ANALYSIS *Do local participation rules benefit countries in the long run? Explain.*

◼

terms commonly included in a partnership agreement are listed in Exhibit 26–1 on the next page. Notice that this list includes an arbitration clause, which is often included in a partnership agreement. (Creating a partnership agreement in another country may involve additional requirements, as this chapter's *Beyond Our Borders* feature explains.)

Duration of the Partnership

The partnership agreement can specify the duration of the partnership by stating that it will continue until a certain date or the completion of a particular project. A partnership that is specifically limited in duration is called a *partnership for a term*. Generally, withdrawing from a partnership for a term prematurely (prior to the expiration date) constitutes a breach of the agreement, and the responsible partner can be held liable for any resulting losses [UPA 602(b)(2)]. If no fixed duration is specified, the partnership is a *partnership at will*.

Partnership by Estoppel

Occasionally, persons who are not partners may nevertheless hold themselves out as partners and make representations that third parties rely on in dealing with them. In such a situation, a court may conclude that a *partnership by estoppel* exists. The law does not confer any partnership rights on these persons, but it may impose liability on them. This is also true when a partner represents, expressly or impliedly, that a nonpartner is a member of the firm. Whenever a third person has reasonably and detrimentally relied on the representation that a nonpartner was part of the partnership, partnership by estoppel is deemed to exist. When this occurs, the nonpartner is regarded as an agent whose acts are binding on the partnership [UPA 308].

◼**EXAMPLE 26.4** Sorento owns a small shop. Knowing that Midland Bank will not make a loan on his credit alone, Sorento represents that Lukas, a financially secure businessperson, is a partner in Sorento's business. Lukas knows of Sorento's misrepresentation but

EXHIBIT 26–1	Common Terms Included in a Partnership Agreement
Basic Structure	1. Name of the partnership.
	2. Names of the partners.
	3. Location of the business and the state law under which the partnership is organized.
	4. Purpose of the partnership.
	5. Duration of the partnership.
Capital Contributions	1. Amount of capital that each partner is contributing.
	2. The agreed-on value of any real or personal property that is contributed instead of cash.
	3. How losses and gains on contributed capital will be allocated, and whether contributions will earn interest.
Sharing of Profits and Losses	1. Percentage of the profits and losses of the business that each partner will receive.
	2. When distributions of profit will be made and how net profit will be calculated.
Management and Control	1. How management responsibilities will be divided among the partners.
	2. Name(s) of the managing partner or partners, and whether other partners have voting rights.
Accounting and Partnership Records	1. Name of the bank in which the partnership will maintain its business and checking accounts.
	2. Statement that an accounting of partnership records will be maintained and that any partner or her or his agent can review these records at any time.
	3. The dates of the partnership's fiscal year (if used) and when the annual audit of the books will take place.
Dissolution	1. Events that will dissolve the partnership, such as the retirement, death, or incapacity of any partner.
	2. How partnership property will be valued and apportioned on dissolution.
	3. Whether an arbitrator will determine the value of partnership property on dissolution and whether that determination will be binding.
Miscellaneous	Whether arbitration is required for any dispute relating to the partnership agreement.

fails to correct it. Midland Bank, relying on the strength of Lukas's reputation and credit, extends a loan to Sorento. Sorento will be liable to the bank for repaying the loan. Lukas could also be held liable to the bank in many states. Because Lukas has impliedly consented to the misrepresentation, she will normally be estopped (prevented) from denying that she is Sorento's partner. A court will treat Lukas as if she were in fact a partner in Sorento's business insofar as this loan is concerned. ■

PARTNERSHIP OPERATION

The rights and duties of partners are governed largely by the specific terms of their partnership agreement. In the absence of provisions to the contrary in the partnership agreement, the law imposes the rights and duties discussed here. The character and nature of the partnership business generally influence the application of these rights and duties.

Rights of Partners

The rights of partners in a partnership relate to the following areas: management, interest in the partnership, compensation, inspection of books, accounting, and property.

Management Rights In a general partnership, all partners have equal rights in managing the partnership [UPA 401(f)]. Unless the partners agree otherwise, each partner has one vote in management matters *regardless of the proportional size of his or her interest in the firm.* Often, in a large partnership, partners will agree to delegate daily management responsibilities to a management committee made up of one or more of the partners.

The majority rule controls decisions in ordinary matters connected with partnership business, unless otherwise specified in the agreement. Decisions that significantly affect the nature of the partnership or that are not apparently for carrying on the ordinary course of the partnership business, or business of the kind, however, require the *unanimous* consent of the partners [UPA 301(2), 401(i), (j)]. Unanimous consent is likely to be required for a decision to undertake any of the following actions[2]:

1 To alter the essential nature of the firm's business as expressed in the partnership agreement or to alter the capital structure of the partnership.

2 To admit new partners or to enter a wholly new business.

3 To assign partnership property to a trust for the benefit of creditors.

4 To dispose of the partnership's goodwill.

5 To confess judgment against the partnership or to submit partnership claims to arbitration. (A **confession of judgment** is the act of a debtor in permitting a judgment to be entered against her or him by a creditor, for an agreed sum, without the institution of legal proceedings.)

6 To undertake any act that would make further conduct of partnership business impossible.

7 To amend the articles of the partnership agreement.

CONFESSION OF JUDGMENT
The act or agreement of a debtor in permitting a judgment to be entered against him or her by a creditor, for an agreed sum, without the institution of legal proceedings.

Interest in the Partnership Each partner is entitled to the proportion of business profits and losses that is designated in the partnership agreement. If the agreement does not apportion profits (indicate how the profits will be shared), the UPA provides that profits will be shared equally. If the agreement does not apportion losses, losses will be shared in the same ratio as profits [UPA 401(b)].

■EXAMPLE 26.5 The partnership agreement for Rico and Brent provides for capital contributions of $60,000 from Rico and $40,000 from Brent, but it is silent as to how Rico and Brent will share profits or losses. In this situation, Rico and Brent will share both profits and losses equally. If their partnership agreement provided for profits to be shared in the same ratio as capital contributions, however, 60 percent of the profits would go to Rico, and 40 percent of the profits would go to Brent. If their partnership agreement was silent as to losses, losses would be shared in the same ratio as profits (60 percent and 40 percent, respectively). ■

Compensation Devoting time, skill, and energy to partnership business is a partner's duty and generally is not a compensable service. Rather, as mentioned, a partner's income

---

2. The previous version of the UPA specifically listed most of these actions as requiring unanimous consent. The current version of the UPA omits the list entirely to allow the courts more flexibility. The Official Comments explain that most of the actions on this list, except for submitting a claim to arbitration, will likely continue to require unanimous consent because they are outside the apparent authority of an individual partner.

Partners examine accounting records. Are there any restrictions on the right of a partner to inspect his or her firm's books and records? Why or why not? (PhotoDisc)

from the partnership takes the form of a distribution of profits according to the partner's share in the business. Partners can, of course, agree otherwise. For example, the managing partner of a law firm often receives a salary in addition to her or his share of profits for performing special administrative duties, such as managing the office or personnel.

Inspection of Books Partnership books and records must be kept accessible to all partners. Each partner has the right to receive (and the corresponding duty to produce) full and complete information concerning the conduct of all aspects of partnership business [UPA 403]. Each firm keeps books for recording and preserving such information. Partners contribute the information, and a bookkeeper or an accountant typically has the duty to preserve it. The books must be kept at the firm's principal business office and cannot be removed without the consent of all of the partners. Every partner, whether active or inactive, is entitled to inspect all books and records on demand and can make copies of the materials. The personal representative of a deceased partner's estate has the same right of access to partnership books and records that the decedent would have had [UPA 403].

Accounting of Partnership Assets or Profits An accounting of partnership assets or profits is required to determine the value of each partner's share in the partnership. An accounting can be performed voluntarily, or it can be compelled by court order. Under UPA 405(b), a partner has the right to bring an action for an accounting during the term of the partnership, as well as on the firm's dissolution and winding up.[3] A partner also has the right to bring an action against the partnership or another partner, with or without a formal accounting, in the following situations:

1 To enforce the partner's rights under the partnership agreement.

2 To enforce the partner's rights under the UPA.

3 To enforce the partner's rights and interests arising independently of the partnership relationship.

Property Rights Property acquired *by* a partnership is the property of the partnership and not of the partners individually [UPA 203]. Partnership property includes all property that was originally contributed to the partnership and anything later purchased by the partnership or in the partnership's name (except in rare circumstances) [UPA 204]. A partner may use or possess partnership property only on behalf of the partnership [UPA 401(g)]. A partner is *not* a co-owner of partnership property and has no right to sell, mortgage, or transfer partnership property to another.[4]

In other words, partnership property is owned by the partnership as an entity and not by the individual partners. Thus, a creditor of an individual partner cannot seek to use partnership property to satisfy the partner's debt. Such a creditor can, however, petition a court for a **charging order** to attach the individual partner's interest in the partnership (her or his proportionate share of the profits and losses) to satisfy the partner's obligation.

CHARGING ORDER
In partnership law, an order granted by a court to a judgment creditor that entitles the creditor to attach profits or assets of a partner on the dissolution of the partnership.

---

3. Under the previous version of the UPA, a partner could bring an action for an accounting in any of the following situations: the partnership agreement provided for it, the partner was wrongfully excluded from the business or its property or books, another partner was in breach of his or her fiduciary duty, or other circumstances rendered it "just and reasonable."

4. Under the previous version of the UPA, partners were *tenants in partnership*. This meant that every partner was a co-owner with all other partners of the partnership property. The current UPA does not recognize this concept.

(A partner can also assign her or his right to a share of the partnership profits to another to satisfy a debt.)

Duties and Liabilities of Partners

The duties and liabilities of partners are basically derived from agency law. Each partner is an agent of every other partner and acts as both a principal and an agent in any business transaction within the scope of the partnership agreement. Each partner is also a general agent of the partnership in carrying out the usual business of the firm "or business of the kind carried on by the partnership" [UPA 301(1)]. Thus, every act of a partner concerning partnership business and "business of the kind," and every contract signed in the partnership's name, bind the firm.

We examine here the fiduciary duties of partners, the authority of partners, the joint and several liability that characterizes partnerships, and the limitations imposed on the liability of incoming partners for preexisting partnership debts.

Fiduciary Duties   The fiduciary duties a partner owes to the partnership and the other partners are the duty of loyalty and the duty of care [UPA 404(a)]. The duty of loyalty requires a partner to account to the partnership for "any property, profit, or benefit" derived by the partner from the partnership's business or the use of its property [UPA 404(b)]. A partner must also refrain from competing with the partnership in business or dealing with the firm as an adverse party. A partner's duty of care involves refraining from "grossly negligent or reckless conduct, intentional misconduct, or a knowing violation of law" [UPA 404(c)].[5]

These duties may not be waived or eliminated in the partnership agreement, and in fulfilling them each partner must act consistently with the obligation of good faith and fair dealing, which applies to all contracts, including partnership agreements [UPA 103(b), 404(d)]. The agreement can specify acts that the partners agree will violate a fiduciary duty.

Note that a partner may pursue his or her own interests without automatically violating these duties [UPA 404(e)]. The key is whether the partner has disclosed the interest to the other partners. For instance, a partner who owns a shopping mall may vote against a partnership proposal to open a competing mall, provided that the partner has fully disclosed her interest in the shopping mall to the other partners at the firm. A partner cannot make secret profits or put self-interest before his or her duty to the interest of the partnership, however.

Authority of Partners   The UPA affirms general principles of agency law that pertain to the authority of a partner to bind a partnership in contract. A partner may also subject the partnership to tort liability under the agency principles. When a partner is carrying on partnership business or business of the kind with third parties in the usual way, both the partner and the firm share liability.

The partnership will not be liable, however, if the third parties know that the partner has no such authority. **■EXAMPLE 26.6** Patricia, a partner in the partnership of Heise, Green, and Stevens, applies for a loan on behalf of the partnership without authorization from the other partners. The bank manager knows that Patricia has no authority. If the bank manager grants the loan, Patricia will be personally bound, but the firm will not be liable. ■

A partnership may file in a designated state office a "statement of partnership authority" to limit the capacity of a partner to act as the firm's agent or transfer property on its

---

5. The previous version of the UPA touched only briefly on the duty of loyalty and left the details of the partners' fiduciary duties to be developed under the law of agency.

behalf [UPA 105, 303]. Any limit on a partner's authority, however, normally does not affect a third party who does not know about the statement (except in real estate transactions when the statement has been recorded with the appropriate state office).

Agency concepts relating to actual (express and implied) authority, apparent authority, and ratification are also applicable to partnerships. The extent of *implied authority* is generally broader for partners than for ordinary agents, though.

The Scope of Implied Powers. The character and scope of the partnership business, the customary nature of the particular business operation, and the ordinary course of business of the kind carried on by the partnership determine the implied powers of the partners. For example, each partner in a trading partnership—essentially, any partnership business that has goods in inventory and makes profits buying and selling those goods—has a wide range of implied powers, such as to advertise products, hire employees, and extend the firm's credit by issuing or indorsing instruments (see Chapters 20 and 21).

In an ordinary partnership, the partners can exercise all implied powers reasonably necessary and customary to carry on that particular business. Some customarily implied powers include the authority to make warranties on goods in the sales business and the power to enter into contracts consistent with the firm's regular course of business. Most partners also have the implied authority to make representations to others concerning partnership affairs and these statements may be admissible as evidence against the partnership. A partner might also have the implied power to convey real property in the firm's name when such conveyances are part of the ordinary course of partnership business.

Authorized versus Unauthorized Actions. If a partner acts within the scope of authority, the partnership is legally bound to honor the partner's commitments to third parties. For example, a partner's authority to sell partnership products carries with it the implied authority to transfer title and to make the usual warranties. Hence, in a partnership that operates a retail tire store, any partner negotiating a contract with a customer for the sale of a set of tires can warrant that "each tire will be warranted for normal wear for 40,000 miles."

This same partner, however, does not have the authority to sell office equipment, fixtures, or the partnership office building without the consent of all of the other partners. In addition, because partnerships are formed to generate profits, a partner generally does not have the authority to make charitable contributions without the consent of the other partners. Such actions are not binding on the partnership unless they are ratified by all of the other partners.

Liability of Partners One significant disadvantage associated with a traditional partnership is that partners are *personally* liable for the debts of the partnership. Moreover, the liability is essentially unlimited because the acts of one partner in the ordinary course of business subject the other partners to personal liability [UPA 305]. The following subsections explain the rules on a partner's liability that are followed by most states. The *Application* feature at the end of this chapter discusses the effect that liability rules are having on the rate of partnership formation.

Joint and Several Liability. Under UPA 306(a), partners are jointly and severally (separately or individually) liable for all partnership obligations, including contracts, torts, and breaches of trust.[6] **Joint and several liability** means that a third party may sue all of the partners together (jointly) or one or more of the partners separately (severally) at his or her

JOINT AND SEVERAL LIABILITY
In partnership law, a doctrine under which a plaintiff may sue, and collect a judgment from, all of the partners together (jointly) or one or more of the partners separately (severally, or individually). This is true even if one of the partners sued did not participate in, ratify, or know about whatever it was that gave rise to the cause of action.

---

6. Under the previous version of the UPA, which is still in effect in a minority of states, partners were jointly liable on partnership debts and contracts, but not on partnership debts arising from torts.

option. This is true even if the partner did not participate in, ratify, or know about whatever it was that gave rise to the cause of action. Generally, under UPA 307(d), however, a creditor cannot bring an action to collect a partnership debt from the partner of a nonbankrupt partnership without first attempting to collect from the partnership or convincing a court that the attempt would be unsuccessful.

A judgment against one partner severally (separately) does not extinguish the others' liability. (Similarly, a release of one partner does not discharge the partners' several liability.) Thus, those partners not sued in the first action may be sued subsequently, unless the first action was conclusive for the partnership on the question of liability. In other words, if an action is brought against one partner and the court holds that the partnership was in no way liable, the third party cannot bring an action against another partner and succeed on the issue of the partnership's liability.

If a third party is successful in a suit against a partner or partners, she or he may collect on the judgment only against the assets of those partners named as defendants. A partner who commits a tort is required to indemnify (compensate) the partnership for any damages it pays. The question in the following case was whether a partnership must indemnify a partner for liability that results from negligent conduct occurring in the ordinary course of the partnership's business.

CASE 26.1   **Moren v. Jax Restaurant**

Minnesota Court of Appeals, 679 N.W.2d 165 (2004).
www.lawlibrary.state.mn.us/archive/cap1st.html[a]

FACTS "Jax Restaurant" is a partnership that operates Jax Restaurant in Foley, Minnesota. One afternoon in October 2000, Nicole Moren, one of the partners, finished her shift at the restaurant at 4:00 P.M. and picked up her two-year-old son, Remington, from day care. About 5:30 P.M., Moren returned to the restaurant with Remington after Amy Benedetti, the other partner and Moren's sister, asked for help. Moren's husband Martin offered to pick up Remington in twenty minutes. Because Moren did not want Remington running around the restaurant, she brought him into the kitchen with her, set him on top of the counter, and began rolling out pizza dough using a dough-pressing machine. As she was making pizzas, Remington reached his hand into the dough press. His hand was crushed, causing permanent injuries. Through his father, Remington filed a suit in a Minnesota state court against the partnership, alleging negligence. The partnership then filed a complaint against Moren, arguing that in the event it was obligated to compensate Remington, it was entitled to indemnity from Moren for her negligence. The court issued a summary judgment dismissing the partnership's complaint

against Moren. The partnership appealed this judgment to a state intermediate appellate court.

ISSUE Must a partnership indemnify a partner for liability that results from negligent conduct occurring in the ordinary course of the partnership's business?

DECISION Yes. The state intermediate appellate court affirmed the lower court's judgment. "Minnesota law requires a partnership to indemnify its partners for the result of their negligence."

REASON The appellate court pointed out that under the UPA, a partnership is liable for an injury caused by a partner who, while acting in the ordinary course of the firm's business, commits a wrongful act or omission, or engages in other misconduct. Thus, according to the court, the firm must indemnify a partner for liability incurred by the partner in the ordinary course of the partnership's business. The court also reasoned that "the conduct of a partner may be partly motivated by personal reasons and still occur in the ordinary course of business of the partnership." In this case, Moren was acting for the benefit of the partnership by making pizzas when her son was injured. Even though she was simultaneously acting in her role as a mother, the court concluded that her conduct remained in the ordinary course of

a. In the "Published" section, click on "M–O." On that page, scroll to the name of the case and click on the docket number to access the opinion. The Minnesota State Law Library maintains this Web site.

CASE 26.1–Continues next page

CASE 26.1–Continued

the partnership business. Therefore "[l]iability for Nicole Moren's negligence rested with the partnership, even if the partner's conduct partly served her personal interests." For this reason, said the court, "her conduct bound the partnership and it owes indemnity to her for her negligence."

WHAT IF THE FACTS WERE DIFFERENT?
Suppose that Moren's predominant motive in bringing her son to the restaurant had been to benefit herself. Would the result have been different? Why or why not?

Liability of Incoming Partner.   A newly admitted partner to an existing partnership normally has limited liability for whatever debts and obligations the partnership incurred *prior to* the new partner's admission. The new partner's liability can be satisfied only from partnership assets [UPA 306(b)]. This means that the new partner usually has no personal liability for these debts and obligations, but any capital contribution that he or she made to the partnership is subject to these debts. **■EXAMPLE 26.7** Smartclub is a partnership with four members. Alex Jaff, a newly admitted partner, contributes $100,000 to the partnership. Smartclub has about $600,000 in debt at the time Jaff joins the firm. Although Jaff's capital contribution of $100,000 can be used to satisfy Smartclub's obligations, Jaff is not personally liable for partnership debts that were incurred before he became a partner. Thus, his personal assets cannot be used to satisfy the partnership's antecedent debt. If, however, the managing partner at Smartclub borrows funds after Jaff becomes a partner, Jaff will be personally liable for those amounts. ■

PARTNER'S DISSOCIATION

DISSOCIATION
The severance of the relationship between a partner and a partnership when the partner ceases to be associated with the carrying on of the partnership business.

Dissociation occurs when a partner ceases to be associated in the carrying on of the partnership business. Although a partner always has the *power* to dissociate from the firm, he or she may not have the *right* to dissociate. Dissociation normally entitles the partner to have his or her interest purchased by the partnership and terminates his or her actual authority to act for the partnership and to participate with the partners in running the business. Otherwise, the partnership continues to do business without the dissociating partner.[7]

Events Causing Dissociation

Under UPA 601, a partner can be dissociated from a partnership in any of the following ways:

1 By the partner's voluntarily giving notice of an "express will to withdraw."

2 By the occurrence of an event agreed to in the partnership agreement.

3 By a unanimous vote of the other partners under certain circumstances, such as when a partner transfers substantially all of her or his interest in the partnership, or when it becomes unlawful to carry on partnership business with that partner.

4 By order of a court or arbitrator if the partner has engaged in wrongful conduct that affects the partnership business, breached the partnership agreement or violated a duty owed to the partnership or the other partners, or engaged in conduct that makes it "not reasonably practicable to carry on the business in partnership with the partner" [UPA 601(5)].

---

7. Under the previous version of the UPA, when a partner dissociated from a partnership, the partnership was considered dissolved, its business had to be wound up, and the proceeds had to be distributed to creditors and among partners. The amendments to the UPA recognize that a partnership may not want to break up just because one partner has left the firm.

5 By the partner's declaring bankruptcy, assigning his or her interest in the partnership for the benefit of creditors, or becoming physically or mentally incapacitated, or by the partner's death. Note that although the bankruptcy or death of a partner represents that partner's "dissociation" from the partnership, it is not an *automatic* ground for the partnership's dissolution (*dissolution* will be discussed shortly).

Wrongful Dissociation

As mentioned, a partner has the power to dissociate from a partnership at any time, but if she or he lacks the right to dissociate, then the dissociation is considered wrongful under the law [UPA 602]. When a partner's dissociation is in breach of the partnership agreement, for instance, it is wrongful. **EXAMPLE 26.8** Suppose that a partnership agreement states that it is a breach of the partnership agreement for any partner to assign partnership property to a creditor without the consent of the others. If a partner, Janis, makes such an assignment, she not only has breached the agreement but has also wrongfully dissociated from the partnership. ■ Similarly, if a partner refuses to perform duties required by the partnership agreement—such as accounting for profits earned from the use of partnership property—this breach can be treated as wrongful dissociation.

With regard to a partnership for a definite term or a particular undertaking, dissociation that occurs before the expiration of the term or the completion of the undertaking may be wrongful. In these types of partnerships, the dissociation normally is considered wrongful if the partner withdraws by express will, is expelled by a court or an arbitrator, or declares bankruptcy [UPA 602].

A partner who wrongfully dissociates is liable to the partnership and to the other partners for damages caused by the dissociation. This liability is in addition to any other obligation of the partner to the partnership or to the other partners. For example, a dissociating partner would be liable for any damage caused by a breach of a partnership agreement. The partner would also be liable to the partnership for costs incurred to replace the partner's expertise or obtain new financing.

Effects of Dissociation

Dissociation (rightful or wrongful) terminates some of the rights of the dissociated partner, creates a mandatory duty for the partnership, and alters the liability of both parties to third parties.

Rights and Duties On a partner's dissociation, his or her right to participate in the management and conduct of the partnership business terminates [UPA 603]. The partner's duty of loyalty also ends. A partner's other fiduciary duties, including the duty of care, continue only with respect to events that occurred before dissociation, unless the partner participates in winding up the partnership's business (to be discussed later in this chapter). **EXAMPLE 26.9** Debbie Pearson, a partner who leaves an accounting firm, Bubb & Pearson, can immediately compete with the firm for new clients. She must exercise care in completing ongoing client transactions, however, and must account to the firm for any fees received from the old clients based on those transactions. ■

After a partner's dissociation, his or her interest in the partnership must be purchased according to the rules in UPA 701. The **buyout price** is based on the amount that would have been distributed to the partner if the partnership were wound up on the date of dissociation. Offset against the price are amounts owed by the partner to the partnership, including any damages for the partner's wrongful dissociation.

In the following case, the court had to decide how the buyout price of a partner's interest should be determined on his dissociation from his family's ranch business, which had been operated as a partnership for more than twenty years.

BUYOUT PRICE
The amount payable to a partner on his or her dissociation from a partnership, based on the amount distributable to that partner if the firm were wound up on that date, and offset by any damages for wrongful dissociation.

CASE 26.2 Warnick v. Warnick

Supreme Court of Wyoming, 2006 WY 58, 133 P.3d 997 (2006).

FACTS In 1978, Wilbur and Dee Warnick and their son Randall Warnick bought a ranch in Sheridan County, Wyoming, for $335,000. To operate the ranch, they formed a partnership—Warnick Ranches. The partners' initial capital contributions totaled $60,000, of which Wilbur paid 36 percent, Dee paid 30 percent, and Randall paid 34 percent. Wilbur and Dee moved onto the ranch in 1981. Randall lived and worked on the ranch during the 1981 and 1982 summer haying seasons and again from 1991 to 1998. The partners each contributed funds to the operation and received cash distributions from the partnership. In the summer of 1999, Randall dissociated from the partnership. When the parties could not agree on a buyout price, Randall filed a suit in a Wyoming state court against the other partners and the partnership to recover what he believed to be a fair price. The court awarded Randall $115,783.13—the amount of his cash contributions, plus 34 percent of the increase in the value of the partnership's assets above all partners' cash contributions, with interest from the date of his dissociation. The defendants appealed to the Wyoming Supreme Court, arguing that in the calculation, $50,000 should be deducted from the appraised value of the ranch, its livestock, and its equipment for the estimated expenses of selling these assets.

ISSUE In determining the buyout price of a dissociated partner, do the costs of liquidating partnership assets include the expenses of a hypothetical sale?

DECISION No. The court affirmed the judgment of the lower court, holding that "purely hypothetical costs of sale are not a required deduction in valuing partnership assets."

REASON The state supreme court explained that under Wyoming Statutes Section 17-21-701 (Wyoming's version of UPA 701) the buyout price is "the amount that would have been paid to the dissociating partner following a settlement of partnership accounts upon the winding up of the partnership, if, on the date of dissociation, the assets of the partnership were sold at a price equal to the greater of the liquidation value or the value based on a sale of the business as a going concern without the dissociating partner." The first step in the calculation is to value the partnership's assets according to the two methods. In making the determination in this case, the defendants "assume that the liquidation value of the ranch is the amount of cash that would remain following a sale." But liquidation value refers to the prices of assets if they are sold separately, as opposed to the value of the business as a whole. For this purpose, an asset's price is the amount that "a willing and informed buyer would pay a willing and informed seller, with neither being under any compulsion to deal." Such a seller would factor the cost of a sale into the price, as the appraiser and the lower court likely did here. Besides "the assets of this partnership were not, in fact, liquidated. Instead, * * * the assets were retained by Warnick Ranches."

FOR CRITICAL ANALYSIS–Economic Consideration
How and why might the value of a partnership interest in a going concern differ from the value of the same interest as a result of a liquidation?

Liability to Third Parties For two years after a partner dissociates from a continuing partnership, the partnership may be bound by the acts of the dissociated partner based on apparent authority [UPA 702]. In other words, the partnership may be liable to a third party with whom a dissociated partner enters into a transaction if the third party reasonably believed that the dissociated partner was still a partner. Similarly, a dissociated partner may be liable for partnership obligations entered into during a two-year period following dissociation [UPA 703].

To avoid this possible liability, a partnership should notify its creditors, customers, and clients of a partner's dissociation. Also, either the partnership or the dissociated partner can file a statement of dissociation in the appropriate state office to limit the dissociated partner's authority to ninety days after the filing [UPA 704]. Filing this statement helps to minimize the firm's potential liability for the former partner and vice versa.

PARTNERSHIP TERMINATION

The same events that cause dissociation can result in the end of the partnership if the remaining partners no longer wish to (or are unable to) continue the partnership business. The termination of a partnership is referred to as **dissolution,** which essentially means the commencement of the winding up process. **Winding up** is the actual process of collecting, liquidating, and distributing the partnership assets.[8] We discuss here the dissolution and winding up of partnership business.

Dissolution

Dissolution of a partnership generally can be brought about by the acts of the partners, by the operation of law, and by judicial decree [UPA 801]. Any partnership (including one for a fixed term) can be dissolved by the partners' agreement. Similarly, if the partnership agreement states that it will dissolve on a certain event, such as a partner's death or bankruptcy, then the occurrence of that event will dissolve the partnership. A partnership for a fixed term or a particular undertaking is dissolved by operation of law at the expiration of the term or on the completion of the undertaking.

Any event that makes it unlawful for the partnership to continue its business will result in dissolution [UPA 801(4)]. Under the UPA, a court may order dissolution when it becomes obviously impractical for the firm to continue—for example, if the business can only be operated at a loss [UPA 801(5)]. Additionally, a partner's impropriety involving partnership business (for example, fraud perpetrated on the other partners) or improper behavior reflecting unfavorably on the firm may provide grounds for a judicial decree of dissolution. Finally, if dissension between partners becomes so persistent and harmful as to undermine the confidence and cooperation necessary to carry on the firm's business, a court may grant a decree of dissolution.

Do former partners remain jointly and severally liable for a partnership's obligations even after the partnership has been dissolved? Yes, at least according to one 2006 case. The plaintiff in the case alleged that when he was about twelve years old, Nelson Faerber, Jr., a school board member and prominent attorney, began sexually molesting him. For almost six years, Faerber, who was a partner at a Florida law firm, purportedly molested the boy on numerous occasions and at various locations, including the law firm's offices and the plaintiff's middle school. Faerber had died before the plaintiff filed the lawsuit, so the suit named several other defendants, including Faerber's wife, the school, and members of Faerber's former law firm. The law firm argued that the court should dismiss the case against it because the firm no longer existed. The court disagreed, however, holding that "[u]nder Florida law, partners remain jointly and severally liable for partnership liability, notwithstanding dissolution and division of property."[9] Although the holding in this case might seem unfair, it illustrates how unlimited liability in general partnerships can extend even beyond the partnership's termination.

ETHICAL ISSUE 26.1

Winding Up

After dissolution, the partnership continues for the limited purpose of the winding up process. The partners cannot create new obligations on behalf of the partnership. They

DISSOLUTION
The formal disbanding of a partnership or a corporation. It can take place by (1) acts of the partners or, in a corporation, acts of the shareholders and board of directors; (2) the subsequent illegality of the firm's business; (3) the expiration of a time period stated in a partnership agreement or a certificate of incorporation; or (4) judicial decree.

WINDING UP
The second of two stages in the termination of a partnership or corporation. Once the firm is dissolved, it continues to exist legally until the process of winding up all business affairs (collecting and distributing the firm's assets) is complete.

DON'T FORGET Secured creditors have priority over unsecured creditors to any assets that serve as collateral for a partnership's debts.

---

8. Although "winding down" would seem to describe more accurately the process of settling accounts and liquidating the assets of a partnership, "winding up" has been traditionally used in English and U.S. statutory and case law to denote this final stage of a partnership's existence.

9. *Doe v. Faerber,* 446 F.Supp.2d 1311 (M.D.Fla. 2006).

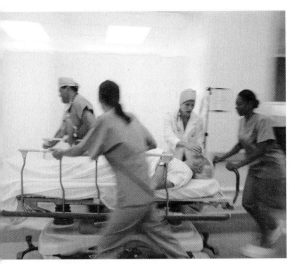

If a partner becomes incapacitated or dies, how does this affect the existence of the partnership?
(PhotoDisc)

have authority only to complete transactions begun but not finished at the time of dissolution and to wind up the business of the partnership [UPA 803, 804(1)]. *Winding up* includes collecting and preserving partnership assets, discharging liabilities (paying debts), and accounting to each partner for the value of her or his interest in the partnership. Partners continue to have fiduciary duties to one another and to the firm during this process. UPA 401(h) provides that a partner is entitled to compensation for services in winding up partnership affairs (and reimbursement for expenses incurred in the process) above and apart from his or her share in the partnership profits.

Both creditors of the partnership and creditors of the individual partners can make claims on the partnership's assets. In general, partnership creditors share proportionately with the partners' individual creditors in the assets of the partners' estates, which include their interests in the partnership. A partnership's assets are distributed according to the following priorities [UPA 807]:

1 Payment of debts, including those owed to partner and nonpartner creditors.
2 Return of capital contributions and distribution of profits to partners.[10]

If the partnership's liabilities are greater than its assets, the partners bear the losses—in the absence of a contrary agreement—in the same proportion in which they shared the profits (rather than, for example, in proportion to their contributions to the partnership's capital).

PREVENTING LEGAL DISPUTES

Usually, when people enter into partnerships, they are getting along with one another. Obviously, the situation can change, and partners often become unable to work together amicably. To prepare for this possibility, businesspersons entering a partnership should agree on how their assets will be valued and divided in the event the partnership dissolves. Make express arrangements during the formation of the partnership to provide for its smooth dissolution. Partners can enter a buy-sell, or buyout, agreement, which provides that one or more partners will buy out the other or others, should the relationship deteriorate. Agreeing beforehand on who buys what, under what circumstances, and, if possible, at what price may eliminate costly negotiations or litigation later. Alternatively, the agreement may specify that one or more partners will determine the value of the interest being sold and that the other or others will decide whether to buy or sell.

LIMITED LIABILITY PARTNERSHIPS

LIMITED LIABILITY PARTNERSHIP (LLP)
A hybrid form of business organization that is used mainly by professionals who normally do business in a partnership. Like a partnership, an LLP is a pass-through entity for tax purposes, but the personal liability of the partners is limited.

The **limited liability partnership (LLP)** is a hybrid form of business designed mostly for professionals who normally do business as partners in a partnership. The major advantage of the LLP is that it allows a partnership to continue as a *pass-through entity* for tax purposes, but limits the personal liability of the partners.

The first state to enact an LLP statute was Texas, in 1991. Other states quickly followed suit, and by 1997, virtually all of the states had enacted LLP statutes. LLPs must be formed

---

10. Under the previous version of the UPA, creditors of the partnership had priority over creditors of the individual partners. Also, in distributing partnership assets, third party creditors were paid before partner creditors, and capital contributions were returned before profits.

and operated in compliance with state statutes, which may include provisions of the UPA. The appropriate form must be filed with a central state agency, usually the secretary of state's office, and the business's name must include either "Limited Liability Partnership" or "LLP" [UPA 1001, 1002]. In addition, an LLP must file an annual report with the state to remain qualified as an LLP in that state [UPA 1003]. In most states, it is relatively easy to convert a traditional partnership into an LLP because the firm's basic organizational structure remains the same. Additionally, all of the statutory and common law rules governing partnerships still apply (apart from those modified by the LLP statute). Normally, LLP statutes are simply amendments to a state's already existing partnership law.

The LLP is especially attractive for two categories of businesses: professional services and family businesses. Professional service firms include law firms and accounting firms. Family limited liability partnerships are basically business organizations in which all of the partners are related.

Liability in an LLP

Many professionals, such as attorneys and accountants, work together using the partnership business form. As discussed previously in this chapter, a major disadvantage of the general partnership is the unlimited personal liability of its owner-partners. Partners in a general partnership are also subject to joint and several (individual) liability for partnership obligations, which exposes each partner to potential liability for the malpractice of another partner.

The LLP allows professionals to avoid personal liability for the malpractice of other partners. A partner in an LLP is still liable for her or his own wrongful acts, such as negligence, however. Also liable is the partner who supervised the party who committed a wrongful act. This is generally true for all types of partners and partnerships, not just LLPs. ■**EXAMPLE 26.10** A group of five lawyers is operating as a partnership. One of the attorneys, Dan Kolcher, is sued for malpractice and loses. If the firm was organized as a general partnership and the firm did not have sufficient malpractice insurance to pay the judgment, the personal assets of other attorneys could be used to satisfy the obligation. Because the firm is organized as a limited liability partnership, however, no other partner at the law firm can be held *personally* liable for Kolcher's malpractice, unless she or he acted as Kolcher's supervisor. In the absence of a supervisor, only Kolcher's personal assets could be used to satisfy the judgment (to the extent that it exceeds the liability insurance coverage). ■

Although LLP statutes vary from state to state, generally each state statute limits the liability of partners in some way. For example, Delaware law protects each innocent partner from the "debts and obligations of the partnership arising from negligence, wrongful acts, or misconduct." In North Carolina, Texas, and Washington, D.C., the statutes protect innocent partners from obligations arising from "errors, omissions, negligence, incompetence, or malfeasance." The UPA more broadly exempts partners from personal liability for any partnership obligation, "whether arising in contract, tort, or otherwise" [UPA 306(c)]. Although the language of these statutes may seem to apply specifically to attorneys, virtually any group of professionals can use the LLP.

Some aspects of this exemption from liability are still uncertain, however. One question is whether limits on liability apply outside the state in which the LLP was formed. Another question involves how liability should be shared when more than one partner is negligent.

Liability outside the State of Formation   When an LLP formed in one state wants to do business in another state, some states require that the LLP must first register in the other state—for example, by filing a statement of foreign qualification [UPA 1102].

ON THE WEB

For an example of a state law (that of Iowa) governing limited liability partnerships, go to

www.sos.state.ia.us/business/ limliabpart.html.

Because state LLP statutes are not uniform, a question arises in this situation. If the LLP statutes in the two states provide different liability protection, which law applies? Most states apply the law of the state in which the LLP was formed, even when the firm does business in another state, which is also the rule under UPA 1101.

Sharing Liability among Partners   When more than one partner in an LLP is negligent, there is a question as to how liability is to be shared. Is each partner jointly and severally liable for the entire result, as a general partner would be in most states? Some states provide for proportionate liability—that is, for separate determinations of the negligence of the partners.[11] The American Institute of Certified Public Accountants (AICPA) supports the enactment of proportionate liability statutes.[12]

■ EXAMPLE 26.11   Accountants Don and Jane are partners in an LLP, with Don supervising Jane. Jane negligently fails to file tax returns for their client, Centaur Tools. Centaur files a suit against Don and Jane. In a state that does not allow for proportionate liability, Don can be held liable for the entire loss. Under a proportionate liability statute, Don will be liable for no more than his portion of the responsibility for the missed tax deadline. (Even if Jane settles the case quickly, Don will still be liable for his portion.) ■

Family Limited Liability Partnerships

A **family limited liability partnership (FLLP)** is a limited liability partnership in which the majority of the partners are persons related to each other, essentially as spouses, parents, grandparents, siblings, cousins, nephews, or nieces. A person acting in a fiduciary capacity for persons so related can also be a partner. All of the partners must be natural persons or persons acting in a fiduciary capacity for the benefit of natural persons.

Probably the most significant use of the FLLP form of business organization is in agriculture. Family-owned farms sometimes find this form to their benefit. The FLLP offers the same advantages as other LLPs with some additional advantages, such as, in Iowa, an exemption from real estate transfer taxes when partnership real estate is transferred among partners.[13]

LIMITED PARTNERSHIPS

We now look at a business organizational form that limits the liability of *some* of its owners—the **limited partnership.** Limited partnerships originated in medieval Europe and have been in existence in the United States since the early 1800s. In many ways, limited partnerships are like the general partnerships discussed at the outset of this chapter, but they differ from general partnerships in several ways. Because of this, they are sometimes referred to as *special partnerships.*

A limited partnership consists of at least one **general partner** and one or more **limited partners.** A general partner assumes management responsibility for the partnership and so has full responsibility for the partnership and for all debts of the partnership. A limited partner contributes cash or other property and owns an interest in the firm but does not undertake any management responsibilities and is not personally liable for partnership debts beyond the amount of his or her investment. A limited partner can forfeit limited

11. See, for example, Colorado Revised Statutes Annotated Section 13-21-111.5(1) and Utah Code Annotated Section 78-27-39.

12. Public Oversight Board of the Securities and Exchange Commission Practice Section, AICPA, *In the Public Interest: Issues Confronting the Accounting Profession* (New York: AICPA, March 5, 1993), Recommendation I-1.

13. Iowa Statutes Section 428A.2.

liability by taking part in the management of the business. Exhibit 26–2 compares characteristics of general and limited partnerships.[14]

Until 1976, the law governing limited partnerships in all states except Louisiana was the Uniform Limited Partnership Act (ULPA). Since 1976, most states and the District of

---

14. Under the UPA, a general partnership can be converted into a limited partnership and vice versa [UPA 902, 903]. The UPA also provides for the merger of a general partnership with one or more general or limited partnerships under rules that are similar to those governing corporate mergers [UPA 905].

EXHIBIT 26–2	**A Comparison of General Partnerships and Limited Partnerships**	
CHARACTERISTIC	**GENERAL PARTNERSHIP (UPA)**	**LIMITED PARTNERSHIP (RULPA)**
Creation	By agreement of two or more persons to carry on a business as co-owners for profit.	By agreement of two or more persons to carry on a business as co-owners for profit. Must include one or more general partners and one or more limited partners. Filing of a certificate with the secretary of state is required.
Sharing of Profits and Losses	By agreement; or, in the absence of agreement, profits are shared equally by the partners, and losses are shared in the same ratio as profits.	Profits are shared as required in the certificate agreement, and losses are shared likewise, up to the amount of the limited partners' capital contributions. In the absence of a provision in the certificate agreement, profits and losses are shared on the basis of percentages of capital contributions.
Liability	Unlimited personal liability of all partners.	Unlimited personal liability of all general partners; limited partners liable only to the extent of their capital contributions.
Capital Contribution	No minimum or mandatory amount; set by agreement.	Set by agreement.
Management	By agreement, or in the absence of agreement, all partners have an equal voice.	General partner or partners only. Limited partners have no voice or else are subject to liability as general partners (but *only* if a third party has reason to believe that the limited partner is a general partner). A limited partner may act as an agent or employee of the partnership and vote on amending the certificate or on the sale or dissolution of the partnership.
Duration	Terminated by agreement of the partners, but can continue to do business even when a partner dissociates from the partnership.	Terminated by agreement in the certificate or by retirement, death, or mental incompetence of a general partner in the absence of the right of the other general partners to continue the partnership. Death of a limited partner, unless he or she is the only remaining limited partner, does not terminate the partnership.
Distribution of Assets on Liquidation– Order of Priorities	1. Payment of debts, including those owed to partner and nonpartner creditors. 2. Return of capital contributions and distribution of profit to partners.	1. Outside creditors and partner creditors. 2. Partners and former partners entitled to distributions or partnership assets. 3. Unless otherwise agreed, return of capital contributions and distribution of profit to partners.

ADAPTING THE LAW TO THE ONLINE ENVIRONMENT — Jurisdiction Issues in Limited Partnerships

Numerous business and investment opportunities are organized as limited partnerships. Often, especially when the business involves the Internet and technology, the limited partners live in different states and have little contact with each other. In this situation, significant jurisdiction issues can arise. Which court has jurisdiction in the event of a dispute? Do the courts of the state in which a limited partnership is organized have jurisdiction over all members of the partnership, regardless of where they live?

The *Werner* Case

The question of jurisdiction over limited partners came before the court in *Werner v. Miller Technology Management, L.P.*[a]

a. 831 A.2d 318 (Del.Ch. 2003).

A New York resident, Marc Werner, invested $250,000 as a limited partner in Interprise Technology Partners (ITP), a Delaware limited partnership. ITP was formed in 1999 to invest in information technology companies (companies engaged in creating, storing, and exchanging information on computers). Under the partnership agreement, the general partner, Miller Technology Management (MTM), was to manage the business with the advice and assistance of an advisory board that consisted of five of ITP's limited partners.

In 2002, Werner sued MTM and ITP's advisory board, claiming a pattern of self-dealing in breach of their fiduciary duties of care, disclosure, and loyalty. As it turned out, in three years of operation, ITP had invested more than $45 million in companies that were affiliated with its general partner (MTM) or with the limited partners on ITP's advisory board. For example, ITP paid more than $17.5 million for consulting services from a company called Answerthink, Inc., which was founded and controlled by the five members of ITP's advisory board. In fact, four of the individuals on ITP's advisory board held top

---

Columbia have adopted the revised version of the ULPA, known as the Revised Uniform Limited Partnership Act (RULPA). Because the RULPA is the dominant law governing limited partnerships in the United States, we will refer to the RULPA in the following discussion of limited partnerships.

Formation of the Limited Partnership

In contrast to the informal, private, and voluntary agreement that usually suffices for a general partnership, the formation of a limited partnership is a public and formal proceeding that must follow statutory requirements. A limited partnership must have at least one general partner and one limited partner, as mentioned previously. Additionally, the partners must sign a **certificate of limited partnership,** which requires information similar to that found in a corporate charter (see Chapter 28). The certificate must be filed with the designated state official—under the RULPA, the secretary of state. The certificate is usually open to public inspection. Does the state in which the limited partnership was formed have jurisdiction over all the partners (limited and general) in the event of a dispute involving the limited partnership? See this chapter's *Adapting the Law to the Online Environment* feature for a discussion of a case involving this issue.

CERTIFICATE OF LIMITED PARTNERSHIP
The basic document filed with a designated state official by which a limited partnership is formed.

Rights and Liabilities of Partners

General partners, unlike limited partners, are personally liable to the partnership's creditors; thus, at least one general partner is necessary in a limited partnership so that someone has personal liability. This policy can be circumvented in states that allow a corporation to be the general partner in a partnership. Because the corporation has limited liability by virtue of corporate laws, if a corporation is the general partner, no one in the limited partnership has personal liability.

positions in Answerthink for which they were paid salaries of more than $500,000 per year. These conflicts of interest were never disclosed to Werner or to any of the other limited partners in ITP.

"Minimum Contacts" Required

Werner contended that the defendants used their positions of control and influence over ITP to engage in transactions that benefited them personally but were detrimental to ITP. Although the self-dealing nature of these transactions seems apparent, the court first had to determine whether Delaware had jurisdiction over the defendants. The advisory board defendants claimed that they did not have "minimum contacts" (discussed in Chapter 3) with Delaware because they were not residents and did not transact any business in that state. Werner argued that because the advisory board was created to participate in the management of a Delaware limited partnership, Delaware had jurisdiction.

Ultimately, the court held that Delaware did not have jurisdiction over the limited partners on ITP's advisory board. Limited partners are not legally entitled to participate in

management. Even if ITP's advisory board had done more than advise MTM, the court held that Werner had not shown that these defendants had any business contacts with Delaware, such as entering contracts or attending meetings. Thus, the court dismissed the case against the limited partners on ITP's advisory board, but it allowed the plaintiff's claim against the general partner (MTM).

FOR CRITICAL ANALYSIS *Given that the general partner and the limited partners on the advisory board engaged in the same pattern of self-dealing and nondisclosure, why did the court have jurisdiction only over the general partner? What policy considerations underlie the court's decision?*

Rights of Limited Partners   Subject to the limitations that will be discussed here, limited partners have essentially the same rights as general partners, including the right of access to partnership books and the right to other information regarding partnership business. On dissolution, limited partners are entitled to a return of their contributions in accordance with the partnership certificate [RULPA 201(a)(10)]. They can also assign their interests subject to the certificate [RULPA 702, 704].

The RULPA provides a limited partner with the right to sue an outside party on behalf of the firm if the general partners with authority to do so have refused to file suit [RULPA 1001]. In addition, investor protection legislation, such as securities laws (discussed in Chapter 30), may give some protection to limited partners.

Liabilities of Limited Partners   In contrast to the personal liability of general partners, the liability of a limited partner is limited to the capital that she or he contributes or agrees to contribute to the partnership [RULPA 502].

A limited partnership is formed by good faith compliance with the requirements for signing and filing the certificate, even if it is incomplete or defective. When a limited partner discovers a defect in the formation of the limited partnership, he or she can avoid future liability by causing an appropriate amendment or certificate to be filed or by renouncing an interest in the profits of the partnership [RULPA 304]. If the limited partner takes neither of these actions on discovering the defect, however, the limited partner can be held personally liable by the firm's creditors. Liability for false statements in a partnership certificate runs in favor of persons relying on the false statements and against members who know of the falsity but still sign the certificate [RULPA 207].

NOTE A limited partner is also liable to the extent of any contribution that she or he made to the partnership but later took back from the firm.

Limited Partners and Management   Limited partners enjoy limited liability so long as they do not participate in management [RULPA 303]. A limited partner who participates in management will be just as liable as a general partner to any creditor who transacts business with the limited partnership and believes, based on a limited partner's conduct, that the limited partner is a general partner [RULPA 303]. How much actual review and advisement a limited partner can engage in before being exposed to liability is an unsettled question.[15] A limited partner who knowingly permits his or her name to be used in the name of the limited partnership is liable to creditors who extend credit to the limited partnership without knowledge that the limited partner is not a general partner [RULPA 102, 303(d)].

Dissolution

A limited partnership is dissolved in much the same way as an ordinary partnership. The retirement, death, or mental incompetence of a general partner can dissolve the partnership, but not if the business can be continued by one or more of the other general partners in accordance with their certificate or by the consent of all of the members [RULPA 801]. The death or assignment of interest of a limited partner does not dissolve the limited partnership [RULPA 702, 704, 705]. A limited partnership can be dissolved by court decree [RULPA 802].

Bankruptcy or the withdrawal of a general partner dissolves a limited partnership. Bankruptcy of a limited partner, however, does not dissolve the partnership unless it causes the bankruptcy of the limited partnership. The retirement of a general partner causes a dissolution unless the members consent to a continuation by the remaining general partners or unless this contingency is provided for in the certificate.

On dissolution, creditors' rights, including those of partners who are creditors, take first priority. Then partners and former partners receive unpaid distributions of partnership assets and, except as otherwise agreed, amounts representing returns on their contributions and amounts proportionate to their shares of the distributions [RULPA 804].

In the following case, one limited partner wanted the business of the partnership to be sold on its dissolution, while another limited partner and the general partner wanted it to continue. In whose favor should the court rule and why?

---

15. It is an unsettled question partly because different states have different laws. Factors to be considered under the RULPA are listed in RULPA 303(b) and (c).

CASE 26.3 **In re Dissolution of Midnight Star Enterprises, L.P.**

Supreme Court of South Dakota, 2006 SD 98, 724 N.W.2d 334 (2006).

FACTS Midnight Star Enterprises, Limited Partnership, consists of a casino, bar, and restaurant in Deadwood, South Dakota. The owners are Midnight Star Enterprises, Limited (MSEL), the general partner, which owns 22 partnership units; actor Kevin Costner, a limited partner, who owns 71.5 partnership units; and Carla and Francis Caneva, limited partners, who own 3.25 partnership units each. Costner also owns MSEL and thus controls 93.5 partnership units. The Canevas were the business's managers, for which they received salaries and bonuses. When MSEL voiced concerns about the management, communication among the partners broke down. MSEL filed a petition in a South Dakota state court to dissolve the partnership. MSEL hired Paul

Thorstenson, an accountant, to determine the firm's fair market value, which he calculated to be $3.1 million. The Canevas solicited a competitor's offer to buy the business for $6.2 million, which the court ruled was the appropriate amount. At the Canevas' request, the court ordered MSEL and Costner to buy the business for that price within ten days or sell it on the open market to the highest bidder. MSEL appealed to the South Dakota Supreme Court.

ISSUE Can a partner force the sale of a limited partnership when the other partners want to continue the business?

DECISION No. The South Dakota Supreme Court reversed the judgment of the lower court and remanded the case to

CASE 26.3–Continued

allow MSEL and Costner to pay the Canevas the value of their 6.5 partnership units after a revaluation of the partnership.

REASON The state supreme court concluded that the partnership agreement did not require the business to be sold on the open market on the partnership's dissolution. Under the agreement, during liquidation, the firm's property could be distributed in kind among the partners if it was first offered for sale to a third party. In other words, only a decision to make an in-kind distribution of assets required that the business be offered for sale on the open market. The court also concluded that the correct value of the business was the accountant's figure, which was based on a fair market value analysis using a hypothetical buyer. This analysis provided a reasonable basis for determining value "by removing the irrationalities,

strategies, and emotions" that exist in an actual offer. Besides, the partnership agreement required a "fair market value" of the assets. Finally, "[s]ince it was error for the [lower] court to value Midnight Star at $6.2 million, it was also error to force the general partners to buy the business for $6.2 million or sell the business." The state supreme court reasoned that "forced sales typically end up in economic waste." A buyout is an acceptable alternative, as long as the partners receive the fair value of their property interest. "Instead of ordering the majority partners to purchase the whole partnership for the appraised value, the majority partners should only be required to pay any interests the withdrawing partner is due."

 FOR CRITICAL ANALYSIS–Ethical Consideration *Under what circumstances might a forced sale of the property of a limited partnership on its dissolution be appropriate?*

Limited Liability Limited Partnerships

A **limited liability limited partnership (LLLP)** is a type of limited partnership. An LLLP differs from a limited partnership in that a general partner in an LLLP has the same liability as a limited partner in a limited partnership. In other words, the liability of all partners is limited to the amount of their investments in the firm.

A few states provide expressly for LLLPs.[16] In states that do not provide for LLLPs but do allow for limited partnerships and limited liability partnerships, a limited partnership should probably still be able to register with the state as an LLLP.

LIMITED LIABILITY LIMITED PARTNERSHIP (LLLP)
A type of limited partnership in which the liability of all of the partners, including general partners, is limited to the amount of their investments.

---

16. See, for example, Colorado Revised Statutes Annotated Section 7-62-109. Other states that provide expressly for limited liability limited partnerships include Delaware, Florida, Missouri, Pennsylvania, Texas, and Virginia.

REVIEWING Partnerships

Grace Tarnavsky and her sons, Manny and Jason, bought a ranch known as the Cowboy Palace in March 2002, and the three verbally agreed to share the business for five years. Grace contributed 50 percent of the investment, and each son contributed 25 percent. Manny agreed to handle the livestock, and Jason agreed to handle the bookkeeping. The Tarnavskys took out joint loans and opened a joint bank account into which they deposited the ranch's proceeds, and from which they made payments toward property, cattle, equipment, and supplies. In September 2007, Manny severely injured his back while baling hay and became permanently unable to handle livestock. Manny therefore hired additional laborers to tend the livestock, causing the Cowboy Palace to incur significant

debt. In September 2008, Al's Feed Barn filed a lawsuit against Jason to collect $12,400 in unpaid debts. Using the information presented in the chapter, answer the following questions.

1 Was this relationship a partnership for a term or a partnership at will?

2 Did Manny have the authority to hire additional laborers to work at the ranch after his injury? Why or why not?

3 Under the UPA, can Al's Feed Barn bring an action against Jason individually for Cowboy Palace's debt? Why or why not?

4 Suppose that after his back injury in 2007, Manny sent his mother and brother a notice indicating his intent to withdraw from the partnership. Can he still be held liable for the debt to Al's Feed Barn? Why or why not?

Why Are Partnerships Declining in Popularity?*

orty years ago there were three basic forms of business organization—the sole proprietorship, the general partnership, and the corporation. The advantages and disadvantages of the sole proprietorship were discussed in Chapter 25, and corporations will be examined in Chapters 28 through 30. Here, we look at the advantages and disadvantages of general partnerships.

What Are Some Advantages of Partnerships?

One advantage of partnerships is their ease of formation. A partnership can be created by agreement. Although a written agreement is highly desirable—and required for enforceability if the agreement falls under the Statute of Frauds—a partnership agreement can be oral, written, or implied by the conduct of the partners. Furthermore, a partnership can be formed and can operate without obtaining a certificate or charter from the state. In addition, partnerships are flexible. A partnership can be explicitly limited in duration, it can be restricted to a stated purpose, or it can be a partnership at will, existing until one or more of the partners terminate it.

Other advantages stem from the fact that partnerships involve more than one person. Thus, the firm is likely to benefit from the expertise and varied strengths of the different partners. Because the partners all contribute capital to the firm, partnerships often are better financed than sole proprietorships, which must depend on only one person for their funding. Similarly, because creditors have assurance of payment from more than one person, a partnership is likely to have less difficulty securing financing than a sole proprietorship would. For these reasons, partnerships may be able to grow larger more quickly than sole proprietorships.

Another advantage is that the partnership entity itself has no income tax liability. Instead, the individual partners pay taxes on the profits derived from the partnership. Thus, partnerships avoid double taxation, which occurs with corporations.

What Are Some Disadvantages of Partnerships?

Despite their many advantages, partnerships also have one very important disadvantage—the unlimited personal liability of the individual partners for the debts of the partnership and for the acts of other partners committed within the scope of

the partnership business. Because partners have joint and several liability, a partner's personal assets can be in jeopardy even though he or she was not involved in the act that gave rise to the liability. Reportedly, Mark Twain lost more than one small fortune due to his participation in unsuccessful partnerships.

Partnerships have some other disadvantages as well. A partnership cannot receive a Chapter 7 discharge in bankruptcy, for example, and one partner's death can sometimes result in the firm's dissolution. Nevertheless, these problems are minor compared to the unlimited liability issue.

A Possible Solution—Limited Liability Entities

Not surprisingly, the many advantages of partnerships combined with their very major disadvantage have created demand for business organizational forms that offer many of the benefits of partnerships while providing limited liability as well. These forms include the limited partnership, limited liability partnership, and limited liability limited partnership (discussed in this chapter); the limited liability company (to be discussed in Chapter 27); and the S corporation (to be discussed in Chapter 28). These limited liability entities have increased dramatically in popularity in recent years at the expense of general partnerships.

CHECKLIST IN FORMING A GENERAL PARTNERSHIP

1 Decide how important ease and informality are to the creation of your business organization. For example, to accomplish a single project within a limited time, a general partnership may be the ideal business form.
2 Choose your partners carefully. Remember that you can be personally liable for their actions.
3 The partnership should carry sufficient insurance to protect against third parties reaching each partner's individual assets and to allow the partnership to continue on a partner's death.
4 Before you form a partnership, decide how profits and losses are to be shared and the amount of each partner's capital contribution. Express these decisions in a written partnership agreement.

* This *Application* is not meant to substitute for the services of an attorney who is licensed to practice law in your state.

KEY TERMS

articles of partnership 726
buyout price 735
certificate of limited
  partnership 742
charging order 730
confession of judgment 729
dissociation 734
dissolution 737

family limited liability
  partnership (FLLP) 740
general partner 740
information return 726
joint and several liability 732
limited liability limited
  partnership (LLLP) 745

limited liability
  partnership (LLP) 738
limited partner 740
limited partnership 740
partnership 724
pass-through entity 726
winding up 737

CHAPTER SUMMARY Partnerships

Partnerships (See pages 723–738.)	1. A partnership is created by agreement of the parties. 2. A partnership is treated as an entity except for limited purposes. 3. Each partner pays a proportionate share of income taxes on the net profits of the partnership, whether or not they are distributed; the partnership files only an information return with the Internal Revenue Service. 4. Each partner has an equal voice in management unless the partnership agreement provides otherwise. 5. In the absence of an agreement, partners share profits equally and share losses in the same ratio as they share profits. 6. The capital contribution of each partner is determined by agreement. 7. Partners have unlimited liability for partnership debts. 8. A partnership can be terminated by agreement or can be dissolved by action of the partners (dissociation from a partnership at will), operation of law (subsequent illegality), or court decree.
Limited Liability Partnerships (LLPs) (See pages 738–740.)	1. *Formation*—A statement of qualification must be filed with the appropriate state agency, usually the secretary of state's office. Typically, an LLP is formed by professionals who work together as partners in a partnership. Under most state LLP statutes, it is relatively easy to convert a traditional partnership into an LLP. 2. *Liability of partners*—LLP statutes vary, but under the UPA, professionals generally can avoid personal liability for acts committed by other partners. The extent to which partners' limited liability will be recognized when the partnership does business in another state depends on the other state's laws. Partners in an LLP continue to be liable for their own wrongful acts and for the wrongful acts of those whom they supervise. 3. *Family limited liability partnership (FLLP)*—A form of LLP in which all of the partners are family members or fiduciaries of family members; the most significant use of the FLLP is by families engaged in agricultural enterprises.
Limited Partnerships (See pages 740–745.)	1. *Formation*—A certificate of limited partnership must be filed with the secretary of state's office or other designated state official. The certificate must include information about the business, similar to the information included in a corporate charter. The partnership consists of one or more general partners and one or more limited partners. 2. *Rights and liabilities of partners*—With some exceptions, the rights of partners are the same as the rights of partners in a general partnership. General partners have unlimited liability for partnership obligations; limited partners are liable only to the extent of their contributions.

(Continued)

CHAPTER SUMMARY Partnerships–Continued

Limited Partnerships–Continued

3. *Limited partners and management*—Only general partners can participate in management. Limited partners have no voice in management; if they do participate in management activities, they risk having general-partner liability.

4. *Dissolution*—Generally, a limited partnership can be dissolved in much the same way as an ordinary partnership. The death or assignment of interest of a limited partner does not dissolve the partnership; bankruptcy of a limited partner also will not dissolve the partnership unless it causes the bankruptcy of the firm.

5. *Limited liability limited partnerships (LLLPs)*—A special type of limited partnership in which the liability of all partners, including general partners, is limited to the amount of their investments.

FOR REVIEW

Answers for the even-numbered questions in this **For Review** *section can be found in Appendix E at the end of this text.*

1 What are the three essential elements of a partnership?

2 What are the rights and duties of partners in an ordinary partnership?

3 What is meant by joint and several liability? Why is this often considered to be a disadvantage of the partnership form of business?

4 What advantages do limited liability partnerships offer to businesspersons that are not offered by general partnerships?

5 What are the key differences between the rights and liabilities of general partners and those of limited partners?

 The following multiple-choice question is representative of the types of questions available in one of the four sections of ThomsonNOW for *Business Law Today*. ThomsonNOW also provides feedback for each response option, whether correct or incorrect, and refers to the location within the chapter where the correct answer can be found.

Generally speaking, a limited partnership will be dissolved if

a a limited partner dies.

b the partnership business relocates.

c a limited partner gets married.

d a general partner goes bankrupt.

QUESTIONS AND CASE PROBLEMS

 **HYPOTHETICAL SCENARIOS**

26.1 Partnership Formation. Daniel is the owner of a chain of shoe stores. He hires Rubya to be the manager of a new store, which is to open in Grand Rapids, Michigan. Daniel, by written contract, agrees to pay Rubya a monthly salary and 20 percent of the profits. Without Daniel's knowledge, Rubya represents himself to Classen as Daniel's partner, showing Classen the agreement to share profits. Classen extends credit to Rubya. Rubya defaults. Discuss whether Classen can hold Daniel liable as a partner.

26.2 Hypothetical Question with Sample Answer. Dorinda, Luis, and Elizabeth form a limited partnership. Dorinda is a general partner, and Luis and Elizabeth are limited partners. Consider each of the separate events below, and discuss fully which event(s) constitute(s) a dissolution of the limited partnership.

1 Luis assigns his partnership interest to Ashley.

2 Elizabeth is petitioned into involuntary bankruptcy.

3 Dorinda dies.

For a sample answer to Question 26.2, go to Appendix F at the end of this text.

26.3 Distribution of Partnership Assets. Shawna and David formed a partnership. At the time of the partnership's formation, Shawna's capital contribution was $10,000, and David's was $15,000. Later, Shawna made a $10,000 loan to the partnership when it needed working capital. The partnership agreement provided that profits were to be shared with 40 percent for Shawna and 60 percent for David. The partnership was dissolved after David's death. At the end of the dissolution and the winding up of the partnership, the partnership's assets were $50,000, and the partnership's debts were $8,000. Discuss fully how the assets should be distributed.

CASE PROBLEMS

26.4 Liability of Partners. Frank Kolk was the manager of Triples American Grill, a sports bar and restaurant. Kolk and John Baines opened bank accounts in the name of the bar, each signing the account signature cards as "owner." Baines was often at the bar and had free access to its office. Baines told others that he was "an owner" and "a partner." Kolk told Steve Mager, the president of Cheesecake Factory, Inc., that Baines was a member of a partnership that owned Triples. On this basis, Cheesecake delivered its goods to Triples on credit. In fact, the bar was owned by a corporation. When the unpaid account totaled more than $20,000, Cheesecake filed a suit in a New Mexico state court against Baines to collect. On what basis might Baines be liable to Cheesecake? What does Cheesecake have to show to win its case? [*Cheesecake Factory, Inc. v. Baines*, 125 N.M. 622, 964 P.2d 183 (App. 1998)]

26.5 Indications of Partnership. In August 1998, Jea Yu contacted Cameron Eppler, president of Design88, Ltd., to discuss developing a Web site that would cater to investors and provide services to its members for a fee. Yu and Patrick Connelly invited Eppler and Ha Tran, another member of Design88, to a meeting to discuss the site. The parties agreed that Design88 would perform certain Web design, implementation, and maintenance functions for 10 percent of the profits from the site, which would be called "The Underground Trader." They signed a "Master Partnership Agreement," which was later amended to include Power Uptik Productions, LLC (PUP). The parties often referred to themselves as partners. From its offices in Virginia, Design88 designed and hosted the site, solicited members through Internet and national print campaigns, processed member applications, provided technical support, monitored access to the site, and negotiated and formed business alliances on the site's behalf. When relations among the parties soured, PUP withdrew. Design88 filed a suit against PUP and the others in a Virginia state court. Did a partnership exist among these parties? Explain. [*Design88, Ltd. v. Power Uptik Productions, LLC*, 133 F.Supp.2d 873 (W.D.Va. 2001)]

26.6 Case Problem with Sample Answer. At least six months before the 1996 Summer Olympic Games in Atlanta, Georgia,

Stafford Fontenot, Steve Turner, Mike Montelaro, Joe Sokol, and Doug Brinsmade agreed to sell Cajun food at the games and began making preparations. Calling themselves "Prairie Cajun Seafood Catering of Louisiana," on May 19 the group applied for a license with the Fulton County, Georgia, Department of Public Health–Environmental Health Services. Later, Ted Norris sold a mobile kitchen for an $8,000 check drawn on the "Prairie Cajun Seafood Catering of Louisiana" account and two promissory notes, one for $12,000 and the other for $20,000. The notes, which were dated June 12, listed only Fontenot "d/b/a Prairie Cajun Seafood" as the maker (*d/b/a* is an abbreviation for "doing business as"). On July 31, Fontenot and his friends signed a partnership agreement, which listed specific percentages of profits and losses. They drove the mobile kitchen to Atlanta, but business was "disastrous." When the notes were not paid, Norris filed a suit in a Louisiana state court against Fontenot, seeking payment. What are the elements of a partnership? Was there a partnership among Fontenot and the others? Who is liable on the notes? Explain. [*Norris v. Fontenot*, 867 So.2d 179 (La.App. 3 Cir. 2004)]

After you have answered Problem 26.6, compare your answer with the sample answer given on the Web site that accompanies this text. Go to www.thomsonedu.com/westbuslaw/blt, select "Chapter 26," and click on "Case Problem with Sample Answer."

26.7 Fiduciary Duties. Charles Chaney and Lawrence Burdett were equal partners in a partnership in Georgia known as BMW Partners. Their agreement was silent as to the effect of a partner's death on the firm. The partnership's sole asset was real property, which the firm leased in 1987 to a corporation that the partners co-owned. Under the lease, the corporation was to pay the partnership $8,000 per month, but after a few years, the corporation began paying $9,000 per month. Chaney died on April 15, 1998. Burdett wanted to continue the partnership business and offered to buy Chaney's estate's interest in it. Meanwhile, claiming that the real property's fair rental value was $4,500 (not $9,000) and that the corporation had overpaid the rent by $80,000, Burdett adjusted the rental payments to recoup this amount. Bonnie Chaney, Charles's widow and his estate's legal representative, filed a suit in a Georgia state court against

Burdett, alleging in part that he had breached his fiduciary duty by adjusting the amount of the rent. Did Burdett's fiduciary duty expire on Chaney's death? Explain. [*Chaney v. Burdett*, 274 Ga. 805, 560 S.E.2d 21 (2002)]

26.8 Partnership Status. Charlie Waugh owned and operated an auto parts junkyard in Georgia. Charlie's son, Mack, started working in the business part-time as a child and full-time when he left school at age sixteen. Mack oversaw the business's finances, depositing the profits in a bank. Charlie gave Mack a one-half interest in the business, telling him that if "something happened" to Charlie, the entire business would be his. In 1994, Charlie and his wife, Alene, transferred to Mack the land on which the junkyard was located. Two years later, however, Alene and her daughters, Gail and Jewel, falsely convinced Charlie, whose mental competence had deteriorated, that Mack had cheated him. Mack was ordered off the land. Shortly thereafter, Charlie died. Mack filed a suit in a Georgia state court against the rest of the family, asserting, among other things, that he and Charlie had been partners and that he was entitled to Charlie's share of the business. Was the relationship between Charlie and Mack a partnership? Is Mack entitled to Charlie's "share"? Explain. [*Waugh v. Waugh*, 265 Ga.App. 799, 595 S.E.2d 647 (2004)]

26.9 Indications of Partnership. In August 2003, Tammy Duncan began working as a waitress at Bynum's Diner, which was owned by her mother, Hazel Bynum, and her stepfather, Eddie Bynum, in Valdosta, Georgia. Less than a month later, the three signed an agreement under which Eddie was to relinquish his management responsibilities, allowing Tammy to be co-manager. At the end of this six-month period, Eddie would revisit this agreement and could then extend it for another six-month period. The diner's bank account was to remain in Eddie's name. There was no provision with regard to the diner's profit, if any, and the parties did not change the business's tax information. Tammy began doing the bookkeeping, as well as waiting tables and performing other duties. On October 30, she slipped off a ladder and injured her knees. At the end of the six-month term, Tammy quit working at the diner. The Georgia State Board of Workers' Compensation determined that she had been the diner's employee and awarded her benefits under

the diner's workers' compensation policy with Cypress Insurance Co. Cypress filed a suit in a Georgia state court against Tammy, arguing that she was not an employee, but a co-owner. What are the essential elements of a partnership? Was Tammy a partner in the business of the diner? Explain. [*Cypress Insurance Co. v. Duncan*, 281 Ga.App. 469, 636 S.E.2d 159 (2006)]

26.10 **A Question of Ethics.** *In 1991, Hassan Mardanlou and Ali Ghaffarian signed a lease for 3960 South State Street in Salt Lake City, Utah. Ghaffarian paid $6,000 for the first and last months' rent, and said to Mardanlou, "We are in this together, partner." Mardanlou bought business cards for "Access Auto" with his and Ghaffarian's names on the cards. Both men were listed on Access Auto's insurance policy. Mardanlou bought the firm's furniture. Ghaffarian did the bookkeeping and bought the inventory. Mardanlou did not have access to the books but wrote checks on the firm's account, sold its inventory, and managed the sales staff. In March 1993, Ghaffarian gave Mardanlou a check for $10,000. Otherwise, Mardanlou was paid a fixed amount each month. Later that year, without telling Mardanlou, Ghaffarian bought the leased property with the firm's funds but titled it in his name. In 1995, Mardanlou learned of this deal and confronted Ghaffarian, who said, "Don't worry, we're partners." Ghaffarian filed the firm's tax returns in his name only, despite Mardanlou's repeated objections. Finally, in 1997, Mardanlou quit the firm and filed a suit in a Utah state court against Ghaffarian to dissolve the partnership and obtain a share of the profits.* [*Mardanlou v. Ghaffarian*, 2006 UT App 165, 135 P.3d 904 (2006)]

1 What factors indicate that Mardanlou and Ghaffarian were partners? What factors indicate that they were not partners? If you were the judge, how would you resolve this dispute?

2 Is Mardanlou entitled to a share of the value of the real property that Ghaffarian bought in his own name? If so, how much? From an ethical point of view, what solution appears to be the fairest? Discuss.

3 Is Mardanlou entitled to a share of Access Auto's profits? Why or why not?

CRITICAL THINKING AND WRITING ASSIGNMENTS

26.11 Critical Legal Thinking. Given the extensive liability of partners, why would any entrepreneur choose to do business with another, or others, as a general partnership?

26.12 Critical Thinking and Writing Assignment for Business. Sandra Lerner met Patricia Holmes at Holmes's horse training facility, and they became friends. One evening, while applying nail polish to Lerner, Holmes layered a raspberry color over black to produce a new color, which Lerner liked. Later, the two created other colors with names like "Bruise," "Smog," and "Oil Slick," and titled their concept "Urban Decay." Lerner and Holmes started a firm to produce and market the polishes but never discussed the sharing of profits and losses. They agreed to build the business and then sell it. Together, they did market research, experimented with colors, worked on a logo and advertising, obtained capital from an investment firm, and hired employees. Then Lerner began working to edge Holmes out of the firm.

1 Lerner claimed that there was no partnership agreement because there was no agreement to divide profits. Was Lerner right? Why or why not?

2 Suppose that Lerner, but not Holmes, had contributed a significant amount of personal funds into developing and marketing the new nail polish. Would this entitle Lerner to receive more of the profits? Explain.

3 Did Lerner violate her fiduciary duty in this scenario? Why or why not?

ONLINE ACTIVITIES

PRACTICAL INTERNET EXERCISES

Go to this text's Web site at **www.thomsonedu.com/westbuslaw/blt**, select "Chapter 26," and click on "Practical Internet Exercises." There you will find the following Internet research exercises that you can perform to learn more about the topics covered in this chapter.

PRACTICAL INTERNET EXERCISE 26-1 LEGAL PERSPECTIVE—Liability of Dissociated Partners

PRACTICAL INTERNET EXERCISE 26-2 ECONOMIC PERSPECTIVE—Taxation of Partnerships

PRACTICAL INTERNET EXERCISE 26-3 MANAGEMENT PERSPECTIVE—Limited Partnerships and Limited Liability Partnerships

BEFORE THE TEST

Go to this text's Web site at **www.thomsonedu.com/westbuslaw/blt**, select "Chapter 26," and click on "Interactive Quizzes." You will find a number of interactive questions relating to this chapter.

CHAPTER 27
Limited Liability Companies and Special Business Forms

LEARNING OBJECTIVES

AFTER READING THIS CHAPTER, YOU SHOULD BE ABLE TO ANSWER THE FOLLOWING QUESTIONS:

1 What advantages do limited liability companies offer to businesspersons that are not offered by sole proprietorships or partnerships?

2 How are limited liability companies formed, and who decides how they will be managed and operated?

3 What are the two options for managing limited liability companies?

4 What is a joint venture? How is it similar to a partnership? How is it different?

5 What are the essential characteristics of joint stock companies, syndicates, business trusts, and cooperatives, respectively?

LIMITED LIABILITY COMPANY (LLC)
A hybrid form of business enterprise that offers the limited liability of a corporation and the tax advantages of a partnership.

F ew would argue with David Ricardo's statement in the chapter-opening quotation that high profits contribute to the "prosperity and happiness of a country." Certainly, this assumption is the basis for this country's public policy of encouraging trade and commerce. To promote commerce and profit-making activities, our government allows entrepreneurs to choose from a variety of business organizational forms when undertaking their business ventures.

In the preceding chapters, we have examined sole proprietorships and various partnership forms. Before we discuss corporations, one of the most prevalent forms of business, we examine a relatively new form of business organization, the **limited liability company (LLC).** The LLC is a hybrid that combines the limited liability aspects of a corporation and the tax advantages of a partnership. Increasingly, LLCs are becoming an organizational form of choice among businesspersons, a trend encouraged by state statutes permitting their use.

In this chapter, we begin by examining the LLC, the origins and evolution of which are discussed in this chapter's *Landmark in the Law* feature on the facing page. Specifically, we look at the following characteristics of the LLC: formation and jurisdictional requirements, the advantages and disadvantages of choosing to do business as an LLC, and management options. The chapter concludes with a discussion of various other special business forms, including joint ventures, syndicates, joint stock companies, business trusts, and cooperatives.

LANDMARK IN THE LAW | Limited Liability Company (LLC) Statutes

In 1977, Wyoming became the first state to pass legislation authorizing the creation of a limited liability company (LLC). Although LLCs emerged in the United States only in 1977, they have been used for more than a century in other areas, including several European and South American nations.

Taxation of LLCs   In the United States, after Wyoming's adoption of an LLC statute, it still was not known how the Internal Revenue Service (IRS) would treat the LLC for tax purposes. In 1988, however, the IRS ruled that Wyoming LLCs would be taxed as partnerships instead of as corporations, providing that certain requirements were met. Prior to this ruling, only one other state—Florida, in 1982—had authorized LLCs. The 1988 IRS ruling encouraged other states to enact LLC statutes, and in less than a decade, all states had done so.

IRS rules that went into effect on January 1, 1997, also encouraged more widespread use of LLCs in the business world. Under these rules, any unincorporated business is automatically taxed as a partnership unless it indicates otherwise on the tax form. The exceptions involve publicly traded companies, companies formed under a state incorporation statute, and certain foreign-owned companies. If a business prefers to be taxed as a corporation, it can check a box on the IRS form to indicate this choice.

Foreign Entities May Be LLC Members   Part of the impetus behind the creation of LLCs in this country is that foreign investors are allowed to become LLC members. Generally, in an era increasingly characterized by global business efforts and investments, the LLC offers U.S. firms and potential investors from other countries greater flexibility and opportunities than are available through partnerships or corporations.

APPLICATION TO TODAY'S WORLD   *Once it became clear that LLCs could be taxed as partnerships, the LLC form of business organization was widely adopted. Members could avoid the personal liability associated with the partnership form of business as well as the "double taxation" of the corporate form of business. Today, LLCs, which were virtually unheard of twenty years ago, are a widely used form of business organization.*

RELEVANT WEB SITES   *To locate information on the Web concerning limited liability company statutes, go to this text's Web site at* **www.thomsonedu.com/westbuslaw/blt**, *select "Chapter 27," and click on "URLs for Landmarks."*

LIMITED LIABILITY COMPANIES

Limited liability companies are governed by state LLC statutes. These laws vary, of course, from state to state. In an attempt to create more uniformity among the states in this respect, in 1995 the National Conference of Commissioners on Uniform State Laws issued the Uniform Limited Liability Company Act (ULLCA).[1] To date, fewer than one-fifth of the states have adopted the ULLCA, and thus the law governing LLCs remains far

---

1. Excerpts from the Uniform Limited Liability Company Act (ULLCA) are presented on the Web site that accompanies this text.

from uniform. Some provisions are common to most state statutes, however, and we base our discussion of LLCs in this section on these common elements.

The Nature of the LLC

Limited liability companies share many characteristics with corporations. Like corporations, LLCs are creatures of the state. In other words, they must be formed and operated in compliance with state law. Like shareholders in a corporation, owners of an LLC, who are called **members,** enjoy limited liability [ULLCA 303]. Also like corporations, LLCs are legal entities apart from their members. As a legal person, the LLC can sue or be sued, enter into contracts, and hold title to property [ULLCA 201]. The terminology used to describe LLCs formed in other states or nations is also similar to the terminology used in corporate law. For example, an LLC formed in one state but doing business in another state is referred to in the second state as a *foreign LLC*.

As you will read in Chapter 28, on occasion the courts will disregard the corporate entity ("pierce the corporate veil") and hold a shareholder personally liable for corporate obligations. At issue in the following case was whether this same principle should be extended to an LLC. Could the managing member of an LLC (the person designated to manage the firm—see the discussion of LLC management options later in this chapter) be held personally liable for property damage caused by the LLC?

CASE 27.1   **Kaycee Land and Livestock v. Flahive**

Wyoming Supreme Court, 2002 WY 73, 46 P.3d 323 (2002).

FACTS Roger Flahive is the managing member of Flahive Oil & Gas, LLC. To exercise mineral rights beneath certain real property, Flahive Oil & Gas entered into a contract with Kaycee Land and Livestock in Johnson County, Wyoming, that allowed Flahive Oil & Gas to use the surface of Kaycee's land. Later, Kaycee alleged environmental contamination of its property and filed a suit in a Wyoming state court against Flahive and his LLC. On discovering that Flahive Oil & Gas had no assets at the time of the suit, Kaycee asked the court to disregard the LLC entity and hold Flahive personally liable for the contamination. Before issuing a judgment in the case, the court submitted this question to the Wyoming Supreme Court: "[I]s a claim to pierce the Limited Liability entity veil or disregard the Limited Liability Company entity in the same manner as a court would pierce a corporate veil or disregard a corporate shield, an available remedy" against an LLC? Unlike some states' statutes, Wyoming's LLC provisions do not address this issue.

ISSUE May a court "pierce the veil" of an LLC and hold a member personally liable?

DECISION Yes. The Wyoming Supreme Court held that an LLC entity could be pierced. The court remanded the case for a determination as to whether piercing the veil was appropriate under the circumstances.

REASON The court pointed out that "[e]very state that has enacted LLC piercing legislation has chosen to follow corporate law standards and not develop a separate LLC standard." The overall purpose of statutes that create corporations and LLCs is to limit the liability of individual investors with a corresponding benefit to economic development. Statutes created the legal fiction of the corporation being a completely separate entity that could act independently from individual persons. "[W]hen corporations fail to follow the statutorily mandated formalities, co-mingle funds, or ignore the restrictions in their articles of incorporation regarding separate treatment of corporate property, the courts deem it appropriate to disregard the separate identity and do not permit shareholders to be sheltered from liability to third parties for damages caused by the corporations' acts." The court concluded, "If the members and officers of an LLC fail to treat it as a separate entity as contemplated by statute, they should not enjoy immunity from individual liability for the LLC's acts that cause damage to third parties."

WHY IS THIS CASE IMPORTANT? *The LLC is a "creature of statute" and thus is governed by the state's statutory law. Businesspersons should be aware, though, that courts can at times apply legal principles that are standard in corporate or partnership law to an LLC, as this case illustrates.*

LLC Formation

To form an LLC, **articles of organization** must be filed with a central state agency—usually the secretary of state's office [ULLCA 202]. Typically, the articles are required to include such information as the name of the business, its principal address, the name and address of a registered agent, the names of the members, and information on how the LLC will be managed [ULLCA 203]. The business's name must include the words *Limited Liability Company* or the initials *LLC* [ULLCA 105a]. In addition to filing the articles of organization, a few states require that a notice of the intention to form an LLC be published in a local newspaper.

About one-fourth of the states specifically require LLCs to have at least two members. The rest of the states usually permit one-member LLCs, although some LLC statutes are silent on this issue. See the *Application* feature at the end of this chapter for a discussion of the factors that entrepreneurs need to consider when choosing between LLCs and limited liability partnerships (LLPs).

Jurisdictional Requirements

One of the significant differences between LLCs and corporations has to do with federal jurisdictional requirements. The federal jurisdiction statute provides that a corporation is deemed to be a citizen of the state where it is incorporated and maintains its principal place of business. The statute does not mention the citizenship of partnerships, LLCs, and other unincorporated associations, but the courts have tended to regard these entities as citizens of every state in which their members are citizens.

The state citizenship of LLCs may come into play when a party sues an LLC based on diversity of citizenship. Remember from Chapter 3 that in some circumstances, such as when parties to a lawsuit are from different states, a federal court can exercise diversity jurisdiction in cases in which the amount in controversy exceeds $75,000. *Total* diversity of citizenship must exist, however. **■EXAMPLE 27.1** Fong, a citizen of New York, wishes to bring a lawsuit against Skycel, an LLC formed under the laws of Connecticut. One of Skycel's members also lives in New York. Fong will not be able to bring the action against Skycel in federal court—on the basis of diversity jurisdiction—because the defendant LLC is also impliedly a citizen of New York. The same would be true if Fong was filing a suit against multiple defendants and one of the defendants lived in New York. ■

Advantages and Disadvantages of the LLC

Although the LLC offers many advantages to businesspersons, this form of business organization also has some disadvantages. We look now at some of the advantages and disadvantages of the LLC. For a discussion of business organizations in other nations that are similar to the LLC, see this chapter's *Beyond Our Borders* feature on the next page.

Advantages of the LLC A key advantage of the LLC is that the liability of members is limited to the amount of their investments. Another advantage is the flexibility of the LLC in regard to both taxation and management.

An LLC that has *two or more members* can choose to be taxed either as a partnership or as a corporation. As you will read in Chapter 28, a corporate entity must pay income taxes on its profits, and the shareholders pay personal income taxes on profits distributed as dividends. An LLC that wants to distribute profits to the members may prefer to be taxed as a partnership to avoid the "double-taxation" characteristic of the corporate entity. Unless an LLC indicates that it wishes to be taxed as a corporation, the IRS automatically taxes it as a partnership. This means that the LLC as an entity pays no taxes; rather, as in a partnership, profits are "passed through" the LLC to the members who then personally

ARTICLES OF ORGANIZATION
The document filed with a designated state official by which a limited liability company is formed.

ON THE WEB

You can find information on how to form an LLC, including the fees charged in each state for filing LLC articles of organization, at the Web site of Bizcorp, Inc. Go to

www.bizcorp.com.

Stan Ovshinsky, founder of Ovonic Hydrogen Systems, LLC, a developer of alternative energy technologies. What are some of the advantages of doing business as an LLC instead of a corporation? Are there any disadvantages? (Photo Courtesy of ECD Ovonics)

BEYOND OUR BORDERS — Limited Liability Companies in Foreign Nations

Limited liability companies are not unique to the United States. Many nations have business forms that provide limited liability, although these organizations may differ significantly from domestic LLCs. In Germany, for example, the *GmbH,* or *Gesellschaft mit beschrankter Haftung* (which means "company with limited liability"), is a type of business entity that has been available since 1892. The GmbH is now the most widely used business form in Germany. A GmbH, however, is owned by shareholders and thus resembles a U.S. corporation in certain respects. German laws also impose numerous restrictions on the operations and business transactions of GmbHs, whereas LLCs in the United States are not even required to have an operating agreement.

Variants of the LLC form of business that limit the liability of owners are available today to businesspersons around the globe. Limited liability companies known as *limitadas* are common in many Latin American nations. In France, a *société à responsabilité limitée* (meaning "society with limited liability") is an entity that provides business owners with limited liability. In 2002, the United Kingdom and Ireland passed laws that allow limited liability. Although these laws use the term *limited liability partnership,* the entities are similar to our domestic LLCs. In 2006, Japan enacted legislation that created a new type of business organization, called the *godo kaisha (GK),* which is also quite similar to a U.S. LLC. In most nations, some type of document that is similar to the LLC's articles of organization must be filed with the government to form the business. Many countries limit the number of owners that such businesses may have, and some also require the member-owners to choose one or more persons who will manage the business affairs.

 FOR CRITICAL ANALYSIS *Clearly, limited liability is an important aspect of doing business globally. Why might a nation limit the number of member-owners in a limited liability company?*

pay taxes on the profits. If an LLC's members want to reinvest the profits in the business, however, rather than distribute the profits to members, they may prefer that the LLC be taxed as a corporation. Corporate income tax rates may be lower than personal tax rates. Part of the attractiveness of the LLC is this flexibility with respect to taxation.

For federal income tax purposes, one-member LLCs are automatically taxed as sole proprietorships unless they indicate that they wish to be taxed as corporations. With respect to state taxes, most states follow the IRS rules. Still another advantage of the LLC for businesspersons is the flexibility it offers in terms of business operations and management—as will be discussed shortly. Finally, because foreign investors can participate in an LLC, the LLC form of business is attractive as a way to encourage investment.

Disadvantages of the LLC   The disadvantages of the LLC are relatively few. Although initially there was uncertainty over how LLCs would be taxed, that disadvantage no longer exists. One remaining disadvantage is that state LLC statutes are not yet uniform. Until all of the states have adopted the ULLCA, an LLC in one state will have to check the rules in the other states in which the firm does business to ensure that it retains its limited liability. Generally, though, most—if not all—states apply to a foreign LLC (an LLC formed in another state) the law of the state where the LLC was formed.

REMEMBER   A uniform law is a "model" law. It does not become the law of any state until the state legislature adopts it, either in part or in its entirety.

Still another disadvantage is the lack of case law dealing with LLCs. How the courts interpret statutes provides important guidelines for businesses. Given the relative newness of the LLC as a business form in the United States, there is not, as yet, a substantial body of case law to provide this kind of guidance.

The LLC Operating Agreement

The members of an LLC can decide how to operate the various aspects of the business by forming an **operating agreement** [ULLCA 103(a)]. Operating agreements typically contain provisions relating to management, how profits will be divided, the transfer of membership interests, whether the LLC will be dissolved on the death or departure of a member, and other important issues.

An operating agreement need not be in writing and indeed need not even be formed for an LLC to exist. Generally, though, LLC members should protect their interests by forming a written operating agreement. As with any business arrangement, disputes may arise over any number of issues. If there is no agreement covering the topic under dispute, such as how profits will be divided, the state LLC statute will govern the outcome. For example, most LLC statutes provide that if the members have not specified how profits will be divided, they will be divided equally among the members.

Generally, when an issue is not covered by an operating agreement or by an LLC statute, the courts apply the principles of partnership law. The following case illustrates what can happen in the absence of a written operating agreement when one of the members of the LLC has a "bad intent."

OPERATING AGREEMENT
In a limited liability company, an agreement in which the members set forth the details of how the business will be managed and operated. State statutes typically give the members wide latitude in deciding for themselves the rules that will govern their organization.

CASE 27.2   **Kuhn v. Tumminelli**

Superior Court of New Jersey, Appellate Division, 366 N.J.Super. 431, 841 A.2d 496 (2004).
lawlibrary.rutgers.edu/search.shtml[a]

FACTS Clifford Kuhn, Jr., and Joseph Tumminelli formed Touch of Class Limousine Service under the New Jersey Limited Liability Company Act in 1999, doing business as Touch of Elegance Limousine Service. They did not sign a written operating agreement but orally agreed that Kuhn would provide the financial backing and procure customers, and that Tumminelli would manage the company's day-to-day operations. Tumminelli embezzled $283,000 from the company after cashing customers' checks at Quick Cash, Inc., a local check-cashing service. Quick Cash deposited the checks in its bank account with First Union National Bank, N.A., which collected on the checks from the drawee banks, Bank of America Corporation and Chase Manhattan Bank, N.A. Kuhn

filed a suit in a New Jersey state court against Tumminelli, the banks, and others to recover the embezzled funds. The court ordered Tumminelli to pay Kuhn and to transfer his interest in Touch of Class to Kuhn, but issued a summary judgment in favor of the other defendants. Kuhn appealed to a state intermediate appellate court, arguing, among other things, that Quick Cash and the banks were liable because Tumminelli did not have the authority to cash the company's checks and convert the funds.

ISSUE In the absence of a written operating agreement to the contrary, does a member of an LLC have the authority to cash the firm's checks?

DECISION Yes. The state intermediate appellate court affirmed the lower court's judgment in favor of Quick Cash and the banks. Tumminelli had the authority to accept, indorse, and cash checks on behalf of Touch of Class, under the LLC statute.

REASON Under New Jersey's LLC statute, when the members of an LLC are its managers, each member has the

a. Scroll to the box below the heading "Search for cases by party name." In the "Which courts do you want to search?" section, click on the small box next to "Appellate Division." In the "Enter Names Here" section, in the "First Name:" box, type "Kuhn," in the "Second Name:" box, type "Tumminelli," and click on "Submit Form." In the result, click on the appropriate link to access the opinion. Rutgers University School of Law in Camden, New Jersey, maintains this Web site.

CASE 27.2–Continues next page

CASE 27.2–Continued

authority to bind the LLC unless the operating agreement provides otherwise. A member or manager can lend to or borrow from the LCC and can act as a surety, guarantor, or indorser for an LLC. The appellate court explained, "The LLC Act is, therefore, quite flexible and permits the LLC members great discretion to establish the company structure and procedures." Tumminelli was thus authorized under the statute to indorse the LLC's checks. The court further reasoned that "considering Tumminelli's position at the LLC, his responsibilities, and daily functions along with the statutory grant of authority, it can be inferred that Tumminelli had actual authority to receive the checks, indorse the checks, and cash them at Quick Cash,

especially because Kuhn knew that Tumminelli was paying business expenses in cash." Tumminelli's "bad intent" to convert the funds to his own use did not affect this authority. If the members had wanted more limited authority, they should have provided for it in a written operating agreement.

WHAT IF THE FACTS WERE DIFFERENT?
Suppose that Kuhn and Tumminelli had signed a written operating agreement that required both members' indorsements when cashing customers' checks. Assuming that Quick Cash would have known of this requirement, would the result have been different? Why or why not?

MANAGEMENT OF AN LLC

Basically, there are two options for managing an LLC. The members may decide in their operating agreement to be either a "member-managed" LLC or a "manager-managed" LLC. Most LLC statutes and the ULLCA provide that unless the articles of organization specify otherwise, an LLC is assumed to be member managed [ULLCA 203(a)(6)].

Participation in Management

In a *member-managed* LLC, all of the members participate in management, and decisions are made by majority vote [ULLCA 404(a)]. In a *manager-managed* LLC, the members designate a group of persons to manage the firm. The management group may consist of only members, both members and nonmembers, or only nonmembers. Managers in a manager-managed LLC owe fiduciary duties to the LLC and its members, including the duty of loyalty and the duty of care [ULLCA 409(a), (h)], just as corporate directors and officers owe fiduciary duties to the corporation and its shareholders.

ETHICAL ISSUE 27.1

Should members who own a majority of the interests in a member-managed LLC owe a fiduciary duty to the minority members? If the managers of a manager-managed LLC owe fiduciary duties to the members, what happens in a member-managed LLC? Do the members owe one another fiduciary duties? That question came before a Tennessee court in a dispute among the members of FuturePoint Administrative Services, LLC. FuturePoint's operating agreement allowed members to be expelled from the LLC—with or without cause—provided that the members holding a majority of interests in the company (majority members) agreed to the expulsion by vote or by written consent. Under the agreement, expelled members were to be paid the same price per share on expulsion as they paid to purchase the interest ($150) when the company was started in 2000.

By September 2001, FuturePoint had generated $63,000 in excess cash. The majority members, wanting to keep the $63,000 among themselves, expelled the minority members from the LLC. They paid the minority members the purchase price of their interests and then resold the interests for more than twice that price to another party. Subsequently, the minority members filed suit claiming that the majority members had breached their fiduciary duties. The majority members argued that Tennessee's LLC statute did not impose any fiduciary obligations on majority shareholders and that the LLC's operating agreement authorized their actions. Ultimately, the appellate court rejected that argument and determined that the majority members in a member-managed LLC do owe fiduciary duties to minority members simply because "[t]hey should."[2]

■

Operating Procedures

The members of an LLC can also set forth in their operating agreement provisions governing decision-making procedures. For instance, the agreement can include procedures for choosing or removing managers. Although most LLC statutes are silent on this issue, the ULLCA provides that members may choose and remove managers by majority vote [ULLCA 404(b)(3)].

The members are also free to include in the agreement provisions designating when and for what purposes they will hold formal members' meetings. Most state LLC statutes have no provisions regarding members' meetings, which is in contrast to most state laws governing corporations, as you will read in Chapter 28.

Members may also specify in their agreement how voting rights will be apportioned. If they do not, LLC statutes in most states provide that voting rights are apportioned according to each member's capital contributions. Some states provide that, in the absence of an agreement to the contrary, each member has one vote.

Members of a manager-managed LLC hold a formal members' meeting. What is the difference between a member-managed LLC and a manger-managed LLC? How are managers typically chosen?
(PhotoDisc)

DISSOCIATION AND DISSOLUTION OF AN LLC

Recall from Chapter 26 that in the context of partnerships, *dissociation* occurs when a partner ceases to be associated in the carrying on of the business. The same concept applies to limited liability companies. A member of an LLC has the *power* to dissociate from the LLC at any time, but he or she may not have the *right* to dissociate. Under the ULLCA, the events that trigger a member's dissociation in an LLC are similar to the events causing a partner to be dissociated under the Uniform Partnership Act (UPA). These include voluntary withdrawal, expulsion by other members or by court order, bankruptcy, incompetence, and death. Generally, even if a member dies or otherwise dissociates from an LLC, the other members may continue to carry on LLC business, unless the operating agreement has contrary provisions.

The Effect of Dissociation

When a member dissociates from an LLC, he or she loses the right to participate in management and the right to act as an agent for the LLC. His or her duty of loyalty to the LLC also terminates, and the duty of care continues only with respect to events that occurred before dissociation. Generally, the dissociated member also has a right to have his or her interest in the LLC bought out by the other members of the LLC. The LLC's operating agreement may contain provisions establishing a buyout price, but if it does not, the member's interest is usually purchased at a fair value. In states that have adopted the ULLCA, the LLC must purchase the interest at "fair" value within 120 days after the dissociation.

If the member's dissociation violates the LLC's operating agreement, it is considered legally wrongful, and the dissociated member can be held liable for damages caused by the dissociation. ■**EXAMPLE 27.2** Chadwick and Barrel are members in an LLC. Chadwick manages the accounts, and Barrel, who has many connections in the community and is a

---

2. *Anderson v. Wilder,* ___ S.W.3d ___ (Tenn.Ct.App. 2003).

skilled investor, brings in the business. If Barrel wrongfully dissociates from the LLC, the LLC's business will suffer, and Chadwick can hold Barrel liable for the loss of business resulting from her withdrawal. ◼

Dissolution

Regardless of whether a member's dissociation was wrongful or rightful, normally the dissociated member has no right to force the LLC to dissolve. The remaining members can opt to either continue or dissolve the business. Members can also stipulate in their operating agreement that certain events will cause dissolution, or they can agree that they have the power to dissolve the LLC by vote. As with partnerships, a court can order an LLC to be dissolved in certain circumstances, such as when the members have engaged in illegal or oppressive conduct, or when it is no longer feasible to carry on the business.

When an LLC is dissolved, any members who did not wrongfully dissociate may participate in the winding up process. To wind up the business, members must collect, liquidate, and distribute the LLC's assets. Members may preserve the assets for a reasonable time to optimize their return, and they continue to have the authority to perform reasonable acts in conjunction with winding up. In other words, the LLC will be bound by the reasonable acts of its members during the winding up process. Once all the LLC's assets have been sold, the proceeds are distributed to pay off debts to creditors first (including debts owed to members who are creditors of the LLC). The member's capital contributions are returned next, and any remaining amounts are then distributed to members in equal shares or according to their operating agreement.

PREVENTING LEGAL DISPUTES

Because disputes often arise among members of an LLC during dissociation and dissolution, businesspersons forming an LLC should carefully draft their operating agreement. Stipulate the events that will cause dissociation and how the fair-value buyout price will be calculated. Set a time limit by which the LLC must pay the dissociated member (or her or his estate) in the event that she or he withdraws, becomes disabled, or dies. Include provisions that clearly limit the authority of dissociated members to act on behalf of the LLC, and provide a right to seek damages from members who exceed the agreed-on parameters. Also, remember to notify third parties if any member dissociates and file a notice of dissociation with the state to limit the extent of the former member's apparent authority to act on behalf of the LLC. It is also advisable to set forth in the operating agreement any events that will automatically cause a dissolution, as well as which members will have a right to participate in—or make decisions about—the winding up.

◼

SPECIAL BUSINESS FORMS

Besides the traditional business forms and limited liability companies discussed in this unit, several other forms can be used to organize a business. For the most part, these special business forms are hybrid organizations—that is, they have characteristics similar to those of partnerships or corporations or combine features of both. These forms include joint ventures, syndicates, joint stock companies, business trusts, and cooperatives.

JOINT VENTURE
A joint undertaking of a specific commercial enterprise by an association of persons. A joint venture normally is not a legal entity and is treated like a partnership for federal income tax purposes.

Joint Ventures

A **joint venture**, sometimes referred to as a *joint adventure*, is a relationship in which two or more persons or business entities combine their efforts or their property for a single transaction or project or a related series of transactions or projects. Unless otherwise agreed, joint venturers share profits and losses equally. For instance, when several contractors combine their resources to build and sell houses in a single development, their relationship is a joint venture.

Joint ventures range in size from very small activities to huge, multimillion-dollar joint actions carried out by some of the world's largest corporations. Large organizations often investigate new markets or new ideas by forming joint ventures with other enterprises. For instance, Intel Corporation and Micron Technology, Inc., formed a joint venture to manufacture NAND flash memory, a data-storage chip widely used in digital cameras, cell phones, and portable music players, including some iPods made by Apple, Inc. Also, Mitsubishi Chemical Corporation formed a joint venture with Exxon Chemical Corporation to start Mytex Polymers, a company that produces certain plastic compounds used by automakers in the United States and Japan.

The firm that financed and built this housing development is organized as a joint venture. What will happen to the joint venture after the last house in the subdivision is sold?
(Elizabeth Golden/Creative Commons)

Similarities to Partnerships The joint venture resembles a partnership and is taxed like a partnership. For this reason, most courts apply the same principles to joint ventures as they apply to partnerships. For instance, the joint venturers owe to each other the same fiduciary duties, including the duty of loyalty, that partners owe each other. If one of the venturers secretly buys land that was to be acquired by the joint venture, the other joint venturers may be awarded damages for the breach of loyalty. A joint venturer can also be held personally liable for the venture's debts (because joint venturers share profits and *losses*).

Like partners, the joint venturers have equal rights to manage the activities of the enterprise. Control of the operation may be given to one of the members, however, without affecting the status of the relationship. ■**EXAMPLE 27.3** Two companies, PGI and Rathe, had separately worked for the Smithsonian Institution on a traveling museum exhibition in the United States. They submit a joint proposal to the Smithsonian to study the feasibility of producing an international tour, and the Smithsonian accepts their offer. They have formed a joint venture for the limited purpose of conducting the study, regardless of the fact that each company has different functions and responsibilities in the undertaking. If the Smithsonian pays Rathe at the conclusion of the project, Rathe must share the profits with PGI.[3] ■

The question in the following case was whether a joint venture existed between two vintage aircraft makers and, if so, how the principles of partnership law applied between them.

CONTRAST A partnership involves a continuing relationship of the partners. A joint venture is often a one-time association.

---

3. *PGI, Inc. v. Rathe Productions, Inc.*, 265 Va. 438, 576 S.E.2d 438 (2003).

CASE 27.3 **SPW Associates, LLP v. Anderson**

Supreme Court of North Dakota, 2006 ND 159, 718 N.W.2d 580 (2006).
www.ndcourts.com/search/opinions.asp[a]

FACTS Murdo Cameron is a commercial airline pilot interested in vintage P-51 Mustang planes. He developed graphite body parts and other components to make replicas of

the P-51, and placed ads in aviation magazines for someone to design and make other parts and build the planes. Douglas Anderson answered the ad, and in 1996, they agreed in writing to collaborate on the manufacture of one P-51 for each of them. They agreed orally to make additional P-51s to sell. For the first plane, which Anderson would build, Cameron would provide an engine, which Anderson would pay for after

a. In the "Title:" box, type "SPW" and then click on "Execute." In the result, click on the name of the case to access the opinion. The North Dakota Supreme Court maintains this Web site.

CASE 27.3–Continues next page

CASE 27.3–Continued

the plane's first flight. In 1997, to finance the making of the P-51s, Anderson borrowed funds from SPW Associates, LLP, using the first plane as the security for the loan. Anderson did not tell SPW about his deal with Cameron nor did he tell Cameron about his deal with SPW. Anderson built one plane before defaulting on the loan. SPW filed a suit in a North Dakota state court against Anderson, Cameron, and others, asking the court to declare that SPW was entitled to the aircraft. The court ruled, among other things, that Anderson and Cameron had entered into a joint venture, the plane was the venture's property, Anderson was authorized to grant SPW a security interest in it, and SPW was entitled to its possession. Cameron appealed to the North Dakota Supreme Court, arguing, in part, that there was no joint venture.

ISSUE Did Anderson and Cameron's enterprise constitute a joint venture?

DECISION Yes. The state supreme court affirmed the conclusions of the lower court.

REASON The state supreme court identified four elements that must exist for an enterprise to constitute a joint venture: (1) a contract showing that the parties agreed to engage in a common undertaking; (2) the parties' contribution of funds, property, time, or skill to further the undertaking; (3) an interest in, and mutual right to control, the property of the venture; and (4) an agreement to share its profits. In this case, there was no dispute that Anderson and Cameron had contracted in writing to build two P-51s; that they had contributed funds, property, time, and skill to this purpose; and that they each had exerted control over the planes' components. As for evidence of an agreement to share profits, Anderson and Cameron's written contract referred to "future aircraft purchases" and "multiple year production runs," and they admitted that they intended to build additional planes to sell to the public. The court recognized that the principles of partnership law apply to joint ventures. Under those principles, "a partner is an agent of, and may bind, the partnership." Applying that rule to this case, the court found that Anderson, as a joint venturer, had the authority to grant a security interest in the venture's property—the first P-51—for the loan from SPW, which was thus entitled to keep the plane in satisfaction of the debt on Anderson's default.

 WHAT IF THE FACTS WERE DIFFERENT? *How might the outcome of this case have been different if Cameron had been merely an aircraft parts supplier, with his only profit to be from the sale of components to Anderson?*

Differences from Partnerships Joint ventures differ from partnerships in several important ways. The members of a joint venture have less implied and apparent authority than the partners in a partnership. As discussed in Chapter 26, each partner is treated as an agent of the other partners. Because the activities of a joint venture are more limited than the business of a partnership, the members of a joint venture are presumed to have less power to bind their co-venturers. Also, unlike most partnerships, a joint venture normally terminates when the project or the transaction for which it was formed has been completed, though the members can specify how long the relationship will last.

Syndicates

A group of individuals or firms that get together to finance a particular project, such as the building of a shopping center or the purchase of a professional basketball franchise, is called a **syndicate** or an *investment group*. The form of such groups varies considerably. A syndicate may exist as a corporation or as a general or limited partnership. In some instances, the members merely purchase and own property jointly but have no legally recognized business arrangement.

Joint Stock Companies

A **joint stock company** is a true hybrid of a partnership and a corporation. It has many characteristics of a corporation in that (1) its ownership is represented by transferable shares of stock, (2) it is usually managed by directors and officers of the company or association, and (3) it can have a perpetual existence. Most of its other features, however, are

SYNDICATE
An investment group of persons or firms brought together for the purpose of financing a project that they would not or could not undertake independently.

JOINT STOCK COMPANY
A hybrid form of business organization that combines characteristics of a corporation and a partnership. Usually, a joint stock company is regarded as a partnership for tax and other legal purposes.

more characteristic of a partnership, and it is usually treated like a partnership. As with a partnership, a joint stock company is formed by agreement (not statute), property is usually held in the names of the members, shareholders have personal liability, and the company generally is not treated as a legal entity for purposes of a lawsuit. In a joint stock company, however, shareholders are not considered to be agents of one another, as would be the case if the company were a true partnership (see Chapter 26).

Business Trusts

A **business trust** is created by a written trust agreement that sets forth the interests of the beneficiaries and the obligations and powers of the trustees. With a business trust, legal ownership and management of the property of the business stay with one or more of the trustees, and the profits are distributed to the beneficiaries.

The business trust was started in Massachusetts in an attempt to obtain the limited liability advantage of corporate status while avoiding certain restrictions on a corporation's ownership of, and ability to develop, real property. A business trust resembles a corporation in many respects. Beneficiaries of the trust, for example, are not personally responsible for the debts or obligations of the business trust. In fact, in a number of states, business trusts must pay corporate taxes.

BUSINESS TRUST
A form of business organization in which investors (trust beneficiaries) transfer cash or property to trustees in exchange for trust certificates that represent their investment shares. The certificate holders share in the trust's profits but have limited liability.

Cooperatives

A **cooperative** is an association that is organized to provide an economic service to its members (or shareholders); it may or may not be incorporated. Most cooperatives are organized under state statutes for cooperatives, general business corporations, or LLCs. Generally, an incorporated cooperative will distribute dividends, or profits, to its owners on the basis of their transactions with the cooperative rather than on the basis of the amount of capital they contributed. Members of incorporated cooperatives have limited liability, as do shareholders of corporations and members of LLCs. Cooperatives that are unincorporated are often treated like partnerships. The members have joint liability for the cooperative's acts.

This form of business is generally adopted by groups of individuals who wish to pool their resources to gain some advantage in the marketplace. Consumer purchasing co-ops are formed to obtain lower prices through quantity discounts. Seller marketing co-ops are formed to control the market and thereby obtain higher sales prices from consumers. Co-ops range in size from small, local, consumer cooperatives to national businesses such as Ace Hardware and Land O'Lakes, the well-known producer of dairy products.

COOPERATIVE
An association, which may or may not be incorporated, that is organized to provide an economic service to its members. Unincorporated cooperatives are often treated like partnerships for tax and other legal purposes. Examples of cooperatives include consumer purchasing cooperatives, credit cooperatives, and farmers' cooperatives.

REVIEWING Limited Liability Companies and Special Business Forms

The city of Papagos, Arizona, had a deteriorating bridge in need of repair on a prominent public roadway. The city posted notices seeking proposals for an artistic bridge design and reconstruction. Davidson Masonry, LLC—owned and managed by Carl Davidson and his wife, Marilyn Rowe—decided to submit a bid for a decorative concrete project that incorporated artistic metalwork. They contacted Shana Lafayette, a local sculptor who specialized in large-scale metal designs, to help them design the bridge. The city selected their bridge design and awarded them the contract for a commission of $184,000. Davidson Masonry and Lafayette then entered into an agreement to work together on the bridge project. Davidson Masonry agreed to install and pay for concrete and structural work, and Lafayette agreed to install the metalwork at her expense. They agreed that overall profits would be split, with 25 percent going to Lafayette and 75 percent going to Davidson Masonry. Lafayette designed numerous metal salmon sculptures that were incorporated into colorful decorative concrete forms designed by Rowe, while Davidson performed the structural engineering. The group worked together successfully until the completion of the project. Using the information presented in the chapter, answer the following questions.

1 Would Davidson Masonry automatically be taxed as a partnership or a corporation?

2 Is Davidson Masonry member managed or manager managed?

3 When Davidson Masonry and Lafayette entered into an agreement to work together, what kind of special business form was created? Explain.

4 Suppose that during construction, Lafayette had entered into an agreement to rent space in a warehouse that was close to the bridge so that she could work on her sculptures near the location at which they would eventually be installed. She entered into the contract without the knowledge or consent of Davidson Masonry. In this situation, would a court be likely to hold that Davidson Masonry was bound by the contract that Lafayette entered? Why or why not?

APPLICATION

How Do You Choose between LLCs and LLPs?*

One of the most important decisions that an entrepreneur makes is the selection of the form in which to do business. To make the best decision, a businessperson should understand all aspects of the various forms, including legal, tax, licensing, and business considerations. It is also important that all of the participants in the business understand their actual relationship, regardless of the organizational structure.

Number of Participants

During the last decade or so, new forms of business organizations, including limited liability partnerships (LLPs—discussed in Chapter 26) and limited liability companies (LLCs), have been added to the options for business entities. An initial consideration in choosing between these forms is the number of participants. An LLP must have two or more partners, but in many states, an LLC can have a single member (owner).

Liability Considerations

The members of an LLC are not liable for the obligations of the organization. Members' liability is limited to the amount of their property (investment) interest. The liability of the partners in an LLP varies from state to state. About half of the states exempt the partners from liability for any obligation of the firm. In some states, the partners are individually liable for the contractual obligations of the firm but are not liable for obligations arising from the torts of others. In either situation, each partner may be on his or her own with respect to liability unless the other partners agree to help.

Distributions from the Firm

Members and partners are generally paid by allowing them to withdraw funds from the firm against their share of the profits. In many states, a member of an LLC must repay so-called wrongful distributions even if she or he did not know that the distributions were wrongful. Under most LLP statutes, by contrast, the partners must repay only distributions that were fraudulent.

Management Structure

Both LLPs and LLCs can set up whatever management structure the participants desire. Also, all unincorporated business organizations, including LLPs and LLCs with two or more members, are treated as partnerships for federal income tax purposes (unless an LLC elects to be treated as a corporation[a]). This means that the firms are not taxed at the entity level. Their income is passed through to the partners or members who must report it on their individual income tax returns. Some states impose additional taxes on LLCs.

---

* This *Application* is not meant to substitute for the services of an attorney who is licensed to practice law in your state.

a. The chief benefits of electing corporate status for tax purposes are that the members generally are not subject to self-employment taxes and that fringe benefits may be provided to employee-members on a tax-reduced basis. The tax laws are complicated, however, and a professional should be consulted about the details.

The Nature of the Business

The business in which a firm engages is another factor to consider in choosing a business form. For example, with a few exceptions, professionals, such as accountants, attorneys, and physicians, may organize as either an LLP or an LLC in any state. In many states, however, the organizational form of an entity that engages in a certain profession and the liability of the owners are prescribed by state law.

Financial and Personal Relationships

Although the legal consequences of choosing a business form are certainly important, they are often secondary to the financial and personal relationships among the participants. Work effort, motivation, ability, and other personal attributes can be significant factors, as may fundamental business concerns such as the expenses and debts of the firm—and the extent of personal liability for these obligations. Another practical factor to consider is the willingness of others to do business with an

LLP or an LLC. A supplier, for example, may not be willing to extend credit to a firm whose partners or members will not accept personal liability for the debt.

CHECKLIST FOR CHOOSING A LIMITED LIABILITY BUSINESS FORM

1 Determine the number of participants, the forms a state allows, and the limits on liability the state provides for the participants.
2 Evaluate the tax considerations.
3 Consider the business in which the firm engages, or will engage, and any restrictions imposed on that type of business.
4 Weigh such practical concerns as the financial and personal relationships among the participants and the willingness of others to do business with a particular organizational form.

KEY TERMS

articles of organization 755
business trust 763
cooperative 763

joint stock company 762
joint venture 760
limited liability company (LLC) 752

member 754
operating agreement 757
syndicate 762

CHAPTER SUMMARY Limited Liability Companies and Special Business Forms

Limited Liability Companies (LLCs)
(See pages 753–760.)

1. *Formation*—Articles of organization must be filed with the appropriate state office—usually the office of the secretary of state—setting forth the name of the business, its principal address, the names of the owners (called *members*), and other relevant information.

2. *Advantages and disadvantages of the LLC*—Advantages of the LLC include limited liability, the option to be taxed as a partnership or as a corporation, and flexibility in deciding how the business will be managed and operated. Disadvantages relate mainly to the absence of uniformity in state LLC statutes and the lack of case law dealing with LLCs.

3. *Operating agreement*—When an LLC is formed, the members decide, in an operating agreement, how the business will be managed and what rules will apply to the organization.

4. *Management*—An LLC may be managed by members only, by some members and some nonmembers, or by nonmembers only.

5. *Dissociation and dissolution*—Members of an LLC have the power to dissociate from the LLC at any time, but they may not have the right to dissociate. Dissociation does not always result in the dissolution of an LLC; the remaining members can choose to continue the business. Dissociated members have a right to have their interest purchased by the other members. If the LLC is dissolved, the business must be wound up and the assets sold. Creditors are paid first; then members' capital investments are returned. Any remaining proceeds are distributed to members.

(Continued)

CHAPTER SUMMARY Limited Liability Companies and Special Business Forms—Continued

Special Business Forms
(See pages 760–763.)

1. *Joint venture*—An organization created by two or more persons in contemplation of a limited activity or a single transaction; similar to a partnership in many respects.

2. *Syndicate*—An investment group that undertakes to finance a particular project; may exist as a corporation or as a general or limited partnership.

3. *Joint stock company*—A business form similar to a corporation in some respects (transferable shares of stock, management by directors and officers, perpetual existence) but otherwise resembling a partnership.

4. *Business trust*—A business form created by a written trust agreement that sets forth the interests of the beneficiaries and the obligations and powers of the trustee(s); similar to a corporation in many respects. Beneficiaries are not personally liable for the debts or obligations of the business trust.

5. *Cooperative*—An association organized to provide an economic service, without profit, to its members; may take the form of a corporation or a partnership.

FOR REVIEW

Answers for the even-numbered questions in this For Review *section can be found in Appendix E at the end of this text.*

1 What advantages do limited liability companies offer to businesspersons that are not offered by sole proprietorships or partnerships?

2 How are limited liability companies formed, and who decides how they will be managed and operated?

3 What are the two options for managing limited liability companies?

4 What is a joint venture? How is it similar to a partnership? How is it different?

5 What are the essential characteristics of joint stock companies, syndicates, business trusts, and cooperatives, respectively?

 The following multiple-choice question is representative of the types of questions available in one of the four sections of ThomsonNOW for *Business Law Today.* **ThomsonNOW also provides feedback for each response option, whether correct or incorrect, and refers to the location within the chapter where the correct answer can be found.**

A limited liability company (LLC) combines the tax characteristics of a

a corporation with the liability of shareholders.

b partnership with the liability of partners.

c corporation with the liability of a partnership.

d partnership with the liability of a corporation.

QUESTIONS AND CASE PROBLEMS

 **HYPOTHETICAL SCENARIOS**

27.1 Limited Liability Companies. John, Lesa, and Trevor form a limited liability company. John contributes 60 percent of the capital, and Lesa and Trevor each contribute 20 percent.

Nothing is decided about how profits will be divided. John assumes that he will be entitled to 60 percent of the profits, in accordance with his contribution. Lesa and Trevor, however, assume that the profits will be divided equally. A dispute over the profits arises, and ultimately a court has to decide the issue. What law will the court apply? In most states, what will result? How could this dispute have been avoided in the first place? Discuss fully.

27.2 Hypothetical Question with Sample Answer. Faraway Corp. is considering entering into two contracts, one with a joint stock company that distributes home products east of the Mississippi River and the other with a business trust formed by a number of sole proprietors who are sellers of home products on the West Coast. Both contracts involve large capital outlays for Faraway, which will supply each business with soft-drink dispensers. In both business organizations, at least two shareholders or beneficiaries are personally wealthy, but each organization has limited financial resources. The owner-managers of Faraway are not familiar with either form of business organization. Because each form resembles a corporation, they are concerned about whether they will be able to collect payments from the wealthy members of the business organizations in the event that either organization breaches the contract by failing to make the payments. Discuss fully Faraway's concern.

 For a sample answer to Question 27.2, go to Appendix F at the end of this text.

27.3 Limited Liability Companies. Joe, a resident of New Jersey, wants to open a restaurant. He asks Kay, his friend, an experienced attorney and a New Yorker, for her business and legal advice in exchange for a 20 percent ownership interest in the restaurant. Kay helps Joe negotiate a lease for the restaurant premises and advises Joe to organize the business as a limited liability company (LLC). Joe forms Café Olé, LLC, and, with Kay's help, obtains financing. Then, the night before the restaurant opens, Joe tells Kay that he is "cutting her out of the deal." The restaurant proves to be a success. Kay wants to file a suit in a federal district court against Joe and the LLC. Can a federal court exercise jurisdiction over the parties based on diversity of citizenship? Explain.

 CASE
PROBLEMS

27.4 Foreign Limited Liability Companies. Walter Matjasich and Cary Hanson organized Capital Care, LLC, in Utah. Capital Care operated, and Matjasich and Hanson managed, Heartland Care Center in Topeka, Kansas. LTC Properties, Inc., held a mortgage on the Heartland facilities. When Heartland failed as a business, its residents were transferred to other facilities. Heartland employees who provided care to the residents for five days during the transfers were not paid wages. The employees filed claims with the Kansas Department of Human Resources for the unpaid wages. Kansas state law provides that a *corporate* officer or manager may be liable for a firm's unpaid wages, but protects LLC members from personal liability generally and states that an LLC cannot be construed as a corporation. Under Utah state law, the members of an LLC can be personally liable for wages due the LLC's employees. Should Matjasich and Hanson be held personally liable for the unpaid wages? Explain. [*Matjasich v. Department of Human Resources,* 271 Kan. 246, 21 P.3d 985 (2001)]

27.5 Limited Liability Companies. Michael Collins entered into a three-year employment contract with E-Magine, LLC. E-Magine was in business for only a brief time, during which it incurred considerable losses. In terminating operations, which ceased before the term of the contract with Collins expired, E-Magine also terminated Collins's services. In exchange for a payment of $24,240, Collins signed a "final payment agreement," which purported to be a settlement of any claims that he might have against E-Magine. Collins filed a suit in a New York state court against E-Magine, its members and managers, and others, alleging, among other things, breach of his employment contract. Collins claimed that signing the "final payment agreement" was the only means for him to obtain what he was owed for past sales commissions and asked the court to impose personal liability on the members and managers of E-Magine for breach of contract. Should the court grant this request? Why or why not? [*Collins v. E-Magine,* LLC, 291 A.D.2d 350, 739 N.Y.S.2d 15 (1 Dept. 2002)]

27.6 Joint Ventures. In 1993, TOG Acquisition Co. attempted to acquire the Orleander Group, a manufacturer of bicycle accessories, but failed for lack of financing. Orleander then granted to Herrick Co. an exclusive right to negotiate for the sale of the business. In August, representatives of TOG, Herrick, and SCS Communications, Inc., signed a letter in which they agreed "to work together to acquire the business of the Orleander Group." The "letter agreement" provided that the parties would contribute "equal amounts of capital" and that all of the terms of the acquisition required the approval of each party. On November 19, TOG and SCS told Herrick that it was out of the deal and, ten days later, acquired Orleander without Herrick. Herrick filed a suit in a federal district court against SCS and others, alleging, among other things, that the "letter agreement" was a contract to establish a joint venture, which TOG and SCS had breached. The defendants filed a motion for summary judgment. In whose favor should the court rule? Why? [*SCS Communications, Inc. v. Herrick Co.,* 360 F.3d 329 (2d Cir. 2004)]

27.7 Case Problem with Sample Answer. Westbury Properties, Inc., and others (collectively the Westbury group) owned, managed, and developed real property. Jerry Stoker and The Stoker Group, Inc. (the Stokers), also developed real property. The Westbury group entered into agreements with the Stokers concerning a large tract of property in Houston County, Georgia. The parties formed limited liability companies (LLCs), including Bellemeade, LLC (the LLC group), to develop various parcels of the tract for residential purposes. The operating agreements provided that "no Member shall be accountable to the [LLC] or to any other Member with respect to [any other] business or activity even if the business or activity competes with the [LLC's] business." The Westbury group entered into agreements with other parties to develop additional parcels within the tract in competition with the LLC group. The Stokers filed a suit in a Georgia state court against the Westbury group, alleging, among other things, breach of fiduciary duty. What duties do the members of an LLC owe to each other? Under what principle might the terms of an operating agreement alter these duties? In whose favor should the court rule? Discuss. [*Stoker v. Bellemeade, LLC*, 272 Ga.App. 817, 615 S.E.2d 1 (2005)]

 After you have answered Problem 27.7, compare your answer with the sample answer given on the Web site that accompanies this text. Go to www.thomsonedu.com/westbuslaw/blt, select "Chapter 27," and click on "Case Problem with Sample Answer."

27.8 Limited Liability Companies. A "Certificate of Formation" (CF) for Grupo Dos Chiles, LLC, was filed with the Delaware secretary of state in February 2000, naming Jamie Rivera as the "initial member." The next month, Jamie's mother, Yolanda Martinez, and Alfred Shriver, who had a personal relationship with Martinez at the time, signed an "LLC Agreement" for Grupo, naming themselves "managing partners." Grupo's business was the operation of Dancing Peppers Cantina, a restaurant in Alexandria, Virginia. Identifying themselves as Grupo's owners, Shriver and Martinez borrowed funds from Advanceme, Inc., a restaurant lender. In June 2003, Grupo lost its LLC status in Delaware for failing to pay state taxes, and by the end of July, Martinez and Shriver had ended their relationship. Shriver filed a suit in a Virginia state court against Martinez

to wind up Grupo's affairs. Meanwhile, without consulting Shriver, Martinez paid Grupo's back taxes. Shriver filed a suit in a Delaware state court against Martinez, asking the court to dissolve the firm. What effect did the LLC Agreement have on the CF? Did Martinez's unilateral act reestablish Grupo's LLC status? Should the Delaware court grant Shriver's request? Why or why not? [*In re Grupo Dos Chiles, LLC*, __ A.2d __ (Del.Ch. 2006)]

27.9 **A Question of Ethics.** *Blushing Brides, L.L.C., a publisher of wedding planning magazines in Columbus, Ohio, opened an account with Gray Printing Co. in July 2000. On behalf of Blushing Brides, Louis Zacks, the firm's member-manager, signed a credit agreement that identified the firm as the "purchaser" and required payment within thirty days. Despite the agreement, Blushing Brides typically took up to six months to pay the full amount for its orders. Gray printed and shipped 10,000 copies of a fall/winter 2001 issue for Blushing Brides but had not been paid when the firm ordered 15,000 copies of a spring/summer 2002 issue. Gray refused to print the new order without an assurance of payment. Zacks signed a promissory note for $14,778, plus interest at 6 percent per year, payable to Gray on June 22. Gray printed the new order but by October had been paid only $7,500. Gray filed a suit in an Ohio state court against Blushing Brides and Zacks to collect the balance.* [Gray Printing Co. v. Blushing Brides, L.L.C., __ Ohio App.3d __, __ N.E.2d __ (10 Dist. 2006)]

1 Under what circumstances is a member of an LLC liable for the firm's debts? In this case, is Zacks personally liable under the credit agreement for the unpaid amount on Blushing Brides' account? Did Zacks's promissory note affect the parties' liability on the account? Explain.

2 Should a member of an LLC assume an ethical responsibility to meet the obligations of the firm? Discuss.

3 Gray shipped only 10,000 copies of the spring/summer 2002 issue of Blushing Brides' magazine, waiting for the publisher to identify a destination for the other 5,000 copies. The magazine had a retail price of $4.50 per copy. Did Gray have a legal or ethical duty to "mitigate the damages" by attempting to sell or otherwise distribute these copies itself? Why or why not?

CRITICAL THINKING AND WRITING ASSIGNMENTS

27.10 Critical Legal Thinking. Although a limited liability entity may be the best organizational form for most businesses, a significant number of firms may be better off as a corporation or some other form of organization. How does the fact that most of the limited liability entities are new forms for

doing business affect the reasons for choosing another form of organization in which to do business? Explain.

27.11 Case Analysis Question. Go to Appendix G at the end of this text and examine Case No. 7 [*Gottsacker v. Monnier*, 281 Wis.2d 361, 697 N.W.2d 436 (2005)]. This case has been excerpted there in great detail. Review and then brief the case, making sure that your brief answers the following questions.

1 What was Gregory's complaint against Julie, Paul, and 2005 New Jersey LLC in this case?

2 What did the Wisconsin Supreme Court conclude with respect to the applicable law in this case, and what was the result?

3 Why did the state supreme court remand the case to the *trial* court instead of the intermediate appellate court?

4 What factors should the court consider in making its findings on remand?

5 What might be an appropriate remedy in this case if the standard set out by the state supreme court is found to have been violated?

ONLINE ACTIVITIES

PRACTICAL INTERNET EXERCISES

Go to this text's Web site at **www.thomsonedu.com/westbuslaw/blt**, select "Chapter 27," and click on "Practical Internet Exercises." There you will find the following Internet research exercises that you can perform to learn more about the topics covered in this chapter.

PRACTICAL INTERNET EXERCISE 27-1 LEGAL PERSPECTIVE—Limited Liability Companies

PRACTICAL INTERNET EXERCISE 27-2 MANAGEMENT PERSPECTIVE—Joint Ventures

BEFORE THE TEST

Go to this text's Web site at **www.thomsonedu.com/westbuslaw/blt**, select "Chapter 27," and click on "Interactive Quizzes." You will find a number of interactive questions relating to this chapter.

CHAPTER 28
Corporate Formation, Merger, and Termination

"A corporation is an artificial being, invisible, intangible, and existing only in contemplation of law."

John Marshall, 1755–1835
(Chief justice of the
United States Supreme Court,
1801–1835)

LEARNING OBJECTIVES

AFTER READING THIS CHAPTER, YOU SHOULD BE ABLE TO ANSWER THE FOLLOWING QUESTIONS:

1 What steps are involved in bringing a corporation into existence? Who is liable for preincorporation contracts?

2 What is the difference between a *de jure* corporation and a *de facto* corporation?

3 In what circumstances might a court disregard the corporate entity ("pierce the corporate veil") and hold the shareholders personally liable?

4 What are the four steps of the merger or consolidation procedure?

5 What are the two ways in which a corporation can be voluntarily dissolved? Under what circumstances might a corporation be involuntarily dissolved by state action?

T he corporation is a creature of statute. As John Marshall indicated in the chapter-opening quotation, a corporation is an artificial being, existing only in law and neither tangible nor visible. Its existence generally depends on state law, although some corporations, especially public organizations, can be created under state or federal law.

Each state has its own body of corporate law, and these laws are not entirely uniform. The Model Business Corporation Act (MBCA) is a codification of modern corporation law that has been influential in the drafting and revision of state corporation statutes. Today, the majority of state statutes are guided by the revised version of the MBCA, which is often referred to as the Revised Model Business Corporation Act (RMBCA).[1] You should keep in mind, however, that there is considerable variation among the statutes of the states that have used the MBCA or the RMBCA as a basis for their statutes, and several states do not follow either act. Consequently, individual state corporation laws should be relied on rather than the MBCA or the RMBCA.

In this chapter, we examine the nature of the corporate form of business enterprise, the various classifications of corporations, and the formation and financing of today's corpo-

---

1. Excerpts from the Revised Model Business Corporation Act (RMBCA) are presented on the Web site that accompanies this text.

rations. We also discuss how a corporation can expand its operations by combining with another corporation through a merger, a consolidation, a purchase of assets, or a purchase of a controlling interest in the other corporation. The last part of this chapter will discuss the typical reasons for—and methods used in—terminating a corporation's existence.

THE NATURE AND CLASSIFICATION OF CORPORATIONS

A **corporation** is a legal entity created and recognized by state law. It can consist of one or more *natural persons* (as opposed to the artificial *legal person* of the corporation) identified under a common name. A corporation can be owned by a single person, or it can have hundreds, thousands, or even millions of owners (shareholders). The corporation substitutes itself for its shareholders in conducting corporate business and in incurring liability, yet its authority to act and the liability for its actions are separate and apart from the individuals who own it.

CORPORATION
A legal entity formed in compliance with statutory requirements that is distinct from its shareholder-owners.

Corporate Personnel

In a corporation, the responsibility for the overall management of the firm is entrusted to a *board of directors*, whose members are elected by the shareholders. The board of directors hires *corporate officers* and other employees to run the daily business operations of the corporation.

When an individual purchases a share of stock in a corporation, that person becomes a shareholder and thus an owner of the corporation. Unlike the members of a partnership, the body of shareholders can change constantly without affecting the continued existence of the corporation. A shareholder can sue the corporation, and the corporation can sue a shareholder. Also, under certain circumstances, a shareholder can sue on behalf of a corporation. The rights and duties of corporate personnel will be examined in detail in Chapter 29.

CONTRAST The death of a sole proprietor or a partner can result in the dissolution of a business. The death of a corporate shareholder, however, rarely, if ever, causes the dissolution of a corporation.

The shareholder form of business organization emerged in Europe at the end of the seventeenth century. These organizations, called *joint stock companies* (see Chapter 27), frequently collapsed because their organizers absconded with the funds or proved to be incompetent. Because of this history of fraud and collapse, organizations resembling corporations were regarded with suspicion in the United States during its early years. Although several business corporations were formed after the Revolutionary War, the corporation did not come into common use for private business until the nineteenth century.

The Constitutional Rights of Corporations

A corporation is recognized as a "person" under state and federal law, and it enjoys many of the same rights and privileges that U.S. citizens enjoy. The Bill of Rights guarantees persons certain protections, and corporations are considered persons in most instances. Accordingly, a corporation as an entity has the same right of access to the courts as a natural person and can sue or be sued. It also has a right to due process before denial of life, liberty, or property, as well as freedom from unreasonable searches and seizures (see Chapter 6 for a discussion of searches and seizures in the business context) and from double jeopardy.

Under the First Amendment, corporations are entitled to freedom of speech. As we pointed out in Chapter 2, however, commercial speech (such as advertising) and political speech (such as contributions to political causes or candidates) receive significantly less protection than noncommercial speech.

Generally, a corporation is not entitled to claim the Fifth Amendment privilege against self-incrimination. Agents or officers of the corporation therefore cannot refuse to produce corporate records on the ground that it might incriminate them.[2] Additionally, the privileges and immunities clause of the U.S. Constitution (Article IV, Section 2) does not protect corporations, nor does it protect an unincorporated association.[3] This clause requires each state to treat citizens of other states equally with respect to certain rights, such as access to the courts and travel rights. This constitutional clause does not apply to corporations because corporations are legal persons only, not natural citizens.

The Limited Liability of Shareholders

One of the key advantages of the corporate form is the limited liability of its owners (shareholders). Corporate shareholders normally are not personally liable for the obligations of the corporation beyond the extent of their investments. In certain limited situations, however, the "corporate veil" can be pierced and liability for the corporation's obligations extended to shareholders—a concept that will be explained later in this chapter. Additionally, to enable the firm to obtain credit, shareholders in small companies sometimes voluntarily assume personal liability, as guarantors, for corporate obligations.

Corporate Taxation

Corporate profits are taxed by various levels of government. Corporations can do one of two things with corporate profits—retain them or pass them on to shareholders in the form of **dividends.** The corporation normally receives no tax deduction for dividends distributed to shareholders. Dividends are again taxable (except when they represent distributions of capital) as income to the shareholder receiving them. This double-taxation feature of the corporation is one of its major disadvantages—although a 2003 law mitigated this double-taxation feature to some extent by providing a reduced federal tax rate on qualifying dividends.[4]

Profits that are not distributed are retained by the corporation. These **retained earnings,** if invested properly, will yield higher corporate profits in the future and thus cause the price of the company's stock to rise. Individual shareholders can then reap the benefits of these retained earnings in the capital gains they receive when they sell their shares.

As you will read later in this chapter, the consequences of a corporation's failure to pay taxes can be severe. The state can suspend corporate status until the taxes are paid, or it can dissolve a corporation for failing to pay taxes.[5]

Another taxation issue of increasing importance to corporations today is whether corporations that sell goods or services to consumers via the Internet are required to collect state sales taxes. See this chapter's *Adapting the Law to the Online Environment* feature on page 774 for a discussion of this issue.

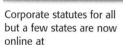
ON THE WEB

Corporate statutes for all but a few states are now online at

www.law.cornell.edu/topics/state_statutes.html#corporations.

DIVIDEND
A distribution to corporate shareholders of corporate profits or income, disbursed in proportion to the number of shares held.

RETAINED EARNINGS
The portion of a corporation's profits that has not been paid out as dividends to shareholders.

HOLDING COMPANY
A company whose business activity is holding shares in another company.

ETHICAL ISSUE 28.1

Is it ethical for a corporation to establish an offshore holding company to reduce U.S. taxes? In recent years, some U.S. corporations have been using holding companies to reduce—or at least defer—their U.S. income taxes. At its simplest, a **holding company** (sometimes referred to as a *parent company*) is a company whose business activity consists of holding shares in another company. Typically, the holding company is established in a low-tax or

---

2. *Braswell v. United States*, 487 U.S. 99, 108 S.Ct. 2284, 101 L.Ed. 98 (1988). A court might allow an officer or employee to assert the Fifth Amendment privilege against self-incrimination in only a few circumstances. See, for example, *In re Three Grand Jury Subpoenas Duces Tecum Dated January 29, 1999*, 191 F.3d 173 (2nd Cir. 1999).
3. *W. C. M. Window Co. v. Bernardi*, 730 F.2d 486 (7th Cir. 1984).
4. The Jobs Growth Tax Relief Reconciliation Act of 2003, Pub. L. No. 108-27, May 28, 2003, codified at 26 U.S.C.A. Section 6429 and 42 U.S.C.A. Section 801.
5. See, for example, *Bullington v. Palangio*, 345 Ark. 320, 45 S.W.3d 834 (2001).

no-tax offshore jurisdiction, such as those shown in Exhibit 28–1. Among the best known are the Cayman Islands, Dubai, Hong Kong, Luxembourg, Monaco, and Panama.

Sometimes, a major U.S. corporation sets up an investment holding company in a low-tax offshore environment. The corporation then transfers its cash, bonds, stocks, and other investments to the holding company. In general, any profits received by the holding company on these investments are taxed at the rate of the offshore jurisdiction in which the company is registered, not the rates applicable to the parent company or its shareholders in their country of residence. Thus, deposits of cash, for example, may earn interest that is taxed at only a minimal rate. Once the profits are brought "onshore," though, they are taxed at the federal corporate income tax rate, and any payments received by the shareholders are also taxable at the full U.S. rates.

Occasionally, a member of Congress or the media learns that a large U.S. corporation has used an offshore holding company to reduce its U.S. tax liability. The company's actions are then decried as both unethical and unpatriotic. Others are not so sure. They point out that those who run corporations have a duty to minimize (legally, of course) taxes owed by the corporation and by its shareholders.

Torts and Criminal Acts

A corporation is liable for the torts committed by its agents or officers within the course and scope of their employment. This principle applies to a corporation exactly as it applies to the ordinary agency relationships discussed in Chapter 24. It follows the doctrine of *respondeat superior*.

EXHIBIT 28–1 **Offshore Low-Tax Jurisdictions**

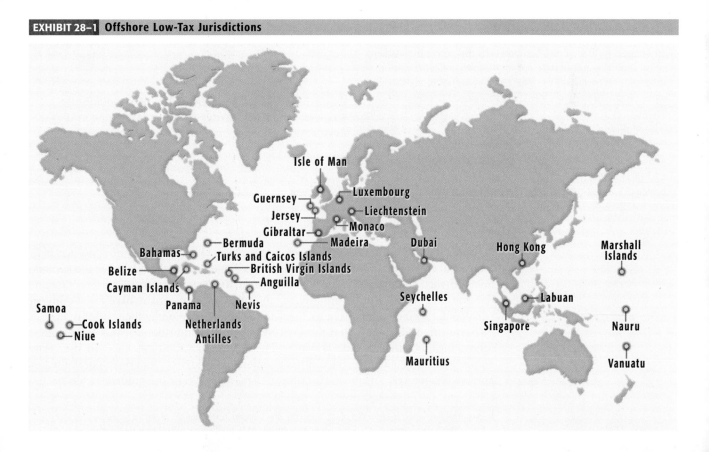

ADAPTING THE LAW TO THE ONLINE ENVIRONMENT — **The Internet Taxation Debate**

Since the advent of the Internet, governments at the state and federal levels have debated the following question: Should state governments be able to collect sales taxes on goods sold via the Internet? Many state governments claim that sales taxes should be imposed on such transactions. They argue that their inability to tax online sales of goods to in-state customers by out-of-state corporations has caused them to suffer significant losses in sales tax revenues. Opponents of Internet taxation argue that taxing online sales will impede the growth of e-commerce. They also claim that because online sellers do not benefit from the state services that are typically paid for by tax revenues (such as fire departments and road construction), they should not be required to collect sales taxes.

The Supreme Court's Approach

According to a United States Supreme Court ruling in 1992, no individual state can compel an out-of-state business that lacks a substantial physical presence within that state to collect and remit state taxes.[a] If the corporation has a warehouse, office, or retail store within the state, though, the state can compel the collection of state taxes. Nevertheless, as the Court recognized in that ruling, Congress has the power to pass legislation requiring out-of-state corporations to collect and remit state sales taxes. Congress so far has chosen not to tax Internet transactions. In fact, in 1998 Congress passed the Internet Tax Freedom Act, which temporarily prohibited states from taxing sales of products conducted over the Internet.[b] An amendment to the act extended the temporary ban until November

2007.[c] Although legislation that would permanently prohibit state and local taxation of Internet sales has been proposed several times, it has not been enacted.

A State Court's Decision

The issue of Internet taxation came before a Tennessee appellate court in *Prodigy Services Corp. v. Johnson.*[d] Prodigy, a Delaware corporation with its principal place of business in New York, is an Internet service provider (ISP) that offers two software programs for purchase online. A Tennessee statute imposes an obligation to collect sales taxes on anyone supplying "telecommunication services" to state residents. The Tennessee Department of Revenue determined that Prodigy's services constituted telecommunication services and assessed sales taxes. Prodigy appealed this tax assessment.

Ultimately, the state appellate court held that Prodigy did not have to charge its Tennessee customers the sales taxes. After looking closely at the wording of the statute and its legislative history, the court reasoned that the legislature had not intended the statute to apply to ISPs. The court also concluded that even if Prodigy had provided some telecommunication services, these services "were not the 'true object' of the Prodigy sale." The customer had to supply her or his own telephone services, and Prodigy had paid to use a telecommunications network to connect the customer to the main computer in New York. Thus, in the court's opinion, Prodigy was a consumer of telecommunication services rather than a provider.

 FOR CRITICAL ANALYSIS *Why should state governments be able to collect taxes from traditional retailers but not from Web-based businesses?*

a. See *Quill Corp. v. North Dakota,* 504 U.S. 298, 112 S.Ct. 1904, 119 L.Ed.2d 91 (1992).
b. Pub. L. No. 105–277; 47 U.S.C. Section 151 n. (1998).
c. Pub. L. No. 108-435.
d. 125 S.W.3d 413 (Tenn.Ct.App. 2003).

Under modern criminal law, a corporation may be held liable for the criminal acts of its agents and employees, provided the punishment is one that can be applied to the corporation. Although corporations cannot be imprisoned, they can be fined. (Of course, corporate directors and officers can be imprisoned, and in recent years, many have faced criminal penalties for their own actions or for the actions of employees under their supervision.)

Recall from Chapter 6 that the U.S. Sentencing Commission created standardized sentencing guidelines for federal crimes. These guidelines went into effect in 1987. The commission subsequently created specific sentencing guidelines for crimes committed by corporate employees (white-collar crimes).[6] The net effect of the guidelines has been a

6. Note that the Sarbanes-Oxley Act of 2002, discussed in Chapter 7, stiffened the penalties for certain types of corporate crime and ordered the U.S. Sentencing Commission to revise the sentencing guidelines accordingly.

significant increase in criminal penalties for crimes committed by corporate personnel. Penalties depend on such factors as the seriousness of the offense, the amount involved, and the extent to which top company executives are implicated. Corporate lawbreakers can face fines amounting to hundreds of millions of dollars, though the guidelines allow judges to impose less severe penalties in certain circumstances.

The question in the following case was whether a corporation could be convicted for its employee's criminal negligence.

CASE 28.1   **Commonwealth v. Angelo Todesca Corp.**

Supreme Judicial Court of Massachusetts, 446 Mass. 128, 842 N.E.2d 930 (2006).
www.findlaw.com/11stategov/ma/maca.html[a]

FACTS   Brian Gauthier worked as a truck driver for Angelo Todesca Corporation, a trucking and paving company. During 2000, Gauthier drove a ten-wheel tri-axle dump truck, which was designated as AT-56. Angelo's safety manual required its trucks to be equipped with back-up alarms, which were to sound automatically whenever the vehicles were in reverse gear. In November, Gauthier discovered that AT-56's alarm was missing. Angelo ordered a new alarm. Meanwhile, Gauthier continued to drive AT-56. On December 1, Angelo assigned Gauthier to haul asphalt to a work site in Centerville, Massachusetts. At the site, as Gauthier backed up AT-56 to dump its load, he struck a police officer who was directing traffic through the site and facing away from the truck. The officer died of his injuries. The commonwealth of Massachusetts charged Gauthier and Angelo in a Massachusetts state court with, among other wrongful acts, vehicular homicide. Angelo was convicted and fined $2,500. On Angelo's appeal, a state intermediate appellate court reversed Angelo's conviction. The state appealed to the Massachusetts Supreme Judicial Court, the state's highest court.

ISSUE   Can a corporation be convicted for its employee's criminal negligence?

DECISION   Yes. The Massachusetts Supreme Judicial Court affirmed Angelo's conviction.

REASON   The court identified three elements required to prove a corporation guilty of a criminal offense: (1) an individual commits a criminal offense; (2) at the time of commission, the individual is engaged in corporate business; and (3) the corporation vested the individual with the authority to engage in that business on its behalf. The focus in this case was on the first element, with the defendant arguing that a "corporation" could not be guilty of vehicular homicide because it cannot "operate" a vehicle. The court recognized that a corporation is not a "living person" but pointed out that it can act through its agents, which may include its employees. The court reasoned that if an employee commits a crime "while engaged in corporate business that the employee has been authorized to conduct," a corporation can be held liable for the crime. The defendant also contended that operating a truck without a back-up alarm is not a crime. The court conceded this point but explained that "the criminal conduct was Gauthier's negligent operation of the defendant's truck, resulting in the victim's death."

 WHY IS THIS CASE IMPORTANT TO BUSINESSPERSONS?   *Other states' courts that have considered the question at issue in this case have concluded that a corporation may be criminally liable for vehicular homicide under those states' statutes. This was the first case in which Massachusetts state courts ruled on the question under a Massachusetts statute.*

a. In the "Supreme Court Opinions" section, in the "2006" row, click on "March." When that page opens, scroll to the name of the case and click on its docket number to access the opinion.

Classification of Corporations

Corporations can be classified in several ways. The classification of a corporation normally depends on its location, purpose, and ownership characteristics, as described in the following subsections.

BMW automobiles are inspected at the Spartanburg, South Carolina, plant. BMW is classified as an alien corporation. What is the difference between an alien corporation and a foreign corporation? (Courtesy of BMW Manufacturing, Inc.)

DOMESTIC CORPORATION
In a given state, a corporation that does business in, and is organized under the law of, that state.

FOREIGN CORPORATION
In a given state, a corporation that does business in the state without being incorporated therein.

ALIEN CORPORATION
A designation in the United States for a corporation formed in another country but doing business in the United States.

NOTE A private corporation is a voluntary association, but a public corporation is not.

Domestic, Foreign, and Alien Corporations A corporation is referred to as a **domestic corporation** by its home state (the state in which it incorporates). A corporation formed in one state but doing business in another is referred to in the second state as a **foreign corporation.** A corporation formed in another country (say, Mexico) but doing business in the United States is referred to in the United States as an **alien corporation.** (For a discussion of when a U.S. court can exercise jurisdiction over an alien corporation, see this chapter's *Beyond Our Borders* feature.)

A corporation does not have an automatic right to do business in a state other than its state of incorporation. In some instances, it must obtain a *certificate of authority* in any state in which it plans to do business. Once the certificate has been issued, the corporation generally can exercise in that state all of the powers conferred on it by its home state. If a foreign corporation does business in a state without obtaining a certificate of authority, the state can impose substantial fines and sanctions on the corporation, and sometimes even on its officers, directors, or agents.[7]

Public and Private Corporations A public corporation is one formed by the government to meet some political or governmental purpose. Cities and towns that incorporate are common examples. In addition, many federal government organizations, such as the U.S. Postal Service, the Tennessee Valley Authority, and AMTRAK, are public corporations. Note that a public corporation is not the same as a *publicly held* corporation (often called a *public company*). A publicly held corporation is any corporation whose shares are publicly traded in securities markets, such as the New York Stock Exchange or the over-the-counter market.

In contrast to public corporations (*not* public companies), private corporations are created either wholly or in part for private benefit. Most corporations are private. Although they may serve a public purpose, as a public electric or gas utility does, they are owned by private persons rather than by the government.[8]

---

7. Note that most state statutes specify certain activities, such as soliciting orders via the Internet, which are not considered doing business within the state. Thus, a foreign corporation normally does not need a certificate of authority to sell goods or services via the Internet or by mail.

8. The United States Supreme Court first recognized the property rights of private corporations and clarified the distinction between public and private corporations in the landmark case *Trustees of Dartmouth College v. Woodward,* 17 U.S. (4 Wheaton) 518, 4 L.Ed. 629 (1819).

BEYOND OUR BORDERS **The Question of Jurisdiction over Alien Corporations**

If a U.S. consumer is injured by a product manufactured by a corporation based in another country, can the consumer sue that corporation in a U.S. state court? Normally, the answer depends on whether the defendant corporation has sufficient "contacts" with the state in which the lawsuit is filed. As we pointed out in Chapter 3, this requirement is satisfied if a corporation does business in the state, advertises or sells its product in the state, or places its goods within the "stream of commerce" with the intent that the goods be sold in the state.

The jurisdiction issue arose in a case involving Weida, a Chinese corporation that is the world's largest manufacturer of drill chucks. Weida sells its drill chucks to Techtronic Industries, a Hong Kong corporation. Techtronic then uses the drill chucks in manufacturing drills under the RIDGID brand. Home Depot has an exclusive contract to sell RIDGID drills in the United States.

A Delaware corporation, Jacobs, also makes drill chucks. It filed suit against Weida in a Texas state court for patent infringement. Weida argued that the court lacked jurisdiction. The Texas state court disagreed, however, stating that it had jurisdiction over alien corporations in such situations. The court concluded that it was reasonably inferable that Weida knew and expected its chucks would be used as components in RIDGID brand drills manufactured and distributed by Techtronic to Home Depot stores in the United States, including Texas.[a]

Sometimes, alien corporations argue that the cost of transporting witnesses, documents, and other evidence would be so great that U.S. courts should not have jurisdiction over them. In response to such arguments, U.S. courts generally hold that alien corporations marketing their goods in the United States should expect to be "haled into court" in this country.[b]

FOR CRITICAL ANALYSIS *How might a foreign manufacturer selling products in the United States avoid being "haled into court" in this country to defend against a product liability action?*

a. *Jacobs Chuck Manufacturing Co. v. Shandong Weida Machinery Co., Ltd.,* 2005 WL 3299718 (E.D.Tex. 2005).
b. *Donnelly Corp. v. Reitter & Schefenacker, GnbH & Co. KG,* 189 F.Supp.2d 696 (W.D.Mich. 2002).

Nonprofit Corporations Corporations formed for purposes other than making a profit are called *nonprofit* or *not-for-profit* corporations. Private hospitals, educational institutions, charities, and religious organizations, for example, are frequently organized as nonprofit corporations. The nonprofit corporation is a convenient form of organization that allows various groups to own property and to form contracts without exposing the individual members to personal liability.

Close Corporations Most corporate enterprises in the United States fall into the category of close corporations. A **close corporation** is one whose shares are held by members of a family or by relatively few persons. Close corporations are also referred to as *closely held, family,* or *privately held* corporations. Usually, the members of the small group constituting

CLOSE CORPORATION
A corporation whose shareholders are limited to a small group of persons, often including only family members. In a close corporation, the shareholders' rights to transfer shares to others are usually restricted.

A drummer plays a set of drums with Zildjian cymbals. Zildjian, founded in 1623, is perhaps the world's longest-running, family-owned business. What steps might a small, family-owned corporation take to ensure that ownership of the company stays within the family? (Photo Courtesy of Drummerworld)

S CORPORATION
A close business corporation that has met certain requirements set out in the Internal Revenue Code and thus qualifies for special income tax treatment. Essentially, an S corporation is taxed the same as a partnership, but its owners enjoy the privilege of limited liability.

a close corporation are personally known to one another. Because the number of shareholders is so small, there is no trading market for the shares.

In practice, a close corporation is often operated like a partnership. Some states have enacted special statutory provisions that apply to close corporations. These provisions expressly permit close corporations to depart significantly from certain formalities required by traditional corporation law.[9]

Additionally, a provision added to the RMBCA in 1991 gives close corporations a substantial amount of flexibility in determining the rules by which they will operate [RMBCA 7.32]. If all of the shareholders of a corporation agree in writing, the corporation can operate without directors, bylaws, annual or special shareholders' or directors' meetings, stock certificates, or formal records of shareholders' or directors' decisions.[10]

Management of Close Corporations. A close corporation has a single shareholder or a closely knit group of shareholders, who usually hold the positions of directors and officers. Management of a close corporation resembles that of a sole proprietorship or a partnership. As a corporation, however, the firm must meet all specific legal requirements set forth in state statutes.

To prevent a majority shareholder from dominating a close corporation, the corporation may require that more than a simple majority of the directors approve any action taken by the board. Typically, this would apply only to extraordinary actions, such as changing the amount of dividends or dismissing an employee-shareholder, and not to ordinary business decisions.

Transfer of Shares in Close Corporations. By definition, a close corporation has a small number of shareholders. Thus, the transfer of one shareholder's shares to someone else can cause serious management problems. The other shareholders may find themselves required to share control with someone they do not know or like.

■EXAMPLE 28.1 Three brothers, Terry, Damon, and Henry Johnson, are the only shareholders of Johnson's Car Wash, Inc. Terry and Damon do not want Henry to sell his shares to an unknown third person. To avoid this situation, the corporation could restrict the transferability of shares to outside persons. Shareholders could be required to offer their shares to the corporation or the other shareholders before selling them to an outside purchaser. In fact, a few states have statutes that prohibit the transfer of close corporation shares unless certain persons—including shareholders, family members, and the corporation—are first given the opportunity to purchase the shares for the same price. ■

Control of a close corporation can also be stabilized through the use of a *shareholder agreement*. A shareholder agreement can provide that when one of the original shareholders dies, her or his shares of stock in the corporation will be divided in such a way that the proportionate holdings of the survivors, and thus their proportionate control, will be maintained. Courts are generally reluctant to interfere with private agreements, including shareholder agreements.

S Corporations A close corporation that meets the qualifying requirements specified in Subchapter S of the Internal Revenue Code can operate as an **S corporation.** If a corporation has S corporation status, it can avoid the imposition of income taxes at the corporate level while retaining many of the advantages of a corporation, particularly limited liability.

---

9. For example, in some states (such as Maryland), a close corporation need not have a board of directors.
10. Shareholders cannot agree, however, to eliminate certain rights of shareholders, such as the right to inspect corporate books and records or the right to bring *derivative actions* (lawsuits on behalf of the corporation—see Chapter 29).

Qualification Requirements for S Corporations. Among the numerous requirements for S corporation status, the following are the most important:

1 The corporation must be a domestic corporation.

2 The corporation must not be a member of an affiliated group of corporations.

3 The shareholders of the corporation must be individuals, estates, or certain trusts. Partnerships and nonqualifying trusts cannot be shareholders. Corporations can be shareholders under certain circumstances.

4 The corporation must have no more than one hundred shareholders.

5 The corporation must have only one class of stock, although all shareholders do not have to have the same voting rights.

6 No shareholder of the corporation may be a nonresident alien.

Benefits of S Corporations. At times, it is beneficial for a regular corporation to elect S corporation status. Benefits include the following:

1 When the corporation has losses, the S election allows the shareholders to use the losses to offset other income.

2 When the shareholder's tax bracket is lower than the corporation's tax bracket, the S election causes the corporation's pass-through net income to be taxed in the shareholder's bracket (because it is taxed as personal income). This is particularly attractive when the corporation wants to accumulate earnings for some future business purpose.

Because of these tax benefits, many close corporations have opted for S corporation status. Today, however, the limited liability company (see Chapter 27) and the limited liability partnership (see Chapter 26) offer similar advantages plus additional benefits, including more flexibility in forming and operating the business. Hence, the S corporation is losing some of its significance.

Professional Corporations Professionals such as physicians, lawyers, dentists, and accountants can incorporate. Professional corporations are typically identified by the letters *S.C.* (service corporation), *P.C.* (professional corporation), or *P.A.* (professional association). In general, the laws governing professional corporations are similar to those governing ordinary business corporations, but three basic areas of liability deserve special attention.

First, some courts may, for liability purposes, regard the professional corporation as a partnership in which each partner can be held liable for any malpractice liability incurred by the others within the scope of the business. The reason for this rule is that professionals, in contrast to shareholders in other types of corporations, should not be allowed to avoid liability for their wrongful acts simply by virtue of incorporating. Second, in many states, professional persons are liable not only for their own negligent acts, but also for the misconduct of any person under their direct supervision who is rendering services on behalf of the corporation. Third, a shareholder in a professional corporation is generally protected from contractual liability and cannot be held liable for the torts—other than malpractice or a breach of duty to clients or patients—that are committed by other professionals at the firm.

CONTRAST Unlike the shareholders of most other corporations, the shareholders of professional corporations must generally be licensed professionals.

CORPORATE POWERS

When a corporation is created, the express and implied powers necessary to achieve its purpose also come into existence. The express powers of a corporation are found in its **articles of incorporation** (a document filed with the state that contains information about

ARTICLES OF INCORPORATION
The document filed with the appropriate governmental agency, usually the secretary of state, when a business is incorporated. State statutes usually prescribe what kind of information must be contained in the articles of incorporation.

the corporation, including its organization and functions), in the law of the state of incorporation, and in the state and federal constitutions.

BYLAWS
A set of governing rules adopted by a corporation or other association.

Corporate **bylaws,** which are internal rules of management adopted by the corporation at its first organizational meeting, also establish the express powers of the corporation. Because state corporation statutes frequently provide default rules that apply if the company's bylaws are silent on an issue, it is important that the bylaws set forth the specific operating rules of the corporation. In addition, after the bylaws are adopted, the corporation's board of directors will pass resolutions that also grant or restrict corporate powers.

The following order of priority is used when conflicts arise among documents involving corporations:

1 The U.S. Constitution.

2 State constitutions.

3 State statutes.

4 The articles of incorporation.

5 Bylaws.

6 Resolutions of the board of directors.

Implied Powers

Certain implied powers attach when a corporation is created. Barring express constitutional, statutory, or other prohibitions, the corporation has the implied power to perform all acts reasonably appropriate and necessary to accomplish its corporate purposes. For this reason, a corporation has the implied power to borrow funds within certain limits, to lend funds, and to extend credit to those with whom it has a legal or contractual relationship.

To borrow funds, the corporation acts through its board of directors to authorize the loan. Most often, the president or chief executive officer of the corporation will execute the necessary papers on behalf of the corporation. In so doing, corporate officers have the implied power to bind the corporation in matters directly connected with the *ordinary* business affairs of the enterprise. There is a limit to what a corporate officer can do, though. A corporate officer does not have the authority to bind the corporation to an action that will greatly affect the corporate purpose or undertaking, such as the sale of substantial corporate assets.

Ultra Vires Doctrine

ULTRA VIRES
A Latin term meaning "beyond the powers"; in corporate law, acts of a corporation that are beyond its express and implied powers to undertake.

The term ***ultra vires*** means "beyond the powers." In corporate law, acts of a corporation that are beyond its express and implied powers are *ultra vires* acts. Most cases dealing with *ultra vires* acts have involved contracts made for unauthorized purposes. **■EXAMPLE 28.2** Suarez is the chief executive officer of SOS Plumbing, Inc. He enters a contract with Carlini for the purchase of fifty cases of brandy. It is difficult to see how this contract is reasonably related to the conduct and furtherance of the corporation's stated purpose of providing plumbing installation and services. Hence, a court would probably find such a contract to be *ultra vires.* ■

Under Section 3.04 of the RMBCA, the shareholders can seek an injunction from a court to prevent (or stop) the corporation from engaging in *ultra vires* acts. The attorney general in the state of incorporation can also bring an action to obtain an injunction against the *ultra vires* transactions or to institute dissolution proceedings against the corporation on the basis of *ultra vires* acts. The corporation or its shareholders (on behalf of the corporation) can seek damages from the officers and directors who were responsible for the *ultra vires* acts.

CORPORATE FORMATION

Up to this point, we have discussed some of the general characteristics of corporations. We now examine the process by which corporations come into existence. Incorporating a business is much simpler today than it was twenty years ago, and many states allow businesses to incorporate online via the Internet.

Note that one of the most common reasons for creating a corporation is the need for additional capital to finance expansion. Many of the Fortune 500 companies were originally sole proprietorships or partnerships before converting to a corporate entity. A sole proprietor in need of funds can seek partners who will bring capital with them. Although a partnership may be able to secure more funds from potential lenders than the sole proprietor could, the amount is still limited. When a firm wants significant growth, simply increasing the number of partners can result in so many partners that the firm can no longer operate effectively. Therefore, incorporation may be the best choice for an expanding business organization because a corporation can obtain more capital by issuing shares of stock.

Promotional Activities

In the past, preliminary steps were taken to organize and promote the business prior to incorporating. Contracts were made with investors and others on behalf of the future corporation. Today, however, due to the relative ease of forming a corporation in most states, persons incorporating their business rarely, if ever, engage in preliminary promotional activities. Nevertheless, it is important for businesspersons to understand that they are personally liable for all preincorporation contracts made with investors, accountants, or others on behalf of the future corporation. This personal liability continues until the corporation assumes the preincorporation contracts by *novation* (discussed in Chapter 12).

■**EXAMPLE 28.3** Jade Sorrel contracts with an accountant, Ray Cooper, to provide tax advice for a proposed corporation, Blackstone, Inc. Cooper provides the services to Sorrel, knowing that the corporation has not yet been formed. Once Blackstone, Inc., is formed, Cooper sends an invoice to the corporation and to Sorrel personally, but the bill is not paid. Because Sorrel is personally liable for the preincorporation contract, Cooper can file a lawsuit against Sorrel for breaching the contract for accounting services. Cooper cannot seek to hold Blackstone, Inc., liable unless he has entered into a novation contract with the corporation. ■

Incorporation Procedures

Exact procedures for incorporation differ among states, but the basic steps are as follows: (1) select a state of incorporation, (2) secure the corporate name by confirming its availability, (3) prepare the articles of incorporation, and (4) file the articles of incorporation with the secretary of state accompanied by payment of the specified fees. If the articles contain all of the information required by statute, the secretary of state stamps the articles "Filed," and the corporation comes into existence. These steps are discussed in more detail in the following subsections.

Selecting the State of Incorporation The first step in the incorporation process is to select a state in which to incorporate. Because state incorporation laws differ, individuals may look for the states that offer the most advantageous tax or incorporation provisions. (See the *Application* feature at the end of this chapter for details on how you can find out each state's requirements and incorporate your business online.) Another consideration is the fee that a particular state charges to incorporate, as well as the annual fees and the fees for specific transactions (such as stock transfers).

"A man to carry on a successful business must have imagination. He must see things as in a vision, a dream of the whole thing."
CHARLES M. SCHWAB,
1862–1939
(American industrialist)

Delaware has historically had the least restrictive laws and provisions that favor corporate management. Consequently, many corporations, including a number of the largest, have incorporated there. Delaware's statutes permit firms to incorporate in that state and conduct business and locate their operating headquarters elsewhere. Most other states now permit this as well. Note, though, that closely held corporations, particularly those of a professional nature, generally incorporate in the state where their principal shareholders live and work. For reasons of convenience and cost, businesses often choose to incorporate in the state in which the corporation's business will primarily be conducted.

ON THE WEB

For answers to "frequently asked questions" on the topic of incorporation, go to www.bizfilings.com/products/ccorp.asp.

Securing the Corporate Name   The choice of a corporate name is subject to state approval to ensure against duplication or deception. State statutes usually require that the secretary of state run a check on the proposed name in the state of incorporation. Some states require that the persons incorporating a firm, at their own expense, run a check on the proposed name, which can often be accomplished via Internet-based services. Once cleared, a name can be reserved for a short time, for a fee, pending the completion of the articles of incorporation. All corporate statutes require the corporation name to include the word *Corporation, Incorporated, Company,* or *Limited,* or abbreviations of these terms.

A new corporation's name cannot be the same as (or deceptively similar to) the name of an existing corporation doing business within the state. The name should also be one that can be used as the business's domain name. **■EXAMPLE 28.4** If an existing corporation is named Digital Synergy, Inc., you cannot choose the name Digital Synergy Company because that name is deceptively similar to the first. The state will be unlikely to allow the corporate name because it could impliedly transfer a part of the goodwill established by the first corporate user to the second corporation. In addition, you would not want to choose the name Digital Synergy Company because you would be unable to acquire a domain name using the name of the business. **■**

Note that if a future firm contemplates doing business in other states—or over the Internet—those incorporating it also need to check on existing corporate names in those states as well. Otherwise, if the firm does business under a name that is the same as or deceptively similar to an existing company's name, it may be liable for trade name infringement.

PREVENTING LEGAL DISPUTES

Businesspersons should be cautious when choosing a corporate name. Recognize that even if a particular state does not require the incorporator to run a name check, doing so is always advisable and can help prevent future disputes. Many states provide online search capabilities, but these searches are usually limited and will only compare the proposed name to the names of active corporations within that state. Trade name disputes, however, are not limited to corporations. Thus, using a business name that is deceptively similar to the name of a partnership or limited liability company can also lead to a dispute. Disputes are even more likely to arise among firms that do business over the Internet. Always check on the availability of a particular domain name before selecting a corporate name. This is an area in which it pays to be overly cautious and incur some additional cost to hire an attorney or specialized firm to conduct a name search. If you learn that another business is using a similar name, you can contact that business and ask for its consent to your proposed name.

■

Preparing the Articles of Incorporation   The primary document needed to incorporate a business is the *articles of incorporation* (see Exhibit 28–2). As mentioned earlier, the articles include basic information about the corporation and serve as a primary source of authority for its future organization and business functions. The person or persons who

EXHIBIT 28–2 **Articles of Incorporation**

ARTICLE ONE   The name of the corporation is _____ .

ARTICLE TWO   The period of its duration is _____ (may be a number of years or until a certain date).

ARTICLE THREE   The purpose (or purposes) for which the corporation is organized is (are) _____
_____
_____ .

ARTICLE FOUR   The aggregate number of shares that the corporation shall have the authority to issue is _____ with the par value of
_____dollar(s) each (or without par value).

ARTICLE FIVE   The corporation will not commence business until it has received for the issuance of its shares consideration of the
value of $1,000 (can be any sum not less than $1,000).

ARTICLE SIX   The address of the corporation's registered office is _____ ,
and the name of its registered agent at such address is _____
_____ .

ARTICLE SEVEN   The number of initial directors is _____ , and the names and addresses of the directors are _____
_____
_____ .

ARTICLE EIGHT   The names and addresses of the incorporators are

_____   _____   _____
(name)   (address)   (signature)

_____   _____   _____
(name)   (address)   (signature)

_____   _____   _____
(name)   (address)   (signature)

Sworn to on_____ by the above-named incorporators.
         (date)

                                                    _____
                                                    Notary Public

(Notary Seal)

execute (sign) the articles are called *incorporators*. Generally, the articles of incorporation
must include the following information [RMBCA 2.02]:

1 The name of the corporation.

2 The number of shares the corporation is authorized to issue.

3 The name and address of the corporation's initial registered agent.

4 The name and address of each incorporator.

In addition, the articles *may* set forth other information, such as the names and addresses
of the initial board of directors, the duration and purpose of the corporation, a par value of

shares of the corporation, and any other information pertinent to the rights and duties of the corporation's shareholders and directors. Articles of incorporation vary widely depending on the size and type of corporation and the jurisdiction. Frequently, the articles do not provide much detail about the firm's operations, which are spelled out in the company's bylaws.

Shares of the Corporation. The articles must specify the number of shares of stock authorized for issuance. For instance, a company might state that the aggregate number of shares that the corporation has the authority to issue is five thousand. Large corporations often state a par value of each share, such as $.20 per share, and specify the various types or classes of stock authorized for issuance (see the discussion of *common* and *preferred stock* later in this chapter). Sometimes, the articles set forth the capital structure of the corporation and other relevant information concerning equity, shares, and credit.

Registered Office and Agent. The corporation must indicate the location and address of its registered office within the state. Usually, the registered office is also the principal office of the corporation. The corporation must also give the name and address of a specific person who has been designated as an *agent* and who can receive legal documents (such as orders to appear in court) on behalf of the corporation.

Incorporators. Each incorporator must be listed by name and must indicate an address. The incorporators need not have any interest at all in the corporation, and sometimes signing the articles is their only duty. Many states do not have residency or age requirements for incorporators. States vary on the required number of incorporators; it can be as few as one or as many as three. Incorporators frequently participate in the first organizational meeting of the corporation.

Duration and Purpose. A corporation has perpetual existence unless stated otherwise in the articles. The owners may want to prescribe a maximum duration, however, after which the corporation must formally renew its existence.

The RMBCA does not require a specific statement of purpose to be included in the articles. A corporation can be formed for any lawful purpose. Some incorporators choose to include a general statement of purpose "to engage in any lawful act or activity," while others opt to specify the intended business activities ("to engage in the production and sale of agricultural products," for example). It is increasingly common for the articles to state that the corporation is organized for "any legal business," with no mention of specifics, to avoid the need for future amendments to the corporate articles. The trend towards general statements of corporate purpose also means that corporations today are less likely to be accused of engaging in *ultra vires* acts.

Internal Organization. The articles can describe the internal management structure of the corporation, although this is usually included in the bylaws adopted after the corporation is formed. The articles of incorporation commence the corporation; the bylaws are formed after commencement by the board of directors. Bylaws cannot conflict with the incorporation statute or the articles of incorporation [RMBCA 2.06].

Under the RMBCA, shareholders may amend or repeal the bylaws. The board of directors may also amend or repeal the bylaws unless the articles of incorporation or provisions of the incorporation statute reserve this power to the shareholders exclusively [RMBCA 10.20]. Typical bylaw provisions describe such matters as voting requirements for shareholders, the election of the board of directors, the methods of replacing directors, and the manner and time of holding shareholders' and board meetings (these corporate activities will be discussed in Chapter 29).

KEEP IN MIND Unlike the articles of incorporation, bylaws do not need to be filed with a state official.

Filing the Articles with the State   Once the articles of incorporation have been prepared, signed, and authenticated by the incorporators, they are sent to the appropriate state official, usually the secretary of state, along with the required filing fee. In most states, as noted previously, the secretary of state then stamps the articles as "Filed" and returns a copy of the articles to the incorporators. Once this occurs, the corporation officially exists. (Note that some states issue a *certificate of incorporation*, which is similar to articles of incorporation, representing the state's authorization for the corporation to conduct business. This procedure was typical under the unrevised MBCA.)

First Organizational Meeting to Adopt Bylaws

After incorporation, the first organizational meeting must be held. If the articles of incorporation named the initial board of directors, then the directors, by majority vote, call for the meeting to adopt the bylaws and complete the company's organization. If the articles did not name the directors (as is typical), then the incorporators hold the meeting to elect the directors, adopt bylaws, and complete the routine business of incorporation (authorizing the issuance of shares and hiring employees, for example). The business transacted depends on the requirements of the state's incorporation statute, the nature of the corporation, the provisions made in the articles, and the desires of the incorporators. Adoption of bylaws—the internal rules of management for the corporation—is usually the most important function of this meeting. As mentioned earlier, the shareholders, directors, and officers must abide by the bylaws in conducting corporate business.

CORPORATE STATUS

The procedures for incorporation are very specific. If they are not followed precisely, others may be able to challenge the existence of the corporation. Errors in the incorporation procedures might become important when, for example, a third party who is attempting to enforce a contract or bring suit for a tort injury learns of them. On the basis of improper incorporation, the plaintiff could attempt to hold the would-be shareholders personally liable. Additionally, when the corporation seeks to enforce a contract against a defaulting party, that party may be able to avoid liability on the ground of a defect in the incorporation procedure.

   To prevent injustice, courts will sometimes attribute corporate status to an improperly formed corporation by holding it to be a *de jure* corporation or a *de facto* corporation. Occasionally, a corporation may be held to exist by estoppel. Additionally, in certain circumstances involving abuse of the corporate form, a court may disregard the corporate entity and hold the shareholders personally liable.

De Jure and De Facto Corporations

If a corporation has substantially complied with all conditions precedent to incorporation, the corporation is said to have *de jure* (rightful and lawful) existence. In most states and under the RMBCA, the secretary of state's filing of the articles of incorporation is conclusive proof that all mandatory statutory provisions have been met [RMBCA 2.03(b)]. Because a *de jure* corporation is one that is properly formed, neither the state nor a third party can attack its existence.[11]

---

11. There is an exception: a few states allow state authorities, in a *quo warranto* proceeding, to bring an action against the corporation for noncompliance with a condition subsequent to incorporation. This might occur if the corporation fails to file annual reports, for example.

Sometimes, there is a defect in complying with statutory mandates—for example, the corporation failed to hold an organizational meeting. Under these circumstances, the corporation may have *de facto* (actual) status, meaning that it will be treated as a legal corporation despite the defect in its formation. A corporation with *de facto* status cannot be challenged by third persons (except for the state). In other words, the shareholders of a *de facto* corporation are still protected by limited liability (provided they are unaware of the defect). The following elements are required for *de facto* status:

1 There must be a state statute under which the corporation can be validly incorporated.

2 The parties must have made a good faith attempt to comply with the statute.

3 The enterprise must already have undertaken to do business as a corporation.

Corporation by Estoppel

If a business association holds itself out to others as being a corporation but has made no attempt to incorporate, the firm normally will be estopped (prevented) from denying corporate status in a lawsuit by a third party. This usually occurs when a third party contracts with an entity that claims to be a corporation but has not filed articles of incorporation—or contracts with a person claiming to be an agent of a corporation that does not in fact exist. When the third party brings a suit naming the so-called corporation as the defendant, the association may not escape liability on the ground that no corporation exists. When justice requires, the courts treat an alleged corporation as if it were an actual corporation for the purpose of determining the rights and liabilities involved in a particular situation. A corporation by estoppel is thus determined by the situation. Recognition of its corporate status does not extend beyond the resolution of the problem at hand.

Disregarding the Corporate Entity

PIERCING THE CORPORATE VEIL
An action in which a court disregards the corporate entity and holds the shareholders personally liable for corporate debts and obligations.

Occasionally, the owners use a corporate entity to perpetrate a fraud, circumvent the law, or in some other way accomplish an illegitimate objective. In these situations, the court will ignore the corporate structure by **piercing the corporate veil** and exposing the shareholders to personal liability. Generally, when the corporate privilege is abused for personal benefit or when the corporate business is treated so carelessly that the corporation and the controlling shareholder are no longer separate entities, the court will require the owner to assume personal liability to creditors for the corporation's debts.

In short, when the facts show that great injustice would result from the use of a corporation to avoid individual responsibility, a court of equity will look behind the corporate structure to the individual shareholder. The following are some of the factors that frequently cause the courts to pierce the corporate veil:

1 A party is tricked or misled into dealing with the corporation rather than the individual.

2 The corporation is set up never to make a profit or always to be insolvent, or it is too "thinly" capitalized—that is, it has insufficient capital at the time of formation to meet its prospective debts or other potential liabilities.

3 Statutory corporate formalities, such as holding required corporation meetings, are not followed.

COMMINGLE
To put funds or goods together into one mass so that they are so mixed that they no longer have separate identities. In corporate law, if personal and corporate interests are commingled to the extent that the corporation has no separate identity, a court may "pierce the corporate veil" and expose the shareholders to personal liability.

4 Personal and corporate interests are **commingled** (mixed together) to such an extent that the corporation has no separate identity.

The potential for corporate assets to be used for personal benefit is especially great in a close corporation, in which the shares are held by a single person or by only a few individuals, usually family members. In such a situation, the separate status of the corporate entity and the sole shareholder (or family-member shareholders) must be carefully preserved. Certain practices invite trouble for the one-person or family-owned corporation: the commingling of corporate and personal funds, the failure to hold board of directors' meetings and record the minutes, or the shareholders' continuous personal use of corporate property (for example, vehicles).

EXAMPLE 28.5 Donald Park incorporated three sports companies—SSP, SSII, and SSI. His mother was the president of SSP and SSII but did not participate in their operations. Park handled most of the corporations' activities out of his apartment and drew funds from their accounts as needed to pay his personal expenses. None of the three corporations had any employees, issued stock or paid dividends, maintained corporate records, or followed other corporate formalities. Then Park—misrepresenting himself as the president of SSP and the vice president of SSII—applied for, and obtained, loans from Dimmitt & Owens Financial, Inc. When the loans were not paid, Dimmitt filed a suit in a federal district court, seeking, among other things, to impose personal liability on Park. Because Park had commingled corporate funds with his personal funds and failed to follow corporate formalities, the court "pierced the corporate veil" and held him personally responsible for the debt.[12] ■

The following case also illustrates some of the factors that may cause a court to pierce the corporate veil in a close corporation.

---

12. *Dimmitt & Owens Financial, Inc. v. Superior Sports Products, Inc.*, 196 F.Supp.2d 731 (N.D.Ill. 2002).

CASE 28.2 **In re Flutie New York Corp.**

United States Bankruptcy Court, Southern District of New York, 310 Bankr. 31 (2004).

FACTS In 1990, Michael Flutie created MFME Model Management Company (MFME), doing business as "Company Management," to represent fashion models for all purposes, including the entertainment business. MFME's offices were in New York City, New York. In 1995, Michael transferred MFME's assets to Flutie New York Corporation (Flutie N.Y.), a company that Michael and his mother, Victoria, had created one year earlier. Flutie N.Y. performed the same services for the same models at the same address and also did business as Company Management. Michael's father, Albert, was the sole shareholder and president of Flutie N.Y., but Michael was responsible for all major decisions involving the company. Flutie N.Y. did not follow any corporate formalities—there were no board meetings, shareholder meetings, or shareholder votes—but did pay Albert's and Michael's personal expenses. In 2001, Michael transferred the assets of Flutie N.Y. to Flutie Media Corporation, a firm that he and Albert had created in 1999. The next year, Flutie N.Y. filed a petition in a federal bankruptcy court to declare bankruptcy. David Kittay, the court-appointed trustee, filed a suit against Michael, seeking, among

other things, to pierce the corporate veil and hold him liable for all of Flutie N.Y.'s debts, including more than $2.7 million in creditors' claims.

ISSUE Is piercing the corporate veil warranted when a party with control over a corporation engages in conduct that causes significant losses for the firm?

DECISION Yes. The court pierced the corporate veil and held Michael liable for all of Flutie N.Y.'s debts. The court concluded, "It is clear that Michael Flutie had exclusive control over the operations of Flutie N.Y., and with this control he committed wrongful acts which resulted in significant losses by Flutie N.Y."

REASON The court pointed out that, among other things, transfers to Michael, as well as the transfers to Albert on Michael's behalf, were made without consideration to Flutie N.Y., as were transfers of model management contracts and arrangements for the services of models to Flutie Media. Piercing the corporate veil was also supported by Flutie N.Y.'s failure to follow corporate formalities—no board of directors'

CASE 28.2–Continues next page

meetings were held, no votes were taken, and no stock certificates were issued. The firm was too thinly capitalized, as shown by the excess of its liabilities over its assets and the losses on its income statements for 1995 through 2000. Furthermore, stated the court, "Michael Flutie looted Flutie N.Y.," using it as a "sham" to deprive its creditors of amounts that they were owed, and Albert "acquiesced in and permitted his son to engage in [this] conduct." They behaved as though the firm's assets belonged to them and ignored the effect of their acts on the firm and its creditors.

 WHAT IF THE FACTS WERE DIFFERENT?
If the corporation had observed corporate formalities, including board meetings, shareholder meetings, and shareholder votes, would the result have been different? Explain.

CORPORATE FINANCING

SECURITIES
Generally, stock certificates, bonds, notes, debentures, warrants, or other documents given as evidence of an ownership interest in a corporation or as a promise of repayment by a corporation.

STOCK
An equity (ownership) interest in a corporation, measured in units of shares.

BOND
A certificate that evidences a corporate (or government) debt. It is a security that involves no ownership interest in the issuing entity.

Part of the process of corporate formation involves corporate financing. Corporations are financed by the issuance and sale of corporate securities. **Securities** (stocks and bonds) evidence the right to participate in earnings and the distribution of corporate property or the obligation to pay funds.

Stocks, or *equity securities*, represent the purchase of ownership in the business firm. **Bonds** (debentures), or *debt securities*, represent the borrowing of funds by firms (and governments). Of course, not all debt is in the form of debt securities. For example, some debt is in the form of accounts payable and notes payable, which typically are short-term debts. Bonds are simply a way for the corporation to split up its long-term debt so that it can market it more easily.

Bonds

Bonds are issued by business firms and by governments at all levels as evidence of the funds they are borrowing from investors. Bonds normally have a designated *maturity date*—the date when the principal, or face, amount of the bond is returned to the investor. They are sometimes referred to as *fixed-income securities* because their owners (that is, the creditors) receive fixed-dollar interest payments, usually semiannually, during the period of time prior to maturity.

BOND INDENTURE
A contract between the issuer of a bond and the bondholder.

Because debt financing represents a legal obligation on the part of the corporation, various features and terms of a particular bond issue are specified in a lending agreement called a **bond indenture.** A corporate trustee, often a commercial bank trust department, represents the collective well-being of all bondholders in ensuring that the corporation meets the terms of the bond issue. The bond indenture specifies the maturity date of the bond and the pattern of interest payments until maturity. The different types of corporate bonds are described in Exhibit 28–3.

Stocks

COMMON STOCK
Shares of ownership in a corporation that give the owner of the stock a proportionate interest in the corporation with regard to control, earnings, and net assets. Shares of common stock are lowest in priority with respect to payment of dividends and distribution of the corporation's assets on dissolution.

Issuing stocks is another way that corporations can obtain financing. The ways in which stocks differ from bonds are summarized in Exhibit 28–4. Basically, as mentioned, stocks represent ownership in a business firm, whereas bonds represent borrowing by the firm.

Exhibit 28–5 on page 790 summarizes the types of stocks issued by corporations. We look now at the two major types of stock—*common stock* and *preferred stock.*

Common Stock The true ownership of a corporation is represented by **common stock.** Common stock provides a proportionate interest in the corporation with regard to (1) con-

EXHIBIT 28-3	Types of Corporate Bonds
Debenture bonds	Bonds for which no specific assets of the corporation are pledged as backing. Rather, they are backed by the general credit rating of the corporation, plus any assets that can be seized if the corporation allows the debentures to go into default.
Mortgage bonds	Bonds that pledge specific property. If the corporation defaults on the bonds, the bondholders can take the property.
Convertible bonds	Bonds that can be exchanged for a specified number of shares of common stock under certain conditions.
Callable bonds	Bonds that may be called in and the principal repaid at specified times or under conditions specified in the bonds when they are issued.

trol, (2) earnings, and (3) net assets. A shareholder's interest is generally in proportion to the number of shares he or she owns out of the total number of shares issued.

Voting rights in a corporation apply to the election of the firm's board of directors and to any proposed changes in the ownership structure of the firm. For example, a holder of common stock generally has the right to vote in a decision on a proposed merger, as mergers can change the proportion of ownership. State corporation law specifies the types of actions for which shareholder approval must be obtained.

Firms are not obligated to return a principal amount per share to each holder of common stock because no firm can ensure that the market price per share of its common stock will not decline over time. The issuing firm also does not have to guarantee a dividend; indeed, some corporations never pay dividends.

Holders of common stock are investors who assume a *residual* position in the overall financial structure of a business. In terms of receiving payment for their investments, they are last in line. They are entitled to the earnings that are left after preferred stockholders,

EXHIBIT 28-4	How Do Stocks and Bonds Differ?	
STOCKS		**BONDS**
1. Stocks represent ownership.		1. Bonds represent debt.
2. Stocks (common) do not have a fixed dividend rate.		2. Interest on bonds must always be paid, whether or not any profit is earned.
3. Stockholders can elect the board of directors, which controls the corporation.		3. Bondholders usually have no voice in, or control over, management of the corporation.
4. Stocks do not have a maturity date; the corporation usually does not repay the stockholder.		4. Bonds have a maturity date, when the corporation is to repay the bondholder the face value of the bond.
5. All corporations issue or offer to sell stocks. This is the usual definition of a corporation.		5. Corporations do not necessarily issue bonds.
6. Stockholders have a claim against the property and income of a corporation after all creditors' claims have been met.		6. Bondholders have a claim against the property and income of a corporation that must be met *before* the claims of stockholders.

EXHIBIT 28–5	Types of Stocks
Common stock	Voting shares that represent ownership interest in a corporation. Common stock has the lowest priority with respect to payment of dividends and distribution of assets on the corporation's dissolution.
Preferred stock	Shares of stock that have priority over common-stock shares as to payment of dividends and distribution of assets on dissolution. Dividend payments are usually a fixed percentage of the face value of the share.
Cumulative preferred stock	Required dividends not paid in a given year must be paid in a subsequent year before any common-stock dividends are paid.
Participating preferred stock	Stock entitling the owner to receive the preferred-stock dividend and additional dividends if the corporation has paid dividends on common stock.
Convertible preferred stock	Stock entitling the owners to convert their shares into a specified number of common shares either in the issuing corporation or, sometimes, in another corporation.
Redeemable, or callable, preferred stock	Preferred shares issued with the express condition that the issuing corporation has the right to repurchase the shares as specified.

bondholders, suppliers, employees, and other groups have been paid. Once those groups are paid, however, the owners of common stock may be entitled to *all* the remaining earnings as dividends. (The board of directors normally is not under any duty to declare the remaining earnings as dividends, however.)

PREFERRED STOCK
Classes of stock that have priority over common stock as to both payment of dividends and distribution of assets on the corporation's dissolution.

Preferred Stock **Preferred stock** is stock with *preferences*. Usually, this means that holders of preferred stock have priority over holders of common stock as to dividends and as to payment on dissolution of the corporation. Holders of preferred stock may or may not have the right to vote.

Preferred stock is not included among the liabilities of a business because it is equity. Like other equity securities, preferred shares have no fixed maturity date on which the firm must pay them off. Although firms occasionally buy back preferred stock, they are not legally obligated to do so. Holders of preferred stock are investors who have assumed a rather cautious position in their relationship to the corporation. They have a stronger position than common shareholders with respect to dividends and claims on assets, but they will not share in the full prosperity of the firm if it grows successfully over time. This is because the value of preferred shares will not rise as rapidly as that of common shares during a period of financial success. Preferred stockholders do receive fixed dividends periodically, however, and they may benefit to some extent from changes in the market price of the shares.

"There are two times in a man's life when he should not speculate: when he can't afford it and when he can."
SAMUEL CLEMENS (MARK TWAIN)
1835–1919
(Amercian author and humorist)

The return and the risk for preferred stock lie somewhere between those for bonds and those for common stock. Preferred stock is more similar to bonds than to common stock, even though preferred stock appears in the ownership section of the firm's balance sheet. As a result, preferred stock is often categorized with corporate bonds as a fixed-income security, even though the legal status is not the same.

MERGER AND CONSOLIDATION

A corporation typically extends its operations by combining with another corporation through a merger, a consolidation, a purchase of assets, or a purchase of a controlling interest in the other corporation. The terms *merger* and *consolidation* are often used interchangeably, but they refer to two legally distinct proceedings. The rights and liabilities of the corporation, its shareholders, and its creditors are the same for both, however.

Merger

A **merger** involves the legal combination of two or more corporations in such a way that only one of the corporations continues to exist. ▇**EXAMPLE 28.6** Corporation A and Corporation B decide to merge. They agree that A will absorb B. Therefore, on merging, B ceases to exist as a separate entity, and A continues as the *surviving corporation*. ▇ Exhibit 28–6 graphically illustrates this process.

After the merger, A is recognized as a single corporation, possessing all the rights, privileges, and powers of itself and B. It automatically acquires all of B's property and assets without the necessity of a formal transfer. Additionally, A becomes liable for all of B's debts and obligations. Finally, A's articles of incorporation are deemed amended to include any changes that are stated in the *articles of merger* (a document setting forth the terms and conditions of the merger that is filed with the secretary of state).

In a merger, the surviving corporation inherits the disappearing corporation's preexisting legal rights and obligations. For example, if the disappearing corporation had a right of action against a third party, the surviving corporation can bring suit after the merger to recover the disappearing corporation's damages. The common law similarly recognizes that, following a merger, a right to bring an action to enforce a property right will vest with the successor (surviving) corporation, and no right of action will remain with the disappearing corporation. The principles regarding successor liability were applied in the following case.

EXHIBIT 28–6 **Merger**

In this illustration, Corporation A and Corporation B decide to merge. They agree that A will absorb B, so after the merger, B no longer exists as a separate entity, and A continues as the surviving corporation.

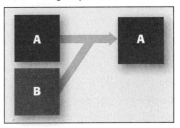

MERGER
A contractual and statutory process in which one corporation (the surviving corporation) acquires all of the assets and liabilities of another corporation (the merged corporation). The shareholders of the merged corporation either are paid for their shares or receive shares in the surviving corporation.

CASE 28.3 **Rodriguez v. Tech Credit Union Corp.**

Court of Appeals of Indiana, 824 N.E.2d 442 (2005).
www.findlaw.com/11stategov/in/inca.html[a]

FACTS Catalina Rodriguez became the general manager of LTV Steel Employees Federal Credit Union in East Chicago, Indiana, in January 2000, subject to an employment contract. At the time, LTV was in poor financial condition, with a large number of delinquent and unpaid loans. In January 2002, LTV's board of directors terminated Rodriguez's employment for, among other things, extending loan payment periods for individuals with whom she had personal relationships and directing some of LTV's insurance business to Airey Insurance and Financial Services, Inc., a brokerage firm for which her son

a. In the "Court of Appeals" section, in the "2005" row, click on "March." In the result, scroll to the name of the case and click on "html" to access the opinion.

worked as a sales representative. On April 27, Tech Credit Union Corporation acquired LTV. The "Agreement of Merger" stated, "The LTV Steel Employees Federal Credit Union shall be merged into TECH Credit Union under the name and charter of TECH Credit Union." The agreement was silent as to whether Tech acquired LTV's liabilities. LTV dissolved. Later, Rodriguez filed a suit in an Indiana state court against Tech and others, alleging, among other things, breach of contract. Tech filed a motion for summary judgment, which the court granted. Rodriguez appealed to a state intermediate appellate court.

ISSUE On a merger, does the surviving corporation acquire the liabilities of the merging corporation if their agreement is silent on the question?

CASE 28.3–Continues next page

CASE 28.3–Continued

DECISION Yes. The state intermediate appellate court affirmed the judgment of the lower court, holding that Tech succeeded to LTV's liabilities. There was no basis for assessing liability against Tech, however.

REASON The court pointed out that the document under which Tech acquired LTV was titled "Agreement of Merger" and that it repeatedly referred to the transaction as a merger. Following a merger between two firms, the surviving corporation succeeds to all the rights, powers, liabilities, and obligations of the merging corporation. Thus, Tech, as the surviving corporation, acquired LTV's liabilities. Because neither LTV nor its board acted wrongfully with respect to Rodriguez, however, there was no basis for assessing liability against Tech. LTV was failing financially when Rodriguez became the general manager and "things did not improve on her watch." There were "[q]uestionable loans and extensions" and "collections efforts were ineffective. In addition, Rodriguez signed a contract with Airey, then presented it to the Board of Directors as a proposal rather than as an existing contract," without revealing her son's employment with Airey. In terminating Rodriguez, the members of the board "exercised their business judgment in good faith and acted in the best interest of the corporation. Thus, the Board Members committed no wrongdoing."

 WHAT IF THE FACTS WERE DIFFERENT? *Suppose that the document under which Tech acquired LTV was not titled "Agreement of Merger" and that it did not refer to the transaction as a merger. Would the result have been different? Explain.*

Consolidation

CONSOLIDATION
A contractual and statutory process in which two or more corporations join to become a completely new corporation. The original corporations cease to exist, and the new corporation acquires all their assets and liabilities.

In a **consolidation**, two or more corporations combine in such a way that each corporation ceases to exist and a new one emerges. ◼**EXAMPLE 28.7** Corporation A and Corporation B consolidate to form an entirely new organization, Corporation C. In the process, A and B both terminate, and C comes into existence as an entirely new entity. Exhibit 28–7 graphically illustrates this process.

The results of a consolidation are essentially the same as the results of a merger. C is recognized as a new corporation and a single entity; A and B cease to exist. C inherits all of the rights, privileges, and powers previously held by A and B. Title to any property and assets owned by A and B passes to C without a formal transfer. C assumes liability for all of the debts and obligations owed by A and B. The *articles of consolidation*, which state the terms of the consolidation, take the place of A's and B's original corporate articles and are thereafter regarded as C's corporate articles. ◼

Procedure for Merger or Consolidation

All states have statutes authorizing mergers and consolidations for domestic (in-state) corporations, and most states allow the combination of domestic and foreign (out-of-state) corporations. Although the procedures vary somewhat among jurisdictions, the basic requirements for an ordinary merger or a consolidation are as follows:

1 The board of directors of *each* corporation involved must approve a merger or consolidation plan.

2 The shareholders of *each* corporation must approve the plan, by vote, at a shareholders' meeting. Most state statutes require the approval of two-thirds of the outstanding shares of voting stock, although some states require only a simple majority, and others require a four-fifths vote. Frequently, statutes require that each class of stock approve the merger; thus, the holders of nonvoting stock must also approve. A corporation's bylaws can provide for a stricter requirement.

3 Once approved by all of the directors and shareholders, the plan (articles of merger or consolidation) is filed, usually with the secretary of state.

EXHIBIT 28–7 **Consolidation**

In this illustration, Corporation A and Corporation B consolidate to form an entirely new organization, Corporation C. In the process, A and B terminate, and C comes into existence as an entirely new entity.

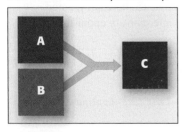

4 When state formalities are satisfied, the state issues a certificate of merger to the surviving corporation or a certificate of consolidation to the newly consolidated corporation.

Section 11.04 of the RMBCA provides for a simplified procedure for the merger of a substantially owned subsidiary corporation into its parent corporation. Under these provisions, a **short-form merger**—also referred to as a **parent-subsidiary merger**—can be accomplished *without the approval of the shareholders* of either corporation. The short-form merger can be used only when the parent corporation owns at least 90 percent of the outstanding shares of each class of stock of the subsidiary corporation. The approval of the board of directors of the parent corporation is all that is required for a short-form merger. The merger plan is filed with the state, and a copy of the plan must be sent to each shareholder of record of the subsidiary corporation.

Shareholder Approval

As mentioned, except in a short-form merger, the shareholders of both corporations must approve a merger or consolidation plan. Shareholders invest in a corporation with the expectation that the board of directors will manage the enterprise and make decisions on ordinary business matters. For extraordinary matters, however, the authorization of both the shareholders and the board of directors is required. In addition, state corporation statutes often require shareholder approval for various other types of extraordinary transactions, such as the sale, lease, or exchange of all or substantially all corporate assets outside the corporation's regular course of business. Amendments to the articles of incorporation and the dissolution of the corporation also generally require shareholder approval.

Hence, when any extraordinary matter arises, the corporation must proceed as authorized by law to obtain the approval of the shareholders and the board of directors. Sometimes, a transaction can be structured in such a way that shareholder approval is not required, but if the shareholders challenge the transaction, a court will use its equity powers to require such approval. To determine the nature of the transaction, the court will look to its consequences as well as its form.

Appraisal Rights

What if a shareholder disapproves of a merger or a consolidation but is outvoted by the other shareholders? The law recognizes that a dissenting shareholder should not be forced to become an unwilling shareholder in a corporation that is new or different from the one in which the shareholder originally invested. The shareholder has the right to dissent and may be entitled to be paid the fair value for the number of shares held on the date of the merger or consolidation. This right is referred to as the shareholder's **appraisal right.**

Appraisal rights are available only when a state statute specifically provides for them. State laws vary on whether appraisal rights are available in close corporations. Appraisal rights normally extend to regular mergers, consolidations, short-form mergers, and sales of substantially all of the corporate assets not in the ordinary course of business. In fact, exercising appraisal rights is often the only remedy available to a minority stockholder who is dissatisfied with a short-form merger.[13]

A marquee for Harrah's hotel and casino is seen across the strip from Caesars Palace in Las Vegas, Nevada. In 2004, Harrah's agreed to buy Caesars for about $5.2 billion, creating the world's largest casino operator. What role do shareholders typically play in a merger or consolidation? ("Pingping"/Creative Commons)

SHORT-FORM (PARENT-SUBSIDIARY) MERGER
A merger of companies in which one company (the parent corporation) owns at least 90 percent of the outstanding shares of each class of stock of the other corporation (the subsidiary corporation). The merger can be accomplished without the approval of the shareholders of either corporation.

REMEMBER State statutes, articles of incorporation, and corporate bylaws can require the approval of more than a majority of shares for some extraordinary matters.

APPRAISAL RIGHT
The right of a dissenting shareholder, who objects to an extraordinary transaction of the corporation (such as a merger or a consolidation), to have his or her shares appraised and to be paid the fair value of those shares by the corporation.

13. See *Glassman v. Unocal Exploration Corp.*, 777 A.2d 242 (Del.Sup.Ct. 2001).

PURCHASE OF ASSETS OR STOCK

When a corporation acquires all or substantially all of the assets of another corporation by direct purchase, the purchasing, or *acquiring*, corporation simply extends its ownership and control over more physical assets. Because no change in the legal entity occurs, the acquiring corporation is not required to obtain shareholder approval for the purchase.[14] The U.S. Department of Justice and the Federal Trade Commission, however, have issued guidelines that significantly constrain and often prohibit mergers that could result from a purchase of assets, including takeover bids. (These guidelines are part of the federal antitrust laws that will be discussed in Chapter 31.)

Note that the corporation that is *selling* all of its assets is substantially changing its business position and perhaps its ability to carry out its corporate purposes. For that reason, the corporation whose assets are being sold must obtain the approval of both the board of directors and the shareholders. In most states and under RMBCA 13.02, a dissenting shareholder of the selling corporation can demand appraisal rights.

Potential Liability in Purchases of Assets

RECALL In a merger or consolidation, the surviving corporation inherits the disappearing corporation's rights *and* obligations.

Generally, a corporation that purchases the assets of another corporation is not responsible for the liabilities of the selling corporation. Exceptions to this rule are made in certain circumstances, however. In any of the following situations, the acquiring corporation will be held to have assumed *both* the assets and the liabilities of the selling corporation.

1 When the purchasing corporation impliedly or expressly assumes the seller's liabilities.

2 When the sale amounts to what is in fact a merger or consolidation.

3 When the purchaser continues the seller's business and retains the same personnel (same shareholders, directors, and officers).

4 When the sale is fraudulently executed to escape liability.

Purchase of Stock and Tender Offers

TARGET CORPORATION
The corporation to be acquired in a corporate takeover; a corporation whose shareholders receive a tender offer.

TAKEOVER
The acquisition of control over a corporation through the purchase of a substantial number of the voting shares of the corporation.

TENDER OFFER
An offer to purchase made by one company directly to the shareholders of another (target) company; sometimes referred to as a *takeover bid.*

An alternative to the purchase of another corporation's assets is the purchase of a substantial number of the voting shares of its stock. This enables the acquiring corporation to control the **target corporation** (the corporation being acquired). The process of acquiring control over a corporation in this way is commonly referred to as a corporate **takeover.**

The acquiring corporation deals directly with the target company's shareholders in seeking to purchase the shares they hold. It does this by making a **tender offer** to all of the shareholders of the target corporation. The tender offer can be conditioned on receiving a specified number of shares by a certain date. The price offered is generally higher than the market price of the target corporation's stock prior to the announcement of the tender offer as a means of inducing shareholders to accept the offer. For instance, in the 2006 merger of AT&T and BellSouth, BellSouth shareholders reportedly received approximately $37.09 per share—a 16 percent premium over the market price of the stock. Federal securities laws strictly control the terms, duration, and circumstances under which most tender offers are made.

---

14. If the acquiring corporation plans to pay for the assets with its own corporate stock and not enough authorized unissued shares are available, the shareholders must vote to approve the issuance of additional shares by amendment of the corporate articles. Additionally, acquiring corporations whose stock is traded on a national stock exchange can be required to obtain their own shareholders' approval if they plan to issue a significant number of shares, such as a number equal to 20 percent or more of the outstanding shares.

A firm may respond to a tender offer in numerous ways. Sometimes, a target firm's board of directors will see a tender offer as favorable and will recommend to the shareholders that they accept it. To resist a takeover, a target company can make a *self-tender*, which is an offer to acquire stock from its own shareholders and thereby retain corporate control. Alternatively, a target corporation might resort to one of several other defensive tactics to resist a takeover (see Exhibit 28–8). In one commonly used tactic, known as a "poison pill," a target company gives its shareholders rights to purchase additional shares at low prices when there is a takeover attempt. The use of poison pills is an attempt to prevent takeovers by making a takeover prohibitively expensive.

TERMINATION

The termination of a corporation's existence has two phases—dissolution and winding up. **Dissolution** is the legal death of the artificial "person" of the corporation. *Winding up* is the process by which corporate assets are liquidated, or converted into cash and distributed among creditors and shareholders.[15]

Voluntary Dissolution

Dissolution can be brought about voluntarily by the directors and the shareholders. State incorporation statutes establish the required procedures to voluntarily dissolve a corporation. Basically, there are two possible methods: by the shareholders' unanimous vote to

DISSOLUTION
The formal disbanding of a partnership or a corporation. Dissolution of a corporation can take place by (1) an act of the state legislature, (2) agreement of the shareholders and the board of directors, (3) the expiration of a time period stated in the certificate of incorporation, or (4) court order.

---

15. Some prefer to call this phase *liquidation*, but we use the term *winding up* to mean all acts needed to bring the legal and financial affairs of the business to an end, including liquidating the assets and distributing them among creditors and shareholders. See RMBCA 14.05.

EXHIBIT 28–8	**The Terminology of Takeover Defenses**
TERM	**DEFINITION**
Crown jewel	When threatened with a takeover, management makes the company less attractive to the acquiring corporation by selling the company's most valuable asset (the "crown jewel") to a third party.
Golden parachute	When a takeover is successful, top management is usually changed. With this in mind, a company may establish special termination or retirement benefits that must be paid to top managers if they are "retired." In other words, a departing high-level manager's parachute will be "golden" when he or she is forced to "bail out" of the company.
Greenmail	To regain control, a target company may pay a higher-than-market price to repurchase the stock that the acquiring corporation bought. When a takeover is attempted through a gradual accumulation of target stock rather than a tender offer, the intent may be to induce the target company to buy back the shares at a premium price—a concept similar to blackmail.
Pac-Man	Named after the Atari video game, this is an aggressive defense in which the target corporation attempts its own takeover of the acquiring corporation.
Poison pill	The target corporation issues to its stockholders rights to purchase additional shares at low prices when there is a takeover attempt. This makes the takeover undesirably or even prohibitively expensive for the acquiring corporation.
White knight	The target corporation solicits a merger with a third party, which then makes a better (often simply a higher) tender offer to the target's shareholders. The third party that "rescues" the target is the "white knight."

initiate dissolution proceedings[16] or by a proposal of the board of directors that is submitted to the shareholders at a shareholders' meeting. When a corporation is dissolved voluntarily, the corporation must file *articles of dissolution* with the state and notify its creditors of the dissolution. The corporation must also establish a date (at least 120 days following the date of dissolution) by which all claims against the corporation must be received [RMBCA 14.06].

Involuntary Dissolution

Because corporations are creatures of statute, the state can also dissolve a corporation in certain circumstances. The secretary of state or the state attorney general can bring an action to dissolve a corporation that has failed to pay its annual taxes or to submit required annual reports, for example. A state court can also dissolve a corporation that has engaged in *ultra vires* acts or committed fraud or misrepresentation to the state during incorporation.

Sometimes, a shareholder or a group of shareholders petitions a court for corporate dissolution. A court may dissolve a corporation if the controlling shareholders or directors have engaged in fraudulent, illegal, or oppressive conduct. ▐**EXAMPLE 28.8** Mt. Princeton Trout Club, Inc. (MPTC), was formed to own land in Colorado and provide fishing and other recreational benefits to its shareholders. The articles of incorporation prohibited MPTC from selling or leasing any of the property and assets of the corporation without the approval of a majority of the directors. Despite this provision, MPTC officers entered into leases and contracts to sell corporate property without even notifying the directors. When a shareholder, Sam Colt, petitioned for dissolution, the court dissolved MPTC based on a finding that its officers had engaged in illegal, oppressive, and fraudulent conduct.[17] ▐

Shareholders may also petition a court for dissolution when the board of directors is deadlocked. Courts hesitate to order involuntary dissolution in such situations unless there is specific statutory authorization to do so. In the following case, the issue was whether the circumstances satisfied the statutory requirements for a court to dissolve a trucking corporation.

---

16. See, for example, Delaware Code Section 275(c). Not every state allows shareholders to initiate corporate dissolution, however.
17. *Colt v. Mt. Princeton Trout Club, Inc.*, 78 P.3d 1115 (Colo.App. 2003).

▐ **CASE 28.4**   **Sartori v. S & S Trucking, Inc.**

Supreme Court of Montana, 2006 MT 164, 332 Mont. 503, 139 P.3d 806 (2006).

FACTS Tony Stacy approached his friend, Justin Sartori, about buying a trucking business and operating it together. Sartori agreed, and because he had a good credit standing and Stacy did not, Sartori borrowed $78,493.68 from First Interstate Bank in Eureka, Montana, to buy the business. In September 2003, they formed S & S Trucking, Inc., and agreed to be its only directors, officers, and shareholders, with each owning an equal number of shares. Within weeks, however, they realized that they were incompatible. For example, Sartori often did not appear when and where Stacy expected, and they differed over the payment of earnings from S & S's income. In October,

Sartori incorporated Brimstone Enterprise to undermine S & S. He had S & S's mail forwarded to Brimstone, transferred S & S's licenses to Brimstone, and attempted to attract S & S's customers to Brimstone. In mid-November, he quit working for S & S and filed a suit in a Montana state court against S & S and Stacy, demanding that the firm be dissolved. The court set a deadline for the dissolution. The defendants appealed to the Montana Supreme Court.

ISSUE Can a court order the dissolution of a corporation without finding that the firm has suffered or is threatened with an injury?

CASE 28.4—Continued

DECISION Yes. The Montana Supreme Court affirmed the decision of the lower court, holding that the order for the dissolution of S & S was correct.

REASON The state supreme court pointed out that under Montana Code Section 35-1-938(2)(a), a court can dissolve a corporation in a proceeding by a shareholder if "the directors are deadlocked in the management of the corporate affairs, the shareholders are unable to break the deadlock, and irreparable injury to the corporation is threatened or being suffered or the business and affairs of the corporation can no longer be conducted to the advantage of the shareholders generally

because of the deadlock." The court conceded that S & S had not suffered an "irreparable injury," but reasoned that the deadlock between Sartori and Stacy had led Sartori to sabotage the corporation. "As a result, the business and affairs of S & S could no longer be conducted to the advantage of the shareholders."

 FOR CRITICAL ANALYSIS–Social Consideration *At the time of the defendants' appeal, S & S had twelve employees and, according to Stacy, its business was thriving. Should the court have taken these factors into consideration when deciding whether to order the dissolution of the firm? Why or why not?*

Winding Up

When dissolution takes place by voluntary action, the members of the board of directors act as trustees of the corporate assets. As trustees, they are responsible for winding up the affairs of the corporation for the benefit of corporate creditors and shareholders. This makes the board members personally liable for any breach of their fiduciary trustee duties.

When the dissolution is involuntary—or if board members do not wish to act as trustees of the assets—the court will appoint a **receiver** to wind up the corporate affairs and liquidate corporate assets. Courts may also appoint a receiver when shareholders or creditors can show that the board of directors should not be permitted to act as trustees of the corporate assets.

RECEIVER
In a corporate dissolution, a court-appointed person who winds up corporate affairs and liquidates corporate assets.

REVIEWING **Corporate Formation, Merger, and Termination**

In November 2002, Mario Bonsetti and Rico Sanchez incorporated Gnarly Vulcan Gear, Inc. (GVG), to manufacture windsurfing equipment. Bonsetti owned 60 percent and Sanchez owned 40 percent of the corporation's stock, and both men served on the board of directors. In January 2005, Hula Boards, Inc., owned solely by Mai Jin Li, made a public offer to Bonsetti and Sanchez to buy GVG stock. Hula offered 30 percent more than the market price per share for the GVG stock, and Bonsetti and Sanchez each sold 20 percent of their stock to Hula. Jin Li became the third member of the GVG board of directors. In April 2007, an irreconcilable dispute arose between Bonsetti and Sanchez over design modifications of their popular Baked Chameleon board. Despite Bonsetti's dissent, Sanchez and Jin Li voted to

merge GVG with Hula Boards under the latter name. Gnarly Vulcan Gear was dissolved, and production of the Baked Chameleon ceased. Using the information presented in the chapter, answer the following questions.

1 What rights does Bonsetti have (in most states) as a minority shareholder dissenting to the merger of GVG and Hula Boards?

2 Could the parties have used a short-form merger procedure in this situation? Why or why not?

3 What is the term used for Hula's offer to purchase GVG stock?

4 Suppose that after the merger, a person who was injured on the Baked Chameleon board sued Hula (the surviving corporation). Can Hula be held liable for the injury? Why or why not?

APPLICATION | **How Can Online Services Facilitate the Incorporation Process?***

Today, just about any-body can form a corporation for any lawful purpose in any state. The requirements differ from state to state. You do not even have to form your corporation in the state where you live or the state where you are doing business. In fact, many individuals form their corporations in the state of Delaware because it has the fewest legal restrictions on corporate formation and operation. Today, Delaware is also the state most often chosen for incorporation via the Internet, often through online companies that offer incorporation services.

Finding Information on Incorporation Requirements

Nearly every state has a Web site at which you can find the individual state's requirements for incorporation. (To locate your state's Web site, go to **www.statelocalgov.net**.) Most state sites post guidelines or instructions on forming corporations (and other business entities), fee schedules, and frequently asked questions (FAQs). Many also provide downloadable corporate forms.

In addition, hundreds of companies now provide incorporation services online, and you can obtain a great deal of information at their Web sites. For example, at the Web site of The Company Corporation (TCC) of Delaware (**www. corporate.com**), you can read about the advantages and costs of incorporating in your state or any other state, as well as the pros and cons of the different types of corporate entities. Similar information is available via an online seminar at the Web site of Harvard Business Services, Inc. (**www.delawareinc.com**). In addition, this site provides free downloadable forms and will act as the corporation's registered agent for a fixed annual fee of $50.

Another useful site is that of the Corporation Service Company (CSC) (**www.incspot.com/public**), which has more than a hundred years' experience in forming corporations. In addition to the standard services, CSC will scan and upload documents related to any corporate transaction or litigation into an online database. This service provides centralized access to important documents for authorized users anywhere in the world and allows multiple parties to track ongoing negotiations.

Incorporating Online

If you wish to incorporate via an online incorporation service, all you need to do is fill out a form online. For example, if you fill out the incorporation forms at the TCC Web site, TCC will then file the forms with the appropriate state office and obtain the state's authorization of the corporation for you. You can also arrange for the online incorporation service to perform other services such as acting as registered agent for your corporation, obtaining a tax identification number, and registering a domain name for your business.

CHECKLIST OF FACTORS TO CONSIDER WHEN INCORPORATING ONLINE OR OFFLINE

1 Determine how important the state of incorporation is to your business.
2 Decide which state's incorporation requirements and restrictions best suit the needs of your business.
3 Find out not only the initial cost of incorporation but also any continuing costs, such as annual fees and possible fees for attorneys and accountants.
4 Learn what formalities are necessary and the amount of record keeping that will be required.
5 Is "do-it-yourself" online incorporation appropriate? (Depending on the nature and potential growth of your business, you may decide to contact an attorney who can take you through the necessary steps in incorporating your business.)

* This *Application* is not meant to substitute for the services of an attorney who is licensed to practice law in your state.

KEY TERMS

alien corporation 776
appraisal right 793
articles of incorporation 779

bond 788
bond indenture 788
bylaws 780

close corporation 777
commingle 786
common stock 788

CHAPTER SUMMARY Corporate Formation, Merger, and Termination

The Nature and Classification of Corporations
(See pages 771–779.)

A corporation is a legal entity distinct from its owners. Formal statutory requirements, which vary somewhat from state to state, must be followed in forming a corporation.

1. *Corporate parties*—The shareholders own the corporation. They elect a board of directors to govern the corporation. The board of directors hires corporate officers and other employees to run the daily business of the firm.

2. *Corporate taxation*—The corporation pays income tax on net profits; shareholders pay income tax on the disbursed dividends that they receive from the corporation (double-taxation feature).

3. *Torts and criminal acts*—The corporation is liable for the torts committed by its agents or officers within the course and scope of their employment (under the doctrine of *respondeat superior*). In some circumstances, a corporation can be held liable (and be fined) for the criminal acts of its agents and employees. In certain situations, corporate officers may be held personally liable for corporate crimes.

4. *Domestic, foreign, and alien corporations*—A corporation is referred to as a *domestic corporation* within its home state (the state in which it incorporates). A corporation is referred to as a *foreign corporation* by any state that is not its home state. A corporation is referred to as an *alien corporation* if it originates in another country but does business in the United States.

5. *Public and private corporations*—A public corporation is one formed by a government (for example, cities, towns, and public projects). A private corporation is one formed wholly or in part for private benefit. Most corporations are private corporations.

6. *Nonprofit corporations*—Corporations formed without a profit-making purpose (for example, charitable, educational, and religious organizations and hospitals).

7. *Close corporations*—Corporations owned by a family or a relatively small number of individuals. Transfer of shares is usually restricted, and the corporation cannot make a public offering of its securities.

8. *S corporations*—Small domestic corporations (must have no more than one hundred shareholders) that, under Subchapter S of the Internal Revenue Code, are given special tax treatment. These corporations allow shareholders to enjoy the limited legal liability of the corporate form but avoid its double-taxation feature (shareholders pay taxes on the income at personal income tax rates, and the S corporation is not taxed separately).

9. *Professional corporations*—Corporations formed by professionals (for example, doctors and lawyers) to obtain the benefits of incorporation (such as tax benefits and limited liability). In most situations, the professional corporation is treated like other corporations, but sometimes the courts will disregard the corporate form and treat the shareholders as partners.

(Continued)

CHAPTER SUMMARY Corporate Formation, Merger, and Termination–Continued

Corporate Powers (See pages 779–780.)	1. *Express powers*—The express powers of a corporation are granted by the following laws and documents (listed according to their priority): federal constitution, state constitutions, state statutes, articles of incorporation, bylaws, and resolutions of the board of directors. 2. *Implied powers*—Barring express constitutional, statutory, or other prohibitions, the corporation has the implied power to do all acts reasonably appropriate and necessary to accomplish its corporate purposes. 3. *Ultra vires doctrine*—Any act of a corporation that is beyond its express or implied powers to undertake is an *ultra vires* act. The corporation (or shareholders on behalf of the corporation) may sue to enjoin or recover damages for *ultra vires* acts of corporate officers or directors. In addition, the state attorney general may bring an action either to obtain an injunction against the transaction or to institute dissolution proceedings against the corporation for the *ultra vires* acts.

Corporate Formation
(See pages 781–785.)
	1. *Promotional activities*—Preliminary promotional activities are rarely if ever taken today. A person who enters contracts with investors and others on behalf of the future corporation is personally liable on all preincorporation contracts. Liability remains until the corporation is formed and assumes the contract by novation.
	
	2. *Incorporation procedures*—Exact procedures for incorporation differ among states, but the basic steps are as follows: (a) select a state of incorporation, (b) secure the corporate name by confirming its availability, (c) prepare the articles of incorporation, and (d) file the articles of incorporation with the secretary of state accompanied by payment of the specified fees.
	
	  a. The articles of incorporation must include the corporate name, the number of shares of stock the corporation is authorized to issue, the registered office and agent, and the names and addresses of the incorporators. The articles may (but are not required to) include additional information about the corporation's nature and purpose, a statement limiting its duration (a corporation has perpetual existence unless the articles state otherwise), and specifics on its internal organization.
	
	  b. The state's filing of the articles of incorporation (corporate charter) authorizes the corporation to conduct business.
	
	  c. The first organizational meeting is held after incorporation. The board of directors is elected, and other business is completed (for example, adopting bylaws and authorizing the issuance of shares).

Corporate Status (See pages 785–788.)	1. *De jure or de facto corporation*—If a corporation has been improperly incorporated, the courts will sometimes impute corporate status to the firm by holding that it is a *de jure* corporation (cannot be challenged by the state or third persons) or a *de facto* corporation (can be challenged by the state but not by third persons). 2. *Corporation by estoppel*—If a firm is neither a *de jure* nor a *de facto* corporation but represents itself to be a corporation and is sued as such by a third party, it may be held to be a corporation by estoppel. 3. *Disregarding the corporate entity*—To avoid injustice, courts may "pierce the corporate veil" and hold a shareholder or shareholders personally liable for a judgment against the corporation. This usually occurs only when the corporation was established to circumvent the law, when the corporate form is used for an illegitimate or fraudulent purpose, or when the controlling shareholder commingles his or her own interests with those of the corporation to such an extent that the corporation no longer has a separate identity.
Corporate Financing–Bonds (See page 788.)	Corporate bonds are securities representing *corporate debt*—money borrowed by a corporation. See Exhibit 28–3 on page 789 for a description of the various types of corporate bonds.

CHAPTER SUMMARY	**Corporate Formation, Merger, and Termination–Continued**
Corporate Financing–Stocks (See pages 788–790.)	Stocks are equity securities issued by a corporation that represent the purchase of ownership in the business firm. Exhibit 28–4 on page 789 describes how stocks differ from bonds, and Exhibit 28–5 on page 790 describes the various types of stocks issued by corporations, including the two main types—common stock and preferred stock.
Merger and Consolidation (See pages 791–793.)	1. *Merger*—The legal combination of two or more corporations, with the result that the surviving corporation acquires all the assets and obligations of the other corporation, which then ceases to exist. 2. *Consolidation*—The legal combination of two or more corporations, with the result that each corporation ceases to exist and a new one emerges. The new corporation assumes all the assets and obligations of the former corporations. 3. *Procedure*—Determined by state statutes. Basic requirements are as follows: a. The board of directors of each corporation involved must approve the merger or consolidation plan. b. The shareholders of each corporation must approve the merger or consolidation plan at a shareholders' meeting. c. Articles of merger or consolidation (the plan) must be filed, usually with the secretary of state. d. The state issues a certificate of merger (or consolidation) to the surviving (or newly consolidated) corporation. 4. *Short-form merger (parent-subsidiary merger)*—Possible when the parent corporation owns at least 90 percent of the outstanding shares of each class of stock of the subsidiary corporation. a. Shareholder approval is not required. b. The merger must be approved only by the board of directors of the parent corporation. c. A copy of the merger plan must be sent to each shareholder of record of the subsidiary corporation. d. The merger plan must be filed with the state. 5. *Appraisal rights*—Rights of dissenting shareholders (given by state statute) to receive the *fair value* for their shares when a merger or consolidation takes place.
Purchase of Assets or Stock (See pages 794–795.)	A purchase of assets occurs when one corporation acquires all or substantially all of the assets of another corporation. A purchase of stock occurs when one corporation acquires a substantial number of the voting shares of the stock of another (target) corporation. 1. *Acquiring corporation*—The acquiring (purchasing) corporation is not required to obtain shareholder approval; the corporation is merely increasing its assets, and no fundamental business change occurs. 2. *Acquired corporation*—The acquired (purchased) corporation is required to obtain the approval of both its directors and its shareholders for the sale of its assets, because the sale will substantially change the corporation's business position. 3. *Tender offer*—A public offer to all shareholders of the target corporation to purchase its stock at a price that is generally higher than the market price of the target stock prior to the announcement of the tender offer. Federal and state securities laws strictly control the terms, duration, and circumstances under which most tender offers are made. 4. *Target responses*—Target corporations may respond to takeover bids in various ways, including a self-tender (the target firm's offer to acquire its own shareholders' stock) and the strategies listed in Exhibit 28–8 on page 795.

CHAPTER SUMMARY Corporate Formation, Merger, and Termination–Continued

Termination (See pages 795–797.)	The termination of a corporation involves the following two phases:
	1. *Dissolution*—The legal death of the artificial "person" of the corporation. Dissolution can be brought about voluntarily by the directors and shareholders or involuntarily by the state or through a court order.
	2. *Winding up (liquidation)*—The process by which corporate assets are converted into cash and distributed to creditors and shareholders according to specified rules of preference. May be supervised by members of the board of directors (when dissolution is voluntary) or by a receiver appointed by the court to wind up corporate affairs.

FOR REVIEW

Answers for the even-numbered questions in this **For Review** *section can be found in Appendix E at the end of this text.*

1 What steps are involved in bringing a corporation into existence? Who is liable for preincorporation contracts?

2 What is the difference between a *de jure* corporation and a *de facto* corporation?

3 In what circumstances might a court disregard the corporate entity ("pierce the corporate veil") and hold the shareholders personally liable?

4 What are the four steps of the merger or consolidation procedure?

5 What are the two ways in which a corporation can be voluntarily dissolved? Under what circumstances might a corporation be involuntarily dissolved by state action?

 The following multiple-choice question is representative of the types of questions available in one of the four sections of ThomsonNOW for *Business Law Today.* **ThomsonNOW also provides feedback for each response option, whether correct or incorrect, and refers to the location within the chapter where the correct answer can be found.**

In corporate law, when a corporation acts beyond the scope of its authority, it is said to

a engage in *respondeat superior.*

b pierce the corporate veil.

c hide the corporate veil.

d engage in *ultra vires* transactions.

QUESTIONS AND CASE PROBLEMS

 **HYPOTHETICAL SCENARIOS**

28.1 Corporate Status. Three brothers inherited a small paper-supply business from their father, who had operated the business as a sole proprietorship. The brothers decided to incorporate under the name of Gomez Corp. and retained an attorney to draw up the necessary documents. The attorney drew up the papers and had the brothers sign them but neglected to file the articles of incorporation with the secretary of state's office. The brothers assumed that all necessary legal work had been completed, so they proceeded to do business as Gomez Corp. One day, a Gomez Corp. employee, while making a delivery to one of Gomez's customers, negligently ran a red light and caused an accident. Baxter, the driver of the other vehicle, was injured as a result and sued Gomez Corp. for damages. Baxter then learned that no state authorization had ever been issued to Gomez Corp., so he sued each of the brothers personally for damages. Can the brothers avoid personal liability for the tort of their employee? Explain.

28.2 Hypothetical Question with Sample Answer. Jolson is the chair of the board of directors of Artel, Inc., and Douglas is the chair of the board of directors of Fox Express, Inc. Artel is a manufacturing corporation, and Fox Express is a transportation corporation. Jolson and Douglas meet to consider the possibility of combining their corporations and activities into a single corporate entity. They consider two alternative courses of action: Artel could acquire all of the stock and assets of Fox Express, or the corporations could combine to form a new corporation, called A&F Enterprises, Inc. Both Jolson and Douglas are concerned about the necessity of a formal transfer of property, liability for existing debts, and the need to amend the articles of incorporation. Discuss what the two proposed combinations are called and the legal effect each has on the transfer of property, the liabili-

ties of the combined corporations, and the need to amend the articles of incorporation.

 For a sample answer to Question 28.2, go to Appendix F at the end of this text.

28.3 Corporate Powers. Kora Nayenga and two business associates formed a corporation called Nayenga Corp. for the purpose of selling computer services. Kora, who owned 50 percent of the corporate shares, served as the corporation's president. Kora wished to obtain a personal loan from his bank for $250,000, but the bank required the note to be cosigned by a third party. Kora cosigned the note in the name of the corporation. Later, Kora defaulted on the note, and the bank sued the corporation for payment. The corporation asserted, as a defense, that Kora had exceeded his authority when he cosigned the note. Had he? Explain.

 **CASE PROBLEMS**

28.4 Torts and Criminal Acts. Greg Allen is an employee, a shareholder, a director, and the president of Greg Allen Construction Co. In 1996, Daniel and Sondra Estelle hired Allen's firm to renovate a home they owned in Ladoga, Indiana. To finance the cost, they obtained a line of credit from Banc One, Indiana, which required periodic inspections to disburse funds. Allen was on the job every day and supervised all of the work. He designed all of the structural changes, including a floor system for the bedroom over the living room, the floor system of the living room, and the stairway to the second floor. He did all of the electrical, plumbing, and carpentry work and installed all of the windows. He did most of the drywall taping and finishing and most of the painting. The Estelles found much of this work to be unacceptable, and the bank's inspector agreed that it was of poor quality. When Allen failed to act on the Estelles' complaints, they filed a suit in an Indiana state court against Allen Construction and Allen personally, alleging, in part, that his individual work on the project was negligent. Can both Allen and his corporation be held liable for this tort? Explain. [*Greg Allen Construction Co. v. Estelle*, 798 N.E.2d 171 (Ind. 2003)]

28.5 Purchase of Assets. Paradise Pools, Inc. (PPI), also known as "Paradise Pools and Spas," was incorporated in 1981. In 1994, PPI entered into a contract with Bromanco, Inc., to build a pool in Vicksburg, Mississippi, as part of a Days Inn Hotel project being developed by Amerihost Development, Inc. PPI built the pool, but Bromanco, the general contractor, defaulted on other parts of the project, so Amerihost completed the construction itself. Litigation ensued in Mississippi state courts, and Amerihost was awarded $12,656.46 against PPI. Meanwhile, Paradise Corp. (PC)

was incorporated in 1995 with the same management as PPI, but different shareholders. PC acquired PPI's assets in 1996, without assuming its liabilities, and soon became known as "Paradise Pools and Spas." Amerihost obtained a writ of garnishment against PC to enforce the judgment against PPI. PC filed a motion to dismiss the writ on the basis that it was "not a party to the proceeding." Should the court dismiss the case? Why or why not? [*Paradise Corp. v. Amerihost Development, Inc.*, 848 So.2d 177 (Miss. 2003)]

28.6 Case Problem with Sample Answer. Thomas Persson and Jon Nokes founded Smart Inventions, Inc., in 1991 to market household consumer products. The success of their first product, the Smart Mop, continued with later products, which were sold through infomercials and other means. Persson and Nokes were the firm's officers and equal shareholders, with Persson responsible for product development and Nokes operating the day-to-day activities. By 1998, they had become dissatisfied with each other's efforts. Nokes represented the firm as financially "dying," "in a grim state, . . . worse than ever," and offered to buy all of Persson's shares for $1.6 million. Persson accepted. On the day that they signed the agreement to transfer the shares, Smart Inventions began marketing a new product—the Tap Light, which was an instant success, generating millions of dollars in revenues. In negotiating with Persson, Nokes had intentionally kept the Tap Light a secret. Persson filed a suit in a California state court against Smart Inventions and others, asserting fraud and other claims. Under what principle might Smart Inventions be liable for Nokes's fraud? Is Smart Inventions liable in this case? Explain. [*Persson v. Smart Inventions, Inc.*, 125 Cal.App.4th 1141, 23 Cal.Rptr.3d 335 (2 Dist. 2005)]

After you have answered Problem 28.6, compare your answer with the sample answer given on the Web site that accompanies this text. Go to www.thomsonedu.com/westbuslaw/blt, select "Chapter 28," and click on "Case Problem with Sample Answer."

28.7 Corporate Powers. InterBel Telephone Co-operative, Inc., is a Montana corporation organized under the Montana Rural Electric and Telephone Cooperative Act. This statute limits the purposes of such corporations to providing "adequate telephone service," but adds that this "enumeration . . . shall not be deemed to exclude like or similar objects, purposes, powers, manners, methods, or things." Mooseweb Corp. is an Internet service provider that has been owned and operated by Fred Weber since 1996. Mooseweb provides Web site hosting, modems, computer installation, technical support, and dial-up access to customers in Lincoln County, Montana. InterBel began to offer Internet service in 1999, competing with Mooseweb in Lincoln County. Weber filed a suit in a Montana state court against InterBel, alleging that its Internet service was *ultra vires.* Both parties filed motions for summary judgment. In whose favor should the court rule, and why? [*Weber v. InterBel Telephone Co-operative, Inc.,* 2003 MT 320, 318 Mont. 295, 80 P.3d 88 (2003)]

28.8 Purchase of Assets. In January 1999, General Star Indemnity Co. agreed to insure Indianapolis Racing League (IRL) racecars against damage during on-track accidents. In connection with the insurance, General Star deposited $400,000 with G Force LLC (GFCO), a Colorado firm, to enable it to buy and provide, without delay, parts for damaged cars. GFCO agreed to return any unspent funds. Near the end of the season, Elan Motorsports Technologies (EMT) acquired GFCO. In 2000, EMT incorporated G Force LLC in Georgia (GFGA), and GFCO ceased to exist. GFGA renewed the arrangement with General Star and engaged in the same operations as GFCO, but EMT employees conducted GFGA's business at EMT's offices. In 2002, EMT assumed ownership of GFGA's assets and continued the business. EMT also assumed GFGA's liabilities, except for the obligation to return General Star's unspent funds. General Star filed a suit in a Georgia state court against EMT, seeking to recover its deposit. What is the rule concerning the liability of a corporation that buys the assets of another? Are there exceptions? Which principles apply in this case? Explain. [*General Star Indemnity Co. v. Elan Motorsports Technologies, Inc.,* 356 F.Supp.2d 1333 (N.D.Ga. 2004)]

28.9 Dissolution. Clara Mahaffey operated Mahaffey's Auto Salvage, Inc., in Dayton, Ohio, as a sole proprietorship. In 1993, Kenneth Stumpff and Mahaffey's son, Richard Harris, joined the firm. Stumpff ran the wrecker and bought the vehicles for salvage. Harris handled the day-to-day operations and the bookkeeping. They became the company's equal 50 percent shareholders on Mahaffey's death in 2002. Harris, who inherited the land on which the firm was located, increased the rent to $1,500 per month. Within two years of Mahaffey's death, and without consulting Stumpff, Harris raised the rent to $2,500. Stumpff's wife died, and he took a leave of absence, during which the company paid him $2,500 a month and provided health insurance. After two years, Harris stopped the payments, discontinued the health benefits, and fired Stumpff, threatening to call the police if he came on the premises. Stumpff withdrew $16,000 from the firm's account, leaving a balance of $113. Harris offered to buy Stumpff's interest in the business, but Stumpff refused and filed a suit in an Ohio state court against Harris. A state statute permits the dissolution of a corporation if the owners are deadlocked in its management. Should the court order the dissolution of Mahaffey's? Why or why not? [*Stumpff v. Harris,* __ N.E.2d __, __ Ohio App.3d __ (2 Dist. 2006)]

28.10 A Question of Ethics. In 1990, *American Design Properties, Inc. (ADP), leased premises at 8604 Olive Boulevard in St. Louis County, Missouri. Under the lease agreement, ADP had the right to terminate the lease on 120 days' written notice, but it did not have the right to sublease the premises without the lessor's (landowner's) consent. ADP had no bank account, no employees, and no funds. ADP had never filed an income tax return or held a directors' or shareholders' meeting. In fact, ADP's only business was to collect and pay the exact amount of rent due under the lease. American Design Group, Inc. (ADG), a wholesale distributor of jewelry and other merchandise, actually occupied 8604 Olive Boulevard. J. H. Blum owned ADG and was an officer and director of both ADG and ADP. Blum's husband, Marvin, was an officer of ADG and signed the lease as an officer of ADP. Marvin's former son-in-law, Matthew Smith, was a salaried employee of ADG, an officer of ADG, and an officer and director of ADP. In 1995, Nusrala Four, Inc. (later known as Real Estate Investors Four, Inc.), purchased the property at 8604 Olive Boulevard and became the lessor. No one told Nusrala that ADG was the occupant of the premises leased by ADP. ADP continued to pay the rent until November 1998, when Smith paid with a check drawn on ADG's account. No more payments were made. On February 26, 1999, Marvin sent Nusrala a note that read, "We have vacated the property at 8604 Olive," which, Nusrala discovered, had been damaged. Nusrala filed a suit in a Missouri state court against ADG and ADP, seeking compensation for the damage. In view of these facts, consider the following questions.* [*Real Estate Investors Four, Inc. v. American Design Group, Inc.,* 46 S.W.3d 51 (Mo.App. E.D. 2001)]

1 Given that ADG had not signed the lease and was not rightfully a sublessee, could ADG be held liable, at least in part, for the damage to the premises? Under what theory might the court ignore the separate corporate identities of ADG and ADP? If you were the judge, how would you rule in this case?

2 Assuming that ADP had few, if any, corporate assets, would it be fair to preclude Nusrala from recovering compensation for the damage from ADG?

3 Is it ever appropriate for a court to ignore the corporate structure? Why or why not?

CRITICAL THINKING AND WRITING ASSIGNMENTS

28.11 Critical Legal Thinking. What are some of the ways in which the limited liability of corporate shareholders serves the public interest? Are there any ways in which this limited liability is harmful to the public interest? Explain.

28.12 **Video Question.** Go to this text's Web site at **www.thomsonedu.com/westbuslaw/blt** and select "Chapter 28." Click on "Video Questions" and view the video titled *Corporation or LLC: Which Is Better?* Then answer the following questions.

1 Compare the liability that Anna and Caleb would be exposed to as shareholders/owners of a corporation versus as members of a limited liability company (LLC).

2 How does the taxation of corporations differ from that of LLCs?

3 Given that Anna and Caleb conduct their business (Wizard Internet) over the Internet, can you think of any drawbacks to forming an LLC?

4 If you were in the position of Anna and Caleb, would you choose to create a corporation or an LLC? Why?

PRACTICAL INTERNET EXERCISES

Go to this text's Web site at **www.thomsonedu.com/westbuslaw/blt**, select "Chapter 28," and click on "Practical Internet Exercises." There you will find the following Internet research exercises that you can perform to learn more about the topics covered in this chapter.

PRACTICAL INTERNET EXERCISE 28–1 LEGAL PERSPECTIVE—Mergers

PRACTICAL INTERNET EXERCISE 28–2 MANAGEMENT PERSPECTIVE—Online Incorporation

BEFORE THE TEST

Go to this text's Web site at **www.thomsonedu.com/westbuslaw/blt**, select "Chapter 28," and click on "Interactive Quizzes." You will find a number of interactive questions relating to this chapter.

CHAPTER 29
Corporate Directors, Officers, and Shareholders

> **"They [corporations] cannot commit treason, nor be outlawed nor excommunicated, because they have no soul."**
>
> Sir Edward Coke, 1552–1634
> (English jurist and legal scholar)

CHAPTER OUTLINE

- ROLES OF DIRECTORS AND OFFICERS
- DUTIES AND LIABILITIES OF DIRECTORS AND OFFICERS
- ROLE OF SHAREHOLDERS
- RIGHTS OF SHAREHOLDERS
- DUTIES AND LIABILITIES OF SHAREHOLDERS
- MAJOR BUSINESS FORMS COMPARED

LEARNING OBJECTIVES

AFTER READING THIS CHAPTER, YOU SHOULD BE ABLE TO ANSWER THE FOLLOWING QUESTIONS:

1 What are the duties of corporate directors and officers?

2 Directors are expected to use their best judgment in managing the corporation. What must directors do to avoid liability for honest mistakes of judgment and poor business decisions?

3 What is a voting proxy? What is cumulative voting?

4 If a group of shareholders perceives that the corporation has suffered a wrong and the directors refuse to take action, can the shareholders compel the directors to act? If so, how?

5 From what sources may dividends be paid legally? In what circumstances is a dividend illegal? What happens if a dividend is illegally paid?

When Sir Edward Coke observed, in the chapter-opening quotation, that a corporation has no "soul," he was referring to the fact that a corporation is not a "natural" person but a legal fiction. No one individual shareholder or director bears sole responsibility for the corporation and its actions. Rather, a corporation joins the efforts and resources of a large number of individuals for the purpose of producing greater returns than those persons could have obtained individually.

Sometimes, actions that benefit the corporation as a whole do not coincide with the separate interests of the individuals making up the corporation. In such situations, it is important to know the rights and duties of all participants in the corporate enterprise. This chapter focuses on the rights and duties of directors, officers, and shareholders and the ways in which conflicts among them are resolved.

ROLES OF DIRECTORS AND OFFICERS

Every business corporation is governed by a board of directors. A director occupies a position of responsibility unlike that of other corporate personnel. Directors are sometimes inappropriately characterized as *agents* because they act on behalf of the corporation. No *individual* director, however, can act as an agent to bind the corporation; and as a group, directors collectively control the corporation in a way that no agent is able to control a principal. Directors are also often incorrectly characterized as *trustees* because they occupy positions of trust and control over the corporation. Unlike trustees, however, they do not own or hold title to property for the use and benefit of others.

Few legal requirements exist concerning directors' qualifications. Only a handful of states impose minimum age and residency requirements. A director may be a shareholder, but this is not necessary, unless required by statute or by the corporate articles or bylaws.

Election of Directors

Subject to statutory limitations, the number of directors is set forth in the corporation's articles or bylaws. Historically, the minimum number of directors has been three, but today many states permit fewer. Indeed, the Revised Model Business Corporation Act (RMBCA), in Section 8.01, permits corporations with fewer than fifty shareholders to eliminate the board of directors.

Normally, the incorporators appoint the initial board of directors at the time the corporation is created, or the corporation itself names the directors in the articles. The first board serves until the first annual shareholders' meeting. Subsequent directors are elected by a majority vote of the shareholders.

The term of office for a director is usually one year—from annual meeting to annual meeting. Longer and staggered terms are permissible under most state statutes. A common practice is to elect one-third of the board members each year for a three-year term. In this way, there is greater management continuity.

Removal of Directors A director can be removed *for cause*—that is, for failing to perform a required duty—either as specified in the articles or bylaws or by shareholder action. Even the board of directors itself may be given power to remove a director for cause, subject to shareholder review. In most states, a director cannot be removed without cause unless the corporation has previously authorized such an action.

Whether shareholders should be able to remove a director without cause is part of an ongoing debate about the balance of power between a corporation and its shareholders. It was also the pivotal question at the heart of the battle for corporate control in the following case.

ON THE WEB

One of the best sources on the Web for information on corporations, including their directors, is the EDGAR database of the Securities and Exchange Commission at

www.sec.gov/edgar.shtml.

BE AWARE The articles of incorporation may provide that a director can be removed only for cause.

CASE 29.1 **Relational Investors, LLC v. Sovereign Bancorp, Inc.**

United States District Court, Southern District of New York, 417 F.Supp.2d 438 (2006).

FACTS In June 2004, Relational Investors, LLC, a Delaware corporation, began acquiring a significant number of shares of stock in Sovereign Bancorp, Inc., a Pennsylvania firm. By 2005, Relational held about 8 percent of Sovereign's stock and had become its largest shareholder. Relational expressed dissatisfaction with Sovereign's management and, in May, announced that it would seek representation on Sovereign's board at the next annual shareholders' meeting in April 2006. (Sovereign elects one-third of its six board members at each annual meeting.) Sovereign then announced that it would sell 19.8 percent of its stock for $2.4 billion to Santander Central Hispano, S.A., a bank incorporated under the laws of Spain. Relational responded that it intended to seek the removal of Sovereign's *entire* board at the next shareholders' meeting. Sovereign filed a suit in a federal district court against Relational, seeking a declaration that its directors could be removed only for cause. Relational filed a motion for judgment on the pleadings.

ISSUE Could Sovereign's shareholders remove its directors without cause?

CASE 29.1—Continues next page

CASE 29.1–Continued

DECISION Yes. The court granted Relational's motion for judgment on the pleadings, declaring that Sovereign's shareholders had the right to remove its directors without cause. "[T]he tension is * * * resolved in favor of shareholder autonomy."

REASON The court pointed out that "[a]t the time of Sovereign's incorporation in 1987, Pennsylvania law expressly provided for the removal of directors without cause." The court acknowledged that "as concerns about hostile corporate takeovers grew, several states began enacting legislation to limit the ability of shareholders to remove directors," and in 1989, Pennsylvania likewise "limit[ed] the ability of shareholders to remove directors without cause to situations where the company's charter and bylaws permitted such actions." In this case, Sovereign's articles of incorporation "clearly and unambiguously" allowed for directors to be

removed without cause. "Article Eighth [of Sovereign's articles of incorporation] provides, simply and clearly, that a majority vote of qualified shareholders may remove directors from office." Sovereign argued that because Article Eighth was adopted before Pennsylvania amended its law to restrict the removal of directors, the article "could not have been intended as an 'opt out' to the revised statute which thereafter provided for a presumption of removal only for cause." The court refused to accept this argument: "The plain language of Article Eighth, and an analysis of the law in effect at the time of its enactment in 1987, makes clear that the original Articles of Incorporation provided for removal without cause. The enactment of [the revised statute] did not alter this original intent."

 FOR CRITICAL ANALYSIS–Social Consideration *If you could dictate a corporation's rule with respect to the removal of its directors, what would you prescribe? Why?*

Vacancies on the Board of Directors Vacancies can occur on the board of directors if a director dies or resigns or if a new position is created through amendment of the articles or bylaws. In these situations, either the shareholders or the board itself can fill the position, depending on state law or on the provisions of the bylaws. Note, however, that even when the bylaws appear to authorize an election, a court can invalidate the election if the directors were attempting to diminish the shareholders' influence in it.

EXAMPLE 29.1 The bylaws of Liquid Audio, a Delaware corporation, authorized a board of five directors. Two directors on the board were elected each year. Another company had offered to buy all of Liquid Audio's stock, but the board of directors rejected this offer. An election was coming, and the directors feared that the shareholders would elect new directors who would allow the other company to purchase Liquid Audio's assets. The directors therefore amended the bylaws to increase the number of directors to seven, thereby diminishing the shareholders' influence in the vote. The shareholders filed an action challenging the election. The Delaware Supreme Court ruled that the directors' actions were illegal because they had attempted to diminish the shareholders' right to vote effectively in an election of directors.[1] ■

Board of Directors' Meetings

The board of directors conducts business by holding formal meetings with recorded minutes. The dates of regular meetings are usually established in the articles or bylaws or by board resolution, and no further notice is customarily required. Special meetings can be called, with notice sent to all directors.

Quorum requirements vary among jurisdictions. (A **quorum** is the minimum number of members of a body of officials or other group that must be present in order for business to be validly transacted.) Many states leave the decision as to quorum requirements to the corporate articles or bylaws. In the absence of specific state statutes, most states provide

QUORUM
The number of members of a decision-making body that must be present before business may be transacted.

---

1. *MM Companies, Inc. v. Liquid Audio, Inc.,* 813 A.2d 1118 (Del.Supr. 2003).

that a quorum is a majority of the number of directors authorized in the articles or bylaws. Voting is done in person (unlike voting at shareholders' meetings, which can be done by proxy, as discussed later in this chapter).[2] The rule is one vote per director. Ordinary matters generally require a simple majority vote; certain extraordinary issues may require a greater-than-majority vote.

Rights of Directors

A director of a corporation has a number of rights, including the rights of participation, inspection, compensation, and indemnification.

Participation and Inspection A corporate director must have certain rights to function properly in that position and make informed policy decisions for the company. The right to participation means that directors are entitled to participate in all board of directors' meetings and have a right to be notified of these meetings. As pointed out earlier in this chapter, the dates of regular board meetings are usually established by the bylaws or by board resolution, and no notice of these meetings is required. If special meetings are called, however, notice is required unless waived by the director.

A director must have access to all of the corporate books and records to make decisions and to exercise the necessary supervision over corporate officers and employees. This right of inspection is virtually absolute and cannot be restricted.

Compensation and Indemnification In the past, directors rarely were paid. Today, in contrast, corporate directors are often paid at least nominal sums and may receive more substantial compensation in large corporations because of the time, work, effort, and especially risk involved. Most states permit the corporate articles or bylaws to authorize compensation for directors; sometimes, the directors are allowed to set their own compensation. In many corporations, directors are also chief corporate officers (president or chief executive officer, for example) and receive compensation in their managerial positions. A director who is also an officer of the corporation is referred to as an **inside director,** whereas a director who does not hold a management position is an **outside director.** Directors also gain through indirect benefits, such as business contacts and prestige, and other rewards, such as stock options.

Corporate directors may become involved in lawsuits by virtue of their positions and their actions as directors. Most states (and RMBCA 8.51) permit a corporation to indemnify (guarantee reimbursement to) a director for legal costs, fees, and judgments involved in defending corporation-related suits. Many states specifically permit a corporation to purchase liability insurance for the directors and officers to cover indemnification. When the statutes are silent on this matter, the power to purchase such insurance is usually considered to be part of the corporation's implied powers.

INSIDE DIRECTOR
A person on the board of directors who is also an officer of the corporation.

OUTSIDE DIRECTOR
A person on the board of directors who does not hold a management position at the corporation.

Whenever businesspersons serve as corporate directors or officers, they should be aware that they may at some point become involved in litigation as a result of their positions. To protect against personal liability, a director or officer should take several steps. First, make sure that the corporate bylaws explicitly give directors and officers a right to indemnification (reimbursement) for any costs incurred as a result of litigation, as well as any judgments or settlements stemming from a lawsuit. Second, have the corporation purchase directors' and officers' liability insurance (D & O insurance). Having D & O insurance policies

PREVENTING LEGAL DISPUTES

---

2. Except in Louisiana, which allows a director to vote by proxy under certain circumstances.

enables the corporation to avoid paying the substantial costs involved in
defending a particular director or officer. The D & O policies offered by most
private insurance companies have maximum coverage limits, so make sure that
the corporation is required to indemnify directors and officers in the event
that the costs exceed the policy limits.

■

Directors' Management Responsibilities

Directors have responsibility for all policymaking decisions necessary to the management
of corporate affairs. Just as shareholders cannot act individually to bind the corporation,
the directors must act as a body in carrying out routine corporate business. The general
areas of responsibility of the board of directors include the following:

1 Declaration and payment of corporate dividends to shareholders.

2 Authorization for major corporate policy decisions—for example, the initiation of proceedings for the sale or lease of corporate assets outside the regular course of business,
the determination of new product lines, and the overseeing of major contract negotiations and major management-labor negotiations.

3 Appointment, supervision, and removal of corporate officers and other managerial
employees and the determination of their compensation.

4 Financial decisions, such as the decision to issue authorized shares and bonds.

CONTRAST Shareholders own a
corporation and directors make
policy decisions, but officers who
run the daily business of the
corporation often have significant
decision-making power.

In most states, the board of directors can delegate some of its functions to an executive
committee or to corporate officers. In doing so, the board is not relieved of its overall
responsibility for directing the affairs of the corporation, but corporate officers and managerial personnel are empowered to make decisions relating to ordinary, daily corporate
affairs within well-defined guidelines.

*Corporate executives discuss the
business of their firm. Can the same
person be both a director and an
officer of a corporation?* (John Terence
Turner/Getty Images)

Corporate Officers and Executives

Corporate officers and other executive employees are hired by the board of directors or,
in rare instances, by the shareholders. In addition to carrying out the duties articulated in
the bylaws, corporate and managerial officers act as agents of the corporation,
and the ordinary rules of agency (discussed in Chapter 24) normally apply to
their employment. The qualifications required of officers and executive
employees are determined at the discretion of the corporation and are
included in the articles or bylaws. In most states, a person can hold more than
one office and can be both an officer and a director of the corporation.

Corporate officers and other high-level managers are employees of the
company, so their rights are defined by employment contracts. The board of
directors, though, normally can remove corporate officers at any time with or
without cause and regardless of the terms of the employment contracts—
although in so doing, the corporation may be liable for breach of contract.
The duties of corporate officers are the same as those of directors because both
groups are involved in decision making and are in similar positions of control.
Hence, officers are viewed as having the same fiduciary duties of care and loyalty in their conduct of corporate affairs as directors have, a subject to which
we now turn.

DUTIES AND LIABILITIES OF DIRECTORS AND OFFICERS

Directors and officers are deemed *fiduciaries* of the corporation because their relationship with the corporation and its shareholders is one of trust and confidence. As fiduciaries, directors and officers owe ethical—and legal—duties to the corporation and to the shareholders as a whole. These fiduciary duties include the duty of care and the duty of loyalty.

Duty of Care

Directors and officers must exercise due care in performing their duties. The standard of *due care* has been variously described in judicial decisions and codified in many corporation codes. Generally, a director or officer is expected to act in good faith, to exercise the care that an ordinarily prudent person would exercise in similar circumstances, and to act in what he or she considers to be the best interests of the corporation [RMBCA 8.30]. Directors and officers who have not exercised the required duty of care can be held liable for the harms suffered by the corporation as a result of their negligence. (Directors and officers also have a duty not to destroy evidence in the event of a lawsuit involving the corporation. The *Application* feature at the end of this chapter discusses how due care can be exercised to preserve electronic evidence by creating an e-document-retention policy.)

Duty to Make Informed and Reasonable Decisions Directors and officers are expected to be informed on corporate matters. To be informed, the director or officer must do what is necessary to become informed: attend presentations, ask for information from those who have it, read reports, and review other written materials such as contracts. In other words, directors and officers must carefully study a situation and its alternatives before making a decision. Depending on the nature of the business, directors and officers are often expected to act in accordance with their own knowledge and training. Nevertheless, most states (and Section 8.30 of the RMBCA) allow a director to make decisions in reliance on information furnished by competent officers or employees, professionals such as attorneys and accountants, or even an executive committee of the board without being accused of acting in bad faith or failing to exercise due care if such information turns out to be faulty.

Directors are also expected to make reasonable decisions. For example, a director should not vote to approve a *merger* with only a moment's consideration and solely on the basis of the market price of the corporation's shares. As discussed in Chapter 28, a merger is the legal combination of two or more corporations into one entity.

Duty to Exercise Reasonable Supervision Directors are also expected to exercise a reasonable amount of supervision when they delegate work to corporate officers and employees. **EXAMPLE 29.2** Dale, a corporate bank director, fails to attend any board of directors' meetings for five years. In addition, Dale never inspects any of the corporate books or records and generally fails to supervise the efforts of the bank president and the loan committee. Meanwhile, Brennan, the bank president, who is a corporate officer, makes various improper loans and permits large overdrafts. In this situation, Dale (the corporate director) can be held liable to the corporation for losses resulting from the unsupervised actions of the bank president and the loan committee. ▣

Dissenting Directors Directors are expected to attend board of directors' meetings, and their votes should be entered into the minutes of the meetings. Unless a dissent is entered, the director is presumed to have assented. Directors who dissent are rarely held individually liable for mismanagement of the corporation. For this reason, a director who is absent from a given meeting sometimes registers with the secretary of the board a dissent to actions taken at the meeting.

Duty of Loyalty

Loyalty can be defined as faithfulness to one's obligations and duties. In the corporate context, the duty of loyalty requires directors and officers to subordinate their personal interests to the welfare of the corporation. Among other things, this means that directors may not use corporate funds or confidential corporate information for personal advantage. They must also refrain from self-dealing. For instance, a director should not oppose a tender offer that is in the corporation's best interest simply because its acceptance may cost the director her or his position. Cases dealing with fiduciary duty may involve one or more of the following:

1 Competing with the corporation.

2 Usurping (taking advantage of) a corporate opportunity.

3 Having an interest that conflicts with the interest of the corporation.

4 Engaging in insider trading (using information that is not public to make a profit trading securities, as discussed in Chapter 30).

5 Authorizing a corporate transaction that is detrimental to minority shareholders.

Conflicts of Interest

The duty of loyalty also requires officers and directors to *fully disclose* to the board of directors any potential conflict of interest that might arise in any corporate transaction. The various state statutes contain different standards, but a contract generally will *not* be voidable if all of the following are true: if the contract was fair and reasonable to the corporation at the time it was made, if there was a full disclosure of the interest of the officers or directors involved in the transaction, and if the contract was approved by a majority of the disinterested directors or shareholders.

     ■EXAMPLE 29.3 Southwood Corporation needs office space. Lambert Alden, one of its five directors, owns the building adjoining the corporation's main office building. He negotiates a lease with Southwood for the space, making a full disclosure to Southwood and the other four board directors. The lease arrangement is fair and reasonable, and it is unanimously approved by the corporation's board of directors. In this situation, Alden has not breached his duty of loyalty to the corporation, and thus the contract is valid. If it were otherwise, directors would be prevented from ever transacting business with the corporations they serve. ■

ETHICAL ISSUE 29.1

What happens to the duty of loyalty when a director sits on the boards of two corporations? Corporate directors often have many business affiliations, and they may even sit on the board of more than one corporation. (Of course, directors generally are precluded from sitting on the boards of directors of competing companies.) The duty of loyalty can become cloudy, though, when corporate directors sit on the boards of more than one corporation. Because of the potential for abuse in transactions negotiated between corporations whose boards have some members in common, courts tend to scrutinize such actions closely.

    For example, suppose that four individuals own a total of 70 percent of the shares of Company A and 100 percent of the shares of Company B. All four of these shareholders sit on the boards of directors of both corporations. Company A decides to purchase all of Company B's stock for $6 million, when in fact it is worth only $3 million. The shareholder-directors of both firms have not breached their duty to Company B because the $6 million price is beneficial to that company. A court would likely hold that the directors breached their duty to the other shareholders of Company A (who owned the remaining 30 percent of Company A's shares), however, because these other shareholders had nothing to gain by the transaction and much to lose by Company A's purchase of Company B at an inflated price.[3]

Liability of Directors and Officers

Directors and officers are exposed to liability on many fronts. Corporate directors and officers may be held liable for the crimes and torts committed by themselves or by corporate employees under their supervision, as discussed in Chapter 6 and Chapter 24, respectively. Additionally, if shareholders perceive that the corporate directors are not acting in the best interests of the corporation, they may sue the directors, in what is called a *shareholder's derivative suit,* on behalf of the corporation. (This type of action is discussed later in this chapter, in the context of shareholders' rights.)

The Business Judgment Rule   A corporate director or officer may be able to avoid liability to the corporation or to its shareholders for poor business judgments under the **business judgment rule.** Directors and officers are expected to exercise due care and to use their best judgment in guiding corporate management, but they are not insurers of business success. Honest mistakes of judgment and poor business decisions on their part do not make them liable to the corporation for resulting losses.

The business judgment rule generally immunizes directors and officers from liability for the consequences of a decision that is within managerial authority, as long as the decision complies with management's fiduciary duties and as long as acting on the decision is within the powers of the corporation. Consequently, if there is a reasonable basis for a business decision, it is unlikely that a court will interfere with that decision, even if the corporation suffers as a result.

BUSINESS JUDGMENT RULE
A rule that immunizes corporate management from liability for actions that result in corporate losses or damages if the actions are undertaken in good faith and are within both the power of the corporation and the authority of management to make.

Requirements for the Rule to Apply   To benefit from the business judgment rule, directors and officers must act in good faith, in what they consider to be the best interests of the corporation, and with the care that an ordinarily prudent person in a similar position would exercise in like circumstances. This requires an informed decision, with a rational basis, and with no conflict between the decision maker's personal interest and the interest of the corporation.

ROLE OF SHAREHOLDERS

The acquisition of a share of stock makes a person an owner and shareholder in a corporation. Shareholders thus own the corporation. Although they have no legal title to corporate property, such as buildings and equipment, they do have an equitable (ownership) interest in the firm.

As a general rule, shareholders have no responsibility for the daily management of the corporation, although they are ultimately responsible for choosing the board of directors, which does have such control. Ordinarily, corporate officers and directors owe no duty to individual shareholders unless some contract or special relationship exists between them

BE AWARE   Shareholders normally are not agents of the corporation.

---

3. See, for example, *Gries Sports Enterprises, Inc. v. Cleveland Browns Football Co.,* 26 Ohio St.3d 15, 496 N.E.2d 959 (1986).

Starbucks Corporation board member James G. Shennan, Jr., waves as he is introduced by Chairman Howard Schultz at the company's annual shareholders' meeting. Shareholders meet to vote on corporate issues. (AP Photo/Elaine Thompson)

in addition to the corporate relationship. Their duty is to act in the best interests of the corporation and its shareholder-owners as a whole. In turn, as you will read later in this chapter, controlling shareholders owe a fiduciary duty to minority shareholders. Normally, there is no legal relationship between shareholders and creditors of the corporation. Shareholders can, in fact, be creditors of the corporation and thus have the same rights of recovery against the corporation as any other creditor.

In this section, we look at the powers and voting rights of shareholders, which are generally established in the articles of incorporation and under the state's general incorporation law.

Shareholders' Powers

Shareholders must approve fundamental changes affecting the corporation before the changes can be implemented. Hence, shareholders are empowered to amend the articles of incorporation (charter) and bylaws, approve a merger or the dissolution of the corporation, and approve the sale of all or substantially all of the corporation's assets. Some of these powers are subject to prior board approval.

Members of the board of directors are elected and removed by a vote of the shareholders. The first board of directors is either named in the articles of incorporation or chosen by the incorporators to serve until the first shareholders' meeting. From that time on, the selection and retention of directors are exclusively shareholder functions.

Directors usually serve their full terms; if they are unsatisfactory, they are simply not reelected. Shareholders have the inherent power, however, to remove a director from office *for cause* (breach of duty or misconduct) by a majority vote.[4] As mentioned earlier, some state statutes (and some corporate articles) even permit removal of directors without cause by the vote of a majority of the holders of outstanding shares entitled to vote.

Shareholders' Meetings

Shareholders' meetings must occur at least annually. In addition, special meetings can be called to deal with urgent matters.

Notice of Meetings Each shareholder must receive written notice of the date, time, and place of a shareholders' meeting.[5] The notice must be received within a reasonable length of time prior to the date of the meeting. Notice of a special meeting must include a statement of the purpose of the meeting, and business transacted at the meeting is limited to that purpose.

---

4. A director can often demand court review of removal for cause.
5. The shareholder can waive the requirement of written notice by signing a waiver form. In some states, a shareholder who does not receive written notice, but who learns of the meeting and attends without protesting the lack of notice, is said to have waived notice by such conduct. State statutes and corporate bylaws typically set forth the time within which notice must be sent, what methods can be used, and what the notice must contain.

Proxies   Because it is usually not practical for owners of only a few shares of stock of publicly traded corporations to attend shareholders' meetings, such shareholders normally give third parties written authorization to vote their shares at the meeting. This authorization is called a **proxy** (from the Latin *procurare*, "to manage, take care of"). Proxies are often solicited by management, but any person can solicit proxies to concentrate voting power. Proxies have been used by a group of shareholders as a device for taking over a corporation (corporate takeovers were discussed in Chapter 28). Proxies are normally revocable (that is, they can be withdrawn), unless they are specifically designated as irrevocable. Under RMBCA 7.22(c), proxies last for eleven months, unless the proxy agreement provides for a longer period.

Proxy Materials and Shareholder Proposals   When shareholders want to change a company policy, they can put their idea up for a shareholder vote. They can do this by submitting a shareholder proposal to the board of directors and asking the board to include the proposal in the proxy materials that are sent to all shareholders before meetings.

The Securities and Exchange Commission (SEC), which regulates the purchase and sale of securities (see Chapter 30), has special provisions relating to proxies and shareholder proposals. SEC Rule 14a-8 provides that all shareholders who own stock worth at least $1,000 are eligible to submit proposals for inclusion in corporate proxy materials. The corporation is required to include information on whatever proposals will be considered at the shareholders' meeting along with proxy materials. Only those proposals that relate to significant policy considerations rather than ordinary business operations must be included. For a discussion of how the SEC is adapting its rules regarding proxy solicitation to take advantage of today's communications technology, see this chapter's *Adapting the Law to the Online Environment* feature on the following two pages.

Shareholder Voting

Shareholders exercise ownership control through the power of their votes. Corporate business matters are presented in the form of *resolutions*, which shareholders vote to approve or disapprove. Each shareholder is entitled to one vote per share, although the voting techniques that will be discussed shortly all enhance the power of the shareholder's vote. The articles of incorporation can exclude or limit voting rights, particularly for certain classes of shares. For example, owners of preferred shares are usually denied the right to vote [RMBCA 7.21]. If a state statute requires specific voting procedures, the corporation's articles or bylaws must be consistent with the statute.

Quorum Requirements   For shareholders to conduct business at a meeting, a quorum must be present. Generally, a quorum exists when shareholders holding more than 50 percent of the outstanding shares are present. In some states, obtaining the unanimous written consent of shareholders is a permissible alternative to holding a shareholders' meeting [RMBCA 7.25].

Once a quorum is present, voting can proceed. A majority vote of the shares represented at the meeting is usually required to pass resolutions.   **EXAMPLE 29.4** Novo Pictures, Inc., has 10,000 outstanding shares of voting stock. Its articles of incorporation set the quorum at 50 percent of outstanding shares and provide that a majority vote of the shares present is necessary to pass resolutions concerning ordinary matters. Therefore, for this firm, a quorum of shareholders representing 5,000 outstanding shares must be present at a shareholders' meeting to conduct business. If exactly 5,000 shares are represented at the meeting, a vote of at least 2,501 of those shares is needed to pass a resolution. If 6,000 shares are represented, a vote of 3,001 will be required, and so on.   ▪

PROXY
In corporate law, a written agreement between a stockholder and another party in which the stockholder authorizes the other party to vote the stockholder's shares in a certain manner.

ON THE WEB

For information on the SEC's rulings, including rulings on proxy materials, go to
www.sec.gov/rules/final.shtml.

BE CAREFUL   Once a quorum is present, a vote can be taken even if some shareholders leave without casting their votes.

ADAPTING THE LAW TO THE ONLINE ENVIRONMENT — The SEC Adopts New E-Proxy Rules

In the past, anyone wishing to solicit proxies from shareholders had to mail each shareholder numerous paper documents relating to the proxy. Required materials often include notice of the meeting, proxy statements and consent solicitation statements, proxy cards, information statements, annual reports, additional soliciting materials, and any amendments made to these materials. Providing all of these documents in paper form can be very costly.

In January 2007, the Securities and Exchange Commission (SEC) adopted voluntary e-proxy rules that went into effect on July 1, 2007.[a] Essentially, the new rules allow companies to furnish proxy materials to shareholders by posting them on a Web site and providing shareholders with notice of the availability of the proxy materials online. This is

a. 17 C.F.R. Parts 240, 249, and 274.

a significant development that will reduce the printing and mailing costs associated with furnishing proxy materials to shareholders. Because the rules are voluntary, a company may still provide paper proxy documents if it so chooses.

The Notice and Access Model

Under the SEC's new rules, a company may now furnish proxy materials to shareholders using the notice and access model, which includes the following steps:

- The company posts the proxy materials on a publicly accessible Web site.
- The company then sends a (paper) notice to each shareholder at least forty calendar days prior to the date of the shareholders' meeting for which the proxy is being solicited.
- No other materials (such as a proxy card) can be sent along with the initial notice (unless the proxy is being combined with a meeting notice required by state law).
- The notice must be written in plain English and include a prominent statement of the following: the date, time, and location of the shareholders' meeting; the specific Web site

---

At times, more than a simple majority vote will be required either by a state statute or by the corporate articles. Extraordinary corporate matters, such as a merger, consolidation, or dissolution of the corporation (as discussed in Chapter 28), require a higher percentage of all corporate shares entitled to vote [RMBCA 7.27].

Voting Lists   The corporation prepares voting lists prior to each meeting of the shareholders. Ordinarily, only persons whose names appear on the corporation's shareholder records as owners are entitled to vote.[6] The voting list contains the name and address of each shareholder as shown on the corporate records on a given cutoff, or record, date. (Under RMBCA 7.07, the record date may be as much as seventy days before the meeting.) The voting list also includes the number of voting shares held by each owner. The list is usually kept at the corporate headquarters and is available for shareholder inspection [RMBCA 7.20].

Cumulative Voting   Most states permit or even require shareholders to elect directors by *cumulative voting,* a voting method designed to allow minority shareholders to be represented on the board of directors.[7] With cumulative voting, the number of board members to be elected is multiplied by the number of voting shares a shareholder owns. The result equals the number of votes the shareholder has, and this total can be cast for one or more nominees for director. All nominees stand for election at the same time. When cumulative voting is not required either by statute or under the articles, the entire board can be elected by a simple majority of shares at a shareholders' meeting.

---

6. When the legal owner is bankrupt, incompetent, deceased, or in some other way under a legal disability, his or her vote can be cast by a person designated by law to control and manage the owner's property.

7. See, for example, California Corporate Code Section 708. Under RMBCA 7.28, however, no cumulative voting rights exist unless the articles of incorporation so provide.

at which the shareholders can access the proxy materials; an explanation of how they can obtain paper copies of the proxy materials at no cost (by calling a toll-free phone number, for instance); and a clear and impartial description of each matter to be considered at the shareholders' meeting.

- After sending the initial notice, the company must wait at least ten days before sending a (paper) proxy card to the shareholders. This ten-day waiting period is designed to provide shareholders with sufficient time to access the proxy materials online or request paper copies.
- If a shareholder requests paper proxy materials, the company must send them to the shareholder within three business days.
- After receiving the initial paper notice, a shareholder can permanently elect to receive all future proxy materials on paper or by e-mail.

Shareholders and other parties conducting their own proxy solicitations can also use the notice and access model with slight modifications. The notice must still be sent forty days before the meeting date and include substantially the same information, but the notice need not be provided to all shareholders. In contrast to company solicitations, other parties can selectively choose the shareholders from whom they wish to solicit proxies without sending information to all other shareholders.

Should E-Proxy Rules Be Mandatory?

The SEC has also proposed making the new e-proxy rules mandatory for all proxy solicitations in the future. The mandatory notice and access model would operate substantially the same as just outlined, except that the initial notice could be accompanied by a paper or e-mail copy of the proxy statement, annual report, and proxy card. The main difference between the mandatory and voluntary models is that under the voluntary rule, the company (or other party seeking proxies) can choose whether to use electronic or paper means, whereas under a mandatory rule, the SEC would require the use of electronic means. Under either rule, the shareholder can always choose to receive paper documents rather than accessing the materials online.

FOR CRITICAL ANALYSIS *Why might a company or other party choose to solicit proxies the old-fashioned way, by providing paper documents instead of Internet access, despite the added costs?*

Cumulative voting can best be understood by an example. **EXAMPLE 29.5** A corporation has 10,000 shares issued and outstanding. One group of shareholders (the minority shareholders) holds only 3,000 shares, and the other group of shareholders (the majority shareholders) holds the other 7,000 shares. Three members of the board are to be elected. The majority shareholders' nominees are Acevedo, Barkley, and Craycik. The minority shareholders' nominee is Drake. Can Drake be elected by the minority shareholders?

If cumulative voting is allowed, the answer is yes. Together, the minority shareholders have 9,000 votes (the number of directors to be elected times the number of shares held by the minority shareholders equals 3 times 3,000, which equals 9,000 votes). All of these votes can be cast to elect Drake. The majority shareholders have 21,000 votes (3 times 7,000 equals 21,000 votes), but these votes have to be distributed among their three nominees. The principle of cumulative voting is that no matter how the majority shareholders cast their 21,000 votes, they will not be able to elect all three directors if the minority shareholders cast all of their 9,000 votes for Drake, as illustrated in Exhibit 29–1 on page 818. ■

Other Voting Techniques Before a shareholders' meeting, a group of shareholders can agree in writing to vote their shares together in a specified manner. Such agreements, called *shareholder voting agreements*, are usually held to be valid and enforceable. A shareholder can also appoint a voting agent and vote by proxy. As mentioned previously, a proxy is a written authorization to cast the shareholder's vote, and a person can solicit proxies from a number of shareholders in an attempt to concentrate voting power.

Another technique is for shareholders to enter into a **voting trust,** which is an agreement (a trust contract) under which legal title (record ownership on the corporate books) is transferred to a trustee who is responsible for voting the shares. The agreement can specify how the trustee is to vote, or it can allow the trustee to use his or her discretion. The trustee takes physical possession of the stock certificate and in return gives the shareholder

VOTING TRUST
An agreement (trust contract) under which legal title to shares of corporate stock is transferred to a trustee who is authorized by the shareholders to vote the shares on their behalf.

EXHIBIT 29–1 **Results of Cumulative Voting**

This exhibit illustrates how cumulative voting gives minority shareholders a greater chance of electing a director of their choice. By casting all of their 9,000 votes for one candidate (Drake), the minority shareholders will succeed in electing Drake to the board of directors.

BALLOT	MAJORITY SHAREHOLDERS' VOTES			MINORITY SHAREHOLDERS' VOTES	DIRECTORS ELECTED
	Acevedo	Barkley	Craycik	Drake	
1	10,000	10,000	1,000	9,000	Acevedo/Barkley/Drake
2	9,001	9,000	2,999	9,000	Acevedo/Barkley/Drake
3	6,000	7,000	8,000	9,000	Barkley/Craycik/Drake

a voting trust certificate. The shareholder retains all of the rights of ownership (for example, the right to receive dividend payments) except for the power to vote the shares.

RIGHTS OF SHAREHOLDERS

Shareholders possess numerous rights. A significant right—the right to vote their shares—has already been discussed. We now look at some additional rights of shareholders.

Stock Certificates

STOCK CERTIFICATE
A certificate issued by a corporation evidencing the ownership of a specified number of shares in the corporation.

PREEMPTIVE RIGHTS
Rights held by shareholders that entitle them to purchase newly issued shares of a corporation's stock, equal in percentage to shares already held, before the stock is offered to any outside buyers. Preemptive rights enable shareholders to maintain their proportionate ownership and voice in the corporation.

Stock certificates are displayed. To be a shareholder, is it necessary to have physical possession of a certificate? Why or why not? (PhotoDisc)

A **stock certificate** is a certificate issued by a corporation that evidences ownership of a specified number of shares in the corporation. In jurisdictions that require the issuance of stock certificates, shareholders have the right to demand that the corporation issue certificates. In most states and under RMBCA 6.26, boards of directors may provide that shares of stock will be uncertificated—that is, no actual, physical stock certificates will be issued. When shares are uncertificated, the corporation may be required to send each shareholder a letter or some other form of notice that contains the same information that would normally appear on the face of stock certificates.

Stock is intangible personal property, and the ownership right exists independently of the certificate itself. If a stock certificate is lost or destroyed, ownership is not destroyed with it. A new certificate can be issued to replace one that has been lost or destroyed.[8] Notice of shareholders' meetings, dividends, and operational and financial reports are all distributed according to the recorded ownership listed in the corporation's books, not on the basis of possession of the certificate.

Preemptive Rights

With **preemptive rights,** which are based on a common law concept, a shareholder receives a preference over all other purchasers to subscribe to or purchase a prorated share of a new issue of stock. In other words, a shareholder who is given preemptive rights can purchase the same percentage of the new shares being issued as she or he already holds in the company. This allows each shareholder to maintain her or his proportionate control, voting power,

---

8. The Uniform Commercial Code (UCC) provides that for a lost or destroyed certificate to be reissued, a shareholder normally must furnish an *indemnity bond.* An indemnity bond is a written promise to reimburse the holder for any actual or claimed loss caused by the issuer's or some other person's conduct. The bond protects the corporation against potential loss should the original certificate reappear at some future time in the hands of a bona fide purchaser [UCC 8–302, 8–405(2)].

or financial interest in the corporation. Most statutes either (1) grant preemptive rights but allow them to be negated in the corporation's articles or (2) deny preemptive rights except to the extent that they are granted in the articles. The result is that the articles of incorporation determine the existence and scope of preemptive rights. Generally, preemptive rights apply only to additional, newly issued stock sold for cash, and the preemptive rights must be exercised within a specified time period, which is usually thirty days.

■EXAMPLE 29.6 Tran Corporation authorizes and issues 1,000 shares of stock. Lebow purchases 100 shares, making her the owner of 10 percent of the company's stock. Subsequently, Tran, by vote of its shareholders, authorizes the issuance of another 1,000 shares (by amending the articles of incorporation). This increases its capital stock to a total of 2,000 shares. If preemptive rights have been provided, Lebow can purchase one additional share of the new stock being issued for each share she already owns—or 100 additional shares. Thus, she can own 200 of the 2,000 shares outstanding, and she will maintain her relative position as a shareholder. If preemptive rights are not allowed, her proportionate control and voting power may be diluted from that of a 10 percent shareholder to that of a 5 percent shareholder because of the issuance of the additional 1,000 shares. ■

Preemptive rights are most important in close corporations because each shareholder owns a relatively small number of shares but controls a substantial interest in the corporation. Without preemptive rights, it would be possible for a shareholder to lose his or her proportionate control over the firm.

Stock Warrants

Usually, when preemptive rights exist and a corporation is issuing additional shares, each shareholder is given **stock warrants,** which are transferable options to acquire a given number of shares from the corporation at a stated price. Warrants are often publicly traded on securities exchanges. When the option to purchase is in effect for a short period of time, the stock warrants are usually referred to as *rights*.

STOCK WARRANT
A certificate that grants the owner the option to buy a given number of shares of stock, usually within a set time period.

Dividends

As mentioned in Chapter 28, a *dividend* is a distribution of corporate profits or income *ordered by the directors* and paid to the shareholders in proportion to their respective shares in the corporation. Dividends can be paid in cash, property, stock of the corporation that is paying the dividends, or stock of other corporations.[9]

State laws vary, but each state determines the general circumstances and legal requirements under which dividends are paid. State laws also control the sources of revenue to be used; only certain funds are legally available for paying dividends. Depending on state law, dividends may be paid from the following sources:

1 *Retained earnings.* All states allow dividends to be paid from the undistributed net profits earned by the corporation, including capital gains from the sale of fixed assets. As mentioned in Chapter 28, the undistributed net profits are called *retained earnings*.

2 *Net profits.* A few states allow dividends to be issued from current net profits without regard to deficits in prior years.

3 *Surplus.* A number of states allow dividends to be paid out of any kind of surplus.

Illegal Dividends   Sometimes, dividends are improperly paid from an unauthorized account, or their payment causes the corporation to become insolvent. Generally, in such

---

9. Technically, dividends paid in stock are not dividends. They maintain each shareholder's proportionate interest in the corporation. On one occasion, a distillery declared and paid a "dividend" in bonded whiskey.

situations, shareholders must return illegal dividends only if they knew that the dividends were illegal when the payment was received. A dividend paid while the corporation is insolvent is automatically an illegal dividend, and shareholders may be required to return the payment to the corporation or its creditors. Whenever dividends are illegal or improper, the board of directors can be held personally liable for the amount of the payment. When directors can show that a shareholder knew that a dividend was illegal when it was received, however, the directors are entitled to reimbursement from the shareholder.

Directors' Failure to Declare a Dividend   When directors fail to declare a dividend, shareholders can ask a court to compel the directors to meet and to declare a dividend. To succeed, the shareholders must show that the directors have acted so unreasonably in withholding the dividend that their conduct is an abuse of their discretion.

Often, a corporation accumulates large cash reserves for a bona fide purpose, such as expansion, research, or other legitimate corporate goals. The mere fact that the firm has sufficient earnings or surplus available to pay a dividend is not enough to compel directors to distribute funds that, in the board's opinion, should not be distributed. The courts are reluctant to interfere with corporate operations and will not compel directors to declare dividends unless abuse of discretion is clearly shown.

Inspection Rights

Shareholders in a corporation enjoy both common law and statutory inspection rights. The shareholder's right of inspection is limited, however, to the inspection and copying of corporate books and records for a *proper purpose*, provided the request is made in advance. The shareholder can inspect in person, or an attorney, accountant, or other type of assistant can do so as the shareholder's agent. The RMBCA requires the corporation to maintain an alphabetical voting list of shareholders with addresses and number of shares owned; this list must be kept open at the annual meeting for inspection by any shareholder of record [RMBCA 7.20].

The power of inspection is fraught with potential abuses, and the corporation is allowed to protect itself from them. For example, a shareholder can properly be denied access to corporate records to prevent harassment or to protect trade secrets or other confidential corporate information. Some states require that a shareholder must have held his or her shares for

A General Motors shareholder asks a question at the company's annual stockholders' meeting. Shareholders also have a limited right to inspect and copy corporate books and records, provided the request is made in advance and is not impromtu in an open forum like a shareholders' meeting. What other limitations are placed on shareholders' inspection rights?
(AP Photo/Chris Gardner)

a minimum period of time immediately preceding the demand to inspect or must hold a minimum number of outstanding shares. The RMBCA provides, though, that every shareholder is entitled to examine specified corporate records [RMBCA 16.02]. A shareholder who is denied the right of inspection can seek a court order to compel the inspection.

The question in the following case was whether a shareholder who obtains access to corporate books and records that the company regards as confidential should be free to disseminate information in those documents publicly.

CASE 29.2   Disney v. Walt Disney Co.

Court of Chancery of Delaware, 857 A.2d 444 (2004).

FACTS Roy Disney is a shareholder of Walt Disney Company, a Delaware corporation with its principal offices in Burbank, California. Roy Disney was a director of the company until he resigned in November 2003. After his resignation, Disney began a campaign to encourage other shareholders to vote "no" on the reelection of Michael Eisner and three other members of the board of directors at the company's March 2004 annual meeting. As part of this effort, in January, Disney sought access to corporate books and records related to compensation for the company's five senior executives. Before honoring this request, the company designated some of the information "confidential" and asked Disney not to disseminate it publicly. He agreed only to hold it in "strict confidence." On review of the material, however, Disney objected to the confidentiality designation. He filed a suit in a Delaware state court against the company, asking the court to rule that the information was not appropriately designated "confidential."

ISSUE Is a shareholder who obtains access to corporate books and records that the company regards as confidential free to disseminate information in those documents publicly?

DECISION No. The court denied Roy Disney's request to remove the confidentiality designation from the documents on which the company had imposed it, and dismissed the case.

REASON The court acknowledged that "Section 220 of the Delaware General Corporation Law provides every stockholder of a Delaware corporation acting for a proper purpose a powerful right to inspect the company's books and records." But the exercise of this right is subject to a "reasonable confidentiality order," which is meant to "protect the corporation's legitimate interests" and "prevent the dissemination of confidential business information." Disney sought the public disclosure of information that related to "the bases for a compensation committee's decisions to award enormous compensation packages to a public company's top executives" so that the company's shareholders could "know the whole truth." The court reasoned that removing the confidentiality limit in this case would lead to the disclosure of nonpublic information in other cases—"snippets of information gleaned from a few e-mails or internal memoranda"—which would cause a company to disclose even more otherwise nonpublic information to place the material in its "proper" context. This would not "advance the best interests of the corporation or its stockholders."

WHAT IF THE FACTS WERE DIFFERENT? *If the information that Disney sought to disseminate publicly—via a Web site, for example—had been previously disclosed in a limited manner, such as in a company newsletter, would the result have been different? Explain.*

Transfer of Shares

Corporate stock represents an ownership right in intangible personal property. The law generally recognizes the right to transfer stock to another person unless there are valid restrictions on its transferability. Although stock certificates are negotiable and freely transferable by indorsement and delivery, transfer of stock in closely held corporations usually is restricted. These restrictions must be reasonable and may be set out in the bylaws or in a shareholder agreement. The existence of any restrictions on transferability must always be indicated on the face of the stock certificate.

Sometimes, corporations or their shareholders restrict transferability by reserving the option to purchase any shares offered for resale by a shareholder. This **right of first refusal** remains with the corporation or the shareholders for only a specified time or a reasonable period. Variations on the purchase option are possible. For example, a shareholder might be required to offer the shares to other shareholders first or to the corporation first.

When shares are transferred, a new entry is made in the corporate stock book to indicate the new owner. Until the corporation is notified and the entry is complete, all rights—including voting rights, the right to notice of shareholders' meetings, and the right to dividend distributions—remain with the current record owner.

Rights on Dissolution

When a corporation is dissolved and its outstanding debts and the claims of its creditors have been satisfied, the remaining assets are distributed to the shareholders in proportion to the percentage of shares owned by each shareholder. Certain classes of preferred stock can be given priority. If no class of stock has been given preferences in the distribution of assets on liquidation, then all of the stockholders share the remaining assets.

In some circumstances, shareholders may petition a court to have the corporation dissolved. If, for example, the minority shareholders know that the board of directors is mishandling corporate assets, those shareholders can petition a court to appoint a *receiver* who will wind up corporate affairs and liquidate the business assets of the corporation (see Chapter 28 for the duties of a receiver). The RMBCA permits any shareholder to initiate such an action in any of the following circumstances [RMBCA 14.30]:

1 The directors are deadlocked in the management of corporate affairs. The shareholders are unable to break that deadlock, and irreparable injury to the corporation is being suffered or threatened.

2 The acts of the directors or those in control of the corporation are illegal, oppressive, or fraudulent.

3 Corporate assets are being misapplied or wasted.

4 The shareholders are deadlocked in voting power and have failed, for a specified period (usually two annual meetings), to elect successors to directors whose terms have expired or would have expired with the election of successors.

The Shareholder's Derivative Suit

When those in control of a corporation—the corporate directors—fail to sue in the corporate name to redress a wrong suffered by the corporation, shareholders are permitted to do so "derivatively" in what is known as a **shareholder's derivative suit.** Before a derivative suit can be brought, some wrong must have been done to the corporation, and the shareholders must have presented their complaint to the board of directors. Only if the directors fail to solve the problem or to take appropriate action can the derivative suit go forward.

The right of shareholders to bring a derivative action is especially important when the wrong suffered by the corporation results from the actions of corporate directors or officers. This is because the directors and officers would probably want to prevent any action against themselves.

The shareholder's derivative suit is unusual in that those suing are not pursuing rights or benefits for themselves personally but are acting as guardians of the corporate entity. Therefore, any damages recovered by the suit normally go into the corporation's treasury, not to the shareholders personally. This is true even if the company is a small, closely held corporation. **EXAMPLE 29.7** Zeon Corporation is owned by two shareholders, each holding 50 percent of the corporate shares. Suppose that one of the shareholders wants to sue the other for misusing corporate assets or usurping corporate opportunities. The plaintiff-

shareholder will have to bring a shareholder's derivative suit (not a suit in his or her own name) because the alleged harm was suffered by Zeon, not by the plaintiff personally. Any damages awarded will go to the corporation, not to the plaintiff-shareholder. (Derivative actions are less common in other countries than in the United States, as this chapter's *Beyond Our Borders* feature explains.)

DUTIES AND LIABILITIES OF SHAREHOLDERS

One of the hallmarks of the corporate organization is that shareholders are not personally liable for the debts of the corporation. If the corporation fails, shareholders can lose their investments, but that is generally the limit of their liability. As discussed in Chapter 28, in certain instances of fraud, undercapitalization, or careless observance of corporate formalities, a court will pierce the corporate veil (disregard the corporate entity) and hold the shareholders individually liable. These situations are the exception, however, not the rule.

A shareholder can also be personally liable in certain other rare instances. One relates to illegal dividends, which were discussed previously. Another relates to *watered stock.* Finally, in certain instances, a majority shareholder who engages in oppressive conduct or attempts to exclude minority shareholders from receiving certain benefits can be held personally liable.

Watered Stock

When a corporation issues shares for less than their fair market value, the shares are referred to as **watered stock.**[10] Usually, the shareholder who receives watered stock must pay the difference to the corporation (the shareholder is personally liable). In some states, the shareholder who receives watered stock may be liable to creditors of the corporation for unpaid corporate debts.

■EXAMPLE 29.8 During the formation of a corporation, Gomez, one of the incorporators, transfers his property, Sunset Beach, to the corporation for 10,000 shares of stock.

WATERED STOCK
Shares of stock issued by a corporation for which the corporation receives, as payment, less than the stated value of the shares.

---

10. The phrase *watered stock* was originally used to describe cattle that were kept thirsty during a long drive and then were allowed to drink large quantities of water just prior to their sale. The increased weight of the "watered stock" allowed the seller to reap a higher profit.

The stock has a specific face value (*par value*) of $100 per share, and thus the total price of the 10,000 shares is $1 million. After the property is transferred and the shares are issued, Sunset Beach is carried on the corporate books at a value of $1 million. On appraisal, it is discovered that the market value of the property at the time of transfer was only $500,000. The shares issued to Gomez are therefore watered stock, and he is liable to the corporation for the difference. ■

Duties of Majority Shareholders

In some instances, a majority shareholder is regarded as having a fiduciary duty to the corporation and to the minority shareholders. This occurs when a single shareholder (or a few shareholders acting in concert) owns a sufficient number of shares to exercise *de facto* (actual) control over the corporation. In these situations, majority shareholders owe a fiduciary duty to the minority shareholders.

A breach of fiduciary duty can also occur when the majority shareholders of a closely held corporation use their control to exclude the minority from certain benefits of participating in the firm. **■EXAMPLE 29.9** Three brothers, Alfred, Carl, and Eugene, each owned a one-third interest in a corporation and had worked for the corporation for most of their adult lives. When a dispute arose concerning discrepancies in the corporation's accounting records, Carl and Eugene fired Alfred and told the company's employees that Alfred had had a nervous breakdown, which was not true. Alfred sued Carl and Eugene, alleging that they had breached their fiduciary duties. The brothers argued that because there was no reduction in the value of the corporation or the value of Alfred's shares in the company, they had not breached their fiduciary duties. The court, however, held that the brothers' conduct was unfairly prejudicial toward Alfred and supported a finding of a breach of fiduciary duty.[11] ■

Such a breach of fiduciary duties by those who control a closely held corporation may constitute *oppressive conduct*. The court in the following case was asked to review a pattern of allegedly oppressive conduct by the person in control and determine whether that conduct fell within a two-year statute of limitations.

---

11. See, for example, *Swanson v. Upper Midwest Industries, Inc.,* ___ N.W.2d ___ (Minn.App. 2002).

CASE 29.3 | **Robbins v. Sanders**

Supreme Court of Alabama, 890 So.2d 998 (2004).

FACTS James and Mary Bailey owned fifty-three acres of land, subject to mortgages totaling $450,000, in Birmingham, Alabama. The Baileys rented buildings on the property and used part of the land as a landfill. In 1988, an underground fire broke out in the landfill. Pete Robbins offered to extinguish the fire and to pay the mortgages. The parties formed Corridor Enterprises, Inc., to which the Baileys contributed the land. Half of the stock—one thousand shares—was issued to Robbins. In 1991, the Baileys agreed to sell their thousand shares to Robbins at the rate of two shares per month. The Baileys both died in 1997. Terrill Sanders was appointed administrator of their estates. Over the next twelve months, Sanders had problems obtaining information from

Robbins and uncovered discrepancies in Corridor's corporate records. On the estates' behalf, Sanders filed a suit in an Alabama state court, alleging, among other things, oppression of minority shareholders. The court assessed more than $4 million in damages against Robbins, who appealed to the Alabama Supreme Court, arguing in part that a two-year statute of limitations barred the suit.

ISSUE Were the minority shareholders entitled to recover for their claim of oppression?

DECISION Yes. The Alabama Supreme Court held that Sanders's claims on behalf of the Baileys' estates were timely. The court remanded the case, though, so that the lower court

CASE 29.3–Continued

could clearly state how the damages should be apportioned among the estates and Corridor.[a]

REASON The state supreme court rejected Robbins's statute-of-limitations argument. The court explained that the Baileys' estates became minority shareholders after the Baileys died in 1997. The court pointed out that Robbins engaged in oppressive conduct after this event. "For example, in 1998, Robbins used funds of Corridor Enterprises to purchase real estate in his own name, to invest in other businesses in his own name, and to purchase personal property for himself; he refused to provide an accounting of the corporate finances when he was requested to do so; he failed to pay the

a. This case was remanded and tried again and appealed again on different issues. The court's holding in this case still stands. The subsequent decision involving the same parties is located at 927 So.2d 777 (Ala.Sup.Ct. 2005).

corporate property and income taxes, failed to have tax returns prepared and filed, and failed to maintain proper corporate records; he entered into a contract to sell property belonging to Corridor Enterprises without notice to or approval of the minority shareholders; and he failed to declare dividends during the entire time the estates were shareholders while he paid himself an exorbitant salary and drained the corporate funds." Sanders initiated this suit on the estates' behalf in the same year that many of these activities occurred. "Therefore, the estates' claims of * * * oppression were not time-barred to the extent those claims sought to recover damages for injuries occurring to the estates."

 FOR CRITICAL ANALYSIS–Economic Consideration
What should be the basis for determining the specific amount of damages to be awarded to the minority shareholders in this case?

MAJOR BUSINESS FORMS COMPARED

As mentioned in Chapter 25, when deciding which form of business organization would be most appropriate, businesspersons normally take into account several factors, including ease of creation, the liability of the owners, tax considerations, and the need for capital. Each major form of business organization offers distinct advantages and disadvantages with respect to these and other factors. Exhibit 29–2 on pages 826 and 827 summarizes the essential advantages and disadvantages of each of the forms of business organization discussed in Chapters 25 through 28, as well as in this chapter.

REVIEWING Corporate Directors, Officers, and Shareholders

David Brock is on the board of directors of Firm Body Fitness, Inc., which owns a string of fitness clubs in New Mexico. Brock owns 15 percent of the Firm Body stock, and he is also employed as a tanning technician at one of the fitness clubs. After the January financial report showed that Firm Body's tanning division was operating at a substantial net loss, the board of directors, led by Marty Levinson, discussed terminating the tanning operations. Brock successfully convinced a majority of the board that the tanning division was necessary to market the club's overall fitness package. By April, the tanning division's financial losses had risen. The board hired a business analyst who conducted surveys and determined that the tanning operations did not significantly increase membership. A shareholder, Diego Peñada, discovered that Brock owned stock in Sunglow, Inc., the company from which Firm Body purchased

its tanning equipment. Peñada notified Levinson, who privately reprimanded Brock. Shortly afterwards, Brock and Mandy Vail, who owned 37 percent of Firm Body stock and also held shares of Sunglow, voted to replace Levinson on the board of directors. Using the information presented in the chapter, answer the following questions.

1 What duties did Brock, as a director, owe to Firm Body?

2 Does the fact that Brock owned shares in Sunglow establish a conflict of interest? Why or why not?

3 Suppose that Firm Body brought an action against Brock claiming that he had breached the duty of loyalty by not disclosing his interest in Sunglow to the other directors. What theory might Brock use in his defense?

4 Now suppose that Firm Body did not bring an action against Brock. What type of lawsuit might Peñada be able to bring based on these facts?

EXHIBIT 29–2 **Major Forms of Business Compared**

CHARACTERISTIC	SOLE PROPRIETORSHIP	PARTNERSHIP	CORPORATION
Method of creation	Created at will by owner.	Created by agreement of the parties.	Authorized by the state under the state's corporation law.
Legal position	Not a separate entity; owner is the business.	Is a separate legal entity in most states.	Always a legal entity separate and distinct from its owners—a legal fiction for the purposes of owning property and being a party to litigation.
Liability	Unlimited liability.	Unlimited liability.	Limited liability of shareholders—shareholders are not liable for the debts of the corporation.
Duration	Determined by owner; automatically dissolved on owner's death.	Terminated by agreement of the partners, but can continue to do business even when a partner dissociates from the partnership.	Can have perpetual existence.
Transferability of interest	Interest can be transferred, but individual's proprietorship then ends.	Although partnership interest can be assigned, assignee does not have full rights of a partner.	Shares of stock can be transferred.
Management	Completely at owner's discretion.	Each general partner has a direct and equal voice in management unless expressly agreed otherwise in the partnership agreement.	Shareholders elect directors, who set policy and appoint officers.
Taxation	Owner pays personal taxes on business income.	Each partner pays pro rata share of income taxes on net profits, whether or not they are distributed.	Double taxation—corporation pays income tax on net profits, with no deduction for dividends, and shareholders pay income tax on disbursed dividends they receive.
Organizational fees, annual license fees, and annual reports	None or minimal.	None or minimal.	All required.
Transaction of business in other states	Generally no limitation.	Generally no limitation.[a]	Normally must qualify to do business and obtain certificate of authority.

a. A few states have enacted statutes requiring that foreign partnerships qualify to do business there.

EXHIBIT 29–2 Major Forms of Business Compared—Continued

CHARACTERISTIC	LIMITED PARTNERSHIP	LIMITED LIABILITY COMPANY	LIMITED LIABILITY PARTNERSHIP
Method of creation	Created by agreement to carry on a business for a profit. At least one party must be a general partner and the other(s) limited partner(s). Certificate of limited partnership is filed. Charter must be issued by the state.	Created by an agreement of the member-owners of the company. Articles of organization are filed. Charter must be issued by the state.	Created by agreement of the partners. A statement of qualification for the limited liability partnership is filed.
Legal position	Treated as a legal entity.	Treated as a legal entity.	Generally, treated same as a general partnership.
Liability	Unlimited liability of all general partners; limited partners are liable only to the extent of capital contributions.	Member-owners' liability is limited to the amount of capital contributions or investments.	Varies, but under the Uniform Partnership Act, liability of a partner for acts committed by other partners is limited.
Duration	By agreement in certificate, or by termination of the last general partner (retirement, death, and the like) or last limited partner.	Unless a single-member LLC, can have perpetual existence (same as a corporation).	Remains in existence until cancellation or revocation.
Transferability of interest	Interest can be assigned (same as general partnership), but if assignee becomes a member with consent of other partners, certificate must be amended.	Member interests are freely transferable.	Interest can be assigned same as in a general partnership.
Management	General partners have equal voice or by agreement. Limited partners may not retain limited liability if they actively participate in management.	Member-owners can fully participate in management, or management is selected by member-owners who manage on behalf of the members.	Same as a general partnership.
Taxation	Generally taxed as a partnership.	LLC is not taxed, and members are taxed personally on profits "passed through" the LLC.	Same as a general partnership.
Organizational fees, annual license fees, and annual reports	Organizational fee required; usually not others.	Organizational fee required; others vary with states.	Fees are set by each state for filing statements of qualification, foreign qualification, and annual reports.
Transaction of business in other states	Generally no limitations.	Generally no limitation, but may vary depending on state.	Must file a statement of foreign qualification before doing business in another state.

APPLICATION

Creating an E-Document-Retention Policy*

If a corporation becomes the target of a civil lawsuit or criminal investigation, the company may be required to turn over any documents in its files relating to the matter during the discovery stage of litigation. These documents may include legal documents, contracts, e-mail, faxes, letters, interoffice memorandums, notebooks, diaries, and other materials, even if they are kept in personal files in the homes of directors or officers. Under the current Federal Rules of Civil Procedure, which govern civil litigation procedures (see Chapter 3), a defendant in a lawsuit must disclose all relevant electronic data compilations and documents, as well as all relevant paper documents.

Although certain documents or data might free a company of any liability arising from a claim, others might serve to substantiate a civil claim or criminal charge. It is also possible that information contained in a document—an interoffice e-mail memo, for example (or even a memo referring to that memo)—could be used to convince a jury that the company or its directors or officers had condoned a certain action that they later denied condoning.

Which E-Documents Should Be Retained?

How does a company decide which e-documents should be retained and which should be destroyed? By law, corporations are required to keep certain types of documents, such as those specified in the *Code of Federal Regulations* and in regulations issued by government agencies, such as the Occupational Safety and Health Administration. Most businesses today have a document-retention policy. Generally, any records that the company is not legally required to keep or that the company is sure it will have no legal need for should be removed from the files and destroyed. A partnership agreement, for example, should be kept. A memo about last year's

company picnic, however, should be removed from the files and destroyed; obviously, it is just taking up storage space.

Modifications May Be Necessary during an Investigation

If the company becomes the target of an investigation, it usually must modify its document-retention policy until the investigation has been completed. Company officers, after receiving a subpoena to produce specific types of documents, should instruct the appropriate employees not to destroy relevant papers or e-documents that would otherwise be disposed of as part of the company's normal document-retention program.

Generally, to avoid being charged with obstruction of justice, company officials must always exercise good faith in deciding which documents should or should not be destroyed when attempting to comply with a subpoena. The specter of criminal prosecution would appear to encourage the retention of even those documents that are only remotely related to the dispute—at least until it has been resolved.

CHECKLIST FOR AN E-DOCUMENT-RETENTION POLICY

1 Develop guidelines that let employees know not only which e-documents should be retained and deleted but also which types of documents should not be created in the first place.

2 Find out which documents must be retained under the *Code of Federal Regulations* and under other government agency regulations to which your corporation is subject.

3 Retain other e-documents only if their retention is in the corporation's interest.

4 If certain corporate documents are subpoenaed, modify your document-retention policy to retain any document that is even remotely related to the dispute until the legal action has been resolved.

* This *Application* is not meant to substitute for the services of an attorney who is licensed to practice law in your state.

KEY TERMS

CHAPTER SUMMARY Corporate Directors, Officers, and Shareholders

Roles of Directors and Officers (See pages 806–810.)	1. *Directors' qualifications*—Few qualifications are required; a director may be a shareholder but is not required to be. 2. *Election of directors*—The first board of directors is usually appointed by the incorporators; thereafter, directors are elected by the shareholders. Directors usually serve a one-year term, although the term can be longer, and staggered terms are permitted under most state statutes. 3. *Board of directors' meetings*—The board of directors conducts business by holding formal meetings with recorded minutes. The date of regular meetings is usually established in the corporate articles or bylaws; special meetings can be called, with notice sent to all directors. Quorum requirements vary from state to state; usually, a quorum is a majority of the corporate directors. Voting must usually be done in person, and in ordinary matters only a majority vote is required. 4. *Rights of directors*—Directors' rights include the rights of participation, inspection, compensation, and indemnification. Compensation is usually specified in the corporate articles or bylaws. 5. *Directors' management responsibilities*—Directors are responsible for declaring and paying corporate dividends to shareholders; authorizing major corporate decisions; appointing, supervising, and removing corporate officers and other managerial employees; determining employees' compensation; and making financial decisions, such as the decision to issue authorized shares and bonds. Directors may delegate some of their responsibilities to executive committees and corporate officers and executives. 6. *Corporate officers and executives*—Corporate officers and other executive employees are normally hired by the board of directors. As employees, corporate officers and executives have the rights defined by their employment contracts. The duties of corporate officers are the same as those of directors.
Duties and Liabilities of Directors and Officers (See pages 811–813.)	1. *Duty of care*—Directors and officers are obligated to act in good faith, to use prudent business judgment in the conduct of corporate affairs, and to act in the corporation's best interests. If a director fails to exercise this duty of care, she or he can be answerable to the corporation and to the shareholders for breaching the duty. 2. *Duty of loyalty*—Directors and officers have a fiduciary duty to subordinate their own interests to those of the corporation in matters relating to the corporation. 3. *Conflicts of interest*—To fulfill their duty of loyalty, directors and officers must make a full disclosure of any potential conflicts between their personal interests and those of the corporation. 4. *Liability of directors and officers*—Corporate directors and officers are personally liable for their own torts and crimes; additionally, they may be held personally liable for the torts and crimes committed by corporate personnel under their supervision (see Chapters 6 and 24). 5. *The business judgment rule*—This rule immunizes directors and officers from liability when they acted in good faith, acted in the best interests of the corporation, and exercised due care. For the rule to apply, the directors and officers must have made an informed, reasonable, and loyal decision.
Role of Shareholders (See pages 813–818.)	1. *Shareholders' powers*—Shareholders' powers include the approval of all fundamental changes affecting the corporation and the election of the board of directors. 2. *Shareholders' meetings*—Shareholders' meetings must occur at least annually; special meetings can be called when necessary. Notice of the date, time, and place of the meeting (and its purpose, if it is specially called) must be sent to shareholders. Shareholders may vote by proxy (authorizing someone else to vote their shares) and may submit proposals to be included in the company's proxy materials sent to shareholders before meetings.

(Continued)

CHAPTER SUMMARY Corporate Directors, Officers, and Shareholders—Continued

Role of Shareholders— Continued	3. *Shareholder voting*—Shareholder voting requirements and procedures are as follows: a. A minimum number of shareholders (a quorum—generally, more than 50 percent of shares held) must be present at a meeting for business to be conducted; resolutions are passed (usually) by simple majority vote. b. The corporation must prepare voting lists of shareholders of record prior to each shareholders' meeting. c. Cumulative voting may or may not be required or permitted. Cumulative voting gives minority shareholders a better chance to be represented on the board of directors. d. A shareholder voting agreement (an agreement of shareholders to vote their shares together) is usually held to be valid and enforceable. e. A shareholder may appoint a proxy (substitute) to vote her or his shares. f. A shareholder may enter into a voting trust agreement by which title (record ownership) of his or her shares is given to a trustee, and the trustee votes the shares in accordance with the trust agreement.
Rights of Shareholders (See pages 818–823.)	Shareholders have numerous rights, which may include the following: 1. The right to a stock certificate, preemptive rights, and the right to stock warrants (depending on the articles of incorporation). 2. The right to obtain a dividend (at the discretion of the directors). 3. Voting rights. 4. The right to inspect the corporate records. 5. The right to transfer shares (this right may be restricted in close corporations). 6. The right to a share of corporate assets when the corporation is dissolved. 7. The right to sue on behalf of the corporation (bring a shareholder's derivative suit) when the directors fail to do so.
Duties and Liabilities of Shareholders (See pages 823–825.)	1. Shareholders may be liable for the retention of illegal dividends and for the value of watered stock. 2. In certain situations, majority shareholders may be regarded as having a fiduciary duty to minority shareholders and will be liable if that duty is breached.

FOR REVIEW

Answers for the even-numbered questions in this For Review *section can be found in Appendix E at the end of this text.*

1 What are the duties of corporate directors and officers?

2 Directors are expected to use their best judgment in managing the corporation. What must directors do to avoid liability for honest mistakes of judgment and poor business decisions?

3 What is a voting proxy? What is cumulative voting?

4 If a group of shareholders perceives that the corporation has suffered a wrong and the directors refuse to take action, can the shareholders compel the directors to act? If so, how?

5 From what sources may dividends be paid legally? In what circumstances is a dividend illegal? What happens if a dividend is illegally paid?

The following multiple-choice question is representative of the types of questions available in one of the four sections of ThomsonNOW for *Business Law Today*. ThomsonNOW also provides feedback for each response option, whether correct or incorrect, and refers to the location within the chapter where the correct answer can be found.

A major power held by shareholders is the power to

a appoint corporate officers.

b manage and supervise daily operations of the corporation.

c declare dividends.

d amend the articles of incorporation or the corporate bylaws.

QUESTIONS AND CASE PROBLEMS

 HYPOTHETICAL SCENARIOS

29.1 Voting Techniques. Algonquin Corp. has issued and has outstanding 100,000 shares of common stock. Four stockholders own 60,000 of these shares, and for the past six years they have nominated a slate of people for membership on the board, all of whom have been elected. Sergio and twenty other shareholders, owning 20,000 shares, are dissatisfied with corporate management and want a representative on the board who shares their views. Explain under what circumstances Sergio and the minority shareholders can elect their representative to the board.

29.2 Hypothetical Question with Sample Answer. Starboard, Inc., has a board of directors consisting of three members (Ellsworth, Green, and Morino) and approximately five hundred shareholders. At a regular meeting of the board, the board selects Tyson as president of the corporation by a two-to-one vote, with Ellsworth dissenting. The minutes of the meeting do not register Ellsworth's dissenting vote. Later, during an audit, it is discovered that Tyson is a former convict and has openly embezzled $500,000 from Starboard. This loss is not covered by insurance. The corporation wants to hold directors Ellsworth, Green, and Morino liable. Ellsworth claims no liability. Discuss the personal liability of the directors to the corporation.

 For a sample answer to Question 29.2, go to Appendix F at the end of this text.

29.3 Lucia has acquired one share of common stock of a multimillion-dollar corporation with more than 500,000 shareholders. Lucia's ownership is so small that she is questioning what her rights are as a shareholder. For example, she wants to know whether owning this one share entitles her to (1) attend and vote at shareholders' meetings, (2) inspect the corporate books, and (3) receive yearly dividends. Discuss Lucia's rights in these three matters.

CASE PROBLEMS

29.4 Business Judgment Rule. Charles Pace and Maria Fuentez were shareholders of Houston Industries, Inc. (HII), and employees of Houston Lighting & Power, a subsidiary of HII, when they lost their jobs because of a companywide reduction in its workforce. Pace, as a shareholder, three times wrote to HII, demanding that the board of directors terminate certain HII directors and officers and file a suit to recover damages for breach of fiduciary duty. Three times, the directors referred the charges to board committees and an outside law firm, which found that the facts did not support the charges. The board also received input from federal regulatory authorities about the facts behind some of the charges. The board notified Pace that it was refusing his demands. In response, Pace and Fuentez filed a shareholder's derivative suit in a Texas state court against Don Jordan and the other HII directors, contending that the board's investigation was inadequate. The defendants filed a motion for summary judgment, arguing that the suit was barred by the business judgment rule. Are the defendants right? How should the court rule? Why? [*Pace v. Jordan*, 999 S.W.2d 615 (Tex.App. — Houston [1 Dist.] 1999)]

29.5 Duties of Majority Shareholders. Atlas Food Systems & Services, Inc., based in South Carolina, was a food vending service that provided refreshments to factories and other businesses. Atlas was a closely held corporation. John Kiriakides was a minority shareholder of Atlas. Alex Kiriakides was the majority shareholder. Throughout most of Atlas's history, Alex was the chair of the board, which included John as a director. In 1995, while John was the president of the firm, the board and shareholders decided to convert Atlas to an S corporation. A few months later, however, Alex, without calling a vote, decided that the firm would not convert. In 1996, a dispute arose over Atlas's contract to buy certain property. John and others decided not to buy it. Without consulting anyone, Alex elected to go through with the sale. Within a few days, Alex refused to allow John to stay on as president. Two months later, Atlas offered to buy John's interest in the firm for almost $2 million. John refused, believing the offer was too low. John filed a suit in a South Carolina state court against Atlas and Alex, seeking, among other things, to force a buyout of John's shares. On what basis might the court grant John's request? Discuss. [*Kiriakides v. Atlas Food Systems & Services, Inc.*, 343 S.C. 587, 541 S.E.2d 257 (2001)]

29.6 Inspection Rights. Craig Johnson founded Distributed Solutions, Inc. (DSI), in 1991 to make software and provide consulting services, including payroll services, for small companies. Johnson was the sole officer and director and the majority shareholder. Jeffrey Hagen was a minority shareholder. In 1993, Johnson sold DSI's payroll services to himself and a few others and set up Distributed Payroll Solutions, Inc. (DPSI). In 1996, DSI had revenues of $739,034 and assets of $541,168. DSI's revenues in 1997 were $934,532. Within a year, however, all of DSI's assets were sold, and Johnson told Hagen that he was dissolving the firm because, among other things, it conducted no business and had no prospects for future business. Hagen asked for corporate records to determine the value of DSI's stock, DSI's financial condition, and "whether unauthorized and oppressive acts had occurred in connection with the operation of the corporation which impacted the value of" the stock. When there was no response, Hagen filed a suit in an Illinois state court against DSI and Johnson, seeking an order to compel the inspection. The defendants filed a motion to dismiss, arguing that Hagen had failed to plead a proper purpose. Should the court grant Hagen's request? Discuss. [*Hagen v. Distributed Solutions, Inc.*, 328 Ill.App.3d 132, 764 N.E.2d 1141, 262 Ill.Dec. 24 (1 Dist. 2002)]

29.7 Case Problem with Sample Answer. Digital Commerce, Ltd., designed software to enable its clients to sell their products or services over the Internet. Kevin Sullivan served as a Digital vice president until 2000, when he became president. Sullivan was dissatisfied that his compensation did not include stock in Digital, but he was unable to negotiate a deal that included equity (referring to shares of ownership in the company). In May, Sullivan solicited ASR Corp.'s business for Digital while he investigated employment opportunities with ASR for himself. When ASR would not include an "equity component" in a job offer, Sullivan refused to

negotiate further on Digital's behalf. A few months later, Sullivan began to form his own firm to compete with Digital, conducting organizational and marketing activities on Digital's time, including soliciting ASR's business. In August, Sullivan resigned after first having all e-mail pertaining to the new firm deleted from Digital's computers. ASR signed a contract with Sullivan's new firm and paid it $400,000 for work through October 2001. Digital filed a suit in a federal district court against Sullivan, claiming that he had usurped a corporate opportunity. Did Sullivan breach his fiduciary duty to Digital? Explain. [*In re Sullivan*, 305 Bankr. 809 (W.D.Mich. 2004)]

After you have answered Problem 29.7, compare your answer with the sample answer given on the Web site that accompanies this text. Go to **www.thomsonedu.com/westbuslaw/blt**, select "Chapter 29," and click on "Case Problem with Sample Answer."

29.8 Duties of Majority Shareholders. Steve and Marie Venturini were involved in the operation of Steve's Sizzling Steakhouse in Carlstadt, New Jersey, from the day their parents opened it in the 1930s. By the 1980s, Steve, Marie, and her husband, Joe, were running it. The business was a corporation with Steve and Marie each owning half of the stock. Steve died in 2001, leaving his stock in equal shares to his sons Steve and Gregg. Son Steve had never worked there. Gregg did occasional maintenance work until his father's death. Despite their lack of participation, the sons were paid more than $750 per week each. In 2002, Marie's son Blaise, who had obtained a college degree in restaurant management while working part-time at the steakhouse, took over its management. When his cousins became threatening, he denied them access to the business and its books. Marie refused Gregg and Steve's offer of about $1.4 million for her stock in the restaurant, and they refused her offer of about $800,000 for theirs. They filed a suit in a New Jersey state court against her, claiming, among other things, a breach of fiduciary duty. Should the court order the aunt to buy out the nephews or the nephews to buy out the aunt, or neither? Why? [*Venturini v. Steve's Steakhouse, Inc.*, __ N.J.Super. __, __ A.2d __ (Ch.Div. 2006)]

29.9 Fiduciary Duties and Liabilities. Harry Hoaas and Larry Griffiths were shareholders in Grand Casino, Inc., which owned and operated a casino in Watertown, South Dakota. Griffiths owned 51 percent of the stock and Hoaas 49 percent. Hoaas managed the casino, which Griffiths typically visited once a week. At the end of 1997, an accounting showed that the cash on hand was less than the amount posted in the casino's books. Later, more shortfalls were discovered. In October 1999, Griffiths did a complete audit. Hoaas was unable to account for $135,500 in missing cash. Griffiths then kept all of the casino's most recent profits, including Hoaas's $9,447.20 share, and, without telling Hoaas, sold the casino for $100,000 and kept all of the proceeds. Hoaas filed a suit in a South Dakota state court against Griffiths, asserting, among other things, a breach of fiduciary duty. Griffiths countered with evidence of Hoaas's misappropriation of corporate cash. What duties did these parties owe each other? Did either Griffiths or Hoaas, or both of them, breach those duties? How should their dispute be resolved? How should their finances be reconciled? Explain. [*Hoaas v. Griffiths,* 2006 SD 27, 714 N.W.2d 61 (2006)]

29.10 **A Question of Ethics.** *New Orleans Paddlewheels, Inc. (NOP), is a Louisiana corporation formed in 1982 when James Smith, Sr., and Warren Reuther were its only shareholders, with each holding 50 percent of the stock. NOP is part of a sprawling enterprise of tourism and hospitality companies in New Orleans. The positions on the board of each company were split equally between the Smith and Reuther families. At Smith's request, his son James Smith, Jr. (JES), became involved in the businesses. In 1999, NOP's board elected JES the president, in charge of day-to-day operations, and Reuther the chief executive officer (CEO), in charge of marketing and development. Over the next few years, animosity developed between Reuther and JES. In October 2001, JES terminated Reuther as CEO and denied him access to the offices and books of NOP and the other companies, literally changing the locks on the doors. At the*

next meetings of the boards of NOP and the overall enterprise, deadlock ensued, with the directors voting along family lines on every issue. Complaining that the meetings were a "waste of time," JES began to run the entire enterprise by taking advantage of an unequal balance of power on the companies' executive committees. In NOP's subsequent bankruptcy proceeding, Reuther filed a motion for the appointment of a trustee to formulate a plan for the firm's reorganization, alleging, among other things, misconduct by NOP's management. [In re New Orleans Paddlewheels, Inc., 350 Bankr. 667 (E.D.La. 2006)]

1 Was Reuther legally entitled to have access to the books and records of NOP and the other companies? JES maintained, among other things, that NOP's books were "a mess." Was JES's denial of that access unethical? Explain.

2 How would you describe JES's attempt to gain control of NOP and the other companies? Were his actions duplicitous and self-serving in the pursuit of personal gain or legitimate and reasonable in the pursuit of a business goal? Discuss.

CRITICAL THINKING
AND WRITING ASSIGNMENTS

29.11 Critical Legal Thinking. In general, courts are reluctant to grant shareholders' petitions for corporate dissolution except in extreme circumstances, such as when corporate directors or shareholders are deadlocked and the corporation suffers as a result. Rather, a court will attempt to "save" the corporate entity whenever possible. Why is this?

ONLINE ACTIVITIES

PRACTICAL
INTERNET EXERCISES

Go to this text's Web site at **www.thomsonedu.com/westbuslaw/blt**, select "Chapter 29," and click on "Practical Internet Exercises." There you will find the following Internet research exercises that you can perform to learn more about the topics covered in this chapter.

PRACTICAL INTERNET EXERCISE 29–1 LEGAL PERSPECTIVE—Liability of Directors and Officers

PRACTICAL INTERNET EXERCISE 29–2 MANAGEMENT PERSPECTIVE—D & O Insurance

BEFORE THE TEST

Go to this text's Web site at **www.thomsonedu.com/westbuslaw/blt**, select "Chapter 29," and click on "Interactive Quizzes." You will find a number of interactive questions relating to this chapter.

CHAPTER 30
Investor Protection, Insider Trading, and Corporate Governance

LEARNING OBJECTIVES

AFTER READING THIS CHAPTER, YOU SHOULD BE ABLE TO ANSWER THE FOLLOWING QUESTIONS:

1 What is meant by the term *securities?*

2 What are the two major statutes regulating the securities industry? When was the Securities and Exchange Commission created, and what are its major purposes and functions?

3 What is insider trading? Why is it prohibited?

4 What are some of the features of state securities laws?

5 What certification requirements does the Sarbanes-Oxley Act impose on corporate executives?

> **❝** It shall be unlawful for any person in the offer or sale of any security . . . to engage in any transaction, practice, or course of business which operates or would operate as a fraud or deceit upon the purchaser. **❞**

Securities Act of 1933, Section 17

SECURITY
Generally, a stock certificate, bond, note, debenture, warrant, or other document or record evidencing an ownership interest in a corporation or a promise to repay a corporation's debt.

After the stock market crash of 1929, many members of Congress argued in favor of regulating securities markets. Basically, legislation for such regulation was enacted to provide investors with more information to help them make buying and selling decisions about **securities**—generally defined as any documents or records evidencing corporate ownership (stock) or debts (bonds)—and to prohibit deceptive, unfair, and manipulative practices. Today, the sale and transfer of securities are heavily regulated by federal and state statutes and by government agencies.

This chapter discusses the nature of federal securities regulation and its effect on the business world. We first examine the major traditional laws governing securities offerings and trading. We then discuss corporate governance and the Sarbanes-Oxley Act of 2002,[1] which affects certain types of securities transactions. Finally, we look at how securities laws are being adapted to the online environment. Before we begin, though, the important role played by the Securities and Exchange Commission (SEC) in the regulation of federal securities laws requires some attention. We examine the origin and functions of the SEC in this chapter's *Landmark in the Law* feature on pages 836 and 837.

SECURITIES ACT OF 1933

The Securities Act of 1933[2] governs initial sales of stock by businesses. The act was designed to prohibit various forms of fraud and to stabilize the securities industry by requiring that all essential information concerning the issuance of securities be made available

---

1. 15 U.S.C. Sections 7201 *et seq.*
2. 15 U.S.C. Sections 77–77aa.

to the investing public. Basically, the purpose of this act is to require disclosure. The 1933 act provides that all securities transactions must be registered with the SEC or be exempt from registration requirements.

What Is a Security?

Section 2(1) of the Securities Act states that securities include the following:

> [A]ny note, stock, treasury stock, bond, debenture, evidence of indebtedness, certificate of interest or participation in any profit-sharing agreement, collateral-trust certificate, preorganization certificate or subscription, transferable share, investment contract, voting-trust certificate, certificate of deposit for a security, fractional undivided interest in oil, gas, or other mineral rights, or, in general, any interest or instrument commonly known as a "security," or any certificate of interest or participation in, temporary or interim certificate for, receipt for, guarantee of, or warrant or right to subscribe to or purchase, any of the foregoing.[3]

The courts have had to interpret what the act's statement of what constitutes a security[4] means by "investment contracts." An investment contract is any transaction in which a person (1) invests (2) in a common enterprise (3) reasonably expecting profits (4) derived *primarily* or *substantially* from others' managerial or entrepreneurial efforts.[5]

During the stock market crash of 1929, hordes of investors crowded Wall Street to find out the latest news. How did this crash affect the future stock market? (National Archives)

For our purposes, it is probably convenient to think of securities in their most common forms—stocks and bonds issued by corporations. Bear in mind, though, that securities can take many forms and have been held to include whiskey, cosmetics, worms, beavers, boats, vacuum cleaners, muskrats, and cemetery lots, as well as investment contracts in condominiums, franchises, limited partnerships, oil or gas or other mineral rights, and farm animals accompanied by care agreements.

■EXAMPLE 30.1 Alpha Telcom sold, installed, and maintained pay-phone systems. As part of its pay-phone program, Alpha guaranteed buyers a 14 percent return on the amount of their purchase. Alpha was operating at a net loss, however, and continually borrowed funds to pay investors the fixed rate of return it had promised. Eventually, the company filed for bankruptcy, and the SEC brought an action alleging that Alpha had violated the Securities Act of 1933. In this situation, a federal court concluded that the pay-phone program was a security because it involved an investment contract.[6] ■

Businesspersons should be aware that securities are not limited to stocks and bonds but can encompass a wide variety of interests. The analysis hinges on the nature of the transaction rather than the instrument or substance involved. Because Congress enacted securities laws to regulate *investments,* in whatever form and by whatever name they are called, virtually any type of security that might be sold as an investment can be subject to securities laws. When in doubt about whether an investment transaction involves securities, businesspersons should always seek the advice of an attorney.

PREVENTING
LEGAL DISPUTES

---

3. 15 U.S.C. Section 77b(1). Amendments in 1982 added stock options.
4. See 15 U.S.C. Section 77b(a)(1).
5. *SEC v. W. J. Howey Co.,* 328 U.S. 293, 66 S.Ct. 1100, 90 L.Ed. 1244 (1946).
6. *SEC v. Alpha Telcom, Inc.,* 187 F.Supp.2d 1250 (2002). See also *SEC v. Edwards,* 540 U.S. 389, 124 S.Ct. 892, 157 L.Ed.2d 813 (2004), in which the United States Supreme Court held that an investment scheme offering contractual entitlement to a fixed rate of return can be an investment contract and therefore can be considered a security under federal law.

LANDMARK IN THE LAW — The Securities and Exchange Commission

In 1931, the U.S. Senate passed a resolution calling for an extensive investigation of securities trading. The investigation led, ultimately, to the passage by Congress of the Securities Act of 1933, which is also known as the *truth-in-securities* bill. In the following year, Congress passed the Securities Exchange Act. This 1934 act created the Securities and Exchange Commission (SEC).

Major Responsibilities of the SEC   The SEC was created as an independent regulatory agency with the function of administering the 1933 and 1934 acts. Its major responsibilities in this respect are as follows:

1 Requiring disclosure of facts concerning offerings of securities listed on national securities exchanges and of certain securities traded over the counter (OTC).
2 Regulating the trade in securities on national and regional securities exchanges and in the OTC markets.
3 Investigating securities fraud.
4 Regulating the activities of securities brokers, dealers, and investment advisers and requiring their registration.
5 Supervising the activities of mutual funds.
6 Recommending administrative sanctions, injunctive remedies, and criminal prosecution against those who violate securities laws. (The SEC can bring enforcement actions for civil violations of federal securities laws. The Fraud Section of the Criminal Division of the U.S. Department of Justice prosecutes criminal violations.)

The SEC's Expanding Regulatory Powers   Since its creation, the SEC's regulatory functions have gradually been increased by legislation granting it authority in different areas. For example, to further curb securities fraud, the Securities Enforcement Remedies and Penny Stock Reform Act of 1990[a] amended existing securities laws to allow SEC administrative law judges to hear cases involving many more types of alleged

a. 15 U.S.C. Section 77g.

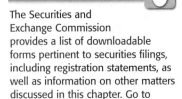

PROSPECTUS
A written document, required by securities laws, that describes the security being sold, the financial operations of the issuing corporation, and the investment or risk attaching to the security. It is designed to provide sufficient information to enable investors to evaluate the risk involved in purchasing the security.

Registration Statement

Section 5 of the Securities Act of 1933 broadly provides that unless a security qualifies for an exemption, that security must be *registered* before it is offered to the public. Issuing corporations must file a *registration statement* with the SEC and must provide all investors with a *prospectus*. A **prospectus** is a written disclosure document that describes the security being sold, the financial operations of the issuing corporation, and the investment or risk attaching to the security. The 1933 act requires a prospectus to be delivered to investors, and issuers use this document as a selling tool. In principle, the registration statement and the prospectus supply sufficient information to enable unsophisticated investors to evaluate the financial risk involved.

Contents of the Registration Statement   The registration statement must be written in plain English and fully describe the following:

securities law violations; the SEC's enforcement options were also greatly expanded. In addition, the act provides that courts can prevent persons who have engaged in securities fraud from serving as officers and directors of publicly held corporations. The Securities Acts Amendments of 1990 authorized the SEC to seek sanctions against those who violate foreign securities laws.[b]

The National Securities Markets Improvement Act of 1996 expanded the power of the SEC to exempt persons, securities, and transactions from the requirements of the securities laws.[c] (This part of the act is also known as the Capital Markets Efficiency Act.) The act also limited the authority of the states to regulate certain securities transactions and particular investment advisory firms.[d] The Sarbanes-Oxley Act of 2002,[e] which you will read about later in this chapter, further expanded the authority of the SEC by directing the agency to issue new rules relating to corporate disclosure requirements and by creating an oversight board to regulate public accounting firms.

APPLICATION TO TODAY'S WORLD *Congress and the SEC have been attempting to streamline the regulatory process generally. The goal is to make it more efficient and more relevant to today's securities trading practices, including those occurring in the online environment. Another goal is to establish more oversight over securities transactions and accounting practices. Additionally, as the number and types of online securities frauds increase, the SEC is trying to keep pace by expanding its online fraud division.*

RELEVANT WEB SITES *To locate information on the Web concerning the SEC, go to this text's Web site at* **www.thomsonedu.com/westbuslaw/blt**, *select "Chapter 30," and click on "URLs for Landmarks."*

b. 15 U.S.C. Section 78a.
c. 15 U.S.C. Sections 77z-3, 78mm.
d. 15 U.S.C. Section 80b-3a.
e. 15 U.S.C. Sections 7201 *et seq.*

Shown here is the New York Stock Exchange. It is only one of the many markets in which securities are publicly traded. Indeed, in today's global context, New York is no longer the "king" of financial markets. In any event, security trading in the United States is heavily regulated. Does this regulation mean that investors face less risk? (Luis Villa del Campo/ Creative Commons)

DON'T FORGET The purpose of the Securities Act of 1933 is disclosure—the SEC does not consider whether a security is worth the investment price.

1 The securities being offered for sale, including their relationship to the registrant's other capital securities.

2 The corporation's properties and business (including a financial statement certified by an independent public accounting firm).

3 The management of the corporation, including managerial compensation, stock options, pensions, and other benefits. Any interests of directors or officers in any material transactions with the corporation must be disclosed.

4 How the corporation intends to use the proceeds of the sale.

5 Any pending lawsuits or special risk factors.

Registration Process The registration statement does not become effective until after it has been reviewed and approved by the SEC. The 1933 act restricts the types of activities that an issuer can engage in at each stage in the registration process. If an issuer violates the restrictions discussed here, investors can rescind their contracts to purchase the securities. During the *prefiling period* (before filing the registration statement), the issuer cannot either sell or offer to sell the securities. No advertising of an upcoming securities offering is allowed during the prefiling period.

Waiting Period. Once the registration statement has been filed, a waiting period of at least twenty days begins during which the SEC reviews the registration statement for completeness. Typically, the staff members at the SEC who review the registration statement ask the registrant to make numerous changes and additions, which can extend the length of the waiting period.[7] During the waiting period, the issuing corporation may make *oral* offers to sell the securities to interested investors and may distribute a *preliminary prospectus*, called a **red herring prospectus.**[8] A red herring prospectus contains most of the information that will be included in the final prospectus but often does not include a price. Only general advertising is permitted, such as a **tombstone ad,** so named because historically the format resembled a tombstone. Such ads simply tell the investor where and how to obtain a prospectus. Normally, any other type of advertising—as well as written offers or actual sales—is prohibited until the registration becomes effective.

Posteffective Period. Once the SEC has reviewed and approved the registration statement and the twenty-day period has elapsed, the registration is effective. The issuer can now offer and sell the securities without restrictions. If the company issued a preliminary prospectus to investors, it must provide those investors with a final prospectus either prior to or at the time they purchase the securities. The issuer can require investors to download the final prospectus from a Web site.

EXAMPLE 30.2 Delphia, Inc., wants to make a public offering of its common stock. The firm files a registration statement and a prospectus with the SEC on May 1. On the same day, the company can make its first *offers* to sell the stock, but an actual sale can take place only *after* the SEC declares the registration to be effective. On May 10, Delphia places tombstone ads in certain trade publications to announce the offering and to tell investors how to get a prospectus. The firm issues a preliminary prospectus on May 15. On May 20, the registration statement becomes effective, and the company makes the final prospectus available to potential buyers. On this date, Delphia can sell the first shares in the issue. ■

Exempt Securities

A number of specific securities are exempt from the registration requirements of the Securities Act of 1933. These securities—which can also generally be resold without being registered—include the following[9]:

1 Government-issued securities.

2 Bank and financial institution securities, which are regulated by banking authorities.

3 Short-term notes and drafts (negotiable instruments that have a maturity date that does not exceed nine months).

RED HERRING PROSPECTUS
A preliminary prospectus that can be distributed to potential investors after the registration statement (for a securities offering) has been filed with the Securities and Exchange Commission. The name derives from the red legend printed across the prospectus stating that the registration has been filed but has not become effective.

TOMBSTONE AD
An advertisement, historically in a format resembling a tombstone, of a securities offering. The ad tells potential investors where and how they may obtain a prospectus.

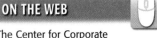

ON THE WEB

The Center for Corporate Law at the University of Cincinnati College of Law examines all of the acts discussed in this chapter. Go to

www.law.uc.edu/CCL.

---

7. It is common for the SEC to require a registrant to provide additional information more than once. After the registration statement has gone through several rounds of changes, the SEC gives its approval. In these circumstances, because the process may have taken months to complete, registrants frequently request an acceleration of the twenty-day waiting period. If the SEC grants the request, registration can become effective without the issuer having to wait the full twenty days.

8. The name *red herring* comes from the red legend printed across the prospectus stating that the registration has been filed but has not become effective.

9. 15 U.S.C. Section 77c.

4 Securities of nonprofit, educational, and charitable organizations.

5 Securities issued by common carriers (railroads and trucking companies).

6 Any insurance, endowment, or annuity contract issued by a state-regulated insurance company.

7 Securities issued in a corporate reorganization in which one security is exchanged for another or in a bankruptcy proceeding.

8 Securities issued in stock dividends and stock splits.

Exhibit 30–1 summarizes the securities and transactions (discussed next) that are exempt from the registration requirements under the Securities Act of 1933 and SEC regulations.

Exempt Transactions

In addition to the exempt securities listed in the previous subsection, certain *transactions* are exempt from registration requirements. These transaction exemptions are very broad

EXHIBIT 30–1 **Exemptions under the 1933 Securities Act**

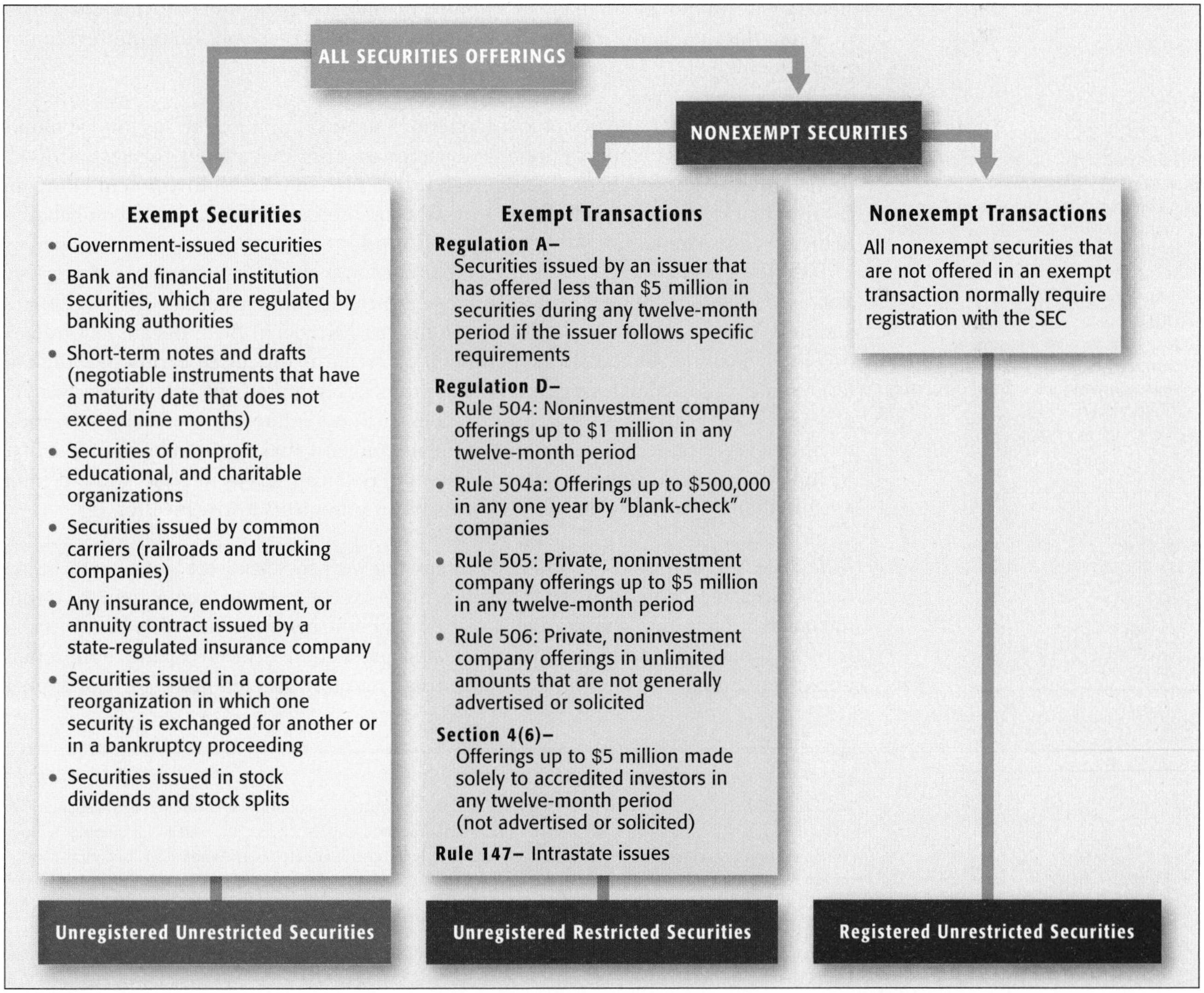

ALL SECURITIES OFFERINGS

NONEXEMPT SECURITIES

Exempt Securities

- Government-issued securities
- Bank and financial institution securities, which are regulated by banking authorities
- Short-term notes and drafts (negotiable instruments that have a maturity date that does not exceed nine months)
- Securities of nonprofit, educational, and charitable organizations
- Securities issued by common carriers (railroads and trucking companies)
- Any insurance, endowment, or annuity contract issued by a state-regulated insurance company
- Securities issued in a corporate reorganization in which one security is exchanged for another or in a bankruptcy proceeding
- Securities issued in stock dividends and stock splits

Unregistered Unrestricted Securities

Exempt Transactions

Regulation A–
Securities issued by an issuer that has offered less than $5 million in securities during any twelve-month period if the issuer follows specific requirements

Regulation D–
- Rule 504: Noninvestment company offerings up to $1 million in any twelve-month period
- Rule 504a: Offerings up to $500,000 in any one year by "blank-check" companies
- Rule 505: Private, noninvestment company offerings up to $5 million in any twelve-month period
- Rule 506: Private, noninvestment company offerings in unlimited amounts that are not generally advertised or solicited

Section 4(6)–
Offerings up to $5 million made solely to accredited investors in any twelve-month period (not advertised or solicited)

Rule 147– Intrastate issues

Unregistered Restricted Securities

Nonexempt Transactions

All nonexempt securities that are not offered in an exempt transaction normally require registration with the SEC

Registered Unrestricted Securities

and can enable an issuer to avoid the high cost and complicated procedures associated with registration. Because the coverage of the exemptions overlaps somewhat, an offering may qualify for more than one. Therefore, many sales occur without registration.

Regulation A Offerings Securities issued by an issuer that has offered less than $5 million in securities during any twelve-month period are exempt from registration.[10] Under Regulation A,[11] the issuer must file with the SEC a notice of the issue and an offering circular, which must also be provided to investors before the sale. This is a much simpler and less expensive process than the procedures associated with full registration. Companies are allowed to "test the waters" for potential interest before preparing the offering circular. To *test the waters* means to determine potential interest without actually selling any securities or requiring any commitment on the part of those who express interest. Small-business issuers (companies with annual revenues of less than $25 million) can also use an integrated registration and reporting system that uses simpler forms than the full registration system.

Small Offerings—Regulation D The SEC's Regulation D contains four separate exemptions from registration requirements for limited offers (offers that either involve a small dollar amount or are made in a limited manner). Regulation D provides that any of these offerings made during any twelve-month period are exempt from the registration requirements.

Rule 504. Noninvestment company offerings up to $1 million in any twelve-month period are exempt.[12] Noninvestment companies are firms that are not engaged primarily in the business of investing or trading in securities. (In contrast, an **investment company** is a firm that buys a large portfolio of securities and professionally manages it on behalf of many smaller shareholders/owners. A **mutual fund** is a type of investment company.)

INVESTMENT COMPANY
A company that acts on behalf of many smaller shareholders/owners by buying a large portfolio of securities and professionally managing that portfolio.

MUTUAL FUND
A specific type of investment company that continually buys or sells to investors shares of ownership in a portfolio.

■EXAMPLE 30.3 Beta, L.P., is a limited partnership that develops commercial property. Beta intends to offer $600,000 of its limited partnership interests for sale between June 1 and next May 31. The buyers will become limited partners in Beta. Because an interest in a limited partnership meets the definition of a security (discussed earlier in this chapter), its sale is subject to the registration and prospectus requirements of the Securities Act of 1933. Under Rule 504, however, the sales of Beta's interests are exempt from these requirements because Beta is a noninvestment company making an offering of less than $1 million in a twelve-month period. Therefore, Beta can sell its interests without filing a registration statement with the SEC or issuing a prospectus to any investor. ■

Rule 504a. Offerings up to $500,000 in any one year by so-called blank-check companies—companies with no specific business plans except to locate and acquire currently unknown businesses or opportunities—are exempt if no general solicitation or advertising is used; the SEC is notified of the sales; and precaution is taken against nonexempt, unregistered resales.[13] The limits on advertising and unregistered resales do not apply if

---

10. 15 U.S.C. Section 77c(b).
11. 17 C.F.R. Sections 230.251–230.263.
12. 17 C.F.R. Section 230.504. Rule 504 is the exemption used by most small businesses, but that could change under new SEC Rule 1001. This rule permits, under certain circumstances, "testing the waters" for offerings of up to $5 million *per transaction*. These offerings can be made only to "qualified purchasers" (knowledgeable, sophisticated investors), though.
13. Precautions to be taken against nonexempt, unregistered resales include asking the investor whether he or she is buying the securities for others; before the sale, disclosing to each purchaser in writing that the securities are unregistered and thus cannot be resold, except in an exempt transaction, without first being registered; and indicating on the certificates that the securities are unregistered and restricted.

the offering is made solely in states that provide for registration and disclosure and the securities are sold in compliance with those provisions.[14]

Rule 505.   Private, noninvestment company offerings up to $5 million in any twelve-month period are exempt, regardless of the number of **accredited investors** (banks, insurance companies, investment companies, the issuer's executive officers and directors, and persons whose income or net worth exceeds certain limits), so long as there are no more than thirty-five unaccredited investors; no general solicitation or advertising is used; the SEC is notified of the sales; and precaution is taken against nonexempt, unregistered resales. If the sale involves *any* unaccredited investors, *all* investors must be given material information about the offering company, its business, and the securities before the sale. Unlike Rule 506 (discussed next), Rule 505 does not require that the issuer believe each unaccredited investor "has such knowledge and experience in financial and business matters that he [or she] is capable of evaluating the merits and the risks of the prospective investment."[15]

Rule 506.   Private, noninvestment company offerings in unlimited amounts that are not generally solicited or advertised are exempt if the SEC is notified of the sales; precaution is taken against nonexempt, unregistered resales; and the issuer believes that each unaccredited investor has sufficient knowledge or experience in financial matters to be capable of evaluating the investment's merits and risks. There may be no more than thirty-five unaccredited investors, but there are no limits on the number of accredited investors. If there are *any* unaccredited investors, the issuer must provide *all* purchasers with material information about itself, its business, and the securities before the sale.[16]

This exemption is perhaps most important to those firms that want to raise funds through the sale of securities without registering them. It is often referred to as the *private placement* exemption because it exempts "transactions not involving any public offering."[17] This provision applies to private offerings to a limited number of persons who are sufficiently sophisticated and able to assume the risk of the investment (and who thus have no need for federal registration protection). It also applies to private offerings to similarly situated institutional investors.

■**EXAMPLE 30.4** Citco Corporation needs to raise capital to expand its operations. Citco decides to make a private $10 million offering of its common stock directly to two hundred accredited investors and a group of thirty highly sophisticated, but unaccredited, investors. Citco provides all of these investors with a prospectus and material information about the firm, including its most recent financial statements. As long as Citco notifies the SEC of the sale, this offering will likely qualify as an exempt transaction under Rule 506. The offering is nonpublic and not generally advertised. There are fewer than thirty-five unaccredited investors, and each of them possesses sufficient knowledge and experience to evaluate the risks involved. The issuer has provided all purchasers with the material information. Thus, Citco will *not* be required to comply with the registration requirements of the Securities Act of 1933. ■

Small Offerings—Section 4(6)   Under Section 4(6) of the Securities Act of 1933, an offer made *solely* to accredited investors is exempt if its amount is not more than $5 million. Any number of accredited investors may participate, but no unaccredited investors may do so. No general solicitation or advertising may be used; the SEC must be notified of all sales; and precautions must be taken against nonexempt, unregistered resales. Precautions are

ACCREDITED INVESTORS
In the context of securities offerings, "sophisticated" investors, such as banks, insurance companies, investment companies, the issuer's executive officers and directors, and persons whose income or net worth exceeds certain limits.

KEEP IN MIND   An investor can be "sophisticated" by virtue of his or her education and experience or by investing through a knowledgeable, experienced representative.

---

14. 17 C.F.R. Section 230.504a.
15. 17 C.F.R. Section 230.505.
16. 17 C.F.R. Section 230.506.
17. 15 U.S.C. Section 77d(2).

necessary because these are *restricted* securities and may be resold only by registration or in an exempt transaction.[18] (The securities purchased and sold by most people who deal in stock are called, in contrast, *unrestricted* securities.)

Intrastate Offerings—Rule 147   Also exempt are intrastate transactions involving purely local offerings.[19] This exemption applies to most offerings that are restricted to residents of the state in which the issuing company is organized and doing business. For nine months after the last sale, virtually no resales may be made to nonresidents, and precautions must be taken against this possibility. These offerings remain subject to applicable laws in the state of issue.

Resales   Most securities can be resold without registration (although some resales may be subject to restrictions, as discussed above in connection with specific exemptions). The Securities Act of 1933 provides exemptions for resales by most persons other than issuers or underwriters. The average investor who sells shares of stock does not have to file a registration statement with the SEC. Resales of restricted securities acquired under Rule 504a, Rule 505, Rule 506, or Section 4(6), however, trigger the registration requirements unless the party selling them complies with Rule 144 or Rule 144A. These rules are sometimes referred to as "safe harbors."

Rule 144.   Rule 144 exempts restricted securities from registration on resale if there is adequate current public information about the issuer, the person selling the securities has owned them for at least one year, they are sold in certain limited amounts in unsolicited brokers' transactions, and the SEC is given notice of the resale.[20] "Adequate current public information" refers to the reports that certain companies are required to file under the Securities Exchange Act of 1934. A person who has owned the securities for at least one year is subject to none of these requirements, unless the person is an affiliate. An *affiliate* is one who controls, is controlled by, or is in common control with the issuer.

CONTRAST   Securities do not have to be held for one year to be exempt from registration on a resale under Rule 144A, as they do under Rule 144.

Rule 144A.   Securities that at the time of issue are not of the same class as securities listed on a national securities exchange or quoted in a U.S. automated interdealer quotation system may be resold under Rule 144A.[21] They may be sold only to a qualified institutional buyer (an institution, such as an insurance company or a bank that owns and invests at least $100 million in securities). The seller must take reasonable steps to ensure that the buyer knows that the seller is relying on the exemption under Rule 144A. A sample restricted stock certificate is shown in Exhibit 30–2.

Violations of the 1933 Act

As mentioned, the SEC has the power to investigate and bring civil enforcement actions against companies that violate federal securities laws. It is a violation of the Securities Act of 1933 to intentionally defraud investors by misrepresenting or omitting facts in a registration statement or prospectus. Liability is also imposed on those who are negligent for not discovering the fraud. Selling securities before the effective date of the registration statement or under an exemption for which the securities do not qualify results in liability.

Criminal violations are prosecuted by the U.S. Department of Justice. Violators may be fined up to $10,000, imprisoned for up to five years, or both. The SEC is authorized

---

18. 15 U.S.C. Section 77d(6).
19. 15 U.S.C. Section 77c(a)(11); 17 C.F.R. Section 230.147.
20. 17 C.F.R. Section 230.144.
21. 17 C.F.R. Section 230.144A.

EXHIBIT 30–2 **A Sample Restricted Stock Certificate**

to seek civil sanctions against those who willfully violate the 1933 act. It can request an injunction to prevent further sales of the securities involved or ask the court to grant other relief, such as an order to a violator to refund profits. Those parties who purchase securities and suffer harm as a result of false or omitted statements may also bring suits in a federal court to recover their losses and other damages.

SECURITIES EXCHANGE ACT OF 1934

The Securities Exchange Act of 1934 provides for the regulation and registration of securities exchanges, brokers, dealers, and national securities associations, such as the National Association of Securities Dealers (NASD). Unlike the 1933 act, which is a one-time disclosure law, the 1934 act provides for continuous periodic disclosures by publicly held corporations to enable the SEC to regulate subsequent trading. The Securities Exchange Act of 1934 applies to companies that have assets in excess of $10 million and five hundred or more shareholders. These corporations are referred to as Section 12 companies because they are required to register their securities under Section 12 of the 1934 act. Section 12 companies are required to file reports with the SEC annually and quarterly, and sometimes even monthly if specified events occur (such as a merger).

The act also authorizes the SEC to engage in market surveillance to deter undesirable market practices such as fraud, market manipulation (attempts at illegally influencing stock prices), and misrepresentation. In addition, the act provides for the SEC's regulation of proxy solicitations for voting (discussed in Chapter 29).

Section 10(b), SEC Rule 10b-5, and Insider Trading

Section 10(b) is one of the most important sections of the Securities Exchange Act of 1934. This section proscribes the use of any manipulative or deceptive device in violation of SEC rules and regulations. Among the rules that the SEC has promulgated pursuant

SEC RULE 10b-5
A rule of the Securities and Exchange Commission that makes it unlawful, in connection with the purchase or sale of any security, to make any untrue statement of a material fact or to omit a material fact if such omission causes the statement to be misleading.

to the 1934 act is **SEC Rule 10b-5,** which prohibits the commission of fraud in connection with the purchase or sale of any security.

Applicability of SEC Rule 10b-5   SEC Rule 10b-5 applies in virtually all cases concerning the trading of securities, whether on organized exchanges, in over-the-counter markets, or in private transactions. The rule covers, among other things, notes, bonds, agreements to form a corporation, and joint-venture agreements. Generally, it covers just about any form of security. It is immaterial whether a firm has securities registered under the 1933 act for the 1934 act to apply.

SEC Rule 10b-5 is applicable only when the requisites of federal jurisdiction—such as the use of stock exchange facilities, U.S. mail, or any means of interstate commerce—are present. Nevertheless, virtually every commercial transaction involves interstate contacts. In addition, the states have corporate securities laws, many of which include provisions similar to SEC Rule 10b-5.

INSIDER TRADING
The purchase or sale of securities on the basis of information that has not been made available to the public.

Insider Trading   One of the major goals of Section 10(b) and SEC Rule 10b-5 is to prevent so-called **insider trading,** which occurs when persons buy or sell securities on the basis of information that is not available to the public. Corporate directors, officers, and others such as majority shareholders, for instance, often have advance inside information that can affect the future market value of the corporate stock. Obviously, if they act on this information, their positions give them a trading advantage over the general public and other shareholders. The 1934 Securities Exchange Act defines inside information and extends liability to those who take advantage of such information in their personal transactions when they know that the information is unavailable to those with whom they are dealing. Section 10(b) of the 1934 act and SEC Rule 10b-5 apply to anyone who has access to or receives information of a nonpublic nature on which trading is based—not just to corporate "insiders."

Evidence in an insider trading case against the former chief executive officer of Qwest Communications gets delivered to a Denver courthouse. Why is insider trading deemed illegal? (AP Photo/ Ed Andrieski)

Disclosure under SEC Rule 10b-5   Any material omission or misrepresentation of material facts in connection with the purchase or sale of a security may violate not only the Securities Act of 1933 but also the antifraud provisions of Section 10(b) of the 1934 act and SEC Rule 10b-5. The key to liability (which can be civil or criminal) under Section 10(b) and SEC Rule 10b-5 is whether the insider's information is *material.*

Examples of Material Facts Calling for Disclosure.   The following are some examples of material facts calling for disclosure under SEC Rule 10b-5:

1 Fraudulent trading in the company stock by a broker-dealer.

2 A dividend change (whether up or down).

3 A contract for the sale of corporate assets.

4 A new discovery, a new process, or a new product.

5 A significant change in the firm's financial condition.

6 Potential litigation against the company.

Note that any one of these facts, by itself, is not *automatically* considered a material fact. Rather, it will be regarded as a material fact if it is significant enough that it would likely affect an investor's decision as to whether to purchase or sell the company's securities. **■EXAMPLE 30.5** Omega Company is the defendant in a class-action product liability lawsuit.

Omega's attorney, Paula Frasier, believes that the company likely will ultimately be held liable for damages, resulting in a considerable loss to the company. She advises Omega's directors, officers, and accountants of this possibility. Omega plans to make a $5 million offering of newly issued stock before the date when the trial in the suit is expected to end. Omega's potential liability in the litigation and the financial consequences to the firm are material facts that must be disclosed because they are significant enough to affect an investor's decision as to whether to purchase the stock. ▣

The following is one of the landmark cases interpreting SEC Rule 10b-5. The SEC sued Texas Gulf Sulphur Company for issuing a misleading press release. The release underestimated the magnitude and value of a mineral discovery. The SEC also sued several of Texas Gulf Sulphur's directors, officers, and employees under SEC Rule 10b-5 for purchasing large amounts of the corporate stock prior to the announcement of the corporation's rich ore discovery.

CASE 30.1 **SEC v. Texas Gulf Sulphur Co.**

LANDMARK AND CLASSIC CASES

United States Court of Appeals, Second Circuit, 401 F.2d 833 (1968).

HISTORICAL AND ENVIRONMENTAL SETTING

No court has ever held that every buyer or seller is entitled to all of the information relating to all of the circumstances in every stock transaction. By the mid-1950s, however, significant understatement of the value of the assets of a company had been held to be materially misleading.[a] In 1957, the Texas Gulf Sulphur Company (TGS) began exploring for minerals in eastern Canada. In March 1959, aerial geophysical surveys were conducted over more than fifteen thousand square miles of the area. The operations revealed numerous and extraordinary variations in the conductivity of the rock, which indicated a remarkable concentration of commercially exploitable minerals. One site of such variations was near Timmins, Ontario. On October 29 and 30, 1963, a ground survey of the site near Timmins indicated a need to drill for further evaluation.

FACTS On November 12, 1963, the Texas Gulf Sulphur Company drilled a hole that appeared to yield a core with an exceedingly high mineral content, although further drilling would be necessary to establish whether there was enough ore to be mined commercially. TGS kept secret the results of the core sample. After learning of the ore discovery, officers and employees of the company made substantial purchases of TGS's stock or accepted stock options. On April 11, 1964, an unauthorized report of the mineral find appeared in the newspapers. On the following day, April 12, TGS issued a press release that played down the discovery and stated that it was

a. *Speed v. Transamerica Corp.,* 99 F.Supp. 808 (D.Del. 1951).

too early to tell whether the ore find would be a significant one. Later on, TGS announced a strike of at least 25 million tons of ore. The news led to a substantial increase in the price of TGS stock. The Securities and Exchange Commission (SEC) brought a suit in a federal district court against the officers and employees of TGS for violating the insider-trading prohibition of SEC Rule 10b-5. The officers and employees argued that the prohibition did not apply. They reasoned that the information on which they had traded was not material, as the find had not been commercially proved. The trial court held that most of the defendants had not violated SEC Rule 10b-5, and the SEC appealed.

ISSUE Did the officers and employees of TGS violate SEC Rule 10b-5 by buying the stock, even though they did not know the full extent and profit potential of the ore discovery at the time of their purchases?

DECISION Yes. The U.S. Court of Appeals for the Second Circuit reversed the lower court's decision and remanded the case for further proceedings, holding that the employees and officers had violated SEC Rule 10b-5's prohibition against insider trading.

REASON For SEC Rule 10b-5 purposes, the test of materiality is whether the information would affect the judgment of reasonable investors. Reasonable investors include speculative as well as conservative investors. "[A] major factor in determining whether the * * * discovery [of the ore] was a material fact is the importance attached to the drilling results by those who knew about it. * * * [T]he

CASE 30.1–Continues next page

CASE 30.1–Continued

timing by those who knew of it of their stock purchases and their purchases of short-term calls [rights to buy shares at a specified price within a specified time period]—purchases in some cases by individuals who had never before purchased calls or even TGS stock—virtually compels the inference that the insiders were influenced by the drilling results. * * * We hold, therefore, that all transactions in TGS stock or calls by individuals apprised of the drilling results * * * were made in violation of Rule 10b-5."

IMPACT OF THIS CASE ON TODAY'S LAW *This landmark case affirmed the principle that the test of whether information is "material," for SEC Rule 10b-5 purposes, is whether it would affect the judgment of reasonable investors. The corporate insiders' purchases of stock and stock options (rights to purchase stock) indicated that they were influenced by the drilling results and that the information about the drilling results was material. The courts continue to cite this case when applying SEC Rule 10b-5 to other cases of alleged insider trading.*

RELEVANT WEB SITES *To locate information on the Web concerning the SEC v. Texas Gulf Suphur Co. decision, go to this text's Web site at **www.thomsonedu.com/westbuslaw/blt**, select "Chapter 30," and click on "URLs for Landmarks."*

The Private Securities Litigation Reform Act of 1995. One of the unintended effects of SEC Rule 10b-5 was to deter the disclosure of some material information, such as financial forecasts. To understand why, consider an example. ▪**EXAMPLE 30.6** A company announces that its projected earnings in a certain time period will be X amount. It turns out that the forecast is wrong. The earnings are in fact much lower, and the price of the company's stock is affected—negatively. The shareholders then bring a class-action suit against the company, alleging that the directors violated SEC Rule 10b-5 by disclosing misleading financial information. ▪

In an attempt to rectify this problem and promote disclosure, Congress passed the Private Securities Litigation Reform Act of 1995. Among other things, the act provides a "safe harbor" for publicly held companies that make forward-looking statements, such as financial forecasts. Those who make such statements are protected against liability for securities fraud as long as the statements are accompanied by "meaningful cautionary statements identifying important factors that could cause actual results to differ materially from those in the forward-looking statement."[22]

After the 1995 act was passed, a number of securities class-action suits were filed in state courts to skirt the requirements of the 1995 federal act. In response to this problem, Congress passed the Securities Litigation Uniform Standards Act of 1998 (SLUSA).[23] The act placed stringent limits on the ability of plaintiffs to bring class-action suits in state courts against firms whose securities are traded on national stock exchanges. Does the SLUSA prevent only the purchasers and sellers of securities from bringing class-action fraud claims under state securities laws? Or does it also apply to those investors who are fraudulently induced to hold on to their securities? That was the question in the following case.

22. 15 U.S.C. Sections 77z-2, 78u-5.
23. Pub. L. No. 105-353. This act amended many sections of Title 15 of the *United States Code.*

CASE 30.2 **Merrill Lynch, Pierce, Fenner & Smith, Inc. v. Dabit**

Supreme Court of the United States, 547 U.S. 71, 126 S.Ct. 1503, 164 L.Ed.2d 179 (2006).
www.findlaw.com/casecode/supreme.html[a]

FACTS Merrill Lynch, Pierce, Fenner & Smith, Inc., offers research and brokerage services to investors. Shadi Dabit, a

a. In the "Browsing" section, click on "2006 Decisions." When that page opens, scroll to the name of the case and click on it to read the opinion.

former Merrill Lynch broker, filed a class-action suit in an Oklahoma state court against the firm on behalf of all its brokers who bought certain stocks for themselves or their clients between December 1, 1999, and December 31, 2000. Basing his claims on state law, Dabit alleged, among other

CASE 30.2–Continued

things, that the firm had issued overly optimistic appraisals of the stocks' values on which its brokers relied to buy and sell their shares and to advise their clients whether or not to sell their holdings. When "the truth was actually revealed," the stocks' prices plummeted. The suit was moved to a federal district court. Merrill Lynch filed a motion to dismiss Dabit's complaint, arguing, among other things, that the SLUSA blocked it. The trial court agreed and dismissed the complaint. Dabit appealed to the U.S. Court of Appeals for the Second Circuit, which vacated the lower court's decision. Merrill Lynch appealed to the United States Supreme Court.

ISSUE Does the SLUSA cover investors who are fraudulently induced not to buy or sell securities but to hold on to their investments?

DECISION Yes. The United States Supreme Court vacated the judgment of the appellate court and remanded the case for further proceedings. The SLUSA prevents state law class-action claims by shareholders who traded their securities based on a "misrepresentation or omission of a material fact in connection with the purchase or sale of a covered security." That is to say, those who buy or hold rights to buy specific stock based on "incorrect" advice cannot file a class-action lawsuit in state court. The act also bars such claims by shareholders who refrained from trading their securities.

REASON The Court reasoned that under the SLUSA, an alleged fraud need only "coincide" with a trade, whether or not the plaintiff is the party who made the purchase or sale. "The requisite showing, in other words, is deception 'in connection with the purchase or sale of any security,' not deception of an identifiable purchaser or seller." This conclusion accorded with the Court's previous decisions and with the SEC's interpretation of the phrase before Congress used it in the SLUSA. "[R]epetition of the same language in a new statute indicates *   *   * the intent to incorporate its *   *   * judicial interpretations." Besides, to limit the SLUSA to purchasers and sellers would run contrary to the act's purpose, which is "to prevent certain State private securities class action lawsuits alleging fraud from being used to frustrate the objectives" of the Private Securities Litigation Reform Act of 1995. This would lead to "parallel class actions proceeding in state and federal court, with different standards governing claims asserted on identical facts. That prospect, which exists to some extent in this very case, squarely conflicts with the congressional preference for national standards for securities class action lawsuits."

WHAT IF THE FACTS WERE DIFFERENT? *If Dabit had filed his suit only on his own behalf, rather than on behalf of other brokers and investors, how might the result in this case have been different?*

Outsiders and SEC Rule 10b-5   The traditional insider-trading case involves true insiders—corporate officers, directors, and majority shareholders who have access to (and trade on) inside information. Increasingly, liability under Section 10(b) of the 1934 act and SEC Rule 10b-5 is being extended to include certain "outsiders"—those persons who trade on inside information acquired indirectly. Two theories have been developed under which outsiders may be held liable for insider trading: the *tipper/tippee theory* and the *misappropriation theory.*

Tipper/Tippee Theory.   Anyone who acquires inside information as a result of a corporate insider's breach of his or her fiduciary duty can be liable under SEC Rule 10b-5. This liability extends to **tippees** (those who receive "tips" from insiders) and even remote tippees (tippees of tippees).

TIPPEE
A person who receives inside information.

  The key to liability under this theory is that the inside information must be obtained as a result of someone's breach of a fiduciary duty to the corporation whose shares are involved in the trading. The tippee is liable under this theory only if (1) there is a breach of a duty not to disclose inside information, (2) the disclosure is in exchange for personal benefit, and (3) the tippee knows (or should know) of this breach and benefits from it.[24]

Misappropriation Theory.   Liability for insider trading may also be established under the misappropriation theory. This theory holds that an individual who wrongfully obtains

---

24. See, for example, *Chiarella v. United States*, 445 U.S. 222, 100 S.Ct. 1108, 63 L.Ed.2d 348 (1980); and *Dirks v. SEC*, 463 U.S. 646, 103 S.Ct. 3255, 77 L.Ed.2d 911 (1983).

(misappropriates) inside information and trades on it for her or his personal gain should be held liable because, in essence, she or he stole information rightfully belonging to another.

The misappropriation theory has been controversial because it significantly extends the reach of SEC Rule 10b-5 to outsiders who ordinarily would not be deemed fiduciaries of the corporations in whose stock they trade. The United States Supreme Court, however, has held that liability under SEC Rule 10b-5 can be based on the misappropriation theory.[25]

It is not always wrong to disclose material, nonpublic information about a company to a person who would not otherwise be privy to it. A corporate officer might discuss business events with his or her spouse, for example, with the understanding that the spouse will not repeat the conversation to anyone. What if the spouse says that she will disclose the information? In the following case, the defendants argued that there should be no liability under the misappropriation theory in this situation.

---

25. *United States v. O'Hagan*, 521 U.S. 642, 117 S.Ct. 2199, 138 L.Ed.2d 724 (1997).

CASE 30.3   **SEC v. Rocklage**

United States Court of Appeals, First Circuit, 470 F.3d 1 (2006).
www.ca1.uscourts.gov[a]

FACTS Patricia Rocklage was the wife of Scott Rocklage, the chairman and chief executive officer of Cubist Pharmaceuticals, Inc. Scott had sometimes disclosed material, nonpublic information about Cubist to Patricia, and she had always kept the information confidential. On December 31, 2001, Scott told Patricia that one of Cubist's key drugs had failed its clinical trial and reminded her not to discuss this information with anyone. Patricia was aware that her brother, William Beaver, owned Cubist stock, and she told Scott that she wanted to tell her brother about the failed trial. Scott tried to discourage her. Patricia had an "understanding" with William, however, and told him that she had heard significant negative news about Cubist. He sold his 5,583 shares of its stock and tipped his friend David Jones, who sold his 7,500 shares. On January 16, 2002, Cubist publicly announced the trial results, and the price of its stock dropped. William and David had avoided losses of $99,527 and $133,222, respectively, by selling when they did. The Securities and Exchange Commission (SEC) filed a suit in a federal district court against Patricia, William, and David, alleging insider trading in violation of Section 10(b) of the Securities Exchange Act of 1934 and SEC Rule 10b-5. The court denied the defendants' motion to

dismiss. They appealed to the U.S. Court of Appeals for the First Circuit.

ISSUE Could Patricia, William, and David avoid liability for insider trading under the misappropriation theory on the ground that Patricia had told Scott she would tell William what Scott had told her?

DECISION No. The U.S. Court of Appeals for the First Circuit affirmed the lower court's decision and remanded the case for further proceedings.

REASON The U.S. Court of Appeals for the First Circuit recognized that the misappropriation theory bases liability on the deception of the source of the information. In this case, "Mrs. Rocklage engaged in deceptive devices, in connection with a securities transaction, when she tricked her husband into revealing confidential information to her so that she could, and did, assist her brother with the sale of his Cubist stock. * * * [B]efore her husband's initial disclosure about the clinical trial, Mrs. Rocklage did absolutely nothing to correct his mistaken understanding that she would keep the trial results confidential." And she did this, "knowing full well that in obtaining that information she would enable her brother to execute a securities transaction. She then actively facilitated a securities transaction by tipping her brother, and securities were in fact sold based on her information." The court conceded that Patricia's disclosure to Scott might have eliminated any deception involved in her tip to William, but it

---

a. Click on "Opinions." On the next page, in the "General Search" section, in the "Short title contains" box, type "Rocklage" and then click on "Submit Search." In the result, in the "Click for Opinion" column, click on the first number to access the opinion. The U.S. Court of Appeals for the First Circuit maintains this Web site.

CASE 30.3–Continued

did not "negate the original deception. * * * [B]ecause of the way in which Mrs. Rocklage first acquired this information, her overall scheme was still deceptive: it had as part of it at least one deceptive device."

 FOR CRITICAL ANALYSIS–Social Consideration *Are there any circumstances in which the disclosure to the source that his or her information will be revealed to others might serve to avoid liability? Explain.*

Insider Reporting and Trading–Section 16(b)

Officers, directors, and certain large stockholders[26] of Section 12 corporations (corporations that are required to register their securities under Section 12 of the 1934 act) must file reports with the SEC concerning their ownership and trading of the corporations' securities.[27] To discourage such insiders from using nonpublic information about their companies for their personal benefit in the stock market, Section 16(b) of the 1934 act provides for the recapture by the corporation of all profits realized by an insider on any purchase and sale or sale and purchase of the corporation's stock within any six-month period.[28] It is irrelevant whether the insider actually uses inside information; *all such* **short-swing profits** *must be returned to the corporation.*

Section 16(b) applies not only to stock but also to warrants, options, and securities convertible into stock. In addition, the courts have fashioned complex rules for determining profits. Note that the SEC exempts a number of transactions under Rule 16b-3.[29] For all of these reasons, corporate insiders are wise to seek specialized counsel prior to trading in the corporation's stock. Exhibit 30–3 compares the effects of SEC Rule 10b-5 and Section 16(b).

ON THE WEB

For information on investor protection, including answers to frequently asked questions on the topic of securities fraud, go to

www.securitieslaw.com.

SHORT-SWING PROFITS
Profits earned within six months of a trade. Section 12 of the 1934 Securities Exchange Act requires company insiders to return any profits made from the purchase and sale of company stock if both transactions occur within a six-month period.

---

26. Those stockholders owning 10 percent of the class of equity securities registered under Section 12 of the 1934 act.
27. 15 U.S.C. Section 78*l*.
28. A person who expects the price of a particular stock to decline can realize profits by "selling short"—selling at a high price and repurchasing later at a lower price to cover the "short sale."
29. 17 C.F.R. Section 240.16b-3.

EXHIBIT 30–3 **Comparison of Coverage, Application, and Liability under SEC Rule 10b–5 and Section 16(b)**

AREA OF COMPARISON	SEC RULE 10b–5	SECTION 16(b)
What is the subject matter of the transaction?	Any security (does not have to be registered).	Any security (does not have to be registered).
What transactions are covered?	Purchase or sale.	Short-swing purchase and sale or short-swing sale and purchase.
Who is subject to liability?	Virtually anyone with inside information under a duty to disclose—including officers, directors, controlling shareholders, and tippees.	Officers, directors, and certain 10 percent shareholders.
Is omission or misrepresentation necessary for liability?	Yes.	No.
Are there any exempt transactions?	No.	Yes, there are a number of exemptions.
Who may bring an action?	A person transacting with an insider, the SEC, or a purchaser or seller damaged by a wrongful act.	A corporation or a shareholder by derivative action.

A proxy statement. Who regulates the content of proxy statements and how? (Courtesy of Prudential Financial)

Proxy Statements

Section 14(a) of the Securities Exchange Act of 1934 regulates the solicitation of proxies from shareholders of Section 12 companies. The SEC regulates the content of proxy statements. As discussed in Chapter 29, a proxy statement is sent to shareholders when corporate officials are requesting authority to vote on behalf of the shareholders in a particular election on specified issues. Whoever solicits a proxy must fully and accurately disclose in the proxy statement all of the facts that are pertinent to the matter on which the shareholders are to vote. SEC Rule 14a-9 is similar to the antifraud provisions of SEC Rule 10b-5. Remedies for violations are extensive; they range from injunctions that prevent a vote from being taken to monetary damages.

Violations of the 1934 Act

As mentioned earlier, violations of Section 10(b) of the Securities Exchange Act of 1934 and SEC Rule 10b-5, including insider trading, may be subject to criminal or civil liability. For either criminal or civil sanctions to be imposed, however, *scienter* must exist—that is, the violator must have had an intent to defraud or knowledge of her or his misconduct (see Chapter 11). *Scienter* can be proved by showing that the defendant made false statements or wrongfully failed to disclose material facts.

Violations of Section 16(b) include the sale by insiders of stock acquired less than six months before the sale (or less than six months after the sale if selling short). These violations are subject to civil sanctions. Liability under Section 16(b) is strict liability. Thus, liability is imposed regardless of whether *scienter* or negligence existed.

Criminal Penalties For violations of Section 10(b) and Rule 10b-5, an individual may be fined up to $5 million, imprisoned for up to twenty years, or both.[30] A partnership or a corporation may be fined up to $25 million. Under Section 807 of the Sarbanes-Oxley Act of 2002, for a *willful* violation of the 1934 act the violator may, in addition to being subject to a fine, be imprisoned for up to twenty-five years.

In a criminal prosecution under the securities laws, a jury is not allowed to speculate on whether a defendant acted willfully—there can be no reasonable doubt that the defendant knew he or she was acting wrongfully. The issue in the following case was whether, in light of this principle, there was enough evidence to present to a jury the question of whether Martha Stewart, founder of a well-known media and homemaking empire, intended to deceive investors.

---

30. These numbers reflect the increased penalties imposed by the Sarbanes-Oxley Act of 2002.

CASE 30.4   **United States v. Stewart**

United States District Court, Southern District of New York, 305 F.Supp.2d 368 (2004).

FACTS Samuel Waksal, the chief executive officer of ImClone Systems, Inc., a biotechnology company, was a client of stockbroker Peter Bacanovic. Bacanovic's other clients included Martha Stewart, then the chief executive officer of Martha Stewart Living Omnimedia (MSLO). On December 27, 2001, Waksal began selling his ImClone stock. Bacanovic allegedly had Stewart informed of Waksal's sales, and she also sold her ImClone shares. The next day, ImClone announced that the Food and Drug Administration had rejected the company's application for approval of the greatly anticipated medication called Erbitux. The government began to

CASE 30.4–Continued

investigate Stewart's ImClone trades, the media began to report on the investigation, and the value of MSLO stock began to drop. In June 2002, at a "Mid-Year Media Review" conference attended by investment professionals and investors, Stewart said that she had previously agreed with Bacanovic to sell her ImClone stock if the price fell to $60 per share. "I have nothing to add on this matter today. And I'm here to talk about our terrific company." Her statements were followed by a forty-minute presentation on MSLO. Subsequently, Stewart was charged with, among other things, fraud in connection with the purchase and sale of MSLO securities in violation of the Securities Exchange Act of 1934. She filed a motion asking for an acquittal on this charge.

ISSUE Could a reasonable juror find beyond a reasonable doubt that Stewart lied to influence the market for the securities of her company?

DECISION No. The court concluded that in Stewart's case, "to find the essential element of criminal intent beyond a reasonable doubt, a rational juror would have to speculate."[a]

---

a. Stewart was later convicted on other charges related to her ImClone trades and was sentenced to five months in prison and five months under house arrest. Although she appealed the decision in an attempt to clear her name, the U.S. Court of Appeals for the Second Circuit upheld her conviction in 2006.

REASON The government argued that Stewart was aware that the negative publicity about her ImClone trade was having an impact on the market value of MSLO securities and that she deliberately directed her statement to investors. The government pointed out that Stewart was aware that she was speaking to analysts and investors at the conference and began by saying that she was embarking on a topic about which her audience was "probably interested." According to the government, Stewart's awareness of her audience (investors and analysts) and the timing of her statement as the price of MSLO stock was falling were sufficient to permit a jury to infer that she intended to deceive investors when she made the statement. The court reasoned, however, that "any inference to be drawn from the makeup of the audience must also take into account the fact that Stewart was only one of several representatives of MSLO, and that MSLO was only one of several corporations making presentations at the conference. * * * There is no evidence that the negative publicity about ImClone influenced Stewart's decision to attend and take advantage of a platform from which to reach investors directly. To the contrary, her statement—a very brief portion of a much longer presentation—indicates otherwise."

 FOR CRITICAL ANALYSIS–Social Consideration *Why might a court require more evidence of* scienter, *or intent, in the context of criminal securities fraud prosecution than it would in the context of civil securities fraud action?*

Civil Sanctions The SEC can also bring suit in a federal district court against anyone violating or aiding in a violation of the 1934 act or SEC rules by purchasing or selling a security while in the possession of material nonpublic information.[31] The violation must occur on or through the facilities of a national securities exchange or from or through a broker or dealer. The court may assess as a penalty as much as triple the profits gained or the loss avoided by the guilty party. Profit or loss is defined as "the difference between the purchase or sale price of the security and the value of that security as measured by the trading price of the security at a reasonable period of time after public dissemination of the nonpublic information."[32]

The Insider Trading and Securities Fraud Enforcement Act of 1988 enlarged the class of persons who may be subject to civil liability for insider-trading violations. This act also gave the SEC authority to award **bounty payments** (rewards given by government officials for acts beneficial to the state) to persons providing information leading to the prosecution of insider-trading violations.[33]

Private parties may also sue violators of Section 10(b) and Rule 10b-5. A private party may obtain rescission (cancellation) of a contract to buy securities or damages to the extent of the violator's illegal profits. Those found liable have a right to seek contribution

BOUNTY PAYMENT
A reward (payment) given to a person or persons who perform a certain service, such as informing legal authorities of illegal actions.

---

31. The Insider Trading Sanctions Act of 1984, 15 U.S.C. Section 78u(d)(2)(A).
32. 15 U.S.C. Section 78u(d)(2)(C).
33. 15 U.S.C. Section 78u-1.

from those who share responsibility for the violations, including accountants, attorneys, and corporations.[34] For violations of Section 16(b), a corporation can bring an action to recover the short-swing profits.

STATE SECURITIES LAWS

BE AWARE Federal securities laws do not take priority over state securities laws.

Today, all states have their own corporate securities laws, or "blue sky laws," that regulate the offer and sale of securities within individual state borders. (As mentioned in Chapter 10, the phrase *blue sky laws* dates to a 1917 decision by the United States Supreme Court in which the Court declared that the purpose of such laws was to prevent "speculative schemes which have no more basis than so many feet of 'blue sky.'")[35] Article 8 of the Uniform Commercial Code, which has been adopted by all of the states, also imposes various requirements relating to the purchase and sale of securities.

Requirements under State Securities Laws

Despite some differences in philosophy, all state blue sky laws have certain features. Typically, state laws have disclosure requirements and antifraud provisions, many of which are patterned after Section 10(b) of the Securities Exchange Act of 1934 and SEC Rule 10b-5. State laws also provide for the registration or qualification of securities offered or issued for sale within the state and impose disclosure requirements. Unless an exemption from registration is applicable, issuers must register or qualify their stock with the appropriate state official, often called a *corporations commissioner.* Additionally, most state securities laws regulate securities brokers and dealers.

Concurrent Regulation

State securities laws apply mainly to intrastate transactions. Since the adoption of the 1933 and 1934 federal securities acts, the state and federal governments have regulated securities concurrently. Issuers must comply with both federal and state securities laws, and exemptions from federal law are not exemptions from state laws.

The dual federal and state system has not always worked well, particularly during the early 1990s, when the securities markets underwent considerable expansion. In response, Congress passed the National Securities Markets Improvement Act of 1996, which eliminated some of the duplicate regulations and gave the SEC exclusive power to regulate most national securities activities. The National Conference of Commissioners on Uniform State Laws then substantially revised the Uniform Securities Act and recommended it to the states for adoption in 2002. Unlike the previous version of this law, the new act is designed to coordinate state and federal securities regulation and enforcement efforts. Eleven states have already adopted the Uniform Securities Act, and several other states are considering adoption.[36]

---

34. The United States Supreme Court has ruled that a private party cannot bring an action against those who "aid and abet" under Section 10(b) and SEC Rule 10b-5. *Central Bank of Denver, N.A. v. First Interstate Bank of Denver, N.A.,* 511 U.S. 164, 114 S.Ct. 1439, 128 L.Ed.2d 119 (1994). Only the SEC can bring actions against so-called aiders and abettors. Nevertheless, some courts have held accountants and attorneys liable as primary violators under Section 10(b), and a conflict exists in the federal circuit courts as to precisely what conduct subjects accountants and attorneys to liability.

35. *Hall v. Geiger-Jones Co.,* 242 U.S. 539, 37 S.Ct. 217, 61 L.Ed. 480 (1917).

36. At the time this book went to press, the Uniform Securities Act had been adopted in Hawaii, Idaho, Iowa, Kansas, Maine, Minnesota, Missouri, Oklahoma, South Carolina, South Dakota, and Vermont, as well as in the U.S. Virgin Islands. Adoption legislation was pending in Indiana and Washington State. You can find current information on state adoptions at **www.nccusl.org**.

BEYOND OUR BORDERS **Corporate Governance in Other Nations**

Corporate governance has become an issue of concern not only for U.S. corporations, but also for corporate entities around the world. With the globalization of business, a corporation's bad acts (or lack of control systems) can have far-reaching consequences.

Different models of corporate governance exist, often depending on the degree of capitalism in the particular nation. In the United States, corporate governance tends to give priority to shareholders' interests. This approach encourages significant innovation and cost and quality competition. In contrast, the coordinated model of governance that prevails in continental Europe and Japan considers the interests of so-called stakeholders—employees, managers, suppliers, customers, and the community—to be a priority. The coordinated model still encourages innovation and cost and quality competition, but not to the same extent as the U.S. model.

 FOR CRITICAL ANALYSIS *Why does the presence of a capitalist system affect a nation's perspective on corporate governance?*

CORPORATE GOVERNANCE

Corporate governance can be narrowly defined as the relationship between a corporation and its shareholders. The Organization for Economic Cooperation and Development (OECD) provides a broader definition:

> Corporate governance is the system by which business corporations are directed and controlled. The corporate governance structure specifies the distribution of rights and responsibilities among different participants in the corporation, such as the board of directors, managers, shareholders, and other stakeholders, and spells out the rules and procedures for making decisions on corporate affairs.[37]

Although this definition has no legal value, it does set the tone for the ways in which modern corporations should be governed. In other words, effective corporate governance requires more than compliance with laws and regulations. The definition and focus of corporate governance principles vary around the world. For a discussion of corporate governance in other nations, see this chapter's *Beyond Our Borders* feature.

The Need for Good Corporate Governance

The need for effective corporate governance arises in large corporations because corporate ownership (by shareholders) is separated from corporate control (by officers and managers). In the real world, officers and managers are tempted to advance their own interests, even when such interests conflict with those of the shareholders. The collapse of Enron Corporation and other well-publicized scandals in the corporate world in the early 2000s provide a clear illustration of the reasons for concern about managerial opportunism.

CORPORATE GOVERNANCE
A set of policies or procedures affecting the way a corporation is directed or controlled.

---

37. *Governance in the 21st Century: Future Studies* (OECD, 2001).

Attempts at Aligning the Interests of Officers with Those of Shareholders

STOCK OPTIONS
An agreement that grants the owner the option to buy a given number of shares of stock, usually within a set time period.

Some corporations have sought to align the financial interests of their offficers with those of the company's shareholders by providing the officers with **stock options,** which enable them to purchase shares of the corporation's stock at a set price. When the market price rises above that level, the officers can sell their shares for a profit. Because a stock's market price generally increases as the corporation prospers, the options give the officers a financial stake in the corporation's well-being and supposedly encourage them to work hard for the benefit of the shareholders.

Options have turned out to be an imperfect device for providing effective governance, however. Executives in some companies have been tempted to "cook" the company's books in order to keep share prices higher so that they could sell their stock for a profit. Executives in other corporations have experienced no losses when share prices dropped; instead, their options were "repriced" so that they did not suffer from the share price decline and could still profit from future increases above the lowered share price. Thus, although stock options theoretically can motivate officers to protect shareholder interests, stock option plans have often become a way for officers to take advantage of shareholders.

With stock options generally failing to work as planned and numerous headline-making scandals occurring within major corporations, there has been an outcry for more "outside" directors (those with no formal employment affiliation with the company). The theory is that independent directors will more closely monitor the actions of corporate officers. Hence, today we see more boards with outside directors. Note, though, that outside directors may not be truly independent of corporate officers; they may be friends or business associates of the leading officers. A study of board appointments found that the best way to increase one's probability of appointment was to "suck up" to the chief executive officer.[38]

Corporate Governance and Corporate Law

Good corporate governance standards are designed to address problems (such as those briefly discussed above) and to motivate officers to make decisions to promote the financial interests of the company's shareholders. Generally, corporate governance entails corporate decision-making structures that monitor employees (particularly officers) to ensure that they are acting for the benefit of the shareholders. Thus, corporate governance involves, at a minimum:

1 The audited reporting of financial progress at the corporation, so that managers can be evaluated.

2 Legal protections for shareholders, so that violators of the law, who attempt to take advantage of shareholders, can be punished for misbehavior and victims may recover damages for any associated losses.

The Practical Significance of Good Corporate Governance Effective corporate governance may have considerable practical significance. A study by researchers at Harvard University and the Wharton School of Business found that firms providing greater shareholder rights had higher profits, higher sales growth, higher firm value, and other economic advantages.[39] Better corporate governance in the form of greater accountability to investors may therefore offer the opportunity to increase corporations' valuations.

---

38. Jennifer Reingold, "Suck Up and Move Fast," *Fast Company*, January 2005, p. 34.
39. Paul A. Gompers, Joy L. Ishii, and Andrew Metrick, "Corporate Governance and Equity Prices," *Quarterly Journal of Economics*, Vol. 118 (2003), p. 107.

Governance and Corporation Law Corporate governance is the essential purpose of corporation law in the United States. These statutes set up the legal framework for corporate governance. Under the corporate law of Delaware, where most major companies incorporate, all corporations must have in place certain structures of corporate governance. The key structure of corporate law is, of course, the board of directors. Directors make the most important decisions about the future of the corporation and monitor the actions of corporate officers. Directors are elected by shareholders to look out for their best interests.

The Board of Directors Some argue that shareholder democracy is key to improving corporate governance. If shareholders could vote on major corporate decisions, shareholders could presumably have more control over the corporation. Essential to shareholder democracy is the concept of electing the board of directors, usually at the corporation's annual meeting. Under corporate law, a corporation must have a board of directors elected by the shareholders. Virtually anyone can become a director, though some organizations, such as the New York Stock Exchange, require certain standards of service for directors of their listed corporations.

Directors have the responsibility of ensuring that officers are operating wisely and in the exclusive interest of shareholders. Directors receive reports from the officers and give them managerial directions. The board in theory controls the compensation of officers (presumably tied to performance). The reality, though, is that corporate directors devote a relatively small amount of time to monitoring officers.

Ideally, shareholders would monitor the directors' supervision of officers. As one leading board monitor commented, "Boards of directors are like subatomic particles—they behave differently when they are observed." Consequently, monitoring of directors, and holding them responsible for corporate failings, can induce the directors to do a better job of monitoring officers and ensuring that the company is being managed in the interest of shareholders. Although the directors can be sued for failing to do their jobs effectively, directors are rarely held personally liable.

Importance of the Audit Committee One crucial board committee is known as the *audit committee*. The audit committee oversees the corporation's accounting and financial reporting processes, including both internal and outside auditors. Unless the committee members have sufficient expertise and are willing to spend the time to carefully examine the corporation's bookkeeping methods, however, the audit committee may be ineffective.

The audit committee also oversees the corporation's "internal controls." These are the measures taken to ensure that reported results are accurate; they are carried out largely by the company's internal auditing staff. As an example, these controls help to determine whether a corporation's debts are collectible. If the debts are not collectible, it is up to the audit committee to make sure that the corporation's financial officers do not simply pretend that payment will eventually be made.

The Compensation Committee Another important committee of the board of directors is the *compensation committee*. This committee monitors and determines the compensation to be paid to the company's officers. As part of this process, it is responsible for assessing the officers' performance and for designing a compensation system that will better align the officers' interests with those of shareholders. (The *Application* feature at the end of this chapter discusses other corporate governance issues that a business owner may encounter.)

The Sarbanes-Oxley Act of 2002

As discussed in Chapter 7, in 2002, following a series of corporate scandals, Congress passed the Sarbanes-Oxley Act. The act separately addresses certain issues relating to corporate governance. Generally, the act attempts to increase corporate accountability by imposing strict disclosure requirements and harsh penalties for violations of securities laws. Among other things, the act requires chief corporate executives to take responsibility for the accuracy of financial statements and reports that are filed with the SEC. Chief executive officers and chief financial officers must personally certify that the statements and reports are accurate and complete.

Additionally, the new rules require that certain financial and stock-transaction reports must be filed with the SEC earlier than was required under the previous rules. The act also mandates SEC oversight over a new entity, called the Public Company Accounting Oversight Board, which regulates and oversees public accounting firms. Other provisions of the act created new private civil actions and expanded the SEC's remedies in administrative and civil actions.

Because of the importance of this act for corporate leaders and for those dealing with securities transactions, we present excerpts and explanatory comments in Appendix D. We also highlight some of its key provisions relating to corporate accountability in Exhibit 30–4.

More Internal Controls and Accountability The Sarbanes-Oxley Act includes some traditional securities law provisions but also introduces direct *federal* corporate governance requirements for public companies (companies whose shares are traded in the public securities markets). The law addresses many of the corporate governance procedures just discussed and creates new requirements in an attempt to make the system work more effectively. The requirements deal with independent monitoring of company officers by both the board of directors and auditors.

Sections 302 and 404 of Sarbanes-Oxley require high-level managers (the most senior officers) to establish and maintain an effective system of internal controls. Moreover, senior management must reassess the system's effectiveness on an annual basis. Some com-

The chairman of the Securities and Exchange Commission (SEC), Christopher Cox, uses a prop when testifying before Congress about the complexity of the Sarbanes-Oxley Act. Notice that the "for Dummies" book is quite thick. Why would the SEC chairman want Congress to simplify an act that his agency must enforce?
(AP Photo/Lawrence Jackson)

EXHIBIT 30–4	Some Key Provisions of the Sarbanes-Oxley Act of 2002 Relating to Corporate Accountability

Certification Requirements—Under Section 906 of the Sarbanes-Oxley Act, the chief executive officers (CEOs) and chief financial officers (CFOs) of most major companies listed on public stock exchanges must now certify financial statements that are filed with the SEC. For virtually all filed financial reports, CEOs and CFOs have to certify that such reports "fully comply" with SEC requirements and that all of the information reported "fairly represents in all material respects, the financial conditions and results of operations of the issuer."

Under Section 302 of the act, for each quarterly and annual filing with the SEC, CEOs and CFOs of reporting companies are required to certify that a signing officer reviewed the report and that it contains no untrue statements of material fact. Also, the signing officer or officers must certify that they have established an internal control system to identify all material information, and that any deficiencies in the system were disclosed to the auditors.

Loans to Directors and Officers—Section 402 prohibits any reporting company, as well as any private company that is filing an initial public offering, from making personal loans to directors and executive officers (with a few limited exceptions, such as for certain consumer and housing loans).

Protection for Whistleblowers—Section 806 protects "whistleblowers"—those employees who report ("blow the whistle" on) securities violations by their employers—from being fired or in any way discriminated against by their employers.

Blackout Periods—Section 306 prohibits certain types of securities transactions during "blackout periods"—periods during which the issuer's ability to purchase, sell, or otherwise transfer funds in individual account plans (such as pension funds) is suspended.

Enhanced Penalties for—

• *Violations of Section 906 Certification Requirements*—A CEO or CFO who certifies a financial report or statement filed with the SEC knowing that the report or statement does not fulfill all of the requirements of Section 906 will be subject to criminal penalties of up to $1 million in fines, ten years in prison, or both. *Willful* violators of the certification requirements may be subject to $5 million in fines, twenty years in prison, or both.

• *Violations of the Securities Exchange Act of 1934*—Penalties for securities fraud under the 1934 act were also increased (as discussed earlier in this chapter). Individual violators may be fined up to $5 million, imprisoned for up to twenty years, or both. *Willful* violators may be imprisoned for up to twenty-five years in addition to being fined.

• *Destruction or Alteration of Documents*—Anyone who alters, destroys, or conceals documents or otherwise obstructs any official proceeding will be subject to fines, imprisonment for up to twenty years, or both.

• *Other Forms of White-Collar Crime*—The act stiffened the penalties for certain criminal violations, such as federal mail and wire fraud, and ordered the U.S. Sentencing Commission to revise the sentencing guidelines for white-collar crimes (see Chapter 6).

Statute of Limitations for Securities Fraud—Section 804 provides that a private right of action for securities fraud may be brought no later than two years after the discovery of the violation or five years after the violation, whichever is earlier.

panies already had strong and effective internal control systems in place before the passage of the act, but others had to take expensive steps to bring their internal controls up to the new federal standard. These include "disclosure controls and procedures" to ensure that company financial reports are accurate and timely. Assessment must involve the documenting of financial results and accounting policies before reporting the results. By the beginning of 2008, hundreds of companies had reported that they had identified and corrected shortcomings in their internal control systems.

Certification and Monitoring Requirements   Section 906 requires that chief executive officers (CEOs) and chief financial officers (CFOs) certify that the information in the corporate financial statements "fairly represents in all material respects, the financial conditions and results of operations of the issuer." These corporate officers are subject to both civil and criminal penalties for violation of this section. This requirement makes officers directly accountable for the accuracy of their financial reporting and avoids any "ignorance defense" if shortcomings are later discovered.

Sarbanes-Oxley also includes requirements to improve directors' monitoring of officers' activities. All members of the corporate audit committee for public companies must be outside directors. The New York Stock Exchange (NYSE) has a similar rule that also extends to the board's compensation committee. The audit committee must have a written charter that sets out its duties and provides for performance appraisal. At least one "financial expert" must serve on the audit committee, which must hold executive meetings without company officers being present. The audit committee must establish procedures for "whistleblowers" to report violations. In addition to reviewing the internal controls, the committee also monitors the actions of the outside auditor.

ETHICAL ISSUE 30.1

Is scienter *required for corporate executives to be liable for securities fraud based on financial statements that contain accounting misstatements or omissions?* Section 906 of the Sarbanes-Oxley Act makes signing officers (CEOs and CFOs) directly accountable for the accuracy of their financial reports. One concern since the passage of the act is whether signing officers can be liable for fraud if the reports contain any errors or inaccurate information. Is mere negligence sufficient for liability, or must the officer have intended to deceive (*scienter*)? State courts have been split on the degree of intent required to impose liability. In 2006, however, a federal appellate court ruled that to be liable for securities fraud, an executive must either have had an intent to deceive or have been severely reckless in certifying a financial report.

The case involved a Georgia company, NDC Health Corporation; six of its executives; and the New York–based accounting firm Ernst & Young. An investor, Robert Garfield, filed a class-action suit claiming that the company's executives had certified financial reports that understated corporate expenses due to errors in amortization and capitalization. The trial court concluded that the specific accounting errors alleged were vague and difficult to evaluate and held that although the signing executives might have been negligent, they could not be liable for securities fraud. The federal appellate court agreed and affirmed the lower court's dismissal of the complaint. The appellate court held that to interpret Sarbanes-Oxley as imposing liability on corporate executives regardless of whether they had any intent to deceive would conflict with the plain language of the Private Securities Litigation Reform Act (discussed earlier in this chapter).[40]

ONLINE SECURITIES OFFERINGS AND DISCLOSURES

The Spring Street Brewing Company, headquartered in New York, made history when it became the first company to attempt to sell securities via the Internet. Through its online initial public offering (IPO), which ended in early 1996, Spring Street raised about $1.6 million—without having to pay any commissions to brokers or underwriters. The offering was made pursuant to Regulation A, which, as mentioned earlier in this chapter, allows small-business issuers to use a simplified registration procedure.

Such online IPOs (sometimes referred to as DPOs, which stands for *direct public offerings*) are particularly attractive to small companies and start-up ventures that may find it difficult to raise capital from institutional investors or through underwriters. By making the offering online under Regulation A, the company can avoid both commissions and the costly and time-consuming filings required for a traditional IPO under federal and state law.

---

40. *Garfield v. NDC Health Corp.*, 466 F.3d 1255 (11th Cir. 2006).

ADAPTING THE LAW TO THE ONLINE ENVIRONMENT | **Should the SEC Recognize Internet Postings and Blogs as a Means of Disseminating Financial Information?**

In 2000, the SEC issued Regulation Fair Disclosure,[a] or Regulation FD, in an attempt to ensure that some investors do not have more information than the general public. Under Regulation FD, when a company gives "material nonpublic information" about its prospects to certain individuals or entities, such as stock analysts or Wall Street professionals, it must also disclose that information to the public. To comply with the regulation, corporate executives typically first meet in person or by phone conference with analysts and then hold a press conference to disseminate the information to the public.

Now at least one corporate executive would like to use the company's Web site to disseminate the required information. On September 25, 2006, Jonathan Schwartz, the CEO of Sun Microsystems, Inc., sent a letter to the chair of the SEC. Pointing out "the utility of the Internet to inform investors," Schwartz said that he wanted to avoid "consuming trees with

a. 17 C.F.R. Section 243.101(e)(2).

press releases." According to Schwartz, Sun Microsystems' Web site (**www.sun.com**), which includes a blog written by Schwartz himself (**www.blogs.sun.com/jonathan**) as well as blogs from almost four thousand employees, receives nearly a million hits per day. His letter stated emphatically, "we believe that the proliferation of the Internet supports a new policy that online communications fully satisfy Regulation FD's broad distribution requirement."[b] As of mid-2007, however, the SEC has not taken a position on whether the "widespread dissemination" required by the regulation can be satisfied by posting the information on the company's Web site or blog.

FOR CRITICAL ANALYSIS *What are the pros and cons of the SEC allowing Web site postings to satisfy the fair disclosure rule? Should blogs be treated differently than Web sites? Why or why not?*

b. Schwartz's letter is posted with a short article titled "One Small Step for the Blogosphere" at **www.blogs.sun.com/jonathan/entry/ one_small_step_for_the**.

Regulations Governing Online Securities Offerings

One of the early questions posed by online offerings was whether the delivery of securities *information* via the Internet met the requirements of the 1933 Securities Act, which traditionally were applied to the delivery of paper documents. In an interpretive release issued in 1995, the SEC stated that "[t]he use of electronic media should be at least an equal alternative to the use of paper-based media" and that anything that can be delivered in paper form under the current securities laws might also be delivered in electronic form.[41]

Basically, there has been no change in the substantive law of disclosure; only the delivery vehicle has changed. When the Internet is used for delivery of a prospectus, the same rules apply as for the delivery of a paper prospectus. Timely and adequate notice is required, however. The only unique consideration is how to provide timely and adequate notice of the delivery of information. Posting a prospectus on a Web site does not constitute adequate notice, but sending separate e-mails or even postcards stating the URL where the prospectus can be viewed will satisfy the SEC's notice requirements.

An issue that has come up in the last few years is whether Web site postings and blogs can satisfy the requirement that companies provide "widespread dissemination" of material information about a stock to investors. See this chapter's *Adapting the Law to the Online Environment* feature for a discussion of this topic.

---

41. "Use of Electronic Media for Delivery Purposes," Securities Act Release No. 33-7233 (October 6, 1995). The rules governing the use of electronic transmissions for delivery purposes were subsequently confirmed in Securities Act Release No. 33-7289 (May 9, 1996) and expanded in Securities Act Release No. 33-7856 (April 28, 2000).

Potential Liability Created by Online Offering Materials

Every printed prospectus indicates that only the information given in the prospectus can be used in making an investment decision about the securities offered. The same wording, of course, appears on Web-based offerings. What happens if an electronic prospectus contains information that conflicts with the information provided in a printed prospectus?

As anyone who is familiar with the Internet knows, the graphics, images, and audio files created by one computer are not always readable by another computer when they are exchanged online. The SEC has issued Rule 304 to deal with this situation.[42] The first part of the rule states that if graphic, image, or audio material in a prospectus cannot be reproduced in an electronic form on the SEC's EDGAR system, the electronic prospectus must include a fair and accurate narrative description of the omitted data. The second part of Rule 304 provides that the graphic, image, and audio material contained in the version of a document delivered to investors is *deemed to be part of the electronic document* filed with the SEC. As a result, a corporation can have two versions of a prospectus—a print version that contains graphics and an electronic version that describes the information shown in the graphics.

Hyperlinks to Other Web Pages Those who create such Web-based offerings may be tempted to insert hyperlinks to other Web pages. They may include links to other sites that have analyzed the future prospects of the company, the products and services sold by the company, or the offering itself. To avoid potential liability, however, online offerors (the entities making the offerings) need to exercise caution when including such hyperlinks. **EXAMPLE 30.7** Suppose that a hyperlink goes to an analyst's Web page that makes optimistic statements concerning the financial outlook of the offering company. Further suppose that after the initial public offering, or IPO, the stock price falls. By including the hyperlink on its Web site, the offering company is impliedly supporting the information presented on the linked page. If it turns out that the company knew the statements made on the analyst's Web page were false or misleading, the company may be liable for violating sections of the Securities Exchange Act of 1934.[43] ▣

Regulation D Offerings Potential problems may also occur with some Regulation D offerings, if the offeror places the offering circular on its Web site for general consumption by anybody on the Internet. Because Regulation D offerings are private placements, general solicitation is restricted. If anyone can have access to the offering circular on the Web, the Regulation D exemption may be disqualified.

Online Securities Offerings by Foreign Companies

Another question raised by Internet transactions has to do with securities offerings by foreign companies. Traditionally, foreign companies have not been able to offer new shares to the U.S. public without first registering them with the SEC. Today, however, anybody in the world can offer shares of stock worldwide via the Web.

The SEC asks that foreign issuers on the Internet implement measures to warn U.S. investors. For instance, a foreign company offering shares of stock on the Internet must add a disclaimer on its Web site stating that it has not gone through the registration procedure in the United States. If the SEC believes that a Web site's offering of foreign secu-

---

42. 17 C.F.R. Section 232.304.

43. See, for example, *In re Syntex Corp. Securities Litigation*, 95 F.3d. 922 (9th Cir. 1996), involving alleged violations of Sections 10(b) and 20(a) of the 1934 act.

rities is targeting U.S. residents, it will pursue that company in an attempt to require it to register in the United States.[44]

ONLINE SECURITIES FRAUD

A major problem facing the SEC today is how to enforce the antifraud provisions of the securities laws in the online environment. In 1999, in the first cases involving illegal online securities offerings, the SEC filed suit against three individuals for illegally offering securities on an Internet auction site.[45] In essence, all three indicated that their companies would go public soon and attempted to sell unregistered securities via the Web auction site. All of these actions were in violation of Sections 5, 17(a)(1), and 17(a)(3) of the 1933 Securities Act. Since then, the SEC has brought a variety of Internet-related fraud cases, including cases involving investment scams and the manipulation of stock prices in Internet chat rooms.

Investment Scams

An ongoing problem is how to curb online investment scams. One fraudulent investment scheme involved twenty thousand investors, who lost, in all, more than $3 million. Some cases have involved false claims about the earnings potential of home business programs, such as the claim that one could "earn $4,000 or more each month." Others have concerned claims of "guaranteed credit repair."

Using Chat Rooms to Manipulate Stock Prices

"Pumping and dumping" occurs when a person who has purchased a particular stock heavily promotes ("pumps up") that stock—thereby creating a great demand for it and driving up its price—and then sells ("dumps") it. The practice of pumping up a stock and then dumping it is quite old. In the online world, however, the process can occur much more quickly and efficiently.

■EXAMPLE 30.8 The most famous case in this area involved Jonathan Lebed, a fifteen-year-old stock trader and Internet user from New Jersey. Lebed was the first minor ever charged with securities fraud by the SEC, but it is unlikely that he will be the last. The SEC charged that Lebed bought thinly traded stocks. After purchasing a stock, he would flood stock-related chat rooms, particularly at Yahoo's finance boards, with messages touting the stock's virtues. He used numerous false names so that no one would know that a single person was posting the messages. He would say that the stock was the most "undervalued stock in history" and that its price would jump by 1,000 percent "very soon." When other investors would then buy the stock, the price would go up quickly, and Lebed would sell out. The SEC forced the teenager to repay almost $300,000 in gains plus interest but allowed him to keep about $500,000 of the profits he made by trading small-company stocks that he also touted on the Internet. ■

The SEC has been bringing an increasing number of cases against those who manipulate stock prices in this way. Many of these online investment scams are perpetrated through mass e-mails (spam), online newsletters, and chat rooms.

Hacking into Online Stock Accounts   The last few years have seen the emergence of a new form of "pumping and dumping" stock involving hackers who break into existing

---

44. International Series Release No. 1125 (March 23, 1998).
45. *In re Davis*, SEC Administrative File No. 3-10080 (October 20, 1999); *In re Haas*, SEC Administrative File No. 3-10081 (October 20, 1999); *In re Sitaras*, SEC Administrative File No. 3-10082 (October 20, 1999).

online stock accounts and make unauthorized transfers. Millions of people now buy and sell investments online through online brokerage companies such as E*Trade and Ameritrade. Sophisticated hackers have learned to use online investing to their advantage.

By installing keystroke-monitoring software on computer terminals in public places, such as hotels, libraries, and airports, hackers can gain access to online account information. All they have to do is wait for a person to access an online trading account and then monitor the next several dozen keystrokes to determine the customer's account number and password. Once they have the log-in information, they can access the customer's account and liquidate her or his existing stock holdings. The hackers then use the customer's funds to purchase thinly traded, microcap securities, also known as penny stocks. The goal is to boost the price of a stock that the hacker has already purchased at a lower price. Then, when the stock price goes up, the hacker sells all the stock and wires the funds to either an offshore account or a dummy corporation, making it difficult for the SEC to trace the transactions and prosecute the offender.

■EXAMPLE 30.9 Aleksey Kamardin, a twenty-one-year-old Florida student, purchased 55,000 shares of stock in Fuego Entertainment using an E*Trade account in his own name. Kamardin then hacked into other customers' accounts at E*Trade, Ameritrade, Schwab, and other brokerage companies, and used their funds to purchase a total of 458,000 shares of Fuego stock. When the stock price rose from $.88 per share to $1.28 per share, Kamardin sold all of his shares of Fuego, making a profit of $9,164.28 in about three hours. Kamardin did this with other thinly traded stocks as well, allegedly making $82,960 in about five weeks, and prompting the SEC to file charges against him in January 2007.[46] ■

So far, the brokerage companies have been covering their customers' losses from this new wave of frauds, but the potential for loss is substantial. E*Trade and Ameritrade have also increased security measures and are changing their software to prevent further intrusions into customers' online stock accounts.

---

46. You can read the SEC's complaint against Kamardin by going to the SEC's Web site at **www.sec.gov**, clicking on the link to litigation releases, and selecting "LR-19981." The case had not been resolved by the time this book went to press.

REVIEWING Investor Protection, Insider Trading, and Corporate Governance

Dale Emerson served as the chief financial officer for Reliant Electric Company, a distributor of electricity serving portions of Montana and North Dakota. Reliant was in the final stages of planning a takeover of Dakota Gasworks, Inc., a natural gas distributor that operated solely within North Dakota. Emerson went on a weekend fishing trip with his uncle, Ernest Wallace. Emerson mentioned to Wallace that he had been putting in a lot of extra hours at the office planning a takeover of Dakota Gasworks. On returning from the fishing trip, Wallace met with a broker from Chambers Investments and purchased $20,000 of Reliant stock. Three weeks later, Reliant made a tender offer to Dakota Gasworks stockholders and purchased 57 percent of Dakota Gasworks stock. Over the next two weeks, the price of Reliant stock rose 72 percent before leveling out. Wallace then sold his Reliant stock for a gross profit of $14,400. Using the information presented in the chapter, answer the following questions.

1 Would registration with the SEC be required for Dakota Gasworks securities? Why or why not?

2 Did Emerson violate Section 10(b) of the Securities Exchange Act of 1934 and SEC Rule 10b-5? Why or why not?

3 What theory or theories might a court use to hold Wallace liable for insider trading?

4 Under the Sarbanes-Oxley Act of 2002, who would be required to certify the accuracy of financial statements filed with the SEC?

APPLICATION

What Venture Capital Financing and Corporate Governance Issues Might a Business Owner Encounter?*

As pointed out in Chapter 28, corporations obtain financing in a variety of ways, including selling corporate securities in the form of stocks and bonds. Nevertheless, a reason that many new businesses fail is that they are undercapitalized. Thus, obtaining proper financing for your new or existing business is extremely important.

Start-Up Businesses

Start-up businesses, particularly in the high-tech industry, are good examples of the need for proper financing. Many new businesses rely for funding on the owners' personal assets, loans from the owners' relatives or friends, and, sometimes, loans from outsiders. If a new business has a viable product or service, it may seek financing from venture capitalists—that is, businesses and individuals who lend funds to a start-up business. Generally, to obtain this "loan," the start-up business gives up a share of its ownership to the venture capitalist.

When venture capitalists provide financing, their primary goals are to enable the business to enhance its product or service; have the business properly incorporated; and, by the proper filing of a registration statement, take the corporation public through an IPO. Most often, it is the issuance and sale of these shares that affords the owners, including the venture capitalists, with operating costs and modest to substantial profits.

The Dangers of Venture Capitalist Financing

There are dangers to this type of financing. First, the start-up must find a venture capitalist willing to invest in the business. Whether this will happen depends largely on how viable the product or service is or will be. Many start-ups die simply because venture capitalists declined to invest, and the owners' personal funds were exhausted. Second, as mentioned, the start-up business will most likely be giving up a percentage of its ownership. Despite the old saying "do not give the farm away," the developers of the product or service may have to give up part of their control over the business or a significant portion of the financial rewards it produces. Third, when the business goes public, investors may not purchase the shares in sufficient amount or at a price that will provide the hoped-for profits.

Corporate Governance Issues

Once the venture capital financing is secured and the corporation has been formed, the owners may become members of the board of directors or officers. Corporate governance is important today regardless of the corporation's size. Increasingly, the SEC and shareholders are closely scrutinizing whether the stock options granted to corporate officers as a form of compensation are excessive or unfair in other ways.

Several corporations have recently come under investigation for "backdating" stock options—that is, for dating the options earlier than they were actually issued in order to lower the set price (the price that the option recipient must pay for stock purchased with the options). For example, suppose that options are issued on December 31 when the market price of the company's stock is $50. In this situation, the set price would be $50. If, however, the options issued on December 31 were backdated to February 1, when the market price was $30 per share, the options recipient would have to pay only $30 per share and would have an immediate profit of $20 per share. Backdating is illegal, however.

If you become an officer or board member, you will have access to information concerning your corporation that is not available to the public. Never use this information to gain an advantage on the stock market or give this information to others who can get a trading advantage. *Insider trading* is illegal, and liability extends to those to whom you give the information.

CHECKLIST FOR VENTURE CAPITAL FINANCING AND CORPORATE GOVERNANCE ISSUES

1 Be sure you have a viable product or service before seeking venture capital financing.
2 If the venture capitalist wants a percentage of the ownership of your business, be sure you "do not give the farm away" (lose control or substantially reduce the value of your interest in the business).
3 Take care when granting stock options as a form of compensation and never backdate the set price for stock options.
4 If you are a corporate officer or director, do not trade on the stock market based on nonpublic information nor give inside information to others.

* This *Application* is not meant to substitute for the services of an attorney who is licensed to practice law in your state.

KEY TERMS

CHAPTER SUMMARY Investor Protection, Insider Trading, and Corporate Governance

Securities Act of 1933
(See pages 834–843.)

Prohibits fraud and stabilizes the securities industry by requiring disclosure of all essential information relating to the issuance of securities to the investing public.

1. *Registration requirements*—Securities, unless exempt, must be registered with the SEC before being offered to the public. The *registration statement* must include detailed financial information about the issuing corporation; the intended use of the proceeds of the securities being issued; and certain disclosures, such as interests of directors or officers and pending lawsuits.

2. *Prospectus*—The issuer must provide investors with a *prospectus* that describes the security being sold, the issuing corporation, and the risk attaching to the security.

3. *Exemptions*—The SEC has exempted certain offerings from the requirements of the Securities Act of 1933. Exemptions may be determined on the basis of the size of the issue, whether the offering is private or public, and whether advertising is involved. Exemptions are summarized in Exhibit 30–1 on page 839.

Securities Exchange Act of 1934
(See pages 843–852.)

Provides for the regulation and registration of securities exchanges, brokers, dealers, and national securities associations (such as the NASD). Maintains a continuous disclosure system for all corporations with securities on the securities exchanges and for those companies that have assets in excess of $10 million and five hundred or more shareholders (Section 12 companies).

1. *SEC Rule 10b-5 [under Section 10(b) of the 1934 act]*—

   a. Applies in virtually all cases concerning the trading of securities—a firm's securities do not have to be registered under the 1933 act for the 1934 act to apply.

   b. Applies only when the requisites of federal jurisdiction (such as use of the mails, stock exchange facilities, or any facility of interstate commerce) are present.

   c. Applies to insider trading by corporate officers, directors, majority shareholders, and any persons receiving inside information (information not available to the investing public) who base their trading on this information.

   d. Liability for violations can be civil or criminal.

   e. May be violated by failing to disclose "material facts" that must be disclosed under this rule.

   f. Liability may be based on the tipper/tippee or the misappropriation theory.

2. *Insider trading [under Section 16(b) of the 1934 act]*—To prevent corporate officers and directors from taking advantage of inside information, the 1934 act requires officers, directors, and shareholders owning 10 percent or more of the issued stock of a corporation to turn over to the corporation all short-term profits (called *short-swing profits*) realized from the purchase and sale or sale and purchase of corporate stock within any six-month period.

3. *Proxies [under Section 14(a) of the 1934 act]*—The SEC regulates the content of proxy statements sent to shareholders by corporate managers of Section 12 companies who are requesting authority to vote on behalf of the shareholders in a particular election on specified issues. Section 14(a) is essentially a disclosure law, with provisions similar to the antifraud provisions of SEC Rule 10b-5.

CHAPTER SUMMARY Investor Protection, Insider Trading, and Corporate Governance–Continued

State Securities Laws (See page 852.)	All states have corporate securities laws (*blue sky laws*) that regulate the offer and sale of securities within state borders; these laws are designed to prevent "speculative schemes which have no more basis than so many feet of 'blue sky.' " States regulate securities concurrently with the federal government. The Uniform Securities Act of 2002, which has been adopted by eleven states and is being considered by several others, is designed to promote coordination and reduce duplication between state and federal securities regulation.
Corporate Governance (See pages 853–858.)	1. *Definition*—Corporate governance is the system by which business corporations are governed, including policies and procedures for making decisions on corporate affairs. 2. *The need for corporate governance*—Corporate governance is necessary in large corporations because corporate ownership (by the shareholders) is separated from corporate control (by officers and managers). This separation of corporate ownership and control can often result in conflicting interests. Corporate governance standards address such issues. 3. *Sarbanes-Oxley Act of 2002*—This act attempts to increase corporate accountability by imposing strict disclosure requirements and harsh penalties for violations of securities laws.
Online Securities Offerings and Disclosures (See pages 858–861.)	In 1995, the SEC announced that anything that can be delivered in paper form under current securities laws may also be delivered in electronic form. Generally, when the Internet is used for the delivery of a prospectus, the same rules apply as for the delivery of a paper prospectus. When securities offerings are made online, the offerors should be careful that any hyperlinked materials do not mislead investors. Caution should also be used when making Regulation D offerings (private placements), because general solicitation is restricted with these offerings.
Online Securities Fraud (See pages 861–862.)	A major problem facing the SEC today is how to enforce the antifraud provisions of the securities laws in the online environment. Internet-related forms of securities fraud include investment scams and the manipulation of stock prices in online chat rooms.

FOR REVIEW

Answers for the even-numbered questions in this **For Review** *section can be found in Appendix E at the end of this text.*

1 What is meant by the term *securities*?

2 What are the two major statutes regulating the securities industry? When was the Securities and Exchange Commission created, and what are its major purposes and functions?

3 What is insider trading? Why is it prohibited?

4 What are some of the features of state securities laws?

5 What certification requirements does the Sarbanes-Oxley Act impose on corporate executives?

 Thomson NOW! The following multiple-choice question is representative of the types of questions available in one of the four sections of ThomsonNOW for *Business Law Today.* ThomsonNOW also provides feedback for each response option, whether correct or incorrect, and refers to the location within the chapter where the correct answer can be found.

The 1933 Securities Act requires that nonexempt organizations file a registration statement with the SEC that contains a

a marketing plan for the organization.

b financial statement certified by a public accounting firm.

c tombstone ad.

d proxy statement applicable for all new shareholders.

QUESTIONS AND CASE PROBLEMS

HYPOTHETICAL SCENARIOS

30.1 Registration Requirements. Langley Brothers, Inc., a corporation incorporated and doing business in Kansas, decides to sell common stock worth $1 million to the public. The stock will be sold only within the state of Kansas. Joseph Langley, the chairman of the board, says the offering need not be registered with the Securities and Exchange Commission. His brother, Harry, disagrees. Who is right? Explain.

30.2 Hypothetical Question with Sample Answer. Huron Corp. has 300,000 common shares outstanding. The owners of these outstanding shares live in several different states. Huron has decided to split the 300,000 shares two for one. Will Huron Corp. have to file a registration statement and prospectus on the 300,000 new shares to be issued as a result of the split? Explain.

 For a sample answer to Question 30.2, go to Appendix F at the end of this text.

CASE PROBLEMS

30.3 Definition of a Security. The W. J. Howey Co. owned large tracts of citrus acreage in Lake County, Florida. For several years, it planted about five hundred acres annually, keeping half of the groves itself and offering the other half to the public to help finance additional development. Howey-in-the-Hills Service, Inc., was a service company engaged in cultivating and developing these groves, including harvesting and marketing the crops. Each prospective customer was offered both a land sales contract and a service contract, after being told that it was not feasible to invest in a grove unless service arrangements were made. Of the acreage sold by Howey, 85 percent was sold with a service contract with Howey-in-the-Hills Service. Howey did not register with the Securities and Exchange Commission (SEC) or meet the other administrative requirements that issuers of securities must fulfill. The SEC sued to enjoin Howey from continuing to offer the land sales and service contracts. Howey responded that no SEC violation existed because no securities had been issued. Evaluate the definition of a security given in this chapter, and then determine whether Howey or the SEC should prevail in court. [*SEC v. W. J. Howey Co.*, 328 U.S. 293, 66 S.Ct. 1100, 90 L.Ed. 1244 (1946)]

30.4 Violations of the 1934 Act. 2TheMart.com, Inc., was conceived in January 1999 to launch an auction Web site to compete with eBay, Inc. On January 19, 2TheMart announced that its Web site was in its "final development" stages and was expected to be active by the end of July as a "preeminent" auction site. The company also said that it had "retained the services of leading Web site design and architecture consultants to design and construct" the site. Based on the announcement, investors rushed to buy 2TheMart's stock, causing a rapid increase in the price. On February 3, 2TheMart entered into an agreement with IBM to take preliminary steps to plan the site. Three weeks later, 2TheMart announced that the site was "currently in final development." On June 1, 2TheMart signed a contract with IBM to design, build, and test the site, with a target delivery date of October 8. When 2TheMart's site did not debut as announced, Mary Harrington and others who had bought the stock filed a suit in a federal district court against the firm's officers, alleging violations of the Securities Exchange Act of 1934. The defendants responded, in part, that any alleged misrepresentations were not material and asked the court to dismiss the suit. How should the court rule, and why? [*In re 2TheMart.com, Inc. Securities Litigation*, 114 F.Supp.2d 955 (C.D.Ca. 2000)]

30.5 Insider Reporting and Trading. Ronald Bleakney, an officer at Natural Microsystems Corp. (NMC), a Section 12 corporation, directed NMC sales in North America, South America, and Europe. In November 1998, Bleakney sold more than 7,500 shares of NMC stock. The following March, Bleakney resigned from the firm, and the next month, he bought more than 20,000 shares of its stock. NMC provided some guidance to employees concerning the rules of insider trading, but with regard to Bleakney's transactions, the corporation said nothing about potential liability. Richard Morales, an NMC shareholder, filed a suit against NMC and Bleakney to compel recovery, under Section 16(b) of the Securities Exchange Act of 1934, of Bleakney's profits from the sale and purchase of his shares. (When Morales died, his executor Deborah Donoghue became the plaintiff.) Bleakney argued that he should not be liable because he relied on NMC's advice. Should the court order Bleakney to disgorge his profits? Explain. [*Donoghue v. Natural Microsystems Corp.*, 198 F.Supp.2d 487 (S.D.N.Y. 2002)]

30.6 Case Problem with Sample Answer. Scott Ginsburg was chief executive officer (CEO) of Evergreen Media Corp., which owned and operated radio stations. In 1996, Evergreen became interested in acquiring EZ Communications, Inc., which also owned radio stations. To initiate negotiations, Ginsburg met with EZ's CEO, Alan Box, on Friday, July 12. Two days later, Scott phoned his brother Mark, who, on Monday, bought 3,800 shares of EZ stock. Mark discussed the deal with their father, Jordan, who bought 20,000 EZ shares on Thursday. On July 25, the day before the EZ bid was due, Scott phoned his parents' home, and Mark bought another 3,200 EZ shares. The same routine was followed over the next few days, with Scott periodically phoning Mark or Jordan, both of whom continued to buy EZ shares. Evergreen's bid was refused, but on August 5, EZ announced its merger with another company. The price of EZ stock rose 30 percent, increasing the value of Mark and Jordan's shares by $664,024 and $412,875, respectively. The Securities and Exchange Commission (SEC) filed a civil suit in a federal district court against Scott. What was the most likely allegation? What is required to impose sanctions for this offense? Should the court hold Scott liable? Why or why not? [*SEC v. Ginsburg*, 362 F.3d 1292 (11th Cir. 2004)]

After you have answered Problem 30.6, compare your answer with the sample answer given on the Web site that accompanies this text. Go to **www.thomsonedu.com/westbuslaw/blt**, select "Chapter 30," and click on "Case Problem with Sample Answer."

30.7 Securities Laws. In 1997, WTS Transnational, Inc., required financing to develop a prototype of an unpatented fingerprint-verification system. At the time, WTS had no revenue, $655,000 in liabilities, and only $10,000 in assets. Thomas Cavanagh and Frank Nicolois, who operated an investment banking company called U.S. Milestone (USM), arranged the financing using Curbstone Acquisition Corp. Curbstone had no assets but had registered approximately 3.5 million shares of stock with the Securities and Exchange Commission (SEC). Under the terms of the deal, Curbstone acquired WTS, and the resulting entity was named Electro-Optical Systems Corp. (EOSC). New EOSC shares were issued to all of the WTS shareholders. Only Cavanagh and others affiliated with USM could sell EOSC stock to the public, however. Over the next few months, these individuals issued false press releases, made small deceptive purchases of EOSC shares at high prices, distributed hundreds of thousands of shares to friends and relatives, and sold their own shares at inflated prices through third party companies they owned. When the SEC began to investigate, the share price fell to its actual value, and innocent investors lost over $15 million. Were any securities laws violated in this case? If so, what might be an appropriate remedy? [*SEC v. Cavanagh*, 445 F.3d 105 (2d Cir. 2006)]

30.8 Securities Trading. Between 1994 and 1998, Richard Svoboda, a credit officer for NationsBank N.A., in Dallas, Texas, evaluated and approved his employer's extensions of credit to clients. These responsibilities gave Svoboda access to nonpublic information about the clients' earnings, performance, acquisitions, and business plans in confidential memos, e-mail, credit applications, and other sources. Svoboda devised a scheme with Michael Robles, an independent accountant, to use this information to trade securities. Pursuant to their scheme, Robles traded in the securities of more than twenty different companies and profited by more than $1 million. Svoboda also executed trades for his own profit of more than $200,000, despite their agreement that Robles would do all of the trading. Aware that their scheme violated NationsBank's policy, they attempted to conduct their trades to avoid suspicion. When NationsBank questioned Svoboda about his actions, he lied, refused to cooperate, and was fired. Did Svoboda or Robles commit any crimes? Are they subject to civil liability? If so, who could file a suit and on what ground? What are the possible sanctions? What might be a defense? How should a court rule? Discuss. [*SEC v. Svoboda*, 409 F.Supp.2d 331 (S.D.N.Y. 2006)]

30.9 A Question of Ethics. *Melvin Lyttle told John Montana and Paul Knight about a "Trading Program" that purportedly would buy and sell securities in deals that were fully insured, as well as monitored and controlled by the Federal Reserve Bank. Without checking the details or even verifying whether the Program existed, Montana and Knight, with Lyttle's help, began to sell interests in the Program to investors. For a minimum investment of $1 million, the investors were promised extraordinary rates of return—from 10 percent to as much as 100 percent per week—without risk. They were told, among other things, that the Program would "utilize banks that can ensure full bank integrity of The Transaction whose undertaking[s] are in complete harmony with international banking rules and protocol and who [sic] guarantee maximum security of a Funder's Capital Placement Amount." Nothing was required but the investors' funds and their silence—the Program was to be kept secret. Over a four-month period in 1999, Montana raised approximately $23 million from twenty-two investors. The promised gains did not accrue, however. Instead, Montana, Lyttle, and Knight depleted investors' funds in high-risk trades or spent the funds on themselves. [SEC v. Montana, 464 F.Supp.2d 772 (S.D.Ind. 2006)]*

1 The Securities and Exchange Commission (SEC) filed a suit in a federal district court against Montana and the others, seeking an injunction, civil penalties, and disgorgement with interest. The SEC alleged, among other things, violations of Section 10(b) of the Securities Exchange Act of 1934 and SEC Rule 10b-5. What is required to establish a violation of these laws? Describe how and why the facts in this case meet, or fail to meet, these requirements.

2 It is often remarked, "There's a sucker born every minute!" Does that phrase describe the Program's investors? Ultimately, about half of the investors recouped the amount they invested. Should the others be considered at least partly responsible for their own losses? Why or why not?

CRITICAL THINKING
AND WRITING ASSIGNMENTS

30.10 Critical Legal Thinking. Do you think that the tipper/tippee and misappropriation theories extend liability under SEC Rule 10b-5 too far? Why or why not?

30.11 Critical Thinking and Writing Assignment for Business. Insider trading, as you learned, is illegal. Not everyone agrees that it should be, though. A small group of legal scholars believe that insider trading should be completely legal. They argue that insider trading, if more widespread, would cause stock prices to almost instantly adjust to new information. They further argue that "insiders," if able to make profits from insider trading, would therefore accept lower salaries and benefits.

1 Why is insider trading illegal in the first place? Who is supposed to be protected and why?

2 What is wrong with the argument advanced by the legal scholars who want insider trading made legal? Or, are they right? Explain your answer.

30.12 **Video Question.** Go to this text's Web site at **www.thomsonedu.com/westbuslaw/blt** and select

"Chapter 30." Click on "Video Questions" and view the video titled *Mergers and Acquisitions*. Then answer the following questions.

1 Analyze whether the purchase of Onyx Advertising is a material fact that the Quigley Company had a duty to disclose under SEC Rule 10b-5.

2 Does it matter whether Quigley personally knew about or authorized the company spokesperson's statements? Why or why not?

3 Which case discussed in the chapter presented issues that are very similar to those raised in the video? Under the holding of that case, would Onyx Advertising be able to maintain a suit against the Quigley Company for violation of SEC Rule 10b-5?

4 Who else might be able to bring a suit against the Quigley Company for insider trading under SEC Rule 10b-5?

ONLINE ACTIVITIES

PRACTICAL
INTERNET EXERCISES

Go to this text's Web site at **www.thomsonedu.com/westbuslaw/blt**, select "Chapter 30," and click on "Practical Internet Exercises." There you will find the following Internet research exercises that you can perform to learn more about the topics covered in this chapter.

PRACTICAL INTERNET EXERCISE 30-1 LEGAL PERSPECTIVE—Electronic Delivery

PRACTICAL INTERNET EXERCISE 30-2 MANAGEMENT PERSPECTIVE—The SEC's Role

BEFORE THE TEST

Go to this text's Web site at **www.thomsonedu.com/westbuslaw/blt**, select "Chapter 30," and click on "Interactive Quizzes." You will find a number of interactive questions relating to this chapter.

John leases an office and buys computer equipment. Initially, to pay for the lease and the equipment, he goes into the business of designing Web pages. He also has an idea for a new software product that he hopes will be more profitable than designing Web pages. Whenever he has time, he works on the software.

1 After six months, Mary and Paul come to work in the office to help develop John's idea. John continues to pay the rent and other expenses, including salaries for Mary and Paul. John does not expect to make a profit until the software is developed, which could take months; even then, there may be very little profit if the product is not marketed successfully. John believes that if the product is successful, however, the firm will be able to follow up with other products. In choosing a form of business organization for this firm, what are the important considerations? What are the advantages and disadvantages of each basic option?

2 It is decided that the organizational form for this firm should provide limited liability for the owners. The owners will include John, Mary, Paul, and some members of their respective families. One of the features of the corporate form is limited liability. Ordinarily, however, corporate income is taxed at both the corporate level and the shareholder level. Which corporate form could the firm use to avoid this double taxation? Which other forms of business organization provide limited liability? What factors, other than liability and taxation, influence a firm's choice among these forms?

3 The firm is incorporated as Digital Software, Inc. (DSI). The software is developed and marketed successfully, and DSI prospers. John, Mary, and Paul become directors of DSI. At a

board meeting, Paul proposes a marketing strategy for DSI's next product, and John and Mary approve it. Implementing the strategy causes DSI's profits to drop. If the shareholders accuse Paul of breaching his fiduciary duty to DSI, what is Paul's most likely defense? If the shareholders accuse John and Mary of the same breach, what is their best defense? In either case, if the shareholders file a suit, how is a court likely to rule?

4 International Investments, Inc., makes a public offer to buy the stock of DSI. The price of the offer is higher than the market price of the stock, but DSI's board believes that the offer should not be accepted and that International's attempt to take over DSI should be resisted. What steps can DSI take to resist the takeover?

5 Mary and Paul withdraw from DSI to set up their own firm. To obtain operating capital, they solicit investors who agree to become "general partners." Mary and Paul designate themselves "managing partners." The investors are spread over a wide area geographically and do not know anything about Mary and Paul's business until they are contacted. Are Mary and Paul truly soliciting partners, or are they selling securities? What are the criteria for determining whether an investment is a security? What are the advantages and disadvantages of selling securities compared to soliciting partners?

United States v. Bhagat

Violations of the securities laws discussed in Chapter 30 may constitute crimes. As explained in Chapter 6 on criminal law and procedure, an indictment formally charges a defendant with a crime. An indictment must refer to the evidence on which a charge is based to allow the accused party to defend against it. Nevertheless, for some purposes, a court may admit evidence not mentioned in an indictment without affecting the legitimacy of a subsequent conviction. For example, such evidence might be admitted to contradict a defendant's testimony. In this extended case study, we examine United States v. Bhagat,[1] a case in which the defendant was charged with criminal violations of securities laws. During the trial, the prosecution asked questions that, in the defendant's view, suggested a basis for conviction supported by evidence not mentioned in the indictment.

1. 436 F.3d 1140 (9th Cir. 2006).

CASE BACKGROUND On Sunday, March 5, 2000, Microsoft Corporation awarded Nvidia Corporation a multimillion-dollar contract to develop the X-Box. Late that night, Nvidia sent a companywide e-mail to tell its employees about the contract. The next morning, also via e-mail, Nvidia advised the employees that the X-Box deal should be kept confidential, that they should not buy Nvidia stock for several days, and that they should cancel any open or outstanding orders for the stock.

Twenty minutes after the last e-mail was sent, Atul Bhagat, a Nvidia engineer, bought one thousand shares of Nvidia stock—the largest purchase of the stock that he had made in three years. Rumors about the X-Box contract began circulating the next day, and the price of Nvidia stock rose sharply. Three days later, the news was made public and the price skyrocketed. Another four days later, Bhagat sold his shares, reaping a substantial profit.

The government indicted Bhagat in a federal district court for criminal violations of securities laws. Among other things, he was charged with insider trading, based solely on Nvidia's e-mail to its employees. After a jury convicted Bhagat, he appealed to the U.S. Court of Appeals for the Ninth Circuit. The most hotly contested issue was whether the government had adequately proved that Bhagat knew of the X-Box contract before he purchased the stock.

MAJORITY OPINION

RAWLINSON, Circuit Judge:

* * * *

The principal theory of the prosecution during the trial was that Bhagat knew about the contract from reading his own e-mail. During cross-examination, however, the prosecutor also questioned Bhagat about conversations among his co-workers that he had heard that morning concerning the X-Box contract. This line of questioning set the stage for what the parties refer to as the "office 'abuzz' theory."

* * * *

During closing arguments, the government referenced the "office abuzz" theory in passing, stating that the jury should consider the fact that the office was "abuzz" with the news of the X-Box contract, and that Bhagat had to walk through the office to reach his cubicle. The government also repeatedly informed the jury that in order to find Bhagat guilty, the government would have to prove that he read the company-wide e-mails prior to purchasing the stock.

* * * *

Bhagat contends that the government's reference to the "office abuzz" theory introduced an alternative theory by which the jury could infer Bhagat's knowledge of the X-Box contract prior to the stock transaction. The government counters that it invoked the "office abuzz" theory for the limited purpose of impeaching [calling into question] Bhagat's credibility when he testified that he had not heard anyone mention the X-Box contract upon entering the office on Monday morning.

The government's conduct throughout the trial is consistent with its contention. The government repeatedly informed the jury that conviction should be based upon a determination that Bhagat had read the companywide e-mails prior to executing his trades. It was only during cross-examination, after Bhagat denied reading the pertinent e-mails, that the government questioned Bhagat about whether he had heard any office chatter regarding the X-Box contract.

* * * *

* * * The record in this case reflects that the reference to the "office abuzz" theory was not intended to and did not amend the indictment. The facts presented were not distinctly different from those in the indictment. Neither was the crime charged in the indictment * * * substantially altered at trial. That being so, no constructive amendment [the court will not legally construe or interpret the theory as an amendment] of the indictment occurred. Rather, the evidence was admitted for impeachment purposes * * * .

* * * *

A material variance exists if a materially different set of facts from those alleged in the indictment is presented at trial, and if that variance affects the defendant's substantial rights. [Emphasis added.]

* * * *

No [such] situation exists in this case. At all times, the pertinent fact was that Bhagat was aware of the e-mails notifying employees of the X-Box contract award. * * * The record does not support a claim of variance.

* * * *

To convict Bhagat of insider trading, the government was required to prove that he traded stock on the basis of material, nonpublic information.

The government offered significant evidence to support the jury's conclusion that Bhagat was aware of the confidential X-Box information before he executed his trades. The X-Box e-mails were sent prior to his purchase. The e-mails were found on his computer. Bhagat was at his office for several hours prior to executing his trade, which provided him the opportunity to read the e-mails. Finally, Bhagat took virtually no action to divest himself of the stock, or to inform his company that he had violated the company's trading blackout.

* * *

* * * *

The government's use of the "office abuzz" theory did not constructively amend the indictment or create a material variance between the facts alleged in the indictment and the evidence presented at trial.

* * * *

CONVICTION AFFIRMED * * * .

DISSENTING OPINION

TASHIMA, Circuit Judge, dissenting.

* * * *

The government's initial theory, consistent with the indictment, was that Defendant read the e-mails when he arrived at work * * * Monday morning, but there is no direct evidence that he did so. Defendant denied that he read the e-mails before placing his buy order and testified that he did not read them until 1:00 P.M., approximately 40 minutes after he made his purchase.

During its cross-examination of Defendant, the government pursued what the parties refer to as the "office abuzz" theory. The government's questioning of Defendant suggested that because of the open cubicle configuration of the office, Defendant could not help but overhear conversations among his co-workers regarding the exciting news of the X-Box contract—that the office was "abuzz" with the news. Defendant denied that he overheard any X-Box office conversation. The district court overruled Defendant's objection that the government should not be allowed to argue the "office abuzz" theory because "there is no evidence in the record the company was abuzz with the news," as indeed there was not, as a basis of liability. * * *

* * * *

This "office abuzz" theory of liability as to how Defendant acquired insider information, an essential element of the charged crime, is factually distinct from the theory charged in the indictment, that Defendant acquired the insider information through reading the companywide e-mails. Because it is a new, uncharged theory, Defendant had no notice of it and no opportunity to defend against it, to rebut it with his own evidence.

* * * *

* * * One of the primary purposes of an indictment is to inform a defendant of what he is accused of doing in violation of the criminal law, so that he can prepare his defense. * * * This purpose was not served here. * * * Accordingly, I would conclude that the variance here affected Defendant's substantial rights and, thus, requires reversal.

QUESTIONS FOR ANALYSIS

1 LAW. What did the majority rule with respect to the dispute in this case? On what rationale did the majority base this ruling?

2 LAW. What was the dissent's position on the issue before the court? What were the dissent's reasons in support of its position?

3 ETHICS. When a case is tried before a jury, the jury determines the credibility of the witnesses, resolves conflicts in the evidence, and draws reasonable inferences from the facts. Is it appropriate for a prosecutor, as in this case, or a defendant to suggest an inference for the jury to make? Explain.

4 SOCIAL DIMENSIONS. Suppose that a corporate insider, without revealing any material, nonpublic information, advises a friend to buy stock in the company. Can the insider legitimately share the profit on the stock's sale? Why or why not?

5 IMPLICATIONS FOR THE INVESTOR. What does the outcome of this case suggest for the employee who wants to buy stock in her or his employer's firm on the basis of a potentially profitable development?

APPENDIX A
How to Brief Cases and Analyze Case Problems

HOW TO BRIEF CASES

To fully understand the law with respect to business, you need to be able to read and understand court decisions. To make this task easier, you can use a method of case analysis that is called *briefing*. There is a fairly standard procedure that you can follow when you "brief" any court case. You must first read the case opinion carefully. When you feel you understand the case, you can prepare a brief of it.

Although the format of a case brief may vary, typically it will present the essentials of the case under headings such as those listed below. This is basically the format followed by the authors when briefing the cases that have been included in this text.

1 Citation. Give the full citation for the case, including the name of the case, the date it was decided, and the court that decided it.

2 Facts. Briefly indicate (a) the reasons for the lawsuit; (b) the identity and arguments of the plaintiff(s) and defendant(s), respectively; and (c) the lower court's decision—if appropriate.

3 Issue. Concisely phrase, in the form of a question, the essential issue before the court. (If more than one issue is involved, you may have two—or even more—questions here.)

4 Decision. Indicate here—with a "yes" or "no," if possible—the court's answer to the question (or questions) in the *Issue* section above.

5 Reason. Summarize as briefly as possible the reasons given by the court for its decision (or decisions) and the case or statutory law relied on by the court in arriving at its decision.

For a case-specific example of what should be included under each of the above headings when briefing a case, see the review of the sample court case presented in the appendix to Chapter 1 of this text.

HOW TO ANALYZE CASE PROBLEMS

In addition to learning how to brief cases, students of business law and the legal environment also find it helpful to know how to analyze case problems. Part of the study of business law and the legal environment usually involves analyzing case problems, such as those included in this text at the end of each chapter.

For each case problem in this book, we provide the relevant background and facts of the lawsuit and the issue before the court. When you are assigned one of these problems, your job will be to determine how the court should decide the issue, and why. In other words, you will need to engage in legal analysis and reasoning. Here we offer some suggestions on how to make this task less daunting. We begin by presenting a sample problem:

> While Janet Lawson, a famous pianist, was shopping in Quality Market, she slipped and fell on a wet floor in one of the aisles. The floor had recently been mopped by one of the store's employees, but there were no signs warning customers that the floor in that area was wet. As a result of the fall, Lawson injured her right arm and was unable to perform piano concerts for the next six months. Had she been able to perform the scheduled concerts, she would have earned approximately $60,000 over that period of time. Lawson sued Quality Market for this amount, plus another $10,000 in medical expenses. She claimed that the store's failure to warn customers of the wet floor constituted negligence and therefore the market was liable for her injuries. Will the court agree with Lawson? Discuss.

Understand the Facts

This may sound obvious, but before you can analyze or apply the relevant law to a specific set of facts, you must clearly understand those facts. In other words, you should read through the case problem carefully and more than once, if necessary, to make sure you understand the identity of the plaintiff(s) and defendant(s) in the case and the progression of events that led to the lawsuit.

In the sample case just given, the identity of the parties is fairly obvious. Janet Lawson is the one bringing the suit; therefore, she is the plaintiff. Quality Market, against whom she is bringing the suit, is the defendant. Some of the case problems you may work on have multiple plaintiffs or defendants. Often, it is helpful to use abbreviations for the parties. To indicate a reference to a plaintiff, for example, the *pi* symbol—π—is often used, and a defendant is denoted by a *delta*—Δ—a triangle.

The events leading to the lawsuit are also fairly straightforward. Lawson slipped and fell on a wet floor, and she contends that Quality Market should be liable for her injuries because it was negligent in not posting a sign warning customers of the wet floor.

When you are working on case problems, realize that the facts should be accepted as they are given. For example, in our sample problem, it should be accepted that the floor was wet and that there was no sign. In other words, avoid making conjectures, such as "Maybe the floor wasn't too wet" or "Maybe an employee was getting a sign to put up," or "Maybe someone stole the sign." Questioning the facts as they are presented only adds confusion to your analysis.

Legal Analysis and Reasoning

Once you understand the facts given in the case problem, you can begin to analyze the case. The **IRAC method** is a helpful tool to use in the legal analysis and reasoning process. IRAC is an acronym for *Issue, Rule, Application, Conclusion*. Applying this method to our sample problem would involve the following steps:

1 First, you need to decide what legal **issue** is involved in the case. In our sample case, the basic issue is whether Quality Market's failure to warn customers of the wet floor constituted negligence. As discussed in Chapter 4, negligence is a *tort*—a civil wrong. In a tort lawsuit, the plaintiff seeks to be compensated for another's wrongful act. A defendant will be deemed negligent if he or she breached a duty of care owed to the plaintiff and the breach of that duty caused the plaintiff to suffer harm.

2 Once you have identified the issue, the next step is to determine what **rule of law** applies to the issue. To make this determination, you will want to review carefully the text of the chapter in which the problem appears to find the relevant rule of law. Our sample case involves the tort of negligence, covered in Chapter 4. The applicable rule of law is the tort law principle that business owners owe a duty to exercise reasonable care to protect their customers ("business invitees"). Reasonable care, in this context, includes either removing—or warning customers of—*foreseeable* risks about which the owner *knew* or *should have known*. Business owners need not warn customers of "open and obvious" risks, however. If a business owner breaches this duty of care (fails to exercise the appropriate degree of care toward customers), and the breach of duty causes a customer to be injured, the business owner will be liable to the customer for the customer's injuries.

3 The next—and usually the most difficult—step in analyzing case problems is the **application** of the relevant rule of law to the specific facts of the case you are studying. In our sample problem, applying the tort law principle just discussed presents few difficulties. An employee of the store had mopped the floor in the aisle where Lawson slipped and fell, but no sign was present indicating that the floor was wet. That a customer might fall on a wet floor is clearly a foreseeable risk. Therefore, the failure to warn customers about the wet floor was a breach of the duty of care owed by the business owner to the store's customers.

4 Once you have completed Step 3 in the IRAC method, you should be ready to draw your **conclusion.** In our sample case, Quality Market is liable to Lawson for her injuries, because the market's breach of its duty of care caused Lawson's injuries.

The fact patterns in the case problems presented in this text are not always as simple as those presented in our sample problem. Often, for example, there may be more than one plaintiff or defendant. There also may be more than one issue involved in a case and more than one applicable rule of law. Furthermore, in some case problems the facts may indicate that the general rule of law should not apply. For example, suppose a store employee advised Lawson not to walk on the floor in the aisle because it was wet, but Lawson decided to walk on it anyway. This fact could alter the outcome of the case because the store could then raise the defense of assumption of risk (see Chapter 4). Nonetheless, a careful review of the chapter should always provide you with the knowledge you need to analyze the problem thoroughly and arrive at accurate conclusions.

The Constitution of the United States

PREAMBLE

We the People of the United States, in Order to form a more perfect Union, establish Justice, insure domestic Tranquility, provide for the common defence, promote the general Welfare, and secure the Blessings of Liberty to ourselves and our Posterity, do ordain and establish this Constitution for the United States of America.

ARTICLE I

Section 1. All legislative Powers herein granted shall be vested in a Congress of the United States, which shall consist of a Senate and House of Representatives.

Section 2. The House of Representatives shall be composed of Members chosen every second Year by the People of the several States, and the Electors in each State shall have the Qualifications requisite for Electors of the most numerous Branch of the State Legislature.

No Person shall be a Representative who shall not have attained to the Age of twenty five Years, and been seven Years a Citizen of the United States, and who shall not, when elected, be an Inhabitant of that State in which he shall be chosen.

Representatives and direct Taxes shall be apportioned among the several States which may be included within this Union, according to their respective Numbers, which shall be determined by adding to the whole Number of free Persons, including those bound to Service for a Term of Years, and excluding Indians not taxed, three fifths of all other Persons. The actual Enumeration shall be made within three Years after the first Meeting of the Congress of the United States, and within every subsequent Term of ten Years, in such Manner as they shall by Law direct. The Number of Representatives shall not exceed one for every thirty Thousand, but each State shall have at Least one Representative; and until such enumeration shall be made, the State of New Hampshire shall be entitled to chuse three, Massachusetts eight, Rhode Island and Providence Plantations one, Connecticut five, New York six, New Jersey four, Pennsylvania eight, Delaware one, Maryland six, Virginia ten, North Carolina five, South Carolina five, and Georgia three.

When vacancies happen in the Representation from any State, the Executive Authority thereof shall issue Writs of Election to fill such Vacancies.

The House of Representatives shall chuse their Speaker and other Officers; and shall have the sole Power of Impeachment.

Section 3. The Senate of the United States shall be composed of two Senators from each State, chosen by the Legislature thereof, for six Years; and each Senator shall have one Vote.

Immediately after they shall be assembled in Consequence of the first Election, they shall be divided as equally as may be into three Classes. The Seats of the Senators of the first Class shall be vacated at the Expiration of the second Year, of the second Class at the Expiration of the fourth Year, and of the third Class at the Expiration of the sixth Year, so that one third may be chosen every second Year; and if Vacancies happen by Resignation, or otherwise, during the Recess of the Legislature of any State, the Executive thereof may make temporary Appointments until the next Meeting of the Legislature, which shall then fill such Vacancies.

No Person shall be a Senator who shall not have attained to the Age of thirty Years, and been nine Years a Citizen of the United States, and who shall not, when elected, be an Inhabitant of that State for which he shall be chosen.

The Vice President of the United States shall be President of the Senate, but shall have no Vote, unless they be equally divided.

The Senate shall chuse their other Officers, and also a President pro tempore, in the Absence of the Vice President, or when he shall exercise the Office of President of the United States.

The Senate shall have the sole Power to try all Impeachments. When sitting for that Purpose, they shall be on Oath or Affirmation. When the President of the United States is tried, the Chief Justice shall preside: And no Person shall be convicted without the Concurrence of two thirds of the Members present.

Judgment in Cases of Impeachment shall not extend further than to removal from Office, and disqualification to hold and enjoy any Office of honor, Trust, or Profit under the United States: but the Party convicted shall nevertheless be liable and subject to Indictment, Trial, Judgment, and Punishment, according to Law.

Section 4. The Times, Places and Manner of holding Elections for Senators and Representatives, shall be prescribed in each State by the Legislature thereof; but the Congress may at any time by Law make or alter such Regulations, except as to the Places of chusing Senators.

The Congress shall assemble at least once in every Year, and such Meeting shall be on the first Monday in December, unless they shall by Law appoint a different Day.

Section 5. Each House shall be the Judge of the Elections, Returns, and Qualifications of its own Members, and a Majority of each shall constitute a Quorum to do Business; but a smaller Number may adjourn from day to day, and may be authorized to compel the Attendance of absent Members, in such Manner, and under such Penalties as each House may provide.

Each House may determine the Rules of its Proceedings, punish its Members for disorderly Behavior, and, with the Concurrence of two thirds, expel a Member.

Each House shall keep a Journal of its Proceedings, and from time to time publish the same, excepting such Parts as may in their Judgment require Secrecy; and the Yeas and Nays of the Members of either House on any question shall, at the Desire of one fifth of those Present, be entered on the Journal.

Neither House, during the Session of Congress, shall, without the Consent of the other, adjourn for more than three days, nor to any other Place than that in which the two Houses shall be sitting.

Section 6. The Senators and Representatives shall receive a Compensation for their Services, to be ascertained by Law, and paid out of the Treasury of the United States. They shall in all Cases, except Treason, Felony and Breach of the Peace, be privileged from Arrest during their Attendance at the Session of their respective Houses, and in going to and returning from the same; and for any Speech or Debate in either House, they shall not be questioned in any other Place.

No Senator or Representative shall, during the Time for which he was elected, be appointed to any civil Office under the Authority of the United States, which shall have been created, or the Emoluments whereof shall have been increased during such time; and no Person holding any Office under the United States, shall be a Member of either House during his Continuance in Office.

Section 7. All Bills for raising Revenue shall originate in the House of Representatives; but the Senate may propose or concur with Amendments as on other Bills.

Every Bill which shall have passed the House of Representatives and the Senate, shall, before it become a Law, be presented to the President of the United States; If he approve he shall sign it, but if not he shall return it, with his Objections to the House in which it shall have originated, who shall enter the Objections at large on their Journal, and proceed to reconsider it. If after such Reconsideration two thirds of that House shall agree to pass the Bill, it shall be sent together with the Objections, to the other House, by which it shall likewise be reconsidered, and if approved by two thirds of that House, it shall become a Law. But in all such Cases the Votes of both Houses shall be determined by Yeas and Nays, and the Names of the Persons voting for and against the Bill shall be entered on the Journal of each House respectively. If any Bill shall not be returned by the President within ten Days (Sundays excepted) after it shall have been presented to him, the Same shall be a Law, in like Manner as if he had signed it, unless the Congress by their Adjournment prevent its Return in which Case it shall not be a Law.

Every Order, Resolution, or Vote, to which the Concurrence of the Senate and House of Representatives may be necessary (except on a question of Adjournment) shall be presented to the President of the United States; and before the Same shall take Effect, shall be approved by him, or being disapproved by him, shall be repassed by two thirds of the Senate and House of Representatives, according to the Rules and Limitations prescribed in the Case of a Bill.

Section 8. The Congress shall have Power To lay and collect Taxes, Duties, Imposts and Excises, to pay the Debts and provide for the common Defence and general Welfare of the United States; but all Duties, Imposts and Excises shall be uniform throughout the United States;

To borrow Money on the credit of the United States;

To regulate Commerce with foreign Nations, and among the several States, and with the Indian Tribes;

To establish an uniform Rule of Naturalization, and uniform Laws on the subject of Bankruptcies throughout the United States;

To coin Money, regulate the Value thereof, and of foreign Coin, and fix the Standard of Weights and Measures;

To provide for the Punishment of counterfeiting the Securities and current Coin of the United States;

To establish Post Offices and post Roads;

To promote the Progress of Science and useful Arts, by securing for limited Times to Authors and Inventors the exclusive Right to their respective Writings and Discoveries;

To constitute Tribunals inferior to the supreme Court;

To define and punish Piracies and Felonies committed on the high Seas, and Offenses against the Law of Nations;

To declare War, grant Letters of Marque and Reprisal, and make Rules concerning Captures on Land and Water;

To raise and support Armies, but no Appropriation of Money to that Use shall be for a longer Term than two Years;

To provide and maintain a Navy;

To make Rules for the Government and Regulation of the land and naval Forces;

To provide for calling forth the Militia to execute the Laws of the Union, suppress Insurrections and repel Invasions;

To provide for organizing, arming, and disciplining, the Militia, and for governing such Part of them as may be employed in the Service of the United States, reserving to the States respectively, the Appointment of the Officers, and the Authority of training the Militia according to the discipline prescribed by Congress;

To exercise exclusive Legislation in all Cases whatsoever, over such District (not exceeding ten Miles square) as may, by Cession of particular States, and the Acceptance of Congress, become the Seat of the Government of the United States, and to exercise like Authority over all Places purchased by the Consent of the Legislature of the State in which the Same shall be, for the Erection of Forts, Magazines, Arsenals, dock-Yards, and other needful Buildings;—And

To make all Laws which shall be necessary and proper for carrying into Execution the foregoing Powers, and all other Powers vested by this Constitution in the Government of the United States, or in any Department or Officer thereof.

Section 9. The Migration or Importation of such Persons as any of the States now existing shall think proper to admit, shall not be prohibited by the Congress prior to the Year one thousand eight hundred and eight, but a Tax or duty may be imposed on such Importation, not exceeding ten dollars for each Person.

The privilege of the Writ of Habeas Corpus shall not be suspended, unless when in Cases of Rebellion or Invasion the public Safety may require it.

No Bill of Attainder or ex post facto Law shall be passed.

No Capitation, or other direct, Tax shall be laid, unless in Proportion to the Census or Enumeration herein before directed to be taken.

No Tax or Duty shall be laid on Articles exported from any State.

No Preference shall be given by any Regulation of Commerce or Revenue to the Ports of one State over those of another: nor shall Vessels bound to, or from, one State be obliged to enter, clear, or pay Duties in another.

No Money shall be drawn from the Treasury, but in Consequence of Appropriations made by Law; and a regular Statement and Account of the Receipts and Expenditures of all public Money shall be published from time to time.

No Title of Nobility shall be granted by the United States: And no Person holding any Office of Profit or Trust under them, shall, without the Consent of the Congress, accept of any present, Emolument, Office, or Title, of any kind whatever, from any King, Prince, or foreign State.

Section 10.   No State shall enter into any Treaty, Alliance, or Confederation; grant Letters of Marque and Reprisal; coin Money; emit Bills of Credit; make any Thing but gold and silver Coin a Tender in Payment of Debts; pass any Bill of Attainder, ex post facto Law, or Law impairing the Obligation of Contracts, or grant any Title of Nobility.

No State shall, without the Consent of the Congress, lay any Imposts or Duties on Imports or Exports, except what may be absolutely necessary for executing its inspection Laws: and the net Produce of all Duties and Imposts, laid by any State on Imports or Exports, shall be for the Use of the Treasury of the United States; and all such Laws shall be subject to the Revision and Controul of the Congress.

No State shall, without the Consent of Congress, lay any Duty of Tonnage, keep Troops, or Ships of War in time of Peace, enter into any Agreement or Compact with another State, or with a foreign Power, or engage in War, unless actually invaded, or in such imminent Danger as will not admit of delay.

ARTICLE II

Section 1.   The executive Power shall be vested in a President of the United States of America. He shall hold his Office during the Term of four Years, and, together with the Vice President, chosen for the same Term, be elected, as follows:

Each State shall appoint, in such Manner as the Legislature thereof may direct, a Number of Electors, equal to the whole Number of Senators and Representatives to which the State may be entitled in the Congress; but no Senator or Representative, or Person holding an Office of Trust or Profit under the United States, shall be appointed an Elector.

The Electors shall meet in their respective States, and vote by Ballot for two Persons, of whom one at least shall not be an Inhabitant of the same State with themselves. And they shall make a List of all the Persons voted for, and of the Number of Votes for each; which List they shall sign and certify, and transmit sealed to the Seat of the Government of the United States, directed to the President of the Senate. The President of the Senate shall, in the Presence of the Senate and House of Representatives, open all the Certificates, and the Votes shall then be counted. The Person having the greatest Number of Votes shall be the President, if such Number be a Majority of the whole Number of Electors appointed; and if there be more than one who have such Majority, and have an equal Number of Votes, then the House of Representatives shall immediately chuse by Ballot one of them for President; and if no Person have a Majority, then from the five highest on the List the said House shall in like Manner chuse the President. But in chusing the President, the Votes shall be taken by States, the Representation from each State having one Vote; A quorum for this Purpose shall consist of a Member or Members from two thirds of the States, and a Majority of all the States shall be necessary to a Choice. In every Case, after the Choice of the President, the Person having the greater Number of Votes of the Electors shall be the Vice President. But if there should remain two or more who have equal Votes, the Senate shall chuse from them by Ballot the Vice President.

The Congress may determine the Time of chusing the Electors, and the Day on which they shall give their Votes; which Day shall be the same throughout the United States.

No person except a natural born Citizen, or a Citizen of the United States, at the time of the Adoption of this Constitution, shall be eligible to the Office of President; neither shall any Person be eligible to that Office who shall not have attained to the Age of thirty five Years, and been fourteen Years a Resident within the United States.

In Case of the Removal of the President from Office, or of his Death, Resignation or Inability to discharge the Powers and Duties of the said Office, the same shall devolve on the Vice President, and the Congress may by Law provide for the Case of Removal, Death, Resignation or Inability, both of the President and Vice President, declaring what Officer shall then act as President, and such Officer shall act accordingly, until the Disability be removed, or a President shall be elected.

The President shall, at stated Times, receive for his Services, a Compensation, which shall neither be increased nor diminished during the Period for which he shall have been elected, and he shall not receive within that Period any other Emolument from the United States, or any of them.

Before he enter on the Execution of his Office, he shall take the following Oath or Affirmation: "I do solemnly swear (or affirm) that I will faithfully execute the Office of President of the United States, and will to the best of my Ability, preserve, protect and defend the Constitution of the United States."

Section 2.   The President shall be Commander in Chief of the Army and Navy of the United States, and of the Militia of the several States, when called into the actual Service of the United States; he may require the Opinion, in writing, of the principal Officer in each of the executive Departments, upon any Subject relating to the Duties of their respective Offices, and he shall have Power to grant Reprieves and Pardons for Offenses against the United States, except in Cases of Impeachment.

He shall have Power, by and with the Advice and Consent of the Senate to make Treaties, provided two thirds of the Senators present concur; and he shall nominate, and by and with the Advice and Consent of the Senate, shall appoint Ambassadors, other public Ministers and Consuls, Judges of the supreme Court, and all other Officers of the United States, whose Appointments are not herein otherwise provided for, and which shall be established by Law; but the Congress may by Law vest the Appointment of such inferior Officers, as they think proper, in the President alone, in the Courts of Law, or in the Heads of Departments.

The President shall have Power to fill up all Vacancies that may happen during the Recess of the Senate, by granting Commissions which shall expire at the End of their next Session.

Section 3.   He shall from time to time give to the Congress Information of the State of the Union, and recommend to their Consideration such Measures as he shall judge necessary and expedient; he may, on extraordinary Occasions, convene both Houses, or either of them, and in Case of Disagreement between them, with Respect to the Time of Adjournment, he may adjourn them to such Time as he shall think proper; he shall receive Ambassadors and other public Ministers; he shall take Care that the Laws be faithfully executed, and shall Commission all the Officers of the United States.

Section 4.   The President, Vice President and all civil Officers of the United States, shall be removed from Office on Impeachment for, and Conviction of, Treason, Bribery, or other high Crimes and Misdemeanors.

ARTICLE III

Section 1. The judicial Power of the United States, shall be vested in one supreme Court, and in such inferior Courts as the Congress may from time to time ordain and establish. The Judges, both of the supreme and inferior Courts, shall hold their Offices during good Behaviour, and shall, at stated Times, receive for their Services a Compensation, which shall not be diminished during their Continuance in Office.

Section 2. The judicial Power shall extend to all Cases, in Law and Equity, arising under this Constitution, the Laws of the United States, and Treaties made, or which shall be made, under their Authority;—to all Cases affecting Ambassadors, other public Ministers and Consuls;—to all Cases of admiralty and maritime Jurisdiction;—to Controversies to which the United States shall be a Party;—to Controversies between two or more States;—between a State and Citizens of another State;—between Citizens of different States;—between Citizens of the same State claiming Lands under Grants of different States, and between a State, or the Citizens thereof, and foreign States, Citizens or Subjects.

In all Cases affecting Ambassadors, other public Ministers and Consuls, and those in which a State shall be a Party, the supreme Court shall have original Jurisdiction. In all the other Cases before mentioned, the supreme Court shall have appellate Jurisdiction, both as to Law and Fact, with such Exceptions, and under such Regulations as the Congress shall make.

The Trial of all Crimes, except in Cases of Impeachment, shall be by Jury; and such Trial shall be held in the State where the said Crimes shall have been committed; but when not committed within any State, the Trial shall be at such Place or Places as the Congress may by Law have directed.

Section 3. Treason against the United States, shall consist only in levying War against them, or, in adhering to their Enemies, giving them Aid and Comfort. No Person shall be convicted of Treason unless on the Testimony of two Witnesses to the same overt Act, or on Confession in open Court.

The Congress shall have Power to declare the Punishment of Treason, but no Attainder of Treason shall work Corruption of Blood, or Forfeiture except during the Life of the Person attainted.

ARTICLE IV

Section 1. Full Faith and Credit shall be given in each State to the public Acts, Records, and judicial Proceedings of every other State. And the Congress may by general Laws prescribe the Manner in which such Acts, Records and Proceedings shall be proved, and the Effect thereof.

Section 2. The Citizens of each State shall be entitled to all Privileges and Immunities of Citizens in the several States.

A Person charged in any State with Treason, Felony, or other Crime, who shall flee from Justice, and be found in another State, shall on Demand of the executive Authority of the State from which he fled, be delivered up, to be removed to the State having Jurisdiction of the Crime.

No Person held to Service or Labour in one State, under the Laws thereof, escaping into another, shall, in Consequence of any Law or Regulation therein, be discharged from such Service or Labour, but shall be delivered up on Claim of the Party to whom such Service or Labour may be due.

Section 3. New States may be admitted by the Congress into this Union; but no new State shall be formed or erected within the Jurisdiction of any other State; nor any State be formed by the Junction of two or more States, or Parts of States, without the Consent of the Legislatures of the States concerned as well as of the Congress.

The Congress shall have Power to dispose of and make all needful Rules and Regulations respecting the Territory or other Property belonging to the United States; and nothing in this Constitution shall be so construed as to Prejudice any Claims of the United States, or of any particular State.

Section 4. The United States shall guarantee to every State in this Union a Republican Form of Government, and shall protect each of them against Invasion; and on Application of the Legislature, or of the Executive (when the Legislature cannot be convened) against domestic Violence.

ARTICLE V

The Congress, whenever two thirds of both Houses shall deem it necessary, shall propose Amendments to this Constitution, or, on the Application of the Legislatures of two thirds of the several States, shall call a Convention for proposing Amendments, which, in either Case, shall be valid to all Intents and Purposes, as part of this Constitution, when ratified by the Legislatures of three fourths of the several States, or by Conventions in three fourths thereof, as the one or the other Mode of Ratification may be proposed by the Congress; Provided that no Amendment which may be made prior to the Year One thousand eight hundred and eight shall in any Manner affect the first and fourth Clauses in the Ninth Section of the first Article; and that no State, without its Consent, shall be deprived of its equal Suffrage in the Senate.

ARTICLE VI

All Debts contracted and Engagements entered into, before the Adoption of this Constitution shall be as valid against the United States under this Constitution, as under the Confederation.

This Constitution, and the Laws of the United States which shall be made in Pursuance thereof; and all Treaties made, or which shall be made, under the Authority of the United States, shall be the supreme Law of the Land; and the Judges in every State shall be bound thereby, any Thing in the Constitution or Laws of any State to the Contrary notwithstanding.

The Senators and Representatives before mentioned, and the Members of the several State Legislatures, and all executive and judicial Officers, both of the United States and of the several States, shall be bound by Oath or Affirmation, to support this Constitution; but no religious Test shall ever be required as a Qualification to any Office or public Trust under the United States.

ARTICLE VII

The Ratification of the Conventions of nine States shall be sufficient for the Establishment of this Constitution between the States so ratifying the Same.

AMENDMENT I [1791]

Congress shall make no law respecting an establishment of religion, or prohibiting the free exercise thereof; or abridging the freedom of speech, or of the press; or the right of the people peaceably to assembly, and to petition the Government for a redress of grievances.

AMENDMENT II [1791]

A well regulated Militia, being necessary to the security of a free State, the right of the people to keep and bear Arms, shall not be infringed.

AMENDMENT III [1791]

No Soldier shall, in time of peace be quartered in any house, without the consent of the Owner, nor in time of war, but in a manner to be prescribed by law.

AMENDMENT IV [1791]

The right of the people to be secure in their persons, houses, papers, and effects, against unreasonable searches and seizures, shall not be violated, and no Warrants shall issue, but upon probable cause, supported by Oath or affirmation, and particularly describing the place to be searched, and the persons or things to be seized.

AMENDMENT V [1791]

No person shall be held to answer for a capital, or otherwise infamous crime, unless on a presentment or indictment of a Grand Jury, except in cases arising in the land or naval forces, or in the Militia, when in actual service in time of War or public danger; nor shall any person be subject for the same offence to be twice put in jeopardy of life or limb; nor shall be compelled in any criminal case to be a witness against himself, nor be deprived of life, liberty, or property, without due process of law; nor shall private property be taken for public use, without just compensation.

AMENDMENT VI [1791]

In all criminal prosecutions, the accused shall enjoy the right to a speedy and public trial, by an impartial jury of the State and district wherein the crime shall have been committed, which district shall have been previously ascertained by law, and to be informed of the nature and cause of the accusation; to be confronted with the witnesses against him; to have compulsory process for obtaining witnesses in his favor, and to have the Assistance of Counsel for his defence.

AMENDMENT VII [1791]

In Suits at common law, where the value in controversy shall exceed twenty dollars, the right of trial by jury shall be preserved, and no fact tried by jury, shall be otherwise re-examined in any Court of the United States, than according to the rules of the common law.

AMENDMENT VIII [1791]

Excessive bail shall not be required, nor excessive fines imposed, nor cruel and unusual punishments inflicted.

AMENDMENT IX [1791]

The enumeration in the Constitution, of certain rights, shall not be construed to deny or disparage others retained by the people.

AMENDMENT X [1791]

The powers not delegated to the United States by the Constitution, nor prohibited by it to the States, are reserved to the States respectively, or to the people.

AMENDMENT XI [1798]

The Judicial power of the United States shall not be construed to extend to any suit in law or equity, commenced or prosecuted against one of the United States by Citizens of another State, or by Citizens or Subjects of any Foreign State.

AMENDMENT XII [1804]

The Electors shall meet in their respective states, and vote by ballot for President and Vice-President, one of whom, at least, shall not be an inhabitant of the same state with themselves; they shall name in their ballots the person voted for as President, and in distinct ballots the person voted for as Vice-President, and they shall make distinct lists of all persons voted for as President, and of all persons voted for as Vice-President, and of the number of votes for each, which lists they shall sign and certify, and transmit sealed to the seat of the government of the United States, directed to the President of the Senate;—The President of the Senate shall, in the presence of the Senate and House of Representatives, open all the certificates and the votes shall then be counted;—The person having the greatest number of votes for President, shall be the President, if such number be a majority of the whole number of Electors appointed; and if no person have such majority, then from the persons having the highest numbers not exceeding three on the list of those voted for as President, the House of Representatives shall choose immediately, by ballot, the President. But in choosing the President, the votes shall be taken by states, the representation from each state having one vote; a quorum for this purpose shall consist of a member or members from two-thirds of the states, and a majority of all states shall be necessary to a choice. And if the House of Representatives shall not choose a President whenever the right of choice shall devolve upon them, before the fourth day of March next following, then the Vice-President shall act as President, as in the case of the death or other constitutional disability of the President.—The person having the greatest number of votes as Vice-President, shall be the Vice-President, if such number be a majority of the whole number of Electors appointed, and if no person have a majority, then from the two highest numbers on the list, the Senate shall choose the Vice-President; a quorum for the purpose shall consist of two-thirds of the whole number of Senators, and a majority of the whole number shall be necessary to a choice. But no person constitutionally ineligible to the office of President shall be eligible to that of Vice-President of the United States.

AMENDMENT XIII [1865]

Section 1.   Neither slavery nor involuntary servitude, except as a punishment for crime whereof the party shall have been duly convicted, shall exist within the United States, or any place subject to their jurisdiction.

Section 2.   Congress shall have power to enforce this article by appropriate legislation.

AMENDMENT XIV [1868]

Section 1. All persons born or naturalized in the United States, and subject to the jurisdiction thereof, are citizens of the United States and of the State wherein they reside. No State shall make or enforce any law which shall abridge the privileges or immunities of citizens of the United States; nor shall any State deprive any person of life, liberty, or property, without due process of law; nor deny to any person within its jurisdiction the equal protection of the laws.

Section 2. Representatives shall be apportioned among the several States according to their respective numbers, counting the whole number of persons in each State, excluding Indians not taxed. But when the right to vote at any election for the choice of electors for President and Vice President of the United States, Representatives in Congress, the Executive and Judicial officers of a State, or the members of the Legislature thereof, is denied to any of the male inhabitants of such State, being twenty-one years of age, and citizens of the United States, or in any way abridged, except for participation in rebellion, or other crime, the basis of representation therein shall be reduced in the proportion which the number of such male citizens shall bear to the whole number of male citizens twenty-one years of age in such State.

Section 3. No person shall be a Senator or Representative in Congress, or elector of President and Vice President, or hold any office, civil or military, under the United States, or under any State, who having previously taken an oath, as a member of Congress, or as an officer of the United States, or as a member of any State legislature, or as an executive or judicial officer of any State, to support the Constitution of the United States, shall have engaged in insurrection or rebellion against the same, or given aid or comfort to the enemies thereof. But Congress may by a vote of two-thirds of each House, remove such disability.

Section 4. The validity of the public debt of the United States, authorized by law, including debts incurred for payment of pensions and bounties for services in suppressing insurrection or rebellion, shall not be questioned. But neither the United States nor any State shall assume or pay any debt or obligation incurred in aid of insurrection or rebellion against the United States, or any claim for the loss or emancipation of any slave; but all such debts, obligations and claims shall be held illegal and void.

Section 5. The Congress shall have power to enforce, by appropriate legislation, the provisions of this article.

AMENDMENT XV [1870]

Section 1. The right of citizens of the United States to vote shall not be denied or abridged by the United States or by any State on account of race, color, or previous condition of servitude.

Section 2. The Congress shall have power to enforce this article by appropriate legislation.

AMENDMENT XVI [1913]

The Congress shall have power to lay and collect taxes on incomes, from whatever source derived, without apportionment among the several States, and without regard to any census or enumeration.

AMENDMENT XVII [1913]

Section 1. The Senate of the United States shall be composed of two Senators from each State, elected by the people thereof, for six years; and each Senator shall have one vote. The electors in each State shall have the qualifications requisite for electors of the most numerous branch of the State legislatures.

Section 2. When vacancies happen in the representation of any State in the Senate, the executive authority of such State shall issue writs of election to fill such vacancies: *Provided,* That the legislature of any State may empower the executive thereof to make temporary appointments until the people fill the vacancies by election as the legislature may direct.

Section 3. This amendment shall not be so construed as to affect the election or term of any Senator chosen before it becomes valid as part of the Constitution.

AMENDMENT XVIII [1919]

Section 1. After one year from the ratification of this article the manufacture, sale, or transportation of intoxicating liquors within, the importation thereof into, or the exportation thereof from the United States and all territory subject to the jurisdiction thereof for beverage purposes is hereby prohibited.

Section 2. The Congress and the several States shall have concurrent power to enforce this article by appropriate legislation.

Section 3. This article shall be inoperative unless it shall have been ratified as an amendment to the Constitution by the legislatures of the several States, as provided in the Constitution, within seven years from the date of the submission hereof to the States by the Congress.

AMENDMENT XIX [1920]

Section 1. The right of citizens of the United States to vote shall not be denied or abridged by the United States or by any State on account of sex.

Section 2. Congress shall have power to enforce this article by appropriate legislation.

AMENDMENT XX [1933]

Section 1. The terms of the President and Vice President shall end at noon on the 20th day of January, and the terms of Senators and Representatives at noon on the 3d day of January, of the years in which such terms would have ended if this article had not been ratified; and the terms of their successors shall then begin.

Section 2. The Congress shall assemble at least once in every year, and such meeting shall begin at noon on the 3d day of January, unless they shall by law appoint a different day.

Section 3. If, at the time fixed for the beginning of the term of the President, the President elect shall have died, the Vice President elect shall become President. If the President shall not have been chosen before the time fixed for the beginning of his term, or if the President elect shall have failed to qualify, then the Vice President elect shall act as President until a President shall have qualified; and the Congress may by law provide for the case wherein neither a President elect nor a Vice President elect shall have qualified, declaring who shall then act as President, or the manner in which one who is to act shall be selected, and such person shall act accordingly until a President or Vice President shall have qualified.

Section 4. The Congress may by law provide for the case of the death of any of the persons from whom the House of Representatives may choose a President whenever the right of choice shall have devolved upon them, and for the case of the death of any of the persons from whom the Senate may choose a

Vice President whenever the right of choice shall have devolved upon them.

Section 5.   Sections 1 and 2 shall take effect on the 15th day of October following the ratification of this article.

Section 6.   This article shall be inoperative unless it shall have been ratified as an amendment to the Constitution by the legislatures of three-fourths of the several States within seven years from the date of its submission.

AMENDMENT XXI [1933]

Section 1.   The eighteenth article of amendment to the Constitution of the United States is hereby repealed.

Section 2.   The transportation or importation into any State, Territory, or possession of the United States for delivery or use therein of intoxicating liquors, in violation of the laws thereof, is hereby prohibited.

Section 3.   This article shall be inoperative unless it shall have been ratified as an amendment to the Constitution by conventions in the several States, as provided in the Constitution, within seven years from the date of the submission hereof to the States by the Congress.

AMENDMENT XXII [1951]

Section 1.   No person shall be elected to the office of the President more than twice, and no person who has held the office of President, or acted as President, for more than two years of a term to which some other person was elected President shall be elected to the office of President more than once. But this Article shall not apply to any person holding the office of President when this Article was proposed by the Congress, and shall not prevent any person who may be holding the office of President, or acting as President, during the term within which this Article becomes operative from holding the office of President or acting as President during the remainder of such term.

Section 2.   This article shall be inoperative unless it shall have been ratified as an amendment to the Constitution by the legislatures of three-fourths of the several States within seven years from the date of its submission to the States by the Congress.

AMENDMENT XXIII [1961]

Section 1.   The District constituting the seat of Government of the United States shall appoint in such manner as the Congress may direct:

A number of electors of President and Vice President equal to the whole number of Senators and Representatives in Congress to which the District would be entitled if it were a State, but in no event more than the least populous state; they shall be in addition to those appointed by the states, but they shall be considered, for the purposes of the election of President and Vice President, to be electors appointed by a state; and they shall meet in the District and perform such duties as provided by the twelfth article of amendment.

Section 2.   The Congress shall have power to enforce this article by appropriate legislation.

AMENDMENT XXIV [1964]

Section 1.   The right of citizens of the United States to vote in any primary or other election for President or Vice President, for electors for President or Vice President, or for Senator or Representative in Congress, shall not be denied or abridged by the United States, or any State by reason of failure to pay any poll tax or other tax.

Section 2.   The Congress shall have power to enforce this article by appropriate legislation.

AMENDMENT XXV [1967]

Section 1.   In case of the removal of the President from office or of his death or resignation, the Vice President shall become President.

Section 2.   Whenever there is a vacancy in the office of the Vice President, the President shall nominate a Vice President who shall take office upon confirmation by a majority vote of both Houses of Congress.

Section 3.   Whenever the President transmits to the President pro tempore of the Senate and the Speaker of the House of Representatives his written declaration that he is unable to discharge the powers and duties of his office, and until he transmits to them a written declaration to the contrary, such powers and duties shall be discharged by the Vice President as Acting President.

Section 4.   Whenever the Vice President and a majority of either the principal officers of the executive departments or of such other body as Congress may by law provide, transmit to the President pro tempore of the Senate and the Speaker of the House of Representatives their written declaration that the President is unable to discharge the powers and duties of his office, the Vice President shall immediately assume the powers and duties of the office as Acting President.

Thereafter, when the President transmits to the President pro tempore of the Senate and the Speaker of the House of Representatives his written declaration that no inability exists, he shall resume the powers and duties of his office unless the Vice President and a majority of either the principal officers of the executive department or of such other body as Congress may by law provide, transmit within four days to the President pro tempore of the Senate and the Speaker of the House of Representatives their written declaration that the President is unable to discharge the powers and duties of his office. Thereupon Congress shall decide the issue, assembling within forty-eight hours for that purpose if not in session. If the Congress, within twenty-one days after receipt of the latter written declaration, or, if Congress is not in session, within twenty-one days after Congress is required to assemble, determines by two-thirds vote of both Houses that the President is unable to discharge the powers and duties of his office, the Vice President shall continue to discharge the same as Acting President; otherwise, the President shall resume the powers and duties of his office.

AMENDMENT XXVI [1971]

Section 1.   The right of citizens of the United States, who are eighteen years of age or older, to vote shall not be denied or abridged by the United States or by any State on account of age.

Section 2.   The Congress shall have power to enforce this article by appropriate legislation.

AMENDMENT XXVII [1992]

No law, varying the compensation for the services of the Senators and Representatives, shall take effect, until an election of Representatives shall have intervened.

APPENDIX C
Uniform Commercial Code (Excerpts)

(Adopted in fifty-two jurisdictions: all fifty States, although Louisiana has adopted only Articles 1, 3, 4, 7, 8, and 9; the District of Columbia; and the Virgin Islands.)

The Uniform Commercial Code consists of the following articles:

1. General Provisions
2. Sales
2A. Leases
3. Negotiable Instruments
4. Bank Deposits and Collections
4A. Funds Transfers
5. Letters of Credit
6. Repealer of Article 6—Bulk Transfers and [Revised] Article 6—Bulk Sales
7. Warehouse Receipts, Bills of Lading and Other Documents of Title
8. Investment Securities
9. Secured Transactions
10. Effective Date and Repealer
11. Effective Date and Transition Provisions

Article 1
GENERAL PROVISIONS

Part 1 General Provisions

§ 1–101. Short Titles.

(a) This [Act] may be cited as Uniform Commercial Code.

(b) This article may be cited as Uniform Commercial Code-Uniform Provisions.

§ 1–102. Scope of Article.

This article applies to a transaction to the extent that it is governed by another article of [the Uniform Commercial Code].

§ 1–103. Construction of [Uniform Commercial Code] to Promote Its Purpose and Policies; Applicability of Supplemental Principles of Law.

(a) [The Uniform Commercial Code] must be liberally construed and applied to promote its underlying purposes and policies, which are:

(1) to simplify, clarify, and modernize the law governing commercial transactions;

(2) to permit the continued expansion of commercial practices through custom, usage, and agreement of the parties; and

(3) to make uniform the law among the various jurisdictions.

(b) Unless displaced by the particular provisions of [the Uniform Commercial Code], the principles of law and equity, including the law merchant and the law relative to capacity to contract, principal and agent, estoppel, fraud, misrepresentation, duress, coercion, mistake, bankruptcy, and other validating or invalidating cause, supplement its provisions.

§ 1–104. Construction Against Implicit Repeal.

This Act being a general act intended as a unified coverage of its subject matter, no part of it shall be deemed to be impliedly repealed by subsequent legislation if such construction can reasonably be avoided.

§ 1–105. Severability.

If any provision or clause of [the Uniform Commercial Code] or its application to any person or circumstance is held invalid, the invalidity does not affect other provisions or applications of [the Uniform Commercial Code] which can be given effect without the invalid provision or application, and to this end the provisions of [the Uniform Commercial Code] are severable.

§ 1–106. Use of Singular and Plural; Gender.

In [the Uniform Commercial Code], unless the statutory context otherwise requires:

(1) words in the singular number include the plural, and those in the plural include the singular; and

(2) words of any gender also refer to any other gender.

§ 1–107. Section Captions.

Section captions are part of [the Uniform Commercial Code].

§ 1–108. Relation to Electronic Signatures in Global and National Commerce Act.

This article modifies, limits, and supersedes the Federal Electronic Signatures in Global and National Commerce Act, 15 U.S.C. Sections 7001 *et seq.*, except that nothing in this article modifies, limits, or supersedes section 7001(c) of that act or authorizes electronic delivery of any of the notices described in section 7003(b) of that Act.

Part 2 General Definitions and Principles of Interpretation

§ 1–201. General Definitions.

Subject to additional definitions contained in the subsequent Articles of this Act which are applicable to specific Articles or Parts thereof, and unless the context otherwise requires, in this Act:

(1) "Action", in the sense of a judicial proceeding, includes recoupment, counterclaim, set-off, suit in equity, and any other proceedings in which rights are determined.

(2) "Aggrieved party" means a party entitled to resort to a remedy.

(3) "Agreement", as distinguished from "contract", means the bargain of the parties in fact, as found in their language or by implication from other circumstances, including course of performance, course of dealing, or usage of trade as provided in Section 1-303.

(4) "Bank" means a person engaged in the business of banking and includes a savings bank, savings and loan association, credit union, and trust company.

(5) "Bearer" means a person in control of a negotiable electronic document of title or a person in possession of a negotiable instrument, negotiable tangible document of title, or certificated security that is payable to bearer or indorsed in blank.

(6) "Bill of lading" means a document of title evidencing the receipt of goods for shipment issued by a person engaged in the business of directly or indirectly transporting or forwarding goods. The term does not include a warehouse receipt.

(7) "Branch" includes a separately incorporated foreign branch of a bank.

(8) "Burden of establishing" a fact means the burden of persuading the trier of fact that the existence of the fact is more probable than its nonexistence.

(9) "Buyer in ordinary course of business" means a person that buys goods in good faith, without knowledge that the sale violates the rights of another person in the goods, and in the ordinary course from a person, other than a pawnbroker, in the business of selling goods of that kind. A person buys goods in the ordinary course if the sale to the person comports with the usual or customary practices in the kind of business in which the seller is engaged or with the seller's own usual or customary practices. A person that sells oil, gas, or other minerals at the wellhead or minehead is a person in the business of selling goods of that kind. A buyer in ordinary course of business may buy for cash, by exchange of other property, or on secured or unsecured credit, and may acquire goods or documents of title under a pre-existing contract for sale. Only a buyer that takes possession of the goods or has a right to recover the goods from the seller under Article 2 may be a buyer in ordinary course of business. A person that acquires goods in a transfer in bulk or as security for or in total or partial satisfaction of a money debt is not a buyer in ordinary course of business.

(10) "Conspicuous", with reference to a term, means so written, displayed, or presented that a reasonable person against which it is to operate ought to have noticed it. Whether a term is "conspicuous" or not is a decision for the court. Conspicuous terms include the following:

(A) a heading in capitals equal to or greater in size than the surrounding text, or in contrasting type, font, or color to the surrounding text of the same or lesser size; and

(B) language in the body of a record or display in larger type than the surrounding text, or in contrasting type, font, or color to the surrounding text of the same size, or set off from surrounding text of the same size by symbols or other marks that call attention to the language.

(11) "Consumer" means an individual who enters into a transaction primarily for personal, family, or household purposes.

(12) "Contract", as distinguished from "agreement", means the total legal obligation that results from the parties' agreement as determined by [the Uniform Commercial Code] as supplemented by any other laws.

(13) "Creditor" includes a general creditor, a secured creditor, a lien creditor and any representative of creditors, including an assignee for the benefit of creditors, a trustee in bankruptcy, a receiver in equity and an executor or administrator of an insolvent debtor's or assignor's estate.

(14) "Defendant" includes a person in the position of defendant in a counterclaim, cross-action, or third-party claim.

(15) "Delivery" with respect to an electronic document of title means voluntary transfer of control and with respect to an instrument, a tangible document of title, or chattel paper means voluntary transfer of possession.

(16) "Document of title" means a record (i) that in regular course of business or financing is treated as adequately evidencing that the person in possession or control of the record is entitled to receive, control, hold, and dispose of the record and the goods the record covers and (ii) that purports to be issued by or addressed to a bailee and to cover goods in the bailee's possession which are either identified or are fungible portions of an identified mass. The term includes a bill of lading, transport document, dock warrant, dock receipt, warehouse receipt, and order for delivery of goods. An electronic document of title means a document of title evidenced by a record consisting of information stored in an electronic medium. A tangible document of title means a document of title evidenced by a record consisting of information that is inscribed on a tangible medium.

(17) "Fault" means a default, breach, or wrongful act or omission.

(18) "Fungible goods" means:

(A) goods of which any unit, by nature or usage of trade, is the equivalent of any other like unit; or

(B) goods that by agreement are treated as equivalent.

(19) "Genuine" means free of forgery or counterfeiting.

(20) "Good faith," except as otherwise provided in Article 5, means honesty in fact and the observance of reasonable commercial standards of fair dealing.

(21) "Holder" means:

(A) the person in possession of a negotiable instrument that is payable either to bearer or to an identified person that is the person in possession;

(B) the person in possession of a negotiable tangible document of title if the goods are deliverable either to bearer or to the order of the person in possession; or

(C) the person in control of a negotiable electronic document of title.

(22) "Insolvency proceeding" includes an assignment for the benefit of creditors or other proceeding intended to liquidate or rehabilitate the estate of the person involved.

(23) "Insolvent" means:

(A) having generally ceased to pay debts in the ordinary course of business other than as a result of bona fide dispute;

(B) being unable to pay debts as they become due; or

(C) being insolvent within the meaning of federal bankruptcy law.

(24) "Money" means a medium of exchange currently authorized or adopted by a domestic or foreign government. The term includes a monetary unit of account established by an intergovernmental organization or by agreement between two or more countries.

(25) "Organization" means a person other than an individual.

(26) "Party", as distinguished from "third party", means a person that has engaged in a transaction or made an agreement subject to [the Uniform Commercial Code].

(27) "Person" means an individual, corporation, business trust, estate, trust, partnership, limited liability company, association, joint venture, government, governmental subdivision, agency, or instrumentality, public corporation, or any other legal or commercial entity.

(28) "Present value" means the amount as of a date certain of one or more sums payable in the future, discounted to the date certain by use of either an interest rate specified by the parties if that rate is not manifestly unreasonable at the time the transaction is entered into or, if an interest rate is not so specified, a commercially reasonable rate that takes into account the facts and circumstances at the time the transaction is entered into.

(29) "Purchase" means taking by sale, lease, discount, negotiation, mortgage, pledge, lien, security interest, issue or reissue, gift, or any other voluntary transaction creating an interest in property.

(30) "Purchaser" means a person that takes by purchase.

(31) "Record" means information that is inscribed on a tangible medium or that is stored in an electronic or other medium and is retrievable in perceivable form.

(32) "Remedy" means any remedial right to which an aggrieved party is entitled with or without resort to a tribunal.

(33) "Representative" means a person empowered to act for another, including an agent, an officer of a corporation or association, and a trustee, executor, or administrator of an estate.

(34) "Right" includes remedy.

(35) "Security interest" means an interest in personal property or fixtures which secures payment or performance of an obligation. "Security interest" includes any interest of a consignor and a buyer of accounts, chattel paper, a payment intangible, or a promissory note in a transaction that is subject to Article 9. "Security interest" does not include the special property interest of a buyer of goods on identification of those goods to a contract for sale under Section 2-401, but a buyer may also acquire a "security interest" by complying with Article 9. Except as otherwise provided in Section 2-505, the right of a seller or lessor of goods under Article 2 or 2A to retain or acquire possession of the goods is not a "security interest", but a seller or lessor may also acquire a "security interest" by complying with Article 9. The retention or reservation of title by a seller of goods notwithstanding shipment or delivery to the buyer under Section 2-401 is limited in effect to a reservation of a "security interest." Whether a transaction in the form of a lease creates a "security interest" is determined pursuant to Section 1-203.

(36) "Send" in connection with a writing, record, or notice means:

(A) to deposit in the mail or deliver for transmission by any other usual means of communication with postage or cost of transmission provided for and properly addressed and, in the case of an instrument, to an address specified thereon or otherwise agreed, or if there be none to any address reasonable under the circumstances; or

(B) in any other way to cause to be received any record or notice within the time it would have arrived if properly sent.

(37) "Signed" includes using any symbol executed or adopted with present intention to adopt or accept a writing.

(38) "State" means a State of the United States, the District of Columbia, Puerto Rico, the United States Virgin Islands, or any territory or insular possession subject to the jurisdiction of the United States.

(39) "Surety" includes a guarantor or other secondary obligor.

(40) "Term" means a portion of an agreement that relates to a particular matter.

(41) "Unauthorized signature" means a signature made without actual, implied, or apparent authority. The term includes a forgery.

(42) "Warehouse receipt" means a document of title issued by a person engaged in the business of storing goods for hire.

(43) "Writing" includes printing, typewriting, or any other intentional reduction to tangible form. "Written" has a corresponding meaning.

As amended in 2003.

* * * *

§ 1–205. **Reasonable Time; Seasonableness.**

(a) Whether a time for taking an action required by [the Uniform Commercial Code] is reasonable depends on the nature, purpose, and circumstances of the action.

(b) An action is taken seasonably if it is taken at or within the time agreed or, if no time is agreed, at or within a reasonable time.

* * * *

Part 3 **Territorial Applicability and General Rules**

* * * *

§ 1–303. **Course of Performance, Course of Dealing, and Usage of Trade.**

(a) A "course of performance" is a sequence of conduct between the parties to a particular transaction that exists if:

(1) the agreement of the parties with respect to the transaction involves repeated occasions for performance by a party; and

(2) the other party, with knowledge of the nature of the performance and opportunity for objection to it, accepts the performance or acquiesces in it without objection.

(b) A "course of dealing" is a sequence of conduct concerning previous transactions between the parties to a particular transaction that is fairly to be regarded as establishing a common basis of understanding for interpreting their expressions and other conduct.

(c) A "usage of trade" is any practice or method of dealing having such regularity of observance in a place, vocation, or trade as to justify an expectation that it will be observed with respect to the transaction in question. The existence and scope of such a usage must be proved as facts. If it is established that such a usage is embodied in a trade code or similar record, the interpretation of the record is a question of law.

(d) A course of performance or course of dealing between the parties or usage of trade in the vocation or trade in which they are engaged or of which they are or should be aware is relevant in ascertaining the meaning of the parties' agreement, may give particular meaning to specific terms of the agreement, and may supplement or qualify the terms of the agreement. A usage of trade applicable in the place in which part of the performance under the agreement is to occur may be so utilized as to that part of the performance.

(e) Except as otherwise provided in subsection (f), the express terms of an agreement and any applicable course of performance, course of dealing, or usage of trade must be construed whenever reasonable as consistent with each other. If such a construction is unreasonable:

(1) express terms prevail over course of performance, course of dealing, and usage of trade;

(2) course of performance prevails over course of dealing and usage of trade; and

(3) course of dealing prevails over usage of trade.

(f) Subject to Section 2-209 and Section 2A-208, a course of performance is relevant to show a waiver or modification of any term inconsistent with the course of performance.

(g) Evidence of a relevant usage of trade offered by one party is not admissible unless that party has given the other party notice that the court finds sufficient to prevent unfair surprise to the other party.

§ 1–304. Obligation of Good Faith.

Every contract or duty within [the Uniform Commercial Code] imposes an obligation of good faith in its performance and enforcement.

* * * *

§ 1–309. Option to Accelerate at Will.

A term providing that one party or that party's successor in interest may accelerate payment or performance or require collateral or additional collateral "at will" or when the party "deems itself insecure," or words of similar import, means that the party has power to do so only if that party in good faith believes that the prospect of payment or performance is impaired. The burden of establishing lack of good faith is on the party against which the power has been exercised.

§ 1–310. Subordinated Obligations.

An obligation may be issued as subordinated to performance of another obligation of the person obligated, or a creditor may subordinate its right to performance of an obligation by agreement with either the person obligated or another creditor of the person obligated. Subordination does not create a security interest as against either the common debtor or a subordinated creditor.

Article 2
SALES

Part 1 Short Title, General Construction and Subject Matter

§ 2–101. Short Title.

This Article shall be known and may be cited as Uniform Commercial Code—Sales.

§ 2–102. Scope; Certain Security and Other Transactions Excluded From This Article.

Unless the context otherwise requires, this Article applies to transactions in goods; it does not apply to any transaction which although in the form of an unconditional contract to sell or present sale is intended to operate only as a security transaction nor does this Article impair or repeal any statute regulating sales to consumers, farmers or other specified classes of buyers.

§ 2–103. Definitions and Index of Definitions.

(1) In this Article unless the context otherwise requires

(a) "Buyer" means a person who buys or contracts to buy goods.

(b) "Good faith" in the case of a merchant means honesty in fact and the observance of reasonable commercial standards of fair dealing in the trade.

(c) "Receipt" of goods means taking physical possession of them.

(d) "Seller" means a person who sells or contracts to sell goods.

(2) Other definitions applying to this Article or to specified Parts thereof, and the sections in which they appear are:

"Acceptance". Section 2–606.
"Banker's credit". Section 2–325.
"Between merchants". Section 2–104.
"Cancellation". Section 2–106(4).
"Commercial unit". Section 2–105.
"Confirmed credit". Section 2–325.
"Conforming to contract". Section 2–106.
"Contract for sale". Section 2–106.
"Cover". Section 2–712.
"Entrusting". Section 2–403.
"Financing agency". Section 2–104.
"Future goods". Section 2–105.
"Goods". Section 2–105.
"Identification". Section 2–501.
"Installment contract". Section 2–612.
"Letter of Credit". Section 2–325.
"Lot". Section 2–105.

"Merchant". Section 2–104.

"Overseas". Section 2–323.

"Person in position of seller". Section 2–707.

"Present sale". Section 2–106.

"Sale". Section 2–106.

"Sale on approval". Section 2–326.

"Sale or return". Section 2–326.

"Termination". Section 2–106.

(3) The following definitions in other Articles apply to this Article:

"Check". Section 3–104.

"Consignee". Section 7–102.

"Consignor". Section 7–102.

"Consumer goods". Section 9–109.

"Dishonor". Section 3–507.

"Draft". Section 3–104.

(4) In addition Article 1 contains general definitions and principles of construction and interpretation applicable throughout this Article.

As amended in 1994 and 1999.

§ 2–104. **Definitions: "Merchant"; "Between Merchants"; "Financing Agency".**

(1) "Merchant" means a person who deals in goods of the kind or otherwise by his occupation holds himself out as having knowledge or skill peculiar to the practices or goods involved in the transaction or to whom such knowledge or skill may be attributed by his employment of an agent or broker or other intermediary who by his occupation holds himself out as having such knowledge or skill.

(2) "Financing agency" means a bank, finance company or other person who in the ordinary course of business makes advances against goods or documents of title or who by arrangement with either the seller or the buyer intervenes in ordinary course to make or collect payment due or claimed under the contract for sale, as by purchasing or paying the seller's draft or making advances against it or by merely taking it for collection whether or not documents of title accompany the draft. "Financing agency" includes also a bank or other person who similarly intervenes between persons who are in the position of seller and buyer in respect to the goods (Section 2–707).

(3) "Between merchants" means in any transaction with respect to which both parties are chargeable with the knowledge or skill of merchants.

§ 2–105. **Definitions: Transferability; "Goods"; "Future" Goods; "Lot"; "Commercial Unit".**

(1) "Goods" means all things (including specially manufactured goods) which are movable at the time of identification to the contract for sale other than the money in which the price is to be paid, investment securities (Article 8) and things in action. "Goods" also includes the unborn young of animals and growing crops and other identified things attached to realty as described in the section on goods to be severed from realty (Section 2–107).

(2) Goods must be both existing and identified before any interest in them can pass. Goods which are not both existing and identified are "future" goods. A purported present sale of future goods or of any interest therein operates as a contract to sell.

(3) There may be a sale of a part interest in existing identified goods.

(4) An undivided share in an identified bulk of fungible goods is sufficiently identified to be sold although the quantity of the bulk is not determined. Any agreed proportion of such a bulk or any quantity thereof agreed upon by number, weight or other measure may to the extent of the seller's interest in the bulk be sold to the buyer who then becomes an owner in common.

(5) "Lot" means a parcel or a single article which is the subject matter of a separate sale or delivery, whether or not it is sufficient to perform the contract.

(6) "Commercial unit" means such a unit of goods as by commercial usage is a single whole for purposes of sale and division of which materially impairs its character or value on the market or in use. A commercial unit may be a single article (as a machine) or a set of articles (as a suite of furniture or an assortment of sizes) or a quantity (as a bale, gross, or carload) or any other unit treated in use or in the relevant market as a single whole.

§ 2–106. **Definitions: "Contract"; "Agreement"; "Contract for Sale"; "Sale"; "Present Sale"; "Conforming" to Contract; "Termination"; "Cancellation".**

(1) In this Article unless the context otherwise requires "contract" and "agreement" are limited to those relating to the present or future sale of goods. "Contract for sale" includes both a present sale of goods and a contract to sell goods at a future time. A "sale" consists in the passing of title from the seller to the buyer for a price (Section 2–401). A "present sale" means a sale which is accomplished by the making of the contract.

(2) Goods or conduct including any part of a performance are "conforming" or conform to the contract when they are in accordance with the obligations under the contract.

(3) "Termination" occurs when either party pursuant to a power created by agreement or law puts an end to the contract otherwise than for its breach. On "termination" all obligations which are still executory on both sides are discharged but any right based on prior breach or performance survives.

(4) "Cancellation" occurs when either party puts an end to the contract for breach by the other and its effect is the same as that of "termination" except that the cancelling party also retains any remedy for breach of the whole contract or any unperformed balance.

§ 2–107. **Goods to Be Severed From Realty: Recording.**

(1) A contract for the sale of minerals or the like (including oil and gas) or a structure or its materials to be removed from realty is a contract for the sale of goods within this Article if they are to be severed by the seller but until severance a purported present sale thereof which is not effective as a transfer of an interest in land is effective only as a contract to sell.

(2) A contract for the sale apart from the land of growing crops or other things attached to realty and capable of severance without material harm thereto but not described in subsection (1) or of timber to be cut is a contract for the sale of goods within this Article whether the subject matter is to be severed by the buyer or by the seller even though it forms part of the realty at the time of contracting, and the parties can by identification effect a present sale before severance.

(3) The provisions of this section are subject to any third party rights provided by the law relating to realty records, and the contract for sale may be executed and recorded as a document transferring

an interest in land and shall then constitute notice to third parties of the buyer's rights under the contract for sale.

As amended in 1972.

Part 2 Form, Formation and Readjustment of Contract

§ 2–201. Formal Requirements; Statute of Frauds.

(1) Except as otherwise provided in this section a contract for the sale of goods for the price of $500 or more is not enforceable by way of action or defense unless there is some writing sufficient to indicate that a contract for sale has been made between the parties and signed by the party against whom enforcement is sought or by his authorized agent or broker. A writing is not insufficient because it omits or incorrectly states a term agreed upon but the contract is not enforceable under this paragraph beyond the quantity of goods shown in such writing.

(2) Between merchants if within a reasonable time a writing in confirmation of the contract and sufficient against the sender is received and the party receiving it has reason to know its contents, its satisfies the requirements of subsection (1) against such party unless written notice of objection to its contents is given within ten days after it is received.

(3) A contract which does not satisfy the requirements of subsection (1) but which is valid in other respects is enforceable

(a) if the goods are to be specially manufactured for the buyer and are not suitable for sale to others in the ordinary course of the seller's business and the seller, before notice of repudiation is received and under circumstances which reasonably indicate that the goods are for the buyer, has made either a substantial beginning of their manufacture or commitments for their procurement; or

(b) if the party against whom enforcement is sought admits in his pleading, testimony or otherwise in court that a contract for sale was made, but the contract is not enforceable under this provision beyond the quantity of goods admitted; or

(c) with respect to goods for which payment has been made and accepted or which have been received and accepted (Sec. 2–606).

§ 2–202. Final Written Expression: Parol or Extrinsic Evidence.

Terms with respect to which the confirmatory memoranda of the parties agree or which are otherwise set forth in a writing intended by the parties as a final expression of their agreement with respect to such terms as are included therein may not be contradicted by evidence of any prior agreement or of a contemporaneous oral agreement but may be explained or supplemented

(a) by course of dealing or usage of trade (Section 1–205) or by course of performance (Section 2–208); and

(b) by evidence of consistent additional terms unless the court finds the writing to have been intended also as a complete and exclusive statement of the terms of the agreement.

§ 2–203. Seals Inoperative.

The affixing of a seal to a writing evidencing a contract for sale or an offer to buy or sell goods does not constitute the writing a sealed

instrument and the law with respect to sealed instruments does not apply to such a contract or offer.

§ 2–204. Formation in General.

(1) A contract for sale of goods may be made in any manner sufficient to show agreement, including conduct by both parties which recognizes the existence of such a contract.

(2) An agreement sufficient to constitute a contract for sale may be found even though the moment of its making is undetermined.

(3) Even though one or more terms are left open a contract for sale does not fail for indefiniteness if the parties have intended to make a contract and there is a reasonably certain basis for giving an appropriate remedy.

§ 2–205. Firm Offers.

An offer by a merchant to buy or sell goods in a signed writing which by its terms gives assurance that it will be held open is not revocable, for lack of consideration, during the time stated or if no time is stated for a reasonable time, but in no event may such period of irrevocability exceed three months; but any such term of assurance on a form supplied by the offeree must be separately signed by the offeror.

§ 2–206. Offer and Acceptance in Formation of Contract.

(1) Unless other unambiguously indicated by the language or circumstances

(a) an offer to make a contract shall be construed as inviting acceptance in any manner and by any medium reasonable in the circumstances;

(b) an order or other offer to buy goods for prompt or current shipment shall be construed as inviting acceptance either by a prompt promise to ship or by the prompt or current shipment of conforming or nonconforming goods, but such a shipment of non-conforming goods does not constitute an acceptance if the seller seasonably notifies the buyer that the shipment is offered only as an accommodation to the buyer.

(2) Where the beginning of a requested performance is a reasonable mode of acceptance an offeror who is not notified of acceptance within a reasonable time may treat the offer as having lapsed before acceptance.

§ 2–207. Additional Terms in Acceptance or Confirmation.

(1) A definite and seasonable expression of acceptance or a written confirmation which is sent within a reasonable time operates as an acceptance even though it states terms additional to or different from those offered or agreed upon, unless acceptance is expressly made conditional on assent to the additional or different terms.

(2) The additional terms are to be construed as proposals for addition to the contract. Between merchants such terms become part of the contract unless:

(a) the offer expressly limits acceptance to the terms of the offer;

(b) they materially alter it; or

(c) notification of objection to them has already been given or is given within a reasonable time after notice of them is received.

(3) Conduct by both parties which recognizes the existence of a contract is sufficient to establish a contract for sale although the

writings of the parties do not otherwise establish a contract. In such case the terms of the particular contract consist of those terms on which the writings of the parties agree, together with any supplementary terms incorporated under any other provisions of this Act.

§ 2–208. Course of Performance or Practical Construction.

(1) Where the contract for sale involves repeated occasions for performance by either party with knowledge of the nature of the performance and opportunity for objection to it by the other, any course of performance accepted or acquiesced in without objection shall be relevant to determine the meaning of the agreement.

(2) The express terms of the agreement and any such course of performance, as well as any course of dealing and usage of trade, shall be construed whenever reasonable as consistent with each other; but when such construction is unreasonable, express terms shall control course of performance and course of performance shall control both course of dealing and usage of trade (Section 1–205).

(3) Subject to the provisions of the next section on modification and waiver, such course of performance shall be relevant to show a waiver or modification of any term inconsistent with such course of performance.

§ 2–209. Modification, Rescission and Waiver.

(1) An agreement modifying a contract within this Article needs no consideration to be binding.

(2) A signed agreement which excludes modification or rescission except by a signed writing cannot be otherwise modified or rescinded, but except as between merchants such a requirement on a form supplied by the merchant must be separately signed by the other party.

(3) The requirements of the statute of frauds section of this Article (Section 2–201) must be satisfied if the contract as modified is within its provisions.

(4) Although an attempt at modification or rescission does not satisfy the requirements of subsection (2) or (3) it can operate as a waiver.

(5) A party who has made a waiver affecting an executory portion of the contract may retract the waiver by reasonable notification received by the other party that strict performance will be required of any term waived, unless the retraction would be unjust in view of a material change of position in reliance on the waiver.

§ 2–210. Delegation of Performance; Assignment of Rights.

(1) A party may perform his duty through a delegate unless otherwise agreed or unless the other party has a substantial interest in having his original promisor perform or control the acts required by the contract. No delegation of performance relieves the party delegating of any duty to perform or any liability for breach.

(2) Except as otherwise provided in Section 9–406, unless otherwise agreed, all rights of either seller or buyer can be assigned except where the assignment would materially change the duty of the other party, or increase materially the burden or risk imposed on him by his contract, or impair materially his chance of obtaining return performance. A right to damages for breach of the whole contract or a right arising out of the assignor's due performance of his entire obligation can be assigned despite agreement otherwise.

(3) The creation, attachment, perfection, or enforcement of a security interest in the seller's interest under a contract is not a transfer that materially changes the duty of or increases materially the burden or risk imposed on the buyer or impairs materially the buyer's chance of obtaining return performance within the purview of subsection (2) unless, and then only to the extent that, enforcement actually results in a delegation of material performance of the seller. Even in that event, the creation, attachment, perfection, and enforcement of the security interest remain effective, but (i) the seller is liable to the buyer for damages caused by the delegation to the extent that the damages could not reasonably by prevented by the buyer, and (ii) a court having jurisdiction may grant other appropriate relief, including cancellation of the contract for sale or an injunction against enforcement of the security interest or consummation of the enforcement.

(4) Unless the circumstances indicate the contrary a prohibition of assignment of "the contract" is to be construed as barring only the delegation to the assignee of the assignor's performance.

(5) An assignment of "the contract" or of "all my rights under the contract" or an assignment in similar general terms is an assignment of rights and unless the language or the circumstances (as in an assignment for security) indicate the contrary, it is a delegation of performance of the duties of the assignor and its acceptance by the assignee constitutes a promise by him to perform those duties. This promise is enforceable by either the assignor or the other party to the original contract.

(6) The other party may treat any assignment which delegates performance as creating reasonable grounds for insecurity and may without prejudice to his rights against the assignor demand assurances from the assignee (Section 2–609).

As amended in 1999.

Part 3 General Obligation and Construction of Contract

§ 2–301. General Obligations of Parties.

The obligation of the seller is to transfer and deliver and that of the buyer is to accept and pay in accordance with the contract.

§ 2–302. Unconscionable Contract or Clause.

(1) If the court as a matter of law finds the contract or any clause of the contract to have been unconscionable at the time it was made the court may refuse to enforce the contract, or it may enforce the remainder of the contract without the unconscionable clause, or it may so limit the application of any unconscionable clause as to avoid any unconscionable result.

(2) When it is claimed or appears to the court that the contract or any clause thereof may be unconscionable the parties shall be afforded a reasonable opportunity to present evidence as to its commercial setting, purpose and effect to aid the court in making the determination.

§ 2–303. Allocations or Division of Risks.

Where this Article allocates a risk or a burden as between the parties "unless otherwise agreed", the agreement may not only shift the allocation but may also divide the risk or burden.

§ 2–304. Price Payable in Money, Goods, Realty, or Otherwise.

(1) The price can be made payable in money or otherwise. If it is payable in whole or in part in goods each party is a seller of the goods which he is to transfer.

(2) Even though all or part of the price is payable in an interest in realty the transfer of the goods and the seller's obligations with reference to them are subject to this Article, but not the transfer of the interest in realty or the transferor's obligations in connection therewith.

§ 2–305. Open Price Term.

(1) The parties if they so intend can conclude a contract for sale even though the price is not settled. In such a case the price is a reasonable price at the time for delivery if

    (a) nothing is said as to price; or

    (b) the price is left to be agreed by the parties and they fail to agree; or

    (c) the price is to be fixed in terms of some agreed market or other standard as set or recorded by a third person or agency and it is not so set or recorded.

(2) A price to be fixed by the seller or by the buyer means a price for him to fix in good faith.

(3) When a price left to be fixed otherwise than by agreement of the parties fails to be fixed through fault of one party the other may at his option treat the contract as cancelled or himself fix a reasonable price.

(4) Where, however, the parties intend not to be bound unless the price be fixed or agreed and it is not fixed or agreed there is no contract. In such a case the buyer must return any goods already received or if unable so to do must pay their reasonable value at the time of delivery and the seller must return any portion of the price paid on account.

§ 2–306. Output, Requirements and Exclusive Dealings.

(1) A term which measures the quantity by the output of the seller or the requirements of the buyer means such actual output or requirements as may occur in good faith, except that no quantity unreasonably disproportionate to any stated estimate or in the absence of a stated estimate to any normal or otherwise comparable prior output or requirements may be tendered or demanded.

(2) A lawful agreement by either the seller or the buyer for exclusive dealing in the kind of goods concerned imposes unless otherwise agreed an obligation by the seller to use best efforts to supply the goods and by the buyer to use best efforts to promote their sale.

§ 2–307. Delivery in Single Lot or Several Lots.

Unless otherwise agreed all goods called for by a contract for sale must be tendered in a single delivery and payment is due only on such tender but where the circumstances give either party the right to make or demand delivery in lots the price if it can be apportioned may be demanded for each lot.

§ 2–308. Absence of Specified Place for Delivery.

Unless otherwise agreed

    (a) the place for delivery of goods is the seller's place of business or if he has none his residence; but

    (b) in a contract for sale of identified goods which to the knowledge of the parties at the time of contracting are in some other place, that place is the place for their delivery; and

    (c) documents of title may be delivered through customary banking channels.

§ 2–309. Absence of Specific Time Provisions; Notice of Termination.

(1) The time for shipment or delivery or any other action under a contract if not provided in this Article or agreed upon shall be a reasonable time.

(2) Where the contract provides for successive performances but is indefinite in duration it is valid for a reasonable time but unless otherwise agreed may be terminated at any time by either party.

(3) Termination of a contract by one party except on the happening of an agreed event requires that reasonable notification be received by the other party and an agreement dispensing with notification is invalid if its operation would be unconscionable.

§ 2–310. Open Time for Payment or Running of Credit; Authority to Ship Under Reservation.

Unless otherwise agreed

    (a) payment is due at the time and place at which the buyer is to receive the goods even though the place of shipment is the place of delivery; and

    (b) if the seller is authorized to send the goods he may ship them under reservation, and may tender the documents of title, but the buyer may inspect the goods after their arrival before payment is due unless such inspection is inconsistent with the terms of the contract (Section 2–513); and

    (c) if delivery is authorized and made by way of documents of title otherwise than by subsection (b) then payment is due at the time and place at which the buyer is to receive the documents regardless of where the goods are to be received; and

    (d) where the seller is required or authorized to ship the goods on credit the credit period runs from the time of shipment but post-dating the invoice or delaying its dispatch will correspondingly delay the starting of the credit period.

§ 2–311. Options and Cooperation Respecting Performance.

(1) An agreement for sale which is otherwise sufficiently definite (subsection (3) of Section 2–204) to be a contract is not made invalid by the fact that it leaves particulars of performance to be specified by one of the parties. Any such specification must be made in good faith and within limits set by commercial reasonableness.

(2) Unless otherwise agreed specifications relating to assortment of the goods are at the buyer's option and except as otherwise provided in subsections (1)(c) and (3) of Section 2–319 specifications or arrangements relating to shipment are at the seller's option.

(3) Where such specification would materially affect the other party's performance but is not seasonably made or where one party's cooperation is necessary to the agreed performance of the other but is not seasonably forthcoming, the other party in addition to all other remedies

    (a) is excused for any resulting delay in his own performance; and

    (b) may also either proceed to perform in any reasonable manner or after the time for a material part of his own performance treat the failure to specify or to cooperate as a breach by failure to deliver or accept the goods.

§ 2–312. Warranty of Title and Against Infringement; Buyer's Obligation Against Infringement.

(1) Subject to subsection (2) there is in a contract for sale a warranty by the seller that

(a) the title conveyed shall be good, and its transfer rightful; and

(b) the goods shall be delivered free from any security interest or other lien or encumbrance of which the buyer at the time of contracting has no knowledge.

(2) A warranty under subsection (1) will be excluded or modified only by specific language or by circumstances which give the buyer reason to know that the person selling does not claim title in himself or that he is purporting to sell only such right or title as he or a third person may have.

(3) Unless otherwise agreed a seller who is a merchant regularly dealing in goods of the kind warrants that the goods shall be delivered free of the rightful claim of any third person by way of infringement or the like but a buyer who furnishes specifications to the seller must hold the seller harmless against any such claim which arises out of compliance with the specifications.

§ 2–313. Express Warranties by Affirmation, Promise, Description, Sample.

(1) Express warranties by the seller are created as follows:

(a) Any affirmation of fact or promise made by the seller to the buyer which relates to the goods and becomes part of the basis of the bargain creates an express warranty that the goods shall conform to the affirmation or promise.

(b) Any description of the goods which is made part of the basis of the bargain creates an express warranty that the goods shall conform to the description.

(c) Any sample or model which is made part of the basis of the bargain creates an express warranty that the whole of the goods shall conform to the sample or model.

(2) It is not necessary to the creation of an express warranty that the seller use formal words such as "warrant" or "guarantee" or that he have a specific intention to make a warranty, but an affirmation merely of the value of the goods or a statement purporting to be merely the seller's opinion or commendation of the goods does not create a warranty.

§ 2–314. Implied Warranty: Merchantability; Usage of Trade.

(1) Unless excluded or modified (Section 2–316), a warranty that the goods shall be merchantable is implied in a contract for their sale if the seller is a merchant with respect to goods of that kind. Under this section the serving for value of food or drink to be consumed either on the premises or elsewhere is a sale.

(2) Goods to be merchantable must be at least such as

(a) pass without objection in the trade under the contract description; and

(b) in the case of fungible goods, are of fair average quality within the description; and

(c) are fit for the ordinary purposes for which such goods are used; and

(d) run, within the variations permitted by the agreement, of even kind, quality and quantity within each unit and among all units involved; and

(e) are adequately contained, packaged, and labeled as the agreement may require; and

(f) conform to the promises or affirmations of fact made on the container or label if any.

(3) Unless excluded or modified (Section 2–316) other implied warranties may arise from course of dealing or usage of trade.

§ 2–315. Implied Warranty: Fitness for Particular Purpose.

Where the seller at the time of contracting has reason to know any particular purpose for which the goods are required and that the buyer is relying on the seller's skill or judgment to select or furnish suitable goods, there is unless excluded or modified under the next section an implied warranty that the goods shall be fit for such purpose.

§ 2–316. Exclusion or Modification of Warranties.

(1) Words or conduct relevant to the creation of an express warranty and words or conduct tending to negate or limit warranty shall be construed wherever reasonable as consistent with each other; but subject to the provisions of this Article on parol or extrinsic evidence (Section 2–202) negation or limitation is inoperative to the extent that such construction is unreasonable.

(2) Subject to subsection (3), to exclude or modify the implied warranty of merchantability or any part of it the language must mention merchantability and in case of a writing must be conspicuous, and to exclude or modify any implied warranty of fitness the exclusion must be by a writing and conspicuous. Language to exclude all implied warranties of fitness is sufficient if it states, for example, that "There are no warranties which extend beyond the description on the face hereof."

(3) Notwithstanding subsection (2)

(a) unless the circumstances indicate otherwise, all implied warranties are excluded by expressions like "as is", "with all faults" or other language which in common understanding calls the buyer's attention to the exclusion of warranties and makes plain that there is no implied warranty; and

(b) when the buyer before entering into the contract has examined the goods or the sample or model as fully as he desired or has refused to examine the goods there is no implied warranty with regard to defects which an examination ought in the circumstances to have revealed to him; and

(c) an implied warranty can also be excluded or modified by course of dealing or course of performance or usage of trade.

(4) Remedies for breach of warranty can be limited in accordance with the provisions of this Article on liquidation or limitation of damages and on contractual modification of remedy (Sections 2–718 and 2–719).

§ 2–317. Cumulation and Conflict of Warranties Express or Implied.

Warranties whether express or implied shall be construed as consistent with each other and as cumulative, but if such construction is unreasonable the intention of the parties shall determine which warranty is dominant. In ascertaining that intention the following rules apply:

(a) Exact or technical specifications displace an inconsistent sample or model or general language of description.

(b) A sample from an existing bulk displaces inconsistent general language of description.

(c) Express warranties displace inconsistent implied warranties other than an implied warranty of fitness for a particular purpose.

§ 2–318. Third Party Beneficiaries of Warranties Express or Implied.

Note: If this Act is introduced in the Congress of the United States this section should be omitted. (States to select one alternative.)

Alternative A

A seller's warranty whether express or implied extends to any natural person who is in the family or household of his buyer or who is a guest in his home if it is reasonable to expect that such person may use, consume or be affected by the goods and who is injured in person by breach of the warranty. A seller may not exclude or limit the operation of this section.

Alternative B

A seller's warranty whether express or implied extends to any natural person who may reasonably be expected to use, consume or be affected by the goods and who is injured in person by breach of the warranty. A seller may not exclude or limit the operation of this section.

Alternative C

A seller's warranty whether express or implied extends to any person who may reasonably be expected to use, consume or be affected by the goods and who is injured by breach of the warranty. A seller may not exclude or limit the operation of this section with respect to injury to the person of an individual to whom the warranty extends.

As amended 1966.

§ 2–319. F.O.B. and F.A.S. Terms.

(1) Unless otherwise agreed the term F.O.B. (which means "free on board") at a named place, even though used only in connection with the stated price, is a delivery term under which

(a) when the term is F.O.B. the place of shipment, the seller must at that place ship the goods in the manner provided in this Article (Section 2–504) and bear the expense and risk of putting them into the possession of the carrier; or

(b) when the term is F.O.B. the place of destination, the seller must at his own expense and risk transport the goods to that place and there tender delivery of them in the manner provided in this Article (Section 2–503);

(c) when under either (a) or (b) the term is also F.O.B. vessel, car or other vehicle, the seller must in addition at his own expense and risk load the goods on board. If the term is F.O.B. vessel the buyer must name the vessel and in an appropriate case the seller must comply with the provisions of this Article on the form of bill of lading (Section 2–323).

(2) Unless otherwise agreed the term F.A.S. vessel (which means "free alongside") at a named port, even though used only in connection with the stated price, is a delivery term under which the seller must

(a) at his own expense and risk deliver the goods alongside the vessel in the manner usual in that port or on a dock designated and provided by the buyer; and

(b) obtain and tender a receipt for the goods in exchange for which the carrier is under a duty to issue a bill of lading.

(3) Unless otherwise agreed in any case falling within subsection (1)(a) or (c) or subsection (2) the buyer must seasonably give any needed instructions for making delivery, including when the term is F.A.S. or F.O.B. the loading berth of the vessel and in an appropriate case its name and sailing date. The seller may treat the failure of needed instructions as a failure of cooperation under this Article (Section 2–311). He may also at his option move the goods in any reasonable manner preparatory to delivery or shipment.

(4) Under the term F.O.B. vessel or F.A.S. unless otherwise agreed the buyer must make payment against tender of the required documents and the seller may not tender nor the buyer demand delivery of the goods in substitution for the documents.

§ 2–320. C.I.F. and C. & F. Terms.

(1) The term C.I.F. means that the price includes in a lump sum the cost of the goods and the insurance and freight to the named destination. The term C. & F. or C.F. means that the price so includes cost and freight to the named destination.

(2) Unless otherwise agreed and even though used only in connection with the stated price and destination, the term C.I.F. destination or its equivalent requires the seller at his own expense and risk to

(a) put the goods into the possession of a carrier at the port for shipment and obtain a negotiable bill or bills of lading covering the entire transportation to the named destination; and

(b) load the goods and obtain a receipt from the carrier (which may be contained in the bill of lading) showing that the freight has been paid or provided for; and

(c) obtain a policy or certificate of insurance, including any war risk insurance, of a kind and on terms then current at the port of shipment in the usual amount, in the currency of the contract, shown to cover the same goods covered by the bill of lading and providing for payment of loss to the order of the buyer or for the account of whom it may concern; but the seller may add to the price the amount of the premium for any such war risk insurance; and

(d) prepare an invoice of the goods and procure any other documents required to effect shipment or to comply with the contract; and

(e) forward and tender with commercial promptness all the documents in due form and with any indorsement necessary to perfect the buyer's rights.

(3) Unless otherwise agreed the term C. & F. or its equivalent has the same effect and imposes upon the seller the same obligations and risks as a C.I.F. term except the obligation as to insurance.

(4) Under the term C.I.F. or C. & F. unless otherwise agreed the buyer must make payment against tender of the required documents and the seller may not tender nor the buyer demand delivery of the goods in substitution for the documents.

§ 2–321. C.I.F. or C. & F.: "Net Landed Weights"; "Payment on Arrival"; Warranty of Condition on Arrival.

Under a contract containing a term C.I.F. or C. & F.

(1) Where the price is based on or is to be adjusted according to "net landed weights", "delivered weights", "out turn" quantity or quality or the like, unless otherwise agreed the seller must reasonably estimate the price. The payment due on tender of the documents called for by the contract is the amount so estimated, but after final adjustment of the price a settlement must be made with commercial promptness.

(2) An agreement described in subsection (1) or any warranty of quality or condition of the goods on arrival places upon the seller the risk of ordinary deterioration, shrinkage and the like in transportation but has no effect on the place or time of identification to the contract for sale or delivery or on the passing of the risk of loss.

(3) Unless otherwise agreed where the contract provides for payment on or after arrival of the goods the seller must before payment allow such preliminary inspection as is feasible; but if the goods are lost delivery of the documents and payment are due when the goods should have arrived.

§ 2–322. Delivery "Ex-Ship".

(1) Unless otherwise agreed a term for delivery of goods "ex-ship" (which means from the carrying vessel) or in equivalent language is not restricted to a particular ship and requires delivery from a ship which has reached a place at the named port of destination where goods of the kind are usually discharged.

(2) Under such a term unless otherwise agreed

(a) the seller must discharge all liens arising out of the carriage and furnish the buyer with a direction which puts the carrier under a duty to deliver the goods; and

(b) the risk of loss does not pass to the buyer until the goods leave the ship's tackle or are otherwise properly unloaded.

§ 2–323. Form of Bill of Lading Required in Overseas Shipment; "Overseas".

(1) Where the contract contemplates overseas shipment and contains a term C.I.F. or C. & F. or F.O.B. vessel, the seller unless otherwise agreed must obtain a negotiable bill of lading stating that the goods have been loaded on board or, in the case of a term C.I.F. or C. & F., received for shipment.

(2) Where in a case within subsection (1) a bill of lading has been issued in a set of parts, unless otherwise agreed if the documents are not to be sent from abroad the buyer may demand tender of the full set; otherwise only one part of the bill of lading need be tendered. Even if the agreement expressly requires a full set

(a) due tender of a single part is acceptable within the provisions of this Article on cure of improper delivery (subsection (1) of Section 2–508); and

(b) even though the full set is demanded, if the documents are sent from abroad the person tendering an incomplete set may nevertheless require payment upon furnishing an indemnity which the buyer in good faith deems adequate.

(3) A shipment by water or by air or a contract contemplating such shipment is "overseas" insofar as by usage of trade or agreement it is subject to the commercial, financing or shipping practices characteristic of international deep water commerce.

§ 2–324. "No Arrival, No Sale" Term.

Under a term "no arrival, no sale" or terms of like meaning, unless otherwise agreed,

(a) the seller must properly ship conforming goods and if they arrive by any means he must tender them on arrival but he assumes no obligation that the goods will arrive unless he has caused the non-arrival; and

(b) where without fault of the seller the goods are in part lost or have so deteriorated as no longer to conform to the contract or arrive after the contract time, the buyer may proceed as if there had been casualty to identified goods (Section 2–613).

§ 2–325. "Letter of Credit" Term; "Confirmed Credit".

(1) Failure of the buyer seasonably to furnish an agreed letter of credit is a breach of the contract for sale.

(2) The delivery to seller of a proper letter of credit suspends the buyer's obligation to pay. If the letter of credit is dishonored, the seller may on seasonable notification to the buyer require payment directly from him.

(3) Unless otherwise agreed the term "letter of credit" or "banker's credit" in a contract for sale means an irrevocable credit issued by a financing agency of good repute and, where the shipment is overseas, of good international repute. The term "confirmed credit" means that the credit must also carry the direct obligation of such an agency which does business in the seller's financial market.

§ 2–326. Sale on Approval and Sale or Return; Rights of Creditors.

(1) Unless otherwise agreed, if delivered goods may be returned by the buyer even though they conform to the contract, the transaction is

(a) a "sale on approval" if the goods are delivered primarily for use, and

(b) a "sale or return" if the goods are delivered primarily for resale.

(2) Goods held on approval are not subject to the claims of the buyer's creditors until acceptance; goods held on sale or return are subject to such claims while in the buyer's possession.

(3) Any "or return" term of a contract for sale is to be treated as a separate contract for sale within the statute of frauds section of this Article (Section 2–201) and as contradicting the sale aspect of the contract within the provisions of this Article or on parol or extrinsic evidence (Section 2–202).

As amended in 1999.

§ 2–327. Special Incidents of Sale on Approval and Sale or Return.

(1) Under a sale on approval unless otherwise agreed

(a) although the goods are identified to the contract the risk of loss and the title do not pass to the buyer until acceptance; and

(b) use of the goods consistent with the purpose of trial is not acceptance but failure seasonably to notify the seller of election to return the goods is acceptance, and if the goods conform to the contract acceptance of any part is acceptance of the whole; and

(c) after due notification of election to return, the return is at the seller's risk and expense but a merchant buyer must follow any reasonable instructions.

(2) Under a sale or return unless otherwise agreed

(a) the option to return extends to the whole or any commercial unit of the goods while in substantially their original condition, but must be exercised seasonably; and

(b) the return is at the buyer's risk and expense.

§ 2–328. **Sale by Auction.**

(1) In a sale by auction if goods are put up in lots each lot is the subject of a separate sale.

(2) A sale by auction is complete when the auctioneer so announces by the fall of the hammer or in other customary manner. Where a bid is made while the hammer is falling in acceptance of a prior bid the auctioneer may in his discretion reopen the bidding or declare the goods sold under the bid on which the hammer was falling.

(3) Such a sale is with reserve unless the goods are in explicit terms put up without reserve. In an auction with reserve the auctioneer may withdraw the goods at any time until he announces completion of the sale. In an auction without reserve, after the auctioneer calls for bids on an article or lot, that article or lot cannot be withdrawn unless no bid is made within a reasonable time. In either case a bidder may retract his bid until the auctioneer's announcement of completion of the sale, but a bidder's retraction does not revive any previous bid.

(4) If the auctioneer knowingly receives a bid on the seller's behalf or the seller makes or procures such as bid, and notice has not been given that liberty for such bidding is reserved, the buyer may at his option avoid the sale or take the goods at the price of the last good faith bid prior to the completion of the sale. This subsection shall not apply to any bid at a forced sale.

Part 4 Title, Creditors and Good Faith Purchasers

§ 2–401. **Passing of Title; Reservation for Security; Limited Application of This Section.**

Each provision of this Article with regard to the rights, obligations and remedies of the seller, the buyer, purchasers or other third parties applies irrespective of title to the goods except where the provision refers to such title. Insofar as situations are not covered by the other provisions of this Article and matters concerning title became material the following rules apply:

(1) Title to goods cannot pass under a contract for sale prior to their identification to the contract (Section 2–501), and unless otherwise explicitly agreed the buyer acquires by their identification a special property as limited by this Act. Any retention or reservation by the seller of the title (property) in goods shipped or delivered to the buyer is limited in effect to a reservation of a security interest. Subject to these provisions and to the provisions of the Article on Secured Transactions (Article 9), title to goods passes from the seller to the buyer in any manner and on any conditions explicitly agreed on by the parties.

(2) Unless otherwise explicitly agreed title passes to the buyer at the time and place at which the seller completes his performance with reference to the physical delivery of the goods, despite any reservation of a security interest and even though a document of title is to be delivered at a different time or place; and in particular and despite any reservation of a security interest by the bill of lading

(a) if the contract requires or authorizes the seller to send the goods to the buyer but does not require him to deliver them at destination, title passes to the buyer at the time and place of shipment; but

(b) if the contract requires delivery at destination, title passes on tender there.

(3) Unless otherwise explicitly agreed where delivery is to be made without moving the goods,

(a) if the seller is to deliver a document of title, title passes at the time when and the place where he delivers such documents; or

(b) if the goods are at the time of contracting already identified and no documents are to be delivered, title passes at the time and place of contracting.

(4) A rejection or other refusal by the buyer to receive or retain the goods, whether or not justified, or a justified revocation of acceptance revests title to the goods in the seller. Such revesting occurs by operation of law and is not a "sale".

§ 2–402. **Rights of Seller's Creditors Against Sold Goods.**

(1) Except as provided in subsections (2) and (3), rights of unsecured creditors of the seller with respect to goods which have been identified to a contract for sale are subject to the buyer's rights to recover the goods under this Article (Sections 2–502 and 2–716).

(2) A creditor of the seller may treat a sale or an identification of goods to a contract for sale as void if as against him a retention of possession by the seller is fraudulent under any rule of law of the state where the goods are situated, except that retention of possession in good faith and current course of trade by a merchant-seller for a commercially reasonable time after a sale or identification is not fraudulent.

(3) Nothing in this Article shall be deemed to impair the rights of creditors of the seller

(a) under the provisions of the Article on Secured Transactions (Article 9); or

(b) where identification to the contract or delivery is made not in current course of trade but in satisfaction of or as security for a pre-existing claim for money, security or the like and is made under circumstances which under any rule of law of the state where the goods are situated would apart from this Article constitute the transaction a fraudulent transfer or voidable preference.

§ 2–403. **Power to Transfer; Good Faith Purchase of Goods; "Entrusting".**

(1) A purchaser of goods acquires all title which his transferor had or had power to transfer except that a purchaser of a limited interest acquires rights only to the extent of the interest purchased. A person with voidable title has power to transfer a good title to a good faith purchaser for value. When goods have been delivered under a transaction of purchase the purchaser has such power even though

(a) the transferor was deceived as to the identity of the purchaser, or

(b) the delivery was in exchange for a check which is later dishonored, or

(c) it was agreed that the transaction was to be a "cash sale", or

(d) the delivery was procured through fraud punishable as larcenous under the criminal law.

(2) Any entrusting of possession of goods to a merchant who deals in goods of that kind gives him power to transfer all rights of the entruster to a buyer in ordinary course of business.

(3) "Entrusting" includes any delivery and any acquiescence in retention of possession regardless of any condition expressed between the parties to the delivery or acquiescence and regardless of whether the procurement of the entrusting or the possessor's disposition of the goods have been such as to be larcenous under the criminal law.

(4) The rights of other purchasers of goods and of lien creditors are governed by the Articles on Secured Transactions (Article 9), Bulk Transfers (Article 6) and Documents of Title (Article 7).

As amended in 1988.

Part 5 Performance

§ 2–501. Insurable Interest in Goods; Manner of Identification of Goods.

(1) The buyer obtains a special property and an insurable interest in goods by identification of existing goods as goods to which the contract refers even though the goods so identified are non-conforming and he has an option to return or reject them. Such identification can be made at any time and in any manner explicitly agreed to by the parties. In the absence of explicit agreement identification occurs

    (a) when the contract is made if it is for the sale of goods already existing and identified;

    (b) if the contract is for the sale of future goods other than those described in paragraph (c), when goods are shipped, marked or otherwise designated by the seller as goods to which the contract refers;

    (c) when the crops are planted or otherwise become growing crops or the young are conceived if the contract is for the sale of unborn young to be born within twelve months after contracting or for the sale of crops to be harvested within twelve months or the next normal harvest season after contracting whichever is longer.

(2) The seller retains an insurable interest in goods so long as title to or any security interest in the goods remains in him and where the identification is by the seller alone he may until default or insolvency or notification to the buyer that the identification is final substitute other goods for those identified.

(3) Nothing in this section impairs any insurable interest recognized under any other statute or rule of law.

§ 2–502. Buyer's Right to Goods on Seller's Insolvency.

(1) Subject to subsections (2) and (3) and even though the goods have not been shipped a buyer who has paid a part or all of the price of goods in which he has a special property under the provisions of the immediately preceding section may on making and keeping good a tender of any unpaid portion of their price recover them from the seller if:

    (a) in the case of goods bought for personal, family, or household purposes, the seller repudiates or fails to deliver as required by the contract; or

    (b) in all cases, the seller becomes insolvent within ten days after receipt of the first installment on their price.

(2) The buyer's right to recover the goods under subsection (1)(a) vests upon acquisition of a special property, even if the seller had not then repudiated or failed to deliver.

(3) If the identification creating his special property has been made by the buyer he acquires the right to recover the goods only if they conform to the contract for sale.

As amended in 1999.

§ 2–503. Manner of Seller's Tender of Delivery.

(1) Tender of delivery requires that the seller put and hold conforming goods at the buyer's disposition and give the buyer any notification reasonably necessary to enable him to take delivery. The manner, time and place for tender are determined by the agreement and this Article, and in particular

    (a) tender must be at a reasonable hour, and if it is of goods they must be kept available for the period reasonably necessary to enable the buyer to take possession; but

    (b) unless otherwise agreed the buyer must furnish facilities reasonably suited to the receipt of the goods.

(2) Where the case is within the next section respecting shipment tender requires that the seller comply with its provisions.

(3) Where the seller is required to deliver at a particular destination tender requires that he comply with subsection (1) and also in any appropriate case tender documents as described in subsections (4) and (5) of this section.

(4) Where goods are in the possession of a bailee and are to be delivered without being moved

    (a) tender requires that the seller either tender a negotiable document of title covering such goods or procure acknowledgment by the bailee of the buyer's right to possession of the goods; but

    (b) tender to the buyer of a non-negotiable document of title or of a written direction to the bailee to deliver is sufficient tender unless the buyer seasonably objects, and receipt by the bailee of notification of the buyer's rights fixes those rights as against the bailee and all third persons; but risk of loss of the goods and of any failure by the bailee to honor the non-negotiable document of title or to obey the direction remains on the seller until the buyer has had a reasonable time to present the document or direction, and a refusal by the bailee to honor the document or to obey the direction defeats the tender.

(5) Where the contract requires the seller to deliver documents

    (a) he must tender all such documents in correct form, except as provided in this Article with respect to bills of lading in a set (subsection (2) of Section 2–323); and

    (b) tender through customary banking channels is sufficient and dishonor of a draft accompanying the documents constitutes non-acceptance or rejection.

§ 2–504. Shipment by Seller.

Where the seller is required or authorized to send the goods to the buyer and the contract does not require him to deliver them at a particular destination, then unless otherwise agreed he must

    (a) put the goods in the possession of such a carrier and make such a contract for their transportation as may be reasonable having regard to the nature of the goods and other circumstances of the case; and

(b) obtain and promptly deliver or tender in due form any document necessary to enable the buyer to obtain possession of the goods or otherwise required by the agreement or by usage of trade; and

(c) promptly notify the buyer of the shipment.

Failure to notify the buyer under paragraph (c) or to make a proper contract under paragraph (a) is a ground for rejection only if material delay or loss ensues.

§ 2–505. Seller's Shipment under Reservation.

(1) Where the seller has identified goods to the contract by or before shipment:

(a) his procurement of a negotiable bill of lading to his own order or otherwise reserves in him a security interest in the goods. His procurement of the bill to the order of a financing agency or of the buyer indicates in addition only the seller's expectation of transferring that interest to the person named.

(b) a non-negotiable bill of lading to himself or his nominee reserves possession of the goods as security but except in a case of conditional delivery (subsection (2) of Section 2–507) a non-negotiable bill of lading naming the buyer as consignee reserves no security interest even though the seller retains possession of the bill of lading.

(2) When shipment by the seller with reservation of a security interest is in violation of the contract for sale it constitutes an improper contract for transportation within the preceding section but impairs neither the rights given to the buyer by shipment and identification of the goods to the contract nor the seller's powers as a holder of a negotiable document.

§ 2–506. Rights of Financing Agency.

(1) A financing agency by paying or purchasing for value a draft which relates to a shipment of goods acquires to the extent of the payment or purchase and in addition to its own rights under the draft and any document of title securing it any rights of the shipper in the goods including the right to stop delivery and the shipper's right to have the draft honored by the buyer.

(2) The right to reimbursement of a financing agency which has in good faith honored or purchased the draft under commitment to or authority from the buyer is not impaired by subsequent discovery of defects with reference to any relevant document which was apparently regular on its face.

§ 2–507. Effect of Seller's Tender; Delivery on Condition.

(1) Tender of delivery is a condition to the buyer's duty to accept the goods and, unless otherwise agreed, to his duty to pay for them. Tender entitles the seller to acceptance of the goods and to payment according to the contract.

(2) Where payment is due and demanded on the delivery to the buyer of goods or documents of title, his right as against the seller to retain or dispose of them is conditional upon his making the payment due.

§ 2–508. Cure by Seller of Improper Tender or Delivery; Replacement.

(1) Where any tender or delivery by the seller is rejected because non-conforming and the time for performance has not yet expired, the seller may seasonably notify the buyer of his intention to cure and may then within the contract time make a conforming delivery.

(2) Where the buyer rejects a non-conforming tender which the seller had reasonable grounds to believe would be acceptable with or without money allowance the seller may if he seasonably notifies the buyer have a further reasonable time to substitute a conforming tender.

§ 2–509. Risk of Loss in the Absence of Breach.

(1) Where the contract requires or authorizes the seller to ship the goods by carrier

(a) if it does not require him to deliver them at a particular destination, the risk of loss passes to the buyer when the goods are duly delivered to the carrier even though the shipment is under reservation (Section 2–505); but

(b) if it does require him to deliver them at a particular destination and the goods are there duly tendered while in the possession of the carrier, the risk of loss passes to the buyer when the goods are there duly so tendered as to enable the buyer to take delivery.

(2) Where the goods are held by a bailee to be delivered without being moved, the risk of loss passes to the buyer

(a) on his receipt of a negotiable document of title covering the goods; or

(b) on acknowledgment by the bailee of the buyer's right to possession of the goods; or

(c) after his receipt of a non-negotiable document of title or other written direction to deliver, as provided in subsection (4)(b) of Section 2–503.

(3) In any case not within subsection (1) or (2), the risk of loss passes to the buyer on his receipt of the goods if the seller is a merchant; otherwise the risk passes to the buyer on tender of delivery.

(4) The provisions of this section are subject to contrary agreement of the parties and to the provisions of this Article on sale on approval (Section 2–327) and on effect of breach on risk of loss (Section 2–510).

§ 2–510. Effect of Breach on Risk of Loss.

(1) Where a tender or delivery of goods so fails to conform to the contract as to give a right of rejection the risk of their loss remains on the seller until cure or acceptance.

(2) Where the buyer rightfully revokes acceptance he may to the extent of any deficiency in his effective insurance coverage treat the risk of loss as having rested on the seller from the beginning.

(3) Where the buyer as to conforming goods already identified to the contract for sale repudiates or is otherwise in breach before risk of their loss has passed to him, the seller may to the extent of any deficiency in his effective insurance coverage treat the risk of loss as resting on the buyer for a commercially reasonable time.

§ 2–511. Tender of Payment by Buyer; Payment by Check.

(1) Unless otherwise agreed tender of payment is a condition to the seller's duty to tender and complete any delivery.

(2) Tender of payment is sufficient when made by any means or in any manner current in the ordinary course of business unless the

seller demands payment in legal tender and gives any extension of time reasonably necessary to procure it.

(3) Subject to the provisions of this Act on the effect of an instrument on an obligation (Section 3–310), payment by check is conditional and is defeated as between the parties by dishonor of the check on due presentment.

As amended in 1994.

§ 2–512. Payment by Buyer Before Inspection.

(1) Where the contract requires payment before inspection non-conformity of the goods does not excuse the buyer from so making payment unless

(a) the non-conformity appears without inspection; or

(b) despite tender of the required documents the circumstances would justify injunction against honor under this Act (Section 5–109(b)).

(2) Payment pursuant to subsection (1) does not constitute an acceptance of goods or impair the buyer's right to inspect or any of his remedies.

As amended in 1995.

§ 2–513. Buyer's Right to Inspection of Goods.

(1) Unless otherwise agreed and subject to subsection (3), where goods are tendered or delivered or identified to the contract for sale, the buyer has a right before payment or acceptance to inspect them at any reasonable place and time and in any reasonable manner. When the seller is required or authorized to send the goods to the buyer, the inspection may be after their arrival.

(2) Expenses of inspection must be borne by the buyer but may be recovered from the seller if the goods do not conform and are rejected.

(3) Unless otherwise agreed and subject to the provisions of this Article on C.I.F. contracts (subsection (3) of Section 2–321), the buyer is not entitled to inspect the goods before payment of the price when the contract provides

(a) for delivery "C.O.D." or on other like terms; or

(b) for payment against documents of title, except where such payment is due only after the goods are to become available for inspection.

(4) A place or method of inspection fixed by the parties is presumed to be exclusive but unless otherwise expressly agreed it does not postpone identification or shift the place for delivery or for passing the risk of loss. If compliance becomes impossible, inspection shall be as provided in this section unless the place or method fixed was clearly intended as an indispensable condition failure of which avoids the contract.

§ 2–514. When Documents Deliverable on Acceptance; When on Payment.

Unless otherwise agreed documents against which a draft is drawn are to be delivered to the drawee on acceptance of the draft if it is payable more than three days after presentment; otherwise, only on payment.

§ 2–515. Preserving Evidence of Goods in Dispute.

In furtherance of the adjustment of any claim or dispute

(a) either party on reasonable notification to the other and for the purpose of ascertaining the facts and preserving evidence has the right to inspect, test and sample the goods including such of them as may be in the possession or control of the other; and

(b) the parties may agree to a third party inspection or survey to determine the conformity or condition of the goods and may agree that the findings shall be binding upon them in any subsequent litigation or adjustment.

Part 6 Breach, Repudiation and Excuse

§ 2–601. Buyer's Rights on Improper Delivery.

Subject to the provisions of this Article on breach in installment contracts (Section 2–612) and unless otherwise agreed under the sections on contractual limitations of remedy (Sections 2–718 and 2–719), if the goods or the tender of delivery fail in any respect to conform to the contract, the buyer may

(a) reject the whole; or

(b) accept the whole; or

(c) accept any commercial unit or units and reject the rest.

§ 2–602. Manner and Effect of Rightful Rejection.

(1) Rejection of goods must be within a reasonable time after their delivery or tender. It is ineffective unless the buyer seasonably notifies the seller.

(2) Subject to the provisions of the two following sections on rejected goods (Sections 2–603 and 2–604),

(a) after rejection any exercise of ownership by the buyer with respect to any commercial unit is wrongful as against the seller; and

(b) if the buyer has before rejection taken physical possession of goods in which he does not have a security interest under the provisions of this Article (subsection (3) of Section 2–711), he is under a duty after rejection to hold them with reasonable care at the seller's disposition for a time sufficient to permit the seller to remove them; but

(c) the buyer has no further obligations with regard to goods rightfully rejected.

(3) The seller's rights with respect to goods wrongfully rejected are governed by the provisions of this Article on Seller's remedies in general (Section 2–703).

§ 2–603. Merchant Buyer's Duties as to Rightfully Rejected Goods.

(1) Subject to any security interest in the buyer (subsection (3) of Section 2–711), when the seller has no agent or place of business at the market of rejection a merchant buyer is under a duty after rejection of goods in his possession or control to follow any reasonable instructions received from the seller with respect to the goods and in the absence of such instructions to make reasonable efforts to sell them for the seller's account if they are perishable or threaten to decline in value speedily. Instructions are not reasonable if on demand indemnity for expenses is not forthcoming.

(2) When the buyer sells goods under subsection (1), he is entitled to reimbursement from the seller or out of the proceeds for reasonable expenses of caring for and selling them, and if the expenses include no selling commission then to such commission as is usual

in the trade or if there is none to a reasonable sum not exceeding ten per cent on the gross proceeds.

(3) In complying with this section the buyer is held only to good faith and good faith conduct hereunder is neither acceptance nor conversion nor the basis of an action for damages.

§ 2–604. Buyer's Options as to Salvage of Rightfully Rejected Goods.

Subject to the provisions of the immediately preceding section on perishables if the seller gives no instructions within a reasonable time after notification of rejection the buyer may store the rejected goods for the seller's account or reship them to him or resell them for the seller's account with reimbursement as provided in the preceding section. Such action is not acceptance or conversion.

§ 2–605. Waiver of Buyer's Objections by Failure to Particularize.

(1) The buyer's failure to state in connection with rejection a particular defect which is ascertainable by reasonable inspection precludes him from relying on the unstated defect to justify rejection or to establish breach

(a) where the seller could have cured it if stated seasonably; or

(b) between merchants when the seller has after rejection made a request in writing for a full and final written statement of all defects on which the buyer proposes to rely.

(2) Payment against documents made without reservation of rights precludes recovery of the payment for defects apparent on the face of the documents.

§ 2–606. What Constitutes Acceptance of Goods.

(1) Acceptance of goods occurs when the buyer

(a) after a reasonable opportunity to inspect the goods signifies to the seller that the goods are conforming or that he will take or retain them in spite of their nonconformity; or

(b) fails to make an effective rejection (subsection (1) of Section 2–602), but such acceptance does not occur until the buyer has had a reasonable opportunity to inspect them; or

(c) does any act inconsistent with the seller's ownership; but if such act is wrongful as against the seller it is an acceptance only if ratified by him.

(2) Acceptance of a part of any commercial unit is acceptance of that entire unit.

§ 2–607. Effect of Acceptance; Notice of Breach; Burden of Establishing Breach After Acceptance; Notice of Claim or Litigation to Person Answerable Over.

(1) The buyer must pay at the contract rate for any goods accepted.

(2) Acceptance of goods by the buyer precludes rejection of the goods accepted and if made with knowledge of a non-conformity cannot be revoked because of it unless the acceptance was on the reasonable assumption that the non-conformity would be seasonably cured but acceptance does not of itself impair any other remedy provided by this Article for non-conformity.

(3) Where a tender has been accepted

(a) the buyer must within a reasonable time after he discovers or should have discovered any breach notify the seller of breach or be barred from any remedy; and

(b) if the claim is one for infringement or the like (subsection (3) of Section 2–312) and the buyer is sued as a result of such a breach he must so notify the seller within a reasonable time after he receives notice of the litigation or be barred from any remedy over for liability established by the litigation.

(4) The burden is on the buyer to establish any breach with respect to the goods accepted.

(5) Where the buyer is sued for breach of a warranty or other obligation for which his seller is answerable over

(a) he may give his seller written notice of the litigation. If the notice states that the seller may come in and defend and that if the seller does not do so he will be bound in any action against him by his buyer by any determination of fact common to the two litigations, then unless the seller after seasonable receipt of the notice does come in and defend he is so bound.

(b) if the claim is one for infringement or the like (subsection (3) of Section 2–312) the original seller may demand in writing that his buyer turn over to him control of the litigation including settlement or else be barred from any remedy over and if he also agrees to bear all expense and to satisfy any adverse judgment, then unless the buyer after seasonable receipt of the demand does turn over control the buyer is so barred.

(6) The provisions of subsections (3), (4) and (5) apply to any obligation of a buyer to hold the seller harmless against infringement or the like (subsection (3) of Section 2–312).

§ 2–608. Revocation of Acceptance in Whole or in Part.

(1) The buyer may revoke his acceptance of a lot or commercial unit whose non-conformity substantially impairs its value to him if he has accepted it

(a) on the reasonable assumption that its nonconformity would be cured and it has not been seasonably cured; or

(b) without discovery of such non-conformity if his acceptance was reasonably induced either by the difficulty of discovery before acceptance or by the seller's assurances.

(2) Revocation of acceptance must occur within a reasonable time after the buyer discovers or should have discovered the ground for it and before any substantial change in condition of the goods which is not caused by their own defects. It is not effective until the buyer notifies the seller of it.

(3) A buyer who so revokes has the same rights and duties with regard to the goods involved as if he had rejected them.

§ 2–609. Right to Adequate Assurance of Performance.

(1) A contract for sale imposes an obligation on each party that the other's expectation of receiving due performance will not be impaired. When reasonable grounds for insecurity arise with respect to the performance of either party the other may in writing demand adequate assurance of due performance and until he receives such assurance may if commercially reasonable suspend any performance for which he has not already received the agreed return.

(2) Between merchants the reasonableness of grounds for insecurity and the adequacy of any assurance offered shall be determined according to commercial standards.

(3) Acceptance of any improper delivery or payment does not prejudice the party's right to demand adequate assurance of future performance.

(4) After receipt of a justified demand failure to provide within a reasonable time not exceeding thirty days such assurance of due performance as is adequate under the circumstances of the particular case is a repudiation of the contract.

§ 2–610. Anticipatory Repudiation.

When either party repudiates the contract with respect to a performance not yet due the loss of which will substantially impair the value of the contract to the other, the aggrieved party may

(a) for a commercially reasonable time await performance by the repudiating party; or

(b) resort to any remedy for breach (Section 2–703 or Section 2–711), even though he has notified the repudiating party that he would await the latter's performance and has urged retraction; and

(c) in either case suspend his own performance or proceed in accordance with the provisions of this Article on the seller's right to identify goods to the contract notwithstanding breach or to salvage unfinished goods (Section 2–704).

§ 2–611. Retraction of Anticipatory Repudiation.

(1) Until the repudiating party's next performance is due he can retract his repudiation unless the aggrieved party has since the repudiation cancelled or materially changed his position or otherwise indicated that he considers the repudiation final.

(2) Retraction may be by any method which clearly indicates to the aggrieved party that the repudiating party intends to perform, but must include any assurance justifiably demanded under the provisions of this Article (Section 2–609).

(3) Retraction reinstates the repudiating party's rights under the contract with due excuse and allowance to the aggrieved party for any delay occasioned by the repudiation.

§ 2–612. "Installment Contract"; Breach.

(1) An "installment contract" is one which requires or authorizes the delivery of goods in separate lots to be separately accepted, even though the contract contains a clause "each delivery is a separate contract" or its equivalent.

(2) The buyer may reject any installment which is non-conforming if the non-conformity substantially impairs the value of that installment and cannot be cured or if the non-conformity is a defect in the required documents; but if the non-conformity does not fall within subsection (3) and the seller gives adequate assurance of its cure the buyer must accept that installment.

(3) Whenever non-conformity or default with respect to one or more installments substantially impairs the value of the whole contract there is a breach of the whole. But the aggrieved party reinstates the contract if he accepts a non-conforming installment without seasonably notifying of cancellation or if he brings an action with respect only to past installments or demands performance as to future installments.

§ 2–613. Casualty to Identified Goods.

Where the contract requires for its performance goods identified when the contract is made, and the goods suffer casualty without fault of either party before the risk of loss passes to the buyer, or in a proper case under a "no arrival, no sale" term (Section 2–324) then

(a) if the loss is total the contract is avoided; and

(b) if the loss is partial or the goods have so deteriorated as no longer to conform to the contract the buyer may nevertheless demand inspection and at his option either treat the contract as voided or accept the goods with due allowance from the contract price for the deterioration or the deficiency in quantity but without further right against the seller.

§ 2–614. Substituted Performance.

(1) Where without fault of either party the agreed berthing, loading, or unloading facilities fail or an agreed type of carrier becomes unavailable or the agreed manner of delivery otherwise becomes commercially impracticable but a commercially reasonable substitute is available, such substitute performance must be tendered and accepted.

(2) If the agreed means or manner of payment fails because of domestic or foreign governmental regulation, the seller may withhold or stop delivery unless the buyer provides a means or manner of payment which is commercially a substantial equivalent. If delivery has already been taken, payment by the means or in the manner provided by the regulation discharges the buyer's obligation unless the regulation is discriminatory, oppressive or predatory.

§ 2–615. Excuse by Failure of Presupposed Conditions.

Except so far as a seller may have assumed a greater obligation and subject to the preceding section on substituted performance:

(a) Delay in delivery or non-delivery in whole or in part by a seller who complies with paragraphs (b) and (c) is not a breach of his duty under a contract for sale if performance as agreed has been made impracticable by the occurrence of a contingency the nonoccurrence of which was a basic assumption on which the contract was made or by compliance in good faith with any applicable foreign or domestic governmental regulation or order whether or not it later proves to be invalid.

(b) Where the causes mentioned in paragraph (a) affect only a part of the seller's capacity to perform, he must allocate production and deliveries among his customers but may at his option include regular customers not then under contract as well as his own requirements for further manufacture. He may so allocate in any manner which is fair and reasonable.

(c) The seller must notify the buyer seasonably that there will be delay or non-delivery and, when allocation is required under paragraph (b), of the estimated quota thus made available for the buyer.

§ 2–616. Procedure on Notice Claiming Excuse.

(1) Where the buyer receives notification of a material or indefinite delay or an allocation justified under the preceding section he may by written notification to the seller as to any delivery concerned, and where the prospective deficiency substantially impairs the value of the whole contract under the provisions of this Article relating to breach of installment contracts (Section 2–612), then also as to the whole,

(a) terminate and thereby discharge any unexecuted portion of the contract; or

(b) modify the contract by agreeing to take his available quota in substitution.

(2) If after receipt of such notification from the seller the buyer fails so to modify the contract within a reasonable time not exceeding thirty days the contract lapses with respect to any deliveries affected.

(3) The provisions of this section may not be negated by agreement except in so far as the seller has assumed a greater obligation under the preceding section.

Part 7 Remedies

§ 2–701. Remedies for Breach of Collateral Contracts Not Impaired.

Remedies for breach of any obligation or promise collateral or ancillary to a contract for sale are not impaired by the provisions of this Article.

§ 2–702. Seller's Remedies on Discovery of Buyer's Insolvency.

(1) Where the seller discovers the buyer to be insolvent he may refuse delivery except for cash including payment for all goods theretofore delivered under the contract, and stop delivery under this Article (Section 2–705).

(2) Where the seller discovers that the buyer has received goods on credit while insolvent he may reclaim the goods upon demand made within ten days after the receipt, but if misrepresentation of solvency has been made to the particular seller in writing within three months before delivery the ten day limitation does not apply. Except as provided in this subsection the seller may not base a right to reclaim goods on the buyer's fraudulent or innocent misrepresentation of solvency or of intent to pay.

(3) The seller's right to reclaim under subsection (2) is subject to the rights of a buyer in ordinary course or other good faith purchaser under this Article (Section 2–403). Successful reclamation of goods excludes all other remedies with respect to them.

§ 2–703. Seller's Remedies in General.

Where the buyer wrongfully rejects or revokes acceptance of goods or fails to make a payment due on or before delivery or repudiates with respect to a part or the whole, then with respect to any goods directly affected and, if the breach is of the whole contract (Section 2–612), then also with respect to the whole undelivered balance, the aggrieved seller may

(a) withhold delivery of such goods;

(b) stop delivery by any bailee as hereafter provided (Section 2–705);

(c) proceed under the next section respecting goods still unidentified to the contract;

(d) resell and recover damages as hereafter provided (Section 2–706);

(e) recover damages for non-acceptance (Section 2–708) or in a proper case the price (Section 2–709);

(f) cancel.

§ 2–704. Seller's Right to Identify Goods to the Contract Notwithstanding Breach or to Salvage Unfinished Goods.

(1) An aggrieved seller under the preceding section may

(a) identify to the contract conforming goods not already identified if at the time he learned of the breach they are in his possession or control;

(b) treat as the subject of resale goods which have demonstrably been intended for the particular contract even though those goods are unfinished.

(2) Where the goods are unfinished an aggrieved seller may in the exercise of reasonable commercial judgment for the purposes of avoiding loss and of effective realization either complete the manufacture and wholly identify the goods to the contract or cease manufacture and resell for scrap or salvage value or proceed in any other reasonable manner.

§ 2–705. Seller's Stoppage of Delivery in Transit or Otherwise.

(1) The seller may stop delivery of goods in the possession of a carrier or other bailee when he discovers the buyer to be insolvent (Section 2–702) and may stop delivery of carload, truckload, planeload or larger shipments of express or freight when the buyer repudiates or fails to make a payment due before delivery or if for any other reason the seller has a right to withhold or reclaim the goods.

(2) As against such buyer the seller may stop delivery until

(a) receipt of the goods by the buyer; or

(b) acknowledgment to the buyer by any bailee of the goods except a carrier that the bailee holds the goods for the buyer; or

(c) such acknowledgment to the buyer by a carrier by reshipment or as warehouseman; or

(d) negotiation to the buyer of any negotiable document of title covering the goods.

(3) (a) To stop delivery the seller must so notify as to enable the bailee by reasonable diligence to prevent delivery of the goods.

(b) After such notification the bailee must hold and deliver the goods according to the directions of the seller but the seller is liable to the bailee for any ensuing charges or damages.

(c) If a negotiable document of title has been issued for goods the bailee is not obliged to obey a notification to stop until surrender of the document.

(d) A carrier who has issued a non-negotiable bill of lading is not obliged to obey a notification to stop received from a person other than the consignor.

§ 2–706. Seller's Resale Including Contract for Resale.

(1) Under the conditions stated in Section 2–703 on seller's remedies, the seller may resell the goods concerned or the undelivered balance thereof. Where the resale is made in good faith and in a commercially reasonable manner the seller may recover the difference between the resale price and the contract price together with any incidental damages allowed under the provisions of this Article (Section 2–710), but less expenses saved in consequence of the buyer's breach.

(2) Except as otherwise provided in subsection (3) or unless otherwise agreed resale may be at public or private sale including sale by way of one or more contracts to sell or of identification to an existing contract of the seller. Sale may be as a unit or in parcels and at any time and place and on any terms but every aspect of the sale including the method, manner, time, place and terms must be commercially reasonable. The resale must be reasonably identified as referring to the broken contract, but it is not necessary that the goods be in existence or that any or all of them have been identified to the contract before the breach.

(3) Where the resale is at private sale the seller must give the buyer reasonable notification of his intention to resell.

(4) Where the resale is at public sale

(a) only identified goods can be sold except where there is a recognized market for a public sale of futures in goods of the kind; and

(b) it must be made at a usual place or market for public sale if one is reasonably available and except in the case of goods which are perishable or threaten to decline in value speedily the seller must give the buyer reasonable notice of the time and place of the resale; and

(c) if the goods are not to be within the view of those attending the sale the notification of sale must state the place where the goods are located and provide for their reasonable inspection by prospective bidders; and

(d) the seller may buy.

(5) A purchaser who buys in good faith at a resale takes the goods free of any rights of the original buyer even though the seller fails to comply with one or more of the requirements of this section.

(6) The seller is not accountable to the buyer for any profit made on any resale. A person in the position of a seller (Section 2–707) or a buyer who has rightfully rejected or justifiably revoked acceptance must account for any excess over the amount of his security interest, as hereinafter defined (subsection (3) of Section 2–711).

§ 2–707. "Person in the Position of a Seller".

(1) A "person in the position of a seller" includes as against a principal an agent who has paid or become responsible for the price of goods on behalf of his principal or anyone who otherwise holds a security interest or other right in goods similar to that of a seller.

(2) A person in the position of a seller may as provided in this Article withhold or stop delivery (Section 2–705) and resell (Section 2–706) and recover incidental damages (Section 2–710).

§ 2–708. Seller's Damages for Non-Acceptance or Repudiation.

(1) Subject to subsection (2) and to the provisions of this Article with respect to proof of market price (Section 2–723), the measure of damages for non-acceptance or repudiation by the buyer is the difference between the market price at the time and place for tender and the unpaid contract price together with any incidental damages provided in this Article (Section 2–710), but less expenses saved in consequence of the buyer's breach.

(2) If the measure of damages provided in subsection (1) is inadequate to put the seller in as good a position as performance would have done then the measure of damages is the profit (including reasonable overhead) which the seller would have made from full performance by the buyer, together with any incidental damages provided in this Article (Section 2–710), due allowance for costs reasonably incurred and due credit for payments or proceeds of resale.

§ 2–709. Action for the Price.

(1) When the buyer fails to pay the price as it becomes due the seller may recover, together with any incidental damages under the next section, the price

(a) of goods accepted or of conforming goods lost or damaged within a commercially reasonable time after risk of their loss has passed to the buyer; and

(b) of goods identified to the contract if the seller is unable after reasonable effort to resell them at a reasonable price or the circumstances reasonably indicate that such effort will be unavailing.

(2) Where the seller sues for the price he must hold for the buyer any goods which have been identified to the contract and are still in his control except that if resale becomes possible he may resell them at any time prior to the collection of the judgment. The net proceeds of any such resale must be credited to the buyer and payment of the judgment entitles him to any goods not resold.

(3) After the buyer has wrongfully rejected or revoked acceptance of the goods or has failed to make a payment due or has repudiated (Section 2–610), a seller who is held not entitled to the price under this section shall nevertheless be awarded damages for non-acceptance under the preceding section.

§ 2–710. Seller's Incidental Damages.

Incidental damages to an aggrieved seller include any commercially reasonable charges, expenses or commissions incurred in stopping delivery, in the transportation, care and custody of goods after the buyer's breach, in connection with return or resale of the goods or otherwise resulting from the breach.

§ 2–711. Buyer's Remedies in General; Buyer's Security Interest in Rejected Goods.

(1) Where the seller fails to make delivery or repudiates or the buyer rightfully rejects or justifiably revokes acceptance then with respect to any goods involved, and with respect to the whole if the breach goes to the whole contract (Section 2–612), the buyer may cancel and whether or not he has done so may in addition to recovering so much of the price as has been paid

(a) "cover" and have damages under the next section as to all the goods affected whether or not they have been identified to the contract; or

(b) recover damages for non-delivery as provided in this Article (Section 2–713).

(2) Where the seller fails to deliver or repudiates the buyer may also

(a) if the goods have been identified recover them as provided in this Article (Section 2–502); or

(b) in a proper case obtain specific performance or replevy the goods as provided in this Article (Section 2–716).

(3) On rightful rejection or justifiable revocation of acceptance a buyer has a security interest in goods in his possession or control for any payments made on their price and any expenses reasonably incurred in their inspection, receipt, transportation, care and custody and may hold such goods and resell them in like manner as an aggrieved seller (Section 2–706).

§ 2–712. "Cover"; Buyer's Procurement of Substitute Goods.

(1) After a breach within the preceding section the buyer may "cover" by making in good faith and without unreasonable delay any reasonable purchase of or contract to purchase goods in substitution for those due from the seller.

(2) The buyer may recover from the seller as damages the difference between the cost of cover and the contract price together with any incidental or consequential damages as hereinafter defined (Section 2–715), but less expenses saved in consequence of the seller's breach.

(3) Failure of the buyer to effect cover within this section does not bar him from any other remedy.

§ 2–713. Buyer's Damages for Non-Delivery or Repudiation.

(1) Subject to the provisions of this Article with respect to proof of market price (Section 2–723), the measure of damages for non-delivery or repudiation by the seller is the difference between the market price at the time when the buyer learned of the breach and the contract price together with any incidental and consequential damages provided in this Article (Section 2–715), but less expenses saved in consequence of the seller's breach.

(2) Market price is to be determined as of the place for tender or, in cases of rejection after arrival or revocation of acceptance, as of the place of arrival.

§ 2–714. Buyer's Damages for Breach in Regard to Accepted Goods.

(1) Where the buyer has accepted goods and given notification (subsection (3) of Section 2–607) he may recover as damages for any non-conformity of tender the loss resulting in the ordinary course of events from the seller's breach as determined in any manner which is reasonable.

(2) The measure of damages for breach of warranty is the difference at the time and place of acceptance between the value of the goods accepted and the value they would have had if they had been as warranted, unless special circumstances show proximate damages of a different amount.

(3) In a proper case any incidental and consequential damages under the next section may also be recovered.

§ 2–715. Buyer's Incidental and Consequential Damages.

(1) Incidental damages resulting from the seller's breach include expenses reasonably incurred in inspection, receipt, transportation and care and custody of goods rightfully rejected, any commercially reasonable charges, expenses or commissions in connection with effecting cover and any other reasonable expense incident to the delay or other breach.

(2) Consequential damages resulting from the seller's breach include

(a) any loss resulting from general or particular requirements and needs of which the seller at the time of contracting had reason to know and which could not reasonably be prevented by cover or otherwise; and

(b) injury to person or property proximately resulting from any breach of warranty.

§ 2–716. Buyer's Right to Specific Performance or Replevin.

(1) Specific performance may be decreed where the goods are unique or in other proper circumstances.

(2) The decree for specific performance may include such terms and conditions as to payment of the price, damages, or other relief as the court may deem just.

(3) The buyer has a right of replevin for goods identified to the contract if after reasonable effort he is unable to effect cover for such goods or the circumstances reasonably indicate that such effort will be unavailing or if the goods have been shipped under reservation and satisfaction of the security interest in them has been made or tendered. In the case of goods bought for personal, family, or household purposes, the buyer's right of replevin vests upon acquisition of a special property, even if the seller had not then repudiated or failed to deliver. As amended in 1999.

§ 2–717. Deduction of Damages From the Price.

The buyer on notifying the seller of his intention to do so may deduct all or any part of the damages resulting from any breach of the contract from any part of the price still due under the same contract.

§ 2–718. Liquidation or Limitation of Damages; Deposits.

(1) Damages for breach by either party may be liquidated in the agreement but only at an amount which is reasonable in the light of the anticipated or actual harm caused by the breach, the difficulties of proof of loss, and the inconvenience or nonfeasibility of otherwise obtaining an adequate remedy. A term fixing unreasonably large liquidated damages is void as a penalty.

(2) Where the seller justifiably withholds delivery of goods because of the buyer's breach, the buyer is entitled to restitution of any amount by which the sum of his payments exceeds

(a) the amount to which the seller is entitled by virtue of terms liquidating the seller's damages in accordance with subsection (1), or

(b) in the absence of such terms, twenty per cent of the value of the total performance for which the buyer is obligated under the contract or $500, whichever is smaller.

(3) The buyer's right to restitution under subsection (2) is subject to offset to the extent that the seller establishes

(a) a right to recover damages under the provisions of this Article other than subsection (1), and

(b) the amount or value of any benefits received by the buyer directly or indirectly by reason of the contract.

(4) Where a seller has received payment in goods their reasonable value or the proceeds of their resale shall be treated as payments for the purposes of subsection (2); but if the seller has notice of the buyer's breach before reselling goods received in part performance, his resale is subject to the conditions laid down in this Article on resale by an aggrieved seller (Section 2–706).

§ 2–719. Contractual Modification or Limitation of Remedy.

(1) Subject to the provisions of subsections (2) and (3) of this section and of the preceding section on liquidation and limitation of damages,

(a) the agreement may provide for remedies in addition to or in substitution for those provided in this Article and may limit or alter the measure of damages recoverable under this Article, as by limiting the buyer's remedies to return of the goods and repayment of the price or to repair and replacement of nonconforming goods or parts; and

(b) resort to a remedy as provided is optional unless the remedy is expressly agreed to be exclusive, in which case it is the sole remedy.

(2) Where circumstances cause an exclusive or limited remedy to fail of its essential purpose, remedy may be had as provided in this Act.

(3) Consequential damages may be limited or excluded unless the limitation or exclusion is unconscionable. Limitation of consequential damages for injury to the person in the case of consumer goods is prima facie unconscionable but limitation of damages where the loss is commercial is not.

§ 2–720. Effect of "Cancellation" or "Rescission" on Claims for Antecedent Breach.

Unless the contrary intention clearly appears, expressions of "cancellation" or "rescission" of the contract or the like shall not be construed as a renunciation or discharge of any claim in damages for an antecedent breach.

§ 2–721. Remedies for Fraud.

Remedies for material misrepresentation or fraud include all remedies available under this Article for non-fraudulent breach. Neither rescission or a claim for rescission of the contract for sale nor rejection or return of the goods shall bar or be deemed inconsistent with a claim for damages or other remedy.

§ 2–722. Who Can Sue Third Parties for Injury to Goods.

Where a third party so deals with goods which have been identified to a contract for sale as to cause actionable injury to a party to that contract

(a) a right of action against the third party is in either party to the contract for sale who has title to or a security interest or a special property or an insurable interest in the goods; and if the goods have been destroyed or converted a right of action is also in the party who either bore the risk of loss under the contract for sale or has since the injury assumed that risk as against the other;

(b) if at the time of the injury the party plaintiff did not bear the risk of loss as against the other party to the contract for sale and there is no arrangement between them for disposition of the recovery, his suit or settlement is, subject to his own interest, as a fiduciary for the other party to the contract;

(c) either party may with the consent of the other sue for the benefit of whom it may concern.

§ 2–723. Proof of Market Price: Time and Place.

(1) If an action based on anticipatory repudiation comes to trial before the time for performance with respect to some or all of the goods, any damages based on market price (Section 2–708 or Section 2–713) shall be determined according to the price of such goods prevailing at the time when the aggrieved party learned of the repudiation.

(2) If evidence of a price prevailing at the times or places described in this Article is not readily available the price prevailing within any reasonable time before or after the time described or at any other place which in commercial judgment or under usage of trade would serve as a reasonable substitute for the one described may be used, making any proper allowance for the cost of transporting the goods to or from such other place.

(3) Evidence of a relevant price prevailing at a time or place other than the one described in this Article offered by one party is not admissible unless and until he has given the other party such notice as the court finds sufficient to prevent unfair surprise.

§ 2–724. Admissibility of Market Quotations.

Whenever the prevailing price or value of any goods regularly bought and sold in any established commodity market is in issue, reports in official publications or trade journals or in newspapers or periodicals of general circulation published as the reports of such market shall be admissible in evidence. The circumstances of the preparation of such a report may be shown to affect its weight but not its admissibility.

§ 2–725. Statute of Limitations in Contracts for Sale.

(1) An action for breach of any contract for sale must be commenced within four years after the cause of action has accrued. By the original agreement the parties may reduce the period of limitation to not less than one year but may not extend it.

(2) A cause of action accrues when the breach occurs, regardless of the aggrieved party's lack of knowledge of the breach. A breach of warranty occurs when tender of delivery is made, except that where a warranty explicitly extends to future performance of the goods and discovery of the breach must await the time of such performance the cause of action accrues when the breach is or should have been discovered.

(3) Where an action commenced within the time limited by subsection (1) is so terminated as to leave available a remedy by another action for the same breach such other action may be commenced after the expiration of the time limited and within six months after the termination of the first action unless the termination resulted from voluntary discontinuance or from dismissal for failure or neglect to prosecute.

(4) This section does not alter the law on tolling of the statute of limitations nor does it apply to causes of action which have accrued before this Act becomes effective.

Article 2A
LEASES

Part 1 General Provisions

§ 2A–101. Short Title.

This Article shall be known and may be cited as the Uniform Commercial Code—Leases.

§ 2A–102. Scope.

This Article applies to any transaction, regardless of form, that creates a lease.

§ 2A–103. Definitions and Index of Definitions.

(1) In this Article unless the context otherwise requires:

(a) "Buyer in ordinary course of business" means a person who in good faith and without knowledge that the sale to him [or her] is in violation of the ownership rights or security interest or leasehold interest of a third party in the goods buys in ordinary course from a person in the business of selling goods of that kind but does not include a pawnbroker. "Buying" may be for cash or by exchange of other property or on secured or unsecured credit and includes receiving goods or documents of title under a pre-existing contract for sale but does not include a transfer in bulk or as security for or in total or partial satisfaction of a money debt.

(b) "Cancellation" occurs when either party puts an end to the lease contract for default by the other party.

(c) "Commercial unit" means such a unit of goods as by commercial usage is a single whole for purposes of lease and division of which materially impairs its character or value on the market or in use. A commercial unit may be a single article, as a machine, or a set of articles, as a suite of furniture or a line of machinery, or a quantity, as a gross or carload, or any other unit treated in use or in the relevant market as a single whole.

(d) "Conforming" goods or performance under a lease contract means goods or performance that are in accordance with the obligations under the lease contract.

(e) "Consumer lease" means a lease that a lessor regularly engaged in the business of leasing or selling makes to a lessee who is an individual and who takes under the lease primarily for a personal, family, or household purpose [, if the total payments to be made under the lease contract, excluding payments for options to renew or buy, do not exceed $_____].

(f) "Fault" means wrongful act, omission, breach, or default.

(g) "Finance lease" means a lease with respect to which:

(i) the lessor does not select, manufacture or supply the goods;

(ii) the lessor acquires the goods or the right to possession and use of the goods in connection with the lease; and

(iii) one of the following occurs:

(A) the lessee receives a copy of the contract by which the lessor acquired the goods or the right to possession and use of the goods before signing the lease contract;

(B) the lessee's approval of the contract by which the lessor acquired the goods or the right to possession and use of the goods is a condition to effectiveness of the lease contract;

(C) the lessee, before signing the lease contract, receives an accurate and complete statement designating the promises and warranties, and any disclaimers of warranties, limitations or modifications of remedies, or liquidated damages, including those of a third party, such as the manufacturer of the goods, provided to the lessor by the person supplying the goods in connection with or as part of the contract by which the lessor acquired the goods or the right to possession and use of the goods; or

(D) if the lease is not a consumer lease, the lessor, before the lessee signs the lease contract, informs the lessee in writing (a) of the identity of the person supplying the goods to the lessor, unless the lessee has selected that person and directed the lessor to acquire the goods or the right to possession and use of the goods from that person, (b) that the lessee is entitled under this Article to any promises and warranties, including those of any third party, provided to the lessor by the person supplying the goods in connection with or as part of the contract by which the lessor acquired the goods or the right to possession and use of the goods, and (c) that the lessee may communicate with the person supplying the goods to the lessor and receive an accurate and complete statement of those promises and warranties, including any disclaimers and limitations of them or of remedies.

(h) "Goods" means all things that are movable at the time of identification to the lease contract, or are fixtures (Section 2A–309), but the term does not include money, documents, instruments, accounts, chattel paper, general intangibles, or

minerals or the like, including oil and gas, before extraction. The term also includes the unborn young of animals.

(i) "Installment lease contract" means a lease contract that authorizes or requires the delivery of goods in separate lots to be separately accepted, even though the lease contract contains a clause "each delivery is a separate lease" or its equivalent.

(j) "Lease" means a transfer of the right to possession and use of goods for a term in return for consideration, but a sale, including a sale on approval or a sale or return, or retention or creation of a security interest is not a lease. Unless the context clearly indicates otherwise, the term includes a sublease.

(k) "Lease agreement" means the bargain, with respect to the lease, of the lessor and the lessee in fact as found in their language or by implication from other circumstances including course of dealing or usage of trade or course of performance as provided in this Article. Unless the context clearly indicates otherwise, the term includes a sublease agreement.

(l) "Lease contract" means the total legal obligation that results from the lease agreement as affected by this Article and any other applicable rules of law. Unless the context clearly indicates otherwise, the term includes a sublease contract.

(m) "Leasehold interest" means the interest of the lessor or the lessee under a lease contract.

(n) "Lessee" means a person who acquires the right to possession and use of goods under a lease. Unless the context clearly indicates otherwise, the term includes a sublessee.

(o) "Lessee in ordinary course of business" means a person who in good faith and without knowledge that the lease to him [or her] is in violation of the ownership rights or security interest or leasehold interest of a third party in the goods, leases in ordinary course from a person in the business of selling or leasing goods of that kind but does not include a pawnbroker. "Leasing" may be for cash or by exchange of other property or on secured or unsecured credit and includes receiving goods or documents of title under a pre-existing lease contract but does not include a transfer in bulk or as security for or in total or partial satisfaction of a money debt.

(p) "Lessor" means a person who transfers the right to possession and use of goods under a lease. Unless the context clearly indicates otherwise, the term includes a sublessor.

(q) "Lessor's residual interest" means the lessor's interest in the goods after expiration, termination, or cancellation of the lease contract.

(r) "Lien" means a charge against or interest in goods to secure payment of a debt or performance of an obligation, but the term does not include a security interest.

(s) "Lot" means a parcel or a single article that is the subject matter of a separate lease or delivery, whether or not it is sufficient to perform the lease contract.

(t) "Merchant lessee" means a lessee that is a merchant with respect to goods of the kind subject to the lease.

(u) "Present value" means the amount as of a date certain of one or more sums payable in the future, discounted to the date certain. The discount is determined by the interest rate specified by the parties if the rate was not manifestly unreasonable at the time the transaction was entered into; otherwise, the discount is determined by a commercially reasonable rate that takes into account the facts and circumstances of each case at the time the transaction was entered into.

(v) "Purchase" includes taking by sale, lease, mortgage, security interest, pledge, gift, or any other voluntary transaction creating an interest in goods.

(w) "Sublease" means a lease of goods the right to possession and use of which was acquired by the lessor as a lessee under an existing lease.

(x) "Supplier" means a person from whom a lessor buys or leases goods to be leased under a finance lease.

(y) "Supply contract" means a contract under which a lessor buys or leases goods to be leased.

(z) "Termination" occurs when either party pursuant to a power created by agreement or law puts an end to the lease contract otherwise than for default.

(2) Other definitions applying to this Article and the sections in which they appear are:

"Accessions". Section 2A–310(1).
"Construction mortgage". Section 2A–309(1)(d).
"Encumbrance". Section 2A–309(1)(e).
"Fixtures". Section 2A–309(1)(a).
"Fixture filing". Section 2A–309(1)(b).
"Purchase money lease". Section 2A–309(1)(c).

(3) The following definitions in other Articles apply to this Article:

"Accounts". Section 9–106.
"Between merchants". Section 2–104(3).
"Buyer". Section 2–103(1)(a).
"Chattel paper". Section 9–105(1)(b).
"Consumer goods". Section 9–109(1).
"Document". Section 9–105(1)(f).
"Entrusting". Section 2–403(3).
"General intangibles". Section 9–106.
"Good faith". Section 2–103(1)(b).
"Instrument". Section 9–105(1)(i).
"Merchant". Section 2–104(1).
"Mortgage". Section 9–105(1)(j).
"Pursuant to commitment". Section 9–105(1)(k).
"Receipt". Section 2–103(1)(c).
"Sale". Section 2–106(1).
"Sale on approval". Section 2–326.
"Sale or return". Section 2–326.
"Seller". Section 2–103(1)(d).

(4) In addition Article 1 contains general definitions and principles of construction and interpretation applicable throughout this Article.

As amended in 1990 and 1999.

§ 2A–104. Leases Subject to Other Law.

(1) A lease, although subject to this Article, is also subject to any applicable:

(a) certificate of title statute of this State: (list any certificate of title statutes covering automobiles, trailers, mobile homes, boats, farm tractors, and the like);

(b) certificate of title statute of another jurisdiction (Section 2A–105); or

(c) consumer protection statute of this State, or final consumer protection decision of a court of this State existing on the effective date of this Article.

(2) In case of conflict between this Article, other than Sections 2A–105, 2A–304(3), and 2A–305(3), and a statute or decision referred to in subsection (1), the statute or decision controls.

(3) Failure to comply with an applicable law has only the effect specified therein.

As amended in 1990.

§ 2A–105. Territorial Application of Article to Goods Covered by Certificate of Title.

Subject to the provisions of Sections 2A–304(3) and 2A–305(3), with respect to goods covered by a certificate of title issued under a statute of this State or of another jurisdiction, compliance and the effect of compliance or noncompliance with a certificate of title statute are governed by the law (including the conflict of laws rules) of the jurisdiction issuing the certificate until the earlier of (a) surrender of the certificate, or (b) four months after the goods are removed from that jurisdiction and thereafter until a new certificate of title is issued by another jurisdiction.

§ 2A–106. Limitation on Power of Parties to Consumer Lease to Choose Applicable Law and Judicial Forum.

(1) If the law chosen by the parties to a consumer lease is that of a jurisdiction other than a jurisdiction in which the lessee resides at the time the lease agreement becomes enforceable or within 30 days thereafter or in which the goods are to be used, the choice is not enforceable.

(2) If the judicial forum chosen by the parties to a consumer lease is a forum that would not otherwise have jurisdiction over the lessee, the choice is not enforceable.

§ 2A–107. Waiver or Renunciation of Claim or Right After Default.

Any claim or right arising out of an alleged default or breach of warranty may be discharged in whole or in part without consideration by a written waiver or renunciation signed and delivered by the aggrieved party.

§ 2A–108. Unconscionability.

(1) If the court as a matter of law finds a lease contract or any clause of a lease contract to have been unconscionable at the time it was made the court may refuse to enforce the lease contract, or it may enforce the remainder of the lease contract without the unconscionable clause, or it may so limit the application of any unconscionable clause as to avoid any unconscionable result.

(2) With respect to a consumer lease, if the court as a matter of law finds that a lease contract or any clause of a lease contract has been induced by unconscionable conduct or that unconscionable conduct has occurred in the collection of a claim arising from a lease contract, the court may grant appropriate relief.

(3) Before making a finding of unconscionability under subsection (1) or (2), the court, on its own motion or that of a party, shall afford the parties a reasonable opportunity to present evidence as to the setting, purpose, and effect of the lease contract or clause thereof, or of the conduct.

(4) In an action in which the lessee claims unconscionability with respect to a consumer lease:

(a) If the court finds unconscionability under subsection (1) or (2), the court shall award reasonable attorney's fees to the lessee.

(b) If the court does not find unconscionability and the lessee claiming unconscionability has brought or maintained an action he [or she] knew to be groundless, the court shall award reasonable attorney's fees to the party against whom the claim is made.

(c) In determining attorney's fees, the amount of the recovery on behalf of the claimant under subsections (1) and (2) is not controlling.

§ 2A–109. Option to Accelerate at Will.

(1) A term providing that one party or his [or her] successor in interest may accelerate payment or performance or require collateral or additional collateral "at will" or "when he [or she] deems himself [or herself] insecure" or in words of similar import must be construed to mean that he [or she] has power to do so only if he [or she] in good faith believes that the prospect of payment or performance is impaired.

(2) With respect to a consumer lease, the burden of establishing good faith under subsection (1) is on the party who exercised the power; otherwise the burden of establishing lack of good faith is on the party against whom the power has been exercised.

Part 2 Formation and Construction of Lease Contract

§ 2A–201. Statute of Frauds.

(1) A lease contract is not enforceable by way of action or defense unless:

(a) the total payments to be made under the lease contract, excluding payments for options to renew or buy, are less than $1,000; or

(b) there is a writing, signed by the party against whom enforcement is sought or by that party's authorized agent, sufficient to indicate that a lease contract has been made between the parties and to describe the goods leased and the lease term.

(2) Any description of leased goods or of the lease term is sufficient and satisfies subsection (1)(b), whether or not it is specific, if it reasonably identifies what is described.

(3) A writing is not insufficient because it omits or incorrectly states a term agreed upon, but the lease contract is not enforceable under subsection (1)(b) beyond the lease term and the quantity of goods shown in the writing.

(4) A lease contract that does not satisfy the requirements of subsection (1), but which is valid in other respects, is enforceable:

(a) if the goods are to be specially manufactured or obtained for the lessee and are not suitable for lease or sale to others in the ordinary course of the lessor's business, and the lessor, before notice of repudiation is received and under circumstances that reasonably indicate that the goods are for the lessee, has made either a substantial beginning of their manufacture or commitments for their procurement;

(b) if the party against whom enforcement is sought admits in that party's pleading, testimony or otherwise in court that a lease contract was made, but the lease contract is not enforceable under this provision beyond the quantity of goods admitted; or

(c) with respect to goods that have been received and accepted by the lessee.

(5) The lease term under a lease contract referred to in subsection (4) is:

(a) if there is a writing signed by the party against whom enforcement is sought or by that party's authorized agent specifying the lease term, the term so specified;

(b) if the party against whom enforcement is sought admits in that party's pleading, testimony, or otherwise in court a lease term, the term so admitted; or

(c) a reasonable lease term.

§ 2A–202. Final Written Expression: Parol or Extrinsic Evidence.

Terms with respect to which the confirmatory memoranda of the parties agree or which are otherwise set forth in a writing intended by the parties as a final expression of their agreement with respect to such terms as are included therein may not be contradicted by evidence of any prior agreement or of a contemporaneous oral agreement but may be explained or supplemented:

(a) by course of dealing or usage of trade or by course of performance; and

(b) by evidence of consistent additional terms unless the court finds the writing to have been intended also as a complete and exclusive statement of the terms of the agreement.

§ 2A–203. Seals Inoperative.

The affixing of a seal to a writing evidencing a lease contract or an offer to enter into a lease contract does not render the writing a sealed instrument and the law with respect to sealed instruments does not apply to the lease contract or offer.

§ 2A–204. Formation in General.

(1) A lease contract may be made in any manner sufficient to show agreement, including conduct by both parties which recognizes the existence of a lease contract.

(2) An agreement sufficient to constitute a lease contract may be found although the moment of its making is undetermined.

(3) Although one or more terms are left open, a lease contract does not fail for indefiniteness if the parties have intended to make a lease contract and there is a reasonably certain basis for giving an appropriate remedy.

§ 2A–205. Firm Offers.

An offer by a merchant to lease goods to or from another person in a signed writing that by its terms gives assurance it will be held open is not revocable, for lack of consideration, during the time stated or, if no time is stated, for a reasonable time, but in no event may the period of irrevocability exceed 3 months. Any such term of assurance on a form supplied by the offeree must be separately signed by the offeror.

§ 2A–206. Offer and Acceptance in Formation of Lease Contract.

(1) Unless otherwise unambiguously indicated by the language or circumstances, an offer to make a lease contract must be construed as inviting acceptance in any manner and by any medium reasonable in the circumstances.

(2) If the beginning of a requested performance is a reasonable mode of acceptance, an offeror who is not notified of acceptance within a reasonable time may treat the offer as having lapsed before acceptance.

§ 2A–207. Course of Performance or Practical Construction.

(1) If a lease contract involves repeated occasions for performance by either party with knowledge of the nature of the performance and opportunity for objection to it by the other, any course of performance accepted or acquiesced in without objection is relevant to determine the meaning of the lease agreement.

(2) The express terms of a lease agreement and any course of performance, as well as any course of dealing and usage of trade, must be construed whenever reasonable as consistent with each other; but if that construction is unreasonable, express terms control course of performance, course of performance controls both course of dealing and usage of trade, and course of dealing controls usage of trade.

(3) Subject to the provisions of Section 2A–208 on modification and waiver, course of performance is relevant to show a waiver or modification of any term inconsistent with the course of performance.

§ 2A–208. Modification, Rescission and Waiver.

(1) An agreement modifying a lease contract needs no consideration to be binding.

(2) A signed lease agreement that excludes modification or rescission except by a signed writing may not be otherwise modified or rescinded, but, except as between merchants, such a requirement on a form supplied by a merchant must be separately signed by the other party.

(3) Although an attempt at modification or rescission does not satisfy the requirements of subsection (2), it may operate as a waiver.

(4) A party who has made a waiver affecting an executory portion of a lease contract may retract the waiver by reasonable notification received by the other party that strict performance will be required of any term waived, unless the retraction would be unjust in view of a material change of position in reliance on the waiver.

§ 2A–209. Lessee under Finance Lease as Beneficiary of Supply Contract.

(1) The benefit of the supplier's promises to the lessor under the supply contract and of all warranties, whether express or implied, including those of any third party provided in connection with or as part of the supply contract, extends to the lessee to the extent of the lessee's leasehold interest under a finance lease related to the supply contract, but is subject to the terms warranty and of the supply contract and all defenses or claims arising therefrom.

(2) The extension of the benefit of supplier's promises and of warranties to the lessee (Section 2A–209(1)) does not: (i) modify the rights and obligations of the parties to the supply contract, whether arising therefrom or otherwise, or (ii) impose any duty or liability under the supply contract on the lessee.

(3) Any modification or rescission of the supply contract by the supplier and the lessor is effective between the supplier and the lessee unless, before the modification or rescission, the supplier has received notice that the lessee has entered into a finance lease related to the supply contract. If the modification or rescission is effective between the supplier and the lessee, the lessor is deemed to have assumed, in addition to the obligations of the lessor to the lessee under the lease contract, promises of the supplier to the lessor and warranties that were so modified or rescinded as they existed and were available to the lessee before modification or rescission.

(4) In addition to the extension of the benefit of the supplier's promises and of warranties to the lessee under subsection (1), the lessee retains all rights that the lessee may have against the supplier which arise from an agreement between the lessee and the supplier or under other law. As amended in 1990.

§ 2A–210. Express Warranties.

(1) Express warranties by the lessor are created as follows:

(a) Any affirmation of fact or promise made by the lessor to the lessee which relates to the goods and becomes part of the basis of the bargain creates an express warranty that the goods will conform to the affirmation or promise.

(b) Any description of the goods which is made part of the basis of the bargain creates an express warranty that the goods will conform to the description.

(c) Any sample or model that is made part of the basis of the bargain creates an express warranty that the whole of the goods will conform to the sample or model.

(2) It is not necessary to the creation of an express warranty that the lessor use formal words, such as "warrant" or "guarantee," or that the lessor have a specific intention to make a warranty, but an affirmation merely of the value of the goods or a statement purporting to be merely the lessor's opinion or commendation of the goods does not create a warranty.

§ 2A–211. Warranties Against Interference and Against Infringement; Lessee's Obligation Against Infringement.

(1) There is in a lease contract a warranty that for the lease term no person holds a claim to or interest in the goods that arose from an act or omission of the lessor, other than a claim by way of infringement or the like, which will interfere with the lessee's enjoyment of its leasehold interest.

(2) Except in a finance lease there is in a lease contract by a lessor who is a merchant regularly dealing in goods of the kind a warranty that the goods are delivered free of the rightful claim of any person by way of infringement or the like.

(3) A lessee who furnishes specifications to a lessor or a supplier shall hold the lessor and the supplier harmless against any claim by way of infringement or the like that arises out of compliance with the specifications.

§ 2A–212. Implied Warranty of Merchantability.

(1) Except in a finance lease, a warranty that the goods will be merchantable is implied in a lease contract if the lessor is a merchant with respect to goods of that kind.

(2) Goods to be merchantable must be at least such as

(a) pass without objection in the trade under the description in the lease agreement;

(b) in the case of fungible goods, are of fair average quality within the description;

(c) are fit for the ordinary purposes for which goods of that type are used;

(d) run, within the variation permitted by the lease agreement, of even kind, quality, and quantity within each unit and among all units involved;

(e) are adequately contained, packaged, and labeled as the lease agreement may require; and

(f) conform to any promises or affirmations of fact made on the container or label.

(3) Other implied warranties may arise from course of dealing or usage of trade.

§ 2A–213. Implied Warranty of Fitness for Particular Purpose.

Except in a finance of lease, if the lessor at the time the lease contract is made has reason to know of any particular purpose for which the goods are required and that the lessee is relying on the lessor's skill or judgment to select or furnish suitable goods, there is in the lease contract an implied warranty that the goods will be fit for that purpose.

§ 2A–214. Exclusion or Modification of Warranties.

(1) Words or conduct relevant to the creation of an express warranty and words or conduct tending to negate or limit a warranty must be construed wherever reasonable as consistent with each other; but, subject to the provisions of Section 2A–202 on parol or extrinsic evidence, negation or limitation is inoperative to the extent that the construction is unreasonable.

(2) Subject to subsection (3), to exclude or modify the implied warranty of merchantability or any part of it the language must mention "merchantability", be by a writing, and be conspicuous. Subject to subsection (3), to exclude or modify any implied warranty of fitness the exclusion must be by a writing and be conspicuous. Language to exclude all implied warranties of fitness is sufficient if it is in writing, is conspicuous and states, for example, "There is no warranty that the goods will be fit for a particular purpose".

(3) Notwithstanding subsection (2), but subject to subsection (4),

(a) unless the circumstances indicate otherwise, all implied warranties are excluded by expressions like "as is" or "with all faults" or by other language that in common understanding calls the lessee's attention to the exclusion of warranties and makes plain that there is no implied warranty, if in writing and conspicuous;

(b) if the lessee before entering into the lease contract has examined the goods or the sample or model as fully as desired or has refused to examine the goods, there is no implied warranty with regard to defects that an examination ought in the circumstances to have revealed; and

(c) an implied warranty may also be excluded or modified by course of dealing, course of performance, or usage of trade.

(4) To exclude or modify a warranty against interference or against infringement (Section 2A–211) or any part of it, the language must be specific, be by a writing, and be conspicuous, unless the circumstances, including course of performance, course of dealing, or usage of trade, give the lessee reason to know that the goods are being leased subject to a claim or interest of any person.

§ 2A–215. Cumulation and Conflict of Warranties Express or Implied.

Warranties, whether express or implied, must be construed as consistent with each other and as cumulative, but if that construction is unreasonable, the intention of the parties determines which warranty is dominant. In ascertaining that intention the following rules apply:

(a) Exact or technical specifications displace an inconsistent sample or model or general language of description.

(b) A sample from an existing bulk displaces inconsistent general language of description.

(c) Express warranties displace inconsistent implied warranties other than an implied warranty of fitness for a particular purpose.

§ 2A–216. Third-Party Beneficiaries of Express and Implied Warranties.

Alternative A

A warranty to or for the benefit of a lessee under this Article, whether express or implied, extends to any natural person who is in the family or household of the lessee or who is a guest in the lessee's home if it is reasonable to expect that such person may use, consume, or be affected by the goods and who is injured in person by breach of the warranty. This section does not displace principles of law and equity that extend a warranty to or for the benefit of a lessee to other persons. The operation of this section may not be excluded, modified, or limited, but an exclusion, modification, or limitation of the warranty, including any with respect to rights and remedies, effective against the lessee is also effective against any beneficiary designated under this section.

Alternative B

A warranty to or for the benefit of a lessee under this Article, whether express or implied, extends to any natural person who may reasonably be expected to use, consume, or be affected by the goods and who is injured in person by breach of the warranty. This section does not displace principles of law and equity that extend a warranty to or for the benefit of a lessee to other persons. The operation of this section may not be excluded, modified, or limited, but an exclusion, modification, or limitation of the warranty, including any with respect to rights and remedies, effective against the lessee is also effective against the beneficiary designated under this section.

Alternative C

A warranty to or for the benefit of a lessee under this Article, whether express or implied, extends to any person who may reasonably be expected to use, consume, or be affected by the goods and who is injured by breach of the warranty. The operation of this section may not be excluded, modified, or limited with respect to injury to the person of an individual to whom the warranty extends, but an exclusion, modification, or limitation of the warranty, including any with respect to rights and remedies, effective against the lessee is also effective against the beneficiary designated under this section.

§ 2A–217. Identification.

Identification of goods as goods to which a lease contract refers may be made at any time and in any manner explicitly agreed to by the parties. In the absence of explicit agreement, identification occurs:

(a) when the lease contract is made if the lease contract is for a lease of goods that are existing and identified;

(b) when the goods are shipped, marked, or otherwise designated by the lessor as goods to which the lease contract refers, if the lease contract is for a lease of goods that are not existing and identified; or

(c) when the young are conceived, if the lease contract is for a lease of unborn young of animals.

§ 2A–218. Insurance and Proceeds.

(1) A lessee obtains an insurable interest when existing goods are identified to the lease contract even though the goods identified are nonconforming and the lessee has an option to reject them.

(2) If a lessee has an insurable interest only by reason of the lessor's identification of the goods, the lessor, until default or insolvency or notification to the lessee that identification is final, may substitute other goods for those identified.

(3) Notwithstanding a lessee's insurable interest under subsections (1) and (2), the lessor retains an insurable interest until an option to buy has been exercised by the lessee and risk of loss has passed to the lessee.

(4) Nothing in this section impairs any insurable interest recognized under any other statute or rule of law.

(5) The parties by agreement may determine that one or more parties have an obligation to obtain and pay for insurance covering the goods and by agreement may determine the beneficiary of the proceeds of the insurance.

§ 2A–219. Risk of Loss.

(1) Except in the case of a finance lease, risk of loss is retained by the lessor and does not pass to the lessee. In the case of a finance lease, risk of loss passes to the lessee.

(2) Subject to the provisions of this Article on the effect of default on risk of loss (Section 2A–220), if risk of loss is to pass to the lessee and the time of passage is not stated, the following rules apply:

(a) If the lease contract requires or authorizes the goods to be shipped by carrier

(i) and it does not require delivery at a particular destination, the risk of loss passes to the lessee when the goods are duly delivered to the carrier; but

(ii) if it does require delivery at a particular destination and the goods are there duly tendered while in the possession of the carrier, the risk of loss passes to the lessee when the goods are there duly so tendered as to enable the lessee to take delivery.

(b) If the goods are held by a bailee to be delivered without being moved, the risk of loss passes to the lessee on acknowledgment by the bailee of the lessee's right to possession of the goods.

(c) In any case not within subsection (a) or (b), the risk of loss passes to the lessee on the lessee's receipt of the goods if the lessor, or, in the case of a finance lease, the supplier, is a merchant; otherwise the risk passes to the lessee on tender of delivery.

§ 2A–220. Effect of Default on Risk of Loss.

(1) Where risk of loss is to pass to the lessee and the time of passage is not stated:

(a) If a tender or delivery of goods so fails to conform to the lease contract as to give a right of rejection, the risk of their loss remains with the lessor, or, in the case of a finance lease, the supplier, until cure or acceptance.

(b) If the lessee rightfully revokes acceptance, he [or she], to the extent of any deficiency in his [or her] effective insurance coverage, may treat the risk of loss as having remained with the lessor from the beginning.

(2) Whether or not risk of loss is to pass to the lessee, if the lessee as to conforming goods already identified to a lease contract repudiates or is otherwise in default under the lease contract, the lessor, or, in the case of a finance lease, the supplier, to the extent of any deficiency in his [or her] effective insurance coverage may treat the risk of loss as resting on the lessee for a commercially reasonable time.

§ 2A–221. Casualty to Identified Goods.

If a lease contract requires goods identified when the lease contract is made, and the goods suffer casualty without fault of the lessee, the lessor or the supplier before delivery, or the goods suffer casualty before risk of loss passes to the lessee pursuant to the lease agreement or Section 2A–219, then:

(a) if the loss is total, the lease contract is avoided; and

(b) if the loss is partial or the goods have so deteriorated as to no longer conform to the lease contract, the lessee may nevertheless demand inspection and at his [or her] option either treat the lease contract as avoided or, except in a finance lease that is not a consumer lease, accept the goods with due allowance from the rent payable for the balance of the lease term for the deterioration or the deficiency in quantity but without further right against the lessor.

Part 3 Effect of Lease Contract

§ 2A–301. Enforceability of Lease Contract.

Except as otherwise provided in this Article, a lease contract is effective and enforceable according to its terms between the parties, against purchasers of the goods and against creditors of the parties.

§ 2A–302. Title to and Possession of Goods.

Except as otherwise provided in this Article, each provision of this Article applies whether the lessor or a third party has title to the goods, and whether the lessor, the lessee, or a third party has possession of the goods, notwithstanding any statute or rule of law that possession or the absence of possession is fraudulent.

§ 2A–303. Alienability of Party's Interest Under Lease Contract or of Lessor's Residual Interest in Goods; Delegation of Performance; Transfer of Rights.

(1) As used in this section, "creation of a security interest" includes the sale of a lease contract that is subject to Article 9, Secured Transactions, by reason of Section 9–109(a)(3).

(2) Except as provided in subsections (3) and Section 9–407, a provision in a lease agreement which (i) prohibits the voluntary or involuntary transfer, including a transfer by sale, sublease, creation or enforcement of a security interest, or attachment, levy, or other judicial process, of an interest of a party under the lease contract or of the lessor's residual interest in the goods, or (ii) makes such a transfer an event of default, gives rise to the rights and remedies provided in subsection (4), but a transfer that is prohibited or is an event of default under the lease agreement is otherwise effective.

(3) A provision in a lease agreement which (i) prohibits a transfer of a right to damages for default with respect to the whole lease contract or of a right to payment arising out of the transferor's due performance of the transferor's entire obligation, or (ii) makes such a transfer an event of default, is not enforceable, and such a transfer is not a transfer that materially impairs the propsect of obtaining return performance by, materially changes the duty of, or materially increases the burden or risk imposed on, the other party to the lease contract within the purview of subsection (4).

(4) Subject to subsection (3) and Section 9–407:

(a) if a transfer is made which is made an event of default under a lease agreement, the party to the lease contract not making the transfer, unless that party waives the default or otherwise agrees, has the rights and remedies described in Section 2A–501(2);

(b) if paragraph (a) is not applicable and if a transfer is made that (i) is prohibited under a lease agreement or (ii) materially impairs the prospect of obtaining return performance by, materially changes the duty of, or materially increases the burden or risk imposed on, the other party to the lease contract, unless the party not making the transfer agrees at any time to the transfer in the lease contract or otherwise, then, except as limited by contract, (i) the transferor is liable to the party not making the transfer for damages caused by the transfer to the extent that the damages could not reasonably be prevented by the party not making the transfer and (ii) a court having jurisdiction may grant other appropriate relief, including cancellation of the lease contract or an injunction against the transfer.

(5) A transfer of "the lease" or of "all my rights under the lease", or a transfer in similar general terms, is a transfer of rights and, unless the language or the circumstances, as in a transfer for security, indicate the contrary, the transfer is a delegation of duties by the transferor to the transferee. Acceptance by the transferee constitutes a promise by the transferee to perform those duties. The promise is enforceable by either the transferor or the other party to the lease contract.

(6) Unless otherwise agreed by the lessor and the lessee, a delegation of performance does not relieve the transferor as against the other party of any duty to perform or of any liability for default.

(7) In a consumer lease, to prohibit the transfer of an interest of a party under the lease contract or to make a transfer an event of default, the language must be specific, by a writing, and conspicuous.

As amended in 1990 and 1999.

§ 2A–304. Subsequent Lease of Goods by Lessor.

(1) Subject to Section 2A–303, a subsequent lessee from a lessor of goods under an existing lease contract obtains, to the extent of the leasehold interest transferred, the leasehold interest in the goods that the lessor had or had power to transfer, and except as provided in subsection (2) and Section 2A–527(4), takes subject to the existing lease contract. A lessor with voidable title has power to transfer a good leasehold interest to a good faith subsequent lessee for value, but only to the extent set forth in the preceding sentence. If goods have been delivered under a transaction of purchase the lessor has that power even though:

(a) the lessor's transferor was deceived as to the identity of the lessor;

(b) the delivery was in exchange for a check which is later dishonored;

(c) it was agreed that the transaction was to be a "cash sale"; or

(d) the delivery was procured through fraud punishable as larcenous under the criminal law.

(2) A subsequent lessee in the ordinary course of business from a lessor who is a merchant dealing in goods of that kind to whom the goods were entrusted by the existing lessee of that lessor before the interest of the subsequent lessee became enforceable against that lessor obtains, to the extent of the leasehold interest transferred, all of that lessor's and the existing lessee's rights to the goods, and takes free of the existing lease contract.

(3) A subsequent lessee from the lessor of goods that are subject to an existing lease contract and are covered by a certificate of title issued under a statute of this State or of another jurisdiction takes no greater rights than those provided both by this section and by the certificate of title statute.

As amended in 1990.

§ 2A–305. Sale or Sublease of Goods by Lessee.

(1) Subject to the provisions of Section 2A–303, a buyer or sublessee from the lessee of goods under an existing lease contract obtains, to the extent of the interest transferred, the leasehold interest in the goods that the lessee had or had power to transfer, and except as provided in subsection (2) and Section 2A–511(4), takes subject to the existing lease contract. A lessee with a voidable leasehold interest has power to transfer a good leasehold interest to a good faith buyer for value or a good faith sublessee for value, but only to the extent set forth in the preceding sentence. When goods have been delivered under a transaction of lease the lessee has that power even though:

(a) the lessor was deceived as to the identity of the lessee;

(b) the delivery was in exchange for a check which is later dishonored; or

(c) the delivery was procured through fraud punishable as larcenous under the criminal law.

(2) A buyer in the ordinary course of business or a sublessee in the ordinary course of business from a lessee who is a merchant dealing in goods of that kind to whom the goods were entrusted by the lessor obtains, to the extent of the interest transferred, all of the lessor's and lessee's rights to the goods, and takes free of the existing lease contract.

(3) A buyer or sublessee from the lessee of goods that are subject to an existing lease contract and are covered by a certificate of title issued under a statute of this State or of another jurisdiction takes no greater rights than those provided both by this section and by the certificate of title statute.

§ 2A–306. Priority of Certain Liens Arising by Operation of Law.

If a person in the ordinary course of his [or her] business furnishes services or materials with respect to goods subject to a lease contract, a lien upon those goods in the possession of that person given by statute or rule of law for those materials or services takes priority over any interest of the lessor or lessee under the lease contract or this Article unless the lien is created by statute and the statute provides otherwise or unless the lien is created by rule of law and the rule of law provides otherwise.

§ 2A–307. Priority of Liens Arising by Attachment or Levy on, Security Interests in, and Other Claims to Goods.

(1) Except as otherwise provided in Section 2A–306, a creditor of a lessee takes subject to the lease contract.

(2) Except as otherwise provided in subsection (3) and in Sections 2A–306 and 2A–308, a creditor of a lessor takes subject to the lease contract unless the creditor holds a lien that attached to the goods before the lease contract became enforceable.

(3) Except as otherwise provided in Sections 9–317, 9–321, and 9–323, a lessee takes a leasehold interest subject to a security interest held by a creditor of the lessor.

As amended in 1990 and 1999.

§ 2A–308. Special Rights of Creditors.

(1) A creditor of a lessor in possession of goods subject to a lease contract may treat the lease contract as void if as against the creditor retention of possession by the lessor is fraudulent under any statute or rule of law, but retention of possession in good faith and current course of trade by the lessor for a commercially reasonable time after the lease contract becomes enforceable is not fraudulent.

(2) Nothing in this Article impairs the rights of creditors of a lessor if the lease contract (a) becomes enforceable, not in current course of trade but in satisfaction of or as security for a pre-existing claim for money, security, or the like, and (b) is made under circumstances which under any statute or rule of law apart from this Article would constitute the transaction a fraudulent transfer or voidable preference.

(3) A creditor of a seller may treat a sale or an identification of goods to a contract for sale as void if as against the creditor retention of possession by the seller is fraudulent under any statute or rule of law, but retention of possession of the goods pursuant to a lease contract entered into by the seller as lessee and the buyer as lessor in connection with the sale or identification of the goods is not fraudulent if the buyer bought for value and in good faith.

§ 2A–309. Lessor's and Lessee's Rights When Goods Become Fixtures.

(1) In this section:

(a) goods are "fixtures" when they become so related to particular real estate that an interest in them arises under real estate law;

(b) a "fixture filing" is the filing, in the office where a mortgage on the real estate would be filed or recorded, of a financing statement covering goods that are or are to become fixtures and conforming to the requirements of Section 9–502(a) and (b);

(c) a lease is a "purchase money lease" unless the lessee has possession or use of the goods or the right to possession or use of the goods before the lease agreement is enforceable;

(d) a mortgage is a "construction mortgage" to the extent it secures an obligation incurred for the construction of an improvement on land including the acquisition cost of the land, if the recorded writing so indicates; and

(e) "encumbrance" includes real estate mortgages and other liens on real estate and all other rights in real estate that are not ownership interests.

(2) Under this Article a lease may be of goods that are fixtures or may continue in goods that become fixtures, but no lease exists under this Article of ordinary building materials incorporated into an improvement on land.

(3) This Article does not prevent creation of a lease of fixtures pursuant to real estate law.

(4) The perfected interest of a lessor of fixtures has priority over a conflicting interest of an encumbrancer or owner of the real estate if:

(a) the lease is a purchase money lease, the conflicting interest of the encumbrancer or owner arises before the goods become fixtures, the interest of the lessor is perfected by a fixture filing before the goods become fixtures or within ten days thereafter, and the lessee has an interest of record in the real estate or is in possession of the real estate; or

(b) the interest of the lessor is perfected by a fixture filing before the interest of the encumbrancer or owner is of record, the lessor's interest has priority over any conflicting interest of a predecessor in title of the encumbrancer or owner, and the lessee has an interest of record in the real estate or is in possession of the real estate.

(5) The interest of a lessor of fixtures, whether or not perfected, has priority over the conflicting interest of an encumbrancer or owner of the real estate if:

(a) the fixtures are readily removable factory or office machines, readily removable equipment that is not primarily used or leased for use in the operation of the real estate, or readily removable replacements of domestic appliances that are goods subject to a consumer lease, and before the goods become fixtures the lease contract is enforceable; or

(b) the conflicting interest is a lien on the real estate obtained by legal or equitable proceedings after the lease contract is enforceable; or

(c) the encumbrancer or owner has consented in writing to the lease or has disclaimed an interest in the goods as fixtures; or

(d) the lessee has a right to remove the goods as against the encumbrancer or owner. If the lessee's right to remove terminates, the priority of the interest of the lessor continues for a reasonable time.

(6) Notwithstanding paragraph (4)(a) but otherwise subject to subsections (4) and (5), the interest of a lessor of fixtures, including the lessor's residual interest, is subordinate to the conflicting interest of an encumbrancer of the real estate under a construction mortgage recorded before the goods become fixtures if the goods become fixtures before the completion of the construction. To the extent given to refinance a construction mortgage, the conflicting interest of an encumbrancer of the real estate under a mortgage has this priority to the same extent as the encumbrancer of the real estate under the construction mortgage.

(7) In cases not within the preceding subsections, priority between the interest of a lessor of fixtures, including the lessor's residual interest, and the conflicting interest of an encumbrancer or owner of the real estate who is not the lessee is determined by the priority rules governing conflicting interests in real estate.

(8) If the interest of a lessor of fixtures, including the lessor's residual interest, has priority over all conflicting interests of all owners and encumbrancers of the real estate, the lessor or the lessee may (i) on default, expiration, termination, or cancellation of the lease agreement but subject to the agreement and this Article, or (ii) if necessary to enforce other rights and remedies of the lessor or lessee under this Article, remove the goods from the real estate, free and clear of all conflicting interests of all owners and encumbrancers of the real estate, but the lessor or lessee must reimburse any encum-

brancer or owner of the real estate who is not the lessee and who has not otherwise agreed for the cost of repair of any physical injury, but not for any diminution in value of the real estate caused by the absence of the goods removed or by any necessity of replacing them. A person entitled to reimbursement may refuse permission to remove until the party seeking removal gives adequate security for the performance of this obligation.

(9) Even though the lease agreement does not create a security interest, the interest of a lessor of fixtures, including the lessor's residual interest, is perfected by filing a financing statement as a fixture filing for leased goods that are or are to become fixtures in accordance with the relevant provisions of the Article on Secured Transactions (Article 9).

As amended in 1990 and 1999.

§ 2A–310. Lessor's and Lessee's Rights When Goods Become Accessions.

(1) Goods are "accessions" when they are installed in or affixed to other goods.

(2) The interest of a lessor or a lessee under a lease contract entered into before the goods became accessions is superior to all interests in the whole except as stated in subsection (4).

(3) The interest of a lessor or a lessee under a lease contract entered into at the time or after the goods became accessions is superior to all subsequently acquired interests in the whole except as stated in subsection (4) but is subordinate to interests in the whole existing at the time the lease contract was made unless the holders of such interests in the whole have in writing consented to the lease or disclaimed an interest in the goods as part of the whole.

(4) The interest of a lessor or a lessee under a lease contract described in subsection (2) or (3) is subordinate to the interest of

    (a) a buyer in the ordinary course of business or a lessee in the ordinary course of business of any interest in the whole acquired after the goods became accessions; or

    (b) a creditor with a security interest in the whole perfected before the lease contract was made to the extent that the creditor makes subsequent advances without knowledge of the lease contract.

(5) When under subsections (2) or (3) and (4) a lessor or a lessee of accessions holds an interest that is superior to all interests in the whole, the lessor or the lessee may (a) on default, expiration, termination, or cancellation of the lease contract by the other party but subject to the provisions of the lease contract and this Article, or (b) if necessary to enforce his [or her] other rights and remedies under this Article, remove the goods from the whole, free and clear of all interests in the whole, but he [or she] must reimburse any holder of an interest in the whole who is not the lessee and who has not otherwise agreed for the cost of repair of any physical injury but not for any diminution in value of the whole caused by the absence of the goods removed or by any necessity for replacing them. A person entitled to reimbursement may refuse permission to remove until the party seeking removal gives adequate security for the performance of this obligation.

§ 2A–311. Priority Subject to Subordination.

Nothing in this Article prevents subordination by agreement by any person entitled to priority.

As added in 1990.

Part 4 Performance of Lease Contract: Repudiated, Substituted and Excused

§ 2A–401. Insecurity: Adequate Assurance of Performance.

(1) A lease contract imposes an obligation on each party that the other's expectation of receiving due performance will not be impaired.

(2) If reasonable grounds for insecurity arise with respect to the performance of either party, the insecure party may demand in writing adequate assurance of due performance. Until the insecure party receives that assurance, if commercially reasonable the insecure party may suspend any performance for which he [or she] has not already received the agreed return.

(3) A repudiation of the lease contract occurs if assurance of due performance adequate under the circumstances of the particular case is not provided to the insecure party within a reasonable time, not to exceed 30 days after receipt of a demand by the other party.

(4) Between merchants, the reasonableness of grounds for insecurity and the adequacy of any assurance offered must be determined according to commercial standards.

(5) Acceptance of any nonconforming delivery or payment does not prejudice the aggrieved party's right to demand adequate assurance of future performance.

§ 2A–402. Anticipatory Repudiation.

If either party repudiates a lease contract with respect to a performance not yet due under the lease contract, the loss of which performance will substantially impair the value of the lease contract to the other, the aggrieved party may:

(a) for a commercially reasonable time, await retraction of repudiation and performance by the repudiating party;

(b) make demand pursuant to Section 2A–401 and await assurance of future performance adequate under the circumstances of the particular case; or

(c) resort to any right or remedy upon default under the lease contract or this Article, even though the aggrieved party has notified the repudiating party that the aggrieved party would await the repudiating party's performance and assurance and has urged retraction. In addition, whether or not the aggrieved party is pursuing one of the foregoing remedies, the aggrieved party may suspend performance or, if the aggrieved party is the lessor, proceed in accordance with the provisions of this Article on the lessor's right to identify goods to the lease contract notwithstanding default or to salvage unfinished goods (Section 2A–524).

§ 2A–403. Retraction of Anticipatory Repudiation.

(1) Until the repudiating party's next performance is due, the repudiating party can retract the repudiation unless, since the repudiation, the aggrieved party has cancelled the lease contract or materially changed the aggrieved party's position or otherwise indicated that the aggrieved party considers the repudiation final.

(2) Retraction may be by any method that clearly indicates to the aggrieved party that the repudiating party intends to perform under the lease contract and includes any assurance demanded under Section 2A–401.

(3) Retraction reinstates a repudiating party's rights under a lease contract with due excuse and allowance to the aggrieved party for any delay occasioned by the repudiation.

§ 2A–404. Substituted Performance.

(1) If without fault of the lessee, the lessor and the supplier, the agreed berthing, loading, or unloading facilities fail or the agreed type of carrier becomes unavailable or the agreed manner of delivery otherwise becomes commercially impracticable, but a commercially reasonable substitute is available, the substitute performance must be tendered and accepted.

(2) If the agreed means or manner of payment fails because of domestic or foreign governmental regulation:

(a) the lessor may withhold or stop delivery or cause the supplier to withhold or stop delivery unless the lessee provides a means or manner of payment that is commercially a substantial equivalent; and

(b) if delivery has already been taken, payment by the means or in the manner provided by the regulation discharges the lessee's obligation unless the regulation is discriminatory, oppressive, or predatory.

§ 2A–405. Excused Performance.

Subject to Section 2A–404 on substituted performance, the following rules apply:

(a) Delay in delivery or nondelivery in whole or in part by a lessor or a supplier who complies with paragraphs (b) and (c) is not a default under the lease contract if performance as agreed has been made impracticable by the occurrence of a contingency the nonoccurrence of which was a basic assumption on which the lease contract was made or by compliance in good faith with any applicable foreign or domestic governmental regulation or order, whether or not the regulation or order later proves to be invalid.

(b) If the causes mentioned in paragraph (a) affect only part of the lessor's or the supplier's capacity to perform, he [or she] shall allocate production and deliveries among his [or her] customers but at his [or her] option may include regular customers not then under contract for sale or lease as well as his [or her] own requirements for further manufacture. He [or she] may so allocate in any manner that is fair and reasonable.

(c) The lessor seasonably shall notify the lessee and in the case of a finance lease the supplier seasonably shall notify the lessor and the lessee, if known, that there will be delay or nondelivery and, if allocation is required under paragraph (b), of the estimated quota thus made available for the lessee.

§ 2A–406. Procedure on Excused Performance.

(1) If the lessee receives notification of a material or indefinite delay or an allocation justified under Section 2A–405, the lessee may by written notification to the lessor as to any goods involved, and with respect to all of the goods if under an installment lease contract the value of the whole lease contract is substantially impaired (Section 2A–510):

(a) terminate the lease contract (Section 2A–505(2)); or

(b) except in a finance lease that is not a consumer lease, modify the lease contract by accepting the available quota in substitution, with due allowance from the rent payable for the balance of the lease term for the deficiency but without further right against the lessor.

(2) If, after receipt of a notification from the lessor under Section 2A–405, the lessee fails so to modify the lease agreement within a reasonable time not exceeding 30 days, the lease contract lapses with respect to any deliveries affected.

§ 2A–407. Irrevocable Promises: Finance Leases.

(1) In the case of a finance lease that is not a consumer lease the lessee's promises under the lease contract become irrevocable and independent upon the lessee's acceptance of the goods.

(2) A promise that has become irrevocable and independent under subsection (1):

(a) is effective and enforceable between the parties, and by or against third parties including assignees of the parties, and

(b) is not subject to cancellation, termination, modification, repudiation, excuse, or substitution without the consent of the party to whom the promise runs.

(3) This section does not affect the validity under any other law of a covenant in any lease contract making the lessee's promises irrevocable and independent upon the lessee's acceptance of the goods.

As amended in 1990.

Part 5 Default

A. In General

§ 2A–501. Default: Procedure.

(1) Whether the lessor or the lessee is in default under a lease contract is determined by the lease agreement and this Article.

(2) If the lessor or the lessee is in default under the lease contract, the party seeking enforcement has rights and remedies as provided in this Article and, except as limited by this Article, as provided in the lease agreement.

(3) If the lessor or the lessee is in default under the lease contract, the party seeking enforcement may reduce the party's claim to judgment, or otherwise enforce the lease contract by self-help or any available judicial procedure or nonjudicial procedure, including administrative proceeding, arbitration, or the like, in accordance with this Article.

(4) Except as otherwise provided in Section 1–106(1) or this Article or the lease agreement, the rights and remedies referred to in subsections (2) and (3) are cumulative.

(5) If the lease agreement covers both real property and goods, the party seeking enforcement may proceed under this Part as to the goods, or under other applicable law as to both the real property and the goods in accordance with that party's rights and remedies in respect of the real property, in which case this Part does not apply.

As amended in 1990.

§ 2A–502. Notice After Default.

Except as otherwise provided in this Article or the lease agreement, the lessor or lessee in default under the lease contract is not entitled to notice of default or notice of enforcement from the other party to the lease agreement.

§ 2A–503. Modification or Impairment of Rights and Remedies.

(1) Except as otherwise provided in this Article, the lease agreement may include rights and remedies for default in addition to or in substitution for those provided in this Article and may limit or alter the measure of damages recoverable under this Article.

(2) Resort to a remedy provided under this Article or in the lease agreement is optional unless the remedy is expressly agreed to be exclusive. If circumstances cause an exclusive or limited remedy to fail of its essential purpose, or provision for an exclusive remedy is unconscionable, remedy may be had as provided in this Article.

(3) Consequential damages may be liquidated under Section 2A–504, or may otherwise be limited, altered, or excluded unless the limitation, alteration, or exclusion is unconscionable. Limitation, alteration, or exclusion of consequential damages for injury to the person in the case of consumer goods is prima facie unconscionable but limitation, alteration, or exclusion of damages where the loss is commercial is not prima facie unconscionable.

(4) Rights and remedies on default by the lessor or the lessee with respect to any obligation or promise collateral or ancillary to the lease contract are not impaired by this Article.

As amended in 1990.

§ 2A–504. Liquidation of Damages.

(1) Damages payable by either party for default, or any other act or omission, including indemnity for loss or diminution of anticipated tax benefits or loss or damage to lessor's residual interest, may be liquidated in the lease agreement but only at an amount or by a formula that is reasonable in light of the then anticipated harm caused by the default or other act or omission.

(2) If the lease agreement provides for liquidation of damages, and such provision does not comply with subsection (1), or such provision is an exclusive or limited remedy that circumstances cause to fail of its essential purpose, remedy may be had as provided in this Article.

(3) If the lessor justifiably withholds or stops delivery of goods because of the lessee's default or insolvency (Section 2A–525 or 2A–526), the lessee is entitled to restitution of any amount by which the sum of his [or her] payments exceeds:

(a) the amount to which the lessor is entitled by virtue of terms liquidating the lessor's damages in accordance with subsection (1); or

(b) in the absence of those terms, 20 percent of the then present value of the total rent the lessee was obligated to pay for the balance of the lease term, or, in the case of a consumer lease, the lesser of such amount or $500.

(4) A lessee's right to restitution under subsection (3) is subject to offset to the extent the lessor establishes:

(a) a right to recover damages under the provisions of this Article other than subsection (1); and

(b) the amount or value of any benefits received by the lessee directly or indirectly by reason of the lease contract.

§ 2A–505. Cancellation and Termination and Effect of Cancellation, Termination, Rescission, or Fraud on Rights and Remedies.

(1) On cancellation of the lease contract, all obligations that are still executory on both sides are discharged, but any right based on prior default or performance survives, and the cancelling party also retains any remedy for default of the whole lease contract or any unperformed balance.

(2) On termination of the lease contract, all obligations that are still executory on both sides are discharged but any right based on prior default or performance survives.

(3) Unless the contrary intention clearly appears, expressions of "cancellation," "rescission," or the like of the lease contract may not be construed as a renunciation or discharge of any claim in damages for an antecedent default.

(4) Rights and remedies for material misrepresentation or fraud include all rights and remedies available under this Article for default.

(5) Neither rescission nor a claim for rescission of the lease contract nor rejection or return of the goods may bar or be deemed inconsistent with a claim for damages or other right or remedy.

§ 2A–506. Statute of Limitations.

(1) An action for default under a lease contract, including breach of warranty or indemnity, must be commenced within 4 years after the cause of action accrued. By the original lease contract the parties may reduce the period of limitation to not less than one year.

(2) A cause of action for default accrues when the act or omission on which the default or breach of warranty is based is or should have been discovered by the aggrieved party, or when the default occurs, whichever is later. A cause of action for indemnity accrues when the act or omission on which the claim for indemnity is based is or should have been discovered by the indemnified party, whichever is later.

(3) If an action commenced within the time limited by subsection (1) is so terminated as to leave available a remedy by another action for the same default or breach of warranty or indemnity, the other action may be commenced after the expiration of the time limited and within 6 months after the termination of the first action unless the termination resulted from voluntary discontinuance or from dismissal for failure or neglect to prosecute.

(4) This section does not alter the law on tolling of the statute of limitations nor does it apply to causes of action that have accrued before this Article becomes effective.

§ 2A–507. Proof of Market Rent: Time and Place.

(1) Damages based on market rent (Section 2A–519 or 2A–528) are determined according to the rent for the use of the goods concerned for a lease term identical to the remaining lease term of the original lease agreement and prevailing at the times specified in Sections 2A–519 and 2A–528.

(2) If evidence of rent for the use of the goods concerned for a lease term identical to the remaining lease term of the original lease agreement and prevailing at the times or places described in this Article is not readily available, the rent prevailing within any reasonable time before or after the time described or at any other place or for a different lease term which in commercial judgment or under usage of trade would serve as a reasonable substitute for the one described may be used, making any proper allowance for the difference, including the cost of transporting the goods to or from the other place.

(3) Evidence of a relevant rent prevailing at a time or place or for a lease term other than the one described in this Article offered by one

party is not admissible unless and until he [or she] has given the other party notice the court finds sufficient to prevent unfair surprise.

(4) If the prevailing rent or value of any goods regularly leased in any established market is in issue, reports in official publications or trade journals or in newspapers or periodicals of general circulation published as the reports of that market are admissible in evidence. The circumstances of the preparation of the report may be shown to affect its weight but not its admissibility.

As amended in 1990.

B. Default by Lessor

§ 2A–508. Lessee's Remedies.

(1) If a lessor fails to deliver the goods in conformity to the lease contract (Section 2A–509) or repudiates the lease contract (Section 2A–402), or a lessee rightfully rejects the goods (Section 2A–509) or justifiably revokes acceptance of the goods (Section 2A–517), then with respect to any goods involved, and with respect to all of the goods if under an installment lease contract the value of the whole lease contract is substantially impaired (Section 2A–510), the lessor is in default under the lease contract and the lessee may:

(a) cancel the lease contract (Section 2A–505(1));

(b) recover so much of the rent and security as has been paid and is just under the circumstances;

(c) cover and recover damages as to all goods affected whether or not they have been identified to the lease contract (Sections 2A–518 and 2A–520), or recover damages for nondelivery (Sections 2A–519 and 2A–520);

(d) exercise any other rights or pursue any other remedies provided in the lease contract.

(2) If a lessor fails to deliver the goods in conformity to the lease contract or repudiates the lease contract, the lessee may also:

(a) if the goods have been identified, recover them (Section 2A–522); or

(b) in a proper case, obtain specific performance or replevy the goods (Section 2A–521).

(3) If a lessor is otherwise in default under a lease contract, the lessee may exercise the rights and pursue the remedies provided in the lease contract, which may include a right to cancel the lease, and in Section 2A–519(3).

(4) If a lessor has breached a warranty, whether express or implied, the lessee may recover damages (Section 2A–519(4)).

(5) On rightful rejection or justifiable revocation of acceptance, a lessee has a security interest in goods in the lessee's possession or control for any rent and security that has been paid and any expenses reasonably incurred in their inspection, receipt, transportation, and care and custody and may hold those goods and dispose of them in good faith and in a commercially reasonable manner, subject to Section 2A–527(5).

(6) Subject to the provisions of Section 2A–407, a lessee, on notifying the lessor of the lessee's intention to do so, may deduct all or any part of the damages resulting from any default under the lease contract from any part of the rent still due under the same lease contract.

As amended in 1990.

§ 2A–509. Lessee's Rights on Improper Delivery; Rightful Rejection.

(1) Subject to the provisions of Section 2A–510 on default in installment lease contracts, if the goods or the tender or delivery fail in any respect to conform to the lease contract, the lessee may reject or accept the goods or accept any commercial unit or units and reject the rest of the goods.

(2) Rejection of goods is ineffective unless it is within a reasonable time after tender or delivery of the goods and the lessee seasonably notifies the lessor.

§ 2A–510. Installment Lease Contracts: Rejection and Default.

(1) Under an installment lease contract a lessee may reject any delivery that is nonconforming if the nonconformity substantially impairs the value of that delivery and cannot be cured or the nonconformity is a defect in the required documents; but if the nonconformity does not fall within subsection (2) and the lessor or the supplier gives adequate assurance of its cure, the lessee must accept that delivery.

(2) Whenever nonconformity or default with respect to one or more deliveries substantially impairs the value of the installment lease contract as a whole there is a default with respect to the whole. But, the aggrieved party reinstates the installment lease contract as a whole if the aggrieved party accepts a nonconforming delivery without seasonably notifying of cancellation or brings an action with respect only to past deliveries or demands performance as to future deliveries.

§ 2A–511. Merchant Lessee's Duties as to Rightfully Rejected Goods.

(1) Subject to any security interest of a lessee (Section 2A–508(5)), if a lessor or a supplier has no agent or place of business at the market of rejection, a merchant lessee, after rejection of goods in his [or her] possession or control, shall follow any reasonable instructions received from the lessor or the supplier with respect to the goods. In the absence of those instructions, a merchant lessee shall make reasonable efforts to sell, lease, or otherwise dispose of the goods for the lessor's account if they threaten to decline in value speedily. Instructions are not reasonable if on demand indemnity for expenses is not forthcoming.

(2) If a merchant lessee (subsection (1)) or any other lessee (Section 2A–512) disposes of goods, he [or she] is entitled to reimbursement either from the lessor or the supplier or out of the proceeds for reasonable expenses of caring for and disposing of the goods and, if the expenses include no disposition commission, to such commission as is usual in the trade, or if there is none, to a reasonable sum not exceeding 10 percent of the gross proceeds.

(3) In complying with this section or Section 2A–512, the lessee is held only to good faith. Good faith conduct hereunder is neither acceptance or conversion nor the basis of an action for damages.

(4) A purchaser who purchases in good faith from a lessee pursuant to this section or Section 2A–512 takes the goods free of any rights of the lessor and the supplier even though the lessee fails to comply with one or more of the requirements of this Article.

§ 2A–512. Lessee's Duties as to Rightfully Rejected Goods.

(1) Except as otherwise provided with respect to goods that threaten to decline in value speedily (Section 2A–511) and subject to any security interest of a lessee (Section 2A–508(5)):

(a) the lessee, after rejection of goods in the lessee's possession, shall hold them with reasonable care at the lessor's or the supplier's disposition for a reasonable time after the lessee's seasonable notification of rejection;

(b) if the lessor or the supplier gives no instructions within a reasonable time after notification of rejection, the lessee may store the rejected goods for the lessor's or the supplier's account or ship them to the lessor or the supplier or dispose of them for the lessor's or the supplier's account with reimbursement in the manner provided in Section 2A–511; but

(c) the lessee has no further obligations with regard to goods rightfully rejected.

(2) Action by the lessee pursuant to subsection (1) is not acceptance or conversion.

§ 2A–513. Cure by Lessor of Improper Tender or Delivery; Replacement.

(1) If any tender or delivery by the lessor or the supplier is rejected because nonconforming and the time for performance has not yet expired, the lessor or the supplier may seasonably notify the lessee of the lessor's or the supplier's intention to cure and may then make a conforming delivery within the time provided in the lease contract.

(2) If the lessee rejects a nonconforming tender that the lessor or the supplier had reasonable grounds to believe would be acceptable with or without money allowance, the lessor or the supplier may have a further reasonable time to substitute a conforming tender if he [or she] seasonably notifies the lessee.

§ 2A–514. Waiver of Lessee's Objections.

(1) In rejecting goods, a lessee's failure to state a particular defect that is ascertainable by reasonable inspection precludes the lessee from relying on the defect to justify rejection or to establish default:

(a) if, stated seasonably, the lessor or the supplier could have cured it (Section 2A–513); or

(b) between merchants if the lessor or the supplier after rejection has made a request in writing for a full and final written statement of all defects on which the lessee proposes to rely.

(2) A lessee's failure to reserve rights when paying rent or other consideration against documents precludes recovery of the payment for defects apparent on the face of the documents.

§ 2A–515. Acceptance of Goods.

(1) Acceptance of goods occurs after the lessee has had a reasonable opportunity to inspect the goods and

(a) the lessee signifies or acts with respect to the goods in a manner that signifies to the lessor or the supplier that the goods are conforming or that the lessee will take or retain them in spite of their nonconformity; or

(b) the lessee fails to make an effective rejection of the goods (Section 2A–509(2)).

(2) Acceptance of a part of any commercial unit is acceptance of that entire unit.

§ 2A–516. Effect of Acceptance of Goods; Notice of Default; Burden of Establishing Default after Acceptance; Notice of Claim or Litigation to Person Answerable Over.

(1) A lessee must pay rent for any goods accepted in accordance with the lease contract, with due allowance for goods rightfully rejected or not delivered.

(2) A lessee's acceptance of goods precludes rejection of the goods accepted. In the case of a finance lease, if made with knowledge of a nonconformity, acceptance cannot be revoked because of it. In any other case, if made with knowledge of a nonconformity, acceptance cannot be revoked because of it unless the acceptance was on the reasonable assumption that the nonconformity would be seasonably cured. Acceptance does not of itself impair any other remedy provided by this Article or the lease agreement for nonconformity.

(3) If a tender has been accepted:

(a) within a reasonable time after the lessee discovers or should have discovered any default, the lessee shall notify the lessor and the supplier, if any, or be barred from any remedy against the party notified;

(b) except in the case of a consumer lease, within a reasonable time after the lessee receives notice of litigation for infringement or the like (Section 2A–211) the lessee shall notify the lessor or be barred from any remedy over for liability established by the litigation; and

(c) the burden is on the lessee to establish any default.

(4) If a lessee is sued for breach of a warranty or other obligation for which a lessor or a supplier is answerable over the following apply:

(a) The lessee may give the lessor or the supplier, or both, written notice of the litigation. If the notice states that the person notified may come in and defend and that if the person notified does not do so that person will be bound in any action against that person by the lessee by any determination of fact common to the two litigations, then unless the person notified after seasonable receipt of the notice does come in and defend that person is so bound.

(b) The lessor or the supplier may demand in writing that the lessee turn over control of the litigation including settlement if the claim is one for infringement or the like (Section 2A–211) or else be barred from any remedy over. If the demand states that the lessor or the supplier agrees to bear all expense and to satisfy any adverse judgment, then unless the lessee after seasonable receipt of the demand does turn over control the lessee is so barred.

(5) Subsections (3) and (4) apply to any obligation of a lessee to hold the lessor or the supplier harmless against infringement or the like (Section 2A–211).

As amended in 1990.

§ 2A–517. Revocation of Acceptance of Goods.

(1) A lessee may revoke acceptance of a lot or commercial unit whose nonconformity substantially impairs its value to the lessee if the lessee has accepted it:

(a) except in the case of a finance lease, on the reasonable assumption that its nonconformity would be cured and it has not been seasonably cured; or

(b) without discovery of the nonconformity if the lessee's acceptance was reasonably induced either by the lessor's assurances or, except in the case of a finance lease, by the difficulty of discovery before acceptance.

(2) Except in the case of a finance lease that is not a consumer lease, a lessee may revoke acceptance of a lot or commercial unit if the lessor defaults under the lease contract and the default substantially impairs the value of that lot or commercial unit to the lessee.

(3) If the lease agreement so provides, the lessee may revoke acceptance of a lot or commercial unit because of other defaults by the lessor.

(4) Revocation of acceptance must occur within a reasonable time after the lessee discovers or should have discovered the ground for it and before any substantial change in condition of the goods which is not caused by the nonconformity. Revocation is not effective until the lessee notifies the lessor.

(5) A lessee who so revokes has the same rights and duties with regard to the goods involved as if the lessee had rejected them.

As amended in 1990.

§ 2A–518. Cover; Substitute Goods.

(1) After a default by a lessor under the lease contract of the type described in Section 2A–508(1), or, if agreed, after other default by the lessor, the lessee may cover by making any purchase or lease of or contract to purchase or lease goods in substitution for those due from the lessor.

(2) Except as otherwise provided with respect to damages liquidated in the lease agreement (Section 2A–504) or otherwise determined pursuant to agreement of the parties (Sections 1–102(3) and 2A–503), if a lessee's cover is by lease agreement substantially similar to the original lease agreement and the new lease agreement is made in good faith and in a commercially reasonable manner, the lessee may recover from the lessor as damages (i) the present value, as of the date of the commencement of the term of the new lease agreement, of the rent under the new lease agreement applicable to that period of the new lease term which is comparable to the then remaining term of the original lease agreement minus the present value as of the same date of the total rent for the then remaining lease term of the original lease agreement, and (ii) any incidental or consequential damages, less expenses saved in consequence of the lessor's default.

(3) If a lessee's cover is by lease agreement that for any reason does not qualify for treatment under subsection (2), or is by purchase or otherwise, the lessee may recover from the lessor as if the lessee had elected not to cover and Section 2A–519 governs.

As amended in 1990.

§ 2A–519. Lessee's Damages for Non-Delivery, Repudiation, Default, and Breach of Warranty in Regard to Accepted Goods.

(1) Except as otherwise provided with respect to damages liquidated in the lease agreement (Section 2A–504) or otherwise determined pursuant to agreement of the parties (Sections 1–102(3) and 2A–503), if a lessee elects not to cover or a lessee elects to cover and the cover is by lease agreement that for any reason does not qualify for treatment under Section 2A–518(2), or is by purchase or otherwise, the measure of damages for non-delivery or repudiation by the lessor or for rejection or revocation of acceptance by the lessee is the present value, as of the date of the default, of the then market rent minus the present value as of the same date of the original rent, computed for the remaining lease term of the original lease agree-

ment, together with incidental and consequential damages, less expenses saved in consequence of the lessor's default.

(2) Market rent is to be determined as of the place for tender or, in cases of rejection after arrival or revocation of acceptance, as of the place of arrival.

(3) Except as otherwise agreed, if the lessee has accepted goods and given notification (Section 2A–516(3)), the measure of damages for non-conforming tender or delivery or other default by a lessor is the loss resulting in the ordinary course of events from the lessor's default as determined in any manner that is reasonable together with incidental and consequential damages, less expenses saved in consequence of the lessor's default.

(4) Except as otherwise agreed, the measure of damages for breach of warranty is the present value at the time and place of acceptance of the difference between the value of the use of the goods accepted and the value if they had been as warranted for the lease term, unless special circumstances show proximate damages of a different amount, together with incidental and consequential damages, less expenses saved in consequence of the lessor's default or breach of warranty.

As amended in 1990.

§ 2A–520. Lessee's Incidental and Consequential Damages.

(1) Incidental damages resulting from a lessor's default include expenses reasonably incurred in inspection, receipt, transportation, and care and custody of goods rightfully rejected or goods the acceptance of which is justifiably revoked, any commercially reasonable charges, expenses or commissions in connection with effecting cover, and any other reasonable expense incident to the default.

(2) Consequential damages resulting from a lessor's default include:

(a) any loss resulting from general or particular requirements and needs of which the lessor at the time of contracting had reason to know and which could not reasonably be prevented by cover or otherwise; and

(b) injury to person or property proximately resulting from any breach of warranty.

§ 2A–521. Lessee's Right to Specific Performance or Replevin.

(1) Specific performance may be decreed if the goods are unique or in other proper circumstances.

(2) A decree for specific performance may include any terms and conditions as to payment of the rent, damages, or other relief that the court deems just.

(3) A lessee has a right of replevin, detinue, sequestration, claim and delivery, or the like for goods identified to the lease contract if after reasonable effort the lessee is unable to effect cover for those goods or the circumstances reasonably indicate that the effort will be unavailing.

§ 2A–522. Lessee's Right to Goods on Lessor's Insolvency.

(1) Subject to subsection (2) and even though the goods have not been shipped, a lessee who has paid a part or all of the rent and security for goods identified to a lease contract (Section 2A–217) on making and keeping good a tender of any unpaid portion of the rent and security due under the lease contract may recover the goods identified from the lessor if the lessor becomes insolvent within 10 days after receipt of the first installment of rent and security.

(2) A lessee acquires the right to recover goods identified to a lease contract only if they conform to the lease contract.

C. Default by Lessee

§ 2A–523. Lessor's Remedies.

(1) If a lessee wrongfully rejects or revokes acceptance of goods or fails to make a payment when due or repudiates with respect to a part or the whole, then, with respect to any goods involved, and with respect to all of the goods if under an installment lease contract the value of the whole lease contract is substantially impaired (Section 2A–510), the lessee is in default under the lease contract and the lessor may:

(a) cancel the lease contract (Section 2A–505(1));

(b) proceed respecting goods not identified to the lease contract (Section 2A–524);

(c) withhold delivery of the goods and take possession of goods previously delivered (Section 2A–525);

(d) stop delivery of the goods by any bailee (Section 2A–526);

(e) dispose of the goods and recover damages (Section 2A–527), or retain the goods and recover damages (Section 2A–528), or in a proper case recover rent (Section 2A–529)

(f) exercise any other rights or pursue any other remedies provided in the lease contract.

(2) If a lessor does not fully exercise a right or obtain a remedy to which the lessor is entitled under subsection (1), the lessor may recover the loss resulting in the ordinary course of events from the lessee's default as determined in any reasonable manner, together with incidental damages, less expenses saved in consequence of the lessee's default.

(3) If a lessee is otherwise in default under a lease contract, the lessor may exercise the rights and pursue the remedies provided in the lease contract, which may include a right to cancel the lease. In addition, unless otherwise provided in the lease contract:

(a) if the default substantially impairs the value of the lease contract to the lessor, the lessor may exercise the rights and pursue the remedies provided in subsections (1) or (2); or

(b) if the default does not substantially impair the value of the lease contract to the lessor, the lessor may recover as provided in subsection (2).

As amended in 1990.

§ 2A–524. Lessor's Right to Identify Goods to Lease Contract.

(1) After default by the lessee under the lease contract of the type described in Section 2A–523(1) or 2A–523(3)(a) or, if agreed, after other default by the lessee, the lessor may:

(a) identify to the lease contract conforming goods not already identified if at the time the lessor learned of the default they were in the lessor's or the supplier's possession or control; and

(b) dispose of goods (Section 2A–527(1)) that demonstrably have been intended for the particular lease contract even though those goods are unfinished.

(2) If the goods are unfinished, in the exercise of reasonable commercial judgment for the purposes of avoiding loss and of effective realization, an aggrieved lessor or the supplier may either complete manufacture and wholly identify the goods to the lease contract or cease manufacture and lease, sell, or otherwise dispose of the goods for scrap or salvage value or proceed in any other reasonable manner. As amended in 1990.

§ 2A–525. Lessor's Right to Possession of Goods.

(1) If a lessor discovers the lessee to be insolvent, the lessor may refuse to deliver the goods.

(2) After a default by the lessee under the lease contract of the type described in Section 2A–523(1) or 2A–523(3)(a) or, if agreed, after other default by the lessee, the lessor has the right to take possession of the goods. If the lease contract so provides, the lessor may require the lessee to assemble the goods and make them available to the lessor at a place to be designated by the lessor which is reasonably convenient to both parties. Without removal, the lessor may render unusable any goods employed in trade or business, and may dispose of goods on the lessee's premises (Section 2A–527).

(3) The lessor may proceed under subsection (2) without judicial process if that can be done without breach of the peace or the lessor may proceed by action.

As amended in 1990.

§ 2A–526. Lessor's Stoppage of Delivery in Transit or Otherwise.

(1) A lessor may stop delivery of goods in the possession of a carrier or other bailee if the lessor discovers the lessee to be insolvent and may stop delivery of carload, truckload, planeload, or larger shipments of express or freight if the lessee repudiates or fails to make a payment due before delivery, whether for rent, security or otherwise under the lease contract, or for any other reason the lessor has a right to withhold or take possession of the goods.

(2) In pursuing its remedies under subsection (1), the lessor may stop delivery until

(a) receipt of the goods by the lessee;

(b) acknowledgment to the lessee by any bailee of the goods, except a carrier, that the bailee holds the goods for the lessee; or

(c) such an acknowledgment to the lessee by a carrier via reshipment or as warehouseman.

(3) (a) To stop delivery, a lessor shall so notify as to enable the bailee by reasonable diligence to prevent delivery of the goods.

(b) After notification, the bailee shall hold and deliver the goods according to the directions of the lessor, but the lessor is liable to the bailee for any ensuing charges or damages.

(c) A carrier who has issued a nonnegotiable bill of lading is not obliged to obey a notification to stop received from a person other than the consignor.

§ 2A–527. Lessor's Rights to Dispose of Goods.

(1) After a default by a lessee under the lease contract of the type described in Section 2A–523(1) or 2A–523(3)(a) or after the lessor refuses to deliver or takes possession of goods (Section 2A–525 or 2A–526), or, if agreed, after other default by a lessee, the lessor may dispose of the goods concerned or the undelivered balance thereof by lease, sale, or otherwise.

(2) Except as otherwise provided with respect to damages liquidated in the lease agreement (Section 2A–504) or otherwise determined pursuant to agreement of the parties (Sections 1–102(3) and

2A–503), if the disposition is by lease agreement substantially similar to the original lease agreement and the new lease agreement is made in good faith and in a commercially reasonable manner, the lessor may recover from the lessee as damages (i) accrued and unpaid rent as of the date of the commencement of the term of the new lease agreement, (ii) the present value, as of the same date, of the total rent for the then remaining lease term of the original lease agreement minus the present value, as of the same date, of the rent under the new lease agreement applicable to that period of the new lease term which is comparable to the then remaining term of the original lease agreement, and (iii) any incidental damages allowed under Section 2A–530, less expenses saved in consequence of the lessee's default.

(3) If the lessor's disposition is by lease agreement that for any reason does not qualify for treatment under subsection (2), or is by sale or otherwise, the lessor may recover from the lessee as if the lessor had elected not to dispose of the goods and Section 2A–528 governs.

(4) A subsequent buyer or lessee who buys or leases from the lessor in good faith for value as a result of a disposition under this section takes the goods free of the original lease contract and any rights of the original lessee even though the lessor fails to comply with one or more of the requirements of this Article.

(5) The lessor is not accountable to the lessee for any profit made on any disposition. A lessee who has rightfully rejected or justifiably revoked acceptance shall account to the lessor for any excess over the amount of the lessee's security interest (Section 2A–508(5)).

As amended in 1990.

§ 2A–528. Lessor's Damages for Non-acceptance, Failure to Pay, Repudiation, or Other Default.

(1) Except as otherwise provided with respect to damages liquidated in the lease agreement (Section 2A–504) or otherwise determined pursuant to agreement of the parties (Section 1–102(3) and 2A–503), if a lessor elects to retain the goods or a lessor elects to dispose of the goods and the disposition is by lease agreement that for any reason does not qualify for treatment under Section 2A–527(2), or is by sale or otherwise, the lessor may recover from the lessee as damages for a default of the type described in Section 2A–523(1) or 2A–523(3)(a), or if agreed, for other default of the lessee, (i) accrued and unpaid rent as of the date of the default if the lessee has never taken possession of the goods, or, if the lessee has taken possession of the goods, as of the date the lessor repossesses the goods or an earlier date on which the lessee makes a tender of the goods to the lessor, (ii) the present value as of the date determined under clause (i) of the total rent for the then remaining lease term of the original lease agreement minus the present value as of the same date of the market rent as the place where the goods are located computed for the same lease term, and (iii) any incidental damages allowed under Section 2A–530, less expenses saved in consequence of the lessee's default.

(2) If the measure of damages provided in subsection (1) is inadequate to put a lessor in as good a position as performance would have, the measure of damages is the present value of the profit, including reasonable overhead, the lessor would have made from full performance by the lessee, together with any incidental damages allowed under Section 2A–530, due allowance for costs reasonably incurred and due credit for payments or proceeds of disposition.

As amended in 1990.

§ 2A–529. Lessor's Action for the Rent.

(1) After default by the lessee under the lease contract of the type described in Section 2A–523(1) or 2A–523(3)(a) or, if agreed, after other default by the lessee, if the lessor complies with subsection (2), the lessor may recover from the lessee as damages:

(a) for goods accepted by the lessee and not repossessed by or tendered to the lessor, and for conforming goods lost or damaged within a commercially reasonable time after risk of loss passes to the lessee (Section 2A–219), (i) accrued and unpaid rent as of the date of entry of judgment in favor of the lessor (ii) the present value as of the same date of the rent for the then remaining lease term of the lease agreement, and (iii) any incidental damages allowed under Section 2A–530, less expenses saved in consequence of the lessee's default; and

(b) for goods identified to the lease contract if the lessor is unable after reasonable effort to dispose of them at a reasonable price or the circumstances reasonably indicate that effort will be unavailing, (i) accrued and unpaid rent as of the date of entry of judgment in favor of the lessor, (ii) the present value as of the same date of the rent for the then remaining lease term of the lease agreement, and (iii) any incidental damages allowed under Section 2A–530, less expenses saved in consequence of the lessee's default.

(2) Except as provided in subsection (3), the lessor shall hold for the lessee for the remaining lease term of the lease agreement any goods that have been identified to the lease contract and are in the lessor's control.

(3) The lessor may dispose of the goods at any time before collection of the judgment for damages obtained pursuant to subsection (1). If the disposition is before the end of the remaining lease term of the lease agreement, the lessor's recovery against the lessee for damages is governed by Section 2A–527 or Section 2A–528, and the lessor will cause an appropriate credit to be provided against a judgment for damages to the extent that the amount of the judgment exceeds the recovery available pursuant to Section 2A–527 or 2A–528.

(4) Payment of the judgment for damages obtained pursuant to subsection (1) entitles the lessee to the use and possession of the goods not then disposed of for the remaining lease term of and in accordance with the lease agreement.

(5) After default by the lessee under the lease contract of the type described in Section 2A–523(1) or Section 2A–523(3)(a) or, if agreed, after other default by the lessee, a lessor who is held not entitled to rent under this section must nevertheless be awarded damages for non-acceptance under Sections 2A–527 and 2A–528.

As amended in 1990.

§ 2A–530. Lessor's Incidental Damages.

Incidental damages to an aggrieved lessor include any commercially reasonable charges, expenses, or commissions incurred in stopping delivery, in the transportation, care and custody of goods after the lessee's default, in connection with return or disposition of the goods, or otherwise resulting from the default.

§ 2A–531. Standing to Sue Third Parties for Injury to Goods.

(1) If a third party so deals with goods that have been identified to a lease contract as to cause actionable injury to a party to the lease contract (a) the lessor has a right of action against the third party,

and (b) the lessee also has a right of action against the third party if the lessee:

> (i) has a security interest in the goods;

> (ii) has an insurable interest in the goods; or

> (iii) bears the risk of loss under the lease contract or has since the injury assumed that risk as against the lessor and the goods have been converted or destroyed.

(2) If at the time of the injury the party plaintiff did not bear the risk of loss as against the other party to the lease contract and there is no arrangement between them for disposition of the recovery, his [or her] suit or settlement, subject to his [or her] own interest, is as a fiduciary for the other party to the lease contract.

(3) Either party with the consent of the other may sue for the benefit of whom it may concern.

§ 2A–532. Lessor's Rights to Residual Interest.

In addition to any other recovery permitted by this Article or other law, the lessor may recover from the lessee an amount that will fully compensate the lessor for any loss of or damage to the lessor's residual interest in the goods caused by the default of the lessee.

As added in 1990.

Revised Article 3
NEGOTIABLE INSTRUMENTS

Part 1 General Provisions and Definitions

§ 3–101. Short Title.

This Article may be cited as Uniform Commercial Code–Negotiable Instruments.

§ 3–102. Subject Matter.

(a) This Article applies to negotiable instruments. It does not apply to money, to payment orders governed by Article 4A, or to securities governed by Article 8.

(b) If there is conflict between this Article and Article 4 or 9, Articles 4 and 9 govern.

(c) Regulations of the Board of Governors of the Federal Reserve System and operating circulars of the Federal Reserve Banks supersede any inconsistent provision of this Article to the extent of the inconsistency.

§ 3–103. Definitions.

(a) In this Article:

> (1) "Acceptor" means a drawee who has accepted a draft.

> (2) "Drawee" means a person ordered in a draft to make payment.

> (3) "Drawer" means a person who signs or is identified in a draft as a person ordering payment.

> (4) "Good faith" means honesty in fact and the observance of reasonable commercial standards of fair dealing.

> (5) "Maker" means a person who signs or is identified in a note as a person undertaking to pay.

> (6) "Order" means a written instruction to pay money signed by the person giving the instruction. The instruction may be addressed to any person, including the person giving the instruction, or to one or more persons jointly or in the alternative but not in succession. An authorization to pay is not an order unless the person authorized to pay is also instructed to pay.

> (7) "Ordinary care" in the case of a person engaged in business means observance of reasonable commercial standards, prevailing in the area in which the person is located, with respect to the business in which the person is engaged. In the case of a bank that takes an instrument for processing for collection or payment by automated means, reasonable commercial standards do not require the bank to examine the instrument if the failure to examine does not violate the bank's prescribed procedures and the bank's procedures do not vary unreasonably from general banking usage not disapproved by this Article or Article 4.

> (8) "Party" means a party to an instrument.

> (9) "Promise" means a written undertaking to pay money signed by the person undertaking to pay. An acknowledgment of an obligation by the obligor is not a promise unless the obligor also undertakes to pay the obligation.

> (10) "Prove" with respect to a fact means to meet the burden of establishing the fact (Section 1–201(8)).

> (11) "Remitter" means a person who purchases an instrument from its issuer if the instrument is payable to an identified person other than the purchaser.

(b) [Other definitions' section references deleted.]

(c) [Other definitions' section references deleted.]

(d) In addition, Article 1 contains general definitions and principles of construction and interpretation applicable throughout this Article.

§ 3–104. Negotiable Instrument.

(a) Except as provided in subsections (c) and (d), "negotiable instrument" means an unconditional promise or order to pay a fixed amount of money, with or without interest or other charges described in the promise or order, if it:

> (1) is payable to bearer or to order at the time it is issued or first comes into possession of a holder;

> (2) is payable on demand or at a definite time; and

> (3) does not state any other undertaking or instruction by the person promising or ordering payment to do any act in addition to the payment of money, but the promise or order may contain (i) an undertaking or power to give, maintain, or protect collateral to secure payment, (ii) an authorization or power to the holder to confess judgment or realize on or dispose of collateral, or (iii) a waiver of the benefit of any law intended for the advantage or protection of an obligor.

(b) "Instrument" means a negotiable instrument.

(c) An order that meets all of the requirements of subsection (a), except paragraph (1), and otherwise falls within the definition of "check" in subsection (f) is a negotiable instrument and a check.

(d) A promise or order other than a check is not an instrument if, at the time it is issued or first comes into possession of a holder, it contains a conspicuous statement, however expressed, to the effect that the promise or order is not negotiable or is not an instrument governed by this Article.

(e) An instrument is a "note" if it is a promise and is a "draft" if it is an order. If an instrument falls within the definition of both "note" and "draft," a person entitled to enforce the instrument may treat it as either.

(f) "Check" means (i) a draft, other than a documentary draft, payable on demand and drawn on a bank or (ii) a cashier's check or teller's check. An instrument may be a check even though it is described on its face by another term, such as "money order."

(g) "Cashier's check" means a draft with respect to which the drawer and drawee are the same bank or branches of the same bank.

(h) "Teller's check" means a draft drawn by a bank (i) on another bank, or (ii) payable at or through a bank.

(i) "Traveler's check" means an instrument that (i) is payable on demand, (ii) is drawn on or payable at or through a bank, (iii) is designated by the term "traveler's check" or by a substantially similar term, and (iv) requires, as a condition to payment, a countersignature by a person whose specimen signature appears on the instrument.

(j) "Certificate of deposit" means an instrument containing an acknowledgment by a bank that a sum of money has been received by the bank and a promise by the bank to repay the sum of money. A certificate of deposit is a note of the bank.

§ 3–105. Issue of Instrument.

(a) "Issue" means the first delivery of an instrument by the maker or drawer, whether to a holder or nonholder, for the purpose of giving rights on the instrument to any person.

(b) An unissued instrument, or an unissued incomplete instrument that is completed, is binding on the maker or drawer, but nonissuance is a defense. An instrument that is conditionally issued or is issued for a special purpose is binding on the maker or drawer, but failure of the condition or special purpose to be fulfilled is a defense.

(c) "Issuer" applies to issued and unissued instruments and means a maker or drawer of an instrument.

§ 3–106. Unconditional Promise or Order.

(a) Except as provided in this section, for the purposes of Section 3–104(a), a promise or order is unconditional unless it states (i) an express condition to payment, (ii) that the promise or order is subject to or governed by another writing, or (iii) that rights or obligations with respect to the promise or order are stated in another writing. A reference to another writing does not of itself make the promise or order conditional.

(b) A promise or order is not made conditional (i) by a reference to another writing for a statement of rights with respect to collateral, prepayment, or acceleration, or (ii) because payment is limited to resort to a particular fund or source.

(c) If a promise or order requires, as a condition to payment, a countersignature by a person whose specimen signature appears on the promise or order, the condition does not make the promise or order conditional for the purposes of Section 3–104(a). If the person whose specimen signature appears on an instrument fails to countersign the instrument, the failure to countersign is a defense to the obligation of the issuer, but the failure does not prevent a transferee of the instrument from becoming a holder of the instrument.

(d) If a promise or order at the time it is issued or first comes into possession of a holder contains a statement, required by applicable statutory or administrative law, to the effect that the rights of a holder or transferee are subject to claims or defenses that the issuer could assert against the original payee, the promise or order is not thereby made conditional for the purposes of Section 3–104(a); but if the promise or order is an instrument, there cannot be a holder in due course of the instrument.

§ 3–107. Instrument Payable in Foreign Money.

Unless the instrument otherwise provides, an instrument that states the amount payable in foreign money may be paid in the foreign money or in an equivalent amount in dollars calculated by using the current bank-offered spot rate at the place of payment for the purchase of dollars on the day on which the instrument is paid.

§ 3–108. Payable on Demand or at Definite Time.

(a) A promise or order is "payable on demand" if it (i) states that it is payable on demand or at sight, or otherwise indicates that it is payable at the will of the holder, or (ii) does not state any time of payment.

(b) A promise or order is "payable at a definite time" if it is payable on elapse of a definite period of time after sight or acceptance or at a fixed date or dates or at a time or times readily ascertainable at the time the promise or order is issued, subject to rights of (i) prepayment, (ii) acceleration, (iii) extension at the option of the holder, or (iv) extension to a further definite time at the option of the maker or acceptor or automatically upon or after a specified act or event.

(c) If an instrument, payable at a fixed date, is also payable upon demand made before the fixed date, the instrument is payable on demand until the fixed date and, if demand for payment is not made before that date, becomes payable at a definite time on the fixed date.

§ 3–109. Payable to Bearer or to Order.

(a) A promise or order is payable to bearer if it:

(1) states that it is payable to bearer or to the order of bearer or otherwise indicates that the person in possession of the promise or order is entitled to payment;

(2) does not state a payee; or

(3) states that it is payable to or to the order of cash or otherwise indicates that it is not payable to an identified person.

(b) A promise or order that is not payable to bearer is payable to order if it is payable (i) to the order of an identified person or (ii) to an identified person or order. A promise or order that is payable to order is payable to the identified person.

(c) An instrument payable to bearer may become payable to an identified person if it is specially indorsed pursuant to Section 3–205(a). An instrument payable to an identified person may become payable to bearer if it is indorsed in blank pursuant to Section 3–205(b).

§ 3–110. Identification of Person to Whom Instrument Is Payable.

(a) The person to whom an instrument is initially payable is determined by the intent of the person, whether or not authorized, signing as, or in the name or behalf of, the issuer of the instrument. The instrument is payable to the person intended by the signer even if that person is identified in the instrument by a name or other identification that is not that of the intended person. If more than one person signs in the name or behalf of the issuer of an instrument and all the signers do not intend the same person as payee, the instrument is payable to any person intended by one or more of the signers.

(b) If the signature of the issuer of an instrument is made by automated means, such as a check-writing machine, the payee of the instrument is determined by the intent of the person who supplied the name or identification of the payee, whether or not authorized to do so.

(c) A person to whom an instrument is payable may be identified in any way, including by name, identifying number, office, or account number. For the purpose of determining the holder of an instrument, the following rules apply:

(1) If an instrument is payable to an account and the account is identified only by number, the instrument is payable to the person to whom the account is payable. If an instrument is payable to an account identified by number and by the name of a person, the instrument is payable to the named person, whether or not that person is the owner of the account identified by number.

(2) If an instrument is payable to:

(i) a trust, an estate, or a person described as trustee or representative of a trust or estate, the instrument is payable to the trustee, the representative, or a successor of either, whether or not the beneficiary or estate is also named;

(ii) a person described as agent or similar representative of a named or identified person, the instrument is payable to the represented person, the representative, or a successor of the representative;

(iii) a fund or organization that is not a legal entity, the instrument is payable to a representative of the members of the fund or organization; or

(iv) an office or to a person described as holding an office, the instrument is payable to the named person, the incumbent of the office, or a successor to the incumbent.

(d) If an instrument is payable to two or more persons alternatively, it is payable to any of them and may be negotiated, discharged, or enforced by any or all of them in possession of the instrument. If an instrument is payable to two or more persons not alternatively, it is payable to all of them and may be negotiated, discharged, or enforced only by all of them. If an instrument payable to two or more persons is ambiguous as to whether it is payable to the persons alternatively, the instrument is payable to the persons alternatively.

§ 3–111. Place of Payment.

Except as otherwise provided for items in Article 4, an instrument is payable at the place of payment stated in the instrument. If no place of payment is stated, an instrument is payable at the address of the drawee or maker stated in the instrument. If no address is stated, the place of payment is the place of business of the drawee or maker. If a drawee or maker has more than one place of business, the place of payment is any place of business of the drawee or maker chosen by the person entitled to enforce the instrument. If the drawee or maker has no place of business, the place of payment is the residence of the drawee or maker.

§ 3–112. Interest.

(a) Unless otherwise provided in the instrument, (i) an instrument is not payable with interest, and (ii) interest on an interest-bearing instrument is payable from the date of the instrument.

(b) Interest may be stated in an instrument as a fixed or variable amount of money or it may be expressed as a fixed or variable rate or rates. The amount or rate of interest may be stated or described in the instrument in any manner and may require reference to information not contained in the instrument. If an instrument provides for interest, but the amount of interest payable cannot be ascertained from the description, interest is payable at the judgment rate in effect at the place of payment of the instrument and at the time interest first accrues.

§ 3–113. Date of Instrument.

(a) An instrument may be antedated or postdated. The date stated determines the time of payment if the instrument is payable at a fixed period after date. Except as provided in Section 4–401(c), an instrument payable on demand is not payable before the date of the instrument.

(b) If an instrument is undated, its date is the date of its issue or, in the case of an unissued instrument, the date it first comes into possession of a holder.

§ 3–114. Contradictory Terms of Instrument.

If an instrument contains contradictory terms, typewritten terms prevail over printed terms, handwritten terms prevail over both, and words prevail over numbers.

§ 3–115. Incomplete Instrument.

(a) "Incomplete instrument" means a signed writing, whether or not issued by the signer, the contents of which show at the time of signing that it is incomplete but that the signer intended it to be completed by the addition of words or numbers.

(b) Subject to subsection (c), if an incomplete instrument is an instrument under Section 3–104, it may be enforced according to its terms if it is not completed, or according to its terms as augmented by completion. If an incomplete instrument is not an instrument under Section 3–104, but, after completion, the requirements of Section 3–104 are met, the instrument may be enforced according to its terms as augmented by completion.

(c) If words or numbers are added to an incomplete instrument without authority of the signer, there is an alteration of the incomplete instrument under Section 3–407.

(d) The burden of establishing that words or numbers were added to an incomplete instrument without authority of the signer is on the person asserting the lack of authority.

§ 3–116. Joint and Several Liability; Contribution.

(a) Except as otherwise provided in the instrument, two or more persons who have the same liability on an instrument as makers, drawers, acceptors, indorsers who indorse as joint payees, or anomalous indorsers are jointly and severally liable in the capacity in which they sign.

(b) Except as provided in Section 3–419(e) or by agreement of the affected parties, a party having joint and several liability who pays the instrument is entitled to receive from any party having the same joint and several liability contribution in accordance with applicable law.

(c) Discharge of one party having joint and several liability by a person entitled to enforce the instrument does not affect the right under subsection (b) of a party having the same joint and several liability to receive contribution from the party discharged.

§ 3–117. Other Agreements Affecting Instrument.

Subject to applicable law regarding exclusion of proof of contemporaneous or previous agreements, the obligation of a party to an instrument to pay the instrument may be modified, supplemented, or nullified by a separate agreement of the obligor and a person entitled to enforce the instrument, if the instrument is issued or the obligation is incurred in reliance on the agreement or as part of the same transaction giving rise to the agreement. To the extent an obligation is modified, supplemented, or nullified by an agreement under this section, the agreement is a defense to the obligation.

§ 3–118. Statute of Limitations.

(a) Except as provided in subsection (e), an action to enforce the obligation of a party to pay a note payable at a definite time must be commenced within six years after the due date or dates stated in the note or, if a due date is accelerated, within six years after the accelerated due date.

(b) Except as provided in subsection (d) or (e), if demand for payment is made to the maker of a note payable on demand, an action to enforce the obligation of a party to pay the note must be commenced within six years after the demand. If no demand for payment is made to the maker, an action to enforce the note is barred if neither principal nor interest on the note has been paid for a continuous period of 10 years.

(c) Except as provided in subsection (d), an action to enforce the obligation of a party to an unaccepted draft to pay the draft must be commenced within three years after dishonor of the draft or 10 years after the date of the draft, whichever period expires first.

(d) An action to enforce the obligation of the acceptor of a certified check or the issuer of a teller's check, cashier's check, or traveler's check must be commenced within three years after demand for payment is made to the acceptor or issuer, as the case may be.

(e) An action to enforce the obligation of a party to a certificate of deposit to pay the instrument must be commenced within six years after demand for payment is made to the maker, but if the instrument states a due date and the maker is not required to pay before that date, the six-year period begins when a demand for payment is in effect and the due date has passed.

(f) An action to enforce the obligation of a party to pay an accepted draft, other than a certified check, must be commenced (i) within six years after the due date or dates stated in the draft or acceptance if the obligation of the acceptor is payable at a definite time, or (ii) within six years after the date of the acceptance if the obligation of the acceptor is payable on demand.

(g) Unless governed by other law regarding claims for indemnity or contribution, an action (i) for conversion of an instrument, for money had and received, or like action based on conversion, (ii) for breach of warranty, or (iii) to enforce an obligation, duty, or right arising under this Article and not governed by this section must be commenced within three years after the [cause of action] accrues.

§ 3–119. Notice of Right to Defend Action.

In an action for breach of an obligation for which a third person is answerable over pursuant to this Article or Article 4, the defendant may give the third person written notice of the litigation, and the person notified may then give similar notice to any other person who is answerable over. If the notice states (i) that the person notified may come in and defend and (ii) that failure to do so will bind the person notified in an action later brought by the person giving the notice as to any determination of fact common to the two litigations, the person notified is so bound unless after seasonable receipt of the notice the person notified does come in and defend.

Part 2 Negotiation, Transfer, and Indorsement

§ 3–201. Negotiation.

(a) "Negotiation" means a transfer of possession, whether voluntary or involuntary, of an instrument by a person other than the issuer to a person who thereby becomes its holder.

(b) Except for negotiation by a remitter, if an instrument is payable to an identified person, negotiation requires transfer of possession of the instrument and its indorsement by the holder. If an instrument is payable to bearer, it may be negotiated by transfer of possession alone.

§ 3–202. Negotiation Subject to Rescission.

(a) Negotiation is effective even if obtained (i) from an infant, a corporation exceeding its powers, or a person without capacity, (ii) by fraud, duress, or mistake, or (iii) in breach of duty or as part of an illegal transaction.

(b) To the extent permitted by other law, negotiation may be rescinded or may be subject to other remedies, but those remedies may not be asserted against a subsequent holder in due course or a person paying the instrument in good faith and without knowledge of facts that are a basis for rescission or other remedy.

§ 3–203. Transfer of Instrument; Rights Acquired by Transfer.

(a) An instrument is transferred when it is delivered by a person other than its issuer for the purpose of giving to the person receiving delivery the right to enforce the instrument.

(b) Transfer of an instrument, whether or not the transfer is a negotiation, vests in the transferee any right of the transferor to enforce the instrument, including any right as a holder in due course, but the transferee cannot acquire rights of a holder in due course by a transfer, directly or indirectly, from a holder in due course if the transferee engaged in fraud or illegality affecting the instrument.

(c) Unless otherwise agreed, if an instrument is transferred for value and the transferee does not become a holder because of lack of indorsement by the transferor, the transferee has a specifically enforceable right to the unqualified indorsement of the transferor, but negotiation of the instrument does not occur until the indorsement is made.

(d) If a transferor purports to transfer less than the entire instrument, negotiation of the instrument does not occur. The transferee obtains no rights under this Article and has only the rights of a partial assignee.

§ 3–204. Indorsement.

(a) "Indorsement" means a signature, other than that of a signer as maker, drawer, or acceptor, that alone or accompanied by other words is made on an instrument for the purpose of (i) negotiating the instrument, (ii) restricting payment of the instrument, or (iii) incurring indorser's liability on the instrument, but regardless of the intent of the signer, a signature and its accompanying words is an indorsement unless the accompanying words, terms of the instrument, place of the signature, or other circumstances unambiguously indicate that the signature was made for a purpose other than indorsement. For the purpose of determining whether a signature is made on an instrument, a paper affixed to the instrument is a part of the instrument.

(b) "Indorser" means a person who makes an indorsement.

(c) For the purpose of determining whether the transferee of an instrument is a holder, an indorsement that transfers a security interest in the instrument is effective as an unqualified indorsement of the instrument.

(d) If an instrument is payable to a holder under a name that is not the name of the holder, indorsement may be made by the holder in the name stated in the instrument or in the holder's name or both, but signature in both names may be required by a person paying or taking the instrument for value or collection.

§ 3–205. Special Indorsement; Blank Indorsement; Anomalous Indorsement.

(a) If an indorsement is made by the holder of an instrument, whether payable to an identified person or payable to bearer, and the indorsement identifies a person to whom it makes the instrument payable, it is a "special indorsement." When specially indorsed, an instrument becomes payable to the identified person and may be negotiated only by the indorsement of that person. The principles stated in Section 3–110 apply to special indorsements.

(b) If an indorsement is made by the holder of an instrument and it is not a special indorsement, it is a "blank indorsement." When indorsed in blank, an instrument becomes payable to bearer and may be negotiated by transfer of possession alone until specially indorsed.

(c) The holder may convert a blank indorsement that consists only of a signature into a special indorsement by writing, above the signature of the indorser, words identifying the person to whom the instrument is made payable.

(d) "Anomalous indorsement" means an indorsement made by a person who is not the holder of the instrument. An anomalous indorsement does not affect the manner in which the instrument may be negotiated.

§ 3–206. Restrictive Indorsement.

(a) An indorsement limiting payment to a particular person or otherwise prohibiting further transfer or negotiation of the instrument is not effective to prevent further transfer or negotiation of the instrument.

(b) An indorsement stating a condition to the right of the indorsee to receive payment does not affect the right of the indorsee to enforce the instrument. A person paying the instrument or taking it for value or collection may disregard the condition, and the rights and liabilities of that person are not affected by whether the condition has been fulfilled.

(c) If an instrument bears an indorsement (i) described in Section 4–201(b), or (ii) in blank or to a particular bank using the words "for deposit," "for collection," or other words indicating a purpose of having the instrument collected by a bank for the indorser or for a particular account, the following rules apply:

(1) A person, other than a bank, who purchases the instrument when so indorsed converts the instrument unless the amount paid for the instrument is received by the indorser or applied consistently with the indorsement.

(2) A depositary bank that purchases the instrument or takes it for collection when so indorsed converts the instrument unless the amount paid by the bank with respect to the instrument is received by the indorser or applied consistently with the indorsement.

(3) A payor bank that is also the depositary bank or that takes the instrument for immediate payment over the counter from a person other than a collecting bank converts the instrument unless the proceeds of the instrument are received by the indorser or applied consistently with the indorsement.

(4) Except as otherwise provided in paragraph (3), a payor bank or intermediary bank may disregard the indorsement and is not liable if the proceeds of the instrument are not received by the indorser or applied consistently with the indorsement.

(d) Except for an indorsement covered by subsection (c), if an instrument bears an indorsement using words to the effect that payment is to be made to the indorsee as agent, trustee, or other fiduciary for the benefit of the indorser or another person, the following rules apply:

(1) Unless there is notice of breach of fiduciary duty as provided in Section 3–307, a person who purchases the instrument from the indorsee or takes the instrument from the indorsee for collection or payment may pay the proceeds of payment or the value given for the instrument to the indorsee without regard to whether the indorsee violates a fiduciary duty to the indorser.

(2) A subsequent transferee of the instrument or person who pays the instrument is neither given notice nor otherwise affected by the restriction in the indorsement unless the transferee or payor knows that the fiduciary dealt with the instrument or its proceeds in breach of fiduciary duty.

(e) The presence on an instrument of an indorsement to which this section applies does not prevent a purchaser of the instrument from becoming a holder in due course of the instrument unless the purchaser is a converter under subsection (c) or has notice or knowledge of breach of fiduciary duty as stated in subsection (d).

(f) In an action to enforce the obligation of a party to pay the instrument, the obligor has a defense if payment would violate an indorsement to which this section applies and the payment is not permitted by this section.

§ 3–207. Reacquisition.

Reacquisition of an instrument occurs if it is transferred to a former holder, by negotiation or otherwise. A former holder who reacquires the instrument may cancel indorsements made after the reacquirer first became a holder of the instrument. If the cancellation causes the instrument to be payable to the reacquirer or to bearer, the reacquirer may negotiate the instrument. An indorser whose indorsement is canceled is discharged, and the discharge is effective against any subsequent holder.

Part 3 Enforcement of Instruments

§ 3–301. Person Entitled to Enforce Instrument.

"Person entitled to enforce" an instrument means (i) the holder of the instrument, (ii) a nonholder in possession of the instrument who has the rights of a holder, or (iii) a person not in possession of the instrument who is entitled to enforce the instrument pursuant to Section 3–309 or 3–418(d). A person may be a person entitled to enforce the instrument even though the person is not the owner of the instrument or is in wrongful possession of the instrument.

§ 3–302. Holder in Due Course.

(a) Subject to subsection (c) and Section 3–106(d), "holder in due course" means the holder of an instrument if:

(1) the instrument when issued or negotiated to the holder does not bear such apparent evidence of forgery or alteration or is not otherwise so irregular or incomplete as to call into question its authenticity; and

(2) the holder took the instrument (i) for value, (ii) in good faith, (iii) without notice that the instrument is overdue or has been dishonored or that there is an uncured default with respect to payment of another instrument issued as part of the same series, (iv) without notice that the instrument contains an unauthorized signature or has been altered, (v) without notice of any claim to the instrument described in Section 3–306, and (vi) without notice that any party has a defense or claim in recoupment described in Section 3–305(a).

(b) Notice of discharge of a party, other than discharge in an insolvency proceeding, is not notice of a defense under subsection (a), but discharge is effective against a person who became a holder in due course with notice of the discharge. Public filing or recording of a document does not of itself constitute notice of a defense, claim in recoupment, or claim to the instrument.

(c) Except to the extent a transferor or predecessor in interest has rights as a holder in due course, a person does not acquire rights of a holder in due course of an instrument taken (i) by legal process or by purchase in an execution, bankruptcy, or creditor's sale or similar proceeding, (ii) by purchase as part of a bulk transaction not in ordinary course of business of the transferor, or (iii) as the successor in interest to an estate or other organization.

(d) If, under Section 3–303(a)(1), the promise of performance that is the consideration for an instrument has been partially performed, the holder may assert rights as a holder in due course of the instrument only to the fraction of the amount payable under the instrument equal to the value of the partial performance divided by the value of the promised performance.

(e) If (i) the person entitled to enforce an instrument has only a security interest in the instrument and (ii) the person obliged to pay the instrument has a defense, claim in recoupment, or claim to the instrument that may be asserted against the person who granted the security interest, the person entitled to enforce the instrument may assert rights as a holder in due course only to an amount payable under the instrument which, at the time of enforcement of the instrument, does not exceed the amount of the unpaid obligation secured.

(f) To be effective, notice must be received at a time and in a manner that gives a reasonable opportunity to act on it.

(g) This section is subject to any law limiting status as a holder in due course in particular classes of transactions.

§ 3–303. Value and Consideration.

(a) An instrument is issued or transferred for value if:

(1) the instrument is issued or transferred for a promise of performance, to the extent the promise has been performed;

(2) the transferee acquires a security interest or other lien in the instrument other than a lien obtained by judicial proceeding;

(3) the instrument is issued or transferred as payment of, or as security for, an antecedent claim against any person, whether or not the claim is due;

(4) the instrument is issued or transferred in exchange for a negotiable instrument; or

(5) the instrument is issued or transferred in exchange for the incurring of an irrevocable obligation to a third party by the person taking the instrument.

(b) "Consideration" means any consideration sufficient to support a simple contract. The drawer or maker of an instrument has a defense if the instrument is issued without consideration. If an instrument is issued for a promise of performance, the issuer has a defense to the extent performance of the promise is due and the promise has not been performed. If an instrument is issued for value as stated in subsection (a), the instrument is also issued for consideration.

§ 3–304. Overdue Instrument.

(a) An instrument payable on demand becomes overdue at the earliest of the following times:

(1) on the day after the day demand for payment is duly made;

(2) if the instrument is a check, 90 days after its date; or

(3) if the instrument is not a check, when the instrument has been outstanding for a period of time after its date which is unreasonably long under the circumstances of the particular case in light of the nature of the instrument and usage of the trade.

(b) With respect to an instrument payable at a definite time the following rules apply:

(1) If the principal is payable in installments and a due date has not been accelerated, the instrument becomes overdue upon default under the instrument for nonpayment of an installment, and the instrument remains overdue until the default is cured.

(2) If the principal is not payable in installments and the due date has not been accelerated, the instrument becomes overdue on the day after the due date.

(3) If a due date with respect to principal has been accelerated, the instrument becomes overdue on the day after the accelerated due date.

(c) Unless the due date of principal has been accelerated, an instrument does not become overdue if there is default in payment of interest but no default in payment of principal.

§ 3–305. Defenses and Claims in Recoupment.

(a) Except as stated in subsection (b), the right to enforce the obligation of a party to pay an instrument is subject to the following:

(1) a defense of the obligor based on (i) infancy of the obligor to the extent it is a defense to a simple contract, (ii) duress, lack of legal capacity, or illegality of the transaction which, under other law, nullifies the obligation of the obligor, (iii) fraud that induced the obligor to sign the instrument with neither knowl-

edge nor reasonable opportunity to learn of its character or its essential terms, or (iv) discharge of the obligor in insolvency proceedings;

(2) a defense of the obligor stated in another section of this Article or a defense of the obligor that would be available if the person entitled to enforce the instrument were enforcing a right to payment under a simple contract; and

(3) a claim in recoupment of the obligor against the original payee of the instrument if the claim arose from the transaction that gave rise to the instrument; but the claim of the obligor may be asserted against a transferee of the instrument only to reduce the amount owing on the instrument at the time the action is brought.

(b) The right of a holder in due course to enforce the obligation of a party to pay the instrument is subject to defenses of the obligor stated in subsection (a)(1), but is not subject to defenses of the obligor stated in subsection (a)(2) or claims in recoupment stated in subsection (a)(3) against a person other than the holder.

(c) Except as stated in subsection (d), in an action to enforce the obligation of a party to pay the instrument, the obligor may not assert against the person entitled to enforce the instrument a defense, claim in recoupment, or claim to the instrument (Section 3–306) of another person, but the other person's claim to the instrument may be asserted by the obligor if the other person is joined in the action and personally asserts the claim against the person entitled to enforce the instrument. An obligor is not obliged to pay the instrument if the person seeking enforcement of the instrument does not have rights of a holder in due course and the obligor proves that the instrument is a lost or stolen instrument.

(d) In an action to enforce the obligation of an accommodation party to pay an instrument, the accommodation party may assert against the person entitled to enforce the instrument any defense or claim in recoupment under subsection (a) that the accommodated party could assert against the person entitled to enforce the instrument, except the defenses of discharge in insolvency proceedings, infancy, and lack of legal capacity.

§ 3–306. Claims to an Instrument.

A person taking an instrument, other than a person having rights of a holder in due course, is subject to a claim of a property or possessory right in the instrument or its proceeds, including a claim to rescind a negotiation and to recover the instrument or its proceeds. A person having rights of a holder in due course takes free of the claim to the instrument.

§ 3–307. Notice of Breach of Fiduciary Duty.

(a) In this section:

(1) "Fiduciary" means an agent, trustee, partner, corporate officer or director, or other representative owing a fiduciary duty with respect to an instrument.

(2) "Represented person" means the principal, beneficiary, partnership, corporation, or other person to whom the duty stated in paragraph (1) is owed.

(b) If (i) an instrument is taken from a fiduciary for payment or collection or for value, (ii) the taker has knowledge of the fiduciary status of the fiduciary, and (iii) the represented person makes a claim to the instrument or its proceeds on the basis that the transaction of the fiduciary is a breach of fiduciary duty, the following rules apply:

(1) Notice of breach of fiduciary duty by the fiduciary is notice of the claim of the represented person.

(2) In the case of an instrument payable to the represented person or the fiduciary as such, the taker has notice of the breach of fiduciary duty if the instrument is (i) taken in payment of or as security for a debt known by the taker to be the personal debt of the fiduciary, (ii) taken in a transaction known by the taker to be for the personal benefit of the fiduciary, or (iii) deposited to an account other than an account of the fiduciary, as such, or an account of the represented person.

(3) If an instrument is issued by the represented person or the fiduciary as such, and made payable to the fiduciary personally, the taker does not have notice of the breach of fiduciary duty unless the taker knows of the breach of fiduciary duty.

(4) If an instrument is issued by the represented person or the fiduciary as such, to the taker as payee, the taker has notice of the breach of fiduciary duty if the instrument is (i) taken in payment of or as security for a debt known by the taker to be the personal debt of the fiduciary, (ii) taken in a transaction known by the taker to be for the personal benefit of the fiduciary, or (iii) deposited to an account other than an account of the fiduciary, as such, or an account of the represented person.

§ 3–308. Proof of Signatures and Status as Holder in Due Course.

(a) In an action with respect to an instrument, the authenticity of, and authority to make, each signature on the instrument is admitted unless specifically denied in the pleadings. If the validity of a signature is denied in the pleadings, the burden of establishing validity is on the person claiming validity, but the signature is presumed to be authentic and authorized unless the action is to enforce the liability of the purported signer and the signer is dead or incompetent at the time of trial of the issue of validity of the signature. If an action to enforce the instrument is brought against a person as the undisclosed principal of a person who signed the instrument as a party to the instrument, the plaintiff has the burden of establishing that the defendant is liable on the instrument as a represented person under Section 3–402(a).

(b) If the validity of signatures is admitted or proved and there is compliance with subsection (a), a plaintiff producing the instrument is entitled to payment if the plaintiff proves entitlement to enforce the instrument under Section 3–301, unless the defendant proves a defense or claim in recoupment. If a defense or claim in recoupment is proved, the right to payment of the plaintiff is subject to the defense or claim, except to the extent the plaintiff proves that the plaintiff has rights of a holder in due course which are not subject to the defense or claim.

§ 3–309. Enforcement of Lost, Destroyed, or Stolen Instrument.

(a) A person not in possession of an instrument is entitled to enforce the instrument if (i) the person was in possession of the instrument and entitled to enforce it when loss of possession occurred, (ii) the loss of possession was not the result of a transfer by the person or a lawful seizure, and (iii) the person cannot reasonably obtain possession of the instrument because the instrument was destroyed, its whereabouts cannot be determined, or it is in the wrongful possession of an unknown person or a person that cannot be found or is not amenable to service of process.

(b) A person seeking enforcement of an instrument under subsection (a) must prove the terms of the instrument and the person's right to enforce the instrument. If that proof is made, Section 3–308 applies to the case as if the person seeking enforcement had produced the instrument. The court may not enter judgment in favor of the person seeking enforcement unless it finds that the person required to pay the instrument is adequately protected against loss that might occur by reason of a claim by another person to enforce the instrument. Adequate protection may be provided by any reasonable means.

§ 3–310. Effect of Instrument on Obligation for Which Taken.

(a) Unless otherwise agreed, if a certified check, cashier's check, or teller's check is taken for an obligation, the obligation is discharged to the same extent discharge would result if an amount of money equal to the amount of the instrument were taken in payment of the obligation. Discharge of the obligation does not affect any liability that the obligor may have as an indorser of the instrument.

(b) Unless otherwise agreed and except as provided in subsection (a), if a note or an uncertified check is taken for an obligation, the obligation is suspended to the same extent the obligation would be discharged if an amount of money equal to the amount of the instrument were taken, and the following rules apply:

(1) In the case of an uncertified check, suspension of the obligation continues until dishonor of the check or until it is paid or certified. Payment or certification of the check results in discharge of the obligation to the extent of the amount of the check.

(2) In the case of a note, suspension of the obligation continues until dishonor of the note or until it is paid. Payment of the note results in discharge of the obligation to the extent of the payment.

(3) Except as provided in paragraph (4), if the check or note is dishonored and the obligee of the obligation for which the instrument was taken is the person entitled to enforce the instrument, the obligee may enforce either the instrument or the obligation. In the case of an instrument of a third person which is negotiated to the obligee by the obligor, discharge of the obligor on the instrument also discharges the obligation.

(4) If the person entitled to enforce the instrument taken for an obligation is a person other than the obligee, the obligee may not enforce the obligation to the extent the obligation is suspended. If the obligee is the person entitled to enforce the instrument but no longer has possession of it because it was lost, stolen, or destroyed, the obligation may not be enforced to the extent of the amount payable on the instrument, and to that extent the obligee's rights against the obligor are limited to enforcement of the instrument.

(c) If an instrument other than one described in subsection (a) or (b) is taken for an obligation, the effect is (i) that stated in subsection (a) if the instrument is one on which a bank is liable as maker or acceptor, or (ii) that stated in subsection (b) in any other case.

§ 3–311. Accord and Satisfaction by Use of Instrument.

(a) If a person against whom a claim is asserted proves that (i) that person in good faith tendered an instrument to the claimant as full satisfaction of the claim, (ii) the amount of the claim was unliq-

uidated or subject to a bona fide dispute, and (iii) the claimant obtained payment of the instrument, the following subsections apply.

(b) Unless subsection (c) applies, the claim is discharged if the person against whom the claim is asserted proves that the instrument or an accompanying written communication contained a conspicuous statement to the effect that the instrument was tendered as full satisfaction of the claim.

(c) Subject to subsection (d), a claim is not discharged under subsection (b) if either of the following applies:

(1) The claimant, if an organization, proves that (i) within a reasonable time before the tender, the claimant sent a conspicuous statement to the person against whom the claim is asserted that communications concerning disputed debts, including an instrument tendered as full satisfaction of a debt, are to be sent to a designated person, office, or place, and (ii) the instrument or accompanying communication was not received by that designated person, office, or place.

(2) The claimant, whether or not an organization, proves that within 90 days after payment of the instrument, the claimant tendered repayment of the amount of the instrument to the person against whom the claim is asserted. This paragraph does not apply if the claimant is an organization that sent a statement complying with paragraph (1)(i).

(d) A claim is discharged if the person against whom the claim is asserted proves that within a reasonable time before collection of the instrument was initiated, the claimant, or an agent of the claimant having direct responsibility with respect to the disputed obligation, knew that the instrument was tendered in full satisfaction of the claim.

§ 3–312. Lost, Destroyed, or Stolen Cashier's Check, Teller's Check, or Certified Check.

(a) In this section:

(1) "Check" means a cashier's check, teller's check, or certified check.

(2) "Claimant" means a person who claims the right to receive the amount of a cashier's check, teller's check, or certified check that was lost, destroyed, or stolen.

(3) "Declaration of loss" means a written statement, made under penalty of perjury, to the effect that (i) the declarer lost possession of a check, (ii) the declarer is the drawer or payee of the check, in the case of a certified check, or the remitter or payee of the check, in the case of a cashier's check or teller's check, (iii) the loss of possession was not the result of a transfer by the declarer or a lawful seizure, and (iv) the declarer cannot reasonably obtain possession of the check because the check was destroyed, its whereabouts cannot be determined, or it is in the wrongful possession of an unknown person or a person that cannot be found or is not amenable to service of process.

(4) "Obligated bank" means the issuer of a cashier's check or teller's check or the acceptor of a certified check.

(b) A claimant may assert a claim to the amount of a check by a communication to the obligated bank describing the check with reasonable certainty and requesting payment of the amount of the check, if (i) the claimant is the drawer or payee of a certified check or the remitter or payee of a cashier's check or teller's check, (ii) the communication contains or is accompanied by a declaration of loss of the claimant with respect to the check, (iii) the communication is received at a time and in a manner affording the bank a reasonable time to act on it before the check is paid, and (iv) the claimant provides reasonable identification if requested by the obligated bank. Delivery of a declaration of loss is a warranty of the truth of the statements made in the declaration. If a claim is asserted in compliance with this subsection, the following rules apply:

(1) The claim becomes enforceable at the later of (i) the time the claim is asserted, or (ii) the 90th day following the date of the check, in the case of a cashier's check or teller's check, or the 90th day following the date of the acceptance, in the case of a certified check.

(2) Until the claim becomes enforceable, it has no legal effect and the obligated bank may pay the check or, in the case of a teller's check, may permit the drawee to pay the check. Payment to a person entitled to enforce the check discharges all liability of the obligated bank with respect to the check.

(3) If the claim becomes enforceable before the check is presented for payment, the obligated bank is not obliged to pay the check.

(4) When the claim becomes enforceable, the obligated bank becomes obliged to pay the amount of the check to the claimant if payment of the check has not been made to a person entitled to enforce the check. Subject to Section 4–302(a)(1), payment to the claimant discharges all liability of the obligated bank with respect to the check.

(c) If the obligated bank pays the amount of a check to a claimant under subsection (b)(4) and the check is presented for payment by a person having rights of a holder in due course, the claimant is obliged to (i) refund the payment to the obligated bank if the check is paid, or (ii) pay the amount of the check to the person having rights of a holder in due course if the check is dishonored.

(d) If a claimant has the right to assert a claim under subsection (b) and is also a person entitled to enforce a cashier's check, teller's check, or certified check which is lost, destroyed, or stolen, the claimant may assert rights with respect to the check either under this section or Section 3–309.

Added in 1991.

Part 4 Liability of Parties

§ 3–401. Signature.

(a) A person is not liable on an instrument unless (i) the person signed the instrument, or (ii) the person is represented by an agent or representative who signed the instrument and the signature is binding on the represented person under Section 3–402.

(b) A signature may be made (i) manually or by means of a device or machine, and (ii) by the use of any name, including a trade or assumed name, or by a word, mark, or symbol executed or adopted by a person with present intention to authenticate a writing.

§ 3–402. Signature by Representative.

(a) If a person acting, or purporting to act, as a representative signs an instrument by signing either the name of the represented person or the name of the signer, the represented person is bound by the signature to the same extent the represented person would be bound if the signature were on a simple contract. If the represented person is bound, the signature of the representative is the "authorized signature of the represented person" and the represented person is liable on the instrument, whether or not identified in the instrument.

(b) If a representative signs the name of the representative to an instrument and the signature is an authorized signature of the represented person, the following rules apply:

(1) If the form of the signature shows unambiguously that the signature is made on behalf of the represented person who is identified in the instrument, the representative is not liable on the instrument.

(2) Subject to subsection (c), if (i) the form of the signature does not show unambiguously that the signature is made in a representative capacity or (ii) the represented person is not identified in the instrument, the representative is liable on the instrument to a holder in due course that took the instrument without notice that the representative was not intended to be liable on the instrument. With respect to any other person, the representative is liable on the instrument unless the representative proves that the original parties did not intend the representative to be liable on the instrument.

(c) If a representative signs the name of the representative as drawer of a check without indication of the representative status and the check is payable from an account of the represented person who is identified on the check, the signer is not liable on the check if the signature is an authorized signature of the represented person.

§ 3–403. Unauthorized Signature.

(a) Unless otherwise provided in this Article or Article 4, an unauthorized signature is ineffective except as the signature of the unauthorized signer in favor of a person who in good faith pays the instrument or takes it for value. An unauthorized signature may be ratified for all purposes of this Article.

(b) If the signature of more than one person is required to constitute the authorized signature of an organization, the signature of the organization is unauthorized if one of the required signatures is lacking.

(c) The civil or criminal liability of a person who makes an unauthorized signature is not affected by any provision of this Article which makes the unauthorized signature effective for the purposes of this Article.

§ 3–404. Impostors; Fictitious Payees.

(a) If an impostor, by use of the mails or otherwise, induces the issuer of an instrument to issue the instrument to the impostor, or to a person acting in concert with the impostor, by impersonating the payee of the instrument or a person authorized to act for the payee, an indorsement of the instrument by any person in the name of the payee is effective as the indorsement of the payee in favor of a person who, in good faith, pays the instrument or takes it for value or for collection.

(b) If (i) a person whose intent determines to whom an instrument is payable (Section 3–110(a) or (b)) does not intend the person identified as payee to have any interest in the instrument, or (ii) the person identified as payee of an instrument is a fictitious person, the following rules apply until the instrument is negotiated by special indorsement:

(1) Any person in possession of the instrument is its holder.

(2) An indorsement by any person in the name of the payee stated in the instrument is effective as the indorsement of the payee in favor of a person who, in good faith, pays the instrument or takes it for value or for collection.

(c) Under subsection (a) or (b), an indorsement is made in the name of a payee if (i) it is made in a name substantially similar to that of the payee or (ii) the instrument, whether or not indorsed, is deposited in a depositary bank to an account in a name substantially similar to that of the payee.

(d) With respect to an instrument to which subsection (a) or (b) applies, if a person paying the instrument or taking it for value or for collection fails to exercise ordinary care in paying or taking the instrument and that failure substantially contributes to loss resulting from payment of the instrument, the person bearing the loss may recover from the person failing to exercise ordinary care to the extent the failure to exercise ordinary care contributed to the loss.

§ 3–405. Employer's Responsibility for Fraudulent Indorsement by Employee.

(a) In this section:

(1) "Employee" includes an independent contractor and employee of an independent contractor retained by the employer.

(2) "Fraudulent indorsement" means (i) in the case of an instrument payable to the employer, a forged indorsement purporting to be that of the employer, or (ii) in the case of an instrument with respect to which the employer is the issuer, a forged indorsement purporting to be that of the person identified as payee.

(3) "Responsibility" with respect to instruments means authority (i) to sign or indorse instruments on behalf of the employer, (ii) to process instruments received by the employer for bookkeeping purposes, for deposit to an account, or for other disposition, (iii) to prepare or process instruments for issue in the name of the employer, (iv) to supply information determining the names or addresses of payees of instruments to be issued in the name of the employer, (v) to control the disposition of instruments to be issued in the name of the employer, or (vi) to act otherwise with respect to instruments in a responsible capacity. "Responsibility" does not include authority that merely allows an employee to have access to instruments or blank or incomplete instrument forms that are being stored or transported or are part of incoming or outgoing mail, or similar access.

(b) For the purpose of determining the rights and liabilities of a person who, in good faith, pays an instrument or takes it for value or for collection, if an employer entrusted an employee with responsibility with respect to the instrument and the employee or a person acting in concert with the employee makes a fraudulent indorsement of the instrument, the indorsement is effective as the indorsement of the person to whom the instrument is payable if it is made in the name of that person. If the person paying the instrument or taking it for value or for collection fails to exercise ordinary care in paying or taking the instrument and that failure substantially contributes to loss resulting from the fraud, the person bearing the loss may recover

from the person failing to exercise ordinary care to the extent the failure to exercise ordinary care contributed to the loss.

(c) Under subsection (b), an indorsement is made in the name of the person to whom an instrument is payable if (i) it is made in a name substantially similar to the name of that person or (ii) the instrument, whether or not indorsed, is deposited in a depositary bank to an account in a name substantially similar to the name of that person.

§ 3–406. Negligence Contributing to Forged Signature or Alteration of Instrument.

(a) A person whose failure to exercise ordinary care substantially contributes to an alteration of an instrument or to the making of a forged signature on an instrument is precluded from asserting the alteration or the forgery against a person who, in good faith, pays the instrument or takes it for value or for collection.

(b) Under subsection (a), if the person asserting the preclusion fails to exercise ordinary care in paying or taking the instrument and that failure substantially contributes to loss, the loss is allocated between the person precluded and the person asserting the preclusion according to the extent to which the failure of each to exercise ordinary care contributed to the loss.

(c) Under subsection (a), the burden of proving failure to exercise ordinary care is on the person asserting the preclusion. Under subsection (b), the burden of proving failure to exercise ordinary care is on the person precluded.

§ 3–407. Alteration.

(a) "Alteration" means (i) an unauthorized change in an instrument that purports to modify in any respect the obligation of a party, or (ii) an unauthorized addition of words or numbers or other change to an incomplete instrument relating to the obligation of a party.

(b) Except as provided in subsection (c), an alteration fraudulently made discharges a party whose obligation is affected by the alteration unless that party assents or is precluded from asserting the alteration. No other alteration discharges a party, and the instrument may be enforced according to its original terms.

(c) A payor bank or drawee paying a fraudulently altered instrument or a person taking it for value, in good faith and without notice of the alteration, may enforce rights with respect to the instrument (i) according to its original terms, or (ii) in the case of an incomplete instrument altered by unauthorized completion, according to its terms as completed.

§ 3–408. Drawee Not Liable on Unaccepted Draft.

A check or other draft does not of itself operate as an assignment of funds in the hands of the drawee available for its payment, and the drawee is not liable on the instrument until the drawee accepts it.

§ 3–409. Acceptance of Draft; Certified Check.

(a) "Acceptance" means the drawee's signed agreement to pay a draft as presented. It must be written on the draft and may consist of the drawee's signature alone. Acceptance may be made at any time and becomes effective when notification pursuant to instructions is given or the accepted draft is delivered for the purpose of giving rights on the acceptance to any person.

(b) A draft may be accepted although it has not been signed by the drawer, is otherwise incomplete, is overdue, or has been dishonored.

(c) If a draft is payable at a fixed period after sight and the acceptor fails to date the acceptance, the holder may complete the acceptance by supplying a date in good faith.

(d) "Certified check" means a check accepted by the bank on which it is drawn. Acceptance may be made as stated in subsection (a) or by a writing on the check which indicates that the check is certified. The drawee of a check has no obligation to certify the check, and refusal to certify is not dishonor of the check.

§ 3–410. Acceptance Varying Draft.

(a) If the terms of a drawee's acceptance vary from the terms of the draft as presented, the holder may refuse the acceptance and treat the draft as dishonored. In that case, the drawee may cancel the acceptance.

(b) The terms of a draft are not varied by an acceptance to pay at a particular bank or place in the United States, unless the acceptance states that the draft is to be paid only at that bank or place.

(c) If the holder assents to an acceptance varying the terms of a draft, the obligation of each drawer and indorser that does not expressly assent to the acceptance is discharged.

§ 3–411. Refusal to Pay Cashier's Checks, Teller's Checks, and Certified Checks.

(a) In this section, "obligated bank" means the acceptor of a certified check or the issuer of a cashier's check or teller's check bought from the issuer.

(b) If the obligated bank wrongfully (i) refuses to pay a cashier's check or certified check, (ii) stops payment of a teller's check, or (iii) refuses to pay a dishonored teller's check, the person asserting the right to enforce the check is entitled to compensation for expenses and loss of interest resulting from the nonpayment and may recover consequential damages if the obligated bank refuses to pay after receiving notice of particular circumstances giving rise to the damages.

(c) Expenses or consequential damages under subsection (b) are not recoverable if the refusal of the obligated bank to pay occurs because (i) the bank suspends payments, (ii) the obligated bank asserts a claim or defense of the bank that it has reasonable grounds to believe is available against the person entitled to enforce the instrument, (iii) the obligated bank has a reasonable doubt whether the person demanding payment is the person entitled to enforce the instrument, or (iv) payment is prohibited by law.

§ 3–412. Obligation of Issuer of Note or Cashier's Check.

The issuer of a note or cashier's check or other draft drawn on the drawer is obliged to pay the instrument (i) according to its terms at the time it was issued or, if not issued, at the time it first came into possession of a holder, or (ii) if the issuer signed an incomplete instrument, according to its terms when completed, to the extent stated in Sections 3–115 and 3–407. The obligation is owed to a person entitled to enforce the instrument or to an indorser who paid the instrument under Section 3–415.

§ 3–413. Obligation of Acceptor.

(a) The acceptor of a draft is obliged to pay the draft (i) according to its terms at the time it was accepted, even though the acceptance

states that the draft is payable "as originally drawn" or equivalent terms, (ii) if the acceptance varies the terms of the draft, according to the terms of the draft as varied, or (iii) if the acceptance is of a draft that is an incomplete instrument, according to its terms when completed, to the extent stated in Sections 3–115 and 3–407. The obligation is owed to a person entitled to enforce the draft or to the drawer or an indorser who paid the draft under Section 3–414 or 3–415.

(b) If the certification of a check or other acceptance of a draft states the amount certified or accepted, the obligation of the acceptor is that amount. If (i) the certification or acceptance does not state an amount, (ii) the amount of the instrument is subsequently raised, and (iii) the instrument is then negotiated to a holder in due course, the obligation of the acceptor is the amount of the instrument at the time it was taken by the holder in due course.

§ 3–414. Obligation of Drawer.

(a) This section does not apply to cashier's checks or other drafts drawn on the drawer.

(b) If an unaccepted draft is dishonored, the drawer is obliged to pay the draft (i) according to its terms at the time it was issued or, if not issued, at the time it first came into possession of a holder, or (ii) if the drawer signed an incomplete instrument, according to its terms when completed, to the extent stated in Sections 3–115 and 3–407. The obligation is owed to a person entitled to enforce the draft or to an indorser who paid the draft under Section 3–415.

(c) If a draft is accepted by a bank, the drawer is discharged, regardless of when or by whom acceptance was obtained.

(d) If a draft is accepted and the acceptor is not a bank, the obligation of the drawer to pay the draft if the draft is dishonored by the acceptor is the same as the obligation of an indorser under Section 3–415(a) and (c).

(e) If a draft states that it is drawn "without recourse" or otherwise disclaims liability of the drawer to pay the draft, the drawer is not liable under subsection (b) to pay the draft if the draft is not a check. A disclaimer of the liability stated in subsection (b) is not effective if the draft is a check.

(f) If (i) a check is not presented for payment or given to a depositary bank for collection within 30 days after its date, (ii) the drawee suspends payments after expiration of the 30-day period without paying the check, and (iii) because of the suspension of payments, the drawer is deprived of funds maintained with the drawee to cover payment of the check, the drawer to the extent deprived of funds may discharge its obligation to pay the check by assigning to the person entitled to enforce the check the rights of the drawer against the drawee with respect to the funds.

§ 3–415. Obligation of Indorser.

(a) Subject to subsections (b), (c), and (d) and to Section 3–419(d), if an instrument is dishonored, an indorser is obliged to pay the amount due on the instrument (i) according to the terms of the instrument at the time it was indorsed, or (ii) if the indorser indorsed an incomplete instrument, according to its terms when completed, to the extent stated in Sections 3–115 and 3–407. The obligation of the indorser is owed to a person entitled to enforce the instrument or to a subsequent indorser who paid the instrument under this section.

(b) If an indorsement states that it is made "without recourse" or otherwise disclaims liability of the indorser, the indorser is not liable under subsection (a) to pay the instrument.

(c) If notice of dishonor of an instrument is required by Section 3–503 and notice of dishonor complying with that section is not given to an indorser, the liability of the indorser under subsection (a) is discharged.

(d) If a draft is accepted by a bank after an indorsement is made, the liability of the indorser under subsection (a) is discharged.

(e) If an indorser of a check is liable under subsection (a) and the check is not presented for payment, or given to a depositary bank for collection, within 30 days after the day the indorsement was made, the liability of the indorser under subsection (a) is discharged.

As amended in 1993.

§ 3–416. Transfer Warranties.

(a) A person who transfers an instrument for consideration warrants to the transferee and, if the transfer is by indorsement, to any subsequent transferee that:

(1) the warrantor is a person entitled to enforce the instrument;

(2) all signatures on the instrument are authentic and authorized;

(3) the instrument has not been altered;

(4) the instrument is not subject to a defense or claim in recoupment of any party which can be asserted against the warrantor; and

(5) the warrantor has no knowledge of any insolvency proceeding commenced with respect to the maker or acceptor or, in the case of an unaccepted draft, the drawer.

(b) A person to whom the warranties under subsection (a) are made and who took the instrument in good faith may recover from the warrantor as damages for breach of warranty an amount equal to the loss suffered as a result of the breach, but not more than the amount of the instrument plus expenses and loss of interest incurred as a result of the breach.

(c) The warranties stated in subsection (a) cannot be disclaimed with respect to checks. Unless notice of a claim for breach of warranty is given to the warrantor within 30 days after the claimant has reason to know of the breach and the identity of the warrantor, the liability of the warrantor under subsection (b) is discharged to the extent of any loss caused by the delay in giving notice of the claim.

(d) A [cause of action] for breach of warranty under this section accrues when the claimant has reason to know of the breach.

§ 3–417. Presentment Warranties.

(a) If an unaccepted draft is presented to the drawee for payment or acceptance and the drawee pays or accepts the draft, (i) the person obtaining payment or acceptance, at the time of presentment, and (ii) a previous transferor of the draft, at the time of transfer, warrant to the drawee making payment or accepting the draft in good faith that:

(1) the warrantor is, or was, at the time the warrantor transferred the draft, a person entitled to enforce the draft or authorized to obtain payment or acceptance of the draft on behalf of a person entitled to enforce the draft;

(2) the draft has not been altered; and

(3) the warrantor has no knowledge that the signature of the drawer of the draft is unauthorized.

(b) A drawee making payment may recover from any warrantor damages for breach of warranty equal to the amount paid by the drawee less the amount the drawee received or is entitled to receive from the drawer because of the payment. In addition, the drawee is entitled to compensation for expenses and loss of interest resulting from the breach. The right of the drawee to recover damages under this subsection is not affected by any failure of the drawee to exercise ordinary care in making payment. If the drawee accepts the draft, breach of warranty is a defense to the obligation of the acceptor. If the acceptor makes payment with respect to the draft, the acceptor is entitled to recover from any warrantor for breach of warranty the amounts stated in this subsection.

(c) If a drawee asserts a claim for breach of warranty under subsection (a) based on an unauthorized indorsement of the draft or an alteration of the draft, the warrantor may defend by proving that the indorsement is effective under Section 3–404 or 3–405 or the drawer is precluded under Section 3–406 or 4–406 from asserting against the drawee the unauthorized indorsement or alteration.

(d) If (i) a dishonored draft is presented for payment to the drawer or an indorser or (ii) any other instrument is presented for payment to a party obliged to pay the instrument, and (iii) payment is received, the following rules apply:

(1) The person obtaining payment and a prior transferor of the instrument warrant to the person making payment in good faith that the warrantor is, or was, at the time the warrantor transferred the instrument, a person entitled to enforce the instrument or authorized to obtain payment on behalf of a person entitled to enforce the instrument.

(2) The person making payment may recover from any warrantor for breach of warranty an amount equal to the amount paid plus expenses and loss of interest resulting from the breach.

(e) The warranties stated in subsections (a) and (d) cannot be disclaimed with respect to checks. Unless notice of a claim for breach of warranty is given to the warrantor within 30 days after the claimant has reason to know of the breach and the identity of the warrantor, the liability of the warrantor under subsection (b) or (d) is discharged to the extent of any loss caused by the delay in giving notice of the claim.

(f) A [cause of action] for breach of warranty under this section accrues when the claimant has reason to know of the breach.

§ 3–418. Payment or Acceptance by Mistake.

(a) Except as provided in subsection (c), if the drawee of a draft pays or accepts the draft and the drawee acted on the mistaken belief that (i) payment of the draft had not been stopped pursuant to Section 4–403 or (ii) the signature of the drawer of the draft was authorized, the drawee may recover the amount of the draft from the person to whom or for whose benefit payment was made or, in the case of acceptance, may revoke the acceptance. Rights of the drawee under this subsection are not affected by failure of the drawee to exercise ordinary care in paying or accepting the draft.

(b) Except as provided in subsection (c), if an instrument has been paid or accepted by mistake and the case is not covered by subsection (a), the person paying or accepting may, to the extent permitted by the law governing mistake and restitution, (i) recover the payment from the person to whom or for whose benefit payment was made or (ii) in the case of acceptance, may revoke the acceptance.

(c) The remedies provided by subsection (a) or (b) may not be asserted against a person who took the instrument in good faith and for value or who in good faith changed position in reliance on the payment or acceptance. This subsection does not limit remedies provided by Section 3–417 or 4–407.

(d) Notwithstanding Section 4–215, if an instrument is paid or accepted by mistake and the payor or acceptor recovers payment or revokes acceptance under subsection (a) or (b), the instrument is deemed not to have been paid or accepted and is treated as dishonored, and the person from whom payment is recovered has rights as a person entitled to enforce the dishonored instrument.

§ 3–419. Instruments Signed for Accommodation.

(a) If an instrument is issued for value given for the benefit of a party to the instrument ("accommodated party") and another party to the instrument ("accommodation party") signs the instrument for the purpose of incurring liability on the instrument without being a direct beneficiary of the value given for the instrument, the instrument is signed by the accommodation party "for accommodation."

(b) An accommodation party may sign the instrument as maker, drawer, acceptor, or indorser and, subject to subsection (d), is obliged to pay the instrument in the capacity in which the accommodation party signs. The obligation of an accommodation party may be enforced notwithstanding any statute of frauds and whether or not the accommodation party receives consideration for the accommodation.

(c) A person signing an instrument is presumed to be an accommodation party and there is notice that the instrument is signed for accommodation if the signature is an anomalous indorsement or is accompanied by words indicating that the signer is acting as surety or guarantor with respect to the obligation of another party to the instrument. Except as provided in Section 3–605, the obligation of an accommodation party to pay the instrument is not affected by the fact that the person enforcing the obligation had notice when the instrument was taken by that person that the accommodation party signed the instrument for accommodation.

(d) If the signature of a party to an instrument is accompanied by words indicating unambiguously that the party is guaranteeing collection rather than payment of the obligation of another party to the instrument, the signer is obliged to pay the amount due on the instrument to a person entitled to enforce the instrument only if (i) execution of judgment against the other party has been returned unsatisfied, (ii) the other party is insolvent or in an insolvency proceeding, (iii) the other party cannot be served with process, or (iv) it is otherwise apparent that payment cannot be obtained from the other party.

(e) An accommodation party who pays the instrument is entitled to reimbursement from the accommodated party and is entitled to enforce the instrument against the accommodated party. An accommodated party who pays the instrument has no right of recourse against, and is not entitled to contribution from, an accommodation party.

§ 3–420. Conversion of Instrument.

(a) The law applicable to conversion of personal property applies to instruments. An instrument is also converted if it is taken by transfer, other than a negotiation, from a person not entitled to enforce the instrument or a bank makes or obtains payment with respect to the instrument for a person not entitled to enforce the instrument or receive payment. An action for conversion of an instrument may not be brought by (i) the issuer or acceptor of the instrument or (ii) a payee or indorsee who did not receive delivery of the instrument either directly or through delivery to an agent or a co-payee.

(b) In an action under subsection (a), the measure of liability is presumed to be the amount payable on the instrument, but recovery may not exceed the amount of the plaintiff's interest in the instrument.

(c) A representative, other than a depositary bank, who has in good faith dealt with an instrument or its proceeds on behalf of one who was not the person entitled to enforce the instrument is not liable in conversion to that person beyond the amount of any proceeds that it has not paid out.

Part 5 Dishonor

§ 3–501. Presentment.

(a) "Presentment" means a demand made by or on behalf of a person entitled to enforce an instrument (i) to pay the instrument made to the drawee or a party obliged to pay the instrument or, in the case of a note or accepted draft payable at a bank, to the bank, or (ii) to accept a draft made to the drawee.

(b) The following rules are subject to Article 4, agreement of the parties, and clearing-house rules and the like:

(1) Presentment may be made at the place of payment of the instrument and must be made at the place of payment if the instrument is payable at a bank in the United States; may be made by any commercially reasonable means, including an oral, written, or electronic communication; is effective when the demand for payment or acceptance is received by the person to whom presentment is made; and is effective if made to any one of two or more makers, acceptors, drawees, or other payors.

(2) Upon demand of the person to whom presentment is made, the person making presentment must (i) exhibit the instrument, (ii) give reasonable identification and, if presentment is made on behalf of another person, reasonable evidence of authority to do so, and (. . .) sign a receipt on the instrument for any payment made or surrender the instrument if full payment is made.

(3) Without dishonoring the instrument, the party to whom presentment is made may (i) return the instrument for lack of a necessary indorsement, or (ii) refuse payment or acceptance for failure of the presentment to comply with the terms of the instrument, an agreement of the parties, or other applicable law or rule.

(4) The party to whom presentment is made may treat presentment as occurring on the next business day after the day of presentment if the party to whom presentment is made has established a cut-off hour not earlier than 2 P.M. for the receipt and processing of instruments presented for payment or acceptance and presentment is made after the cut-off hour.

§ 3–502. Dishonor.

(a) Dishonor of a note is governed by the following rules:

(1) If the note is payable on demand, the note is dishonored if presentment is duly made to the maker and the note is not paid on the day of presentment.

(2) If the note is not payable on demand and is payable at or through a bank or the terms of the note require presentment, the note is dishonored if presentment is duly made and the note is not paid on the day it becomes payable or the day of presentment, whichever is later.

(3) If the note is not payable on demand and paragraph (2) does not apply, the note is dishonored if it is not paid on the day it becomes payable.

(b) Dishonor of an unaccepted draft other than a documentary draft is governed by the following rules:

(1) If a check is duly presented for payment to the payor bank otherwise than for immediate payment over the counter, the check is dishonored if the payor bank makes timely return of the check or sends timely notice of dishonor or nonpayment under Section 4–301 or 4–302, or becomes accountable for the amount of the check under Section 4–302.

(2) If a draft is payable on demand and paragraph (1) does not apply, the draft is dishonored if presentment for payment is duly made to the drawee and the draft is not paid on the day of presentment.

(3) If a draft is payable on a date stated in the draft, the draft is dishonored if (i) presentment for payment is duly made to the drawee and payment is not made on the day the draft becomes payable or the day of presentment, whichever is later, or (ii) presentment for acceptance is duly made before the day the draft becomes payable and the draft is not accepted on the day of presentment.

(4) If a draft is payable on elapse of a period of time after sight or acceptance, the draft is dishonored if presentment for acceptance is duly made and the draft is not accepted on the day of presentment.

(c) Dishonor of an unaccepted documentary draft occurs according to the rules stated in subsection (b)(2), (3), and (4), except that payment or acceptance may be delayed without dishonor until no later than the close of the third business day of the drawee following the day on which payment or acceptance is required by those paragraphs.

(d) Dishonor of an accepted draft is governed by the following rules:

(1) If the draft is payable on demand, the draft is dishonored if presentment for payment is duly made to the acceptor and the draft is not paid on the day of presentment.

(2) If the draft is not payable on demand, the draft is dishonored if presentment for payment is duly made to the acceptor and payment is not made on the day it becomes payable or the day of presentment, whichever is later.

(e) In any case in which presentment is otherwise required for dishonor under this section and presentment is excused under Section 3–504, dishonor occurs without presentment if the instrument is not duly accepted or paid.

(f) If a draft is dishonored because timely acceptance of the draft was not made and the person entitled to demand acceptance consents to a late acceptance, from the time of acceptance the draft is treated as never having been dishonored.

§ 3–503. Notice of Dishonor.

(a) The obligation of an indorser stated in Section 3–415(a) and the obligation of a drawer stated in Section 3–414(d) may not be enforced unless (i) the indorser or drawer is given notice of dishonor of the instrument complying with this section or (ii) notice of dishonor is excused under Section 3–504(b).

(b) Notice of dishonor may be given by any person; may be given by any commercially reasonable means, including an oral, written, or electronic communication; and is sufficient if it reasonably identifies the instrument and indicates that the instrument has been dishonored or has not been paid or accepted. Return of an instrument given to a bank for collection is sufficient notice of dishonor.

(c) Subject to Section 3–504(c), with respect to an instrument taken for collection by a collecting bank, notice of dishonor must be given (i) by the bank before midnight of the next banking day following the banking day on which the bank receives notice of dishonor of the instrument, or (ii) by any other person within 30 days following the day on which the person receives notice of dishonor. With respect to any other instrument, notice of dishonor must be given within 30 days following the day on which dishonor occurs.

§ 3–504. Excused Presentment and Notice of Dishonor.

(a) Presentment for payment or acceptance of an instrument is excused if (i) the person entitled to present the instrument cannot with reasonable diligence make presentment, (ii) the maker or acceptor has repudiated an obligation to pay the instrument or is dead or in insolvency proceedings, (iii) by the terms of the instrument presentment is not necessary to enforce the obligation of indorsers or the drawer, (iv) the drawer or indorser whose obligation is being enforced has waived presentment or otherwise has no reason to expect or right to require that the instrument be paid or accepted, or (v) the drawer instructed the drawee not to pay or accept the draft or the drawee was not obligated to the drawer to pay the draft.

(b) Notice of dishonor is excused if (i) by the terms of the instrument notice of dishonor is not necessary to enforce the obligation of a party to pay the instrument, or (ii) the party whose obligation is being enforced waived notice of dishonor. A waiver of presentment is also a waiver of notice of dishonor.

(c) Delay in giving notice of dishonor is excused if the delay was caused by circumstances beyond the control of the person giving the notice and the person giving the notice exercised reasonable diligence after the cause of the delay ceased to operate.

§ 3–505. Evidence of Dishonor.

(a) The following are admissible as evidence and create a presumption of dishonor and of any notice of dishonor stated:

(1) a document regular in form as provided in subsection (b) which purports to be a protest;

(2) a purported stamp or writing of the drawee, payor bank, or presenting bank on or accompanying the instrument stating that acceptance or payment has been refused unless reasons for

the refusal are stated and the reasons are not consistent with dishonor;

(3) a book or record of the drawee, payor bank, or collecting bank, kept in the usual course of business which shows dishonor, even if there is no evidence of who made the entry.

(b) A protest is a certificate of dishonor made by a United States consul or vice consul, or a notary public or other person authorized to administer oaths by the law of the place where dishonor occurs. It may be made upon information satisfactory to that person. The protest must identify the instrument and certify either that presentment has been made or, if not made, the reason why it was not made, and that the instrument has been dishonored by nonacceptance or nonpayment. The protest may also certify that notice of dishonor has been given to some or all parties.

Part 6 Discharge and Payment

§ 3–601. Discharge and Effect of Discharge.

(a) The obligation of a party to pay the instrument is discharged as stated in this Article or by an act or agreement with the party which would discharge an obligation to pay money under a simple contract.

(b) Discharge of the obligation of a party is not effective against a person acquiring rights of a holder in due course of the instrument without notice of the discharge.

§ 3–602. Payment.

(a) Subject to subsection (b), an instrument is paid to the extent payment is made (i) by or on behalf of a party obliged to pay the instrument, and (ii) to a person entitled to enforce the instrument. To the extent of the payment, the obligation of the party obliged to pay the instrument is discharged even though payment is made with knowledge of a claim to the instrument under Section 3–306 by another person.

(b) The obligation of a party to pay the instrument is not discharged under subsection (a) if:

(1) a claim to the instrument under Section 3–306 is enforceable against the party receiving payment and (i) payment is made with knowledge by the payor that payment is prohibited by injunction or similar process of a court of competent jurisdiction, or (ii) in the case of an instrument other than a cashier's check, teller's check, or certified check, the party making payment accepted, from the person having a claim to the instrument, indemnity against loss resulting from refusal to pay the person entitled to enforce the instrument; or

(2) the person making payment knows that the instrument is a stolen instrument and pays a person it knows is in wrongful possession of the instrument.

§ 3–603. Tender of Payment.

(a) If tender of payment of an obligation to pay an instrument is made to a person entitled to enforce the instrument, the effect of tender is governed by principles of law applicable to tender of payment under a simple contract.

(b) If tender of payment of an obligation to pay an instrument is made to a person entitled to enforce the instrument and the tender

is refused, there is discharge, to the extent of the amount of the tender, of the obligation of an indorser or accommodation party having a right of recourse with respect to the obligation to which the tender relates.

(c) If tender of payment of an amount due on an instrument is made to a person entitled to enforce the instrument, the obligation of the obligor to pay interest after the due date on the amount tendered is discharged. If presentment is required with respect to an instrument and the obligor is able and ready to pay on the due date at every place of payment stated in the instrument, the obligor is deemed to have made tender of payment on the due date to the person entitled to enforce the instrument.

§ 3–604. Discharge by Cancellation or Renunciation.

(a) A person entitled to enforce an instrument, with or without consideration, may discharge the obligation of a party to pay the instrument (i) by an intentional voluntary act, such as surrender of the instrument to the party, destruction, mutilation, or cancellation of the instrument, cancellation or striking out of the party's signature, or the addition of words to the instrument indicating discharge, or (ii) by agreeing not to sue or otherwise renouncing rights against the party by a signed writing.

(b) Cancellation or striking out of an indorsement pursuant to subsection (a) does not affect the status and rights of a party derived from the indorsement.

§ 3–605. Discharge of Indorsers and Accommodation Parties.

(a) In this section, the term "indorser" includes a drawer having the obligation described in Section 3–414(d).

(b) Discharge, under Section 3–604, of the obligation of a party to pay an instrument does not discharge the obligation of an indorser or accommodation party having a right of recourse against the discharged party.

(c) If a person entitled to enforce an instrument agrees, with or without consideration, to an extension of the due date of the obligation of a party to pay the instrument, the extension discharges an indorser or accommodation party having a right of recourse against the party whose obligation is extended to the extent the indorser or accommodation party proves that the extension caused loss to the indorser or accommodation party with respect to the right of recourse.

(d) If a person entitled to enforce an instrument agrees, with or without consideration, to a material modification of the obligation of a party other than an extension of the due date, the modification discharges the obligation of an indorser or accommodation party having a right of recourse against the person whose obligation is modified to the extent the modification causes loss to the indorser or accommodation party with respect to the right of recourse. The loss suffered by the indorser or accommodation party as a result of the modification is equal to the amount of the right of recourse unless the person enforcing the instrument proves that no loss was caused by the modification or that the loss caused by the modification was an amount less than the amount of the right of recourse.

(e) If the obligation of a party to pay an instrument is secured by an interest in collateral and a person entitled to enforce the instrument impairs the value of the interest in collateral, the obligation of an indorser or accommodation party having a right of recourse against the obligor is discharged to the extent of the impairment. The value of an interest in collateral is impaired to the extent (i) the value of the interest is reduced to an amount less than the amount of the right of recourse of the party asserting discharge, or (ii) the reduction in value of the interest causes an increase in the amount by which the amount of the right of recourse exceeds the value of the interest. The burden of proving impairment is on the party asserting discharge.

(f) If the obligation of a party is secured by an interest in collateral not provided by an accommodation party and a person entitled to enforce the instrument impairs the value of the interest in collateral, the obligation of any party who is jointly and severally liable with respect to the secured obligation is discharged to the extent the impairment causes the party asserting discharge to pay more than that party would have been obliged to pay, taking into account rights of contribution, if impairment had not occurred. If the party asserting discharge is an accommodation party not entitled to discharge under subsection (e), the party is deemed to have a right to contribution based on joint and several liability rather than a right to reimbursement. The burden of proving impairment is on the party asserting discharge.

(g) Under subsection (e) or (f), impairing value of an interest in collateral includes (i) failure to obtain or maintain perfection or recordation of the interest in collateral, (ii) release of collateral without substitution of collateral of equal value, (iii) failure to perform a duty to preserve the value of collateral owed, under Article 9 or other law, to a debtor or surety or other person secondarily liable, or (iv) failure to comply with applicable law in disposing of collateral.

(h) An accommodation party is not discharged under subsection (c), (d), or (e) unless the person entitled to enforce the instrument knows of the accommodation or has notice under Section 3–419(c) that the instrument was signed for accommodation.

(i) A party is not discharged under this section if (i) the party asserting discharge consents to the event or conduct that is the basis of the discharge, or (ii) the instrument or a separate agreement of the party provides for waiver of discharge under this section either specifically or by general language indicating that parties waive defenses based on suretyship or impairment of collateral.

ADDENDUM TO REVISED ARTICLE 3

Notes to Legislative Counsel

1. If revised Article 3 is adopted in your state, the reference in Section 2–511 to Section 3–802 should be changed to Section 3–310.

2. If revised Article 3 is adopted in your state and the Uniform Fiduciaries Act is also in effect in your state, you may want to consider amending Uniform Fiduciaries Act § 9 to conform to Section 3–307(b)(2)(iii) and (4)(iii). See Official Comment 3 to Section 3–307.

Revised Article 4
BANK DEPOSITS AND COLLECTIONS

Part 1 General Provisions and Definitions

§ 4–101. Short Title.

This Article may be cited as Uniform Commercial Code—Bank Deposits and Collections.

As amended in 1990.

§ 4–102. Applicability.

(a) To the extent that items within this Article are also within Articles 3 and 8, they are subject to those Articles. If there is conflict, this Article governs Article 3, but Article 8 governs this Article.

(b) The liability of a bank for action or non-action with respect to an item handled by it for purposes of presentment, payment, or collection is governed by the law of the place where the bank is located. In the case of action or non-action by or at a branch or separate office of a bank, its liability is governed by the law of the place where the branch or separate office is located.

§ 4–103. Variation by Agreement; Measure of Damages; Action Constituting Ordinary Care.

(a) The effect of the provisions of this Article may be varied by agreement, but the parties to the agreement cannot disclaim a bank's responsibility for its lack of good faith or failure to exercise ordinary care or limit the measure of damages for the lack or failure. However, the parties may determine by agreement the standards by which the bank's responsibility is to be measured if those standards are not manifestly unreasonable.

(b) Federal Reserve regulations and operating circulars, clearinghouse rules, and the like have the effect of agreements under subsection (a), whether or not specifically assented to by all parties interested in items handled.

(c) Action or non-action approved by this Article or pursuant to Federal Reserve regulations or operating circulars is the exercise of ordinary care and, in the absence of special instructions, action or non-action consistent with clearing-house rules and the like or with a general banking usage not disapproved by this Article, is prima facie the exercise of ordinary care.

(d) The specification or approval of certain procedures by this Article is not disapproval of other procedures that may be reasonable under the circumstances.

(e) The measure of damages for failure to exercise ordinary care in handling an item is the amount of the item reduced by an amount that could not have been realized by the exercise of ordinary care. If there is also bad faith it includes any other damages the party suffered as a proximate consequence.

As amended in 1990.

§ 4–104. Definitions and Index of Definitions.

(a) In this Article, unless the context otherwise requires:

(1) "Account" means any deposit or credit account with a bank, including a demand, time, savings, passbook, share draft, or like account, other than an account evidenced by a certificate of deposit;

(2) "Afternoon" means the period of a day between noon and midnight;

(3) "Banking day" means the part of a day on which a bank is open to the public for carrying on substantially all of its banking functions;

(4) "Clearing house" means an association of banks or other payors regularly clearing items;

(5) "Customer" means a person having an account with a bank or for whom a bank has agreed to collect items, including a bank that maintains an account at another bank;

(6) "Documentary draft" means a draft to be presented for acceptance or payment if specified documents, certificated securities (Section 8–102) or instructions for uncertificated securities (Section 8–102), or other certificates, statements, or the like are to be received by the drawee or other payor before acceptance or payment of the draft;

(7) "Draft" means a draft as defined in Section 3–104 or an item, other than an instrument, that is an order;

(8) "Drawee" means a person ordered in a draft to make payment;

(9) "Item" means an instrument or a promise or order to pay money handled by a bank for collection or payment. The term does not include a payment order governed by Article 4A or a credit or debit card slip;

(10) "Midnight deadline" with respect to a bank is midnight on its next banking day following the banking day on which it receives the relevant item or notice or from which the time for taking action commences to run, whichever is later;

(11) "Settle" means to pay in cash, by clearing-house settlement, in a charge or credit or by remittance, or otherwise as agreed. A settlement may be either provisional or final;

(12) "Suspends payments" with respect to a bank means that it has been closed by order of the supervisory authorities, that a public officer has been appointed to take it over, or that it ceases or refuses to make payments in the ordinary course of business.

(b) [Other definitions' section references deleted.]

(c) [Other definitions' section references deleted.]

(d) In addition, Article 1 contains general definitions and principles of construction and interpretation applicable throughout this Article.

§ 4–105. "Bank"; "Depository Bank"; "Payor Bank"; "Intermediary Bank"; "Collecting Bank"; "Presenting Bank".

In this Article:

(1) "Bank" means a person engaged in the business of banking, including a savings bank, savings and loan association, credit union, or trust company;

(2) "Depository bank" means the first bank to take an item even though it is also the payor bank, unless the item is presented for immediate payment over the counter;

(3) "Payor bank" means a bank that is the drawee of a draft;

(4) "Intermediary bank" means a bank to which an item is transferred in course of collection except the depositary or payor bank;

(5) "Collecting bank" means a bank handling an item for collection except the payor bank;

(6) "Presenting bank" means a bank presenting an item except a payor bank.

§ 4–106. Payable Through or Payable at Bank: Collecting Bank.

(a) If an item states that it is "payable through" a bank identified in the item, (i) the item designates the bank as a collecting bank and does not by itself authorize the bank to pay the item, and (ii) the item may be presented for payment only by or through the bank.

Alternative A

(b) If an item states that it is "payable at" a bank identified in the item, the item is equivalent to a draft drawn on the bank.

Alternative B

(b) If an item states that it is "payable at" a bank identified in the item, (i) the item designates the bank as a collecting bank and does not by itself authorize the bank to pay the item, and (ii) the item may be presented for payment only by or through the bank.

(c) If a draft names a nonbank drawee and it is unclear whether a bank named in the draft is a co-drawee or a collecting bank, the bank is a collecting bank.

As added in 1990.

§ 4–107. Separate Office of Bank.

A branch or separate office of a bank is a separate bank for the purpose of computing the time within which and determining the place at or to which action may be taken or notices or orders shall be given under this Article and under Article 3.

As amended in 1962 and 1990.

§ 4–108. Time of Receipt of Items.

(a) For the purpose of allowing time to process items, prove balances, and make the necessary entries on its books to determine its position for the day, a bank may fix an afternoon hour of 2 P.M. or later as a cutoff hour for the handling of money and items and the making of entries on its books.

(b) An item or deposit of money received on any day after a cutoff hour so fixed or after the close of the banking day may be treated as being received at the opening of the next banking day.

As amended in 1990.

§ 4–109. Delays.

(a) Unless otherwise instructed, a collecting bank in a good faith effort to secure payment of a specific item drawn on a payor other than a bank, and with or without the approval of any person involved, may waive, modify, or extend time limits imposed or permitted by this [act] for a period not exceeding two additional banking days without discharge of drawers or indorsers or liability to its transferor or a prior party.

(b) Delay by a collecting bank or payor bank beyond time limits prescribed or permitted by this [act] or by instructions is excused if (i) the delay is caused by interruption of communication or computer facilities, suspension of payments by another bank, war, emergency conditions, failure of equipment, or other circumstances beyond the control of the bank, and (ii) the bank exercises such diligence as the circumstances require.

§ 4–110. Electronic Presentment.

(a) "Agreement for electronic presentment" means an agreement, clearing-house rule, or Federal Reserve regulation or operating circular, providing that presentment of an item may be made by transmission of an image of an item or information describing the item ("presentment notice") rather than delivery of the item itself. The agreement may provide for procedures governing retention, presentment, payment, dishonor, and other matters concerning items subject to the agreement.

(b) Presentment of an item pursuant to an agreement for presentment is made when the presentment notice is received.

(c) If presentment is made by presentment notice, a reference to "item" or "check" in this Article means the presentment notice unless the context otherwise indicates.

As added in 1990.

§ 4–111. Statute of Limitations.

An action to enforce an obligation, duty, or right arising under this Article must be commenced within three years after the [cause of action] accrues.

As added in 1990.

Part 2 Collection of Items: Depositary and Collecting Banks

§ 4–201. Status of Collecting Bank as Agent and Provisional Status of Credits; Applicability of Article; Item Indorsed "Pay Any Bank".

(a) Unless a contrary intent clearly appears and before the time that a settlement given by a collecting bank for an item is or becomes final, the bank, with respect to an item, is an agent or sub-agent of the owner of the item and any settlement given for the item is provisional. This provision applies regardless of the form of indorsement or lack of indorsement and even though credit given for the item is subject to immediate withdrawal as of right or is in fact withdrawn; but the continuance of ownership of an item by its owner and any rights of the owner to proceeds of the item are subject to rights of a collecting bank, such as those resulting from outstanding advances on the item and rights of recoupment or setoff. If an item is handled by banks for purposes of presentment, payment, collection, or return, the relevant provisions of this Article apply even though action of the parties clearly establishes that a particular bank has purchased the item and is the owner of it.

(b) After an item has been indorsed with the words "pay any bank" or the like, only a bank may acquire the rights of a holder until the item has been:

(1) returned to the customer initiating collection; or

(2) specially indorsed by a bank to a person who is not a bank.

As amended in 1990.

§ 4–202. Responsibility for Collection or Return; When Action Timely.

(a) A collecting bank must exercise ordinary care in:

(1) presenting an item or sending it for presentment;

(2) sending notice of dishonor or nonpayment or returning an item other than a documentary draft to the bank's transferor after learning that the item has not been paid or accepted, as the case may be;

(3) settling for an item when the bank receives final settlement; and

(4) notifying its transferor of any loss or delay in transit within a reasonable time after discovery thereof.

(b) A collecting bank exercises ordinary care under subsection (a) by taking proper action before its midnight deadline following receipt of an item, notice, or settlement. Taking proper action within a reasonably longer time may constitute the exercise of ordinary care, but the bank has the burden of establishing timeliness.

(c) Subject to subsection (a)(1), a bank is not liable for the insolvency, neglect, misconduct, mistake, or default of another bank or person or for loss or destruction of an item in the possession of others or in transit.

As amended in 1990.

§ 4–203. Effect of Instructions.

Subject to Article 3 concerning conversion of instruments (Section 3–420) and restrictive indorsements (Section 3–206), only a collecting bank's transferor can give instructions that affect the bank or constitute notice to it, and a collecting bank is not liable to prior parties for any action taken pursuant to the instructions or in accordance with any agreement with its transferor.

§ 4–204. Methods of Sending and Presenting; Sending Directly to Payor Bank.

(a) A collecting bank shall send items by a reasonably prompt method, taking into consideration relevant instructions, the nature of the item, the number of those items on hand, the cost of collection involved, and the method generally used by it or others to present those items.

(b) A collecting bank may send:

(1) an item directly to the payor bank;

(2) an item to a nonbank payor if authorized by its transferor; and

(3) an item other than documentary drafts to a nonbank payor, if authorized by Federal Reserve regulation or operating circular, clearing-house rule, or the like.

(c) Presentment may be made by a presenting bank at a place where the payor bank or other payor has requested that presentment be made.

As amended in 1990.

§ 4–205. Depositary Bank Holder of Unindorsed Item.

If a customer delivers an item to a depositary bank for collection:

(1) the depositary bank becomes a holder of the item at the time it receives the item for collection if the customer at the time of delivery was a holder of the item, whether or not the customer indorses the item, and, if the bank satisfies the other requirements of Section 3–302, it is a holder in due course; and

(2) the depositary bank warrants to collecting banks, the payor bank or other payor, and the drawer that the amount of the item was paid to the customer or deposited to the customer's account.

As amended in 1990.

§ 4–206. Transfer Between Banks.

Any agreed method that identifies the transferor bank is sufficient for the item's further transfer to another bank.

As amended in 1990.

§ 4–207. Transfer Warranties.

(a) A customer or collecting bank that transfers an item and receives a settlement or other consideration warrants to the transferee and to any subsequent collecting bank that:

(1) the warrantor is a person entitled to enforce the item;

(2) all signatures on the item are authentic and authorized;

(3) the item has not been altered;

(4) the item is not subject to a defense or claim in recoupment (Section 3–305(a)) of any party that can be asserted against the warrantor; and

(5) the warrantor has no knowledge of any insolvency proceeding commenced with respect to the maker or acceptor or, in the case of an unaccepted draft, the drawer.

(b) If an item is dishonored, a customer or collecting bank transferring the item and receiving settlement or other consideration is obliged to pay the amount due on the item (i) according to the terms of the item at the time it was transferred, or (ii) if the transfer was of an incomplete item, according to its terms when completed as stated in Sections 3–115 and 3–407. The obligation of a transferor is owed to the transferee and to any subsequent collecting bank that takes the item in good faith. A transferor cannot disclaim its obligation under this subsection by an indorsement stating that it is made "without recourse" or otherwise disclaiming liability.

(c) A person to whom the warranties under subsection (a) are made and who took the item in good faith may recover from the warrantor as damages for breach of warranty an amount equal to the loss suffered as a result of the breach, but not more than the amount of the item plus expenses and loss of interest incurred as a result of the breach.

(d) The warranties stated in subsection (a) cannot be disclaimed with respect to checks. Unless notice of a claim for breach of warranty is given to the warrantor within 30 days after the claimant has reason to know of the breach and the identity of the warrantor, the warrantor is discharged to the extent of any loss caused by the delay in giving notice of the claim.

(e) A cause of action for breach of warranty under this section accrues when the claimant has reason to know of the breach.

As amended in 1990.

§ 4–208. Presentment Warranties.

(a) If an unaccepted draft is presented to the drawee for payment or acceptance and the drawee pays or accepts the draft, (i) the person obtaining payment or acceptance, at the time of presentment, and (ii) a previous transferor of the draft, at the time of transfer, warrant to the drawee that pays or accepts the draft in good faith that:

(1) the warrantor is, or was, at the time the warrantor transferred the draft, a person entitled to enforce the draft or authorized to obtain payment or acceptance of the draft on behalf of a person entitled to enforce the draft;

(2) the draft has not been altered; and

(3) the warrantor has no knowledge that the signature of the purported drawer of the draft is unauthorized.

(b) A drawee making payment may recover from a warrantor damages for breach of warranty equal to the amount paid by the drawee less the amount the drawee received or is entitled to receive from the drawer because of the payment. In addition, the drawee is entitled to compensation for expenses and loss of interest resulting from the breach. The right of the drawee to recover damages under this subsection is not affected by any failure of the drawee to exercise ordinary care in making payment. If the drawee accepts the draft (i) breach of warranty is a defense to the obligation of the acceptor, and

(ii) if the acceptor makes payment with respect to the draft, the acceptor is entitled to recover from a warrantor for breach of warranty the amounts stated in this subsection.

(c) If a drawee asserts a claim for breach of warranty under subsection (a) based on an unauthorized indorsement of the draft or an alteration of the draft, the warrantor may defend by proving that the indorsement is effective under Section 3–404 or 3–405 or the drawer is precluded under Section 3–406 or 4–406 from asserting against the drawee the unauthorized indorsement or alteration.

(d) If (i) a dishonored draft is presented for payment to the drawer or an indorser or (ii) any other item is presented for payment to a party obliged to pay the item, and the item is paid, the person obtaining payment and a prior transferor of the item warrant to the person making payment in good faith that the warrantor is, or was, at the time the warrantor transferred the item, a person entitled to enforce the item or authorized to obtain payment on behalf of a person entitled to enforce the item. The person making payment may recover from any warrantor for breach of warranty an amount equal to the amount paid plus expenses and loss of interest resulting from the breach.

(e) The warranties stated in subsections (a) and (d) cannot be disclaimed with respect to checks. Unless notice of a claim for breach of warranty is given to the warrantor within 30 days after the claimant has reason to know of the breach and the identity of the warrantor, the warrantor is discharged to the extent of any loss caused by the delay in giving notice of the claim.

(f) A cause of action for breach of warranty under this section accrues when the claimant has reason to know of the breach.

As amended in 1990.

§ 4–209. Encoding and Retention Warranties.

(a) A person who encodes information on or with respect to an item after issue warrants to any subsequent collecting bank and to the payor bank or other payor that the information is correctly encoded. If the customer of a depositary bank encodes, that bank also makes the warranty.

(b) A person who undertakes to retain an item pursuant to an agreement for electronic presentment warrants to any subsequent collecting bank and to the payor bank or other payor that retention and presentment of the item comply with the agreement. If a customer of a depositary bank undertakes to retain an item, that bank also makes this warranty.

(c) A person to whom warranties are made under this section and who took the item in good faith may recover from the warrantor as damages for breach of warranty an amount equal to the loss suffered as a result of the breach, plus expenses and loss of interest incurred as a result of the breach.

As added in 1990.

§ 4–210. Security Interest of Collecting Bank in Items, Accompanying Documents and Proceeds.

(a) A collecting bank has a security interest in an item and any accompanying documents or the proceeds of either:

(1) in case of an item deposited in an account, to the extent to which credit given for the item has been withdrawn or applied;

(2) in case of an item for which it has given credit available for withdrawal as of right, to the extent of the credit given, whether

or not the credit is drawn upon or there is a right of charge-back; or

(3) if it makes an advance on or against the item.

(b) If credit given for several items received at one time or pursuant to a single agreement is withdrawn or applied in part, the security interest remains upon all the items, any accompanying documents or the proceeds of either. For the purpose of this section, credits first given are first withdrawn.

(c) Receipt by a collecting bank of a final settlement for an item is a realization on its security interest in the item, accompanying documents, and proceeds. So long as the bank does not receive final settlement for the item or give up possession of the item or accompanying documents for purposes other than collection, the security interest continues to that extent and is subject to Article 9, but:

(1) no security agreement is necessary to make the security interest enforceable (Section 9–203(1)(a));

(2) no filing is required to perfect the security interest; and

(3) the security interest has priority over conflicting perfected security interests in the item, accompanying documents, or proceeds.

As amended in 1990 and 1999.

§ 4–211. When Bank Gives Value for Purposes of Holder in Due Course.

For purposes of determining its status as a holder in due course, a bank has given value to the extent it has a security interest in an item, if the bank otherwise complies with the requirements of Section 3–302 on what constitutes a holder in due course.

As amended in 1990.

§ 4–212. Presentment by Notice of Item Not Payable by, Through, or at Bank; Liability of Drawer or Indorser.

(a) Unless otherwise instructed, a collecting bank may present an item not payable by, through, or at a bank by sending to the party to accept or pay a written notice that the bank holds the item for acceptance or payment. The notice must be sent in time to be received on or before the day when presentment is due and the bank must meet any requirement of the party to accept or pay under Section 3–501 by the close of the bank's next banking day after it knows of the requirement.

(b) If presentment is made by notice and payment, acceptance, or request for compliance with a requirement under Section 3–501 is not received by the close of business on the day after maturity or, in the case of demand items, by the close of business on the third banking day after notice was sent, the presenting bank may treat the item as dishonored and charge any drawer or indorser by sending it notice of the facts.

As amended in 1990.

§ 4–213. Medium and Time of Settlement by Bank.

(a) With respect to settlement by a bank, the medium and time of settlement may be prescribed by Federal Reserve regulations or circulars, clearing-house rules, and the like, or agreement. In the absence of such prescription:

(1) the medium of settlement is cash or credit to an account in a Federal Reserve bank of or specified by the person to receive settlement; and

(2) the time of settlement is:

(i) with respect to tender of settlement by cash, a cashier's check, or teller's check, when the cash or check is sent or delivered;

(ii) with respect to tender of settlement by credit in an account in a Federal Reserve Bank, when the credit is made;

(iii) with respect to tender of settlement by a credit or debit to an account in a bank, when the credit or debit is made or, in the case of tender of settlement by authority to charge an account, when the authority is sent or delivered; or

(iv) with respect to tender of settlement by a funds transfer, when payment is made pursuant to Section 4A–406(a) to the person receiving settlement.

(b) If the tender of settlement is not by a medium authorized by subsection (a) or the time of settlement is not fixed by subsection (a), no settlement occurs until the tender of settlement is accepted by the person receiving settlement.

(c) If settlement for an item is made by cashier's check or teller's check and the person receiving settlement, before its midnight deadline:

(1) presents or forwards the check for collection, settlement is final when the check is finally paid; or

(2) fails to present or forward the check for collection, settlement is final at the midnight deadline of the person receiving settlement.

(d) If settlement for an item is made by giving authority to charge the account of the bank giving settlement in the bank receiving settlement, settlement is final when the charge is made by the bank receiving settlement if there are funds available in the account for the amount of the item.

As amended in 1990.

§ 4–214. Right of Charge-Back or Refund; Liability of Collecting Bank: Return of Item.

(a) If a collecting bank has made provisional settlement with its customer for an item and fails by reason of dishonor, suspension of payments by a bank, or otherwise to receive settlement for the item which is or becomes final, the bank may revoke the settlement given by it, charge back the amount of any credit given for the item to its customer's account, or obtain refund from its customer, whether or not it is able to return the item, if by its midnight deadline or within a longer reasonable time after it learns the facts it returns the item or sends notification of the facts. If the return or notice is delayed beyond the bank's midnight deadline or a longer reasonable time after it learns the facts, the bank may revoke the settlement, charge back the credit, or obtain refund from its customer, but it is liable for any loss resulting from the delay. These rights to revoke, charge back, and obtain refund terminate if and when a settlement for the item received by the bank is or becomes final.

(b) A collecting bank returns an item when it is sent or delivered to the bank's customer or transferor or pursuant to its instructions.

(c) A depositary bank that is also the payor may charge back the amount of an item to its customer's account or obtain refund in accordance with the section governing return of an item received by a payor bank for credit on its books (Section 4–301).

(d) The right to charge back is not affected by:

(1) previous use of a credit given for the item; or

(2) failure by any bank to exercise ordinary care with respect to the item, but a bank so failing remains liable.

(e) A failure to charge back or claim refund does not affect other rights of the bank against the customer or any other party.

(f) If credit is given in dollars as the equivalent of the value of an item payable in foreign money, the dollar amount of any charge-back or refund must be calculated on the basis of the bank-offered spot rate for the foreign money prevailing on the day when the person entitled to the charge-back or refund learns that it will not receive payment in ordinary course.

As amended in 1990.

§ 4–215. Final Payment of Item by Payor Bank; When Provisional Debits and Credits Become Final; When Certain Credits Become Available for Withdrawal.

(a) An item is finally paid by a payor bank when the bank has first done any of the following:

(1) paid the item in cash;

(2) settled for the item without having a right to revoke the settlement under statute, clearing-house rule, or agreement; or

(3) made a provisional settlement for the item and failed to revoke the settlement in the time and manner permitted by statute, clearing-house rule, or agreement.

(b) If provisional settlement for an item does not become final, the item is not finally paid.

(c) If provisional settlement for an item between the presenting and payor banks is made through a clearing house or by debits or credits in an account between them, then to the extent that provisional debits or credits for the item are entered in accounts between the presenting and payor banks or between the presenting and successive prior collecting banks seriatim, they become final upon final payment of the item by the payor bank.

(d) If a collecting bank receives a settlement for an item which is or becomes final, the bank is accountable to its customer for the amount of the item and any provisional credit given for the item in an account with its customer becomes final.

(e) Subject to (i) applicable law stating a time for availability of funds and (ii) any right of the bank to apply the credit to an obligation of the customer, credit given by a bank for an item in a customer's account becomes available for withdrawal as of right:

(1) if the bank has received a provisional settlement for the item, when the settlement becomes final and the bank has had a reasonable time to receive return of the item and the item has not been received within that time;

(2) if the bank is both the depositary bank and the payor bank, and the item is finally paid, at the opening of the bank's second banking day following receipt of the item.

(f) Subject to applicable law stating a time for availability of funds and any right of a bank to apply a deposit to an obligation of the depositor, a deposit of money becomes available for withdrawal as of right at the opening of the bank's next banking day after receipt of the deposit.

As amended in 1990.

§ 4–216. Insolvency and Preference.

(a) If an item is in or comes into the possession of a payor or collecting bank that suspends payment and the item has not been finally paid, the item must be returned by the receiver, trustee, or agent in charge of the closed bank to the presenting bank or the closed bank's customer.

(b) If a payor bank finally pays an item and suspends payments without making a settlement for the item with its customer or the presenting bank which settlement is or becomes final, the owner of the item has a preferred claim against the payor bank.

(c) If a payor bank gives or a collecting bank gives or receives a provisional settlement for an item and thereafter suspends payments, the suspension does not prevent or interfere with the settlement's becoming final if the finality occurs automatically upon the lapse of certain time or the happening of certain events.

(d) If a collecting bank receives from subsequent parties settlement for an item, which settlement is or becomes final and the bank suspends payments without making a settlement for the item with its customer which settlement is or becomes final, the owner of the item has a preferred claim against the collecting bank.

As amended in 1990.

Part 3 Collection of Items: Payor Banks

§ 4–301. Deferred Posting; Recovery of Payment by Return of Items; Time of Dishonor; Return of Items by Payor Bank.

(a) If a payor bank settles for a demand item other than a documentary draft presented otherwise than for immediate payment over the counter before midnight of the banking day of receipt, the payor bank may revoke the settlement and recover the settlement if, before it has made final payment and before its midnight deadline, it

(1) returns the item; or

(2) sends written notice of dishonor or nonpayment if the item is unavailable for return.

(b) If a demand item is received by a payor bank for credit on its books, it may return the item or send notice of dishonor and may revoke any credit given or recover the amount thereof withdrawn by its customer, if it acts within the time limit and in the manner specified in subsection (a).

(c) Unless previous notice of dishonor has been sent, an item is dishonored at the time when for purposes of dishonor it is returned or notice sent in accordance with this section.

(d) An item is returned:

(1) as to an item presented through a clearing house, when it is delivered to the presenting or last collecting bank or to the clearing house or is sent or delivered in accordance with clearing-house rules; or

(2) in all other cases, when it is sent or delivered to the bank's customer or transferor or pursuant to instructions.

As amended in 1990.

§ 4–302. Payor Bank's Responsibility for Late Return of Item.

(a) If an item is presented to and received by a payor bank, the bank is accountable for the amount of:

(1) a demand item, other than a documentary draft, whether properly payable or not, if the bank, in any case in which it is not also the depositary bank, retains the item beyond midnight of the banking day of receipt without settling for it or, whether or not it is also the depositary bank, does not pay or return the item or send notice of dishonor until after its midnight deadline; or

(2) any other properly payable item unless, within the time allowed for acceptance or payment of that item, the bank either accepts or pays the item or returns it and accompanying documents.

(b) The liability of a payor bank to pay an item pursuant to subsection (a) is subject to defenses based on breach of a presentment warranty (Section 4–208) or proof that the person seeking enforcement of the liability presented or transferred the item for the purpose of defrauding the payor bank.

As amended in 1990.

§ 4–303. When Items Subject to Notice, Stop-Payment Order, Legal Process, or Setoff; Order in Which Items May Be Charged or Certified.

(a) Any knowledge, notice, or stop-payment order received by, legal process served upon, or setoff exercised by a payor bank comes too late to terminate, suspend, or modify the bank's right or duty to pay an item or to charge its customer's account for the item if the knowledge, notice, stop-payment order, or legal process is received or served and a reasonable time for the bank to act thereon expires or the setoff is exercised after the earliest of the following:

(1) the bank accepts or certifies the item;

(2) the bank pays the item in cash;

(3) the bank settles for the item without having a right to revoke the settlement under statute, clearing-house rule, or agreement;

(4) the bank becomes accountable for the amount of the item under Section 4–302 dealing with the payor bank's responsibility for late return of items; or

(5) with respect to checks, a cutoff hour no earlier than one hour after the opening of the next banking day after the banking day on which the bank received the check and no later than the close of that next banking day or, if no cutoff hour is fixed, the close of the next banking day after the banking day on which the bank received the check.

(b) Subject to subsection (a), items may be accepted, paid, certified, or charged to the indicated account of its customer in any order.

As amended in 1990.

Part 4 Relationship Between Payor Bank and Its Customer

§ 4–401. When Bank May Charge Customer's Account.

(a) A bank may charge against the account of a customer an item that is properly payable from the account even though the charge creates an overdraft. An item is properly payable if it is authorized by the customer and is in accordance with any agreement between the customer and bank.

(b) A customer is not liable for the amount of an overdraft if the customer neither signed the item nor benefited from the proceeds of the item.

(c) A bank may charge against the account of a customer a check that is otherwise properly payable from the account, even though payment was made before the date of the check, unless the customer has given notice to the bank of the postdating describing the check with reasonable certainty. The notice is effective for the period stated in Section 4–403(b) for stop-payment orders, and must be received at such time and in such manner as to afford the bank a reasonable opportunity to act on it before the bank takes any action with respect to the check described in Section 4–303. If a bank charges against the account of a customer a check before the date stated in the notice of postdating, the bank is liable for damages for the loss resulting from its act. The loss may include damages for dishonor of subsequent items under Section 4–402.

(d) A bank that in good faith makes payment to a holder may charge the indicated account of its customer according to:

(1) the original terms of the altered item; or

(2) the terms of the completed item, even though the bank knows the item has been completed unless the bank has notice that the completion was improper.

As amended in 1990.

§ 4–402. Bank's Liability to Customer for Wrongful Dishonor; Time of Determining Insufficiency of Account.

(a) Except as otherwise provided in this Article, a payor bank wrongfully dishonors an item if it dishonors an item that is properly payable, but a bank may dishonor an item that would create an overdraft unless it has agreed to pay the overdraft.

(b) A payor bank is liable to its customer for damages proximately caused by the wrongful dishonor of an item. Liability is limited to actual damages proved and may include damages for an arrest or prosecution of the customer or other consequential damages. Whether any consequential damages are proximately caused by the wrongful dishonor is a question of fact to be determined in each case.

(c) A payor bank's determination of the customer's account balance on which a decision to dishonor for insufficiency of available funds is based may be made at any time between the time the item is received by the payor bank and the time that the payor bank returns the item or gives notice in lieu of return, and no more than one determination need be made. If, at the election of the payor bank, a subsequent balance determination is made for the purpose of reevaluating the bank's decision to dishonor the item, the account balance at that time is determinative of whether a dishonor for insufficiency of available funds is wrongful.

As amended in 1990.

§ 4–403. Customer's Right to Stop Payment; Burden of Proof of Loss.

(a) A customer or any person authorized to draw on the account if there is more than one person may stop payment of any item drawn on the customer's account or close the account by an order to the bank describing the item or account with reasonable certainty received at a time and in a manner that affords the bank a reasonable opportunity to act on it before any action by the bank with respect to the item described in Section 4–303. If the signature of more than one person is required to draw on an account, any of these persons may stop payment or close the account.

(b) A stop-payment order is effective for six months, but it lapses after 14 calendar days if the original order was oral and was not confirmed in writing within that period. A stop-payment order may be renewed for additional six-month periods by a writing given to the bank within a period during which the stop-payment order is effective.

(c) The burden of establishing the fact and amount of loss resulting from the payment of an item contrary to a stop-payment order or order to close an account is on the customer. The loss from payment of an item contrary to a stop-payment order may include damages for dishonor of subsequent items under Section 4–402.

As amended in 1990.

§ 4–404. Bank Not Obliged to Pay Check More Than Six Months Old.

A bank is under no obligation to a customer having a checking account to pay a check, other than a certified check, which is presented more than six months after its date, but it may charge its customer's account for a payment made thereafter in good faith.

§ 4–405. Death or Incompetence of Customer.

(a) A payor or collecting bank's authority to accept, pay, or collect an item or to account for proceeds of its collection, if otherwise effective, is not rendered ineffective by incompetence of a customer of either bank existing at the time the item is issued or its collection is undertaken if the bank does not know of an adjudication of incompetence. Neither death nor incompetence of a customer revokes the authority to accept, pay, collect, or account until the bank knows of the fact of death or of an adjudication of incompetence and has reasonable opportunity to act on it.

(b) Even with knowledge, a bank may for 10 days after the date of death pay or certify checks drawn on or before the date unless ordered to stop payment by a person claiming an interest in the account.

As amended in 1990.

§ 4–406. Customer's Duty to Discover and Report Unauthorized Signature or Alteration.

(a) A bank that sends or makes available to a customer a statement of account showing payment of items for the account shall either return or make available to the customer the items paid or provide information in the statement of account sufficient to allow the customer reasonably to identify the items paid. The statement of account provides sufficient information if the item is described by item number, amount, and date of payment.

(b) If the items are not returned to the customer, the person retaining the items shall either retain the items or, if the items are destroyed, maintain the capacity to furnish legible copies of the items until the expiration of seven years after receipt of the items. A customer may request an item from the bank that paid the item, and that bank must provide in a reasonable time either the item or, if the item has been destroyed or is not otherwise obtainable, a legible copy of the item.

(c) If a bank sends or makes available a statement of account or items pursuant to subsection (a), the customer must exercise reasonable promptness in examining the statement or the items to determine whether any payment was not authorized because of an alteration of an item or because a purported signature by or on behalf of the customer was not authorized. If, based on the statement or items provided, the customer should reasonably have dis-

covered the unauthorized payment, the customer must promptly notify the bank of the relevant facts.

(d) If the bank proves that the customer failed, with respect to an item, to comply with the duties imposed on the customer by subsection (c), the customer is precluded from asserting against the bank:

(1) the customer's unauthorized signature or any alteration on the item, if the bank also proves that it suffered a loss by reason of the failure; and

(2) the customer's unauthorized signature or alteration by the same wrongdoer on any other item paid in good faith by the bank if the payment was made before the bank received notice from the customer of the unauthorized signature or alteration and after the customer had been afforded a reasonable period of time, not exceeding 30 days, in which to examine the item or statement of account and notify the bank.

(e) If subsection (d) applies and the customer proves that the bank failed to exercise ordinary care in paying the item and that the failure substantially contributed to loss, the loss is allocated between the customer precluded and the bank asserting the preclusion according to the extent to which the failure of the customer to comply with subsection (c) and the failure of the bank to exercise ordinary care contributed to the loss. If the customer proves that the bank did not pay the item in good faith, the preclusion under subsection (d) does not apply.

(f) Without regard to care or lack of care of either the customer or the bank, a customer who does not within one year after the statement or items are made available to the customer (subsection (a)) discover and report the customer's unauthorized signature on or any alteration on the item is precluded from asserting against the bank the unauthorized signature or alteration. If there is a preclusion under this subsection, the payor bank may not recover for breach or warranty under Section 4–208 with respect to the unauthorized signature or alteration to which the preclusion applies.

As amended in 1990.

§ 4–407. Payor Bank's Right to Subrogation on Improper Payment.

If a payor has paid an item over the order of the drawer or maker to stop payment, or after an account has been closed, or otherwise under circumstances giving a basis for objection by the drawer or maker, to prevent unjust enrichment and only to the extent necessary to prevent loss to the bank by reason of its payment of the item, the payor bank is subrogated to the rights

(1) of any holder in due course on the item against the drawer or maker;

(2) of the payee or any other holder of the item against the drawer or maker either on the item or under the transaction out of which the item arose; and

(3) of the drawer or maker against the payee or any other holder of the item with respect to the transaction out of which the item arose.

As amended in 1990.

Part 5 Collection of Documentary Drafts

§ 4–501. Handling of Documentary Drafts; Duty to Send for Presentment and to Notify Customer of Dishonor.

A bank that takes a documentary draft for collection shall present or send the draft and accompanying documents for presentment and, upon learning that the draft has not been paid or accepted in due course, shall seasonably notify its customer of the fact even though it may have discounted or bought the draft or extended credit available for withdrawal as of right.

As amended in 1990.

§ 4–502. Presentment of "On Arrival" Drafts.

If a draft or the relevant instructions require presentment "on arrival", "when goods arrive" or the like, the collecting bank need not present until in its judgment a reasonable time for arrival of the goods has expired. Refusal to pay or accept because the goods have not arrived is not dishonor; the bank must notify its transferor of the refusal but need not present the draft again until it is instructed to do so or learns of the arrival of the goods.

§ 4–503. Responsibility of Presenting Bank for Documents and Goods; Report of Reasons for Dishonor; Referee in Case of Need.

Unless otherwise instructed and except as provided in Article 5, a bank presenting a documentary draft:

(1) must deliver the documents to the drawee on acceptance of the draft if it is payable more than three days after presentment, otherwise, only on payment; and

(2) upon dishonor, either in the case of presentment for acceptance or presentment for payment, may seek and follow instructions from any referee in case of need designated in the draft or, if the presenting bank does not choose to utilize the referee's services, it must use diligence and good faith to ascertain the reason for dishonor, must notify its transferor of the dishonor and of the results of its effort to ascertain the reasons therefor, and must request instructions.

However, the presenting bank is under no obligation with respect to goods represented by the documents except to follow any reasonable instructions seasonably received; it has a right to reimbursement for any expense incurred in following instructions and to prepayment of or indemnity for those expenses.

As amended in 1990.

§ 4–504. Privilege of Presenting Bank to Deal With Goods; Security Interest for Expenses.

(a) A presenting bank that, following the dishonor of a documentary draft, has seasonably requested instructions but does not receive them within a reasonable time may store, sell, or otherwise deal with the goods in any reasonable manner.

(b) For its reasonable expenses incurred by action under subsection (a) the presenting bank has a lien upon the goods or their proceeds, which may be foreclosed in the same manner as an unpaid seller's lien.

As amended in 1990.

Article 4A
FUNDS TRANSFERS

Part 1 Subject Matter and Definitions

§ 4A–101. Short Title.

This Article may be cited as Uniform Commercial Code—Funds Transfers.

§ 4A–102. Subject Matter.

Except as otherwise provided in Section 4A–108, this Article applies to funds transfers defined in Section 4A–104.

§ 4A–103. Payment Order–Definitions.

(a) In this Article:

(1) "Payment order" means an instruction of a sender to a receiving bank, transmitted orally, electronically, or in writing, to pay, or to cause another bank to pay, a fixed or determinable amount of money to a beneficiary if:

(i) the instruction does not state a condition to payment to the beneficiary other than time of payment,

(ii) the receiving bank is to be reimbursed by debiting an account of, or otherwise receiving payment from, the sender, and

(iii) the instruction is transmitted by the sender directly to the receiving bank or to an agent, funds-transfer system, or communication system for transmittal to the receiving bank.

(2) "Beneficiary" means the person to be paid by the beneficiary's bank.

(3) "Beneficiary's bank" means the bank identified in a payment order in which an account of the beneficiary is to be credited pursuant to the order or which otherwise is to make payment to the beneficiary if the order does not provide for payment to an account.

(4) "Receiving bank" means the bank to which the sender's instruction is addressed.

(5) "Sender" means the person giving the instruction to the receiving bank.

(b) If an instruction complying with subsection (a)(1) is to make more than one payment to a beneficiary, the instruction is a separate payment order with respect to each payment.

(c) A payment order is issued when it is sent to the receiving bank.

§ 4A–104. Funds Transfer–Definitions.

In this Article:

(a) "Funds transfer" means the series of transactions, beginning with the originator's payment order, made for the purpose of making payment to the beneficiary of the order. The term includes any payment order issued by the originator's bank or an intermediary bank intended to carry out the originator's payment order. A funds transfer is completed by acceptance by the beneficiary's bank of a payment order for the benefit of the beneficiary of the originator's payment order.

(b) "Intermediary bank" means a receiving bank other than the originator's bank or the beneficiary's bank.

(c) "Originator" means the sender of the first payment order in a funds transfer.

(d) "Originator's bank" means (i) the receiving bank to which the payment order of the originator is issued if the originator is not a bank, or (ii) the originator if the originator is a bank.

§ 4A–105. Other Definitions.

(a) In this Article:

(1) "Authorized account" means a deposit account of a customer in a bank designated by the customer as a source of

payment of payment orders issued by the customer to the bank. If a customer does not so designate an account, any account of the customer is an authorized account if payment of a payment order from that account is not inconsistent with a restriction on the use of that account.

(2) "Bank" means a person engaged in the business of banking and includes a savings bank, savings and loan association, credit union, and trust company. A branch or separate office of a bank is a separate bank for purposes of this Article.

(3) "Customer" means a person, including a bank, having an account with a bank or from whom a bank has agreed to receive payment orders.

(4) "Funds-transfer business day" of a receiving bank means the part of a day during which the receiving bank is open for the receipt, processing, and transmittal of payment orders and cancellations and amendments of payment orders.

(5) "Funds-transfer system" means a wire transfer network, automated clearing house, or other communication system of a clearing house or other association of banks through which a payment order by a bank may be transmitted to the bank to which the order is addressed.

(6) "Good faith" means honesty in fact and the observance of reasonable commercial standards of fair dealing.

(7) "Prove" with respect to a fact means to meet the burden of establishing the fact (Section 1–201(8)).

(b) Other definitions applying to this Article and the sections in which they appear are:

"Acceptance"	Section 4A–209
"Beneficiary"	Section 4A–103
"Beneficiary's bank"	Section 4A–103
"Executed"	Section 4A–301
"Execution date"	Section 4A–301
"Funds transfer"	Section 4A–104
"Funds-transfer system rule"	Section 4A–501
"Intermediary bank"	Section 4A–104
"Originator"	Section 4A–104
"Originator's bank"	Section 4A–104
"Payment by beneficiary's bank to beneficiary"	Section 4A–405
"Payment by originator to beneficiary"	Section 4A–406
"Payment by sender to receiving bank"	Section 4A–403
"Payment date"	Section 4A–401
"Payment order"	Section 4A–103
"Receiving bank"	Section 4A–103
"Security procedure"	Section 4A–201
"Sender"	Section 4A–103

(c) The following definitions in Article 4 apply to this Article:

"Clearing house"	Section 4–104
"Item"	Section 4–104
"Suspends payments"	Section 4–104

(d) In addition, Article 1 contains general definitions and principles of construction and interpretation applicable throughout this Article.

§ 4A–106. Time Payment Order Is Received.

(a) The time of receipt of a payment order or communication cancelling or amending a payment order is determined by the rules applicable to receipt of a notice stated in Section 1–201(27). A receiving bank may fix a cut-off time or times on a funds-transfer business day for the receipt and processing of payment orders and communications cancelling or amending payment orders. Different cut-off times may apply to payment orders, cancellations, or amendments, or to different categories of payment orders, cancellations, or amendments. A cut-off time may apply to senders generally or different cut-off times may apply to different senders or categories of payment orders. If a payment order or communication cancelling or amending a payment order is received after the close of a funds-transfer business day or after the appropriate cut-off time on a funds-transfer business day, the receiving bank may treat the payment order or communication as received at the opening of the next funds-transfer business day.

(b) If this Article refers to an execution date or payment date or states a day on which a receiving bank is required to take action, and the date or day does not fall on a funds-transfer business day, the next day that is a funds-transfer business day is treated as the date or day stated, unless the contrary is stated in this Article.

§ 4A–107. Federal Reserve Regulations and Operating Circulars.

Regulations of the Board of Governors of the Federal Reserve System and operating circulars of the Federal Reserve Banks supersede any inconsistent provision of this Article to the extent of the inconsistency.

§ 4A–108. Exclusion of Consumer Transactions Governed by Federal Law.

This Article does not apply to a funds transfer any part of which is governed by the Electronic Fund Transfer Act of 1978 (Title XX, Public Law 95–630, 92 Stat. 3728, 15 U.S.C. § 1693 et seq.) as amended from time to time.

Part 2 Issue and Acceptance of Payment Order

§ 4A–201. Security Procedure.

"Security procedure" means a procedure established by agreement of a customer and a receiving bank for the purpose of (i) verifying that a payment order or communication amending or cancelling a payment order is that of the customer, or (ii) detecting error in the transmission or the content of the payment order or communication. A security procedure may require the use of algorithms or other codes, identifying words or numbers, encryption, callback procedures, or similar security devices. Comparison of a signature on a payment order or communication with an authorized specimen signature of the customer is not by itself a security procedure.

§ 4A–202. Authorized and Verified Payment Orders.

(a) A payment order received by the receiving bank is the authorized order of the person identified as sender if that person authorized the order or is otherwise bound by it under the law of agency.

(b) If a bank and its customer have agreed that the authenticity of payment orders issued to the bank in the name of the customer as sender will be verified pursuant to a security procedure, a payment order received by the receiving bank is effective as the order of the customer, whether or not authorized, if (i) the security procedure is a commercially reasonable method of providing security against unauthorized payment orders, and (ii) the bank proves that it accepted the payment order in good faith and in compliance with the security procedure and any written agreement or instruction of the customer restricting acceptance of payment orders issued in the name of the customer. The bank is not required to follow an instruction that violates a written agreement with the customer or notice of which is not received at a time and in a manner affording the bank a reasonable opportunity to act on it before the payment order is accepted.

(c) Commercial reasonableness of a security procedure is a question of law to be determined by considering the wishes of the customer expressed to the bank, the circumstances of the customer known to the bank, including the size, type, and frequency of payment orders normally issued by the customer to the bank, alternative security procedures offered to the customer, and security procedures in general use by customers and receiving banks similarly situated. A security procedure is deemed to be commercially reasonable if (i) the security procedure was chosen by the customer after the bank offered, and the customer refused, a security procedure that was commercially reasonable for that customer, and (ii) the customer expressly agreed in writing to be bound by any payment order, whether or not authorized, issued in its name and accepted by the bank in compliance with the security procedure chosen by the customer.

(d) The term "sender" in this Article includes the customer in whose name a payment order is issued if the order is the authorized order of the customer under subsection (a), or it is effective as the order of the customer under subsection (b).

(e) This section applies to amendments and cancellations of payment orders to the same extent it applies to payment orders.

(f) Except as provided in this section and in Section 4A–203(a)(1), rights and obligations arising under this section or Section 4A–203 may not be varied by agreement.

§ 4A–203. Unenforceability of Certain Verified Payment Orders.

(a) If an accepted payment order is not, under Section 4A–202(a), an authorized order of a customer identified as sender, but is effective as an order of the customer pursuant to Section 4A–202(b), the following rules apply:

   (1) By express written agreement, the receiving bank may limit the extent to which it is entitled to enforce or retain payment of the payment order.

   (2) The receiving bank is not entitled to enforce or retain payment of the payment order if the customer proves that the order was not caused, directly or indirectly, by a person (i) entrusted at any time with duties to act for the customer with respect to payment orders or the security procedure, or (ii) who obtained access to transmitting facilities of the customer or who obtained, from a source controlled by the customer and without authority of the receiving bank, information facilitating breach of the security procedure, regardless of how the information was obtained or whether the customer was at fault. Information includes any access device, computer software, or the like.

(b) This section applies to amendments of payment orders to the same extent it applies to payment orders.

§ 4A–204. Refund of Payment and Duty of Customer to Report with Respect to Unauthorized Payment Order.

(a) If a receiving bank accepts a payment order issued in the name of its customer as sender which is (i) not authorized and not effective as the order of the customer under Section 4A–202, or (ii) not enforceable, in whole or in part, against the customer under Section 4A–203, the bank shall refund any payment of the payment order received from the customer to the extent the bank is not entitled to enforce payment and shall pay interest on the refundable amount calculated from the date the bank received payment to the date of the refund. However, the customer is not entitled to interest from the bank on the amount to be refunded if the customer fails to exercise ordinary care to determine that the order was not authorized by the customer and to notify the bank of the relevant facts within a reasonable time not exceeding 90 days after the date the customer received notification from the bank that the order was accepted or that the customer's account was debited with respect to the order. The bank is not entitled to any recovery from the customer on account of a failure by the customer to give notification as stated in this section.

(b) Reasonable time under subsection (a) may be fixed by agreement as stated in Section 1–204(1), but the obligation of a receiving bank to refund payment as stated in subsection (a) may not otherwise be varied by agreement.

§ 4A–205. Erroneous Payment Orders.

(a) If an accepted payment order was transmitted pursuant to a security procedure for the detection of error and the payment order (i) erroneously instructed payment to a beneficiary not intended by the sender, (ii) erroneously instructed payment in an amount greater than the amount intended by the sender, or (iii) was an erroneously transmitted duplicate of a payment order previously sent by the sender, the following rules apply:

   (1) If the sender proves that the sender or a person acting on behalf of the sender pursuant to Section 4A–206 complied with the security procedure and that the error would have been detected if the receiving bank had also complied, the sender is not obliged to pay the order to the extent stated in paragraphs (2) and (3).

   (2) If the funds transfer is completed on the basis of an erroneous payment order described in clause (i) or (iii) of subsection (a), the sender is not obliged to pay the order and the receiving bank is entitled to recover from the beneficiary any amount paid to the beneficiary to the extent allowed by the law governing mistake and restitution.

   (3) If the funds transfer is completed on the basis of a payment order described in clause (ii) of subsection (a), the sender is not obliged to pay the order to the extent the amount received by the beneficiary is greater than the amount intended by the sender. In that case, the receiving bank is entitled to recover from the beneficiary the excess amount received to the extent allowed by the law governing mistake and restitution.

(b) If (i) the sender of an erroneous payment order described in subsection (a) is not obliged to pay all or part of the order, and (ii) the sender receives notification from the receiving bank that the order was accepted by the bank or that the sender's account was debited with respect to the order, the sender has a duty to exercise ordinary care, on the basis of information available to the sender, to discover the error with respect to the order and to advise the bank of the relevant facts within a reasonable time, not exceeding 90 days, after the bank's notification was received by the sender. If the bank proves that the sender failed to perform that duty, the sender is liable to the bank for the loss the bank proves it incurred as a result of the failure, but the liability of the sender may not exceed the amount of the sender's order.

(c) This section applies to amendments to payment orders to the same extent it applies to payment orders.

§ 4A–206. Transmission of Payment Order through Funds-Transfer or Other Communication System.

(a) If a payment order addressed to a receiving bank is transmitted to a funds-transfer system or other third party communication system for transmittal to the bank, the system is deemed to be an agent of the sender for the purpose of transmitting the payment order to the bank. If there is a discrepancy between the terms of the payment order transmitted to the system and the terms of the payment order transmitted by the system to the bank, the terms of the payment order of the sender are those transmitted by the system. This section does not apply to a funds-transfer system of the Federal Reserve Banks.

(b) This section applies to cancellations and amendments to payment orders to the same extent it applies to payment orders.

§ 4A–207. Misdescription of Beneficiary.

(a) Subject to subsection (b), if, in a payment order received by the beneficiary's bank, the name, bank account number, or other identification of the beneficiary refers to a nonexistent or unidentifiable person or account, no person has rights as a beneficiary of the order and acceptance of the order cannot occur.

(b) If a payment order received by the beneficiary's bank identifies the beneficiary both by name and by an identifying or bank account number and the name and number identify different persons, the following rules apply:

(1) Except as otherwise provided in subsection (c), if the beneficiary's bank does not know that the name and number refer to different persons, it may rely on the number as the proper identification of the beneficiary of the order. The beneficiary's bank need not determine whether the name and number refer to the same person.

(2) If the beneficiary's bank pays the person identified by name or knows that the name and number identify different persons, no person has rights as beneficiary except the person paid by the beneficiary's bank if that person was entitled to receive payment from the originator of the funds transfer. If no person has rights as beneficiary, acceptance of the order cannot occur.

(c) If (i) a payment order described in subsection (b) is accepted, (ii) the originator's payment order described the beneficiary inconsistently by name and number, and (iii) the beneficiary's bank pays the person identified by number as permitted by subsection (b)(1), the following rules apply:

(1) If the originator is a bank, the originator is obliged to pay its order.

(2) If the originator is not a bank and proves that the person identified by number was not entitled to receive payment from the originator, the originator is not obliged to pay its order unless the originator's bank proves that the originator, before acceptance of the originator's order, had notice that payment of a payment order issued by the originator might be made by the beneficiary's bank on the basis of an identifying or bank account number even if it identifies a person different from the named beneficiary. Proof of notice may be made by any admissible evidence. The originator's bank satisfies the burden of proof if it proves that the originator, before the payment order was accepted, signed a writing stating the information to which the notice relates.

(d) In a case governed by subsection (b)(1), if the beneficiary's bank rightfully pays the person identified by number and that person was not entitled to receive payment from the originator, the amount paid may be recovered from that person to the extent allowed by the law governing mistake and restitution as follows:

(1) If the originator is obliged to pay its payment order as stated in subsection (c), the originator has the right to recover.

(2) If the originator is not a bank and is not obliged to pay its payment order, the originator's bank has the right to recover.

§ 4A–208. Misdescription of Intermediary Bank or Beneficiary's Bank.

(a) This subsection applies to a payment order identifying an intermediary bank or the beneficiary's bank only by an identifying number.

(1) The receiving bank may rely on the number as the proper identification of the intermediary or beneficiary's bank and need not determine whether the number identifies a bank.

(2) The sender is obliged to compensate the receiving bank for any loss and expenses incurred by the receiving bank as a result of its reliance on the number in executing or attempting to execute the order.

(b) This subsection applies to a payment order identifying an intermediary bank or the beneficiary's bank both by name and an identifying number if the name and number identify different persons.

(1) If the sender is a bank, the receiving bank may rely on the number as the proper identification of the intermediary or beneficiary's bank if the receiving bank, when it executes the sender's order, does not know that the name and number identify different persons. The receiving bank need not determine whether the name and number refer to the same person or whether the number refers to a bank. The sender is obliged to compensate the receiving bank for any loss and expenses incurred by the receiving bank as a result of its reliance on the number in executing or attempting to execute the order.

(2) If the sender is not a bank and the receiving bank proves that the sender, before the payment order was accepted, had notice that the receiving bank might rely on the number as the proper identification of the intermediary or beneficiary's bank even if it identifies a person different from the bank identified by name, the rights and obligations of the sender and the receiving bank are governed by subsection (b)(1), as though the sender were a bank. Proof of notice may be made by any admissible evidence. The receiving bank satisfies the burden of proof if it proves that the sender, before the payment order was

accepted, signed a writing stating the information to which the notice relates.

(3) Regardless of whether the sender is a bank, the receiving bank may rely on the name as the proper identification of the intermediary or beneficiary's bank if the receiving bank, at the time it executes the sender's order, does not know that the name and number identify different persons. The receiving bank need not determine whether the name and number refer to the same person.

(4) If the receiving bank knows that the name and number identify different persons, reliance on either the name or the number in executing the sender's payment order is a breach of the obligation stated in Section 4A–302(a)(1).

§ 4A–209. Acceptance of Payment Order.

(a) Subject to subsection (d), a receiving bank other than the beneficiary's bank accepts a payment order when it executes the order.

(b) Subject to subsections (c) and (d), a beneficiary's bank accepts a payment order at the earliest of the following times:

(1) When the bank (i) pays the beneficiary as stated in Section 4A–405(a) or 4A–405(b), or (ii) notifies the beneficiary of receipt of the order or that the account of the beneficiary has been credited with respect to the order unless the notice indicates that the bank is rejecting the order or that funds with respect to the order may not be withdrawn or used until receipt of payment from the sender of the order;

(2) When the bank receives payment of the entire amount of the sender's order pursuant to Section 4A–403(a)(1) or 4A–403(a)(2); or

(3) The opening of the next funds-transfer business day of the bank following the payment date of the order if, at that time, the amount of the sender's order is fully covered by a withdrawable credit balance in an authorized account of the sender or the bank has otherwise received full payment from the sender, unless the order was rejected before that time or is rejected within (i) one hour after that time, or (ii) one hour after the opening of the next business day of the sender following the payment date if that time is later. If notice of rejection is received by the sender after the payment date and the authorized account of the sender does not bear interest, the bank is obliged to pay interest to the sender on the amount of the order for the number of days elapsing after the payment date to the day the sender receives notice or learns that the order was not accepted, counting that day as an elapsed day. If the withdrawable credit balance during that period falls below the amount of the order, the amount of interest payable is reduced accordingly.

(c) Acceptance of a payment order cannot occur before the order is received by the receiving bank. Acceptance does not occur under subsection (b)(2) or (b)(3) if the beneficiary of the payment order does not have an account with the receiving bank, the account has been closed, or the receiving bank is not permitted by law to receive credits for the beneficiary's account.

(d) A payment order issued to the originator's bank cannot be accepted until the payment date if the bank is the beneficiary's bank, or the execution date if the bank is not the beneficiary's bank. If the

originator's bank executes the originator's payment order before the execution date or pays the beneficiary of the originator's payment order before the payment date and the payment order is subsequently cancelled pursuant to Section 4A–211(b), the bank may recover from the beneficiary any payment received to the extent allowed by the law governing mistake and restitution.

§ 4A–210. Rejection of Payment Order.

(a) A payment order is rejected by the receiving bank by a notice of rejection transmitted to the sender orally, electronically, or in writing. A notice of rejection need not use any particular words and is sufficient if it indicates that the receiving bank is rejecting the order or will not execute or pay the order. Rejection is effective when the notice is given if transmission is by a means that is reasonable in the circumstances. If notice of rejection is given by a means that is not reasonable, rejection is effective when the notice is received. If an agreement of the sender and receiving bank establishes the means to be used to reject a payment order, (i) any means complying with the agreement is reasonable and (ii) any means not complying is not reasonable unless no significant delay in receipt of the notice resulted from the use of the noncomplying means.

(b) This subsection applies if a receiving bank other than the beneficiary's bank fails to execute a payment order despite the existence on the execution date of a withdrawable credit balance in an authorized account of the sender sufficient to cover the order. If the sender does not receive notice of rejection of the order on the execution date and the authorized account of the sender does not bear interest, the bank is obliged to pay interest to the sender on the amount of the order for the number of days elapsing after the execution date to the earlier of the day the order is cancelled pursuant to Section 4A–211(d) or the day the sender receives notice or learns that the order was not executed, counting the final day of the period as an elapsed day. If the withdrawable credit balance during that period falls below the amount of the order, the amount of interest is reduced accordingly.

(c) If a receiving bank suspends payments, all unaccepted payment orders issued to it are are deemed rejected at the time the bank suspends payments.

(d) Acceptance of a payment order precludes a later rejection of the order. Rejection of a payment order precludes a later acceptance of the order.

§ 4A–211. Cancellation and Amendment of Payment Order.

(a) A communication of the sender of a payment order cancelling or amending the order may be transmitted to the receiving bank orally, electronically, or in writing. If a security procedure is in effect between the sender and the receiving bank, the communication is not effective to cancel or amend the order unless the communication is verified pursuant to the security procedure or the bank agrees to the cancellation or amendment.

(b) Subject to subsection (a), a communication by the sender cancelling or amending a payment order is effective to cancel or amend the order if notice of the communication is received at a time and in a manner affording the receiving bank a reasonable opportunity to act on the communication before the bank accepts the payment order.

(c) After a payment order has been accepted, cancellation or amendment of the order is not effective unless the receiving bank agrees or a funds-transfer system rule allows cancellation or amendment without agreement of the bank.

(1) With respect to a payment order accepted by a receiving bank other than the beneficiary's bank, cancellation or amendment is not effective unless a conforming cancellation or amendment of the payment order issued by the receiving bank is also made.

(2) With respect to a payment order accepted by the beneficiary's bank, cancellation or amendment is not effective unless the order was issued in execution of an unauthorized payment order, or because of a mistake by a sender in the funds transfer which resulted in the issuance of a payment order (i) that is a duplicate of a payment order previously issued by the sender, (ii) that orders payment to a beneficiary not entitled to receive payment from the originator, or (iii) that orders payment in an amount greater than the amount the beneficiary was entitled to receive from the originator. If the payment order is cancelled or amended, the beneficiary's bank is entitled to recover from the beneficiary any amount paid to the beneficiary to the extent allowed by the law governing mistake and restitution.

(d) An unaccepted payment order is cancelled by operation of law at the close of the fifth funds-transfer business day of the receiving bank after the execution date or payment date of the order.

(e) A cancelled payment order cannot be accepted. If an accepted payment order is cancelled, the acceptance is nullified and no person has any right or obligation based on the acceptance. Amendment of a payment order is deemed to be cancellation of the original order at the time of amendment and issue of a new payment order in the amended form at the same time.

(f) Unless otherwise provided in an agreement of the parties or in a funds-transfer system rule, if the receiving bank, after accepting a payment order, agrees to cancellation or amendment of the order by the sender or is bound by a funds-transfer system rule allowing cancellation or amendment without the bank's agreement, the sender, whether or not cancellation or amendment is effective, is liable to the bank for any loss and expenses, including reasonable attorney's fees, incurred by the bank as a result of the cancellation or amendment or attempted cancellation or amendment.

(g) A payment order is not revoked by the death or legal incapacity of the sender unless the receiving bank knows of the death or of an adjudication of incapacity by a court of competent jurisdiction and has reasonable opportunity to act before acceptance of the order.

(h) A funds-transfer system rule is not effective to the extent it conflicts with subsection (c)(2).

§ 4A–212. Liability and Duty of Receiving Bank Regarding Unaccepted Payment Order.

If a receiving bank fails to accept a payment order that it is obliged by express agreement to accept, the bank is liable for breach of the agreement to the extent provided in the agreement or in this Article, but does not otherwise have any duty to accept a payment order or, before acceptance, to take any action, or refrain from taking action, with respect to the order except as provided in this Article or by express agreement. Liability based on acceptance arises only when acceptance occurs as stated in Section 4A–209, and liability is limited to that provided in this Article. A receiving bank is not the agent of the sender or beneficiary of the payment order it accepts, or of any other party to the funds transfer, and the bank owes no duty to any party to the funds transfer except as provided in this Article or by express agreement.

Part 3 Execution of Sender's Payment Order by Receiving Bank

§ 4A–301. Execution and Execution Date.

(a) A payment order is "executed" by the receiving bank when it issues a payment order intended to carry out the payment order received by the bank. A payment order received by the beneficiary's bank can be accepted but cannot be executed.

(b) "Execution date" of a payment order means the day on which the receiving bank may properly issue a payment order in execution of the sender's order. The execution date may be determined by instruction of the sender but cannot be earlier than the day the order is received and, unless otherwise determined, is the day the order is received. If the sender's instruction states a payment date, the execution date is the payment date or an earlier date on which execution is reasonably necessary to allow payment to the beneficiary on the payment date.

§ 4A–302. Obligations of Receiving Bank in Execution of Payment Order.

(a) Except as provided in subsections (b) through (d), if the receiving bank accepts a payment order pursuant to Section 4A–209(a), the bank has the following obligations in executing the order:

(1) The receiving bank is obliged to issue, on the execution date, a payment order complying with the sender's order and to follow the sender's instructions concerning (i) any intermediary bank or funds-transfer system to be used in carrying out the funds transfer, or (ii) the means by which payment orders are to be transmitted in the funds transfer. If the originator's bank issues a payment order to an intermediary bank, the originator's bank is obliged to instruct the intermediary bank according to the instruction of the originator. An intermediary bank in the funds transfer is similarly bound by an instruction given to it by the sender of the payment order it accepts.

(2) If the sender's instruction states that the funds transfer is to be carried out telephonically or by wire transfer or otherwise indicates that the funds transfer is to be carried out by the most expeditious means, the receiving bank is obliged to transmit its payment order by the most expeditious available means, and to instruct any intermediary bank accordingly. If a sender's instruction states a payment date, the receiving bank is obliged to transmit its payment order at a time and by means reasonably necessary to allow payment to the beneficiary on the payment date or as soon thereafter as is feasible.

(b) Unless otherwise instructed, a receiving bank executing a payment order may (i) use any funds-transfer system if use of that system is reasonable in the circumstances, and (ii) issue a payment order to the beneficiary's bank or to an intermediary bank through which a payment order conforming to the sender's order can expeditiously be issued to the beneficiary's bank if the receiving bank exercises ordinary care in the selection of the intermediary bank. A receiving bank is not required to follow an instruction of the sender designating a funds-transfer system to be used in carrying out the funds transfer if the receiving bank, in good faith, determines that it is not feasible to follow the instruction or that following the instruction would unduly delay completion of the funds transfer.

(c) Unless subsection (a)(2) applies or the receiving bank is otherwise instructed, the bank may execute a payment order by transmitting its payment order by first class mail or by any means reasonable in the circumstances. If the receiving bank is instructed to execute the sender's order by transmitting its payment order by a particular means, the receiving bank may issue its payment order by the means stated or by any means as expeditious as the means stated.

(d) Unless instructed by the sender, (i) the receiving bank may not obtain payment of its charges for services and expenses in connection with the execution of the sender's order by issuing a payment order in an amount equal to the amount of the sender's order less the amount of the charges, and (ii) may not instruct a subsequent receiving bank to obtain payment of its charges in the same manner.

§ 4A–303. Erroneous Execution of Payment Order.

(a) A receiving bank that (i) executes the payment order of the sender by issuing a payment order in an amount greater than the amount of the sender's order, or (ii) issues a payment order in execution of the sender's order and then issues a duplicate order, is entitled to payment of the amount of the sender's order under Section 4A–402(c) if that subsection is otherwise satisfied. The bank is entitled to recover from the beneficiary of the erroneous order the excess payment received to the extent allowed by the law governing mistake and restitution.

(b) A receiving bank that executes the payment order of the sender by issuing a payment order in an amount less than the amount of the sender's order is entitled to payment of the amount of the sender's order under Section 4A–402(c) if (i) that subsection is otherwise satisfied and (ii) the bank corrects its mistake by issuing an additional payment order for the benefit of the beneficiary of the sender's order. If the error is not corrected, the issuer of the erroneous order is entitled to receive or retain payment from the sender of the order it accepted only to the extent of the amount of the erroneous order. This subsection does not apply if the receiving bank executes the sender's payment order by issuing a payment order in an amount less than the amount of the sender's order for the purpose of obtaining payment of its charges for services and expenses pursuant to instruction of the sender.

(c) If a receiving bank executes the payment order of the sender by issuing a payment order to a beneficiary different from the beneficiary of the sender's order and the funds transfer is completed on the basis of that error, the sender of the payment order that was erroneously executed and all previous senders in the funds transfer are not obliged to pay the payment orders they issued. The issuer of the erroneous order is entitled to recover from the beneficiary of the order the payment received to the extent allowed by the law governing mistake and restitution.

§ 4A–304. Duty of Sender to Report Erroneously Executed Payment Order.

If the sender of a payment order that is erroneously executed as stated in Section 4A–303 receives notification from the receiving bank that the order was executed or that the sender's account was debited with respect to the order, the sender has a duty to exercise ordinary care to determine, on the basis of information available to the sender, that the order was erroneously executed and to notify the bank of the relevant facts within a reasonable time not exceed-

ing 90 days after the notification from the bank was received by the sender. If the sender fails to perform that duty, the bank is not obliged to pay interest on any amount refundable to the sender under Section 4A–402(d) for the period before the bank learns of the execution error. The bank is not entitled to any recovery from the sender on account of a failure by the sender to perform the duty stated in this section.

§ 4A–305. Liability for Late or Improper Execution or Failure to Execute Payment Order.

(a) If a funds transfer is completed but execution of a payment order by the receiving bank in breach of Section 4A–302 results in delay in payment to the beneficiary, the bank is obliged to pay interest to either the originator or the beneficiary of the funds transfer for the period of delay caused by the improper execution. Except as provided in subsection (c), additional damages are not recoverable.

(b) If execution of a payment order by a receiving bank in breach of Section 4A–302 results in (i) noncompletion of the funds transfer, (ii) failure to use an intermediary bank designated by the originator, or (iii) issuance of a payment order that does not comply with the terms of the payment order of the originator, the bank is liable to the originator for its expenses in the funds transfer and for incidental expenses and interest losses, to the extent not covered by subsection (a), resulting from the improper execution. Except as provided in subsection (c), additional damages are not recoverable.

(c) In addition to the amounts payable under subsections (a) and (b), damages, including consequential damages, are recoverable to the extent provided in an express written agreement of the receiving bank.

(d) If a receiving bank fails to execute a payment order it was obliged by express agreement to execute, the receiving bank is liable to the sender for its expenses in the transaction and for incidental expenses and interest losses resulting from the failure to execute. Additional damages, including consequential damages, are recoverable to the extent provided in an express written agreement of the receiving bank, but are not otherwise recoverable.

(e) Reasonable attorney's fees are recoverable if demand for compensation under subsection (a) or (b) is made and refused before an action is brought on the claim. If a claim is made for breach of an agreement under subsection (d) and the agreement does not provide for damages, reasonable attorney's fees are recoverable if demand for compensation under subsection (d) is made and refused before an action is brought on the claim.

(f) Except as stated in this section, the liability of a receiving bank under subsections (a) and (b) may not be varied by agreement.

Part 4 Payment

§ 4A–401. Payment Date.

"Payment date" of a payment order means the day on which the amount of the order is payable to the beneficiary by the beneficiary's bank. The payment date may be determined by instruction of the sender but cannot be earlier than the day the order is received by the beneficiary's bank and, unless otherwise determined, is the day the order is received by the beneficiary's bank.

§ 4A–402. Obligation of Sender to Pay Receiving Bank.

(a) This section is subject to Sections 4A–205 and 4A–207.

(b) With respect to a payment order issued to the beneficiary's bank, acceptance of the order by the bank obliges the sender to pay the bank the amount of the order, but payment is not due until the payment date of the order.

(c) This subsection is subject to subsection (e) and to Section 4A–303. With respect to a payment order issued to a receiving bank other than the beneficiary's bank, acceptance of the order by the receiving bank obliges the sender to pay the bank the amount of the sender's order. Payment by the sender is not due until the execution date of the sender's order. The obligation of that sender to pay its payment order is excused if the funds transfer is not completed by acceptance by the beneficiary's bank of a payment order instructing payment to the beneficiary of that sender's payment order.

(d) If the sender of a payment order pays the order and was not obliged to pay all or part of the amount paid, the bank receiving payment is obliged to refund payment to the extent the sender was not obliged to pay. Except as provided in Sections 4A–204 and 4A–304, interest is payable on the refundable amount from the date of payment.

(e) If a funds transfer is not completed as stated in subsection (c) and an intermediary bank is obliged to refund payment as stated in subsection (d) but is unable to do so because not permitted by applicable law or because the bank suspends payments, a sender in the funds transfer that executed a payment order in compliance with an instruction, as stated in Section 4A–302(a)(1), to route the funds transfer through that intermediary bank is entitled to receive or retain payment from the sender of the payment order that it accepted. The first sender in the funds transfer that issued an instruction requiring routing through that intermediary bank is subrogated to the right of the bank that paid the intermediary bank to refund as stated in subsection (d).

(f) The right of the sender of a payment order to be excused from the obligation to pay the order as stated in subsection (c) or to receive refund under subsection (d) may not be varied by agreement.

§ 4A–403. Payment by Sender to Receiving Bank.

(a) Payment of the sender's obligation under Section 4A–402 to pay the receiving bank occurs as follows:

(1) If the sender is a bank, payment occurs when the receiving bank receives final settlement of the obligation through a Federal Reserve Bank or through a funds-transfer system.

(2) If the sender is a bank and the sender (i) credited an account of the receiving bank with the sender, or (ii) caused an account of the receiving bank in another bank to be credited, payment occurs when the credit is withdrawn or, if not withdrawn, at midnight of the day on which the credit is withdrawable and the receiving bank learns of that fact.

(3) If the receiving bank debits an account of the sender with the receiving bank, payment occurs when the debit is made to the extent the debit is covered by a withdrawable credit balance in the account.

(b) If the sender and receiving bank are members of a funds-transfer system that nets obligations multilaterally among participants, the receiving bank receives final settlement when settlement is complete in accordance with the rules of the system. The obligation of the sender to pay the amount of a payment order transmitted through the funds-transfer system may be satisfied, to the extent permitted by the rules of the system, by setting off and applying against the sender's obligation the right of the sender to receive payment from the receiving bank of the amount of any other payment order transmitted to the sender by the receiving bank through the funds-transfer system. The aggregate balance of obligations owed by each sender to each receiving bank in the funds-transfer system may be satisfied, to the extent permitted by the rules of the system, by setting off and applying against that balance the aggregate balance of obligations owed to the sender by other members of the system. The aggregate balance is determined after the right of setoff stated in the second sentence of this subsection has been exercised.

(c) If two banks transmit payment orders to each other under an agreement that settlement of the obligations of each bank to the other under Section 4A–402 will be made at the end of the day or other period, the total amount owed with respect to all orders transmitted by one bank shall be set off against the total amount owed with respect to all orders transmitted by the other bank. To the extent of the setoff, each bank has made payment to the other.

(d) In a case not covered by subsection (a), the time when payment of the sender's obligation under Section 4A–402(b) or 4A–402(c) occurs is governed by applicable principles of law that determine when an obligation is satisfied.

§ 4A–404. Obligation of Beneficiary's Bank to Pay and Give Notice to Beneficiary.

(a) Subject to Sections 4A–211(e), 4A–405(d), and 4A–405(e), if a beneficiary's bank accepts a payment order, the bank is obliged to pay the amount of the order to the beneficiary of the order. Payment is due on the payment date of the order, but if acceptance occurs on the payment date after the close of the funds-transfer business day of the bank, payment is due on the next funds-transfer business day. If the bank refuses to pay after demand by the beneficiary and receipt of notice of particular circumstances that will give rise to consequential damages as a result of nonpayment, the beneficiary may recover damages resulting from the refusal to pay to the extent the bank had notice of the damages, unless the bank proves that it did not pay because of a reasonable doubt concerning the right of the beneficiary to payment.

(b) If a payment order accepted by the beneficiary's bank instructs payment to an account of the beneficiary, the bank is obliged to notify the beneficiary of receipt of the order before midnight of the next funds-transfer business day following the payment date. If the payment order does not instruct payment to an account of the beneficiary, the bank is required to notify the beneficiary only if notice is required by the order. Notice may be given by first class mail or any other means reasonable in the circumstances. If the bank fails to give the required notice, the bank is obliged to pay interest to the beneficiary on the amount of the payment order from the day notice should have been given until the day the beneficiary learned of receipt of the payment order by the bank. No other damages are recoverable. Reasonable attorney's fees are also recoverable if demand for interest is made and refused before an action is brought on the claim.

(c) The right of a beneficiary to receive payment and damages as stated in subsection (a) may not be varied by agreement or a funds-transfer system rule. The right of a beneficiary to be notified as stated in subsection (b) may be varied by agreement of the beneficiary or by a funds-transfer system rule if the beneficiary is notified of the rule before initiation of the funds transfer.

§ 4A–405. Payment by Beneficiary's Bank to Beneficiary.

(a) If the beneficiary's bank credits an account of the beneficiary of a payment order, payment of the bank's obligation under Section 4A–404(a) occurs when and to the extent (i) the beneficiary is notified of the right to withdraw the credit, (ii) the bank lawfully applies the credit to a debt of the beneficiary, or (iii) funds with respect to the order are otherwise made available to the beneficiary by the bank.

(b) If the beneficiary's bank does not credit an account of the beneficiary of a payment order, the time when payment of the bank's obligation under Section 4A–404(a) occurs is governed by principles of law that determine when an obligation is satisfied.

(c) Except as stated in subsections (d) and (e), if the beneficiary's bank pays the beneficiary of a payment order under a condition to payment or agreement of the beneficiary giving the bank the right to recover payment from the beneficiary if the bank does not receive payment of the order, the condition to payment or agreement is not enforceable.

(d) A funds-transfer system rule may provide that payments made to beneficiaries of funds transfers made through the system are provisional until receipt of payment by the beneficiary's bank of the payment order it accepted. A beneficiary's bank that makes a payment that is provisional under the rule is entitled to refund from the beneficiary if (i) the rule requires that both the beneficiary and the originator be given notice of the provisional nature of the payment before the funds transfer is initiated, (ii) the beneficiary, the beneficiary's bank, and the originator's bank agreed to be bound by the rule, and (iii) the beneficiary's bank did not receive payment of the payment order that it accepted. If the beneficiary is obliged to refund payment to the beneficiary's bank, acceptance of the payment order by the beneficiary's bank is nullified and no payment by the originator of the funds transfer to the beneficiary occurs under Section 4A–406.

(e) This subsection applies to a funds transfer that includes a payment order transmitted over a funds-transfer system that (i) nets obligations multilaterally among participants, and (ii) has in effect a loss-sharing agreement among participants for the purpose of providing funds necessary to complete settlement of the obligations of one or more participants that do not meet their settlement obligations. If the beneficiary's bank in the funds transfer accepts a payment order and the system fails to complete settlement pursuant to its rules with respect to any payment order in the funds transfer, (i) the acceptance by the beneficiary's bank is nullified and no person has any right or obligation based on the acceptance, (ii) the beneficiary's bank is entitled to recover payment from the beneficiary, (iii) no payment by the originator to the beneficiary occurs under Section 4A–406, and (iv) subject to Section 4A–402(e), each sender in the funds transfer is excused from its obligation to pay its payment order under Section 4A–402(c) because the funds transfer has not been completed.

§ 4A–406. Payment by Originator to Beneficiary; Discharge of Underlying Obligation.

(a) Subject to Sections 4A–211(e), 4A–405(d), and 4A–405(e), the originator of a funds transfer pays the beneficiary of the originator's payment order (i) at the time a payment order for the benefit of the beneficiary is accepted by the beneficiary's bank in the funds transfer and (ii) in an amount equal to the amount of the order accepted by the beneficiary's bank, but not more than the amount of the originator's order.

(b) If payment under subsection (a) is made to satisfy an obligation, the obligation is discharged to the same extent discharge would result from payment to the beneficiary of the same amount in money, unless (i) the payment under subsection (a) was made by a means prohibited by the contract of the beneficiary with respect to the obligation, (ii) the beneficiary, within a reasonable time after receiving notice of receipt of the order by the beneficiary's bank, notified the originator of the beneficiary's refusal of the payment, (iii) funds with respect to the order were not withdrawn by the beneficiary or applied to a debt of the beneficiary, and (iv) the beneficiary would suffer a loss that could reasonably have been avoided if payment had been made by a means complying with the contract. If payment by the originator does not result in discharge under this section, the originator is subrogated to the rights of the beneficiary to receive payment from the beneficiary's bank under Section 4A–404(a).

(c) For the purpose of determining whether discharge of an obligation occurs under subsection (b), if the beneficiary's bank accepts a payment order in an amount equal to the amount of the originator's payment order less charges of one or more receiving banks in the funds transfer, payment to the beneficiary is deemed to be in the amount of the originator's order unless upon demand by the beneficiary the originator does not pay the beneficiary the amount of the deducted charges.

(d) Rights of the originator or of the beneficiary of a funds transfer under this section may be varied only by agreement of the originator and the beneficiary.

Part 5 Miscellaneous Provisions

§ 4A–501. Variation by Agreement and Effect of Funds-Transfer System Rule.

(a) Except as otherwise provided in this Article, the rights and obligations of a party to a funds transfer may be varied by agreement of the affected party.

(b) "Funds-transfer system rule" means a rule of an association of banks (i) governing transmission of payment orders by means of a funds-transfer system of the association or rights and obligations with respect to those orders, or (ii) to the extent the rule governs rights and obligations between banks that are parties to a funds transfer in which a Federal Reserve Bank, acting as an intermediary bank, sends a payment order to the beneficiary's bank. Except as otherwise provided in this Article, a funds-transfer system rule governing rights and obligations between participating banks using the system may be effective even if the rule conflicts with this Article and indirectly affects another party to the funds transfer who does not consent to the rule. A funds-transfer system rule may also govern rights and obligations of parties other than participating banks using the system to the extent stated in Sections 4A–404(c), 4A–405(d), and 4A–507(c).

§ 4A–502. Creditor Process Served on Receiving Bank; Setoff by Beneficiary's Bank.

(a) As used in this section, "creditor process" means levy, attachment, garnishment, notice of lien, sequestration, or similar process issued by or on behalf of a creditor or other claimant with respect to an account.

(b) This subsection applies to creditor process with respect to an authorized account of the sender of a payment order if the creditor process is served on the receiving bank. For the purpose of determining rights with respect to the creditor process, if the receiving bank accepts the payment order the balance in the authorized account is deemed to be reduced by the amount of the payment order to the extent the bank did not otherwise receive payment of the order, unless the creditor process is served at a time and in a manner affording the bank a reasonable opportunity to act on it before the bank accepts the payment order.

(c) If a beneficiary's bank has received a payment order for payment to the beneficiary's account in the bank, the following rules apply:

(1) The bank may credit the beneficiary's account. The amount credited may be set off against an obligation owed by the beneficiary to the bank or may be applied to satisfy creditor process served on the bank with respect to the account.

(2) The bank may credit the beneficiary's account and allow withdrawal of the amount credited unless creditor process with respect to the account is served at a time and in a manner affording the bank a reasonable opportunity to act to prevent withdrawal.

(3) If creditor process with respect to the beneficiary's account has been served and the bank has had a reasonable opportunity to act on it, the bank may not reject the payment order except for a reason unrelated to the service of process.

(d) Creditor process with respect to a payment by the originator to the beneficiary pursuant to a funds transfer may be served only on the beneficiary's bank with respect to the debt owed by that bank to the beneficiary. Any other bank served with the creditor process is not obliged to act with respect to the process.

§ 4A–503. Injunction or Restraining Order with Respect to Funds Transfer.

For proper cause and in compliance with applicable law, a court may restrain (i) a person from issuing a payment order to initiate a funds transfer, (ii) an originator's bank from executing the payment order of the originator, or (iii) the beneficiary's bank from releasing funds to the beneficiary or the beneficiary from withdrawing the funds. A court may not otherwise restrain a person from issuing a payment order, paying or receiving payment of a payment order, or otherwise acting with respect to a funds transfer.

§ 4A–504. Order in Which Items and Payment Orders May Be Charged to Account; Order of Withdrawals from Account.

(a) If a receiving bank has received more than one payment order of the sender or one or more payment orders and other items that are payable from the sender's account, the bank may charge the sender's account with respect to the various orders and items in any sequence.

(b) In determining whether a credit to an account has been withdrawn by the holder of the account or applied to a debt of the holder of the account, credits first made to the account are first withdrawn or applied.

§ 4A–505. Preclusion of Objection to Debit of Customer's Account.

If a receiving bank has received payment from its customer with respect to a payment order issued in the name of the customer as sender and accepted by the bank, and the customer received notification reasonably identifying the order, the customer is precluded from asserting that the bank is not entitled to retain the payment unless the customer notifies the bank of the customer's objection to the payment within one year after the notification was received by the customer.

§ 4A–506. Rate of Interest.

(a) If, under this Article, a receiving bank is obliged to pay interest with respect to a payment order issued to the bank, the amount payable may be determined (i) by agreement of the sender and receiving bank, or (ii) by a funds-transfer system rule if the payment order is transmitted through a funds-transfer system.

(b) If the amount of interest is not determined by an agreement or rule as stated in subsection (a), the amount is calculated by multiplying the applicable Federal Funds rate by the amount on which interest is payable, and then multiplying the product by the number of days for which interest is payable. The applicable Federal Funds rate is the average of the Federal Funds rates published by the Federal Reserve Bank of New York for each of the days for which interest is payable divided by 360. The Federal Funds rate for any day on which a published rate is not available is the same as the published rate for the next preceding day for which there is a published rate. If a receiving bank that accepted a payment order is required to refund payment to the sender of the order because the funds transfer was not completed, but the failure to complete was not due to any fault by the bank, the interest payable is reduced by a percentage equal to the reserve requirement on deposits of the receiving bank.

§ 4A–507. Choice of Law.

(a) The following rules apply unless the affected parties otherwise agree or subsection (c) applies:

(1) The rights and obligations between the sender of a payment order and the receiving bank are governed by the law of the jurisdiction in which the receiving bank is located.

(2) The rights and obligations between the beneficiary's bank and the beneficiary are governed by the law of the jurisdiction in which the beneficiary's bank is located.

(3) The issue of when payment is made pursuant to a funds transfer by the originator to the beneficiary is governed by the law of the jurisdiction in which the beneficiary's bank is located.

(b) If the parties described in each paragraph of subsection (a) have made an agreement selecting the law of a particular jurisdiction to govern rights and obligations between each other, the law of that jurisdiction governs those rights and obligations, whether or not the payment order or the funds transfer bears a reasonable relation to that jurisdiction.

(c) A funds-transfer system rule may select the law of a particular jurisdiction to govern (i) rights and obligations between participating banks with respect to payment orders transmitted or processed through the system, or (ii) the rights and obligations of some or all parties to a funds transfer any part of which is carried out by means of the system. A choice of law made pursuant to clause (i) is binding on participating banks. A choice of law made pursuant to clause (ii) is binding on the originator, other sender, or a receiving bank having notice that the funds-transfer system might be used in the funds transfer and of the choice of law by the system when the originator, other sender, or receiving bank issued or accepted a payment order. The beneficiary of a funds transfer is bound by the choice of law if, when the funds transfer is initiated, the beneficiary has notice that the funds-transfer system might be used in the funds transfer and of the choice of law by the system. The law of a jurisdiction selected pursuant to this subsection may govern, whether or not that law bears a reasonable relation to the matter in issue.

(d) In the event of inconsistency between an agreement under subsection (b) and a choice-of-law rule under subsection (c), the agreement under subsection (b) prevails.

(e) If a funds transfer is made by use of more than one funds-transfer system and there is inconsistency between choice-of-law rules of the systems, the matter in issue is governed by the law of the selected jurisdiction that has the most significant relationship to the matter in issue.

Revised Article 9
SECURED TRANSACTIONS

Part 1 General Provisions

[Subpart 1. Short Title, Definitions, and General Concepts]

§ 9–101. Short Title.

This article may be cited as Uniform Commercial Code—Secured Transactions.

§ 9–102. Definitions and Index of Definitions.

(a) In this article:

(1) "Accession" means goods that are physically united with other goods in such a manner that the identity of the original goods is not lost.

(2) "Account", except as used in "account for", means a right to payment of a monetary obligation, whether or not earned by performance, (i) for property that has been or is to be sold, leased, licensed, assigned, or otherwise disposed of, (ii) for services rendered or to be rendered, (iii) for a policy of insurance issued or to be issued, (iv) for a secondary obligation incurred or to be incurred, (v) for energy provided or to be provided, (vi) for the use or hire of a vessel under a charter or other contract, (vii) arising out of the use of a credit or charge card or information contained on or for use with the card, or (viii) as winnings in a lottery or other game of chance operated or sponsored by a State, governmental unit of a State, or person licensed or authorized to operate the game by a State or governmental unit of a State. The term includes health-care insurance receivables. The term does not include (i) rights to payment evidenced by chattel paper or an instrument, (ii) commercial tort claims, (iii) deposit accounts, (iv) investment property, (v) letter-of-credit rights or letters of credit, or (vi) rights to payment for money or funds advanced or sold, other than rights arising out of the use of a credit or charge card or information contained on or for use with the card.

(3) "Account debtor" means a person obligated on an account, chattel paper, or general intangible. The term does not include persons obligated to pay a negotiable instrument, even if the instrument constitutes part of chattel paper.

(4) "Accounting", except as used in "accounting for", means a record:

(A) authenticated by a secured party;

(B) indicating the aggregate unpaid secured obligations as of a date not more than 35 days earlier or 35 days later than the date of the record; and

(C) identifying the components of the obligations in reasonable detail.

(5) "Agricultural lien" means an interest, other than a security interest, in farm products:

(A) which secures payment or performance of an obligation for:

(i) goods or services furnished in connection with a debtor's farming operation; or

(ii) rent on real property leased by a debtor in connection with its farming operation;

(B) which is created by statute in favor of a person that:

(i) in the ordinary course of its business furnished goods or services to a debtor in connection with a debtor's farming operation; or

(ii) leased real property to a debtor in connection with the debtor's farming operation; and

(C) whose effectiveness does not depend on the person's possession of the personal property.

(6) "As-extracted collateral" means:

(A) oil, gas, or other minerals that are subject to a security interest that:

(i) is created by a debtor having an interest in the minerals before extraction; and

(ii) attaches to the minerals as extracted; or

(B) accounts arising out of the sale at the wellhead or minehead of oil, gas, or other minerals in which the debtor had an interest before extraction.

(7) "Authenticate" means:

(A) to sign; or

(B) to execute or otherwise adopt a symbol, or encrypt or similarly process a record in whole or in part, with the present intent of the authenticating person to identify the person and adopt or accept a record.

(8) "Bank" means an organization that is engaged in the business of banking. The term includes savings banks, savings and loan associations, credit unions, and trust companies.

(9) "Cash proceeds" means proceeds that are money, checks, deposit accounts, or the like.

(10) "Certificate of title" means a certificate of title with respect to which a statute provides for the security interest in question to be indicated on the certificate as a condition or result of the security interest's obtaining priority over the rights of a lien creditor with respect to the collateral.

(11) "Chattel paper" means a record or records that evidence both a monetary obligation and a security interest in specific goods, a

security interest in specific goods and software used in the goods, a security interest in specific goods and license of software used in the goods, a lease of specific goods, or a lease of specific goods and license of software used in the goods. In this paragraph, "monetary obligation" means a monetary obligation secured by the goods or owed under a lease of the goods and includes a monetary obligation with respect to software used in the goods. The term does not include (i) charters or other contracts involving the use or hire of a vessel or (ii) records that evidence a right to payment arising out of the use of a credit or charge card or information contained on or for use with the card. If a transaction is evidenced by records that include an instrument or series of instruments, the group of records taken together constitutes chattel paper.

(12) "Collateral" means the property subject to a security interest or agricultural lien. The term includes:

(A) proceeds to which a security interest attaches;

(B) accounts, chattel paper, payment intangibles, and promissory notes that have been sold; and

(C) goods that are the subject of a consignment.

(13) "Commercial tort claim" means a claim arising in tort with respect to which:

(A) the claimant is an organization; or

(B) the claimant is an individual and the claim:

(i) arose in the course of the claimant's business or profession; and

(ii) does not include damages arising out of personal injury to or the death of an individual.

(14) "Commodity account" means an account maintained by a commodity intermediary in which a commodity contract is carried for a commodity customer.

(15) "Commodity contract" means a commodity futures contract, an option on a commodity futures contract, a commodity option, or another contract if the contract or option is:

(A) traded on or subject to the rules of a board of trade that has been designated as a contract market for such a contract pursuant to federal commodities laws; or

(B) traded on a foreign commodity board of trade, exchange, or market, and is carried on the books of a commodity intermediary for a commodity customer.

(16) "Commodity customer" means a person for which a commodity intermediary carries a commodity contract on its books.

(17) "Commodity intermediary" means a person that:

(A) is registered as a futures commission merchant under federal commodities law; or

(B) in the ordinary course of its business provides clearance or settlement services for a board of trade that has been designated as a contract market pursuant to federal commodities law.

(18) "Communicate" means:

(A) to send a written or other tangible record;

(B) to transmit a record by any means agreed upon by the persons sending and receiving the record; or

(C) in the case of transmission of a record to or by a filing office, to transmit a record by any means prescribed by filing-office rule.

(19) "Consignee" means a merchant to which goods are delivered in a consignment.

(20) "Consignment" means a transaction, regardless of its form, in which a person delivers goods to a merchant for the purpose of sale and:

(A) the merchant:

(i) deals in goods of that kind under a name other than the name of the person making delivery;

(ii) is not an auctioneer; and

(iii) is not generally known by its creditors to be substantially engaged in selling the goods of others;

(B) with respect to each delivery, the aggregate value of the goods is $1,000 or more at the time of delivery;

(C) the goods are not consumer goods immediately before delivery; and

(D) the transaction does not create a security interest that secures an obligation.

(21) "Consignor" means a person that delivers goods to a consignee in a consignment.

(22) "Consumer debtor" means a debtor in a consumer transaction.

(23) "Consumer goods" means goods that are used or bought for use primarily for personal, family, or household purposes.

(24) "Consumer-goods transaction" means a consumer transaction in which:

(A) an individual incurs an obligation primarily for personal, family, or household purposes; and

(B) a security interest in consumer goods secures the obligation.

(25) "Consumer obligor" means an obligor who is an individual and who incurred the obligation as part of a transaction entered into primarily for personal, family, or household purposes.

(26) "Consumer transaction" means a transaction in which (i) an individual incurs an obligation primarily for personal, family, or household purposes, (ii) a security interest secures the obligation, and (iii) the collateral is held or acquired primarily for personal, family, or household purposes. The term includes consumer-goods transactions.

(27) "Continuation statement" means an amendment of a financing statement which:

(A) identifies, by its file number, the initial financing statement to which it relates; and

(B) indicates that it is a continuation statement for, or that it is filed to continue the effectiveness of, the identified financing statement.

(28) "Debtor" means:

(A) a person having an interest, other than a security interest or other lien, in the collateral, whether or not the person is an obligor;

(B) a seller of accounts, chattel paper, payment intangibles, or promissory notes; or

(C) a consignee.

(29) "Deposit account" means a demand, time, savings, passbook, or similar account maintained with a bank. The term does not include investment property or accounts evidenced by an instrument.

(30) "Document" means a document of title or a receipt of the type described in Section 7–201(2).

(31) "Electronic chattel paper" means chattel paper evidenced by a record or records consisting of information stored in an electronic medium.

(32) "Encumbrance" means a right, other than an ownership interest, in real property. The term includes mortgages and other liens on real property.

(33) "Equipment" means goods other than inventory, farm products, or consumer goods.

(34) "Farm products" means goods, other than standing timber, with respect to which the debtor is engaged in a farming operation and which are:

    (A) crops grown, growing, or to be grown, including:

        (i) crops produced on trees, vines, and bushes; and

        (ii) aquatic goods produced in aquacultural operations;

    (B) livestock, born or unborn, including aquatic goods produced in aquacultural operations;

    (C) supplies used or produced in a farming operation; or

    (D) products of crops or livestock in their unmanufactured states.

(35) "Farming operation" means raising, cultivating, propagating, fattening, grazing, or any other farming, livestock, or aquacultural operation.

(36) "File number" means the number assigned to an initial financing statement pursuant to Section 9–519(a).

(37) "Filing office" means an office designated in Section 9–501 as the place to file a financing statement.

(38) "Filing-office rule" means a rule adopted pursuant to Section 9–526.

(39) "Financing statement" means a record or records composed of an initial financing statement and any filed record relating to the initial financing statement.

(40) "Fixture filing" means the filing of a financing statement covering goods that are or are to become fixtures and satisfying Section 9–502(a) and (b). The term includes the filing of a financing statement covering goods of a transmitting utility which are or are to become fixtures.

(41) "Fixtures" means goods that have become so related to particular real property that an interest in them arises under real property law.

(42) "General intangible" means any personal property, including things in action, other than accounts, chattel paper, commercial tort claims, deposit accounts, documents, goods, instruments, investment property, letter-of-credit rights, letters of credit, money, and oil, gas, or other minerals before extraction. The term includes payment intangibles and software.

(43) "Good faith" means honesty in fact and the observance of reasonable commercial standards of fair dealing.

(44) "Goods" means all things that are movable when a security interest attaches. The term includes (i) fixtures, (ii) standing timber that is to be cut and removed under a conveyance or contract for sale, (iii) the unborn young of animals, (iv) crops grown, growing, or to be grown, even if the crops are produced on trees, vines, or bushes, and (v) manufactured homes. The term also includes a computer program embedded in goods and any supporting information provided in connection with a transaction relating to the program if (i) the program is associated with the goods in such a manner that it customarily is considered part of the goods, or (ii) by becoming the owner of the goods, a person acquires a right to use the program in connection with the goods. The term does not include a computer program embedded in goods that consist solely of the medium in which the program is embedded. The term also does not include accounts, chattel paper, commercial tort claims, deposit accounts, documents, general intangibles, instruments, investment property, letter-of-credit rights, letters of credit, money, or oil, gas, or other minerals before extraction.

(45) "Governmental unit" means a subdivision, agency, department, county, parish, municipality, or other unit of the government of the United States, a State, or a foreign country. The term includes an organization having a separate corporate existence if the organization is eligible to issue debt on which interest is exempt from income taxation under the laws of the United States.

(46) "Health-care-insurance receivable" means an interest in or claim under a policy of insurance which is a right to payment of a monetary obligation for health-care goods or services provided.

(47) "Instrument" means a negotiable instrument or any other writing that evidences a right to the payment of a monetary obligation, is not itself a security agreement or lease, and is of a type that in ordinary course of business is transferred by delivery with any necessary indorsement or assignment. The term does not include (i) investment property, (ii) letters of credit, or (iii) writings that evidence a right to payment arising out of the use of a credit or charge card or information contained on or for use with the card.

(48) "Inventory" means goods, other than farm products, which:

    (A) are leased by a person as lessor;

    (B) are held by a person for sale or lease or to be furnished under a contract of service;

    (C) are furnished by a person under a contract of service; or

    (D) consist of raw materials, work in process, or materials used or consumed in a business.

(49) "Investment property" means a security, whether certificated or uncertificated, security entitlement, securities account, commodity contract, or commodity account.

(50) "Jurisdiction of organization", with respect to a registered organization, means the jurisdiction under whose law the organization is organized.

(51) "Letter-of-credit right" means a right to payment or performance under a letter of credit, whether or not the beneficiary has demanded or is at the time entitled to demand payment or performance. The term does not include the right of a beneficiary to demand payment or performance under a letter of credit.

(52) "Lien creditor" means:

(A) a creditor that has acquired a lien on the property involved by attachment, levy, or the like;

(B) an assignee for benefit of creditors from the time of assignment;

(C) a trustee in bankruptcy from the date of the filing of the petition; or

(D) a receiver in equity from the time of appointment.

(53) "Manufactured home" means a structure, transportable in one or more sections, which, in the traveling mode, is eight body feet or more in width or 40 body feet or more in length, or, when erected on site, is 320 or more square feet, and which is built on a permanent chassis and designed to be used as a dwelling with or without a permanent foundation when connected to the required utilities, and includes the plumbing, heating, air-conditioning, and electrical systems contained therein. The term includes any structure that meets all of the requirements of this paragraph except the size requirements and with respect to which the manufacturer voluntarily files a certification required by the United States Secretary of Housing and Urban Development and complies with the standards established under Title 42 of the United States Code.

(54) "Manufactured-home transaction" means a secured transaction:

(A) that creates a purchase-money security interest in a manufactured home, other than a manufactured home held as inventory; or

(B) in which a manufactured home, other than a manufactured home held as inventory, is the primary collateral.

(55) "Mortgage" means a consensual interest in real property, including fixtures, which secures payment or performance of an obligation.

(56) "New debtor" means a person that becomes bound as debtor under Section 9–203(d) by a security agreement previously entered into by another person.

(57) "New value" means (i) money, (ii) money's worth in property, services, or new credit, or (iii) release by a transferee of an interest in property previously transferred to the transferee. The term does not include an obligation substituted for another obligation.

(58) "Noncash proceeds" means proceeds other than cash proceeds.

(59) "Obligor" means a person that, with respect to an obligation secured by a security interest in or an agricultural lien on the collateral, (i) owes payment or other performance of the obligation, (ii) has provided property other than the collateral to secure payment or other performance of the obligation, or (iii) is otherwise accountable in whole or in part for payment or other performance of the obligation. The term does not include issuers or nominated persons under a letter of credit.

(60) "Original debtor", except as used in Section 9–310(c), means a person that, as debtor, entered into a security agreement to which a new debtor has become bound under Section 9–203(d).

(61) "Payment intangible" means a general intangible under which the account debtor's principal obligation is a monetary obligation.

(62) "Person related to", with respect to an individual, means:

(A) the spouse of the individual;

(B) a brother, brother-in-law, sister, or sister-in-law of the individual;

(C) an ancestor or lineal descendant of the individual or the individual's spouse; or

(D) any other relative, by blood or marriage, of the individual or the individual's spouse who shares the same home with the individual.

(63) "Person related to", with respect to an organization, means:

(A) a person directly or indirectly controlling, controlled by, or under common control with the organization;

(B) an officer or director of, or a person performing similar functions with respect to, the organization;

(C) an officer or director of, or a person performing similar functions with respect to, a person described in subparagraph (A);

(D) the spouse of an individual described in subparagraph (A), (B), or (C); or

(E) an individual who is related by blood or marriage to an individual described in subparagraph (A), (B), (C), or (D) and shares the same home with the individual.

(64) "Proceeds", except as used in Section 9–609(b), means the following property:

(A) whatever is acquired upon the sale, lease, license, exchange, or other disposition of collateral;

(B) whatever is collected on, or distributed on account of, collateral;

(C) rights arising out of collateral;

(D) to the extent of the value of collateral, claims arising out of the loss, nonconformity, or interference with the use of, defects or infringement of rights in, or damage to, the collateral; or

(E) to the extent of the value of collateral and to the extent payable to the debtor or the secured party, insurance payable by reason of the loss or nonconformity of, defects or infringement of rights in, or damage to, the collateral.

(65) "Promissory note" means an instrument that evidences a promise to pay a monetary obligation, does not evidence an order to pay, and does not contain an acknowledgment by a bank that the bank has received for deposit a sum of money or funds.

(66) "Proposal" means a record authenticated by a secured party which includes the terms on which the secured party is willing to accept collateral in full or partial satisfaction of the obligation it secures pursuant to Sections 9–620, 9–621, and 9–622.

(67) "Public-finance transaction" means a secured transaction in connection with which:

(A) debt securities are issued;

(B) all or a portion of the securities issued have an initial stated maturity of at least 20 years; and

(C) the debtor, obligor, secured party, account debtor or other person obligated on collateral, assignor or assignee of a secured obligation, or assignor or assignee of a security interest is a State or a governmental unit of a State.

(68) "Pursuant to commitment", with respect to an advance made or other value given by a secured party, means pursuant to the secured party's obligation, whether or not a subsequent event of default or other event not within the secured party's control has relieved or may relieve the secured party from its obligation.

(69) "Record", except as used in "for record", "of record", "record or legal title", and "record owner", means information that is inscribed on a tangible medium or which is stored in an electronic or other medium and is retrievable in perceivable form.

(70) "Registered organization" means an organization organized solely under the law of a single State or the United States and as to which the State or the United States must maintain a public record showing the organization to have been organized.

(71) "Secondary obligor" means an obligor to the extent that:

(A) the obligor's obligation is secondary; or

(B) the obligor has a right of recourse with respect to an obligation secured by collateral against the debtor, another obligor, or property of either.

(72) "Secured party" means:

(A) a person in whose favor a security interest is created or provided for under a security agreement, whether or not any obligation to be secured is outstanding;

(B) a person that holds an agricultural lien;

(C) a consignor;

(D) a person to which accounts, chattel paper, payment intangibles, or promissory notes have been sold;

(E) a trustee, indenture trustee, agent, collateral agent, or other representative in whose favor a security interest or agricultural lien is created or provided for; or

(F) a person that holds a security interest arising under Section 2–401, 2–505, 2–711(3), 2A–508(5), 4–210, or 5–118.

(73) "Security agreement" means an agreement that creates or provides for a security interest.

(74) "Send", in connection with a record or notification, means:

(A) to deposit in the mail, deliver for transmission, or transmit by any other usual means of communication, with postage or cost of transmission provided for, addressed to any address reasonable under the circumstances; or

(B) to cause the record or notification to be received within the time that it would have been received if properly sent under subparagraph (A).

(75) "Software" means a computer program and any supporting information provided in connection with a transaction relating to the program. The term does not include a computer program that is included in the definition of goods.

(76) "State" means a State of the United States, the District of Columbia, Puerto Rico, the United States Virgin Islands, or any territory or insular possession subject to the jurisdiction of the United States.

(77) "Supporting obligation" means a letter-of-credit right or secondary obligation that supports the payment or performance

of an account, chattel paper, a document, a general intangible, an instrument, or investment property.

(78) "Tangible chattel paper" means chattel paper evidenced by a record or records consisting of information that is inscribed on a tangible medium.

(79) "Termination statement" means an amendment of a financing statement which:

(A) identifies, by its file number, the initial financing statement to which it relates; and

(B) indicates either that it is a termination statement or that the identified financing statement is no longer effective.

(80) "Transmitting utility" means a person primarily engaged in the business of:

(A) operating a railroad, subway, street railway, or trolley bus;

(B) transmitting communications electrically, electromagnetically, or by light;

(C) transmitting goods by pipeline or sewer; or

(D) transmitting or producing and transmitting electricity, steam, gas, or water.

(b) The following definitions in other articles apply to this article:

"Applicant."	Section 5–102
"Beneficiary."	Section 5–102
"Broker."	Section 8–102
"Certificated security."	Section 8–102
"Check."	Section 3–104
"Clearing corporation."	Section 8–102
"Contract for sale."	Section 2–106
"Customer."	Section 4–104
"Entitlement holder."	Section 8–102
"Financial asset."	Section 8–102
"Holder in due course."	Section 3–302
"Issuer" (with respect to a letter of credit or letter-of-credit right).	Section 5–102
"Issuer" (with respect to a security).	Section 8–201
"Lease."	Section 2A–103
"Lease agreement."	Section 2A–103
"Lease contract."	Section 2A–103
"Leasehold interest."	Section 2A–103
"Lessee."	Section 2A–103
"Lessee in ordinary course of business."	Section 2A–103
"Lessor."	Section 2A–103
"Lessor's residual interest."	Section 2A–103
"Letter of credit."	Section 5–102
"Merchant."	Section 2–104
"Negotiable instrument."	Section 3–104
"Nominated person."	Section 5–102

"Note."	Section 3–104
"Proceeds of a letter of credit."	Section 5–114
"Prove."	Section 3–103
"Sale."	Section 2–106
"Securities account."	Section 8–501
"Securities intermediary."	Section 8–102
"Security."	Section 8–102
"Security certificate."	Section 8–102
"Security entitlement."	Section 8–102
"Uncertificated security."	Section 8–102

(c) Article 1 contains general definitions and principles of construction and interpretation applicable throughout this article.

Amended in 1999 and 2000.

§ 9–103. Purchase-Money Security Interest; Application of Payments; Burden of Establishing.

(a) In this section:

(1) "purchase-money collateral" means goods or software that secures a purchase-money obligation incurred with respect to that collateral; and

(2) "purchase-money obligation" means an obligation of an obligor incurred as all or part of the price of the collateral or for value given to enable the debtor to acquire rights in or the use of the collateral if the value is in fact so used.

(b) A security interest in goods is a purchase-money security interest:

(1) to the extent that the goods are purchase-money collateral with respect to that security interest;

(2) if the security interest is in inventory that is or was purchase-money collateral, also to the extent that the security interest secures a purchase-money obligation incurred with respect to other inventory in which the secured party holds or held a purchase-money security interest; and

(3) also to the extent that the security interest secures a purchase-money obligation incurred with respect to software in which the secured party holds or held a purchase-money security interest.

(c) A security interest in software is a purchase-money security interest to the extent that the security interest also secures a purchase-money obligation incurred with respect to goods in which the secured party holds or held a purchase-money security interest if:

(1) the debtor acquired its interest in the software in an integrated transaction in which it acquired an interest in the goods; and

(2) the debtor acquired its interest in the software for the principal purpose of using the software in the goods.

(d) The security interest of a consignor in goods that are the subject of a consignment is a purchase-money security interest in inventory.

(e) In a transaction other than a consumer-goods transaction, if the extent to which a security interest is a purchase-money security interest depends on the application of a payment to a particular obligation, the payment must be applied:

(1) in accordance with any reasonable method of application to which the parties agree;

(2) in the absence of the parties' agreement to a reasonable method, in accordance with any intention of the obligor manifested at or before the time of payment; or

(3) in the absence of an agreement to a reasonable method and a timely manifestation of the obligor's intention, in the following order:

(A) to obligations that are not secured; and

(B) if more than one obligation is secured, to obligations secured by purchase-money security interests in the order in which those obligations were incurred.

(f) In a transaction other than a consumer-goods transaction, a purchase-money security interest does not lose its status as such, even if:

(1) the purchase-money collateral also secures an obligation that is not a purchase-money obligation;

(2) collateral that is not purchase-money collateral also secures the purchase-money obligation; or

(3) the purchase-money obligation has been renewed, refinanced, consolidated, or restructured.

(g) In a transaction other than a consumer-goods transaction, a secured party claiming a purchase-money security interest has the burden of establishing the extent to which the security interest is a purchase-money security interest.

(h) The limitation of the rules in subsections (e), (f), and (g) to transactions other than consumer-goods transactions is intended to leave to the court the determination of the proper rules in consumer-goods transactions. The court may not infer from that limitation the nature of the proper rule in consumer-goods transactions and may continue to apply established approaches.

§ 9–104. Control of Deposit Account.

(a) A secured party has control of a deposit account if:

(1) the secured party is the bank with which the deposit account is maintained;

(2) the debtor, secured party, and bank have agreed in an authenticated record that the bank will comply with instructions originated by the secured party directing disposition of the funds in the deposit account without further consent by the debtor; or

(3) the secured party becomes the bank's customer with respect to the deposit account.

(b) A secured party that has satisfied subsection (a) has control, even if the debtor retains the right to direct the disposition of funds from the deposit account.

§ 9–105. Control of Electronic Chattel Paper.

A secured party has control of electronic chattel paper if the record or records comprising the chattel paper are created, stored, and assigned in such a manner that:

(1) a single authoritative copy of the record or records exists which is unique, identifiable and, except as otherwise provided in paragraphs (4), (5), and (6), unalterable;

(2) the authoritative copy identifies the secured party as the assignee of the record or records;

(3) the authoritative copy is communicated to and maintained by the secured party or its designated custodian;

(4) copies or revisions that add or change an identified assignee of the authoritative copy can be made only with the participation of the secured party;

(5) each copy of the authoritative copy and any copy of a copy is readily identifiable as a copy that is not the authoritative copy; and

(6) any revision of the authoritative copy is readily identifiable as an authorized or unauthorized revision.

§ 9–106. Control of Investment Property.

(a) A person has control of a certificated security, uncertificated security, or security entitlement as provided in Section 8–106.

(b) A secured party has control of a commodity contract if:

(1) the secured party is the commodity intermediary with which the commodity contract is carried; or

(2) the commodity customer, secured party, and commodity intermediary have agreed that the commodity intermediary will apply any value distributed on account of the commodity contract as directed by the secured party without further consent by the commodity customer.

(c) A secured party having control of all security entitlements or commodity contracts carried in a securities account or commodity account has control over the securities account or commodity account.

§ 9–107. Control of Letter-of-Credit Right.

A secured party has control of a letter-of-credit right to the extent of any right to payment or performance by the issuer or any nominated person if the issuer or nominated person has consented to an assignment of proceeds of the letter of credit under Section 5–114(c) or otherwise applicable law or practice.

§ 9–108. Sufficiency of Description.

(a) Except as otherwise provided in subsections (c), (d), and (e), a description of personal or real property is sufficient, whether or not it is specific, if it reasonably identifies what is described.

(b) Except as otherwise provided in subsection (d), a description of collateral reasonably identifies the collateral if it identifies the collateral by:

(1) specific listing;

(2) category;

(3) except as otherwise provided in subsection (e), a type of collateral defined in [the Uniform Commercial Code];

(4) quantity;

(5) computational or allocational formula or procedure; or

(6) except as otherwise provided in subsection (c), any other method, if the identity of the collateral is objectively determinable.

(c) A description of collateral as "all the debtor's assets" or "all the debtor's personal property" or using words of similar import does not reasonably identify the collateral.

(d) Except as otherwise provided in subsection (e), a description of a security entitlement, securities account, or commodity account is sufficient if it describes:

(1) the collateral by those terms or as investment property; or

(2) the underlying financial asset or commodity contract.

(e) A description only by type of collateral defined in [the Uniform Commercial Code] is an insufficient description of:

(1) a commercial tort claim; or

(2) in a consumer transaction, consumer goods, a security entitlement, a securities account, or a commodity account.

[Subpart 2. Applicability of Article]

§ 9–109. Scope.

(a) Except as otherwise provided in subsections (c) and (d), this article applies to:

(1) a transaction, regardless of its form, that creates a security interest in personal property or fixtures by contract;

(2) an agricultural lien;

(3) a sale of accounts, chattel paper, payment intangibles, or promissory notes;

(4) a consignment;

(5) a security interest arising under Section 2–401, 2–505, 2–711(3), or 2A–508(5), as provided in Section 9–110; and

(6) a security interest arising under Section 4–210 or 5–118.

(b) The application of this article to a security interest in a secured obligation is not affected by the fact that the obligation is itself secured by a transaction or interest to which this article does not apply.

(c) This article does not apply to the extent that:

(1) a statute, regulation, or treaty of the United States preempts this article;

(2) another statute of this State expressly governs the creation, perfection, priority, or enforcement of a security interest created by this State or a governmental unit of this State;

(3) a statute of another State, a foreign country, or a governmental unit of another State or a foreign country, other than a statute generally applicable to security interests, expressly governs creation, perfection, priority, or enforcement of a security interest created by the State, country, or governmental unit; or

(4) the rights of a transferee beneficiary or nominated person under a letter of credit are independent and superior under Section 5–114.

(d) This article does not apply to:

(1) a landlord's lien, other than an agricultural lien;

(2) a lien, other than an agricultural lien, given by statute or other rule of law for services or materials, but Section 9–333 applies with respect to priority of the lien;

(3) an assignment of a claim for wages, salary, or other compensation of an employee;

(4) a sale of accounts, chattel paper, payment intangibles, or promissory notes as part of a sale of the business out of which they arose;

(5) an assignment of accounts, chattel paper, payment intangibles, or promissory notes which is for the purpose of collection only;

(6) an assignment of a right to payment under a contract to an assignee that is also obligated to perform under the contract;

(7) an assignment of a single account, payment intangible, or promissory note to an assignee in full or partial satisfaction of a preexisting indebtedness;

(8) a transfer of an interest in or an assignment of a claim under a policy of insurance, other than an assignment by or to a health-care provider of a health-care-insurance receivable and any subsequent assignment of the right to payment, but Sections 9–315 and 9–322 apply with respect to proceeds and priorities in proceeds;

(9) an assignment of a right represented by a judgment, other than a judgment taken on a right to payment that was collateral;

(10) a right of recoupment or set-off, but:

(A) Section 9–340 applies with respect to the effectiveness of rights of recoupment or set-off against deposit accounts; and

(B) Section 9–404 applies with respect to defenses or claims of an account debtor;

(11) the creation or transfer of an interest in or lien on real property, including a lease or rents thereunder, except to the extent that provision is made for:

(A) liens on real property in Sections 9–203 and 9–308;

(B) fixtures in Section 9–334;

(C) fixture filings in Sections 9–501, 9–502, 9–512, 9–516, and 9–519; and

(D) security agreements covering personal and real property in Section 9–604;

(12) an assignment of a claim arising in tort, other than a commercial tort claim, but Sections 9–315 and 9–322 apply with respect to proceeds and priorities in proceeds; or

(13) an assignment of a deposit account in a consumer transaction, but Sections 9–315 and 9–322 apply with respect to proceeds and priorities in proceeds.

§ 9–110. Security Interests Arising under Article 2 or 2A.

A security interest arising under Section 2–401, 2–505, 2–711(3), or 2A–508(5) is subject to this article. However, until the debtor obtains possession of the goods:

(1) the security interest is enforceable, even if Section 9–203(b)(3) has not been satisfied;

(2) filing is not required to perfect the security interest;

(3) the rights of the secured party after default by the debtor are governed by Article 2 or 2A; and

(4) the security interest has priority over a conflicting security interest created by the debtor.

Part 2 Effectiveness of Security Agreement; Attachment of Security Interest; Rights of Parties to Security Agreement

[Subpart 1. Effectiveness and Attachment]

§ 9–201. General Effectiveness of Security Agreement.

(a) Except as otherwise provided in [the Uniform Commercial Code], a security agreement is effective according to its terms between the parties, against purchasers of the collateral, and against creditors.

(b) A transaction subject to this article is subject to any applicable rule of law which establishes a different rule for consumers and

[insert reference to (i) any other statute or regulation that regulates the rates, charges, agreements, and practices for loans, credit sales, or other extensions of credit and (ii) any consumer-protection statute or regulation].

(c) In case of conflict between this article and a rule of law, statute, or regulation described in subsection (b), the rule of law, statute, or regulation controls. Failure to comply with a statute or regulation described in subsection (b) has only the effect the statute or regulation specifies.

(d) This article does not:

(1) validate any rate, charge, agreement, or practice that violates a rule of law, statute, or regulation described in subsection (b); or

(2) extend the application of the rule of law, statute, or regulation to a transaction not otherwise subject to it.

§ 9–202. Title to Collateral Immaterial.

Except as otherwise provided with respect to consignments or sales of accounts, chattel paper, payment intangibles, or promissory notes, the provisions of this article with regard to rights and obligations apply whether title to collateral is in the secured party or the debtor.

§ 9–203. Attachment and Enforceability of Security Interest; Proceeds; Supporting Obligations; Formal Requisites.

(a) A security interest attaches to collateral when it becomes enforceable against the debtor with respect to the collateral, unless an agreement expressly postpones the time of attachment.

(b) Except as otherwise provided in subsections (c) through (i), a security interest is enforceable against the debtor and third parties with respect to the collateral only if:

(1) value has been given;

(2) the debtor has rights in the collateral or the power to transfer rights in the collateral to a secured party; and

(3) one of the following conditions is met:

(A) the debtor has authenticated a security agreement that provides a description of the collateral and, if the security interest covers timber to be cut, a description of the land concerned;

(B) the collateral is not a certificated security and is in the possession of the secured party under Section 9–313 pursuant to the debtor's security agreement;

(C) the collateral is a certificated security in registered form and the security certificate has been delivered to the secured party under Section 8–301 pursuant to the debtor's security agreement; or

(D) the collateral is deposit accounts, electronic chattel paper, investment property, or letter-of-credit rights, and the secured party has control under Section 9–104, 9–105, 9–106, or 9–107 pursuant to the debtor's security agreement.

(c) Subsection (b) is subject to Section 4–210 on the security interest of a collecting bank, Section 5–118 on the security interest of a letter-of-credit issuer or nominated person, Section 9–110 on a security interest arising under Article 2 or 2A, and Section 9–206 on security interests in investment property.

(d) A person becomes bound as debtor by a security agreement entered into by another person if, by operation of law other than this article or by contract:

(1) the security agreement becomes effective to create a security interest in the person's property; or

(2) the person becomes generally obligated for the obligations of the other person, including the obligation secured under the security agreement, and acquires or succeeds to all or substantially all of the assets of the other person.

(e) If a new debtor becomes bound as debtor by a security agreement entered into by another person:

(1) the agreement satisfies subsection (b)(3) with respect to existing or after-acquired property of the new debtor to the extent the property is described in the agreement; and

(2) another agreement is not necessary to make a security interest in the property enforceable.

(f) The attachment of a security interest in collateral gives the secured party the rights to proceeds provided by Section 9–315 and is also attachment of a security interest in a supporting obligation for the collateral.

(g) The attachment of a security interest in a right to payment or performance secured by a security interest or other lien on personal or real property is also attachment of a security interest in the security interest, mortgage, or other lien.

(h) The attachment of a security interest in a securities account is also attachment of a security interest in the security entitlements carried in the securities account.

(i) The attachment of a security interest in a commodity account is also attachment of a security interest in the commodity contracts carried in the commodity account.

§ 9–204. After-Acquired Property; Future Advances.

(a) Except as otherwise provided in subsection (b), a security agreement may create or provide for a security interest in after-acquired collateral.

(b) A security interest does not attach under a term constituting an after-acquired property clause to:

(1) consumer goods, other than an accession when given as additional security, unless the debtor acquires rights in them within 10 days after the secured party gives value; or

(2) a commercial tort claim.

(c) A security agreement may provide that collateral secures, or that accounts, chattel paper, payment intangibles, or promissory notes are sold in connection with, future advances or other value, whether or not the advances or value are given pursuant to commitment.

§ 9–205. Use or Disposition of Collateral Permissible.

(a) A security interest is not invalid or fraudulent against creditors solely because:

(1) the debtor has the right or ability to:

(A) use, commingle, or dispose of all or part of the collateral, including returned or repossessed goods;

(B) collect, compromise, enforce, or otherwise deal with collateral;

(C) accept the return of collateral or make repossessions; or

(D) use, commingle, or dispose of proceeds; or

(2) the secured party fails to require the debtor to account for proceeds or replace collateral.

(b) This section does not relax the requirements of possession if attachment, perfection, or enforcement of a security interest depends upon possession of the collateral by the secured party.

§ 9–206. Security Interest Arising in Purchase or Delivery of Financial Asset.

(a) A security interest in favor of a securities intermediary attaches to a person's security entitlement if:

(1) the person buys a financial asset through the securities intermediary in a transaction in which the person is obligated to pay the purchase price to the securities intermediary at the time of the purchase; and

(2) the securities intermediary credits the financial asset to the buyer's securities account before the buyer pays the securities intermediary.

(b) The security interest described in subsection (a) secures the person's obligation to pay for the financial asset.

(c) A security interest in favor of a person that delivers a certificated security or other financial asset represented by a writing attaches to the security or other financial asset if:

(1) the security or other financial asset:

(A) in the ordinary course of business is transferred by delivery with any necessary indorsement or assignment; and

(B) is delivered under an agreement between persons in the business of dealing with such securities or financial assets; and

(2) the agreement calls for delivery against payment.

(d) The security interest described in subsection (c) secures the obligation to make payment for the delivery.

[Subpart 2. Rights and Duties]

§ 9–207. Rights and Duties of Secured Party Having Possession or Control of Collateral.

(a) Except as otherwise provided in subsection (d), a secured party shall use reasonable care in the custody and preservation of collateral in the secured party's possession. In the case of chattel paper or an instrument, reasonable care includes taking necessary steps to preserve rights against prior parties unless otherwise agreed.

(b) Except as otherwise provided in subsection (d), if a secured party has possession of collateral:

(1) reasonable expenses, including the cost of insurance and payment of taxes or other charges, incurred in the custody, preservation, use, or operation of the collateral are chargeable to the debtor and are secured by the collateral;

(2) the risk of accidental loss or damage is on the debtor to the extent of a deficiency in any effective insurance coverage;

(3) the secured party shall keep the collateral identifiable, but fungible collateral may be commingled; and

(4) the secured party may use or operate the collateral:

(A) for the purpose of preserving the collateral or its value;

(B) as permitted by an order of a court having competent jurisdiction; or

(C) except in the case of consumer goods, in the manner and to the extent agreed by the debtor.

(c) Except as otherwise provided in subsection (d), a secured party having possession of collateral or control of collateral under Section 9–104, 9–105, 9–106, or 9–107:

(1) may hold as additional security any proceeds, except money or funds, received from the collateral;

(2) shall apply money or funds received from the collateral to reduce the secured obligation, unless remitted to the debtor; and

(3) may create a security interest in the collateral.

(d) If the secured party is a buyer of accounts, chattel paper, payment intangibles, or promissory notes or a consignor:

(1) subsection (a) does not apply unless the secured party is entitled under an agreement:

(A) to charge back uncollected collateral; or

(B) otherwise to full or limited recourse against the debtor or a secondary obligor based on the nonpayment or other default of an account debtor or other obligor on the collateral; and

(2) subsections (b) and (c) do not apply.

§ 9–208. Additional Duties of Secured Party Having Control of Collateral.

(a) This section applies to cases in which there is no outstanding secured obligation and the secured party is not committed to make advances, incur obligations, or otherwise give value.

(b) Within 10 days after receiving an authenticated demand by the debtor:

(1) a secured party having control of a deposit account under Section 9–104(a)(2) shall send to the bank with which the deposit account is maintained an authenticated statement that releases the bank from any further obligation to comply with instructions originated by the secured party;

(2) a secured party having control of a deposit account under Section 9–104(a)(3) shall:

(A) pay the debtor the balance on deposit in the deposit account; or

(B) transfer the balance on deposit into a deposit account in the debtor's name;

(3) a secured party, other than a buyer, having control of electronic chattel paper under Section 9–105 shall:

(A) communicate the authoritative copy of the electronic chattel paper to the debtor or its designated custodian;

(B) if the debtor designates a custodian that is the designated custodian with which the authoritative copy of the electronic chattel paper is maintained for the secured party, communicate to the custodian an authenticated record releasing the designated custodian from any further obligation to comply with instructions originated by the secured party and instructing the custodian to comply with instructions originated by the debtor; and

(C) take appropriate action to enable the debtor or its designated custodian to make copies of or revisions to the authoritative copy which add or change an identified assignee of the authoritative copy without the consent of the secured party;

(4) a secured party having control of investment property under Section 8–106(d)(2) or 9–106(b) shall send to the securities intermediary or commodity intermediary with which the security entitlement or commodity contract is maintained an authenticated record that releases the securities intermediary or commodity intermediary from any further obligation to comply with entitlement orders or directions originated by the secured party; and

(5) a secured party having control of a letter-of-credit right under Section 9–107 shall send to each person having an unfulfilled obligation to pay or deliver proceeds of the letter of credit to the secured party an authenticated release from any further obligation to pay or deliver proceeds of the letter of credit to the secured party.

§ 9–209. Duties of Secured Party If Account Debtor Has Been Notified of Assignment.

(a) Except as otherwise provided in subsection (c), this section applies if:

(1) there is no outstanding secured obligation; and

(2) the secured party is not committed to make advances, incur obligations, or otherwise give value.

(b) Within 10 days after receiving an authenticated demand by the debtor, a secured party shall send to an account debtor that has received notification of an assignment to the secured party as assignee under Section 9–406(a) an authenticated record that releases the account debtor from any further obligation to the secured party.

(c) This section does not apply to an assignment constituting the sale of an account, chattel paper, or payment intangible.

§ 9–210. Request for Accounting; Request Regarding List of Collateral or Statement of Account.

(a) In this section:

(1) "Request" means a record of a type described in paragraph (2), (3), or (4).

(2) "Request for an accounting" means a record authenticated by a debtor requesting that the recipient provide an accounting of the unpaid obligations secured by collateral and reasonably identifying the transaction or relationship that is the subject of the request.

(3) "Request regarding a list of collateral" means a record authenticated by a debtor requesting that the recipient approve or correct a list of what the debtor believes to be the collateral securing an obligation and reasonably identifying the transaction or relationship that is the subject of the request.

(4) "Request regarding a statement of account" means a record authenticated by a debtor requesting that the recipient approve or correct a statement indicating what the debtor believes to be the aggregate amount of unpaid obligations secured by collateral as of a specified date and reasonably identifying the transaction or relationship that is the subject of the request.

(b) Subject to subsections (c), (d), (e), and (f), a secured party, other than a buyer of accounts, chattel paper, payment intangibles, or promissory notes or a consignor, shall comply with a request within 14 days after receipt:

(1) in the case of a request for an accounting, by authenticating and sending to the debtor an accounting; and

(2) in the case of a request regarding a list of collateral or a request regarding a statement of account, by authenticating and sending to the debtor an approval or correction.

(c) A secured party that claims a security interest in all of a particular type of collateral owned by the debtor may comply with a request regarding a list of collateral by sending to the debtor an authenticated record including a statement to that effect within 14 days after receipt.

(d) A person that receives a request regarding a list of collateral, claims no interest in the collateral when it receives the request, and claimed an interest in the collateral at an earlier time shall comply with the request within 14 days after receipt by sending to the debtor an authenticated record:

(1) disclaiming any interest in the collateral; and

(2) if known to the recipient, providing the name and mailing address of any assignee of or successor to the recipient's interest in the collateral.

(e) A person that receives a request for an accounting or a request regarding a statement of account, claims no interest in the obligations when it receives the request, and claimed an interest in the obligations at an earlier time shall comply with the request within 14 days after receipt by sending to the debtor an authenticated record:

(1) disclaiming any interest in the obligations; and

(2) if known to the recipient, providing the name and mailing address of any assignee of or successor to the recipient's interest in the obligations.

(f) A debtor is entitled without charge to one response to a request under this section during any six-month period. The secured party may require payment of a charge not exceeding $25 for each additional response.

As amended in 1999.

Part 3 Perfection and Priority

[Subpart 1. Law Governing Perfection and Priority]

§ 9–301. Law Governing Perfection and Priority of Security Interests.

Except as otherwise provided in Sections 9–303 through 9–306, the following rules determine the law governing perfection, the effect of perfection or nonperfection, and the priority of a security interest in collateral:

(1) Except as otherwise provided in this section, while a debtor is located in a jurisdiction, the local law of that jurisdiction governs perfection, the effect of perfection or nonperfection, and the priority of a security interest in collateral.

(2) While collateral is located in a jurisdiction, the local law of that jurisdiction governs perfection, the effect of perfection or nonperfection, and the priority of a possessory security interest in that collateral.

(3) Except as otherwise provided in paragraph (4), while negotiable documents, goods, instruments, money, or tangible chattel paper is located in a jurisdiction, the local law of that jurisdiction governs:

(A) perfection of a security interest in the goods by filing a fixture filing;

(B) perfection of a security interest in timber to be cut; and

(C) the effect of perfection or nonperfection and the priority of a nonpossessory security interest in the collateral.

(4) The local law of the jurisdiction in which the wellhead or minehead is located governs perfection, the effect of perfection or nonperfection, and the priority of a security interest in as-extracted collateral.

§ 9–302. Law Governing Perfection and Priority of Agricultural Liens.

While farm products are located in a jurisdiction, the local law of that jurisdiction governs perfection, the effect of perfection or nonperfection, and the priority of an agricultural lien on the farm products.

§ 9–303. Law Governing Perfection and Priority of Security Interests in Goods Covered by a Certificate of Title.

(a) This section applies to goods covered by a certificate of title, even if there is no other relationship between the jurisdiction under whose certificate of title the goods are covered and the goods or the debtor.

(b) Goods become covered by a certificate of title when a valid application for the certificate of title and the applicable fee are delivered to the appropriate authority. Goods cease to be covered by a certificate of title at the earlier of the time the certificate of title ceases to be effective under the law of the issuing jurisdiction or the time the goods become covered subsequently by a certificate of title issued by another jurisdiction.

(c) The local law of the jurisdiction under whose certificate of title the goods are covered governs perfection, the effect of perfection or nonperfection, and the priority of a security interest in goods covered by a certificate of title from the time the goods become covered by the certificate of title until the goods cease to be covered by the certificate of title.

§ 9–304. Law Governing Perfection and Priority of Security Interests in Deposit Accounts.

(a) The local law of a bank's jurisdiction governs perfection, the effect of perfection or nonperfection, and the priority of a security interest in a deposit account maintained with that bank.

(b) The following rules determine a bank's jurisdiction for purposes of this part:

(1) If an agreement between the bank and the debtor governing the deposit account expressly provides that a particular jurisdiction is the bank's jurisdiction for purposes of this part, this article, or [the Uniform Commercial Code], that jurisdiction is the bank's jurisdiction.

(2) If paragraph (1) does not apply and an agreement between the bank and its customer governing the deposit account expressly provides that the agreement is governed by the law of a particular jurisdiction, that jurisdiction is the bank's jurisdiction.

(3) If neither paragraph (1) nor paragraph (2) applies and an agreement between the bank and its customer governing the deposit account expressly provides that the deposit account is maintained at an office in a particular jurisdiction, that jurisdiction is the bank's jurisdiction.

(4) If none of the preceding paragraphs applies, the bank's jurisdiction is the jurisdiction in which the office identified in an account statement as the office serving the customer's account is located.

(5) If none of the preceding paragraphs applies, the bank's jurisdiction is the jurisdiction in which the chief executive office of the bank is located.

§ 9–305. Law Governing Perfection and Priority of Security Interests in Investment Property.

(a) Except as otherwise provided in subsection (c), the following rules apply:

(1) While a security certificate is located in a jurisdiction, the local law of that jurisdiction governs perfection, the effect of perfection or nonperfection, and the priority of a security interest in the certificated security represented thereby.

(2) The local law of the issuer's jurisdiction as specified in Section 8–110(d) governs perfection, the effect of perfection or nonperfection, and the priority of a security interest in an uncertificated security.

(3) The local law of the securities intermediary's jurisdiction as specified in Section 8–110(e) governs perfection, the effect of perfection or nonperfection, and the priority of a security interest in a security entitlement or securities account.

(4) The local law of the commodity intermediary's jurisdiction governs perfection, the effect of perfection or nonperfection, and the priority of a security interest in a commodity contract or commodity account.

(b) The following rules determine a commodity intermediary's jurisdiction for purposes of this part:

(1) If an agreement between the commodity intermediary and commodity customer governing the commodity account expressly provides that a particular jurisdiction is the commodity intermediary's jurisdiction for purposes of this part, this article, or [the Uniform Commercial Code], that jurisdiction is the commodity intermediary's jurisdiction.

(2) If paragraph (1) does not apply and an agreement between the commodity intermediary and commodity customer governing the commodity account expressly provides that the agreement is governed by the law of a particular jurisdiction, that jurisdiction is the commodity intermediary's jurisdiction.

(3) If neither paragraph (1) nor paragraph (2) applies and an agreement between the commodity intermediary and commodity customer governing the commodity account expressly provides that the commodity account is maintained at an office in a particular jurisdiction, that jurisdiction is the commodity intermediary's jurisdiction.

(4) If none of the preceding paragraphs applies, the commodity intermediary's jurisdiction is the jurisdiction in which the office identified in an account statement as the office serving the commodity customer's account is located.

(5) If none of the preceding paragraphs applies, the commodity intermediary's jurisdiction is the jurisdiction in which the chief executive office of the commodity intermediary is located.

(c) The local law of the jurisdiction in which the debtor is located governs:

(1) perfection of a security interest in investment property by filing;

(2) automatic perfection of a security interest in investment property created by a broker or securities intermediary; and

(3) automatic perfection of a security interest in a commodity contract or commodity account created by a commodity intermediary.

§ 9–306. Law Governing Perfection and Priority of Security Interests in Letter-of-Credit Rights.

(a) Subject to subsection (c), the local law of the issuer's jurisdiction or a nominated person's jurisdiction governs perfection, the effect of perfection or nonperfection, and the priority of a security interest in a letter-of-credit right if the issuer's jurisdiction or nominated person's jurisdiction is a State.

(b) For purposes of this part, an issuer's jurisdiction or nominated person's jurisdiction is the jurisdiction whose law governs the liability of the issuer or nominated person with respect to the letter-of-credit right as provided in Section 5–116.

(c) This section does not apply to a security interest that is perfected only under Section 9–308(d).

§ 9–307. Location of Debtor.

(a) In this section, "place of business" means a place where a debtor conducts its affairs.

(b) Except as otherwise provided in this section, the following rules determine a debtor's location:

(1) A debtor who is an individual is located at the individual's principal residence.

(2) A debtor that is an organization and has only one place of business is located at its place of business.

(3) A debtor that is an organization and has more than one place of business is located at its chief executive office.

(c) Subsection (b) applies only if a debtor's residence, place of business, or chief executive office, as applicable, is located in a jurisdiction whose law generally requires information concerning the existence of a nonpossessory security interest to be made generally available in a filing, recording, or registration system as a condition or result of the security interest's obtaining priority over the rights of a lien creditor with respect to the collateral. If subsection (b) does not apply, the debtor is located in the District of Columbia.

(d) A person that ceases to exist, have a residence, or have a place of business continues to be located in the jurisdiction specified by subsections (b) and (c).

(e) A registered organization that is organized under the law of a State is located in that State.

(f) Except as otherwise provided in subsection (i), a registered organization that is organized under the law of the United States and a branch or agency of a bank that is not organized under the law of the United States or a State are located:

(1) in the State that the law of the United States designates, if the law designates a State of location;

(2) in the State that the registered organization, branch, or agency designates, if the law of the United States authorizes the registered organization, branch, or agency to designate its State of location; or

(3) in the District of Columbia, if neither paragraph (1) nor paragraph (2) applies.

(g) A registered organization continues to be located in the jurisdiction specified by subsection (e) or (f) notwithstanding:

(1) the suspension, revocation, forfeiture, or lapse of the registered organization's status as such in its jurisdiction of organization; or

(2) the dissolution, winding up, or cancellation of the existence of the registered organization.

(h) The United States is located in the District of Columbia.

(i) A branch or agency of a bank that is not organized under the law of the United States or a State is located in the State in which the branch or agency is licensed, if all branches and agencies of the bank are licensed in only one State.

(j) A foreign air carrier under the Federal Aviation Act of 1958, as amended, is located at the designated office of the agent upon which service of process may be made on behalf of the carrier.

(k) This section applies only for purposes of this part.

[Subpart 2. Perfection]

§ 9–308. When Security Interest or Agricultural Lien Is Perfected; Continuity of Perfection.

(a) Except as otherwise provided in this section and Section 9–309, a security interest is perfected if it has attached and all of the applicable requirements for perfection in Sections 9–310 through 9–316 have been satisfied. A security interest is perfected when it attaches if the applicable requirements are satisfied before the security interest attaches.

(b) An agricultural lien is perfected if it has become effective and all of the applicable requirements for perfection in Section 9–310 have been satisfied. An agricultural lien is perfected when it becomes effective if the applicable requirements are satisfied before the agricultural lien becomes effective.

(c) A security interest or agricultural lien is perfected continuously if it is originally perfected by one method under this article and is later perfected by another method under this article, without an intermediate period when it was unperfected.

(d) Perfection of a security interest in collateral also perfects a security interest in a supporting obligation for the collateral.

(e) Perfection of a security interest in a right to payment or performance also perfects a security interest in a security interest, mortgage, or other lien on personal or real property securing the right.

(f) Perfection of a security interest in a securities account also perfects a security interest in the security entitlements carried in the securities account.

(g) Perfection of a security interest in a commodity account also perfects a security interest in the commodity contracts carried in the commodity account.

Legislative Note: Any statute conflicting with subsection (e) must be made expressly subject to that subsection.

§ 9–309. Security Interest Perfected upon Attachment.

The following security interests are perfected when they attach:

(1) a purchase-money security interest in consumer goods, except as otherwise provided in Section 9–311(b) with respect to consumer goods that are subject to a statute or treaty described in Section 9–311(a);

(2) an assignment of accounts or payment intangibles which does not by itself or in conjunction with other assignments to the same assignee transfer a significant part of the assignor's outstanding accounts or payment intangibles;

(3) a sale of a payment intangible;

(4) a sale of a promissory note;

(5) a security interest created by the assignment of a health-care-insurance receivable to the provider of the health-care goods or services;

(6) a security interest arising under Section 2–401, 2–505, 2–711(3), or 2A–508(5), until the debtor obtains possession of the collateral;

(7) a security interest of a collecting bank arising under Section 4–210;

(8) a security interest of an issuer or nominated person arising under Section 5–118;

(9) a security interest arising in the delivery of a financial asset under Section 9–206(c);

(10) a security interest in investment property created by a broker or securities intermediary;

(11) a security interest in a commodity contract or a commodity account created by a commodity intermediary;

(12) an assignment for the benefit of all creditors of the transferor and subsequent transfers by the assignee thereunder; and

(13) a security interest created by an assignment of a beneficial interest in a decedent's estate; and

(14) a sale by an individual of an account that is a right to payment of winnings in a lottery or other game of chance.

§ 9–310. When Filing Required to Perfect Security Interest or Agricultural Lien; Security Interests and Agricultural Liens to Which Filing Provisions Do Not Apply.

(a) Except as otherwise provided in subsection (b) and Section 9–312(b), a financing statement must be filed to perfect all security interests and agricultural liens.

(b) The filing of a financing statement is not necessary to perfect a security interest:

(1) that is perfected under Section 9–308(d), (e), (f), or (g);

(2) that is perfected under Section 9–309 when it attaches;

(3) in property subject to a statute, regulation, or treaty described in Section 9–311(a);

(4) in goods in possession of a bailee which is perfected under Section 9–312(d)(1) or (2);

(5) in certificated securities, documents, goods, or instruments which is perfected without filing or possession under Section 9–312(e), (f), or (g);

(6) in collateral in the secured party's possession under Section 9–313;

(7) in a certificated security which is perfected by delivery of the security certificate to the secured party under Section 9–313;

(8) in deposit accounts, electronic chattel paper, investment property, or letter-of-credit rights which is perfected by control under Section 9–314;

(9) in proceeds which is perfected under Section 9–315; or

(10) that is perfected under Section 9–316.

(c) If a secured party assigns a perfected security interest or agricultural lien, a filing under this article is not required to continue the perfected status of the security interest against creditors of and transferees from the original debtor.

§ 9–311. Perfection of Security Interests in Property Subject to Certain Statutes, Regulations, and Treaties.

(a) Except as otherwise provided in subsection (d), the filing of a financing statement is not necessary or effective to perfect a security interest in property subject to:

(1) a statute, regulation, or treaty of the United States whose requirements for a security interest's obtaining priority over the rights of a lien creditor with respect to the property preempt Section 9–310(a);

(2) [list any certificate-of-title statute covering automobiles, trailers, mobile homes, boats, farm tractors, or the like, which provides for a security interest to be indicated on the certificate as a condition or result of perfection, and any non-Uniform Commercial Code central filing statute]; or

(3) a certificate-of-title statute of another jurisdiction which provides for a security interest to be indicated on the certificate as a condition or result of the security interest's obtaining priority over the rights of a lien creditor with respect to the property.

(b) Compliance with the requirements of a statute, regulation, or treaty described in subsection (a) for obtaining priority over the rights of a lien creditor is equivalent to the filing of a financing statement under this article. Except as otherwise provided in subsection (d) and Sections 9–313 and 9–316(d) and (e) for goods covered by a certificate of title, a security interest in property subject to a statute, regulation, or treaty described in subsection (a) may be perfected only by compliance with those requirements, and a security interest so perfected remains perfected notwithstanding a change in the use or transfer of possession of the collateral.

(c) Except as otherwise provided in subsection (d) and Section 9–316(d) and (e), duration and renewal of perfection of a security interest perfected by compliance with the requirements prescribed by a statute, regulation, or treaty described in subsection (a) are governed by the statute, regulation, or treaty. In other respects, the security interest is subject to this article.

(d) During any period in which collateral subject to a statute specified in subsection (a)(2) is inventory held for sale or lease by a person or leased by that person as lessor and that person is in the business of selling goods of that kind, this section does not apply to a security interest in that collateral created by that person.

Legislative Note: This Article contemplates that perfection of a security interest in goods covered by a certificate of title occurs upon receipt by appropriate State officials of a properly tendered application for a certificate of title on which the security interest is to be indicated, without a relation back to an earlier time. States whose certificate-of-title statutes provide for perfection at a different time or contain a relation-back provision should amend the statutes accordingly.

§ 9–312. Perfection of Security Interests in Chattel Paper, Deposit Accounts, Documents, Goods Covered by Documents, Instruments, Investment Property, Letter-of-Credit Rights, and Money; Perfection by Permissive Filing; Temporary Perfection without Filing or Transfer of Possession.

(a) A security interest in chattel paper, negotiable documents, instruments, or investment property may be perfected by filing.

(b) Except as otherwise provided in Section 9–315(c) and (d) for proceeds:

(1) a security interest in a deposit account may be perfected only by control under Section 9–314;

(2) and except as otherwise provided in Section 9–308(d), a security interest in a letter-of-credit right may be perfected only by control under Section 9–314; and

(3) a security interest in money may be perfected only by the secured party's taking possession under Section 9–313.

(c) While goods are in the possession of a bailee that has issued a negotiable document covering the goods:

(1) a security interest in the goods may be perfected by perfecting a security interest in the document; and

(2) a security interest perfected in the document has priority over any security interest that becomes perfected in the goods by another method during that time.

(d) While goods are in the possession of a bailee that has issued a nonnegotiable document covering the goods, a security interest in the goods may be perfected by:

(1) issuance of a document in the name of the secured party;

(2) the bailee's receipt of notification of the secured party's interest; or

(3) filing as to the goods.

(e) A security interest in certificated securities, negotiable documents, or instruments is perfected without filing or the taking of possession for a period of 20 days from the time it attaches to the extent that it arises for new value given under an authenticated security agreement.

(f) A perfected security interest in a negotiable document or goods in possession of a bailee, other than one that has issued a negotiable document for the goods, remains perfected for 20 days without filing if the secured party makes available to the debtor the goods or documents representing the goods for the purpose of:

(1) ultimate sale or exchange; or

(2) loading, unloading, storing, shipping, transshipping, manufacturing, processing, or otherwise dealing with them in a manner preliminary to their sale or exchange.

(g) A perfected security interest in a certificated security or instrument remains perfected for 20 days without filing if the secured party delivers the security certificate or instrument to the debtor for the purpose of:

(1) ultimate sale or exchange; or

(2) presentation, collection, enforcement, renewal, or registration of transfer.

(h) After the 20-day period specified in subsection (e), (f), or (g) expires, perfection depends upon compliance with this article.

§ 9–313. When Possession by or Delivery to Secured Party Perfects Security Interest without Filing.

(a) Except as otherwise provided in subsection (b), a secured party may perfect a security interest in negotiable documents, goods, instruments, money, or tangible chattel paper by taking possession of the collateral. A secured party may perfect a security interest in certificated securities by taking delivery of the certificated securities under Section 8–301.

(b) With respect to goods covered by a certificate of title issued by this State, a secured party may perfect a security interest in the goods by taking possession of the goods only in the circumstances described in Section 9–316(d).

(c) With respect to collateral other than certificated securities and goods covered by a document, a secured party takes possession of collateral in the possession of a person other than the debtor, the secured party, or a lessee of the collateral from the debtor in the ordinary course of the debtor's business, when:

(1) the person in possession authenticates a record acknowledging that it holds possession of the collateral for the secured party's benefit; or

(2) the person takes possession of the collateral after having authenticated a record acknowledging that it will hold possession of collateral for the secured party's benefit.

(d) If perfection of a security interest depends upon possession of the collateral by a secured party, perfection occurs no earlier than the time the secured party takes possession and continues only while the secured party retains possession.

(e) A security interest in a certificated security in registered form is perfected by delivery when delivery of the certificated security occurs under Section 8–301 and remains perfected by delivery until the debtor obtains possession of the security certificate.

(f) A person in possession of collateral is not required to acknowledge that it holds possession for a secured party's benefit.

(g) If a person acknowledges that it holds possession for the secured party's benefit:

(1) the acknowledgment is effective under subsection (c) or Section 8–301(a), even if the acknowledgment violates the rights of a debtor; and

(2) unless the person otherwise agrees or law other than this article otherwise provides, the person does not owe any duty to the secured party and is not required to confirm the acknowledgment to another person.

(h) A secured party having possession of collateral does not relinquish possession by delivering the collateral to a person other than the debtor or a lessee of the collateral from the debtor in the ordinary course of the debtor's business if the person was instructed before the delivery or is instructed contemporaneously with the delivery:

(1) to hold possession of the collateral for the secured party's benefit; or

(2) to redeliver the collateral to the secured party.

(i) A secured party does not relinquish possession, even if a delivery under subsection (h) violates the rights of a debtor. A person to which collateral is delivered under subsection (h) does not owe any duty to the secured party and is not required to confirm the delivery to another person unless the person otherwise agrees or law other than this article otherwise provides.

§ 9–314. Perfection by Control.

(a) A security interest in investment property, deposit accounts, letter-of-credit rights, or electronic chattel paper may be perfected by control of the collateral under Section 9–104, 9–105, 9–106, or 9–107.

(b) A security interest in deposit accounts, electronic chattel paper, or letter-of-credit rights is perfected by control under Section 9–104, 9–105, or 9–107 when the secured party obtains control and remains perfected by control only while the secured party retains control.

(c) A security interest in investment property is perfected by control under Section 9–106 from the time the secured party obtains control and remains perfected by control until:

(1) the secured party does not have control; and

(2) one of the following occurs:

(A) if the collateral is a certificated security, the debtor has or acquires possession of the security certificate;

(B) if the collateral is an uncertificated security, the issuer has registered or registers the debtor as the registered owner; or

(C) if the collateral is a security entitlement, the debtor is or becomes the entitlement holder.

§ 9–315. Secured Party's Rights on Disposition of Collateral and in Proceeds.

(a) Except as otherwise provided in this article and in Section 2–403(2):

(1) a security interest or agricultural lien continues in collateral notwithstanding sale, lease, license, exchange, or other disposition thereof unless the secured party authorized the disposition free of the security interest or agricultural lien; and

(2) a security interest attaches to any identifiable proceeds of collateral.

(b) Proceeds that are commingled with other property are identifiable proceeds:

(1) if the proceeds are goods, to the extent provided by Section 9–336; and

(2) if the proceeds are not goods, to the extent that the secured party identifies the proceeds by a method of tracing, including application of equitable principles, that is permitted under law other than this article with respect to commingled property of the type involved.

(c) A security interest in proceeds is a perfected security interest if the security interest in the original collateral was perfected.

(d) A perfected security interest in proceeds becomes unperfected on the 21st day after the security interest attaches to the proceeds unless:

(1) the following conditions are satisfied:

(A) a filed financing statement covers the original collateral;

(B) the proceeds are collateral in which a security interest may be perfected by filing in the office in which the financing statement has been filed; and

(C) the proceeds are not acquired with cash proceeds;

(2) the proceeds are identifiable cash proceeds; or

(3) the security interest in the proceeds is perfected other than under subsection (c) when the security interest attaches to the proceeds or within 20 days thereafter.

(e) If a filed financing statement covers the original collateral, a security interest in proceeds which remains perfected under subsection (d)(1) becomes unperfected at the later of:

(1) when the effectiveness of the filed financing statement lapses under Section 9–515 or is terminated under Section 9–513; or

(2) the 21st day after the security interest attaches to the proceeds.

§ 9–316. Continued Perfection of Security Interest Following Change in Governing Law.

(a) A security interest perfected pursuant to the law of the jurisdiction designated in Section 9–301(1) or 9–305(c) remains perfected until the earliest of:

(1) the time perfection would have ceased under the law of that jurisdiction;

(2) the expiration of four months after a change of the debtor's location to another jurisdiction; or

(3) the expiration of one year after a transfer of collateral to a person that thereby becomes a debtor and is located in another jurisdiction.

(b) If a security interest described in subsection (a) becomes perfected under the law of the other jurisdiction before the earliest time or event described in that subsection, it remains perfected thereafter. If the security interest does not become perfected under the law of the other jurisdiction before the earliest time or event, it becomes unperfected and is deemed never to have been perfected as against a purchaser of the collateral for value.

(c) A possessory security interest in collateral, other than goods covered by a certificate of title and as-extracted collateral consisting of goods, remains continuously perfected if:

(1) the collateral is located in one jurisdiction and subject to a security interest perfected under the law of that jurisdiction;

(2) thereafter the collateral is brought into another jurisdiction; and

(3) upon entry into the other jurisdiction, the security interest is perfected under the law of the other jurisdiction.

(d) Except as otherwise provided in subsection (e), a security interest in goods covered by a certificate of title which is perfected by any method under the law of another jurisdiction when the goods become covered by a certificate of title from this State remains perfected until the security interest would have become unperfected under the law of the other jurisdiction had the goods not become so covered.

(e) A security interest described in subsection (d) becomes unperfected as against a purchaser of the goods for value and is deemed never to have been perfected as against a purchaser of the goods for value if the applicable requirements for perfection under Section 9–311(b) or 9–313 are not satisfied before the earlier of:

(1) the time the security interest would have become unperfected under the law of the other jurisdiction had the goods not become covered by a certificate of title from this State; or

(2) the expiration of four months after the goods had become so covered.

(f) A security interest in deposit accounts, letter-of-credit rights, or investment property which is perfected under the law of the bank's jurisdiction, the issuer's jurisdiction, a nominated person's jurisdiction, the securities intermediary's jurisdiction, or the commodity intermediary's jurisdiction, as applicable, remains perfected until the earlier of:

(1) the time the security interest would have become unperfected under the law of that jurisdiction; or

(2) the expiration of four months after a change of the applicable jurisdiction to another jurisdiction.

(g) If a security interest described in subsection (f) becomes perfected under the law of the other jurisdiction before the earlier of the time or the end of the period described in that subsection, it remains perfected thereafter. If the security interest does not become perfected under the law of the other jurisdiction before the earlier of that time or the end of that period, it becomes unperfected and is deemed never to have been perfected as against a purchaser of the collateral for value.

[Subpart 3. Priority]

§ 9–317. Interests That Take Priority over or Take Free of Security Interest or Agricultural Lien.

(a) A security interest or agricultural lien is subordinate to the rights of:

(1) a person entitled to priority under Section 9–322; and

(2) except as otherwise provided in subsection (e), a person that becomes a lien creditor before the earlier of the time:

(A) the security interest or agricultural lien is perfected; or

(B) one of the conditions specified in Section 9–203(b)(3) is met and a financing statement covering the collateral is filed.

(b) Except as otherwise provided in subsection (e), a buyer, other than a secured party, of tangible chattel paper, documents, goods, instruments, or a security certificate takes free of a security interest or agricultural lien if the buyer gives value and receives delivery of the collateral without knowledge of the security interest or agricultural lien and before it is perfected.

(c) Except as otherwise provided in subsection (e), a lessee of goods takes free of a security interest or agricultural lien if the lessee gives value and receives delivery of the collateral without knowledge of the security interest or agricultural lien and before it is perfected.

(d) A licensee of a general intangible or a buyer, other than a secured party, of accounts, electronic chattel paper, general intangibles, or investment property other than a certificated security takes free of a security interest if the licensee or buyer gives value without knowledge of the security interest and before it is perfected.

(e) Except as otherwise provided in Sections 9–320 and 9–321, if a person files a financing statement with respect to a purchase-money security interest before or within 20 days after the debtor receives delivery of the collateral, the security interest takes priority over the rights of a buyer, lessee, or lien creditor which arise between the time the security interest attaches and the time of filing.

As amended in 2000.

§ 9–318. No Interest Retained in Right to Payment That Is Sold; Rights and Title of Seller of Account or Chattel Paper with Respect to Creditors and Purchasers.

(a) A debtor that has sold an account, chattel paper, payment intangible, or promissory note does not retain a legal or equitable interest in the collateral sold.

(b) For purposes of determining the rights of creditors of, and purchasers for value of an account or chattel paper from, a debtor that has sold an account or chattel paper, while the buyer's security interest is unperfected, the debtor is deemed to have rights and title to the account or chattel paper identical to those the debtor sold.

§ 9–319. Rights and Title of Consignee with Respect to Creditors and Purchasers.

(a) Except as otherwise provided in subsection (b), for purposes of determining the rights of creditors of, and purchasers for value of goods from, a consignee, while the goods are in the possession of the consignee, the consignee is deemed to have rights and title to the goods identical to those the consignor had or had power to transfer.

(b) For purposes of determining the rights of a creditor of a consignee, law other than this article determines the rights and title of a consignee while goods are in the consignee's possession if, under this part, a perfected security interest held by the consignor would have priority over the rights of the creditor.

§ 9–320. Buyer of Goods.

(a) Except as otherwise provided in subsection (e), a buyer in ordinary course of business, other than a person buying farm products from a person engaged in farming operations, takes free of a security interest created by the buyer's seller, even if the security interest is perfected and the buyer knows of its existence.

(b) Except as otherwise provided in subsection (e), a buyer of goods from a person who used or bought the goods for use primarily for personal, family, or household purposes takes free of a security interest, even if perfected, if the buyer buys:

(1) without knowledge of the security interest;

(2) for value;

(3) primarily for the buyer's personal, family, or household purposes; and

(4) before the filing of a financing statement covering the goods.

(c) To the extent that it affects the priority of a security interest over a buyer of goods under subsection (b), the period of effectiveness of a filing made in the jurisdiction in which the seller is located is governed by Section 9–316(a) and (b).

(d) A buyer in ordinary course of business buying oil, gas, or other minerals at the wellhead or minehead or after extraction takes free of an interest arising out of an encumbrance.

(e) Subsections (a) and (b) do not affect a security interest in goods in the possession of the secured party under Section 9–313.

§ 9–321. Licensee of General Intangible and Lessee of Goods in Ordinary Course of Business.

(a) In this section, "licensee in ordinary course of business" means a person that becomes a licensee of a general intangible in good faith, without knowledge that the license violates the rights of another person in the general intangible, and in the ordinary course from a person in the business of licensing general intangibles of that kind. A person becomes a licensee in the ordinary course if the license to the person comports with the usual or customary practices in the kind of business in which the licensor is engaged or with the licensor's own usual or customary practices.

(b) A licensee in ordinary course of business takes its rights under a nonexclusive license free of a security interest in the general intangible created by the licensor, even if the security interest is perfected and the licensee knows of its existence.

(c) A lessee in ordinary course of business takes its leasehold interest free of a security interest in the goods created by the lessor, even if the security interest is perfected and the lessee knows of its existence.

§ 9–322. Priorities among Conflicting Security Interests in and Agricultural Liens on Same Collateral.

(a) Except as otherwise provided in this section, priority among conflicting security interests and agricultural liens in the same collateral is determined according to the following rules:

(1) Conflicting perfected security interests and agricultural liens rank according to priority in time of filing or perfection. Priority dates from the earlier of the time a filing covering the collateral is first made or the security interest or agricultural lien is first perfected, if there is no period thereafter when there is neither filing nor perfection.

(2) A perfected security interest or agricultural lien has priority over a conflicting unperfected security interest or agricultural lien.

(3) The first security interest or agricultural lien to attach or become effective has priority if conflicting security interests and agricultural liens are unperfected.

(b) For the purposes of subsection (a)(1):

(1) the time of filing or perfection as to a security interest in collateral is also the time of filing or perfection as to a security interest in proceeds; and

(2) the time of filing or perfection as to a security interest in collateral supported by a supporting obligation is also the time of filing or perfection as to a security interest in the supporting obligation.

(c) Except as otherwise provided in subsection (f), a security interest in collateral which qualifies for priority over a conflicting security interest under Section 9–327, 9–328, 9–329, 9–330, or 9–331 also has priority over a conflicting security interest in:

(1) any supporting obligation for the collateral; and

(2) proceeds of the collateral if:

(A) the security interest in proceeds is perfected;

(B) the proceeds are cash proceeds or of the same type as the collateral; and

(C) in the case of proceeds that are proceeds of proceeds, all intervening proceeds are cash proceeds, proceeds of the same type as the collateral, or an account relating to the collateral.

(d) Subject to subsection (e) and except as otherwise provided in subsection (f), if a security interest in chattel paper, deposit accounts, negotiable documents, instruments, investment property, or letter-of-credit rights is perfected by a method other than filing, conflicting perfected security interests in proceeds of the collateral rank according to priority in time of filing.

(e) Subsection (d) applies only if the proceeds of the collateral are not cash proceeds, chattel paper, negotiable documents, instruments, investment property, or letter-of-credit rights.

(f) Subsections (a) through (e) are subject to:

(1) subsection (g) and the other provisions of this part;

(2) Section 4–210 with respect to a security interest of a collecting bank;

(3) Section 5–118 with respect to a security interest of an issuer or nominated person; and

(4) Section 9–110 with respect to a security interest arising under Article 2 or 2A.

(g) A perfected agricultural lien on collateral has priority over a conflicting security interest in or agricultural lien on the same collateral if the statute creating the agricultural lien so provides.

§ 9–323. Future Advances.

(a) Except as otherwise provided in subsection (c), for purposes of determining the priority of a perfected security interest under Section 9–322(a)(1), perfection of the security interest dates from the time an advance is made to the extent that the security interest secures an advance that:

(1) is made while the security interest is perfected only:

(A) under Section 9–309 when it attaches; or

(B) temporarily under Section 9–312(e), (f), or (g); and

(2) is not made pursuant to a commitment entered into before or while the security interest is perfected by a method other than under Section 9–309 or 9–312(e), (f), or (g).

(b) Except as otherwise provided in subsection (c), a security interest is subordinate to the rights of a person that becomes a lien creditor to the extent that the security interest secures an advance made more than 45 days after the person becomes a lien creditor unless the advance is made:

(1) without knowledge of the lien; or

(2) pursuant to a commitment entered into without knowledge of the lien.

(c) Subsections (a) and (b) do not apply to a security interest held by a secured party that is a buyer of accounts, chattel paper, payment intangibles, or promissory notes or a consignor.

(d) Except as otherwise provided in subsection (e), a buyer of goods other than a buyer in ordinary course of business takes free of a security interest to the extent that it secures advances made after the earlier of:

(1) the time the secured party acquires knowledge of the buyer's purchase; or

(2) 45 days after the purchase.

(e) Subsection (d) does not apply if the advance is made pursuant to a commitment entered into without knowledge of the buyer's purchase and before the expiration of the 45-day period.

(f) Except as otherwise provided in subsection (g), a lessee of goods, other than a lessee in ordinary course of business, takes the leasehold interest free of a security interest to the extent that it secures advances made after the earlier of:

(1) the time the secured party acquires knowledge of the lease; or

(2) 45 days after the lease contract becomes enforceable.

(g) Subsection (f) does not apply if the advance is made pursuant to a commitment entered into without knowledge of the lease and before the expiration of the 45-day period.

As amended in 1999.

§ 9–324. Priority of Purchase-Money Security Interests.

(a) Except as otherwise provided in subsection (g), a perfected purchase-money security interest in goods other than inventory or livestock has priority over a conflicting security interest in the same goods, and, except as otherwise provided in Section 9–327, a perfected security interest in its identifiable proceeds also has priority, if the purchase-money security interest is perfected when the debtor receives possession of the collateral or within 20 days thereafter.

(b) Subject to subsection (c) and except as otherwise provided in subsection (g), a perfected purchase-money security interest in inventory has priority over a conflicting security interest in the same inventory, has priority over a conflicting security interest in chattel paper or an instrument constituting proceeds of the inventory and in proceeds of the chattel paper, if so provided in Section 9–330, and, except as otherwise provided in Section 9–327, also has priority in identifiable cash proceeds of the inventory to the extent the identifiable cash proceeds are received on or before the delivery of the inventory to a buyer, if:

(1) the purchase-money security interest is perfected when the debtor receives possession of the inventory;

(2) the purchase-money secured party sends an authenticated notification to the holder of the conflicting security interest;

(3) the holder of the conflicting security interest receives the notification within five years before the debtor receives possession of the inventory; and

(4) the notification states that the person sending the notification has or expects to acquire a purchase-money security interest in inventory of the debtor and describes the inventory.

(c) Subsections (b)(2) through (4) apply only if the holder of the conflicting security interest had filed a financing statement covering the same types of inventory:

(1) if the purchase-money security interest is perfected by filing, before the date of the filing; or

(2) if the purchase-money security interest is temporarily perfected without filing or possession under Section 9–312(f), before the beginning of the 20-day period thereunder.

(d) Subject to subsection (e) and except as otherwise provided in subsection (g), a perfected purchase-money security interest in livestock that are farm products has priority over a conflicting security interest in the same livestock, and, except as otherwise provided in Section 9–327, a perfected security interest in their identifiable proceeds and identifiable products in their unmanufactured states also has priority, if:

(1) the purchase-money security interest is perfected when the debtor receives possession of the livestock;

(2) the purchase-money secured party sends an authenticated notification to the holder of the conflicting security interest;

(3) the holder of the conflicting security interest receives the notification within six months before the debtor receives possession of the livestock; and

(4) the notification states that the person sending the notification has or expects to acquire a purchase-money security interest in livestock of the debtor and describes the livestock.

(e) Subsections (d)(2) through (4) apply only if the holder of the conflicting security interest had filed a financing statement covering the same types of livestock:

(1) if the purchase-money security interest is perfected by filing, before the date of the filing; or

(2) if the purchase-money security interest is temporarily perfected without filing or possession under Section 9–312(f), before the beginning of the 20-day period thereunder.

(f) Except as otherwise provided in subsection (g), a perfected purchase-money security interest in software has priority over a conflicting security interest in the same collateral, and, except as otherwise provided in Section 9–327, a perfected security interest in its identifiable proceeds also has priority, to the extent that the purchase-money security interest in the goods in which the software was acquired for use has priority in the goods and proceeds of the goods under this section.

(g) If more than one security interest qualifies for priority in the same collateral under subsection (a), (b), (d), or (f):

(1) a security interest securing an obligation incurred as all or part of the price of the collateral has priority over a security interest securing an obligation incurred for value given to enable the debtor to acquire rights in or the use of collateral; and

(2) in all other cases, Section 9–322(a) applies to the qualifying security interests.

§ 9–325. Priority of Security Interests in Transferred Collateral.

(a) Except as otherwise provided in subsection (b), a security interest created by a debtor is subordinate to a security interest in the same collateral created by another person if:

(1) the debtor acquired the collateral subject to the security interest created by the other person;

(2) the security interest created by the other person was perfected when the debtor acquired the collateral; and

(3) there is no period thereafter when the security interest is unperfected.

(b) Subsection (a) subordinates a security interest only if the security interest:

(1) otherwise would have priority solely under Section 9–322(a) or 9–324; or

(2) arose solely under Section 2–711(3) or 2A–508(5).

§ 9–326. Priority of Security Interests Created by New Debtor.

(a) Subject to subsection (b), a security interest created by a new debtor which is perfected by a filed financing statement that is effective solely under Section 9–508 in collateral in which a new debtor has or acquires rights is subordinate to a security interest in the same

collateral which is perfected other than by a filed financing statement that is effective solely under Section 9–508.

(b) The other provisions of this part determine the priority among conflicting security interests in the same collateral perfected by filed financing statements that are effective solely under Section 9–508. However, if the security agreements to which a new debtor became bound as debtor were not entered into by the same original debtor, the conflicting security interests rank according to priority in time of the new debtor's having become bound.

§ 9–327. Priority of Security Interests in Deposit Account.

The following rules govern priority among conflicting security interests in the same deposit account:

(1) A security interest held by a secured party having control of the deposit account under Section 9–104 has priority over a conflicting security interest held by a secured party that does not have control.

(2) Except as otherwise provided in paragraphs (3) and (4), security interests perfected by control under Section 9–314 rank according to priority in time of obtaining control.

(3) Except as otherwise provided in paragraph (4), a security interest held by the bank with which the deposit account is maintained has priority over a conflicting security interest held by another secured party.

(4) A security interest perfected by control under Section 9–104(a)(3) has priority over a security interest held by the bank with which the deposit account is maintained.

§ 9–328. Priority of Security Interests in Investment Property.

The following rules govern priority among conflicting security interests in the same investment property:

(1) A security interest held by a secured party having control of investment property under Section 9–106 has priority over a security interest held by a secured party that does not have control of the investment property.

(2) Except as otherwise provided in paragraphs (3) and (4), conflicting security interests held by secured parties each of which has control under Section 9–106 rank according to priority in time of:

(A) if the collateral is a security, obtaining control;

(B) if the collateral is a security entitlement carried in a securities account and:

(i) if the secured party obtained control under Section 8–106(d)(1), the secured party's becoming the person for which the securities account is maintained;

(ii) if the secured party obtained control under Section 8–106(d)(2), the securities intermediary's agreement to comply with the secured party's entitlement orders with respect to security entitlements carried or to be carried in the securities account; or

(iii) if the secured party obtained control through another person under Section 8–106(d)(3), the time on which priority would be based under this paragraph if the other person were the secured party; or

(C) if the collateral is a commodity contract carried with a commodity intermediary, the satisfaction of the requirement for control specified in Section 9–106(b)(2) with respect to commodity contracts carried or to be carried with the commodity intermediary.

(3) A security interest held by a securities intermediary in a security entitlement or a securities account maintained with the securities intermediary has priority over a conflicting security interest held by another secured party.

(4) A security interest held by a commodity intermediary in a commodity contract or a commodity account maintained with the commodity intermediary has priority over a conflicting security interest held by another secured party.

(5) A security interest in a certificated security in registered form which is perfected by taking delivery under Section 9–313(a) and not by control under Section 9–314 has priority over a conflicting security interest perfected by a method other than control.

(6) Conflicting security interests created by a broker, securities intermediary, or commodity intermediary which are perfected without control under Section 9–106 rank equally.

(7) In all other cases, priority among conflicting security interests in investment property is governed by Sections 9–322 and 9–323.

§ 9–329. Priority of Security Interests in Letter-of-Credit Right.

The following rules govern priority among conflicting security interests in the same letter-of-credit right:

(1) A security interest held by a secured party having control of the letter-of-credit right under Section 9–107 has priority to the extent of its control over a conflicting security interest held by a secured party that does not have control.

(2) Security interests perfected by control under Section 9–314 rank according to priority in time of obtaining control.

§ 9–330. Priority of Purchaser of Chattel Paper or Instrument.

(a) A purchaser of chattel paper has priority over a security interest in the chattel paper which is claimed merely as proceeds of inventory subject to a security interest if:

    (1) in good faith and in the ordinary course of the purchaser's business, the purchaser gives new value and takes possession of the chattel paper or obtains control of the chattel paper under Section 9–105; and

    (2) the chattel paper does not indicate that it has been assigned to an identified assignee other than the purchaser.

(b) A purchaser of chattel paper has priority over a security interest in the chattel paper which is claimed other than merely as proceeds of inventory subject to a security interest if the purchaser gives new value and takes possession of the chattel paper or obtains control of the chattel paper under Section 9–105 in good faith, in the ordinary course of the purchaser's business, and without knowledge that the purchase violates the rights of the secured party.

(c) Except as otherwise provided in Section 9–327, a purchaser having priority in chattel paper under subsection (a) or (b) also has priority in proceeds of the chattel paper to the extent that:

    (1) Section 9–322 provides for priority in the proceeds; or

    (2) the proceeds consist of the specific goods covered by the chattel paper or cash proceeds of the specific goods, even if the purchaser's security interest in the proceeds is unperfected.

(d) Except as otherwise provided in Section 9–331(a), a purchaser of an instrument has priority over a security interest in the instrument perfected by a method other than possession if the purchaser gives value and takes possession of the instrument in good faith and without knowledge that the purchase violates the rights of the secured party.

(e) For purposes of subsections (a) and (b), the holder of a purchase-money security interest in inventory gives new value for chattel paper constituting proceeds of the inventory.

(f) For purposes of subsections (b) and (d), if chattel paper or an instrument indicates that it has been assigned to an identified secured party other than the purchaser, a purchaser of the chattel paper or instrument has knowledge that the purchase violates the rights of the secured party.

§ 9–331. Priority of Rights of Purchasers of Instruments, Documents, and Securities under Other Articles; Priority of Interests in Financial Assets and Security Entitlements under Article 8.

(a) This article does not limit the rights of a holder in due course of a negotiable instrument, a holder to which a negotiable document of title has been duly negotiated, or a protected purchaser of a security. These holders or purchasers take priority over an earlier security interest, even if perfected, to the extent provided in Articles 3, 7, and 8.

(b) This article does not limit the rights of or impose liability on a person to the extent that the person is protected against the assertion of a claim under Article 8.

(c) Filing under this article does not constitute notice of a claim or defense to the holders, or purchasers, or persons described in subsections (a) and (b).

§ 9–332. Transfer of Money; Transfer of Funds from Deposit Account.

(a) A transferee of money takes the money free of a security interest unless the transferee acts in collusion with the debtor in violating the rights of the secured party.

(b) A transferee of funds from a deposit account takes the funds free of a security interest in the deposit account unless the transferee acts in collusion with the debtor in violating the rights of the secured party.

§ 9–333. Priority of Certain Liens Arising by Operation of Law.

(a) In this section, "possessory lien" means an interest, other than a security interest or an agricultural lien:

    (1) which secures payment or performance of an obligation for services or materials furnished with respect to goods by a person in the ordinary course of the person's business;

    (2) which is created by statute or rule of law in favor of the person; and

    (3) whose effectiveness depends on the person's possession of the goods.

(b) A possessory lien on goods has priority over a security interest in the goods unless the lien is created by a statute that expressly provides otherwise.

§ 9–334. Priority of Security Interests in Fixtures and Crops.

(a) A security interest under this article may be created in goods that are fixtures or may continue in goods that become fixtures. A security interest does not exist under this article in ordinary building materials incorporated into an improvement on land.

(b) This article does not prevent creation of an encumbrance upon fixtures under real property law.

(c) In cases not governed by subsections (d) through (h), a security interest in fixtures is subordinate to a conflicting interest of an encumbrancer or owner of the related real property other than the debtor.

(d) Except as otherwise provided in subsection (h), a perfected security interest in fixtures has priority over a conflicting interest of an encumbrancer or owner of the real property if the debtor has an interest of record in or is in possession of the real property and:

(1) the security interest is a purchase-money security interest;

(2) the interest of the encumbrancer or owner arises before the goods become fixtures; and

(3) the security interest is perfected by a fixture filing before the goods become fixtures or within 20 days thereafter.

(e) A perfected security interest in fixtures has priority over a conflicting interest of an encumbrancer or owner of the real property if:

(1) the debtor has an interest of record in the real property or is in possession of the real property and the security interest:

(A) is perfected by a fixture filing before the interest of the encumbrancer or owner is of record; and

(B) has priority over any conflicting interest of a predecessor in title of the encumbrancer or owner;

(2) before the goods become fixtures, the security interest is perfected by any method permitted by this article and the fixtures are readily removable:

(A) factory or office machines;

(B) equipment that is not primarily used or leased for use in the operation of the real property; or

(C) replacements of domestic appliances that are consumer goods;

(3) the conflicting interest is a lien on the real property obtained by legal or equitable proceedings after the security interest was perfected by any method permitted by this article; or

(4) the security interest is:

(A) created in a manufactured home in a manufactured-home transaction; and

(B) perfected pursuant to a statute described in Section 9–311(a)(2).

(f) A security interest in fixtures, whether or not perfected, has priority over a conflicting interest of an encumbrancer or owner of the real property if:

(1) the encumbrancer or owner has, in an authenticated record, consented to the security interest or disclaimed an interest in the goods as fixtures; or

(2) the debtor has a right to remove the goods as against the encumbrancer or owner.

(g) The priority of the security interest under paragraph (f)(2) continues for a reasonable time if the debtor's right to remove the goods as against the encumbrancer or owner terminates.

(h) A mortgage is a construction mortgage to the extent that it secures an obligation incurred for the construction of an improvement on land, including the acquisition cost of the land, if a recorded record of the mortgage so indicates. Except as otherwise provided in subsec-

tions (e) and (f), a security interest in fixtures is subordinate to a construction mortgage if a record of the mortgage is recorded before the goods become fixtures and the goods become fixtures before the completion of the construction. A mortgage has this priority to the same extent as a construction mortgage to the extent that it is given to refinance a construction mortgage.

(i) A perfected security interest in crops growing on real property has priority over a conflicting interest of an encumbrancer or owner of the real property if the debtor has an interest of record in or is in possession of the real property.

(j) Subsection (i) prevails over any inconsistent provisions of the following statutes:

[List here any statutes containing provisions inconsistent with subsection (i).]

Legislative Note: States that amend statutes to remove provisions inconsistent with subsection (i) need not enact subsection (j).

§ 9–335. Accessions.

(a) A security interest may be created in an accession and continues in collateral that becomes an accession.

(b) If a security interest is perfected when the collateral becomes an accession, the security interest remains perfected in the collateral.

(c) Except as otherwise provided in subsection (d), the other provisions of this part determine the priority of a security interest in an accession.

(d) A security interest in an accession is subordinate to a security interest in the whole which is perfected by compliance with the requirements of a certificate-of-title statute under Section 9–311(b).

(e) After default, subject to Part 6, a secured party may remove an accession from other goods if the security interest in the accession has priority over the claims of every person having an interest in the whole.

(f) A secured party that removes an accession from other goods under subsection (e) shall promptly reimburse any holder of a security interest or other lien on, or owner of, the whole or of the other goods, other than the debtor, for the cost of repair of any physical injury to the whole or the other goods. The secured party need not reimburse the holder or owner for any diminution in value of the whole or the other goods caused by the absence of the accession removed or by any necessity for replacing it. A person entitled to reimbursement may refuse permission to remove until the secured party gives adequate assurance for the performance of the obligation to reimburse.

§ 9–336. Commingled Goods.

(a) In this section, "commingled goods" means goods that are physically united with other goods in such a manner that their identity is lost in a product or mass.

(b) A security interest does not exist in commingled goods as such. However, a security interest may attach to a product or mass that results when goods become commingled goods.

(c) If collateral becomes commingled goods, a security interest attaches to the product or mass.

(d) If a security interest in collateral is perfected before the collateral becomes commingled goods, the security interest that attaches to the product or mass under subsection (c) is perfected.

(e) Except as otherwise provided in subsection (f), the other provisions of this part determine the priority of a security interest that attaches to the product or mass under subsection (c).

(f) If more than one security interest attaches to the product or mass under subsection (c), the following rules determine priority:

(1) A security interest that is perfected under subsection (d) has priority over a security interest that is unperfected at the time the collateral becomes commingled goods.

(2) If more than one security interest is perfected under subsection (d), the security interests rank equally in proportion to the value of the collateral at the time it became commingled goods.

§ 9–337. Priority of Security Interests in Goods Covered by Certificate of Title.

If, while a security interest in goods is perfected by any method under the law of another jurisdiction, this State issues a certificate of title that does not show that the goods are subject to the security interest or contain a statement that they may be subject to security interests not shown on the certificate:

(1) a buyer of the goods, other than a person in the business of selling goods of that kind, takes free of the security interest if the buyer gives value and receives delivery of the goods after issuance of the certificate and without knowledge of the security interest; and

(2) the security interest is subordinate to a conflicting security interest in the goods that attaches, and is perfected under Section 9–311(b), after issuance of the certificate and without the conflicting secured party's knowledge of the security interest.

§ 9–338. Priority of Security Interest or Agricultural Lien Perfected by Filed Financing Statement Providing Certain Incorrect Information.

If a security interest or agricultural lien is perfected by a filed financing statement providing information described in Section 9–516(b)(5) which is incorrect at the time the financing statement is filed:

(1) the security interest or agricultural lien is subordinate to a conflicting perfected security interest in the collateral to the extent that the holder of the conflicting security interest gives value in reasonable reliance upon the incorrect information; and

(2) a purchaser, other than a secured party, of the collateral takes free of the security interest or agricultural lien to the extent that, in reasonable reliance upon the incorrect information, the purchaser gives value and, in the case of chattel paper, documents, goods, instruments, or a security certificate, receives delivery of the collateral.

§ 9–339. Priority Subject to Subordination.

This article does not preclude subordination by agreement by a person entitled to priority.

[Subpart 4. Rights of Bank]

§ 9–340. Effectiveness of Right of Recoupment or Set-Off against Deposit Account.

(a) Except as otherwise provided in subsection (c), a bank with which a deposit account is maintained may exercise any right of recoupment or set-off against a secured party that holds a security interest in the deposit account.

(b) Except as otherwise provided in subsection (c), the application of this article to a security interest in a deposit account does not affect a right of recoupment or set-off of the secured party as to a deposit account maintained with the secured party.

(c) The exercise by a bank of a set-off against a deposit account is ineffective against a secured party that holds a security interest in the deposit account which is perfected by control under Section 9–104(a)(3), if the set-off is based on a claim against the debtor.

§ 9–341. Bank's Rights and Duties with Respect to Deposit Account.

Except as otherwise provided in Section 9–340(c), and unless the bank otherwise agrees in an authenticated record, a bank's rights and duties with respect to a deposit account maintained with the bank are not terminated, suspended, or modified by:

(1) the creation, attachment, or perfection of a security interest in the deposit account;

(2) the bank's knowledge of the security interest; or

(3) the bank's receipt of instructions from the secured party.

§ 9–342. Bank's Right to Refuse to Enter into or Disclose Existence of Control Agreement.

This article does not require a bank to enter into an agreement of the kind described in Section 9–104(a)(2), even if its customer so requests or directs. A bank that has entered into such an agreement is not required to confirm the existence of the agreement to another person unless requested to do so by its customer.

Part 4   Rights of Third Parties

§ 9–401. Alienability of Debtor's Rights.

(a) Except as otherwise provided in subsection (b) and Sections 9–406, 9–407, 9–408, and 9–409, whether a debtor's rights in collateral may be voluntarily or involuntarily transferred is governed by law other than this article.

(b) An agreement between the debtor and secured party which prohibits a transfer of the debtor's rights in collateral or makes the transfer a default does not prevent the transfer from taking effect.

§ 9–402. Secured Party Not Obligated on Contract of Debtor or in Tort.

The existence of a security interest, agricultural lien, or authority given to a debtor to dispose of or use collateral, without more, does not subject a secured party to liability in contract or tort for the debtor's acts or omissions.

§ 9–403. Agreement Not to Assert Defenses against Assignee.

(a) In this section, "value" has the meaning provided in Section 3–303(a).

(b) Except as otherwise provided in this section, an agreement between an account debtor and an assignor not to assert against an assignee any claim or defense that the account debtor may have against the assignor is enforceable by an assignee that takes an assignment:

(1) for value;

(2) in good faith;

(3) without notice of a claim of a property or possessory right to the property assigned; and

(4) without notice of a defense or claim in recoupment of the type that may be asserted against a person entitled to enforce a negotiable instrument under Section 3–305(a).

(c) Subsection (b) does not apply to defenses of a type that may be asserted against a holder in due course of a negotiable instrument under Section 3–305(b).

(d) In a consumer transaction, if a record evidences the account debtor's obligation, law other than this article requires that the record include a statement to the effect that the rights of an assignee are subject to claims or defenses that the account debtor could assert against the original obligee, and the record does not include such a statement:

(1) the record has the same effect as if the record included such a statement; and

(2) the account debtor may assert against an assignee those claims and defenses that would have been available if the record included such a statement.

(e) This section is subject to law other than this article which establishes a different rule for an account debtor who is an individual and who incurred the obligation primarily for personal, family, or household purposes.

(f) Except as otherwise provided in subsection (d), this section does not displace law other than this article which gives effect to an agreement by an account debtor not to assert a claim or defense against an assignee.

§ 9–404. Rights Acquired by Assignee; Claims and Defenses against Assignee.

(a) Unless an account debtor has made an enforceable agreement not to assert defenses or claims, and subject to subsections (b) through (e), the rights of an assignee are subject to:

(1) all terms of the agreement between the account debtor and assignor and any defense or claim in recoupment arising from the transaction that gave rise to the contract; and

(2) any other defense or claim of the account debtor against the assignor which accrues before the account debtor receives a notification of the assignment authenticated by the assignor or the assignee.

(b) Subject to subsection (c) and except as otherwise provided in subsection (d), the claim of an account debtor against an assignor may be asserted against an assignee under subsection (a) only to reduce the amount the account debtor owes.

(c) This section is subject to law other than this article which establishes a different rule for an account debtor who is an individual and who incurred the obligation primarily for personal, family, or household purposes.

(d) In a consumer transaction, if a record evidences the account debtor's obligation, law other than this article requires that the record include a statement to the effect that the account debtor's recovery against an assignee with respect to claims and defenses against the assignor may not exceed amounts paid by the account debtor under the record, and the record does not include such a statement, the extent to which a claim of an account debtor against the assignor may

be asserted against an assignee is determined as if the record included such a statement.

(e) This section does not apply to an assignment of a health-care-insurance receivable.

§ 9–405. Modification of Assigned Contract.

(a) A modification of or substitution for an assigned contract is effective against an assignee if made in good faith. The assignee acquires corresponding rights under the modified or substituted contract. The assignment may provide that the modification or substitution is a breach of contract by the assignor. This subsection is subject to subsections (b) through (d).

(b) Subsection (a) applies to the extent that:

(1) the right to payment or a part thereof under an assigned contract has not been fully earned by performance; or

(2) the right to payment or a part thereof has been fully earned by performance and the account debtor has not received notification of the assignment under Section 9–406(a).

(c) This section is subject to law other than this article which establishes a different rule for an account debtor who is an individual and who incurred the obligation primarily for personal, family, or household purposes.

(d) This section does not apply to an assignment of a health-care-insurance receivable.

§ 9–406. Discharge of Account Debtor; Notification of Assignment; Identification and Proof of Assignment; Restrictions on Assignment of Accounts, Chattel Paper, Payment Intangibles, and Promissory Notes Ineffective.

(a) Subject to subsections (b) through (i), an account debtor on an account, chattel paper, or a payment intangible may discharge its obligation by paying the assignor until, but not after, the account debtor receives a notification, authenticated by the assignor or the assignee, that the amount due or to become due has been assigned and that payment is to be made to the assignee. After receipt of the notification, the account debtor may discharge its obligation by paying the assignee and may not discharge the obligation by paying the assignor.

(b) Subject to subsection (h), notification is ineffective under subsection (a):

(1) if it does not reasonably identify the rights assigned;

(2) to the extent that an agreement between an account debtor and a seller of a payment intangible limits the account debtor's duty to pay a person other than the seller and the limitation is effective under law other than this article; or

(3) at the option of an account debtor, if the notification notifies the account debtor to make less than the full amount of any installment or other periodic payment to the assignee, even if:

(A) only a portion of the account, chattel paper, or payment intangible has been assigned to that assignee;

(B) a portion has been assigned to another assignee; or

(C) the account debtor knows that the assignment to that assignee is limited.

(c) Subject to subsection (h), if requested by the account debtor, an assignee shall seasonably furnish reasonable proof that the assignment has been made. Unless the assignee complies, the account debtor may discharge its obligation by paying the assignor, even if the account debtor has received a notification under subsection (a).

(d) Except as otherwise provided in subsection (e) and Sections 2A–303 and 9–407, and subject to subsection (h), a term in an agreement between an account debtor and an assignor or in a promissory note is ineffective to the extent that it:

(1) prohibits, restricts, or requires the consent of the account debtor or person obligated on the promissory note to the assignment or transfer of, or the creation, attachment, perfection, or enforcement of a security interest in, the account, chattel paper, payment intangible, or promissory note; or

(2) provides that the assignment or transfer or the creation, attachment, perfection, or enforcement of the security interest may give rise to a default, breach, right of recoupment, claim, defense, termination, right of termination, or remedy under the account, chattel paper, payment intangible, or promissory note.

(e) Subsection (d) does not apply to the sale of a payment intangible or promissory note.

(f) Except as otherwise provided in Sections 2A–303 and 9–407 and subject to subsections (h) and (i), a rule of law, statute, or regulation that prohibits, restricts, or requires the consent of a government, governmental body or official, or account debtor to the assignment or transfer of, or creation of a security interest in, an account or chattel paper is ineffective to the extent that the rule of law, statute, or regulation:

(1) prohibits, restricts, or requires the consent of the government, governmental body or official, or account debtor to the assignment or transfer of, or the creation, attachment, perfection, or enforcement of a security interest in the account or chattel paper; or

(2) provides that the assignment or transfer or the creation, attachment, perfection, or enforcement of the security interest may give rise to a default, breach, right of recoupment, claim, defense, termination, right of termination, or remedy under the account or chattel paper.

(g) Subject to subsection (h), an account debtor may not waive or vary its option under subsection (b)(3).

(h) This section is subject to law other than this article which establishes a different rule for an account debtor who is an individual and who incurred the obligation primarily for personal, family, or household purposes.

(i) This section does not apply to an assignment of a health-care-insurance receivable.

(j) This section prevails over any inconsistent provisions of the following statutes, rules, and regulations:

[List here any statutes, rules, and regulations containing provisions inconsistent with this section.]

Legislative Note: States that amend statutes, rules, and regulations to remove provisions inconsistent with this section need not enact subsection (j).

As amended in 1999 and 2000.

§ 9–407. Restrictions on Creation or Enforcement of Security Interest in Leasehold Interest or in Lessor's Residual Interest.

(a) Except as otherwise provided in subsection (b), a term in a lease agreement is ineffective to the extent that it:

(1) prohibits, restricts, or requires the consent of a party to the lease to the assignment or transfer of, or the creation, attachment, perfection, or enforcement of a security interest in an interest of a party under the lease contract or in the lessor's residual interest in the goods; or

(2) provides that the assignment or transfer or the creation, attachment, perfection, or enforcement of the security interest may give rise to a default, breach, right of recoupment, claim, defense, termination, right of termination, or remedy under the lease.

(b) Except as otherwise provided in Section 2A–303(7), a term described in subsection (a)(2) is effective to the extent that there is:

(1) a transfer by the lessee of the lessee's right of possession or use of the goods in violation of the term; or

(2) a delegation of a material performance of either party to the lease contract in violation of the term.

(c) The creation, attachment, perfection, or enforcement of a security interest in the lessor's interest under the lease contract or the lessor's residual interest in the goods is not a transfer that materially impairs the lessee's prospect of obtaining return performance or materially changes the duty of or materially increases the burden or risk imposed on the lessee within the purview of Section 2A–303(4) unless, and then only to the extent that, enforcement actually results in a delegation of material performance of the lessor.

As amended in 1999.

§ 9–408. Restrictions on Assignment of Promissory Notes, Health-Care-Insurance Receivables, and Certain General Intangibles Ineffective.

(a) Except as otherwise provided in subsection (b), a term in a promissory note or in an agreement between an account debtor and a debtor which relates to a health-care-insurance receivable or a general intangible, including a contract, permit, license, or franchise, and which term prohibits, restricts, or requires the consent of the person obligated on the promissory note or the account debtor to, the assignment or transfer of, or creation, attachment, or perfection of a security interest in, the promissory note, health-care-insurance receivable, or general intangible, is ineffective to the extent that the term:

(1) would impair the creation, attachment, or perfection of a security interest; or

(2) provides that the assignment or transfer or the creation, attachment, or perfection of the security interest may give rise to a default, breach, right of recoupment, claim, defense, termination, right of termination, or remedy under the promissory note, health-care-insurance receivable, or general intangible.

(b) Subsection (a) applies to a security interest in a payment intangible or promissory note only if the security interest arises out of a sale of the payment intangible or promissory note.

(c) A rule of law, statute, or regulation that prohibits, restricts, or requires the consent of a government, governmental body or official, person obligated on a promissory note, or account debtor to the assignment or transfer of, or creation of a security interest in, a promissory note, health-care-insurance receivable, or general intangible, including a contract, permit, license, or franchise between an account debtor and a debtor, is ineffective to the extent that the rule of law, statute, or regulation:

(1) would impair the creation, attachment, or perfection of a security interest; or

(2) provides that the assignment or transfer or the creation, attachment, or perfection of the security interest may give rise to

a default, breach, right of recoupment, claim, defense, termination, right of termination, or remedy under the promissory note, health-care-insurance receivable, or general intangible.

(d) To the extent that a term in a promissory note or in an agreement between an account debtor and a debtor which relates to a health-care-insurance receivable or general intangible or a rule of law, statute, or regulation described in subsection (c) would be effective under law other than this article but is ineffective under subsection (a) or (c), the creation, attachment, or perfection of a security interest in the promissory note, health-care-insurance receivable, or general intangible:

(1) is not enforceable against the person obligated on the promissory note or the account debtor;

(2) does not impose a duty or obligation on the person obligated on the promissory note or the account debtor;

(3) does not require the person obligated on the promissory note or the account debtor to recognize the security interest, pay or render performance to the secured party, or accept payment or performance from the secured party;

(4) does not entitle the secured party to use or assign the debtor's rights under the promissory note, health-care-insurance receivable, or general intangible, including any related information or materials furnished to the debtor in the transaction giving rise to the promissory note, health-care-insurance receivable, or general intangible;

(5) does not entitle the secured party to use, assign, possess, or have access to any trade secrets or confidential information of the person obligated on the promissory note or the account debtor; and

(6) does not entitle the secured party to enforce the security interest in the promissory note, health-care-insurance receivable, or general intangible.

(e) This section prevails over any inconsistent provisions of the following statutes, rules, and regulations:

[List here any statutes, rules, and regulations containing provisions inconsistent with this section.]

Legislative Note: States that amend statutes, rules, and regulations to remove provisions inconsistent with this section need not enact subsection (e).

As amended in 1999.

§ 9–409. Restrictions on Assignment of Letter-of-Credit Rights Ineffective.

(a) A term in a letter of credit or a rule of law, statute, regulation, custom, or practice applicable to the letter of credit which prohibits, restricts, or requires the consent of an applicant, issuer, or nominated person to a beneficiary's assignment of or creation of a security interest in a letter-of-credit right is ineffective to the extent that the term or rule of law, statute, regulation, custom, or practice:

(1) would impair the creation, attachment, or perfection of a security interest in the letter-of-credit right; or

(2) provides that the assignment or the creation, attachment, or perfection of the security interest may give rise to a default, breach, right of recoupment, claim, defense, termination, right of termination, or remedy under the letter-of-credit right.

(b) To the extent that a term in a letter of credit is ineffective under subsection (a) but would be effective under law other than this article or a custom or practice applicable to the letter of credit, to the transfer of a right to draw or otherwise demand performance under the letter of credit, or to the assignment of a right to proceeds of the letter of credit, the creation, attachment, or perfection of a security interest in the letter-of-credit right:

(1) is not enforceable against the applicant, issuer, nominated person, or transferee beneficiary;

(2) imposes no duties or obligations on the applicant, issuer, nominated person, or transferee beneficiary; and

(3) does not require the applicant, issuer, nominated person, or transferee beneficiary to recognize the security interest, pay or render performance to the secured party, or accept payment or other performance from the secured party.

As amended in 1999.

Part 5 Filing

[Subpart 1. Filing Office; Contents and Effectiveness of Financing Statement]

§ 9–501. Filing Office.

(a) Except as otherwise provided in subsection (b), if the local law of this State governs perfection of a security interest or agricultural lien, the office in which to file a financing statement to perfect the security interest or agricultural lien is:

(1) the office designated for the filing or recording of a record of a mortgage on the related real property, if:

(A) the collateral is as-extracted collateral or timber to be cut; or

(B) the financing statement is filed as a fixture filing and the collateral is goods that are or are to become fixtures; or

(2) the office of [ ] [or any office duly authorized by [ ]], in all other cases, including a case in which the collateral is goods that are or are to become fixtures and the financing statement is not filed as a fixture filing.

(b) The office in which to file a financing statement to perfect a security interest in collateral, including fixtures, of a transmitting utility is the office of [ ]. The financing statement also constitutes a fixture filing as to the collateral indicated in the financing statement which is or is to become fixtures.

Legislative Note: The State should designate the filing office where the brackets appear. The filing office may be that of a governmental official (e.g., the Secretary of State) or a private party that maintains the State's filing system.

§ 9–502. Contents of Financing Statement; Record of Mortgage as Financing Statement; Time of Filing Financing Statement.

(a) Subject to subsection (b), a financing statement is sufficient only if it:

(1) provides the name of the debtor;

(2) provides the name of the secured party or a representative of the secured party; and

(3) indicates the collateral covered by the financing statement.

(b) Except as otherwise provided in Section 9–501(b), to be sufficient, a financing statement that covers as-extracted collateral or timber to be cut, or which is filed as a fixture filing and covers goods that are or are to become fixtures, must satisfy subsection (a) and also:

(1) indicate that it covers this type of collateral;

(2) indicate that it is to be filed [for record] in the real property records;

(3) provide a description of the real property to which the collateral is related [sufficient to give constructive notice of a mortgage under the law of this State if the description were contained in a record of the mortgage of the real property]; and

(4) if the debtor does not have an interest of record in the real property, provide the name of a record owner.

(c) A record of a mortgage is effective, from the date of recording, as a financing statement filed as a fixture filing or as a financing statement covering as-extracted collateral or timber to be cut only if:

(1) the record indicates the goods or accounts that it covers;

(2) the goods are or are to become fixtures related to the real property described in the record or the collateral is related to the real property described in the record and is as-extracted collateral or timber to be cut;

(3) the record satisfies the requirements for a financing statement in this section other than an indication that it is to be filed in the real property records; and

(4) the record is [duly] recorded.

(d) A financing statement may be filed before a security agreement is made or a security interest otherwise attaches.

Legislative Note: Language in brackets is optional. Where the State has any special recording system for real property other than the usual grantor-grantee index (as, for instance, a tract system or a title registration or Torrens system) local adaptations of subsection (b) and Section 9–519(d) and (e) may be necessary. See, e.g., Mass. Gen. Laws Chapter 106, Section 9–410.

§ 9–503. Name of Debtor and Secured Party.

(a) A financing statement sufficiently provides the name of the debtor:

(1) if the debtor is a registered organization, only if the financing statement provides the name of the debtor indicated on the public record of the debtor's jurisdiction of organization which shows the debtor to have been organized;

(2) if the debtor is a decedent's estate, only if the financing statement provides the name of the decedent and indicates that the debtor is an estate;

(3) if the debtor is a trust or a trustee acting with respect to property held in trust, only if the financing statement:

(A) provides the name specified for the trust in its organic documents or, if no name is specified, provides the name of the settlor and additional information sufficient to distinguish the debtor from other trusts having one or more of the same settlors; and

(B) indicates, in the debtor's name or otherwise, that the debtor is a trust or is a trustee acting with respect to property held in trust; and

(4) in other cases:

(A) if the debtor has a name, only if it provides the individual or organizational name of the debtor; and

(B) if the debtor does not have a name, only if it provides the names of the partners, members, associates, or other persons comprising the debtor.

(b) A financing statement that provides the name of the debtor in accordance with subsection (a) is not rendered ineffective by the absence of:

(1) a trade name or other name of the debtor; or

(2) unless required under subsection (a)(4)(B), names of partners, members, associates, or other persons comprising the debtor.

(c) A financing statement that provides only the debtor's trade name does not sufficiently provide the name of the debtor.

(d) Failure to indicate the representative capacity of a secured party or representative of a secured party does not affect the sufficiency of a financing statement.

(e) A financing statement may provide the name of more than one debtor and the name of more than one secured party.

§ 9–504. Indication of Collateral.

A financing statement sufficiently indicates the collateral that it covers if the financing statement provides:

(1) a description of the collateral pursuant to Section 9–108; or

(2) an indication that the financing statement covers all assets or all personal property.

As amended in 1999.

§ 9–505. Filing and Compliance with Other Statutes and Treaties for Consignments, Leases, Other Bailments, and Other Transactions.

(a) A consignor, lessor, or other bailor of goods, a licensor, or a buyer of a payment intangible or promissory note may file a financing statement, or may comply with a statute or treaty described in Section 9–311(a), using the terms "consignor", "consignee", "lessor", "lessee", "bailor", "bailee", "licensor", "licensee", "owner", "registered owner", "buyer", "seller", or words of similar import, instead of the terms "secured party" and "debtor".

(b) This part applies to the filing of a financing statement under subsection (a) and, as appropriate, to compliance that is equivalent to filing a financing statement under Section 9–311(b), but the filing or compliance is not of itself a factor in determining whether the collateral secures an obligation. If it is determined for another reason that the collateral secures an obligation, a security interest held by the consignor, lessor, bailor, licensor, owner, or buyer which attaches to the collateral is perfected by the filing or compliance.

§ 9–506. Effect of Errors or Omissions.

(a) A financing statement substantially satisfying the requirements of this part is effective, even if it has minor errors or omissions, unless the errors or omissions make the financing statement seriously misleading.

(b) Except as otherwise provided in subsection (c), a financing statement that fails sufficiently to provide the name of the debtor in accordance with Section 9–503(a) is seriously misleading.

(c) If a search of the records of the filing office under the debtor's correct name, using the filing office's standard search logic, if any, would disclose a financing statement that fails sufficiently to provide the name of the debtor in accordance with Section 9–503(a), the name provided does not make the financing statement seriously misleading.

(d) For purposes of Section 9–508(b), the "debtor's correct name" in subsection (c) means the correct name of the new debtor.

§ 9–507. Effect of Certain Events on Effectiveness of Financing Statement.

(a) A filed financing statement remains effective with respect to collateral that is sold, exchanged, leased, licensed, or otherwise disposed of and in which a security interest or agricultural lien continues, even if the secured party knows of or consents to the disposition.

(b) Except as otherwise provided in subsection (c) and Section 9–508, a financing statement is not rendered ineffective if, after the financing statement is filed, the information provided in the financing statement becomes seriously misleading under Section 9–506.

(c) If a debtor so changes its name that a filed financing statement becomes seriously misleading under Section 9–506:

(1) the financing statement is effective to perfect a security interest in collateral acquired by the debtor before, or within four months after, the change; and

(2) the financing statement is not effective to perfect a security interest in collateral acquired by the debtor more than four months after the change, unless an amendment to the financing statement which renders the financing statement not seriously misleading is filed within four months after the change.

§ 9–508. Effectiveness of Financing Statement If New Debtor Becomes Bound by Security Agreement.

(a) Except as otherwise provided in this section, a filed financing statement naming an original debtor is effective to perfect a security interest in collateral in which a new debtor has or acquires rights to the extent that the financing statement would have been effective had the original debtor acquired rights in the collateral.

(b) If the difference between the name of the original debtor and that of the new debtor causes a filed financing statement that is effective under subsection (a) to be seriously misleading under Section 9–506:

(1) the financing statement is effective to perfect a security interest in collateral acquired by the new debtor before, and within four months after, the new debtor becomes bound under Section 9B–203(d); and

(2) the financing statement is not effective to perfect a security interest in collateral acquired by the new debtor more than four months after the new debtor becomes bound under Section 9–203(d) unless an initial financing statement providing the name of the new debtor is filed before the expiration of that time.

(c) This section does not apply to collateral as to which a filed financing statement remains effective against the new debtor under Section 9–507(a).

§ 9–509. Persons Entitled to File a Record.

(a) A person may file an initial financing statement, amendment that adds collateral covered by a financing statement, or amendment that adds a debtor to a financing statement only if:

(1) the debtor authorizes the filing in an authenticated record or pursuant to subsection (b) or (c); or

(2) the person holds an agricultural lien that has become effective at the time of filing and the financing statement covers only collateral in which the person holds an agricultural lien.

(b) By authenticating or becoming bound as debtor by a security agreement, a debtor or new debtor authorizes the filing of an initial financing statement, and an amendment, covering:

(1) the collateral described in the security agreement; and

(2) property that becomes collateral under Section 9–315(a)(2), whether or not the security agreement expressly covers proceeds.

(c) By acquiring collateral in which a security interest or agricultural lien continues under Section 9–315(a)(1), a debtor authorizes the filing of an initial financing statement, and an amendment, covering the collateral and property that becomes collateral under Section 9–315(a)(2).

(d) A person may file an amendment other than an amendment that adds collateral covered by a financing statement or an amendment that adds a debtor to a financing statement only if:

(1) the secured party of record authorizes the filing; or

(2) the amendment is a termination statement for a financing statement as to which the secured party of record has failed to file or send a termination statement as required by Section 9–513(a) or (c), the debtor authorizes the filing, and the termination statement indicates that the debtor authorized it to be filed.

(e) If there is more than one secured party of record for a financing statement, each secured party of record may authorize the filing of an amendment under subsection (d).

As amended in 2000.

§ 9–510. Effectiveness of Filed Record.

(a) A filed record is effective only to the extent that it was filed by a person that may file it under Section 9–509.

(b) A record authorized by one secured party of record does not affect the financing statement with respect to another secured party of record.

(c) A continuation statement that is not filed within the six-month period prescribed by Section 9–515(d) is ineffective.

§ 9–511. Secured Party of Record.

(a) A secured party of record with respect to a financing statement is a person whose name is provided as the name of the secured party or a representative of the secured party in an initial financing statement that has been filed. If an initial financing statement is filed under Section 9–514(a), the assignee named in the initial financing statement is the secured party of record with respect to the financing statement.

(b) If an amendment of a financing statement which provides the name of a person as a secured party or a representative of a secured party is filed, the person named in the amendment is a secured party of record. If an amendment is filed under Section 9–514(b), the assignee named in the amendment is a secured party of record.

(c) A person remains a secured party of record until the filing of an amendment of the financing statement which deletes the person.

§ 9–512. Amendment of Financing Statement.

[Alternative A]

(a) Subject to Section 9–509, a person may add or delete collateral covered by, continue or terminate the effectiveness of, or, subject to subsection (e), otherwise amend the information provided in, a financing statement by filing an amendment that:

(1) identifies, by its file number, the initial financing statement to which the amendment relates; and

(2) if the amendment relates to an initial financing statement filed [or recorded] in a filing office described in Section 9–501(a)(1), provides the information specified in Section 9–502(b).

[Alternative B]

(a) Subject to Section 9–509, a person may add or delete collateral covered by, continue or terminate the effectiveness of, or, subject to subsection (e), otherwise amend the information provided in, a financing statement by filing an amendment that:

(1) identifies, by its file number, the initial financing statement to which the amendment relates; and

(2) if the amendment relates to an initial financing statement filed [or recorded] in a filing office described in Section 9–501(a)(1), provides the date [and time] that the initial financing statement was filed [or recorded] and the information specified in Section 9–502(b).

[End of Alternatives]

(b) Except as otherwise provided in Section 9–515, the filing of an amendment does not extend the period of effectiveness of the financing statement.

(c) A financing statement that is amended by an amendment that adds collateral is effective as to the added collateral only from the date of the filing of the amendment.

(d) A financing statement that is amended by an amendment that adds a debtor is effective as to the added debtor only from the date of the filing of the amendment.

(e) An amendment is ineffective to the extent it:

(1) purports to delete all debtors and fails to provide the name of a debtor to be covered by the financing statement; or

(2) purports to delete all secured parties of record and fails to provide the name of a new secured party of record.

Legislative Note: States whose real-estate filing offices require additional information in amendments and cannot search their records by both the name of the debtor and the file number should enact Alternative B to Sections 9–512(a), 9–518(b), 9–519(f), and 9–522(a).

§ 9–513. Termination Statement.

(a) A secured party shall cause the secured party of record for a financing statement to file a termination statement for the financing statement if the financing statement covers consumer goods and:

(1) there is no obligation secured by the collateral covered by the financing statement and no commitment to make an advance, incur an obligation, or otherwise give value; or

(2) the debtor did not authorize the filing of the initial financing statement.

(b) To comply with subsection (a), a secured party shall cause the secured party of record to file the termination statement:

(1) within one month after there is no obligation secured by the collateral covered by the financing statement and no commitment to make an advance, incur an obligation, or otherwise give value; or

(2) if earlier, within 20 days after the secured party receives an authenticated demand from a debtor.

(c) In cases not governed by subsection (a), within 20 days after a secured party receives an authenticated demand from a debtor, the secured party shall cause the secured party of record for a financing statement to send to the debtor a termination statement for the financing statement or file the termination statement in the filing office if:

(1) except in the case of a financing statement covering accounts or chattel paper that has been sold or goods that are the subject of a consignment, there is no obligation secured by the collateral covered by the financing statement and no commitment to make an advance, incur an obligation, or otherwise give value;

(2) the financing statement covers accounts or chattel paper that has been sold but as to which the account debtor or other person obligated has discharged its obligation;

(3) the financing statement covers goods that were the subject of a consignment to the debtor but are not in the debtor's possession; or

(4) the debtor did not authorize the filing of the initial financing statement.

(d) Except as otherwise provided in Section 9–510, upon the filing of a termination statement with the filing office, the financing statement to which the termination statement relates ceases to be effective. Except as otherwise provided in Section 9–510, for purposes of Sections 9–519(g), 9–522(a), and 9–523(c), the filing with the filing office of a termination statement relating to a financing statement that indicates that the debtor is a transmitting utility also causes the effectiveness of the financing statement to lapse.

As amended in 2000.

§ 9–514. Assignment of Powers of Secured Party of Record.

(a) Except as otherwise provided in subsection (c), an initial financing statement may reflect an assignment of all of the secured party's power to authorize an amendment to the financing statement by providing the name and mailing address of the assignee as the name and address of the secured party.

(b) Except as otherwise provided in subsection (c), a secured party of record may assign of record all or part of its power to authorize an amendment to a financing statement by filing in the filing office an amendment of the financing statement which:

(1) identifies, by its file number, the initial financing statement to which it relates;

(2) provides the name of the assignor; and

(3) provides the name and mailing address of the assignee.

(c) An assignment of record of a security interest in a fixture covered by a record of a mortgage which is effective as a financing statement filed as a fixture filing under Section 9–502(c) may be made only by an assignment of record of the mortgage in the manner provided by law of this State other than [the Uniform Commercial Code].

§ 9–515. Duration and Effectiveness of Financing Statement; Effect of Lapsed Financing Statement.

(a) Except as otherwise provided in subsections (b), (e), (f), and (g), a filed financing statement is effective for a period of five years after the date of filing.

(b) Except as otherwise provided in subsections (e), (f), and (g), an initial financing statement filed in connection with a public-finance transaction or manufactured-home transaction is effective for a period of 30 years after the date of filing if it indicates that it is filed in connection with a public-finance transaction or manufactured-home transaction.

(c) The effectiveness of a filed financing statement lapses on the expiration of the period of its effectiveness unless before the lapse a continuation statement is filed pursuant to subsection (d). Upon lapse, a financing statement ceases to be effective and any security interest or agricultural lien that was perfected by the financing statement becomes unperfected, unless the security interest is perfected otherwise. If the security interest or agricultural lien becomes unperfected upon lapse, it is deemed never to have been perfected as against a purchaser of the collateral for value.

(d) A continuation statement may be filed only within six months before the expiration of the five-year period specified in subsection (a) or the 30-year period specified in subsection (b), whichever is applicable.

(e) Except as otherwise provided in Section 9–510, upon timely filing of a continuation statement, the effectiveness of the initial financing statement continues for a period of five years commencing on the day on which the financing statement would have become ineffective in the absence of the filing. Upon the expiration of the five-year period, the financing statement lapses in the same manner as provided in subsection (c), unless, before the lapse, another continuation statement is filed pursuant to subsection (d). Succeeding continuation statements may be filed in the same manner to continue the effectiveness of the initial financing statement.

(f) If a debtor is a transmitting utility and a filed financing statement so indicates, the financing statement is effective until a termination statement is filed.

(g) A record of a mortgage that is effective as a financing statement filed as a fixture filing under Section 9–502(c) remains effective as a financing statement filed as a fixture filing until the mortgage is released or satisfied of record or its effectiveness otherwise terminates as to the real property.

§ 9–516. What Constitutes Filing; Effectiveness of Filing.

(a) Except as otherwise provided in subsection (b), communication of a record to a filing office and tender of the filing fee or acceptance of the record by the filing office constitutes filing.

(b) Filing does not occur with respect to a record that a filing office refuses to accept because:

(1) the record is not communicated by a method or medium of communication authorized by the filing office;

(2) an amount equal to or greater than the applicable filing fee is not tendered;

(3) the filing office is unable to index the record because:

(A) in the case of an initial financing statement, the record does not provide a name for the debtor;

(B) in the case of an amendment or correction statement, the record:

(i) does not identify the initial financing statement as required by Section 9–512 or 9–518, as applicable; or

(ii) identifies an initial financing statement whose effectiveness has lapsed under Section 9–515;

(C) in the case of an initial financing statement that provides the name of a debtor identified as an individual or an amendment that provides a name of a debtor identified as an individual which was not previously provided in the financing statement to which the record relates, the record does not identify the debtor's last name; or

(D) in the case of a record filed [or recorded] in the filing office described in Section 9–501(a)(1), the record does not provide a sufficient description of the real property to which it relates;

(4) in the case of an initial financing statement or an amendment that adds a secured party of record, the record does not provide a name and mailing address for the secured party of record;

(5) in the case of an initial financing statement or an amendment that provides a name of a debtor which was not previously provided in the financing statement to which the amendment relates, the record does not:

(A) provide a mailing address for the debtor;

(B) indicate whether the debtor is an individual or an organization; or

(C) if the financing statement indicates that the debtor is an organization, provide:

(i) a type of organization for the debtor;

(ii) a jurisdiction of organization for the debtor; or

(iii) an organizational identification number for the debtor or indicate that the debtor has none;

(6) in the case of an assignment reflected in an initial financing statement under Section 9–514(a) or an amendment filed under Section 9–514(b), the record does not provide a name and mailing address for the assignee; or

(7) in the case of a continuation statement, the record is not filed within the six-month period prescribed by Section 9–515(d).

(c) For purposes of subsection (b):

(1) a record does not provide information if the filing office is unable to read or decipher the information; and

(2) a record that does not indicate that it is an amendment or identify an initial financing statement to which it relates, as required by Section 9–512, 9–514, or 9–518, is an initial financing statement.

(d) A record that is communicated to the filing office with tender of the filing fee, but which the filing office refuses to accept for a reason other than one set forth in subsection (b), is effective as a filed record except as against a purchaser of the collateral which gives value in reasonable reliance upon the absence of the record from the files.

§ 9–517. Effect of Indexing Errors.

The failure of the filing office to index a record correctly does not affect the effectiveness of the filed record.

§ 9–518. Claim Concerning Inaccurate or Wrongfully Filed Record.

(a) A person may file in the filing office a correction statement with respect to a record indexed there under the person's name if the person believes that the record is inaccurate or was wrongfully filed.

[Alternative A]

(b) A correction statement must:

(1) identify the record to which it relates by the file number assigned to the initial financing statement to which the record relates;

(2) indicate that it is a correction statement; and

(3) provide the basis for the person's belief that the record is inaccurate and indicate the manner in which the person believes the record should be amended to cure any inaccuracy or provide the basis for the person's belief that the record was wrongfully filed.

[Alternative B]

(b) A correction statement must:

(1) identify the record to which it relates by:

(A) the file number assigned to the initial financing statement to which the record relates; and

(B) if the correction statement relates to a record filed [or recorded] in a filing office described in Section 9–501(a)(1), the date [and time] that the initial financing statement was filed [or recorded] and the information specified in Section 9–502(b);

(2) indicate that it is a correction statement; and

(3) provide the basis for the person's belief that the record is inaccurate and indicate the manner in which the person believes the record should be amended to cure any inaccuracy or provide the basis for the person's belief that the record was wrongfully filed.

[End of Alternatives]

(c) The filing of a correction statement does not affect the effectiveness of an initial financing statement or other filed record.

Legislative Note: States whose real-estate filing offices require additional information in amendments and cannot search their records by both the name of the debtor and the file number should enact Alternative B to Sections 9–512(a), 9–518(b), 9–519(f), and 9–522(a).

[Subpart 2. Duties and Operation of Filing Office]

§ 9–519. Numbering, Maintaining, and Indexing Records; Communicating Information Provided in Records.

(a) For each record filed in a filing office, the filing office shall:

(1) assign a unique number to the filed record;

(2) create a record that bears the number assigned to the filed record and the date and time of filing;

(3) maintain the filed record for public inspection; and

(4) index the filed record in accordance with subsections (c), (d), and (e).

(b) A file number [assigned after January 1, 2002,] must include a digit that:

(1) is mathematically derived from or related to the other digits of the file number; and

(2) aids the filing office in determining whether a number communicated as the file number includes a single-digit or transpositional error.

(c) Except as otherwise provided in subsections (d) and (e), the filing office shall:

(1) index an initial financing statement according to the name of the debtor and index all filed records relating to the initial financing statement in a manner that associates with one another an initial financing statement and all filed records relating to the initial financing statement; and

(2) index a record that provides a name of a debtor which was not previously provided in the financing statement to which the record relates also according to the name that was not previously provided.

(d) If a financing statement is filed as a fixture filing or covers as-extracted collateral or timber to be cut, [it must be filed for record and] the filing office shall index it:

(1) under the names of the debtor and of each owner of record shown on the financing statement as if they were the mortgagors under a mortgage of the real property described; and

(2) to the extent that the law of this State provides for indexing of records of mortgages under the name of the mortgagee, under the name of the secured party as if the secured party were the mortgagee thereunder, or, if indexing is by description, as if the financing statement were a record of a mortgage of the real property described.

(e) If a financing statement is filed as a fixture filing or covers as-extracted collateral or timber to be cut, the filing office shall index an assignment filed under Section 9–514(a) or an amendment filed under Section 9–514(b):

(1) under the name of the assignor as grantor; and

(2) to the extent that the law of this State provides for indexing a record of the assignment of a mortgage under the name of the assignee, under the name of the assignee.

[Alternative A]

(f) The filing office shall maintain a capability:

(1) to retrieve a record by the name of the debtor and by the file number assigned to the initial financing statement to which the record relates; and

(2) to associate and retrieve with one another an initial financing statement and each filed record relating to the initial financing statement.

[Alternative B]

(f) The filing office shall maintain a capability:

(1) to retrieve a record by the name of the debtor and:

(A) if the filing office is described in Section 9–501(a)(1), by the file number assigned to the initial financing statement to which the record relates and the date [and time] that the record was filed [or recorded]; or

(B) if the filing office is described in Section 9–501(a)(2), by the file number assigned to the initial financing statement to which the record relates; and

(2) to associate and retrieve with one another an initial financing statement and each filed record relating to the initial financing statement.

[End of Alternatives]

(g) The filing office may not remove a debtor's name from the index until one year after the effectiveness of a financing statement naming the debtor lapses under Section 9–515 with respect to all secured parties of record.

(h) The filing office shall perform the acts required by subsections (a) through (e) at the time and in the manner prescribed by filing-office rule, but not later than two business days after the filing office receives the record in question.

[(i) Subsection[s] [(b)] [and] [(h)] do[es] not apply to a filing office described in Section 9–501(a)(1).]

Legislative Notes:

1. States whose filing offices currently assign file numbers that include a verification number, commonly known as a "check digit," or can implement this requirement before the effective date of this Article should omit the bracketed language in subsection (b).

2. In States in which writings will not appear in the real property records and indices unless actually recorded the bracketed language in subsection (d) should be used.

3. States whose real-estate filing offices require additional information in amendments and cannot search their records by both the name of the debtor and the file number should enact Alternative B to Sections 9–512(a), 9–518(b), 9–519(f), and 9–522(a).

4. A State that elects not to require real-estate filing offices to comply with either or both of subsections (b) and (h) may adopt an applicable variation of subsection (i) and add "Except as otherwise provided in subsection (i)," to the appropriate subsection or subsections.

§ 9–520. Acceptance and Refusal to Accept Record.

(a) A filing office shall refuse to accept a record for filing for a reason set forth in Section 9–516(b) and may refuse to accept a record for filing only for a reason set forth in Section 9–516(b).

(b) If a filing office refuses to accept a record for filing, it shall communicate to the person that presented the record the fact of and reason for the refusal and the date and time the record would have been filed had the filing office accepted it. The communication must be made at the time and in the manner prescribed by filing-office rule but [, in the case of a filing office described in Section 9–501(a)(2),] in no event more than two business days after the filing office receives the record.

(c) A filed financing statement satisfying Section 9–502(a) and (b) is effective, even if the filing office is required to refuse to accept it for filing under subsection (a). However, Section 9–338 applies to a filed financing statement providing information described in Section 9–516(b)(5) which is incorrect at the time the financing statement is filed.

(d) If a record communicated to a filing office provides information that relates to more than one debtor, this part applies as to each debtor separately.

Legislative Note: A State that elects not to require real-property filing offices to comply with subsection (b) should include the bracketed language.

§ 9–521. Uniform Form of Written Financing Statement and Amendment.

(a) A filing office that accepts written records may not refuse to accept a written initial financing statement in the following form and format except for a reason set forth in Section 9–516(b):

[NATIONAL UCC FINANCING STATEMENT (FORM UCC1)(REV. 7/29/98)]

[NATIONAL UCC FINANCING STATEMENT ADDENDUM (FORM UCC1Ad)(REV. 07/29/98)]

(b) A filing office that accepts written records may not refuse to accept a written record in the following form and format except for a reason set forth in Section 9–516(b):

[NATIONAL UCC FINANCING STATEMENT AMENDMENT (FORM UCC3)(REV. 07/29/98)]

[NATIONAL UCC FINANCING STATEMENT AMENDMENT ADDENDUM (FORM UCC3Ad)(REV. 07/29/98)]

§ 9–522. Maintenance and Destruction of Records.

[Alternative A]

(a) The filing office shall maintain a record of the information provided in a filed financing statement for at least one year after the effectiveness of the financing statement has lapsed under Section 9–515 with respect to all secured parties of record. The record must be retrievable by using the name of the debtor and by using the file number assigned to the initial financing statement to which the record relates.

[Alternative B]

(a) The filing office shall maintain a record of the information provided in a filed financing statement for at least one year after the effectiveness of the financing statement has lapsed under Section 9–515 with respect to all secured parties of record. The record must be retrievable by using the name of the debtor and:

(1) if the record was filed [or recorded] in the filing office described in Section 9–501(a)(1), by using the file number assigned to the initial financing statement to which the record relates and the date [and time] that the record was filed [or recorded]; or

(2) if the record was filed in the filing office described in Section 9–501(a)(2), by using the file number assigned to the initial financing statement to which the record relates.

[End of Alternatives]

(b) Except to the extent that a statute governing disposition of public records provides otherwise, the filing office immediately may destroy any written record evidencing a financing statement. However, if the filing office destroys a written record, it shall maintain another record of the financing statement which complies with subsection (a).

Legislative Note: States whose real-estate filing offices require additional information in amendments and cannot search their records by both the name of the debtor and the file number should enact Alternative B to Sections 9–512(a), 9–518(b), 9–519(f), and 9–522(a).

§ 9–523. Information from Filing Office; Sale or License of Records.

(a) If a person that files a written record requests an acknowledgment of the filing, the filing office shall send to the person an image of the record showing the number assigned to the record pursuant to Section 9–519(a)(1) and the date and time of the filing of the record. However, if the person furnishes a copy of the record to the filing office, the filing office may instead:

(1) note upon the copy the number assigned to the record pursuant to Section 9–519(a)(1) and the date and time of the filing of the record; and

(2) send the copy to the person.

(b) If a person files a record other than a written record, the filing office shall communicate to the person an acknowledgment that provides:

(1) the information in the record;

(2) the number assigned to the record pursuant to Section 9–519(a)(1); and

(3) the date and time of the filing of the record.

(c) The filing office shall communicate or otherwise make available in a record the following information to any person that requests it:

(1) whether there is on file on a date and time specified by the filing office, but not a date earlier than three business days before the filing office receives the request, any financing statement that:

(A) designates a particular debtor [or, if the request so states, designates a particular debtor at the address specified in the request];

(B) has not lapsed under Section 9–515 with respect to all secured parties of record; and

(C) if the request so states, has lapsed under Section 9–515 and a record of which is maintained by the filing office under Section 9–522(a);

(2) the date and time of filing of each financing statement; and

(3) the information provided in each financing statement.

(d) In complying with its duty under subsection (c), the filing office may communicate information in any medium. However, if requested, the filing office shall communicate information by issuing [its written certificate] [a record that can be admitted into evidence in the courts of this State without extrinsic evidence of its authenticity].

(e) The filing office shall perform the acts required by subsections (a) through (d) at the time and in the manner prescribed by filing-office rule, but not later than two business days after the filing office receives the request.

(f) At least weekly, the [insert appropriate official or governmental agency] [filing office] shall offer to sell or license to the public on a nonexclusive basis, in bulk, copies of all records filed in it under this part, in every medium from time to time available to the filing office.

Legislative Notes:

1. States whose filing office does not offer the additional service of responding to search requests limited to a particular address should omit the bracketed language in subsection (c)(1)(A).

2. A State that elects not to require real-estate filing offices to comply with either or both of subsections (e) and (f) should specify in the appropriate subsection(s) only the filing office described in Section 9–501(a)(2).

§ 9–524. Delay by Filing Office.

Delay by the filing office beyond a time limit prescribed by this part is excused if:

(1) the delay is caused by interruption of communication or computer facilities, war, emergency conditions, failure of equipment, or other circumstances beyond control of the filing office; and

(2) the filing office exercises reasonable diligence under the circumstances.

§ 9–525. Fees.

(a) Except as otherwise provided in subsection (e), the fee for filing and indexing a record under this part, other than an initial financing statement of the kind described in subsection (b), is [the amount specified in subsection (c), if applicable, plus]:

(1) $[X] if the record is communicated in writing and consists of one or two pages;

(2) $[2X] if the record is communicated in writing and consists of more than two pages; and

(3) $[½X] if the record is communicated by another medium authorized by filing-office rule.

(b) Except as otherwise provided in subsection (e), the fee for filing and indexing an initial financing statement of the following kind is [the amount specified in subsection (c), if applicable, plus]:

(1) $_____ if the financing statement indicates that it is filed in connection with a public-finance transaction;

(2) $_____ if the financing statement indicates that it is filed in connection with a manufactured-home transaction.

[Alternative A]

(c) The number of names required to be indexed does not affect the amount of the fee in subsections (a) and (b).

[Alternative B]

(c) Except as otherwise provided in subsection (e), if a record is communicated in writing, the fee for each name more than two required to be indexed is $_____.

[End of Alternatives]

(d) The fee for responding to a request for information from the filing office, including for [issuing a certificate showing] [communicating] whether there is on file any financing statement naming a particular debtor, is:

(1) $_____ if the request is communicated in writing; and

(2) $_____ if the request is communicated by another medium authorized by filing-office rule.

(e) This section does not require a fee with respect to a record of a mortgage which is effective as a financing statement filed as a fixture filing or as a financing statement covering as-extracted collateral or timber to be cut under Section 9–502(c). However, the recording and satisfaction fees that otherwise would be applicable to the record of the mortgage apply.

Legislative Notes:

1. To preserve uniformity, a State that places the provisions of this section together with statutes setting fees for other services should do so without modification.

2. A State should enact subsection (c), Alternative A, and omit the bracketed language in subsections (a) and (b) unless its indexing system entails a substantial additional cost when indexing additional names.

As amended in 2000.

§ 9–526. Filing-Office Rules.

(a) The [insert appropriate governmental official or agency] shall adopt and publish rules to implement this article. The filing-office rules must be[:

(1)] consistent with this article[; and

(2) adopted and published in accordance with the [insert any applicable state administrative procedure act]].

(b) To keep the filing-office rules and practices of the filing office in harmony with the rules and practices of filing offices in other jurisdictions that enact substantially this part, and to keep the technology used by the filing office compatible with the technology used by filing offices in other jurisdictions that enact substantially this part, the [insert appropriate governmental official or agency], so far as is consistent with the purposes, policies, and provisions of this article, in adopting, amending, and repealing filing-office rules, shall:

(1) consult with filing offices in other jurisdictions that enact substantially this part; and

(2) consult the most recent version of the Model Rules promulgated by the International Association of Corporate Administrators or any successor organization; and

(3) take into consideration the rules and practices of, and the technology used by, filing offices in other jurisdictions that enact substantially this part.

§ 9–527. Duty to Report.

The [insert appropriate governmental official or agency] shall report [annually on or before _____] to the [Governor and Legislature] on the operation of the filing office. The report must contain a statement of the extent to which:

(1) the filing-office rules are not in harmony with the rules of filing offices in other jurisdictions that enact substantially this part and the reasons for these variations; and

(2) the filing-office rules are not in harmony with the most recent version of the Model Rules promulgated by the International Association of Corporate Administrators, or any successor organization, and the reasons for these variations.

Part 6 Default

[Subpart 1. Default and Enforcement of Security Interest]

§ 9–601. Rights after Default; Judicial Enforcement; Consignor or Buyer of Accounts, Chattel Paper, Payment Intangibles, or Promissory Notes.

(a) After default, a secured party has the rights provided in this part and, except as otherwise provided in Section 9–602, those provided by agreement of the parties. A secured party:

(1) may reduce a claim to judgment, foreclose, or otherwise enforce the claim, security interest, or agricultural lien by any available judicial procedure; and

(2) if the collateral is documents, may proceed either as to the documents or as to the goods they cover.

(b) A secured party in possession of collateral or control of collateral under Section 9–104, 9–105, 9–106, or 9–107 has the rights and duties provided in Section 9–207.

(c) The rights under subsections (a) and (b) are cumulative and may be exercised simultaneously.

(d) Except as otherwise provided in subsection (g) and Section 9–605, after default, a debtor and an obligor have the rights provided in this part and by agreement of the parties.

(e) If a secured party has reduced its claim to judgment, the lien of any levy that may be made upon the collateral by virtue of an execution based upon the judgment relates back to the earliest of:

(1) the date of perfection of the security interest or agricultural lien in the collateral;

(2) the date of filing a financing statement covering the collateral; or

(3) any date specified in a statute under which the agricultural lien was created.

(f) A sale pursuant to an execution is a foreclosure of the security interest or agricultural lien by judicial procedure within the meaning of this section. A secured party may purchase at the sale and thereafter hold the collateral free of any other requirements of this article.

(g) Except as otherwise provided in Section 9–607(c), this part imposes no duties upon a secured party that is a consignor or is a buyer of accounts, chattel paper, payment intangibles, or promissory notes.

§ 9–602. Waiver and Variance of Rights and Duties.

Except as otherwise provided in Section 9–624, to the extent that they give rights to a debtor or obligor and impose duties on a secured party, the debtor or obligor may not waive or vary the rules stated in the following listed sections:

(1) Section 9–207(b)(4)(C), which deals with use and operation of the collateral by the secured party;

(2) Section 9–210, which deals with requests for an accounting and requests concerning a list of collateral and statement of account;

(3) Section 9–607(c), which deals with collection and enforcement of collateral;

(4) Sections 9–608(a) and 9–615(c) to the extent that they deal with application or payment of noncash proceeds of collection, enforcement, or disposition;

(5) Sections 9–608(a) and 9–615(d) to the extent that they require accounting for or payment of surplus proceeds of collateral;

(6) Section 9–609 to the extent that it imposes upon a secured party that takes possession of collateral without judicial process the duty to do so without breach of the peace;

(7) Sections 9–610(b), 9–611, 9–613, and 9–614, which deal with disposition of collateral;

(8) Section 9–615(f), which deals with calculation of a deficiency or surplus when a disposition is made to the secured party, a person related to the secured party, or a secondary obligor;

(9) Section 9–616, which deals with explanation of the calculation of a surplus or deficiency;

(10) Sections 9–620, 9–621, and 9–622, which deal with acceptance of collateral in satisfaction of obligation;

(11) Section 9–623, which deals with redemption of collateral;

(12) Section 9–624, which deals with permissible waivers; and

(13) Sections 9–625 and 9–626, which deal with the secured party's liability for failure to comply with this article.

§ 9–603. Agreement on Standards Concerning Rights and Duties.

(a) The parties may determine by agreement the standards measuring the fulfillment of the rights of a debtor or obligor and the duties of a secured party under a rule stated in Section 9–602 if the standards are not manifestly unreasonable.

(b) Subsection (a) does not apply to the duty under Section 9–609 to refrain from breaching the peace.

§ 9–604. Procedure If Security Agreement Covers Real Property or Fixtures.

(a) If a security agreement covers both personal and real property, a secured party may proceed:

(1) under this part as to the personal property without prejudicing any rights with respect to the real property; or

(2) as to both the personal property and the real property in accordance with the rights with respect to the real property, in which case the other provisions of this part do not apply.

(b) Subject to subsection (c), if a security agreement covers goods that are or become fixtures, a secured party may proceed:

(1) under this part; or

(2) in accordance with the rights with respect to real property, in which case the other provisions of this part do not apply.

(c) Subject to the other provisions of this part, if a secured party holding a security interest in fixtures has priority over all owners and encumbrancers of the real property, the secured party, after default, may remove the collateral from the real property.

(d) A secured party that removes collateral shall promptly reimburse any encumbrancer or owner of the real property, other than the debtor, for the cost of repair of any physical injury caused by the removal. The secured party need not reimburse the encumbrancer or owner for any diminution in value of the real property caused by the absence of the goods removed or by any necessity of replacing them. A person entitled to reimbursement may refuse permission to remove until the secured party gives adequate assurance for the performance of the obligation to reimburse.

§ 9–605. Unknown Debtor or Secondary Obligor.

A secured party does not owe a duty based on its status as secured party:

(1) to a person that is a debtor or obligor, unless the secured party knows:

(A) that the person is a debtor or obligor;

(B) the identity of the person; and

(C) how to communicate with the person; or

(2) to a secured party or lienholder that has filed a financing statement against a person, unless the secured party knows:

(A) that the person is a debtor; and

(B) the identity of the person.

§ 9–606. Time of Default for Agricultural Lien.

For purposes of this part, a default occurs in connection with an agricultural lien at the time the secured party becomes entitled to enforce the lien in accordance with the statute under which it was created.

§ 9–607. Collection and Enforcement by Secured Party.

(a) If so agreed, and in any event after default, a secured party:

(1) may notify an account debtor or other person obligated on collateral to make payment or otherwise render performance to or for the benefit of the secured party;

(2) may take any proceeds to which the secured party is entitled under Section 9–315;

(3) may enforce the obligations of an account debtor or other person obligated on collateral and exercise the rights of the debtor with respect to the obligation of the account debtor or other person obligated on collateral to make payment or otherwise render performance to the debtor, and with respect to any property that secures the obligations of the account debtor or other person obligated on the collateral;

(4) if it holds a security interest in a deposit account perfected by control under Section 9–104(a)(1), may apply the balance of the deposit account to the obligation secured by the deposit account; and

(5) if it holds a security interest in a deposit account perfected by control under Section 9–104(a)(2) or (3), may instruct the bank to pay the balance of the deposit account to or for the benefit of the secured party.

(b) If necessary to enable a secured party to exercise under subsection (a)(3) the right of a debtor to enforce a mortgage nonjudicially, the secured party may record in the office in which a record of the mortgage is recorded:

(1) a copy of the security agreement that creates or provides for a security interest in the obligation secured by the mortgage; and

(2) the secured party's sworn affidavit in recordable form stating that:

(A) a default has occurred; and

(B) the secured party is entitled to enforce the mortgage nonjudicially.

(c) A secured party shall proceed in a commercially reasonable manner if the secured party:

(1) undertakes to collect from or enforce an obligation of an account debtor or other person obligated on collateral; and

(2) is entitled to charge back uncollected collateral or otherwise to full or limited recourse against the debtor or a secondary obligor.

(d) A secured party may deduct from the collections made pursuant to subsection (c) reasonable expenses of collection and enforcement, including reasonable attorney's fees and legal expenses incurred by the secured party.

(e) This section does not determine whether an account debtor, bank, or other person obligated on collateral owes a duty to a secured party.

As amended in 2000.

§ 9–608. Application of Proceeds of Collection or Enforcement; Liability for Deficiency and Right to Surplus.

(a) If a security interest or agricultural lien secures payment or performance of an obligation, the following rules apply:

(1) A secured party shall apply or pay over for application the cash proceeds of collection or enforcement under Section 9–607 in the following order to:

(A) the reasonable expenses of collection and enforcement and, to the extent provided for by agreement and not prohibited by law, reasonable attorney's fees and legal expenses incurred by the secured party;

(B) the satisfaction of obligations secured by the security interest or agricultural lien under which the collection or enforcement is made; and

(C) the satisfaction of obligations secured by any subordinate security interest in or other lien on the collateral subject to the security interest or agricultural lien under which the collection or enforcement is made if the secured party receives an authenticated demand for proceeds before distribution of the proceeds is completed.

(2) If requested by a secured party, a holder of a subordinate security interest or other lien shall furnish reasonable proof of the interest or lien within a reasonable time. Unless the holder complies, the secured party need not comply with the holder's demand under paragraph (1)(C).

(3) A secured party need not apply or pay over for application noncash proceeds of collection and enforcement under Section 9–607 unless the failure to do so would be commercially unreasonable. A secured party that applies or pays over for application noncash proceeds shall do so in a commercially reasonable manner.

(4) A secured party shall account to and pay a debtor for any surplus, and the obligor is liable for any deficiency.

(b) If the underlying transaction is a sale of accounts, chattel paper, payment intangibles, or promissory notes, the debtor is not entitled to any surplus, and the obligor is not liable for any deficiency.

As amended in 2000.

§ 9–609. Secured Party's Right to Take Possession after Default.

(a) After default, a secured party:

(1) may take possession of the collateral; and

(2) without removal, may render equipment unusable and dispose of collateral on a debtor's premises under Section 9–610.

(b) A secured party may proceed under subsection (a):

(1) pursuant to judicial process; or

(2) without judicial process, if it proceeds without breach of the peace.

(c) If so agreed, and in any event after default, a secured party may require the debtor to assemble the collateral and make it available to the secured party at a place to be designated by the secured party which is reasonably convenient to both parties.

§ 9–610. Disposition of Collateral after Default.

(a) After default, a secured party may sell, lease, license, or otherwise dispose of any or all of the collateral in its present condition or following any commercially reasonable preparation or processing.

(b) Every aspect of a disposition of collateral, including the method, manner, time, place, and other terms, must be commercially reasonable. If commercially reasonable, a secured party may dispose of collateral by public or private proceedings, by one or more contracts, as a unit or in parcels, and at any time and place and on any terms.

(c) A secured party may purchase collateral:

(1) at a public disposition; or

(2) at a private disposition only if the collateral is of a kind that is customarily sold on a recognized market or the subject of widely distributed standard price quotations.

(d) A contract for sale, lease, license, or other disposition includes the warranties relating to title, possession, quiet enjoyment, and the like which by operation of law accompany a voluntary disposition of property of the kind subject to the contract.

(e) A secured party may disclaim or modify warranties under subsection (d):

(1) in a manner that would be effective to disclaim or modify the warranties in a voluntary disposition of property of the kind subject to the contract of disposition; or

(2) by communicating to the purchaser a record evidencing the contract for disposition and including an express disclaimer or modification of the warranties.

(f) A record is sufficient to disclaim warranties under subsection (e) if it indicates "There is no warranty relating to title, possession, quiet enjoyment, or the like in this disposition" or uses words of similar import.

§ 9–611. Notification before Disposition of Collateral.

(a) In this section, "notification date" means the earlier of the date on which:

(1) a secured party sends to the debtor and any secondary obligor an authenticated notification of disposition; or

(2) the debtor and any secondary obligor waive the right to notification.

(b) Except as otherwise provided in subsection (d), a secured party that disposes of collateral under Section 9–610 shall send to the persons specified in subsection (c) a reasonable authenticated notification of disposition.

(c) To comply with subsection (b), the secured party shall send an authenticated notification of disposition to:

(1) the debtor;

(2) any secondary obligor; and

(3) if the collateral is other than consumer goods:

(A) any other person from which the secured party has received, before the notification date, an authenticated notification of a claim of an interest in the collateral;

(B) any other secured party or lienholder that, 10 days before the notification date, held a security interest in or other lien on the collateral perfected by the filing of a financing statement that:

  (i) identified the collateral;

  (ii) was indexed under the debtor's name as of that date; and

  (iii) was filed in the office in which to file a financing statement against the debtor covering the collateral as of that date; and

(C) any other secured party that, 10 days before the notification date, held a security interest in the collateral perfected by compliance with a statute, regulation, or treaty described in Section 9–311(a).

(d) Subsection (b) does not apply if the collateral is perishable or threatens to decline speedily in value or is of a type customarily sold on a recognized market.

(e) A secured party complies with the requirement for notification prescribed by subsection (c)(3)(B) if:

(1) not later than 20 days or earlier than 30 days before the notification date, the secured party requests, in a commercially reasonable manner, information concerning financing statements indexed under the debtor's name in the office indicated in subsection (c)(3)(B); and

(2) before the notification date, the secured party:

  (A) did not receive a response to the request for information; or

  (B) received a response to the request for information and sent an authenticated notification of disposition to each secured party or other lienholder named in that response whose financing statement covered the collateral.

§ 9–612. Timeliness of Notification before Disposition of Collateral.

(a) Except as otherwise provided in subsection (b), whether a notification is sent within a reasonable time is a question of fact.

(b) In a transaction other than a consumer transaction, a notification of disposition sent after default and 10 days or more before the earliest time of disposition set forth in the notification is sent within a reasonable time before the disposition.

§ 9–613. Contents and Form of Notification before Disposition of Collateral: General.

Except in a consumer-goods transaction, the following rules apply:

(1) The contents of a notification of disposition are sufficient if the notification:

  (A) describes the debtor and the secured party;

  (B) describes the collateral that is the subject of the intended disposition;

  (C) states the method of intended disposition;

  (D) states that the debtor is entitled to an accounting of the unpaid indebtedness and states the charge, if any, for an accounting; and

  (E) states the time and place of a public disposition or the time after which any other disposition is to be made.

(2) Whether the contents of a notification that lacks any of the information specified in paragraph (1) are nevertheless sufficient is a question of fact.

(3) The contents of a notification providing substantially the information specified in paragraph (1) are sufficient, even if the notification includes:

  (A) information not specified by that paragraph; or

  (B) minor errors that are not seriously misleading.

(4) A particular phrasing of the notification is not required.

(5) The following form of notification and the form appearing in Section 9–614(3), when completed, each provides sufficient information:

NOTIFICATION OF DISPOSITION OF COLLATERAL

To: [*Name of debtor, obligor, or other person to which the notification is sent*]

From: [*Name, address, and telephone number of secured party*]

Name of Debtor(s): [*Include only if debtor(s) are not an addressee*]

  [*For a public disposition:*]

  We will sell [or lease or license, *as applicable*] the [*describe collateral*] [to the highest qualified bidder] in public as follows:

  Day and Date: _____

  Time: _____

  Place: _____

  [*For a private disposition:*]

  We will sell [or lease or license, *as applicable*] the [*describe collateral*] privately sometime after [*day and date*].

  You are entitled to an accounting of the unpaid indebtedness secured by the property that we intend to sell [or lease or license, *as applicable*] [for a charge of $_____]. You may request an accounting by calling us at [*telephone number*].

[End of Form]

As amended in 2000.

§ 9–614. Contents and Form of Notification before Disposition of Collateral: Consumer-Goods Transaction.

In a consumer-goods transaction, the following rules apply:

(1) A notification of disposition must provide the following information:

  (A) the information specified in Section 9–613(1);

  (B) a description of any liability for a deficiency of the person to which the notification is sent;

  (C) a telephone number from which the amount that must be paid to the secured party to redeem the collateral under Section 9–623 is available; and

  (D) a telephone number or mailing address from which additional information concerning the disposition and the obligation secured is available.

(2) A particular phrasing of the notification is not required.

(3) The following form of notification, when completed, provides sufficient information:

  [*Name and address of secured party*]

  [*Date*]

NOTICE OF OUR PLAN TO SELL PROPERTY

[*Name and address of any obligor who is also a debtor*]

Subject: [*Identification of Transaction*]

We have your [*describe collateral*], because you broke promises in our agreement.

[*For a public disposition:*]

We will sell [*describe collateral*] at public sale. A sale could include a lease or license. The sale will be held as follows:

Date: _____

Time: _____

Place: _____

You may attend the sale and bring bidders if you want.

[*For a private disposition:*]

We will sell [*describe collateral*] at private sale sometime after [*date*]. A sale could include a lease or license.

The money that we get from the sale (after paying our costs) will reduce the amount you owe. If we get less money than you owe, you [*will or will not, as applicable*] still owe us the difference. If we get more money than you owe, you will get the extra money, unless we must pay it to someone else.

You can get the property back at any time before we sell it by paying us the full amount you owe (not just the past due payments), including our expenses. To learn the exact amount you must pay, call us at [*telephone number*].

If you want us to explain to you in writing how we have figured the amount that you owe us, you may call us at [*telephone number*] [or write us at [*secured party's address*]] and request a written explanation. [We will charge you $_____ for the explanation if we sent you another written explanation of the amount you owe us within the last six months.]

If you need more information about the sale call us at [*telephone number*] [or write us at [*secured party's address*]].

We are sending this notice to the following other people who have an interest in [*describe collateral*] or who owe money under your agreement:

[*Names of all other debtors and obligors, if any*]

[End of Form]

(4) A notification in the form of paragraph (3) is sufficient, even if additional information appears at the end of the form.

(5) A notification in the form of paragraph (3) is sufficient, even if it includes errors in information not required by paragraph (1), unless the error is misleading with respect to rights arising under this article.

(6) If a notification under this section is not in the form of paragraph (3), law other than this article determines the effect of including information not required by paragraph (1).

§ 9–615. Application of Proceeds of Disposition; Liability for Deficiency and Right to Surplus.

(a) A secured party shall apply or pay over for application the cash proceeds of disposition under Section 9–610 in the following order to:

(1) the reasonable expenses of retaking, holding, preparing for disposition, processing, and disposing, and, to the extent provided for by agreement and not prohibited by law, reasonable attorney's fees and legal expenses incurred by the secured party;

(2) the satisfaction of obligations secured by the security interest or agricultural lien under which the disposition is made;

(3) the satisfaction of obligations secured by any subordinate security interest in or other subordinate lien on the collateral if:

(A) the secured party receives from the holder of the subordinate security interest or other lien an authenticated demand for proceeds before distribution of the proceeds is completed; and

(B) in a case in which a consignor has an interest in the collateral, the subordinate security interest or other lien is senior to the interest of the consignor; and

(4) a secured party that is a consignor of the collateral if the secured party receives from the consignor an authenticated demand for proceeds before distribution of the proceeds is completed.

(b) If requested by a secured party, a holder of a subordinate security interest or other lien shall furnish reasonable proof of the interest or lien within a reasonable time. Unless the holder does so, the secured party need not comply with the holder's demand under subsection (a)(3).

(c) A secured party need not apply or pay over for application noncash proceeds of disposition under Section 9–610 unless the failure to do so would be commercially unreasonable. A secured party that applies or pays over for application noncash proceeds shall do so in a commercially reasonable manner.

(d) If the security interest under which a disposition is made secures payment or performance of an obligation, after making the payments and applications required by subsection (a) and permitted by subsection (c):

(1) unless subsection (a)(4) requires the secured party to apply or pay over cash proceeds to a consignor, the secured party shall account to and pay a debtor for any surplus; and

(2) the obligor is liable for any deficiency.

(e) If the underlying transaction is a sale of accounts, chattel paper, payment intangibles, or promissory notes:

(1) the debtor is not entitled to any surplus; and

(2) the obligor is not liable for any deficiency.

(f) The surplus or deficiency following a disposition is calculated based on the amount of proceeds that would have been realized in a disposition complying with this part to a transferee other than the secured party, a person related to the secured party, or a secondary obligor if:

(1) the transferee in the disposition is the secured party, a person related to the secured party, or a secondary obligor; and

(2) the amount of proceeds of the disposition is significantly below the range of proceeds that a complying disposition to a person other than the secured party, a person related to the secured party, or a secondary obligor would have brought.

(g) A secured party that receives cash proceeds of a disposition in good faith and without knowledge that the receipt violates the rights of the holder of a security interest or other lien that is not subordinate to the security interest or agricultural lien under which the disposition is made:

(1) takes the cash proceeds free of the security interest or other lien;

(2) is not obligated to apply the proceeds of the disposition to the satisfaction of obligations secured by the security interest or other lien; and

(3) is not obligated to account to or pay the holder of the security interest or other lien for any surplus.

As amended in 2000.

§ 9–616. Explanation of Calculation of Surplus or Deficiency.

(a) In this section:

(1) "Explanation" means a writing that:

(A) states the amount of the surplus or deficiency;

(B) provides an explanation in accordance with subsection (c) of how the secured party calculated the surplus or deficiency;

(C) states, if applicable, that future debits, credits, charges, including additional credit service charges or interest, rebates, and expenses may affect the amount of the surplus or deficiency; and

(D) provides a telephone number or mailing address from which additional information concerning the transaction is available.

(2) "Request" means a record:

(A) authenticated by a debtor or consumer obligor;

(B) requesting that the recipient provide an explanation; and

(C) sent after disposition of the collateral under Section 9–610.

(b) In a consumer-goods transaction in which the debtor is entitled to a surplus or a consumer obligor is liable for a deficiency under Section 9–615, the secured party shall:

(1) send an explanation to the debtor or consumer obligor, as applicable, after the disposition and:

(A) before or when the secured party accounts to the debtor and pays any surplus or first makes written demand on the consumer obligor after the disposition for payment of the deficiency; and

(B) within 14 days after receipt of a request; or

(2) in the case of a consumer obligor who is liable for a deficiency, within 14 days after receipt of a request, send to the consumer obligor a record waiving the secured party's right to a deficiency.

(c) To comply with subsection (a)(1)(B), a writing must provide the following information in the following order:

(1) the aggregate amount of obligations secured by the security interest under which the disposition was made, and, if the amount reflects a rebate of unearned interest or credit service charge, an indication of that fact, calculated as of a specified date:

(A) if the secured party takes or receives possession of the collateral after default, not more than 35 days before the secured party takes or receives possession; or

(B) if the secured party takes or receives possession of the collateral before default or does not take possession of the collateral, not more than 35 days before the disposition;

(2) the amount of proceeds of the disposition;

(3) the aggregate amount of the obligations after deducting the amount of proceeds;

(4) the amount, in the aggregate or by type, and types of expenses, including expenses of retaking, holding, preparing for disposition, processing, and disposing of the collateral, and attorney's fees secured by the collateral which are known to the secured party and relate to the current disposition;

(5) the amount, in the aggregate or by type, and types of credits, including rebates of interest or credit service charges, to which the obligor is known to be entitled and which are not reflected in the amount in paragraph (1); and

(6) the amount of the surplus or deficiency.

(d) A particular phrasing of the explanation is not required. An explanation complying substantially with the requirements of subsection (a) is sufficient, even if it includes minor errors that are not seriously misleading.

(e) A debtor or consumer obligor is entitled without charge to one response to a request under this section during any six-month period in which the secured party did not send to the debtor or consumer obligor an explanation pursuant to subsection (b)(1). The secured party may require payment of a charge not exceeding $25 for each additional response.

§ 9–617. Rights of Transferee of Collateral.

(a) A secured party's disposition of collateral after default:

(1) transfers to a transferee for value all of the debtor's rights in the collateral;

(2) discharges the security interest under which the disposition is made; and

(3) discharges any subordinate security interest or other subordinate lien [other than liens created under [cite acts or statutes providing for liens, if any, that are not to be discharged]].

(b) A transferee that acts in good faith takes free of the rights and interests described in subsection (a), even if the secured party fails to comply with this article or the requirements of any judicial proceeding.

(c) If a transferee does not take free of the rights and interests described in subsection (a), the transferee takes the collateral subject to:

(1) the debtor's rights in the collateral;

(2) the security interest or agricultural lien under which the disposition is made; and

(3) any other security interest or other lien.

§ 9–618. Rights and Duties of Certain Secondary Obligors.

(a) A secondary obligor acquires the rights and becomes obligated to perform the duties of the secured party after the secondary obligor:

(1) receives an assignment of a secured obligation from the secured party;

(2) receives a transfer of collateral from the secured party and agrees to accept the rights and assume the duties of the secured party; or

(3) is subrogated to the rights of a secured party with respect to collateral.

(b) An assignment, transfer, or subrogation described in subsection (a):

    (1) is not a disposition of collateral under Section 9–610; and

    (2) relieves the secured party of further duties under this article.

§ 9–619. Transfer of Record or Legal Title.

(a) In this section, "transfer statement" means a record authenticated by a secured party stating:

    (1) that the debtor has defaulted in connection with an obligation secured by specified collateral;

    (2) that the secured party has exercised its post-default remedies with respect to the collateral;

    (3) that, by reason of the exercise, a transferee has acquired the rights of the debtor in the collateral; and

    (4) the name and mailing address of the secured party, debtor, and transferee.

(b) A transfer statement entitles the transferee to the transfer of record of all rights of the debtor in the collateral specified in the statement in any official filing, recording, registration, or certificate-of-title system covering the collateral. If a transfer statement is presented with the applicable fee and request form to the official or office responsible for maintaining the system, the official or office shall:

    (1) accept the transfer statement;

    (2) promptly amend its records to reflect the transfer; and

    (3) if applicable, issue a new appropriate certificate of title in the name of the transferee.

(c) A transfer of the record or legal title to collateral to a secured party under subsection (b) or otherwise is not of itself a disposition of collateral under this article and does not of itself relieve the secured party of its duties under this article.

§ 9–620. Acceptance of Collateral in Full or Partial Satisfaction of Obligation; Compulsory Disposition of Collateral.

(a) Except as otherwise provided in subsection (g), a secured party may accept collateral in full or partial satisfaction of the obligation it secures only if:

    (1) the debtor consents to the acceptance under subsection (c);

    (2) the secured party does not receive, within the time set forth in subsection (d), a notification of objection to the proposal authenticated by:

        (A) a person to which the secured party was required to send a proposal under Section 9–621; or

        (B) any other person, other than the debtor, holding an interest in the collateral subordinate to the security interest that is the subject of the proposal;

    (3) if the collateral is consumer goods, the collateral is not in the possession of the debtor when the debtor consents to the acceptance; and

    (4) subsection (e) does not require the secured party to dispose of the collateral or the debtor waives the requirement pursuant to Section 9–624.

(b) A purported or apparent acceptance of collateral under this section is ineffective unless:

    (1) the secured party consents to the acceptance in an authenticated record or sends a proposal to the debtor; and

    (2) the conditions of subsection (a) are met.

(c) For purposes of this section:

    (1) a debtor consents to an acceptance of collateral in partial satisfaction of the obligation it secures only if the debtor agrees to the terms of the acceptance in a record authenticated after default; and

    (2) a debtor consents to an acceptance of collateral in full satisfaction of the obligation it secures only if the debtor agrees to the terms of the acceptance in a record authenticated after default or the secured party:

        (A) sends to the debtor after default a proposal that is unconditional or subject only to a condition that collateral not in the possession of the secured party be preserved or maintained;

        (B) in the proposal, proposes to accept collateral in full satisfaction of the obligation it secures; and

        (C) does not receive a notification of objection authenticated by the debtor within 20 days after the proposal is sent.

(d) To be effective under subsection (a)(2), a notification of objection must be received by the secured party:

    (1) in the case of a person to which the proposal was sent pursuant to Section 9–621, within 20 days after notification was sent to that person; and

    (2) in other cases:

        (A) within 20 days after the last notification was sent pursuant to Section 9–621; or

        (B) if a notification was not sent, before the debtor consents to the acceptance under subsection (c).

(e) A secured party that has taken possession of collateral shall dispose of the collateral pursuant to Section 9–610 within the time specified in subsection (f) if:

    (1) 60 percent of the cash price has been paid in the case of a purchase-money security interest in consumer goods; or

    (2) 60 percent of the principal amount of the obligation secured has been paid in the case of a non-purchase-money security interest in consumer goods.

(f) To comply with subsection (e), the secured party shall dispose of the collateral:

    (1) within 90 days after taking possession; or

    (2) within any longer period to which the debtor and all secondary obligors have agreed in an agreement to that effect entered into and authenticated after default.

(g) In a consumer transaction, a secured party may not accept collateral in partial satisfaction of the obligation it secures.

§ 9–621. Notification of Proposal to Accept Collateral.

(a) A secured party that desires to accept collateral in full or partial satisfaction of the obligation it secures shall send its proposal to:

    (1) any person from which the secured party has received, before the debtor consented to the acceptance, an authenticated notification of a claim of an interest in the collateral;

    (2) any other secured party or lienholder that, 10 days before the debtor consented to the acceptance, held a security interest in or other lien on the collateral perfected by the filing of a financing statement that:

        (A) identified the collateral;

(B) was indexed under the debtor's name as of that date; and

(C) was filed in the office or offices in which to file a financing statement against the debtor covering the collateral as of that date; and

(3) any other secured party that, 10 days before the debtor consented to the acceptance, held a security interest in the collateral perfected by compliance with a statute, regulation, or treaty described in Section 9–311(a).

(b) A secured party that desires to accept collateral in partial satisfaction of the obligation it secures shall send its proposal to any secondary obligor in addition to the persons described in subsection (a).

§ 9–622. Effect of Acceptance of Collateral.

(a) A secured party's acceptance of collateral in full or partial satisfaction of the obligation it secures:

(1) discharges the obligation to the extent consented to by the debtor;

(2) transfers to the secured party all of a debtor's rights in the collateral;

(3) discharges the security interest or agricultural lien that is the subject of the debtor's consent and any subordinate security interest or other subordinate lien; and

(4) terminates any other subordinate interest.

(b) A subordinate interest is discharged or terminated under subsection (a), even if the secured party fails to comply with this article.

§ 9–623. Right to Redeem Collateral.

(a) A debtor, any secondary obligor, or any other secured party or lienholder may redeem collateral.

(b) To redeem collateral, a person shall tender:

(1) fulfillment of all obligations secured by the collateral; and

(2) the reasonable expenses and attorney's fees described in Section 9–615(a)(1).

(c) A redemption may occur at any time before a secured party:

(1) has collected collateral under Section 9–607;

(2) has disposed of collateral or entered into a contract for its disposition under Section 9–610; or

(3) has accepted collateral in full or partial satisfaction of the obligation it secures under Section 9–622.

§ 9–624. Waiver.

(a) A debtor or secondary obligor may waive the right to notification of disposition of collateral under Section 9–611 only by an agreement to that effect entered into and authenticated after default.

(b) A debtor may waive the right to require disposition of collateral under Section 9–620(e) only by an agreement to that effect entered into and authenticated after default.

(c) Except in a consumer-goods transaction, a debtor or secondary obligor may waive the right to redeem collateral under Section 9–623 only by an agreement to that effect entered into and authenticated after default.

[Subpart 2. Noncompliance with Article]

§ 9–625. Remedies for Secured Party's Failure to Comply with Article.

(a) If it is established that a secured party is not proceeding in accordance with this article, a court may order or restrain collection, enforcement, or disposition of collateral on appropriate terms and conditions.

(b) Subject to subsections (c), (d), and (f), a person is liable for damages in the amount of any loss caused by a failure to comply with this article. Loss caused by a failure to comply may include loss resulting from the debtor's inability to obtain, or increased costs of, alternative financing.

(c) Except as otherwise provided in Section 9–628:

(1) a person that, at the time of the failure, was a debtor, was an obligor, or held a security interest in or other lien on the collateral may recover damages under subsection (b) for its loss; and

(2) if the collateral is consumer goods, a person that was a debtor or a secondary obligor at the time a secured party failed to comply with this part may recover for that failure in any event an amount not less than the credit service charge plus 10 percent of the principal amount of the obligation or the time-price differential plus 10 percent of the cash price.

(d) A debtor whose deficiency is eliminated under Section 9–626 may recover damages for the loss of any surplus. However, a debtor or secondary obligor whose deficiency is eliminated or reduced under Section 9–626 may not otherwise recover under subsection (b) for noncompliance with the provisions of this part relating to collection, enforcement, disposition, or acceptance.

(e) In addition to any damages recoverable under subsection (b), the debtor, consumer obligor, or person named as a debtor in a filed record, as applicable, may recover $500 in each case from a person that:

(1) fails to comply with Section 9–208;

(2) fails to comply with Section 9–209;

(3) files a record that the person is not entitled to file under Section 9–509(a);

(4) fails to cause the secured party of record to file or send a termination statement as required by Section 9–513(a) or (c);

(5) fails to comply with Section 9–616(b)(1) and whose failure is part of a pattern, or consistent with a practice, of noncompliance; or

(6) fails to comply with Section 9–616(b)(2).

(f) A debtor or consumer obligor may recover damages under subsection (b) and, in addition, $500 in each case from a person that, without reasonable cause, fails to comply with a request under Section 9–210. A recipient of a request under Section 9–210 which never claimed an interest in the collateral or obligations that are the subject of a request under that section has a reasonable excuse for failure to comply with the request within the meaning of this subsection.

(g) If a secured party fails to comply with a request regarding a list of collateral or a statement of account under Section 9–210, the secured party may claim a security interest only as shown in the list or statement included in the request as against a person that is reasonably misled by the failure.

As amended in 2000.

§ 9–626. Action in Which Deficiency or Surplus Is in Issue.

(a) In an action arising from a transaction, other than a consumer transaction, in which the amount of a deficiency or surplus is in issue, the following rules apply:

(1) A secured party need not prove compliance with the provisions of this part relating to collection, enforcement, disposition, or acceptance unless the debtor or a secondary obligor places the secured party's compliance in issue.

(2) If the secured party's compliance is placed in issue, the secured party has the burden of establishing that the collection, enforcement, disposition, or acceptance was conducted in accordance with this part.

(3) Except as otherwise provided in Section 9–628, if a secured party fails to prove that the collection, enforcement, disposition, or acceptance was conducted in accordance with the provisions of this part relating to collection, enforcement, disposition, or acceptance, the liability of a debtor or a secondary obligor for a deficiency is limited to an amount by which the sum of the secured obligation, expenses, and attorney's fees exceeds the greater of:

(A) the proceeds of the collection, enforcement, disposition, or acceptance; or

(B) the amount of proceeds that would have been realized had the noncomplying secured party proceeded in accordance with the provisions of this part relating to collection, enforcement, disposition, or acceptance.

(4) For purposes of paragraph (3)(B), the amount of proceeds that would have been realized is equal to the sum of the secured obligation, expenses, and attorney's fees unless the secured party proves that the amount is less than that sum.

(5) If a deficiency or surplus is calculated under Section 9–615(f), the debtor or obligor has the burden of establishing that the amount of proceeds of the disposition is significantly below the range of prices that a complying disposition to a person other than the secured party, a person related to the secured party, or a secondary obligor would have brought.

(b) The limitation of the rules in subsection (a) to transactions other than consumer transactions is intended to leave to the court the determination of the proper rules in consumer transactions. The court may not infer from that limitation the nature of the proper rule in consumer transactions and may continue to apply established approaches.

§ 9–627. Determination of Whether Conduct Was Commercially Reasonable.

(a) The fact that a greater amount could have been obtained by a collection, enforcement, disposition, or acceptance at a different time or in a different method from that selected by the secured party is not of itself sufficient to preclude the secured party from establishing that the collection, enforcement, disposition, or acceptance was made in a commercially reasonable manner.

(b) A disposition of collateral is made in a commercially reasonable manner if the disposition is made:

(1) in the usual manner on any recognized market;

(2) at the price current in any recognized market at the time of the disposition; or

(3) otherwise in conformity with reasonable commercial practices among dealers in the type of property that was the subject of the disposition.

(c) A collection, enforcement, disposition, or acceptance is commercially reasonable if it has been approved:

(1) in a judicial proceeding;

(2) by a bona fide creditors' committee;

(3) by a representative of creditors; or

(4) by an assignee for the benefit of creditors.

(d) Approval under subsection (c) need not be obtained, and lack of approval does not mean that the collection, enforcement, disposition, or acceptance is not commercially reasonable.

§ 9–628. Nonliability and Limitation on Liability of Secured Party; Liability of Secondary Obligor.

(a) Unless a secured party knows that a person is a debtor or obligor, knows the identity of the person, and knows how to communicate with the person:

(1) the secured party is not liable to the person, or to a secured party or lienholder that has filed a financing statement against the person, for failure to comply with this article; and

(2) the secured party's failure to comply with this article does not affect the liability of the person for a deficiency.

(b) A secured party is not liable because of its status as secured party:

(1) to a person that is a debtor or obligor, unless the secured party knows:

(A) that the person is a debtor or obligor;

(B) the identity of the person; and

(C) how to communicate with the person; or

(2) to a secured party or lienholder that has filed a financing statement against a person, unless the secured party knows:

(A) that the person is a debtor; and

(B) the identity of the person.

(c) A secured party is not liable to any person, and a person's liability for a deficiency is not affected, because of any act or omission arising out of the secured party's reasonable belief that a transaction is not a consumer-goods transaction or a consumer transaction or that goods are not consumer goods, if the secured party's belief is based on its reasonable reliance on:

(1) a debtor's representation concerning the purpose for which collateral was to be used, acquired, or held; or

(2) an obligor's representation concerning the purpose for which a secured obligation was incurred.

(d) A secured party is not liable to any person under Section 9–625(c)(2) for its failure to comply with Section 9–616.

(e) A secured party is not liable under Section 9–625(c)(2) more than once with respect to any one secured obligation.

Part 7 Transition

§ 9–701. Effective Date.

This [Act] takes effect on July 1, 2001.

§ 9–702. Savings Clause.

(a) Except as otherwise provided in this part, this [Act] applies to a transaction or lien within its scope, even if the transaction or lien was entered into or created before this [Act] takes effect.

(b) Except as otherwise provided in subsection (c) and Sections 9–703 through 9–709:

(1) transactions and liens that were not governed by [former Article 9], were validly entered into or created before this [Act] takes effect, and would be subject to this [Act] if they had been entered into or created after this [Act] takes effect, and the rights, duties, and interests flowing from those transactions and liens remain valid after this [Act] takes effect; and

(2) the transactions and liens may be terminated, completed, consummated, and enforced as required or permitted by this [Act] or by the law that otherwise would apply if this [Act] had not taken effect.

(c) This [Act] does not affect an action, case, or proceeding commenced before this [Act] takes effect.

As amended in 2000.

§ 9–703. Security Interest Perfected before Effective Date.

(a) A security interest that is enforceable immediately before this [Act] takes effect and would have priority over the rights of a person that becomes a lien creditor at that time is a perfected security interest under this [Act] if, when this [Act] takes effect, the applicable requirements for enforceability and perfection under this [Act] are satisfied without further action.

(b) Except as otherwise provided in Section 9–705, if, immediately before this [Act] takes effect, a security interest is enforceable and would have priority over the rights of a person that becomes a lien creditor at that time, but the applicable requirements for enforceability or perfection under this [Act] are not satisfied when this [Act] takes effect, the security interest:

(1) is a perfected security interest for one year after this [Act] takes effect;

(2) remains enforceable thereafter only if the security interest becomes enforceable under Section 9–203 before the year expires; and

(3) remains perfected thereafter only if the applicable requirements for perfection under this [Act] are satisfied before the year expires.

§ 9–704. Security Interest Unperfected before Effective Date.

A security interest that is enforceable immediately before this [Act] takes effect but which would be subordinate to the rights of a person that becomes a lien creditor at that time:

(1) remains an enforceable security interest for one year after this [Act] takes effect;

(2) remains enforceable thereafter if the security interest becomes enforceable under Section 9–203 when this [Act] takes effect or within one year thereafter; and

(3) becomes perfected:

(A) without further action, when this [Act] takes effect if the applicable requirements for perfection under this [Act] are satisfied before or at that time; or

(B) when the applicable requirements for perfection are satisfied if the requirements are satisfied after that time.

§ 9–705. Effectiveness of Action Taken before Effective Date.

(a) If action, other than the filing of a financing statement, is taken before this [Act] takes effect and the action would have resulted in priority of a security interest over the rights of a person that becomes a lien creditor had the security interest become enforceable before

this [Act] takes effect, the action is effective to perfect a security interest that attaches under this [Act] within one year after this [Act] takes effect. An attached security interest becomes unperfected one year after this [Act] takes effect unless the security interest becomes a perfected security interest under this [Act] before the expiration of that period.

(b) The filing of a financing statement before this [Act] takes effect is effective to perfect a security interest to the extent the filing would satisfy the applicable requirements for perfection under this [Act].

(c) This [Act] does not render ineffective an effective financing statement that, before this [Act] takes effect, is filed and satisfies the applicable requirements for perfection under the law of the jurisdiction governing perfection as provided in [former Section 9–103]. However, except as otherwise provided in subsections (d) and (e) and Section 9–706, the financing statement ceases to be effective at the earlier of:

(1) the time the financing statement would have ceased to be effective under the law of the jurisdiction in which it is filed; or

(2) June 30, 2006.

(d) The filing of a continuation statement after this [Act] takes effect does not continue the effectiveness of the financing statement filed before this [Act] takes effect. However, upon the timely filing of a continuation statement after this [Act] takes effect and in accordance with the law of the jurisdiction governing perfection as provided in Part 3, the effectiveness of a financing statement filed in the same office in that jurisdiction before this [Act] takes effect continues for the period provided by the law of that jurisdiction.

(e) Subsection (c)(2) applies to a financing statement that, before this [Act] takes effect, is filed against a transmitting utility and satisfies the applicable requirements for perfection under the law of the jurisdiction governing perfection as provided in [former Section 9–103] only to the extent that Part 3 provides that the law of a jurisdiction other than the jurisdiction in which the financing statement is filed governs perfection of a security interest in collateral covered by the financing statement.

(f) A financing statement that includes a financing statement filed before this [Act] takes effect and a continuation statement filed after this [Act] takes effect is effective only to the extent that it satisfies the requirements of Part 5 for an initial financing statement.

§ 9–706. When Initial Financing Statement Suffices to Continue Effectiveness of Financing Statement.

(a) The filing of an initial financing statement in the office specified in Section 9–501 continues the effectiveness of a financing statement filed before this [Act] takes effect if:

(1) the filing of an initial financing statement in that office would be effective to perfect a security interest under this [Act];

(2) the pre-effective-date financing statement was filed in an office in another State or another office in this State; and

(3) the initial financing statement satisfies subsection (c).

(b) The filing of an initial financing statement under subsection (a) continues the effectiveness of the pre-effective-date financing statement:

(1) if the initial financing statement is filed before this [Act] takes effect, for the period provided in [former Section 9–403] with respect to a financing statement; and

(2) if the initial financing statement is filed after this [Act] takes effect, for the period provided in Section 9–515 with respect to an initial financing statement.

(c) To be effective for purposes of subsection (a), an initial financing statement must:

(1) satisfy the requirements of Part 5 for an initial financing statement;

(2) identify the pre-effective-date financing statement by indicating the office in which the financing statement was filed and providing the dates of filing and file numbers, if any, of the financing statement and of the most recent continuation statement filed with respect to the financing statement; and

(3) indicate that the pre-effective-date financing statement remains effective.

§ 9–707. Amendment of Pre-Effective-Date Financing Statement.

(a) In this section, "Pre-effective-date financing statement" means a financing statement filed before this [Act] takes effect.

(b) After this [Act] takes effect, a person may add or delete collateral covered by, continue or terminate the effectiveness of, or otherwise amend the information provided in, a pre-effective-date financing statement only in accordance with the law of the jurisdiction governing perfection as provided in Part 3. However, the effectiveness of a pre-effective-date financing statement also may be terminated in accordance with the law of the jurisdiction in which the financing statement is filed.

(c) Except as otherwise provided in subsection (d), if the law of this State governs perfection of a security interest, the information in a pre-effective-date financing statement may be amended after this [Act] takes effect only if:

(1) the pre-effective-date financing statement and an amendment are filed in the office specified in Section 9–501;

(2) an amendment is filed in the office specified in Section 9–501 concurrently with, or after the filing in that office of, an initial financing statement that satisfies Section 9–706(c); or

(3) an initial financing statement that provides the information as amended and satisfies Section 9–706(c) is filed in the office specified in Section 9–501.

(d) If the law of this State governs perfection of a security interest, the effectiveness of a pre-effective-date financing statement may be continued only under Section 9–705(d) and (f) or 9–706.

(e) Whether or not the law of this State governs perfection of a security interest, the effectiveness of a pre-effective-date financing statement filed in this State may be terminated after this [Act] takes effect by filing a termination statement in the office in which the pre-effective-date financing statement is filed, unless an initial financing statement that satisfies Section 9–706(c) has been filed in the office specified by the law of the jurisdiction governing perfection as provided in Part 3 as the office in which to file a financing statement.

As amended in 2000.

§ 9–708. Persons Entitled to File Initial Financing Statement or Continuation Statement.

A person may file an initial financing statement or a continuation statement under this part if:

(1) the secured party of record authorizes the filing; and

(2) the filing is necessary under this part:

(A) to continue the effectiveness of a financing statement filed before this [Act] takes effect; or

(B) to perfect or continue the perfection of a security interest.

As amended in 2000.

§ 9–709. Priority.

(a) This [Act] determines the priority of conflicting claims to collateral. However, if the relative priorities of the claims were established before this [Act] takes effect, [former Article 9] determines priority.

(b) For purposes of Section 9–322(a), the priority of a security interest that becomes enforceable under Section 9–203 of this [Act] dates from the time this [Act] takes effect if the security interest is perfected under this [Act] by the filing of a financing statement before this [Act] takes effect which would not have been effective to perfect the security interest under [former Article 9]. This subsection does not apply to conflicting security interests each of which is perfected by the filing of such a financing statement.

As amended in 2000.

APPENDIX D
The Sarbanes-Oxley Act of 2002
(Excerpts and Explanatory Comments)

Note: The author's explanatory comments appear in italics following the excerpt from each section.

SECTION 302
Corporate responsibility for financial reports[1]

(a) Regulations required

The Commission shall, by rule, require, for each company filing periodic reports under section 13(a) or 15(d) of the Securities Exchange Act of 1934 (15 U.S.C. 78m, 78o(d)), that the principal executive officer or officers and the principal financial officer or officers, or persons performing similar functions, certify in each annual or quarterly report filed or submitted under either such section of such Act that—

(1) the signing officer has reviewed the report;

(2) based on the officer's knowledge, the report does not contain any untrue statement of a material fact or omit to state a material fact necessary in order to make the statements made, in light of the circumstances under which such statements were made, not misleading;

(3) based on such officer's knowledge, the financial statements, and other financial information included in the report, fairly present in all material respects the financial condition and results of operations of the issuer as of, and for, the periods presented in the report;

(4) the signing officers—

(A) are responsible for establishing and maintaining internal controls;

(B) have designed such internal controls to ensure that material information relating to the issuer and its consolidated subsidiaries is made known to such officers by others within those entities, particularly during the period in which the periodic reports are being prepared;

(C) have evaluated the effectiveness of the issuer's internal controls as of a date within 90 days prior to the report; and

(D) have presented in the report their conclusions about the effectiveness of their internal controls based on their evaluation as of that date;

(5) the signing officers have disclosed to the issuer's auditors and the audit committee of the board of directors (or persons fulfilling the equivalent function)—

(A) all significant deficiencies in the design or operation of internal controls which could adversely affect the issuer's ability to record, process, summarize, and report financial data and have identified for the issuer's auditors any material weaknesses in internal controls; and

(B) any fraud, whether or not material, that involves management or other employees who have a significant role in the issuer's internal controls; and

(6) the signing officers have indicated in the report whether or not there were significant changes in internal controls or in other factors that could significantly affect internal controls subsequent to the date of their evaluation, including any corrective actions with regard to significant deficiencies and material weaknesses.

(b) Foreign reincorporations have no effect

Nothing in this section shall be interpreted or applied in any way to allow any issuer to lessen the legal force of the statement required under this section, by an issuer having reincorporated or having engaged in any other transaction that resulted in the transfer of the corporate domicile or offices of the issuer from inside the United States to outside of the United States.

(c) Deadline

The rules required by subsection (a) of this section shall be effective not later than 30 days after July 30, 2002.

*　*　*　*

EXPLANATORY COMMENTS: *Section 302 requires the chief executive officer (CEO) and chief financial officer (CFO) of each public company to certify that they have reviewed the company's quarterly and annual reports to be filed with the Securities and Exchange Commission (SEC). The CEO and CFO must certify that, based on their knowledge, the reports do not contain any untrue statement of a material fact or any half-truth that would make the report misleading, and that the information contained in the reports fairly presents the company's financial condition.*

In addition, this section also requires the CEO and CFO to certify that they have created and designed an internal control system for their company and have recently evaluated that system to ensure that it is effectively providing them with relevant and accurate financial information. If the signing officers have found any significant deficiencies or weaknesses in the company's system or have discovered any evidence of fraud, they must have reported the situation, and any corrective actions they have taken, to the auditors and the audit committee.

---

1. This section of the Sarbanes-Oxley Act is codified at 15 U.S.C. Section 7241.

SECTION 306

Insider trades during pension fund blackout periods[2]

(a) Prohibition of insider trading during pension fund blackout periods

(1) In general

Except to the extent otherwise provided by rule of the Commission pursuant to paragraph (3), it shall be unlawful for any director or executive officer of an issuer of any equity security (other than an exempted security), directly or indirectly, to purchase, sell, or otherwise acquire or transfer any equity security of the issuer (other than an exempted security) during any blackout period with respect to such equity security if such director or officer acquires such equity security in connection with his or her service or employment as a director or executive officer.

(2) Remedy

(A) In general

Any profit realized by a director or executive officer referred to in paragraph (1) from any purchase, sale, or other acquisition or transfer in violation of this subsection shall inure to and be recoverable by the issuer, irrespective of any intention on the part of such director or executive officer in entering into the transaction.

(B) Actions to recover profits

An action to recover profits in accordance with this subsection may be instituted at law or in equity in any court of competent jurisdiction by the issuer, or by the owner of any security of the issuer in the name and in behalf of the issuer if the issuer fails or refuses to bring such action within 60 days after the date of request, or fails diligently to prosecute the action thereafter, except that no such suit shall be brought more than 2 years after the date on which such profit was realized.

(3) Rulemaking authorized

The Commission shall, in consultation with the Secretary of Labor, issue rules to clarify the application of this subsection and to prevent evasion thereof. Such rules shall provide for the application of the requirements of paragraph (1) with respect to entities treated as a single employer with respect to an issuer under section 414(b), (c), (m), or (o) of Title 26 to the extent necessary to clarify the application of such requirements and to prevent evasion thereof. Such rules may also provide for appropriate exceptions from the requirements of this subsection, including exceptions for purchases pursuant to an automatic dividend reinvestment program or purchases or sales made pursuant to an advance election.

(4) Blackout period

For purposes of this subsection, the term "blackout period", with respect to the equity securities of any issuer—

(A) means any period of more than 3 consecutive business days during which the ability of not fewer than 50 percent of the participants or beneficiaries under all individual account plans maintained by the issuer to purchase, sell, or otherwise acquire

or transfer an interest in any equity of such issuer held in such an individual account plan is temporarily suspended by the issuer or by a fiduciary of the plan; and

(B) does not include, under regulations which shall be prescribed by the Commission—

(i) a regularly scheduled period in which the participants and beneficiaries may not purchase, sell, or otherwise acquire or transfer an interest in any equity of such issuer, if such period is—

(I) incorporated into the individual account plan; and

(II) timely disclosed to employees before becoming participants under the individual account plan or as a subsequent amendment to the plan; or

(ii) any suspension described in subparagraph (A) that is imposed solely in connection with persons becoming participants or beneficiaries, or ceasing to be participants or beneficiaries, in an individual account plan by reason of a corporate merger, acquisition, divestiture, or similar transaction involving the plan or plan sponsor.

(5) Individual account plan

For purposes of this subsection, the term "individual account plan" has the meaning provided in section 1002(34) of Title 29, except that such term shall not include a one-participant retirement plan (within the meaning of section 1021(i)(8)(B) of Title 29).

(6) Notice to directors, executive officers, and the Commission

In any case in which a director or executive officer is subject to the requirements of this subsection in connection with a blackout period (as defined in paragraph (4)) with respect to any equity securities, the issuer of such equity securities shall timely notify such director or officer and the Securities and Exchange Commission of such blackout period.

*　*　*　*

EXPLANATORY COMMENTS: *Corporate pension funds typically prohibit employees from trading shares of the corporation during periods when the pension fund is undergoing significant change. Prior to 2002, however, these blackout periods did not affect the corporation's executives, who frequently received shares of the corporate stock as part of their compensation. During the collapse of Enron, for example, its pension plan was scheduled to change administrators at a time when Enron's stock price was falling. Enron's employees therefore could not sell their shares while the price was dropping, but its executives could and did sell their stock, consequently avoiding some of the losses. Section 306 was Congress's solution to the basic unfairness of this situation. This section of the act required the SEC to issue rules that prohibit any director or executive officer from trading during pension fund blackout periods. (The SEC later issued these rules, entitled Regulation Blackout Trading Restriction, or Reg BTR.) Section 306 also provided shareholders with a right to file a shareholder's derivative suit against officers and directors who have profited from trading during these blackout periods (provided that the corporation has failed to bring a suit). The officer or director can be forced to return to the corporation any profits received, regardless of whether the director or officer acted with bad intent.*

---

2. Codified at 15 U.S.C. Section 7244.

SECTION 402

Periodical and other reports[3]

* * * *

(i) Accuracy of financial reports

Each financial report that contains financial statements, and that is required to be prepared in accordance with (or reconciled to) generally accepted accounting principles under this chapter and filed with the Commission shall reflect all material correcting adjustments that have been identified by a registered public accounting firm in accordance with generally accepted accounting principles and the rules and regulations of the Commission.

(j) Off-balance sheet transactions

Not later than 180 days after July 30, 2002, the Commission shall issue final rules providing that each annual and quarterly financial report required to be filed with the Commission shall disclose all material off-balance sheet transactions, arrangements, obligations (including contingent obligations), and other relationships of the issuer with unconsolidated entities or other persons, that may have a material current or future effect on financial condition, changes in financial condition, results of operations, liquidity, capital expenditures, capital resources, or significant components of revenues or expenses.

(k) Prohibition on personal loans to executives

(1) In general

It shall be unlawful for any issuer (as defined in section 7201 of this title), directly or indirectly, including through any subsidiary, to extend or maintain credit, to arrange for the extension of credit, or to renew an extension of credit, in the form of a personal loan to or for any director or executive officer (or equivalent thereof) of that issuer. An extension of credit maintained by the issuer on July 30, 2002, shall not be subject to the provisions of this subsection, provided that there is no material modification to any term of any such extension of credit or any renewal of any such extension of credit on or after July 30, 2002.

(2) Limitation

Paragraph (1) does not preclude any home improvement and manufactured home loans (as that term is defined in section 1464 of Title 12), consumer credit (as defined in section 1602 of this title), or any extension of credit under an open end credit plan (as defined in section 1602 of this title), or a charge card (as defined in section 1637(c)(4)(e) of this title), or any extension of credit by a broker or dealer registered under section 78o of this title to an employee of that broker or dealer to buy, trade, or carry securities, that is permitted under rules or regulations of the Board of Governors of the Federal Reserve System pursuant to section 78g of this title (other than an extension of credit that would be used to purchase the stock of that issuer), that is—

(A) made or provided in the ordinary course of the consumer credit business of such issuer;

(B) of a type that is generally made available by such issuer to the public; and

(C) made by such issuer on market terms, or terms that are no more favorable than those offered by the issuer to the general public for such extensions of credit.

(3) Rule of construction for certain loans

Paragraph (1) does not apply to any loan made or maintained by an insured depository institution (as defined in section 1813 of Title 12), if the loan is subject to the insider lending restrictions of section 375b of Title 12.

(l) Real time issuer disclosures

Each issuer reporting under subsection (a) of this section or section 78o(d) of this title shall disclose to the public on a rapid and current basis such additional information concerning material changes in the financial condition or operations of the issuer, in plain English, which may include trend and qualitative information and graphic presentations, as the Commission determines, by rule, is necessary or useful for the protection of investors and in the public interest.

EXPLANATORY COMMENTS: *Corporate executives during the Enron era typically received extremely large salaries, significant bonuses, and abundant stock options, even when the companies for which they worked were suffering. Executives were also routinely given personal loans from corporate funds, many of which were never paid back. The average large company during that period loaned almost $1 million a year to top executives, and some companies, including Tyco International and Adelphia Communications Corporation, loaned hundreds of millions of dollars to their executives every year. Section 402 amended the 1934 Securities Exchange Act to prohibit public companies from making personal loans to executive officers and directors. There are a few exceptions to this prohibition, such as home-improvement loans made in the ordinary course of business. Note also that while loans are forbidden, outright gifts are not. A corporation is free to give gifts to its executives, including cash, provided that these gifts are disclosed on its financial reports. The idea is that corporate directors will be deterred from making substantial gifts to their executives by the disclosure requirement—particularly if the corporation's financial condition is questionable—because making such gifts could be perceived as abusing their authority.*

SECTION 403

Directors, officers, and principal stockholders[4]

(a) Disclosures required

(1) Directors, officers, and principal stockholders required to file

Every person who is directly or indirectly the beneficial owner of more than 10 percent of any class of any equity security (other than an exempted security) which is registered pursuant to section 78l of this title, or who is a director or an officer of the issuer of such security, shall file the statements required by this subsection with the Commission (and, if such security is registered on a national securities exchange, also with the exchange).

(2) Time of filing

The statements required by this subsection shall be filed—

---

3. This section of the Sarbanes-Oxley Act amended some of the provisions of the 1934 Securities Exchange Act and added the paragraphs reproduced here at 15 U.S.C. Section 78m.

4. This section of the Sarbanes-Oxley Act amended the disclosure provisions of the 1934 Securities Exchange Act, at 15 U.S.C. Section 78p.

(A) at the time of the registration of such security on a national securities exchange or by the effective date of a registration statement filed pursuant to section 78l(g) of this title;

(B) within 10 days after he or she becomes such beneficial owner, director, or officer;

(C) if there has been a change in such ownership, or if such person shall have purchased or sold a security-based swap agreement (as defined in section 206(b) of the Gramm-Leach-Bliley Act (15 U.S.C. 78c note)) involving such equity security, before the end of the second business day following the day on which the subject transaction has been executed, or at such other time as the Commission shall establish, by rule, in any case in which the Commission determines that such 2-day period is not feasible.

(3) Contents of statements

A statement filed—

(A) under subparagraph (A) or (B) of paragraph (2) shall contain a statement of the amount of all equity securities of such issuer of which the filing person is the beneficial owner; and

(B) under subparagraph (C) of such paragraph shall indicate ownership by the filing person at the date of filing, any such changes in such ownership, and such purchases and sales of the security-based swap agreements as have occurred since the most recent such filing under such subparagraph.

(4) Electronic filing and availability

Beginning not later than 1 year after July 30, 2002—

(A) a statement filed under subparagraph (C) of paragraph (2) shall be filed electronically;

(B) the Commission shall provide each such statement on a publicly accessible Internet site not later than the end of the business day following that filing; and

(C) the issuer (if the issuer maintains a corporate website) shall provide that statement on that corporate website, not later than the end of the business day following that filing.

❋   ❋   ❋   ❋

EXPLANATORY COMMENTS: *This section dramatically shortens the time period provided in the Securities Exchange Act of 1934 for disclosing transactions by insiders. The prior law stated that most transactions had to be reported within ten days of the beginning of the following month, although certain transactions did not have to be reported until the following fiscal year (within the first forty-five days). Because some of the insider trading that occurred during the Enron fiasco did not have to be disclosed (and was therefore not discovered) until long after the transactions, Congress added this section to reduce the time period for making disclosures. Under Section 403, most transactions by insiders must be electronically filed with the SEC within two business days. Also, any company that maintains a Web site must post these SEC filings on its site by the end of the next business day. Congress enacted this section in the belief that if insiders are required to file reports of their transactions promptly with the SEC, companies will do more to police themselves and prevent insider trading.*

SECTION 404

Management assessment of internal controls[5]

(a) Rules required

The Commission shall prescribe rules requiring each annual report required by section 78m(a) or 78o(d) of this title to contain an internal control report, which shall—

(1) state the responsibility of management for establishing and maintaining an adequate internal control structure and procedures for financial reporting; and

(2) contain an assessment, as of the end of the most recent fiscal year of the issuer, of the effectiveness of the internal control structure and procedures of the issuer for financial reporting.

(b) Internal control evaluation and reporting

With respect to the internal control assessment required by subsection (a) of this section, each registered public accounting firm that prepares or issues the audit report for the issuer shall attest to, and report on, the assessment made by the management of the issuer. An attestation made under this subsection shall be made in accordance with standards for attestation engagements issued or adopted by the Board. Any such attestation shall not be the subject of a separate engagement.

❋   ❋   ❋   ❋

EXPLANATORY COMMENTS: *This section was enacted to prevent corporate executives from claiming they were ignorant of significant errors in their companies' financial reports. For instance, several CEOs testified before Congress that they simply had no idea that the corporations' financial statements were off by billions of dollars. Congress therefore passed Section 404, which requires each annual report to contain a description and assessment of the company's internal control structure and financial reporting procedures. The section also requires that an audit be conducted of the internal control assessment, as well as the financial statements contained in the report. This section goes hand in hand with Section 302 (which, as discussed previously, requires various certifications attesting to the accuracy of the information in financial reports).*

Section 404 has been one of the more controversial and expensive provisions in the Sarbanes-Oxley Act because it requires companies to assess their own internal financial controls to make sure that their financial statements are reliable and accurate. A corporation might need to set up a disclosure committee and a coordinator, establish codes of conduct for accounting and financial personnel, create documentation procedures, provide training, and outline the individuals who are responsible for performing each of the procedures. Companies that were already well managed have not experienced substantial difficulty complying with this section. Other companies, however, have spent millions of dollars setting up, documenting, and evaluating their internal financial control systems. Although initially creating the internal financial control system is a one-time-only expense, the costs of maintaining and evaluating it are ongoing. Some corporations that spent considerable sums complying with Section 404 have been able to offset these costs by discovering and correcting inefficiencies or frauds within their systems. Nevertheless, it is unlikely that any corporation will find compliance with this section to be inexpensive.

---

5. Codified at 15 U.S.C. Section 7262.

SECTION 802(a)

Destruction, alteration, or falsification of records in Federal investigations and bankruptcy[6]

Whoever knowingly alters, destroys, mutilates, conceals, covers up, falsifies, or makes a false entry in any record, document, or tangible object with the intent to impede, obstruct, or influence the investigation or proper administration of any matter within the jurisdiction of any department or agency of the United States or any case filed under title 11, or in relation to or contemplation of any such matter or case, shall be fined under this title, imprisoned not more than 20 years, or both.

Destruction of corporate audit records[7]

(a) (1) Any accountant who conducts an audit of an issuer of securities to which section 10A(a) of the Securities Exchange Act of 1934 (15 U.S.C. 78j-1(a)) applies, shall maintain all audit or review workpapers for a period of 5 years from the end of the fiscal period in which the audit or review was concluded.

(2) The Securities and Exchange Commission shall promulgate, within 180 days, after adequate notice and an opportunity for comment, such rules and regulations, as are reasonably necessary, relating to the retention of relevant records such as workpapers, documents that form the basis of an audit or review, memoranda, correspondence, communications, other documents, and records (including electronic records) which are created, sent, or received in connection with an audit or review and contain conclusions, opinions, analyses, or financial data relating to such an audit or review, which is conducted by any accountant who conducts an audit of an issuer of securities to which section 10A(a) of the Securities Exchange Act of 1934 (15 U.S.C. 78j-1(a)) applies. The Commission may, from time to time, amend or supplement the rules and regulations that it is required to promulgate under this section, after adequate notice and an opportunity for comment, in order to ensure that such rules and regulations adequately comport with the purposes of this section.

(b) Whoever knowingly and willfully violates subsection (a)(1), or any rule or regulation promulgated by the Securities and Exchange Commission under subsection (a)(2), shall be fined under this title, imprisoned not more than 10 years, or both.

(c) Nothing in this section shall be deemed to diminish or relieve any person of any other duty or obligation imposed by Federal or State law or regulation to maintain, or refrain from destroying, any document.

* * * *

EXPLANATORY COMMENTS: *Section 802(a) enacted two new statutes that punish those who alter or destroy documents. The first statute is not specifically limited to securities fraud cases. It provides that anyone who alters, destroys, or falsifies records in federal investigations or bankruptcy may be criminally prosecuted and sentenced to a fine or to up to twenty years in prison, or both. The second statute requires auditors of public companies to keep all audit or review working papers for five years but expressly allows the SEC to amend or supplement these requirements as it sees fit. The SEC has, in fact,*

amended this section by issuing a rule that requires auditors who audit reporting companies to retain working papers for seven years from the conclusion of the review. Section 802(a) further provides that anyone who knowingly and willfully violates this statute is subject to criminal prosecution and can be sentenced to a fine, imprisoned for up to ten years, or both if convicted.

This portion of the Sarbanes-Oxley Act implicitly recognizes that persons who are under investigation often are tempted to respond by destroying or falsifying documents that might prove their complicity in wrongdoing. The severity of the punishment should provide a strong incentive for these individuals to resist the temptation.

SECTION 804

Time limitations on the commencement of civil actions arising under Acts of Congress[8]

(a) Except as otherwise provided by law, a civil action arising under an Act of Congress enacted after the date of the enactment of this section may not be commenced later than 4 years after the cause of action accrues.

(b) Notwithstanding subsection (a), a private right of action that involves a claim of fraud, deceit, manipulation, or contrivance in contravention of a regulatory requirement concerning the securities laws, as defined in section 3(a)(47) of the Securities Exchange Act of 1934 (15 U.S.C. 78c(a)(47)), may be brought not later than the earlier of—

(1) 2 years after the discovery of the facts constituting the violation; or

(2) 5 years after such violation.

* * * *

EXPLANATORY COMMENTS: *Prior to the enactment of this section, Section 10(b) of the Securities Exchange Act of 1934 had no express statute of limitations. The courts generally required plaintiffs to have filed suit within one year from the date that they should (using due diligence) have discovered that a fraud had been committed but no later than three years after the fraud occurred. Section 804 extends this period by specifying that plaintiffs must file a lawsuit within two years after they discover (or should have discovered) a fraud but no later than five years after the fraud's occurrence. This provision has prevented the courts from dismissing numerous securities fraud lawsuits.*

SECTION 806

Civil action to protect against retaliation in fraud cases[9]

(a) Whistleblower protection for employees of publicly traded companies.—

No company with a class of securities registered under section 12 of the Securities Exchange Act of 1934 (15 U.S.C. 78l), or that is required to file reports under section 15(d) of the Securities Exchange Act of 1934 (15 U.S.C. 78o(d)), or any officer, employee, contractor, subcontractor, or agent of such company, may discharge, demote, suspend, threaten, harass, or in any other manner discriminate against an

---

6. Codified at 15 U.S.C. Section 1519.
7. Codified at 15 U.S.C. Section 1520.

8. Codified at 28 U.S.C. Section 1658.
9. Codified at 18 U.S.C. Section 1514A.

employee in the terms and conditions of employment because of any lawful act done by the employee—

(1) to provide information, cause information to be provided, or otherwise assist in an investigation regarding any conduct which the employee reasonably believes constitutes a violation of section 1341, 1343, 1344, or 1348, any rule or regulation of the Securities and Exchange Commission, or any provision of Federal law relating to fraud against shareholders, when the information or assistance is provided to or the investigation is conducted by—

(A) a Federal regulatory or law enforcement agency;

(B) any Member of Congress or any committee of Congress; or

(C) a person with supervisory authority over the employee (or such other person working for the employer who has the authority to investigate, discover, or terminate misconduct); or

(2) to file, cause to be filed, testify, participate in, or otherwise assist in a proceeding filed or about to be filed (with any knowledge of the employer) relating to an alleged violation of section 1341, 1343, 1344, or 1348, any rule or regulation of the Securities and Exchange Commission, or any provision of Federal law relating to fraud against shareholders.

(b) Enforcement action.—

(1) In general.—A person who alleges discharge or other discrimination by any person in violation of subsection (a) may seek relief under subsection (c), by—

(A) filing a complaint with the Secretary of Labor; or

(B) if the Secretary has not issued a final decision within 180 days of the filing of the complaint and there is no showing that such delay is due to the bad faith of the claimant, bringing an action at law or equity for de novo review in the appropriate district court of the United States, which shall have jurisdiction over such an action without regard to the amount in controversy.

(2) Procedure.—

(A) In general.—An action under paragraph (1)(A) shall be governed under the rules and procedures set forth in section 42121(b) of title 49, United States Code.

(B) Exception.—Notification made under section 42121(b)(1) of title 49, United States Code, shall be made to the person named in the complaint and to the employer.

(C) Burdens of proof.—An action brought under paragraph (1)(B) shall be governed by the legal burdens of proof set forth in section 42121(b) of title 49, United States Code.

(D) Statute of limitations.—An action under paragraph (1) shall be commenced not later than 90 days after the date on which the violation occurs.

(c) Remedies.—

(1) In general.—An employee prevailing in any action under subsection (b)(1) shall be entitled to all relief necessary to make the employee whole.

(2) Compensatory damages.—Relief for any action under paragraph (1) shall include—

(A) reinstatement with the same seniority status that the employee would have had, but for the discrimination;

(B) the amount of back pay, with interest; and

(C) compensation for any special damages sustained as a result of the discrimination, including litigation costs, expert witness fees, and reasonable attorney fees.

(d) Rights retained by employee.—Nothing in this section shall be deemed to diminish the rights, privileges, or remedies of any employee under any Federal or State law, or under any collective bargaining agreement.

EXPLANATORY COMMENTS: *Section 806 is one of several provisions that were included in the Sarbanes-Oxley Act to encourage and protect whistleblowers—that is, employees who report their employer's alleged violations of securities law to the authorities. This section applies to employees, agents, and independent contractors who work for publicly traded companies or testify about such a company during an investigation. It sets up an administrative procedure at the U.S. Department of Labor for individuals who claim that their employer retaliated against them (fired or demoted them, for example) for blowing the whistle on the employer's wrongful conduct. It also allows the award of civil damages— including back pay, reinstatement, special damages, attorneys' fees, and court costs—to employees who prove that they suffered retaliation. Since this provision was enacted, whistleblowers have filed numerous complaints with the U.S. Department of Labor under this section.*

SECTION 807

Securities fraud[10]

Whoever knowingly executes, or attempts to execute, a scheme or artifice—

(1) to defraud any person in connection with any security of an issuer with a class of securities registered under section 12 of the Securities Exchange Act of 1934 (15 U.S.C. 78l) or that is required to file reports under section 15(d) of the Securities Exchange Act of 1934 (15 U.S.C. 78o(d)); or

(2) to obtain, by means of false or fraudulent pretenses, representations, or promises, any money or property in connection with the purchase or sale of any security of an issuer with a class of securities registered under section 12 of the Securities Exchange Act of 1934 (15 U.S.C. 78l) or that is required to file reports under section 15(d) of the Securities Exchange Act of 1934 (15 U.S.C. 78o(d)); shall be fined under this title, or imprisoned not more than 25 years, or both.

*　　*　　*　　*

EXPLANATORY COMMENTS: *Section 807 adds a new provision to the federal criminal code that addresses securities fraud. Prior to 2002, federal securities law had already made it a crime—under Section 10(b) of the Securities Exchange Act of 1934 and SEC Rule 10b-5, both of which are discussed in Chapter 30—to intentionally defraud someone in connection with a purchase or sale of securities, but the offense was not listed in the federal criminal code. Also, paragraph 2 of Section 807 goes beyond what is prohibited under securities law by making it a crime to obtain by means of false or fraudulent pretenses any money or property from the purchase or sale of securities. This new provision allows violators to be punished by up to twenty-five years in prison, a fine, or both.*

---

10. Codified at 18 U.S.C. Section 1348.

SECTION 906

Failure of corporate officers to certify financial reports[11]

(a) Certification of periodic financial reports.—Each periodic report containing financial statements filed by an issuer with the Securities Exchange Commission pursuant to section 13(a) or 15(d) of the Securities Exchange Act of 1934 (15 U.S.C. 78m(a) or 78o(d)) shall be accompanied by a written statement by the chief executive officer and chief financial officer (or equivalent thereof) of the issuer.

(b) Content.—The statement required under subsection (a) shall certify that the periodic report containing the financial statements fully complies with the requirements of section 13(a) or 15(d) of the Securities Exchange Act of 1934 (15 U.S.C. 78m or 78o(d)) and that information contained in the periodic report fairly presents, in all material respects, the financial condition and results of operations of the issuer.

(c) Criminal penalties.—Whoever—

(1) certifies any statement as set forth in subsections (a) and (b) of this section knowing that the periodic report accompanying the statement does not comport with all the requirements set forth in this section shall be fined not more than $1,000,000 or imprisoned not more than 10 years, or both; or

(2) willfully certifies any statement as set forth in subsections (a) and (b) of this section knowing that the periodic report accompanying the statement does not comport with all the requirements set forth in this section shall be fined not more than $5,000,000, or imprisoned not more than 20 years, or both.

EXPLANATORY COMMENTS: *As previously discussed, under Section 302 a corporation's CEO and CFO are required to certify that they believe the quarterly and annual reports their company files with the SEC are accurate and fairly present the company's financial condition. Section 906 adds "teeth" to these requirements by authorizing criminal penalties for those officers who intentionally certify inaccurate SEC filings. Knowing violations of the requirements are punishable by a fine of up to $1 million, ten years' imprisonment, or both. Willful violators may be fined up to $5 million, sentenced to up to twenty years' imprisonment, or both. Although the difference between a knowing and a willful violation is not entirely clear, the section is obviously intended to remind corporate officers of the serious consequences of certifying inaccurate reports to the SEC.*

---

11. Codified at 18 U.S.C. Section 1350.

APPENDIX E
Answers to the Even-Numbered
For Review Questions

CHAPTER 1

2A. *Common law tradition*
Because of our colonial heritage, much of American law is based on the English legal system. In that system, after the Norman Conquest, the king's courts sought to establish a uniform set of rules for the entire country. What evolved in these courts was the common law—a body of general legal principles that applied throughout the entire English realm. Courts developed the common law rules from the principles underlying judges' decisions in actual legal controversies.

4A. *Remedies*
An award of compensation in either money or property, including land, is a remedy at law. Remedies in equity include a decree for *specific performance* (an order to perform what was promised), an *injunction* (an order directing a party to do or refrain from doing a particular act), and *rescission* (cancellation) of a contract (and a return of the parties to the positions that they held before the contract's formation). As a rule, courts will grant an equitable remedy only when the remedy at law (money damages) is inadequate. Remedies in equity on the whole are more flexible than remedies at law.

CHAPTER 2

2A. *Commercial activities*
To prevent states from establishing laws and regulations that would interfere with trade and commerce among the states, the Constitution expressly delegated to the national government the power to regulate interstate commerce. The commerce clause (Article I, Section 8, of the U.S. Constitution) expressly permits Congress "[t]o regulate Commerce with foreign Nations, and among the several States, and with the Indian Tribes."

4A. *Bill of Rights*
The Bill of Rights consists of the first ten amendments to the U.S. Constitution. Adopted in 1791, the Bill of Rights embodies protections for individuals against interference by the federal government. Some of the protections also apply to business entities. The First Amendment guarantees the freedoms of religion, speech, and the press, and the rights to assemble peaceably and to petition the government.

CHAPTER 3

2A. *Jurisdiction*
To hear a case, a court must have jurisdiction over the person against whom the suit is brought or over the property involved in the suit. The court must also have jurisdiction over the subject matter.

Generally, courts apply a "sliding-scale" standard to determine when it is proper to exercise jurisdiction over a defendant whose only connection with the jurisdiction is the Internet.

4A. *Pleadings, discovery, and electronic filing*
The pleadings include a plaintiff's complaint and a defendant's answer (and the counterclaim and reply). The pleadings inform each party of the other's claims and specify the issues involved in a case. Discovery is the process of obtaining information and evidence about a case from the other party or third parties. Discovery entails gaining access to witnesses, documents, records, and other types of evidence. Electronic discovery differs in its subject (e-media rather than traditional sources of information). Electronic filing involves the filing of court documents in electronic media, typically over the Internet.

CHAPTER 4

2A. *Purpose and categories of torts*
Generally, the purpose of tort law is to provide remedies for the invasion of legally recognized and protected interests (personal safety, freedom of movement, property, and some intangibles, including privacy and reputation). The two broad categories of torts are intentional and unintentional.

4A. *Strict liability*
Strict liability is liability without fault. Strict liability for damages proximately caused by an abnormally dangerous or exceptional activity, or the keeping of dangerous animals, is an application of this doctrine. Another significant application of strict liability is in the area of product liability.

CHAPTER 5

2A. *Trademarks and patents*
As stated in Article I, Section 8, of the Constitution, Congress is authorized "[t]o promote the Progress of Science and useful Arts, by securing for limited Times to Authors and Inventors the exclusive Right to their respective Writings and Discoveries." Laws protecting patents and trademarks, as well copyrights, are designed to protect and reward inventive and artistic creativity.

4A. *Trade secrets*
Trade secrets are business processes and information that are not or cannot be patented, copyrighted, or trademarked. Trade secrets consist of generally anything that makes an individual company unique and that would have value to a competitor. The Uniform Trade Secrets Act, the Economic Espionage Act, and the common law offer trade secrets protection.

CHAPTER 6

2A. *Types of crime and white-collar crime*
Traditionally, crimes have been grouped into the following categories: violent crime (crimes against persons), property crime, public order crime, white-collar crime, and organized crime. White-collar crime is an illegal act or series of acts committed by an individual or business entity using some nonviolent means usually in the course of a legitimate occupation.

4A. *Constitutional safeguards and criminal process*
Under the Fourth Amendment, before searching or seizing private property, law enforcement officers must obtain a search warrant, which requires probable cause. Under the Fifth Amendment, no one can be deprived of "life, liberty, or property without due process of law." The Fifth Amendment also protects persons against double jeopardy and self-incrimination. The Sixth Amendment guarantees the right to a speedy trial, the right to a jury trial, the right to a public trial, the right to confront witnesses, and the right to counsel. All evidence obtained in violation of the Fourth, Fifth, and Sixth Amendments must be excluded from the trial, as well as all evidence derived from the illegally obtained evidence. Individuals who are arrested must be informed of certain constitutional rights, including their Fifth Amendment right to remain silent and their Sixth Amendment right to counsel. The Eighth Amendment prohibits excessive bail and fines, and cruel and unusual punishment. The basic steps in the criminal process include an arrest, the booking, the initial appearance, a preliminary hearing, a grand jury or magistrate's review, the arraignment, a plea bargain (if any), and the trial or guilty plea.

CHAPTER 7

2A. *Ensuring legal and ethical behavior*
Ethical leadership is important to create and maintain an ethical workplace. Managers can set standards, and apply those standards to themselves and their firm's employees.

4A. *Sources of ethical standards*
Duty-based ethical standards are derived from religious precepts or philosophical principles. Outcome-based ethics focus on the consequences of an action, not on the nature of the action or on a set of pre-established moral values or religious beliefs.

CHAPTER 8

2A. *Elements of a contract*
The basic elements for the formation of a valid contract are an agreement, consideration, contractual capacity, and legality. Defenses to the enforcement of an otherwise valid contract include the lack of genuineness of assent and improper form.

4A. *Void, voidable, and unenforceable contracts*
A void contract is not a valid contract; it is no contract. A voidable contract is a valid contract, but one that can be avoided at the option of one or both of the parties. An unenforceable contract is one that cannot be enforced because of certain legal defenses against it.

CHAPTER 9

2A. *Irrevocable offers*
An offeror may not effectively revoke an offer if the offeree has changed position in justifiable reliance on the offer. Also, an option contract takes away the offeror's power to revoke an offer for the period of time specified in the option (or, if unspecified, for a reasonable time).

4A. *Consideration and its legal sufficiency*
Consideration is the value exchanged for a promise. To be legally sufficient, consideration must be "something of legal value" and either detrimental to the promisee or beneficial to the promisor. This may include (1) a promise to do something that one has no prior legal duty to do, (2) the performance of an act that one is otherwise not obligated to do, or (3) the refraining from an act that one has a legal right to do.

CHAPTER 10

2A. *Intoxication*
If a person who is sufficiently intoxicated to lack mental capacity enters into a contract, the contract is voidable at the option of that person. It must be proved that the person's reason and judgment were impaired to the extent that he or she did not comprehend the legal consequences of entering into the contract.

4A. *Covenant not to compete*
If a covenant not to compete is ancillary to an agreement to sell an ongoing business (enabling the seller to sell, and the purchaser to buy, the "goodwill" and "reputation" of the business) or is contained in an employment contract, and is reasonable in terms of time and geographic area, it will be enforceable. A covenant not to compete that is not ancillary to an agreement to sell an ongoing business will be void, because it unreasonably restrains trade and is contrary to public policy.

CHAPTER 11

2A. *Mistake of value versus mistake of fact*
A mistake as to the value of a deal is an ordinary risk of business for which a court normally will not provide relief. A mistake concerning a fact important to the subject matter of a contract, however, may provide a basis for relief.

4A. *Contracts that must be in writing to be enforceable*
Contracts that are normally required to be in writing or evidenced by a written memorandum include contracts involving interests in land; contracts that cannot by their terms be performed within one year from the date of formation; collateral contracts, such as promises to answer for the debt or duty of another; promises made in consideration of marriage; and contracts for the sale of goods priced at $500 or more.

CHAPTER 12

2A. *Rights that can be assigned*
A contract cannot prevent an assignment of the right to receive money. The assignment of ownership rights in real estate may not be prohibited because it is contrary to public policy in most states. The assignment of negotiable instruments cannot be prohibited. In a contract for a sale of goods, the right to receive damages for breach or for payment of an account owed may be assigned even if the contract prohibits it.

4A. *Discharge*
The most common way to discharge, or terminate, a contract is by the performance of contractual duties.

CHAPTER 13

2A. *Measure of damages*

In a contract for the sale of goods, the usual measure of compensatory damages is an amount equal to the difference between the contract price and the market price. When the buyer breaches and the seller has not yet produced the goods, compensatory damages normally equal the lost profits on the sale rather than the difference between the contract price and the market price. On the breach of a contract for a sale of land, when specific performance is not available, the measure of damages is also the difference between the contract and the market price. The measure on the breach of a construction contract depends on who breaches, and when. Recovery for an innocent contractor is generally based on funds expended or expected profit, or both; and for a nonbreaching owner, the cost to complete the project.

4A. *Specific performance*

Specific performance might be granted as a remedy when damages is an inadequate remedy and the subject matter of the contract is unique.

CHAPTER 14

2A. *Shrink-wrap and click-on agreements*

A shrink-wrap agreement is an agreement whose terms are expressed inside a box in which the goods are packaged. Generally, courts have enforced the terms of shrink-wrap agreements the same as the terms of other contracts, applying the traditional common law of contracts.

4A. *Partnering agreement*

A partnering agreement is an agreement between a seller and a buyer who often do business on the terms and conditions that apply to all of their transactions conducted electronically. Such an agreement reduces the likelihood of a dispute and provides for the resolution of any dispute that does arise.

CHAPTER 15

2A. *Merchant's firm offer*

A firm offer by a merchant to sell, buy, or lease goods arises when a merchant-offeror gives *assurances* in a *signed writing* that an offer will remain open. This offer is irrevocable without consideration for the stated period or, if no definite period is stated, a reasonable period (neither period to exceed three months).

4A. *Statute of Frauds exceptions*

An oral contract is enforceable if it is for (1) goods that are specially manufactured for a particular buyer or specially manufactured or obtained for a particular lessee, (2) the goods are not suitable for resale or lease to others in the ordinary course of the seller's or lessor's business, and (3) the seller or lessor has substantially started to make the goods or has committed to the manufacture or procurement of the goods. An oral contract for a sale or lease of goods is enforceable if the party against whom enforcement of a contract is sought admits in pleadings, testimony, or other court proceedings that a contract was made (but it is limited to the quantity of goods admitted). An oral contract for a sale or lease of goods is enforceable if payment has been made and accepted or goods have been received and accepted.

CHAPTER 16

2A. *Passage of title*

In the absence of a contrary agreement, title passes to the buyer at the time and the place that the seller physically delivers the goods. Delivery terms can determine this point: under a shipment contract title passes to the buyer at the time and place of shipment, while under a destination contract title passes to the buyer when the goods are tendered at the destination.

4A. *Void versus voidable title*

If a seller is a thief, the seller's title is void—legally, no title exists. A buyer would acquire no title or other interest in the goods, and the real owner can reclaim the goods. A seller has voidable title if the goods were obtained by fraud, paid for with a check that is later dishonored, purchased from a minor, or purchased on credit when the seller was insolvent. A seller with voidable title has the power to transfer good title or other interest to a good faith purchaser for value. The real, or original, owner cannot recover goods from the good faith purchaser.

CHAPTER 17

2A. *Perfect tender rule*

Under the perfect tender rule, the seller or lessor has an obligation to ship or tender conforming goods, and if goods or tender of delivery fail in any respect, the buyer or lessee has the right to accept the goods, reject the entire shipment, or accept part and reject part. Exceptions to the perfect tender rule may be established by agreement. When tender is rejected because of nonconforming goods and the time for performance has not yet expired, the seller or lessor can notify the buyer or lessee promptly of the intention to cure and can then do so within the contract time for performance. Once the time for performance has expired, the seller or lessor can, for a reasonable time, exercise the right to cure if he or she had, at the time of delivery, reasonable grounds to believe that the nonconforming tender would be acceptable to the buyer or lessee. When an agreed-on manner of delivery becomes impracticable or unavailable through no fault of either party, a seller may choose a commercially reasonable substitute. In an installment contract, a buyer or lessee can reject an installment only if the nonconformity substantially impairs the value of the installment and cannot be cured. Delay in delivery or nondelivery in whole or in part is not a breach when performance is commercially impracticable. If an unexpected event totally destroys goods identified at the time the contract is formed through no fault of either party and before risk passes to the buyer or lessee, the parties are excused from performance. If a party has reasonable grounds to believe that the other party will not perform, he or she may in writing demand assurance of performance from the other party. Until such assurance is received, he or she may suspend further performance. Finally, when required cooperation is not forthcoming, the cooperative party can suspend her or his own performance without liability.

4A. *Remedies for breach*

Depending on the circumstances at the time of a buyer's breach, a seller may have the right to cancel the contract, withhold delivery, resell or dispose of the goods subject to the contract, recover the purchase price (or lease payments), recover damages, stop delivery in transit, or reclaim the goods. Similarly, on a seller's breach, a buyer may have the right to cancel the contract, recover the goods, obtain specific performance, obtain cover, replevy the goods, recover damages, reject the goods, withhold delivery, resell or dispose of the goods, stop delivery, or revoke acceptance.

CHAPTER 18

2A. *Implied warranties*
Implied warranties that arise under the UCC include the implied warranty of merchantability, the implied warranty of fitness for a particular purpose, and implied warranties that may arise from, or be excluded or modified by, course of dealing, course of performance, or usage of trade.

4A. *Strict product liability*
Under Section 402A of the *Restatement (Second) of Torts*, the elements of an action for strict product liability are (1) the product must be in a defective condition when the defendant sells it; (2) the defendant must normally be engaged in the business of selling (or distributing) that product; (3) the product must be unreasonably dangerous to the user or consumer because of its defective condition (in most states); (4) the plaintiff must incur physical harm to self or property by use or consumption of the product; (5) the defective condition must be the proximate cause of the injury or damage; and (6) the goods must not have been substantially changed from the time the product was sold to the time the injury was sustained.

CHAPTER 19

2A. *Requirements for negotiability*
For an instrument to be negotiable, it must (1) be in writing, (2) be signed by the maker or the drawer, (3) be an unconditional promise or order to pay, (4) state a fixed amount of money, (5) be payable on demand or at a definite time, and (6) be payable to order or to bearer, unless it is a check.

4A. *Blank versus special indorsements*
A blank indorsement specifies no particular indorsee and can consist of a mere signature. A special indorsement indicates the specific person to whom the indorser intends to make the instrument payable.

CHAPTER 20

2A. *HDC rights and privileges*
A person who does not qualify as an HDC can acquire the rights and privileges of an HDC by deriving his or her title through an HDC.

4A. *Defenses against HDCs*
Universal, or real, defenses are good against the claims of all holders, including HDCs. These defenses include forgery of a maker's or drawer's signature, fraud in the execution of an instrument, material alteration of an instrument, discharge in bankruptcy, minority to the extent recognized by state law, illegality to the extent that state law makes a transaction void, mental incapacity if a person has been so adjudged in a state proceeding, and extreme duress.

CHAPTER 21

2A. *Dishonor*
A bank may dishonor a customer's check without liability to the customer when the customer's account contains insufficient funds to pay the check, providing the bank did not agree to cover overdrafts. A bank may also properly dishonor a stale check, a timely check subject to a valid stop-payment order, a check drawn after the customer's death, and forged or altered checks. If a bank wrongfully

dishonors a customer's check, the bank is liable to the customer for damages for the failure to pay.

4A. *EFTs and consumers*
The four most common types of EFT systems used by bank customers are automated teller machines, point-of-sale systems, systems handling direct deposits and withdrawals of funds, and pay-by-telephone systems. The EFTA provides a basic framework for the rights, liabilities, and responsibilities of users of these EFT systems. For consumers, the terms and conditions of EFTs must be disclosed in readily understandable language, a receipt must be provided at an e-terminal at the time of a transfer, periodic statements must describe transfers for each account through which an EFT system provides access, and some preauthorized payments can be stopped within three days before they are made.

CHAPTER 22

2A. *Requirements for an enforceable security interest*
(1) Either (a) the collateral must be in the possession of the secured party in accordance with an agreement, or (b) there must be a written or authenticated security agreement that describes the collateral subject to the security interest and is signed or authenticated by the debtor. (2) The secured party must give to the debtor something of value. (3) The debtor must have "rights" in the collateral.

4A. *Priority of perfected security interests*
When two or more secured parties have perfected security interests in the same collateral, the first to perfect has priority, unless an applicable state statute provides otherwise.

CHAPTER 23

2A. *Garnishment*
Garnishment occurs when a creditor is permitted to collect a debt by seizing property of the debtor that is being held by a third party (such as a paycheck held by an employer or a checking account held by a bank). Closely regulated, garnishment is used in some cases in which debts are not paid.

4A. *Exceptions and objections to discharge*
An *exception* to discharge is a claim that is not dischargeable in bankruptcy (such as a government claim for unpaid taxes). An *objection* to discharge is a circumstance that causes a discharge to be denied (such as concealing assets).

CHAPTER 24

2A. *Agency relationships*
Agency relationships normally are consensual: they arise by voluntary consent and agreement between the parties.

4A. *Liability to third parties*
A disclosed or partially disclosed principal is liable to a third party for a contract made by an agent who is acting within the scope of her or his authority. If the agent exceeds the scope of authority and the principal fails to ratify the contract, the agent may be liable (and the principal may not). When neither the fact of agency nor the identity of the principal is disclosed, the agent is liable, and if an agent has acted within the scope of his or her authority, the undisclosed principal is also liable. Each party is liable for his or her own torts and crimes. A principal may also be liable for an agent's torts committed within the course or scope of employment. A principal

is liable for an agent's crime if the principal participated by conspiracy or other action.

CHAPTER 25

2A. Franchise definition
A *franchise* is any arrangement in which the owner of a trademark, a trade name, or a copyright licenses others to use the trademark, trade name, or copyright in the selling of goods or services. The majority of franchises are distributorships, chain-style business operations, or manufacturing or processing-plant arrangements.

4A. Franchise contract
A franchise contract typically covers such issues as the franchisee's payment for the franchise, any lease or purchase of the business premises, any lease or purchase of equipment, the location of the franchise, the territory to be served, the business organization of the franchisee, quality standards to be met, the degree of supervision and control by the franchisor, pricing arrangements, and termination of the franchise.

CHAPTER 26

2A. Rights and duties of partners
The rights and duties of partners may be whatever the partners declare them to be. In the absence of partners' agreements to the contrary, the law imposes certain rights and duties. These include a sharing of profits and losses in equal measure, the ability to assign a partnership interest, equal rights in managing the firm (subject to majority rule), access to all of the firm's books and records, an accounting of assets and profits, and a sharing of the firm's property. The duties include fiduciary duties, being bound to third parties through contracts entered into with other partners, and liability for the firm's debts and liabilities.

4A. Advantages of limited liability partnerships
Advantages of limited liability partnerships over general partnerships include that, depending on the applicable state statute, the liability of their partners for partnership and partners' debts and torts can be limited to the amount of the partners' investments. Another advantage is the flexibility of these entities in regard to taxation and management.

CHAPTER 27

2A. Formation and operation of limited liability companies
To form a limited liability company (LLC), articles of organization must be filed with a central state agency (usually the secretary of state's office). A few states also require that a notice of the intention to form an LLC be published in a local newspaper. The members can decide how to operate the business. If there is no agreement, the state LLC statute will govern the outcome, and if there is no statute on the issue, partnership law principles apply.

4A. Joint ventures
A *joint venture* is an enterprise in which two or more persons or business entities combine their efforts or their property for a single transaction or project, or a related series of transactions or projects. Generally, partnership law applies to joint ventures, although joint venturers have less implied and apparent authority than partners because they have less power to bind the members of their organization.

CHAPTER 28

2A. De jure and de facto corporations
A *de jure* corporation is one that is properly formed, and its status as a corporation is not subject to attack. A *de facto* corporation is one that exists, but as to which there is a defect that, although it will not support an attack by a third party, could subject the firm to a challenge by the state.

4A. Merger and consolidation procedure
First, the board of directors of each corporation involved must approve the merger or consolidation plan. Second, the shareholders of each corporation must approve the plan, by vote, at a shareholders' meeting. Third, the plan (articles of merger or consolidation) is filed, usually with the secretary of state. And fourth, the state issues a certificate of merger to the surviving corporation or a certificate of consolidation to the newly consolidated corporation.

CHAPTER 29

2A. Business judgment rule
Directors and officers must exercise due care in performing their duties. They are expected to be informed on corporate matters. They are expected to act in accord with their own knowledge and training. Directors are expected to exercise a reasonable amount of supervision when they delegate work to others. Directors are expected to attend board of directors' meetings. In general, directors and officers must act in good faith, in what they consider to be the best interests of the corporation, and with the care that an ordinarily prudent person in a similar position would exercise in similar circumstances. This requires an informed decision, with a rational basis, and with no conflict between the decision maker's personal interest and the interest of the corporation.

4A. Shareholder's derivative suit
The shareholders cannot compel the directors to act to redress a wrong suffered by the corporation, but if the directors refuse to act, the shareholders can act on behalf of the firm by filing what is known as a shareholder's derivative suit. Any damages recovered by the suit normally go into the corporation's treasury, not to the shareholders personally.

CHAPTER 30

2A. Major statutes and Securities and Exchange Commission
The major statutes regulating the securities industry are the Securities Act of 1933 and the Securities Exchange Act of 1934, which created the Securities and Exchange Commission (SEC). The SEC's major functions are to (1) require the disclosure of facts concerning offerings of securities listed on national securities exchanges and of certain securities traded over the counter; (2) regulate the trade in securities on the national and regional securities exchanges and in the over-the-counter markets; (3) investigate securities fraud; (4) regulate the activities of securities brokers, dealers, and investment advisers and requiring their registration; (5) supervise the activities of mutual funds; and (6) recommend administrative sanctions, injunctive remedies, and criminal prosecution against those who violate securities laws.

4A. State securities laws
Typically, state laws have disclosure requirements and antifraud provisions patterned after Section 10(b) of the Securities Exchange Act of 1934 and SEC Rule 10b-5. State laws provide for the registration or qualification of securities offered or issued for sale within the state with the appropriate state official. Also, most state securities laws regulate securities brokers and dealers.

CHAPTER 31

2A. *Sherman Act*
Section 1 prohibits agreements that are anticompetitively restrictive—that is, agreements that have the wrongful purpose of restraining competition. Section 2 prohibits the misuse, and attempted misuse, of monopoly power in the marketplace.

4A. *Enforcing agencies*
The federal agencies that enforce the federal antitrust laws are the U.S. Department of Justice and the Federal Trade Commission.

CHAPTER 32

2A. *Credit transactions*
Federal statutes that protect consumers in credit transactions include the various titles of the Consumer Credit Protection Act—the Truth-in-Lending Act, of which the Equal Credit Opportunity Act and the Consumer Leasing Act are a part, is discussed in the text—as well as the Fair Credit Reporting Act and the Fair Debt Collection Practices Act.

4A. *Environmental impact statements*
An environmental impact statement (EIS) analyzes (1) the impact on the environment that an action will have, (2) any adverse effects on the environment and alternative actions that might be taken, and (3) irreversible effects the action might generate. For every major federal action that significantly affects the quality of the environment, an EIS must be prepared. An action is "major" if it involves a substantial commitment of resources (monetary or otherwise). An action is "federal" if a federal agency has the power to control it.

CHAPTER 33

2A. *Hours, wages, and unions*
The Fair Labor Standards Act is the most significant federal statute governing working hours and wages. Labor unions and collective bargaining are covered under the Norris-LaGuardia Act, the National Labor Relations Act, the Labor-Management Relations Act, and the Labor-Management Reporting and Disclosure Act.

4A. *Family and Medical Leave Act*
Under the Family and Medical Leave Act, an employee may take family leave to care for a newborn baby, an adopted child, or a foster child, and medical leave when the employee or the employee's spouse, child, or parent has a "serious health condition" requiring care. For most absences, the health condition must require continued treatment by a health-care provider and include a period of incapacity of more than three days.

CHAPTER 34

2A. *Disparate-treatment and disparate-impact discrimination*
Intentional discrimination by an employer against an employee is known as *disparate-treatment discrimination. Disparate-impact discrimination* occurs when, as a result of educational or other job requirements or hiring procedures, an employer's work force does not reflect the percentage of nonwhites, women, or members of other protected classes that characterizes qualified individuals in the local labor market. Disparate-impact discrimination does not require evidence of intent.

4A. *Discrimination based on age and disability*
The Age Discrimination in Employment Act of 1967 and the Americans with Disabilities Act of 1990 prohibit discrimination on the basis of age and disability, respectively.

CHAPTER 35

2A. *Auditor's liability to third parties*
An auditor may be liable to a third party on the ground of negligence, when the auditor knew or should have known that the third party would benefit from the auditor's work. Depending on the jurisdiction, liability may be imposed (1) only if the auditor is in privity, or near privity, with the third party; (2) only if the third party's reliance on the auditor's work was foreseen, or the third party was within a class of known or foreseeable users; or (3) if the third party's use of the auditor's work was reasonably foreseeable.

4A. *Crimes under the Internal Revenue Code*
Crimes under the Internal Revenue (IR) Code include (1) aiding or assisting in the preparation of a false tax return; (2) aiding or abetting an individual's understatement of tax liability; (3) negligently or willfully understating a client's tax liability, or recklessly or intentionally disregarding IR rules or regulations; (4) failing to provide a taxpayer with a copy of a tax return, failing to sign the return, or failing to furnish the appropriate tax identification numbers.

CHAPTER 36

2A. *Fee simple, joint tenancy, and tenancy in common*
An owner in fee simple is entitled to use, possess, or dispose of the property as he or she chooses during his or her lifetime, and on this owner's death, the interests in the property descend to his or her heirs. A *tenancy in common* is a form of co-ownership in which each of two or more persons owns an undivided interest in the whole property. On the death of a tenant in common, that tenant's interest passes to his or her heirs. In a *joint tenancy,* each of two or more persons owns an undivided interest in the property, and a deceased joint tenant's interest passes to the surviving joint tenant or tenants. This right distinguishes the joint tenancy from the tenancy in common.

4A. *Elements of a bailment*
A bailment is formed by the delivery of personal property, without transfer of title, by a bailor to a bailee, under an agreement, often for a particular purpose.

CHAPTER 37

2A. *Adverse possession*
The adverse possessor's possession must be (1) actual and exclusive; (2) open, visible, and notorious, not secret or clandestine; (3) continuous and peaceable for the statutory period of time; and (4) hostile and adverse.

4A. *Leasehold estates*
A *leasehold estate* is property in the possession of a tenant. Leasehold estates include tenancies for years, periodic tenancies, tenancies at will, and tenancies at sufferance.

CHAPTER 38

2A. *Broker*
A broker is the agent of an insurance applicant.

4A. Per stirpes *and* per capita
Per stirpes distribution dictates that grandchildren share the part of the estate that their deceased parent (and descendant of the deceased grandparent) would have been entitled to inherit. *Per capita* distribution dictates that each of these grandchildren takes an equal share of the estate.

CHAPTER 39

2A. *Act of state doctrine*

The *act of state doctrine* is a judicially created doctrine that provides that the judicial branch of one country will not examine the validity of public acts committed by a recognized foreign government within its own territory. This doctrine is often employed in cases involving expropriation or confiscation.

4A. *Antitrust laws*

U.S. courts will apply U.S. antitrust laws extraterritorially when it is shown that an alleged violation has a substantial effect on U.S. commerce.

APPENDIX F
Sample Answers for End-of-Chapter *Hypothetical Questions* with *Sample Answer*

1.4A. HYPOTHETICAL QUESTION WITH SAMPLE ANSWER

1. The U.S. Constitution—The U.S. Constitution is the supreme law of the land. A law in violation of the Constitution, no matter what its source, will be declared unconstitutional and will not be enforced.
2. The federal statute—Under the U.S. Constitution, when there is a conflict between federal law and state law, federal law prevails.
3. The state statute—State statutes are enacted by state legislatures. Areas not covered by state statutory law are governed by state case law.
4. The U.S. Constitution—State constitutions are supreme within their respective borders unless they conflict with the U.S. Constitution, which is the supreme law of the land.
5. The federal administrative regulation—Under the U.S. Constitution, when there is a conflict between federal law and state law, federal law prevails.

2.2A. HYPOTHETICAL QUESTION WITH SAMPLE ANSWER

As the text points out, Thomas has a constitutionally protected right to his religion and the free exercise of it. In denying his unemployment benefits, the state violated these rights. Employers are obligated to make reasonable accommodations for their employees' beliefs, right or wrong, that are openly and sincerely held. Thomas's beliefs were openly and sincerely held. By placing him in a department that made military goods, his employer effectively put him in a position of having to choose between his job and his religious principles. This unilateral decision on the part of the employer was the reason Thomas left his job and why the company was required to compensate Thomas for his resulting unemployment.

3.2A. HYPOTHETICAL QUESTION WITH SAMPLE ANSWER

Marya can bring suit in all three courts. The trucking firm did business in Florida, and the accident occurred there. Thus, the state of Florida would have jurisdiction over the defendant. Because the firm was headquartered in Georgia and had its principal place of business in that state, Marya could also sue in a Georgia court. Finally, because the amount in controversy exceeds $75,000, the suit could be brought in federal court on the basis of diversity of citizenship.

4.2A. HYPOTHETICAL QUESTION WITH SAMPLE ANSWER

The correct answer is (2). The *Restatement (Second) of Torts* defines negligence as "conduct that falls below the standard established by law for the protection of others against unreasonable risk of harm." The standard established by law is that of a reasonable person acting with due care in the circumstances. Mary was well aware that the medication she took would make her drowsy, and her failure to observe due care (that is, refrain from driving) under the circumstances was negligent. Answer (1) is incorrect because Mary had no reason to believe the golf club was defective, and she could not have prevented the injury by the exercise of due care.

5.2A. HYPOTHETICAL QUESTION WITH SAMPLE ANSWER

1. Making a photocopy of an article in a scholarly journal "for purposes such as * * * scholarship, or research, is not an infringement of copyright" under Section 107 of the Copyright Act.
2. This is an example of trademark infringement. Whenever a trademark is copied to a substantial degree or used in its entirety by one who is not entitled to its use, the trademark has been infringed.
3. This is the most likely example of copyright infringement. Generally, determining whether the reproduction of copyrighted material constitutes copyright infringement is made on a case-by-case basis under the "fair use" doctrine, as expressed in Section 107 of the Copyright Act. Courts look at such factors as the "purpose and character" of a use, such as whether it is "of a commercial nature;" "the amount and substantiality of the portion used in relation to the copyrighted work as a whole;" and "the effect of the use on the potential market" for the copied work. In this question, the DVD store owner is copying copyright-protected works in their entirety for commercial purposes, thereby affecting the market for the works.
4. Taping a television program "for purposes such as * * * teaching * * * is not an infringement of copyright" under Section 107 of the Copyright Act.

6.2A. HYPOTHETICAL QUESTION WITH SAMPLE ANSWER

1. Sarah has wrongfully taken and carried away the personal property of another with the intent to permanently deprive the owner of such property. She has committed the crime of larceny.
2. Sarah has unlawfully and forcibly taken the personal property of another. She has committed the crime of robbery.
3. Sarah has broken and entered a dwelling with the intent to commit a felony. She has committed the crime of burglary. (Most states have dispensed with the requirement that the act take place at night.)

Note the basic differences: Burglary requires breaking and entering into a building without the use of force against a person. Robbery does not involve any breaking and entering, but force is required. Larceny is the taking of personal property without force and without breaking and entering into a building. Generally, because force is used, robbery is considered the most serious of these crimes and carries the most severe penalties. Larceny involves no force or threat to human life; therefore, it carries the least severe penalty of the three. Burglary, because it involves breaking and entering, frequently where people live, carries a lesser penalty than robbery but a greater penalty than larceny.

7.2A. HYPOTHETICAL QUESTION WITH SAMPLE ANSWER

This question essentially asks whether good behavior can ever be unethical. The answer to this question depends on which approach to ethical reasoning you are using. Under the outcome-based approach of utilitarianism, it is simply not possible for selfish motives to be unethical if they result in good conduct. A good outcome is moral regardless of the nature of the action itself or the reason for the action. Under a duty-based approach, motive would be more relevant in assessing whether a firm's conduct was ethical. You would need to analyze the firm's conduct in terms of religious truths or to determine whether human beings were being treated with the inherent dignity that they deserve. Although a good motive would not justify a bad act to a religious ethicist, in this situation the actions were good and the motive was questionable (because the firm was simply seeking to increase its profit). Nevertheless, unless one's religion prohibited making a profit, the firm's actions would likely not be considered unethical. Applying Kantian ethics would require you to evaluate the firm's actions in light of what would happen if everyone in society acted that way (categorical imperative). Here, because the conduct was good, it would be positive for society if every firm acted that way. Hence, the profit-seeking motive would be irrelevant in a Kantian analysis. In a debate between motive and conduct, then, conduct is almost always given greater weight in evaluating ethics.

8.2A. HYPOTHETICAL QUESTION WITH SAMPLE ANSWER

According to the question, Janine was apparently unconscious or otherwise unable to agree to a contract for the nursing services she received while she was in the hospital. As you read in the chapter, however, sometimes the law will create a fictional contract in order to prevent one party from unjustly receiving a benefit at the expense of another. This is known as a quasi contract and provides a basis for Nursing Services to recover the value of the services it provided while Janine was in the hospital. As for the at-home services that were provided to Janine, because Janine was aware that those services were being provided for her, Nursing Services can recover for those services under an implied-in-fact contract. Under this type of contract, the conduct of the parties creates and defines the terms. Janine's acceptance of the services constitutes her agreement to form a contract, and she will probably be required to pay Nursing Services in full.

9.2A. HYPOTHETICAL QUESTION WITH SAMPLE ANSWER

1. Death of either the offeror or the offeree prior to acceptance automatically terminates a revocable offer. The basic legal reason is that the offer is personal to the parties and cannot be passed on to others, not even to the estate of the deceased. This rule applies even if the other party is unaware of the death. Thus, Cherneck's offer terminates on Cherneck's death, and Bollow's later acceptance does not constitute a contract.

2. An offer is automatically terminated by the destruction of the specific subject matter of the offer prior to acceptance. Thus, Bollow's acceptance after the fire does not constitute a contract.

3. When the offer is irrevocable, under an option contract, death of the offeror does not terminate the option contract, and the offeree can accept the offer to sell the equipment, binding the offeror's estate to performance. Performance is not personal to Cherneck, as the estate can transfer title to the equipment. Knowledge of the death is immaterial to the offeree's right of acceptance. Thus, Bollow can hold Cherneck's estate to a contract for the purchase of the equipment.

4. When the offer is irrevocable, under an option contract, death of the offeree also does not terminate the offer. Because the option is a separate contract, the contract survives and passes to the offeree's estate, which can exercise the option by acceptance within the option period. Thus, acceptance by Bollow's estate binds Cherneck to a contract for the sale of the equipment.

10.2A. HYPOTHETICAL QUESTION WITH SAMPLE ANSWER

Contracts in restraint of trade are usually illegal and unenforceable. An exception to this rule applies to a covenant not to compete that is ancillary to certain types of business contracts in which some fair protection is deemed appropriate (such as in the sale of a business). The covenant, however, must be reasonable in terms of time and area to be legally enforceable. If either term is excessive, the court can declare that the restraint goes beyond what is necessary for reasonable protection. In this event, the court can either declare the covenant illegal or it can reform the covenant to make the terms of time and area reasonable and then enforce it. Suppose the court declares the covenant illegal and unenforceable. Because the covenant is ancillary and severable from the primary contract, the primary contract is not affected by such a ruling. In the case of Hotel Lux, the primary contract concerns employment; the covenant is ancillary and desirable for the protection of the hotel. The time period of one year may be considered reasonable for a chef with an international reputation. The reasonableness of the three-state area restriction may be questioned, however. If it is found to be reasonable, the covenant probably will be enforced. If it is not found to be reasonable, the court could declare the entire covenant illegal, allowing Perlee to be employed by any restaurant or hotel, including one in direct competition with Hotel Lux. Alternatively, the court could reform the covenant, making its terms reasonable for protecting Hotel Lux's normal customer market area.

11.2A. HYPOTHETICAL QUESTION WITH SAMPLE ANSWER

In this situation, Gemma becomes what is known as a *guarantor* on the loan. That is, she guarantees the hardware store that she will pay for the mower if her brother fails to do so. This kind of collateral promise, in which the guarantor states that he or she will become responsible *only* if the primary party does not perform, must be in writing to be enforceable. There is an exception, however. If the main purpose in accepting secondary liability is to secure a personal benefit—for example, if Gemma's brother bought the mower for her—the contract need not be in writing. The assumption is that a court can infer from the circumstances of the case whether the main purpose was to secure a personal benefit and thus, in effect, to answer for the guarantor's own debt.

12.3A. HYPOTHETICAL QUESTION WITH SAMPLE ANSWER

As a general rule any right(s) flowing from a contract can be assigned. There are, however, exceptions, such as when the contract expressly and specifically prohibits or limits the right of assignment. Because of the principle of freedom of contract, this type of prohibition is enforced—unless it is deemed contrary to public policy. For example, courts have held that a prohibition clause against assignment that restrains the alienation of property is invalid by virtue of being against public policy. Authorities differ on how a case like Aron's should be decided. Some courts would enforce the prohibition completely, holding that Aron's assignment to Erica is completely ineffective without the landlord's consent. Others would permit the assignment to be effective, with the landlord's remedies limited to the normal contract remedies ensuing from Aron's breach.

13.2A. HYPOTHETICAL QUESTION WITH SAMPLE ANSWER

Generally, the equitable remedy of specific performance will be granted only if two criteria are met: monetary damages (under the circumstances) must be inadequate as a remedy, and the subject matter of the contract must be unique.

1. In the sale of land, the buyer's contract is for a specific piece of real property. The land under contract is unique, because no two pieces of real property have the same legal description. In addition, monetary damages would not compensate a buyer adequately, as the same land cannot be purchased elsewhere. Specific performance is an appropriate remedy.

2. The basic criteria for specific performance do not apply well to personal service contracts. If the identical service contracted for is readily available from others, the service is not unique and monetary damages for nonperformance are adequate. If, however, the services are so personal that only the contracted party can perform them, the contract meets the test of uniqueness; but the courts will refuse to decree specific performance based on either of two theories. First, the enforcement of specific performance requires involuntary servitude (prohibited by the Thirteenth Amendment to the U. S. Constitution). Second, it is impractical to attempt to force meaningful performance by someone against his or her will. In the case of Marita and Horace, specific performance is not an appropriate remedy.

3. A rare coin is unique, and monetary damages for breach are inadequate, as Juan cannot obtain a substantially identical substitute in the market. This is a typical case where specific performance is an appropriate remedy.

4. The key fact for consideration here is that this is a closely held corporation. Therefore, the stock is not available in the market, and the shares become unique. The uniqueness of these shares is enhanced by the fact that if Cary sells his 4 percent of the shares to De Valle, De Valle will have a controlling voice in the corporation. Because of this, monetary damages for De Valle are totally inadequate as a remedy. Specific performance is an appropriate remedy.

14.2A. HYPOTHETICAL QUESTION WITH SAMPLE ANSWER

Anne has entered into an enforceable contract to subscribe to *E-Commerce Weekly*. In this problem, the offer to deliver, via e-mail, the newsletter was presented by the offeror with a statement of how to accept—by clicking on the "SUBSCRIBE" button.

Consideration was in the promise to deliver the newsletter and at the price that the subscriber agreed to pay. The offeree had an opportunity to read the terms of the subscription agreement before making the contract. Whether or not she actually read those terms does not matter.

15.3A. HYPOTHETICAL QUESTION WITH SAMPLE ANSWER

The entire answer falls under UCC 2–206(1)(b), because the situation deals with a buyer's order to buy goods for prompt shipment. The law is that such an order or offer invites acceptance by a prompt *promise* to ship conforming goods. If the promise (acceptance) is sent by a medium reasonable under the circumstances, the acceptance is effective when sent. Therefore, a contract was formed on October 8, and it required Fulsom to ship one hundred Model Color-X television sets. Fulsom's shipment is nonconforming, and Salinger is correct in claiming that Fulsom is in breach. Fulsom's claim would be valid if Fulsom had not sent its promise of shipment. The Code provides that shipment of nonconforming goods constitutes an acceptance *unless* the seller seasonably notifies the buyer that such shipment is sent only as an accommodation. Thus, had a contract not been formed on October 8, the nonconforming shipment on the 28th would not be treated as an acceptance, and no contract would be in existence to breach.

16.2A. HYPOTHETICAL QUESTION WITH SAMPLE ANSWER

1. In a destination contract, the risk of loss passes to the buyer when the goods are tendered to the buyer at the specified destination—in this case, San Francisco.

2. In a shipment contract, if the seller is required or authorized to ship goods by carrier, but the contract specifies no locale, the risk of loss passes to the buyer when the goods are duly delivered to the carrier.

3. If the seller is a merchant, risk of loss to goods held by the seller passes to the buyer when the buyer actually takes physical possession of the goods. If the seller is not a merchant, the risk of loss to goods held by the seller passes to the buyer on tender of delivery.

4. When a bailee is holding goods for a person who has contracted to sell them and the goods are to be delivered without being moved, risk of loss passes to the buyer when (1) the buyer receives a negotiable document of title for the goods, (2) the bailee acknowledges the buyer's right to possess the goods, or (3) the buyer receives a nonnegotiable document of title and has had a reasonable time to present the document to the bailee and demand the goods. (If the bailee refuses to honor the document, the risk of loss remains with the seller.) If the goods are to be delivered by being moved, but the contract does not specify whether it is a destination or a shipment contract, it is presumed to be a shipment contract. If no locale is specified in the contract, risk of loss passes to the buyer when the seller delivers the goods to the carrier.

17.2A. HYPOTHETICAL QUESTION WITH SAMPLE ANSWER

No. Cummings had not breached the sales contract because the C.O.D. shipment had deprived him of his absolute right, in the absence of agreement, to inspect the goods before accepting them. Had Cummings requested or agreed to the C.O.D. method of shipment, the result would have been different. Because he had not agreed to the C.O.D. shipment, he was fully within his rights to refuse to accept the goods because he could not inspect them prior to acceptance. In this case, it was the seller who had breached the contract by shipping the goods C.O.D. without Cummings's consent.

18.3A. Hypothetical Question with Sample Answer

Yes. To disclaim the implied warranty of fitness for a particular purpose, the disclaimer must be in writing and be conspicuous. Although the implied warranty of merchantability can be disclaimed orally, if the disclaimer is in writing it must be conspicuously written. This means that the disclaimer must—either by different color or type size or some other technique—stand out from the context in which it is printed so as to readily alert the reader of the document of the disclaimer. In this case, the disclaimer was printed in the same size and color of type as the rest of the contract and was not conspicuous. If this was the only warranty disclaimer, it is not effective and Tandy can recover.

19.2A. Hypothetical Question with Sample Answer

For an instrument to be negotiable, it must meet the following requirements:

1. Be in writing.
2. Be signed by the maker or the drawer.
3. Be an unconditional promise or order to pay.
4. State a fixed amount of money.
5. Be payable on demand or at a definite time.
6. Be payable to order or to bearer, unless it is a check.

The instrument in this case meets the writing requirement in that it is handwritten and on something with a degree of permanence that is transferable. The instrument meets the requirement of being signed by the maker, as Muriel Evans's signature (her name in her handwriting) appears in the body of the instrument. The instrument's payment is not conditional and contains Muriel Evans's definite promise to pay. In addition, the sum of $100 is both a fixed amount and payable in money (U.S. currency). Because the instrument is payable on demand and to bearer (Karen Marvin or any holder), the instrument is negotiable.

20.2A. Hypothetical Question with Sample Answer

No. Material alteration of a negotiable instrument may be a real defense against payment on the instrument. As against a holder in due course, the raising of the amount (material alteration) is only a defense as to the altered amount, and the HDC can recover according to the original tenor of the instrument [UCC 3–407(b)]. In this case, however, Williams materially contributed to the alteration by his negligence in writing the check in pencil. Thus, the defense of material alteration was not available to him, and Williams is liable to Boz for the $10,000 [UCC 3–406]. If Williams had written the check in ink, and Stein had altered the amount in such a clever fashion that Boz could take the check without notice and become an HDC, then Williams would have a real defense against paying $10,000. In the latter case, Boz, as an HDC, could collect only $1,000, the original amount of the check.

21.2A. Hypothetical Question with Sample Answer

Under the Home Mortgage Disclosure Act (HMDA) and the Community Reinvestment Act of 1977, which were passed to prevent discrimination in lending practices, a bank is required to define its market area. This area must be established contiguous to the bank's branch offices. It must be mapped using the existing boundaries of the counties or the standard metropolitan areas (SMAs) in which the offices are located. A bank must delineate the community served, and annually review this delineation. The issue here is how a successful Internet-only bank could delineate its community. Does an Internet bank have a physically limited market area or serve a physically distinct community? Will the Federal Reserve Board, the government agency charged with enforcing this law, allow a bank to describe its market area as a "cybercommunity"?

22.2A. Hypothetical Question with Sample Answer

Mendez has a security interest in Arabian Knight and is a perfected secured party. He has met all the necessary criteria listed under UCC 9–203 to be a secured creditor. Mendez has given value of $5,000 and has taken possession of the collateral, Arabian Knight, owned by Marsh (who has rights in the collateral). Thus, he has a security interest even though Marsh did not sign a security agreement. Once a security interest attaches, a transfer of possession of the collateral to the secured party can perfect the party's security interest without a filing [UCC 9–310(b)(6); 9–313]. Thus, a security interest was created and perfected at the time Marsh transferred Arabian Knight to Mendez as security for the loan.

23.2A. Hypothetical Question with Sample Answer

The Bankruptcy Code establishes a payment priority of claims from the debtor's estate. Each class of debt in this priority list must be fully paid before the next class in priority is entitled to any of the proceeds. If insufficient funds remain to pay an entire class, the proceeds are distributed on a pro rata basis to each creditor within that class. The order of priority for claims listed in this problem is as follows:

1. Administrative bankruptcy costs (Martinez)—$500.
2. Claims for back wages, limited to $4,300 per claimant, provided wages were earned within ninety days of petition (Kohak)—$4,300.
3. Taxes and penalties due and owing (Micanopa County)—$1,000.
4. General creditors, $10,000 (First Bank of Sunny Acres—$5,000; Calvin—$2,500; balance of Kohak wages owed—$2,500).

Because the amount remaining after paying (a), (b), and (c) is only $1,200, the general creditors will share on a pro rata basis. First Bank of Sunny Acres will receive $600 ($5,000/$10,000 × $1,200 = $600), and Calvin and Kohak will each receive $300 ($2,500/$10,000 × $1,200 = $300).

24.2A. Hypothetical Question with Sample Answer

Agency is usually a consensual relationship in that the principal and agent agree that the agent will have the authority to act for the principal, binding the principal to any contract with a third party. If no agency in fact exists, the purported agent's contracts with third parties are not binding on the principal. In this case, no agency by agreement was created. Brown may claim that an agency by estoppel was created; however, this argument will fail. Agency by estoppel is applicable only when a *principal* causes a third person to believe that another person is the principal's agent. Then the third party's actions in dealing with the agent are in reliance upon the principal's words or actions and the third party's reasonable belief that the agent has authority. This is said to estop the principal from claiming that in fact no agency existed.

Acts and declarations of the *agent*, however, do not in and of themselves create an agency by estoppel, because such actions should not reasonably lead a third person to believe that the purported agent has authority. In this case, Wade's declarations and allegations alone led Brown to believe that Wade was an agent. Gett's actions were not involved. It is not reasonable to believe that someone is an agent solely because he or she is a friend of the principal. Therefore, Brown cannot hold Gett liable unless Gett ratifies Wade's contract—which is unlikely, as Wade has disappeared with the rare coin.

25.2A. HYPOTHETICAL QUESTION WITH SAMPLE ANSWER

The court would likely consider the terms of any contracts between the parties and whether or not the parties were acting in good faith. One way to avoid conflicts such as those described in this problem is to institute a Web site in conjunction with a franchisor's franchisees. When a Web site directs interested parties to a franchisee, for example, all parties would seem to benefit. Because territorial conflicts can occur not only between a franchisor and its franchisees but also between competing franchisees, some companies have instituted specific "no compete" pledges.

26.2A. HYPOTHETICAL QUESTION WITH SAMPLE ANSWER

1. A limited partner's interest is assignable. In fact, assignment allows the assignee to become a substituted limited partner with the consent of the remaining partners. The assignment, however, does not dissolve the limited partnership.
2. Bankruptcy of the limited partnership itself causes dissolution, but bankruptcy of one of the limited partners does not dissolve the partnership unless it causes the bankruptcy of the firm.
3. The retirement, death, or insanity of a general partner dissolves the partnership unless the business can be continued by the remaining general partners. Because Dorinda was the only general partner, her death dissolves the limited partnership.

27.2A. HYPOTHETICAL QUESTION WITH SAMPLE ANSWER

Although a joint stock company has characteristics of a corporation, it is usually treated as a partnership. Therefore, although the joint stock company issues transferable shares of stock and is managed by directors and officers, the shareholders have personal liability. Unless the shareholders transfer their stock and ownership to a third party, not only are the joint stock company's assets available for damages caused by a breach, but the individual shareholders' estates are also subject to such liability. The business trust resembles and is treated like a corporation in many respects. One is the limited liability of the beneficiaries. Unless by state law the beneficiaries are treated as partners, making them liable to business trust creditors, Faraway Corp. can look to only business trust assets in the event of breach.

28.2A. HYPOTHETICAL QUESTION WITH SAMPLE ANSWER

If Artel acquires the stocks and assets of Fox Express, a *merger* will take place. Artel will be the surviving corporation, and Fox Express will disappear as a corporation. If Artel and Fox Express combine so that both corporations cease to exist and a new corporation, A&F Enterprises, is formed, a *consolidation* will take place. In either case, title to the property of the corporation that ceases to exist will pass automatically to the surviving or new corporation without a formal transfer being necessary. In addition, in a merger, the debt liabilities

of Fox Express become the liabilities of Artel. Artel's articles of incorporation are deemed to be amended to include the terms stated in the articles of merger. If a consolidation takes place, A&F Enterprises will automatically acquire title to the properties of both Artel and Fox Express without a formal transfer being necessary. A&F Enterprises also will assume liability for the debts and obligations of Artel and Fox Express. The articles of consolidation take the place of the articles of incorporation of Artel and Fox Express, and they will be regarded thereafter as the articles of incorporation of A&F Enterprises.

29.2A. HYPOTHETICAL QUESTION WITH SAMPLE ANSWER

Directors are personally answerable to the corporation and the shareholders for breach of their duty to exercise reasonable care in conducting the affairs of the corporation. Reasonable care is defined as being the degree of care that a reasonably prudent person would use in the conduct of personal business affairs. When directors delegate the running of the corporate affairs to officers, the directors are expected to use reasonable care in the selection and supervision of such officers. Failure to do so will make the directors liable for negligence or mismanagement. A director who dissents to an action by the board is not personally liable for losses resulting from that action. Unless the dissent is entered into the board meeting minutes, however, the director is presumed to have assented. Therefore, the first issue in the case of Starboard, Inc., is whether the board members failed to use reasonable care in the selection of the president, Tyson. If so, and particularly if the board failed to provide a reasonable amount of supervision (and openly embezzled funds indicate that failure), the directors will be personally liable. This liability will include Ellsworth unless she can prove that she dissented and that she tried to reasonably supervise Tyson. Considering the facts in this case, it is questionable that Ellsworth could prove this.

30.2A. HYPOTHETICAL QUESTION WITH SAMPLE ANSWER

No. Under federal securities law, a stock split is exempt from registration requirements. This is because no *sale* of stock is involved. The existing shares are merely being split, and no consideration is received by the corporation for the additional shares created.

31.2A. HYPOTHETICAL QUESTION WITH SAMPLE ANSWER

Yes. The major antitrust law being violated is the Sherman Act, Section 1. Allitron and Donovan are engaged in interstate commerce, and the agreement to divide marketing territories between them is a contract in restraint of trade. The U.S. Department of Justice could seek fines of up to $1 million for each corporation, and the officers or directors responsible could be imprisoned for up to three years. In addition, the U.S. Department of Justice could institute civil proceedings to restrain this conduct.

32.2A. HYPOTHETICAL QUESTION WITH SAMPLE ANSWER

The Truth-in-Lending Act (TILA) deals specifically with lost or stolen credit cards and their unauthorized use. For credit cards *solicited* by the cardholder and then lost or stolen, the act limits the liability of the cardholder to $50 for unauthorized charges made prior to the time the creditor is notified. There is no liability for any unauthorized charges made after the date of notice. In the case of the Midtown Department Store credit card stolen on May 31, the $500 charge made on June 1, which is prior to Ochoa's notice, causes Ochoa to be liable for the $50 limit. For the June 3 charge of $200 made after the notification, Ochoa has no liability. TILA also deals with unsolicited credit cards. Unless a credit cardholder accepts an unsolicited card (such as by using it), the cardholder is not liable for any unauthorized charges. Moreover, the act prohibits the issuance of unsolicited credit cards. No notice by the cardholder of an unsolicited, unaccepted credit card is required to absolve the cardholder from liability for unauthorized charges. Therefore, Ochoa owes $50 to the Midtown Department Store and nothing to High-Flying Airlines.

33.2A. HYPOTHETICAL QUESTION WITH SAMPLE ANSWER

The Occupational Safety and Health Act (OSHA) requires employers to provide safe working conditions for employees. The act prohibits employers from discharging or discriminating against any employee who refuses to work when the employee believes in good faith that he or she will risk death or great bodily harm by undertaking the employment activity. Denton and Carlo had sufficient reason to believe that the maintenance job required of them by their employer involved great risk, and therefore, under OSHA, their discharge was wrongful. Denton and Carlo can turn to the Occupational Safety and Health Administration, which is part of the U.S. Department of Labor, for assistance.

34.2A. HYPOTHETICAL QUESTION WITH SAMPLE ANSWER

Educational requirements can be legally imposed provided that the educational requirement is directly related to, and necessary for, performance of the job. The requirement of a high school diploma is not a direct, job-related requirement in this case. Chinawa obviously comes under the 1964 Civil Rights Act, Title VII, as amended, and the educational requirement under the circumstances is definitely discriminatory against minorities.

35.2A. HYPOTHETICAL QUESTION WITH SAMPLE ANSWER

Assuming that the circuit court has abandoned the *Ultramares* rule, it is likely that the accounting firm of Goldman, Walters, Johnson & Co. will be held liable to Happydays State Bank for negligent preparation of financial statements. This hypothetical scenario is partially derived from *Citizens State Bank v. Timm, Schmidt & Co.* In *Citizens State Bank* the Supreme Court of Wisconsin enunciated various policy reasons for holding accountants liable to third parties even in the absence of privity. The court suggested that this potential liability would make accountants more careful in the preparation of financial statements. Moreover, in some situations the accountants may be the only solvent defendants, and hence, unless liability is imposed on accountants, third parties who reasonably rely on financial statements may go unprotected. The court further asserted that accountants, rather than third parties, are in better positions to spread the risks. If third parties such as banks have to absorb the costs of bad loans made as a result of negligently prepared financial statements, then the cost of credit to the public in general will increase. In contrast, the court suggests that accountants are in a better position to spread the risk by purchasing liability insurance.

36.3A. HYPOTHETICAL QUESTION WITH SAMPLE ANSWER

For Curtis to recover against the hotel, he must first prove that a bailment relationship was created between himself and the hotel as to the car or the fur coat, or both. For a bailment to exist, there must be a delivery of the personal property that gives the bailee exclusive possession of the property, and the bailee must knowingly accept the bailed property. If either element is lacking, there is no bailment relationship and no liability on the part of the bailee hotel. The facts clearly indicate that the bailee hotel took exclusive possession and control of Curtis's car, and it knowingly accepted the car when the attendant took the car from Curtis and parked it in the underground guarded garage, retaining the keys. Thus, a bailment was created as to the car, and, because a mutual benefit bailment was created, the hotel owes Curtis the duty to exercise reasonable care over the property and to return the bailed car at the end of the bailment. Failure to return the car creates a presumption of negligence (lack of reasonable care), and unless the hotel can rebut this presumption, the hotel is liable to Curtis for the loss of the car. As to the fur coat, the hotel neither knew nor expected that the trunk contained an expensive fur coat. Thus, although the hotel knowingly took exclusive possession of the car, the hotel did not do so with the fur coat. (But for a regular coat and other items likely to be in the car, the hotel would be liable.) Because no bailment of the expensive fur coat was created, the hotel has no liability for its loss.

37.2A. HYPOTHETICAL QUESTION WITH SAMPLE ANSWER

Wiley understandably wants a general warranty deed, as this type of deed will give him the most extensive protection against any defects of title claimed against the property transferred. The general warranty would have Gemma warranting the following covenants:

1. Covenant of seisin and right to convey—a warranty that the seller has good title and power to convey.
2. Covenant against encumbrances—a guaranty by the seller that, unless stated, there are no outstanding encumbrances or liens against the property conveyed.
3. Covenant of quiet possession—a warranty that the grantee's possession will not be disturbed by others claiming a prior legal right. Gemma, however, is conveying only ten feet along a property line that may not even be accurately surveyed. Gemma therefore does not wish to make these warranties. Consequently, she is offering a quitclaim deed, which does not convey any warranties but conveys only whatever interest, if any, the grantor owns. Although title is passed by the quitclaim deed, the quality of the title is not warranted. Because Wiley really needs the property, it appears that he has three choices: he can accept the quitclaim deed; he can increase his offer price to obtain the general warranty deed he wants; or he can offer to have a title search made, which should satisfy both parties.

38.2A. HYPOTHETICAL QUESTION WITH SAMPLE ANSWER

1. In most states, for a will to be valid, it must be in writing, signed by the testator, and witnessed (attested to) according to the statutes of the state. In some states the testator is also required to publish (declare) that the document is his or her last will and testament. (Such is not required under the Uniform Probate Code.) In the case of Benjamin, the will is unquestionably written (typewritten) and signed by the testator. The only problem is with the witnesses. Some states require three witnesses, and some invalidate a will if a named beneficiary is also a witness. The Uniform Probate Code provides that a will is valid even if attested to by an interested witness. Therefore, whether the will is valid depends on the state laws dealing with witness qualifications.

2. If the will is declared invalid, Benjamin's estate will pass in accordance with the state's intestacy laws. These statutes provide for distribution of an estate when there is no valid will. The intent of the statutes is to distribute the estate in the way that the deceased person would have wished. Generally, the estate is divided between a surviving spouse and all surviving children. Because Benjamin is a widower, if his only surviving child is Edward, the entire estate will go to Edward, and Benjamin's grandchildren, Perry and Paul, will receive nothing from the estate.

3. If the will is valid, the estate will be divided between Benjamin's two children, Patricia and Edward. Should either or both predecease Benjamin, leaving children (Benjamin's grandchildren), the grandchildren take *per stirpes* the share that would have gone to their parent. In this case Edward, as a surviving child of Benjamin, would receive one-half of the estate, and Perry and Paul, as grandchildren, would each receive *per stirpes* one-fourth of the estate (one-half of the share that would have gone to their deceased mother, Patricia).

39.2A. HYPOTHETICAL QUESTION WITH SAMPLE ANSWER

Each system has its advantages and its disadvantages. In a common law system, the courts independently develop the rules governing certain areas of law, such as torts and contracts. This judge-made law exists in addition to the laws passed by a legislature. Judges must follow precedential decisions in their jurisdictions, but courts may modify or even overturn precedents when deemed necessary. Also, if there is no case law to guide a court, the court may create a new rule of law. In a civil law system, the only official source of law is a statutory code. Courts are required to interpret the code and apply the rules to individual cases, but courts may not depart from the code and develop their own laws. In theory, the law code will set forth all the principles needed for the legal system. Common law and civil law systems are not wholly distinct. For example, the United States has a common law system, but crimes are defined by statute as in civil law systems. Civil law systems may allow considerable room for judges to develop law: law codes cannot be so precise as to address every contested issue, so the judiciary must interpret the codes. There are also significant differences among common law countries. The judges of different common law nations have produced differing common law principles. The roles of judges and lawyers under the different systems should be taken into account. Among other factors that should be considered in establishing a business law system and in deciding what regulations to impose are the goals that the system and its regulations are intended to achieve and the expectations of those to whom both will apply, including foreign and domestic investors.

APPENDIX G
Case Excerpts for
Case Analysis Questions

CASE NO. 1 ■ FOR CHAPTER 3

Circuit City Stores, Inc. v. Adams
532 U.S. 105, 121 S.Ct. 1302, 149 L.Ed.2d 234 (2001).

MAJORITY OPINION

Justice *KENNEDY* delivered the opinion of the Court.

Section 1 of the Federal Arbitration Act (FAA) excludes from the Act's coverage "contracts of employment of seamen, railroad employees, or any other class of workers engaged in foreign or interstate commerce." * * *

* * * *

I

In October 1995, respondent Saint Clair Adams applied for a job at petitioner Circuit City Stores, Inc., a national retailer of consumer electronics. Adams signed an employment application which included the following provision:

"I agree that I will settle any and all previously unasserted claims, disputes or controversies arising out of or relating to my application or candidacy for employment, employment and/or cessation of employment with Circuit City, *exclusively* by final and binding *arbitration* before a neutral Arbitrator. By way of example only, such claims include claims under federal, state, and local statutory or common law, such as the Age Discrimination in Employment Act, Title VII of the Civil Rights Act of 1964, as amended, including the amendments of the Civil Rights Act of 1991, the Americans with Disabilities Act, the law of contract and the law of tort." [Emphasis in original.]

Adams was hired as a sales counselor in Circuit City's store in Santa Rosa, California.

Two years later, Adams filed an employment discrimination lawsuit against Circuit City in state court, asserting claims under * * * California law. Circuit City filed suit in the United States District Court for the Northern District of California, seeking to enjoin the state-court action and to compel arbitration of respondent's claims pursuant to the FAA. The District Court entered the requested order. Respondent, the court concluded, was obligated by the arbitration agreement to submit his claims against the employer to binding arbitration. An appeal followed.

* * * [T]he Court of Appeals held the arbitration agreement between Adams and Circuit City was contained in a "contract of employment," and so was not subject to the FAA. Circuit City petitioned this Court * * * . We granted *certiorari* to resolve the issue.

II

A

* * * [T]he FAA compels judicial enforcement of a wide range of written arbitration agreements. * * *

* * * *

The instant case [the case now before the Court] * * * involves * * * the exemption from coverage under [Section] 1. * * * Most Courts of Appeals conclude the exclusion provision is limited to transportation workers, defined, for instance, as those workers "actually engaged in the movement of goods in interstate commerce." * * * [T]he Court of Appeals for the Ninth Circuit takes a different view and interprets the [Section] 1 exception to exclude all contracts of employment from the reach of the FAA. * * *

B

* * * *

Respondent, endorsing the reasoning of the Court of Appeals for the Ninth Circuit that the provision excludes all employment contracts, relies on the asserted breadth of the words "contracts of employment of * * * any other class of workers engaged in * * * commerce." * * * [R]espondent contends [Section] 1's interpretation should have a like reach, thus exempting all employment contracts. The two provisions, it is argued, are coterminous; under this view the "involving commerce" provision brings within the FAA's scope all contracts within the Congress' commerce power, and the "engaged in * * * commerce" language in [Section] 1 in turn exempts from the FAA all employment contracts falling within that authority.

This reading of [Section] 1, however, runs into an immediate and, in our view, insurmountable textual obstacle [a problem in interpreting the text of Section 1 of the FAA]. * * * [T]he words "any other class of workers engaged in * * * commerce" constitute a residual phrase, following, in the same sentence, explicit reference to "seamen" and "railroad employees." Construing the residual phrase to exclude all employment contracts fails to give independent effect to the statute's enumeration of the specific categories of workers which precedes it; there would be no need for Congress to use the phrases "seamen" and "railroad employees" if those same classes of workers were subsumed within the meaning of the "engaged in * * * commerce" residual clause. The wording of [Section] 1 calls for the application of * * * the statutory canon [rule for interpreting statutes] that "[w]here general words follow specific words in a statutory enumeration, the general words are construed to embrace only objects similar in nature to those objects enumerated by the preced-

Case No. 1–Continued

ing specific words." Under this rule of construction the residual clause should be read to give effect to the terms "seamen" and "railroad employees," and should itself be controlled and defined by reference to the enumerated categories of workers which are recited just before it; the interpretation of the clause pressed by respondent fails to produce these results.

＊　＊　＊ [E]ven if the term "engaged in commerce" stood alone in [Section] 1, we would not construe the provision to exclude all contracts of employment from the FAA. Congress uses different modifiers to the word "commerce" in the design and enactment of its statutes. The phrase "affecting commerce" indicates Congress' intent to regulate to the outer limits of its authority under the Commerce Clause. The "involving commerce" phrase, the operative words for the reach of the basic coverage provision in [Section] 2, was at issue in [a previous Supreme Court case]. ＊　＊　＊ Considering the usual meaning of the word "involving," and the pro-arbitration purposes of the FAA, [we] held the word "involving," like "affecting," signals an intent to exercise Congress' commerce power to the full. Unlike those phrases, however, the general words "in commerce" and the specific phrase "engaged in commerce" are understood to have a more limited reach. ＊　＊　＊ [T]he words "in commerce" are often-found words of art that we have not read as expressing congressional intent to regulate to the outer limits of authority under the Commerce Clause.

＊　＊　＊　＊

In sum, the text of the FAA forecloses the construction of [Section] 1 followed by the Court of Appeals in the case under review, a construction which would exclude all employment contracts from the FAA. ＊　＊　＊

＊　＊　＊　＊

For the foregoing reasons, the judgment of the Court of Appeals for the Ninth Circuit is reversed, and the case is remanded for further proceedings consistent with this opinion.

It is so ordered.

DISSENTING OPINION
Justice *STEVENS* ＊　＊　＊, dissenting.

＊　＊　＊　＊

＊　＊　＊ History amply supports the proposition that [the exclusion] was an uncontroversial provision that merely confirmed the fact that no one interested in the enactment of the FAA ever intended or expected that [Section] 2 would apply to employment contracts. ＊　＊　＊

The irony of the Court's reading of [Section] 2 to include contracts of employment is compounded by its cramped interpretation of the exclusion inserted into [Section] 1. As proposed and enacted, the exclusion fully responded to the concerns of the Seamen's Union and other labor organizations that [Section] 2 might encompass employment contracts by expressly exempting not only the labor agreements of "seamen" and "railroad employees," but also of *"any other class of workers* engaged in foreign or interstate commerce." Today, however, the Court fulfills the original—and originally unfounded—fears of organized labor by essentially rewriting the text of [Section] 1 to exclude the employment contracts solely of "seamen, railroad employees, or any other class of *transportation* workers engaged in foreign or interstate commerce." In contrast, whether one views the legislation before or after the amendment to [Section] 1, it is clear that it was not intended to apply to employment contracts at all. [Emphasis added.]

CASE NO. 2 ■ FOR CHAPTER 5

New York Times Co. v. Tasini
533 U.S. 483, 121 S.Ct. 2381, 150 L.Ed.2d 500 (2001).

MAJORITY OPINION
Justice *GINSBURG* delivered the opinion of the Court.

＊　＊　＊　＊

Respondents Jonathan Tasini, Mary Kay Blakely, Barbara Garson, Margot Mifflin, Sonia Jaffe Robbins, and David S. Whitford are authors (Authors). Between 1990 and 1993, they wrote the 21 articles (Articles) on which this dispute centers. Tasini, Mifflin, and Blakely contributed 12 Articles to *The New York Times*, the daily newspaper published by petitioner The New York Times Company (Times), [and 9 articles to other periodicals]. ＊　＊　＊ The Authors registered copyrights in each of the Articles. The Times [and the other publishers] (Print Publishers) registered collective work copyrights in each periodical edition in which an Article originally appeared. The Print Publishers engaged the Authors as independent contractors (freelancers) under contracts that in no instance secured consent from an Author to placement of an Article in an electronic database.

At the time the Articles were published, [the] Print Publishers had agreements with petitioner LEXIS/NEXIS ＊　＊　＊, owner and operator of NEXIS, a computerized database that stores information in a text-only format. NEXIS contains articles from hundreds of journals (newspapers and periodicals) spanning many years. The Print Publishers have licensed to LEXIS/NEXIS the text of articles appearing in [the] periodicals. The licenses authorize LEXIS/NEXIS to copy and sell any portion of those texts.

＊　＊　＊　＊

The Times ＊　＊　＊ also has licensing agreements with petitioner University Microfilms International (UMI). The agreements authorize reproduction of Times materials on two CD-ROM products, the *New York Times OnDisc* (NYTO) and *General Periodicals OnDisc* (GPO).

＊　＊　＊　＊

On December 16, 1993, the Authors filed this civil action in the United States District Court for the Southern District of New York. The Authors alleged that their copyrights were infringed when, as permitted and facilitated by the Print Publishers, LEXIS/NEXIS and UMI (Electronic Publishers) placed the Articles in the NEXIS, NYTO, and GPO databases (Databases). The Authors sought declaratory and injunctive relief, and damages. In response to the Authors' complaint, the Print and Electronic Publishers raised the reproduction and distribution privilege accorded collective work copyright owners by [the Copyright Act]. ＊　＊　＊

The ＊　＊　＊ Court granted summary judgment for the Publishers ＊　＊　＊.

The Authors appealed, and the [U.S. Court of Appeals for the] Second Circuit reversed. ＊　＊　＊

We granted *certiorari* to determine whether the copying of the Authors' Articles in the Databases is privileged by [the Copyright Act]. ＊　＊　＊

＊　＊　＊　＊

Under the Copyright Act, as amended in 1976, "[c]*opyright protection subsists* ＊　＊　＊ *in original works of authorship fixed in any tangible medium of expression* ＊　＊　＊ *from which they can be perceived, reproduced, or otherwise communicated.*" When, as in this case, a freelance author has contributed an article to a "collective work" such as

(Continued)

Case No. 2—Continued

a newspaper or magazine, the statute recognizes two distinct copyrighted works: "Copyright in *each separate contribution to a collective work* is distinct from copyright in *the collective work as a whole* * * *" (emphasis added [by the Court]). Copyright in the separate contribution "vests initially in the author of the contribution" (here, the freelancer). Copyright in the collective work vests in the collective author (here, the newspaper or magazine publisher) and extends only to the creative material contributed by that author, not to "the preexisting material employed in the work." [Emphasis added.]

* * * *

A newspaper or magazine publisher is thus privileged to reproduce or distribute an article contributed by a freelance author, absent a contract otherwise providing, only "as part of" any (or all) of three categories of collective works: (a) "that collective work" to which the author contributed her work, (b) "any revision of that collective work," or (c) "any later collective work in the same series." In accord with Congress' prescription, a publishing company could reprint a contribution from one issue in a later issue of its magazine, and could reprint an article from a 1980 edition of an encyclopedia in a 1990 revision of it; the publisher could not revise the contribution itself or include it in a new anthology or an entirely different magazine or other collective work.

* * * *

In determining whether the Articles have been reproduced and distributed "as part of" a "revision" of the collective works in issue, we focus on the Articles as presented to, and perceptible by, the user of the Databases. In this case, the * * * Databases present articles to users clear of the context provided either by the original periodical editions or by any revision of those editions. The Databases first prompt users to search the universe of their contents: thousands of millions of files containing individual articles from thousands of collective works (*i.e.*, editions), either in one series (the *Times*, in NYTO) or in scores of series (the sundry titles in NEXIS and GPO). When the user conducts a search, each article appears as a separate item within the search result. In NEXIS and NYTO, an article appears to a user without the graphics, formatting, or other articles with which the article was initially published. In GPO, the article appears with the other materials published on the same page or pages, but without any material published on other pages of the original periodical. In either circumstance, we cannot see how the Database perceptibly reproduces and distributes the article "as part of" either the original edition or a "revision" of that edition.

One might view the articles as parts of a new compendium—namely, the entirety of works in the Database. In that compendium, each edition of each periodical represents only a min[u]scule fraction of the ever-expanding Database. The Database no more constitutes a "revision" of each constituent edition than a 400-page novel quoting a sonnet in passing would represent a "revision" of that poem. * * *

* * * *

We conclude that the Electronic Publishers infringed the Authors' copyrights by reproducing and distributing the Articles in a manner not authorized by the Authors and not privileged by [the Copyright Act]. We further conclude that the Print Publishers infringed the Authors' copyrights by authorizing the Electronic Publishers to place the Articles in the Databases and by aiding the Electronic Publishers in that endeavor. We therefore affirm the judgment of the Court of Appeals.

It is so ordered.

DISSENTING OPINION
Justice STEVENS * * * dissenting.

* * * *

* * * [W]hat is sent from the New York Times to the Electronic Databases * * * is simply a collection of ASCII text files representing the editorial content of the *New York Times* for a particular day. * * *

* * * *

No one doubts that the New York Times has the right to reprint its issues in Braille, in a foreign language, or in microform, even though such revisions might look and feel quite different from the original. Such differences, however, would largely result from the different medium being employed. Similarly, the decision to convert the single collective work newspaper into a collection of individual ASCII files can be explained as little more than a decision that reflects the different nature of the electronic medium. Just as the paper version of the *New York Times* is divided into "sections" and "pages" in order to facilitate the reader's navigation and manipulation of large batches of newsprint, so too the decision to subdivide the electronic version of that collective work into individual article files facilitates the reader's use of the electronic information.

CASE NO. 3 ■ FOR CHAPTER 8

AmeriPro Search, Inc. v. Fleming Steel Co.
2001 Pa.Super. 325, 787 A.2d 988 (2001).

DEL SOLE, President Judge.

Fleming Steel Company ("Fleming") appeals from the judgment entered against it, and in favor of AmeriPro Search, Inc. ("AmeriPro"). Upon review, we reverse.

* * * AmeriPro is an employment referral firm that places professional employees with interested employers. Fleming is a steel fabricator. In May of 1993, Elaine Brauninger, an agent of AmeriPro, contacted Fleming and inquired about Fleming's need for professional employees. * * * Fleming was seeking an employee with an engineering background. * * * Ms. Brauninger was advised that [she] would have to speak to Seth Kohn, president of Fleming, who alone made all decisions relating to employment and salaries.

* * * Ms. Brauninger advised Mr. Kohn that if her services were accepted she would be entitled to a fee equal to 30% of the candidate's first year's salary. Mr. Kohn did not agree because he believed the fee to be too high. Mr. Kohn told Ms. Brauninger that the fee would be as determined by him and AmeriPro only after an agreement to hire a candidate was made. Ms. Brauninger agreed and told Mr. Kohn that she would work with him on the amount of the fee.

One of the candidates referred to Fleming was Dominic Barracchini. Ms. Brauninger had contacted Mr. Barracchini in November of 1993 to determine whether Mr. Barracchini would be interested in a position at Fleming. * * * Despite Mr. Barracchini's statement of interest, an interview could not be arranged with Fleming and Mr. Barracchini took employment with [another] company. In April of 1994, Ms. Brauninger again contacted Mr. Barracchini and informed him that she could arrange for an interview with Fleming. Mr. Kohn interviewed Mr. Barracchini on April 8, 1994. Fleming did not hire Mr. Barracchini because Mr. Barracchini's salary request was too high.

Case No. 3—Continued

* * * [In February of 1995,] Mr. Barracchini called Ms. Brauninger to inquire whether Fleming was still trying to fill the position for which he had previously interviewed. Ms. Brauninger never got back to Mr. Barracchini regarding his inquiry. Mr. Barracchini then contacted Fleming on his own. * * * Fleming hired Mr. Barracchini as an engineer on June 19, 1995.

On September 6, 1995, AmeriPro sent an invoice to Fleming claiming entitlement to $14,400.00 for placement of Mr. Barracchini with Fleming. Fleming refused to pay * * *.

* * * *

The trial court determined that there was no express contract formed in this case. * * * The trial court did, however, find that there was a contract implied in law, or a quasi-contract, in this case. It was on this basis that the trial court ordered Fleming to pay AmeriPro the fee for placement of Barracchini.

* * * *

A quasi-contract imposes a duty, not as a result of any agreement, whether express or implied, but in spite of the absence of an agreement, when one party receives unjust enrichment at the expense of another. In determining if the doctrine applies, we focus not on the intention of the parties, but rather on whether the defendant has been unjustly enriched. * * * The most significant element of the doctrine is whether the enrichment of the defendant is unjust * * *.

We cannot find that Fleming was unjustly enriched in this case. Mr. Barracchini was referred to Fleming and the first interview was arranged by AmeriPro. Fleming did not hire Mr. Barracchini at that time because the candidate's salary requirements were too high. Approximately ten months after Mr. Barracchini's initial interview with Fleming, he was laid off from Montage. He contacted Ms. Brauninger to inquire about the job at Fleming and whether it was still open. Ms. Brauninger never responded to Mr. Barracchini's inquiry. As a result, Mr. Barracchini contacted Fleming directly to determine whether the position for which he had previously interviewed was still available. * * * After interviewing Mr. Barracchini in June of 1995, Fleming hired him.

The events leading to the hiring of Mr. Barracchini were separate from any actions taken by Ms. Brauninger and AmeriPro on his behalf. While it is true that AmeriPro and Brauninger first introduced Barracchini to Fleming and the available position, that connection was broken when Fleming refused to hire Barracchini after the interview in April of 1994. * * * Mr. Barracchini's subsequent independent interaction with Mr. Kohn, which led to his actual employment by Fleming, was removed from previous actions taken by AmeriPro on his behalf.

While it may be argued that Fleming received a benefit from AmeriPro because Barracchini would not have known about the position at Fleming without the initial interaction involving AmeriPro, the doctrine of quasi-contract does not apply simply because the defendant may have benefited as a result of the actions of the plaintiff. Regardless of any benefit Fleming received by AmeriPro's action of first introducing Mr. Barracchini to Fleming, the enrichment of Fleming was not unjust. Mr. Barracchini approached Fleming the second time on his own and the two parties came to an agreement regarding Mr. Barracchini's employment without any involvement by AmeriPro. Fleming did nothing to wrongly secure the benefit of Mr. Barracchini's employment. * * * Because Fleming was not unjustly enriched, we find that there was no quasi-contract, or contract implied in law. Thus, Fleming owes AmeriPro nothing in restitution.

Judgment reversed. * * *

CASE NO. 4 ■ FOR CHAPTER 15

Wilson Fertilizer & Grain, Inc. v. ADM Milling Co.
654 N.E.2d 848 (Ind.App. 1995).

MAJORITY OPINION
BARTEAU, Judge.

FACTS

Wilson [Fertilizer & Grain, Inc.] and ADM [Milling Company] entered into a contract under which Wilson shipped grain to ADM. A broker facilitated the deal between Wilson and ADM, and sent each party a confirmation of trade. The confirmation of trade did not contain an arbitration provision. ADM sent a purchase confirmation to Wilson that contained boiler plate language which states: "This contract is also subject to the Trade Rules of the National Grain and Feed Association currently in effect." Wilson did not object to this language and did not respond to ADM's purchase confirmation.

A dispute arose under the contract and Wilson filed suit against ADM in [an Indiana state court]. ADM moved to dismiss the action, claiming that the Trade Rules of the National Grain and Feed Association require the parties to arbitrate the dispute. Wilson argued that the arbitration provisions were not included within the terms of its agreement with ADM. The trial court granted ADM's motion and ordered the parties to arbitration.

DISCUSSION

A party seeking to compel arbitration must satisfy a two-prong burden of proof. First, the party must demonstrate an enforceable agreement to arbitrate the dispute. Second, the party must prove that the disputed matter is the type of claim that the parties agreed to arbitrate. In this case, the second prong of our analysis is not in dispute, since neither party contends that the arbitration provisions do not encompass Wilson's claim. The only question presented herein is under the first prong: whether the additional terms are included in the contract between Wilson and ADM.

Whether the additional provisions are part of the contract is controlled by [Indiana Code Section 26-1-2-207, Indiana's version of UCC 2-207], which provides in part:

(1) A definite and seasonable expression of acceptance or a written confirmation which is sent within a reasonable time operates as an acceptance even though it states terms additional to or different from those offered or agreed upon, unless acceptance is expressly made conditional on assent to the additional or different terms.

(2) The additional terms are to be construed as proposals for addition to the contract. Between merchants such terms become part of the contract unless:

(a) the offer expressly limits acceptance to the terms of the offer;

(b) they materially alter it; or

(c) notification of objection to them has already been given or is given within a reasonable time after notice of them is received.

* * * *

The test for whether additional terms materially alter an agreement is whether their incorporation into the contract without express awareness by the other party would result in surprise or hardship. * * *

(Continued)

Case No. 4—Continued

Some jurisdictions that have considered this issue have adopted the "New York rule" holding that additional arbitration provisions create a material alteration *per se*. This rule is based on New York's well-established law that parties will not be compelled to arbitrate in the absence of an express, unequivocal agreement to that effect; absent such an explicit commitment neither party may be compelled to arbitrate. * * *

* * * Wilson argues that we should follow the New York rule and find that * * * ADM's additional arbitration provisions materially alter the agreement as a matter of law.

* * * [W]e reject Wilson's argument * * * and decline to adopt the New York rule. Instead, whether included arbitration provisions result in hardship or surprise depends upon the facts and circumstances of each case. * * *

* * * [R]equiring a party to arbitrate a dispute does not *necessarily* place a hardship on the party. To the contrary, arbitration may work to the party's benefit by facilitating an efficient and potentially favorable resolution to a dispute. Many trades employ arbitration as a usual and customary dispute resolution mechanism. In light of this, even New York courts have deviated from their *per se* rule and have held that *an additional arbitration clause is not a material alteration if the party had reason to know that such a clause was customarily used in the trade.* [Emphasis added.]

* * *

Turning to the facts presented, Wilson argues that the trial court erroneously determined that the additional provisions did not materially alter its agreement with ADM because the evidence conclusively shows that inclusion of the provisions imposes hardship on Wilson. Specifically, Wilson argues that the National Grain and Feed Association Rules of Arbitration significantly reduce the time period during which it may file its complaint against ADM from Indiana's six-year statute of limitation to one year. Wilson argues that this results in hardship because, now that its claim has been dismissed * * *, time has run for Wilson to file its claim under the arbitration rules. We disagree for two reasons.

First of all, contractually reducing the time period during which parties may bring complaints is permitted under the Uniform Commercial Code. * * * [The UCC] specifically permits parties to a contract for sale to reduce the time for filing claims to one year, and Wilson has not shown that the one-year limitation is not within the customary limits of the trade.

Second, and even more significantly, we are persuaded by Wilson's apparent ability to have submitted its claim for arbitration within the one-year limit. The contract between Wilson and ADM was formed on October 20, 1992. There is nothing in the record indicating when Wilson delivered its grain to ADM, or when ADM's alleged breach occurred. However, Wilson filed its complaint for damages * * * on September 24, 1993, within one year after the contract was formed. Thus, Wilson filed its complaint within one year after the cause of action accrued because, as a matter of logic, an action for breach of contract can only accrue after the contract was formed. If Wilson was able to file its complaint in court within one year after the cause of action accrued, we fail to see how a contract provision requiring Wilson to submit its claim for arbitration in the same time period imposes a hardship.

* * * *

The trial court's finding that the additional term in ADM's purchase confirmation did not materially alter the agreement is supported by the evidence and is not clearly erroneous.

AFFIRMED.

DISSENTING OPINION

KIRSCH, Judge, * * * dissenting.

I fully concur with the rule of law set forth in the majority opinion. From its application to the facts of this case, however, I respectfully dissent.

* * * *

* * * [T]here are two factual issues which should be determined by the trial court: The first issue is whether ADM's confirmation even constituted an acceptance within the meaning of UCC [Section] 2–207. If the confirmation sent by the broker to Wilson was sent prior to ADM's confirmation, it constitutes the acceptance of the offer; the contract was fully formed by that confirmation. The later confirmation sent by ADM would only be a proposal to modify the contract as formed and UCC [Section] 2–207 would not apply. Second, even if ADM's confirmation constitutes the acceptance and [Section] 2–207 does apply, there is an unresolved question of fact as to whether the additional term contained in such confirmation results in hardship or surprise and thus constitutes a material alteration. In either event, these unresolved factual issues make the dismissal of this case inappropriate.

ADM Milling Company played the latest version of "Legal Gotcha." And it won. It has received the grain which it ordered and escaped paying for it.

I would reverse the dismissal and remand to the trial court to conduct an evidentiary hearing.

CASE NO. 5 ■ FOR CHAPTER 19

Flatiron Linen, Inc. v. First American State Bank
23 P.3d 1209 (Colo.Sup.Ct. 2001).

Justice *KORLIS* delivered the Opinion of the Court.

In this case, we granted *certiorari* to address questions related to the legal status of a cashier's check under Articles 3 and 4 of the Uniform Commercial Code (U.C.C.). Specifically, we address the issue of whether an obligated bank that accepts an endorsed personal check on the account of one of its customers and issues a cashier's check in the same amount can later refuse to honor that cashier's check on the basis that its customer had previously placed a stop payment order on the check and its employee, the cashier, failed to notice the stop payment order on the computer records. * * *

* * * *

In 1996, Flatiron received a personal check for $4,100, drawn on an account at First American. Flatiron attempted to deposit the check the same day, but First American returned the check to Flatiron due to insufficient funds in the issuer's account. The next day, the issuer of the check contacted First American and requested a stop payment order on the dishonored check.

Five months later, without knowledge of the stop payment order, Flatiron contacted First American and inquired whether the dishonored check would clear. An employee of First American responded that the account contained sufficient funds for the check to clear. Flatiron then took the check to a First American branch and presented it for payment. * * * The teller failed to notice the stop

Case No. 5—Continued

payment order on the check and, in exchange for the check, issued the plaintiff a cashier's check for $4,100.

Flatiron then went to its own bank, Colorado National Bank (CNB), deposited the cashier's check, and immediately withdrew the same amount of funds in the form of * * * [a] cashier's check * * *. Meanwhile, First American discovered the stop payment order on the original check * * * called and wrote to Flatiron, informing Flatiron of First American's mistake in issuing the cashier's check * * * and informing Flatiron that it intended to dishonor the cashier's check upon presentment.

The next day, CNB contacted Flatiron and informed it that First American had indeed dishonored the cashier's check. CNB charged back Flatiron's account for the amount of the cashier's check, resulting in an overdraft in Flatiron's account.

Flatiron filed this action, alleging fraudulent misrepresentation and negligence against the issuer of the original check and one of its officers. * * *

* * * *

II.

We begin by discussing the proper classification of cashier's checks. *Our analysis of this case turns on whether we treat a cashier's check as an ordinary negotiable instrument or whether we treat it as equivalent to cash.* [Emphasis added.]

A.

Courts are split on this issue. A minority of courts treat a cashier's check as a note, subject to the provisions of the U.C.C.

Both the trial court and the court of appeals adopted this approach. Under this reasoning, courts then turn to the U.C.C. to determine which defenses the bank may assert against the holder of a cashier's check. [Colorado Revised Statutes] Section 4-3-305 [Colorado's version of UCC 3–305] outlines the availability of defenses to the payment of negotiable instruments under the revised U.C.C. and differentiates between defenses that may be asserted only against a holder in due course and those that may be asserted against a holder not in due course. The only defenses available against a holder in due course are the "real defenses." When the instrument is held by a holder not in due course, the obligor can raise not only the real defenses, but also the general contract defenses and the defenses included in the U.C.C. Failure of consideration is a defense that "would be available if the person entitled to enforce the instrument were enforcing a right to payment under a simple contract." Therefore, such a defense cannot be used against a holder in due course. Section 4-3-302 [UCC 3–302] outlines the requirements to establish the status of a holder in due course. The basic prerequisites of a holder in due course are: receiving the instrument for value, in good faith, and without notice of defects or claims against it. Hence, under this theory, in order for Flatiron to have holder in due course status, it must prove that it acted in good faith when it presented the personal check, that it had no knowledge of the stop payment order, and that the personal check had intrinsic value.

The majority of courts hold that a cashier's check is the equivalent of cash, accepted when issued. Those courts do not treat the cashier's check as a check on the bank's account, but rather as the equivalent of cash. Courts following this approach have held that a cashier's check is a bill of exchange drawn by a bank upon itself. Therefore, it is accepted in advance by the act of its issuance, and it cannot be dishonored by the issuing bank.

We agree with the majority of courts that a cashier's check is equivalent to cash.

B.

We begin with an analysis of the U.C.C.'s treatment of cashier's checks. Although the U.C.C. does not specifically state how cashier's checks should be classified, it does provide some guidance. Section 4-3-104(g) [UCC 3–104(g)] defines a cashier's check as "a draft with respect to which the drawer and drawee are the same bank or branches of the same bank." Because the bank serves as both the drawer and the drawee of the cashier's check, the check becomes a promise by the bank to draw the amount of the check from its own resources and to pay the check upon demand. Thus, the issuance of the cashier's check constitutes an acceptance by the issuing bank and the cashier's check itself becomes the primary obligation of the bank. Once the bank issues and delivers the cashier's check to the payee, the transaction is complete as far as the payee is concerned. *Because the issuing bank is obligated to pay the cashier's check upon presentment, we conclude that a cashier's check is essentially the same as cash.* [Emphasis added.]

* * * *

C.

* * * The commercial world treats cashier's checks as the equivalent of cash. People accept cashier's checks as a substitute for cash because the bank, not an individual, stands behind it. By issuing a cashier's check, the bank becomes a guarantor of the value of the check and pledges its resources to the payment of the amount represented upon presentation. To allow the bank to stop payment on such an instrument would be inconsistent with the representation it makes in issuing the check. Such a rule would undermine the public confidence in the bank and its checks and thereby deprive the cashier's check of the essential incident which makes it useful.

Cashier's checks play a unique role in the American economy because they are widely recognized as a cash equivalent. The public uses cashier's checks because they are a reliable vehicle for transferring funds, are as negotiable as cash, and are free of the risks of loss and theft that accompany cash.

In short, we conclude that cashier's checks represent the unconditional obligation of the issuing bank to pay, and therefore, banks may not dishonor their cashier's checks once issued.

* * * *

IV.

In conclusion, we hold that when First American issued the cashier's check, it became an unconditional promise to pay the amount of the check—as the equivalent of cash. Accordingly, First American was not entitled to stop payment on the cashier's check. * * * Therefore, we reverse the judgment of the court of appeals, and remand the case with directions to return it to the trial court for proceedings consistent with this opinion.

CASE NO. 6 ■ FOR CHAPTER 23

Shanks v. Lowe
364 Md. 538, 774 A.3d 411 (2001).

MAJORITY OPINION
WILNER, Judge:

The issue before us is whether tips earned by a waitress (or other person who earns tips) constitute "wages" for purposes of the

(Continued)

Case No. 6—Continued

Maryland wage garnishment law, Maryland Code [Sections] 15-601 through 15-607 * * * . Principally at issue is whether tips fall within the definition of "wages" in [Section] 15-601(c): "all monetary remuneration paid to any employee for his employment." * * *

* * * In January, 1995, petitioner, Laura Shanks, recovered a judgment for $6,000 against Susan Dolle, in [a Maryland state court]. In April, 1998, Ms. Shanks caused a wage garnishment to be issued by the * * * Court and served on Kibby's Restaurant & Lounge, Dolle's employer [in Baltimore, Maryland]. The writ of garnishment directed Kibby's to withhold Dolle's "attachable wages" for any workweek until either the judgment * * * [was] satisfied or Kibby's was otherwise notified by the court. The writ also stated, in relevant part, that exempt from the garnishment was the greater of (1) the product of $154.50 multiplied by the number of weeks in which "the wages due were earned," or (2) 75% of "the disposable wages due." The term "disposable wages" was defined to mean "the part of wages that remain after deduction of any amount required to be withheld by law."

On June 5, 1998, Kibby's sent the writ of garnishment back to the court with a handwritten note stating that Dolle's "disposable income average per week is approx $35–$40," which fell below the allowable exemption of $154.50. Kibby's said that, if that situation changed, it would comply with the court order, but it requested that the garnishment action be dismissed. * * *

* * * Kibby's acknowledged that, in addition to the money that it paid to her, Dolle earned tips, but, because those tips were paid directly to her by restaurant patrons, it denied that they constituted "wages" for purposes of the wage garnishment law. In that regard, it claimed that Kibby's only obligation to Dolle was to pay the agreed-upon hourly wage, that it had no obligation to pay her the tips she earned directly from customers, and that, even if the tips *did* constitute * * * wages for purposes of [Section] 15-601, Kibby's could not comply with the duty to withhold because it never had possession of them. * * * [T]he * * * Court found merit in Kibby's response. It * * * held that Kibby's was "not responsible for the collection of any tips paid directly to its employee * * * ."

Petitioner appealed that decision to [a state intermediate appellate] Court, which affirmed * * * . Some greater detail regarding Dolle's gross and net earnings was revealed at the [appellate] Court level through payroll and Federal tax records * * * . This can be easily illustrated by looking at one representative week—that of November 27, 1998. In that week, Kibby's reported $92.44 in wages due Dolle and $153.50 in tips, for a total taxable wage of $245.94. From that amount, it deducted $29.25 in Federal taxes, $18.82 [in Social Security contributions under the Federal Insurance Contributions Act (FICA)], and $13.87 in State taxes, leaving a net pay, from the $92.44 it owed Dolle, of $30.50.

Kibby's never had possession of the tips paid to Dolle; she received and retained the full gross amount of those tips. What Kibby's did, however, was to withhold from the wage that *it* owed to Dolle the Federal, State, and FICA taxes attributable to the tips, which served to reduce the net pay owing to Dolle below what it would have been had the withholdings been based solely on the amount of wage payable by Kibby's.

We granted *certiorari* * * * .

* * * Maryland Code, [Section] 3-413(1) * * * requires each employer in Maryland to pay its employees the minimum wage

required by the Federal Fair Labor Standards Act. The term "wage" is defined in [Section] 3-401(e) as "all compensation that is due to an employee for employment" * * * . Section 3-419 takes specific account of tips and, as to any employee who regularly receives more than $30/month in tips, * * * provides, in relevant part, that an employer may include, "as part of the wage of an employee to whom this section applies," an amount that the employer sets to represent the tips of the employee, up to $2.77/hour. This is consistent with the Federal law, which defines a "tipped employee" as an employee engaged in an occupation in which he or she customarily and regularly receives more than $30/month in tips and, in relevant part, calculates the required minimum wage for such an employee as the actual cash wage paid by the employer plus an additional amount on account of tips equal to the difference between that actual cash wage and the minimum wage * * * . Thus, for purposes of the State and Federal minimum wage laws, tips are regarded as part of wages.

Significantly, tips are included within the meaning of wages for purposes of the unemployment insurance and workers' compensation laws, each of which provide benefits based on the employee's wages. * * * Were Ms. Dolle to file a claim for either unemployment insurance or workers' compensation benefits, any benefits to which she might be entitled would be determined on the basis of the aggregate amounts she received from both Kibby's and its customers.

* * * *

These statutes illustrate a consistent view by the General Assembly [Maryland's legislature] that, in using terms such as "wage" or "wages," it intended to include all forms of remuneration, whether or not paid directly by the employer, except to the extent specifically excluded. When it desired to limit the scope of a statute to the remuneration paid in the form of a salary or other periodic payment by an employer, it made that intent clear. * * *

* * * *

For these reasons, we reverse the judgment of the [appellate] Court and remand to that court with instructions to reverse the judgment of the [trial] Court and remand to that court for further proceedings * * * .

DISSENTING OPINION

ELDRIDGE, Judge, dissenting.

I disagree with the Court's conclusion that cash tips paid directly to an employee by a customer constitute "wages" for the purpose of Maryland's wage garnishment law. * * *

* * * *

* * * [T]he debtor-employee could not maintain an action against the garnishee-employer for payment of these tips because the employer is not liable to the employee for cash tips paid directly to the employee by her customers. Under no scenario is the employer liable to the employee for cash tips which the employer never possesses or controls. Since the debtor has no right to recover from her employer cash tips paid to her directly from her customers, the judgment creditor has no right to such a recovery. Where the creditor fails to prove that such a liability existed, there must be a verdict for the garnishee.

* * * *

* * * [Also] I fail to understand how [the] statutes [that the majority cites] have any bearing on garnishment proceedings. * * * Garnishment is a tool by which a judgment creditor can reach the assets of a judgment debtor in the hands of a third party, the gar-

Case No. 6–Continued

nishee. The purpose of garnishment is the seizure of money or other property actually in the hands of the garnishee, and if that money or property is not there, then it cannot be garnished. * * * [T]hose statutes which expressly include tips and gratuities within the definition of wages do not support the Court's theory. To the contrary, the statutory language on which the Court relies demonstrates that the General Assembly knows how to draft a statute to include tips within the meaning of wages if it so desires.

* * *

* * * If notions of fairness justify treating cash tips, paid directly by the customer to a waitress or waiter, as garnishable wages in the hands of the employer, it is for the General Assembly, and not for this Court, to say so.

CASE NO. 7 ■ FOR CHAPTER 27

Gottsacker v. Monnier
281 Wis.2d 361, 697 N.W.2d 436 (2005).

MAJORITY OPINION
ANN WALSH BRADLEY, J. [Justice]

* * *

On September 4, 1998, Julie Monnier * * * formed New Jersey LLC as a vehicle to own investment real estate. Ten days later, the company acquired a 40,000-square-foot warehouse located at 2005 New Jersey Avenue in Sheboygan, Wisconsin. * * * New Jersey LLC purchased the property for $510,000, with the financing arranged for and guaranteed by Monnier.

Brothers Paul Gottsacker * * * and Gregory Gottsacker * * * became members of New Jersey LLC in January 1999. They entered into a Member's Agreement, which expressed their intent to operate under Wisconsin's limited liability company laws. That document stated in relevant part:

(4) Julie A. Monnier shall own a 50% interest in the capital, profits and losses of Company and shall have 50% of the voting rights of Company.
(5) Paul Gottsacker and Gregory Gottsacker, collectively, shall own a 50% interest * * * and shall have 50% of the voting rights * * * .

New Jersey LLC later purchased additional property in Sheboygan on Wilson Avenue. When it was sold, the proceeds were distributed to the members as follows: 50% to Julie, 25% to Paul, and 25% to Gregory. After the sale of the Wilson Avenue property, the only remaining asset of New Jersey LLC was the warehouse on New Jersey Avenue.

Relationships among the members of New Jersey LLC subsequently became strained. In May 2000, Paul and Gregory had a falling-out, allegedly due to Gregory's lack of contribution to the enterprise. Thereafter, communication between the brothers was virtually nonexistent. Monnier also testified that she had not spoken with Gregory since 1998.

On June 7, 2001, Monnier executed a * * * deed transferring the warehouse * * * to a new limited liability company called 2005 New Jersey LLC for $510,000, the same amount as the original purchase price. The new limited liability company consisted of two members: Monnier with a 60% ownership interest and Paul with a 40% ownership interest. Neither one had discussed the transfer with Gregory * * * .

Following the transfer, Monnier sent a check to Gregory for $22,000, which purportedly represented his 25% interest in the ware-

house property previously owned by New Jersey LLC. Gregory did not cash the check. Monnier and Paul, meanwhile, did not receive any cash payment but instead left their equity in the recently created 2005 New Jersey LLC.

Gregory commenced suit [in a Wisconsin state court] against Monnier, Paul, and 2005 New Jersey LLC, alleging that they had engaged in an illegal transaction * * * . [The trial] court agreed

* * * .

* * * Monnier, Paul, and 2005 New Jersey LLC appealed

* * * .

[A state intermediate appellate court] affirmed the decision * * * . [The defendants appealed to the Wisconsin Supreme Court.]

* * *

The first issue we address is whether the [defendants] possessed the majority necessary to authorize the transfer in question. * * *

* * *

We conclude that the Member's Agreement here is ambiguous as to the voting rights of Paul and Gregory. To begin, the term "collectively" is not defined in the document. * * *

* * *

* * * [W]e are satisfied that the term "collectively" refers to the sum of the brothers' individual 25% interests. To conclude otherwise would require unanimous approval by the members in order to perform any act that concerns the business of the company. Here, there is no express language indicating that the parties intended such a result. Construing the Member's Agreement to allow one minority member to effectively deadlock the LLC is unreasonable absent express language.

* * *

* * * [W]e consider next whether [the defendants] were nonetheless prohibited from voting to transfer the property because of a material conflict of interest. Here, the [trial] court found that "the conveyance of the property by Julie Monnier and Paul Gottsacker to themselves in the guise of a newly created LLC, unquestionably, represents a material conflict of interest." This finding is supported by the facts of the case. Not only did Monnier and Paul engage in self-dealing, but in doing so they also increased their individual interests in the new LLC which received the property. Monnier's ownership improved from 50% to 60%, while Paul's interest improved from 25% to 40%.

The question therefore becomes what, if any, impact did this conflict of interest have on Monnier and Paul's ability to vote to transfer the property. [Wisconsin Statutes Section] 183.0404 governs voting in LLCs and contemplates situations that would prevent a member from exercising that voting power. Subsection (3) of the statute explicitly states that members can be "precluded from voting." However, that subsection does not address how or when that preclusion would occur. * * *

* * *

* * * Wis. Stat. [Section] 183.0402 * * * anticipates members having a material conflict of interest and requires them to "deal fairly" with the LLC and its other members. * * *

* * *

Reading Wis. Stat. [Sections] 183.0404 and 183.0402 together in harmony, we determine that the [Wisconsin LLC Law] does not preclude members with a material conflict of interest from voting their ownership interest with respect to a given matter. Rather, it prohibits

(Continued)

Case No. 7—Continued

members with a material conflict of interest from acting in a manner that constitutes a willful failure to deal fairly with the LLC or its other members. * * *

Here, the [trial] court made no express determination as to whether the petitioners willfully failed to deal fairly in spite of the conflict of interest. * * *

* * * *

Accordingly, we remand the case to the [trial] court for further findings and application of the foregoing standard. * * * If it is determined by the [trial] court that this [standard] was violated, then the court will determine the appropriate remedy under the circumstances.

* * * *

The decision of the court of appeals is reversed * * *.

* * * *

DISSENTING OPINION
LOUIS B. BUTLER, JR., J. [Justice] (dissenting).

* * * *

* * * It was the parties that specified [in the members' agreement] the two separate 50 percent interests in New Jersey LLC. It was the parties that specified the two separate voting blocks. They could have chosen to draft the agreement to take into account each person's individual interest and voting rights, but the parties chose not to do so. If the parties choose to set forth an agreement that requires the brothers to vote together as one interest, this court should not stand in their way. If the drafters of [the Wisconsin LLC Law] emphasized the importance of flexibility and freedom of contract, then we ought to respect the flexibility and freedom of this agreement. In short, the trial court got it right when it concluded that Paul Gottsacker lacked the authority to act without the assent of his brother.

Gregory Gottsacker did not agree to or even know about the transfer of the warehouse engineered by petitioners in this matter. * * * I therefore agree with the trial court that the warehouse should be returned from 2005 New Jersey LLC to New Jersey LLC. Accordingly, I respectfully dissent.

CASE NO. 8 ■ FOR CHAPTER 34

Sutton v. United Airlines, Inc.
527 U.S. 471, 119 S.Ct. 2139, 144 L.Ed.2d 450 (1999).

MAJORITY OPINION
Justice *O'CONNOR* delivered the opinion of the Court.

* * * *

Petitioners [Karen and Kimberly Sutton] are twin sisters, both of whom have severe myopia. Each petitioner's uncorrected visual acuity is 20/200 or worse in her right eye and 20/400 or worse in her left eye, but with the use of corrective lenses, each * * * has vision that is 20/20 or better. Consequently, without corrective lenses, each effectively cannot see to conduct numerous activities such as driving a vehicle, watching television or shopping in public stores, but with corrective measures, such as glasses or contact lenses, both function identically to individuals without a similar impairment.

In 1992, petitioners applied to respondent [United Airlines, Inc.,] for employment as commercial airline pilots. They met respondent's basic age, education, experience, and Federal Aviation Administration certification qualifications. After submitting their applications for employment, both petitioners were invited by respondent to an interview and to flight simulator tests. Both were told during their interviews, however, that a mistake had been made in inviting them to interview because petitioners did not meet respondent's minimum vision requirement, which was uncorrected visual acuity of 20/100 or better. Due to their failure to meet this requirement, petitioners' interviews were terminated, and neither was offered a pilot position.

In light of respondent's proffered [offered] reason for rejecting them, petitioners filed a charge of disability discrimination under the [Americans with Disabilities Act of 1990 (ADA)] with the Equal Employment Opportunity Commission (EEOC). After receiving a right to sue letter, petitioners filed suit in the United States District Court for the District of Colorado, alleging that respondent had discriminated against them "on the basis of their disability, or because [respondent] regarded [petitioners] as having a disability" in violation of the ADA. Specifically, petitioners alleged that due to their severe myopia they actually have a substantially limiting impairment or are regarded as having such an impairment and are thus disabled under the Act.

The District Court dismissed petitioners' complaint for failure to state a claim upon which relief could be granted. * * * [T]he Court of Appeals for the Tenth Circuit affirmed the District Court's judgment. * * * We granted *certiorari* * * *.

* * * *

* * * The Act defines a "disability" as "a physical or mental impairment that *substantially limits* one or more of the major life activities" of an individual. [Emphasis added.] Because the phrase "substantially limits" appears in the Act in the present indicative verb form, we think the language is properly read as requiring that a person be presently—not potentially or hypothetically—substantially limited in order to demonstrate a disability. A "disability" exists only where an impairment "substantially limits" a major life activity, not where it "might," "could," or "would" be substantially limiting if mitigating measures were not taken. A person whose physical or mental impairment is corrected by medication or other measures does not have an impairment that presently "substantially limits" a major life activity. To be sure, *a person whose physical or mental impairment is corrected by mitigating measures still has an impairment, but if the impairment is corrected it does not "substantially limi[t]" a major life activity.* [Emphasis added.]

* * * *

* * * The use of a corrective device does not, by itself, relieve one's disability. Rather, one has a disability under [the ADA] if, notwithstanding the use of a corrective device, that individual is substantially limited in a major life activity. For example, individuals who use prosthetic limbs or wheelchairs may be mobile and capable of functioning in society but still be disabled because of a substantial limitation on their ability to walk or run. The same may be true of individuals who take medicine to lessen the symptoms of an impairment so that they can function but nevertheless remain substantially limited. Alternatively, one whose high blood pressure is "cured" by medication may be regarded as disabled by a covered entity, and thus disabled under [the ADA]. *The use or nonuse of a corrective device does not determine whether an individual is disabled; that determination depends on whether the limitations an individual with an impairment actually faces are in fact substantially limiting.* [Emphasis added.]

Applying this reading of the Act to the case at hand, we conclude that the Court of Appeals correctly resolved the issue of disability in respondent's favor. As noted above, petitioners allege that with cor-

Case No. 8—Continued

rective measures, their visual acuity is 20/20 and that they "function identically to individuals without a similar impairment." In addition, petitioners concede that they "do not argue that the use of corrective lenses in itself demonstrates a substantially limiting impairment." Accordingly, because we decide that disability under the Act is to be determined with reference to corrective measures, we agree with the [lower] courts * * * that petitioners have not stated a claim that they are substantially limited in any major life activity.

* * * *

Our conclusion that petitioners have failed to state a claim that they are actually disabled under [the ADA's] disability definition does not end our inquiry. * * * [The ADA] provides that having a disability includes "being regarded as having a physical or mental impairment that substantially limits one or more of the major life activities of such individual." There are two apparent ways in which individuals may fall within this statutory definition: (1) a covered entity mistakenly believes that a person has a physical impairment that substantially limits one or more major life activities, or (2) a covered entity mistakenly believes that an actual, non-limiting impairment substantially limits one or more major life activities. In both cases, it is necessary that a covered entity entertain misperceptions about the individual—it must believe either that one has a substantially limiting impairment that one does not have or that one has a substantially limiting impairment when, in fact, the impairment is not so limiting. These misperceptions often result from stereotypic assumptions not truly indicative of * * * individual ability.

* * * *

* * * By its terms, the ADA allows employers to prefer some physical attributes over others and to establish physical criteria. *An employer runs afoul of the ADA when it makes an employment decision based on a physical or mental impairment, real or imagined, that is regarded as substantially limiting a major life activity.* * * * [Emphasis added.]

* * * The EEOC has codified regulations interpreting the term "substantially limits" * * * to mean "[u]nable to perform" or "[s]ignificantly restricted." When the major life activity under consideration is that of working, the statutory phrase "substantially limits" requires, at a minimum, that plaintiffs allege they are unable to work in a broad class of jobs. * * * The inability to perform a single, particular job does not constitute a substantial limitation in the major life activity of working.

* * * *

* * * [P]etitioners have failed to allege adequately that their poor eyesight is regarded as an impairment that substantially limits them in the major life activity of working. They allege only that respondent regards their poor vision as precluding them from holding positions as a "global airline pilot." Because the position of global airline pilot is a single job, this allegation does not support the claim that respondent regards petitioners as having a *substantially limiting* impairment. Indeed, there are a number of other positions utilizing petitioners' skills, such as regional pilot and pilot instructor to name a few, that are available to them. * * *

* * * *

For these reasons, the judgment of the Court of Appeals for the Tenth Circuit is affirmed.

It is so ordered.

DISSENTING OPINION
Justice STEVENS * * * dissenting.

* * * [I]f we apply customary tools of statutory construction, it is quite clear that the threshold question whether an individual is "disabled" within the meaning of the Act * * * focuses on her past or present physical condition without regard to mitigation that has resulted from rehabilitation, self-improvement, prosthetic devices, or medication. One might reasonably argue that the general rule should not apply to an impairment that merely requires a near-sighted person to wear glasses. But I believe that, in order to be faithful to the remedial purpose of the Act, we should give it a generous, rather than a miserly, construction.

* * * *

* * * [E]ach of the three Executive agencies charged with implementing the Act has consistently interpreted the Act as mandating that the presence of disability turns on an individual's uncorrected state. * * *

* * * *

* * * In my judgment * * * [t]he Act generally protects individuals who have "correctable" substantially limiting impairments from unjustified employment discrimination on the basis of those impairments. * * *

* * * *

* * * [V]isual impairments should be judged by the same standard as hearing impairments or any other medically controllable condition.

* * * *

* * * Only two percent of the population suffers from such myopia. Such acuity precludes a person from driving, shopping in a public store, or viewing a computer screen from a reasonable distance. Uncorrected vision, therefore, can be "substantially limiting" in the same way that unmedicated epilepsy or diabetes can be. Because Congress obviously intended to include individuals with the latter impairments in the Act's protected class, we should give petitioners the same protection.

* * * *

Accordingly * * * I am persuaded that [the petitioners] have a disability covered by the ADA. I therefore respectfully dissent.

CASE NO. 9 ■ FOR CHAPTER 37

City of Monterey v. Del Monte Dunes at Monterey
526 U.S. 687, 119 S.Ct. 1624, 143 L.Ed.2d 882 (1999).

Justice *KENNEDY* delivered the opinion of the Court.

This case began with attempts by respondent Del Monte Dunes and its predecessor in interest to develop a parcel of land within the jurisdiction of the petitioner, the city of Monterey. The city, in a series of repeated rejections, denied proposals to develop the property, each time imposing more rigorous demands on the developers. Del Monte Dunes brought suit in the United States District Court for the Northern District of California, under Rev. Stat. [Section] 1979, 42 U.S.C. [Section] 1983. After protracted litigation, the case was submitted to the jury on Del Monte Dunes' theory that the city effected a regulatory taking or otherwise injured the property by unlawful acts, without paying compensation or providing an adequate postdeprivation remedy for the loss. The jury found for Del Monte Dunes, and the Court of Appeals affirmed.

* * * The controlling question is whether * * * the matter was properly submitted to the jury.

(Continued)

Case No. 9—Continued

* * * * * * *

* * * [I]n suits sounding in tort for money damages [suits brought not for the recovery of things, such as land or goods, but for damages only], questions of liability were [historically] decided by the jury, rather than the judge, in most cases. * * *

In *Williamson County Regional Planning Commission v. Hamilton Bank of Johnson City*, 473 U.S. 172, 105 S.Ct. 3108, 87 L.Ed.2d 126 (1985), we * * * review[ed] a regulatory takings case in which the plaintiff landowner sued a county planning commission in federal court for money damages * * * . Whether the commission had denied the plaintiff all economically viable use of the property had been submitted to the jury. Although the Court did not consider the point, it assumed the propriety of this procedure.

* * * * * * *

In actions at law predominantly factual issues are in most cases allocated to the jury. The allocation rests on a firm historical foundation and serves to preserve the right to a jury's resolution of the ultimate dispute.

Almost from the inception of our regulatory takings doctrine, we have held that whether a regulation of property goes so far that there must be an exercise of eminent domain and compensation to sustain the act * * * depends upon the particular facts. Consistent with this understanding, we have described determinations of liability in regulatory takings cases as essentially * * * factual inquiries, requiring complex factual assessments of the purposes and economic effects of government actions.

In accordance with these pronouncements, we hold that the issue whether a landowner has been deprived of all economically viable use of his property is a predominantly factual question. As our implied acknowledgment of the procedure in *Williamson* suggests, in actions at law otherwise within the purview of the Seventh Amendment, this question is for the jury.

The jury's role in determining whether a land-use decision substantially advances legitimate public interests within the meaning of our regulatory takings doctrine presents a more difficult question. Although our cases make clear that this inquiry involves an essential factual component, it no doubt has a legal aspect as well, and is probably best understood as a mixed question of fact and law.

In this case, the narrow question submitted to the jury was whether, when viewed in light of the context and protracted history of the development application process, the city's decision to reject a particular development plan bore a reasonable relationship to its proffered justifications. As the [U.S. Court of Appeals for the Ninth Circuit] recognized, this question was "essentially fact-bound [in] nature." Under these circumstances, we hold that it was proper to submit this narrow, factbound question to the jury.

* * * * * * *

* * * [T]he judgment of the Court of Appeals is affirmed.

CASE NO. 10 ▪ FOR CHAPTER 39

JP Morgan Chase Bank v. Alto Hornos de Mexico, S.A. de C.V.
__ F.Supp.2d __ (S.D.N.Y. 2004), affirmed on appeal, 412 F.3d 418 (2d Cir. 2005).

BAER, J. [Judge]

* * * * * *

On April 11, 1997, Altos Hornos, Mexico's largest liquid steel producer, entered into a $330-million loan agreement with JPMCB [JP Morgan Chase Bank] and twenty-seven other lending banks. * * * In addition to being one of the lending banks, JPMCB was designated as the "Facility Agent" to act on behalf of the banks. * * * The Loan Agreement, among other things, established a "special cash collection account" ("Collection Account") held at JPMCB's office in New York into which certain payments under the Loan Agreement were to be made and from which JPMCB, as Facility Agent, would distribute funds to the other lending banks. * * * Altos Hornos [instructed] three of its customers * * * to make payments to the Collection Account. * * * [E]ach of the Loan Documents contained a forum-selection and choice-of-law clause in favor of New York.

* * * * * *

Due to adverse developments in the global steel market in the late 1990s caused largely by the financial crisis in Asia, Altos Hornos, already in financial difficulty, suffered additional significant operating losses. As a result, Altos Hornos missed a payment required by the Loan Agreement and JPMCB declared Altos Hornos in default. On May 24, 1999, Altos Hornos filed a petition * * * [in] Mexico to be declared in *suspension de pagos* [suspension of payments, or SOP, which is somewhat analogous to a reorganization under Chapter 11 of the U.S. Bankruptcy Code]. * * * [A]fter the Mexican court granted the petition, the three steel customers paid into the Collection Account approximately $4.7 million for purchases they had made prior to the SOP in the ordinary course of Altos Hornos's business. Morgan did not distribute these proceeds to the lending banks, as was provided in the Loan Agreement. * * *

* * * Altos Hornos made the equivalent in Mexico of a motion to order JPMCB to reimburse the $4.7 million to Altos Hornos for distribution in the SOP proceeding on the ground that this money is part of Altos Hornos's equity and properly belongs to it as an asset to be equitably distributed in this SOP proceeding. * * * JPMCB commenced this action seeking a declaration that the funds in the Collection Account are not property of Altos Hornos's estate.

[Altos Hornos contends that this matter should be dismissed on the grounds of comity.] Under the principle of comity, American courts defer to proceedings in foreign countries so long as the foreign court had proper jurisdiction and enforcement does not prejudice the rights of the United States citizens or violate domestic public policy. We have repeatedly noted the importance of extending comity to foreign bankruptcy proceedings. [Because] the equitable and orderly distribution of a debtor's property requires assembling all claims against the limited assets in a single proceeding, American courts regularly defer to such actions. The decision whether or not to extend comity is generally a matter of discretion. * * * "Comity," in the legal sense, is neither a matter of absolute obligation, on the one hand, nor of mere courtesy and good will, upon the other. *But it is the recognition which one nation allows within its territory to the legislative, executive, or judicial acts of another nation, having due regard both to international duty and convenience, and to the rights of its own citizens, or of other persons who are under the protection of its laws.* [Emphasis added.]

As to whether under Mexican law U.S. courts can, should, or must resolve the issue [in this case] JPMCB posits [suggests, proposes] the thought that under Mexican law the ownership of this property is more appropriately resolved by a U.S. court, given that * * * the SOP court lacks jurisdiction * * * .

Case No. 10—Continued

* * * [T]his argument is what psychiatrists might characterize as rationalization. Article 126 of the Mexican bankruptcy law establishes the scope of claims that must be heard by the bankruptcy court. It provides as follows:

> All pending suits against the bankrupt shall be tried jointly with the bankruptcy proceedings, except * * * [t]hose dealing with secured claims or collateral.

Assuming that JPMCB is correct that the assets in the Collection Account are assets that deal with secured claims or collateral and thus fall within the exception * * * the SOP court has jurisdiction. * * *

* * * *

* * * I do not believe that there is anything in Mexican law that would require the issue of ownership of the Collection Account to be resolved in a Mexican court; nor is there any principle in Mexican law that would be offended by this Court's resolution of the issue. In short, Mexican law appears to be quite agnostic on this issue—it does not dictate one way or the other where the dispute must be decided.

* * * *

JPMCB contends that the forum-selection and choice-of-law clause * * * operate to prevent Altos Hornos from objecting to jurisdiction here. * * *

It is settled law that the presence of such a forum-selection and choice-of-law clause does not preclude comity where it is otherwise warranted. * * * [C]onsiderations associated with comity trump the parties' express wishes. That the parties here appear to have stated their intentions * * * does not change the fact that there are important considerations that may not have concerned the parties [at the time of their contract] but which must concern this Court now—for example, Altos Hornos's other creditors and the importance of a unified administration rather than a piecemeal administration of its estate in the SOP proceeding. * * *

* * * *

For the foregoing reasons, Altos Hornos's motion to dismiss the complaint on the basis of comity is granted.

Glossary

A

actual malice ■ The deliberate intent to cause harm, which exists when a person makes a statement either knowing that it is false or showing a reckless disregard for whether it is true. In defamation law, a statement made about a public figure normally must be made with actual malice for the plaintiff to recover damages.

abandoned property ■ Property with which the owner has voluntarily parted, with no intention of recovering it.

acceleration clause ■ A clause that allows a payee or other holder of a time instrument to demand payment of the entire amount due, with interest, if a certain event occurs, such as a default in the payment of an installment when due.

acceptance ■ In contract law, a voluntary act by the offeree that shows assent, or agreement, to the terms of an offer; may consist of words or conduct. In negotiable instruments law, the drawee's signed agreement to pay a draft when it is presented.

acceptor ■ A drawee that is legally obligated to pay an instrument when it is presented later for payment.

accession ■ Occurs when an individual adds value to personal property by the use of either labor or materials. In some situations, a person may acquire ownership rights in another's property through accession.

accommodation party ■ A person who signs an instrument for the purpose of lending her or his name as credit to another party on the instrument.

accord and satisfaction ■ A common means of settling a disputed claim, whereby a debtor offers to pay a lesser amount than the creditor purports is owed. The creditor's acceptance of the offer creates an accord (agreement), and when the accord is executed, satisfaction occurs.

accredited investors ■ In the context of securities offerings, "sophisticated" investors, such as banks, insurance companies, investment companies, the issuer's executive officers and directors, and persons whose income or net worth exceeds certain limits.

act of state doctrine ■ A doctrine providing that the judicial branch of one country will not examine the validity of public acts committed by a recognized foreign government within its own territory.

actionable ■ Capable of serving as the basis of a lawsuit. An actionable claim can be pursued in a lawsuit or other court action.

actus reus ■ A guilty (prohibited) act. The commission of a prohibited act is one of the two essential elements required for criminal liability, the other element being the intent to commit a crime.

adhesion contract ■ A "standard-form" contract, such as that between a large retailer and a consumer, in which the stronger party dictates the terms.

adjudicate ■ To render a judicial decision. In administrative law, adjudication is the trial-like proceeding in which an administrative law judge hears and decides issues that arise when an administrative agency charges a person or a firm with violating a law or regulation enforced by the agency.

administrative agency ■ A federal or state government agency established to perform a specific function. Administrative agencies are authorized by legislative acts to make and enforce rules in order to administer and enforce the acts.

administrative law ■ The body of law created by administrative agencies (in the form of rules, regulations, orders, and decisions) in order to carry out their duties and responsibilities.

administrative law judge (ALJ) ■ One who presides over an administrative agency hearing and has the power to administer oaths, take testimony, rule on questions of evidence, and make determinations of fact.

administrative process ■ The procedure used by administrative agencies in the administration of law.

administrator ■ One who is appointed by a court to handle the probate (disposition) of a person's estate if that person dies intestate (without a valid will) or if the executor named in the will cannot serve.

adverse possession ■ The acquisition of title to real property by occupying it openly, without the consent of the owner, for a period of time specified by a state statute. The occupation must be actual, open, notorious, exclusive, and in opposition to all others, including the owner.

affirmative action ■ Job-hiring policies that give special consideration to members of protected classes in an effort to overcome present effects of past discrimination.

after-acquired property ■ Property that is acquired by the debtor after the execution of a security agreement.

agency ■ A relationship between two parties in which one party (the agent) agrees to represent or act for the other (the principal).

agent ■ A person who agrees to represent or act for another, called the principal.

agreement ■ A meeting of two or more minds in regard to the terms of a contract; usually broken down into two events—an offer by one party to form a contract and an acceptance of the offer by the person to whom the offer is made.

alien corporation ■ A designation in the United States for a corporation formed in another country but doing business in the United States.

alienation ■ The process of transferring land out of one's possession (thus "alienating" the land from oneself).

allonge ■ A piece of paper firmly attached to a negotiable instrument, on which transferees can make indorsements if there is no room left on the instrument itself.

alternative dispute resolution (ADR) ■ The resolution of disputes in ways other than those involved in the traditional judicial process. Negotiation, mediation, and arbitration are forms of ADR.

answer ■ Procedurally, a defendant's response to the plaintiff's complaint.

anticipatory repudiation ■ An assertion or action by a party indicating that he or she will not perform an obligation that the party is contractually obligated to perform at a future time.

antitrust law ■ Laws protecting commerce from unlawful restraints.

apparent authority ■ Authority that is only apparent, not real. In agency law, a person may be deemed to have had the power to act as an agent for another party if the other party's manifestations to a third party led the third party to believe that an agency existed when, in fact, it did not.

appraisal right ■ The right of a dissenting shareholder, who objects to an extraordinary transaction of the corporation (such as a merger or a consolidation), to have his or her shares appraised and to be paid the fair value of those shares by the corporation.

appropriation ■ In tort law, the use by one person of another person's name, likeness, or other identifying characteristic without permission and for the benefit of the user.

arbitration ■ The settling of a dispute by submitting it to a disinterested third party (other than a court), who renders a decision that is (most often) legally binding.

arbitration clause ■ A clause in a contract that provides that, in the event of a dispute, the parties will submit the dispute to arbitration rather than litigate the dispute in court.

arson ■ The intentional burning of another's dwelling. Some statutes have expanded this to include any real property regardless of ownership and the destruction of property by other means—for example, by explosion.

articles of incorporation ■ The document filed with the appropriate governmental agency, usually the secretary of state, when a business is incorporated. State statutes usually prescribe what kind of information must be contained in the articles of incorporation.

articles of organization ■ The document filed with a designated state official by which a limited liability company is formed.

articles of partnership ■ A written agreement that sets forth each partner's rights and obligations with respect to the partnership.

artisan's lien ■ A possessory lien given to a person who has made improvements and added value to another person's personal property as security for payment for services performed.

assault ■ Any word or action intended to make another person fearful of immediate physical harm; a reasonably believable threat.

assignee ■ A party to whom the rights under a contract are transferred, or assigned.

assignment ■ The act of transferring to another all or part of one's rights arising under a contract.

assignor ■ A party who transfers (assigns) his or her rights under a contract to another party (called the *assignee*).

assumption of risk ■ A doctrine under which a plaintiff may not recover for injuries or damage suffered from risks he or she knows of and has voluntarily assumed.

attachment ■ In a secured transaction, the process by which a secured creditor's interest "attaches" to the property of another (collateral) and the creditor's security interest becomes enforceable. In the context of judicial liens, a court-ordered seizure and taking into custody of property prior to the securing of a judgment for a past-due debt.

attempted monopolization ■ Any actions by a firm to eliminate competition and gain monopoly power.

authorization card ■ A card signed by an employee that gives a union permission to act on his or her behalf in negotiations with management.

automatic stay ■ In bankruptcy proceedings, the suspension of virtually all litigation and other action by creditors against the debtor or the debtor's property. The stay is effective the moment the debtor files a petition in bankruptcy.

award ■ In litigation, the amount of monetary compensation awarded to a plaintiff in a civil lawsuit as damages. In the context of alternative dispute resolution, the decision rendered by an arbitrator.

B

bailee ■ One to whom goods are entrusted by a bailor.

bailment ■ A situation in which the personal property of one person (a bailor) is entrusted to another (a bailee), who is obligated to return the bailed property to the bailor or dispose of it as directed.

bailor ■ One who entrusts goods to a bailee.

bait-and-switch advertising ■ Advertising a product at a very attractive price (the "bait") and then, once the consumer is in the store, saying that the advertised product is either not available or is of poor quality. The customer is then urged to purchase ("switched" to) a more expensive item.

bankruptcy court ■ A federal court of limited jurisdiction that handles only bankruptcy proceedings, which are governed by federal bankruptcy law.

battery ■ The unprivileged, intentional touching of another.

bearer ■ A person in possession of an instrument payable to bearer or indorsed in blank.

bearer instrument ■ Any instrument that is not payable to a specific person, including instruments payable to the bearer or to "cash."

bequest ■ A gift of personal property by will (from the verb *to bequeath*).

beyond a reasonable doubt ■ The standard of proof used in criminal cases. If there is any reasonable doubt that a criminal defendant committed the crime with which she or he has been charged, then the verdict must be "not guilty."

bilateral contract ■ A type of contract that arises when a promise is given in exchange for a return promise.

bill of rights ■ The first ten amendments to the U.S. Constitution.

binding authority ■ Any source of law that a court must follow when deciding a case.

blank indorsement ■ An indorsement that specifies no particular indorsee and can consist of a mere signature. An order instrument that is indorsed in blank becomes a bearer instrument.

blue laws ■ State or local laws that prohibit the performance of certain types of commercial activities on Sunday.

blue sky laws ■ State laws that regulate the offering and sale of securities.

bona fide occupational qualification (BFOQ) ■ Identifiable characteristics reasonably necessary to the normal operation of a particular business. These characteristics can include gender, national origin, and religion, but not race.

bond ■ A certificate that evidences a corporate (or government) debt. It is a security that involves no ownership interest in the issuing entity.

bond indenture ■ A contract between the issuer of a bond and the bondholder.

bounty payment ■ A reward (payment) given to a person or persons who perform a certain service, such as informing legal authorities of illegal actions.

breach ■ The failure to perform a legal obligation.

breach of contract ■ The failure, without legal excuse, of a promisor to perform the obligations of a contract.

brief ■ A formal legal document prepared by a party's attorney and submitted to an appellate court when a case is appealed, which outlines the facts and issues of the case that are in dispute.

browse-wrap terms ■ Terms and conditions of use that are presented to an Internet user at the time certain products, such as software, are being downloaded but that need not be agreed to (by clicking "I agree," for example) before the user is able to install or use the product.

burglary ■ The unlawful entry or breaking into a building with the intent to commit a felony (or any crime, in some states).

business ethics ■ Ethics in a business context; a consensus as to what constitutes right or wrong behavior in the world of business and the application of moral principles to situations that arise in a business setting.

business invitee ■ A person, such as a customer or a client, who is invited onto business premises by the owner of those premises for business purposes.

business judgment rule ■ A rule that immunizes corporate management from liability for actions that result in corporate losses or damages if the actions are undertaken in good faith and are within both the power of the corporation and the authority of management to make.

business necessity ■ A defense to allegations of employment discrimination in which the employer demonstrates that an employment practice that discriminates against members of a protected class is related to job performance.

business tort ■ Wrongful interference with another's business rights.

business trust ■ A form of business organization in which investors (trust beneficiaries) transfer cash or property to trustees in exchange for trust certificates that represent their investment shares. The certificate holders share in the trust's profits but have limited liability.

buyout price ■ The amount payable to a partner on his or her dissociation from a partnership, based on the amount distributable to that partner if the firm were wound up on that date, and offset by any damages for wrongful dissociation.

C

case law ■ The rules of law announced in court decisions. Case law includes the aggregate of reported cases that interpret judicial precedents, statutes, regulations, and constitutional provisions.

cashier's check ■ A check drawn by a bank on itself.

categorical imperative ■ A concept developed by the philosopher Immanuel Kant as an ethical guideline for behavior. In deciding whether an action is right or wrong, or desirable or undesirable, a person should evaluate the action in terms of what would happen if everybody else in the same situation, or category, acted the same way.

causation in fact ■ An act or omission without which an event would not have occurred.

cease-and-desist order ■ An administrative or judicial order prohibiting a person or business firm from conducting activities that an agency or court has deemed illegal.

certificate of deposit (CD) ■ A note issued by a bank in which the bank acknowledges the receipt of funds from a party and promises to repay that amount, with interest, to the party on a certain date.

certificate of limited partnership ■ The basic document filed with a designated state official by which a limited partnership is formed.

certification mark ■ A mark used by one or more persons, other than the owner, to certify the region, materials, mode of manufacture, quality, or other characteristic of specific goods or services.

certified check ■ A check that has been accepted in writing by the bank on which it is drawn. Essentially, the bank, by certifying (accepting) the check, promises to pay the check at the time the check is presented.

charging order ■ In partnership law, an order granted by a court to a judgment creditor that entitles the creditor to attach profits or assets of a partner on the dissolution of the partnership.

charitable trust ■ A trust in which the property held by the trustee must be used for a charitable purpose, such as the advancement of health, education, or religion.

chattel ■ All forms of personal property.

check ■ A draft drawn by a drawer ordering the drawee bank or financial institution to pay a certain amount of money to the holder on demand.

checks and balances ■ The principle under which the powers of the national government are divided among three separate branches—the executive, legislative, and judicial branches—each of which exercises a check on the actions of the others.

choice-of-language clause ■ A clause in a contract designating the official language by which the contract will be interpreted in the event of a future disagreement over the contract's terms.

choice-of-law clause ■ A clause in a contract designating the law (such as the law of a particular state or nation) that will govern the contract.

citation ■ A reference to a publication in which a legal authority—such as a statute or a court decision—or other source can be found.

civil law ■ The branch of law dealing with the definition and enforcement of all private or public rights, as opposed to criminal matters.

civil law system ■ A system of law derived from that of the Roman Empire and based on a code rather than case law; the predominant system of law in the nations of continental Europe and the nations that were once their colonies.

clearinghouse ■ A system or place where banks exchange checks and drafts drawn on each other and settle daily balances.

click-on agreement ■ An agreement that arises when a buyer, engaging in a transaction on a computer, indicates assent to be bound by the terms of an offer by clicking on a button that says, for example, "I agree"; sometimes referred to as a *click-on license* or a *click-wrap agreement.*

close corporation ■ A corporation whose shareholders are limited to a small group of persons, often including only family members.

closed shop ■ A firm that requires union membership by its workers as a condition of employment. The closed shop was made illegal by the Labor-Management Relations Act of 1947.

codicil ■ A written supplement or modification to a will. A codicil must be executed with the same formalities as a will.

collateral ■ Under Article 9 of the UCC, the property subject to a security interest, including accounts and chattel paper that have been sold.

collateral promise ■ A secondary promise that is ancillary (subsidiary) to a principal transaction or primary contractual relationship, such as a promise made by one person to pay the debts of another if the latter fails to perform. A collateral promise normally must be in writing to be enforceable.

collecting bank ■ Any bank handling an item for collection, except the payor bank.

collective bargaining ■ The process by which labor and management negotiate the terms and conditions of employment, including working hours and workplace conditions.

collective mark ■ A mark used by members of a cooperative, association, union, or other organization to certify the region, materials, mode of manufacture, quality, or other characteristic of specific goods or services.

comity ■ The principle by which one nation defers to and gives effect to the laws and judicial decrees of another nation. This recognition is based primarily on respect.

commerce clause ■ The provision in Article I, Section 8, of the U.S. Constitution that gives Congress the power to regulate interstate commerce.

commercial impracticability ■ A doctrine under which a party may be excused from performing a contract when (1) a contingency occurs, (2) the contingency's occurrence makes performance impracticable, and (3) the nonoccurrence of the contingency was a basic assumption on which the contract was made.

commingle ■ To put funds or goods together into one mass so that they are so mixed that they no longer have separate identities. In corporate law, if personal and corporate interests are commingled to the extent that the corporation has no separate identity, a court may "pierce the corporate veil" and expose the shareholders to personal liability.

common law ■ The body of law developed from custom or judicial decisions in English and U.S. courts, not attributable to a legislature.

common stock ■ Shares of ownership in a corporation that give the owner of the stock a proportionate interest in the corporation with regard to control, earnings, and net assets. Shares of common stock are lowest in priority with respect to payment of dividends and distribution of the corporation's assets on dissolution.

community property ■ A form of concurrent ownership of property in which each spouse technically owns an undivided one-half interest in property acquired during the marriage.

comparative negligence ■ A rule followed by most states in tort cases that reduces the plaintiff's recovery in proportion to the plaintiff's degree of fault, rather than barring recovery completely.

compensatory damages ■ A monetary award equivalent to the actual value of injuries or damage sustained by the aggrieved party.

complaint ■ The pleading made by a plaintiff alleging wrongdoing on the part of the defendant; the document that, when filed with a court, initiates a lawsuit.

computer crime ■ Any act that is directed against computers and computer parts, that uses computers as instruments of crime, or that involves computers and constitutes abuse.

concurrent conditions ■ Conditions that must occur or be performed at the same time; they are mutually dependent. No obligations arise until these conditions are simultaneously performed.

concurrent jurisdiction ■ Jurisdiction that exists when two different courts have the power to hear a case. For example, some cases can be heard in a federal or a state court.

concurrent ownership ■ Joint ownership.

condemnation ■ The process of taking private property for public use through the government's power of eminent domain.

condition ■ A qualification, provision, or clause in a contractual agreement, the occurrence or nonoccurrence of which creates, suspends, or terminates the obligations of the contracting parties.

condition precedent ■ In a contractual agreement, a condition that must be met before a party's promise becomes absolute.

condition subsequent ■ A condition in a contract that, if not fulfilled, operates to terminate a party's absolute promise to perform.

confession of judgment ■ The act or agreement of a debtor in permitting a judgment to be entered against him or her by a creditor, for an agreed sum, without the institution of legal proceedings.

confiscation ■ A government's taking of a privately owned business or personal property without a proper public purpose or an award of just compensation.

confusion ■ The mixing together of goods belonging to two or more owners so that the separately owned goods cannot be identified.

consent ■ Voluntary agreement to a proposition or an act of another; a concurrence of wills.

consequential damages ■ Special damages that compensate for a loss that does not directly or immediately result from the breach (for example, lost profits). For the plaintiff to collect consequential damages, they must have been reasonably foreseeable at the time the breach or injury occurred.

consideration ■ Generally, the value given in return for a promise; involves two elements—the giving of something of legally sufficient value and a bargained-for exchange. The consideration must result in a detriment to the promisee or a benefit to the promisor.

consignment ■ A transaction in which an owner of goods (the consignor) delivers the goods to another (the consignee) for the consignee to sell. The consignee pays the consignor only for the goods that are sold by the consignee.

consolidation ■ A contractual and statutory process in which two or more corporations join to become a completely new corporation. The original corporations cease to exist, and the new corporation acquires all their assets and liabilities.

constitutional law ■ The body of law derived from the U.S. Constitution and the constitutions of the various states.

constructive delivery ■ An act equivalent to the actual, physical delivery of property that cannot be physically delivered because of difficulty or impossibility. For example, the transfer of a key to a safe constructively delivers the contents of the safe.

constructive discharge ■ A termination of employment brought about by making the employee's working conditions so intolerable that the employee reasonably feels compelled to leave.

constructive eviction ■ A form of eviction that occurs when a landlord fails to perform adequately any of the duties (such as providing heat in the winter) required by the lease, thereby making the tenant's further use and enjoyment of the property exceedingly difficult or impossible.

constructive trust ■ An equitable trust that is imposed in the interests of fairness and justice when someone wrongfully holds legal title to property. A court may require the owner to hold the property in trust for the person or persons who should rightfully own the property.

consumer-debtor ■ An individual whose debts are primarily consumer debts (debts for purchases made primarily for personal, family, or household use).

continuation statement ■ A statement that, if filed within six months prior to the expiration date of the original financing statement, continues the perfection of the original security interest for another five years. The perfection of a security interest can be continued in the same manner indefinitely.

contract ■ An agreement that can be enforced in court; formed by two or more competent parties who agree, for consideration, to perform or to refrain from performing some legal act now or in the future.

contributory negligence ■ A rule in tort law that completely bars the plaintiff from recovering any damages if the damage suffered is partly the plaintiff's own fault; used in a minority of states.

conversion ■ Wrongfully taking or retaining possession of an individual's personal property and placing it in the service of another.

conveyance ■ The transfer of title to land from one person to another by deed; a document (such as a deed) by which an interest in land is transferred from one person to another.

"cooling-off" laws ■ Laws that allow buyers a period of time, such as three days, in which to cancel door-to-door sales contracts.

cooperative ■ An association, which may or may not be incorporated, that is organized to provide an economic service to its members. Examples of cooperatives include consumer purchasing cooperatives, credit cooperatives, and farmers' cooperatives.

copyright ■ The exclusive right of an author or originator of a literary or artistic production (including computer programs) to publish, print, or sell that production for a statutory period of time.

corporate governance ■ A set of policies or procedures affecting the way a corporation is directed or controlled.

corporate social responsibility ■ The idea that corporations can and should act ethically and be accountable to society for their actions.

corporation ■ A legal entity formed in compliance with statutory requirements that is distinct from its shareholder-owners.

correspondent bank ■ A bank in which another bank has an account (and vice versa) for the purpose of facilitating fund transfers.

cost-benefit analysis ■ A decision-making technique that involves weighing the costs of a given action against the benefits of that action.

co-surety ■ A joint surety; a person who assumes liability jointly with another surety for the payment of an obligation.

counteradvertising ■ New advertising that is undertaken pursuant to a Federal Trade Commission order for the purpose of correcting earlier false claims that were made about a product.

counterclaim ■ A claim made by a defendant in a civil lawsuit against the plaintiff. In effect, the defendant is suing the plaintiff.

counteroffer ■ An offeree's response to an offer in which the offeree rejects the original offer and at the same time makes a new offer.

course of dealing ■ Prior conduct between the parties to a contract that establishes a common basis for their understanding.

course of performance ■ The conduct that occurs under the terms of a particular agreement. Such conduct indicates what the parties to an agreement intended it to mean.

covenant not to compete ■ A contractual promise of one party to refrain from conducting business similar to that of another party for a certain period of time and within a specified geographic area. Courts commonly enforce such covenants if they are reasonable in terms of time and geographic area and are part of, or supplemental to, a contract for the sale of a business or an employment contract.

covenant not to sue ■ An agreement to substitute a contractual obligation for some other type of legal action based on a valid claim.

cover ■ Under the UCC, a remedy that allows the buyer or lessee, on the seller's or lessor's breach, to purchase goods from another seller or lessor and substitute them for the goods due under the contract. If the cost of cover exceeds the cost of the contract goods, the buyer or lessee can recover the difference, plus incidental and consequential damages.

cram-down provision ■ A provision of the Bankruptcy Code that allows a court to confirm a debtor's Chapter 11 reorganization plan even though only one class of creditors has accepted it.

creditors' composition agreement ■ An agreement formed between a debtor and his or her creditors in which the creditors agree to accept a lesser sum than that owed by the debtor in full satisfaction of the debt.

crime ■ A wrong against society proclaimed in a statute and, if committed, punishable by society through fines and/or imprisonment—and, in some cases, death.

criminal law ■ Law that defines and governs actions that constitute crimes. Generally, criminal law has to do with wrongful actions committed against society for which society demands redress.

cross-collateralization ■ The use of an asset that is not the subject of a loan to collateralize that loan.

cure ■ The right of a party who tenders nonconforming performance to correct that performance within the contract period [UCC 2–508(1)].

cyber mark ■ A trademark in cyberspace.

cyber tort ■ A tort committed in cyberspace.

cyberlaw ■ An informal term used to refer to all laws governing electronic communications and transactions, particularly those conducted via the Internet.

cybernotary ■ A legally recognized authority that can certify the validity of digital signatures.

cybersquatting ■ The act of registering a domain name that is the same as, or confusingly similar to, the trademark of another and then offering to sell that domain name back to the trademark owner.

cyberterrorist ■ A hacker whose purpose is to exploit a target computer for a serious impact, such as corrupting a program to sabotage a business.

D

damages ■ Money sought as a remedy for a breach of contract or a tortious action.

debtor ■ Under Article 9 of the UCC, any party who owes payment or performance of a secured obligation, whether or not the party actually owns or has rights in the collateral.

debtor in possession (DIP) ■ In Chapter 11 bankruptcy proceedings, a debtor who is allowed to continue in possession of the estate in property (the business) and to continue business operations.

deceptive advertising ■ Advertising that misleads consumers, either by making unjustified claims concerning a product's performance or by omitting a material fact concerning the product's composition or performance.

deed ■ A document by which title to property (usually real property) is passed.

defalcation ■ Embezzlement; the misappropriation of funds by a party, such as a corporate officer or public official, in a fiduciary relationship with another.

defamation ■ Anything published or publicly spoken that causes injury to another's good name, reputation, or character.

default ■ Failure to observe a promise or discharge an obligation; commonly used to refer to failure to pay a debt when it is due.

default judgment ■ A judgment entered by a court against a defendant who has failed to appear in court to answer or defend against the plaintiff's claim.

defendant ■ One against whom a lawsuit is brought; the accused person in a criminal proceeding.

defense ■ A reason offered and alleged by a defendant in an action or suit as to why the plaintiff should not recover or establish what she or he seeks.

deficiency judgment ■ A judgment against a debtor for the amount of a debt remaining unpaid after the collateral has been repossessed and sold.

delegatee ■ A party to whom contractual obligations are transferred, or delegated.

delegation of duties ■ The act of transferring to another all or part of one's duties arising under a contract.

delegator ■ A party who transfers (delegates) her or his obligations under a contract to another party (called the *delegatee*).

depositary bank ■ The first bank to receive a check for payment.

deposition ■ The testimony of a party to a lawsuit or a witness taken under oath before a trial.

destination contract ■ A contract for the sale of goods in which the seller is required or authorized to ship the goods by carrier and tender delivery of the goods at a particular destination. The seller assumes liability for any losses or damage to the goods until they are tendered at the destination specified in the contract.

devise ■ As a noun, a gift of real property by will; as a verb, to make a gift of real property by will.

devisee ■ One designated in a will to receive a gift of real property.

digital cash ■ Funds contained on computer software, in the form of secure programs stored on microchips and on other computer devices.

disaffirmance ■ The legal avoidance, or setting aside, of a contractual obligation.

discharge ■ The termination of an obligation. In contract law, discharge occurs when the parties have fully performed their contractual obligations or when other events occur that release the parties from performance. In bankruptcy proceedings, discharge is the extinction of the debtor's dischargeable debts, thereby relieving the debtor of the obligation to pay the debts.

disclosed principal ■ A principal whose identity is known to a third party at the time the agent makes a contract with the third party.

discovery ■ A phase in the litigation process during which the opposing parties may obtain information from each other and from third parties prior to trial.

dishonor ■ A negotiable instrument is dishonored when payment or acceptance of the instrument, whichever is required, is refused even though the instrument is presented in a timely and proper manner.

disparagement of property ■ An economically injurious falsehood made about another's product or property; a general term for torts that are more specifically referred to as slander of quality or slander of title.

disparate-impact discrimination ■ A form of employment discrimination that results from certain employer practices or procedures that, although not discriminatory on their face, have a discriminatory effect.

disparate-treatment discrimination ■ A form of employment discrimination that results when an employer intentionally discriminates against employees who are members of protected classes.

dissociation ■ The severance of the relationship between a partner and a partnership when the partner ceases to be associated with the carrying on of the partnership business.

dissolution ■ The formal disbanding of a partnership or a corporation. It can take place by (1) acts of the partners or, in a corporation, acts of the shareholders and board of directors; (2) the subsequent illegality of the firm's business; (3) the expiration of a time period stated in a partnership agreement or a certificate of incorporation; or (4) judicial decree.

distributed network ■ A network that can be used by persons located (distributed) around the country or the globe to share computer files.

distribution agreement ■ A contract between a seller and a distributor of the seller's products setting out the terms and conditions of the distributorship.

diversity of citizenship ■ Under Article III, Section 2, of the U.S. Constitution, a basis for federal district court jurisdiction over a lawsuit between (1) citizens of different states, (2) a foreign country and citizens of a state or of different states, or (3) citizens of a state.

divestiture ■ The act of selling one or more of a company's divisions or parts, such as a subsidiary or plant; often mandated by the courts in merger or monopolization cases.

dividend ■ A distribution to corporate shareholders of corporate profits or income, disbursed in proportion to the number of shares held.

docket ■ The list of cases entered on a court's calendar and thus scheduled to be heard by the court.

document of title ■ A paper exchanged in the regular course of business that evidences the right to possession of goods (for example, a bill of lading or a warehouse receipt).

domain name ■ The last part of an Internet address, such as "westlaw.edu." The top level (the part of the name to the right of the period) indicates the type of entity that operates the site ("edu" is an abbreviation for "educational"). The second level (the part of the name to the left of the period) is chosen by the entity.

domestic corporation ■ In a given state, a corporation that does business in, and is organized under the law of, that state.

dominion ■ Ownership rights in property, including the right to possess and control the property.

double jeopardy ■ A situation occurring when a person is tried twice for the same criminal offense; prohibited by the Fifth Amendment to the Constitution.

draft ■ Any instrument drawn on a drawee that orders the drawee to pay a certain sum of money, usually to a third party (the payee), on demand or at a definite future time.

dram shop act ■ A state statute that imposes liability on the owners of bars and taverns, as well as those who serve alcoholic drinks to the public, for injuries resulting from accidents caused by intoxicated persons when the sellers or servers of alcoholic drinks contributed to the intoxication.

drawee ■ The party that is ordered to pay a draft or check. With a check, a bank or a financial institution is always the drawee.

drawer ■ The party that initiates a draft (such as a check), thereby ordering the drawee to pay.

due diligence ■ A required standard of care that certain professionals, such as accountants, must meet to avoid liability for securities violations.

due process clause ■ The provisions in the Fifth and Fourteenth Amendments to the Constitution that guarantee that no person shall be deprived of life, liberty, or property without due process of law. Similar clauses are found in most state constitutions.

dumping ■ The selling of goods in a foreign country at a price below the price charged for the same goods in the domestic market.

duress ■ Unlawful pressure brought to bear on a person, causing the person to perform an act that she or he would not otherwise perform.

duty of care ■ The duty of all persons, as established by tort law, to exercise a reasonable amount of care in their dealings with others. Failure to exercise due care, which is normally determined by the reasonable person standard, constitutes the tort of negligence.

E

e-agent ■ A computer program that by electronic or other automated means can independently initiate an action or respond to electronic messages or data without review by an individual.

easement ■ A nonpossessory right to use another's property in a manner established by either express or implied agreement.

e-contract ■ A contract that is formed electronically.

e-evidence ■ Evidence that consists of computer-generated or electronically recorded information, including e-mail, voice mail, spreadsheets, word-processing documents, and other data.

electronic fund transfer (EFT) ■ A transfer of funds with the use of an electronic terminal, a telephone, a computer, or magnetic tape.

emancipation ■ In regard to minors, the act of being freed from parental control; occurs when a child's parent or legal guardian relinquishes the legal right to exercise control over the child or when a minor who leaves home to support himself or herself.

embezzlement ■ The fraudulent appropriation of funds or other property by a person to whom the funds or property has been entrusted.

eminent domain ■ The power of a government to take land from private citizens for public use on the payment of just compensation.

e-money ■ Prepaid funds recorded on a computer or a card (such as a smart card or a stored-value card).

employment at will ■ A common law doctrine under which either party may terminate an employment relationship at any time for any reason, unless a contract specifies otherwise.

employment contract ■ A contract between an employer and an employee in which the terms and conditions of employment are stated.

employment discrimination ■ Treating employees or job applicants unequally on the basis of race, color, national origin, religion, gender, age, or disability; prohibited by federal statutes.

enabling legislation ■ A statute enacted by Congress that authorizes the creation of an administrative agency and specifies the name, composition, purpose, and powers of the agency being created.

entrapment ■ In criminal law, a defense in which the defendant claims that he or she was induced by a public official—usually an undercover agent or police officer—to commit a crime that he or she would otherwise not have committed.

entrepreneur ■ One who initiates and assumes the financial risk of a new business enterprise and undertakes to provide or control its management.

environmental impact statement (EIS) ■ A statement required by the National Environmental Policy Act for any major federal action that will significantly affect the quality of the environment. The statement must analyze the action's impact on the environment and explore alternative actions that might be taken.

equal dignity rule ■ In most states, a rule stating that express authority given to an agent must be in writing if the contract to be made on behalf of the principal is required to be in writing.

equal protection clause ■ The provision in the Fourteenth Amendment to the Constitution that guarantees that no state will "deny to any person within its jurisdiction the equal protection of the laws." This clause mandates that the state governments must treat similarly situated individuals in a similar manner.

equitable principles and maxims ■ General propositions or principles of law that have to do with fairness (equity).

e-signature ■ As defined by the Uniform Electronic Transactions Act, "an electronic sound, symbol, or process attached to or logically associated with a record and executed or adopted by a person with the intent to sign the record."

establishment clause ■ The provision in the First Amendment to the Constitution that prohibits the government from establishing any state-sponsored religion or enacting any law that promotes religion or favors one religion over another.

estate in property ■ In bankruptcy proceedings, all of the debtor's interests in property currently held, wherever located, together with certain jointly owned property, property transferred in transactions voidable by the trustee, proceeds and profits from the property of the estate, and certain property interests to which the debtor becomes entitled within 180 days after filing for bankruptcy.

estopped ■ Barred, impeded, or precluded.

estray statute ■ A statute defining finders' rights in property when the true owners are unknown.

ethics ■ Moral principles and values applied to social behavior.

eviction ■ A landlord's act of depriving a tenant of possession of the leased premises.

exclusionary rule ■ In criminal procedure, a rule under which any evidence that is obtained in violation of the accused's constitutional rights guaranteed by the Fourth, Fifth, and Sixth Amendments, as well as any evidence derived from illegally obtained evidence, will not be admissible in court.

exclusive distributorship ■ A distributorship in which the seller and the distributor of the seller's products agree that the distributor will distribute only the seller's products.

exclusive jurisdiction ■ Jurisdiction that exists when a case can be heard only in a particular court or type of court.

exclusive-dealing contract ■ An agreement under which a seller forbids a buyer to purchase products from the seller's competitors.

exculpatory clause ■ A clause that releases a contractual party from liability in the event of monetary or physical injury, no matter who is at fault.

executed contract ■ A contract that has been completely performed by both parties.

execution ■ An action to carry into effect the directions in a court decree or judgment.

executive agency ■ An administrative agency within the executive branch of government. At the federal level, executive agencies are those within the cabinet departments.

executor ■ A person appointed by a testator in a will to see that her or his will is administered appropriately.

executory contract ■ A contract that has not as yet been fully performed.

export ■ The goods and services that domestic firms sell to buyers located in other countries.

express contract ■ A contract in which the terms of the agreement are stated in words, oral or written.

express warranty ■ A seller's or lessor's oral or written promise or affirmation of fact, ancillary to an underlying sales or lease agreement, as to the quality, description, or performance of the goods being sold or leased.

expropriation ■ The seizure by a government of a privately owned business or personal property for a proper public purpose and with just compensation.

extension clause ■ A clause in a time instrument that allows the instrument's date of maturity to be extended into the future.

F

family limited liability partnership (FLLP) ■ A type of limited liability partnership owned by family members or fiduciaries of family members.

federal form of government ■ A system of government in which the states form a union and the sovereign power is divided between the central government and the member states.

federal question ■ A question that pertains to the U.S. Constitution, acts of Congress, or treaties. A federal question provides a basis for federal jurisdiction.

federal reserve system ■ A network of twelve district banks and related branches located around the country and headed by the Federal Reserve Board of Governors. Most banks in the United States have Federal Reserve accounts.

fee simple ■ An absolute form of property ownership entitling the property owner to use, possess, or dispose of the property as he or she chooses during his or her lifetime. On death, the interest in the property descends to the owner's heirs.

fee simple absolute ■ An ownership interest in land in which the owner has the greatest possible aggregation of rights, privileges, and power. Ownership in fee simple absolute is limited absolutely to a person and her or his heirs.

felony ■ A crime—such as arson, murder, rape, or robbery—that carries the most severe sanctions, ranging from one year in a state or federal prison to the death penalty.

fictitious payee ■ A payee on a negotiable instrument whom the maker or drawer does not intend to have an interest in the instrument. Indorsements by fictitious payees are treated as authorized indorsements under Article 3 of the UCC.

fiduciary ■ As a noun, a person having a duty created by his or her undertaking to act primarily for another's benefit in matters connected with the undertaking. As an adjective, a relationship founded on trust and confidence.

filtering software ■ A computer program that is designed to block access to certain Web sites based on their content. The software blocks the retrieval of a site whose URL or key words are on a list within the program.

financing statement ■ A document prepared by a secured creditor and filed with the appropriate state or local official, to give notice to the public that the creditor has a security interest in collateral belonging to the debtor named in the statement. Financing statement's must contain the names and addresses of both the debtor and the secured party and must describe the collateral.

firm offer ■ An offer (by a merchant) that is irrevocable without the necessity of consideration for a stated period of time or, if no definite period is stated, for a reasonable time (neither period to exceed three months). A firm offer by a merchant must be in writing and must be signed by the offeror.

fixed-term tenancy ■ A type of tenancy under which property is leased for a specified period of time, such as a month, a year, or a period of years; also called a *tenancy for years.*

fixture ■ A thing that was once personal property but has become attached to real property in such a way that it takes on the characteristics of real property and becomes part of that real property.

floating lien ■ A security interest in proceeds, after-acquired property, or collateral subject to future advances by the secured party (or all three); a security interest in collateral that is retained even when the collateral changes in character, classification, or location.

forbearance ■ The act of refraining from an action that one has a legal right to undertake.

force majeure clause ■ A provision in a contract stipulating that certain unforeseen events—such as war, political upheavals, or acts of God—will excuse a party from liability for nonperformance of contractual obligations.

foreign corporation ■ In a given state, a corporation that does business in the state without being incorporated therein.

foreign exchange market ■ A worldwide system in which foreign currencies are bought and sold.

forgery ■ The fraudulent making or altering of any writing in a way that changes the legal rights and liabilities of another.

formal contract ■ A contract that by law requires a specific form, such as being executed under seal, for its validity.

forum-selection clause ■ A provision in a contract designating the court, jurisdiction, or tribunal that will decide any disputes arising under the contract.

franchise ■ Any arrangement in which the owner of a trademark, trade name, or copyright licenses another to use that trademark, trade name, or copyright in the selling of goods or services.

franchisee ■ One receiving a license to use another's (the franchisor's) trademark, trade name, or copyright in the sale of goods and services.

franchisor ■ One licensing another (the franchisee) to use the owner's trademark, trade name, or copyright in the selling of goods or services.

fraudulent misrepresentation ■ Any misrepresentation, either by misstatement or by omission of a material fact, knowingly made with the intention of deceiving another and on which a reasonable person would and does rely to his or her detriment.

free exercise clause ■ The provision in the First Amendment to the Constitution that prohibits the government from interfering with people's religious practices or forms of worship.

frustration of purpose ■ A court-created doctrine under which a party to a contract will be relieved of her or his duty to perform when the objective purpose for performance no longer exists (due to reasons beyond that party's control).

fungible goods ■ Goods that are alike by physical nature, by agreement, or by trade usage (for example, wheat, oil, and wine that are identical in type and quality). When owners of fungible goods hold the goods as tenants in common, title and risk can pass without actually separating the goods being sold from the mass of fungible goods.

G

garnishment ■ A legal process used by a creditor to collect a debt by seizing property of the debtor (such as wages) that is being held by a third party (such as the debtor's employer).

general partner ■ In a limited partnership, a partner who assumes responsibility for the management of the partnership and liability for all partnership debts.

generally accepted accounting principles (GAAP) ■ The conventions, rules, and procedures that define accepted accounting practices at a particular time. The source of the principles is the Financial Accounting Standards Board.

generally accepted auditing standards (GAAS) ■ Standards concerning an auditor's professional qualities and the judgment exercised by him or her in the performance of an audit and report. The source of the standards is the American Institute of Certified Public Accountants.

gift *causa mortis* ■ A gift made in contemplation of death. If the donor does not die of that ailment, the gift is revoked.

gift ■ Any voluntary transfer of property made without consideration, past or present.

gift *inter vivos* ■ A gift made during one's lifetime and not in contemplation of imminent death, in contrast to a gift *causa mortis.*

good faith purchaser ■ A purchaser who buys without notice of any circumstance that would cause a person of ordinary prudence to inquire as to whether the seller has valid title to the goods being sold.

good samaritan statute ■ A state statute stipulating that persons who provide emergency services to, or rescue, someone in peril cannot be sued for negligence, unless they act recklessly, thereby causing further harm.

grand jury ■ A group of citizens called to decide, after hearing the state's evidence, whether a reasonable basis (probable cause) exists for believing that a crime has been committed and that a trial ought to be held.

group boycott ■ The refusal by a group of competitors to deal with a particular person or firm; prohibited by the Sherman Act.

guarantor ■ A person who agrees to satisfy the debt of another (the debtor) only after the principal debtor defaults. Thus, a guarantor's liability is secondary.

H

hacker ■ A person who uses one computer to break into another. Professional computer programmers refer to such persons as "crackers."

historical school ■ A school of legal thought that emphasizes the evolutionary process of law and looks to the past to discover what the principles of contemporary law should be.

holder ■ Any person in possession of an instrument drawn, issued, or indorsed to him or her, to his or her order, to bearer, or in blank.

holder in due course (HDC) ■ A holder who acquires a negotiable instrument for value; in good faith; and without notice that the instrument is overdue, that it has been dishonored, that any person has a defense against it or a claim to it, or that the instrument contains unauthorized signatures, has been altered, or is so irregular or incomplete as to call into question its authenticity.

holding company ■ A company whose business activity is holding shares in another company.

holographic will ■ A will written entirely in the signer's handwriting and usually not witnessed.

homestead exemption ■ A law permitting a debtor to retain the family home, either in its entirety or up to a specified dollar amount, free from the claims of unsecured creditors or trustees in bankruptcy.

horizontal merger ■ A merger between two firms that are competing in the same marketplace.

horizontal restraint ■ Any agreement that in some way restrains competition between rival firms competing in the same market.

hot-cargo agreement ■ An agreement in which employers voluntarily agree with unions not to handle, use, or deal in other employers' goods that were not produced by union employees; a type of secondary boycott explicitly prohibited by the Labor-Management Reporting and Disclosure Act of 1959.

I

identification ■ In a sale of goods, the express designation of the goods provided for in the contract.

identity theft ■ The act of stealing another's identifying information—such as a name, date of birth, or Social Security number—and using that information to access the victim's financial resources.

implied warranty ■ A warranty that arises by law because of the circumstances of a sale, rather than by the seller's express promise.

implied warranty of fitness for a particular purpose ■ A warranty that goods sold or leased are fit for a particular purpose. The warranty arises when any seller or lessor knows the particular purpose for which a buyer or lessee will use the goods and knows that the buyer or lessee is relying on the skill and judgment of the seller or lessor to select suitable goods.

implied warranty of habitability ■ An implied promise by a landlord that rented residential premises are fit for human habitation—that is, in a condition that is safe and suitable for people to live there.

implied warranty of merchantability ■ A warranty that goods being sold or leased are reasonably fit for the general purpose for which they are sold or leased, are properly packaged and labeled, and are of proper quality. The warranty automatically arises in every sale or lease of goods made by a merchant who deals in goods of the kind sold or leased.

implied-in-fact contract ■ A contract formed in whole or in part from the conduct of the parties (as opposed to an express contract).

impossibility of performance ■ A doctrine under which a party to a contract is relieved of her or his duty to perform when performance becomes objectively impossible or totally impracticable (through no fault of either party).

imposter ■ One who, by use of the mails, Internet, telephone, or personal appearance, induces a maker or drawer to issue an instrument in the name of an impersonated payee. Indorsements by imposters are treated as authorized indorsements under Article 3 of the UCC.

incidental beneficiary ■ A third party who incidentally benefits from a contract but whose benefit was not the reason the contract was formed. An incidental beneficiary has no rights in a contract and cannot sue to have the contract enforced.

incidental damages ■ Damages awarded to compensate for reasonable expenses that are directly incurred because of a breach of contract—such as the cost of obtaining performance from another source.

independent contractor ■ One who works for, and receives payment from, an employer but whose working conditions and methods are not controlled by the employer. An independent contractor is not an employee but may be an agent.

independent regulatory agency ■ An administrative agency that is not considered part of the government's executive branch and is not subject to the authority of the president. Independent agency officials cannot be removed without cause.

indictment ■ A charge by a grand jury that a named person has committed a crime.

indorsee ■ The person to whom a negotiable instrument is transferred by indorsement.

indorsement ■ A signature placed on an instrument for the purpose of transferring one's ownership rights in the instrument.

indorser ■ A person who transfers an instrument by signing (indorsing) it and delivering it to another person.

informal contract ■ A contract that does not require a specified form or formality to be valid.

information return ■ A tax return submitted by a partnership that only reports the income and losses earned by the business. The partnership as an entity does not pay taxes on the income received by the partnership. A partner's profit from the partnership (whether distributed or not) is taxed as individual income to the individual partner.

information ■ A formal accusation or complaint (without an indictment) issued in certain types of actions (usually criminal actions involving lesser crimes) by a government prosecutor.

inside director ■ A person on the board of directors who is also an officer of the corporation.

insider trading ■ The purchase or sale of securities on the basis of *inside information* (information that has not been made available to the public).

insolvent ■ Under the UCC, a term describing a person who ceases to pay "his [or her] debts in the ordinary course of business or cannot pay his [or her] debts as they become due or is insolvent within the meaning of federal bankruptcy law" [UCC 1–201(23)].

installment contract ■ Under the UCC, a contract that requires or authorizes delivery in two or more separate lots to be accepted and paid for separately.

insurable interest ■ In regard to the sale or lease of goods, a property interest in the goods that is sufficiently substantial to permit a party to insure against damage to the goods. In the context of insurance, an interest either in a person's life or well-being that is sufficiently substantial to justify insuring against injury to (or death of) the person.

insurance ■ A contract in which, for a stipulated consideration, one party agrees to compensate the other for loss on a specific subject by a specified peril.

intangible property ■ Property that cannot be seen or touched but exists only conceptually, such as corporate stocks and bonds, patents and copyrights, and ordinary contract rights. Article 2 of the UCC does not govern intangible property.

integrated contract ■ A written contract that constitutes the final expression of the parties' agreement. If a contract is integrated, evidence extraneous to the contract that contradicts or alters the meaning of the contract in any way is inadmissible.

intellectual property ■ Property resulting from intellectual, creative processes.

intended beneficiary ■ A third party for whose benefit a contract is formed. An intended beneficiary can sue the promisor if such a contract is breached.

intentional tort ■ A wrongful act knowingly committed.

inter vivos **trust** ■ A trust created by the grantor (settlor) and effective during the grantor's lifetime; a trust not established by a will.

intermediary bank ■ Any bank to which an item is transferred in the course of collection, except the depositary or payor bank.

international law ■ The law that governs relations among nations. National laws, customs, treaties, and international conferences and organizations are generally considered to be the most important sources of international law.

interrogatories ■ A series of written questions for which written answers are prepared by a party to a lawsuit, usually with the assistance of the party's attorney, and then signed under oath.

intestacy laws ■ State statutes that specify how property will be distributed when a person dies intestate (without a valid will); also called *statutes of descent and distribution*.

intestate ■ As a noun, one who has died without having created a valid will; as an adjective, the state of having died without a will.

investment company ■ A company that acts on behalf of many smaller shareholders/owners by buying a large portfolio of securities and professionally managing that portfolio.

J

joint and several liability ■ In partnership law, a doctrine under which a plaintiff may sue, and collect a judgment from, all of the partners together (jointly) or one or more of the partners separately (severally, or individually). This is true even if one of the partners sued did not participate in, ratify, or know about whatever it was that gave rise to the cause of action.

joint stock company ■ A hybrid form of business organization that combines characteristics of a corporation and a partnership. Usually, a joint stock company is regarded as a partnership for tax and other legal purposes.

joint tenancy ■ The joint ownership of property by two or more co-owners in which each co-owner owns an undivided portion of the property. On the death of one of the joint tenants, his or her interest automatically passes to the surviving joint tenant(s).

joint venture ■ A joint undertaking of a specific commercial enterprise by an association of persons. A joint venture normally is not a legal entity and is treated like a partnership for federal income tax purposes.

judicial review ■ The process by which a court decides on the constitutionality of legislative enactments and actions of the executive branch.

junior lienholder ■ A party that holds a lien that is subordinate to one or more other liens on the same property.

jurisdiction ■ The authority of a court to hear and decide a specific case.

jurisprudence ■ The science or philosophy of law.

justiciable controversy ■ A controversy that is not hypothetical or academic but real and substantial; a requirement that must be satisfied before a court will hear a case.

L

larceny ■ The wrongful taking and carrying away of another person's personal property with the intent to permanently deprive the owner of the property. Some states classify larceny as either grand or petit, depending on the property's value.

law ■ A body of enforceable rules governing relationships among individuals and between individuals and their society.

lease ■ Under Article 2A of the UCC, a transfer of the right to possess and use goods for a period of time in exchange for payment.

lease agreement ■ In regard to the lease of goods, an agreement in which one person (the lessor) agrees to transfer the right to the possession and use of property to another person (the lessee) in exchange for rental payments.

leasehold estate ■ An estate in realty held by a tenant under a lease. In every leasehold estate, the tenant has a qualified right to possess and/or use the land.

legacy ■ A gift of personal property under a will.

legal positivism ■ A school of legal thought centered on the assumption that there is no law higher than the laws created by a national government. Laws must be obeyed, even if they are unjust, to prevent anarchy.

legal realism ■ A school of legal thought of the 1920s and 1930s that generally advocated a less abstract and more realistic approach to the law, an approach that takes into account customary practices and the circumstances in which transactions take place. This school left a lasting imprint on American jurisprudence.

legatee ■ One designated in a will to receive a gift of personal property.

lessee ■ A person who acquires the right to the possession and use of another's goods in exchange for rental payments.

lessor ■ A person who transfers the right to the possession and use of goods to another in exchange for rental payments.

letter of credit ■ A written instrument, usually issued by a bank on behalf of a customer or other person, in which the issuer promises to honor drafts or other demands for payment by third persons in accordance with the terms of the instrument.

levy ■ The obtaining of funds by legal process through the seizure and sale of nonsecured property, usually done after a writ of execution has been issued.

libel ■ Defamation in writing or other form having the quality of permanence (such as a digital recording).

license ■ A revocable right or privilege of a person to come onto another person's land. In the context of intellectual property law, an agreement permitting the use of a trademark, copyright, patent, or trade secret for certain limited purposes.

lien ■ An encumbrance on a property to satisfy a debt or protect a claim for payment of a debt.

life estate ■ An interest in land that exists only for the duration of the life of some person, usually the holder of the estate.

limited liability company (LLC) ■ A hybrid form of business enterprise that offers the limited liability of a corporation and the tax advantages of a partnership.

limited liability limited partnership (LLLP) ■ A type of limited partnership in which the liability of all of the partners, including general partners, is limited to the amount of their investments.

limited liability partnership (LLP) ■ A hybrid form of business organization that is used mainly by professionals who normally do business in a partnership. Like a partnership, an LLP is a pass-through entity for tax purposes, but the personal liability of the partners is limited.

limited partner ■ In a limited partnership, a partner who contributes capital to the partnership but has no right to participate in the management and operation of the business. The limited partner assumes no liability for partnership debts beyond the capital contributed.

limited partnership ■ A partnership consisting of one or more general partners (who manage the business and are liable to the full extent of their personal assets for debts of the partnership) and one or more limited partners (who contribute only assets and are liable only up to the extent of their contributions).

liquidated damages ■ An amount, stipulated in a contract, that the parties to the contract believe to be a reasonable estimation of the damages that will occur in the event of a breach.

liquidated debt ■ A debt for which the amount has been ascertained, fixed, agreed on, settled, or exactly determined. If the amount of the debt is in dispute, the debt is considered unliquidated.

liquidation ■ The sale of all of the nonexempt assets of a debtor and the distribution of the proceeds to the debtor's creditors. Chapter 7 of the Bankruptcy Code provides for liquidation bankruptcy proceedings.

litigation ■ The process of resolving a dispute through the court system.

long arm statute ■ A state statute that permits a state to obtain personal jurisdiction over nonresident defendants. A defendant must have certain "minimum contacts" with that state for the statute to apply.

lost property ■ Property with which the owner has involuntarily parted and then cannot find or recover.

M

mailbox rule ■ A rule providing that an acceptance of an offer becomes effective on dispatch (on being placed in an official mailbox), if mail is, expressly or impliedly, an authorized means of communication of acceptance to the offeror.

maker ■ One who promises to pay a fixed amount of money to the holder of a promissory note or a certificate of deposit (CD).

malpractice ■ Professional misconduct or unreasonable lack of skill. The failure of a professional to use the degree of care common to the average reputable members of the profession or to apply the skills and learning the professional claims to possess, resulting in injury, loss, or damage to those relying on the professional.

market concentration ■ The degree to which a small number of firms control a large percentage share of a relevant market; determined by calculating the percentages held by the largest firms in that market.

market power ■ The power of a firm to control the market price of its product. A monopoly has the greatest degree of market power.

market-share liability ■ A theory of sharing liability among all firms that manufactured and distributed a particular product during a certain period of time. This form of liability sharing is used only in some jurisdictions and only when the true source of the harmful product in unidentifiable.

market-share test ■ The primary measure of monopoly power. A firm's market share is the percentage of a market that the firm controls.

mechanic's lien ■ A statutory lien on the real property of another, created to ensure payment for work performed and materials furnished in the repair or improvement of real property, such as a building.

mediation ■ A method of settling disputes outside of court by using the services of a neutral third party, who acts as a communicating agent between the parties and assists them in negotiating a settlement.

member ■ The term used to designate a person who has an ownership interest in a limited liability company.

mens rea ■ Mental state, or intent. A wrongful mental state is as necessary as a wrongful act to establish criminal liability. What constitutes a mental state varies according to the wrongful action. Thus, for murder, the *mens rea* is the intent to take a life.

merchant ■ A person who is engaged in the purchase and sale of goods. Under the UCC, a person who deals in goods of the kind involved in the sales contract or who holds herself or himself out as having skill or knowledge peculiar to the practices or goods being purchased or sold [UCC 2–104].

merger ■ A contractual and statutory process in which one corporation (the surviving corporation) acquires all of the assets and liabilities of another corporation (the merged corporation). The shareholders of the merged corporation either are paid for their shares or receive shares in the surviving corporation.

meta tag ■ A key word in a document that can serve as an index reference to the document. On the Web, search engines return results based, in part, on the tags in Web documents.

minimum wage ■ The lowest wage, either by government regulation or union contract, that an employer may pay an hourly worker.

mirror image rule ■ A common law rule that requires that the terms of the offeree's acceptance adhere exactly to the terms of the offeror's offer for a valid contract to be formed.

misdemeanor ■ A lesser crime than a felony, punishable by a fine or incarceration in jail for up to one year.

mislaid property ■ Property with which the owner has voluntarily parted and then cannot find or recover.

mitigation of damages ■ A rule requiring a plaintiff to do whatever is reasonable to minimize the damages caused by the defendant.

money laundering ■ Falsely reporting income that has been obtained through criminal activity as income obtained through a legitimate business enterprise—in effect, "laundering" the "dirty money."

monopolization ■ The possession of monopoly power in the relevant market and the willful acquisition or maintenance of that power, as distinguished from growth or development as a consequence of a superior product, business acumen, or historic accident.

monopoly power ■ The ability of a monopoly to dictate what takes place in a given market.

monopoly ■ A term generally used to describe a market in which there is a single seller or a very limited number of sellers.

moral minimum ■ The minimum degree of ethical behavior expected of a business firm, which is usually defined as compliance with the law.

mortgage ■ A written instrument giving a creditor an interest in (lien on) the debtor's real property as security for payment of a debt.

mortgagee ■ Under a mortgage agreement, the creditor who takes a security interest in the debtor's property.

mortgagor ■ Under a mortgage agreement, the debtor who gives the creditor a security interest in the debtor's property in return for a mortgage loan.

motion for a directed verdict ■ In a jury trial, a motion for the judge to take the decision out of the hands of the jury and to direct a verdict for the party who filed the motion on the ground that the other party has not produced sufficient evidence to support her or his claim.

motion for a new trial ■ A motion asserting that the trial was so fundamentally flawed (because of error, newly discovered evidence, prejudice, or another reason) that a new trial is necessary to prevent a miscarriage of justice.

motion for judgment n.o.v. ■ A motion requesting the court to grant judgment in favor of the party making the motion on the ground that the jury's verdict against him or her was unreasonable and erroneous.

motion for judgment on the pleadings ■ A motion by either party to a lawsuit at the close of the pleadings requesting the court to decide the issue solely on the pleadings without proceeding to trial. The motion will be granted only if no facts are in dispute.

motion for summary judgment ■ A motion requesting the court to enter a judgment without proceeding to trial. The motion can be based on evidence outside the pleadings and will be granted only if no facts are in dispute.

motion to dismiss ■ A pleading in which a defendant asserts that the plaintiff's claim fails to state a cause of action (that is, has no basis in law) or that there are other grounds on which a suit should be dismissed. Although the defendant normally is the party requesting a dismissal, either the plaintiff or the court can also make a motion to dismiss the case.

mutual fund ■ A specific type of investment company that continually buys or sells to investors shares of ownership in a portfolio.

N

national law ■ Law that pertains to a particular nation (as opposed to international law).

natural law ■ The belief that government and the legal system should reflect universal moral and ethical principles that are inherent in human nature. The natural law school is the oldest and one of the most significant schools of legal thought.

necessaries ■ Necessities required for life, such as food, shelter, clothing, and medical attention; may include whatever is believed to be necessary to maintain a person's standard of living or financial and social status.

negligence ■ The failure to exercise the standard of care that a reasonable person would exercise in similar circumstances.

negligence per se ■ An action or failure to act in violation of a statutory requirement.

negotiable instrument ■ A signed writing (record) that contains an unconditional promise or order to pay an exact sum on demand or at an exact future time to a specific person or order, or to bearer.

negotiation ■ A process in which parties attempt to settle their dispute informally, with or without attorneys to represent them. In the context of negotiable instruments, the transfer of an instrument in such form that the transferee (the person to whom the instrument is transferred) becomes a holder.

nominal damages ■ A small monetary award (often one dollar) granted to a plaintiff when no actual damage was suffered.

nonpossessory interest ■ In the context of real property, an interest in land that does not include any right to possess the property.

normal trade relations (NTR) status ■ A status granted in an international treaty by a provision stating that the citizens of the contracting nations may enjoy the privileges accorded by either party to citizens of its NTR nations. Generally, this status is designed to establish equality of international treatment.

notary public ■ A public official authorized to attest to the authenticity of signatures.

novation ■ The substitution, by agreement, of a new contract for an old one, with the rights under the old one being terminated. Typically, novation involves the substitution of a new person who is responsible for the contract and the removal of the original partyrights and duties under the contract.

nuisance ■ A common law doctrine under which persons may be held liable for using their property in a manner that unreasonably interferes with others' rights to use or enjoy their own property.

nuncupative will ■ An oral will (often called a *deathbed will*) made before witnesses; usually limited to transfers of personal property.

O

objective theory of contracts ■ A theory under which the intent to form a contract will be judged by outward, objective facts (what the party said when entering into the contract, how the party acted or appeared, and the circumstances surrounding the transaction) as interpreted by a reasonable person, rather than by the party's own secret, subjective intentions.

obligee ■ One to whom an obligation is owed.

obligor ■ One who owes an obligation to another.

offer ■ A promise or commitment to perform or refrain from performing some specified act in the future.

offeree ■ A person to whom an offer is made.

offeror ■ A person who makes an offer.

online dispute resolution (ODR) ■ The resolution of disputes with the assistance of organizations that offer dispute-resolution services via the Internet.

operating agreement ■ In a limited liability company, an agreement in which the members set forth the details of how the business will be managed and operated. State statutes typically give the members wide latitude in deciding for themselves the rules that will govern their organization.

option contract ■ A contract under which the offeror cannot revoke the offer for a stipulated time period. During this period, the offeree can accept or reject the offer without fear that the offer will be made to another person. The offeree must give consideration for the option (the irrevocable offer) to be enforceable.

order for relief ■ A court's grant of assistance to a complainant. In bankruptcy proceedings, the order relieves the debtor of the immediate obligation to pay the debts listed in the bankruptcy petition.

order instrument ■ A negotiable instrument that is payable "to the order of an identified person" or "to an identified person or order."

ordinance ■ A regulation enacted by a city or county legislative body that becomes part of that state's statutory law.

output contract ■ An agreement in which a seller agrees to sell and a buyer agrees to buy all or up to a stated amount of what the seller produces.

outside director ■ A person on the board of directors who does not hold a management position at the corporation.

overdraft ■ A check that is paid by the bank when the checking account on which the check is written contains insufficient funds to cover the check.

P

parol evidence rule ■ A rule under which a court will not receive into evidence the parties' prior negotiations, prior agreements, or contemporaneous oral agreements if that evidence contradicts or varies the terms of the parties' written contract.

partially disclosed principal ■ A principal whose identity is unknown by a third party, but the third party knows that the agent is or may be acting for a principal at the time the agent and the third party form a contract.

partnering agreement ■ An agreement between a seller and a buyer who frequently do business with each other concerning the terms and conditions that will apply to all subsequently formed electronic contracts.

partnership ■ An agreement by two or more persons to carry on, as co-owners, a business for profit.

pass-through entity ■ A business entity that has no tax liability. The entity's income is passed through to the owners, and the owners pay taxes on the income.

past consideration ■ An act that takes place before the contract is made and that ordinarily, by itself, cannot be consideration for a later promise to pay for the act.

patent ■ A government grant that gives an inventor the exclusive right or privilege to make, use, or sell his or her invention for a limited time period.

payee ■ A person to whom an instrument is made payable.

payor bank ■ The bank on which a check is drawn (the drawee bank).

peer-to-peer (P2P) networking ■ The sharing of resources (such as files, hard drives, and processing styles) among multiple computers without necessarily requiring a central network server.

penalty ■ A contractual clause that states that a certain amount of monetary damages will be paid in the event of a future default or breach of contract. The damages are a punishment for a default and not a measure of compensation for the contract's breach. The agreement as to the penalty amount will not be enforced, and recovery will be limited to actual damages.

per capita ■ A Latin term meaning "per person." In the law governing estate distribution, a method of distributing the property of an intestate's estate so that each heir in a certain class (such as grandchildren) receives an equal share.

per se **violation** ■ A type of anticompetitive agreement that is considered to be so injurious to the public that there is no need to determine whether it actually injures market competition. Rather, it is in itself (*per se*) a violation of the Sherman Act.

per stirpes ■ A Latin term meaning "by the roots." In estate law, a method of distributing an intestate's estate so that each heir in a certain class (such as grandchildren) takes the share to which her or his deceased ancestor (such as a mother or father) would have been entitled.

perfection ■ The legal process by which secured parties protect themselves against the claims of third parties who may wish to have their debts satisfied out of the same collateral; usually accomplished by filing a financing statement with the appropriate government official.

performance ■ In contract law, the fulfillment of one's duties arising under a contract with another; the normal way of discharging one's contractual obligations.

periodic tenancy ■ A lease interest in land for an indefinite period involving payment of rent at fixed intervals, such as week to week, month to month, or year to year.

personal defenses ■ Defenses that can be used to avoid payment to an ordinary holder of a negotiable instrument but not a holder in due course (HDC) or a holder with the rights of an HDC.

personal property ■ Property that is movable; any property that is not real property.

persuasive authority ■ Any legal authority or source of law that a court may look to for guidance but on which it need not rely in making its decision. Persuasive authorities include cases from other jurisdictions and secondary sources of law.

petition in bankruptcy ■ The document that is filed with a bankruptcy court to initiate bankruptcy proceedings. The official forms required for a petition in bankruptcy must be completed accurately, sworn to under oath, and signed by the debtor.

petty offense ■ In criminal law, the least serious kind of criminal offense, such as a traffic or building-code violation.

piercing the corporate veil ■ An action in which a court disregards the corporate entity and holds the shareholders personally liable for corporate debts and obligations. ■

plaintiff ■ One who initiates a lawsuit.

plea bargaining ■ The process by which a criminal defendant and the prosecutor in a criminal case work out a mutually satisfactory disposition of the case, subject to court approval; usually involves the defendant's pleading guilty to a lesser offense in return for a lighter sentence.

pleadings ■ Statements made by the plaintiff and the defendant in a lawsuit that detail the facts, charges, and defenses involved in the litigation. The complaint and answer are part of the pleadings.

pledge ■ A common law security device (retained in Article 9 of the UCC) in which personal property is transferred into the possession of the creditor as security for the payment of a debt and retained by the creditor until the debt is paid.

police powers ■ Powers possessed by the states as part of their inherent sovereignty. These powers may be exercised to protect or promote the public order, health, safety, morals, and general welfare.

policy ■ In insurance law, a contract between the insurer and the insured in which, for a stipulated consideration, the insurer agrees to compensate the insured for loss on a specific subject by a specified peril.

positive law ■ The body of conventional, or written, law of a particular society at a particular point in time.

potentially responsible party (PRP) ■ A party liable for the costs of cleaning up a hazardous waste–disposal site under the Comprehensive Environmental Response, Compensation, and Liability Act (CERCLA). Any person who generated the hazardous waste, transported it, owned or operated the waste site at the time of disposal, or owns or operates the site at the present time may be responsible for some or all of the clean-up costs.

power of attorney ■ A written document, which is usually notarized, authorizing another to act as one's agent; can be special (permitting the agent to do specified acts only) or general (permitting the agent to transact all business for the principal).

precedent ■ A court decision that furnishes an example or authority for deciding subsequent cases involving identical or similar facts.

predatory behavior ■ Business behavior that is undertaken with the intention of unlawfully driving competitors out of the market.

predatory pricing ■ The pricing of a product below cost with the intent to drive competitors out of the market.

predominant-factor test ■ A test courts use to determine whether a contract is primarily for the sale of goods or for the sale of services.

preemption ■ A doctrine under which certain federal laws preempt, or take precedence over, conflicting state or local laws.

preemptive rights ■ Rights held by shareholders that entitle them to purchase newly issued shares of a corporation's stock, equal in percentage to shares already held, before the stock is offered to any outside buyers. Preemptive rights enable shareholders to maintain their proportionate ownership and voice in the corporation.

preference ■ In bankruptcy proceedings, property transfers or payments made by the debtor that favor (give preference to) one creditor over others. The bankruptcy trustee is allowed to recover payments made both voluntarily and involuntarily to one creditor in preference over another.

preferred creditor ■ In the context of bankruptcy, a creditor who has received a preferential transfer from a debtor.

preferred stock ■ Classes of stock that have priority over common stock as to both payment of dividends and distribution of assets on the corporation's dissolution.

premium ■ In insurance law, the price paid by the insured for insurance protection for a specified period of time.

prenuptial agreement ■ An agreement made before marriage that defines each partner's ownership rights in the other partner's property. Prenuptial agreements must be in writing to be enforceable.

presentment ■ The act of presenting an instrument to the party liable on the instrument to collect payment. Presentment also occurs when a person presents an instrument to a drawee for a required acceptance.

presentment warranties ■ Implied warranties, made by any person who presents an instrument for payment or acceptance, that (1) the person obtaining payment or acceptance is entitled to enforce the instrument or is authorized to obtain payment or acceptance on behalf of a person who is entitled to enforce the instrument, (2) the instrument has not been altered, and (3) the person obtaining payment or acceptance has no knowledge that the signature of the drawer of the instrument is unauthorized.

price discrimination ■ Setting prices in such a way that two competing buyers pay two different prices for an identical product or service.

price-fixing agreement ■ An agreement between competitors to fix the prices of products or services at a certain level.

prima facie **case** ■ A case in which the plaintiff has produced sufficient evidence of his or her claim that the case can go to a jury; a case in which the evidence compels a decision for the plaintiff if the defendant produces no affirmative defense or evidence to disprove the plaintiff's assertion.

primary source of law ■ A document that establishes the law on a particular issue, such as a constitution, a statute, an administrative rule, or a court decision.

principal ■ In agency law, a person who agrees to have another, called the agent, act on her or his behalf.

principle of rights ■ The principle that human beings have certain fundamental rights (to life, freedom, and the pursuit of happiness, for example). Those who adhere to this "rights theory" believe that a key factor in determining whether a business decision is ethical is how that decision affects the rights of various groups. These groups include the firm's owners, its employees, the consumers of its products or services, its suppliers, the community in which it does business, and society as a whole.

privilege ■ A legal right, exemption, or immunity granted to a person or a class of persons. In the context of defamation, an absolute privilege immunizes the person making the statements from a lawsuit, regardless of whether the statements were malicious.

privity of contract ■ The relationship that exists between the promisor and the promisee of a contract.

probable cause ■ Reasonable grounds for believing that a person should be arrested or searched.

probate ■ The process of proving and validating a will and settling all matters pertaining to an estate.

probate court ■ A state court of limited jurisdiction that conducts proceedings relating to the settlement of a deceased person's estate.

procedural law ■ Law that establishes the methods of enforcing the rights established by substantive law.

proceeds ■ Under Article 9 of the UCC, whatever is received when collateral is sold or otherwise disposed of, such as by exchange.

product liability ■ The legal liability of manufacturers, sellers, and lessors of goods to consumers, users, and bystanders for injuries or damages that are caused by the goods.

profit ■ In real property law, the right to enter onto and remove things from the property of another (for example, the right to enter onto a person's land and remove sand and gravel).

promise ■ An assertion that something either will or will not happen in the future.

promisee ■ A person to whom a promise is made.

promisor ■ A person who makes a promise.

promissory estoppel ■ A doctrine that applies when a promisor makes a clear and definite promise on which the promisee justifiably relies. Such a promise is binding if justice will be better served by the enforcement of the promise.

promissory note ■ A written promise made by one person (the maker) to pay a fixed amount of money to another person (the payee or a subsequent holder) on demand or on a specified date.

property ■ Legally protected rights and interests in anything with an ascertainable value that is subject to ownership.

prospectus ■ A written document, required by securities laws, that describes the security being sold, the financial operations of the issuing corporation, and the investment or risk attaching to the security. It is designed to provide sufficient information to enable investors to evaluate the risk involved in purchasing the security.

protected class ■ A group of persons protected by specific laws because of the group's defining characteristics. Under laws prohibiting employment discrimination, these characteristics include race, color, religion, national origin, gender, age, and disability.

proximate cause ■ Legal cause; exists when the connection between an act and an injury is strong enough to justify imposing liability.

puffery ■ A salesperson's often exaggerated claims concerning the quality of property offered for sale. Such claims involve opinions rather than facts and are not considered to be legally binding promises or warranties.

punitive damages ■ Monetary damages that may be awarded to a plaintiff to punish the defendant and deter future similar conduct.

purchase-money security interest (PMSI) ■ A security interest that arises when a seller or lender extends credit for part or all of the purchase price of goods purchased by a buyer.

Q

qualified indorsement ■ An indorsement on a negotiable instrument in which the indorser disclaims any contract liability on the instrument. The notation "without recourse" is commonly used to create a qualified indorsement.

quasi contract ■ A fictional contract imposed on the parties by a court in the interests of fairness and justice; usually imposed to avoid the unjust enrichment of one party at the expense of another.

question of fact ■ In a lawsuit, an issue that involves only disputed facts, and not what the law is on a given point. Questions of fact are decided by the jury in a jury trial (by the judge if there is no jury).

question of law ■ In a lawsuit, an issue involving the application or interpretation of a law. Only a judge, not a jury, can rule on questions of law.

quitclaim deed ■ A deed intended to pass any title, interest, or claim that the grantor may have in the property without warranting that such title is valid. A quitclaim deed offers the least amount of protection against defects in the title.

quota ■ A set limit on the amount of goods that can be imported.

R

ratification ■ The act of accepting and giving legal force to an obligation that previously was not enforceable.

reaffirmation agreement ■ An agreement between a debtor and a creditor in which the debtor voluntarily agrees to pay, or reaffirm, a debt dischargeable in bankruptcy. To be enforceable, the agreement must be made before the debtor is granted a discharge.

real property ■ Land and everything attached to it, such as trees and buildings.

reasonable person standard ■ The standard of behavior expected of a hypothetical "reasonable person"; the standard against which negligence is measured and that must be observed to avoid liability for negligence.

receiver ■ In a corporate dissolution, a court-appointed person who winds up corporate affairs and liquidates corporate assets.

record ■ According to the Uniform Electronic Transactions Act, information that is either inscribed on a tangible medium or stored in an electronic or other medium and is retrievable.

recording statutes ■ Statutes that allow deeds, mortgages, and other real property transactions to be recorded so as to provide notice to future purchasers or creditors of an existing claim on the property.

red herring prospectus ■ A preliminary prospectus that can be distributed to potential investors after the registration statement (for a securities offering) has been filed with the Securities and Exchange Commission. The name derives from the red legend printed across the prospectus stating that the registration has been filed but has not become effective.

reformation ■ A court-ordered correction of a written contract so that it reflects the true intentions of the parties.

regulation e ■ A set of rules issued by the Federal Reserve System's Board of Governors to protect users of elecronic fund transfer systems.

regulation z ■ A set of rules promulgated by the Federal Reserve Board of Governors to implement the provisions of the Truth-in-Lending Act.

release ■ A contract in which one party forfeits the right to pursue a legal claim against the other party.

remedy ■ The relief given to an innocent party to enforce a right or compensate for the violation of a right.

replevin ■ An action to recover identified goods in the hands of a party who is wrongfully withholding them from the other party. Under the UCC, this remedy is usually available only if the buyer or lessee is unable to cover.

reply ■ Procedurally, a plaintiff's response to a defendant's answer.

requirements contract ■ An agreement in which a buyer agrees to purchase and the seller agrees to sell all or up to a stated amount of what the buyer needs or requires.

res ipsa loquitur ■ A doctrine under which negligence may be inferred simply because an event occurred, if it is the type of event that would not occur in the absence of negligence. Literally, the term means "the facts speak for themselves."

resale price maintenance agreement ■ An agreement between a manufacturer and a retailer in which the manufacturer specifies what the retail prices of its products must be.

rescission ■ A remedy whereby a contract is canceled and the parties are returned to the positions they occupied before the contract was made; may be effected through the mutual consent of the parties, by the parties' conduct, or by court decree.

respondeat superior ■ Latin for "let the master respond." A doctrine under which a principal or an employer is held liable for the wrongful acts committed by agents or employees while acting within the course and scope of their agency or employment.

restitution ■ An equitable remedy under which a person is restored to his or her original position prior to loss or injury, or placed in the position he or she would have been in had the breach not occurred.

restrictive indorsement ■ Any indorsement on a negotiable instrument that requires the indorsee to comply with certain instructions regarding the funds involved. A restrictive indorsement does not prohibit the further negotiation of the instrument.

resulting trust ■ An implied trust arising from the conduct of the parties. A trust in which a party holds the actual legal title to another's property but only for that person's benefit.

retained earnings ■ The portion of a corporation's profits that has not been paid out as dividends to shareholders.

revocation ■ In contract law, the withdrawal of an offer by an offeror. Unless the offer is irrevocable, it can be revoked at any time prior to acceptance without liability.

right of contribution ■ The right of a co-surety who pays more than her or his proportionate share on a debtor's default to recover the excess paid from other co-sureties.

right of first refusal ■ The right to purchase personal or real property—such as corporate shares or real estate—before the property is offered for sale to others.

right of reimbursement ■ The legal right of a person to be restored, repaid, or indemnified for costs, expenses, or losses incurred or expended on behalf of another.

right of subrogation ■ The right of a person to stand in the place of (be substituted for) another, giving the substituted party the same legal rights that the original party had.

right-to-work law ■ A state law providing that employees may not be required to join a union as a condition of retaining employment.

risk management ■ Planning that is undertaken to protect one's interest should some event threaten to undermine its security. In the context of insurance, risk management involves transferring certain risks from the insured to the insurance company.

risk ■ A prediction concerning potential loss based on known and unknown factors.

robbery ■ The act of forcefully and unlawfully taking personal property of any value from another. Force or intimidation is usually necessary for an act of theft to be considered robbery.

rule of four ■ A rule of the United States Supreme Court under which the Court will not issue a writ of certiorari unless at least four justices approve of the decision to issue the writ.

rule of reason ■ A test by which a court balances the positive effects (such as economic efficiency) of an agreement against its potentially anticompetitive effects. In antitrust litigation, many practices are analyzed under the rule of reason.

rulemaking ■ The process undertaken by an administrative agency when formally adopting a new regulation or amending an old one. Rulemaking involves notifying the public of a proposed rule or change and receiving and considering the public's comments.

S

s corporation ■ A close business corporation that has met certain requirements set out in the Internal Revenue Code and thus qualifies for special income tax treatment. Essentially, an S corporation is taxed the same as a partnership, but its owners enjoy the privilege of limited liability.

sale ■ The passing of title to property from the seller to the buyer for a price.

sale on approval ■ A type of conditional sale in which the buyer may take the goods on a trial basis. The sale becomes absolute only when the buyer approves of (or is satisfied with) the goods being sold.

sale or return ■ A type of conditional sale in which title and possession pass from the seller to the buyer, but the buyer retains the option to return the goods during a specified period even though the goods conform to the contract.

sales contract ■ A contract for the sale of goods under which the ownership of goods is transferred from a seller to a buyer for a price.

scienter ■ Knowledge by the misrepresenting party that material facts have been falsely represented or omitted with an intent to deceive.

search warrant ■ An order granted by a public authority, such as a judge, that authorizes law enforcement personnel to search a particular premise or property.

seasonably ■ Within a specified time period or, if no period is specified, within a reasonable time.

sec rule 10b-5 ■ A rule of the Securities and Exchange Commission that makes it unlawful, in connection with the purchase or sale of any security, to make any untrue statement of a material fact or to omit a material fact if such omission causes the statement to be misleading.

secondary boycott ■ A union's refusal to work for, purchase from, or handle the products of a secondary employer, with whom the union has no dispute, in order to force that employer to stop doing business with the primary employer, with whom the union has a labor dispute.

secondary source of law ■ A publication that summarizes or interprets the law, such as a legal encyclopedia, a legal treatise, or an article in a law review.

secured party ■ A lender, seller, or any other person in whose favor there is a security interest, including a person to whom accounts or chattel paper have been sold.

secured transaction ■ Any transaction in which the payment of a debt is guaranteed, or secured, by personal property owned by the debtor or in which the debtor has a legal interest.

securities ■ Generally, stock certificates, bonds, notes, debentures, warrants, or other documents given as evidence of an ownership interest in a corporation or as a promise of repayment by a corporation.

security ■ Generally, a stock certificate, bond, note, debenture, warrant, or other document or record evidencing an ownership interest in a corporation or a promise to repay a corporation's debt.

security agreement ■ An agreement that creates or provides for a security interest between the debtor and a secured party.

security interest ■ Any interest in personal property or fixtures that secures payment or performance of an obligation.

self-defense ■ The legally recognized privilege to protect oneself or one's property against injury by another. The privilege of self-defense usually applies only to acts that are reasonably necessary to protect oneself, one's property, or another person.

self-incrimination ■ The giving of testimony that may subject the testifier to criminal prosecution. The Fifth Amendment to the Constitution protects against self-incrimination by providing that no person "shall be compelled in any criminal case to be a witness against himself."

seniority system ■ In regard to employment relationships, a system in which those who have worked longest for the employer are first in line for promotions, salary increases, and other benefits. They are also the last to be laid off if the workforce must be reduced.

service mark ■ A mark used in the sale or the advertising of services to distinguish the services of one person from those of others. Titles, character names, and other distinctive features of radio and television programs may be registered as service marks.

sexual harassment ■ In the employment context, the demanding of sexual favors in return for job promotions or other benefits, or language or conduct that is so sexually offensive that it creates a hostile working environment.

shareholder's derivative suit ■ A suit brought by a shareholder to enforce a corporate cause of action against a third person.

shelter principle ■ The principle that the holder of a negotiable instrument who cannot qualify as a holder in due course (HDC), but who derives his or her title through an HDC, acquires the rights of an HDC.

shipment contract ■ A contract for the sale of goods in which the seller is required or authorized to ship the goods by carrier. The seller assumes liability for any losses or damage to the goods until they are delivered to the carrier.

short-form (parent-subsidiary) merger ■ A merger of companies in which one company (the parent corporation) owns at least 90 percent of the outstanding shares of each class of stock of the other corporation (the subsidiary corporation). The merger can be accomplished without the approval of the shareholders of either corporation.

short-swing profits ■ Profits earned within six months of a trade. Section 12 of the 1934 Securities Exchange Act requires company insiders to return any profits made from the purchase and sale of company stock if both transactions occur within a six-month period.

shrink-wrap agreement ■ An agreement whose terms are expressed in a document located inside a box in which goods (usually software) are packaged; sometimes called a *shrink-wrap license.*

signature ■ Under the UCC, "any symbol executed or adopted by a party with a present intention to authenticate a writing."

slander ■ Defamation in oral form.

slander of quality (trade libel) ■ The publication of false information about another's product, alleging that it is not what its seller claims.

slander of title ■ The publication of a statement that denies or casts doubt on another's legal ownership of any property, causing financial loss to that property's owner.

small claims court ■ A special court in which parties may litigate small claims (such as $5,000 or less). Attorneys are not required in small claims courts and, in some states, are not allowed to represent the parties.

smart card ■ A card containing a microprocessor that permits storage of funds via security programming, can communicate with other computers, and does not require online authorization for fund transfers.

sociological school ■ A school of legal thought that views the law as a tool for promoting justice in society.

sole proprietorship ■ The simplest form of business organization, in which the owner is the business. The owner reports business income on his or her personal income tax return and is legally responsible for all debts and obligations incurred by the business.

sovereign immunity ■ A doctrine that immunizes foreign nations from the jurisdiction of U.S. courts when certain conditions are satisfied.

spam ■ Bulk, unsolicited ("junk") e-mail.

special indorsement ■ An indorsement on an instrument that indicates the specific person to whom the indorser intends to make the instrument payable; that is, it names the indorsee.

special warranty deed ■ A deed in which the grantor warrants only that the grantor or seller held good title during his or her ownership of the property and does not warrant that there were no defects of title when the property was held by previous owners.

specific performance ■ An equitable remedy requiring exactly the performance that was specified; usually granted only when monetary damages would be an inadequate remedy and the subject matter of the contract is unique.

spendthrift trust ■ A trust created to protect the beneficiary from spending all the funds to which she or he is entitled. Only a certain portion of the total amount is given to the beneficiary at any one time, and most states prohibit creditors from attaching assets of the trust.

stale check ■ A check, other than a certified check, that is presented for payment more than six months after its date.

standing to sue ■ The requirement that an individual must have a sufficient stake in a controversy before he or she can bring a lawsuit. The plaintiff must demonstrate that he or she has been either injured or threatened with injury.

stare decisis ■ A common law doctrine under which judges are obligated to follow the precedents established in prior decisions.

statute of frauds ■ A state statute under which certain types of contracts must be in writing to be enforceable.

statute of limitations ■ A federal or state statute setting the maximum time period during which a certain action can be brought or certain rights enforced.

statute of repose ■ Basically, a statute of limitations that is not dependent on the happening of a cause of action. Statutes of repose generally begin to run at an earlier date and run for a longer period of time than statutes of limitations.

statutory law ■ The body of law enacted by legislative bodies (as opposed to constitutional law, administrative law, or case law).

stock ■ An equity (ownership) interest in a corporation, measured in units of shares.

stock certificate ■ A certificate issued by a corporation evidencing the ownership of a specified number of shares in the corporation.

stock options ■ An agreement that grants the owner the option to buy a given number of shares of stock, usually within a set time period.

stock warrant ■ A certificate that grants the owner the option to buy a given number of shares of stock, usually within a set time period.

stop-payment order ■ An order by a bank customer to his or her bank not to pay or certify a certain check.

stored-value card ■ A card bearing a magnetic strip that holds magnetically encoded data, providing access to stored funds.

strict liability ■ Liability regardless of fault. In tort law, strict liability is imposed on a manufacturer or seller that introduces into commerce a good that is unreasonably dangerous when in a defective condition.

strike ■ An action undertaken by unionized workers when collective bargaining fails. The workers leave their jobs, refuse to work, and (typically) picket the employer's workplace.

sublease ■ A lease executed by the lessee of real estate to a third person, conveying the same interest that the lessee enjoys but for a shorter term than that held by the lessee.

substantive law ■ Law that defines, describes, regulates, and creates legal rights and obligations.

summary jury trial (SJT) ■ A method of settling disputes, used in many federal courts, in which a trial is held, but the jury's verdict is not binding. The verdict acts only as a guide to both sides in reaching an agreement during the mandatory negotiations that immediately follow the summary jury trial.

summons ■ A document informing a defendant that a legal action has been commenced against him or her and that the defendant must appear in court on a certain date to answer the plaintiff's complaint.

supremacy clause ■ The provision in Article VI of the Constitution that provides that the Constitution, laws, and treaties of the United States are "the supreme Law of the Land." Under this clause, state and local laws that directly conflict with federal law will be rendered invalid.

surety ■ A person, such as a cosigner on a note, who agrees to be primarily responsible for the debt of another.

suretyship ■ An express contract in which a third party to a debtor-creditor relationship (the surety) promises to be primarily responsible for the debtor's obligation.

symbolic speech ■ Nonverbal expressions of beliefs. Symbolic speech, which includes gestures, movements, and articles of clothing, is given substantial protection by the courts.

syndicate ■ An investment group of persons or firms brought together for the purpose of financing a project that they would not or could not undertake independently.

T

takeover ■ The acquisition of control over a corporation through the purchase of a substantial number of the voting shares of the corporation.

taking ■ The taking of private property by the government for public use. The government may not take private property for public use without "just compensation."

tangible property ■ Property that has physical existence and can be distinguished by the senses of touch or sight. A car is tangible property; a patent right is intangible property.

target corporation ■ The corporation to be acquired in a corporate takeover; a corporation whose shareholders receive a tender offer.

tariff ■ A tax on imported goods.

tenancy at sufferance ■ A type of tenancy under which a tenant who, after rightfully being in possession of leased premises, continues (wrongfully) to occupy the property after the lease has terminated. The tenant has no rights to possess the property and occupies it only because the person entitled to evict the tenant has not done so.

tenancy at will ■ A type of tenancy that either party can terminate without notice; usually arises when a tenant who has been under a tenancy for years retains possession, with the landlord's consent, after the tenancy for years has terminated.

tenancy by the entirety ■ The joint ownership of property by a husband and wife. Neither party can transfer her or his interest in the property without the consent of the other.

tenancy in common ■ Co-ownership of property in which each party owns an undivided interest that passes to her or his heirs at death.

tender ■ An unconditional offer to perform an obligation by a person who is ready, willing, and able to do so.

tender offer ■ An offer to purchase made by one company directly to the shareholders of another (target) company; sometimes referred to as a *takeover bid*.

testamentary trust ■ A trust that is created by will and therefore does not take effect until the death of the testator.

testate ■ Having left a will at death.

testator ■ One who makes and executes a will.

third party beneficiary ■ One for whose benefit a promise is made in a contract but who is not a party to the contract.

tippee ■ A person who receives inside information.

tombstone ad ■ An advertisement, historically in a format resembling a tombstone, of a securities offering. The ad tells potential investors where and how they may obtain a prospectus.

tort ■ A civil wrong not arising from a breach of contract; a breach of a legal duty that proximately causes harm or injury to another.

tortfeasor ■ One who commits a tort.

totten trust ■ A trust created by the deposit of a person's own funds in his or her own name as a trustee for another. It is a tentative trust, revocable at will until the depositor dies or completes the gift in his or her lifetime by some unequivocal act or declaration.

toxic tort ■ A civil wrong arising from exposure to a toxic substance, such as asbestos, radiation, or hazardous waste.

trade dress ■ The image and overall appearance of a product—for example, the distinctive decor, menu, layout, and style of service of a particular restaurant. Basically, trade dress is subject to the same protection as trademarks.

trade name ■ A term that is used to indicate part or all of a business's name and that is directly related to the business's reputation and goodwill. Trade names are protected under the common law (and under trademark law, if the name is the same as the firm's trademarked product).

trade secrets ■ Information or processes that give a business an advantage over competitors that do not know the information or processes.

trademark ■ A distinctive mark, motto, device, or emblem that a manufacturer stamps, prints, or otherwise affixes to the goods it produces so that they may be identified on the market and their origins made known. Once a trademark is established (under the common law or through registration), the owner is entitled to its exclusive use.

transfer warranties ■ Implied warranties, made by any person who transfers an instrument for consideration to subsequent transferees and holders who take the instrument in good faith, that (1) the transferor is entitled to enforce the instrument; (2) all signatures are authentic and authorized; (3) the instrument has not been altered; (4) the instrument is not subject to a defense or claim of any party that can be asserted against the transferor; and (5) the transferor has no knowledge of any insolvency proceedings against the maker, the acceptor, or the drawer of the instrument.

traveler's check ■ A check that is payable on demand, drawn on or payable through a financial institution (bank), and designated as a traveler's check.

treble damages ■ Damages that, by statute, are three times the amount that the fact finder determines is owed.

trespass to land ■ The entry onto, above, or below the surface of land owned by another without the owner's permission or legal authorization.

trespass to personal property ■ The unlawful taking or harming of another's personal property; interference with another's right to the exclusive possession of his or her personal property.

trust ■ An arrangement in which title to property is held by one person (a trustee) for the benefit of another (a beneficiary).

trust indorsement ■ An indorsement for the benefit of the indorser or a third person; also known as an *agency indorsement*. The indorsement results in legal title vesting in the original indorsee.

tying arrangement ■ An agreement between a buyer and a seller in which the buyer of a specific product or service becomes obligated to purchase additional products or services from the seller.

U

U.S. trustee ■ A government official who performs certain administrative tasks that a bankruptcy judge would otherwise have to perform.

ultra vires ■ A Latin term meaning "beyond the powers"; in corporate law, acts of a corporation that are beyond its express and implied powers to undertake.

unconscionable contract (or unconscionable clause) ■ A contract or clause that is void on the basis of public policy because one party, as a result of disproportionate bargaining power, is forced to accept terms that are unfairly burdensome and that unfairly benefit the dominating party.

underwriter ■ In insurance law, the insurer, or the one assuming a risk in return for the payment of a premium.

undisclosed principal ■ A principal whose identity is unknown by a third person, and the third person has no knowledge that the agent is acting for a principal at the time the agent and the third person form a contract.

unenforceable contract ■ A valid contract rendered unenforceable by some statute or law.

uniform law ■ A model law created by the National Conference of Commissioners on Uniform State Laws and/or the American Law Institute for the states to consider adopting. If the state adopts the law, it becomes statutory law in that state. Each state has the option of adopting or rejecting all or part of a uniform law.

unilateral contract ■ A contract that results when an offer can be accepted only by the offeree's performance.

union shop ■ A firm that requires all workers, once employed, to become union members within a specified period of time as a condition of their continued employment.

universal defenses ■ Defenses that are valid against all holders of a negotiable instrument, including holders in due course (HDCs) and holders with the rights of HDCs.

unreasonably dangerous product ■ In product liability law, a product that is defective to the point of threatening a consumer's health and safety. A product will be considered unreasonably dangerous if it is dangerous beyond the expectation of the ordinary consumer or if a less dangerous alternative was economically feasible for the manufacturer, but the manufacturer failed to produce it.

usage of trade ■ Any practice or method of dealing having such regularity of observance in a place, vocation, or trade as to justify an expectation that it will be observed with respect to the transaction in question.

usury ■ Charging an illegal rate of interest.

utilitarianism ■ An approach to ethical reasoning that evaluates behavior in light of the consequences of that behavior for those who will be affected by it, rather than on the basis of any absolute ethical or moral values. In utilitarian reasoning, a "good" decision is one that results in the greatest good for the greatest number of people affected by the decision.

V

valid contract ■ A contract that results when the elements necessary for contract formation (agreement, consideration, legal purpose, and contractual capacity) are present.

venue ■ The geographic district in which a legal action is tried and from which the jury is selected.

vertical merger ■ The acquisition by a company at one level in a marketing chain of a company at a higher or lower level in the chain (such as a company merging with one of its suppliers or retailers).

vertical restraint ■ Any restraint on trade created by agreements between firms at different levels in the manufacturing and distribution process.

vertically integrated firm ■ A firm that carries out two or more functional phases (manufacture, distribution, and retailing, for example) of the chain of production.

vesting ■ The creation of an absolute or unconditional right or power.

vicarious liability ■ Legal responsibility placed on one person for the acts of another; indirect liability imposed on a supervisory party (such as an employer) for the actions of a subordinate (such as an employee) because of the relationship between the two parties.

void contract ■ A contract having no legal force or binding effect.

voidable contract ■ A contract that may be legally avoided (canceled, or annulled) at the option of one or both of the parties.

voir dire ■ An old French phrase meaning "to speak the truth." In legal terms, it refers to the process in which the attorneys question prospective jurors to learn about their backgrounds, attitudes, biases, and other characteristics that may affect their ability to serve as impartial jurors.

voting trust ■ An agreement (trust contract) under which legal title to shares of corporate stock is transferred to a trustee who is authorized by the shareholders to vote the shares on their behalf.

W

warranty deed ■ A deed in which the grantor assures (warrants to) the grantee that the grantor has title to the property conveyed in the deed, that there are no encumbrances on the property other than what the grantor has represented, and that the grantee will enjoy quiet possession of the property; a deed that provides the greatest amount of protection for the grantee.

watered stock ■ Shares of stock issued by a corporation for which the corporation receives, as payment, less than the stated value of the shares.

wetlands ■ Water-saturated areas of land that are designated by a government agency (such as the Environmental Protection Agency) as protected areas that support wildlife and therefore cannot be filled in or dredged by private contractors or parties without a permit.

whistleblowing ■ An employee's disclosure to government authorities, upper-level managers, or the press that the employer is engaged in unsafe or illegal activities.

white-collar crime ■ Nonviolent crime committed by individuals or corporations to obtain a personal or business advantage.

will ■ An instrument directing what is to be done with the testator's property on his or her death, made by the testator and revocable during his or her lifetime. No interests in the testator's property pass until the testator dies.

will substitutes ■ Various documents that attempt to dispose of an estate in the same or similar manner as a will, such as trusts or life insurance plans.

winding up ■ The second of two stages in the termination of a partnership or corporation. Once the firm is dissolved, it continues to exist legally until the process of winding up all business affairs (collecting and distributing the firm's assets) is complete.

workers' compensation laws ■ State statutes establishing an administrative procedure for compensating workers' injuries that arise out of—or in the course of—their employment, regardless of fault.

working papers ■ The various documents used and developed by an accountant during an audit, such as notes and computations, that make up the work product of an accountant's services to a client.

workout ■ An out-of-court agreement between a debtor and creditors in which the parties work out a payment plan or schedule under which the debtor's debts can be discharged.

writ of attachment ■ A court's order, issued prior to a trial to collect a debt, directing the sheriff or other public officer to seize nonexempt property of the debtor. If the creditor prevails at trial, the seized property can be sold to satisfy the judgment.

writ of certiorari ■ A writ from a higher court asking the lower court for the record of a case.

writ of execution ■ A court's order, issued after a judgment has been entered against a debtor, directing the sheriff to seize (levy) and sell any of the debtor's nonexempt real or personal property. The proceeds of the sale are used to pay off the judgment, accrued interest, and costs of the sale; any surplus is paid to the debtor.

wrongful discharge ■ An employer's termination of an employee's employment in violation of the law.

Table of Cases

Index